June 10–14, 2012
Washington, DC, USA

Association for
Computing Machinery

Advancing Computing as a Science & Profession

JCDL'12

Proceedings of the 12th ACM/IEEE-CS
Joint Conference on Digital Libraries

Sponsored by:

ACM SIGIR, ACM SIGWEB, IEEE CS, & TCDL

Supported by:

CROWLEY, NSF, Institute of Museum and Library Services, The George Washington University, Library of Congress, ALCTS, ARL, ASIS&T, Coalition for Academic Scientific Computation, CNI, DLF, & OCLC

Association for
Computing Machinery

Advancing Computing as a Science & Profession

The Association for Computing Machinery
2 Penn Plaza, Suite 701
New York, New York 10121-0701

ISBN: 978-1-4503-1154-0 (Digital)

ISBN: 978-1-4503-1731-3 (Print)

Additional copies may be ordered prepaid from:

ACM Order Department
PO Box 30777
New York, NY 10087-0777, USA

Phone: 1-800-342-6626 (USA and Canada)
+1-212-626-0500 (Global)
Fax: +1-212-944-1318
E-mail: acmhelp@acm.org
Hours of Operation: 8:30 am – 4:30 pm ET

Printed in the USA

Foreword

It is our great pleasure to welcome you to Washington, D.C., for the 12th ACM/IEEE Joint Conference on Digital Libraries (JCDL 2012). JCDL is the premiere international conference focused on digital libraries, and associated organizational, practical, social, and technical issues. The event addresses a broad spectrum of topical areas, and is open to all emerging and established educators, industry leaders, researchers, and students working in the field of digital library research and development. This year's conference is hosted by The George Washington University and co-organized with The Library of Congress.

We have chosen a number of keynotes to amplify our conference themes of *#preserving #linking #using #sharing*. The opening keynote will be given by Jason Scott of textfiles.com. On the second day the keynote will be delivered by Carole Goble of the University of Manchester, and on the third day a closing keynote will be presented by George Dyson, a frequent contributor to The Edge Foundation.

This year, we received 201 submissions (with authors from 32 countries) that went through a rigorous review process with Program Committee members from 22 countries. The result is a program that reflects the high quality of research being conducted in the breadth of disciplines that comprise digital libraries. We accepted 25 of 91 full paper submissions (27%) and 22 of 70 short papers (34%). In addition, there will be 43 posters and 9 demos following the now legendary "minute madness" on the first day of the conference. The Vannevar Bush Best Paper Award and the Best Student Paper Award will be presented at the conference banquet.

JCDL 2012 continues the tradition of supporting digital library developers with four tutorials that cover a range of timely issues including user studies, building digital libraries, and teaching about digital libraries. The program also includes five workshops, which provide a venue for a cross-section of disciplines to explore focused, cutting-edge topics including disciplinary repositories, emergency informatics, and institutional repositories. JCDL 2012 opens with a Doctoral Consortium, a forum where Ph.D. students receive feedback and advice from a committee of internationally recognized researchers and practitioners.

We would like to thank the Program Committee for their dedication to creating a program that reflects the conference themes of *#preserving #linking #using #sharing*. We would also like to thank all the committee members and student volunteers who supported the conference in its various stages. We hope that the conference will provide a valuable opportunity to share ideas with other researchers and practitioners from institutions around the world. Finally, we would like to thank the cooperating and sponsoring organizations for their significant support.

Program Co-Chairs:

Michael L. Nelson
Old Dominion University

Herbert Van de Sompel
Los Alamos National Laboratory

Ingeborg Sølvberg
Norwegian University of Science and Technology

General Co-Chairs:

Karim B. Boughida
George Washington University

Barrie Howard
Library of Congress

Table of Contents

JCDL 2012 Conference Organization xii

JCDL 2012 Sponsors & Supporters xvi

Session 1: Preservation

- **On the Institutional Archiving of Social Media** 1
  Catherine C. Marshall *(Microsoft Research, Silicon Valley)*, Frank M. Shipman *(Texas A&M University)*,
- **To Envisage and Design the Transition from a Digital Archive System Developed for Domain Experts to one for Non-domain Users** 11
  Maristella Agosti, Nicola Orio *(University of Padua)*,
- **Visualizing Digital Collections at Archive-It** 15
  Kalpesh Padia, Yasmin AlNoamany, Michele C. Weigle *(Old Dominion University)*
- **Data, Data Use, and Scientific Inquiry: Two Case Studies of Data Practices** 19
  Laura A. Wynholds, Jillian C. Wallis, Christine L. Borgman, Ashley Sands, Sharon Traweek *(University of California, Los Angeles)*
- **Digital Preservation and Knowledge Discovery Based on Documents from an International Health Science Program** 23
  Dharitri Misra, Robert H. Hall, Susan M. Payne, George R. Thoma *(National Institutes of Health)*

Session 2: Education

- **Teacher Sociality and Information Diffusion in Educational Digital Libraries** 27
  Ogheneovo Dibie, Keith E. Maull, Tamara Sumner *(University of Colorado Boulder)*
- **Is It Time to Change the OER Repositories Role?** 31
  Christo Dichev, Darina Dicheva *(Winston Salem State University)*
- **Identifying Core Concepts in Educational Resources** 35
  James M. Foster, Md. Arafat Sultan *(University of Colorado, Boulder)*, Holly Devaul *(University Corporation for Atmospheric Research)*, Ifeyinwa Okoye, Tamara Sumner *(University of Colorado, Boulder)*
- **Deduced Social Networks for an Educational Digital Library** 43
  Monika Akbar, Clifford A. Shaffer, Edward A. Fox *(Virginia Tech)*
- **A Tale of Two Studies: Is Dissemination Working?** 47
  Flora McMartin, Sarah Giersch *(Broad-based Knowledge, LLC)*, Joseph Tront *(Virginia Polytechnic University)*, Wesley Shumar *(Drexel University)*

Session 3: Bibliographic Networks

- **To Better Stand on the Shoulder of Giants** 51
  Rui Yan *(Peking University & National University of Taiwan)*, Congrui Huang *(Peking University)*, Jie Tang *(Tsinghua University)*, Yan Zhang *(Peking University)*, Xiaoming Li *(Peking University & Beihang University)*
- **BibRank: A Language-Based Model for Co-Ranking Entities in Bibliographic Networks** 61
  Laure Soulier, Lamjed Ben Jabeur, Lynda Tamine, Wahiba Bahsoun *(IRIT - Paul Sabatier University)*
- **Modeling and Exploiting Heterogeneous Bibliographic Networks for Expertise Ranking** 71
  Hongbo Deng, Jiawei Han *(University of Illinois at Urbana-Champaign)*, Michael R. Lyu, Irwin King *(The Chinese University of Hong Kong)*

Session 5: Architecture

- **Live Television in a Digital Library** 81
  Maxime Roüast, David Bainbridge *(University of Waikato)*
- **Transforming Japanese Archives into Accessible Digital Books** 91
  Tatsuya Ishihara, Toshinari Itoko, Daisuke Sato *(IBM Research — Tokyo)*,
  Asaf Tzadok *(IBM Research — Haifa)*, Hironobu Takagi *(IBM Research — Tokyo)*
- **IPKB: A Digital Library for Invertebrate Paleontology** 101
  Yuanliang Meng, Junyan Li, Patrick Denton *(The University of Kansas)*,
  Yuxin Chen *(Swiss Federal Institute of Technology)*,
  Bo Luo, Paul Selden, Xue-wen Chen *(The University of Kansas)*

Session 6: Metadata

- **Descriptive Metadata, Iconclass, and Digitized Emblem Literature** 111
  Timothy W. Cole, Myung-Ja K. Han, Jordan A. Vannoy *(University of Illinois at Urbana-Champaign)*
- **Categorization of Computing Education Resources with Utilization of Crowdsourcing** 121
  Yinlin Chen *(Virginia Tech)*, Paul Logasa Bogen II *(Oak Ridge National Laboratory)*,
  Haowei Hsieh *(University of Iowa)*, Edward A. Fox *(Virginia Tech)*, Lillian N. Cassel *(Villanova University)*
- **Re-ranking Bibliographic Records for Personalized Library Search** 125
  Tadashi Nomoto *(National Institute of Japanese Literature)*
- **Generating Ground Truth for Music Mood Classification Using Mechanical Turk** 129
  Jin Ha Lee *(University of Washington)*, Xiao Hu *(University of Denver)*

Session 7: Data

- **Content-Based Layouts for Exploratory Metadata Search in Scientific Research Data** 139
  Jürgen Bernard, Tobias Ruppert *(Fraunhofer Institute for Computer Graphics Research)*,
  Maximilian Scherer *(TU Darmstadt)*, Jörn Kohlhammer *(Fraunhofer Institute for Computer Graphics Research)*,
  Tobias Schreck *(University of Konstanz)*
- **Refactoring HUBzero for Linked Data** 149
  Michael Witt *(Purdue University Libraries)*, Yongyang Yu *(Purdue University)*
- **Treating Data Like Software: A Case for Production Quality Data** 153
  Jennifer M. Schopf *(Woods Hole Oceanographic Institution)*
- **A Quantitative Evaluation of Techniques for Detection of Abnormal Change Events in Blogs** 157
  Paul Logasa Bogen II *(Oak Ridge National Laboratory)*, Frank Shipman, Richard Furuta *(Texas A&M University)*

Session 9: Named Entities

- **'Similar Researcher Search' in Academic Environments** 167
  Sujatha Das Gollapalli, Prasenjit Mitra, C. Lee Giles *(The Pennsylvania State University)*
- **An Analysis of the Named Entity Recognition Problem in Digital Library Metadata** 171
  Nuno Freire *(IST/INESC-ID & National Library of the Netherlands)*,
  José Borbinha, Pável Calado *(IST/INESC-ID)*
- **Active Associative Sampling for Author Name Disambiguation** 175
  Anderson A. Ferreira *(Universidade Federal de Minas Gerais & Universidade Federal de Ouro Preto)*,
  Rodrigo Silva, Marcos André Gonçalves, Adriano Veloso,
  Alberto H. F. Laender *(Universidade Federal de Minas Gerais)*
- **AckSeer: A Repository and Search Engine for Automatically Extracted Acknowledgments from Digital Libraries** 185
  Madian Khabsa, Pucktada Treeratpituk, C. Lee Giles *(The Pennsylvania State University)*

Session 10: Books and Reading

- **Learning Topics and Related Passages in Books** 195
  David Newman *(University of California, Irvine)*, Youn Noh *(Yale University)*, Kat Hagedorn *(University of Michigan)*, Arun Balagopalan *(University of California, Irvine)*
- **Emphasis on Examining Results in Fiction Searches Contributes to Finding Good Novels** 199
  Suvi Oksanen, Pertti Vakkari *(University of Tampere)*
- **The "City of Lit" Digital Library — A Case Study of Interdisciplinary Research and Collaboration** 203
  Haowei Hsieh *(The University of Iowa)*, Bridget Draxler *(Monmouth College)*, Nicole J. Dudley, Jon Winet *(The University of Iowa)*
- **Student Researchers, Citizen Scholars and the Trillion Word Library** 213
  Gregory Crane, Bridget Almas, Alison Babeu, Lisa Cerrato, Matthew Harrington *(Tufts University)*, David Bamman *(Carnegie Mellon University)*, Harry Diakoff *(Alpheios Project)*

Session 11: Concepts and Topics

- **Event-Centric Search and Exploration in Document Collections** 223
  Jannik Strötgen, Michael Gertz *(Heidelberg University)*
- **Dynamic Online Views of Meta-Indexes** 233
  Michael Huggett, Edie Rasmussen *(University of British Columbia)*
- **Topic Models for Taxonomies** 237
  Anton Bakalov, Andrew McCallum, Hanna Wallach *(University of Massachusetts, Amherst)*, David Mimno *(Princeton University)*
- **Concept Chaining Utilizing Meronyms in Text Characterization** 241
  Lori Watrous-deVersterre, Chong Wang, Min Song *(New Jersey Institute of Technology)*

Session 12: Search

- **Improving Multi-Faceted Book Search by Incorporating Sparse Latent Semantic Analysis of Click-Through Logs** 249
  Deng Yi, Yin Zhang, Haihan Yu, Yanfei Yin, Jing Pan, Baogang Wei *(Zhejiang University)*
- **Personalized Query Expansion in the QIC System** 259
  Prat Tanapaisankit, Lori Watrous-deVersterre, Min Song *(New Jersey Institute of Technology)*
- **Investigating Keyphrase Indexing with Text Denoising** 263
  Rushdi Shams, Robert E. Mercer *(University of Western Ontario)*
- **Exploiting Real-Time Information Retrieval in the Microblogosphere** 267
  Feng Liang, Runwei Qiang, Jianwu Yang *(Peking University)*

Session 13: Citations

- **Improving Algorithm Search Using the Algorithm Co-Citation Network** 277
  Suppawong Tuarob, Prasenjit Mitra, C. Lee Giles *(The Pennsylvania State University)*
- **Evaluating and Ranking Patents Using Weighted Citations** 281
  Sooyoung Oh, Zhen Lei, Prasenjit Mitra, John Yen *(The Pennsylvania State University)*
- **A Hybrid Two-Stage Approach for Discipline-Independent Canonical Representation Extraction from References** 285
  Sung Hee Park, Roger W. Ehrich, Edward A. Fox *(Virginia Tech)*
- **Web-Based Citation Parsing, Correction and Augmentation** 295
  Liangcai Gao, Xixi Qi *(Peking University)*, Zhi Tang *(State Key Laboratory of Digital Publishing Technology)*, Xiaofan Lin *(A9.com)*, Ying Liu *(Korea Advanced Institute of Science and Technology)*

Session 14: User Behavior

- **Book Selection Behavior in the Physical Library: Implications for eBook Collections** 305
  Annika Hinze *(University of Waikato)*, Dana McKay *(Swinburne University of Technology)*, Nicholas Vanderschantz, Claire Timpany, Sally Jo Cunningham *(University of Waikato)*
- **How Do People Organize Their Photos in Each Event and How Does It Affect Storytelling, Searching and Interpretation Tasks?** 315
  Jesse Prabawa Gozali, Min-Yen Kan *(National University of Singapore)*, Hari Sundaram *(Arizona State University)*
- **Co-Reading: Investigating Collaborative Group Reading** 325
  Jennifer Pearson, Tom Owen, Harold Thimbleby *(Swansea University)*, George Buchanan *(City University, London)*

Posters ....

- **A Digital Library for Water Main Break Identification and Visualization** 335
  Sunshin Lee, Noha Elsherbiny, Edward A. Fox *(Virginia Tech)*
- **A Preliminary Analysis of FRBR's Bibliographic Relationships for Path Based Associative Rules** 337
  Ya-Ning Chen *(National Taiwan Normal University & Academia Sinica)*, Hui-Pin Chen, Fei-Yen Tu *(Academia Sinica)*
- **A Qualitative Analysis of Information Dissemination Through Twitter in a Digital Library** 339
  Hae Min Kim, Christopher C. Yang, Eileen G. Abels, Mi Zhang *(Drexel University)*
- **A Study of Automation from Seed URL Generation to Focused Web Archive Development: The CTRnet Context** 341
  Seungwon Yang, Kiran Chitturi, Gregory Wilson, Mohamed Magdy Gharib Farag, Edward A. Fox *(Virginia Tech)*
- **A System for Indexing Tables, Algorithms and Figures** 343
  Pradeep B. Teregowda, Madian Khabsa, C. Lee Giles *(The Pennsylvania State University)*
- **A Technique for Suggesting Related Wikipedia Articles Using Link Analysis** 345
  Christopher Markson, Min Song *(New Jersey Institute of Technology)*
- **An Exploration of the Research Trends in the Digital Library Evaluation Domain** 347
  Giannis Tsakonas, Angelos Mitrelis, Leonidas Papachristopoulos, Christos Papatheodorou *(Ionian University)*
- **An Iterative Reliability Measure for Semi-Anonymous Annotators** 349
  Peter Organisciak *(University of Illinois at Urbana-Champaign)*
- **An Unsupervised Technical Difficulty Ranking Model Based on Conceptual Terrain in the Latent Space** 351
  Shoaib Jameel, Wai Lam, Xiaojun Qian *(The Chinese University of Hong Kong)*, Ching-man Au Yeung *(ASTRI)*
- **Longitudinal Analysis of Historical Texts' Readability** 353
  Adam Jatowt *(Kyoto University & Japan Science and Technology Agency)*, Katsumi Tanaka *(Kyoto University)*
- **Bi2SoN — A Digital Library for Supporting Biomedical Research** 355
  Benjamin Köhncke, Sascha Tönnies *(L3S Research Center)*, Wolf-Tilo Balke *(IFIS TU Braunschweig)*
- **CADAL Digital Calligraphy System** 357
  Gao Pengcheng, Wu Jiangqin, Xia Yang, Lin Yuan *(Zhejiang University)*
- **Characterize Scientific Domain and Domain Context** 359
  Jinsong Zhang *(Dalian Maritime University)*, Chun Guo, Xiaozhong Liu *(Indiana University)*
- **Collaboration and Communication Tools Used by the Biodiversity Heritage Library: Refining Strategies for Success** 361
  Trish-Rose Sandler *(Missouri Botanical Garden 4344)*, Constance Rinaldo *(Harvard University)*, William Ulate *(Missouri Botanical Garden)*, Keri Thompson, Martin Kalfatovic *(Smithsonian Institution)*

- **Data Determination, Disambiguation, and Referencing in Molecular Biology** 363
  Shuheng Wu, Besiki Stvilia, Dong Joon Lee *(Florida State University)*
- **Digital Libraries for Computational Journalism** 365
  Luis Francisco-Revilla *(The University of Texas at Austin)*
- **Comparison of Three Digital Library Interfaces: Open Library, Google Books, and Hathi Trust** 367
  Matthew Miller, Gilok Choi, Lindsay Chell *(Pratt Institute)*
- **Digital Preservation in a Box: Outreach Resources for Digital Stewardship** 369
  Butch Lazorchak, Susan Manus *(Library of Congress)*, Dever Powell *(National Library of Medicine)*, Jane Zhang *(Catholic University of America)*
- **Distinguishing Venues by Writing Styles** 371
  Zaihan Yang, Brian D. Davison *(Lehigh University)*
- **Do Public Library Websites Consider the Disabled or Senior Citizens?** 373
  Yong Jeong Yi, Ji Hei Kang *(The Florida State University)*
- **Electronic Records Processing: It's a CINCH!** 375
  Amy Rudersdorf, Dean Farrell, Lisa Gregory *(State Library of North Carolina)*
- **Exploiting Canonical Structures to Transmit Complex Objects from a Digital Library to a Portal** 377
  Scott Britell *(Portland State University)*, Lois M.L. Delcambre *(Portland State University)*, Lillian N. Cassel *(Villanova University)*, Edward A. Fox *(Virginia Tech)*, Richard Furuta *(Texas A&M University)*
- **Global Web Archive Integration with Memento** 379
  Robert Sanderson *(Los Alamos National Laboratory)*
- **GROTOAP: GROund Truth for Open Access Publications** 381
  Dominika Tkaczyk, Artur Czeczko, Krzysztof Rusek, Łukasz Bolikowski, Roman Bogacewicz *(University of Warsaw)*
- **Has it Been Already Digitized? How to Find Information about Digitized Documents** 383
  Tomas Foltyn *(National Library of the Czech Republic)*, Martin Lhotak *(Academy of Sciences Library)*, Pavel Kocourek *(INCAD, spol. s r. o.)*
- **How Can Spreaders Affect the Indirect Infuence on Twitter?** 385
  Xin Shuai, Ying Ding, Jerome Busemeyer *(Indiana University)*
- **Improving a Hybrid Literary Book Recommendation System Through Author Ranking** 387
  Paula Cristina Vaz *(INESC-ID/IST – Portugal)*, David Martins de Matos *(INESC-ID/IST – Portugal)*, Bruno Martins, Pavel Calado *(IST/INESC-ID – Portugal)*
- **Introducing High Performance Computing in Digital Library Processing Workflows** 389
  Bill Barth, Maria Esteva, Jon Gibson, Ladd Hanson, Christopher Jordan *(University of Texas at Austin)*
- **Investigating User Perceptions of Engagement and Information Quality in Mobile Human Computation Games** 391
  Dion H. Goh, Khasfariyati Razikin, Chei Sian Lee, Alton Y.K. Chua *(Nanyang Technological University)*
- **Lessons Learned from Developing and Evaluating a Comprehensive Digital Library for Engineering Education** 393
  Yunlu Zhang *(Wuhan University)*, Alice Merner Agogino *(University of California, Berkeley)*, Shijun Li *(Wuhan University)*
- **Meta-Line: Lineage Information for Improved Metadata Quality** 395
  Sascha Tönnies, Benjamin Köhncke *(L3S Research Center)*, Wolf-Tilo Balke *(IFIS TU Braunschweig)*

- **Multi-View of the ACM Classification System** 397
  Xia Lin, Mi Zhang, Haozhen Zhao, Jan Buzydlowski *(Drexel University)*
- **National Digital Newspaper Program: A Case Study in Sharing, Linking, and Using Data** 399
  Nathan Yarasavage, Robin Butterhof, Christopher Ehrman *(Library of Congress)*
- **Responsibility for Research Data Quality in Open Access: A Slovenian Case** 401
  Janez Štebe *(University of Ljubljana)*
- **Scientific Cyberlearning Resources Referential Metadata Creation Via Information Retrieval** 403
  Xiaozhong Liu, Han Jia *(Indiana University Bloomington)*
- **Sheer Curation for Experimental Data and Provenance** 405
  Tobias Blanke, Mark Hedges *(King's College London)*
- **Web2MARC: Sharing and Using STEM Digital Content in School Libraries** 407
  Marcia A. Mardis, Casey McLaughlin, Grant Gingell *(The Florida State University)*
- **Social Network-Based Recommendation: A Graph Random Walk Kernel Approach** 409
  Xin Li, Xin Su, Mengyue Wang *(City University of Hong Kong)*
- **The David Livingstone Spectral Imaging Project** 411
  Stephen Davison *(University of California, Los Angeles)*, Adrian Wisnicki *(Indiana University of Pennsylvania)*, Elizabeth McAulay *(University of California, Los Angeles)*
- **The Logical Form of the Proposition Expressed by a Metadata Record** 413
  Karen M. Wickett, Allen H. Renear *(University of Illinois at Urbana-Champaign)*
- **Toponym Extraction and Resolution in a Digital Library** 415
  James Creel, Katherine Weimer *(Texas A&M University)*
- **Pinterest: Social Collecting for #linking #using #sharing** 417
  Michael Zarro, Catherine Hall *(Drexel University)*
- **YADDA2 — Assemble Your Own Digital Library Application from Lego Bricks** 419
  Wojtek Sylwestrzak, Tomasz Rosiek, Łukasz Bolikowski *(University of Warsaw)*

Demonstrations

- **An Integrated Participatory Platform for Human Evaluation of Machine Translation** 421
  Jiangping Chen, Olajumoke Azogu, Wenqian Zhao *(University of North Texas)*
- **'Erasmus': an Organization- and User-Centered Dublin Core Metadata Tool** 423
  Michael Khoo, Craig M. MacDonald, Joon Park *(Drexel University)*
- **Faceted Search for Heterogeneous Digital Collections** 425
  Hui Zhang, Jon Dunn, Will Cowan, Mike Durbin, Brian Wheeler *(Indiana University)*
- **NLM Video Search** 427
  John P. Doyle *(U.S. National Library of Medicine)*, Doron Shalvi, Edward C. Luczak *(U.S. National Library of Medicine (contractor))*
- **Research Discovery Through Linked Open Data** 429
  Paul Albert *(Weill Cornell Medical College)*, Kristi L. Holmes *(Washington University in St. Louis)*, Katy Börner *(Indiana University)*, Mike Conlon *(University of Florida)*
- **Structured Audio Content Analysis and Metadata in a Digital Library** 431
  David Bainbridge *(University of Waikato)*, J. Stephen Downie, Andreas F. Ehmann *(University of Illinois)*
- **The Profiles in Science Digital Library: Behind the Scenes** 433
  Marie E. Gallagher, Christie Moffatt *(U.S. National Library of Medicine)*

- **The ResultsSpace Collaborative Search Environment** 435
  Robert Capra, Jaime Arguello, Annie T. Chen, Katie Hawthorne, Gary Marchionini,
  Lee Shaw *(University of North Carolina at Chapel Hill)*
- **WARCreate - Create Wayback-Consumable WARC Files from Any Webpage** 437
  Mat Kelly, Michele C. Weigle *(Old Dominion University)*

Author Index 439

JCDL 2012 Conference Organization

General Co-chairs: Karim B. Boughida *(The George Washington University, USA)*
Barrie Howard *(The Library of Congress, USA)*

Program Co-chairs: Michael L. Nelson *(Old Dominion University, USA)*
Herbert Van de Sompel *(Los Alamos National Laboratory, USA)*
Ingeborg Sølvberg *(Norwegian University of Science & Technology, Norway)*

Doctoral Consortium Co-chairs: Luanne Freund *(University of British Columbia, Canada)*
Mounia Lalmas *(Yahoo! Research, Spain)*

Tutorials Co-chairs: Richard Marciano *(University of North Carolina at Chapel Hill, USA)*
Gregory Crane *(Tufts University, USA)*

Panels Co-chairs: Haowei Hsieh *(University of Iowa, USA)*
Noha Adly *(Bibliotheca Alexandrina, Egypt)*

Posters/Demos Co-chairs: José Borbinha *(Instituto Superior Técnic, Portugal)*
Bill Kules *(The Catholic University of America, USA)*

Workshops Co-chairs: Shigeo Sugimato *(University of Tsukuba, Japan)*
Ingrid Hsieh-Yee *(The Catholic University of America, USA)*

Local Arrangements Co-chairs: Gina Jones *(The Library of Congress, USA)*
Sue Manus *(The Library of Congress, USA)*

Student Volunteers Coordinator: Sue Yeon Syn *(The Catholic University of America, USA)*

Publicity Co-chairs: Rachel Frick *(Digital Library Federation, USA)*
Anne Washington *(George Mason University, USA)*

Publications Co-chairs: Jackie Shieh *(The George Washington University, USA)*
Dan Chudnov *(The George Washington University, USA)*

Webmaster: Christian Aldridge *(The George Washington University, USA)*

Sponsorship Chair: Robert H. McDonald *(Indiana University, USA)*

Treasurer: Martha Whittaker *(The George Washington University, USA)*

JCDL Steering Committee: Ed Fox *(Virginia Polytechnic Institute and State University, USA)*
Edie Rasmussen *(University of British Columbia, Canada)*
David Hicks *(Aalborg University, Esbjerg, Denmark)*
Richard Furuta *(Texas A &M University, USA)*
Sally Jo Cunningham *(University of Waikato, New Zealand)*
Ronald Larsen *(University of Pittsburgh, USA)*
Rudi Schmiede *(Technische Universität Darmstadt, Germany)*
Ingeborg Sølvberg *(Norwegian University of Science & Technology, Norway)*
Shigeo Sugimato *(University of Tsukuba, Japan)*

Senior Program Committee: Maristella Agosti *(University of Padova, Italy)*
Nicholas Belkin *(Rutgers University, USA)*
Johan Bollen *(Indiana University, USA)*
Christine Borgman *(UCLA, USA)*
Edward Fox *(Virginia Tech, USA)*
Richard Furuta *(Texas A&M University, USA)*
C. Lee Giles *(Pennsylvania State University, USA)*
Marcos Goncalvez *(Federal University of Minas Gerais, Brazil)*
Geneva Henry *(Rice University, USA)*
Jane Hunter *(University of Queensland, Australia)*
Min-Yen Kan *(National University of Singapore, Singapore)*
Carl Lagoze *(Cornell University, USA)*
Ray Larson *(University of California, Berkeley, USA)*
Gary Marchionini *(University of North Carolina at Chapel Hill, USA)*
Reagan Moore *(University of North Carolina at Chapel Hill, USA)*
Edie Rasmussen *(University of British Columbia, Canada)*
Andreas Rauber *(Vienna University of Technology, Austria)*

Program Committee: Eytan Adar *(University of Michigan, USA)*
Robert Allen *(Victoria University of Wellington, New Zealand)*
David Bainbridge *(University of Waikato, New Zealand)*
Sean Bechhofer *(University of Manchester, United Kingdom)*
Sabine Bergler *(Concordia University, Canada)*
Steven Bethard *(Katholieke Universiteit Leuven, Belgium)*
Chris Bizer *(FU Berlin, Germany)*
José Borbinha *(National Library Portugal, Portugal)*
Hennie Brugman *(Meertens Institut, The Netherlands)*
George Buchanan *(City University London, United Kingdom)*
Robert Capra *(University of North Carolina at Chapel Hill, USA)*
Lillian Cassel *(Villanova University, USA)*
James Caverlee *(Texas A&M University, USA)*
Youngok Choi *(The Catholic University of America, USA)*
Gregory Crane *(Tufts University, USA)*
Sally Jo Cunningham *(Waikato University, New Zealand)*
Lois Delcambre *(Portland State University, USA)*
Anne Diekema *(Utah State University, USA)*
J. Stephen Downie *(University of Illinois, USA)*
Miles Efron *(University of Illinois, USA)*
Nicola Ferro *(University of Padova, Italy)*
Schubert Foo *(Nanyang Technological University, Singapore)*
Luis Francisco-Revilla *(University of Texas at Austin, USA)*
Luanne Freund *(University of British Columbia, Canada)*
Stephane Gancarski *(Laboratoire d'Informatique de Paris 6, France)*
Gary Geisler *(University of Texas at Austin, USA)*
Gene Golovchinsky *(University of Texas at Austin, USA)*

Program Committee (continued):

Stefan Gradmann *(Humboldt Universitat Berlin, Germany)*
Jane Greenberg *(University of North Carolina at Chapel Hill, USA)*
Bradley Hemminger *(University of North Carolina at Chapel Hill, USA)*
Sarah Holsted *(Broad-based Knowledge, USA)*
Ingrid Hsieh-Yee *(The Catholic University of America, USA)*
Xiao Hu *(University of Denver, USA)*
Jimmy Huang *(York University, Canada)*
Antoine Isaac *(Vrije Universiteit Amsterdam, The Netherlands)*
Adam Jatowt *(Kyoto University, Japan)*
Unmil Karadkar *(University of Texas at Austin, USA)*
Andruid Kerne *(Texas A&M University, USA)*
Michael Khoo *(Drexel University, USA)*
Wolfgang Klas *(University of Vienna, Austria)*
Martin Klein *(Los Alamos National Laboratory, USA)*
Rick Kopak *(University of British Columbia, Canada)*
Bill Kules *(The Catholic University of America, USA)*
Ronald Larsen *(University of Pittsburgh, USA)*
Dongwon Lee *(Pennsylvania State University, USA)*
Daniel Lemire *(Université du Québec à Montréal, Canada)*
Joan Lippincott *(Coalition for Networked Information, USA)*
Paul Logasa Bogen II *(Oak Ridge National Laboratory, USA)*
Richard Marciano *(University of North Carolina at Chapel Hill, USA)*
Byron Marshall *(Oregon State University, USA)*
Frank McCown *(Harding University, USA)*
Jerome Mcdonough *(University of Illinois, USA)*
David Mimno *(University of Massachusetts, USA)*
William Moen *(University of North Texas, USA)*
Uma Murthy *(URC Ventures, USA)*
Erich Neuhold *(University of Vienna, Austria)*
Glen Newton *(Carleton University, Canada)*
Christos Papatheodorou *(Ionian University, Greece)*
Mimi Recker *(Utah State University, USA)*
Thomas Risse *(L3S Research Center, Germany)*
Robert Sanderson *(Los Alamos National Laboratory, USA)*
Rudi Schmiede *(Darmstadt University of Technology, Germany)*
Heiko Schuldt *(University of Basel, Switzerland)*
Frank Shipman *(Texas A&M University, USA)*
Ali Shiri *(University of Alberta, Canada)*
Joan Smith *(Emory University, USA)*
Min Song *(New Jersey Institute of Technology, USA)*
Lisa Spiro *(Rice University, USA)*
Gail Steinhart *(Cornell University, USA)*
Shigeo Sugimato *(University of Tsukuba, Japan)*
Kazunari Sugiyama *(National University of Singapore, Singapore)*
Hussein Suleman *(University of Cape Town, South Africa)*

Program Committee (continued):

Tamara Sumner *(University of Colorado at Boulder, USA)*
Sue Yeon Syn *(The Catholic University of America, USA)*
J. Alfredo Sánchez *(Universidad de las Américas Puebla, Mexico)*
Andre Vellino *(University of Ottawa, Canada)*
Simeon Warner *(Cornell University, USA)*
Michele Weigle *(Old Dominion University, USA)*
Michael Witt *(Purdue University, USA)*
René Witte *(Concordia University, Canada)*
Ian Witten *(Waikato University, New Zealand)*
Mike Wright *(University Corporation for Atmospheric Research, USA)*

Additional reviewers:

Scott Ainsworth
Ihab Al Kabary
Sawood Alam
Abdulla Alasaadi
Zahra Amin Nayeri
Md. Arafat Sultan
Myriam Ben Saad
Justin Brunelle
Jan Buzydlowski
On Byung-Won
Catherine C. Marshall
Chuck Cartledge
Hau-Wen Chang
Eli Cortez
Soheil Danesh
Sujatha Das
Ogheneovo Dibie
Anne Doucet
Seyda Ertekin
Yee Fan Tan
Gerhard Gossen
Stephen Griffin
Saurabh Kataria
Mat Kelly
Woo-Cheol Kim
Haibin Liu
Nic Lupfer
Ivano Masiero
Keith Maull
Matt Mayernik
Alyona Medelyan
Marie-Jean Meurs
Jun Miao
David Nichols
Ifeyinwa Okoye
Zeynep Pehlivan
Simone Peruzzo
Yin Qu
Arcot Rajasekar
Heri Ramampiaro
Hany Salaheldeen
Andres Sanoja
Andrew Schaefer
Michalis Sfakakis
Gianmaria Silvello
Albena Strupchanska
Nina Tahmasebi
Pucktada Treeratpituk
Giannis Tsakonas
Lin Tzy Li
Andrew Webb
Zhaohui Wu
Su Yan
Tao Yang
Zheng Ye
Soyoung Yu
Dayu Yuan
Jiashu Zhao

JCDL 2012 Sponsors & Supporters

Sponsors:

SIGIR
Special Interest Group
on Information Retrieval

sig web

Technical Supporters:

IEEE

IEEE
COMPUTER
SOCIETY

TCDL

acm

Corporate Donor:

CROWLEY

IMAGING PRODUCTS ■ CONVERSION SERVICES

Grant Funder:

NSF

INSTITUTE of
Museum and Library
SERVICES

Conference Co-hosts:

THE GEORGE WASHINGTON UNIVERSITY
WASHINGTON DC

LIBRARY OF
CONGRESS

Cooperating Organizations:

ALCTS
Association for Library Collections & Technical Services

ARL
Association of Research Libraries

asis&t

Coalition for Academic Scientific Computation

cni
Coalition for Networked Information

DLF
Digital Library Federation

OCLC
OCLC Research

On the Institutional Archiving of Social Media

Catherine C. Marshall
Microsoft Research, Silicon Valley
1065 La Avenida
Mountain View, CA 94043
1-650-693-1308
cathymar@microsoft.com

Frank M. Shipman
Department of Computer Science
Texas A&M University
College Station, TX 77843-3112
1-979-862-3216
shipman@cs.tamu.edu

ABSTRACT

Social media records the thoughts and activities of countless cultures and subcultures around the globe. Yet institutional efforts to archive social media content remain controversial. We report on 988 responses across six surveys of social media users that included questions to explore this controversy. The quantitative and qualitative results show that the way people think about the issue depends on how personal and ephemeral they view the content to be. They use concepts such as creator privacy, content characteristics, technological capabilities, perceived legal rights, and intrinsic social good to reason about the boundaries of institutional social media archiving efforts.

Categories and Subject Descriptors

H4.3 Information Systems: Communications Applications.

General Terms

Design, Experimentation, Human Factors.

Keywords

Library of Congress, archiving, information rights, survey.

1. INTRODUCTION

Several years ago, as part of the National Digital Information Infrastructure Preservation Program (NDIIPP), the Library of Congress held workshops about information permanence with students, representatives of a first generation of so-called digital natives. When one of these students was asked what she thought should be saved, she speculated, "*They should just save Facebook. That is our generation's scrapbook, yearbook, Guinness World Record.*" [15] Indeed, social media plays an important function in how many of us negotiate our everyday lives, in how news and gossip are disseminated, and in how we record personal events large and small. It is no wonder that in 2010 the Library of Congress embarked on a project to archive public tweets after Twitter, a privately-held corporation, donated this content; arguably tweets can be an irreplaceable resource for documenting trends, breaking news, public reactions, and the more mundane aspects of peoples' lives [10].

Yet the project was not without controversy. Not only was there consternation in some quarters about the potential worthlessness of most tweets, but also there was outcry about the effect this acquisition would have on personal privacy. In his blog, social media privacy researcher Fred Stutzman posed a scenario that illustrated why we might be concerned:

> *"This is what makes Twitter's "gift" troubling. It assumes that all content shared publicly is truly public and for posterity. ... [Consider this scenario:] Bob wants to be practically obscure – private in public – without going to all the trouble of setting up complicated privacy controls. So what happens, two years from now, when Bob accidentally discloses his handle in the wrong context, and he needs to remove some Tweets?"* [24]

Erosion of personal privacy is only one aspect of the institutional archiving of social media that makes it a complex endeavor. Most transfer of personal materials to institutions used to be done by explicit design, though donor agreements that linked individuals and their families with specific archives or libraries that had the resources to maintain such collections, and possibly to provide future generations of historians and researchers access to them.

Expectations have changed. The curation of personal materials has become more difficult [21]; individuals have orders of magnitude more digital stuff than they did print media and physical belongings. They are seldom fully aware of what they have and where they've kept it. Furthermore, the ownership and control of these digital belongings is significantly more entangled: individuals may no longer own what they have stored online, nor are their assets centralized. Instead, digital belongings may be subject to the terms and conditions of many different agreements and competing legal and social interests [23].

Specifically, users of social media services such as Twitter and Facebook agree to terms and conditions that put the content they contribute into the hands of the service providers; thus the content is legally owned and controlled by these corporations as part of their assets. Because the content is shared socially and may be re-used more broadly, its de facto ownership is fluid, and its reach may extend far beyond a contributor's original intent.

Moreover, the content has potential archival value as it moves through time and space. A personal tweet from a day of rioting may become part of a larger exchange that reflects a country's growing political unrest; a vacation photo of a landmark may become a reference image that is used to illustrate dozens of minor publications; a book review, movie rating, or crowdsourced biographical information may become metadata for a resource like the Internet Movie Database (IMDB). As this kind of value grows and is recognized, a service's content may be acquired by a public institution such as the Library of Congress, a non-profit such as the Internet Archive, or a for-profit corporation that perceives the value of the service's content (for example, consider Yahoo's acquisition of Flickr, the photo-sharing service).

In spite of general recognition of the historical or cultural value of such acquisitions by public institutions, as we saw earlier, they are not without controversy. Just because a user cannot figure out Facebook's privacy controls, are her posts and profile public? To

JCDL'12, June 10–14, 2012, Washington, DC, USA.

whom do they belong when she stops using the service? If a friend copies a photo, does she lose control of it into perpetuity?

We performed a series of six scenario-based surveys to explore the attitudes of Internet-fluent (but not necessarily technologically trained) people to the issues that arise when public institutions acquire social media. The surveys also cover other aspects of the ownership and control of individually-contributed online content, including respondents' own practices, but in this paper, we focus on the results that pertain to institutional archiving of social media. In addition to identifying emergent issues, we sought answers to the following questions:

(1) How pervasive are the attitudes that we observed when the public Twitter feed was donated to the Library of Congress?

(2) Do different media types raise new concerns for the institutions doing the archiving?

(3) Are there ways an institution can mitigate the anxiety that may arise? (e.g., will limiting access help?)

We begin this paper by describing the surveys themselves; we especially focus on three recent surveys that were aimed at eliciting explanations of what the respondents perceive to be off-limits for institutional archiving efforts. We then summarize salient results from earlier surveys and discuss new results from the most recent surveys. Finally we explore the implications of the cumulative results for future institutional archiving efforts.

2. SIX SURVEYS: METHODS AND DATA

In this paper, we discuss and compare data collected in six different scenario-based surveys; a total of 988 valid responses (out of 1060 total) form the basis for our findings. Each survey covers a significant genre of user-contributed content, including tweets, photos, reviews, recorded videoconferences, podcasts, and educational media.

2.1 Using Mechanical Turk

The surveys were conducted using Mechanical Turk to solicit and screen respondents and to collect the data. We limited prospective respondents to the English speaking US-based Mechanical Turk community for three reasons: First, limiting the respondent pool simplified justifiable concerns about scenario comprehension and legal and cultural norms; in other words, we wanted to ensure that the situations we presented were understood in comparable ways to provide us with a firm basis for data analysis. Second, past studies have confirmed that US-based Turkers participate in the community out of interest and for entertainment, rather than for meaningful compensation [8]. This motivation is evident in their lucid and detailed responses to open-ended questions; it is unlikely they were influenced by the small payment. Finally, US-based Turkers have demographic characteristics that suggest they are representative of a larger, fairly diverse population of Internet users who are fluent in social media; we felt Mechanical Turk was a good way to reach a broad set of respondents.

Our own previous experiences with Mechanical Turk, coupled with documented best practices [4][9][10], enabled us to screen respondents and assemble reliable high-quality datasets. In particular, we made certain that respondents performed adequately on reading comprehension questions embedded in each survey; that they spent sufficient time completing the surveys; and that they responded fully to the open-ended questions that formed an important qualitative component of the data. We paid respondents for survey completion at a level commensurate with other similar Mechanical Turk tasks; respondents were paid regardless of whether their data was discarded.

2.2 Surveys and Respondents

This paper describes the results of the institutional archiving portions of four unpublished surveys, in addition to summarizing and contrasting these new results with results from two earlier studies of microblog entries (Twitter tweets) [16] and personal photos (photos with identifiable human subjects) [17]. The methods sections of the earlier papers contain additional details about the implementation of the surveys and how we ensured data reliability. The new surveys build on and refine the methods used in the early surveys. Most significantly, we added two types of open-ended questions: we asked about respondents' *current practices* (focusing on specific instances of media creation and reuse) and about their *ethical concerns* with social media reuse and archiving. We also added three practice-based questions that we felt would be good indicators of respondents' current privacy behavior; we are aware that abstract questions about future privacy behavior are apt to yield aspirational results [1][3].

Table 1 summarizes the surveys we have fielded to-date. The table documents the number of responses we received for each survey, how long it took respondents on average to complete the survey, and some key demographic properties of each set of respondents. Since the surveys were offered over comparable durations (two weeks of active responses, until the survey reached 250 participants), and we required respondents be users of the survey's social media type, the number of responses is likely to reflect the relative popularity of the media type. Hence photos are probably the most familiar media type among the prospective respondents, and recorded videoconferences are the least.

Table 1. Summary of survey respondents and demographics

Survey Media	screened responses (out of total)	average completion time	% female/ male/ no response	have college degree	have some college	current students	born before 1960	born 1960-1969	born 1970-1979	born 1980–1989	born after 1989
Twitter	173 (of 190)	8 minutes 44 seconds	61/39/0 (105/68/0)	54% (94)	88% (152)	did not ask	4% (7)	4% (7)	17% (29)	64% (110)	11% (19)
Photos	242 (of 250)	13 minutes 7 seconds	71/27/1 (173/66/3)	55% (133)	91% (221)	34% (82)	2% (4)	10% (25)	22% (53)	56% (135)	10% (23)
Reviews	203 (of 216)	14 minutes 23 seconds	59/41/0 (119/84/0)	62% (125)	92% (186)	32% (64)	3% (7)	12% (25)	23% (47)	50% (101)	9% (19)
Podcasts	170 (of 180)	11 minutes 30 seconds	46/53/1 (78/90/2)	59% (101)	91% (154)	32% (55)	2% (4)	9% (15)	22% (37)	52% (88)	15% (25)
Videos	98 (of 107)	10 minutes 7 seconds	55/43/2 (54/42/2)	72% (71)	94% (92)	24% (24)	5% (5)	8% (8)	26% (25)	47% (46)	13% (13)
Educational recordings	102 (of 117)	11 minutes 52 seconds	57/43/0 (58/44/0)	65% (66)	96% (98)	31% (32)	8% (8)	11% (11)	21% (21)	50% (51)	9% (9)
Total	988 (of 1060)		59/40/1 (587/394/7)	60% (590)	91% (903)		4% (35)	9% (91)	21% (212)	54% (531)	11% (108)

If we look at the relative demographic participation for each survey, we can pinpoint certain distinctions: The photo survey has the greatest proportion of female respondents (at 71%) and the podcast survey has the least (at 46%). As is true of surveys in general, and Mechanical Turk surveys in particular, women tend to participate in higher numbers [8]. Current students constituted about a third of the participation in most of the surveys, with the exception of the videoconference survey. We believe this can be attributed to the fact that we limited participation to Turkers familiar with videoconferences (rather than Turkers familiar with Skype); upon reflection, the term 'videoconference' is associated with the workplace, which may discourage prospective respondents who use Skype (or a similar application) to chat with their friends and families. The surveys were dominated by respondents in their twenties and thirties, although they all had participants who were over fifty and under twenty.

The surveys identified strong participation in diverse types of social media creation and use. Some respondents limited their contributions to basic profile information, "*name, address, email, phone number, bank info for shopping, anything I need to basically*" [EDU106]; others focused on fairly specific topics and genres, "*Labor law articles for work*" [EDU103]. Still others seemed fairly expansive, and revealed the respondent's interests and media creation skills: "*Music oriented information, including, music and music gear reviews, videos on how to work musical gear, and reviews on music*" [EDU257]. This broad sample of Internet users was important to us.

The six surveys each had a parallel structure. The first part of the survey elicited demographic and background information about the respondent. The second set of questions was scenario-driven. Respondents read about a social media situation. Then they were presented with a series of statements, and were asked whether they agreed or disagreed with the statement according to a 7-point Likert scale (where 1 point means "disagree strongly" and 7 points means "agree strongly"). Next they answered questions about their own experiences with the type of social media that was the survey topic (e.g., podcasts). Finally we asked an open-ended question designed to reveal their bigger-picture ethical attitudes.

Naturally, the surveys covered significant ground apart from the topic of this paper; the portions of the survey that we direct our attention to here are those connected with institutional archiving of social media. Table 2 summarizes these questions. The table also recaps the scenarios, since we are aware that both the media type and the scenario details may have some bearing on the responses to general questions. For the sake of brevity, and because the questions we are analyzing here are not scenario-specific, most of the details have been omitted from the table.

Table 2. Scenarios and questions about institutional archiving on each survey

Survey media	Types of Scenarios	Scenarios and Likert scale statements about institutional archiving	Open-ended questions about institutional archiving
Twitter	Storing and reposting personal tweets and conversations; removal of libelous tweets.	*LoC is archiving public Twitter feed.* • LoC can give researchers access. • LoC can give everyone access. • LoC can give everyone access after 50 years has passed.	*none*
Photos	Storing and reposting personal photo of subjects and bystanders, including a minor; removal of photos and metadata.	*LoC is archiving public Flickr photos.* • LoC can give researchers access. • LoC can give everyone access. • LoC can give everyone access after 50 years has passed.	*none (although there are open-ended questions about actual and hypothetical photo reuse)*
Reviews	Storing and reposting reviews of an award-winning children's book, including one that is anonymous (possibly fraudulent). Removal of reviews and comments.	*Qualified academic reviewer writes useful review of children's book* • LoC can use review as metadata. *LoC is archiving Amazon's book reviews.* • LoC can give researchers access. LoC can give everyone access. LoC can give everyone access after 50 years has passed. • Reviewer can remove review after 50 years has passed. • Reviews should be anonymized. • Reviews should be archived only if reviewers real name is on them.	*none (although there is a general open-ended question about reuse of content on the Internet)*
Podcasts	Storing and reposting an entertainment-oriented podcast. Removal of tags and comments. Re-use of audio snippets.	*LoC is archiving iTunes comedy podcasts.* • LoC can give researchers access. • LoC can give everyone access. • LoC can give everyone access after 50 years has passed.	Are there types of social media that the Library of Congress (or other public institutions) should not be able to archive? What are they (and why)? (*There are also open-ended questions about reuse of audio snippets.*)
Video-conference recordings	Storing and reposting of different versions of a recorded job interview, made with varying levels of consent and purpose (including satire). Reuse of video snippets, comments, and tags.	*LoC is archiving selected YouTube videos.* • LoC can archive a recording made without explicit subject consent. • LoC can archive a recording that shows only the side of a conversation where there's consent. • LoC can archive a recording that has been satirically repurposed. • LoC can give researchers access. • LoC can give everyone access. • LoC can give everyone access after 50 years has passed.	Are there types of social media that the Library of Congress (or other public institutions) should not be able to archive? What are they (and why)?
Educational recordings	Storing and reposting of an astronaut's commencement address with and without permission. Posting of a rebuttal from a qualified scientist. Posting, sharing and removal of reviews.	*LoC is archiving educational lectures from iTunes.* • LoC can give researchers access. • LoC can give everyone access. • LoC can give everyone access after 50 years has passed. • LoC can save reviews of the lectures without asking permission from the reviews authors. • LoC should not archive anonymous reviews.	Are there types of social media that the Library of Congress (or other public institutions) should not be able to archive? What are they (and why)?

2.3 Survey Structure

All 6 surveys included an institutional archiving scenario based on the form of social media that the survey covered. The scenario posited that a major social media company had donated its assets to the Library of Congress. Then the respondent was asked to evaluate three access variations—immediate universal access to the social media repository; deferred universal access to the social media repository; or immediate access that was limited to researchers. After we had analyzed the results to our first survey (about Twitter content), we began adding depth to these questions. Was anonymity permissible? Was permission necessary? Should comments be archived along with primary content? The most recent three surveys included an open-ended question, "Are there types of social media that the Library of Congress (or other public institutions) should not be able to archive? What are they (and why)?" Two of the earlier surveys had asked an open-ended question about respondents' reuse of online content; the answers were so interesting and provocative (see [16][17]) that we felt that respondents might express similarly diverse multi-dimensional attitudes about the institutional archiving of social media.

In the surveys, we used the Library of Congress as a proxy for any large public institution (or non-profit) capable of archiving social media. We chose the Library of Congress for three reasons. First, respondents may be familiar with the Library's Twitter effort; it makes sense to extend this project to other types of social media. Second, it seemed necessary to select an institution with sufficient resources and expertise to make the scenario plausible. We could have used the Internet Archive, but respondents were slightly less likely to be familiar with its successful efforts to date. Finally, we wanted to use a public governmental institution so there would be no overriding questions about the scenario's legality; it is easy for respondents to get distracted by peripheral aspects of a scenario.

3. RESULTS

The surveys elicited concerns about institutional archiving of social media content in two ways: Likert-scale responses to specific statements about the scenarios, which yielded quantitative data, and an open-ended question at the end of the survey that asked respondents what they felt should be excluded from a hypothetical Library of Congress social media archive. We first discuss the survey-specific quantitative results; these responses are all in the context of our media type-based scenarios.

3.1 Media Type-Specific Results

We present the media-specific results from four new surveys on reviews, educational recordings, podcasts, and videoconferences, so the results can be compared to our survey results for tweets [16], photos [17], and build on an earlier paper comparing the simple institutional archiving scenarios for those two types [18].

Amazon book reviews. The third survey of the series posed scenarios that involved reviews of the classic children's book, *Where the Wild Things Are*; the reviews—including one written by an expert on early childhood education, and one purportedly written by a child—were published on Amazon's online bookstore, and had amassed comments and ratings. The survey also included our standard institutional archiving scenario: this time, the Library of Congress archive was using the Amazon reviews as metadata to help describe books in its collection. We asked respondents about how they felt access to this archive of reviews should be regulated: should it be publicly available, available to researchers only, or publicly available after a significant period of time (50 years) had elapsed.

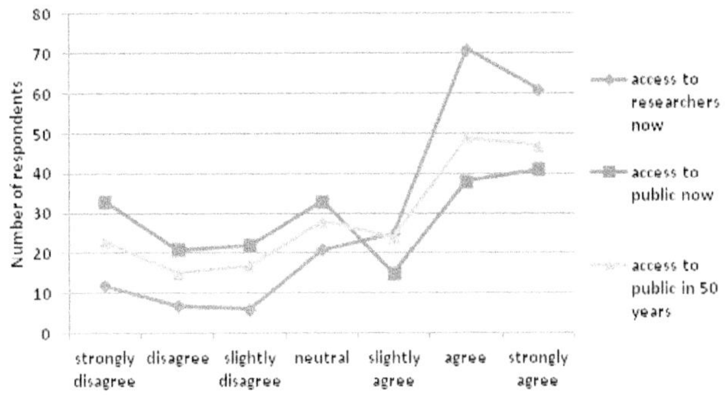

Figure 1. Three access conditions for archive of reviews

Figure 1 shows respondents' relative attitudes toward the three access conditions; the differences between them are statistically significant (Wilcoxon's Signed Rank, $p<.001$ for closest). Current access by researchers elicits the most positive reaction; current access by the public elicits the least positive reaction and the most controversy (as evidenced by the bimodal distribution of responses). Deferring public access for 50 years is both less controversial than immediate access, and less well-received than limiting access to researchers.

We tested the concept of permission with two questions. In one, the review on Amazon's website was written by a child (who is anonymous), and in the other, the review was written by an adult, a credentialed scholar in early childhood education who is authenticated by the system. Is permission necessary before the Library of Congress ingests either review into its repository? The status of the review (and reviewer) does not seem to affect respondents' attitudes toward permission. The concept is controversial, with respondents just about evenly split in both cases. The means are 3.98 and 3.93 (4 is neutral) for the child's review and the scholar's review respectively, and the distributions are flat.

Educational recording results. The final three surveys covered different types of recorded media. First we will examine the results for the scenario about institutional archiving of educational recordings, such as those found in iTunes University. To set the stage, the scenarios earlier in the survey posited a recorded commencement lecture delivered by an astronaut and a recorded rebuttal posted by a noted geologist. As Table 2 notes, we also tested concepts of permission and anonymity in this survey; these results are discussed when we compare results across surveys.

Responses to our standard access probes—access to researchers now, access to the public now, and access to the public in 50 years—revealed that the public access conditions (now and in 50 years) were statistically indistinguishable. However, access to researchers now tested more positively than either public access scenario (with statistical significance, Wilcoxon Signed Rank, $.05>p>.02$ for both).

Podcast results. Next we look at the institutional archiving results for the podcast scenario (the scenario that posited entertainment-oriented podcasts donated to the public institution by an iTunes-like service). Again, granting immediate access to researchers was significantly different than the responses to the two public access scenarios (Wilcoxon Signed Rank, $p<.001$ for both). There was no significant difference between the two public access scenarios.

Videoconference results. Finally we look at the institutional archiving results for the videoconference scenarios (several scenarios that posited recordings of job interviews that were manipulated and published with a variety of purposes in mind, including instruction, satire, and vlog-like personal commentary). Given popular YouTube videos as the archival genre, we found no significant difference between the three access scenarios. This result may have been because the videoconference recording survey attracted fewer respondents. Nonetheless, access to the material looks generally uncontroversial and trends positive.

In addition to testing our standard access conditions, we also explored the institutional archiving of a videoconference given varying levels of consent (to being recorded) and anonymity. In one scenario, a job interview conducted over Skype is recorded by the interviewee (Bill) without explicit consent of the interviewer (or his company). In the second scenario, the interviewer's side of the conversation has been removed from the final video, as well as any traces of corporate identity. In the third case, the recording has been satirically repurposed; again, the interviewer's side of the conversation has been replaced on the video, and any traces of corporate identity have been removed. Respondents were asked to evaluate whether it was appropriate to archive each of the three versions of the videoconference, and whether anonymity would influence this decision (i.e. if consent could not be obtained from the video's creator). Figure 2 shows the results of these conceptual probes about consent, permission, and anonymity.

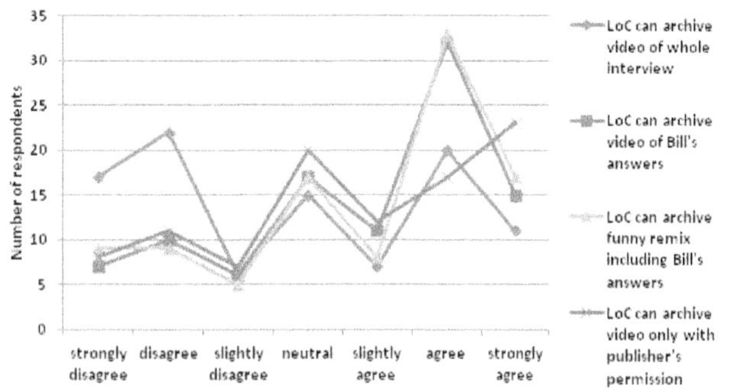

Figure 2. Conceptual probes of consent, permission, and anonymity

The results show that respondents were skeptical about the Library of Congress's right to archive the video of the whole interview. Both of the edited versions fared better; respondents assessed the institutional archiving effort positively. The differences between the full video and the two edited videos are significant (Wilcoxon's Signed Rank, $p<.001$ for both). There is no significant difference in the responses for the two edited versions of the video; in other words, the differing genres and purposes of the videos (instruction in one case and satire in the other) did not appear to influence respondents' sense of whether the video could be archived by a public institution.

A final condition—whether the Library of Congress could archive a video only if it was able to get the creator's consent—elicited similar responses to two edited video conditions, albeit slightly less enthusiastic. We should note that in the other cases, Bill's consent was only implied because he made the video public on websites like YouTube and FunnyOrDie; his permission was never explicitly solicited. This seems consistent with the response to the open-ended question we included at the end of the survey (and discussed in a later subsection)—some respondents feel that publishing content implies this sort of consent.

3.2 Cross-Media Results

In our past research, we used the Library of Congress scenario (the Library of Congress is building an archive of the media type used in the survey's other scenarios) to test three conditions (immediate public access, delayed public access, and immediate researcher access). In particular, we compared responses to the Twitter survey and the Flickr/personal photo survey. We found that the responses seemed to vary across media types [17]. How would this finding play out over six media types and genres?

Researcher access now. Unsurprisingly, the most positive responses are elicited by researcher access to an institutional archive that consists of the four most 'published' media types and genres—educational content comes out on top, followed closely by reviews and podcasts, with YouTube videos slightly below. Educational recordings are also the least controversial.

Which media types are controversial, given this scenario of immediate researcher access? More personal (and possibly less valuable) material proved to be more controversial: tweets and photos. Figure 3 shows this ordering.

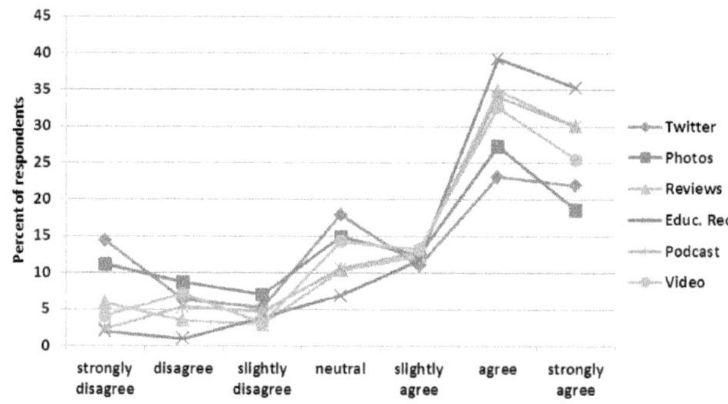

Figure 3. Immediate researcher access by media type

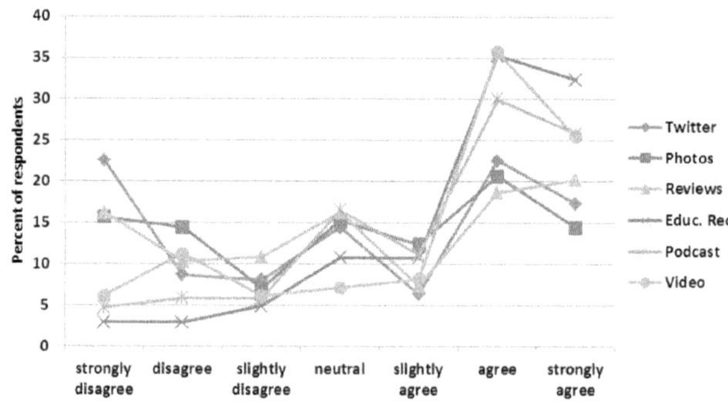

Figure 4. Immediate public access by media type

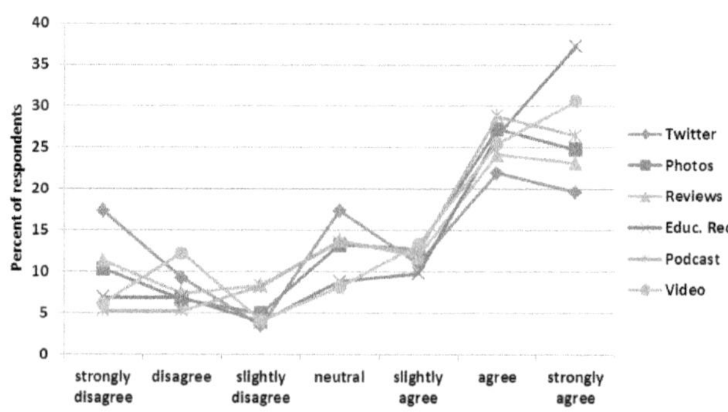

Figure 5. Public access in 50 years by media type

Public access now. Given the broadened purpose of public access to these media type-based institutional archives, we might expect positive outcomes to remain the same and negative responses to be exaggerated. We might also expect a heightened sense of controversy. Indeed, Figure 4 shows the responses to immediate public access to educational recordings, podcasts, and popular videos to trend positively, and the respondents to be in rough agreement.

On the other hand, public access to tweets, photos, and product reviews elicit less agreement, with tweets being the most controversial type. What might cause this controversy? Tweets and photos may rely on 'privacy through obscurity', but surely reviews rely less on this effect. Later, through the open-ended responses, we may speculate that the controversy may be engendered by the respondents' sense of the ultimate value (or lack of value) of this content.

Public access in 50 years. Does the passage of time mitigate privacy concerns? If it did, tweets might no longer be controversial relative to the other media types. Figure 5 shows that this reordering does not occur. Instead tweets remain controversial (and educational recordings remain benign). As we saw in our earlier comparison across types [17], concerns about access to photos are indeed diminished by waiting 50 years to provide access to them. Yet access to popular videos (across video genres) shows continuing concern. These effects again may be explained in the responses to the opened ended questions—characteristics such as social value may be amplified with time, especially as the perceived expense of maintaining an archive grows.

Anonymity. One of the features we were interested in exploring was anonymity. User-contributed content sometimes relies on relinquishing anonymity; some social media sites demand 'real user' authentication. Is content valuable if its creator cannot be identified? Might anonymity mitigate some of the privacy loss that individuals experience when social media is archived? We included some questions about creator anonymity in our institutional archiving scenarios.

Figure 6 aggregates the responses to three related questions about anonymity. First, respondents reacted in a positive way to the requirement that the Library of Congress anonymize book (or product) reviews it archives from Amazon by removing the name or pseudonym of the reviewer. We speculate that respondents feel this may address concerns about privacy loss. The two other results confirm this finding about reviewer anonymity; respondents were ambivalent about restricting the ability of the Library of Congress to archive anonymous reviews of educational recordings. Furthermore, respondents tended to disagree with limits placed on the Library of Congress's efforts to archive Amazon book reviews to only those with real names attached.

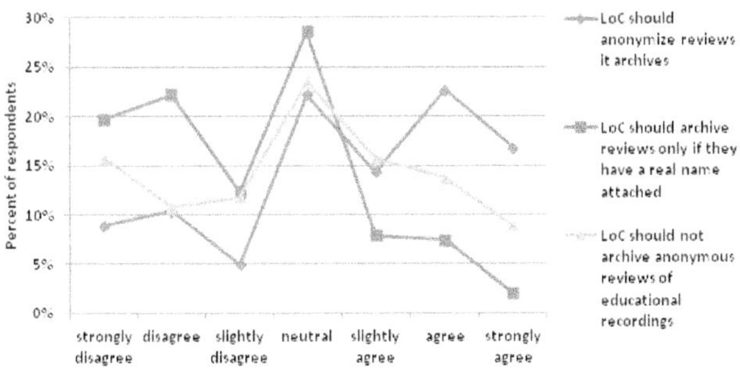

Figure 6. Exploring creator anonymity

These results also underscore the prevailing current of thought among respondents that a public institution should have an overriding ability to archive material for the public good. We will discuss this perspective in the next section.

Archiving associated content. One important property of social media—be it user-contributed photos, videos, reviews, or recordings—is that it may have associated content such as comments, ratings, tags, and other annotations that add value to the original item. Which restrictions should be imposed on archiving this additional content?

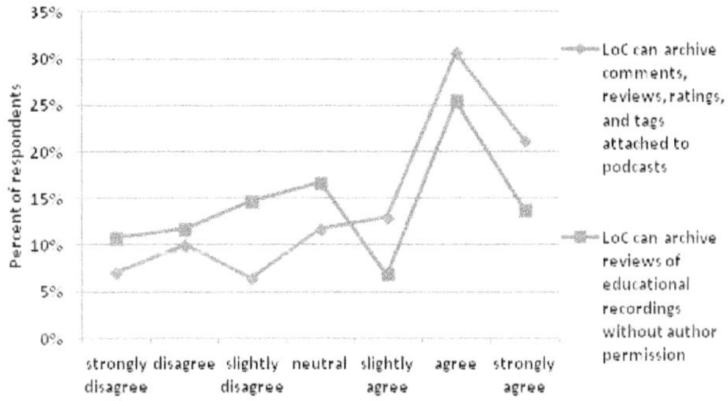

Figure 7. Archiving associated content

Figure 7 aggregates responses to two representative questions about whether the Library of Congress can archive this type of social metadata, with and without author permission. In the podcast survey, respondents were asked to evaluate whether the Library of Congress can archive the reviews, ratings, and tags that listeners associate with a podcast. They generally agreed that social metadata can be ingested along with the primary media. When we added the caveat that the social metadata would be ingested without asking the authors' permission (when educational recordings were archived), the effort became more controversial. In fact, many respondents raised the idea of creator permission when they answered the open-ended question described in the next section, possibly without realizing that social metadata contributors often cede their rights to the content as per the terms and conditions of many social media services.

3.3 Exclusion

The final open-ended question of the three recorded media surveys asked respondents to consider the general problem of archiving social media. Should the Library of Congress simply be able to archive any social media that's available today on the public Internet? If not, what should be excluded and why?

The surveys were lengthy, yet most of the respondents gave this question some thought; they seemed anxious to express their own opinions about whether institutions should be archiving social media as part of their mission, or whether this sort of archiving was an opportunistic incursion into individuals' private lives.

How did respondents reason about this question? How did they determine what should be excluded? Some (about 1/3 of the respondents) considered the purpose and mission of the Library of Congress as a public institution, often appealing to an aspirational notion of social good and everyday culture (although a few respondents, as we will discuss, did not think this sort of archiving fell within the Library's purview). Other respondents reasoned from the creator's perspective: about 1/5 thought that surely the Library should be obtaining permission from the media's creator. Still others considered the value—and, potentially, the veracity—of the material: is it worth it to gather seemingly trivial cultural detritus? A small number (about 5%) noted that the technology itself offers remedies to this problem: privacy settings and other mechanisms telegraph the individual's intent; these respondents thought the Library of Congress should use existing technological affordances to guide their efforts. Finally, about 10% of the respondents situated their answers in the legal concept of public domain, primarily indicating their belief that the Internet affords no copyright protection. We examine each of these stances in turn.

We began our analysis by open-coding the responses, attempting to capture the theme of each respondent's primary argument (and how it differed from the arguments other respondents had offered) [24]. Many of the respondents reasoned from several different vantage points, creating a nuanced set of exceptions and edge cases; we try to indicate a rough sense of how prevalent various perspectives were in the arguments. Generally, we only report on a particular point of view if it occurs in a meaningful number of responses (more than 1%); this way, we are able to indicate if a response is a true outlier. We identify the respondents according the survey (EDU, PC, or VC) and a respondent-specific ID number. Thus if the ID number matches, e.g. EDU007 and PC007, it means that Respondent 007 completed both the EDU and PC surveys. Duplicate responses from a single person completing different surveys are only counted once in computing the relative prominence of a response type.

3.3.1 The Creator's Perspective

It is not difficult to understand why many respondents took the creator's perspective, especially given the current climate of anti-piracy legislation, and the controversy surrounding the Library of Congress's efforts to archive the public Twitter feed. Respondents brought up two main facets of this perspective: permission and the implicit privacy of personal content, especially when it is emotionally resonant or may be damaging to the individual. Needless to say, there are many variations of each type of response; we explore only the main ones.

Permission. The need to obtain creator permission arose in about 20% of the responses. One respondent argued, "*The Library of Congress should not be able to archive personal imagery or opinionated media (audio, video, textual or otherwise) without the given consent of its owners. This is because everything created deserves to have proper credit by its creator, and if the creator doesn't want it archived that should be an available choice. The Library of Congress doesn't automatically own something just because they want it.*" [PC007]

Naturally respondents identified exceptions. Several respondents brought up mitigating factors such as the prevention of pedophilia or national security needs. A few also inserted consent earlier into the publication process: *"Maybe, if the media company supplies an option to opt out of future archiving then it should be honored.*" [EDU187] or later "*The Library of Congress should be able to archive anything that is freely available on the internet, but should provide the ability for the content creator to remove the content from the archive.*" [PC074] Currently this consent is part of many service providers' terms and conditions, but respondents remind us that institutional archiving is not something that's on their minds, even if they've read the fine print.

Anonymity is the flip side of permission: if a contributor does not dignify content with attribution, why would a public institution archive it? "*Anonymous videos or videos without consent should not be archived, as they violate freedom of speech.*" [VC005] Such arguments were relatively rare (only 4 occurred in the 3 surveys); these respondents seemed to be drawing on encounters with abusive anonymous comments on YouTube or blogs, and several also may have misunderstood 'freedom of speech.'

Privacy. About 1 in 7 respondents express a desire to protect the creator's privacy. These respondents argued that personal material shared as social media is *per se* private: "*Facebook pages, Twitter accounts, and any other social media on a personal level should not be archived. It is that person's private account and should not be messed with.*" [PC020] About 1 in 10 argued further that some social media types—e.g video, personal correspondence, or Facebook posts—are more private than others: "*…Videos are a lot more personal than anything written on paper so they should be treated more cautiously.*" [PC245]

A common theme running through privacy arguments—one that echoes Stutzman's example—is that this personal material is intended to be transient. That this transient material may become permanent is disquieting to about 3% of respondents, and to some, seemingly unfair: *"…It just seems wrong that something made when you are 15 would follow you forever"* [VC114]

Similarly, a few respondents pointed out that comments on social media were created in a context—in open discussion at a particular time, in a particular forum—and preserving them in an archive would serve to decontextualize them in such a way that is unfair to the creator: *"…Even though the comments are public, people making them think they will remain on that site and for the site members, not be archived."* [PC107]

Other creator-derived concerns. In addition to the need to obtain the creator's permission and a desire to protect the creator's privacy, a few respondents brought up other concerns such as the subjects' privacy (drawn from photography) and the concomitant need to seek the subjects' permission. Respondents also raised the potential need to protect the contributor's interests if the content is commercially valuable.

3.3.2 The Content Perspective

If a public institution is to invest significant resources in an archiving effort, to many it follows that the effort should be worthwhile; the content should be sufficiently valuable to merit attention or, from the standpoint of protecting society, it should not perpetrate harm. In this case, the content's creator or source is not a factor; rather, the content speaks for itself. We explore elements of the two major content perceptions: the content should be intrinsically valuable and the content should cause no harm.

High-value content. Some respondents (under 10%) thought in terms of inherent value to society, while others posed examples of content or content genres worthy of archival efforts. For example, PC153 argued that the Library of Congress should not archive "*Anything that is not considered public record, or that does not provide some inherent value to society. No one cares what status updates someone in Colorado writes about the sandwich they ate for lunch.*" Others kept their responses generic. For example, EDU078 responded, "*I think if [social media content] could benefit someone else, then yes, [it] should be archived."*

Because the scenarios focused on recorded material, some respondents thought in terms of recorded genres: *"If the Library of Congress deems something is worth archiving, I believe they should be able use it. Things only available online, perhaps even youtube. If the recordings offer educational opportunities for the future posterity, I think its [sic] a good thing.*" [EDU046] Note the emphasis on unique content: EDU046 is consciously excluding material that has migrated from published physical media—the respondent may be thinking of movie clips, commercials, or excerpts from published forms like movies or TV shows. Another respondent's reaction demonstrates a lack of understanding about the value of archives, "*Youtube is so popular there would be no point in archiving any of the videos that are already available to public unless it pertains to specific things that may be helpful.*" [VC048]

Some respondents did not feel all public content should be archived; specific types were excluded as *per se* valueless. Tweets and YouTube videos were particular targets of this reasoning, e.g. "*Although things like Twitter are generally public, I think the Library of Congress archiving individuals' accounts is tacky and in poor taste. A podcast or an essay is different than a tweet.*" [PC166] and "*Personal videos because I find it excessive and unnecessary.*" [VC083]

Others argued that the content of social media services such as Facebook is trivial, or that the few nuggets are obscured by the weight of the mundane, e.g.: "*People who really post worthwhile information usually don't bother with facebook. Of course there may be exceptions, and I believe that those should be taken into account, but as a general rule it is not worthwhile to comb through millions of facebook posts just for the few good ones.*" [PC025]

Thus arguments about social media content value frequently shifted the ground to what might be historically important (and what would make it so, say Obama's tweets). Here the respondent sometimes considered the content creator as a property of the content, not as a stakeholder in the archival process, e.g.: "*...social media from the average citizen [should only be saved] if the person is a political power or somehow of historical significance (IE President of the nation, a nobel prize winner etc). Otherwise I think recording the average persons tweets etc would just be a colossal waste of time.*" [EDU035]

Content veracity. Content veracity was tied to value in a little over 7% of the responses. Opinions, these respondents opined, are not worth the bits they are stored as: "*I don't think opinions should be archived if they are not useful to future generations.... This is the reason I don't read blogs. If a person does not have sound experience and knowledge in the topic being presented (say a podcast for example), then I have no interest in wasting my time reading about how they 'feel' about said podcast.*" [PC008]

Do no harm. Content veracity also formed the linchpin to many arguments about the harm done by social media. Inaccurate content, about 6% of respondents argued, is inherently pernicious. "*Personal profiles [on Facebook] can be a deception.*" [PC131] We might speculate that either bad experiences with inaccurate information, or accounts of such experiences, led some respondents to limit archival information to that which has been verified: "*I'm not sure why the Library of Congress would be involved in social media. ... I think the Library of Congress is more useful by keeping information that has reasonably been researched to know is true, as some of these things out there are not real.*" [EDU180] Using the same logic, several respondents argued against keeping anything that is incomplete.

Just as inaccurate information may be regarded as pernicious, so too is material that is considered either biased, slanderous, offensive, racially-charged, or would incite lawless behavior, e.g. "*I think social media that contains racial bias or any kind of prejudiced based content shouldn't be archived.*" [PC043] and "*...Items that could incite lawlessness, promote illegal activities or provide information that could be used detrimentally against the welfare of others may be candidates for information that should be withheld.*" [EDU040]

Pornography was called out as a particular type of social media content that shouldn't be archived by a public institution (social media sites themselves seem to expend considerable effort on anti-pornography policies). Some respondents were concerned that no offensive material be accidentally (or purposefully) harvested in the name of social media preservation, e.g., "*[no] Porn, off-color, anything that could harm a child or person if shown [should be included in social media archive].*" [VC024]

Again, many of these perceptions seem misaligned with the purpose of archives, or perhaps confounding the idea of an archive with the notion of a reference like Wikipedia.

3.3.3 The Technology Perspective

Social media services usually include mechanisms such as user authorization and privacy settings designed to protect their users' interests. Some sites (like Facebook) even do a certain amount of policing to encourage their users to stick with their real identities, and not to adopt personas based on fictitious characters (e.g. Nomi Malone from *Showgirls*), so the authorization is a meaningful association of a real person with the content they contribute.

Only 5% of the responses suggested that institutional archiving efforts should simply rely on authorization mechanisms and privacy settings to guide collection policies, e.g.: "*[Institutional archives should exclude] social media that has expressly been blocked by the user, such as Twitter profiles that are kept private. These types of profiles indicate the user's express wish not to have their information accessible to everyone.*" [PC246] Another response revealed concern about 'friends of friends' and the uncontrolled (and, practically speaking, uncontrollable) flow of personal information through these services:

> "*The Library of Congress should not be able to archive any types of social media content that is accessed through an authorized user but not available to the general public (i.e. Facebook, Myspace). I believe that information which users knowingly make available to everyone is fair game, but the line should be drawn when content is distributed to the Library of Congress by individuals with access to information not available to everyone. A user's friend on Facebook, for example, should not be able to share information not intended for the general public with the Library of Congress without the original poster's permission.*" [EDU154]

The permeability of privacy settings and other mechanisms to control personal information seemed to convince respondents that these mechanisms provide insufficient guidance to determine which content is intentionally public.

3.3.4 The Legal Perspective

As we saw in earlier studies, a significant portion of respondents consider material posted on the Internet to be in the public domain; around 10% explicitly say so, and as many as 1/3 imply it. In this case, they may feel that anything public should have no restrictions, especially in view of the Library of Congress's role as a governmental institution. We divide these arguments into two (uneven) camps: the small number of respondents (under 3%) who feel that the Library of Congress is charged with maintaining the public record, and the much larger number who feel that anything on the Internet that is publicly accessible falls into the public domain.

Public record. Public record arguments have at their heart the idea that institutions like the Library of Congress are free to gather published (and public) information as they see fit, as per their defined role as archival institutions, and that this overrides interests of the individual. In other words, the Library of Congress is serving a role which gives it special dispensation to curate the public record. PC059 maintained that archiving should proceed without restrictions: "*Though the LoC is performing these actions with public fund, people should consider that anything digitally recorded and uploaded to the internet may exist outside their control "forever"*". Similarly, PC170 said, "*...the Library of*

Congress should be able to archive any public information they would like. Due to public information status." PC258 simply declared, "*I feel all social media is public record.*" Finally, VC231 likened YouTube videos to print books: "*Once the video is published for all to see, then the Library of Congress should treat videos as they treat printed material.*"

Alternatively, a small number of respondents (around 3%) were concerned about how copyright law applied to this type of endeavor. In so doing, they often revealed a fairly loose grasp of copyright and its purpose: "*They should not be able to archive media, like music, that is copyrighted because it is not in their jurisdiction.*" [PC081] There is also a perception that the Library of Congress serves a regulatory function, and that the materials it gathers are some sort of yardstick for measuring the truth (this goes hand in hand with our earlier discussion that this type of archive should somehow be factual and accurate): "*I think it is important for the Lobrary [sic] of Congress to regulate material.*" [PC244] One respondent even felt a social media archive would have an evidentiary role: "*they can go to their archive files for evidence.*" [PC095] It is not clear who 'they' refers to, although several respondents took 'they' to mean Congress (in keeping with history, whether by intention or accident).

Public domain. On the flip side of this public record argument, other respondents reasoned that because some social media is part of the public Internet, the content is all in the public domain. Why should restrictions be imposed on the Library of Congress that are beyond those applied to everyday users? "*Once something is on the Web, it belongs to the Web users,*" wrote VC141. VC169 explained, "*I think if someone puts something publicly on the internet, they have no control over how it is used in future. Therefore, anything that an individual chooses to put on the public domain is in fact public. If someone does not want something archived they should keep it in the private domain.*" Public domain, private domain: if the content is accessible to any of us, it is ours.

3.3.5 Social Good

Although many respondents implicitly considered the role of the Library of Congress in their reasoning about what should be in a social media archive, some evoked it explicitly. What are the intentions of a public institution when it gathers material that is potentially private, that is often personal, and that might be damaging to individuals? "*They should be able to [archive social media] if they have good intentions as far as what they will do with that info...*" [PC112]

Around 10% of the respondents argued that the Library of Congress should be able to archive everything as a matter of principle ("*If they archive some they should get them all!*" [EDU156]), either because it all has documentary importance ("*... it will all be useful for research.*" [PC049]) or because taken as a whole, social media content has unique cultural value ("*...future generations can use all types of social media to learn about our current time.*" [PC071]). However, respondents also acknowledged counterarguments about content value, e.g.:

> "*If given the space, most things should be documented. However trivial it may be.*" [PC030]

> "*...Podcasts... interviews... even goofy user videos are all part of society/culture and worth archiving for future accessibility.*" [PC157]

> "*The Library of Congress should really keep at least a sample of everything. We are creating culture and history. No matter how some people feel about a certain subject or genre, nothing should be excluded.*" [PC181]

> "*The Library of Congress is charged with (among other things), recording our history. History is made by citizens every day and social media is a good way to capture this history.*" [PC193]

One way to mitigate perceived damage is to separate preservation and access. Several respondents made this separation explicit—that not everyone should have access to the archive—and wrote that the data should be "*well protected.*" [PC112]

Naturally in the current political climate there will be nay-sayers about the value and mission of governmental institutions. Two responses questioned not just the effort's Herculean nature, but also whether archival institutions should exist and be involved in the affairs of individuals. "*I don't believe the LoC should exist as it's not a private institution.*" [PC117] Another respondent restored the responsibility to the individual (without considering that the archive would fulfill a larger role than keeping personal material safe for oneself): "*I feel that this should be a person's own responsibility and that the government should have nothing to do with this... There are plenty of private digital vaults around for anyone to avail themselves of, if they wished.*" [PC255]

4. DISCUSSION

Personal experience with social media, coupled with a growing unease about larger issues such as privacy, piracy, the control of user contributed content, and the ubiquity of technology in modern life, has greatly complicated institutional efforts to archive social media. [11] By fielding a set of six surveys, we have been able to paint a more complete and nuanced picture of attitudes toward current and future efforts.

First, we have learned that content type matters: different content types evoke different responses when we propose that they be saved on a grand scale for posterity. Two dimensions guide and constrain how respondents react to different content types:

(1) How personal is the genre or type perceived to be? On one hand, the more personal (and seemingly transient) the information is, the more it raises the threat of additional privacy loss, and on the other hand, the less certain respondents are about its long-term value to society. We have also seen that not all elements of a social media genre are equal. Comments, for example, may seem more private than the primary media.

(2) How familiar is the genre or type? How much experience do respondents have with it in their everyday lives? Have they created it as well as simply consumed it? In our photo survey, we learned that respondents were well able to rationalize individual instances of reuse when they understood the motivation and had engaged in it themselves [17]. In this set of surveys, we have become increasingly convinced that it is familiarity with the creation and reuse of a genre or type that leads respondents to come up with plausible examples to reason from. Furthermore, the scenarios that we use to set the stage seem to have a substantial effect on respondents' attitudes to more general questions about institutional archiving.

Next, we have seen a need to tease apart collection-building and access. These distinctions do not occur to respondents naturally. When will a collection be used, by whom, and for what? Certain limitations on access would seem to ease anxieties about gathering, ingesting, and processing the content in the first place.

"*This is just too hard of a problem*" complained one respondent. The idea of this survey was not to throw the question back onto individuals, but rather to help institutions frame archiving efforts so that boundaries match the public's expectations. What are the features that people care about? For example, the idea of harm (either emotional or professional) arises when respondents imagine their social media content taken out of context; that they are ambivalent about the preservation of hate speech seems a reflection of larger cultural impetuses, but not necessarily aligned with the mission of any archiving effort.

In the end, the surveys highlight most profoundly the need to help people envision boundaries—collection boundaries, access boundaries, issues of identity and attribution, of permission and reuse. Most importantly, characterizing current attitudes will help us determine if these attitudes are changing with time and experience, and whether they are tied to demographic properties.

In practice, precautions like obtaining permission are not straightforward. The Preserving Virtual Worlds project noted that its efforts to obtain in-world permission were fraught with difficulty; they cite an at-best permission rate of 10% and at worst their efforts were met with hostility [19]. This reaction seems to stem from peoples' problems envisioning constructive reuse. Although constructive reuse by artists [13] and scholars [22] is within reach, our study suggests that respondents' imaginations about everyday reuse are shaped and constrained by their own experiences.

Broader still—extending beyond institutional archiving—is the perspective that much of this new content is viewed by its creators and consumers as largely personal, even as it is increasingly entangled in relationships with service providers that render it more closely akin to published content. Just as the web caused us to rethink the rhythm of fixity and fluidity [14], so too has social media caused us to reconsider the relationship between personal, shared, public, and published media.

5. ACKNOWLEDGEMENTS

This work was supported in part by National Science Foundation grant DUE-0938074.

6. REFERENCES

[1] Acquisti, A. and Grossklags, J. Privacy Attitudes and Privacy Behavior, in J. Camp and S. Lewis (Eds.) *The Economics of Information Security*, Kluwer, Boston, pp. 165-178.

[2] Boyle, J. *The Public Domain: Enclosing the Commons of the Mind*, Yale University Press, New Haven & London, 2008.

[3] Connelly K, Khalil A, Liu Y. "Do I Do What I Say?: Observed Versus Stated Privacy Preferences," *Proc. INTERACT 2007.*

[4] Downs, J., Holbrook, M., Sheng, S., and Cranor, L. Are your participants gaming the system?: Screening Mechanical Turk workers. *Proc. of CHI'10.* ACM, 2399-2402.

[5] Faridani, S., Bitton, E., Ryokai, K., and Goldberg, K. 2010. Opinion space: a scalable tool for browsing online comments. *Proc. of CHI '10.* ACM, 1175-1184.

[6] Gilbert, E. and Karahalios, K. Understanding Deja Reviewers. *Proc. of CSCW '10*, 225-228.

[7] Hill, B., Monroy-Hernandez, A., and Olson, K. Responses to Remixing on a Social Media Website. *Proc. AAAI Conference on Weblogs and Social Media.* 2010. 74-81.

[8] Ipeirotis, P. Analyzing the Amazon Mechanical Turk Marketplace. *ACM XRDS 17*, 2, Winter 2010.

[9] Jakobsson, M. (2009) Experimenting on Mechanical Turk: 5 How Tos. *ITWorld*, September 3, 2009.

[10] Java, A., Song, X., Finin, T. and Tseng, B. Why We Twitter: Understanding Microblogging Usage and Communities, *Proc. KDD'07*, ACM, 56-65.

[11] John, J.L., Rowlands, I., Williams, P., Dean, K. *Digital Lives >> An Initial Synthesis version 0.2.* Digital Lives Research Paper Series, British Library, 3 March 2010.

[12] Kittur, A., Chi, E., and Suh, B. Crowdsourcing User Studies with Mechanical Turk. *Proc. of CHI'08.* ACM, 453-456.

[13] Lessig, L. *Remix: Making Art and Commerce Thrive in the Hybrid Economy*, Penguin, New York, 2008.

[14] Levy, D. "Fixed or Fluid: Document Stability and New Media." *Proc. ECHT'94*, 1994, 24-31.

[15] Library of Congress: Digital Preservation Video Series. 2010. *Digital Natives Explore Digital Preservation.*

[16] Marshall, C.C., and Shipman, F.M. 2011. Social media ownership: using Twitter as a window onto current attitudes and beliefs. *Proc. of CHI'11.* ACM, 1081-1090.

[17] Marshall, C.C., and Shipman, F.M. 2011. The ownership and reuse of visual media. *Proc. of JCDL'11.* ACM, 157-166.

[18] Marshall, C.C., and Shipman, F.M. 2011. Attitudes about Institutional Archiving of Social Media. Proc Archiving'11.

[19] McDonough, J., Olendorf, R., Kirschenbaum, M., Kraus, K., Reside, D., Donahue, R., Phelps, A., Egert, C., Lowood, H., Rojo, S. *Preserving Virtual Worlds Final Report.* 8/ 31/2010.

[20] Munson, S., Avrahami, D., Consolvo, S., Fogarty, J., Friedman, B., Smith, I. Attitudes toward online availability of US public records. dg.o '11, ACM Press, 2-9.

[21] Odom, W., Sellen, A., Harper, R., Thereska, E. Lost in Translation: Understanding the Possession of Digital Things in the Cloud. to appear in *Proc CHI 2012.*

[22] Owens, T. Tripadvisor rates Einstein: using the social web to unpack the public meanings of a cultural heritage site. *IJWC 8*, 1, 40 – 56.

[23] Shinen, B. Twitterlogical: The Misunderstandings of Ownership. http://www.canyoucopyrightatweet.com/

[24] Strauss, A. and Corbin, J. *Basics of Qualitative Research*, Sage Publications, 1998.

[25] Stutzman, F. Twitter and the Library of Congress. http://fstutzman.com/2010/04/14/twitter-and-the-library-of-congress/.

To Envisage and Design the Transition from a Digital Archive System Developed for Domain Experts to one for Non-domain Users

Maristella Agosti
Department of Information Engineering
University of Padua
Via Gradenigo, 6/a
Padua, Italy
maristella.agosti@unipd.it

Nicola Orio
Department of Cultural Heritage
University of Padua
Piazza Capitaniato, 7
Padua, Italy
nicola.orio@unipd.it

ABSTRACT

Diverse digital resources are commonly used by different types of users. It is common practice to develop those application having in mind a set of requirements for a specific target category of users. We envisaged and designed the IPSA archive and system using a similar approach: the identification of a set of requirements for researchers in illuminated manuscripts as a target group of domain professional users. The IPSA system has been in use as a research tool by domain professionals. The consideration that the content of the archive managed by the IPSA system could be of interest for other types of users suggested reconsidering its approach to envisage a new system designed around the same archive of illuminated manuscripts for their access by diverse categories of users. The paper reports on the work that was conducted to re-design and re-engineer the system to match requirements and expectations of non-domain users.

Categories and Subject Descriptors

H.3.7 [**Information Storage and Retrieval**]: Digital Libraries - User issues

General Terms

Human Factors, Design, Experimentation

Keywords

Digital Archives, Illuminated Manuscripts, Digital Archive Systems, Evaluation, Categories of Users

1. INTRODUCTION AND MOTIVATIONS

The availability of digital multimedia resources of cultural heritage poses challenging questions about the kind of interaction that needs to be foreseen to make them available to distinct categories of users. This interaction is likely to depend on the level of expertise of the users, which may range from a general interest towards multimedia resources to a deep knowledge through scientific research.

IPSA (*Imaginum Patavinae Scientiae Archivum*: archive of images of the Paduan science) is a digital archive and system of illuminated manuscripts that was envisaged and developed as a scientific tool for the analysis of the role played by the Paduan school during the Middle Ages and the Renaissance in the spread of the new scientific method in different sciences, from medicine to astronomy and botany, through the study of illuminated manuscripts [5]. IPSA was developed for use by professional researchers who are scholars in history of medieval art specialised in history of illumination. The aims and the results of IPSA of interest for the digital library area are presented in [1, 2, 3].

IPSA is a combination of digitised images of manuscripts and related metadata information, and its content can be of interest to a much larger group of users than the initial target of the work. In line with this consideration, IPSA was selected, together with the collection named "1641 Depositions" of the Trinity College Dublin (Ireland), to contribute to the design, development and evaluation of the innovative research environment that is under design and development in the context of CULTURA (Cultivating Understanding and Research through Adaptivity)[1], an EU funded STREP project which was launched in February 2011 and which is now under development [4].

CULTURA aims at personalisation and community-aware adaptivity for digital humanities through the implementation of innovative adaptive services in an interactive environment, which generality is going to be demonstrated by the fact of supporting both the IPSA and 1641 Deposition collections, which differ in morphology, language, modality and metadata [6]. The intention is to offer genuine user empowerment and different levels of engagement with digital cultural heritage collections and communities. The groups that are taken into account include:

- Professional researchers: scholars, academics, tutors and historical curators.
- Non-domain professional researchers: same as above though in a different domain.

[1] `http://www.cultura-strep.eu/`

- Student community: post-doctoral, postgraduate and undergraduate students.
- Non-professional researchers: members of a historical/cultural society, authors, publishers, members of the public with an interest in history or in arts.
- Interested members of the general public. This can include both adults and school children.

The study of making IPSA, the 1641 Depositions collections and the software applications available to non-domain users will provide useful input for two different objectives: 1) the re-designing of those applications to generalise them for future use with pertinent but diverse cultural heritage collections, and 2) the injection into the CULTURA project of new knowledge on user requirements for designing and developing a new software environment which will be of interest and use to new types of user groups who have never previously had experience with this sort of collection.

2. IPSA DIGITAL ARCHIVE SYSTEM

The IPSA digital archive system was made available on its stabilised form in 2005 and from then on it has been used for research purposes by history of art researchers. Over the years the collection of manuscripts and images has been incremented.

Following the launch of the CULTURA project, the IPSA digital archive system was re-engineered to bring it up-to-date with the new technologies that in the meanwhile have been made available, while the underlying model of content management has been for the moment kept as reported in [2]. One challenging aspect of the work that is under development is to check if the actual functionalities – search facilities, content organization inside the graphical interface, navigation tools – are sufficient to meet the requirements of new categories of users. If the functionalities prove to be insufficient to deal with the new requirements, the model will also be reviewed and a new model will be developed.

Taking into consideration that users mainly focus their attention on the graphical interface when interacting with a digital resource, the system interface has been re-designed to make it more in-line with recent advancements. The new IPSA user interface aimed at simplicity and easy user accessibility. For instance, the search functionality based on cataloguing records has been paired with a free-text search engine, which is expected to be more intuitive for non specialist users.

Figure 1 shows a screenshot of how illustrations are presented by the present IPSA Web interface. It displays relevant metadata, general information and a link to the manuscript containing the illumination, as well as a tool for visually exploring the digital image. Through the interface it is also possible to create links between similar images; for instance, Figure 1 shows in its lower-right part an existing link with a similar illumination that belongs to a different manuscript.

3. NON-DOMAIN USER EXPERIMENTS

As part of the goals of the CULTURA project, we investigated whether IPSA features, which were developed for domain professional researchers, can be of interest also to non-domain users. To this end, we selected a group of five non-domain researchers divided into two classes: one expert in a related research area – i.e. painting of the same historical period – and four master students in archival science, without a specific interest in the content of the digital archive. During the interaction with IPSA, the participants were asked to try out all the search facilities, browse the illustrations of manuscripts, and access the metadata related to both images and manuscripts. We preferred to let the participants freely interact with the IPSA digital archive, without fulfilling particular research tasks because this might have biased the evaluation.

Participant feedback was gathered through open interviews which were carried out after the participants had extensively tested the IPSA digital archive. As general guidelines, participants were asked to describe their initial expectations, to report problems encountered during the interaction, and to provide suggestions on how additional functionalities could enhance their access to the digital collection.

We analyzed the transcriptions of the interviews with the main goal of highlighting possible overlaps between the requirements of the users of the two considered classes. In the rest of this section we report the findings of this effort and in Section 4 we report the re-engineering results on the IPSA system after having generalised the findings to give directions in re-designing some aspects of user interaction with the system.

3.1 Effect of Computer Skills

The first outcome of the experiment with non-domain users is that competence in the use of automatic tools plays an important role in the way users interact with the system. In particular, specialists in other research areas show a *resistance to change* the way they interact with digital resources. The presence of multimedia content available for inspection and analysis was considered an additional difficulty in the interaction, because users were accustomed to searching for bibliographic values rather than obtaining and studying images directly through the interface to the digital archive. This shift in the interaction paradigm may give rise to a lack of interest towards the collection. This result can be taken into consideration by specialists designing a new multimedia digital archive.

In contrast, master students are more accustomed to interact with multimedia systems, and did not find it problematic to access multimedia information directly from the digital archive. Their approach with the digital archive content was biased by their habit of interacting with large multimedia collections available on the Web. Their requirements were more related to the need for search facilities that are typically available in multimedia systems. For instance they highlight the possibility of obtaining recommendations based on users' tags, although social tagging does not easily apply to the cultural heritage domain because of the kind of digital objects and the limited number of users.

3.2 Navigation Tools

An additional set of requirements regarded the exploitation of links within and outside the digital archive. This finding extends the requirements of specialized users, who probably already have other tools to access the relevant literature or other digital resources. In the case of non-domain users, the need to retrieve additional information can be explained by the fact that non-domain users have only a general in-

Figure 1: Example of the IPSA Web application displaying the image of a grapevine, pertinent metadata and the link towards a similar image.

terest towards the digital content of the archive, which can be enhanced by providing a larger amount of information, even if it goes beyond the goals of the digital archive itself. In particular, the possibility of using the digital archive as a starting point to browse other related collection was considered of interest.

The possibility of exploiting links to navigate the digital archive content was considered of interest as well. In particular, non-domain users need different ways to retrieve multimedia information. To this end, the possibility of expressing relations between images, which was a requirement also for domain professional users, may become a valuable tool which allows casual users to retrieve information of interest. A lack of knowledge on the domain of the cultural heritage resources managed by the archive system may prevent users from retrieving information, while the presence of annotations made by experts can fill this gap.

3.3 Need for Textual Information

A final outcome, which might be extended to other collections in the cultural heritage domain, is that multimedia information – digital images in the case of IPSA – is not sufficient to raise interest when it is not paired with accompanying textual information. Both non-domain specialists and master students suggested directions in which the digital archive should be enriched to be more attractive.

Non-domain specialists asked for analytic descriptions of all the multimedia content of the digital archive, to make users aware of every characteristic of the images studied, to highlight relations with other research fields, and basically to follow and understand the research process of specialized users. The possibility of obtaining different graphical representations and to personalize the digital archive content is of interest mainly if it is mediated by specialized users. Although this finding can be related to the degree of computer skills, it is important to note that non-domain researchers are more interested in how the digital archive can track the research process than in the content itself.

Master students in archival science had a bias, as can be expected, towards bibliographic values. In particular, they showed an interest in the way bibliographic records were created, their authorship, the motivations behind attributions and so on. Also in this case, the approach to IPSA content depended on the particular field of interest of non-domain users, where the research work of specialized users played a major role, notwithstanding the fact that the content of the digital archive was perceived of important cultural value.

4. INITIAL FEEDBACK ON THE DIGITAL ARCHIVE SYSTEM

In relation to what has emerged from the initial experiments that have been completed, most of the IPSA system functions have been considered of interest, but some of the interaction functions needed to be re-engineered and they are at present used for the development of new system features. In particular, some new presentation features were requested and have been developed.

The search results are presented as a paginated list of results in textual format as for many search engines or information access systems, in this case the list also contains the illustration subject, the signature mark of the work and the links to the illustration and to the general information on the manuscript. A new alternative visualisation of results was envisaged where the results need to be presented as a "wall" of thumbnails of the illustrations, incrementally loaded in slots at user request, without generating a new page request.

The page showing a single work contains the textual metadata of the work and the thumbnails of the illustrations for each page of the work. Initially, this wall of illustrations was designed for showing all thumbnails at a time. This organization proved to be very inefficient because it caused server overloading when manuscripts contaning hundreds of llustrations were displayed. Now it has been reorganized to incrementally load the images at user request in slots of thirty thumbnails.

A different problem emerged in the page showing a single illustration. The page shows the textual metadata of the illustration and allows the user to explore the image. By mousing over the thumbnail, the user can explore and zoom a magnified version of the image. The magnified image was rendered at the loading of the page, scaling on the server-side the full version of the image. This allowed a personalized rendering, customized according to the screen resolution and the domain professional user preferences. Unfortunately this process was too slow for an effective user experience and too heavily loaded the server in the presence of many concurrent requests of non-domain users. So we decided to pre-render the magnified image, using a predeterminate fixed screen resolution. This now allows fluid navigation with very fast page loading and much improved user satisfaction.

Other improvements are planned in the near future for the feature of creating links between images, and for a totally new feature that will allow easy navigation and comparison of a set of images. For these features users need more space on the screen for viewing more than a single image at the maximum possible size, and for maintaining a clear context during these multi-step operations. So we are planning for a design that could use all the horizontal space available in the page.

Lastly, a contextual online help system is going to be introduced for non-domain users. The help on single elements of the page will be shown in tooltips. The help of a feature, usually attached to a page, will be shown in a sidebar that the user will activate or hire as he needs. All the help text will be multi-lingual and managed through an internal content management system.

5. CONCLUSIONS AND FUTURE WORK

Multimedia resources for cultural heritage play a double role. On the one hand, they allow specialized users to carry out their research, keeping track of their research results. On the other hand, they play a major role in the dissemination of cultural heritage to a wider public. In order to highlight the requirements a digital resource for cultural heritage has to meet, we carried out an initial evaluation with two groups of non-domain users of the IPSA digital archive system, initially developed as a research tool for domain professional users. Through the initial evaluation, non-domain users highlighted a number of functionalities that might enhance their experience with multimedia content, and those findings are used at present to complete an initial extension of the IPSA system.

The second evaluation with the other groups that have to be taken into account in the context of the CULTURA environment is going to be conducted to collect new information on the way non-domain users are interested in interacting with digital culture heritage resources. We imagine that the findings of this second evaluation will produce other insights to be taken into consideration in the design of innovative adaptive services. When the results in terms of data and method will be available, it will be possible to consider if the method is general enough to be applied in other contexts.

Finally, an important outcome of this evaluation was the role of specialized users as mediators between the general public and the digital content. The same tools used by researchers to carry out their studies should be exploited to enhance the interaction of non-domain users, who can take advantage of the results of scientific research to improve their enjoyment of multimedia content.

Acknowledgements

The authors are most grateful to the anonymous referees for their very helpful comments.

The work reported has been partially supported by the CULTURA project, as part of the Seventh Framework Programme of the European Commission, grant agreement no. 269973. The authors would like to thank the CULTURA partners for the useful discussions on aspects related to the evaluation with non-domain users.

6. REFERENCES

[1] M. Agosti, L. Benfante, and N. Orio. IPSA: A Digital Archive of Herbals to Support Scientific Research. In T. M. T. Sembok and alii, editors, *Proc. of the Int. Conf. on Asian Digital Libraries*, volume 2911 of *LNCS*, pages 253–264. Springer, 2003.

[2] M. Agosti, N. Ferro, and N. Orio. Annotating Illuminated Manuscripts: an Effective Tool for Research and Education. In M. Marlino and alii, editors, *Proc. 5th ACM/IEEE Joint Conf. on Digital Libraries*, pages 121–130. ACM Press, New York, USA, 2005.

[3] M. Agosti, N. Ferro, and N. Orio. Graph-based Automatic Suggestion of Relationships among Images of Illuminated Manuscripts. In H. Haddad, editor, *Proc. of the ACM Symposium on Applied Computing*, pages 1063–1067. ACM Press, New York, USA, 2006.

[4] M. Agosti and N. Orio. The CULTURA project: CULTivating Understanding and Research through Adaptivity. In *Digital Libraries and Archives - 7th Italian Research Conference, IRCDL 2011. Revised Papers*, pages 111–114. Springer, 2011.

[5] G. Mariani Canova. La cultura universitaria padovana e la nascita del realismo nell'immagine botanica. *Atti e memorie dell'Accademia di Storia della Farmacia*, XX(3):198–212, 2002.

[6] E. O'Neill, M. Sweetnam, O. Conlan, S. Lawless, A. O'Connor, M. Ó'Siochrú, J. Ohlmeyer, and V. Wade. Towards Multi-Dimensional Adaptation of Digitised Historical Content. In *Proc. of the Supporting Digital Humanities 2011 Conf.*, Copenhagen, DK, 2011.

Visualizing Digital Collections at Archive-It

Kalpesh Padia
kpadia@cs.odu.edu

Yasmin AlNoamany
yasmin@cs.odu.edu

Michele C. Weigle
mweigle@cs.odu.edu

Department of Computer Science
Old Dominion University
Norfolk, VA 23529

ABSTRACT

Archive-It, a subscription service from the Internet Archive, allows users to create, maintain and view digital collections of web resources. The current interface of Archive-It is largely text-based, supporting drill-down navigation using lists of URIs. To provide an overview of each collection and highlight the collection's underlying characteristics, we present four alternate visualizations (image plot with histogram, wordle, bubble chart and timeline). The sites in an Archive-It collection may be organized by the collection curator into groups for easier navigation. However, many collections do not have such groupings, making them difficult to explore. We introduce a heuristics-based categorization for such collections.

Categories and Subject Descriptors

H.3.5 [**On-line Information Services**]: Commercial services; H.3.7 [**Digital Libraries**]: Collection; H.5.2 [**User Interfaces**]: Graphical user interfaces

General Terms

Human Factors

Keywords

Digital collections, information visualization, bubble chart, timeline, image plot, wordle

1. INTRODUCTION

Archive-It[1] is a subscription service developed by the Internet Archive to allow institutions to harvest and preserve collections of digital content. For each collection, Archive-It provides a listing of all URIs in the collection along with the number of times and dates over which each site was archived. Archive-It also provides full-text search of archived sites, allowing users to quickly search for topics of interest within a collection or spanning multiple collections. However, the organization of a collection is dependent upon the collection's curator. If the curator has organized URIs into groups and assigned subjects, coverage, and creator tags, Archive-It provides filtering of the URIs on the left-side of the listing page (Figure 1, foreground, Human Rights collection[2]). If the curator has not defined such groups or tags, then there are no filtering options available (Figure 1, background, Pakistan Floods collection[3]). If there are no groups defined or if there are a large number of sites in a group, exploration of the collection can be cumbersome.

Figure 1: Archive-It's interface

We present an alternate interface for exploring Archive-It collections. This interface consists of multiple visualizations, namely image plot with histogram, wordle, bubble chart, and timeline. These visualizations help to provide an overview of each collection and highlight the collection's underlying characteristics, allowing the user to progressively gain insight into the collection. For those collections that lack a curator-defined grouping, we provide a heuristics-based categorization to make the new visualizations more meaningful. To test this interface, we picked several Archive-It collections that differ widely from each other. The collections used and their characteristics are listed in Table 1.

[1]http://www.archive-it.org

[2]http://archive-it.org/collections/1068

[3]http://archive-it.org/collections/2836

2. RELATED WORK

Considerable research has been dedicated towards developing visualizations for viewing and querying documents, and towards graphical querying and browsing of results [1, 2]. Jatowt et al. [3] describe a browser for viewing past web resources with changes animated on a timeline. Popular web archives such as Archive-It, Internet Archive[4], California Digital Library[5], and Library of Congress[6] provide a good user interface for searching through the collections, however they still use list view as their main interface which makes it difficult for users to gain insight about the whole collection. One exception, the UK Web Archive[7], provides a 3D wall visualization for selected collections, allowing interaction through zooming.

3. DESIGN

Our approach for an alternate interface for viewing Archive-It collections consists of visualizations and heuristics-based categorization of sites.

3.1 Visualizations

We have created four different visualizations for collections in Archive-It viz. image plot with histogram, wordle, bubble chart, and timeline, presented in an integrated interface allowing users to switch between visualizations via the filters tab (Figure 2, black band at bottom).

3.1.1 Image plot with histogram

The *image plot with histogram* view (Figure 2) is an implementation of an inverted stacked bar chart to represent all sites in a collection in a graphical manner. The chart is divided based on the collection's defined groups. This representation allows the user to explore the collection by viewing a screenshot of a recent version of each archived site. Each screenshot is linked to Archive-It's list of archived versions of that site. The inverted representation allows the user to see both larger and smaller groups side by side. Since it is likely that not all sites will be viewable in a single window, a resizable histogram in the bottom right corner shows the number of sites in each group, so that the user gains an overview of the distribution of sites over the groups.

3.1.2 Wordle

Hovering over any image in the image plot reveals a *wordle* [5] (Figure 2 overlay) summarizing the content discussed on the site. For multimedia content in the collection, the wordle summarizes the comments (if present). This wordle representation aids the understanding of a site in the collection by supplementing the visual representation provided by the image plot. Analyzing various wordles allows the user to quickly grasp the key ideas of the collection.

3.1.3 Bubble chart

The *bubble chart* visualization (Figure 3) provides a quick summary of the collection by displaying each group in the collection as a bubble, where the size of the bubble represents the number of sites in each group. The number of total sites, archived copies, and duration over which the collection has been constructed is also visible to the user below the bubble chart. Each bubble links to Archive-It's default list of sites in that group, allowing the user to quickly filter through the collection by group.

[4]http://www.archive.org
[5]http://www.cdlib.org
[6]http://lcweb2.loc.gov/diglib/lcwa/html/lcwa-home.html
[7]http://www.webarchive.org.uk/ukwa

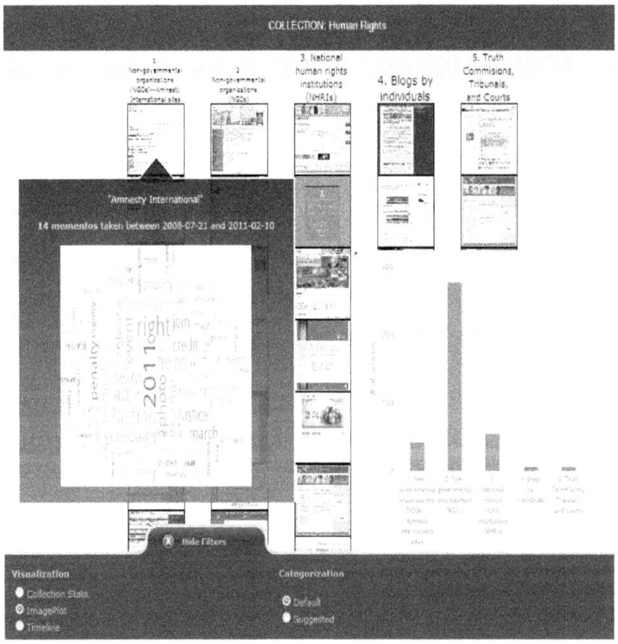

Figure 2: Image plot with histogram visualization for the Human Rights collection, showing the wordle for the highlighted site.

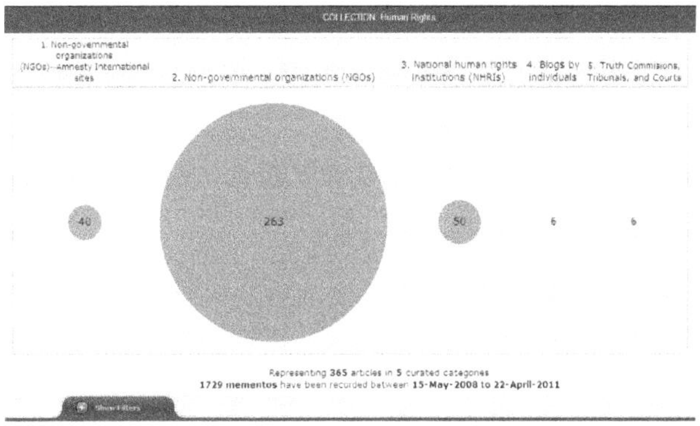

Figure 3: Bubble chart visualization for the Human Rights collection.

3.1.4 Timeline

The previous visualizations provide a quick statistical summary (bubble chart) and content summary (image plot with histogram, wordle) of the collection. However, curators may be interested in discovering how the collection developed over time to correlate events in history with the organization of the collection. We provide a *timeline* visualization (Figure 4) for visualizing the development of the collection over time. In this visualization, each site is represented as a single horizontal line, the length of which denotes the duration over which its archived copies have been captured.

ID	Collection Name	Time Span	Groups	URI Domains	Sites
11	South Dakota Government	3 Days	1	50	88
12	State Minnesota Sites	3 Weeks	1	6	6
13	Ari Salomon Archive	1 Day	1	1	1
194	NC State Government Web Site Archive	4 Months	1	451	609
499	Archive Montana: Preserving State Agency Websites	15 Years	36	132	144
667	The New York Greens	1 Day	1	1	1
677	Actors Equity Association	1 Day	1	1	1
1068	Human Rights	3 Years	5	341	365
1621	Chile Earthquake	1 Day	1	13	19
2323	Jasmine Revolution - Tunisia 2011	5 Months	4	147	223
2836	Pakistan Floods (2011)	20 Days	1	253	623

Table 1: Example collections used for developing and testing the visualizations.

Each point on the line represents an archived copy of the site. Hovering over a point displays a list of archives of other sites captured on that same day. A curator can easily see the growth of a collection over time by looking at site density and analyzing the addition (or removal) of sites from the collection.

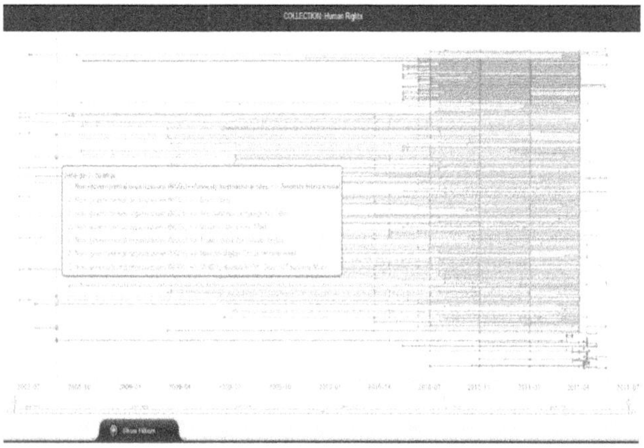

Figure 4: Timeline visualization for the Human Rights collection.

3.2 Heuristics-based categorization

Several Archive-It collections do not have the sites of the collection organized into groups (*e.g.*, Pakistan Floods collection), making it difficult for the user to explore the collection. Thus, we provide an option of exploring the collection using a heuristics-based categorization. The usefulness of URIs for webpage classification has been demonstrated before [4]. We implement a similar approach. Our rules for heuristics-based categorization are based on the hostname component of URI. While most rules were run on all collections, certain rules were applied only to specific collections. Examples of our categorization rules are below:

- If the hostname contains facebook, twitter, or wiki, group the site under "Social Media".
- If the hostname indicates a news site, such as bbc, cnn, nytimes, group the site under "News Web Sites".
- If the hostname contains blog or wordpress, group the site under "Blogs".
- If the hostname contains youtube or dailymotion, group the site under "Videos".

We also developed rules based on the top level domain name (TLD) of a website. For example, the sites in Collection 11, South Dakota Government, were grouped based on the TLD. All sites with a TLD ".gov" were grouped as government web sites and those with the TLD ".edu" were grouped as education web sites. We also developed specific rules for particular collections. For example, Collection 194, NC State Government, has specific rules for the "North Carolina Web Sites" group. If we were unable to group a site using any predefined (either generic or specific) rule, it was grouped under "Others". Such heuristics-based categorization is helpful in organizing the collection, and also in helping users understand which sources and what media types contribute the most to a collection.

4. CASE STUDIES

From the list of collections in Table 1, we highlight two collections to demonstrate how our interface can expose hidden characteristics and provide meaningful insight about the collection to both users and curators. One collection is well-curated and one did not have any curator-defined groups.

4.1 Collection: Human Rights

The Human Rights collection (ID:1068) is a large collection built over a period of 3 years and is an example of a well-curated collection. Due to its large size (365 sites, 1729 archived copies, 5 groups), it can be overwhelming for the user to understand the common topics discussed in the collection, identify the most active sites (and groups), and observe the collection's growth over time.

Figures 2-4 show the various visualizations for this collection (image plot, bubble chart, and timeline, respectively). By looking at the image representation of sites in the collection (Figure 2), the user can get visual feedback and easily locate a site of interest. Upon hovering over any site, the associated wordle effectively summarizes the content, allowing the user to quickly understand the basic content without going to the site. This summary saves time during preliminary exploration. Also the histogram in the bottom right corner quickly summarizes the size of each group, informing the user of the largest (and perhaps the most important) group in the collection.

Since this collection spans a long time, it is interesting for a curator to see how the collection evolved over time using the timeline view (Figure 4). There are a few insights that can be gained through this visualization:

- The "Non-governmental organizations (NGOs)" group

has been the largest since the beginning of the collection.

- Short green lines on the left of the visualization indicate that a few sites were initially added to the collection but quickly removed.
- A handful of sites have remained in the collection since the beginning, and regular archived copies have been made. This is indicated by long lines with frequent data points. This hints at the high importance of these sites in the collection and perhaps are ones the user should explore first.
- A change in the composition of the collection is evident from the abrupt ending of many long lines on the right-hand side of timeline (at 2011-04 time marker) with only a few remaining until the end.

4.2 Collection: Pakistan Floods (2011)

The Pakistan Floods (2011) collection is a good representative of collections with a large number of sites but no curator-defined grouping. The collection contains 655 archived copies of 623 sites collected over a period of 20 days. The absence of any grouping makes it difficult for the user to selectively explore the collection.

After running our heuristics-based categorization, the collection was organized into 8 groups: Blogs (35 sites), News Websites (259 sites), Pakistan News Sites (47 sites), Relief Websites (5 sites), Social Media (105 sites), Television (3 sites), Videos (18 sites) and Others (151 sites). This categorization is shown in the bubble chart (Figure 5). Since this collection is concerned with a natural disaster, we added specific rules to categorize news websites from Pakistan and websites discussing relief operations into their own groups. A large number of websites were categorized as "Others" because the URIs did not meet any specified rule. After this categorization, the composition of the collection can be presented more clearly to the user. Also by looking at the statistics below the bubble chart, the user can infer almost immediately that this collection is still in its early stages because for most of the sites there is only 1 archived copy.

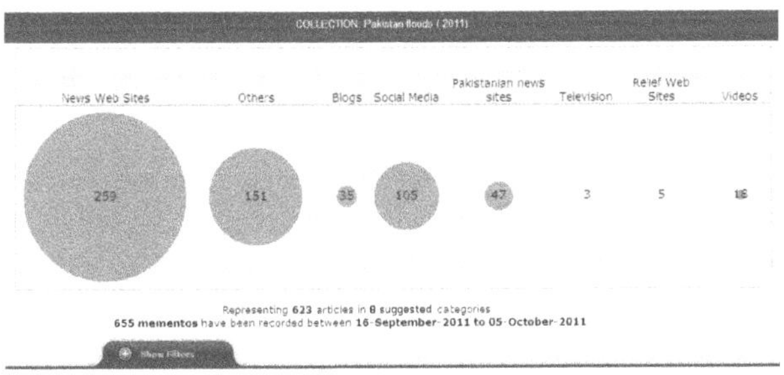

Figure 5: Bubble chart visualization for the Pakistan Floods (2011) collection.

As before, the timeline visualization is effective in visualizing the growth of the collection over time. Figure 6 shows that only one site has contributed consistently to the collection and a large number of sites were added on a single day. By looking at the visualization, one can infer that this collection was perhaps meant to be an archive of various news items related to the disaster and not as a repository of events taking place over time (as with the Human Rights collection).

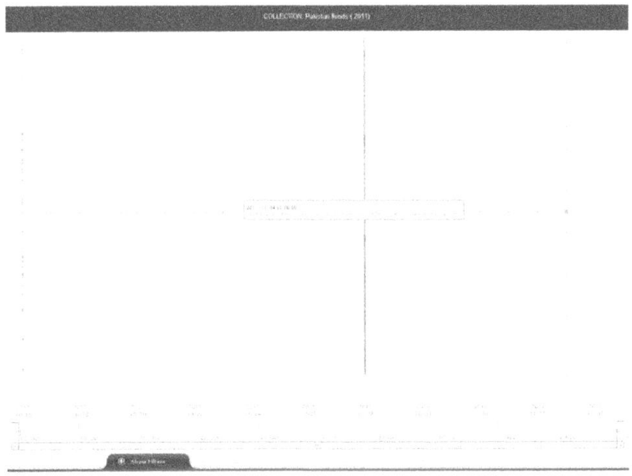

Figure 6: Timeline visualization for the Pakistan Floods (2011) collection.

5. CONCLUSION AND FUTURE WORK

We have developed a novel visual interface for exploring digital collections at Archive-It. The various visualizations that constitute this interface provide insight into the collections. We have found the timeline visualization to be particularly useful in understanding the structure of a collection. The bubble chart provides a quick look at the collection statistics, while the image plot allows for visual exploration of the collection. Also, the wordles enable understanding of the collection by providing a summary of the selected site.

These visualizations are helpful in exploring the digital collections and offer insight into the collections over the textual interface. Based on feedback from Archive-It partners and collection curators, we plan to further develop these visualization techniques, and integrate them with the existing Archive-It interface. Also, the heuristics-based categorization is still in a naive stage and we plan to further develop it to include a broad range of collection types.

6. REFERENCES

[1] C. Ahlberg and B. Shneiderman. Visual information seeking: tight coupling of dynamic query filters with starfield displays. In *Proceedings of ACM SIGCHI*, CHI '94, pages 313–317, 1994.

[2] M. Hearst, A. Elliott, J. English, R. Sinha, K. Swearingen, and K. Yee. Finding the flow in web site search. *Communications of the ACM*, 45(9):42–49, 2002.

[3] A. Jatowt, Y. Kawai, S. Nakamura, Y. Kidawara, and K. Tanaka. A browser for browsing the past web. In *Proceedings of WWW*, pages 877–878, 2006.

[4] M.-Y. Kan and H. O. N. Thi. Fast webpage classification using URL features. In *Proceedings of ACM CIKM*, pages 325–326, 2005.

[5] F. Viégas, M. Wattenberg, and J. Feinberg. Participatory visualization with wordle. *IEEE Transactions on Visualization and Computer Graphics*, 15(6):1137–1144, 2009.

Data, Data Use, and Scientific Inquiry: Two Case Studies of Data Practices

Laura A. Wynholds, Jillian C. Wallis, Christine L. Borgman, Ashley Sands, Sharon Traweek*
Department of Information Studies, University of California, Los Angeles
*History and Gender Studies Departments, University of California, Los Angeles
wynholds@ucla.edu, jwallisi@ucla.edu, borgman@gseis.ucla.edu, ashleysa@ucla.edu, traweek@history.ucla.edu

ABSTRACT

Data are proliferating far faster than they can be captured, managed, or stored. What types of data are most likely to be used and reused, by whom, and for what purposes? Answers to these questions will inform information policy and the design of digital libraries. We report findings from semi-structured interviews and field observations to investigate characteristics of data use and reuse and how those characteristics vary within and between scientific communities. The two communities studied are researchers at the Center for Embedded Network Sensing (CENS) and users of the Sloan Digital Sky Survey (SDSS) data. The data practices of CENS and SDSS researchers have implications for data curation, system evaluation, and policy. Some data that are important to the conduct of research are not viewed as sufficiently valuable to keep. Other data of great value may not be mentioned or cited, because those data serve only as background to a given investigation. Metrics to assess the value of documents do not map well to data.

Categories and Subject Descriptors

H.3.7 [Digital Libraries]: User Issues.

General Terms

Documentation, Design, Human Factors, Standardization.

Keywords

Scientific data, data practices, data sharing, data citation.

1. INTRODUCTION

Data curation is an immediate concern of the digital libraries community and a theme of this conference. Data are proliferating far faster than they can be captured, managed, or stored – all of which are prerequisites to actual curation. A major motivation for data curation is keeping data for future use and reuse. Data curation faces the challenge that the data must be housed, managed, and made accessible prior to use, but actual uses may not be known until after sizeable investments are made. Data curation research has been engaged with outstanding questions of use: How are data used and how are they reused? What types of data are most likely to be reused, by whom, and for what purposes? Answers to these questions are needed to inform information policy and the design of digital libraries to support the capture, management, use, and reuse of data.

Prior work in information studies has not focused on these questions of use and reuse. Information needs and uses studies, which have a long tradition in the information science literature [4, 10], are more concerned with how people seek documents than with the uses they make of the content therein. Research on the seeking and use of documents does not transfer directly to the seeking and use of research data. The science and technology studies literature is more concerned with the processes by which publications and data are created than with subsequent curation activities [6–8]. Little of the research in the social studies of science on data origins has been applied to problems of data management and curation. The present study assesses scientific data use with the intent to inform information policy and the design of digital libraries for data.

Over the last decade we have been conducting interview and field studies to investigate scientific data practices in environmental sciences, marine biology, ecology, seismology, computer science, engineering, and astronomy[1, 3, 14–19]. Portions of the studies included questions about how data were collected by individuals, teams, other parties. This paper addresses two research questions, at two research sites:

1. What are the characteristics of data use and reuse within each research community?
2. How do characteristics of data use and reuse vary within and between research communities?

We identify the characteristics of the "use" of various types of data from the perspectives of individual researchers and of teams. The same data may be used in multiple ways, depending on the research activity. "Uses" may be understood much differently by researchers than by digital library designers, librarians, and archivists. Explanations of "data use" will inform information policy and the design of digital libraries.

2. BACKGROUND

Each scientific community differentiates equipment, data, analytic tools, and findings that currently are regarded as stable (widely used and no longer under active debate) and the search for new kinds of questions, methods, equipment, data, and analytic strategies in each field [9, 11]. Data curation must accommodate stability and instability of daily work and of data sources, large and small.

Scientists pursue research questions, develop hypotheses and theories, and gather data as evidence to support their inquiry. The forms and types of data will vary by many factors, including the stage of inquiry, characteristics of the research domain, and how much is known about the research problem [5, 7, 8]. Choices of data, metadata, analytic tools, and specializations are constantly being revised [19]. Many, if not most, scientific fields are becoming more data-intensive with advances in instrumentation such as sensor networks. As new instruments and forms of data become available and as communities respond to new requirements for data management plans, scientific practices are

JCDL'12, June 10–14, 2012, Washington, DC, USA.

in flux. The flux creates opportunities to study data production, use, and reuse.

Policies such as requirements for data management plans are predicated on the expectation that data will have future value for reuse. The question of use in relation to scientific data is particularly important for digital libraries. Conceptual frameworks of what constitutes use have a long history in relation to documents, bibliographic sources, and texts [13], but less so for data. These frameworks have been formalized into metrics that have become enormously important in assessing scholarly work. It remains unclear, however, how these concepts and metrics of use will apply to data and whether the same constructs can be applied without modification. Efforts to standardize data citation try to map extant publishing frameworks to data, revealing the considerable differences in granularity and stability.

The ubiquity and generality of "use" as a term makes it particularly difficult to study. Even in the context of documents, information use is difficult to capture and has been called 'theoretically underdeveloped' [12]. Use metrics such as citations and download counts are popular indicators of the use of scholarly works. Citations are at best imprecise indicators of the use of information-bearing objects [2]. Comparisons between uses of documents and of data offer a starting point for analyses. Data are more complex and varied than documents. Data are amorphous, taking forms that range from physical specimens to bit streams. While the use of publications has a different basis than the use of data, publications are central to scientific practice and are the means by which most data are reported. The relationship between citations and data is further complicated by the difficulty of differentiating references to publications versus references publications that contain or describe data.

3. RESEARCH METHODS

The research reported here compares findings from parallel studies in sensor networks and astronomy. Since 2002 we have studied data practices, management, and curation in the Center for Embedded Network Sensing (CENS), a multi-disciplinary, science and technology research center. Research protocols and interview questions used in the CENS data practices studies were later adapted to research on astronomers. Our astronomy focus in this paper is builders and users of the Sloan Digital Sky Survey (SDSS), a large, long-term, and well-known data-driven project.

CENS research is "small science," with small teams and emergent data collection methods [3], whereas the SDSS research is "big science," with large teams and elaborate data collection methods. However, the two sites have much in common, allowing us to make a series of comparisons. CENS and SDSS share these attributes: decade-long projects with multiple sources of funding, collaborations of multiple institutions, and multiple teams that have evolved over the course of their research cycles. They are obligated by their funders to share data and findings. Participants collaborate within and across disciplines at each site. Scientists and technology researchers also collaborate to develop instruments and software. Both types of collaborations require substantial infrastructure investments for data collection.

Our CENS and SDSS studies employed semi-structured interviews and field observations to investigate data use and reuse within these communities. Interviews ranged from 45 minutes to 2 hours, with an average of 60 minutes per interview. Participants were asked about their data and data practices. In most cases, their data were observations or output from models; in some cases data may be code, software, or computer systems.

All interviews were recorded and transcribed. Interviewees and interviews were assigned unique identifiers and names redacted upon request per Institutional Review Board procedures. Interviews were coded using NVivo software. The initial codebook was developed for the first round of CENS interviews in 2006 and significantly revised for the second round of CENS interviews in 2009. The SDSS codebook was developed from the CENS 2006 codebook and adapted to the specifics of the astronomy research questions. Inter-coder reliability tests were performed by our team on both projects. Findings presented below are based on selected questions and relevant responses to questions about data types, data sources, and uses of data.

4. RESULTS

The following results are organized by the two study sites, CENS and SDSS. Within each of these two sections, results first are described for data sources and types, then by type of inquiry, and lastly by uses and reuses of data within each community. Comparisons between these sites are presented in the discussion section.

4.1 Center for Embedded Networked Sensing

CENS researchers collect observational, experimental, and simulation data. We have classified CENS data into four categories of data collected during sensor network deployments: sensor-collected application science data, sensor-collected network health data, sensor-collected proprioceptive data, and hand-collected application science data [16], see Figure 1. Researchers supplemented their data with external data including national observatories such as NOAA, where they find tidal estimates, or NASA's MODIS satellite, which provides remote sensing images, and the USGS for gravitational information [1].

Figure 1: CENS data organized by collection method and use.

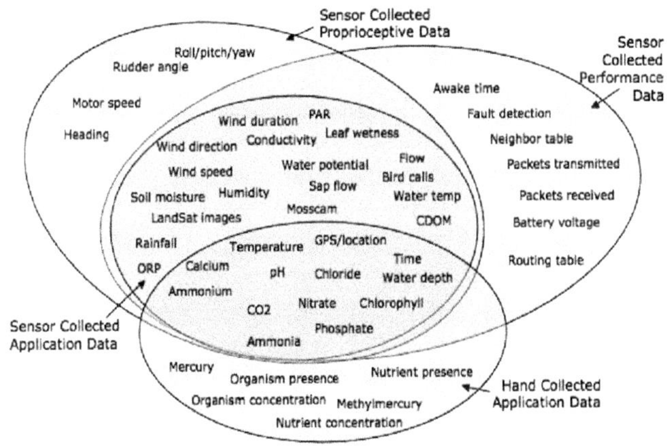

Inquiry at CENS falls into three, sequential categories: (i) proof-of-concept development of new equipment, algorithms, and systems, (ii) refining equipment, algorithms, and systems for use by the application scientists, and (iii) scientific discovery on the part of the application scientists using CENS equipment, algorithms, and systems. The first and third types of inquiry are performed by the technology and scientific researchers, respectively, and counts as scholarship to each community. The second type is characterized by technology and application science researchers working closely together in the field to transform proof-of-concept technologies into research-grade or commercial-grade technologies that the application scientists employ in field or laboratory environments.

Despite the diversity of the CENS community with respect to the phenomena they study, the data they collect, and the actions they apply to data, a number of commonalities exist. Almost all the participants mentioned the importance of their data in identifying patterns or trends, which includes identifying interesting locations and phenomena for further study. From these patterns and trends, most of the researchers would then construct hypotheses or models. When out in the field, about half the participants mentioned relying on data to provide real-time feedback to ensure that they are capturing phenomena of interest. Electrical engineering researchers feed scientific data to algorithms that drive data-collection robots or that redistribute networked sensors to improve data capture. Raw data from the sensors must be processed through scientific models that represent "the real world" prior to analysis. Transformations include adjusting data with calibration and "ground-truthing" measures collected about each sensor, feeding data into algorithms or simulations to generate new data, and translating indirect measures to data about phenomena that can measured only by proxy. Data analyses may include inductive correlations, deductive hypotheses, or model testing. Other possible analyses are performance evaluation of equipment, algorithms, methods, systems, and meta-analysis. We identified six dimensions of CENS data: (a) background and foreground, (b) observation, experimental, and simulation data, (c) old and new, (d) collection in lab or field , (e) raw versus processed, and (f) collection by the team or obtained from external sources.

4.2 Sloan Digital Sky Survey

The researchers we interviewed provided examples of observational, experimental, and simulation data that they relied upon in the course of their research. Most participants reported drawing data from multiple sources; notably, many drew from sources across multiple wavelengths. Researchers distinguished between the physical instrument as a data source and data obtained from venues such as repositories or catalogs. For example, a researcher might acquire Hubble Space Telescope (instrument) data that had been processed and published in a journal article (venue). Figure 2 summarizes the types of data products mentioned in the interviews.

Figure 2: Types of data products used.

Data Type	Example
Instrument Outputs	Ground Based Telescopes Space Based Telescopes
Model Outputs	Simulation Outputs
Structured Data Products	Sky Surveys Value Added Catalogs
Federated Queries	Virtual Observatory Services

Scientists' interactions with their data depend upon the specific activity and stage of research. Inquiry types identified in our interviews included hypothesis testing, open-ended inquiry, known object inquiry, and multi-faceted inquiries. Open-ended inquiry refers to cases where the scientists were looking for previously unknown or undescribed phenomena. One astronomer articulated this mode as, *"let's populate it with my data and I'll see what's in there."* Other scholars described more precise, known-object queries which included looking for physical properties such as white dwarf spin periods or calculating the intrinsic flux of specific galaxies. Researchers are more concerned with demonstrating innovative inquiry than with creating good, long-range, well-calibrated data products.

Researchers had a number of different ways to approach original and cutting-edge science based on their data, including identifying phenomena not previously observable, obtaining observations at a scale not previously possible, comparisons of data from multiple studies, and asking scientific questions that could not have been asked previously. The approaches were strongly linked with concepts of use, the type of inquiry, and their definition of data. Researchers foregrounded their analysis in discussions of use, listing only data associated with certain types of use. Background uses included obtaining baseline data from established sources, using data to calibrate instruments or analyses, and creating simulations and models. Often the background uses were not mentioned in discussions of data sources, but rather mentioned during discussions of instrument design, data processing, or analysis. Another mode of interaction with the data is to reproduce results to extend or to verify the validity of prior research. Foreground uses, in contrast, are those that drive the scientific inquiry.

5. DISCUSSION

We have reported on our findings for two research questions, based on interviews in two complementary communities, the Center for Embedded Networked Sensing (CENS) and users of Sloan Digital Sky Survey (SDSS) data. Our goal was to identify uses and reuses from the perspective of the individual researchers and their communities, and to apply those findings to information policy and to the design of digital libraries.

We found that CENS researchers and astronomers alike describe their data with respect to the purposes for which they are used. Their data exist only in relation to their research question, hypothesis, model, instrument, or study. Importantly, these researchers also act on data in ways that would be considered "use" by librarians, archivists, digital library developers, information policy makers, and other researchers, and yet are not viewed as "use" by the actors themselves. Such uses include seeking data from external sources and employing them as comparisons or calibration metrics.

Reuse suggests using data repeatedly, whether for the same or different purposes. We identified cases in CENS, particularly, where researchers would maintain some laboratory or field data for later analysis, either alone or in combination with new data. Rarely were these data deposited publicly; rather, they were kept for reuse within the research team. Additionally, both CENS and SDSS users drew upon public repositories of data for background information. Some SDSS users also used data from external sources for foreground purposes to drive their inquiry. Thus taking data from public repositories and sky surveys are reuses in the sense of "using again," but not in the sense of maintaining a team's empirical data in ways that those data might be exploited by others in the future.

Some data that are essential to the research process are not kept at all, and thus are not available for future use by the research team or others. In CENS, these include data produced during the long processes of iterative testing and evaluation of sensor networks, which is the most collaborative part of this type of research. Among SDSS users, these may include similar iterative testing and evaluation of instruments, calibration, and merging of data from multiple sources.

6. CONCLUSIONS

"Use" is a term with little value unless qualified. "Data" adds another level of complexity to the understanding of use. Data are extremely varied and rather than being fixed, they shimmer. Data uses vary by type of inquiry, type of data, and interactions between them.

Scientific inquiry varies widely in methods and sources of evidence. Data and data practices vary accordingly. Practices vary by domain, by lab, and by individual. CENS and SDSS research sites are exemplars of small science and big science. Both sites are long-term projects, with individuals participating in the science, technology, or both types of research. The individuals we studied included astronomers, computer scientists, electrical engineers, environmental engineers, habitat ecologists, marine biologists, seismologists, and researchers in several related fields.

The complexity of these interactions has multiple implications for data sharing and for the design of digital libraries. One implication is that data that are important to the conduct of research often are not viewed by the researchers themselves as sufficiently valuable to keep. Thus those data are invisible. They may never be available for capture in digital libraries, much less for sharing and reuse.

Another implication is that data in the foreground of a research problem are most likely to be captured, described, and cited. The same data, when viewed as background to a research problem, may not be mentioned in a research report, nor cited explicitly. Yet these data, such as the density and distribution of phenomena, are essential to the research process and expensive to create and maintain. Since scientists vary between disciplines and even between projects on their understanding of "use," measuring the value of a data repository based on citations may grossly underestimate the collection. For example, our findings suggest that researchers may cite foreground but not background uses, even though both uses are essential to their research process.

Our findings also reinforce concerns from the social studies of science that making data "mobile" may remove so much of their context as to make them useless [8][10][19]. Data sharing efforts, data management plans, and data citation practices all require a more nuanced understanding of data "use" to be effective.

7. ACKNOWLEDGEMENTS

Research reported here is supported in part by grants from the National Science Foundation (NSF) and the Alfred P. Sloan Foundation (Sloan): (1) The Center for Embedded Networked Sensing (CENS) is funded by NSF Cooperative Agreement #CCR-0120778; (2) Towards a Virtual Organization for Data Cyberinfrastructure, NSF #OCI-0750529; (3) Monitoring, Modeling & Memory: Dynamics of Data and Knowledge in Scientific Cyberinfrastructures: NSF #0827322; (4) The Data Conservancy, NSF Cooperative Agreement (DataNet) award OCI0830976; and (5)The Transformation of Knowledge, Culture, and Practice in Data-Driven Science: A Knowledge Infrastructures Perspective, Sloan Award # 20113194.

8. REFERENCES

[1] Borgman, C., Wallis, J.C. and Enyedy, N. 2006. Building Digital Libraries for Scientific Data: An Exploratory Study of Data Practices in Habitat Ecology. *Proceedings of the 10th European Conference on Research and Advanced Technology for Digital Libraries* (Alicante, Spain, Sep. 2006), 170–183.

[2] Borgman, C.L. ed. 1990. *Scholarly Communication and Bibliometrics*. Sage.

[3] Borgman, C.L., Wallis, J.C. and Enyedy, N. 2007. Little Science confronts the data deluge: Habitat ecology, embedded sensor networks, and digital libraries. *International Journal on Digital Libraries*. 7, 1-2 (2007), 17–30.

[4] Case, D.O. 2006. *Looking for Information: A Survey of Research on Information Seeking, Needs, and Behavior*. Academic Press.

[5] Furner, J. 2003. Little book, big book: Before and after Little Science, Big Science: A review article, Part I. *Journal of Librarianship and Information Science*. 35, 2 (2003), 115–125.

[6] Latour, B. 1987. *Science in Action: How to Follow Scientists and Engineers through Society*. Harvard University Press.

[7] Latour, B. and Woolgar, S. 1979. *Laboratory life: The Social Construction of Scientific Facts*. Sage Publications.

[8] Lynch, M. and Woolgar, S. eds. 1988. *Representation in scientific practice*. MIT Press.

[9] Maurer, B.A. 2004. Models of Scientific Inquiry and Statistical Practice: Implications for the structure of scientific knowledge. *The Nature of Scientific Evidence: Statistical, philosophical, and empirical considerations*. The University of Chicago Press. 17–50.

[10] Paisley, W.J. 1968. Information needs and uses. *Annual Review of Information Science and Technology*. 3, (1968), 1–30.

[11] Reid, R. and Traweek, S. eds. 2000. *Cultural Studies of Science, Technology, and Medicine*. Routledge.

[12] Savolainen, R. 2009. Epistemic work and knowing in practice as conceptualizations of information use. *Information Research: An International Electronic Journal*. 14, 1 (Mar. 2009).

[13] Smith, L.C. 1981. Citation analysis. *Library Trends*. 30, 1 (1981), 83–106.

[14] Wallis, J.C. and Borgman, C.L. 2011. Who is responsible for data? An exploratory study of data authorship, ownership, and responsibility. *Proceedings of the Annual Meeting of the American Society for Information Science and Technology* (New Orleans, LA, 2011).

[15] Wallis, J.C., Borgman, C.L., Mayernik, M.S. and Pepe, A. 2008. Moving archival practices upstream: An exploration of the life cycle of ecological sensing data in collaborative field research. *International Journal of Digital Curation*. 3, 1 (2008), 114–126.

[16] Wallis, J.C., Borgman, C.L., Mayernik, M.S., Pepe, A., Ramanathan, N. and Hansen, M. 2007. Know Thy Sensor: Trust, Data Quality, and Data Integrity in Scientific Digital Libraries. *Proceedings of the 11th European Conference on Research and Advanced Technology for Digital Libraries* (Budapest, Hungary, Sep. 2007), 380–391.

[17] Wallis, J.C., Mayernik, M.S., Borgman, C.L. and Pepe, A. 2010. Digital libraries for scientific data discovery and reuse: from vision to practical reality. *Proceedings of the 10th Annual Joint Conference on Digital Libraries* (Gold Coast, Queensland, Australia, 2010), 333–340.

[18] Wynholds, L. 2011. Linking to Scientific Data: Identity Problems of Unruly and Poorly Bounded Digital Objects. *International Journal of Digital Curation*. 6, 1 (Mar. 2011), 214–225.

[19] Wynholds, L., Fearon, D.S., Jr., Borgman, C.L. and Traweek, S. 2011. When use cases are not useful: Data practices, astronomy, and digital libraries. *Proceedings of the 11th Annual Joint Conference on Digital Libraries* (Ottawa, Canada, Jun. 2011), 383–386.

Digital Preservation and Knowledge Discovery Based on Documents from an International Health Science Program

Dharitri Misra
National Library of Medicine
Bethesda, MD, USA 20894
dmisra@mail.nih.gov

Robert H. Hall
National Institute of Allergy and Infectious Diseases
Bethesda, MD, USA 20892
robert.hall@nih.gov

Susan M. Payne
National Institute of Allergy and Infectious Diseases
Bethesda, MD, USA 20892
susan.payne@nih.gov

George R. Thoma
National Library of Medicine
Bethesda, MD, USA 20894
gthoma@mail.nih.gov

ABSTRACT

Important biomedical information is often recorded, published or archived in unstructured and semi-structured textual form. Artificial intelligence and knowledge discovery techniques may be applied to large volumes of such data to identify and extract useful metadata, not only for providing access to these documents, but also for conducting analyses and uncovering patterns and trends in a field. The System for Preservation of Electronic Resources (SPER), an information management tool developed at the U.S. National Library of Medicine, provides these capabilities by integrating machine learning, data mining and digital preservation techniques. In this paper, we present an overview of SPER and its ability to retrieve information from one such dataset. We show how SPER was applied to the semi-structured records of an international health science program, the 46-year continuous archive of conference publications and related documents from the Joint Cholera Panel of the U.S.-Japan Cooperative Medical Science Program (CMSP). We explain the techniques by which metadata was extracted automatically from the semi-structured document contents to preserve these publications, and show how such data was used to quantitatively describe the activity of a research community toward a preliminary study of a subset of its specific health science program goals.

Categories and Subject Descriptors

H.3 **[Information Storage and Retrieval]**: H3.3 Information Search and Retrieval. H3.4 Systems and Software. H3.7 Digital Libraries I.5 **[Pattern Recognition]** I.5.2 Design Methodology - Feature evaluation and selection.

General Terms

Algorithms, Management, Design, Experimentation

Keywords

Metadata, Automated Metadata Extraction, Machine Learning, Digital Preservation, Data Analysis, Knowledge Discovery

1. INTRODUCTION

Medical information, founded on a massive archive of knowledge in biomedical literature, research articles, case studies, and reviews, often carry additional information related to research policies, participants and the contemporary understanding of health science, but potentially valuable health science data are easily overlooked as the retrieval of semantic information from them is often highly labor-intensive. However, automated machine learning techniques have made it possible to identify and retrieve important metadata elements such as article titles, authors, institutions from semi-structured document sets, which can be used for archiving the documents and providing access to them. Furthermore, these metadata fields, in combination with indexed document text, can be used to discover patterns and trends, and to quantify relations among technical terms, individuals, institutions, and other concepts, making it feasible to draw inferences accessible to target communities for specific purposes such as policy formulation and peer review.

In this paper we describe how such data analysis is made possible for a historic health science collection from the Joint Cholera Panel of the U.S.-Japan Cooperative Medical Science Program (CMSP) by using an R&D system called SPER (System for the Preservation of Electronic Resources) developed at the U.S. National Library of Medicine [1].

In the following sections, we provide a brief description of SPER, discuss the CMSP collection and its analysis goals, describe the techniques used by SPER toward meeting such goals, and display some preliminary analytical results. Finally, we outline ongoing knowledge discovery work using SPER.

2. BACKGROUND AND RELATED WORK

The SPER system was originally developed to identify, locate and retrieve collection-specific metadata cost-effectively, using machine learning, from the contents of semi-structured textual documents. It was expanded to research other aspects of digital preservation, including archiving the document collections using the extracted metadata in an OAIS-compliant repository [2]. The system has been successfully used to extract domain-specific metadata for a historic medico-legal document collection from the U.S. Food and Drug Administration, and build a digital repository to access the collection [3]. Recently, we have expanded SPER to use such context-sensitive metadata to conduct semantic queries, perform quantitative analysis, and determine patterns and trends.

3. SPER SYSTEM OVERVIEW

SPER is an evolving system to research and implement digital preservation and information retrieval functions, with focus on:

1. Automated metadata extraction (AME) from textual documents using machine learning
2. Preservation of and access to documents in a digital archive
3. Support of knowledge discovery from the archived data

SPER provides an end-to-end platform for preserving and analyzing document sets by integrating these functions into its workflow. It is implemented as a Java-based, customizable framework, into which new functionalities may be added as deemed appropriate.

3.1 Function Description

a) **Automated Metadata Extraction**: This important functionality is used for locating and extracting domain-specific metadata from the textual contents of a document collection using supervised machine learning techniques. Textlines are classified using Support Vector Machines (SVMs) [4] as the static feature classifier - either singly, or in combination with stochastic language models such as Hidden Markov Models (HMMs) [5] when different textline classes overlap in feature space. From these classified textlines, corresponding metadata elements are extracted either using field tokenizers, or through regular expression matching.

   Paper documents are usually scanned to TIFF images, prior to submission to SPER, where it is input to an optical character recognition (OCR) engine such as the ABBYY FineReader; and the output is used for the AME operations. SPER allows the extracted metadata to be reviewed and validated by an operator for quality assurance, prior to being used for ingesting the document into a digital repository.

b) **Document Preservation and Access:** The preservation of items in a digital collection is performed by SPER using DSpace [6] as the underlying infrastructure. The source pages, derivatives (such as PDFs), metadata for individual items, as well as the indexed text are stored in a high-volume storage device with an accompanying MySQL database.

   Access to archived embedded in the documents but not directly retrievable items is provided via a Web browser using a configurable DSpace Web interface, allowing browse/search of the collection's domain-specific metadata.

c) **Knowledge Discovery:** Discovery of additional information, through standard search mechanisms, requires the following:

   (a) Identification of additional metadata elements prior to AME operations so that they may be located and extracted from the documents during AME phase.

   (b) Post-processing of metadata to transform stored elements to a suitable form for data analysis and trend discovery.

3.2 SPER System Architecture

The architecture and main dataflows within SPER are shown in Figure 1. The main system component, the SPER Server, runs as a Web application and is used to perform AME and build the archive from a collection of digitized documents. A user of the system, an operator or archivist, uses a SPER Client, installed at their site, to download the digitized documents and initiate these functions.

The AME Engine incorporates the automated metadata extraction functions, including invoking the OCR tool for recognition of text in the input documents. Once the data is ingested to the repository, the Data Analysis Engine may be used to first post-process the metadata, then to receive the semantic queries, operate on the data sets, and return the results. Access to the repository is provided by a separate DSpace-based Web application, not shown in the figure.

The AME Engine and the Data Analysis Engine are collection-specific components, whereas the rest of the SPER system is reusable and configurable for each new collection.

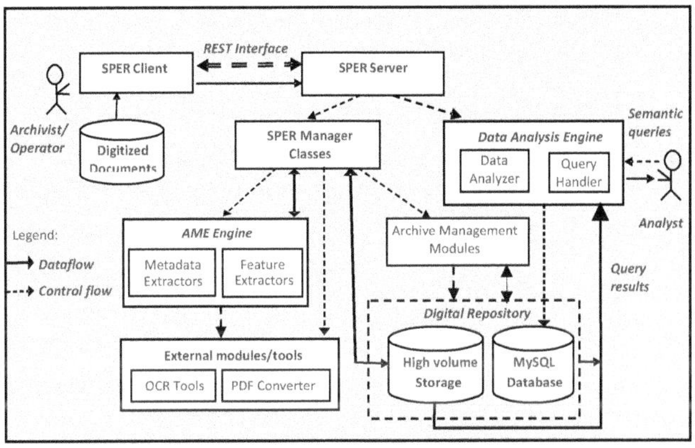

Figure 1. SPER system architecture.

4. The CMSP Program and Publications

The CMSP program [7] was founded in 1965 as a joint commitment by U.S. President Lyndon B. Johnson and Japanese Prime Minister Eisaku Sato to address health problems in South and Southeast Asia through an expanded medical research effort. Joint Panels on Cholera were founded to control cholera through vaccine development, by making effective therapy available, and by international research collaboration. Participants met annually (in meetings sponsored alternately by the U.S. and Japan), and made presentations to report progress. These presentations, published as abstract books, provide an extraordinary window into efforts against a disease that continues to cause major public health problems today.

The CMSP Joint Cholera Panel archive, held by the National Institute of Allergy and Infectious Diseases (NIAID), consists of the conference proceedings from 1965 through 2009, along with the proceedings of an earlier formative conference held in 1960. Also included are annual progress reports from a related NIAID research program within the International Centers for Medical Research and Training (ICMRT), and a list of Study Section reviewers from year 2003 to 2010.

4.1 Goal of Processing the CMSP Publications

The overall goals of processing the CMSP publications were: (a) to preserve the document collection in a digital repository, and (b) to collect statistical data, through metadata analyses, to produce metrics for evaluating the responsiveness of the research program to its strategic objectives.

The specific data for analysis were established as:

- Number of presentations on cholera research in USA, Japan, and developing countries, both individually and through international collaboration
- Levels of innovation in specific fields, such as vaccines, therapeutics, and diagnostics
- The time intervals between presentation of research discoveries in a conference forum and their subsequent appearance in formal peer-reviewed publications
- Identification of the most active and influential authors in terms of the number of presented abstracts, levels of collaboration, and overall impact

4.2 CMSP Metadata

The metadata elements required for access and/or analysis of the CMSP dataset are contained in the research articles and various rosters, within the conference proceedings and Study Section lists, and are shown in Table 1.

Table 1. Metadata fields in different CMSP documents.

Document	Type	Metadata
Conference Proceedings	Presentation	Title, Author Names, Affiliated Institutions, Keywords, Page location
	Panelist Info	Panel (U.S./Japan), Panelist Name, Affiliation, Address
	Attendee List	Attendee Name, Affiliation, Address
Study Section Rosters	Reviewer List	Reviewer Name, Affiliation, Address

An example of metadata occurrence in one sample CMSP record (containing a list of panelists in a conference proceedings page) is shown as a set of rectangular boxes in Figure 2.

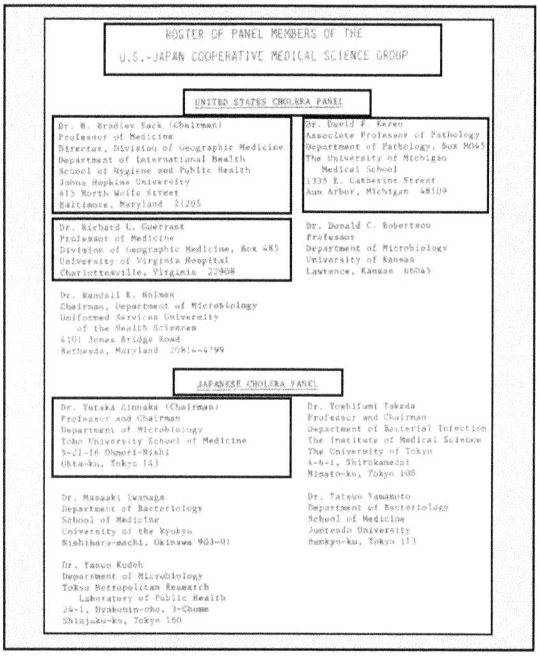

ROSTER OF PANEL MEMBERS OF THE
U.S.-JAPAN COOPERATIVE MEDICAL SCIENCE GROUP

UNITED STATES CHOLERA PANEL

Dr. R. Bradley Sack (Chairman)
Professor of Medicine
Director, Division of Geographic Medicine
Department of International Health
School of Hygiene and Public Health
Johns Hopkins University
615 North Wolfe Street
Baltimore, Maryland 21205

Dr. David F. Keren
Associate Professor of Pathology
Department of Pathology, Box M045
The University of Michigan
Medical School
1335 E. Catherine Street
Ann Arbor, Michigan 48109

Dr. Richard L. Guerrant
Professor of Medicine
Division of Geographic Medicine, Box 485
University of Virginia Hospital
Charlottesville, Virginia 22908

Dr. Donald C. Robertson
Professor
Department of Microbiology
University of Kansas
Lawrence, Kansas 66045

Dr. Randall K. Holmes
Chairman, Department of Microbiology
Uniformed Services University
of the Health Sciences
4301 Jones Bridge Road
Bethesda, Maryland 20814-4799

JAPANESE CHOLERA PANEL

Dr. Yutaka Zinnaka (Chairman)
Professor and Chairman
Department of Microbiology
Toho University School of Medicine
5-21-16 Ohmori-Nishi
Ohta-ku, Tokyo 143

Dr. Yoshifumi Takeda
Professor and Chairman
Department of Bacterial Infection
The Institute of Medical Science
The University of Tokyo
4-6-1, Shirokanedai
Minato-ku, Tokyo 108

Dr. Masaaki Iwanaga
Department of Bacteriology
School of Medicine
University of the Ryukyu
Nishihara-machi, Okinawa 903-01

Dr. Tatsuo Yamamoto
Department of Bacteriology
School of Medicine
Juntendo University
Bunkyo-ku, Tokyo 113

Dr. Yasuo Kudoh
Department of Microbiology
Tokyo Metropolitan Research
Laboratory of Public Health
24-1, Hyakunin-cho, 3-Chome
Shinjuku-ku, Tokyo 160

Figure 2. Metadata location for Panelists in a sample record.

4.3 AME Technique and Feature Generation

The problem of recognizing metadata fields in the CMSP documents falls mainly under the general technique known as "named entity recognition" (NER) [8].

The recognition features selected for locating metadata elements in the CMSP documents [9] fall into six categories: dictionary (name) features, text features, punctuation features, special word features, contextual features (e.g. features from neighboring words) and weight features (e.g. clustering, ordering or frequency of specific features in a line). For our algorithms, a feature is based upon a category or a set of words representing a concept, rather than all equivalent words found for that concept. This improves the performance of the textline classifier, without significantly lowering the accuracy, by reducing the dimension of the feature space for the SVM implementation. Three separate metadata models were developed to handle AME for articles, panelist/attendees and Study Section reviewers respectively.

There were a number of challenges in locating and retrieving required metadata from the CMSP publications. Some examples are: illegibility of the text, wide variations in the format, layout and relative position of data elements (such as individual name, institution and title), occurrence of a country's non-English native language terms, and the occurrence of same words in the context of persons, institutions or addresses. These problems were reduced by developing language-specific "special word" features, field-specific tokenizers, and textline class validators.

Table 2 shows some statistics related to the CMSP collection, as derived from the extracted metadata.

Table 2. CMSP collection related statistics.

Year Span	1960-2009
Number of Conference Proceedings	55
Number of Presentations	2,556
Instances of Author	11,736
Instances of Panelist	589
Instances of Conference Attendee	4,239
Instances of Participating Institution	4,416
Instances of Study Section Reviewer	3,110
Number of Individuals (Participants)	6,923

5. ACCESS TO CMSP REPOSITORY

CMSP documents, along with the corresponding validated metadata and searchable PDFs, were ingested to the CMSP repository by the SPER server. The OCR'ed text for the entire corpus was then indexed using Apache/Lucene and stored in the archive.

SPER provides access to the archived CMSP documents, through title, author, year of publication and keyword searches, by customization of the standard DSpace-based Web interface. Furthermore, it also supports browse and search on Participants.

6. DATA ANALYSIS

The metadata retrieved from the documents do not directly contain all required information for data analysis. The "Data Analysis Engine" for CMSP, therefore, performs post-processing in the following two areas:

(a) Mapping an institution to the corresponding country, and a "Country Group." Special dictionaries were created to do this for institutions where no country was specified.
There were three specific country groups, referenced here as: USG (U.S. + other high GDP countries), Jpn (Japan), and Dev (Developing countries)

(b) Identifying an individual (with a unique first name, last name) corresponding to a contributor, whose "published name" varied widely in the document set. Special utilities and manual authentication were used to accomplish this.

6.1 Trends and Patterns

The analysis of the CMSP data enabled a long-standing health science program to be examined against specific policy goals. A detailed evaluation of the program and its policies is outside the scope of this paper, and will be presented elsewhere.

Nevertheless, the examples in Figure 3 a-c illustrate the results produced by SPER to help assess the stated CMSP Program goals. These results include examination of the U.S. sponsored meetings only, which occurred in alternating years, except 1969 and 2001, when there were no meetings.

Figure 3a shows that one specific important discovery (glucose-based oral rehydration therapy) was presented at conferences eight years before peer-review publications in PubMed [10] in 1968. It further reveals that conference activity on glucose-based oral therapy for cholera remained at a low level from 1979.

Figure 3b shows the trends in research activities over the CMSP

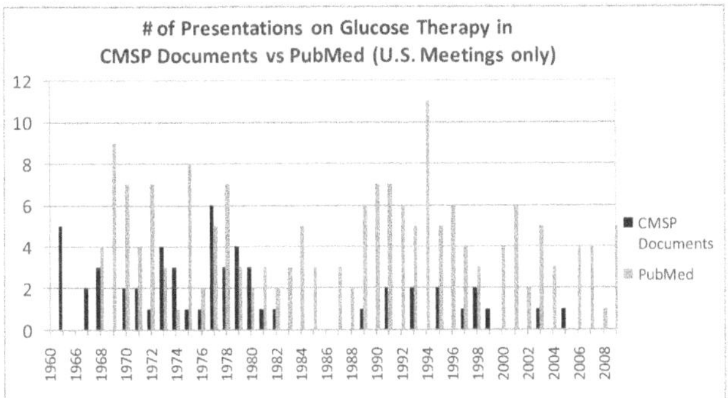

Figure 3a. Research activity on glucose in rehydration therapy reported at CMSP vs. PubMed.

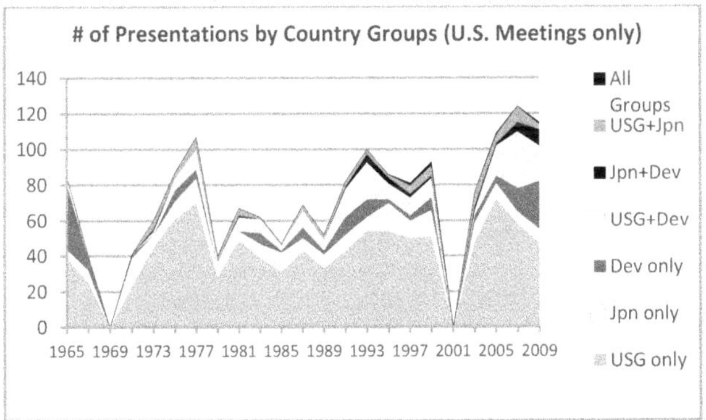

Figure 3b. Contribution of and level of collaboration by different country groups (indicated by # of presentations) in U.S. meetings (with no meetings in 1969 and 2001).

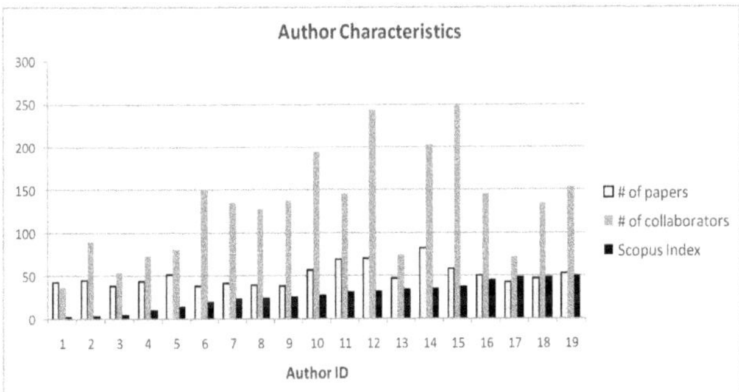

Figure 3c. Publication and collaboration by Authors.

time span, and highlights increased activity and international collaboration from 2003 that coincided with support from stakeholders and a new translational research agenda. (These results include examination of the U.S. sponsored meetings only, which occurred in alternating years, except 1969 and 2001).

Figure 3c identifies the most active authors who collaborated heavily with others for their research, and published their findings in the peer-reviewed journal Scopus.

7. CONCLUSION AND FUTURE WORK

Our work continues in further analysis of the CMSP collection in other related areas, and in providing improved semantic query capabilities by (a) building a full CMSP cholera knowledgebase, and (b) making the knowledge discovery system selectively accessible through a CMSP portal. In future, we also aim to apply the technique to other important biomedical collections, with domain-specific metadata, so as to uncover useful information for researchers and other targeted user communities.

8. ACKNOWLEDGEMENTS

The authors acknowledge Abdulmekik Shifa and Tobias T. Hall for their contributions to compiling the CMSP Joint Cholera Panels' records, and Dr. Xiaoli Zhang for her work in building the metadata models for the automated extraction.

This research was supported by the Intramural Research Program of the National Institutes of Health (NIH), National Library of Medicine (NLM), and Lister Hill National Center for Biomedical Communications (LHNCBC).

9. REFERENCES

[1] Misra, D., Mao, S., Rees, J., Thoma, G.R. 2007. Archiving a Historic Medico-legal Collection: Automation and Workflow Customization, *Proc. IS&T Archiving Conference*, Washington DC, pg 157-161. (2007).

[2] Reference Model for an Open Archival Information System (OAIS). 2002. http://www.ccsds.org/documents/pdf/CCSDS-650.0-R-2.pdf

[3] Misra, D., Chen, S., Thoma, G.R. 2009. **A** System for Automated Extraction of Metadata from Scanned Documents Using Layout Recognition and String Pattern Search Models, Proc. *IS&T Archiving Conference*. Arlin. pg 107-111. (2009).

[4] Cortes C., Vapnik V. 1995. Support-vector Network. Machine Learning. Vol. 20, pages 273-297, (1995).

[5] Rabiner, L. R., Juang, B. H. 1993. Fundamentals of Speech Recognition. Englewood Cliffs, NJ: Prentice-Hall. (1993).

[6] DSpace, MIT (http://www.dspace.org).

[7] The U.S.-Japan Cooperative Medical Science Program (http://www.niaid.nih.gov/topics/globalresearch/usjapan/Pages/history.aspx

[8] Named Entity Recognition (NER) and Information Extraction (IE) (http://www-nlp.stanford.edu/ner/)

[9] Zhang, X., Zou, J., Le, DX., Thoma, G.R. 2010. Investigator Name Recognition From Medical Journal Articles: A Comparative Study of SVM and Structural SVM., *International Workshop on Document Analysis Systems,* pg 121-128. (2010).

[10] PubMed (http://www.ncbi.nlm.nih.gov/pubmed/).

Teacher Sociality and Information Diffusion in Educational Digital Libraries

Ogheneovo Dibie
University of Colorado
Institute of Cognitive Science
Dept. of Computer Science
Boulder, Colorado USA
ogheneovo.dibie@colorado.edu

Keith E. Maull
University of Colorado
Institute of Cognitive Science
Dept. of Computer Science
Boulder, Colorado USA
maull@colorado.edu

Tamara Sumner
University of Colorado
Institute of Cognitive Science
Dept. of Computer Science
Boulder, Colorado USA
sumner@colorado.edu

ABSTRACT

Understanding the social aspects of digital resource utilization is an area of active research. In this study, we examine the digital library resource utilization and social behaviors of middle and high school Earth Science teachers of a large United States urban school district. We present the results of three analysis based on teachers using an online curriculum planning tool called the Curriculum Customization Service (CCS), and examine the social networks that emerge among the participating teachers. We explore these networks in the context of the digital library resources that were part of the CCS and the use of socio-centric features around those resources. Our initial findings show promise toward developing a broader understanding of the social networks of teachers, their behaviors around and usage of digital library resources, as well as the diffusion of information through those networks.

Categories and Subject Descriptors

H.3.7 [**Digital Libraries**]: Collection—*digital resources*; H.3.7 [**Digital Libraries**]: User Issues—*social networks*; H.4.m [**Information Systems**]: Information Systems Applications—*educational resources applications*

Keywords

Social network analysis, information diffusion, teacher collaboration

1. INTRODUCTION

Digital library resources are an important component of the pedagogical strategies used by teachers and schools. Many school districts are making significant investment in gaining access to digital libraries and repositories because the quality and educational relevance of the resources within such digital libraries often times better support their curricular needs and specialized pedagogical goals. As these libraries take a prominent place in the educational landscape, new challenges emerge in understanding the use of digital libraries. For example, it is no longer enough to know what resources within a library are being sought after and by whom. Instead it is now necessary to understand the usage context of resources, for example, whether the resources are used for teaching or as background material. Moreover, as digital libraries transform into social places – where users interact not only with the resources therein, but with other users of the same (or related) resources – developing analytic methods to determine the *social* aspects of digital libraries will be a crucial step in extending their end user value and utility. Thus, within the scope of digital libraries we are primarily concerned with examining: (1) the socio-centric functionality of objects (e.g. resources) within the library, (2) how such functionalities mediate social behaviors and networks, (3) the analytic tools that can be used to understand the networks, and (4) how such behaviors might inform the administration, promotion, design and utility of the digital library and its resources. In this paper, we present the preliminary results of a study of a social network of educators using digital library resources for their curriculum planning and classroom instruction activities.

JCDL'12, June 10–14, 2012, Washington, DC, USA.

2. RELATED WORK

Social network research is broadly tasked with analyzing the social relations and behaviors of individuals or groups. One of the core assumptions of social connectivity is that groups or individuals share some common relation or characteristic (e.g. interest, goal, affiliation, common relationship, etc.), and this is no less true in educational contexts. For example, a social network of school principals might be composed of the connectivity among just principals, where they share the characteristic of being the principal administrator of one or more schools within a common school district. Once social networks are established, an important area of research aims at examining *information diffusion* [11] between members in the network. That is, once a network has been identified, what are the characteristics of the movement of information within the network?

Online social networks have become a prominent area of research in part due to the rise of collaborative Web 2.0 technologies that support and encourage socio-centric behaviors. As people spend more time using social network and information sharing platforms such as Facebook, Google+, Twitter, etc., studying social networks reaches well beyond discovering *who* is in the network and *their relations*, but also *what* they mutually interact with and *how*. As these social platforms expand, communities develop around the shared concerns, goals and objectives of the participants within those communities. For example, users of online video sharing systems such as YouTube, spend time interacting with one another discussing the details of a particular video, yet they also rate, tag, annotate and share videos of interest. These kinds of social sharing behaviors frame the video as an "object of sociality" [2] which is at the heart of research aimed at understanding networks through objects that mediate social behaviors and activities within the network.

Social networks of educators have been recently studied in the context of communities of practice and participation [8, 6], teacher professional development [1], educational effectiveness and evaluation [9], as well as social learning [4]. An underlying motivation for studying these networks of educators is to understand the benefits of the network to its participants. For example, new teachers often rely on more experienced teachers to get through their first few years of teaching, and it is not clear how online social networks will change or influence these crucial professional interactions. Yet, as online communities of teachers grow, it will be important to understand the usage patterns of teachers within these communities, the kinds of information that is being exchanged within them, and the impact these communities have on communication, learner outcomes, teacher practice, effectiveness, productivity and satisfaction.

3. METHODOLOGY

The broad focus of this research is on analytic mechanisms for understanding how socio-centric digital library functionality mediates social behaviors and networks. However, this paper is aimed at a specific group: Earth Science school teachers; over a specific category of digital library resources: Earth systems resources. We are principally concerned about the characteristics and details of how networks of educators are formed, what the socio-centric behaviors are of the people within the network and how these behaviors can be analyzed in the context of socio-centric digital library tools and functionalities. Our guiding research questions, methods and data used in this research are : (1) *What do the social networks of teachers look like?* **Methods:** Analyze the social networks of Earth science teachers, **Data:** Pre-/post- survey questions, school affiliation, (2) *What online social behaviors can be observed in teachers using Earth science digital library resources?* **Methods:** Analyze the usage of socio-centric digital library functionality, **Data:** CCS online usage log data, and (3) *What can those online behaviors reveal about their social connections and visa versa?*, **Methods:** Analyze social networks in the context of the usage data, **Data:** Social network and usage data.

3.1 Data

For this study, we used data from over 100 same-district middle and high school Earth science teachers who, during the 2009-2010 academic year, participated in a field trial of an online curriculum planning and personalization system called the Curriculum Customization Service (CCS) [10]. The CCS is a web-based tool that provides teachers access to digital versions of publisher textbooks, teacher manuals and curriculum guides for Earth science curricula for both Grade 6 and Grade 9. Furthermore, these digital materials are linked to and associated with digital resources from the Digital Library for Earth System Education (DLESE), which is a collection of Earth science related digital resources that are part of the National Sciences Digital Library (NSDL). The CCS also provides functionality for teachers to upload their own materials so that they may be accessed easily in the future. As part of this uploading functionality, teachers may also share such materials into a common "Shared Stuff" area that other users of the system may access, rate, tag and further save into their own private collection of materials. For the duration of the academic year, we collected the detailed clickstream behavior of the participating teachers who logged into the system at least once, and further restricted this data to system functionalities that were relevant to socio-centric behaviors such as public sharing.

As part of the field trial, surveys were administered to the CCS participants that asked a number of questions about their teaching practices, digital library resource awareness and utilization, as well as their professional ties to other teachers. Three surveys were administered throughout the school year, but in this paper we analyzed the first (pre) and last (post) surveys. The pre-survey was conducted prior to the field trial and the post-survey was conducted at the end of the school year. Both surveys asked the same social network question: "Name THREE people [...] whom you most frequently consult regarding teaching-related issues. Please list individuals' names, not titles or descriptors such as department chair." The answers to these questions were normalized to correct for accuracy, such as misspelled names, duplicate or empty entries. The responses of 70 teachers from both surveys were found to be valid. By valid, we mean that each of the 70 teachers from both surveys mentioned at least one other teacher they consult regarding teacher-related issues. Finally, each respondent was matched to the school they were affiliated with so that a common relation could be later used to connect them within a social network.

3.2 Analysis

Our research methodology was divided into three analyses. The first analysis explored the social network that emerged from the survey question of section 3.1. The social network was built and analyzed for its structure and for changes from the pre- and post-survey. The second analysis analyzed the socio-centric sharing behavior of the teachers who both used the system *and* were either a survey participant or mentioned in the answer to the survey question (either pre- or post-). This analysis was designed to provide insight to the behavior of the actual users of the system. The third analysis analyzed the behavior of teachers who were participants in the survey *and* mentioned another teacher in their survey who was also a user of the system. A network of teachers was built and analyzed in the context of the specific sharing behavior of these users.

3.2.1 Pre-Post Survey Network Analysis

A directed network graph was constructed for both pre- and post- surveys with vertices indicating all individuals participating and mentioned in the surveys. A directed edge between two vertices represented the relation that the originating vertex was the individual that mentioned the destination vertex as someone being consulted for help. The network graphs of the pre- and post-survey were analyzed and both resulted in disconnected graphs made up of smaller connected sub-components (sub-graphs). Table 1 shows the summary of the connected components metrics for all teachers.

Table 1: Summary of analysis of the connected components (CC) in the pre- and post- survey.

	Pre-survey	Post-survey
Number of vertices	204	209
Number of CCs	30	35
Minimum CC size	2	3
Maximum CC size	53	28
Average CC size	6.8	5.97

A general trend discovered in both surveys was that vertices in smaller connected components (2-6 vertices) were primarily composed of teachers who worked in the same school. This is expected, as teachers who work in the same school are probably familiar with each other and comfortable seeking assistance from each other. However, in larger connected components were made up of districts from multiple schools. We elucidate on this more in later analysis.

In order to better understand the changes in the social network between each survey, we constrained the network to survey respondents who took both surveys. This was necessary to account for staffing changes (e.g. attrition) that may have occurred between both surveys. Table 2 shows the analysis of 51 teachers who participated in both surveys.

Table 2: Summary of analysis of the connected components (CC) in the pre- and post- survey of teachers who took both surveys.

	Pre-survey	Post-survey
Number of vertices	169	165
Number of CCs	28	30
Minimum CC size	2	3
Maximum CC size	38	20
Average CC size	6.0	5.5

This analysis showed similar trends with our first analysis summarized in Table 1. An interesting observation is that the largest sub-graph of the pre-survey had a network of 10 connected schools, while the largest sub-graph of the post-survey consisted of only four schools. This may be due to the larger fragmentation of the post survey compared to the pre survey (30 to 28 connected components). We also noticed in certain instances that the references of quite a few teachers changed between both surveys. This may be due to discovery of other teachers work from the CCS's social features or other factors outside the CCS.

Graph metrics such as Degree, Betweenness Centrality, PageRank, Closeness Centrality, etc. were measured for both survey networks to understand the relationships between the vertices in the graphs. PageRank (a measure of vertex importance based on the number of incoming links) and Betweenness Centrality (the number of shortest paths from all vertices to all others passing through a vertex) together provide information about 'hubs' and connectedness within a graph. Figure 1 shows a vertex representing an individual with the highest PageRank and Betweenness Centrality in a sub-graph. This vertex appears to be a hub connecting multiple schools. It has five incoming edges representing a connection with teachers from five different schools. The position of these hub vertices in the network may highlight their importance as conduits of information diffusion in the network.

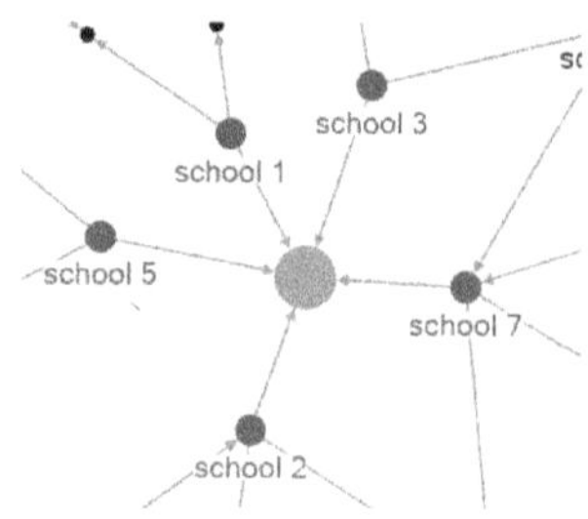

Figure 1: A connected sub-graph demonstrating a hub vertex connecting multiple schools, suggesting a potential channel of influence and information flow.

3.2.2 *System Usage Analysis*

As mentioned in section 3.1, the CCS provides socio-centric features such as tagging, rating and sharing digital resources that are part of the system. In our second analysis, we further analyzed the teachers in the social networks of the previous analysis to determine the usage of the socio-centric features of the CCS.

For this analysis, we limited our network to the subset of individuals who used and accessed the 'Shared Stuff' feature of the CCS. A user's 'Shared Stuff' behavior was determined by the number of clicks they had in that sub-component of the system, including uploads of educational materials and URLs intended to be shared with others. Also, click actions were counted that included viewing the materials shared by other teachers.

Much smaller networks resulted from the analysis of the pre- and post-survey when just considering actual users of the 'Shared Stuff' features of the system. The pre-survey network consisted of 17 vertices divided among 7 connected components, while the post-survey consisted of 20 vertices divided among 9 connected components. As in earlier analyses, most connected components in both pre- and post-survey networks were confined to teachers in the same school. Table 3 shows the usage behavior of the top five users in the post-survey network of the second analysis.

Table 3: The active sharing column indicates the number of contributed digital resources (materials uploaded or links shared) to 'Shared Stuff', while the total sharing column is an aggregate measure of all sharing behavior, including accesses to resources shared by others.

Vertex	Active sharing	Total sharing activity
A	0	147
B	3	431
C	5	194
D	23	279
E	34	185

3.2.3 *System Usage and Network Analysis*

In the third analysis, the socio-centric CCS usage of each teacher was overlayed onto the network structures from the pre- and post-surveys. Specifically, a network was constructed of just the teachers who mentioned each other and who were also users of the 'Shared Stuff' feature of CCS. Each teacher's click activity in the 'Shared Stuff' component of the system was computed, and a network graph was then constructed and each vertex scaled around the proportion of click activity in 'Shared Stuff'. The intuition of this analysis was that if two vertices are connected in the network, then their socio-centric behaviors within the system might indicate an information flow relationship. For example, if two vertices A and B were connected, and vertex A had more sharing behavior than B, then B could very well be relying on the shared resources of A – or at the very least have interest in them. Such a relationship might therefore reveal a potential flow of information through a known social connection.

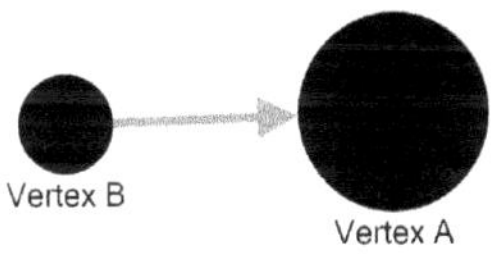

Figure 2: A connected sub-graph showing the relative sharing activity. Vertex A is larger relative to B because more sharing was going on, yet vertex B's edge is incident on A indicating B mentioned A as a resource they relied on in the survey question. Analysis from usage logs shows 70% of resources accessed by B were contributed by A.

In the post-survey results, the position of a vertex in a connected component within the network correlated to its sharing activity within the system. For example, vertices with incoming edges had much larger sharing activity within the CCS compared to vertices with just outgoing edges. This suggests that indeed there may be a relationship between the social relation between users in a network and the kinds of sharing activity that is going on between them. Figure 2 shows an example of the relationship that emerged from the third analysis.

4. DISCUSSION AND FUTURE WORK

In this paper, we have presented the preliminary results of a study of the social networks of teachers using digital library resources. The insights gained from studying the social behavior around objects of sociality, such as educational digital library resources in environments like the CCS, could be useful in three important ways. First, understanding information diffusion within a social network could help determine who and where the hubs of influence are within a network. For example, knowing that a teacher is more likely to view shared digital resources of another teacher (or group of teachers) may provide intuition into developing search interfaces or activity feeds that highlight shared resources of these teachers. Second, this knowledge on information flow within teacher social networks could be valuable in understanding information and communication bottlenecks, particularly in the case where information is *not* flowing. For example, teacher isolation in schools is a significant problem that could be addressed by network knowledge that might highlight teachers who are not connected or not collaborating with others within their expected or ideal networks [7]. Recent research also show a correlation between teacher isolation and lower student learning outcomes [3], yet many administrators do not recognize such isolation until after poor outcomes have been noticed or because the perception of their school's social network is often different from reality [5]. Finally, as digital library resources continue to grow as important tools in educational settings, library administrators and collection managers might develop a broader sense of the value of their resources if they understood the social behaviors that form around them, thus improving decision making from interface design to curation to communication.

5. ACKNOWLEDGMENTS

This material is based upon work supported in part by the NSDL program in the National Science Foundation under Awards #0734875 and #0840744 and by the University of Colorado at Boulder.

6. REFERENCES

[1] E. Bonsignore, D. Hansen, A. Galyardt, T. Aleahmad, and S. Hargadon. The power of social networking for professional development. In T. Gray and H. Silver-Pacuilla, editors, *Breakthrough Teaching and Learning*, pages 25–52. Springer, New York, NY, 2011.

[2] K. K. Cetina. Sociality with objects: Social relations in postsocial knowledge societies. *Theory, Culture & Society*, 14(4):1–30, Nov. 1997.

[3] K. Chenoweth. It can be done, it's being done, and here's how. *Phi Delta Kappan*, 91(1):38–43, 2009.

[4] D. Churchill, W. Wong, N. Law, D. Salter, and B. Tai. Social Bookmarking-Repository-Networking: possibilities for support of teaching and learning in higher education. *Serials Review*, 35(3):142–148, Sept. 2009.

[5] A. Daly and K. Finnigan. A bridge between worlds: Understanding network structure to understand change strategy. *Journal of Educational Change*, 11(2):111–138, 2010.

[6] P. A. Kirschner and K. Lai. Online communities of practice in education. *Technology, Pedagogy and Education*, 16:127–131, July 2007.

[7] N. M. Moolenaar, P. J. Sleegers, and A. J. Daly. Teaming up: Linking collaboration networks, collective efficacy, and student achievement. *Teaching and Teacher Education*, 28(2):251–262, Feb. 2012.

[8] J. A. Moore and B. Chae. Beginning teachers' use of online resources and communities. *Technology, Pedagogy and Education*, 16:215–224, July 2007.

[9] W. R. Penuel, W. Sussex, C. Korbak, and C. Hoadley. Investigating the potential of using social network analysis in educational evaluation. *American Journal of Evaluation*, 27(4):437–451, Dec. 2006.

[10] T. Sumner and C. Team. Customizing science instruction with educational digital libraries. In *Proceedings of the 10th annual joint conference on Digital libraries*, JCDL '10, pages 353–356, New York, NY, USA, 2010. ACM.

[11] J. Yang and J. Leskovec. Modeling information diffusion in implicit networks. In *IEEE International Conference on Data Mining*, pages 599–608, Los Alamitos, CA, USA, 2010. IEEE Computer Society.

Is It Time to Change the OER Repositories Role?

Christo Dichev
Computer Science Department
Winston Salem State University
Winston Salem, NC
dichevc@wssu.edu

Darina Dicheva
Computer Science Department
Winston Salem State University
Winston Salem, NC
dichevad@wssu.edu

ABSTRACT

The growing number of digital libraries providing open educational resources (OER) requires effective resource discovery mechanisms to optimally exploit the benefits of their openness. This paper discusses the OER repositories role and presents a study aimed at understanding how educators find OER by seeking answers to questions such as: what proportion of users seeking OER go directly to OER repositories and what proportion uses search engines or some other means and why. Understanding how and with what tools users discover and access resources can have an impact on the OER repositories strategic development.

Categories and Subject Descriptors

K.3.2 [**Computers and Education**]: Computer and Information Science Education; H.3.5 [**Information Storage and Retrieval**] On-line Information Services

General Terms

Design, Human Factors

Keywords

Open Education, Open Educational Repositories, Discoverability

1. INTRODUCTION

Open Educational Resources (OER) are learning materials that are freely available to use, adapt, remix, and redistribute. There has been a significant investment in the release of OER. As a result, the scope and availability of OER is expanding. The need for OER has a compelling logic. Even if we all embrace the idea of making teaching and learning content freely available, some institutions will ultimately have to pay for it. Therefore, such an investment should be justified by needs along with an adequacy to meet those needs. Although there are some reports on how institutional repositories such as MIT OCW and Open University OpenLearn have been used [1, 2], we are not aware of a large scale analysis addressing issues such as who is using OER and how. OER repositories, as a recent type of digital collections, include only part of the available online learning content. A wealth of useful content is also available on social sites such as YouTube and SlideShare along with large numbers of learning resources published on personal web sites. There are also many sites offering free tutorials and examples. Since search engines make this content findable, it is up to the user to decide which source to use. An interesting question in this context is how people find needed learning content. What is the source of that content? These questions become more pertinent, in light of the fact that out of every 10 people, 9 access online information through a search engine [3].

To gain insight into OER discovery and use we have collected qualitative data from actual and potential OER users via surveys. The first phase of our study was focused on assessing the need and utilization of OER in Computer Science education [4]. The objective was to identify the type of resources in demand, the major criteria for selecting resources and when and how the OER are used. With regards to OER utilization, predictably two groups of users were identified: one that is not aware of any OER repositories besides MIT OCW and another that is aware of some. More interesting was the fact that OER reuse happens in both groups. This raised questions such as: What proportion of users seeking OER go directly to OER repositories and when? What proportion use search engines and what some other means?

These questions motivated us to conduct a second survey to gather data about the current practices related to OER discovery and use. An additional factor was the growing evidence that instructors and students prefer search engines rather than selected and catalogued collections [5]. Additionally, we witness high overall use of search engines by various groups in our society [3]. If search engines dominate users' OER seeking behavior, this would require parallel efforts to make learning content 'search engine-friendly' or visible. A related question is what parts of the fragmented OER landscape attracts more users. Understanding how users discover and access learning resources and with what tools can have an impact on the OER development. In this sense, the survey results can shed light on the OER role and provide empirical evidence to help with decisions about future investments in the OER infrastructure.

The overall goal of this work is to study the actual role of OER repositories in comparison to other sources of open content. Although the emphasis is on Computer Science resources, the study has a broader scope. The next section compares the current alternatives for OER discovery and utilization and lays the motivation for our second study. Section 3 presents the results of the survey and is followed by a discussion and conclusion.

2. REPOSITORIES AND ALTENATIVES

Previous studies [e.g. 4, 6] and our research experience [7] indicate that in general OER repositories are underused. We have identified several possible reasons for this phenomenon. Most of the current OER repositories are based on learning object repositories, which in turn use earlier models of research repositories. However, the model of a research-style collection does not fit well in the routine practices of current day teachers

[8]. This observation is in line with the growing number of instructors who upload teaching material to systems such as YouTube, iTunes U and Slideshare, but are reluctant to do so in dedicated OER repositories. The differences between research and educational repositories arise from their dissimilar purposes:

- *Publicity*. Researchers want their research papers promoted and publicized. There are many incentives for that. However, there are few incentives to publish teaching materials. Some teachers prefer restricted access (e.g. to selected peers or students).
- *Structuring:* Teachers might prefer to classify their material under course titles, and subdivide by course topics rather than following a specific domain classification scheme.
- *Versions*. Research papers are generally a finished product. In contrast, many different versions of an individual learning resource may exist: versions from previous years or variations.
- *Retention*. There is a tradition of preservation and archiving of academic publications whereas there are no similar concerns about retaining and archiving teaching materials.
- *Publication type*. There is considerable variety in the source of learning material (e.g., text, images, videos, audio files, etc.), its format, and how it is used. In contrast, scholarly publications are of a more uniform type and format.
- *Audience*. Research papers are intended for other academics and researchers while learning materials are mainly intended for students and other instructors.

Some re-thinking of the repositories infrastructure is needed, which has to also address the problem of finding content in a collection distributed across separate repositories. Since they are perceived as isolated islands, one would currently either have to know a priori where to find the relevant content or search all repositories separately.

Search engines are an attractive alternative to the highly fragmented landscape that forces users to visit multiple distributed repositories. In [9] the authors observe that users frequently arrive at repository items from outside search engines rather than by browsing through the repository's organizational structure. Additionally, scientists are increasingly relying on Google to find scholarly literature, and college students overwhelmingly use search engines as a starting point of their information searches [3].

Another end of the OER spectrum are the individuals sharing content. There will always be some OER outside of the repository space. Therefore one of the key challenges discovery tools face is how to find and index OERs scattered across institutional repositories, social sites and individuals' pages. Besides, how to decide what is OER and what is not. Many believe that some type of structured data is necessary to improve search outcomes for educational materials. The Learning Resources Metadata Initiative (LRMI) [10] was formed in response to the growing need of making online learning resources more discoverable. It has been driven partly by the opportunity created by the schema.org project to develop and encourage use of metadata vocabularies, which can be used to enhance search results.

Future investments in the infrastructure of the OER repositories should be justified by comparing the amount of investment with other alternatives. This requires assessing the value of the repositories, their content and services. While much emphasis has been placed on creating various OER repositories, there has been little work on evaluating their outputs. Metrics such as the number of citations, downloads, citation/download correlations, and hub/authority indicators have been used in research repositories' assessment. In commercial sites, the level of success is measured by the ability to drive targeted traffic to the site. However, there are no metrics established for evaluating educational repositories. Relevant sources for measurement might be the number of resources, the number of resources added annually, who is using the repository and how satisfied users are. Yet, with few exceptions, there are no such reports.

For that reason, our survey was intended to inform the community about the current OER discovery and utilization strategies and to extrapolate based on the gathered information. In areas where quantitative data are incomplete or unavailable, surveys yield useful information. Despite their weaknesses, surveys can help diagnose a problem - a necessary prerequisite to resolving it.

3. THE STUDY

The purpose of the study was to obtain empirical evidence on how users typically discover OER content. Instructors are both producers and consumers of the content. Our study largely targets OER consumers, however, since our resource discovery objectives are more relevant to that group of users. We have chosen to explore the OER discovery in Computer Science teaching. Among the reasons are: it is a discipline where the content gets outdated quickly; it will allow us to analyze the results in the context of our previous study [4]. The survey was distributed to Computer Science instructors. Students were not targeted because sometimes their motivation for searching online resources is different from that of the instructors. In the survey we ask questions about the users' current or past behaviors. Drawing on previous experience, the idea is to extrapolate about future situations.

The survey was done through surveymonkey.com and consisted of fifteen questions - the first three targeting demographic information and the remaining focusing on OER discovery. An invitation for participation was sent through SIGCSE, OCW/OER, UK OER, research mailing lists, LinkedIn groups, selected departments, and individual emails. A total of 374 instructors responded. The data came from various university categories: doctoral/research universities (38.3%), masters (27.8%) and baccalaureate (21.6%) colleges and universities, associate colleges (7.3%) and other (5.1%). The list of survey participants includes instructors from various geographic regions: North America (145), Europe (101), Asia, Australia and NZ (54), South/Central America and Caribbean (40), and Africa (32). The profile of the respondents confirmed that we reached our intended audience with 79.6% of respondents identifying themselves as educators with five or more years and 20.4% with less than five years computer science teaching experience.

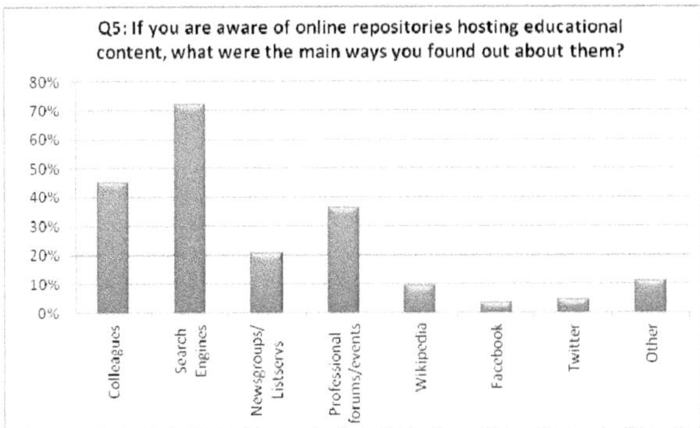

Figure 1. Answers of Question #5

Before exploring the way OER resources are discovered and used, we needed to establish teachers' awareness of repositories hosting such resources. The survey results indicate that 92.1% of the respondents are aware of the existence of OER repositories. Somewhat unexpected were the answers to the question about the main ways users found out about online repositories hosting educational content, in which the majority of the respondents (72.3%) reported that they became aware of repositories through search engines (see Fig. 1). The answers to this question signal that search engines are contributing to the popularization of OER. This fact can be exploited to increase the traffic and reputation of the repositories and their supporting institutions. A fair amount of respondents became aware of repositories through colleagues (45.2%), professional forums (36.5%) and newsgroups (20.6%).

The next question addressed OER repositories utilization. Of the respondents who were aware of OER repositories, 85.8% have used OER content in their teaching materials (we label the remaining part as "potential users"). Thus the survey confirmed that Computer Science instructors do use open content. However, the next question "*If you use open educational content what is the typical source of that content?*" (Fig. 2) revealed that the most common source of such content were personal web sites (68.4%). The use of materials from OER repositories is less common (48.3%). An interesting observation is that the use of online textbook materials and wiki-based learning content, blogs, and social sites, is comparable with the use of educational repositories/institutional sites as a source of teaching materials. The pattern of OER repository use that emerged was that the majority of respondents knew about repositories, but less than half have used them to locate CS materials. This fact makes repository existence in the present form questionable.

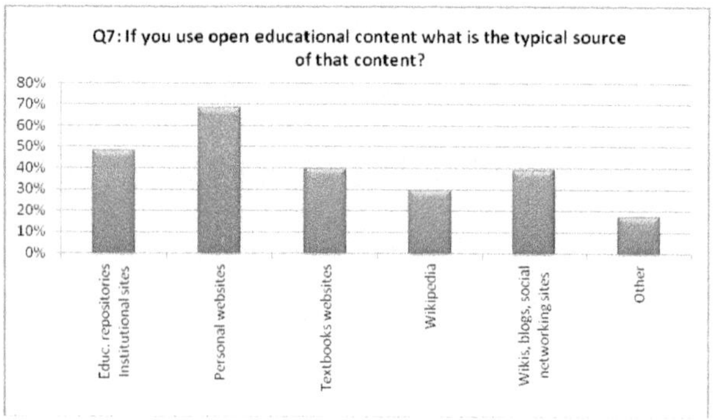

Figure 2. Answers of Question #7

As to the typical level of granularity of open content sought by instructors, the survey shows that most of them (57.1%) seek components that are part of a lecture or activity. The next group (29.7%) is of those who seek larger units (at a lecture/activity level: notes, assignments, tests, etc.), while only 11.9% seek course level content. This fact demonstrates the need for opening repositories up for external (e.g. full text search), so that educators can identify components of interest inside the stored materials.

The question "*How do you typically search for open educational content?*" is central to our survey. The responses to this question, shown in Fig. 3, confirm that search engines are by far the most popular way educators look for open content, with 53.5% of all respondents declaring they use exclusively search engines. Using mainly search engines, but sometimes navigating and searching OER repositories or going to familiar/recommended sites, was the second alternative (21%). About 12% of educators typically go to familiar/recommended sites and sometimes use search engines or navigate OER repositories. Interestingly, the least popular way of searching for OER (3.5%) is by navigating and searching OER repositories only. This observation suggests that the use of OER repositories content is largely due to the traffic that search engines direct to them and that the use of OER material resulting from direct visits to the repositories is insignificant.

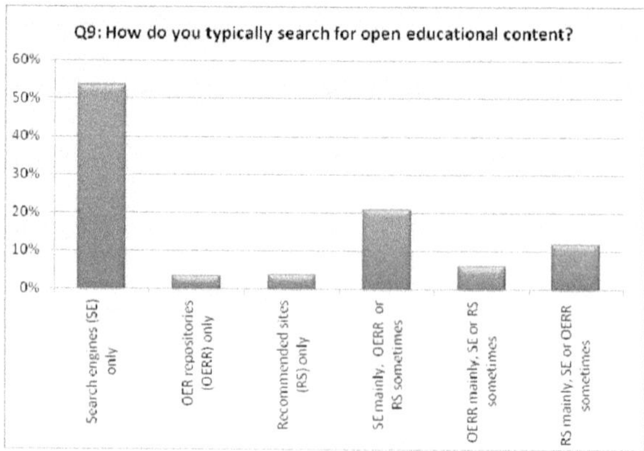

Figure 3. Answers of Question #9

As to the search engines' features that make them a preferable tool for locating educational resources, almost 78% of the respondents felt that "Ability to search for any resource" is the most attractive feature. Next in the list are "Convenience, immediacy and ease of use" (60.3%), followed by "Ability to accomplish my search tasks successfully in most cases" (49.8%). Lower in the list but not insignificant are "Ability to narrow and expand searches" (21.3%) and "Reliability and efficiency" (21%). Only about 10% of the responses pointed "Popularity and reputation" as a factor for choosing search engines as a primary tool for locating OER. The majority of the respondents (48.5%) tend to not use advanced options when searching for learning resources. Less than one third claimed that they used advanced search and 23.1% claimed that they used this option sometimes.

Of the respondents who declared going to OER repositories when looking for learning materials, 68.1% felt that "Quality control of the hosted material" is the central feature of the repositories. The next are "Release of the content under open content licenses" (54.3%) and "Ability for the users to explore resources in their own way" (36.2%). Less than a third of the respondents (27.7%) think that "Intuitive classification that supports organized browsing/exploration" is a critical feature of the OER repositories.

Concerning the start time for searching needed OER, 38.9% of the respondents declared that they start searching days before their actual use, 22.6% - only hours, and 26.4% - weeks before the use of the resources. Only a small number of the respondents (10.2%) claimed starting looking for OER months before their actual use. When limited time is a factor in the preparation of class materials, the immediacy and familiarity of search engines play a major role in choosing them as a tool for finding OER content. The fact that a significant number of instructors search for OER just hours before their use in class suggests that they look for updates or adaptation of existing material. This implies choosing a tool that allows quick location of *content fragments*. At present, search engines offer better support than OER repositories for locating fragments within a document.

The responses to the question "*How do you find needed online information relating to your professional development?*" confirms that the search engines (esp. Google) dominate every aspect of information discovery for both teaching and research. About 74% of the respondents use search engines, 23.8% use search engines and repositories, while just 2% use only repositories. The prevalent presence of the search engines (esp. Google) in the daily professional activities influences the choices instructors make about how to find teaching materials.

The open question asking for comments at the end generated interesting observations most of which are particularly relevant to the current practice of seeking OER content. The expressed opinions are dominated by the following viewpoints:

- The content organization and search mechanisms provided by current OER repositories are inadequate.
- Instructors depend increasingly on web search engines for locating relevant information including OER materials.
- The primary tool for finding OER is Google.

The following comment made in the survey is a concise summary of the mix of opinions expressed by respondents.

I don't care if the material that I need for my class comes from a repository, personal or corporate site. What I care is to be able to find it quickly with my search engine.

The majority of respondents seem to share the opinion communicated by another participant (see the complete survey results at http://iiscs.wssu.edu/drupal/?q=node/1641).

Open Content is only one part of the OER structure. The remaining parts are equally important. Making quality content appear in the Google top pages would be one of the greatest enablers for widespread use of Open Educational Resources.

4. DISCUSSION AND CONCLUSION

OER content is equally valuable, no matter where it resides - in institutional repositories, social/web2.0 or personal sites. This implies a need of an aggregated representation of available OER. Perhaps the most visible and well funded part of the open education movement is the generation of free, open content. Quality content is a vital part of establishing a practice of use, re-use and remix. However, content is worth a lot less on its own than in conjunction with practices, and appropriate infrastructure.

The survey results suggest that finding OER content should be easy and convenient - as easy and convenient as Google's Boolean search. The emerging pattern of locating OER content is through search engines. The survey data signals that the focus should be shifted on tools and standards that enable efficient finding of all types of resources independently of their location. This implies mechanisms allowing users (and agents) to know which content is open and which not. A promising direction is to encourage the use of metadata vocabularies developed under initiatives (such as LRMI) based on the schema.org project, which is intended to enhance web search results.

The second important finding is that the bulk of the used OER content comes from non-repository sites, despite the fact that the OER movement seems to favor institution-centric practice. Since attempts trying to enforce behavioral changes typically fail [11], a better strategy would be to shift the repositories' role from maintaining browsable and searchable catalogs of resources to maintaining integrity, archiving, high visibility, and stewardship of those resources.

The fact that the majority of respondents declared that they search for fragments of lectures or activities indicates that repositories should be opened up for full text search or properly annotated. Facilitating the location of relevant fragments would aid content repurposing and remixing. Besides, incorporating features from Distributed Version Control Systems would allow tracing a document's origin, as well as how it was changed and distributed.

A significant proportion of instructors reported using wiki and social site based materials, which indicates that community-driven repositories, such as Wikiversity, Wikieducator, YouTube, iTunes U, Slideshare, etc., are also parts of the OER mosaic, linked to the OER infrastructure mainly though search engines. The wiki/social model is sustainable, since it is community-driven: people and groups sharing for their own benefit. An additional source of open content may come through Learning Management Systems (LMS) that contain a significant amount of locked up content. LMS still have weak links to external repositories. Supported export can open new content for reuse. Instructors who are reluctant to invest time for publishing their content as OER can do it through LMS.

Knowing how people seek OER content can lead to more informed decisions on the investments aimed at maximizing the use of the existing resources. Overall, the results of this study suggest that there might be a need for re-thinking the role of the OER repositories, so that they are increasingly used for archiving and preservation and as components of a global network of resources with high visibility, while discovering is performed largely through search engines. Based on our study, we conclude that repositories can increase their resources' utilization by conforming to the prevalent searching behavior of OER users. Using standard metadata (e.g. schema.org extensions) can make the content understood by search engines and thus regularly found by users.

The power in OER is not in their production; it is in their reuse by other educators and learners. This study was inspired by our belief that if OER discovery is improved and simplified, many OER aspirations such as widespread remix, repurposing, and redistribution could become part of the educational practice.

5. ACKNOWLEDGMENTS

This material is based upon work supported by the NSF Grant No. DUE-1044224 "NSDL: Social Bookmarking for Digital Libraries: Improving Resource Sharing and Discoverability".

6. REFERENCES

[1] http://www.bb.ustc.edu.cn/ocw/NR/rdonlyres/1118F4F3-AA41-4CB4-B71F-F6E058AD22AA/0/MIT_OCW_Approach_10_5_04.pdf (visited Jan. 27, 2012).

[2] http://archive.futurelab.org.uk/resources/publications-reports-articles/web-articles/Web-Article693.

[3] Jamali H.R, Asadi S. Google and the scholar: the role of Google in scientists' information-seeking behavior. *Online Information Review*, Vol. 34, No. 2, 282-294, 2010.

[4] Dichev C., Dicheva D. Open Educational Resources in Computer Science Teaching, *In Proc. SIGCSE'12*, Raleigh, NC, 2012.

[5] McKnight S. (ed.) *Envisioning Future Library Services: Initiatives, Ideas and Challenges*, Facet Publishing, 2010.

[6] Mitchell, S. M. and Lutters, W. G. Assessing the Value of Computer Science Course Material Repositories. In *Proc. of CSEETW'06*, IEEE Computer Society, 2006.

[7] Dicheva D., Dichev, Ch. A Framework for Concept-Based Digital Course Libraries. *Journal of Interactive Learning Research (JILR)*, 15(4), 347-364, 2004.

[8] Rothery A. and Hayes S. Is there a role for online repositories in e-Learning? In *Proc. EUNIS 2008 VISION IT*: Aarhus University, Denmark, June 24-27, 2008.

[9] Mercer H., Koenig J., McGeachin R., Tucker S. Structure, Features, and Faculty Content in ARL Member Repositories. *Journal of Academic Librarianship* 37:4, 333-342, 2011.

[10] http://creativecommons.org/tag/lrmi (visited April 9, 2012).

[11] Lynch C. A. Institutional Repositories: Essential Infrastructure for Scholarship in the Digital Age. *ARL (226)*, 1–7, 2003.

Identifying Core Concepts in Educational Resources

James M. Foster, Md. Arafat Sultan, Holly Devaul[2], Ifeyinwa Okoye, Tamara Sumner
Institute of Cognitive Science
University of Colorado, Boulder, CO 80309
Digital Learning Sciences[2]
University Corporation for Atmospheric Research, 80307
{james.m.foster, arafat.sultan, ifeyinwa.okoye, sumner}@colorado.edu
devaul@ucar.edu[2]

ABSTRACT

This paper describes the results of a study designed to assess human expert ratings of educational concept features for use in automatic core concept extraction systems. Digital library resources provided the content base for human experts to annotate automatically extracted concepts on seven dimensions: coreness, local importance, topic, content, phrasing, structure, and function. The annotated concepts were used as training data to build a machine learning classifier as part of a tool used to predict the core concepts in the document. These predictions were compared with the experts' judgment of concept coreness.

Categories and Subject Descriptors

H.3.7 [**Digital Libraries**]: Collection – *digital resources;* I.2.7 [**Natural Language Processing**]: Text Analysis – *multi-document summarization;* K.3.1. [**Computers and Education**]: Computer Uses in Education – *Computer-aided instruction.*

General Terms

Algorithms, Design, Experimentation, Human Factors, Measurement, Performance

Keywords

Core Concepts, Multi-document Summarization

1. INTRODUCTION

Users of digital libraries can be overwhelmed by the amount of information available. Although digital libraries address the issue of information overload present on the larger Internet, it is still a significant cognitive task to evaluate and choose resources appropriate for particular educational purposes. Scalable automatic techniques can help filter the information most relevant and important to users. Multi-document summarization offers ways of automatically distilling digital resources into summaries. Our research builds on summarization systems by identifying core concepts that are central ideas in a scientific domain. Core concepts are the critical ideas necessary to support deep science learning and understanding.

Focusing on core concepts is an important strategy for developing enduring understanding that transfers to new domains [15], hence selecting educational resources that address these concepts is a critical task in supporting learners. This work examines a range of high and intermediate level features of digital resources, and uses human expert annotations to determine what features can be used to develop an algorithm that can identify core concepts within a resource. The features that were considered include intermediate level features that require some training to extract: local importance, topic, content, phrasing, structure, and function. Low level features are those that would be straightforward to extract from text, such as sentence length.

We used human domain experts to annotate a corpus of digital educational resources to provide data on human assessment of coreness, as well as the intermediate level features. The key questions this paper addresses are: Can domain experts agree on coreness ratings of educational concepts? How well can intermediate level features be used to predict those coreness ratings?

We find that domain experts can agree on concept coreness ratings, and that intermediate-level annotated features can be used to computationally predict these coreness ratings.

In the remainder of this paper we first review related work in concept coreness and multi-document summarization. We then describe the concept annotation methodology and coding protocol. Finally we present an analysis of the annotations and results of a machine learning approach to predicting concept coreness.

2. RELATED WORK

Multi-document summarization systems try to extract important concepts and cover the breadth of information present in a set of digital documents [12]. Systems such as MEAD [14] focus on summarizing news articles. MEAD has been augmented with additional features customized for educational resources and released as COGENT [9].

COGENT was developed in the context of a cognitive personalization service called CLICK, the Customized Learning ServIce for Concept Knowledge [5]. "Cognitive personalization tools support student learning by matching students with sets of educational resources that they, as individual learners with a unique profile of prior knowledge and misunderstandings, need in order to develop a more complete and coherent understanding of the topic at hand (p. 125-126) [5]." The goal of CLICK is to automatically diagnose learner misunderstandings and generate personalized instruction plans using digital libraries. CLICK first constructs a knowledge map of a scientific domain such as plate tectonics using the COGENT multi-document summarization and concept linking algorithms. This map serves as a representation of domain competency. Learners write an essay on what they know about a topic, e.g., earthquakes. Based on this essay, CLICK constructs another knowledge map representing the learner's knowledge.

The reference map and student map are compared in order to identify misconceptions, knowledge gaps, and fragmented knowledge with the Concept Map Comparison Engine [2]. The relevant nodes in the reference map are used as queries to find the

JCDL'12, June 10-14, 2012, Washington, DC, USA.

specific digital library resources most relevant to the learner's needs. With many possible remediations, there is a need to prioritize which learner conceptual needs to respond to with personalized resource recommendations. The ability to identify core concepts is needed to help prioritize instructional interventions and provide pedagogical feedback to enable robust student learning.

Integrating the ability to identify core concept will refine CLICK's interactions with students in three ways. First, we can ignore certain student difficulties by filtering those that are not associated with core concepts in the domain. Second, we can prioritize the remaining difficulties according to their relative positions within a learning progression as encoded in the core concept prioritization. Finally, we can tailor our response to the student knowledge problem by exploiting the types of concepts being addressed.

The goal of this research is to computationally identify the core concepts in the set of concepts that have been extracted by a summarization system. Core concept identification differs from summarization in that the concepts produced by summarization don't necessarily emphasize the understandings central to a domain but may include a range of ideas of varying importance. *Big ideas* or *linchpin ideas* are "the core concepts, principles, theories, and processes that should serve as the focal point of curricula, instruction, and assessment ...are important and enduring, and are transferable beyond the scope of a particular unit, ... are the building material of understandings, ... and are the meaningful patterns that enable one to connect the dots of otherwise fragmented knowledge (p. 338-339) [15]."

Our approach to identifying core concepts as distinct from less important concepts leverages vetted national education learning standards that articulate core science concepts across numerous domains. Specifically, we used the AAAS Project 2061 Benchmarks for Science Literacy and the National Science Education Standards [1, 13]. The standards and benchmarks embody the notion of critical central ideas in science. They are accepted as representing the core ideas of science understandings at specific grade levels.

An example of a core concept from the biological evolution domain is "The central idea of biological evolution is that all life on Earth shares a common ancestor, just as you and your cousins share a common grandmother." Another core concept from plate tectonics is "The Earth's internal heat source provides the energy for our dynamic planet, supplying it with the driving force for plate-tectonic motion, and for on-going catastrophic events such as earthquakes and volcanic eruptions." Note all examples of educational concepts are from the Digital Library for Earth Science Education (DLESE.org).

Our adaptations of prior work on concept features resulted in a specification of concept features. In addition to coreness, we considered structure, function, local importance, content, phrasing, and topic. These features embody the importance, presentation, intent, context, content, and expression of educational concepts.

A core concept must also be presented effectively to a learner to support understanding. Concept presentation is specified in the concept *structure* feature. In order to successfully teach concepts learners need a definition, an example, a non-example, and an analogy [7]. A definition is a statement of the critical features associated with a concept. An example is an instance of a concept. An analogy is a representation that corresponds with a concept in function or form but which is otherwise dissimilar. Analogies are typically drawn from a domain different from that of the target material being learned. Non-examples are examples that are not instances of the concept. We used these descriptors to guide us in developing a set of terms for human experts to classify the structure of concepts extracted from resources. We did not expect non-examples in the educational resources and so did not include non-example in this protocol. Instead we added the term "explanation" which is a description or analysis of a concept. Analysis can include comparison of ideas (e.g., plate tectonics vs. continental drift), or making connections with other concepts. These terms (definition, example, explanation and analogy) were used to classify the *structure* of how a concept is presented.

To clarify the structure feature, example concepts for each structure type follow. Definition: "The place where two plates meet is called a plate boundary." Example: "The San Andreas fault in CA is a transform boundary where an oceanic plate is sliding past a continental plate." Analogy: "Plate material moves in a conveyer-belt fashion as it is continuously added at one end of a plate and sinks into the earth's interior or crumples up to form mountains at the other end of the plate." Explanation: "The earth is incredibly dynamic - mountain chains build and erode away, volcanoes erupt and go extinct, seas advance and recede - and these changes are all a result of the processes of plate tectonics."

The type of knowledge a concept is intended to elicit is another important dimension relevant to concept coreness. Farnham-Diggory identifies five types of knowledge: declarative (verbal learning), procedural (skill learning), conceptual (concept attainment), analogical (one-trial learning), and logical (problem solving) [10]. We adapted this typology for our annotation protocol to describe the concept *function* feature to include the terms declarative, conceptual, analogical, or scientific method. These functions are described in more detail in the Codes section. The procedural and logical categories were considered not relevant to our educational concept annotation and were not included.

Example concepts for each function type follow. Declarative: "There are four types of plate boundaries." Conceptual: "Paleomagnetism is based on the principle that in molten igneous rocks, or unlithified sediments, magnetic particles will align themselves with the Earth's magnetic field." Relational: "Mountain ranges sometimes are formed by the stress of plates pushing against each other." Scientific Method: "Scientists were able to prove that the rocks nearest the mid-ocean mountains were younger than the rocks farther away by using the magnetic information recorded in rocks to find their age."

The full set of concept features is detailed in the Codes section. The seven features are: coreness, local importance, topic, content, phrasing, structure, and function.

3. METHODOLOGY

First, we selected resources from the Digital Library for Earth System Education from three domains (Plate Tectonics, Weather and Climate, and Biological Evolution) (DLESE.org). Then we ran the COGENT concept extraction algorithm on the resources [9]. Concepts extracted by the algorithm were highlighted in their original context of the resource. A graphical description of our methodology is provided in Figure 1.

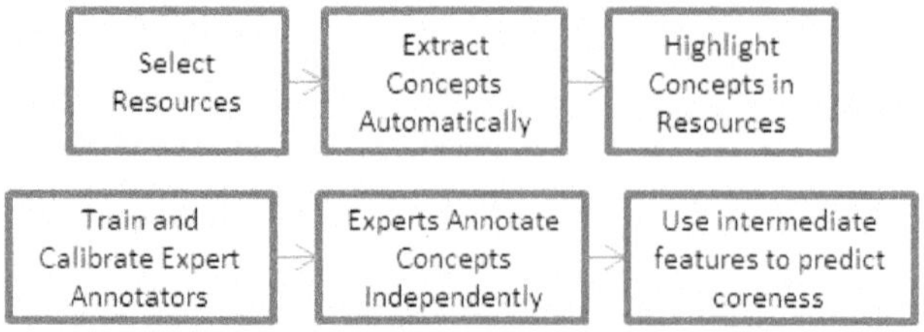

Figure 1. Methodology sequence. Automatically extracted concepts were annotated by experts and then used in a coreness classifier.

Then we trained and calibrated two experts from each domain on the annotation protocol, which is described in the following sections. Each expert then independently annotated concepts that were automatically extracted from his or her domain. Each expert was randomly assigned extracted concepts to annotate with nearly 20% of concepts being double annotated to allow inter-rater reliability to be calculated. The experts used a browser plugin to log in and annotate one highlighted concept at a time along the seven dimensions (coreness, local importance, topic, content, phrasing, structure, and function) after reading the text of the entire resource. Then we analyzed the annotations and used a machine learning classifier to predict coreness ratings.

3.1 Preparation of Materials

The selected resources are the data foundation for the automatic extraction, linking, and labeling of concepts in CLICK. Twenty resources were selected by a science education expert for each of three domains: Plate Tectonics, Weather and Climate, and Biological Evolution.

The criteria for selection were similar to those used by de la Chica et al. [9]. First, resources appropriate for the targeted grade levels of middle and high school (i.e., grades 6 through 12) were identified. Second, the expert selected resources to provide comprehensive coverage about the topic (Plate Tectonics, Weather and Climate, or Biological Evolution) for students in grades 6 through 12. Comprehensive coverage was defined by the benchmarks and standards for these topics in both the National Science Education Standards and the AAAS Benchmarks for Science Literacy for middle and high school. Finally, from this group, resources that contained good, expository, machine-readable text were selected.

The COGENT extraction algorithm is thoroughly described in [9]. It builds on the MEAD multi-document summarization and evaluation platform [14] with additional features based on domain content, document structure, and sentence length. These features are similarity of sentence to educational standards, gazetteer keywords, hypertext structure, and content word density.

Our current work builds on COGENT with a core concept identification module that predicts expert coreness ratings and is described in the Computational Results section.

3.2 Expert Annotation

The rationale of the annotation was to create high-quality training datasets for use in the automatic extraction of important concepts from digital resources. We focus on high-level concept "coreness" and intermediate-level information of its topic, context, structure and function, content, and phrasing. The ultimate machine learning goal is to use automatically extracted low-level features to identify intermediate-level information, which in turn help to identify high-level information. These data will be used to augment the existing COGENT extraction algorithm.

Our experts were recruited based on their training and experience in the relevant domains. All had Masters or PhD level science content degrees and professional or academic experience in science education.

3.3 Codes

Coreness is the importance of the concept to the domain as a whole as described by the learning standards. It was annotated on a scale of 1 to 4, where 1 means least important and 4 means most important. We chose a 4 point scale to prevent annotators from being undecided on the valence of coreness (core or not core).

The local importance feature indicates the importance of the concept to the particular resource from which it was extracted. It contrasts with coreness in that local importance is centrality to the *resource*, while coreness is centrality to the domain as described by the *learning standards*.

The topic feature aligns concepts to their most closely related learning standard. The topic categorization is useful in clustering related concepts and linking related nodes together in a knowledge map.

The content feature is intended to indicate independence or dependence of the concept's meaning. Is the concept useful by itself? Or is it only useful when presented with other concepts? For the purposes of extraction, concepts are considered to be synonymous with sentences. Of course, concepts may also be expressed with multiple sentences. The content feature was intended to indicate if extraction should expand concept scope to multiple sentences.

The phrasing feature indicates whether the expression of the concept makes sense on its own, out of context of the rest of the resource or surrounding paragraph. Since only single sentences are extracted and included in the knowledge map, it is important to be able to replace pronouns with their referents, i.e., anaphora resolution. For the purposes of the content feature, we allowed annotators to consider the pronoun referents. Table 1 shows the list of the first five features with their possible values, a description of the feature, and the intended purpose of the feature.

As detailed in the related work section, the structure feature indicates how the concept is presented: as a definition, explanation, example, or analogy. Table 2 describes the structure feature and its possible values.

The function feature indicates the type of learning intended: declarative, conceptual, relational, or scientific method. We limited relational concepts to cause and effect relations only because relational is too broad a category on its own. Scientific method was added to capture concepts that illustrate the process of science itself, rather than specific domain knowledge. Scientific method concepts emphasize reasoning, analysis, and synthesis skills. Table 3 shows the function feature and its possible values.

Table 1. Explanation of coreness, local importance, topic, content, and phrasing features

Feature	Values	Description	Purpose
Coreness	1 (least important) to 4 (most important)	Centrality (degree of alignment) to the learning standards for this domain.	Identifying key concepts in the domain.
Local Importance	1 (least important) to 4 (most important)	Centrality of the concept to this resource.	Identifying key concepts in the resource.
Topic	Set of AAAS and NSES learning standards	Which AAAS or NSES learning goal does this concept best align with?	Used for grouping related concepts.
Content	Independent or Dependent	Is this concept useful by itself or only useful when presented with other concepts?	Used to assess concept scope.
Phrasing	Independent or Dependent	Does the phrasing of the sentence make sense on its own – out of context?	Used to indicate need for anaphora resolution.

Table 2. Possible values of the structure feature

Structure Feature (how concept is presented)	**Description**
Definition	A statement of the critical features associated with a concept.
Explanation	A description or analysis of a concept. Analysis can include comparison of ideas (e.g., plate tectonics vs. continental drift), or making connections with other concepts.
Example	A real instance of the concept.
Analogy	A representation that corresponds with a concept in function or form but which is otherwise dissimilar. Analogies are typically drawn from a domain different from that of the target material being learned.

Table 3. Possible values of the function feature

Function Feature (type of learning intended)	**Description**
Declarative	Factual knowledge that can be declared, usually in words or mathematical notation.
Conceptual	Semantic knowledge that requires abstract understanding of systems or processes.
Relational	Description of a cause and its effect.
Scientific Method	Concepts that illustrate the process of science, such as hypothesis testing, gathering evidence, analyzing data, and theory building.

4. RESULTS

First we describe the results of the annotation study in Section 4.1. Then we present the results of our computational analysis of the annotation data in Section 4.2.

4.1 Annotation Study Results

In total, 352 unique concepts were annotated, with 61 double-annotated (17% instead of 20% because one weather and climate annotator didn't finish). There were 116 concepts annotated in Plate Tectonics, 170 in Weather and Climate, and 127 in Biological Evolution. The next two tables present inter-rater reliability data. We interpret these results to indicate that expert annotators can agree, to an extent. Topic agreement was not calculated because the educational standards overlap so there are multiple correct answers.

Coreness and Local Importance were annotated on a numerical scale from 1 to 4 so we used Spearman's rho measure of agreement. The other features were categorical and so we used Cohen's kappa measure of agreement. Table 4 and Table 5 show inter-rater reliability statistics.

We calculated average coreness at different extraction percentages. Figure 2 shows the results (subject domains are represented by their acronyms in this and subsequent figures: *PT* for *Plate Tectonics*, *BE* for *Biological Evolution* and *WC* for *Weather & Climate*). As the figure shows, for plate tectonics, increasing the number of sentences extracted decreased the average coreness. This result helps validate the extraction algorithm's effectiveness in plate tectonics. For weather and climate and biological evolution, the average coreness did not seem to depend on the number of sentences extracted. These results are likely explained because the COGENT extraction algorithm was developed and tuned for plate tectonics. We wanted to evaluate the generalizability of the algorithm on a near domain that is similar to Plate Tectonics, and a far domain that is less similar. The algorithm performs nearly as well on the near-domain of weather and climate. Biological Evolution is our far-domain test bed and the algorithm performs worse as expected.

Table 4. Inter-rater reliability of coreness and local importance features

Feature	Spearman's rho	Strength see [8]
Coreness	0.38	Medium
Local Importance	0.51	Strong

Table 5. Inter-rater reliability of structure, function, content, and phrasing features

Feature	Cohen's kappa	Strength see [4]
Structure	0.49	Moderate
Function	0.52	Moderate
Content	0.25	Fair
Phrasing	0.62	Good

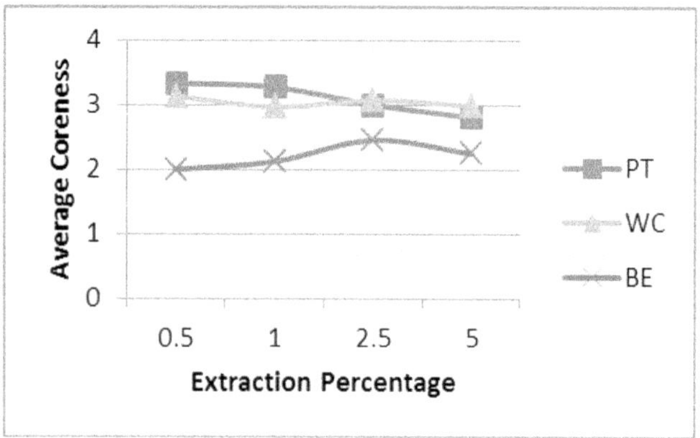

Figure 2. Average coreness at different extraction percentages.

Figure 3 shows the number of concepts annotated with each learning goal (i.e., topic). Each colored line represents a different domain. There is no relationship between the numbering of topics between domains. Plate Tectonics had 18 topics, Weather and Climate had 27 topics, and Biological Evolution had 19 topics. Certain standards appear to be widely covered by the extraction while others seem to lack coverage. This large variability could be caused by bias in the raters towards certain standards, bias in the extraction algorithm, or redundancy in the learning standards since we aggregated both the AAAS Benchmarks and the National Science Education Standards into our topic list.

4.2 Computational Study Results

Computational analysis of the annotation data has produced interesting and significant results related to concept coreness and the intermediate-level concept features. In this section, we report the results of this computational analysis along the following three dimensions:

1. Distribution of different feature values across different subject domains.

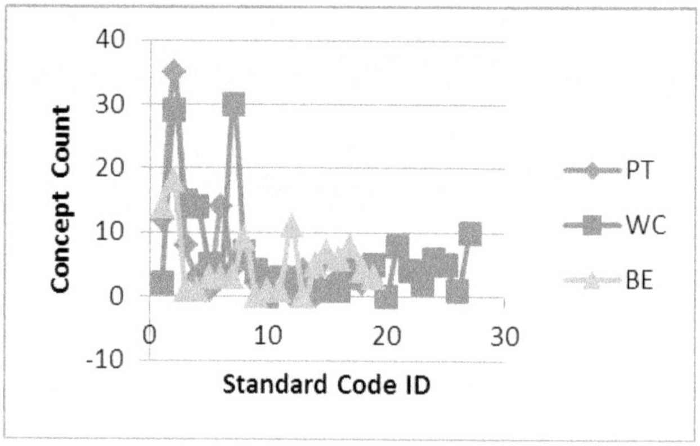

Figure 3. Concept coverage of AAAS Benchmarks and National Science Education Standards topics. There is no relation between Standard Code Ids among domains.

2. Relationship between each individual feature (i.e. the intermediate-level features) of a concept and its coreness.
3. Prediction of concept coreness as a multivariate function of the intermediate-level features.

4.2.1 Feature-Value Distribution in Three Subject Domains

We have examined the behavior of the concepts in the three subject domains (*Plate Tectonics*, *Biological Evolution* and *Weather and Climate*) in terms of six concept features: *content*, *phrasing*, *structure*, *function*, *local importance* and *coreness*. Each part of Figure 4 shows the distribution of a feature's values (in percentage) in all the three dimensions. For example Figure 4(a) shows that over 60% concepts in *Plate Tectonics* are independent in content and the rest are dependent on other concepts in the resource. On the other hand, in *Biological Evolution*, just over 20% of the concepts are independent in their content.

It is evident from Figure 4 that concept features follow very different distributions in different domains. But as we will see in Section 4.2.3, this variability does not affect the effectiveness of the concept features as predictors of concept coreness, as in each of the domains our feature-based predictor performs significantly better than the baseline. We argue that this variability demonstrated by the set of our selected domains makes this set sufficiently general and proves the applicability of our feature set in concept coreness prediction over subject domains of varying nature.

4.2.2 Individual Concept Features as Predictors of Coreness

In this experiment, we examine the individual effectiveness of each feature in extracting highly core concepts from a resource. The aim of this analysis is not to come to a conclusion about the relationship between our predictive features and the coreness of a concept. Rather, we are trying to see here if the results are promising enough so as to encourage a deeper and more powerful next step of analysis.

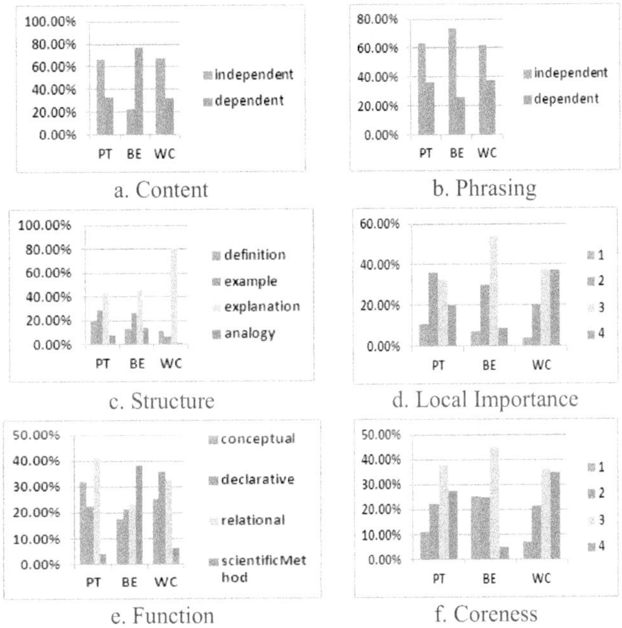

Figure 4. Distribution of feature values in three subject domains. Our selected domains significantly varied in their distribution of concept features.

Specifically, we have analyzed how well each value of a feature does in extracting concepts with high coreness rating. For example, if we label all "independent-content" annotated concepts as core concepts, we ask the question – "how good is this hypothesis?" We ask the same question for "dependent-content" concepts. If any of the features are strongly related with concept coreness, then this analysis will likely discover that relationship.

Table 6 shows the results. For this analysis, we define a *coreness threshold* of 3, essentially treating concepts with coreness 1 and 2 to be less important and concepts with coreness 3 and 4 to be of high importance. We report the results in terms of *precision* and *recall*. Precision is the proportion of instances where the prediction was correct, and recall is the proportion of all core concepts (i.e., concepts with coreness 3 and 4) covered by the prediction.

Table 6: Performance of individual concept features as indicators of high coreness

Feature	Value	Precision	Recall
Content	Independent	**0.72**	**0.60**
	Dependent	0.55	0.39
Phrasing	Independent	**0.63**	**0.67**
	Dependent	0.61	0.33
Structure	Definition	0.58	0.14
	Example	0.46	0.14
	Explanation	**0.67**	**0.64**
	Analogy	0.72	0.08
Function	Declarative	0.53	0.25
	Conceptual	0.69	0.27
	Relational	0.69	0.35
	Scientific Method	0.53	0.13
Local Importance	1	**0.10**	**0.01**
	2	**0.33**	**0.14**
	3	**0.77**	**0.50**
	4	**0.90**	**0.34**

Our experimental setup implies that higher values of precision and recall in this table are indicative of high coreness, since a large proportion of the selected concepts are indeed of high coreness and a large proportion of highly core concepts were covered by the selection. For similar reasons, lower values of precision and recall indicate low coreness.

For example, if we label all "independent content" annotated concepts as core concepts, according to Table 6, we are correct 72% of the time and cover 60% of the core concepts. This is indicative of the fact that there is indeed a strong co-occurrence relationship between content-independence and high coreness. Similarly, if we label all the concepts with a local importance value of 1 to be high-coreness, then we are correct only 10% of the time and this selection covers only 1% of the highly core concepts. This result implies that concepts that are less locally important actually have low coreness values.

As the results in Table 6 show, there are features and their values which are indicative of high or low coreness. Precision and recall for each such feature-value is shown boldfaced in the table. For example, the independent nature of content and phrasing, explanatory concept structure and high local importance are indicative of high coreness. On the other hand, less locally important concepts have low coreness score.

The implication of the fact that some of the feature-values are highly indicative of certain coreness levels is the potential viability of feature-based prediction of concept coreness. In Section 4.2.3 we will present a more powerful predictive modeling technique that uses combinations of these intermediate-level features to more accurately predict concept coreness.

4.2.3 Prediction of Concept Coreness as a Function of the Intermediate-Level Features

One of the aims of annotating each concept with intermediate-level feature values was to find out if and how the high-level notion of coreness is related to these features. Promising results in this first step will trigger our next step – automatic extraction of the intermediate-level features from documents, possibly using low-level concept features (e.g., lexical and semantic properties of the sentences). In this section, we first discuss the computational analysis we performed on these features in combination and then the results.

The specific objective of this phase of our computational analysis is to examine if coreness can be predicted as a (possibly multivariate) function of the intermediate-level features. We formulated this problem as a supervised learning problem where concept coreness can have a finite set of possible values, or labels in supervised learning terminology (these coreness labels are discussed in detail in the next paragraph). The expert-annotated dataset was then used to train a set of classifiers which can predict the coreness value of a given concept from its values along the other dimensions (i.e. the intermediate-level features). A classifier is a supervised learning model that attempts to learn the behavior of a function having a finite (and usually small) range from a set of training examples. Here, we are treating coreness as a function of the intermediate-level features (the behavior of which we want to learn) and the annotation dataset is our set of training examples.

The experimentation was done in two different setups: with two and four levels of coreness. The four-coreness-levels setup is the original one, i.e., it follows the exact expert annotations for concept coreness. With two coreness levels, we regrouped the original coreness 1 and 2 concepts into one class and the rest into another class. This is the same setup with coreness threshold 3 as mentioned in Section 4.2. This new grouping allows us to assess classification results in two different granularity levels in order to judge the potential of these features in predicting coreness.

We applied several classification algorithms (Artificial Neural Network, Decision Tree, Logistic Regression and Support Vector Machine) on the data set using the data mining tool Weka [11]. 10-fold cross validation was applied to determine the accuracy of classification in each case. We computed the accuracy of classification in the three subject domains (*Plate Tectonics*, *Biological Evolution*, *Weather & Climate*) separately and then over all the domains. The combined assessment of the classifiers over all three domains was done by accumulating all the training examples (from all three domains) into one larger set and feeding it to the classifiers as the training dataset.

The best results were found for an RBF-kernel Support Vector Machine (SVM) implemented in LibSVM [6]. An SVM is a binary classifier that views a training example with n features as a point in an n-dimensional space. It aims at constructing the (n-1)-dimensional hyperplane that achieves a maximal separation of the two classes in the n-dimensional space. Later, techniques like one-against-one comparison among different class labels are used (as in LibSVM) to extend the binary classifier to be able to operate in multi-class scenarios.

With both two and four coreness levels, the set of features which predicted coreness the best was {*content*, *structure*, *local importance*}. To evaluate the effectiveness of this feature set, we compare the results with those found using a *majority classifier* used as the baseline. A majority classifier classifies all the examples as a member of the class containing the most number of examples, which means that it does not depend on any feature set and therefore is a good baseline to test the effectiveness of a new feature set.

We present the results in Figure 5 and Figure 6 for two and four coreness levels respectively. We plot the subject domains along the X-axis and classification accuracies along the Y-axis. For each domain, the first bar shows the baseline classifier's prediction accuracy and the second bar shows the accuracy of SVM using the feature set {*content*, *structure*, *local importance*}.

For example, Figure 5 shows that in *Biological Evolution* concepts, the baseline classifier achieves only 50.41% classification accuracy whereas SVM with our feature set achieves a much higher 85.12%. Figure 6 shows classification accuracies for four coreness levels: 44.63% for the baseline and 71.07% for SVM in *Biological Evolution*, for example.

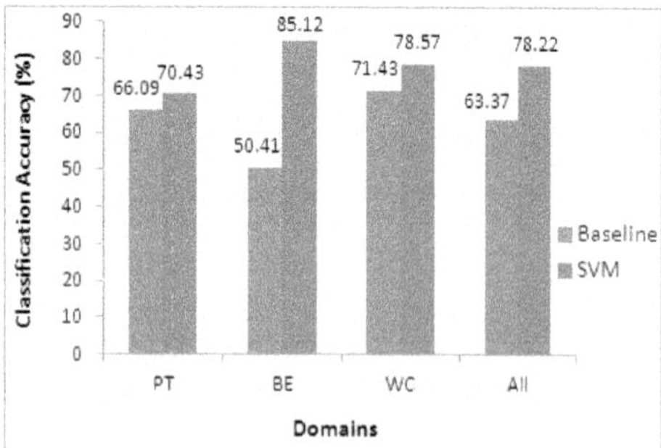

Figure 5. Classification results with two coreness levels.

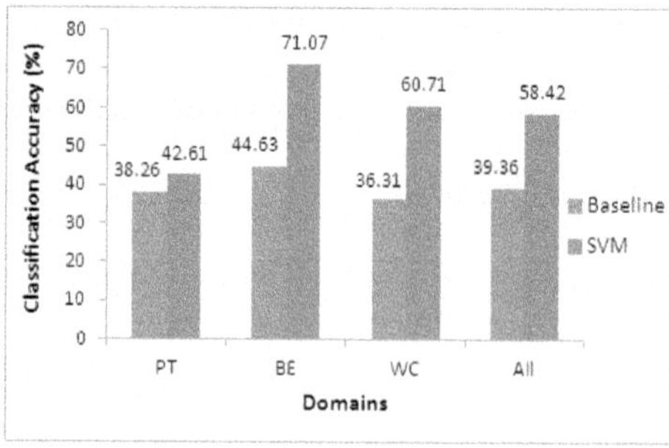

Figure 6. Classification results with four coreness levels.

As we can see, in all the cases our classifier achieves greater accuracy compared to the baseline. The degree to which the accuracy improves over the baseline varies to some extent but in most of the cases (most importantly, in the combined domain), the improvement is significant.

5. CONCLUSIONS AND FUTURE WORK

Our study of coreness as annotated by human experts reveals a significant (but not complete) consensus among human annotators about concept coreness, indicating the viability of automated techniques to do the same. We have further shown that a carefully selected set of intermediate-level features can improve identification of core concepts as compared to a baseline measure over a sufficiently general set of subject domains. These intermediate-level feature values were provided by the same human expert annotation study. The fact that concept coreness can be characterized in terms of more concrete concept features is encouraging enough for us to delve deeper into the question and to try and design an automated system capable of extracting core concepts from digital library resources.

A possible direction for future work is to characterize these intermediate-level features computationally in order to automate the entire process. The basic idea is to use lower-level (i.e. automatically extractable using existing natural language processing techniques) concept features as predictors of the intermediate-level features. This automatic extraction of low-level features can be aided by standard NLP techniques like text summarization (e.g., extracting local importance of concepts within a given resource), textual and semantic similarity between the concepts and the learning standards.

As part of the complete automation of the core concepts extraction system, we have begun to work on identification and automatic extraction of an appropriate set of low-level concept features including textual and semantic similarities with learning standards and concept scores produced by text summarization tools like MEAD and COGENT. We hope that this step of the study will result in an effective automated system for core concept identification which has potential to be an important component of digital library management systems.

6. ACKNOWLEDGMENTS

This material is based in part upon work supported by the National Science Foundation under Grant Numbers EHR/0835393 and EHR/0835381. Any opinions, findings, and conclusions or recommendations expressed in this material are those of the author(s) and do not necessarily reflect the views of the National Science Foundation.

7. REFERENCES

[1] AAAS. 2001. Atlas of Science Literacy. Project 2061, American Association for the Advancement of Science, and the National Science Teachers Association, Washington, DC.

[2] Ahmad, F. 2008. Generating Conceptually Personalized Interactions for Educational Digital Libraries Using Concept Maps. *PhD Dissertation, University of Colorado.*

[3] Ahmad, F., de la Chica, S., Butcher, K., Sumner, T., & Martin, J. H. 2007. Towards automatic conceptual personalization tools. Proceedings of the 7th ACM/IEEE-CS joint conference on Digital libraries (pp. 452–461).

[4] Altman, D. G. 1991. *Practical statistics for medical research*. Chapman & Hall/CRC.

[5] Butcher, K. R., & Sumner, T. 2011. Self-directed learning and the sensemaking paradox. *Human–Computer Interaction*, *26*(1-2), 123–159.

[6] Chang, C. C., & Lin, C. J. 2011. LIBSVM: a library for support vector machines. *ACM Transactions on Intelligent Systems and Technology (TIST)*, *2*(3), 27.

[7] Clark, R. C., & Shadden, M. 2001. Developing Technical Training: Structured Approach for Developing Classroom and Computer-Based Instructional Materials. *Performance Improvement*, *40*(4), 41–43.

[8] Cohen, J., & others. 1960. A coefficient of agreement for nominal scales. *Educational and psychological measurement*, *20*(1), 37–46.

[9] de la Chica, S., Ahmad, F., Sumner, T., Martin, J. H., & Butcher, K. 2008. Computational foundations for personalizing instruction with digital libraries. *International Journal on Digital Libraries*, *9*(1), 3–18.

[10] Farnham-Diggory, S. 1994. Paradigms of knowledge and instruction. *Review of Educational Research*, *64*(3), 463.

[11] Hall, M., Frank, E., Holmes, G., Pfahringer, B., Reutemann, P., & Witten, I. H. 2009. The WEKA data mining software: an update. *ACM SIGKDD Explorations Newsletter*, *11*(1), 10–18.

[12] Mani, I. 2001. *Automatic summarization* (Vol. 3). John Benjamins Pub Co.

[13] National Research Council. 1996. "National Science Education Standards: An Overview." *National Science Education Standards*. Washington, DC: The National Academies Press.

[14] Radev, D.R., Jing, H. and Budzikowska, M. 2000. Centroid-based summarization of multiple documents: sentence extraction, utility-based evaluation, and user studies. In Proceedings of the ANLP/NAACL 2000 Workshop on Summarization, (2000), pages 21-30.

[15] Wiggins, G. P., & McTighe, J. 2005. *Understanding by design*. Association for Supervision and Curriculum Development (ACSD). Alexandria, VA.

Deduced Social Networks for an Educational Digital Library

Monika Akbar
Dept. of Computer Science
Virginia Tech, Blacksburg, VA
amonika@vt.edu

Clifford A. Shaffer
Dept. of Computer Science
Virginia Tech, Blacksburg, VA
shaffer@vt.edu

Edward A. Fox
Dept. of Computer Science
Virginia Tech, Blacksburg, VA
fox@vt.edu

ABSTRACT

By analyzing the behavior of previous users, digital libraries can be made to provide new users with more support to find the best information. The AlgoViz Portal collects metadata on algorithm visualizations and associated research literature. We show how logs can be used to discover latent relationships between users, deducing an implicit social network. By clustering the log data, we find different page-viewing patterns, which provide practical information about the different groups of users.

Categories and Subject Descriptors

H.3.7 [**Information Storage and Retrieval**]: Digital Libraries

General Terms

Design, Measurement

Keywords

Deduced social network, digital library, log data

1. INTRODUCTION

Educational digital libraries (DLs) provide a gateway to educational resources. An abundance of resources provides opportunities but also creates a problem for users when searching for high quality material. While users of educational DLs can play a critical role by providing their feedback and ratings on the content, not many choose to do so. Lack of active participation is a key problem for building online community [3]. Even when DLs provide community space, willingness to participate can decide the success of a portal.

One example of a project that combines an educational portal with online community is the AlgoViz Portal (`http://algoviz.org`). In the absence of adequate explicit user feedback, AlgoViz usage data has helped us to generate networks and find common usage patterns. A portal built for a specific user community (in our case, the educators) may support disparate groups of users. An example of such groups results from linking users via shared resources (e.g., a co-author network). Analysis of these networks and their contextual information can reveal interesting user behavior, different user roles, and communities with similar interests. In this paper, we present a methodology for using log data to deduce connections between users and identify user interests. Applications of such information include refining existing services and providing recommendations on content. While most of the current recommendation systems rely on active user data (e.g., feedback, review, ratings, buying history), we depend solely on passive user data (e.g., clicks, pageviews, times in pages, etc.). Unfortunately, our target audience is mostly anonymous users. Yet, we are able to identify what these users are interested in. We believe our approach can be used in other DLs that have little active user participation but abundant passive user activities.

2. RELATED WORK

Many existing educational portals are built upon a DL framework. Social aspects of DLs were described in [2]. Early DL research pointed out the importance of understanding the needs of the target audience and of building online communities [2, 11]. Researchers have documented the various types of participation, and discovered factors that motivate users to actively participate in those communities [15]. Social navigation methods are used to guide users in an unfamiliar information space, but these methods largely depend on previous user feedback/rating [14]. In cases where user feedback is scarce, rating-based systems can prove insufficient to derive useful usage information. While Amazon has a successful recommendation system [12], it is targeted for e-commerce and depends heavily on user feedback. For educational sites, domain-based recommendation systems for e-learning were explored in [4]. In cases where user activity is less, recommendation systems based on social patterns were proposed in [6].

3. DETECTING COMMUNITIES AND INTERESTS IN A DIGITAL LIBRARY

In this paper, we use the term 'group' to refer to some users with a special interest towards specific content. Our approach has four segments: Filtering, Network Generation, Finding Groups, and Topic Modeling for all User Groups. We will briefly describe each segment next. Further details can be found in Section 4 where we present a case study.

Table 1: **Sample entries of AlgoViz log data.**

Session ID	Page Title	Internal Path/Page URL	IP Address‡	User ID	Timestamp
ievav83	Lifting the hood of the computer...	node/1413	9x.1y8.111.25	0	1276272047
t5fuuba	biblio/export/tagged/118/popup	research.cs.vt.edu/algoviz/biblio	2xy.2z.2a8.192	5	1276260935
ivuks8s	Has an AV helped you learn a topic in computer science?	research.cs.vt.edu/algoviz/poll/	1x1.yz.145.90	0	1276260943

‡ IPs are masked to protect user identity.

Filtering Log Data: Many online systems log their user activity for various purposes. These data, when coupled with user account information, provide useful insight on various factors. Unfortunately, logs also describe activity by crawlers, spammers, and bots along with that of legitimate users. Thus the first step for further analysis is to filter the logs to remove anomalous data.

Generating Networks within a DL: Once the log has been filtered, we cluster users based on their passive activities within the DL. A network built using passive data such as pageviews can be called a passive social network. In contrast to active social networks, passive social networks are not created explicitly by the users but are generated based on user activities. Passive social networks inherit more object-centric approach rather than the relationship-centric approach of active social networks. A wide range of objects can be used in a DL to define a passive social network. For example, we can define a Deduced Social Network (DSN) where users will be the nodes, and an edge links two users who viewed the same page. Our case study in Section 4 contains details on constructing such DSNs. Formally, we define a DSN as:

Definition 1. A **Deduced Social Network (DSN) is a Graph with tuple** G=(*Entity*, *Connection*, *Object*, k), **where:**

- *Entity* **is a node of the network, and** *Connection* **is an edge between two** *Entities*,
- *Object* **is an attribute of** *Entity*, **where one** *Entity* **can have multiple** *Object(s)*; **and**
- k **is a function that returns the minimum number of** *Object(s)* **that must be common between two** *Entities* **to create a** *Connection* **between them.**

Finding Groups within a DSN: Based on DSN characteristics, we may need further analysis to identify groups of users. Depending on connection factors, the DSN can be dense or sparse, thus having different network characteristics (e.g., degree distribution, betweenness centrality).

Identifying Group Interest: Once groups of users are identified, the next step is to find their areas of interest. Characterization of each group can be done by exploring the contents of the pages visited by the members of the group. Instead of such mundane exploration of pages for each group, it is also possible to characterize groups using cluster enrichment techniques (e.g., hypergeometric distribution [9]), classification techniques (e.g., Naive Bayes text classification [13] and Support Vector Machine-based classification), or topic modeling (e.g., Latent Dirichlet Allocation (LDA) [1]).

4. CASE STUDY: THE ALGOVIZ PORTAL

The AlgoViz portal collects within its database several aspects of user history. The Accesslog table is given in Table 1, showing data on the session, user IDs, IPs, timestamps for when the page was visited, etc. AlgoViz content is open for public viewing, hence it is possible for users to not register and so not receive a user ID. These users are referred to as Anonymous users and have a default user ID of 0. Despite a small number of registered users, AlgoViz project leaders are interested in understanding the trends of its overall user base. So instead of IDs, we rely on other methods to identify users whether registered or unregistered.

We used IP addresses to denote users. For any given IP, we are able to view which pages were viewed in that session and the time when the page loaded. We used these data to deduce a behavioral social network. The Accesslog table uses access-id (AID) as the primary key. It also stores session information. Each page viewed in a session generates a new AID row in the table.

We selected the log data of two months (September and October from 2010) for processing. An average month generates 100,000 rows in the table. Much of the data are generated by spammers, crawlers, bots, etc. We followed a three-step process to filter the log data of such outliers. The process involves filtering data based on page title, internal path of the page, and session information.

4.1 Deduced Social Networks

The filtered data were then used to connect pairs of users based on their common pageviews. These connections created a DSN. Nodes represent a user and edges indicate that the users have viewed similar pages. We used the *connection threshold* parameter to vary the network strength. A *connection threshold* of size k for an edge indicates that two users have viewed at least k common pages. Figure 1 shows DSNs based on AlgoViz log data for the months of September and October 2010 with a connection threshold of 10. Two users were connected only if they viewed at least 10 similar pages within a month. We varied k from 1 to 20. With lower k, the network starts to get dense and it becomes difficult to effectively identify interesting user groups. At k=8, we start observing special segments within the network which remain similar until k reaches 15. Then the network starts to lose some smaller segments. So, we selected k=10 for our analysis. Also, from a user's point of view, it is possible and likely that s/he may view ten or more pages in a month (or within a session). Once we selected k, we used a force-directed graph layout algorithm [5] to draw these networks. The network shown in Figure 1 (i) has 195 nodes and 2255 edges, and (ii) has 130 nodes with 1180 edges.

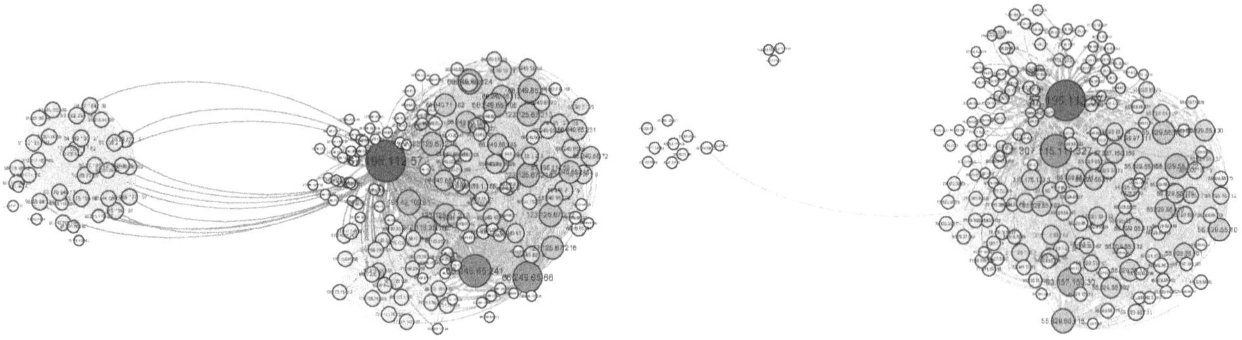

(i) Deduced social network for AlgoViz (September 2010) (ii) Deduced social network for AlgoViz (October 2010)

Figure 1: Using log to find user groups with similar interest (connection threshold k=10). Node size is proportional to the degree of each node. IPs are masked to protect user identity.

4.2 Network Analysis

Network analysis can help us to understand hidden trends and user preferences. Depending on the network characteristics, a number of approaches can be used to analyze the network. For example, for dense graphs, graph partitioning can help us to find smaller sub-graphs that might reveal interesting information. We describe below some approaches that might be useful for analyzing the passive networks discussed in the previous section.

Graph partitioning — Detecting Groups: There are a number of ways in which graphs can be analyzed, graph partitioning being one. Graph partitioning breaks the graph into disjoint subsets such that the number of connections within the subsets is high but the number of connections between the subsets is low. Relevant graph partitioning techniques have been studied in areas such as web science [10], epidemiology[8], sensor networks [16], etc.

Modularity, introduced by Girvan and Newman [7], is a quality measure for clustering that has been successfully adopted in many areas. Modularity clustering is dependent on edge betweenness — a measure that assigns weights on an edge as the number of shortest paths between pairs of vertices containing this edge. If a network contains multiple communities then the number of edges connecting the communities will be less than the number of edges within the community, and all shortest paths between those communities will contain one of those edges that connect the communities. Thus, the edges that connect the communities will have relatively higher edge betweenness values.

As we see from Figure 1, the graphs are very dense, making it difficult to analyze user trends. Graph-partitioning methods are used to find sub-graphs or groups within such dense graphs. We used Modularity clustering which has been successfully used to find communities within large networks in other domains. The result of the clustering is given in Figure 2. While most of the clusters of September 2010 DSN (Figure 2 (left)) are closely situated, clusters 2 and 4 are clearly separable from the rest of the clusters. Similarly, in October 2010 DSN (Figure 2 (right)), clusters 4 and 6 are distinguishable from the rest of the clusters. This indicates that while some clusters are closely related, others address different topics.

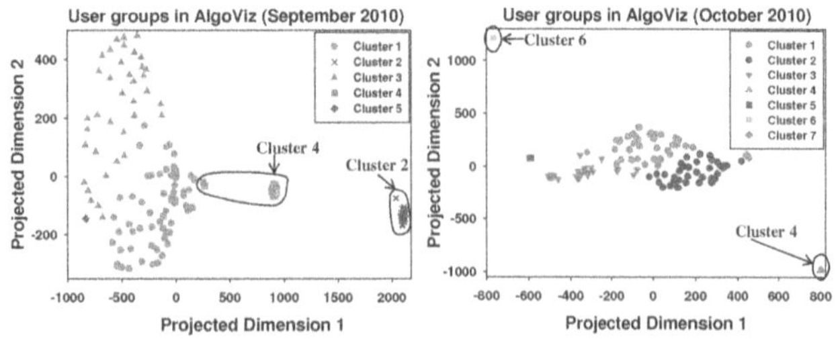

Figure 2: Clusters found in the DSNs of Figure 1.

Topic modeling — Identifying Group Interests: Finding clusters is useful for detecting groups and their sizes but it is not sufficient to understand patterns within the groups. Topic modeling allows us to get an overview of the subjects addressed in the clusters. Probabilistic models such as Latent Dirichlet Allocation (LDA) [1] have been used extensively to detect topics for a document corpus.

The clustering results in the previous subsection were used to identify topics within the clusters. We used the Mallet API[1] which utilizes the LDA approach to find topics appearing in the page titles of that cluster. While building models, we set the number of topics similar to the number of clusters that were generated for each month. For example, in September 2010, there were five clusters and we opted for five topics for those clusters. The number of sampling iterations for the topic model of each month was 200.

Two of the top-most topics in the September 2010 DSN include words related to AlgoViz bibliography entries (i.e., biblio). One of the prominent collections of AlgoViz is the bibliography of publications related to algorithm visualizations. The collection can be sorted by author, title, publication type, or publication year. Also, these entries can be exported in RTF, bibtex, and XML format. The last three topics are less related to bibliography entries. Two are related to sorting, tree, programming, etc.

Table 2 shows the topic distribution within the clusters in the September 2010 DSN. The first column shows the cluster ID, while the subsequent pairs of columns show the topic ID and its proportion in the cluster. We show the top three topics for each cluster that has at least 10% topic proportion value within the cluster. For example, in cluster 1, topics 3 and 5 are most dominant. Cluster 4 has a similar topic distribution. Cluster 5 has three dominant topics (i.e., topics 2, 1, and 4).

The topic distribution for the October 2010 DSN is shown in Table 3. Cluster 1 consists of biblio entries (e.g., biblio, export, rtf), and other content pages (e.g., linked, functional). Topics 3, 6, and 7 are mostly related to bibliography entries and these topics are dominant in cluster 7. Topics

[1]`http://mallet.cs.umass.edu/`

Table 2: Topic distribution of Sept-10 DSN, T=5.

Clust. #	Top Topic (1)	Contr - ibution	Top Topic (2)	Contr - ibution	Top Topic (3)	Contr - ibution
1	3	0.667	5	0.25		
2	3	0.312	1	0.212	5	0.209
3	1	0.539	2	0.193	4	0.119
4	3	0.75	5	0.156		
5	2	0.254	1	0.216	4	0.213

Table 3: Topic distribution of Oct-10 DSN, T=7.

Clust. #	Top Topic (1)	Contr - ibution	Top Topic (2)	Contr - ibution	Top Topic (3)	Contr - ibution
1	3	0.987				
2	1	0.828	2	0.138		
3	6	0.421	5	0.145	3	0.12
4	1	0.815				
5	5	0.253	4	0.217	6	0.137
6	3	0.264	6	0.161	4	0.144
7	6	0.306	3	0.221	7	0.119

1, 2, 4, and 5 are mostly related to AlgoViz catalog entries. These topics are prominent in clusters 2, 4 and 5.

5. APPLICATIONS

The clustering results along with the topics highlighted in the previous section indicate that AlgoViz users have clusters of interests when it comes to using online resources related to algorithm visualizations. Some users are mainly interested in bibliography entries. Other users are more interested in catalog entries; of these, interest clusters around sorting or graph visualizations. Along with their interests, we are able to detect the size of each cluster. Knowing the groups, their interests, and size gives us leverage on better serving the target audience.

In AlgoViz we used the results in two ways: (1) within the content recommendation block that suggests a list of entries based on the DSN analysis results and (2) within the ranking function that generates the ordered list of entries for users during browse and search operations. In both cases, for any given time span, if an entry E in AlgoViz received a certain number of views within a cluster whose topics were highly related to that of E, then E would be weighted more compared to other entries of similar type.

6. CONCLUSIONS AND FUTURE WORK

The focus of this paper was to define DSN, present exploratory analysis, and describe developed prototypes. In the future, we plan to evaluate the prototypes and their variations. One variation on the prototype applications is to customize the search and browsing results for each anonymous user based on their pageviews. We also plan to use the page content, instead of the page titles, to model the topics within each cluster and compare it with the existing result. Creating navigation networks of pages based on common viewers is another area we plan to pursue.

7. ACKNOWLEDGMENTS

This material is based upon work supported by the National Science Foundation under Grant Numbers DUE-0836940, DUE-0937863, and DUE-0840719.

8. REFERENCES

[1] D. M. Blei, A. Y. Ng, and M. I. Jordan. Latent Dirichlet Allocation. *The Journal of Machine Learning Research*, 3:993–1022, 2003.

[2] C. L. Borgman. Social Aspects of Digital Libraries (working session). In *Proceedings of the First ACM Internationl Conference on Digital Libraries*, page 170, 1996.

[3] B. S. Butler. Membership Size, Communication Activity, and Sustainability: A Resource-Based Model of Online Social Structures. *Information Systems Research*, 12(4):346–362, 2001.

[4] A. Dong and B. Wang. Domain-Based Recommendation and Retrieval of Relevant Materials in E-learning. In *IWSCA '08*, pages 103–108, 2008.

[5] P. Eades and M. L. Huang. Navigating Clustered Graphs using Force-Directed Methods. *Journal of Graph Algorithms and Applications*, 4:157–181, 2000.

[6] J. Freyne, R. Farzan, and M. Coyle. Toward the Exploitation of Social Access Patterns for Recommendation. In *RecSys*, pages 179–182, 2007.

[7] M. Girvan and M. E. J. Newman. Community Structure in Social and Biological Networks. *National Academy of Science*, 99(12):7821–7826, 2002.

[8] J. Hadidjojo and S. A. Cheong. Equal Graph Partitioning on Estimated Infection Network as an Effective Epidemic Mitigation Measure. *PLoS ONE*, 6(7):e22124, 2011.

[9] A. Hald. The Compound Hypergeometric Distribution and a System of Single Sampling Inspection Plans Based on Prior Distributions and Costs. *Technometrics*, 2(3):275–340, 1960.

[10] H. Ino, M. Kudo, and A. Nakamura. Partitioning of Web Graphs by Community Topology. In *WWW*, pages 661–669, 2005.

[11] K. Lightle, E. Almasy, L. Barbato, S. Clark, Y. George, S. Hsi, C. Lowe, P. Mackinney, and E. McIlvain. Draft Report: Metrics Recommendations and Resources for NSDL Projects. `https://www.nsdlnetwork.org/sites/default/files/Draft%20Report-Metrics_Recommendations.pdf`, (last accessed on April 2012), 2009.

[12] G. Linden, B. Smith, and J. York. Amazon.com Recommendations: Item-to-Item Collaborative Filtering. *Internet Computing*, 7(1):76 – 80, 2003.

[13] C. D. Manning, P. Raghavan, and H. Schütze. *Introduction to Information Retrieval*. Cambridge University Press, 2008.

[14] P. Melville, R. J. Mooney, and R. Nagarajan. Content-boosted Collaborative Filtering for Improved Recommendations. In *National Conference on Artificial Intelligence*, pages 187–192, 2002.

[15] O. Nov, M. Naaman, and C. Ye. Analysis of Participation in an Online Photo-sharing Community: A Multidimensional Perspective. *Journal of the American Society for Information Science and Technology*, 61(3):555–566, 2010.

[16] S. Roy, Y. Wan, and A. Saberi. A Flexible Algorithm for Sensor Network Partitioning and Self-partitioning Problems. In *Algorithmic Aspects of Wireless Sensor Networks*, volume 4240, pages 152–163. 2006.

A Tale of Two Studies: Is Dissemination Working?

Flora McMartin
Sarah Giersch
Broad-based Knowledge, LLC
5935 Orchard Ave
Richmond, CA
+011 515-237-4795
flora.mcmartin;
sgiersch@gmail.com

Joe Tront
Virginia Polytechnic University
359 Durham Hall
Blacksburg, VA 24061-0111
+011 540-231-5067
jgtront@exchange.vt.edu

Wesley Shumar
Drexel University
3141 Chestnut Street
Philadelphia, PA 19104
+011 215-895-2060
shumarw@drexel.edu

ABSTRACT
In this paper we describe preliminary results from two ongoing research projects that investigate the dissemination practices surrounding digital STEM learning materials for undergraduates. This research consists of two related studies, : 1) survey research about the dissemination practices of NSF-funded PIs; and, 2) a case study on the dissemination practices of courseware developers who won the *Premier Award for Excellence in Engineering Education.* The vast majority of PIs reported in the survey that they do not take advantage of digital dissemination methods such as education digital libraries. *Premier Award*-winning innovators reported using multiple dissemination methods – traditional and digital. Recommendations are provided regarding how digital library developers might work with PIs to improve dissemination.

Categories and Subject Descriptors
K.3.0 [**Computing Milieux**]: Computers and Education – *General*

General Terms
Measurement, Documentation

Keywords
Digital Libraries; Dissemination; Survey; Case Study; Promotion; Tenure

1. INTRODUCTION
One of the aims of the National Science Foundation (NSF) division of Education & Human Resources (EHR) is to support curricular innovation in Science, Technology, Engineering and Mathematics (STEM) education. Since 1999, NSF has provided hundreds of millions of dollars of funding to well over 3,000 projects and Principal Investigators (PIs) to improve the quality of STEM education for K-12 and undergraduate students. This funding has primarily been dispersed in two NSF programs, Transforming Undergraduate Education in STEM (TUES; formerly the Course Curriculum and Lab Improvement (CCLI) program) and the National Science Digital Library (NSDL) now known as National Science Distributed Learning program. The TUES/CCLI program funds PIs to create, test and encourage the adoption of innovations to improve teaching and learning at the undergraduate level [10]. The NSDL provides the STEM education community access to these innovative educational resources. Although both programs, especially the NSDL, are designed to encourage the spread of educational innovations and digital learning materials from the local to regional and national levels, they have not proved to be especially successful in doing so. CCLI innovations are for the most part not widely adopted by STEM instructors as designed [2,4,6,9]. And a significant number of STEM faculty members and instructors do not know about the NSDL or its component collections or use them as mechanisms to search for innovations, nor do they submit materials to these education digital libraries (DLs) as a means for sharing their own innovations. [1,7,8,9].

JCDL'12, June 10–14, 2012, Washington, DC, USA.

Over the past three years, two studies were undertaken to explore the issues that affect PI's dissemination practices of digital STEM learning materials. The CCLI Survey (administered in 2009) was a study of all PIs who received funding from the NSF's CCLI program from 2000 to 2009 (the program nomenclature was changed to TUES in 2010) and focused on uncovering PI's perspectives of their own dissemination activities: their views and opinions about dissemination efforts; vehicles and strategies they used and those they believed were most effective [9]. A Case Study (2011-ongoing), is examining the careers of faculty who developed digital courseware and who have been awarded the *Premier Award for Excellence in Engineering Education Courseware*. The *Premier Award (PA)* was initiated by NEEDS – (now the Engineering Pathway) in 1996 and has been sponsored by John Wiley and Sons, Microsoft Research, and others The *PA* also received support from the NSF. The purpose of the *Premier Award* is "to recognize high-quality, non-commercial courseware designed to enhance engineering education."[3] Since its inception, over 120 courseware submissions have been reviewed and 27 award winners and three finalist candidates selected. The aim of the later study is to better understand the spread and impact of technical and pedagogical innovations across engineering and other related disciplines including the contexts within which faculty attempt to disseminate their materials and the barriers they face.

The CCLI Survey results provide a broad description of the dissemination efforts of a large population of PIs' who received CCLI funding, and it is anticipated that the qualitative research associated with the Case Study of *PA*, winners will provide a deep and rich description of digital courseware developers' dissemination contexts. Taken together, the two studies provide a broad and deep set of data that may lead to a more complete understanding of the process of dissemination, the context in which it occurs and the digital and non-digital tools and mechanisms that are successful in supporting adoption of digital teaching and learning materials.

In this paper, we briefly describe the methodology for both studies, report and discuss some of the preliminary results, synthesize findings, and discuss implications for DL developers.

2. METHODS

2.1 Survey Study of CCLI PIs

In 2009, the 2,463 PIs who had received funding under NSF's CCLI program since 2000 were surveyed regarding their beliefs about effective dissemination, their dissemination activities, and their opinions about dissemination practices and barriers. Approximately half (49%) of those surveyed completed the entire survey. The survey consisted of 14 questions, including demographics. PIs were asked their opinions about dissemination practices, those they used and preferred, and those they thought were most effective. They also described what they believed to be the successful outcome for dissemination and estimates of the numbers of adopters or users of their materials. Using a five point Likert scale (Not at all Successful – Extremely Successful) respondents were asked to indicate opinions about the success of various dissemination methods; respondents who did not use that method were directed to select a Not Applicable response. The dissemination methods were divided into two categories: 1) traditional, academic ways of sharing knowledge, (i.e., peer reviewed papers or conference papers), and 2) web-based options (i.e., hosting a website or contributing to a DL.) Next, respondents were asked about barriers to dissemination. Here, too, a five point Likert scale was used (Not at All Important – Extremely Important). Respondents provided open-ended details about dissemination efforts and barriers to dissemination.

2.2 Case Study of *Premier Award* Winners

The mixed method research design for the Case Study relies upon citation analysis, interviews, and content analysis of transcripts and documents to answer several questions including "*What kinds of dissemination activities and mechanisms are successful in promoting successful adoption and use of courseware?*" The data presented in this paper about *PA* awardees' dissemination practices is derived from a preliminary analysis of interview transcripts and documents.

The sources for the document analysis are dossiers that *PA* applicants submit for judging. Dossiers include narratives that address the *PA* Evaluation Criteria (Instructional Design, Software Design and Engineering Content) [3]. We included 19 award-winners from 1998-2010 in the sample plus 10 of the non-winners to ensure that our findings were indicative of the broader field of engineering courseware applicants. Two researchers on our team developed and tested the reliability of the *PA* Dossier Codebook and then split the review of documents in our sample.

The other data source is interviews, which are semi-structured, retrospective, one-on-one conversations between a researcher and an awardee. To date we have conducted 10 telephone interviews (55% of awardees) with one applicant declining to be interviewed. The interviews are recorded and transcribed. Researchers are currently coding them using the coding software NVIVO.

3. RESULTS & ANALYSIS OF STUDIES

3.1 CCLI PI Dissemination Practices

Tables 1 and 2 list dissemination methods and the percentage of the CCLI survey respondents who reported using the methods. Respondents were asked to rate the level of success for traditional dissemination methods, listed in Table 1. The highest rated method, in terms of success, was also the method used most frequently – "Paper/presentation at a professional conference[1]" - with 75% of the respondents rating this method as *successful* or *extremely successful*. The next most successful methods, rated at 55% and 54% respectively, were "Workshops/seminar held on home campus[2]" and "Poster at a professional conference[3]." The remaining methods all received ratings below 50%.

Table 1. % of Respondents Using Traditional Dissemination Methods and the Top Three Methods Rated Most Successful

Traditional Dissemination Method	% Using Method
Paper/presentation at professional conference [1]	75
Poster at professional conference [3]	73
Paper for publication in peer reviewed journal	65
Workshop/seminar held on home campus [2]	58
Paper/presentation posted to website	56
Workshop/seminar at professional conference	54
Invited workshop/seminar at another campus	45
Promotional materials, i.e., book mark, flyer	31
White paper	22
Booth at professional conference	20

To put these numbers in perspective, respondents were also asked to describe successful dissemination in their own words. The majority of responders described success as some form of adoption or use by other instructors that culminated in student interaction or use of the innovation.

Table 2. % of Respondents Using Digital Dissemination Methods and Top Two Most Successful Methods

Digital Dissemination Methods	% Using Method
Hosting a website on your campus with info about the educational innovation (EI) [1]	70
Contributing to a DL collection in your discipline [2]	29
Contributing to a DL collection i.e., NSDL	22
Contributing to a DL collection or institutional repository on your campus	20
Contributing to an open courseware collection	17
Posting a video to YouTube or similar site describing the EI	13
Using a social network site, e.g., Facebook, to promote the EI	11
Hosting a blog about the EI	11
Posting to a blog about the EI	13
Posting to Wikipedia about the EI	9

Next respondents rated their use of digital dissemination methods (Table 2). Respondents reported much less use of the Web (and services found there) for dissemination when compared to traditional methods. While the vast majority (70%) reported using a local website to make their digital materials available, their usage of DLs was significantly lower. Usage rates range from 20% for "Contributing to a DL collection or institutional repository on your campus" to a high of 29% for "Contributing to a DL within their discipline." "Contributing to a DL collection i.e., the NSDL" (22%) ranked barely above using a campus DL. Note that this choice might be conflated with a PI choosing to use a discipline-based DL without realizing that a number of STEM DLs (i.e., COMPADRE (physics); BEN (biology)) are also

Pathways collections of the NSDL. It is also possible that PIs simply did not know what the phrase 'DL' meant, but did submit materials to a collection [8].

When asked to rate the effectiveness of digital dissemination methods, the respondents did not believe any of the methods were particularly successful. The highest rated method was "Hosting a website locally on the PI's campus[1]" with 48% rating this method as successful or highly successful. "Contributing to a DL in the PI's discipline[2]" was rated next at 19%. Less than 12% of the PIs felt that contributing to any other form of DL, or an open courseware collection or Wikipedia, was effective. It should be noted that since the majority of PIs had not contributed to a DL, their opinions may not have been based on the actual experience of contributing to a DL, leaving open the question: on what basis did they form this opinion? Use of any type of social media was rated extremely low with 7% believing YouTube to be successful, and all other forms (i.e., blogs or Facebook) rated at 4%.

3.2 *Premier Award* Dissemination Practices

The *PA* competition was instituted with two primary goals: to recognize and reward the efforts of faculty (and students) developing courseware and to provide an external measure of the quality of the courseware [3]. The designers of the *PA* saw it as a way to disseminate models of high quality courseware, believing in the long run, that the *PA* would impact promotion and tenure criteria *and* engineering teaching practice by establishing a metric to value teaching and learning innovation. Applicants and winners have spanned the disciplines of architecture, biology, computer science, math, and engineering. Analysis of the dossiers in our sample indicates the number of times different types of courseware were submitted: Curricula (9); Tools (7); Simulations and Databases (2); and, Animation and Case Study (1).

Analysis of the *PA* dossiers indicates that the Web is consistently used as a dissemination mechanism. Every award-winning applicant, save one, had a website hosted on their campus, and the websites contained supporting materials such as instructors guides in addition to access to the courseware.

Table 3. Top Four Dissemination Methods of *PA* Winners

Dissemination Methods	Winner (n)	Non-winner (n)
Conference paper	26	7
NEEDS DL / Engineering Pathway	19	4
Journal article	11	1
Face-to-face Workshop	7	0

The dossiers also showed that applicants, like CCLI PIs, predominantly employed traditional dissemination methods such as writing and presenting conference papers and journal articles (Table 3). Other dissemination methods included: a local computer lab installation, professional society endorsement and promotion, author's personal website, and printed fliers. Dissemination methods such as books, conference posters, online workshops, local and other DLs were rarely used, if at all. The *PA* winners were required as part of the award, to submit their courseware to the NEEDS/EP DL, inflating this number in Table 3. In other words, had they not won the award, it is likely that their use of DLs might more closely match that of the CCLI PIs.

Based on the interviews to date, it appears that *PA* winners have for the most part, put a great deal of effort into disseminating their courseware. Several discussed the time and effort it takes to employ traditional methods. As one interviewee explained: *We...do some kind of workshop, or symposium at...[our discipline's] major conferences...at least once a year....Recently we have been trying to hit other strategic venues.* They also leveraged campus opportunities...*because the people at [our campus learning] center are...more aware of what I am doing. As they interact with other groups, they know...I am a resource in this area.*

Others expressed a sense of frustration about the level of effort required to be successful in encouraging courseware adoption: *It requires continual effort. You basically have to do stuff every year to keep things growing....We tried...to do things that were different than just ... publish some conference papers....We tried to build a community driven website....Then we branched out into offering workshops at...education conferences because that would be the main target audience for our particular courseware.*

A number of interviewees discussed how they felt that winning the *PA* would help with their dissemination efforts:

Interviewee D: *I remember thinking it would be nice if we got this recognition and other people heard about [the courseware] through the Premier Award as way to promote the tool use more broadly.*

Interviewee E: *So I thought that was really a great opportunity for me...I was fielding calls from people to make a copy of the [courseware] CD and then send it to them. And I said [to myself] that was not doable [in the long-term].*

And the *PA* program did put sustained effort into disseminating the winners' materials: distributing over 25,000 CDs containing award winning materials; highlighting winning courseware at the NEEDS and Engineering Pathways DL sites; and, publically recognizing the winners with an awards luncheon at the annual Frontiers in Education (FIE) conference.

However, interviewees also described barriers to dissemination that can be classified as institutional or cultural, indicating that while they might have been 'following the rules' by using traditional means to disseminate, they found that their efforts were not valued.

Interviewee B: *[Our courseware] pre-proposal [to NSF] was turned down and the principal rationale for turning it down...was that NSF will not fund a contest as a way of disseminating an educational product. It was a philosophical rejection of the idea of using competition as a way to spur the interest that would cause the educational product to be disseminated*

Interviewee D: *In all honesty, we did have some publications. They aren't of the same stature of the journals...that really carry sort of the prestige or...the recognition that you would need to be able to tell an administrator..."we're doing good things." I don't know....We could publish and we did, but it just - it wasn't significant enough to really mean anything.*

4. SYNTHESIS - IMPLICATIONS FOR DLS

Both studies indicate that dissemination is largely an individual activity for the PI or awardee with little support from funding agencies or organizations that initially supported development of STEM digital resource or courseware and there are divergent views as to what constituted successful dissemination practices. The survey data suggest that this lack of support may encourage CCLI PIs to take a minimalist approach to fulfilling dissemination requirements, (i.e., writing a paper or making a conference presentation). The interview results indicate *PA* awardees' actual dissemination activities are more nuanced. Awardees noted that concerted individual effort might lead to little professional reward but that persistent effort was also required, as was making connections with DLs (in this case the NEEDS/EP DL) and professional societies. Our interviewees' dissemination stories showed that combining traditional and digital dissemination methods seemed to lead to more widely disseminated materials.

The CCLI Survey results highlight an apparent contradiction between what CCLI PI's report as successful dissemination methods and the practices they employ, e.g., paper presentations, targeted at the relatively small educational research community within their disciplines. This contradiction is not surprising. Most faculty members at four-year institutions must write papers for peer reviewed journals and must publish to get tenure and keep their jobs. This fact directly impacts DLs because faculty who might wish to submit to or publish in a DL perceive little or no value in doing so, in part because of the lack of direct rewards (i.e., scholarly recognition; reach to other instructors or the lack of institutionally- or culturally-accepted methods of gatekeeping that validate their contribution, such as traditionally valued peer review).

The DL developers and the faculty members, then, are involved in a cycle where, because education DLs cannot give faculty and instructors the kinds of rewards recognized by their institution or discipline participation remains low, and because participation remains low, education DLs cannot establish credibility.

Several efforts have been made to strengthen the credibility of educational DLs through site-specific peer review as a way to promote the quality, and therefore the value, of STEM resources created by faculty and teachers and these show promise [5]. Other STEM educational DLs (e.g., BEN and the APS Archive) accept only peer-reviewed materials. With their focus on scholarship, these DLs are becoming recognized in the biology education community for providing quality resources.

In addition to the slow work of changing cultural and institutional attitudes towards valuing DLs as dissemination methods comparable to papers, another solution might be to reward dissemination methods much like we reward research or teaching. For example, research on dissemination efforts might become another path for faculty to pursue. By studying dissemination efforts and adoption practices associated with their digital resources or courseware, faculty members would add significantly to a growing knowledge base around adoption of innovation within their discipline or field. DLs could assist research efforts by developing, systematically collecting, and making available metrics on dissemination.

Lastly, DL developers might institute awards programs for resources in their DLs, similar to the *Premier Award*. This type of award emphasizes peer review of innovative ideas and the impact of digital resources or courseware on a field. As an interviewee noted, *...the [PA] plays a very different role than some of the other awards within IEEE or the ACM... which happen generally pretty late in someone's career after they have made [a] considerable impact.... The Premier Award for me is the only one that really focuses on the quality... of educational software....*

As several *PA* winners noted, dissemination is difficult, and it requires sustained effort plus the use of traditional and digital methods to be effective, including partnerships with professional societies. We have suggested how DLs and developers can help faculty with dissemination in order to effect change in the reward system to provide much needed recognition to the faculty, scholars and students who so justly deserve recognition for their contributions to STEM DLs and education.

ACKNOWLEDGMENTS

The following research has been supported by grants from the National Science Foundation: DUE #0937784; CCLI #0938513

5. REFERENCES

[1] Bikson T., Kalra, N., Galway, L., & Agnew, G. (2010, October). Steps toward a formative evaluation of NSDL: Executive summary. Retrieved 2011, June 11 from: http://www.gohnow.com/goh/wp-content/uploads/2011/PM-3516-NSF_ExecSUmm_10221.pdf .

[2] Borrego, M. Froyd, J. & Simin Hall, T. (2010). Diffusion of engineering education innovations: A survey of awareness and adoption rates in US engineering departments. Journal of Engineering Education, pp. 185 - 207.

[3] Engineering Pathway. Premier Award 2012. Retrieved 2012, January 18 from: http://www.engineeringpathway.com/ep/premier/2012/general.jhtml;jsessionid=DEUIZTATROUTHABAVRSSFEQ .

[4] Fairweather, J. (2008). Linking evidence and promising practices in science, technology, engineering and mathematics (STEM) undergraduate education. Workshop on Promising Practices – Innovation in Undergraduate STEM Education, National Academies Board on Science Education. URL: http://www7.nationalacademies.org/bose/Fairweather_CommissionedPaper.pdf .

[5] Giersch, Leary, Palmer, Recker. (2008). Developing a review rubric for online educational resources to support re-use and meaningful learning. Open Education Conference, Logan, Utah, September 24-26, 2008.

[6] Henderson, C., & Dancy, M. (2007). Barriers to the use of research□based instructional strategies: The influence of both individual and situational characteristics. *Physical Review Special Topics: Physics Education Research, 3*(2), 020102.

[7] Morgan, G., McMartin, F., Wolf, A., and Harley, D. (2006). Moving beyond the innovators: Expanding the use of digital resources in undergraduate education. Western Cooperative of Educational Telecommunications – WCET annual conference, November 2006.

[8] Morgan, G., McMartin, F., Iverson, E., Manduca, C., Wolf, A. & Morrill, J. (2007). Use of digital learning materials and digital libraries: Comparison by discipline. Proceedings of the International Conferences on Digital Libraries.

[9] Tront, J., McMartin, F. & Muramatsu, B. (2011). Improving the dissemination of CCLI (TUES) Educational Innovations. Proceedings from the 41st ASEE/IEEE Frontiers in Education Conference, October 12 - 15, Rapid City, SD.

[10] TUES (2011). Transforming Undergraduate Education in Science, Technology, Engineering and Mathematics (TUES). Program solicitation of the Division of Undergraduate Education (DUE) (No. 10533). Arlington, VA: National Science Foundation

To Better Stand on the Shoulder of Giants

Rui Yan[†,♮], Congrui Huang[†], Jie Tang[§], Yan Zhang[†,*] and Xiaoming Li[†,‡]
[†] School of Electronics Engineering and Computer Science, Peking University, Beijing 100871, China
[‡] State Key Laboratory of Virtual Reality Technology and Systems, Beihang University, Beijing 100083, China
[§] Department of Computer Science and Technology, Tsinghua University, Beijing 100084, China
[♮] Department of Computer Science and Information Engineering, National Taiwan University, Taipei 10617, Taiwan
{r.yan,hcr,lxm}@pku.edu.cn, jietang@tsinghua.edu.cn, zhy@cis.pku.edu.cn

ABSTRACT

Usually scientists breed research ideas inspired by previous publications, but they are unlikely to follow all publications in the unbounded literature collection. The volume of literature keeps on expanding extremely fast, whilst not all papers contribute equal impact to the academic society. Being aware of potentially influential literature would put one in an advanced position in choosing important research references. Hence, estimation of potential influence is of great significance. We study a challenging problem of identifying potentially influential literature. We examine a set of hypotheses on what are the fundamental characteristics for highly cited papers and find some interesting patterns. Based on these observations, we learn to identify potentially influential literature via Future Influence Prediction (FIP), which aims to estimate the future influence of literature. The system takes a series of features of a particular publication as input and produces as output the estimated citation counts of that article after a given time period. We consider several regression models to formulate the learning process and evaluate their performance based on the coefficient of determination (R^2). Experimental results on a real-large data set show a mean average predictive performance of 83.6% measured in R^2. We apply the learned model to the application of bibliography recommendation and obtain prominent performance improvement in terms of Mean Average Precision (MAP).

Categories and Subject Descriptors

H.3.7 [**Information Storage and Retrieval**]: Digital Libraries; H.3.3 [**Information Storage and Retrieval**]: Information Search and Retrieval; H.4 [**Information Systems Applications**]: General

General Terms

Algorithms, Experimentation, Performance

Keywords

Citation pattern analysis, influence prediction, digital libraries

*Corresponding Author.

JCDL'12, June 10–14, 2012, Washington, DC, USA.

1. INTRODUCTION

Effective scientific research requires keeping up with a large, ever-growing body of literature because scientists need to "stand on the shoulder of giants" (knowledge learnt from *Isaac Newton*). But how? Searching for meaningful work is tedious and it is very possible to miss important developments in areas outside a researcher's specialty. More critically, it may miss some potentially influential literature. In fact, considerable research work starts from a small number of initial papers and then explores papers near (citing or cited by) those papers. Therefore, to identify influential literature has long been viewed as one of the most important challenges in data mining for scientific literature. The rapid evolution of scientific research has been creating a huge volume of publications every year, and the explosive trend continues. Figure 1 shows statistics on a large literature database in Computer Science[1]. Figure 1.(a) visualizes the explosive increase on the volume of publications in the past years, in particular recent years. The number of publications in 2009 almost triples than that of 10 years before [28].

Given the large literature population, however, it is natural that not all publications contribute equal impact to academia. It is useful to identify influential literature to make better utilization of "giant shoulders" against unbounded publications. To measure such literature influence is non-trivial due to the numerous complicated methodologies from different perspectives, among which *citation count* is one of the most simple, standard and objective measurements. Citation count is calculated by how many times a particular publication is cited by other articles. In this study, we use the *citation count* to represent *influence* of literature for a simple and quick start, and both terminologies are used interchangeably.

The assumption of "different influence" is verified by showing the highly skewed citation pattern which follows a power law distribution: a huge number of research papers attract only a few citations, and a few research papers accumulate a large number of citations [28]. In all, there are 2.36% papers with more than 2000 citation counts and 68% papers have less than 5 citations! We also illustrate the changes of the citation distributions in different years in Figure 1.(b). The plots indicate more and more citations agglomerate to smaller percentage of literature from 2000 to 2010. This phenomenon coincides with the dotted line shown in Figure 1.(a) where the ratio of influential papers is decreasing year by year[2].

To measure the current influence by citation counts is not difficult but has been proved to be useful. In several bibliography search systems, current citation count is listed as one of the major factors to rank the candidate articles for the retrieval purpose [1]. Intuitively, we might consider the large probability of high future influence will also help select worthy candidates for literature search or recommendation systems (and indeed is verified by

[1]`http://arnetminer.org`.
[2]Here "**influential papers**" denotes papers with citations over 100.

our experiments), but no previous system is able to examine the effect of future impact. Another ambition for future influence prediction is that this technique encourages researchers to pay attention to and keep up with future influential works at an early stage. Our statistics shows that more than 20 papers received more than 100 citations merely after 5 years. Many of these influential papers finally lead to new research sub-fields. Obviously, being aware of these influential literature would put one in an advanced position in choosing new research topics and avoiding missing important references. One step ahead probably enables better and earlier "stand on the shoulder of giants". To answer the question we claimed in the beginning, identifying potentially influential literature via Future Influence Prediction (FIP) provides a possible option.

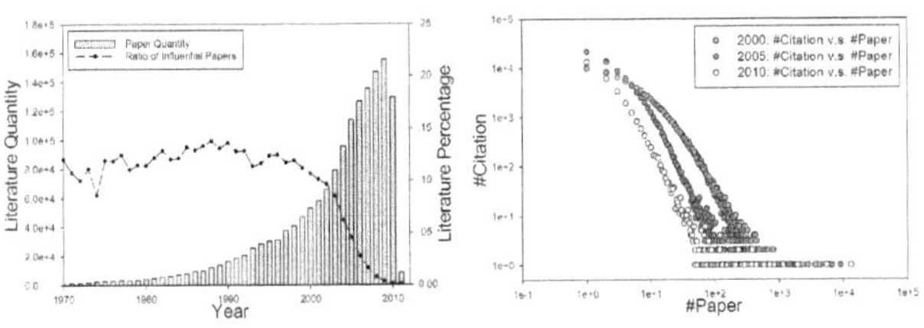

(a). The growing volume of literatures. (b). Distribution of literature citation.

Figure 1: Statistics of literature data from ArnetMiner.

It is challenging for FIP to identify fundamental factors correlated with future citations and to combine them under a unified predictive model. For identification of influential literature in the future, this paper has following contributions:

• The **1st** contribution is that we have explored a series of effective features important to future influence from several aspects, such as paper content, author expertise, venue impact, and more especially, **temporal dimension**, which has never been considered before. Furthermore, we examine these features based on experimental observations, not merely based on theoretical assumptions and show interesting discoveries in citation behaviors. We also analyze different roles in the combination of all features.

• The **2nd** contribution of our work is to model all relevant features to identify the potentially influential papers. Unlike previous studies, we put more focus on identification of highly cited literature, instead of treating them equally, i.e., giving emphasis on "giant shoulders". Given multiple features relevant to influence, i.e., citation counts in this study, we incorporate literature weights into regression models to estimate future impacts of scientific papers.

• The **3rd** contribution is that we integrate the factor of future influence into real practical application of bibliography recommendation system. The improved system outperforms its rivals and hence demonstrates the practical utility and benefits of FIP.

2. RELATED WORK

Influence, for evaluating research achievements, has long been heavily discussed by fundamental research journals (e.g. *Science*, *Nature* and *PNAS*). Impact Factor by Eugene Garfield is a measurement reflecting articles influence and is still pervasive [25, 10]. Journals with higher impact factors are deemed to be more important than those with lower ones [8]. However, impact factor can not reflect the influence of individual papers [7, 23] and hence needs a normalization from the audience of citing sides [30]. As to author aspects, the *h-index* is a useful index that attempts to measure both the productivity and impact of the published work of a scientist or scholar [13, 12]. However, both impact factor and h-index reflect the macro characteristics but the influence of a specific collection (all papers from a particular author or venue) may be skewed by individuals from our observations.

Citations indicate the influence of authors, papers and venues, and several works have conducted to analyze citation behaviors [1, 22, 26] and have perceived interesting discoveries for impact [21, 27]. In recent years, several researchers have investigated the prediction of citation counts. Their work differs primarily as regards the features used for prediction.

The 2003 KDD Cup includes a citation prediction task resembling the one we undertake on this paper. The citation prediction task includes estimating the *change* in the number of citations of papers between two different periods of time [11]. Several papers predict the number of citations using information gathered *after* publication. Brody et al. used download data within 6 months after publication as a predictive feature [4]. However, the aim was to show the Open Access advantage. Castillo et al. used a linear regression for the number of citations, the authors' reputation and the source of the paper citations (author related information) after a short period of time as predictive features [5]. Lokker et al. used features related to the article and journal, like number of authors, pages, references and so on [16]. These three works used measures taken after the paper was published to predict its citation count in the future. The main disadvantage of using this feature is that the required values are not available until after publication, and such features are difficult to access.

On the other hand, Fu et al. attempt to forecast citation counts using features which are are available at the time of publication [9]. Support vector machine regression models are used as the learning algorithm. Ibáñez et al. take into account several regression methods and analyze which one provides better predictions for the problem especially to predict annual time horizons [14]. Predictions in these works are made for a simple binary response variable that is defined by a set of citation thresholds to determine if an article is labeled positively or negatively [6]. Unlike their works, we do not deal with the response variables as several fixed thresholds, but to predict the exact citation count for each individual article. We also exploit the information output by the model, like the identification of key features that increase the chances of citation. This method can actually inform publishers about which articles will have larger influence in the future **before** they are published.

Unlike previous studies, we formally research into a predictive task of FIP and we add more relevant features into consideration. The relevance of features is investigated based on real world observations. We also integrate future influence into real world application of bibliography and obtain prominent improvement. To the best of our knowledge, we are the first to formally research into identification of potentially influential literature and to incorporate FIP into real applications such as literature recommendation.

3. FUTURE INFLUENCE PREDICTION

3.1 Problem Definition

In this section, we first present several necessary definitions and a formal representation of the influence prediction problem.

Influence. *Given the literature corpus **D**, the Influence ($INF(.)$) of a literature article **d**$\in D$ is defined as the citation count of d:*

$$\begin{aligned} citing(d) &= \{d' \in D : d' cites\ d\} \\ INF(d) &= |citing(d)| \end{aligned} \tag{1}$$

Learning task: Given a set of article features, $\vec{X} = x_1, x_2, \ldots, x_n$, our goal is to learn a predictive function $\mathbb{F}(.)$ to predict the influence of an article *d* after a give time period Δt. Formally, we have

$$INF_{FIP}(d|\Delta t) = \mathbb{F}(d|\vec{X}, \Delta t) \tag{2}$$

Given the literature collection *D*, the learned influence predictive function is actually to minimize the following objective cost function $\mathcal{O}(D)$, and the FIP task changes into an optimization problem for an optimal predictive function $\mathbb{F}^*(.)$:

$$\begin{aligned}\mathbb{F}^*(d) &= \operatorname*{argmin}_{\mathbb{F}} \mathcal{O}(D) \\ &= \operatorname*{argmin}_{\mathbb{F}} \sum_{d\in D} |INF_{FIP}(d) - INF(d)| \\ &= \operatorname*{argmin}_{\mathbb{F}} \sum_{d\in D} |\mathbb{F}(d) - INF(d)|\end{aligned} \quad (3)$$

The cost function $\mathcal{O}(D)$ in Equation (3) is to some extent insufficient because it assumes that all papers are equally important. However, our goal is to identify the highly influential ones. Due to the influence distribution in Figure 1.(b), we model the skewed literature weight into cost function $\mathcal{O}(D)$, i.e., to increase the cost for errors on highly influential literature during training, and we change $\mathcal{O}(D)$ into:

$$\mathcal{O}(D) = \sum_{d\in D} \Psi(d) \cdot |INF_{FIP}(d) - INF(d)| \quad (4)$$

where $\Psi(d)$ is the weight of the paper d. The weight can be defined as a normalization to [0, 1] based on the influence distribution on data set D. We emphasize the weight for highly influential papers which are known, and punish the ordinary papers. The weight $\Psi(d)$ is defined as follows:

$$\Psi(d) = \frac{log(1 + INF(d)) - log(1 + INF_{MIN})}{log(1 + INF_{MAX}) - log(1 + INF_{MIN})} \quad (5)$$

where $INF_{MAX/MIN}$ means the maximum and minimum citation counts which are known to us.

The optimal predictive function $\mathbb{F}^*(.)$ becomes:

$$\mathbb{F}^*(d) = \operatorname*{argmin}_{\mathbb{F}} \sum_{d\in D} \Psi(d) \cdot |\mathbb{F}(d) - INF(d)| \quad (6)$$

Before proposing our approach for FIP, we first probe a series of analysis by focusing on the following aspects of input literature articles, and then present the interesting citation patterns observed. Ideally, we ought to consider as many factors as possible. All features in consideration (except for temporal information which is special and is discussed in details) can be grouped into three facets: (1) paper contents, (2) author expertise, and (3) venue impact. Finally, it is important to find unified models which are able to consider all the features simultaneously.

3.2 Contents Feature Definition

3.2.1 *Novelty*

Novelty is a key criterion to evaluate paper quality, and is measured by similarity between a particular article and the other publications. An assumption is that a low similarity means a high novelty. We investigate whether higher novelty attracts more citations.

Novelty can be measured by similarity against all other literatures. However, such metric leads to an overestimated novelty because most papers from different research fields have naturally low similarity. Therefore, we measure an article's novelty against all its references: these papers are generally from the same sub-area and are supposed to have strong relevance. If the article d is significantly different from its references, we presume this phenomenon secures prominent novelty, which is calculated by Kullback-Leibler divergence D_{KL}:

$$Novelty(d) = \frac{\sum_{d'\in D_R} D_{KL}(\Theta_d||\Theta_{d'})}{|D_R|} \quad (7)$$

where $D_R = \{d'|d' \in referring(d)\}$, which is the collection of the reference papers cited by article d, and $referring(d) = \{d' \in D : d\ cites\ d'\}$. Θ_d is the word distribution of article d. V is the vocabulary set and $p(w|\Theta_d) = \frac{tf(w,\Theta_d)}{\sum_{w'\in V} tf(w',\Theta_d)}$ where *tf* denotes the term frequency for word w.

$$D_{KL}(\Theta_d||\Theta_{d'}) = \sum_{w\in V} p(w|\Theta_d)\log\frac{p(w|\Theta_d)}{p(w|\Theta_{d'})} \quad (8)$$

KL-divergence is asymmetric. To measure such novelty, it makes more sense to use $D_{KL}(\Theta_d||\Theta_{d'})$ than $D_{KL}(\Theta_{d'}||\Theta_d)$ because article d is inspired and motivated by all its references $d' \in D_R$.

Figure 2.(1) is interesting: the plot increases in the beginning, showing that the citation counts positively correlate with novelty and then after a certain threshold, the plot decays. This phenomenon indicates that **for articles which are divergent too far away from mass focus, they are unlikely to attract many citations**.

3.2.2 *Topic Rank*

Topics have long been investigated as a significant feature for literature contents [15, 18]. We utilize the unsupervised Latent Dirichlet Allocation [2] to discover topics[3]. Ideally, topics should be trained on the set of full contents of all papers. Because no such data is readily available, here we use the following proxy: we treat the title and the abstract of an article as the approximation.

We empirically train a 100-topic models and obtain the probability distribution over topics assigned to a literature article d, i.e., $p(topic_i|d)$, the inferred probability of topic i in document d. To calculate the influence of a particular topic from article d, denoted by $INF(topic_i|d)$, we distribute the influence of the article $INF(d)$ according to the topic distribution, i.e., $INF(topic_i|d) = INF(d) \times p(topic_i|d)$ and we obtain the influence of all topics by:

$$INF(topic_i) = \sum_{d\in D} INF(topic_i|d) \quad (9)$$

where D is the whole literature collection. We rank topics by average citation counts. From Figure 2.(5), we see different topics have different expected average citation counts. **Popular topics accumulate more citation counts than unpopular ones: topic popularity is relevant to literature influence**.

3.2.3 *Diversity*

Diversity indicates the breadth of an article from its topic distributions. This is important for identifying methodology papers, which are often cited by a wider topical range of articles. When an article has a vast range of audience, it is likely to be cited by authors from various research fields, and hence attract high citation counts. To measure the topical breadth of an article, we calculate the entropy of the document's topic distribution:

$$Diversity(d) = \sum_{i=1}^{|\mathcal{T}|=100} -p(topic_i|d) \cdot \log p(topic_i|d) \quad (10)$$

We hereby calculate the correlation between paper diversity and corresponding average citation counts shown in Figure 2.(3), which is quite interesting because the plot indicates **few papers belong a narrow focused area and in general expected citation counts increase as diversity enlarges**.

3.3 Author Feature Definition

In this section, we will answer the question that how an author's expertise correlates with the number of citation and how to measure

[3]We use Stanford TMT (`http://nlp.stanford.edu/software/tmt/`), with default settings for all parameters.

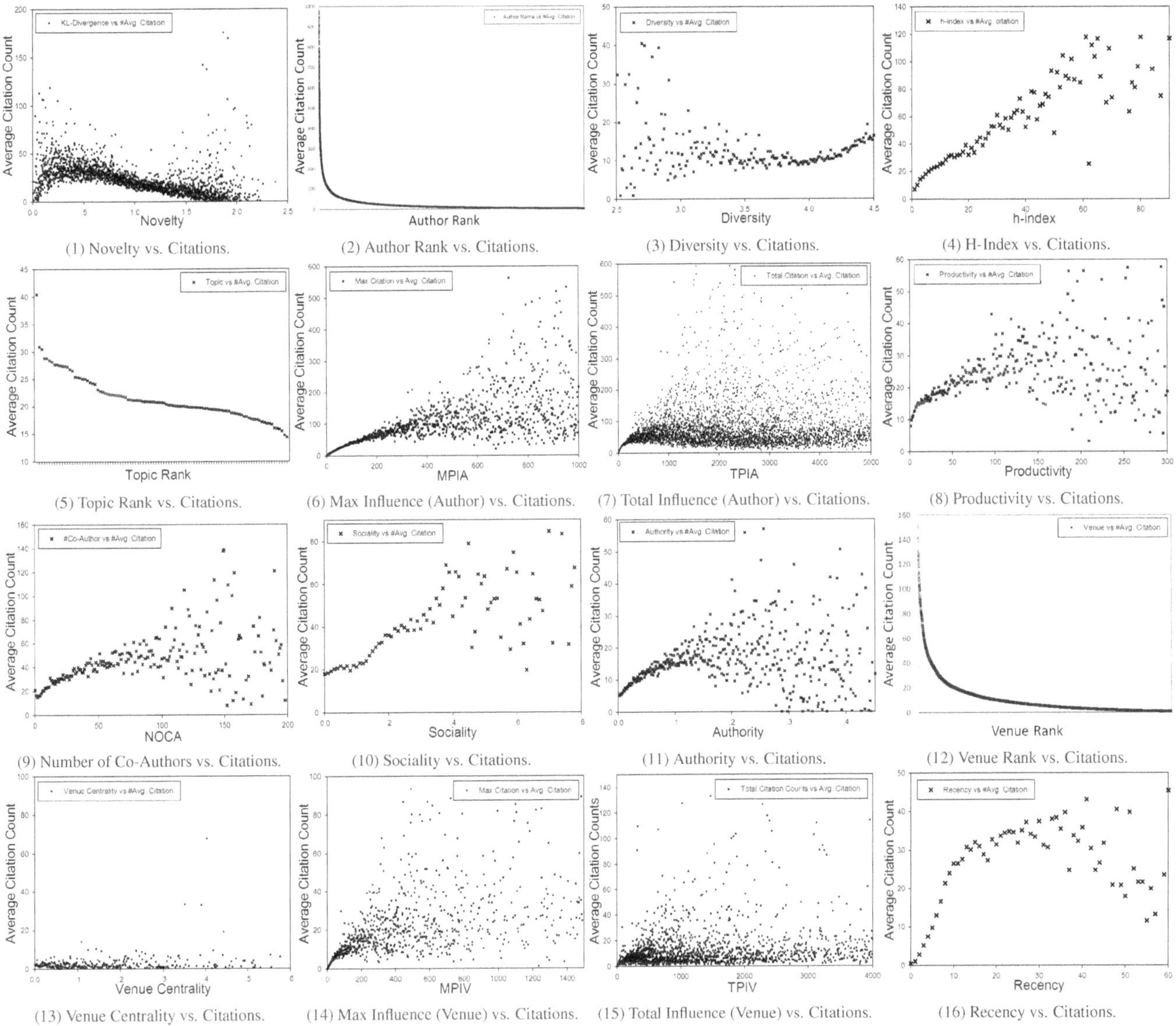

(1) Novelty vs. Citations. (2) Author Rank vs. Citations. (3) Diversity vs. Citations. (4) H-Index vs. Citations.

(5) Topic Rank vs. Citations. (6) Max Influence (Author) vs. Citations. (7) Total Influence (Author) vs. Citations. (8) Productivity vs. Citations.

(9) Number of Co-Authors vs. Citations. (10) Sociality vs. Citations. (11) Authority vs. Citations. (12) Venue Rank vs. Citations.

(13) Venue Centrality vs. Citations. (14) Max Influence (Venue) vs. Citations. (15) Total Influence (Venue) vs. Citations. (16) Recency vs. Citations.

Figure 2: The feature-average citation correlations: x-axis denotes the value of a particular feature (e.g. sociality, authority, etc.), and there are a group of papers with the same value of the examined feature. We take the average citations of these papers as y-value.

such expertise quantitatively. To be self-contained, we first briefly review some of the features introduced in [28], together with our new insights, and then analyze these citation patterns.

3.3.1 Author Rank

Yan *et al.* assume that the "fame" of an author ensures the amount of citations [28]. We calculate the average citations for every author, and then assign an author rank value to him/her according to the rank number by his/her expected citation counts. As shown in Figure 2.(2), the plot of **expected citations is highly skewed, but for most of the authors, their expected citation counts are nearly the same and are rather small**.

3.3.2 H-index

The h-index is useful which attempts to measure both the productivity and impact of the published work of a scientist [12]. Therefore, we examine the correlation between h-index and citation counts. From Figure 2.(4), we observe a highly positive correlation between h-index and average citation counts: the correlation is almost linear, which proves **h-index an effective indicator of influence**.

3.3.3 Past Influence of Authors

Past influence probably indicates future influence. It is reasonable to assume the previous high influence for an author may result in the future high influence, which explains how reputation establishes. There are two ways to measure author past influence: previous (1) maximum citation counts and (2) total citation counts.

• *Maximum Past Influence of Authors (MPIA).* In the real world, one well-known publication helps to recognize academic reputation. The correlation between average citation counts and maximum citation counts is shown in Figure 2.(6), indicating expected citations strongly correlate with MPIA and **one widely acknowledged paper indeed benefits author reputation**.

An interesting observation is that for authors with more than 500 MPIA, the correlations seems to be a chaos with large variances. There are two possible reasons for this situation: 1) the distribution of MPIA per author follows the power law, which means most of the authors have a relatively small MPIA while few authors have a large MPIA. Therefore, for few authors with high MPIA, there is probably lack of average effect and as a result, large variances emerge. 2) The noise of author statistics for high MPIA ranges.

• *Total Past Influence of Authors (TPIA)*. Another measurement of past influence is to calculate total citations per author. From Figure 2.(7) we conclude the weak correlation between expected citations and TPIA: the fitted curve is almost parallel to the x-axis, indicating **total citation of an author might not be predictive**.

3.3.4 Productivity

According to [1], authors have tendencies to cite their own papers: the more productive an author is, the larger chances for his/her papers to be cited. Due to such self-citation behavior analysis, we examine the predictive power of productivity in Figure 2.(8). We notice that productivity and citation counts have a positive correlation: **the more papers an author have published, the higher average citation counts he/she could expect**. Similar to Figure 2.(6), the large variances in the high value range might be due to noisy data and lack of average effect for these few authors.

3.3.5 Sociality

Researchers tend to cite papers from whom the author(s) have co-authored [1]. Hence a widely connected author is more likely to be highly cited by his/her wide variety of co-authors. A straightforward social measurement of Number of Co-Authors (NOCA) is introduced in [28] and we examine the correlation between NOCA and average citation counts. As shown in Figure 2.(9), the plot implies a prominent positive correlation.

However, sociality measured by the co-author numbers is simple and reflects insufficient social relationships: authors have different social weights. Collaboration with the same amount of authors of high (or low) sociality might lead to different influence but "the number of co-authors" fails to distinguish such difference. We then measure sociality based on the real academic social network. We establish a co-author network graph $G_c(V, E)$ to discover the research communities, where V is the set of vertices and each vertex v_i in V represents an author. E is the set of edges which is a subset of $V \times V$. Each edge denotes the co-authorship and is associated with an author affinity weight $A_{aff}(v_i, v_j)$ between vertex v_i and v_j ($i \neq j$). The weights of the edges are calculated by the times of collaboration, i.e., $A_{aff}(v_i, v_j) = |D_{co}|$ where co-authored paper set $D_{co} = \{d|(author(d) \cap (v_i \cup v_j)) \neq \varnothing\}$. The transition probability between v_i and v_j is then defined by normalizing the corresponding affinity weight [28].

We use the row-normalized matrix $M = M_{i,j_{|V|\times|V|}}$ to describe G_c with entry corresponding to the transition probability, i.e., $M_{i,j} = p(v_i, v_j)$. Based on the matrix M, the sociality of an author v_i (denoted as $Sociality(v_i)$) can be deduced from all other authors linked with him/her, which can be formulated in a recursive form as in the PageRank algorithm.

$$Sociality(v_i) = \mu \sum_{j \neq i} Sociality(v_j) \cdot M_{j,i} + \frac{1-\mu}{|V|} \quad (11)$$

where μ=0.85. We conduct an examination of the correlation between sociality and average citation counts. **The positive effect of sociality has been confirmed in Figure 2.(10)**.

3.3.6 Authority

Besides the co-authorship network, another heterogenous social network for academia is established from the "citing - cited" relationships among literature articles. A widely cited paper indicates peer acknowledgements, and hence indicates author authority. We transmit paper authority to all its authors. We build a graph of $G_a(V, E)$, where V denotes the paper collection and E denotes the *citing-cited* linkage with directions. The out-degrees measure how many times a paper is cited while in-degrees indicate the references of a particular paper. Each paper is represented as a term vector of semantic words from the vocabulary, and we calculate the standard cosine similarity between two papers as the weight of the paper affinity in the graph, i.e., $P_{aff}(v_i, v_j) = sim_{cos}(v_i, v_j)$. After a similar PageRank procedure as Equation (11), we obtain the authority score $Authority(d)$ of each paper d. We define the authority of an author a as:

$$Authority(a) = \sum_{d \in D_a} Authority(d) \quad (12)$$

where $D_a = \{d|a \subseteq author(d)\}$. We examine the correlation between these two variants in Figure 2.(11). **The strong correlation between authority and average citations is hence verified**.

3.3.7 Versatility

Like paper contents, a wide topic breadth of an author's research implies large amount of audience from various research fields, which is similar to *diversity* to identify highly influential papers cited by a wider topical range of articles. When an author has a vast range of audience, his/her papers are likely to be highly cited. To measure the topical breadth of an author a, namely *versatility*, we calculate the entropy of the author's topic distribution:

$$Versatility(a) = \sum_{i=1}^{\mathcal{T}=100} -p(topic_i|a) \cdot \log p(topic_i|a) \quad (13)$$

where

$$p(topic_i|a) = \frac{\sum_{d \in D_a} p(topic_i|d)}{|D_a|} \quad (14)$$

where $D_a = \{d|a \subseteq author(d)\}$. We hereby calculate the correlation between author versatility and corresponding average citation counts. The pattern distribution is quite similar to Figure 2.(3) and due to page limits we omit the near-duplication of Figure 2.(3). **Few authors have a narrow focus and the expected citation counts increase as versatility enlarges**.

3.4 Venue Feature Definition

Like authors, venues also have academic reputations. From our observations, some venues have larger probability to be highly cited than others. We hereby investigate the venue impact on citations.

3.4.1 Venue Rank

Prestigious venues attract more focus just as the author rank pattern. As shown in Figure 2.(12), the reputation of a venue ensures different citations. Compared with Figure 2.(2), although plot in Figure 2.(12) is not that skewed, **the differences of expected citations for different venues are prominent enough**.

3.4.2 Venue Centrality

High citations of a particular conference or journal indicate peer acknowledgement from other venues, and we aim to find such central venues. Venues are connected by paper *citing-cited* linkage. We establish a venue connective graph $G_v(V, E)$ where V denotes the venues and the edges E denote the citing-cited relationships between venues. Like $G_a(V, E)$, $G_v(V, E)$ also has directions: the out-degrees measure how many times a venue is cited by papers from other venues while in-degrees denote citations. The weight of each edge is calculated by the number of citations between two venues. Hence, the venue centrality can be calculated via a similar

PageRank algorithm as Equation (11) and we examine the correlations between venue centrality and average citation counts, illustrated in Figure 2.(13). **To our surprise, the feature of venue centrality seems to imply little relevance with citations.**

3.4.3 Past Influence of Venues

Similar to author expertise, past venue influence might indicate probable future success. It is natural to assume the previous high influence for a venue may result in the future high influence. We still use (1) maximum past influence of venues (MPIV) and (2) total past influence of venues (TPIV) to measure past venue influence, showing in Figure 2.(14) and 2.(15). **Interestingly, plots of MPIV and TPIV share similar patterns with Figure 2.(6) and 2.(7).**

3.5 Temporal Feature

Temporal dimension has long been proved to be significant in literature studies [1, 29]. Intuitively the citation counts accumulate as time passes by, thus a measure of the age of an article is important. We include as a feature the number of years since the article was published. We expect a positive correlation on temporal recency - the longer an article is published, the more citations it may receive.

As indicated in Figure 2.(16), the effect of temporal recency is highly prominent for the first 10 to 20 years. The average citation counts sheerly increase for the first decades when the articles get published. The increase rate slows down for the following years: it is natural that articles are attractive when they are to some extent "new" to researchers. Only few classic works accumulate citation counts steadily for decades. We notice that for literatures published more than 40 years ago, the citation counts decay and have a larger variance. This situation may be due to the noise for the aged publications when online literature libraries were not available. The decay may also be due to literatures attracts citations from temporal recent publications, but as shown in Figure 1.(a), the proportion of aged publications (e.g., more than 40 years) is rather small. Large amount of new articles are not likely to cite aged literatures. Therefore, aged literatures have low citations in general.

Growing Factor. Nothing can catch people's eyes more than a rising phenomenon. For instance, an author with rapid accumulation of citations or publications in recent years might indicate high influence to the academia. Therefore, it is reasonable to incorporate growing factor of preference for new scientists, new venues and newly developed research topics. For the growing effect analysis, we create another dataset constituted by literature of recent N years only, namely **RData**. Now we have two datasets: RData and the full dataset by literature of all years (**FData**). We study all features and examine different patterns on these two datasets, as well as the combination of both sets.

Decaying Factor. As the scenario of future influence prediction requires invisibility of future literature patterns, it is natural that the influence calculated from current situation decays after a particular given time period Δt. For simplicity, we use the traditional decay function for the temporal dimension, i.e., the decayed influence is measured as $INF(d) \times e^{-\gamma \Delta t}$, where $\gamma \in [0,1]$ is a scaling factor and $\Delta t = t_f - t_p$. t_p is the publish year and t_f is the future year to predict citations counts.

In all we have 32 features to predict future citation counts (listed in Table 3), including *full-feature* and *recent-feature*. Considering growing factor by distinguishing FData and RData doubles the number of available features. All recent-features are calculated based on the RData. Note that the 100 topics for FData and RData are the same, and hence we do not introduce a duplicate feature of *recent diversity*. Similarly, *recent recency* is fully covered by *recency*. Note that there may be multiple authors for a single paper, and it is inappropriate to use the first author only because all authors are assumed to have contributions to the influence of the paper. We create a **virtual author** whose feature values are averaged based on all authors of the paper. We experiment different combinations of these features.

3.6 Predictive Models

3.6.1 Gaussian Process Regression

Given a compact feature representation amenable for learning, our objective is to estimate an article's expected citation counts. Note that predicting the times that an article will get cited is an extremely hard problem. Due to the complex mechanism of future influence estimation, it is likely that they are a non-linear function of all features used to represent the data. Gaussian Processes provide a Bayesian formulation for non-linear regression, where the prior information about the regression parameters can be easily encoded. This property makes them suitable for our problem formulation.

A Gaussian Process is a collection of random variables, any finite number of which have a joint Gaussian distribution [20]. Given the feature vector X, the estimated citation $INF(d)$ for d is:

$$INF(d) = K(X, X_T)[K(X_T, X_T) + \sigma^2 I]^{-1} INF(d_T), \quad (15)$$

where K is a kernel function returning a kernel matrix, X_T is a matrix of feature vectors for the training papers, σ is a noise parameter, I the identity matrix and $INF(d_T)$ the vector of citation counts of the training article d_T. Note that we only use the mean and not the variance estimated by the GP. We use a Gaussian kernel in our experiments. We notice that the performance of GP has a weak dependence on σ and set it to 0.5.

3.6.2 CART Model

We then fit a Classification and Regression Tree (CART) model [3], in which a greedy optimization process recursively partitions the feature space, resulting in a piecewise-constant function where the value in each partition is fit to the mean of the corresponding training data. Folded cross-validation [19] is used to terminate partitioning to prevent over-fitting. Our model included 32 features summarized in the last section as predictors.

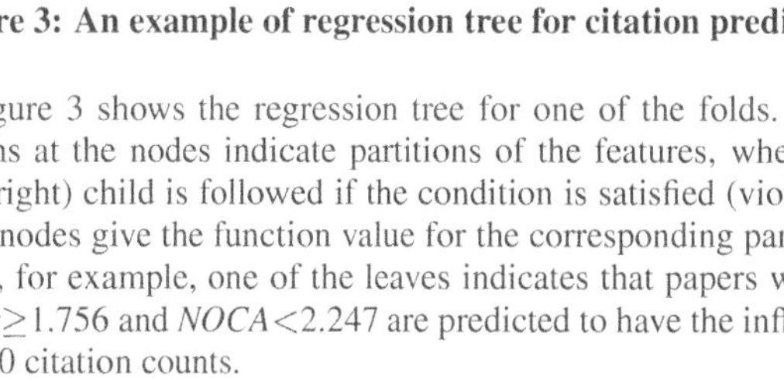

Figure 3: An example of regression tree for citation prediction.

Figure 3 shows the regression tree for one of the folds. Conditions at the nodes indicate partitions of the features, where the left (right) child is followed if the condition is satisfied (violated). Leaf nodes give the function value for the corresponding partition. Thus, for example, one of the leaves indicates that papers with *h-index*≥1.756 and *NOCA*<2.247 are predicted to have the influence of 180 citation counts.

4. EXPERIMENTS AND EVALUATION

4.1 Data Description

We perform influence prediction on the real-world data set[4], which is extracted from academic search and mining platform ArnetMiner.

[4]Downloaded from `http://arnetminer.org/citation`.

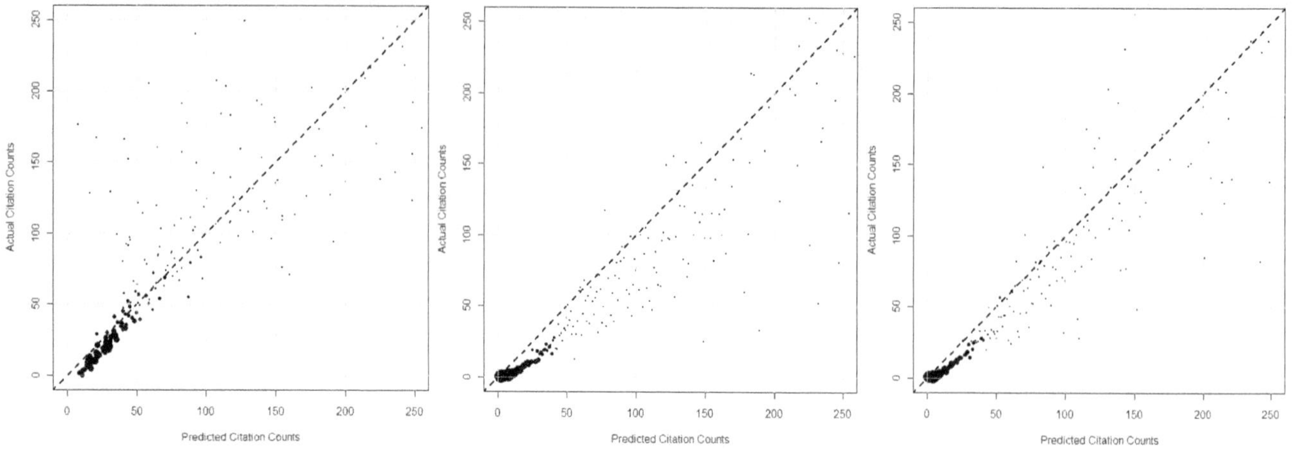

(1). 5-Year unweighted FIP for Year 2005, regression = GPR.(2). 5-Year weighted FIP for Year 2005, regression = GPR.(3). 10-Year weighted FIP for Year 2000, regression = GPR.

Figure 4: Actual vs. predicted citation counts: the performance for FIP with full features. The dotted line $y = x$ means the best result of predicted citation counts = actual citation counts. Figure 4.(2)-4.(3) incorporate literature weights while 4.(1) does not.

It covers 1,558,499 papers from major Computer Science publication venues and has gathered 916,946 researchers for more than 50 years (from 1960 to 2010). Two heterogeneous networks are included: one is the co-author collaboration network and the other is the paper citation network. The full graph of co-author network has 916,946 vertices (authors) and 3,063,257 edges (co-authorship), and the full graph of citation network has 1,558,499 vertices (literature papers) and 20,083,947 edges (citations).

To predict the citation counts after one year, we randomly take 10,000 papers from the literature collection from Year 2009 as the test set, and another random 10,000 papers from the Year 2009 as the development set. Note that for all training and evaluation, we only used features calculated over previous years. For example, when predicting articles published in Year 2009, all the articles up through Year 2008 are processed, and only the articles from the Year 2009 are available (as test set). Thus, these time dependent features would only include papers published in 2008 and earlier. Structuring the evaluation in this way is more realistic - when presented with new coming articles, the system can only predict possible future influence based on the patterns it has previously observed. We take the same procedure to predict citation counts after 5 (and 10) years with 10,000 test papers and 10,000 development papers from Year 2005 (and Year 2000). For unobserved feature values, e.g., new authors or new venues, we use the minimum feature values instead of N/A: anything has a start. We compare predicted citation counts with actual influence from the test data.

4.2 Algorithms for Comparison

We implement the following citation prediction algorithms as the baseline systems. All baselines are originally designed for traditional influence prediction problem rather than identify the influential ones. For fairness we apply the same biased objective function and the same pre-processing procedure for all algorithms.

• **kNN.** k-Nearest Neighbor (kNN) is used to predict citation by Ibáñez et al [14], which predicts the influence value for the paper d to be the average of the values of its k-nearest neighbors and the distance function measuring neighbors is based on a similarity calculation method such as cosine similarity. The neighbors are taken from training set for which real citation counts are known.

• **LR.** Lovaglia et al. propose a Linear Regression model to predict citation counts [17].

• **SVR.** Based on Support Vector Machine (SVM) model, Fu et al. build a Support Vector Regression (SVR) model to predict citation counts of biomedical publications using only predictive information available at publication time [9].

• **CART.** The CART method was used by Yan et al. on a limited feature space without incorporation of literature weight [28].

• **GPR.** The GPR method is our newly proposed approach for FIP problem, using the Gaussian Process for prediction.

4.3 Evaluation Metric

The coefficient of determination R^2 [24] is used in the context of statistical models whose main purpose is the prediction of future outcomes on the basis of related features. It is the proportion of variability in a data set that is accounted for by the statistical model, which provides a measure of how well future outcomes are likely to be predicted by the model. The definition of R^2 is:

$$R^2 = \frac{\sum\limits_{d \in D_T} (INF_{FIP}(d) - INF(D_T))^2}{\sum\limits_{d \in D_T} (INF(d) - INF(D_T))^2} \quad (16)$$

where $INF_{FIP}(d)$ is the predicted citations for article d in the test set D_T and $INF(D_T) = \frac{1}{|D_T|} \sum_{d \in D_T} INF(d)$ is the mean of the observed citation counts for an article in D_T. $R^2 \in [0, 1]$, and a larger R^2 indicates better performance and hence is desired.

4.4 Performance and Strategy Analysis

The performance of FIP for different years is visualized in Figure 4, and the detailed results are summarized in Table 1. The size of circles indicates the number of points in each predicted citation counts. Most circles are gathered within in the range of [0, 50], indicating most of the papers have relatively low citations. Among different prediction tasks, 10-year prediction has the most remarkable performance. Furthermore, we notice a probable trend among these series of experiments: accuracy increases as Δt increases. We will examine the sensibility of Δt in the next section. The system is not quite ideally performed in predicting short term influence but it is still of great significance because it is likely to estimate the long term influence for a paper more accurately, but the ultimate influence determines the achievements of literature.

Comparing FIP with and without literature weights, we notice that both strategies have merits. When $\Psi(d)$ is not incorporated, the overall accuracy of FIP is slightly better because it predicts low citations very well and the lowly cited literature is the most major

Table 1: The performance of various prediction techniques for different feature combinations on the test set.

	1-Year FIP (Δt=1)			5-Year FIP (Δt=5)			10-Year FIP (Δt=10)		
Methods	FData	RData	Combined	FData	RData	Combined	FData	RData	Combined
kNN	0.515	0.311	0.593	0.681	0.268	0.734	0.649	0.161	0.767
LR	0.625	0.479	0.692	0.798	0.134	0.811	0.885	0.123	0.912
SVR	0.590	0.268	0.644	0.723	0.162	0.771	0.813	0.111	0.861
CART	0.679	0.441	**0.713**	0.797	0.203	0.834	0.852	0.128	0.905
GPR	0.601	0.349	0.668	0.823	0.153	**0.869**	0.894	0.130	**0.927**

Table 2: The performance of various prediction techniques for different feature combinations on the test set. "+" indicates the single feature group in isolation while "-" indicates the drop of the feature group from the full combination.

	1-Year FIP (Δt=1)					5-Year FIP (Δt=5)					10-Year FIP (Δt=10)				
Methods	kNN	LR	SVR	CART	GPR	kNN	LR	SVR	CART	GPR	kNN	LR	SVR	CART	GPR
+Content	0.061	0.097	0.101	0.104	0.110	0.065	0.100	0.107	0.105	0.103	0.114	0.152	0.137	0.174	0.168
+Author	0.563	0.586	0.582	0.603	0.589	0.601	0.619	0.611	0.627	0.631	0.616	0.637	0.623	0.652	0.659
+Venue	0.236	0.331	0.333	0.362	0.331	0.315	0.347	0.340	0.369	0.372	0.345	0.380	0.371	0.402	0.417
-Content	0.623	0.711	0.706	**0.727**	0.719	0.651	0.760	0.735	0.769	0.781	0.684	0.795	0.773	0.820	0.867
-Author	0.267	0.323	0.327	0.412	0.419	0.340	0.409	0.427	0.441	0.432	0.406	0.435	0.412	0.468	0.455
-Venue	0.571	0.583	0.588	0.606	0.597	0.605	0.617	0.609	0.632	0.625	0.621	0.650	0.628	0.667	0.672
Combined	0.593	0.692	0.644	0.713	0.668	0.734	0.811	0.771	0.834	**0.869**	0.767	0.912	0.861	0.905	**0.927**

part of the whole collection. When literature weights modeled, FIP biases to find the highly influential papers. We notice that in Figure 4.(2)-(3), the scattered circles in the high citation range are much less, and are much closer to the criterion line $y = x$ than those in Figure 4.(1). **Particular, few circles are in the upper triangle area (i.e., when $y > x$), which indicates few significant literature is missed.** However, for FIP with literature weights, the prediction effect in the low citation range is compromised. Although for lowly cited publications, the error of mis-prediction does not cost as much as those highly cited ones, it remains to be the insufficiency of FIP and can be further improved.

Different predictive models have different performances on these three individual tasks in our experiments. In general, non-linear regression achieves better performance. From Table 1, we notice that kNN has the worst performance. The result is as expected because kNN merely seeks the most similar neighbors and takes the neighbors' citation counts as the predictive influence while utilizes little information from the enormous training data. LR, by linear combination of all features, and CART and GPR by non-linear regressions have comparable performances and proves the generality of our extracted features. GPR is the best and CART, compared with GPR, has a little unstable performance. We also examine the growing factor in Table 1. Generally, the introduction of recent feature distributions benefit the performance of future influence prediction. Although the RData alone does not bring with excellent results, the combination of features from FData and from RData enhance the performance of what FData is capable of.

We then examine the different aspects of feature groups: paper content, author expertise and venue impact in Table 2. Author expertise is proved to be the most influential feature group in influence prediction, with the highest performance of R^2=0.659 in isolation and the lowest performance of R^2=0.419 for GPR when left out from full feature combination. It is understandable that authors are likely to cite papers written by reputable and influential authors. Venue impact is also influential. Papers from prestigious venues are likely to be highly cited. Unexpectedly, paper content is proved to have the least significance, with the average performance of R^2=0.130 in isolation. We assume (1) authors have biases to choose their bibliography: they sometimes merely consider author/venue reputation; (2) it seems that paper quality is represented by author/venue which create the paper. Influential authors or venues seem to overwhelm the impact of paper content itself;

Table 3: Feature analysis: R^2 result when with the pending feature ("+Add"), and result in R^2 when dropped from the all-features model ("-Drop").

	FData		RData	
Feature	+Add	−Drop	+Add	−Drop
Novelty	0.059	0.754	0.066	0.751
T.Rank	0.079	0.783	0.135	0.678
Diversity	0.157	0.661		
A.Rank	**0.593**	**0.406**	0.227	0.626
H-Index	0.244	0.611	0.186	0.663
Productivity	0.198	0.652	0.187	0.684
MPIA	0.585	0.419	**0.363**	**0.596**
TPIA	0.048	0.805	0.037	0.811
NOCA	0.056	0.794	0.158	0.643
Sociality	0.249	0.597	0.181	0.632
Authority	0.155	0.668	0.178	0.615
Versatility	0.160	0.649	0.139	0.665
Recency	0.101	0.738		
V.Rank	0.337	0.603	0.225	0.648
V.Centrality	0.049	0.793	0.067	0.776
MPIV	0.329	0.616	0.196	0.667
TPIV	0.023	0.815	0.021	0.823

(3) it might also be due to the insufficient feature distilling for contents, e.g. using abstracts as approximation may not be enough for topic/diversity discovery.

We also conduct to a detailed experiment on all separate features in Table 3, and the visualization is presented in Figure 5. We mark the most prominent changes of performance in bold characters in Table 3. For the FData, the absence of *Author Rank*, *MPIA* and *Sociality* lead to unfavorable decrease; for the RData, the absence of *MPIA*, *Authority* and *Author Rank* results in similar effects. Hence, the performance is different for the same feature from RData and FData. For instance, the recent productivity is superior than the overall productivity according to the experiments. The visual example of Figure 5 better illustrates the comparisons between different features and their combinations. *TPIA* and *TPIV* are the least powerful prediction factors for both FData and RData, and the results confirm Figure 2.(7) and Figure 2.(15). Another interesting discovery is that *Novelty* and *Recent Novelty* lead to similar per-

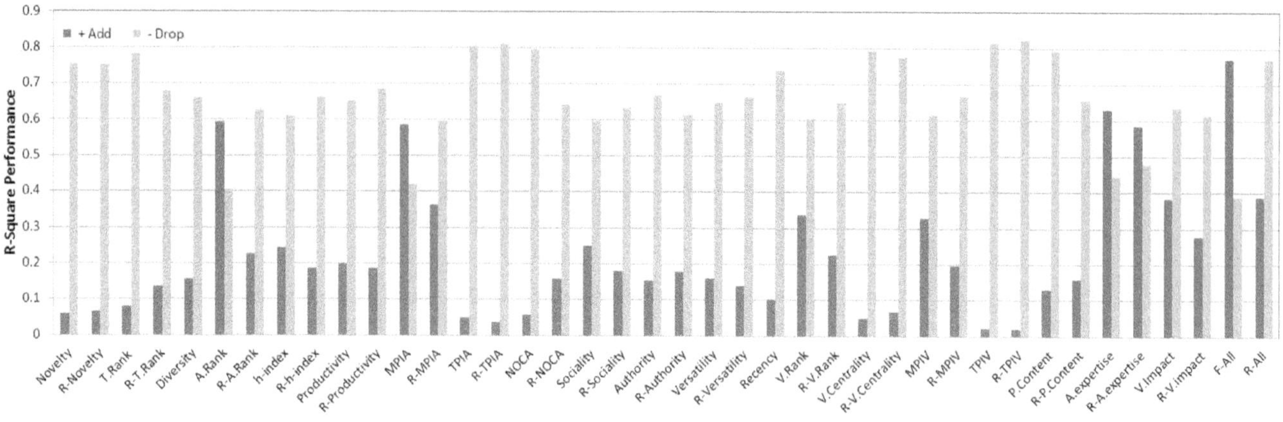

Figure 5: Performance comparison in R^2 for feature analysis. "*R-*" denotes the feature measured on the RData. *A.Rank/V.Rank* denotes author/venue rank, and *F-All/R-All* denotes all features measures on the FData or on the RData.

formances, perhaps due to the temporally recent bibliographies for reference papers. We also find graph-based *sociality* is better than simple *NOCA*.

4.5 Parameter Tuning

We have two free parameters in the temporal features. N is to control the size of RData and when N=0, the consideration of growing factor is off. γ controls the decay of the influence value after a given period of years. When γ=0, the decaying factor is off. We have tested several values, summarized in Table 4. The consideration of feature decay brings positive outcomes, but the penalization should better not be too much: γ=1 harms the performance. We choose N=5 in our experiments because a RData where N=1 hardly makes any difference. From our observations and experiments, the larger N is, the similar feature pattern it would be to the pattern on FData. Based on performance tuning on development set, we set k-NN as 5-NN empirically.

Table 4: Tuning temporal influence on growing factor/decaying factors. $N = 0$ means no growing factor of RData and $\gamma = 0$ means no decaying factor for future feature values.

Decay \ Grow	Off: N=0	N=1	N=5	N=10
Off: γ=0	0.799	0.812	0.833	0.808
γ=0.01	0.803	0.817	0.836	0.806
γ=0.1	0.747	0.765	0.791	0.752
γ=1	0.718	0.739	0.767	0.720

Strictly, Δt is not a parameter to tune but we can see a increasing trend for the performance as Δt enlarges. A possible explanation for such a increasing trend along with Δt is that for papers with certain features (such as high *author rank*, high *MPIA*, etc.) are predicted to have high influence. However, as Figure 2.(16) shows, citation accumulation takes time (about 10 to 20 years). The predicted citation counts will be overestimated for a short period of years: hence in Figure 4, many circles are below the line $y = x$.

4.6 Application: Bibliography Recommendation by Re-Ranking Mechanism

Future influence prediction not only estimates literature quality, but also can be used as auxiliary information in practical applications such as literature recommendation. Although our major focus is on citation estimation, we also implement the prototype of literature recommendation/search system proposed in [1] to prove the benefits of FIP. The system calculates the appropriate candidate reference papers for each article d and hence ranks the reference list by the ranking score, but it takes no consideration of future influence. We combine these estimated citation counts with the original ranking score to obtain the re-ranking score. In particular, the ranking score S_{FIP} for future influence is:

$$S_{FIP}(d) = \frac{log(1 + INF(d)) - log(1 + INF_{min})}{log(1 + INF_{max}) - log(1 + INF_{min})} \quad (17)$$

where $INF_{max/min}$ means the maximum/minimum predicted influence calculated. The score is scaled to [0, 1] so as to be comparable with the original ranking score $S_O(d)$ in [1]. Finally we model the re-ranking score S as the linear combination:

$$S(d) = \lambda \cdot S_O(d) + (1 - \lambda) \cdot S_{FIP}(d) \quad (18)$$

Table 5: Result comparison in MAP for original and combined ranking scores. λ is tuned at 0.3 from development set.

Method	Dev MAP	Test MAP
Original Score	12.51%	12.38%
Combined Score with FIP	15.66%	15.87%

As to evaluation, we train the model on the development set until it achieves the highest Mean Average Precision (MAP) [1]. The performance of bibliography recommendation is listed in Table 6, from where we notice that a 3.49% of improvement. This phenomenon does not necessarily indicate that authors intend to cite future influential papers, but can be explained by citation patterns: papers from reputable authors/venues are more likely to be chosen as bibliography and these papers are predicted to be higher influential, which is not a coincidence.

5. CONCLUSION AND FUTURE WORK

In this paper we propose a novel solution for the task of Future Influence Prediction (FIP), which identifies the potentially influential publications. Given a particular paper and its corresponding features relevant with citation patterns (such as paper content, author expertise and venue impact), FIP predicts its possible citation counts. We formally formulate FIP task as a learning problem utilizing several regression models, and evaluate the prediction performance by coefficient of determination (R^2). We also implement a practical system of bibliography recommendation via re-ranking mechanism. The system outperform the baseline system, indicating papers with influential characteristics are likely to attract author attentions when they choose references.

From our experiments, we find that authors have biases in citing references. Author expertise and venue impact are the distinguishing factors for the consideration of bibliography, among which, *Author Rank*, *Maximum Past Influence of Authors* make paper influential. Content features are not predictive perhaps due to (1) citation bias, (2) paper quality is covered by authors/venues, or (3) insufficient content modeling. As FData and RData have different feature patterns, the combination of both result in better performance. In general, the prediction after a longer period can achieve the best accuracy (R^2=0.927 when $\Delta t = 10$). Currently, we consider a particular paper itself without considering any of its audience (citing papers). However, the impact of audience can also be modeled because once a paper is cited by an influential audience, it is likely to be influential as well. As considering the audience will result in a *multi-step influence diffusion* problem and increase the complexity in measurement. In this study, we do not consider the audience's influence when measuring the influence of the cited literature, while it can be further studied in the future.

6. ACKNOWLEDGMENTS

We thank the anonymous reviewers for their constructive comments. The work was partially supported by the Natural Science Foundation of China (Grant No. 60933004, Grant No. 61073081) and the Open Fund of the State Key Laboratory of Virtual Reality Technology and Systems. Jie Tang was supported by the Natural Science Foundation of China (Grant No. 61073073), Chinese National Key Foundation Research (No. 60933013, No.61035004). Rui Yan was supported by the MediaTek fellowship.

7. REFERENCES

[1] S. Bethard and D. Jurafsky. Who should I cite: learning literature search models from citation behavior. In *Proceedings of CIKM*, CIKM'10, pages 609–618. ACM, 2010.

[2] D. M. Blei, A. Y. Ng, and M. I. Jordan. Latent dirichlet allocation. *J. Mach. Learn. Res.*, 3:993–1022, March 2003.

[3] L. Breiman. *Classification and regression trees*. Chapman & Hall/CRC, 1984.

[4] T. Brody, S. Harnad, and L. Carr. Earlier web usage statistics as predictors of later citation impact. *Journal of the American Society for Information Science and Technology*, 57(8):1060–1072, 2006.

[5] C. Castillo, D. Donato, and A. Gionis. Estimating number of citations using author reputation. In *String processing and information retrieval*, pages 107–117. Springer, 2007.

[6] L. Dietz, S. Bickel, and T. Scheffer. Unsupervised prediction of citation influences. In *Proceedings of ICML'07*, pages 233–240, 2007.

[7] J. Dimitrov, S. Kaveri, and J. Bayry. Metrics: journal's impact factor skewed by a single paper. *Nature*, 466(7303):179–179, 2010.

[8] A. Fersht. The most influential journals: Impact Factor and Eigenfactor. *Proceedings of the National Academy of Sciences*, 106(17):6883, 2009.

[9] L. D. Fu and C. Aliferis. Models for predicting and explaining citation count of biomedical articles. In *AMIA Annual Symposium*, pages 222–226, 2008.

[10] E. Garfield. Impact factors, and why they won't go away. *Nature*, 411(6837):522–522, 2001.

[11] J. Gehrke, P. Ginsparg, and J. Kleinberg. Overview of the 2003 kdd cup. *SIGKDD Explor. Newsl.*, 5:149–151, December 2003.

[12] J. Hirsch. An index to quantify an individual's scientific research output. *Proceedings of the National Academy of Sciences of the United States of America*, 102(46):16569, 2005.

[13] J. Hirsch. Does the h index have predictive power? *Proceedings of the National Academy of Sciences*, 104(49):19193, 2007.

[14] A. Ibáñez, P. Larrañaga, and C. Bielza. Predicting citation count of bioinformatics papers within four years of publication. *Bioinformatics*, 25(24):3303–3309, 2009.

[15] L. Liu, J. Tang, J. Han, M. Jiang, and S. Yang. Mining topic-level influence in heterogeneous networks. In *Proceedings of CIKM'10*, CIKM '10, pages 199–208, 2010.

[16] C. Lokker, K. McKibbon, R. McKinlay, N. Wilczynski, and R. Haynes. Prediction of citation counts for clinical articles at two years using data available within three weeks of publication: retrospective cohort study. *BMJ*, 336(7645):655–657, 2008.

[17] M. Lovaglia. Predicting citations to journal articles: The ideal number of references. *The American Sociologist*, 22(1):49–64, 1991.

[18] R. M. Nallapati, A. Ahmed, E. P. Xing, and W. W. Cohen. Joint latent topic models for text and citations. In *Proceeding of SIGKDD*, KDD '08, pages 542–550, New York, NY, USA, 2008. ACM.

[19] R. Picard and R. Cook. Cross-validation of regression models. *Journal of the American Statistical Association*, 79:575–583, 1984.

[20] C. Rasmussen. Gaussian processes in machine learning. *Advanced Lectures on Machine Learning*, pages 63–71, 2004.

[21] X. Shi, J. Leskovec, and D. A. McFarland. Citing for high impact. In *Proceedings of the 10th annual joint conference on Digital libraries*, JCDL '10, pages 49–58, 2010.

[22] A. Siddharthan and S. Teufel. Whose idea was this, and why does it matter? attributing scientific work to citations. In *HLT-NAACL*, pages 316–323, 2007.

[23] K. Simons. The misused impact factor. *Science*, 322:165, 2008.

[24] R. Steel and J. Torrie. *Principles and procedures of statistics*, volume 633. McGraw-Hill New York, 1980.

[25] Y. Sun and C. Giles. Popularity weighted ranking for academic digital libraries. *Advances in Information Retrieval*, pages 605–612.

[26] Y. Sun, T. Wu, Z. Yin, H. Cheng, J. Han, X. Yin, and P. Zhao. Bibnetminer: mining bibliographic information networks. In *Proceedings of SIGMOD*, SIGMOD '08, pages 1341–1344, 2008.

[27] J. Tang, J. Sun, C. Wang, and Z. Yang. Social influence analysis in large-scale networks. In *Proceedings of SIGKDD*, KDD '09, pages 807–816, New York, NY, USA, 2009. ACM.

[28] R. Yan, J. Tang, X. Liu, D. Shan, and X. Li. Citation count prediction: Learning to estimate future citations for literature. In *Proceeding of CIKM*, CIKM '11, 2011.

[29] D. Zhou, X. Ji, H. Zha, and C. L. Giles. Topic evolution and social interactions: how authors effect research. In *Proceedings of CIKM'06*, pages 248–257, 2006.

[30] M. Zitt. Citing-side normalization of journal impact: A robust variant of the Audience Factor. *Journal of Informetrics*, 4(3):392–406, 2010.

BibRank: a Language-Based Model for Co-Ranking Entities in Bibliographic Networks

Laure Soulier
IRIT - Paul Sabatier University
118 route de Narbonne
31062 Toulouse, France
soulier@irit.fr

Lamjed Ben Jabeur
IRIT - Paul Sabatier University
118 route de Narbonne
31062 Toulouse, France
jabeur@irit.fr

Lynda Tamine
IRIT - Paul Sabatier University
118 route de Narbonne
31062 Toulouse, France
tamine@irit.fr

Wahiba Bahsoun
IRIT - Paul Sabatier University
118 route de Narbonne
31062 Toulouse, France
wbahsoun@irit.fr

ABSTRACT

Bibliographic documents are basically associated with many entities including authors, venues, affiliations, etc. While bibliographic search engines addressed mainly relevant document ranking according to a query topic, ranking other related relevant bibliographic entities is still challenging. Indeed, document relevance is the primary level that allows inferring the relevance of the other entities regardless of the query topic. In this paper, we propose a novel integrated ranking model, called BibRank, that aims at ranking both document and author entities in bibliographic networks. The underlying algorithm propagates entity scores through the network by means of citation and authorship links. Moreover, we propose to weight these relationships using content-based indicators that estimate the topical relatedness between entities. In particular, we estimate the common similarity between homogeneous entities by analyzing marginal citations. We also compare document and author language models in order to evaluate the level of author's knowledge on the document topic and the document representativeness of author's knowledge. Experiment results on the representative CiteSeerX dataset show that BibRank model outperforms baseline ranking models with a significant improvement.

Categories and Subject Descriptors

H.3.3 [**Information Systems**]: Information Search and Retrieval

General Terms

Algorithms, Experimentation, Performance

Keywords

Multi-entity Ranking, Bibliographic Network, Heterogeneous Information Network, Homogeneous Information Network

1. INTRODUCTION

Bibliographic indexers and scientific search engines, such as CiteSeerX[1] and Google Scholar[2] have largely contributed to develop sophisticated models for bibliographic access and scientific document ranking. For this purpose, several features such as citation links and document recency are used in order to rank bibliographic resources. Meanwhile, these approaches remain document-centered and do not consider other entities participating in scientific activities.

From a larger point of view, the bibliographic resources involve several entities comprising documents, authors, venues, research institutions, etc. In addition to the traditional keyword-based search that aims at retrieving documents discussing a specific topic, scientists express usually their need for accessing to relevant information related to other different bibliographic entities. For instance, they are interested in finding authors working on a specific topic, relevant venues to their research activity and specialized institutions in some research area. These information needs reveal a new information retrieval task that consists on ranking jointly different bibliographic entities considering a particular topic.

To tackle this problem, previous approaches in the area of literature access propose to either estimate the relevance of a bibliographic entity from related ones or jointly rank the multiple types of entities that interact with each other. In the first category of approaches, some work propose to estimate the importance of an author from his/her co-authorship links [18]. Likewise, the importance of documents can be estimated from their corresponding authors [11, 15]. The second category of approaches models bibliographic entities using heterogeneous networks and ranks entities according to their relationships to both similar and different types of entities [23, 27, 28, 30, 31]. This category differs from the first one by producing multiple ranking sets

[1]http://www.citeseer.ist.psu.edu/
[2]http://www.scholar.google.com/

as much as the number of entity types are embedded within the network.

In this paper, we are mainly interested in ranking both documents and authors considering a specific topic. We propose a novel ranking model that jointly ranks author and document entities according to their relationships. This model integrates content-based features to evaluate the topical relatedness between connected entities. In particular, a language model is used in order to estimate the author's knowledge on document topic and the document representativeness of author's knowledge.

The rest of this paper is structured as follows. Section 2 reviews related work. Section 3 introduces problem definition and used notations. We present in section 4 our BibRank algorithm for co-ranking bibliographic entities and we detail the proposed link-based and content-based indicators. Section 5 describes experiments carried out using CiteSeerX dataset and discusses the obtained results. In section 6, we conclude the paper and outline research directions for future work.

2. RELATED WORK

A bibliographic information retrieval system aims at retrieving and ranking bibliographic resources considering a particular topic. Previous work in the domain have investigated bibliometric indicators in order to evaluate the scientific quality of documents and therefore rank the search results by their importance [8, 10, 25]. These indicators help to evaluate document quality [25] as well as the prestige of corresponding authors [2, 6, 10, 13, 29] and journals [3, 8, 24]. In this context, the importance of a document is derived from related entities such as authors, journals, venues, etc. These entities mutually reinforce the quality of each other.

Having the meaningful relationships shown between the different bibliographic entities, some work propose to represent bibliographic resources using bibliographic networks. Such representation allows modeling the different relationships between entities. Two categories of bibliographic network models are proposed in the literature. The first category relies on representing bibliographic resources using a *homogenous network* including only one type of entities. The network model introduced in [16, 17, 20] represents documents and citation links between them. Work in [18] propose to model the bibliographic resources with a co-authorship network. The second category of models represents bibliographic resources using a *heterogeneous network* involving several entities. Zang et al [30] propose to include documents, authors and venues in the network. These entities are associated to both similar and different entities in the network.

Based on bibliographic network models introduced above and aiming at evaluating the scientific quality of bibliographic entities, related work have proposed alternative indicators for entity ranking. These indicators take into account the entity position in the network. In the case of homogeneous networks, link analysis algorithms such as PageRank [20], HITS [16] and Salsa [17] have been investigated for computing authority indicators for bibliographic entities [5, 7]. In the case of heterogeneous networks, previous approaches propose to either rank one type of entities by considering its relationships or jointly rank several types of entities. The first category of approaches are called *mono-type entity ranking approaches in heterogeneous bibliographic networks*. The second category is known as *multi-type entity ranking approaches in heterogeneous bibliographic networks*.

Focusing on mono-type entity ranking approaches in heterogeneous networks, previous work propose to rank bibliographic entities based on their topical relevance in response to the query and also according to their position in the network. In this context, bibliographic networks have been addressed from a social network point of view where documents are ranked by combining their topical relevance and the social importance of their corresponding authors [11, 15]. Liu et al. [18] propose to apply a revisited PageRank on a co-authorship network, where edges are weighted by co-authorship frequency, to evaluate the impact of an author in the network.

In comparison to mono-type entity ranking approaches in heterogeneous bibliographic networks, multi-type entity ranking approaches in the same networks jointly rank different types of entities based on the possible relationships between them. Arnetminer[3], Microsoft Academic Search[4] and Rexa[5] are typical examples of search engines that rank at least two types of entities, generally authors and documents. Related work for multi-type entity ranking models propose to either use link analysis approaches [27, 28, 31] or integrate topical indicators to represent entity-query similarity [23, 30].

Considering the link analysis for multi-type entity ranking approaches, Yan and Din [27] propose to jointly rank documents, authors and journals presuming that important authors publish important documents and important entities cite important ones. This model computes entity scores based on the relationships between them by propagating connected entity scores. Document scores are computed differently. First, an initial score is attributed to each document based on the score of other connected entities. Afterwards, a PageRank score is computed on the homogeneous network of documents. Yang et al. [28] propose to extend the Topical PageRank Model, previously introduced in [19], in order to highlight topical authorities in the bibliographic network. This algorithm propagates scores through the network by simulating the surfer behavior. Three actions are considered: stay on the same topic *"Follow-stay"*, move to a different topic *"Follow-jump"* or move to a random topic *"Jump-jump"*. In the same line, Zhou et al. [31] propose to rank jointly different types of entities by combining a PageRank score, expressing the authority of an entity in the homogeneous network, and a *BiWalk* score that emphasizes the authority of an entity through inter-graph relationships.

Beside the previous link analysis-based approaches, some work propose to integrate topical-based indicators in order to rank entities in a bibliographic network. Zang et al. [30] propose to recommend entities in the bibliographic network by combining two scores. The first, namely the topical score, is computed with a language model-based information retrieval framework [21]. The second score evaluates the authority of the entity in the heterogeneous network using a PageRank-like algorithm. *"Author-Topic-Conference"* (ACT) model, proposed by Tang et al. [23] and used in Arnetminer search engine, represents entities thanks to topic distributions inferred by the Latent Dirichlet Allocation

[3]http://www.arnetminer.org/

[4]http://www.academic.research.microsoft.com/

[5]http://www.rexa.info/

(LDA) model [26]. The ACT model ranks authors, documents and venues using a PageRank-like algorithm.

In this paper, we propose a novel ranking algorithm for heterogeneous bibliographic networks. In comparison to previous related work, our approach is different in at least three respects:

- First, we propose an integrated approach for ranking bibliographic entities unlike modular approaches that combine distinct relevance scores [11, 15, 30, 31]. The aim of the integrated approach is to consider, at the same time and within a unified process, both topical and link-based features.
- Second, our approach is based on content-based and link analysis features unlike previous work [27, 28, 31] that consider only link-based indicators. We propose in this work a ranking model that estimates, by means of a language model, the author's knowledge on the document topic and the document representativeness to author's knowledge. We also propose to consider marginal citations to discredit non topical relationships unlike work presented in [23] that models entities through topical distributions.
- Third, the core idea of our approach relies on the use of a language model-based approach to estimate the strength and/or weakness of the topical relationship between the bi-type entities jointly with the link-based relatedness. In contrast, [30] focuses on the link-based relatedness between entities and the topical feature is only addressed at the query level.

3. PROBLEM DEFINITION AND NOTATIONS

In this work, we propose to model bibliographic resources using a bi-type network that integrates documents and authors of scientific publications. In response to a user query Q, each type of entities is ranked according to a relevance score computed using a co-ranking function called *BibRank*. Below, we introduce some definitions and notations.

Definition 1. Document: A scientific document, noted d_i, is represented by a weighted vector of terms $\vec{d_i} = (w_{i1}, \ldots, w_{ip}, \ldots, w_{iT})$. w_{ip} denotes the weight of the pth term occurring in document d_i. T is the number of indexed terms.

Definition 2. Author: A scientific author a_j may publish one or more documents. Let $\mathcal{D}(a_j)$ be the set of documents authored by $\vec{a_j}$. An author a_j is represented by a weighted vector including terms present in all his/her documents $\vec{a_j} = \sum_{d_i \in \mathcal{D}(a_j)} \vec{d_i}$.

Definition 3. Bi-type bibliographic network: Bibliographic resources are represented by a directed graph $G = (V, E)$ where nodes $V = A \cup D$ denote bibliographic entities with D and A corresponding to document set $D = \{d_1, ..., d_n\}$ and author set $A = \{a_1, ..., a_m\}$ respectively. The set of edges $E : V \times V$ represents bibliographic relationships between entities. A directed edge from $x \in V$ to $y \in V$ is represented by the pair $e = (x, y)$.

Definition 4. Document subgraph and author subgraph: Document and author subgraphs are directed graphs which include the subset of homogeneous nodes represented in the bi-type bibliographic network G. The document subgraph $G_D = (D, D \times D) \in G$ represents bibliographic documents and possible relationships between them. The author subgraph $G_A = (A, A \times A) \in G$ represents authors of bibliographic documents and all possible relationships between them.

Definition 5. Bibliographic relationships: In a bi-type bibliographic network and homogeneous related subgraphs, relationships are represented by edges that model semantic links between entities. Three types of relationships are identified:

Document citation associations: Two documents d_i and d_k are connected by a document citation association if document d_i *cites* document d_k. This relationship is modeled by an edge $(d_i, d_k) \in D \times D$.

Author citation associations: Two authors a_j and a_l are connected by an author citation association if one of the publications of author a_j *cites* at least one of the publications of author a_l. This relationship is modeled by and edge $(a_j, a_l) \in A \times A$.

Authorship associations: An author a_j and a document d_i are connected by an authorship association if author a_j *has authored* document d_i. This relationship is established in both directions and is modeled by a couple of edges $(d_i, a_j) \in D \times A$ and $(a_j, d_i) \in A \times D$.

Definition 6. Intra-graph and inter-graph relationships: A relationship (x, y) is called *intra-graph* association if both source node $x \in X$ and target node $y \in X$ are included in the same subgraph G_X where $X \in \{A, D\}$. Document and author citation associations are intra-graph relationships.
A relationship (u, v) is called *inter-graph* association if source node $u \in X$ and target node $v \in Y$ belong to two different subgraphs G_X and G_Y with $X \in \{A, D\}$, $Y \in \{A, D\}$ and $X \neq Y$. Authorship associations are inter-graph relationships.

Figure 1 presents an example of a bibliographic network and illustrates a graphical representation of the extracted bi-type bibliographic network.

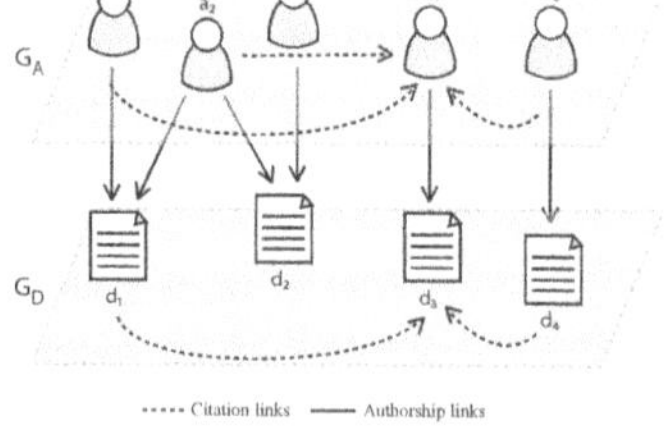

Figure 1: Bi-type bibliographic graph G

Definition 7. Entity Rank: A *Relevance Status Value* $RSV(d_i, Q)$ evaluates the document $d_i \in D$ relevance considering a query Q. This function measures the query-document similarity. Extending this notation, an entity-query similarity between a bibliographic entity $x \in A \cup D$ and a query Q is represented by a *Relevance Status Value*

$RSV(x, Q)$. This function ranks entities according to a relevance score. Let $rank(x)$ be the rank of entity x. The reciprocal rank is defined as follows:

$$r_x = \frac{1}{rank(x)} \quad (1)$$

Definition 8. BibRank function
Considering a bi-type bibliographic network $G = (V, E)$ and a query Q, BibRank function co-ranks author and document entities. A ranked list is produced for each type of entities. BibRank function is defined as follows:

$$\begin{aligned} BibRank : \{Q, G\} &\longrightarrow \{R_A, R_D\} \quad (2) \\ \forall a_j \in A,\ 0 < R_A(a_j) &< 1, \textstyle\sum_{a_j \in A} R_A(a_j) = 1 \\ \forall d_i \in D,\ 0 < R_D(d_i) &< 1, \textstyle\sum_{d_i \in D} R_D(d_i) = 1 \end{aligned}$$

with R_D is the set of document scores. R_A is the set of author scores. $R_D(d_i)$ associates to each document d_i the corresponding score in R_D. Respectively, $R_A(a_j)$ associates to each author a_j the corresponding score in R_A.

4. BIBRANK ALGORITHM

In this section, we present our BibRank algorithm which computes a co-relevance score for both document and author entities of a bi-type bibliographic network. We notice that basic assumptions introduced in [28, 30, 31] are also maintained by our algorithm, particularly the assumption that important entities are cited by important ones. Indeed, BibRank algorithm introduces transition probabilities between the two homogeneous subgraphs and propagates relevance scores through connected entities. In addition to transition probabilities, content-based indicators are defined between connected entities to model the topical relatedness between them. Figure 2 illustrates transition probabilities and content-based indicators in the bi-type bibliographic network. These features are detailed in the next sub-sections.

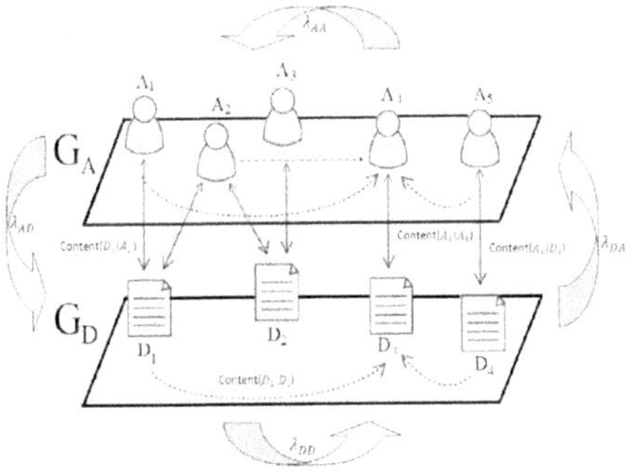

Figure 2: Transition probabilities and content-based indicator in a bi-type bibliographic network

4.1 Computing Transition Probabilities between Homogeneous Document and Author Subgraphs

Transition probabilities measure the possibility that a surfer moves from a subgraph to another one. Accessing a document node, the surfer has two choices: either stay on the same subgraph or move to the author subgraph. Therefore, we estimate the probability of moving from a subgraph to another one based on the current position of the surfer. We compute the transition probability from a subgraph G_X with $X \in \{A, D\}$ to a subgraph G_Y with $Y \in \{A, D\}$ as follows:

$$\begin{aligned} \lambda_{XY} &= \frac{|\{\forall (x,y) \in X \times Y\}|}{|E|} \quad (3) \\ \lambda_{AD} + \lambda_{AA} &= 1 \\ \lambda_{DA} + \lambda_{DD} &= 1 \end{aligned}$$

where $|E|$ is the number of edges in the bibliographic network. The transition probabilities of staying on the same subgraph G_X with $X \in A \cup D$ is represented by λ_{XX}. Four types of transition probabilities are identified in the bi-type bibliographic network: λ_{AA}, λ_{DD}, λ_{DA} and λ_{AD}. The intra-graph transition probabilities are represented by λ_{AA} and λ_{DD}. The inter-graph transition probabilities are represented by λ_{AD} and λ_{DA}.

4.2 Computing Content-Based Indicators

The content-based indicators measure the topical relatedness between two connected entities. Our bi-type bibliographic network is characterized by two types of relationships: inter-graph and intra-graph relationships. Accordingly, two content-based indicators are proposed. A first score is attributed to inter-graph relationships based on the topical relatedness between entities. This score is measured by a language model indicator that expresses, depending on the sense of the bi-directed edge, the document representativeness of author's knowledge and the author's knowledge on the document topic. Second, we attribute a content-based score for intra-graph relationships that estimates the significance of citation links and detects marginal citations. This score expresses the common interest of the two connected entities that they address regarding the query topic.

4.2.1 *Document Representativeness of Author's Knowledge*

For each author a_j, a content-based score is attributed to his/her authored document $d_i \in \mathcal{D}(a_j)$. This score determines the likelihood for document d_i to be representative for the author's knowledge. The content-based score $Content(d_i|a_j)$ from author a_j to document d_i is computed as follows:

$$Content(d_i|a_j) = \frac{P(a_j|M_{d_i})}{\max\limits_{\forall (a_l, d_k) \in A \times D} P(a_l|M_{d_k})} \quad (4)$$

$P(a_j|M_{d_i})$ is the probability of observing author a_j considering the language model M_{d_i} of document d_i. This probability is computed using the Jelineck-Mercer formula [12]:

$$P(a_j|M_{d_i}) = \prod_{t \in \vec{a_j}} [(1-\lambda)P(t|M_{a_j}) + \lambda P(t|M_{d_i})]^{n(t, \vec{a_j})} \quad (5)$$

$n(t, \vec{a_j})$ is the number of times that term t appears in $\vec{a_j}$. $P(t|M_{a_j})$ is the probability of observing term t having the language model M_{a_j} of author a_j. $P(t|M_{d_i})$ is the probability of observing term t having the language model M_{d_i} of document d_i.

For convenience, the probability $P(t|M_x)$ of a term t according to language model of entity $x \in A \cup D$ is computed as follows:

$$P(t|M_x) = \frac{tf(t, x)}{|x|} \quad (6)$$

where $tf(t,x)$ is the frequency of term t in x and $|x|$ is the number of terms included in x.

4.2.2 Author's Knowledge on the Document Topic

For a document d_i, we note the set of corresponding authors $\mathcal{A}(d_i)$. The likelihood of each author $a_j \in \mathcal{A}(d_i)$ considering the topic of document d_i is computed by a content-based score $Content(a_j|d_i)$:

$$Content(a_j|d_i) = \frac{P(d_i|M_{a_j})}{\max\limits_{\forall(a_l,d_k)\in A\times D} P(d_k|M_{a_l})} \quad (7)$$

$P(d_i|M_{a_j})$ is the probability of observing document d_i according to the language model M_{a_j} of author a_j. This probability is computed as follows:

$$P(d_i|M_{a_j}) = \prod_{t\in\vec{d_i}} [(1-\lambda)P(t|M_c) + \lambda P(t|M_{a_j})]^{n(t,\vec{d_j})} \quad (8)$$

where the collection c is represented by the weighted vector of terms included in all documents of the collection $c = \sum_{d_i\in D} \vec{d_i}$. Let $n(t,\vec{d_i})$ be the number of times that term t appears in $\vec{d_i}$. $P(t|M_c)$ is the probability of observing term t having to the language model M_c of collection c. This probability is computed as follows:

$$P(t|M_c) = \frac{tf(t,c)}{|c|} \quad (9)$$

where $tf(t,c)$ is the frequency of term t in the collection c and $|c|$ is the number of terms included in the collection c.

4.2.3 Marginal Citations

Marginal citations are detected by semantic links between two homogeneous entities. We assume that the significance of a citation link can be estimated by the relevance of each entity considering the query topic. The content-based indicator detects semantically related entities for intra-graph relationships. For this aim, we propose to discredit thus marginal citations and emphasize significant citation links by comparing the rank of each cited and citing entity in the result set. The closer the ranks of entities are, more significant the citation link is. The common similarity between two entities x, y of a homogeneous subgraph G_X with $X \in \{D, A\}$ is measured by the closeness of entity ranks:

$$Sim_{com}(x,y) = \frac{1}{|rank(x) - rank(y)|} \quad (10)$$

Similarly to inter-graph relationships, a content-based score $Content(x|y)$ of entity x from entity y is computed for intra-graph relationships:

$$Content(x|y) = \frac{Sim_{com}(x,y)}{\max\limits_{(v,w)\in X\times X} Sim_{com}(v,w)} \quad (11)$$

4.3 Detailed Algorithm

BibRank is a PageRank-like algorithm that ranks jointly document and author entities using both topical-based and link-based features. BibRank algorithm is processed in three main steps. First, it attributes for all the entities in the homogeneous subgraph an initial score based on the total number of similar nodes. Then, it propagates entity scores through the graph proportionally to the transition probabilities defined in formula 3. At each iteration, a new score is attributed to document and author entities as the sum of the predecessor node scores. These scores are weighted using a topical-based feature, modeled by the reciprocal rank defined in formula 1, and content-based indicators, as presented in formula 4, 7 and 11. Finally, a ranked list is produced for each type of entities.

Algorithm 1: BibRank

Data: Q, $G = (V, E)$
Result: *BibRank* : $\{Q, G\} \longrightarrow \{R_D, R_A\}$
begin
  `/* Step 1: Initialize */`
  $\theta \leftarrow 0$
  $R_D^\theta(d_i) \leftarrow \frac{1}{|D|}$
  $R_A^\theta(a_j) \leftarrow \frac{1}{|A|}$
  `/* Step 2: Propagate scores using transition probabilities, query input, graph structure and content-based scores */`
  repeat
    `/* Computing document scores */`
    $R_D^{\theta+1}(d_i) \leftarrow \frac{d}{|V|} + (1-d)\times$
    $(\lambda_{AD} \sum\limits_{\substack{a_l;\\(a_l,d_i)}} \frac{R_A^\theta(a_l).w_{a_l}^{d_i}}{O(a_l)} + \lambda_{DD} \sum\limits_{\substack{d_k;\\(d_k,d_i)}} \frac{R_D^\theta(d_k).w_{d_k}^{d_i}}{O(d_k)})$
    $R_D^{\theta+1}(d_i) = Norm(R_D^{\theta+1}(d_i))$
    `/* Computing author scores */`
    $R_A^{\theta+1}(a_j) \leftarrow \frac{d}{|V|} + (1-d)\times$
    $(\lambda_{DA} \sum\limits_{\substack{d_k;\\(d_k,a_j)}} \frac{R_D^\theta(d_k).w_{d_k}^{a_j}}{O(d_k)} + \lambda_{AA} \sum\limits_{\substack{a_l;\\(a_l,a_j)}} \frac{R_A^\theta(a_l).w_{a_l}^{a_j}}{O(a_l)})$
    $R_A^{\theta+1}(a_j) = Norm(R_A^{\theta+1}(a_j))$
    $\theta \leftarrow \theta + 1$
  until *convergence*
  `/* Step 3: Ranking result sets */`
  $R_D \leftarrow Rank(R_D)$
  $R_A \leftarrow Rank(R_A)$
  Return $\{R_D, R_A\}$

where

- θ is the iteration number,
- $d \in [0,1]$ is a damping factor fixed to $d = 0.15$,
- $w_{a_l}^{d_i}$, $w_{d_k}^{d_i}$, $w_{a_l}^{a_j}$ and $w_{d_k}^{a_j}$ are the weighted factor for relationships (a_l, d_i), (d_k, d_i), (a_l, a_j) and (d_k, a_j) respectively. For convenience, the weighted factor w_x^y from entity $x \in A \cup D$ to entity $y \in A \cup D$ is computed as below:

$$w_x^y = r_x * Content(y|x) \quad (12)$$

- the normalization functions $Norm(R_D^{\theta+1}(d_i))$ and $Norm(R_A^{\theta+1}(a_j))$ normalize document and author scores as follows:

$$Norm(R_D^{\theta+1}(d_i)) = \frac{R_D^{\theta+1}(d_i)}{\sum_{k=1}^{|D|} R_D^{\theta+1}(d_k)} \quad (13)$$

$$Norm(R_A^{\theta+1}(a_j)) = \frac{R_A^{\theta+1}(a_j)}{\sum_{l=1}^{|A|} R_A^{\theta+1}(a_l)}$$

- the ranking functions $Rank(R_D)$ and $Rank(R_A)$ rank respectively document set and author set according to their BibRank score $R_D(d_i)$ and $R_A(a_j)$.

5. EXPERIMENTAL EVALUATION

We conduct a series of experiments in order to evaluate the effectiveness of BibRank ranking model within the task of accessing a bibliographic corpus. This section describes the experimental setup and discusses the obtained results.

5.1 Experimental Framework

5.1.1 Data Collection Description

We use in this experimental evaluation the CiteSeerX[6] dataset downloaded in April 2011. This collection includes document title, abstract, the list of authors and outgoing citation links. We notice that the citation links between authors are extracted from document citation links by applying an exact matching on the name of authors. Table 1 and Figures 3, 4 and 5 show general statistics about the dataset and the extracted bibliographic network. Analyzing the distribution of nodes and relationships in the network, we note that the giant component includes about 73% of documents and authors entailed in the network. We also notice that author citation links represent 71.1% of the relationships in the network.

Documents	1 472 735
Authors	1 366 540
Citation links between documents	16 598 502
Citation links between authors	51 306 409
Document citation links per document	11.270
Author citation links per author	37.545
Authorship links	4 209 980
Documents per author	3.081
Authors per document	2.858

Table 1: CiteSeerX collection statistics

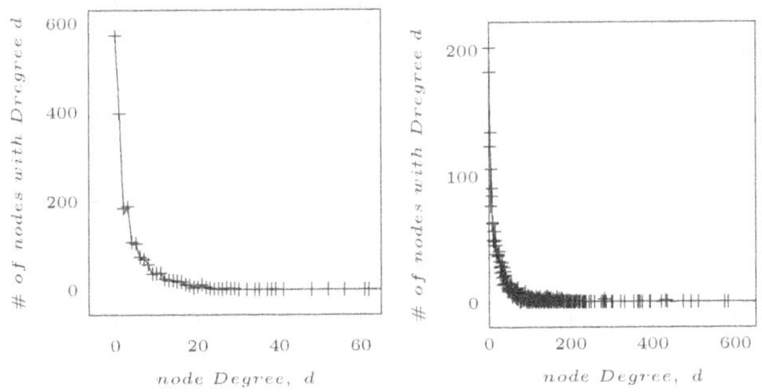

(a) Document citation network (b) Author citation network

Figure 3: Citation network density

5.1.2 Topics and Assessments

We used the Latent Dirichlet Allocation (LDA) model [1] to extract first automatically a set of 200 topics. The LDA

[6]http://citeseer.ist.psu.edu/

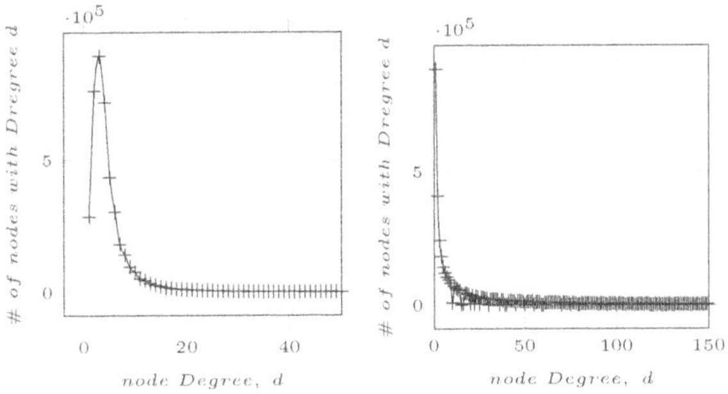

(a) Authors per document (b) Documents per authors

Figure 4: Distribution of authors and documents in the authorship network

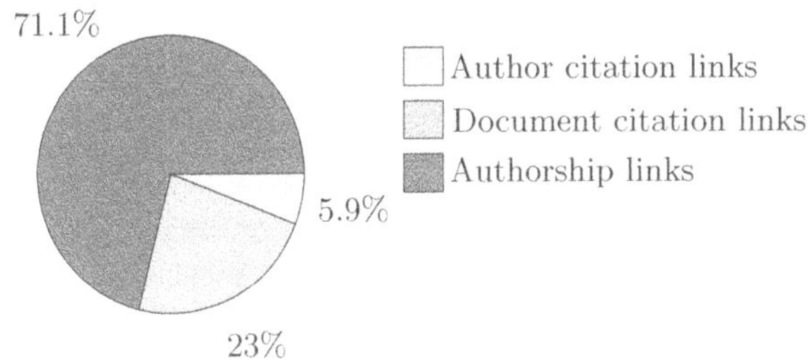

Figure 5: Distribution of links in the network

algorithm analyzes word-topic distributions and document-topic distributions. These probabilities allow determining the optimal number of extracted topics from the dataset, in our case a set of 200 topics. Starting from this set, we manually identified generic topics. Then, we extracted manually a subset of 35 topics. Each topic is represented by a list of terms that have been annotated manually to generate a query as shown in Table 2. For instance, three of the 35 topics are "web services", "intelligent agent system", and "markov chain model". For each topic, a subgraph including top documents and their authors is extracted.
Considering the query "intelligent agent system", Figure 6 illustrates, for an entity, its number of incoming citation links regarding its rank obtained with the BibRank model. It appears the most cited entities are highly ranked entities, that highlights the impact of graph structure in our ranking algorithm. Taking into account the fact that a subgraph is extracted from a query topic on one side, and the impact of graph structure on our ranking algorithm on the other side, we can confirm through observed values that the final relevance score is a combination of a *topical relevance assessment* and an *authority relevance one*.

The topical relevance assessment expresses the similarity of the document content to address the query topic. It was performed using a pool-based process. First of all, BibRank ranking and baseline rankings have been computed. We have merged the top 20 documents obtained in each ranking model. We then asked 25 colleagues to assign to documents a binary topical relevance score considering the query topic. Among assessors, we count 9 assistant professors, 13 Phd students, 2 Master students and 1 engineer. Each query is assessed by two different judges. The average agreement between assessors, measured by the Kappa indicator [4], is a

words	word-topic distributions	query
agent	0.244	
intelligent	0.243	
system	0.083	
artificial	0.067	
autonomy	0.039	intelligent agent
negotiation	0.032	system
cooperation	0.029	
behavior	0.027	
automation	0.023	
coordination	0.022	

Table 2: Topic extraction

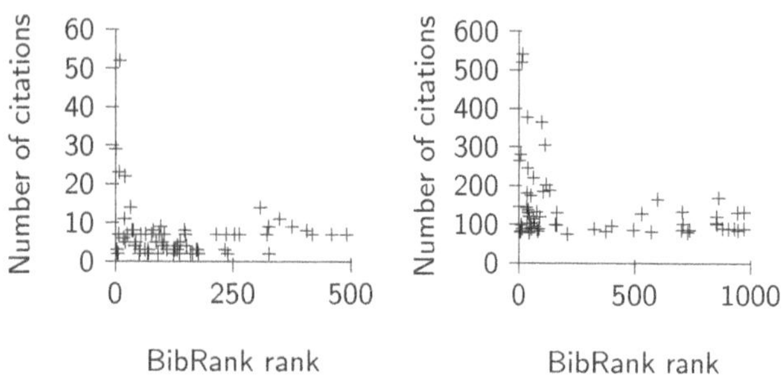

(a) Document entities (b) Author entities

Figure 6: Number of incoming citation links according to the BibRank ranking for the query "intelligent agent system"

moderate agreement of $k = 0.57$. Finally, a topical relevance score is automatically computed for each author as the topical assessment score average of his/her documents in the collection.

The authority relevance assessment expresses how much the author expertise covers the query topic. It was inferred from a PageRank score classification computed in each homogeneous subgraph. Entity authority relevance is equal to 1 if the PageRank score is higher than the average PageRank score or equals to 0 otherwise.

5.1.3 Baselines

We compare the retrieval effectiveness of our model to three baselines:

- **the BM25 model** [22] denotes a classical IR matching model that computes the query-entity similarity by a probabilistic model.

- **the Language Model (LM)** [9] denotes a classical IR matching model that computes the query-entity similarity by a smoothed language model, namely the Hiemstra model. The language model is used in our model to compute the content-based score.

- **the PRank model** [27] denotes a matching model for ranking entities in a bibliographic network. This model has been adapted considering author and document nodes rather than author, document and journal nodes.

5.2 Results and Discussion

We have analyzed the retrieval effectiveness of the BibRank algorithm for ranking both document and author entities. To evaluate the retrieval effectiveness for each entity type ranking and considering the two-levels assessment, we use the Normalized Discount Cumulative Gain at 20th document, denoted NDCG@20 as the effectiveness metric that normalizes the n-top retrieved results by the ideal ranking. Improvement significance was computed using student t-test.

We underline that document and author rankings are jointly produced by the BibRank model as outlined in algorithm 1 but for convenience, they are presented below and discussed separately.

5.2.1 Document Ranking Effectiveness

We compare in Table 3 the effectiveness of BibRank algorithm with state-of-the-art and traditional ranking models. *"% change"* column denotes the percentage of BibRank improvement regarding the baselines. We notice significant improvements between 7.03% for PRank model and 113.13% for the Hiemstra language model. The difference of NDCG@20 values for BibRank and PRank rankings is less important comparing to other baseline rankings because PRank is the closest one since it aims at ranking jointly heterogeneous entities, as BibRank algorithm, whereas BM25 and LM are devoted to rank only one type of entities. We also conclude that considering only a topical feature, as in baselines BM25 and LM, or only graph structure, as in PRank algorithm, is not sufficient to estimate the relevance of documents. Compared to these three baselines, our algorithm integrates jointly in addition to these features a content-based score that analyzes the topical relatedness between linked entities.

Model	NDCG@20	% change	
BM25	0.429	**59.77%**	***
LM	0.322	**113.13%**	***
PRank	0.641	**7.03%**	*
BibRank	**0.686**		

Table 3: Document ranking retrieval effectiveness. % change: BibRank improvement. Student test significance *: $0.01 < t \leqslant 0.05$; **: $0.001 < t \leqslant 0.01$; ***: $t \leqslant 0.001$

Figure 7 illustrates the NDCG values at different levels of rank. We notice that the BibRank curve is always over the baseline ones and more particularly when NDCG is computed before rank 5. This means that our algorithm returns in the top 5 results the most relevant documents.

5.2.2 Author Ranking Effectiveness

Considering the ranking of author entities, our model overpasses significantly the different baselines, as shown in Table 4. This confirms the benefit of integrating bibliographic topical and content features in addition to the graph structure for ranking entities in a bibliographic network. However, we notice that NDCG@20 values for author ranking are less important than for document ranking. It can be explained by the way of modeling topical relevance assessments. As said previously, author topical relevance have been inferred from document topical one.

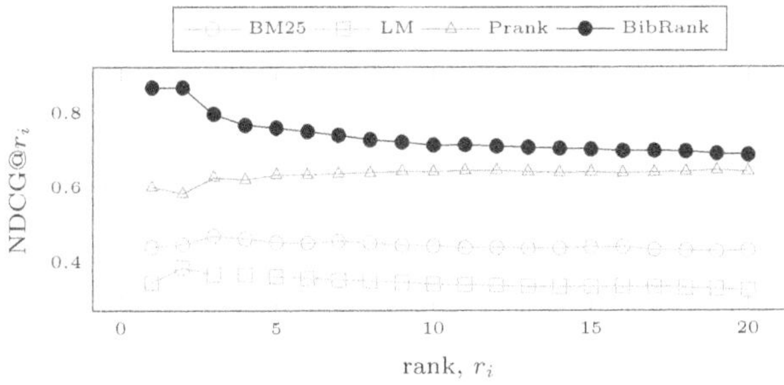

Figure 7: NDCG at different document entity rankings

Model	NDCG@20	% change	
BM25	0.376	**38.26%**	***
LM	0.428	**21.47%**	**
PRank	0.455	**14.29%**	*
BibRank	**0.520**		

Table 4: Author ranking retrieval effectiveness. % change: BibRank improvement. Student test significance *: $0.01 < t \leqslant 0.05$; **: $0.001 < t \leqslant 0.01$; ***: $t \leqslant 0.001$

As for document ranking, Figure 8 introduces the NDCG values computed at different levels of rank. BibRank curve rises above the baseline ones. Compared to document rankings where the BibRank curve remains higher than the baseline ones but declines, this latter grows for author ranking, probably also due to the way of inferring topical relevance assessments for authors.

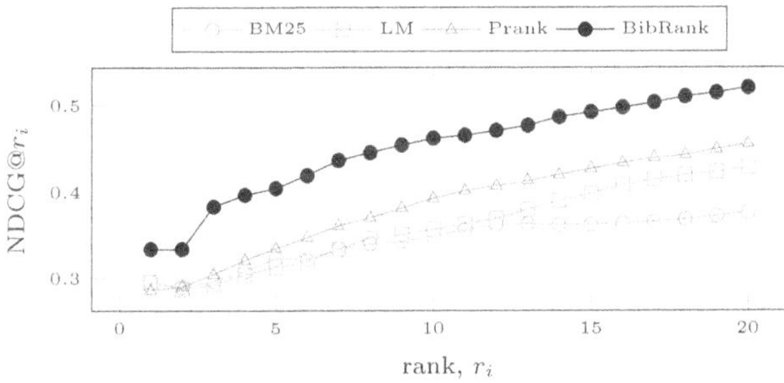

Figure 8: NDCG at different author entity rankings

5.2.3 *Ranking Correlation Analysis*

Ranking correlation analysis is performed through the Kendall's tau (τ) rank correlation coefficient [14] that analyzes the agreement between two ranking models considering concordant and discordant pairs. The more similar (respectively reversed) the rankings are, the more the correlation coefficient τ approaches 1 (respectively -1). If ranking models are independent τ is null.

Table 5 shows entity ranking coefficient correlation τ. For both document and author rankings, a couple of ranking models is particularly correlated: BibRank and PRank models. They both integrate graph structure and have close rankings. Nevertheless, we have noticed in Table 3 that PRank and BibRank ranking effectivenesses are significantly different.

For document ranking, BM25 and Hiemstra models are weakly correlated. Indeed, they are both classical matching models that rank entities according to a query. Other couples of ranking models are not particularly correlated. In other words, the different rankings between these models considered by pairs are not similar.

For author ranking, we notice that some couples of ranking models are weakly correlated by a negative value, that means that one model ranks authors in a decreasing order regarding the other model.

For instance, Figure 9 shows an instance of rank correlation coefficient for a particular query "intelligent agent system". Both axes represent entity rank for a given ranking model (BM25, LM, PRank or BibRank). *LM-BM25*, for instance, compares BM25 ranking to LM ranking.

For document ranking, most of the scatter plots have points distributed in the whole graph, it explains therefore the weak coefficients reported in Table 5. The graph that opposes BibRank and PRank rankings illustrates a diagonal line that emphasizes the Kendall rank correlation value of 0.594 reported in Table 5.

For author ranking, scatter plots have a different point repartition with the diagonal line only in graph opposing BibRank and PRank which represents indeed the most correlated couple of ranking models. In the other graphs, points are not correlated and present moreover a vertical trend, related to a negative value for Kendall rank correlation coefficient in Table 5. We also notice that some points are concentrated along the abscissa axis as in Figures (b)-(2) to (b)-(5). This expresses the fact that the authors returned by the ranking model represented within the abscissa axis are not returned by the ranking model represented within the ordinate axis. This confirms the negative correlation between the ranking models. This fact is emphasized particularly, as shown in Figures (b)-(2) to (b)-(5), in the case of BM25 and LM ranking models that return few results regarding only the query.

6. CONCLUSION AND FUTURE WORK

In this paper, we proposed a bi-type entity ranking algorithm for bibliographic networks, called BibRank. This algorithm propagates entity scores by considering both link-based and content-based features in the network. For this purpose, we estimate the significance of citation links by measuring the common similarity between homogeneous entities regarding a topic and we also evaluate, using a language model, the document representativeness to author's knowledge and the author's knowledge on document topic.

We conducted a series of experiments on CiteSeerX dataset that shows a significant improvement in comparison to other models for both document and author rankings. We also conclude that matching models based only on the query topic are not sufficient for ranking entities in heterogeneous subgraphs. Analyzing ranking correlations, we note that PRank and BibRank algorithms present correlated entity rankings. Meanwhile, this correlation agreement is counterbalanced by a significant improvement for BibRank algorithm.

For future research work, we plan to extend our model to large-scale bibliographic networks including more entity types and relationships, such as co-authorship, the author's affiliation to an institution. We also plan to integrate temporal aspects of citation links in order to measure the author-

	BM25	LM	PRank	BibRank
BM25	1	**0.160**	0.002	0.015
LM		1	0.022	0.039
PRank			1	**0.594**
BibRank				1

(a) Document rankings

	BM25	LM	PRank	BibRank
BM25	1	-0.187	-0.082	-0.160
LM		1	-0.072	-0.151
PRank			1	**0.600**
BibRank				1

(b) Author rankings

Table 5: Rank correlation coefficient for document and author rankings

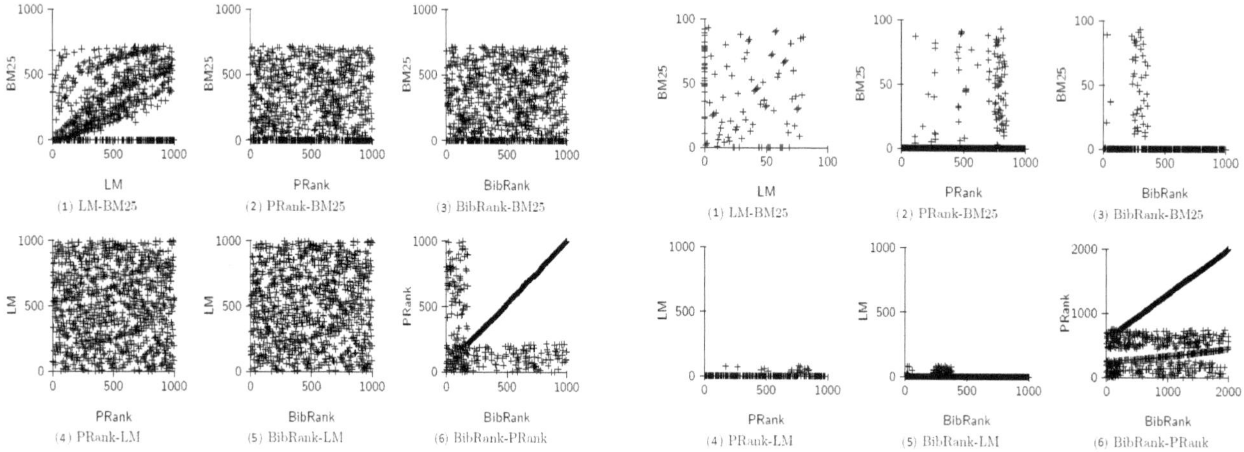

(a) Document rankings

(b) Author rankings

Figure 9: Comparison of document and author rankings for query "intelligent agent system"

ity acquired by a document regarding its publication date. In this mind, the importance of documents is not therefore measured by the number of in-coming links but by the average number of citation links per year. We expect that this revised approach would favour efficient entities rather than basically most cited ones.

7. REFERENCES

[1] E. Agichtein, E. Brill, and S. Dumais. Improving web search ranking by incorporating user behavior information. In *Proceedings of the 29th annual international ACM SIGIR conference on Research and development in information retrieval*, SIGIR '06, pages 19–26, New York, NY, USA, 2006. ACM.

[2] S. Alonso, F. J. Cabrerizo, E. H. Viedma, and F. Herrera. hg-index: a new index to characterize the scientific output of researchers based on the h- and g-indices. *Scientometrics*, 82:391–400, 2010.

[3] C. T. Bergstrom, J. D. West, and M. A. Wiseman. The eigenfactor metrics. *Journal of Neuroscience*, 28(45):11433–11434, 2008.

[4] J. Cohen. A coefficient of agreement for nominal scales. *Educational and Psychological Measurement*, 20(1):37–46, 1960.

[5] A. Dahlan and B. Sitohang. Combining pagerank and citation analysis to measure information credibility in internet. In *Proceedings of iiWAS*, pages 375–382, 2007.

[6] L. Egghe. An improvement of the h-index: the g-index. *ISSI Newsletter*, 2:8–9, 2006.

[7] M. Frické and D. Fallis. Indicators of accuracy for answers to ready reference questions on the internet. *J. Am. Soc. Inf. Sci. Technol.*, 55:238–245, 2004.

[8] E. Garfield. The history and meaning of the journal impact factor. *JAMA: The Journal of the American Medical Association*, 1, 2006.

[9] D. Hiemstra. A linguistically motivated probabilistic model of information retrieval. In *Proceedings of the Second European Conference on Research and Advanced Technology for Digital Libraries*, ECDL '98, pages 569–584, London, UK, 1998. Springer-Verlag.

[10] J. E. Hirsch. An index to quantify an individual's scientific research output. *Proceedings of the National Academy of Sciences of the United States of America*, 102:16569–16572, 2005.

[11] L. B. Jabeur, L. Tamine, and M. Boughanem. A social model for literature access: towards a weighted social network of authors. In *Proceedings of Adaptivity, Personalization and Fusion of Heterogeneous Information*, RIAO '10, pages 32–39, 2010.

[12] F. Jelinek and R. L. Mercer. Interpolated estimation of markov source parameters from sparse data. In *Proceedings of the Workshop on Pattern Recognition in Practice*, pages 381–397, Amsterdam, The Netherlands: North-Holland, 1980.

[13] B. Jin, L. Liang, R. Rousseau, and L. Egghe. The r- and ar-indices: Complementing the h-index. *Chinese Science Bulletin*, 52:855–863, 2007.

[14] M. G. Kendall. A new measure of rank correlation. *Biometrika*, 30(1/2):81–93, 1938.

[15] S. M. Kirsch, A. Prof, D. Armin, B. Cremers, and S. I.

A. D. Rheinischen. Social information retrieval, 2005.

[16] J. M. Kleinberg. Authoritative sources in a hyperlinked environment. *J. ACM*, 46:604–632, 1999.

[17] R. Lempel and S. Moran. The stochastic approach for link-structure analysis (salsa) and the tkc effect. *Comput. Netw.*, 33:387–401, 2000.

[18] X. Liu, J. Bollen, M. L. Nelson, and H. Van de Sompel. Co-authorship networks in the digital library research community. *Inf. Process. Manage.*, 41:1462–1480, 2005.

[19] L. Nie, B. D. Davison, and X. Qi. Topical link analysis for web search. In *Proceedings of the 29th annual international ACM SIGIR conference on Research and development in information retrieval*, SIGIR '06, pages 91–98, New York, NY, USA, 2006. ACM.

[20] L. Page, S. Brin, R. Motwani, and T. Winograd. The pagerank citation ranking: Bringing order to the web. Technical Report 1999-66, Stanford InfoLab, November 1999.

[21] J. M. Ponte and W. B. Croft. A language modeling approach to information retrieval. In *Proceedings of the 21st annual international ACM SIGIR conference on Research and development in information retrieval*, SIGIR '98, pages 275–281. ACM, 1998.

[22] S. E. Robertson and S. Walker. Some simple effective approximations to the 2-poisson model for probabilistic weighted retrieval. In *Proceedings of the 17th annual international ACM SIGIR conference on Research and development in information retrieval*, SIGIR '94, pages 232–241, New York, NY, USA, 1994. Springer-Verlag New York, Inc.

[23] J. Tang, R. Jin, and J. Zhang. A topic modeling approach and its integration into the random walk framework for academic search. In *Proceedings of the 2008 Eighth IEEE International Conference on Data Mining*, pages 1055–1060, Washington, DC, USA, 2008. IEEE Computer Society.

[24] S. Uddin, L. Hossain, A. A., and K. Rasmussen. Trend and efficiency analysis of co-authorship network. *Scientometrics*, In press, 2011.

[25] D. Walker, H. Xie, K.-K. Yan, and S. Maslov. Ranking scientific publications using a simple model of network traffic. *Society*, pages 1–5, 2006.

[26] X. Wei and W. B. Croft. Lda-based document models for ad-hoc retrieval. In *Proceedings of the 29th annual international ACM SIGIR conference on Research and development in information retrieval*, SIGIR '06, pages 178–185, New York, NY, USA, 2006. ACM.

[27] E. Yan and Y. Ding. Measuring scholarly impact in heterogeneous networks. In *Proceedings of the 73rd ASIS&T Annual Meeting on Navigating Streams in an Information Ecosystem - Volume 47*, ASIS&T '10, pages 1–7, Silver Springs, MD, USA, 2010. American Society for Information Science.

[28] Z. Yang, L. Hong, and B. D. Davison. Topic-driven multi-type citation network analysis. In *Proceedings of Adaptivity, Personalization and Fusion of Heterogeneous Information*, RIAO '10, pages 24–31, 2010.

[29] C.-T. Zhang. The e-index, complementing the h-index for excess citations. *PLoS ONE*, 4, 2009.

[30] J. Zhang, J. Tang, B. Liang, Z. Yang, S. Wang, J. Zuo, and J. Li. Recommendation over a heterogeneous social network. In *Proceedings of the 2008 The Ninth International Conference on Web-Age Information Management*, WAIM '08, pages 309–316, Washington, DC, USA, 2008. IEEE Computer Society.

[31] D. Zhou, S. A. Orshanskiy, H. Zha, and C. L. Giles. Co-ranking authors and documents in a heterogeneous network. In *Proceedings of the 2007 Seventh IEEE International Conference on Data Mining*, pages 739–744, Washington, DC, USA, 2007. IEEE Computer Society.

Modeling and Exploiting Heterogeneous Bibliographic Networks for Expertise Ranking

Hongbo Deng[1], Jiawei Han[1], Michael R. Lyu[2], and Irwin King[2]
[1] Dept. of Computer Science, University of Illinois at Urbana-Champaign
[2] Dept. of Computer Science and Engineering, The Chinese University of Hong Kong
hbdeng@uiuc.edu, hanj@cs.uiuc.edu, lyu@cse.cuhk.edu.hk, king@cse.cuhk.edu.hk

ABSTRACT

Recently expertise retrieval has received increasing interests in both academia and industry. Finding experts with demonstrated expertise for a given query is a nontrivial task especially from a large-scale Web 2.0 systems, such as question answering and bibliography data, where users are actively publishing useful content online, interacting with each other, and forming social networks in various ways, leading to heterogeneous networks in addition to the large amounts of textual content information. Many approaches have been proposed and shown to be useful for expertise ranking. However, most of these methods only consider the textual documents while ignoring heterogeneous network structures or can merely integrate with one additional kind of information. None of them can fully exploit the characteristics of heterogeneous networks. In this paper, we propose a joint regularization framework to enhance expertise retrieval by modeling heterogeneous networks as regularization constraints on top of document-centric model. We argue that multi-typed linking edges reveal valuable information which should be treated differently. Motivated by this intuition, we formulate three hypotheses to capture unique characteristics for different graphs, and mathematically model those hypotheses jointly with the document and other information. To illustrate our methodology, we apply the framework to expert finding applications using a bibliography dataset with 1.1 million papers and 0.7 million authors. The experimental results show that our proposed approach can achieve significantly better results than the baseline and other enhanced models.

Categories and Subject Descriptors: H.3.3 [**Information Storage and Retrieval**]: Information Search and Retrieval—*retrieval models*; H.2.8 [**Database Management**]: Database Applications—*data mining*

General Terms: Algorithm, Experimentation

Keywords: Expertise ranking, probabilistic model, heterogeneous bibliographic network, graph regularization

JCDL'12, June 10–14, 2012, Washington, DC, USA.

1. INTRODUCTION

In the age of Web 2.0, online users play more and more important roles in the internet, where they actively publish text information online, participate in communities, post comments, compose blogs, populate tags, and perform many informative functions. In interactive applications of finding experts, the knowledge and skills of experts have, in most cases, made a significant and invaluable contribution to online society as well as our real life. Moreover, the human expertise is one of the most valuable resources in the world, therefore it is natural to advance the information retrieval from traditional document retrieval to advanced expertise retrieval, which has recently received increasing interests in both academia and industry. However, finding expertise in real life requires a mix of individual, social and collaborative practices, thus finding experts with demonstrated expertise for a given query is a nontrivial task which remains much harder than the generic document retrieval task.

In addition to the large amounts of textual content information, users usually interact with each other and form social networks in various ways, which lead to heterogeneous networks along with the users. Taking community-based question answering as an example, since users post various questions and answers on online portals, we can find a wide coverage of topics, a social network among the users, as well as heterogeneous relationships among the questions/answers, categories and users. In another scenario, as researchers are regularly publishing papers in various venues (e.g., conferences, journals, etc.), we not only obtain textual information of the documents, but also have access to co-authorship network, citation network and heterogeneous networks among documents, authors as well as other properties. A sample heterogeneous network is shown in Figure 1(a). One can easily imagine many other examples of the Web 2.0 applications that consist of a large number of interacting, multi-typed components as well as users. Therefore, it would be interesting to study how we can exploit and incorporate the heterogeneous sources for expertise ranking.

Many approaches have been proposed and shown to be useful for expertise ranking. The most popular and successful approaches obtain their estimator of personal expertise by aggregating the relevance scores of documents directly associated with a person, which could be classified as *document-centric* models [1, 7, 10, 18]. These methods share the underlying claiming that the relevance of the textual context of a person adds up to the evidence of his/her expertness, but they only consider the textual documents while ignoring the relations between experts as well as valu-

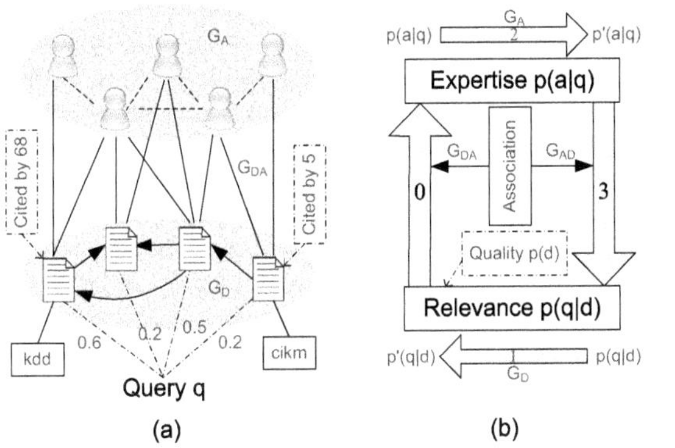

Figure 1: Illustrations of (a) a sample heterogeneous network and (b) a basic framework of our model.

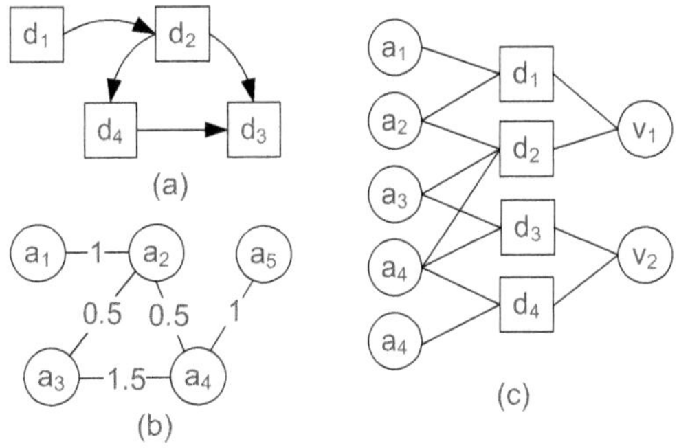

Figure 2: Three kinds of graphs in the heterogeneous network: (a) citation graph or directed affinity graph of documents, (b) co-authorship graph or social network of authors, and (c) author-paper-venue relationship tripartite graph.

able heterogeneous networks. Recently, several studies have been proposed to extend the expertise retrieval by considering one or two additional kinds of information, for example, the quality of documents [7], organizational hierarchy [13] and social network [28] of persons. However, the characteristics of the heterogeneous networks as shown in Figure 1(a) are not fully exploited by these methods. On one hand, the link structures among persons and documents are different which should be treated differently. For example, the citation graph among documents is a directed graph and the co-authorship graph among persons is an undirected graph. On the other hand, it is nontrivial to utilize and combine multiple graphs as well as different information sources effectively.

In this paper, we propose a joint regularization framework to enhance expertise retrieval by modeling heterogeneous networks as regularization constraints on top of document-centric model. We focus on scientific disciplines although the ideas developed in this paper can be applied to other domains. Figure 1(a) presents an example heterogeneous network according to a scientific bibliography, with undirected authorship graph G_{DA} linking authors and papers, undirected publishing edges linking papers and venues, and directed graph G_D linking papers to other papers, as well as co-authorship graph G_A linking authors and other authors. The linking edges among these components reveal a lot of valuable information about the potential relevance and expertise propagation over the network. Our idea is that different types of edges provide different information which should be treated differently. A basic framework of our model is illustrated in Figure 1(b). First, the citation graph G_D can be used to refine the relevance in the document level, then the relevance of documents of a person adds up to the evidence of his/her expertise based on the undirected authorship graph G_{DA}. Second, the co-authorship graph G_A can be used to refine the expertise in the person level. Third, it is essential to check whether the expertise of persons can reinforce the relevance of their associated documents with respect to a query.

To exploit these heterogeneous networks efficiently, we formulate three hypotheses to capture unique characteristics of different graphs, including directed and undirected graphs, and then mathematically model those hypotheses by developing regularization constraints on top of document-centric model. Moreover, we propose a joint regularization framework to incorporate these hypotheses together with the textual content information. Finally, we conduct extensive experiments for the expertise ranking task on the DBLP bibliography dataset. We test each of our hypotheses individually and validate the joint hypotheses, which shows the effectiveness of the joint regularization framework.

The remainder of this paper is organized as follows. In Section 2 we present the baseline model for expertise ranking and describe some preliminaries. In Section 3, we outline our proposed methods that exploit the heterogeneous bibliographic networks, formulate our hypotheses, and provide the mathematical modeling. We then describe and report the experimental evaluation in Section 4, and briefly review some related work in Section 5. Finally, we present our conclusions and future work in Section 6.

2. BACKGROUND AND PRELIMINARIES

2.1 Baseline Model for Expertise Ranking

The basic idea of the document-centric model [1, 7] is to estimate the expertise of a candidate by summing the relevance of the associated documents. In the probabilistic model, for a given query q, the problem of identifying experts is defined by estimating the probability of a candidate a_i being an expert $p(a_i|q)$,

$$p(a_i|q) = \sum_{d \in \mathcal{D}_{a_i}} p(a_i|d)p(d|q) \propto \sum_{d \in \mathcal{D}_{a_i}} p(a_i|d)p(q|d)p(d), \quad (1)$$

where $\mathcal{D}_{a_i}$ denotes the subset of documents related to a_i.

In this model, $p(a_i|d)$ represents the association between the candidates and the documents, where we assume that query q is conditionally independent to author a_i given the document d. Here the proof of the relation is an authorship. Suppose document d_j has n_{d_j} authors, each of whom is assumed to share the same knowledge/expertise described in the document, thus $p(a_i|d_j) = 1/n_{d_j}$ if a_i is an author of d_j, and zero otherwise. In Eq. (1), $p(q|d)$ measures the relevance between q and d, which can be determined using the language model [22, 26]. We infer a document language model θ_d for each document,

$$p(q|d) = p(q|\theta_d) = \prod_{t_i \in q} p(t_i|\theta_d),$$

where $p(t|\theta_d)$ represents the maximum likelihood estimator of the word t in a document d. In order to assign nonzero probabilities to unseen words, we employ Jelinek-Mercer smoothing [26] and use the venue context [8] instead of the whole collection for the statistical language model. In addition, the prior probability $p(d)$ can be viewed as the quality of a document, which is generally set to be uniform. Indeed, $p(d)$ can also be set to be how popular the d is (a variant of the citation count, much like a PageRank [3] for papers). In many situations, this may improve the expert retrieval. In this paper, we followed the model proposed by Deng et al. [7] to estimate $p(d)$ using the natural logarithm of the citation count c_d of the document: $p(d) \propto \ln(e + c_d)$, which achieved much better results than the uniform setting.

For simplicity, let $\mathbf{x}$ be the relevance vector with $x_i = p(q|d_i)$, $\mathbf{y}$ be the expertise vector with $y_j = p(a_j|q)$, and $\mathbf{Q}_D \in \mathbb{R}^{|D|\times|D|}$ be a diagonal matrix with $\mathbf{Q}_{D_{ii}} = p(d_i)$. The *baseline* model as shown in Eq. (1) can be rewritten as:

$$\mathbf{y} = \mathbf{P}_{DA}^T \mathbf{Q}_D \mathbf{x}, \tag{2}$$

where $\mathbf{P}_{DA} \in \mathbb{R}^{|D|\times|A|}$ is the transition matrix from documents $\mathcal{D}$ to authors $\mathcal{A}$ with $\mathbf{P}_{DA_{ij}} = p(a_j|d_i)$. The underlying intuition of this baseline model is to *estimate the expertise of a candidate based on the relevance and quality of associated documents*, which is illustrated as the left up-arrow in Figure 1(b).

2.2 Preliminaries

In this subsection, we define the problem of expertise ranking in a heterogeneous network and introduce several related concepts and notations.

A bibliographic heterogeneous network consists of three types of object sets, including an author set $\mathcal{A} = \{a_1, a_2, ..., a_m\}$, a document set $\mathcal{D} = \{d_1, d_2, ..., d_n\}$ and a venue set $\mathcal{C} = \{c_1, c_2, ..., c_l\}$, as well as the textual content information for each document. Such a heterogeneous network of authors, documents and venues can be denoted as $G = (V, E)$ where $V = V_A \cup V_D \cup V_C$ and $E = E_A \cup E_D \cup E_{A,D} \cup E_{D,C}$. As mentioned before, different types of edges should be treated differently, thus three kinds of graphs are formed as shown in Figure 2. G_D is an unweighted directed graph of documents, G_A is an undirected graph (co-authorship graph or social network) of authors, while $G_{A,D,C}$ is the tripartite graph representing authorship and publishing relationships.

Basically, G_D can be constructed based on a directed citation graph of papers or an affinity graph of documents. With respect to citation graph, a unidirectional link is formed from d_i to $d_j (i \neq j)$, denoted by $\mathbf{W}_{ij} = 1$, if document d_i cites document d_j, and otherwise no link is constructed. Thus, we construct a directed graph G_D with adjacency matrix $\mathbf{W} \in \mathbb{R}^{|D|\times|D|}$. For a given bibliography dataset (e.g., DBLP bibliography), it is very easy to obtain the bipartite graph $G_{D,A}$ and its matrix $\mathbf{R} \in \mathbb{R}^{|D|\times|A|}$, where $\mathbf{R}_{ij} = 1$ if d_i is associated with a_j. In addition, we use $\mathbf{P}_{DA} \in \mathbb{R}^{|D|\times|A|}$ to denote the transition matrix from documents to authors, where $\mathbf{P}_{DA} = \mathbf{D}_R^{-1}\mathbf{R}$ and $\mathbf{D}_R \in \mathbb{R}^{|D|\times|D|}$ is a diagonal matrix with $\mathbf{D}_{R_{ii}} = \sum_j R_{ij}$, thus it satisfies $\mathbf{P}_{DA_{ij}} = p(a_j|d_i)$. Similarly, $\mathbf{P}_{AD} \in \mathbb{R}^{|A|\times|D|}$ is defined as the transition matrix from authors to documents with $\mathbf{P}_{AD} = \mathbf{D}_{R^T}^{-1}\mathbf{R}^T$.

Based on $G_{D,A}$, we can construct the co-authorship graph G_A as well as its corresponding matrix $\mathbf{A}$. To quantify the edge weight, we chose the co-authorship frequency [15] that is the sum of values for all papers co-authored by a_i and a_j, $\mathbf{A}_{ij} = \sum_{k=1}^{N} \frac{\delta_i^k \delta_j^k}{n_{d_k} - 1}$, where $\delta_i^k = 1$ if a_i is one of the authors of paper d_k, $\delta_i^k = 0$ otherwise, and n_{d_k} is the number of authors in paper d_k. Figure 2(b) illustrates the weighted co-authorship graph of the example as shown in Figure 2(c). In this way, the more the co-authored papers, the higher the edge weight between two persons.

Now we can formulate our *expertise ranking* problem as: Given a heterogeneous network G, and the textual content information of documents $\mathcal{D}$, for a query q, we want to identify the relevant and knowledgable experts with expertise in a particular field. Previous work has explored the textual content information of documents $\mathcal{D}$ for ranking expertise based on document-centric model. In the following section, we investigate how to enhance the expertise ranking performance by modeling and exploiting the heterogeneous network G on top of the baseline model.

3. MODELING HETEROGENEOUS NETWORKS

Generally, documents and authors are closely connected in the heterogeneous bibliographic network, and much more information is available in addition to the textual document information. In this section we discuss several ways of incorporating different types of graphs into expertise ranking by developing regularization constraints.

3.1 Basic Hypotheses

We now describe our hypotheses to incorporate the heterogeneous bibliographic networks, and investigate how these hypotheses can be applied in enhancing the performance of expertise ranking. In Section 4 we validate them experimentally on real-world data, and demonstrate that they hold for the data sets we consider, which can also be generalized to other domains with similar semantics. Based on common sense and our observations on real data, we have the following three basic hypotheses:

Document Consistency Hypothesis: *Usually similar documents will be of similar relevance to a given query.* In a citation (or affinity) graph, it is reasonable to assume the neighbors of a document d are those documents that are considered similar to it. If the neighbors of a document are highly relevant to a query, this document is more likely to be relevant to the query; otherwise, if none of the neighbors of a document is relevant to the query, the document is unlikely to be relevant to the query.

Co-Authorship Consistency Hypothesis: *If two persons have co-authored many relevant papers with respect to a given query, then their expertise in the queried field should be similar in some sense.* Suppose author a_1 is an expert in a specific research topic, e.g., "information retrieval", and has co-published many papers related to this topic with author a_2, then author a_2 is more likely to be knowledgeable about this topic.

Document-Author Consistency Hypothesis: *The expertise of a researcher is consistent with that of the documents he/she published.* In this case, author a_i is knowledgeable about a specific topic only if author a_i has published papers related to the topic. Similarly, paper d_j may be related to the specific topic if paper d_j is written by authors who are experts in this area.

3.2 Regularization Framework

We now describe how we enforce the above hypotheses by defining the regularization constraints for the expertise ranking model.

3.2.1 Document Consistency

Here the goal is to refine the relevance score vector $\mathbf{x}$ based on the document consistency that *similar documents are likely to have the same ranking scores for a given query.* Suppose we are given a document citation graph $G_D = (V_D, E_D)$ as illustrated in Figure 2(a), which is a directed graph. Suppose the pairwise similarities among the documents are described by the matrix $\mathbf{S}_D \in \mathbb{R}^{|D|\times|D|}$ measured based on G_D. In the baseline model, the relevance of documents is calculated using the language model for a given query, denoted by the initial relevance vector $\mathbf{x}^0$. Thus we formulate to minimize a regularization loss function [29] as follows:

$$\Omega_1 = \mathbf{x}^T(I - \mathbf{S}_D)\mathbf{x} + \mu_d \left\|\mathbf{x} - \mathbf{x}^0\right\|^2, \tag{3}$$

where $\mu_d > 0$ is the regularization parameter. The first term of the cost function defines the *document consistency*, which prefers small difference in relevance scores between neighbor documents, while the second term defines the *fitting constraint* that measures the difference between the final scores $\mathbf{x}$ and the initial relevance scores $\mathbf{x}^0$.

Minimizing Ω_1 will force the neighbor documents to receive similar relevance scores. Differentiating Eq. (3) and setting $\partial\Omega_1/\partial\mathbf{x} = 0$, we can see that the optimal solution $\mathbf{x}^*$ may be written as

$$\mathbf{x}^* = (1-\alpha)(I - \alpha\mathbf{S}_D)^{-1}\mathbf{x}^0, \tag{4}$$

where $\alpha = 1/(1+\mu_d)$. Accordingly, it needs to calculate the inverse matrix $(I - \alpha\mathbf{S}_D)^{-1}$ to get the optimal solution. Fortunately, the matrix $\mathbf{S}_D$ is usually very sparse, then the complexity time of the sparse matrix inversion can be reduced to be linear with the number of nonzero matrix elements. One alternative solution to the above can be obtained using a powerful iterative method [29, 31]: $\mathbf{x}(t+1) = \alpha\mathbf{S}_D\mathbf{x}(t) + (1-\alpha)\mathbf{x}^0$, where $\mathbf{x}^* = \mathbf{x}(\infty)$ is the solution. In general, the iterative algorithm can converge after 10 iterations in most cases, which means the regularization problem can be solved efficiently with the iterative method. Then the expertise vector $\mathbf{y}^*$ can be inferred according to Eq. (2), so as to affect the results of expertise ranking.

Now the interesting question is how to calculate $\mathbf{S}_D$ among the set $\mathcal{D}$. For graph data, a number of recent work [31] has been given on obtaining the similarity measures. For a directed graph G_D, where the adjacency matrix $\mathbf{W}$ is first normalized as a random walk transition matrix $\mathbf{P}_D = \mathbf{D}_W^{-1}\mathbf{W}$, the similarity measure $\mathbf{S}_D$ is calculated as:

$$\mathbf{S}_D = \frac{\Pi_D^{1/2}\mathbf{P}_D\Pi_D^{-1/2} + \Pi_D^{-1/2}\mathbf{P}_D^T\Pi_D^{1/2}}{2},$$

where Π_D is a diagonal matrix formed from the stationary probability distribution of the adjacency matrix, and $\mathbf{D}_W$ is a diagonal matrix with $\mathbf{D}_{D_{ii}} = \sum_j \mathbf{W}_{ij}$. For undirected graph, $\mathbf{S}_D$ is simply the normalized adjacency matrix: $\mathbf{S}_D = \mathbf{D}_W^{-1/2}\mathbf{W}\mathbf{D}_W^{-1/2}$. In this paper, we consider two different document graphs: One is the citation graph which is a directed graph as shown in Figure 2(a), and the other is the co-conference graph which is an undirected graph with $\mathbf{W}_{ij} = 1$ if d_i and d_j appear in a same conference.

3.2.2 Co-Authorship Consistency

The objective of co-authorship consistency is to *enforce the expertise scores of candidates to be closer if they co-authored more papers related to a given query.* Suppose we are given the co-authorship graph $G_A = (V_A, E_A)$, which is a weighted undirected graph. Let $\mathbf{A} \in \mathbb{R}^{|A|\times|A|}$ be the co-authorship matrix based on G_A. The regularization for the co-authorship consistency is very similar to the one for the document consistency, which can be defined as

$$\Omega_2 = \mathbf{y}^T(I - \mathbf{S}_A)\mathbf{y} + \mu_a \left\|\mathbf{y} - \mathbf{y}^0\right\|^2, \tag{5}$$

$$s.t. \quad \mathbf{y}^0 = \mathbf{P}_{DA}^T\mathbf{Q}_D\mathbf{x}, \tag{6}$$

where $\mathbf{S}_A = \mathbf{D}_A^{-1/2}\mathbf{A}\mathbf{D}_A^{-1/2}$ is the normalized matrix, $\mathbf{x}$ can either be the initial relevance scores $\mathbf{x}^0$, or the optimal solution $\mathbf{x}^*$ refined by document consistency. Intuitively, the first term of Eq. (5) defines the *co-authorship consistency*, which will push the expertise of an author a_i to be close to his/her co-authors if they published many relevant papers together, while the second term is the constraint to fit the expertise scores obtained by the baseline (or refined) model.

The solution of minimizing Ω_2 can be achieved with the closed form solution:

$$\begin{aligned}\mathbf{y}^* &= (1-\beta)(I - \beta\mathbf{S}_\mathbf{A})^{-1}\mathbf{y}^0, \\ &= (1-\beta)(I - \beta\mathbf{S}_\mathbf{A})^{-1}\mathbf{P}_{DA}^T\mathbf{Q}_D\mathbf{x},\end{aligned} \tag{7}$$

where $\beta = 1/(1+\mu_a)$. Similarly, the iterative solution becomes: $\mathbf{y}(t+1) = \beta\mathbf{S}_A\mathbf{y}(t) + (1-\beta)\mathbf{P}_{DA}^T\mathbf{Q}_D\mathbf{x}$, where $\mathbf{y}^* = \mathbf{y}(\infty)$ is the solution. By setting $\mathbf{x} = \mathbf{x}^*$, the above optimization problem can be interpreted as considering the document consistency and co-authorship consistency sequentially in a two-stage process. Although the co-authorship consistency is derived by considering the co-authorship graph, some other information, for example, co-worker information in a same department, can be transformed into a co-authorship graph to some extent, which means our model can handle more general information sources instead of the co-authorship.

3.2.3 Document-Author Consistency and Joint Regularization Framework

The key point of the document-author consistency is that *the expertise of an author is consistent with the relevance of associated documents.* In the above, we have given the methods for incorporating the document consistency and the co-authorship consistency into expertise ranking, respectively. Actually, the document-author consistency has been explicitly used in these methods as well as the baseline model, according to Eq. (2). It can be viewed as a propagation from documents (relevance) to authors (expertise) based on the transition matrix $\mathbf{P}_{DA}$ from $\mathcal{D}$ to $\mathcal{A}$.

In contrast, it is essential to investigate whether the expertise of authors could reinforce the relevance of their associated documents with respect to a query, based on another transition matrix $\mathbf{P}_{AD}$ from $\mathcal{A}$ to $\mathcal{D}$. The underlying assumption is that the expertise/knowledge of an author could propagate to the associated documents according to $\mathbf{Q}_D\mathbf{x} = \mathbf{P}_{AD}^T\mathbf{y}$. Therefore, we can encode the support from the associated authors with the initial relevance scores, so as to define the following new value:

$$\hat{\mathbf{x}}^0 = (1-\gamma)\mathbf{x}^0 + \gamma\mathbf{Q}_D^{-1}\mathbf{P}_{AD}^T\mathbf{y}, \tag{8}$$

where γ is the parameter to control the balance between the initial relevance scores and the propagated scores. Note that *if $\gamma = 0$ we only consider the propagation from documents to authors, while ignore the propagation from authors to documents.* When $\gamma > 0$, we take both propagations into account, which can be denoted as *Mutual Document-Author Consistency.*

To incorporate all the three hypotheses on a heterogeneous network, formally, a joint objective function is defined to be

$$\begin{aligned}\Omega_3 &= \Omega_1 + \Omega_2, \\ &= \mathbf{x}^T(I - \mathbf{S}_D)\mathbf{x} + \mu_d \left\|\mathbf{x} - \hat{\mathbf{x}}^0\right\|^2 \\ &\quad + \mathbf{y}^T(I - \mathbf{S}_A)\mathbf{y} + \mu_a \left\|\mathbf{y} - \mathbf{y}^0\right\|^2. \qquad (9)\end{aligned}$$

along with the constraints as defined in Eq. (6) and Eq. (8). One can understand the above optimization problem in this way: Here Ω_1 is responsible for the *document consistency* within documents, while Ω_2 is responsible for the *co-authorship consistency* within authors. In the meanwhile, the constraints can be considered as the *document-author consistency* between documents and authors.

The optimization illustrated above can be solved using the standard conjugate gradient method, and a closed-form solution can be derived (The proof is omitted due to space limit). However, for a large-scale information retrieval, an iterative algorithm would be more effective and preferable to solve the optimization problem. Suppose $\mathbf{x}(0) = \mathbf{x}^0$ and $\mathbf{y}(0) = \mathbf{P}_{DA}^T\mathbf{Q}_D\mathbf{x}^0$, in the $(t+1)$-th iteration, we first compute $\mathbf{x}(t+1)$ using $\mathbf{x}(t)$ and $\mathbf{y}(t)$:

$$\begin{aligned}\mathbf{x}(t+1) &= \alpha\mathbf{S}_D\mathbf{x}(t) + (1-\alpha)\left((1-\gamma)\mathbf{x}^0 + \gamma\mathbf{Q}_D^{-1}\mathbf{P}_{AD}^T\mathbf{y}(t)\right) \\ &+ \alpha\frac{1-\beta}{\beta}\mathbf{Q}_D\mathbf{P}_{DA}\left(\mathbf{y}(t) - \mathbf{P}_{DA}^T\mathbf{Q}_D\mathbf{x}(t)\right), \qquad (10)\end{aligned}$$

and then compute $\mathbf{y}(t+1)$ based on $\mathbf{x}(t+1)$ and $\mathbf{y}(t)$:

$$\begin{aligned}\mathbf{y}(t+1) &= \beta\mathbf{S}_A\mathbf{y}(t) + (1-\beta)\mathbf{P}_{DA}^T\mathbf{Q}_D\mathbf{x}(t+1) \qquad (11) \\ &+ \beta\frac{1-\alpha}{\alpha}\mathbf{P}_{AD}\mathbf{Q}_D^{-1}\left(\mathbf{x}(t+1) - (1-\gamma)\mathbf{x}^0 - \gamma\mathbf{Q}_D^{-1}\mathbf{P}_{AD}^T\mathbf{y}(t)\right).\end{aligned}$$

Essentially, the values of $\mathbf{x}$ and $\mathbf{y}$ will be updated iteratively according to the parameter setting and the heterogeneous graphs until they converge. The trade-off among these hypotheses is controlled by the parameters $\alpha = 1/(1+\mu_d)$, $\beta = 1/(1+\mu_a)$ and γ, where each of them ranges from 0 to 1. In this paper, we employ a grid-search on the parameters α, β and γ using cross-validation [12], and report the performance in Section 4.

3.3 Connections and Discussions

Here we establish connections between the joint regularization framework and other methods in Table 1. Suppose $\alpha = 0$ ($\mu_d \to \infty$), $\beta = 0$ ($\mu_a \to \infty$), $\gamma = 0$, as shown in Eq. (9), Ω_1 puts all weight $\mu_d \to \infty$ on the second term $\left\|\mathbf{x} - \hat{\mathbf{x}}^0\right\|^2$ to ensure that the final scores are equal to the initial scores $\mathbf{x}^0$ and then propagate to the candidates. Similarly, Ω_2 puts all weight $\mu_a \to \infty$ on the term $\left\|\mathbf{y} - \mathbf{y}^0\right\|^2$, so as to ensure that the final scores are equal to $\mathbf{y}^0$. In this case, the optimal results are $\langle\mathbf{x}^0, \mathbf{P}_{DA}^T\mathbf{Q}_D\mathbf{x}^0\rangle$, and the regularization framework boils down to the *baseline* model.

To incorporate the consistency of each of the three hypothesis individually, it is equivalent to explore one of the parameters α, β, γ and fix the other two parameters to 0 as shown in Table 1. For example, by setting $\alpha > 0$, $\beta = \gamma = 0$, Eq. (11) becomes $\mathbf{y}(t+1) = \mathbf{P}_{DA}^T\mathbf{Q}_D\mathbf{x}(t+1)$, and then Eq. (10) is simplified to the iterative solution of Eq. (3), which means the model only considers the *document consistency* in the regularization framework. Suppose $\gamma > 0$, $\alpha = \beta = 0$, the model consider the *mutual document-author consistency*, and the iterative solution becomes:

$$\mathbf{x}(t+1) = (1-\gamma)\mathbf{x}^0 + \gamma\mathbf{Q}_D^{-1}\mathbf{P}_{AD}^T\mathbf{y}(t),\ \mathbf{y}(t+1) = \mathbf{P}_{DA}^T\mathbf{Q}_D\mathbf{x}(t+1),$$

Table 1: Connections with other methods.

Parameters: α, β, γ	Description
$\alpha = 0,\ \beta = 0,\ \gamma = 0$	*Baseline* probabilistic model
$\alpha > 0,\ \beta = 0,\ \gamma = 0$	Document consistency[a]
$\alpha = 0,\ \beta > 0,\ \gamma = 0$	Co-authorship consistency[a]
$\alpha = 0,\ \beta = 0,\ \gamma > 0$	Mutual document-author consistency
$\alpha > 0,\ \beta > 0,\ \gamma > 0$	Joint Regularization

[a] Note that document-author consistency is also partially used in these models as described in Section 3.2.3.

Table 2: Statistics of the DBLP network.

Nodes		Edges	
# of authors	695,906	# edges in G_A	4,272,319
# of papers	1,152,512	# edges in G_D	5,695,135
# of venues	3,311	# edges in $G_{D,A}$	2,944,797

which is similar to HITS algorithm [14]. Finally, we will investigate the general case (i.e., $\alpha > 0$, $\beta > 0$, $\gamma > 0$) which combines multiple consistency hypotheses jointly.

To compute the model efficiently, we only need to retrieve a subset of documents $\hat{D}$ with top-k relevant documents, and then identify the subset of authors $\hat{A}$ associated with $\hat{D}$, so as to perform our model on the subgraph with most relevant documents and authors. We can benefit from this trick to reduce computational cost and enhance the accuracy by avoiding topic drift in the whole graph. However, the selection of k can also be an issue, which is empirically studied in Section 4.2.4. In addition, it is worth mentioning that the key contribution of this paper is to exploit heterogeneous networks for enhancing expertise ranking model, and our model is built on top of the baseline model.

4. EXPERIMENTS

4.1 Experimental Setup and Metrics

4.1.1 Data Collection

We evaluate our models on the real-world DBLP bibliography data[1], which contains over 1,100,000 XML records. Each record consists of several elements, such as "author", "title", "conference". Using these records, we could easily build the paper-author bipartite graph $G_{D,A}$, the paper-venue bipartite graph $G_{D,C}$ and the co-authorship graph G_A. The citation graph G_D and abstract information were obtained from Arnetminer[2]. In addition, we can construct the document co-conference graph G'_D according to the bipartite graph $G_{D,C}$ for another alternative instead of citation graph.

From the statistics in Table 2, we get totally 1,152,512 papers and 695,906 authors in our data collection. After the construction of the heterogeneous graph, we observe that there are relatively few edges, indicating the resulting matrices are sparse matrices. As for G_A, each author has 6.13 co-authors on average. In G_D we only get about 5 citations per paper. This is because the citations of some papers may not be available in the repository. It can be imagined that we could achieve better results with the whole citation graph, but it is enough to illustrate the performance of our

[1] http://www.informatik.uni-trier.de/~ley/db/
[2] http://arnetminer.org/lab-datasets/citation/

Table 3: Benchmark dataset of 20 queries.

Topic	#Expert
Information Extraction	20
Intelligent Agents	29
Machine Learning	42
Natural Language Processing	41
Planning	34
Semantic Web	45
Support Vector Machine	31
Boosting	56
Ontology Alignment	53
Probabilistic Relevance Model	13
Information Retrieval	23
Language Model for Information Retrieval	12
Face Recognition	21
Semi Supervised Learning	21
Reinforcement Learning	17
Kernel Methods	21
Privacy Preservation	17
Skyline	12
Sensor RFID data management	13
Stream	16

proposed model using the current citation graph. With regard to $G_{D,A}$, on average there are 4.22 papers per author, and 2.55 authors per paper. Since these matrices are very sparse but they represent real-world situations, our proposed algorithm can efficiently solve for the results.

The evaluation of expert finding performance in such a large data collection is very challenging due to the scarcity of ground truth that can be examined publicly. Furthermore, it is impractical to obtain expert ratings for all authors. In order to measure the performance of our proposed methods, a benchmark dataset with 20 query topics and expert lists is manually created as shown in Table 3. The top 9 topics and expert lists in the left table were collected by Zhang et al. [28, 7], which are available at `http://keg.cs.tsinghua.edu.cn/project/PSN/dataset.html#new_expert_list`. The rest 11 topics and relevance judgments for the corresponding expert lists were created and evaluated by 10 researchers and senior graduate students of CUHK [8]. Specifically, these 11 topics were created by the assessors based on their own research topics. We tried to cover not only broad queries but also specific queries to see whether our methods could handle both of them effectively.

Following general relevance judgments, for each query, a list of relevant experts is collected through the method of pooled relevance judgments with human assessment efforts. The top ranked/retrieved authors from the computer science bibliography search engines (such as CiteSeer, Libra, Rexa and ArnetMiner), and the committees of the top conferences related the query topic were taken to construct the pools which contained around 300 authors. Moreover, since the query topics were created by the assessors who had conducted research in the related field for several years, they were quite familiar with the experts in that research field and could make reliable relevance judgments and even nominate some missing experts. The assessments were carried out mainly in terms of the number of top conference/journal papers an expert candidate had published, the number of related publications for the given query, and what distinguished awards he/she had received. There are four grade scores (3, 2, 1, and 0) which were assigned respectively to represent top expert, expert, marginal expert, and non-expert. Basically, each query and the corresponding expert list are judged by at least 3 (to 5) assessors, and we intentionally obtained a small number of experts by marking around 20 top ranked experts as top experts (although the number of experts could be quite large). Finally, the judgment scores (at levels 3 and 2) were averaged to construct the final ground truth with 20 to 50 experts for each query as shown in Table 3. This dataset based on DBLP [8] has been widely used for evaluating expert finding.

4.1.2 Evaluation Metrics

For the evaluation of the task, several popular IR metrics are employed to measure the performance of our proposed models, including precision at rank n ($P@n$), Mean Average Precision (MAP), bpref [4, 24], and Mean Reciprocal Rank (MRR). $P@n$ measures the fraction of the top-n retrieved results that are relevant experts for the given query, which is defined as $P@n = \frac{\#\text{ relevant in top } n \text{ results}}{n}$. R-precision (R-prec) is defined as the precision at rank R where R is the number of relevant candidates for the given query. Average precision (AP) emphasizes returning more relevant documents earlier. For a single query, AP is defined as the average of the $P@n$ values for all relevant documents: $AP = \frac{\sum_{n=1}^{N}(P@n * \text{rel}(n))}{R}$, where n is the rank, N the number retrieved, and $\text{rel}(n)$ is a binary function indicating the relevance of a given rank. MAP is the mean value of the average precisions computed for all queries. The Mean Reciprocal Rank(MRR) of each individual query is the reciprocal of the rank at which the first relevant answer was returned.

Beside the measurement of precisions, Bpref [4] is a good score function that evaluates the performance from a different view, i.e., the number of non-relevant candidates. It is formulated as $\text{bpref} = \frac{1}{R}\sum_{r=1}^{N}(1 - \frac{\# n \text{ ranked higher than } r}{R})$, where r is a relevant candidate and n is a member of the first R candidates judged non-relevant as retrieved by the system.

4.2 Experimental Results

In this subsection, we evaluate our proposed model for expertise ranking. First, the experiments are performed to compare with several state-of-the-art methods, and also to validate our model under various hypotheses. Then we investigate the parameter effect of these hypotheses. Finally, we analyze the detailed results with some case studies.

4.2.1 Comparison of Different Methods

To demonstrate how the expertise ranking performance can be improved by our proposed approaches, we implemented several state-of-the-art methods as follows:

Balog's Model2 [1] is a popular document-centric model for expert finding. It is one of the best-performing models by only utilizing the documents. The source code is available at `http://code.google.com/p/ears`.

BL [7, 8] is our baseline probabilistic model as described in Section 2.1. This model estimates the expertise of a candidate based on both the relevance and quality of associated documents.

EnhancedBL [8] is an enhanced model for expertise ranking with two community-aware strategies. More specifically, it incorporates the co-authorship graph with query-

Table 4: Evaluation and comparison with other methods. Best scores are in boldface.

Methods / Metrics	P@5	P@10	P@20	R-prec	MAP	bpref	MRR
Baseline models							
Balog's Model2 [1]	0.64	0.575	0.46	0.439	0.3915	0.3815	0.9167
BL	0.7	0.67	0.4975	0.4942	0.4803	0.4716	0.9
(vs **Balog's Model2**)	+8.57%	+14.18%	+7.54%	+11.17%	+18.48%*	+19.1%*	-1.85%
Enhanced models based on **BL**							
EnhancedBL [8]	0.73	0.68	0.535	0.5109	0.4906	0.4876	0.91
(vs **BL**)	+4.29%	+1.49%	+7.54%	+3.37%	+2.15%	+3.40%	+1.11%
Co-Ranking [30]	0.77	0.655	0.5125	0.4953	0.5049	0.4707	0.91
(vs **BL**)	+10%	-2.24%	+3.02%	+0.21%	+5.12%	-0.19%	+1.11%
JointHyp	**0.84**	**0.72**	**0.57**	**0.5513**	**0.5661**	**0.5394**	**1**
(vs **EnhancedBL**)	+15.07%*	+5.88%	+6.54%	+7.92%	+15.39%*	+10.63%*	+9.89%
(vs **Co-Ranking**)	+9.09%	+9.92%*	+11.22%*	+11.32%*	+12.13%*	+14.61%*	+9.89%

* indicates the improvement is statistically significant ($p < 0.05$).

Table 5: Experimental results of our proposed methods under various hypotheses. The percentages of relative improvements (%) over the baseline are also shown in the table. Best scores are in boldface.

Methods / Metrics	P@5	P@10	P@20	R-prec	MAP	bpref	MRR
BL	0.7	0.67	0.4975	0.4942	0.4803	0.4716	0.9
Individual hypothesis							
Hyp:Doc(G_D)	0.76	0.72	0.5525	0.5297	0.5318	0.5089	1
(vs **BL**)	+8.57%	+7.46%	+11.06%*	+7.18%*	+10.73%*	+7.93%*	+11.11%*
Hyp:Doc(G'_D)	0.73	0.695	0.5375	0.5238	0.5185	0.4997	0.95
(vs **BL**)	+4.29%	+3.73%	+8.04%*	+5.98%*	+7.96%*	+5.96%*	+5.56%
Hyp:Author	0.77	0.675	0.5525	0.5244	0.5302	0.5135	0.9017
(vs **BL**)	+10%*	+0.75%	+11.06%*	+8.27%*	+10.40%*	+8.9%*	+0.19%
Hyp:DocAuthor	0.73	0.685	0.52	0.4987	0.4921	0.4795	0.8833
(vs **BL**)	+4.29%	+2.24%	+4.52%*	+0.91%	+2.46%	+1.68%	-1.85%
Joint hypotheses							
JointHyp	**0.84**	**0.72**	**0.57**	**0.5513**	**0.5661**	**0.5394**	**1**
(vs **BL**)	+20%*	+7.46%	+14.57%*	+11.56%*	+17.87%*	14.39%*	+11.11%*
(vs **Hyp:Doc**(G_D))	+10.53%*	0%	+3.17%	+4.08%	+6.45%*	+5.99%*	0%
(vs **Hyp:Author**)	+9.09%*	+6.67%	+3.17%	+5.14%	+6.76%*	+5.04%*	+10.91%*

* indicates the improvement is statistically significant ($p < 0.05$).

dependent community on top of **BL** model, which is quite relevant to our model.

Co-Ranking [30] can utilize the heterogeneous networks to rank authors and documents simultaneously, however, Co-Ranking cannot be directly used for expertise ranking since it is query-independent. Here we first constructed a query-specific subgraph based on the relevant documents and authors, and then performed Co-Ranking with empirically best parameters.

To make the comparison fair, we used the same benchmark dataset and reported the best performance of these models with *leave-one-out cross-validation*. Table 4 reports the evaluation results of these methods and our proposed model **JointHyp**. The relative improvement over baseline or other models is also shown in the table. As we can see, the results of our baseline model (BL) are much better than Balog's Model2, especially for MAP and bpref with 18%+ improvements. The reason is that BL model can benefit from the quality of documents in addition to the relevance which is used in Balog's Model2. This indicates our baseline model BL is a very competitive baseline. In terms of the enhanced models based on BL, both EnhancedBL and Co-Ranking can achieves slightly better performances over BL, since these two models integrate with some additional information. However, both enhanced models fail to outperform our proposed model JointHyp in all the metrics. Additionally, JointHyp gains significantly better performance over both EnhancedBL and Co-Ranking, e.g., 10%+ improvements for P@5, MAP and bpref. These observations demonstrate the effectiveness of our model by exploiting different information as well as heterogeneous networks successfully.

4.2.2 Comparison of Different Hypotheses

As discussed before, we develop three kinds of graph consistency hypotheses to enhance the baseline model by adding the regularization constraints. Based on the baseline model **BL**, we consider the following methods to validate three individual and the joint hypotheses, respectively.

- **Hyp:Doc**(G_D): Exploiting document consistency hypothesis with citation graph G_D (Equation 3)
- **Hyp:Doc**(G'_D): Exploiting document consistency hypothesis with co-conference graph G'_D (Equation 3)
- **Hyp:Author**: Exploiting co-authorship consistency hypothesis (Equation 5)
- **Hyp:DocAuthor**: Exploiting mutual document-author consistency hypothesis (Equation 9 & $\alpha = 0, \beta = 0$)
- **JointHyp**: Exploiting three hypotheses jointly (Equation 9).

For each case, we employ a grid-search and leave-one-out cross-validation approach [12] to learn the parameters

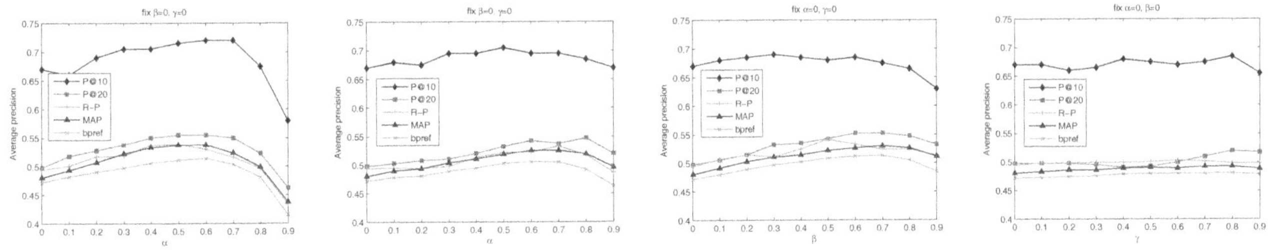

(a) Hyp:Doc(G_D) (b) Hyp:Doc(G'_D) (c) Hyp:Author (d) Hyp:DocAuthor

Figure 3: The effect of three individual hypotheses by varying α, β and γ.

that obtain the best performance. The experimental results of our proposed models are summarized in Table 5 where we show the precision and the relative improvement over baseline. For document consistency hypothesis, we consider two kinds of graphs, i.e., Hyp:Doc(G_D) and Hyp:Doc(G'_D), and we can see both of them have significant improvements over BL for most of the metrics, which indicates that document consistency is very useful. As expected, Hyp:Doc(G_D) appears to be more effective than Hyp:Doc(G'_D) since the directed citation graph provides more valuable information than the co-conference graph although the citation graph we used is not complete. We can imagine to achieve better performance with the complete citation graph. In the joint hypotheses testing, we only show the results using the citation graph due to space limit. For co-authorship consistency hypothesis, we observe that Hyp:Author also has significant improvement over BL, which shows the effectiveness of this hypothesis.

Now we test the mutual document-author consistency. Note that the propagation from documents' relevance to authors' expertise has been used in the baseline model, which is also the foundation of document-centric models for expert finding. The objective of this mutual hypothesis is to validate the effectiveness of the back propagation from authors to documents, i.e., whether the expertise scores of authors can be propagated to or reinforce the relevance scores of associated documents. As shown in Table 5, Hyp:DocAuthor only has slight improvement over BL. The possible reason is that the document-author consistency has partially used in BL, therefore additional value provided by the mutual document-author consistency may be limited in some sense. In general, the results of Hyp:Doc(G_D) and Hyp:Author are comparable, which are better than the mutual document-author consistency.

Since all the individual consistency hypotheses are effective, it is more interesting to check how the joint model JointHyp will perform by incorporating all the three hypotheses together. As we can see from Table 5, JointHyp outperforms BL, Hyp:Doc(G_D) and Hyp:Author with significant improvements[3]. This supports the joint hypothesis that different information and heterogeneous graphs should be modeled and exploited differently, so as to contribute additional value in the joint regularization model.

In summary, these individual consistency hypotheses make a great contribution to enhance the baseline probabilistic model. And meanwhile the joint regularization model can further improve the performance by incorporating all these hypotheses together.

[3]The improvement can be viewed as significant if the method has significant improvements based on MAP and bpref.

4.2.3 *Parameter Effect of Different Hypotheses*

In previous subsections, we learned the best parameters for the joint regularization framework using the grid-search and cross-validation approach. As for JointHyp, the best performance reported above is obtained by setting the parameters with $\alpha = 0.5$, $\beta = 0.6$ and $\gamma = 0.2$. Here we empirically investigate the parameter effect of different hypotheses. Validating the consistency of each of the three individual hypotheses is equivalent to explore one of the parameters α, β and γ after fixing other two parameters to 0, respectively. According to Table 1, if $\alpha = \beta = \gamma = 0$, the joint regularization framework reduces to the baseline model.

We first validate the *document consistency hypothesis* by varying α from 0 to 0.9 and fixing $\gamma = 0$, $\beta = 0$. Here the parameter α controls the balance between the document relevance consistency over the document graph (i.e., citation graph G_D or co-conference graph G'_D) and the initial relevance scores $\mathbf{x}^0$ of the probabilistic model. Figures 3(a) and (b) illustrate the experimental results of Hyp:Doc(G_D) and Hyp:Doc(G'_D) for different α, in which $\alpha = 0$ corresponds to the baseline **BL**. We can see the performance is improved over **BL** when incorporating the document relevance consistency ($\alpha > 0$). Generally, the performance becomes better with the increase of α until it puts too much weight on the term of document consistency. We observe that the performance is relatively stable and promising when α is set between 0.4 and 0.7. The first observation is that considering document consistency hypothesis could improve significantly over the baseline probabilistic model.

Then we evaluate the *co-authorship consistency hypothesis* by varying β from 0 to 0.9 and fixing $\alpha = 0$, $\gamma = 0$. The parameter β controls the importance of the co-authorship consistency. In Figure 3(c), the performance of Hyp:Author is improved along with the increase of β, and it is relatively stable between 0.4 and 0.7. These experiments indicate that the co-authorship consistency can be successfully used to refine expertise scores among authors.

Finally we evaluate the *mutual document-author consistency hypothesis* on top of **BL** by varying γ from 0 to 0.9, corresponding to Hyp:DocAuthor. The objective of this hypothesis is to validate whether the expertise scores of authors can be propagated to or reinforce the relevance scores of associated documents. As shown in Figures 3(d), the performance of Hyp:DocAuthor is stable and almost the same as the baseline. The possible reason is that experts usually have broad, diverse and cross-disciplinary research topics, for example, a data mining expert may have published many papers related to bioinformatics, therefore the propagation from experts to documents may result in topic drift. Another reason is that the document-author relationship has

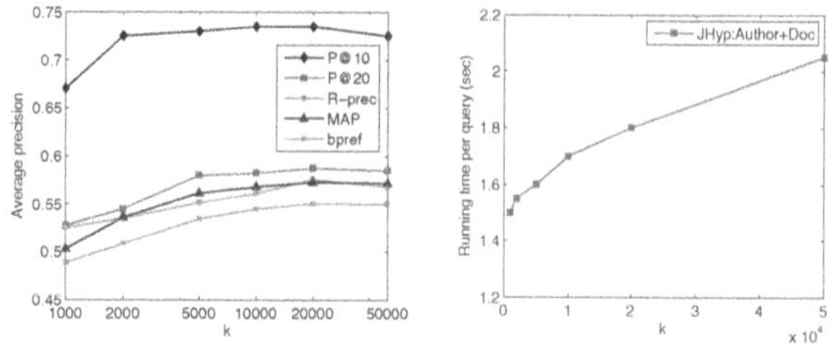

(a) Performance (b) Running time per query

Figure 4: The performance and running time of model JHyp:Author+Doc by varying the parameter k with top-k relevant documents.

been implicitly used in the probabilistic model, therefore it may not contribute new information to the model and only small changes occur in the results by considering the propagation from authors to documents.

4.2.4 *Detailed Results and Analysis*

As mentioned in Section 3.3, we only need to retrieve a subset with top-k relevant documents, so as to construct a query-specific subgraph for efficient computation of our model. The parameter k used in previous experiments is set to 5,000. To investigate the effect of this parameter, we chose **JointHyp**, and evaluated it with 5 different k values from 1,000 to 50,000. The performance and running time[4] per query are depicted in Figures 4(a) and (b), respectively. We can see the performance becomes better for greater k, then levels off as $k > 10,000$. It is reasonable that more documents can better capture the complete expertise. In the meantime, the running time was found to increase less than linearly with the increase of k. Hence a good tradeoff is to set $k = 5,000$.

To gain a better insight into the proposed algorithm, we chose two queries "Probabilistic Relevance Model[5]" and "Kernel Methods[6]" as the example cases to show more detailed results. The top-10 author lists ranked by the models **BL** and **JointHyp** are shown in Table 6, where the relevant experts are in boldface. It is obvious that the results of JHyp:Author+Doc make more sense than the baseline. Taking the query "Kernel Methods" as an example, we find that JHyp:Author+Doc can boost some relevant researchers like "John Shawe-Taylor" and "Jason Weston" into top 10. Similarly, the results of another query shows the same observations. This is because of the document consistency and co-authorship consistency hypotheses. After looking into the details, one important observation is that the joint regularization framework can successfully constrain some irrelevant expertise and return mostly relevant results.

5. RELATED WORK

Generally, there are two principal models for expertise retrieval: profile-based model [16] and document-based model [1, 7, 10, 18]. In contrast, the document-based approach preserves all information contained in the collection and performs better than the profile-based approach. Besides these two categories, there are some other methods [13, 8, 23] proposed to extend the expertise retrieval. The organizational hierarchy [13] and community information [8] are utilized to enhance expert finding. However, these methods analyze the content of each document separately or merely extend the model with another additional kind of information. Our work is different from theirs, as we model and exploit heterogeneous networks in a joint regularization framework along with several hypotheses, which not only distinguishes the propagation between documents and authors, but also treats directed and undirected graphs in a different way.

The work is also concerned with predicting the quality of users or their generated content in social media by calculating their centrality in the organizational social network, including community-based question answering [2], document recommendation [31], collaborative tagging system [21, 11], and other online communities [5, 27]. Zhang et al. [27] analyzed an online forum, seeking to identify users with high expertise while ignoring the relevance of documents. The authors in [2] proposed a co-training idea that jointly models the quality of the author and the review. Noll et al. [21] proposed a graph-based method like HITS algorithm, through assigning different weights to link users and documents, for ranking users in a collaborative tagging system. However, most of these works are based on some generalization of PageRank [3] and HITS [14], and ignore the relevance of documents, which are inferior in performance to the state-of-the-art query-dependent expert finding methods.

There are some other related studies for combining heterogeneous information. PopRank model [20] is developed to integrate heterogenous relationships between objects, which showed authority score of one type of objects could be a combination of scores from different types of objects. Zhou et al. [30] proposed a method for co-ranking authors and their publications using several networks. In addition, Sun et al. [25] proposed a ranking-based clustering method for heterogeneous network analysis, which aims at clustering and ranking objects within clusters simultaneously. However, our work is different from theirs, as their tasks are mainly used in query-independent settings, while we focus on expertise ranking on query-dependent settings.

Table 6: The top-10 experts retrieved by BL and JHyp:Author+Doc. Relevant experts are in boldface.

Baseline (BL)	JointHyp
Query: Kernel Methods	
Bernhard Schölkopf	**Bernhard Schölkopf**
Nello Cristianini	**Nello Cristianini**
Alexander J. Smola	**John Shawe-Taylor**
Francesco Camastra	**Alexander J. Smola**
Colin Campbell	Francesco Camastra
Tong Zhang	**Michael I. Jordan**
Stéphane Canu	**Colin Campbell**
Alessandro Verri	**Tong Zhang**
Shotaro Akaho	**Massimiliano Pontil**
Peter Sussner	**Jason Weston**
Query: Probabilistic Relevance Model	
Norbert Fuhr	**Norbert Fuhr**
Stephen E. Robertson	**Stephen E. Robertson**
Friedrich Gebhardt	**W. Bruce Croft**
M. E. Maron	**M. E. Maron**
J. L. Kuhns	**ChengXiang Zhai**
ChengXiang Zhai	**C. J. van Rijsbergen**
C. J. van Rijsbergen	Friedrich Gebhardt
Azadeh Shakery	**J. L. Kuhns**
W. Bruce Croft	**Chris Buckley**
Victor Lavrenko	**William S. Cooper**

[4]The testing hardware environment is on a Windows PC with 2.4GHz CPU and 4GB physical memory.

[5]`http://dx.doi.org/10.1561/1500000019`

[6]`http://en.wikipedia.org/wiki/Kernel_methods`

Our joint regularization framework using graphs is closely related to graph-based semi-supervised learning [32, 29], which usually assumes label smoothness over the graph. These types of graph regularization methods have been successfully applied in topic modeling [19, 6], ad-hoc information retrieval [9], and review quality prediction [17] tasks. Mei et al. [19] extended the graph harmonic function for topic modeling with network regularization. Diaz [9] used score regularization to adjust ad-hoc retrieval scores from an initial retrieval. Although there have been some existing explorations, to our knowledge, the presented work is the first extensive study of a unified graph-based regularization method by explore the heterogeneous network in the field of expertise retrieval.

6. CONCLUSION AND FUTURE WORK

In this paper we studied the expertise ranking problem through modeling and exploiting heterogeneous network together with the textual content information. We formulate three types of hypotheses that capture different information in the heterogeneous network with respect to different types of edges. We not only mathematically model those hypotheses, but also validate them individually and jointly in a regularization framework. The experimental results show that our proposed approach can achieve significantly better results than the baseline and other state-of-the-art models.

The method we propose is quite generalizable and applicable for expertise ranking tasks in social media with heterogeneous network structure, for example, community-based question answering and online forum. In future work, it would be interesting to apply our techniques in these tasks.

7. ACKNOWLEDGMENTS

The work was supported in part by the U.S. National Science Foundation grants IIS-0905215, by the U.S. Army Research Laboratory under Cooperative Agreement No. W911NF-09-2-0053 (NS-CTA), and by two grants from the Research Grants Council of the Hong Kong SAR (No. CUHK 413210 and No. CUHK 415410). The views and conclusions contained in this document are those of the authors and should not be interpreted as representing the official policies, either expressed or implied, of the Army Research Laboratory or the U.S. Government. The U.S. Government is authorized to reproduce and distribute reprints for Government purposes notwithstanding any copyright notation here on.

8. REFERENCES

[1] K. Balog, L. Azzopardi, and M. de Rijke. Formal models for expert finding in enterprise corpora. In *SIGIR*, pages 43–50, 2006.

[2] J. Bian, Y. Liu, D. Zhou, E. Agichtein, and H. Zha. Learning to recognize reliable users and content in social media with coupled mutual reinforcement. In *WWW*, pages 51–60, 2009.

[3] S. Brin and L. Page. The anatomy of a large-scale hypertextual web search engine. *Computer Networks*, 30(1-7):107–117, 1998.

[4] C. Buckley and E. M. Voorhees. Retrieval evaluation with incomplete information. In *SIGIR*, pages 25–32, 2004.

[5] C. S. Campbell, P. P. Maglio, A. Cozzi, and B. Dom. Expertise identification using email communications. In *CIKM*, pages 528–531, 2003.

[6] H. Deng, J. Han, B. Zhao, Y. Yu and C. X. Lin. Probabilistic topic models with biased propagation on heterogeneous information networks. In *KDD*, pages 1271-1279, 2011.

[7] H. Deng, I. King, and M. R. Lyu. Formal models for expert finding on dblp bibliography data. In *ICDM*, pages 163–172, 2008.

[8] H. Deng, I. King, and M. R. Lyu. Enhanced models for expertise retrieval using community-aware strategies. *IEEE Trans. SMC-B*, pages 93–106, 2012.

[9] F. Diaz. Regularizing ad hoc retrieval scores. In *CIKM*, pages 672–679, 2005.

[10] H. Fang and C. Zhai. Probabilistic models for expert finding. In *ECIR*, pages 418–430, 2007.

[11] Z. Guan, J. Bu, Q. Mei, C. Chen, and C. Wang. Personalized tag recommendation using graph-based ranking on multi-type interrelated objects. In *SIGIR*, 2009.

[12] C.W. Hsu, C.C. Chang, and C.J. Lin. A practical guide to support vector classification. In *Technical Report*, 2003.

[13] M. Karimzadehgan, R. W. White, and M. Richardson. Enhancing expert finding using organizational hierarchies. In *ECIR*, pages 177–188, 2009.

[14] J. M. Kleinberg. Authoritative sources in a hyperlinked environment. *JACM*, 46(5):604–632, 1999.

[15] X. Liu, J. Bollen, M. L. Nelson, and H. V. de Sompel. Co-authorship networks in the digital library research community. *IPM*, 41(6):1462–1480, 2005.

[16] X. Liu, W. B. Croft, and M. B. Koll. Finding experts in community-based question-answering services. In *CIKM*, pages 315–316, 2005.

[17] Y. Lu, P. Tsaparas, A. Ntoulas, and L. Polanyi. Exploiting social context for review quality prediction. In *WWW*, pages 691–700, 2010.

[18] C. Macdonald and I. Ounis. Voting for candidates: adapting data fusion techniques for an expert search task. In *CIKM*, pages 387–396, 2006.

[19] Q. Mei, D. Cai, D. Zhang, and C. Zhai. Topic modeling with network regularization. In *WWW*, pages 101–110, 2008.

[20] Z. Nie, Y. Zhang, J.-R. Wen, and W.-Y. Ma. Object-level ranking: bringing order to web objects. In *WWW*, pages 567–574, 2005.

[21] M. G. Noll, C. man Au Yeung, N. Gibbins, C. Meinel, and N. Shadbolt. Telling experts from spammers: expertise ranking in folksonomies. In *SIGIR*, pages 612–619, 2009.

[22] J. M. Ponte and W. B. Croft. A language modeling approach to information retrieval. In *SIGIR*, 1998.

[23] E. Smirnova and K. Balog. A user-oriented model for expert finding. In *ECIR*, pages 580–592, 2011.

[24] I. Soboroff, A. de Vries, and N. Craswell. Overview of the TREC-2006 enterprise track. In *Proc. of TREC 2006*.

[25] Y. Sun, Y. Yu, and J. Han. Ranking-based clustering of heterogeneous information networks with star network schema. In *KDD*, pages 797–806, 2009.

[26] C. Zhai and J. D. Lafferty. A study of smoothing methods for language models applied to information retrieval. *ACM Trans. Inf. Syst.*, 22(2):179–214, 2004.

[27] J. Zhang, M. S. Ackerman, and L. Adamic. Expertise networks in online communities: structure and algorithms. In *WWW*, pages 221–230, 2007.

[28] J. Zhang, J. Tang, and J.-Z. Li. Expert finding in a social network. In *DASFAA*, pages 1066–1069, 2007.

[29] D. Zhou, O. Bousquet, T. N. Lal, J. Weston, and B. Schölkopf. Learning with local and global consistency. In *NIPS*, 2003.

[30] D. Zhou, S. A. Orshanskiy, H. Zha, and C. L. Giles. Co-ranking authors and documents in a heterogeneous network. In *ICDM*, pages 739–744, 2007.

[31] D. Zhou, S. Zhu, K. Yu, X. Song, B. L. Tseng, H. Zha, and C. L. Giles. Learning multiple graphs for document recommendations. In *WWW*, pages 141–150, 2008.

[32] X. Zhu, Z. Ghahramani, and J. D. Lafferty. Semi-supervised learning using gaussian fields and harmonic functions. In *ICML*, pages 912–919, 2003.

Live Television in a Digital Library

Maxime Roüast
University of Waikato
Hamilton, New Zealand
max@cs.waikato.ac.nz

David Bainbridge
University of Waikato
Hamilton, New Zealand
davidb@cs.waikato.ac.nz

ABSTRACT

The number of channels of digital television is increasing, particularly the number that are free-to-air. However due to the nature of broadcasting, this morass of information is not, for the main part, organized—it is principally a succession of images and sound transmitted as multiplexed streams of data. Compare this deluge that terrestrially bombards our homes with the information available in the digital libraries we access over the Internet—stored using software purpose built to help organize carefully curated sets of documents. This project brings together these two seemingly incompatible concepts to develop a software environment that concurrently captures *all* the available live television channels—so a user does not need to proactively choose what to record—and segments them into files which are then imported into a digital video library with a user interface designed to work from a multimedia remote control. A shifting time-based "window" of all recordings is maintained—we settled on from the last two weeks so as to be practicably operable on a regular desktop PC. The system leverages off the information contained in the electronic program guide and the video recordings to generate metadata suitable for the digital library. A user evaluation of the developed prototype showed a high level of participant satisfaction across a range of attributes, notably date-based searching.

Categories and Subject Descriptors

H.3.7 [**Information storage & retrieval**]: Digital Libraries

General Terms

Design and Experimentation

Keywords

Video Data Streams; Digital Libraries; User Evaluation

1. INTRODUCTION

Watching television on demand is increasingly common in people's homes [6]. Solutions range from Internet based catch-up TV services such as the BBC's iPlayer to more closely integrated TV solutions such as Tivo. Each of these solutions enrich the viewer's experience, however there are also commercial factors involved that mean there are also deliberate limitations in what is provided. For example, the Tivo system does not allow the recorded content to be directly viewed from (streamed to) another television or computer inside the same house. It also requires a broadband service to receive the 14 days "enriched version" of electronic program guide to operate, even if this information is available for 7 days in a basic form directly from the TV signal [16]; furthermore, the facilities provided in these types of products to support searching and browsing are of a poor quality, given what we know about the importance of these activities from over a decade of research in the field of digital libraries.

Inspired, then, by the capabilities of digital library software as a way to overcome such limitations, this work aims to look beyond what is currently available in the digital set-top boxes of today and explore the full potential—unencumbered by commercial market constraints—of what is possible by exploiting the raw technology. We start this paper with the requirements of the project, followed by a brief overview of the developed software called ReplayMe!, or RM for short. Next, related work (both academic and commercial) that informed our design is identified and reviewed, and the results of performance tests that established that real-time operation was achievable, are reported. In Section 5 we detail the design and provide some examples of the system in operation, followed by the result of a user evaluation study conducted over a 3 month period. The penultimate section places the work in a broader context, and details how it aligns with a digital library content model specifically designed for media repositories, before concluding with a summary of our findings.

2. OVERVIEW

The context to this work is to see what can be developed in regard to organizing and maintaining TV content using a regular desktop PC based in a person's home. More specifically the sought after software environment must operate:

- In real-time;
- Without an Internet connection;

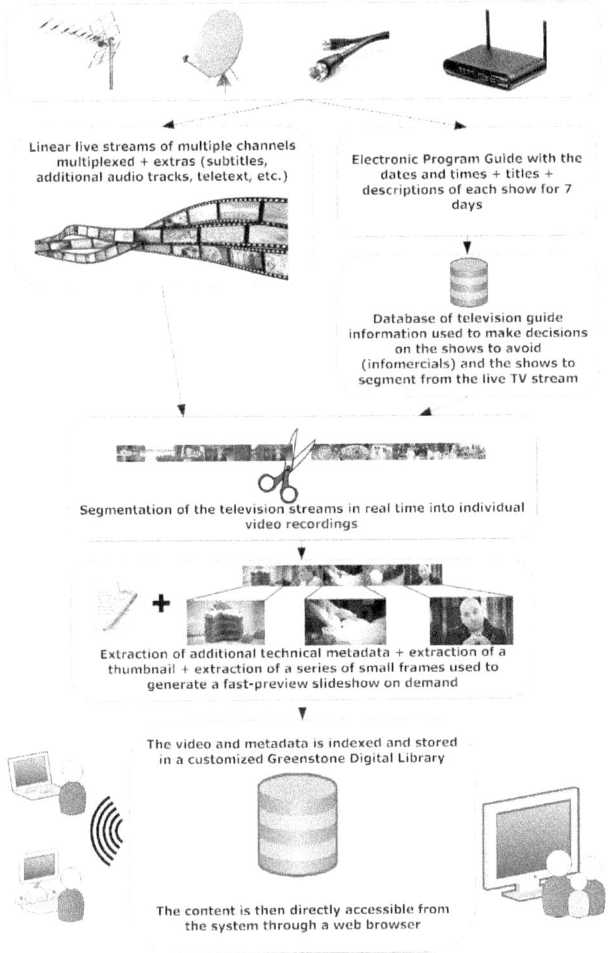

Figure 1: Overview of the ReplayMe! System.

- With continuous recording of all TV channels;
- With automated organization of continuous TV streams;
- Allow manual management of collected TV shows; and
- Allow simultaneous playback from multiple locations within the home, whilst still recording.

The key concept to the envisaged software is one where a user need never think about what to record ahead of time as with other systems. This contrasts with even the latest integrated TV systems where the "season-pass" function—which allows a person to automatically record an entire series of shows—requires the user to proactively select record at the initial stage. Also, to many subscribers' chagrin, the series link information can contain errors that result in missed recordings. In comparison, the approach sought here is a situation where the software is always actively recording, maintaining a shifting time-based "window" of every TV show that has aired in (say) the last fortnight, coupled with the features of the digital library to provide access to—and manage of over time—this rich resource of TV content. Equally, because the envisaged software records all channels broadcast, users no longer need to know which TV company transmitted a show to locate it, unlike the current situation with company-specific Video on Demand web sites.

Figure 1 provides an overview of the ReplayMe! system. The three key components are: the Antenna, the Electronic Program Guide (EPG) and the Digital Library (DL) software. Greenstone was selected for the latter given its flexible architecture and the authors' familiarity with the software. Fedora would have been an equally suitable choice.

The Antenna is the source of all the content coming in to the digital library: this can be a terrestrial antenna, a satellite dish, a cable TV source or even IPTV coming from an ADSL or fiber connected box (if available/desired). The EPG provides information that is used to allow RM to automatically segment the different television channels. It also contains metadata that is used when the content is processed by the digital library software.

Individual channels are continuously de-multiplexed from the video source which RM segments as individual video recordings. In fact, each show is pre-recorded by 3 minutes and post-recorded by 5 minutes in order to make sure that the entire program is recorded even if the broadcaster is not exactly on schedule. There is also the option of using a blacklist that filters the TV shows that should never be recorded—for instance, advertising programs (often called "infomercials") and other unwanted shows like the waiting loops used by the channels that do not broadcast 24 hours per day. This feature effectively lengthens the moving "window" of time that shows can be kept for.

Once finished recording, each individual raw video recording is sent to Greenstone for processing, along with associated metadata that came from the EPG such as the title, descriptions, airing date/time, and the channel name. Through this ingest process the raw content of the video file is also processed in order to extract additional video metadata that is used to determine attributes such as the quality of the video (standard or high definition), and whether subtitles are present or not.

As part of this processing, a series of small pictures (thumbnails) are extracted from the video at regular intervals to create a fast preview slide-show activated on user request. Once the digital library has finished ingesting the recording, all this extra data is used in the web browser based graphical user interface to provide the end user with the maximum details about each video to facilitate searching, browsing and watching.

The video library is accessible directly on the host computer which could be in the living room connected to, say, the main television allowing users to browse and watch their selected program at their own pace. Since the underlying digital library software utilizes a client/server based architecture, it equally allows other computers connected to the home network to take advantage of RM since they can directly stream different television recordings from the host machine simultaneously.

Notwithstanding the real-time operation requirement, in doing all of the above the functional capabilities described encapsulates the project's requirements—indeed, they go beyond what is required. In the case of the household having a broadband connection, then the devised system is capable of providing password protected remote access, should a member of the household be away from home for some reason. In terms of real-time operation, empirical testing is provided in Section 4 to show that this too is satisfied by the design; however, before this we review related work that informed our work.

3. RELATED WORK

In dealing with the "information explosion" authoring and searching tools have been developed that take advantage of the increasing volume of multimedia content [4]. To date, the most efficient methods in terms of accuracy for searching within the video medium remains text-based techniques, often involving manual efforts to write transcripts and other text annotations which is prohibitively expensive for very large collections [3, 7, 8, 12, 13].

This is the approach, for instance, taken by the Open Video DL, with its "Sharium" [9]—the idea being to directly involve the participation of people in order to leverage human time (resource and effort) to contribute to the digital library, by way of digitizing content, entering metadata, and selecting video surrogates from which to build a storyboard [10]. In comparison, the Informedia project [5] has been exploring techniques that allow for the complete automation of this process: leveraging from (amongst other things) speech recognition applied to the audio streams, and optical character recognition applied to the frames of the video streams to identify (and extract) text. Such video processing algorithms, however, are not perfect and they have high computing requirements, in some cases taking longer than real-time to process a video [2].

The burgeoning area of Video On Demand (VOD) also brings into focus the issues of efficient management, retrieval and rapid video viewing. In reality, VOD systems are about finding mechanisms to access video content often from enormous amounts of data. According to Bolle *et al.*, they should allow the viewers to easily filter out unwanted information instead of being forced to watch video in a linear fashion [2].

Visual summaries, such as the surrogates in the Open Video DL, are an interesting solution to help viewers quickly select a video of interest from a library as they give an idea of what a candidate video is about. They also permit random video access since it gives the user clues on the visual content and possibly the length of the video [2]. As a result, a synergy between text-based and visual searching is beneficial since they both indicate a different description of the same content, although there is still room for improvement in this area [4]. Furthermore, visual summaries also play a key role for bandwidth optimization in digital video environments. In fact, they are usually in low resolution so users can browse with pictorial descriptions quickly, whilst still keeping their bandwidth usage down, before finalizing their video selection to watch in high resolution.

3.1 Discussion

In comparing the aspiration of ReplayMe! with the Open Video DL, a key difference is the target audience: RM is targeting home users whereas the Open Video DL targets mainly educational institutions and the wider public, therefore the number of simultaneous visitors could be significant for the latter while RM only serves members of a family within a home environment. This leads to very different computer requirements: RM must be designed to run on a single residential desktop computer. The Open Video DL in comparison is a heavy weight contender—it leverages the power and storage of distributed servers and a professional production set with enterprise grade tools for processing the new videos.

Although the Open Video DL makes use of clever video surrogates with undeniable benefits for the users seeking video content, it does not have a real-time requirement and the generation of these interesting metadata enriched features are still a lengthy and manual process for some parts. On the other hand, RM needs to cope with a continual flow of new recordings from multiple TV channels and needs to be able to process them in real-time to avoid an exponentially growing queue of recordings waiting to be processed. As a result only the minimum of processing for each video file can be afforded in RM, ideally using the most efficient methods available, without requiring any human intervention at any stage.

The Informedia Digital Video Library (like the Open Video DL) is an equally impressive project which has demonstrated that "previously inaccessible data can be derived automatically and used to describe and index video segments" [14]. However, unlike RM and similar to the Open Video DL, their project was not required to operate in real-time. In their design this permitted them to use large vocabulary sets for voice recognition and computationally intensive algorithms for video processing [15].

The Informedia Digital Video Library project is similar to RM in the fact that they are both designed to operate fully automatically. In their "News On Demand" collection, only the news stories from Cable News Network (CNN) were recorded. This left sufficient time between each recording to allow the application of several computational intensive video and audio processing techniques, although even here some of the operations were parallelized on several machines to decrease the time required for processing [14]. The ReplayMe! project, in comparison, has different requirements as it should be able to operate considerably faster than real-time in order to process all the newly recorded TV shows on several channels simultaneously on a single desktop computer. Still, it is irrefutable that the results from state of the art processing used by the Informedia project to get enriched metadata are a true advantage when it comes to searching within videos.

3.2 Commercial Approaches

In terms of commercial solutions, in the introduction we cited some limitations of set-top boxes as one of the factors that motivated this work. Beyond the limits deliberately put in (ostensibly) for market reasons, searching in particular is poorly represented. While the MySky system boasts this feature, for example, it turns out to be nothing more than support for searching for programs by title starting with an *initial* letter, resulting in all the matching shows in the EPG being listed alphabetically. The user is left to page through the list, which in the case of searching by the letter "T" includes all the shows starting with the word *The*. The EPG guide typically contains a week of TV show listings from 40+ channels, making the returned lists tediously long to page through (even for letters of the alphabet other then "T"!) and this search feature is only available for the complete EPG guide. There is no way to limit the search to a subset (e.g., only search shows that are on that day, or that the user subscribes to), nor is possible to use the feature to search other groupings of shows in the system, such as the set of shows the user has recorded.

Moving on from set-top boxes, Personal Video Recorders (PVRs) is the name given to software solutions that run on a PC that allow people to watch live television and record any show with a click of a button. There are many options

	Encoding only		Encoding + De-interlacing filter	
	Encode duration	Speed Δ	Encode duration	Speed Δ
SD sample Duration: 00:12:02	00:03:35	3.3x real time	00:04:55	2.4x real time
HD sample Duration: 00:11:34	00:07:30	1.5x real time	00:10:32	1.1x real time

Table 1: Time elapsed during transcoding and filtering video samples to H.264.

available, both commercial and open source. The Microsoft Windows Media Center (WMC) is perhaps the best known example of this type of software, and has been bundled with the company's operating system since Windows Vista. Like the set-top boxes, however, users still need to remember to record shows beforehand in order to watch them at a more convenient time

Stepping up a gear to technical solutions that continually record multiple channels there are a few projects that meet this criteria. The solution provided by the company SnapStream is representative of these. The delivered solution makes use of rack-mounted servers to record the multiple TV broadcasts. The servers are also responsible for extracting text from any closed captions contained in the transmissions, which is then made available to the end user for searching purposes. However, this capability comes at a price, quite literally. A basic install of a SnapStream server (10 channels recorded), for instance, costs roughly US $50,000, going up to over US $100,000 for a solution capable of recording 50 channels and running on equipment roughly the size of a household refrigerator. Customers, not surprisingly, are large scale organizations. In terms of the requirements for this project, clearly these costs (and equipment size) are not compatible with a solution for the home. We return to this point and discuss it further in the conclusion.

4. PERFORMANCE TESTING

To meet the real-time requirement for this project a series of performance tests were conducted to establish what was achievable in real-time, from which a system design could then be developed. The two key experiments were: the time required to convert TV broadcast signals to a form suitable for streaming; and the CPU load when recording multiple channels at the same time.

Table 1 shows the time taken using an Intel Core i5, 3.33 GHz PC running Windows to convert both Standard Definition (SD) and High Definition (HD) formats to a low-bitrate H.264 format suitable for Internet-friendly streaming to a web browser. This experiment highlighted the high computational cost to achieve the required transcoding and filtering: SD was only 2.4 times faster than real-time, with HD, at 1.1, barely faster than real-time.

Clearly this does not scale well to the recording of multiple channels of live video streams at the point of arrival to the PC. To counter this, from the principle that (in the vernacular) "disk space is cheap" this lead to the decision to avoid any conversion of the incoming video signal (other than demultiplexing it) and import this raw data directly into the video collection. This has the benefit of preserving every sub-stream associated with the video such as the subtitles, multiple audio tracks and most importantly the video quality is kept at its best. It also fitted nicely with the option of a household having a local area network, as the data rate of the video could comfortably be transmitted over this sort of network, allowing a user to view content in different locations. Returning to the case of a family member accessing the digital library when away from home, a corollary to the conversion experiment is that it does show that there is capacity for the host computer to convert individual content on demand, if needed.

In terms of disk storage, recording a Standard Definition channel—720 × 576 pixels, 25fps (4Mbps)—takes 43.2GB per day, or slightly over 300GB to store a week; a High Definition channel—1920 × 1080 pixels, 25fps (10Mbps)—108GB per day, or 756GB to store a week. Freeview|HD (the digital TV channels available to us for our experiments) at the time when this work was undertaken was comprised of 3 HD and 13 SD channels. It would require about 12TB of hard disk space to be able to record all these channels for a fortnight without interruption. However taking in account the fact that not all channels broadcast 24 hours a day, and that some of these channels are duplicates of other channels, but in SD or delayed by an hour in transmission, we have shown—choosing the SD version in preference to the HD ones—that the required disk-space needed can be reduced to roughly 6TB.

For our next performance test we sampled the CPU load over a 15 minute period, first simultaneously recording 4 channels, then 8, then 16. Predictably the 16 channel test yielded the highest load, however, in contrast to the conversion test, this process utilized minimal processing, with a maximum peak of 5.05% of the computer's CPU.

This was a useful result as it meant there was a comfortable margin of CPU capacity in which to perform the other two key point-of-recording tasks—namely, extracting a sequence of thumbnails from a completed program, and then incrementally ingesting it into the digital library. Figure 2 shows in flowchart form how these two processes interact, where a two folder system is used, with an optional queuing mechanism for when a program being recorded finishes, but the Greenstone digital library is busy ingesting another recording, and cannot process it immediately. Each time a Greenstone ingest operation completes, it checks the Video Queue, and if there are any outstanding items in the list a new ingest operation is initiated.

5. DESIGN AND IMPLEMENTATION

We now turn our attention to the implementation of ReplayMe!, and detail the salient points to its design. As noted previously, this was informed by our review of related research, tempered by the project's requirements. Even with the initial performance testing to establish if real-time operation was practicable (Section 4), this requirement was ever pressing as the technical development proceeded; however, ultimately it would always be the user interface developed that would hold the key to whether or not the delivered application was successful or not. We therefore also include in this section some sample snapshots of the developed interface, in preparation for presenting the results of its evaluation in Section 6.

As the overview to RM shown in Figure 1 depicts, the starting point to the software is the processing of the live

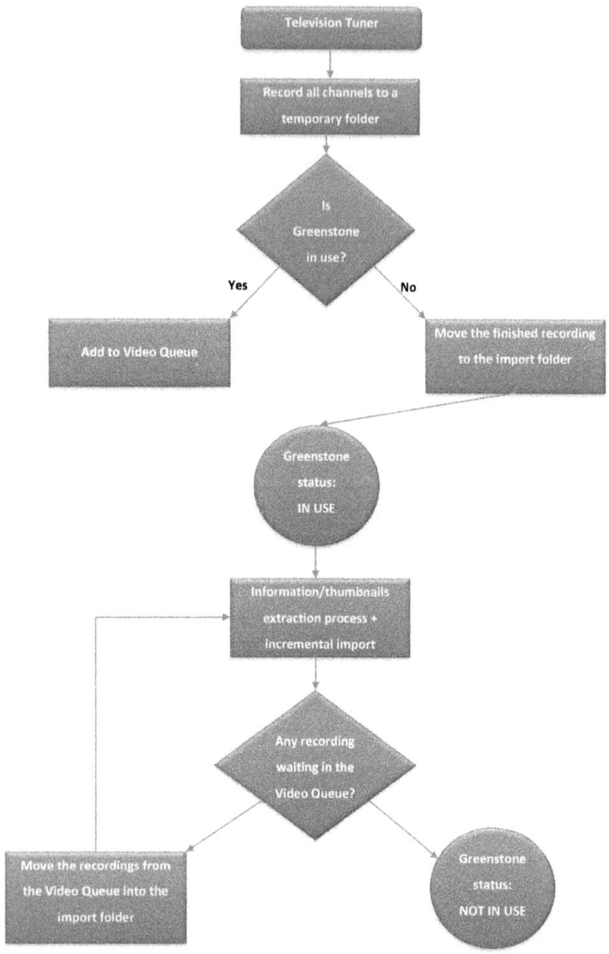

Figure 2: ReplayMe!'s recordings queuing system.

TV signals captured by the digital tuners. In our implementation this was accomplished by repurposing PVR software MediaPortal—an open source home media center software solution principally designed to allow users to watch free-to-air TV on their PC—through its extensible plugin architecture. By encapsulating the work within MediaPortal a benefit that came for free was that our developed software also works in any of the major TV zones around the world, without modification.

A common practice in existing TV decoding-capable software, such as Microsoft's Windows Media Center, is to dedicate one tuner per channel recorded. While conceptually simple, this mapping is highly wasteful given how digital TV is broadcast, and in fact would render the whole ReplayMe! project impractical as it would require 8 dual tuners to capture all the necessary channels, when a general purpose PC typically only has 4 PC slots.

Fortunately given the way TV signals are multiplexed, there is a way to achieve a far more effective utilization of the hardware resources available. Figure 3a shows the approach we devised, which yields the optimal mapping of TV channels to hardware tuners. The key is to spontaneously re-evaluate the set of options available based on a user's selection and display this immediate to the user through visual updates in the interface—a classic principal of HCI design [11].

More specifically, the interface displays two lists of channels on the main tab of its configuration pane as pictured in Figure 3a. As each selection is made, RM tests all the non-selected channels remaining in the left-hand list to find any channels that cannot be physically recorded due to both the user's selection and the tuners' configurations, and these are grayed out from the list of available channels. If a tuner is already committed to demultiplexing a signal that the newly selected channel is carried by, then the system assigns it to that tuner. In the case of the test PC used in our user evaluation experiment, which was equipped with two dual digital TV tuners, only 3 of the 4 digital tuners are needed using this approach to capture the 16 free-to-air satellite TV channels available, leaving one tuner free to extract the Electronic Program Guide.

With the channels selected, all that needs to happen to start ReplayMe! is for the user to press the "Start Recording" button. Before this, they might choose to visit the Blacklist tab to register shows that should not be recorded, but this is optional. The user is even free to quit the MediaPortal application if they so desire as the activated process is designed to run as a Windows service. It is this service that is responsible for instigating the incremental rebuilding of the digital library once a recording is finished (subject to the queuing algorithm described above).

Moving on to the digital library interface, Figure 4 shows the browsing capability of the system, based on the titles of the programs recorded. Using existing capabilities of the digital library software, browsing has been configured to pass over lead words such as "The" when alphabetically sorting. When more than one program of the same title is recored, they are grouped under a folder, sorted by time of broadcast. A thumbnail from the recording is shown, along with summarized textual metadata including when and on which channel the show was broadcast, and how long the recording is. The extraction process for the thumbnail used a simple fixed position value, so as to operate within the real-time requirement. After some experimentation to increase the chance of getting a relevant image describing the content, the extraction position was set at 35%. Boolean metadata such as whether the show was broadcast with closed captions (CC), or in SD or HD are displayed graphically using pictorial representations commonly encountered in connection with TV content. Hovering over the thumbnail instigates a "flick through" storyboard to be shown. Clicking on the thumbnail starts the show playing (explained in more detail below).

This figure is also useful for orientating ourselves with what other functionality is available in general in the digital library. For instance icons next to each recorded show allow the user to manually specify if the show should be deleted immediately (click on the trash-can), or permanently kept (click on the padlock) even when the date of the broadcast exceeds the shifting time-based window of recordings. More global versions of these operations (delete all, keep all) are accessible through the recurring header section to the pages served up from the digital library, along with access to user preferences, help information, and a return to the home page link.

Interaction with the web interface can be done directly with the PC (keyboard and mouse), through a multimedia

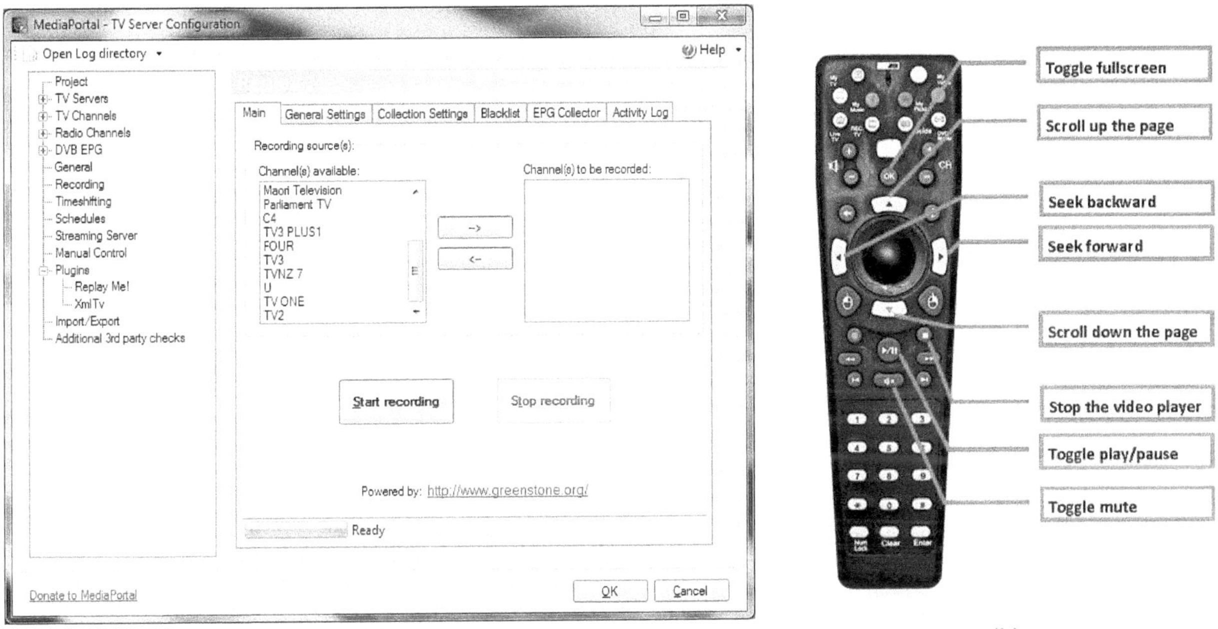

(a) (b)

Figure 3: Priming and accessing ReplayMe! (a) Selecting the channels to record through the MediaPortal plugin (b) the mapping of interface functionality to a multimedia remote control.

Figure 4: Browsing content in ReplayMe!

remote control such as the one shown in Figure 3b, or using a tablet-based universal remote App; the latter two being more convenient choices in terms of portability/mobility.

Viewing a video has the usual navigation features found in a web-browser video player—play or pause, mute, toggle full-screen, seek forwards or backwards, and a time-line within which a user can randomly seek to a new part of the program—as shown in Figure 5. When a user closes the video player, if it is partway through showing a program, the current position is remembered (stored as metadata accompanying the document in the digital library) and used to resume playing from that point in the event the user returns to this show at a later date. This echoes the functionality found in set-top boxes such as MySky.

Figure 5: Viewing a show.

Of note in this area of the system's design, the underlying video player technology used is not Flash-based as in most other systems, as this solution does not have the ability to play the transport streams generated by demultiplexing the TV signals. Instead, a native video player solution based around the open source video player VLC was used, embedded as a web browser plugin.

Originally in our design we chose to open up the video player at a conservative size (smaller than full-screen, so the user would be aware of the context to this operation). From our pilot study we quickly learned that users were frustrated by this, and would immediately toggle the player to be full-screen, and so we switched the default to full-size. Such a default differs from most video websites, such as YouTube, where the majority of the content is in a lower quality than that stored in RM for reasons of bandwidth. In contrast to this situation we have high quality records and (effectively) no network bandwidth concerns within the home, so as one of our participants put it, if you are going to watch a show using the system "why wouldn't you want to view it full size by default?"

In Figure 6 we see the searching interface in action. The top part of the page solicits fielded information by which to search: title, keyword, notes, and so forth. To reduce the likelihood of data entry errors whilst at the same time promoting recognition rather than recall [11], the entry of values such as dates, times and TV channel were done through interactive widgets. For instance in the case of entering a date, these were ultimately displayed "long hand" to the user, but in a read-only format; clicking on such a field results in an interactive calendar picker appearing (similar to the ones encountered on hotel booking sites, for instance) through which the required date can be selected.

In guiding the development of this part of the interface, a set of scenarios were developed. Examples that motivated the implementation of the search capability presented here include:

- A user returns home from work and wants to watch the latest news bulletin. S/he searches the DL by keyword for "news" and sorts the returned results by time.
- A user returning home as before has a similar need, but has a preferred news format they like to watch. S/he constructs the query as before, only this time uses the drop down menu to select the TV station they like to watch the news on.
- A new comedy show, which had aired the previous night, is recommended by a colleague at work to our user. Upon their return home, they perform a title based search to locate the show, and begin watching it. In the event a few episodes of the show have already screened, the user can sort the results by time and start by watching the episodes in chronological order.

The final feature to ReplayMe! we illustrate in this section is its manual metadata enrichment ability of recorded shows. Figure 7 shows the relevant excerpt of the interface, where the user has zeroed in on an episode of *The Simpsons* they have just finished watching. The video is currently marked as uncategorized. This can be changed to: movies, series, cartoons, documentaries, sports, or entertainment at a click of a button. The underlying metadata in the digital library is updated accordingly. Similarly the user can record how much they enjoyed the show by setting a star rating. The graphical element associated with this is a row of stars: initially the stars and sunken empty imprints, however they fill up from left to right as the user moves the cursor over this area of the interface. Clicking when the desired number of stars are showing records the user's rating of the show. As a catch all provision, the user may also type in whatever notes they care to write about the show. All these metadata fields are accessible on the search page, and can be exploited in the formulation of future queries.

6. EVALUATION

To evaluate ReplayMe! a user-study was undertaken. A pilot study was used to trial the procedure before scaling up to the main study. For this, 13 participants were recruited from different backgrounds, with ages ranging from 20 to 65 and over. For each subject, a house visit was made to set up the equipment, and the necessary consent forms signed. In cases where a household had children, the installed system was password protected to prevent access to inappropriate content. Each subject used the system for a week, and completed a questionnaire when the experiment ended. To aid understanding of how a subject utilized RM the installed software was a modified version that automatically logged all interactions with the interface.

Overall, people found ReplayMe! useful and intuitive—in particular its key concept of having everything from all channels accessible anytime was universally liked. Comments made by participants specifically on that point included: "I do not have to think which shows I have to record since everything is already recorded," and "I can watch things I haven't explicitly recorded. This is the best feature." In terms of altering people's existing television watching habits: "I also found lots of other interesting things to watch that I hadn't known were there," and "I could stay longer at work without missing a program." Quantitatively, 62% of participants rated the usefulness of the general system with the top mark of 5/5, 31% of participants rated RM at 4/5 and 7% at 3/5. Most, if not all, of the participants regretted not being able to keep the system.

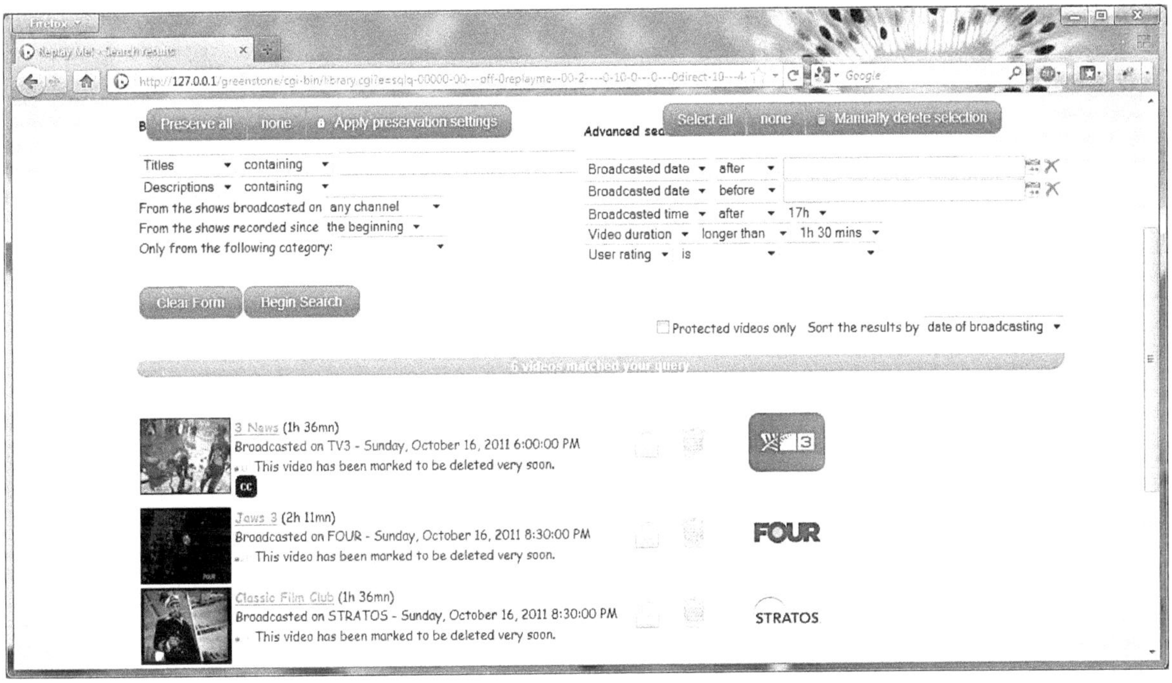

Figure 6: Utilizing the search capability of ReplayMe!

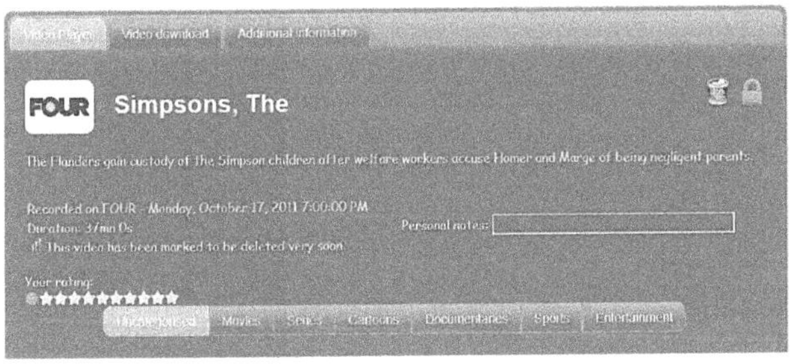

Figure 7: Support for rating, categorizing and annotating with a note.

In terms of the features used within RM, Figure 8 shows how they were proportionally utilized by participants, calculated from the captured activity logs. The fast skipping function, used to precisely skip ahead or backwards for a predefined number of seconds, was by far the most used function. It alone accounts for 62% of usage, and it was frequently used by participants to skip advertisements (1,751 occurrences in total across all participants).[1] The second most used function was video playback with 16%; this shows that people did successfully find their way around the system to locate programs that they considered worth watching. The seeking slider bar on the video player used to directly seek into parts of a recording to find interesting parts was the third most used function accounting for 9% of overall usage. Following this, browsing and searching were particularly close—they respectively accounted for 5% and 4% of overall usage. Pausing the video playback accounted for the final 4% of usage.

The questionnaire was designed to assess the level of satisfaction of the user across the various features to the interface. A Likeart scale was used, ranging 1–5, where 5 represented the highest level of satisfaction. Figure 9 shows a summary of the results. The main functions appreciated by all the participants in order of preference were:

- Resuming the playback of a video from the last known position;
- Keeping the recorded videos until manual deletion;
- Fast skipping forwards and backwards (usually used to skip advertisements);
- Fast selection of a date range in searching (show only videos recorded since the beginning/yesterday/etc.);
- Quick sorting of the search results to only display the recordings that have been manually marked as keep;
- Sorting options during search such as by channel, by date, or alphabetically; and
- Placing video recordings into predefined categories which can then be browsed to (or searched across).

However some other functions appeared to be less interesting to the participants:

- Adding personal notes to recordings,
- Searching videos by duration, and
- Setting a rating for TV recordings.

[1] It is worth noting that it takes several clicks in the interface to skip an advert—for example, for a typical advert break 4 clicks forward for 4 minutes, and then a couple of clicks back at 15 seconds each to home in on the resumption of the show. This, in part, accounts for why this category is so much higher than the other categories.

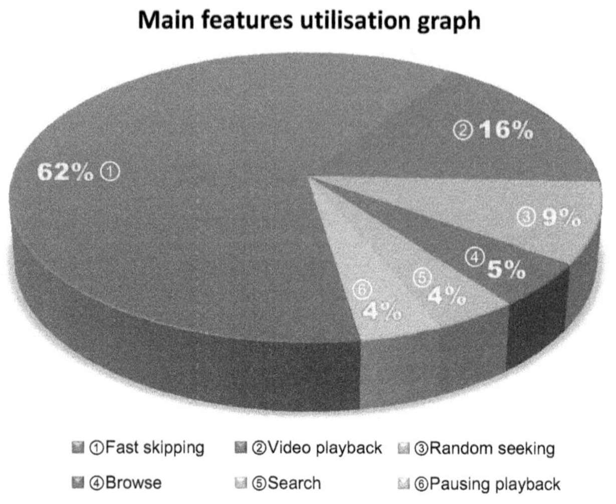

Figure 8: Utilization graph of the main features of ReplayMe! by all the participants.

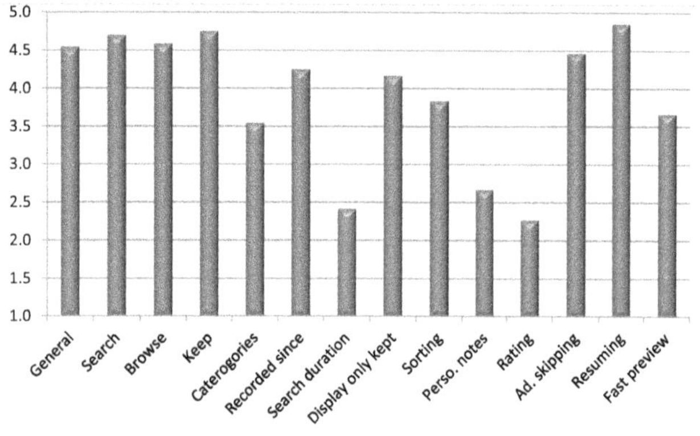

Figure 9: Satisfaction results graph from all the participants.

Most likely, the real situation is more complex as analysis of the global results also shows where some participants found the search by duration function really helpful to find, for instance, movies or main sports events from the digital video collection. This could be an indication that the main goal of this functionality was not clear enough to the target users, and should probably be presented in another way in the future. The data was segmented by age and by gender but no discernible differences were found.

7. BROADER CONTEXT

The work presented in this article has been primarily centered on how the field of digital libraries informed the design and implementation of ReplayMe! For example, techniques developed in earlier video DL research—such as the Open Video DL and Informedia—recur in this work, albeit tempered by the real-time requirement for this project, which was not a factor in the previous work.

In terms of a wider DL context, ReplayMe! fits the content model for media repositories detailed by Beer *et al.* [1]. With respect to this model, the documents in ReplayMe! center strongly on audio-visual material (the video recordings), combined with descriptive/contextual objects (metadata from the EPG, automatically derived metadata from the video content, and manually assigned metadata). The main form of relationships also centers on metadata (such as category, or TV channel), and is used to group together (for browsing) or filter (for searching) lists of items.

Several aspects to the content model simplify as a result of the domain of application being personal video recording. As a side-effect of the logistics and expense of broadcasting terrestrial TV content, there is an implicit provenance associated with the content that is ingested into the digital library. Moreover, because the audio-visual content is homogeneous in nature, a uniform approach to metadata is straightforward to achieve. Finally, while copyright laws vary from country to country, the basic mode of operation of the software is in line with existing internationally acceptable PVR solutions.

8. CONCLUSION

Today, it is clear that watching TV through a device dedicated to the purpose is still a popular choice for people; however, this popular leisure-time pursuit is evolving, the quantity of digital content reaching us is increasing, and the trend for video on demand technologies is growing rapidly, something the current configuration is not well suited to adapt to. Digital set-top boxes go some way to improve the situation—and are even being built-in to newer television sets—but the approach taken still relies on a person perusing the broadcast schedules ahead of time, and actively selecting the items they want to record beforehand. Moreover, these solution often require additional technological to function, such as a 24/7 broadband Internet connection.

Compounding the user experience, existing products intentionally restrict some functionality for commercial reasons, such as not allowing recorded content to be streamed to another location—even if all the owner of the set-top box wants to do is view a show from another location within their house—as this would be a way of the content "leaking" out of the providers closed system, at which point the company would loose control of what the viewer does with it. In addition to this, the organization and maintenance functionality provided is rather impoverished, something that is exacerbated by the increasing volume of content available, especially when compared with what digital libraries have shown is possible.

Motivated by this observation, the work presented here details a practical new approach that provides improved access and control by going beyond what residential digital set-top boxes provide and recording all channels, simultaneously. The approach developed is centered around operation in real-time on a single PC with no Internet connection. Digital library functionality is used to organize, access and maintain the content over time, with the interface redesigned for optional support through a multimedia remote control or tablet interface. For the purposes of experimentation and evaluation the PC acts as a surrogate set-top box—one could easily imagine, in time, the approach being repacked as the latter.

Based on our initial performance testing (reported in Section 4), and further informal tests run we have run with the completed ReplayMe! system, the scaling of the design to record 50 digital channels could still be handled by a single PC. Even with conservative estimates, the required configuration would be met by:

- An Intel Core i5, 3.33 GHz PC (i.e., the same CPU as before);
- 4 dual tuners (a multiplexed signal can carry up to 8 channels); and
- 6 x 3TB HDD in a RAID array (to store 50 standard definition channels for a week).

In many ways the system developed in this project (surprising even to the authors!) competes closely in functionality with current enterprise solutions available (such as the SnapStream server mentioned in Section 3), despite using much more modest equipment. A key difference though is that ReplayMe! does not extract any text from the closed captions. While it is unclear from the information available about the SnapStream solution whether it derives its text from the symbolic or image form of closed captions in the ATSC (Advanced Television Systems Committee) standard used, the trend in broadcasting is towards using the image form since this more naturally supports internationalization. Certainly a fairly straightforward performance test could be devised to see if an OCRing component could be added to the ReplayMe! and still retain its real-time processing capability, but it seems likely that increasing the processor from being a dual-core to quad-core would be a useful, modest adjustment that would go some way to carry the additional load.

In summary, the aim of this project has been achieved since the implementation and user testing of digital library inspired ReplayMe! has indeed permitted us to look beyond what is currently available on the market today and to explore more fully the potential to what the raw technology can provide. Overall, people found the developed software useful and intuitive—in particular its key concept of having everything from all channels accessible anytime was universally liked. The approach essentially frees users from the schedules imposed by broadcasters, and puts them back in control of the choice of the television programs they choose to watch since everything is available locally, on demand, with no loss of quality.

9. ACKNOWLEDGMENTS

We would like to thank the participants of our user-evaluation study for their time and feedback. Our thanks also to the reviewers of this paper for their helpful suggestions.

10. REFERENCES

[1] C. A. Beer, P. D. Pinch, and K. Cariani. Developing a flexible content model for media repositories: a case study. In *Proc. of the 9th ACM/IEEE joint conference on Digital Libraries*, pages 97–100, 2009.

[2] R. M. Bolle, B.-L. Yeo, and M. M. Yeung. Video query: Research directions. *IBM Journal of Research and Development*, pages 233–252, 1998.

[3] J. Bollen. Usage derived recommendations for a video digital library. *Journal of network and computer applications*, pages 1059–1083, 2007.

[4] S.-F. Chang, J. R. Smith, H. J. Meng, H. Wang, and D. Zhong. Finding images/video in large archives: Columbia's content-based visual query project. *D-Lib Magazine*, February 1997.

[5] M. Christel, T. Kanade, M. Mauldin, R. Reddy, M. Sirbu, S. Stevens, and H. Wactlar. Informedia digital video library. *Communications of the ACM*, pages 57–58, 1995.

[6] D. Elsweiler, S. Mandl, and B. Kirkegaard-Lunn. Understanding casual-leisure information needs: a diary study in the context of television viewing. In *Proceedings of the third symposium on Information interaction in context (IIiX '10)*, pages 25–34. ACM, 2010.

[7] D. A. Grossmman and O. Frieder. *Algorithms and heuristics.* Kluwer Academic Publishers, Boston, USA, 1998.

[8] S. Ioannou, G. Moschovitis, K. Ntalianis, K. Karpouzis, and S. Kollias. Effective access to large audiovisual assets based on user preferences. In *Proceedings of the ACM workshop on multimedia*, pages 227–232, 2000.

[9] G. Marchionini. Augmenting library services: Toward the Sharium. In *Proceedings of International Symposium on Digital Libraries*, pages 40–47, Tsukuba, 1999.

[10] G. Marchionini. The open video digital library: A Möbius strip of research and practice. *Journal of the American Society for Information Science and Technology*, pages 1626–1643, 2006.

[11] B. Shneiderman. Dynamic queries for visual information seeking. *IEEE Software*, pages 70–77, 1994.

[12] M.-L. Shyu, S.-C. Chen, M. Chen, C. Zhang, and K. Sarinnapakorn. Image database retrieval utilizing affinity relationships. In *Proceedings of the 1st ACM international workshop on Multimedia databases*, pages 78–85, 2003.

[13] J. Sun, Z. Wang, H. Yu, F. Nishino, Y. Katsuyama, and S. Naoi. Effective text extraction and recognition for WWW images. In *Proceedings of the ACM symposium on Document engineering*, pages 115–117, 2003.

[14] H. Wactlar, M. Christel, Y. Gong, and A. Hauptmann. Lessons learned from building a terabyte digital video library. *Computer*, pages 66–73, 1999.

[15] H. Wactlar, T. Kanade, and M. S. Smith. Intelligent access to digital video: Informedia project. *Computer*, pages 46–52, 1996.

[16] A. P. Wilson. Digital video recording: Personalized television. *Public Libraries*, pages 210–212, July/August 2005.

Transforming Japanese Archives into Accessible Digital Books

Tatsuya Ishihara[†] Toshinari Itoko[†] Daisuke Sato[†]
Asaf Tzadok[‡] Hironobu Takagi[†]

[†]IBM Research – Tokyo
1623-14 Shimo-tsuruma, Yamato, Kanagawa, 242-8502, Japan.

[‡]IBM Research – Haifa
Haifa University, Mount Camel, Haifa HA 31905, Israel

+81-46-215-4978 +81-46-215-4372 +81-46-215-4793 +972-4-829-6533 +81-46-215-4557
tisihara@jp.ibm.com itoko@jp.ibm.com dsato@jp.ibm.com asaf@il.ibm.com takagih@jp.ibm.com

ABSTRACT
Digitized physical books offer access to tremendous amounts of knowledge, even for people with print-related disabilities. Various projects and standard activities are underway to make all of our past and present books accessible. However digitizing books requires extensive human efforts such as correcting the results of OCR (optical character recognition) and adding structural information such as headings. Some Asian languages need extra efforts for the OCR errors because of their many and varied character sets. Japanese has used more than 10,000 characters compared with a few hundred in English. This heavy workload is inhibiting the creation of accessible digital books. To facilitate digitization, we are developing a new system for processing physical books. We reduce and disperse the human efforts and accelerate conversions by combining automatic inference and human capabilities. Our system preserves the original page images for the entire digitization process to support gradual refinement and distributes the work as micro-tasks. We conducted trials with the Japanese National Diet Library (NDL) to evaluate the required effort for digitizing books with a variety of layouts and years of publication. The results showed old Japanese books had specific problems when correcting the OCR errors and adding structures. Drawing on our results, we discuss further workload reductions and future directions for international digitization systems.

Categories and Subject Descriptors
H.3.7 [**Digital Libraries**]: Digital Libraries; H.5.3 [**Group and Organization Interfaces**]: Collaborative computing; I.7.5 [**Document Capture**]: Document analysis

General Terms
Design, Experimentation, Languages.

Keywords
Digital books, crowd-sourcing, accessibility, Japanese digitization.

JCDL'12, June 10–14, 2012, Washington, DC, USA.

1. INTRODUCTION
We all grew up with books. Books are important information sources for our daily lives and for acquiring knowledge right from childhood, and this will not change in the era of digital books. Digital books can allow more people to access this knowledge, including people with print-related disabilities. Problematic disabilities include visual impairments, dyslexia, or even problems in turning the pages. As digital books become more popular, libraries around the world want to digitize their large archives into searchable and accessible digital formats. This is part of their larger dream of reaching a broader range of patrons, such as these people with print-related disabilities.

That is why various efforts have focused on the accessibility of books. The global standard DAISY [1] addresses various needs of people who have print-related disabilities. The general digital book format EPUB [2] was recently updated with accessibility features from the DAISY format to make mainstream digital books more accessible. Such improvements in the key standards may encourage (or even push) publishers around the world to create more digital books that consider accessibility requirements. The grand challenge in this field is our legacy of older books, going back hundreds of years. These are not just piles of old books, but a key part of our cultural heritage.

The holistic view of those activities gives us high expectations for a bright future of accessible books. The main barrier is the workload in the transformation. Even basic text correction and adding non-paper controls for the reading order (which we will describe as "reading order compensation") are often unacceptably time consuming for classic books, especially for languages with thousands of characters (such as Japanese and Chinese) and for books with visually complicated layouts. In addition, digital books should be appropriately structurized with headings, tables of contents, indexes, and references to support navigation. The most useful books should also have appropriate alternative content for images, photos, graphics, and diagrams.

To reduce the workload without lowering the quality of the original books (or even to enhance their presentation) we are working on a digital book transformation system called EBIS (E-Book Improvement System). This system transforms physical books into highly accessible books in four steps: OCR, text correction, structurization, and conversion into various digital book formats.

The subsystems are connected with standard XML to preserve full-page mappings of the characters to the original images. By preserving the mapping of the text and the original image, our system supports gradual refinement of the quality of the digitized books. Whenever participants find apparent errors in the text, they can easily check with the original images. In particular, reading order compensation is much accurate with a visualization method that overlays a text sequence over the original images. The external metadata approach also allows the system to rerun the OCR without losing the current results of the structurization. The system uses a crowd-sourcing strategy for this text correction work, based on reducing the effort for text correction by fragmenting the large task into small chunks.

In this paper, we will review related work and discuss previous approaches for digitization. Then we describe our new approach and the prototype system. The results of trial sessions with the Japanese National Diet Library (NDL) and the workload of digitization are discussed. We consider lessons from digitizing older Japanese books that we learned in our trials. Finally, we discuss the design implications of future digitization systems that can be applied for digitizing books all over the world.

2. RELATED WORK

2.1 Digitization Projects

Public networks have created new possibilities for collaborative digitization. Project Gutenberg [3] is one of the oldest projects where volunteers support to create a collection of digital books. Currently, it has more than 38,000 books. In the initial stages of the project, the text was entered manually. When OCR became available, many new books were digitized by relying on volunteers. The OCR results are collaboratively corrected by Distributed Proofreaders [4], which has greatly accelerated the work. In this system, the verification process is a side-by-side display, with the original image on one side and a text editor with the OCR transcription on the other. The registered proofreaders look at each page of each book to correct the OCR errors. More than 20,000 books have been added this way, and there are more than 1,000 active users. The project originally focused on the textual content without saving the original images.

Bookshare [5] is a collaborative Web service that is creating a collection of accessible digital books from physical books. Volunteers can upload scanned books to the server and registered users can access those books. In 2012, there were over 125,000 books and over 150,000 users. Many volunteers work on the converted digital books to improve the quality of the OCR results. The project started by focusing on the text of each book, and all of the processes are designed for text information. This led to problems when correcting published books. For example, although a text description for a non-textual object is necessary for visually impaired people, Bookshare cannot add metadata for images and diagrams after the digitization process is done because the servers do not retain the original scanned images.

2.2 Distributed Tasks in Digitization

IMPACT [6] is a research project funded by the EU. They developed software tools to improve OCR. One of the focuses of this project is a Web-based collaborative OCR error correction system, CONCERT (Collaborative eNgine for Correction of ExtRacted Text) [7], which became part of our system.

Trove [8] is another Web-based collaborative correction system for OCR results. Users can correct the OCR results from newspapers while viewing the original scanned images. A key feature of this system is that anyone can participate in correcting the OCR results by registering for a user ID, and there is little concern about possible vandalism. This is a trust-based system similar to Wikipedia. This concept is widely accepted, and over 35 million lines were corrected in 2011.

The reCAPTCHA™ system [9] uses minimal OCR error corrections as CAPTCHA tests. In each test, two images of different words are shown to the user, who is asked to type both words. The system has an answer for one word, but is unsure about the other. If the user inputs the correct word for the known word, then the other typed word is used for OCR error correction. This system gains participants by combining the OCR error correction task with an unrelated but similar task for a different purpose. The results of this system are used to support digitization for Google Books™ [10].

Digitalkoot [11] distributes OCR error correction tasks via a different approach. It provides a gaming interface for digitization. It does OCR error correction by matching the results of two types of game. Almost 5,000 volunteers played for over 2,740 hours in seven weeks and completed 2 million tasks.

2.3 Structurization in Digitization

There are digitization projects that add structure information. For example, Chaudhury et al. [12] analyzed the layouts of scanned images of newspaper articles and automatically adds heading information. Also, Liangcai et al. [13] proposed a system to automatically extract structures from a digital book format, PDF. These projects focus on automatically creating structures from scanned images or digital books. There has been other work on creating accessible books from physical books. Tsonos et al. [14] proposed a system to automatically convert a physical book to a Digital Talking Book (DTB) by analyzing the layout to create metadata for the DTB.

Because automatic conversion can inexpensively create nearly accurate content for properly scanned images, book structure extraction is becoming a hot research topic, as shown by the competition at ICDAR [15]. However, it is not realistic to automatically create highly accessible digital books because it is fundamentally difficult to correctly recognize all of the text content and structural information. In particular, older books pose greater difficulties for automatic recognition, because the quality of the older books is lower. For those digitization projects that seek to preserve historical texts as part of our cultural heritage, more accurate transformations are necessary and human efforts are needed to ensure the quality.

2.4 Workload for Japanese Digitization

In [16], the workload to digitize Japanese books for visually impaired people was evaluated. In their experiment, three people who had 3 to 4 years of experience in correcting digitized books used existing OCR software to correct the OCR results for modern Japanese books. Books with graphics, tables, and some English text needed from 25 to 81 minutes for work units of about 13,000 digitized characters. They did not add structures for accessibility, such as links for the tables of contents or for headings. They evaluated the average workload for digitization by these skilled subjects. In contrast, we took a crowd-sourcing approach with non-skilled workers.

3. ACCESSIBLE DIGITAL BOOKS

The goal of this work is to create fully accessible digital books from Japanese physical books of any age with as low a cost as possible. "Fully accessible" indicates that each created digital book includes not only text but also appropriate document structure.

The process of creating fully accessible digital books from older Japanese books faces two major problems. The first problem is the workload of correcting the OCR errors. Some Asian languages, such as Chinese, Korean, and Japanese have the common feature of using many types of characters. For Japanese, the number of characters is over 10,000. Because of this feature of Asian languages, the OCR results include more recognition errors. Also, as books become older, their condition deteriorates, which worsens the results. Meanwhile, these historic books have many archaic characters that are no longer used or that have new forms. Even when these archaic characters are registered in the Unicode table, they are hard to correct because of the difficulty of entering such non-standard characters with standard Japanese input methods.

The second problem is the heavy workload of adding structure information into the digital books. This is a general issue for every language when creating accessible digital content such as a digital book or a webpage. The document structure is important information for assistive technologies such as screen readers [17]. Given the current state of the art, automated algorithms cannot create appropriate structure information. Only human beings can describe good document structures for the digital books.

3.1 Workload

A digital book can be regarded as combining the text information with a rich set of structural metadata. The human workload for this digital book transformation is focused on the creation of the text information and on authoring the metadata. There are six major steps in creating digital books from physical books:

1. Text correction of the OCR results
2. Reading order compensation
3. Add structures for blocks of content
   i. Headings
   ii. Table structures
   iii. Paragraphs
   iv. Foot notes
4. Add structures to support navigation
   i. Table of contents
   ii. References
   iii. Physical page numbers
5. Add descriptions or structures for non-text objects
   i. Alternative text for graphics
   ii. Associated labels for graphic objects
   iii. Convert images to vector graphics
6. Add information for complex text block
   i. Mathematical formulas
   ii. Ruby (pronunciation hints for Japanese characters)
   iii. Sections in other languages

This work inhibits the creation of large numbers of accessible digital books. Publishers can basically ignore most of these steps for image-only digital books. In contrast, if they want a reflowable digital book, one that can adapt to various screen sizes, then they cannot ignore Steps 1-4. Beyond that, Steps 5 and 6 are required for accessible digital books. (See [18] for details about various Japanese-specific text layouts.)

3.2 Accessible Digital Book Format

Various digital book formats exist, such as EPUB or PDF. DAISY is the standard file format that was originally created for print-related disabilities. To provide accessibility features for different types of print-related disabilities, DAISY defines various types of structure information for accessibility purposes [19]. Also, [20] describes the advantages of DAISY over standard audio books for visually impaired people. Because of such advantages, there are already many commercial digital players that support DAISY.

In addition, DAISY is compatible with the major digital book format, EPUB. An EPUB text can be defined with the DTBook part of the DAISY standard. Therefore, we can automatically convert DAISY files to EPUB that can be read by most digital book readers. For these reasons, we decided on DAISY as our output format.

4. EBIS

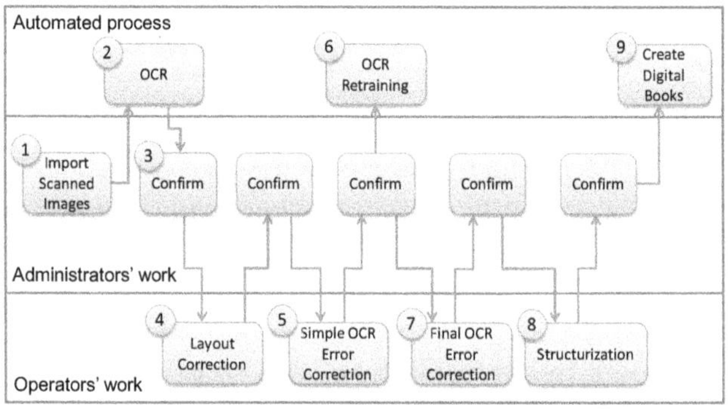

Figure 1. Process of Digitization by EBIS

To achieve the goals described in Section 3, we devised a system called EBIS (E-Book Improvement System) to convert paper books into accessible digital books. Figure 1 is the creation of an accessible digital book with this system. As illustrated in the figure, here are the processes our system uses.

(1) The physical books are scanned into images and the images are imported into the system. (2) The images are processed by an OCR engine to recognize the characters in each page. (3) The administrators check each step of the operators work and each automated process. (4) If the OCR engine does not recognize the page layout correctly, those blocks of text are corrected manually. (5) Operators correct OCR errors. Each task of this step is decomposed down to the character level. (6) The system retrains the OCR engine with these corrections. (7) The operators correct more complex OCR errors such as improperly divided or connected characters and missing or extra characters. Each task of this step is handled at the page level. (8) The operators add document structures as metadata into the digitized text. (9) Accessible digital books are generated from these results.

There are two key characteristics of our system:

4.1 Page Image Preservation

Much of the prior work in major transformation projects simply stripped text data out of the original pages and no links to the images were preserved. In contrast, our system preserves links between the characters and their original locations in the page images. Preserving the full page mappings of characters with original images has two advantages.

First, we can gradually improve the quality of digital books by going back to a previous digitization process at any time and correcting those errors. This feature is especially desirable when digitizing physical books in a language with many characters, such as Japanese, because these books yield more OCR recognition errors. Also, it is useful when creating accessible digital books for various print-related disabilities, because we need to add various kinds and amounts of metadata. In these cases, we need to do lots of work and it is difficult to avoid all human errors. That is why gradual refinement is a realistic approach.

The second advantage of using the page images is that it can decrease the work in various stages of the transformations. Participants can easily check the original page image for suspected errors. Advanced features such as reading order visualization may require the original page images.

4.1.1 Standard for OCR Results

To preserve the page images throughout the process, the ALTO [21] format was used as the internal exchange format. ALTO is a standard XML format for storing OCR results and source images and does not depend on specific OCR software. The system provides an interface to correct the OCR results down to the character level. To do this, we used an extended ALTO format with features to store each character position and multiple candidate characters for that character as determined by the OCR. This extension of the ALTO format was proposed by the IMPACT project.

We added other functions to handle specific Japanese problems. For example, Japanese text can run in several directions besides left to right and top to bottom. Most books actually use a vertical layout, and a few older books even use a right-to-left horizontal layout. To represent these text layouts, we defined a value for writing-mode in the CSS Writing Modes Module Level 3 [22] within ALTO. In our extended ALTO, each text block has a writing-mode attribute for the layout of the text.

4.1.2 Metadata for OCR Results

With a metadata approach, we can reuse the same structural metadata even if the OCR results are updated. We defined external metadata to add structure information to the ALTO files. To store the structure metadata in the repository, we basically used the schema of the Accessibility Commons [23], which was originally defined to improve Web Accessibility. Accessibility Commons is used by Social Accessibility [24] which was developed to improve the accessibility of Web through crowd-sourcing. It uses URIs and XPath to address specific HTML elements. However, applying the same XPath addressing patterns to the ALTO elements is not reliable because elements may easily change. For example, the order of ALTO elements will change if noise regions from the OCR are removed in layout correction. Therefore, for robust addressing of the book elements, we use rectangle regions on the original page images, so that a sequence of characters bounded by a rectangular area is the target of the metadata.

When creating a digital book from metadata and ALTO files in the final stage of digitization, the characters referenced by each piece of metadata are extracted and the metadata is applied to them. Table 1 shows the types of structure metadata used in our prototype, and how it is used in the DAISY file. For the heading metadata, heading levels should also be provided to support hierarchical navigation in DAISY. In the current system, we did not provide functions to add metadata to all of the structures described in Section 3.1.

Table 1. Types of structure metadata used in pilot service

Metadata Type	DAISY conversion
Page number	Remove text content in page number
Running title	Remove text content in running title
Heading	Insert heading tag
Table of contents	Insert table of contents tag
Link source of table of contents	Add link to table of contents tag
Link target of table of contents	Associate link from table of contents tag with heading tag

4.2 Crowd-sourcing

Crowd-sourcing can be used if a large complicated task can be broken into smaller chunks assigned to a crowd of volunteers. Responsibility is not with a specific person, but a motivated volunteer can step up for each task. An advantage of crowd-sourcing is the averaged productivity. By transforming tasks into primitive tasks that use human cognition, the overall productivity can be improved by accumulating the results of simple tasks. Another advantage is that it can collect a larger workforce because more people can participate using small slices of time.

Digital book transformations involve various types of repetitive work, such as correcting texts and adjusting the inferences about the structure information. We want to transform these tasks into smaller tasks that fit a crowd-sourcing strategy.

4.2.1 Decompose OCR Error Correction Tasks

To make the OCR error correction tasks suitable for crowd-sourcing, we separated the OCR correction work into two steps as shown in Figure 1. The first step of OCR error correction (Step 5 in Figure 1) handles only the OCR errors that can be corrected with a simple interface. The operators work on only the results where the character positions were correctly detected. If the character positions are incorrect, then the operators need to merge or separate the character areas. In these cases, they just skip these tasks and proceed to other tasks. Therefore, operators of the first step can focus on simple tasks.

In the second step of OCR error correction (Step 7 in Figure 1), all errors in the OCR results should be corrected. In addition to correcting characters whose locations are correctly detected by the OCR engine, the operators can merge or split character areas that are recognized incorrectly. Also, the operators can add new character regions if the OCR cannot detect them automatically.

4.2.2 Support Input of Japanese Characters

The Japanese language has thousands of characters. Most of these characters are rarely used in modern books, and even educated

Japanese are unfamiliar with them. When typing text in Japanese, people need to know how to pronounce such a character to input the character with a typical Japanese input method. When users do not know how to pronounce a character, they can input the character by using a handwritten character recognition function. Entering characters by using this approach is much slower than entering them by their pronunciation using a keyboard. Because of this problem, we provided two special functions to support the input of Japanese characters in the final OCR error correction step.

First, users can see candidate characters that were nominated by the OCR engine. Even if the final recognition result output by the OCR is the wrong character, the correct answer is often included in the candidate characters. If the correct character is included in this list, users can input it by just selecting the character in the list. This is much faster than using a handwritten character recognition function.

Secondly, we provided a function to see the history of the corrected characters in the same book. Users can input a character by selecting it from this list. Since specific fonts are used in a book, OCR engines tend to repeat the same recognition errors. With this function, users can often avoid handwritten character recognition.

5. IMPLEMENTATION

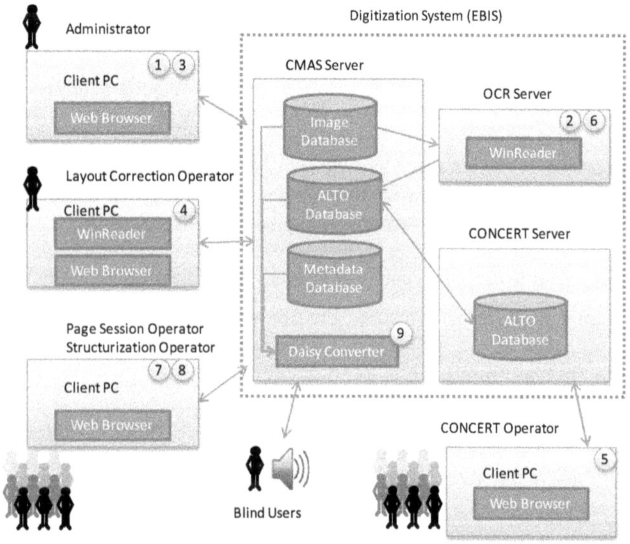

Figure 2. Overview Architecture of EBIS

Figure 2 shows an architectural overview of EBIS. The numbers in right upper corner of the components in Figure 2 correspond to the numbers in the digitization process shown in Figure 1.

From the beginning to the end of the digitization process, EBIS consistently uses the ALTO format for the OCR results. For OCR, we used WinReader Pro v12.0 because it has one of the highest recognition rates in Japanese, and it runs on an OCR server. After OCR processing, the XML files from WinReader are converted to the ALTO format and stored in an EBIS repository.

We also used WinReader to correct the layout for each page. Operators who do layout corrections must install WinReader on their client PC, and download the OCR results to their client. After the layout correction, the operators upload the results of the layout correction to the server.

The first step of the OCR results correction is done by CONCERT [7], which was originally developed in the IMPACT project and designed for English and European languages. CONCERT provides functions to correct OCR error at the character level.

A Collaborative Metadata Authoring System (CMAS) was newly developed to create accessible digital books by applying social computing strategies. CMAS is designed to provide two functions: a function for final OCR error correction at the page level, which we call a "page session" and a structurization function.

After finishing all of the digitization steps, the metadata created by our system is attached to the ALTO file and a DAISY file is created. Users download the DAISY files from the CMAS server.

5.1 User Interfaces

CONCERT provides a simple interface for correction [7]. In each task, a group of characters that is recognized by the OCR as a certain character is shown to an operator as thumbnails. In each character correction session, the character that the OCR selected as the answer is shown. If all of the characters are correct, then the user will see the screen filled with the similar thumbnails. In that case, the user just clicks the submit button and accepts the OCR answers. By leveraging human visual capability, any incorrectly recognized character can be detected with a brief glance. The user selects the incorrect characters and can assign them to a correct classification. The correct answers input by each user are shown above each character image. If there are any characters that users cannot confirm (perhaps due to poor image quality, incorrect character location, or missing parts of the character), they can reject those characters by clicking the mouse on those images. Such characters are not corrected by CONCERT, but the rejected characters will be handled in a page session.

The left side of Figure 3 shows the interface of CMAS that adds structure metadata. Users can add new metadata by selecting a type for the metadata from the toolbar and drawing a box on the page image with the mouse. The gray rectangles on the page image show the reference of each piece of structure metadata. The popup characters next to the rectangular metadata regions show the types of the metadata.

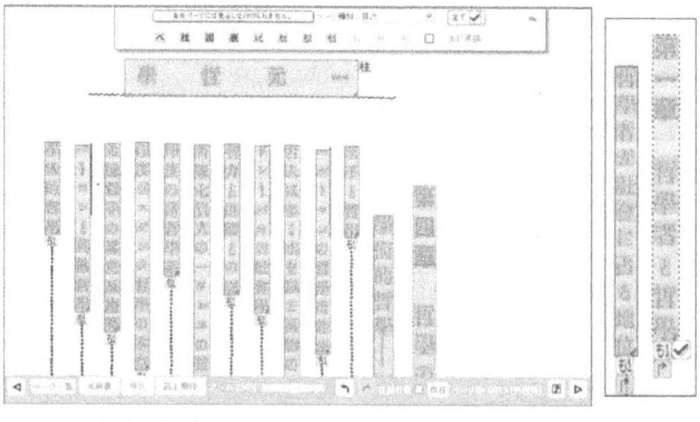

Figure 3. Left: Interface to Add Structure Metadata, Right: Interface to Validate the Automatically Created Metadata

To reduce the workload for structurization, we provided two types of inference functions: Fully automatic (for all six types in Table 1) and manually supported (for page numbers and running titles). The fully automatic engines work by using only the information in ALTO, such as positions of the characters and the text. The manually supported engines run when an operator appends specific metadata to a page and the system infers that the same type of metadata appears on other pages. All of these inference engines use rule-based heuristics, such as string pattern matching. In addition, we use a tuned Viterbi algorithm, which is a dynamic programming algorithm, to infer linkage between headings and the table of contents.

As shown in the right image of Figure 3, a check box is attached to each rectangle of automatically created metadata. If the operator unselects the checkbox, that metadata is validated and used when creating DAISY. If the automatic inference is incorrect, the operator can remove that metadata and add correct metadata.

Our system also provides an intuitive user interface for correcting the reading order of the text (See Figure 4). This interface is based on an interface that was devised for improving the reading order of Web content [25]. The arrows between characters show which characters are read next. Users can change the reading order by dragging and dropping the circles on characters. Modifications of the reading order are also saved as metadata. In addition to the intuitive user interface, we implemented a function to infer the correct reading order. As shown in Figure 4, the reading order can be corrected by inference for typical layouts, and the workload of reading order correction can be greatly reduced.

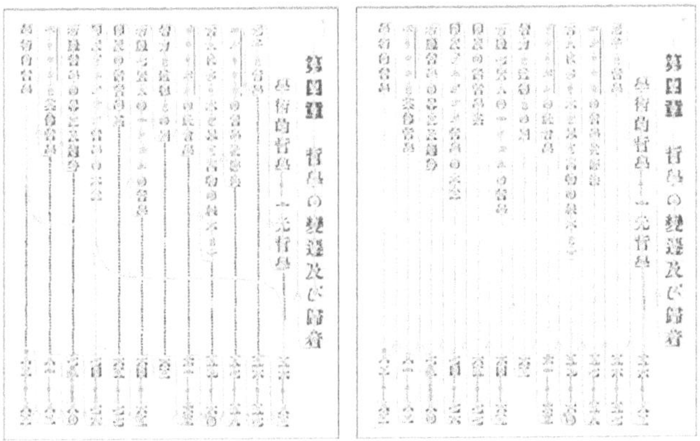

Figure 4. Interface to Correct Reading Order. Left: Original Reading Order, Right: Proper Reading Order

6. EXPERIMENTAL RESULTS

6.1 Settings

We evaluated our system in a trial session lasting approximately one month. More than 21 people participated in this trial period.

In this experiment, we selected data with a variety of layouts and years of publication from 23 books (the years of publication ranged from 1870 to 2003), generally focusing on the first 60 pages of most books (but four small books were completely digitized). The first 60 pages were usually adequate to include the table of contents and some of the main content. In total, we digitized 3,021 pages during this period.

Because the operators doing the layout correction needed to install WinReader on their PCs, this step was not part of the open trial sessions. Only three people worked on this step.

6.2 Workload Evaluation by Different Eras

By analyzing the logged data from the CONCERT server and the CMAS server, we evaluated how much time was needed to digitize books. We also evaluated how the workload depends on the age of the books. Table 2 shows the workload for 10,000 characters averaged for all of the books used in the experiment.

Table 2. Average workload for each step of digitization (hours for 10,000 characters)

	Mean (SD)	Min.	Max.
Layout Correction	0.944 (0.853)	0.096	4.216
CONCERT	4.887 (3.458)	0.908	12.109
Page Session	3.309 (2.271)	0.508	8.564
Structurization	2.456 (1.904)	0.446	6.928

The four charts in Figure 5 show the relationship between the year of publication and the workload for the four digitization steps. In all of the charts, each plot shows the workload for 10,000 characters of one book. The vertical axis is a logarithmic transformation of the hours for 10,000 characters. The horizontal axis shows the year when the books were published.

The top left chart of Figure 5 shows the relationship between the year of publication and the workload of layout correction. There is a moderately negative correlation ($r = -0.670$, $p = 0.0009 < 0.01$) between the year of publication and the log of the workload for layout correction.

The top right chart of Figure 5 shows the relationship between the year of publication and the CONCERT workload. There is a moderately negative correlation ($r = -0.665$, $p = 0.001 < 0.01$) between the year of publication and the log of the CONCERT workload. The older books cause more OCR errors and require more correction time.

The bottom left chart of Figure 5 shows the relationship between the year of publication and the workload in page session. There is a significant negative correlation ($r = -0.796$, $p = 7.9e\text{-}05 < 0.01$) between the year of publication and the log of the workload in

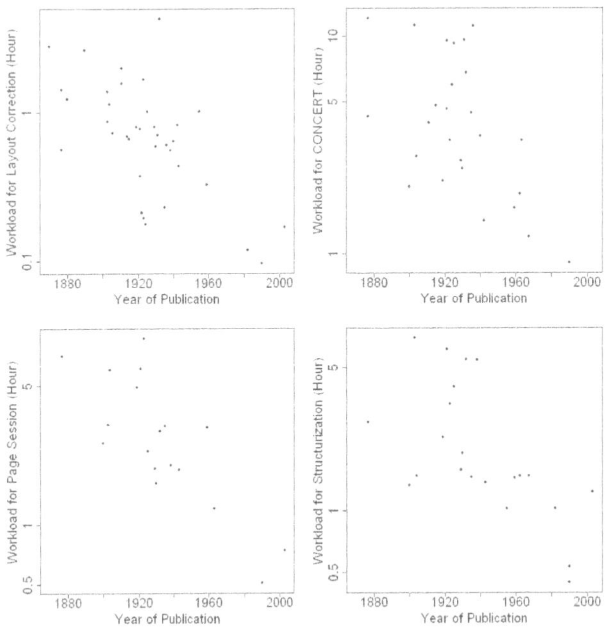

Figure 5. Relationships of Workloads for Each Digitization Step and the Year of Publication (Top Left: Layout Correction Workload, Top Right: CONCERT Workload, Bottom Left: Workload in Page Session, Bottom Right: Structurization Workload)

page session. As with the CONCERT results, the older books need more correction time because there are more OCR errors.

The bottom right chart of Figure 5 shows the relationship between the year of publication and the structurization workload. There is a moderately negative correlation ($r = -0.625$, $p = 0.002 < 0.01$) between the year of publication and the log of the structurization workload. Similar to OCR error corrections, the older books need more time for structurization.

6.3 Estimating OCR Error Correction Workload

Because Japanese has more than 10,000 characters and most of them are rarely used in modern books, we investigated whether the workload for OCR error correction is larger when correcting the less familiar characters. Here, we define the familiarity of characters based on the modern usage frequencies. To collect a sufficiently large amount of modern text, we used Wikipedia. First, we collected all of the Japanese articles from Wikipedia and then we counted the frequencies for all of the characters that are used in Wikipedia articles.

We evaluated the relationship between the familiarity of a candidate character that was recognized by the OCR and the average workload for that character in CONCERT. Figure 6 shows the results. Each plot shows the average CONCERT processing time for one candidate character as output by the OCR. The vertical axis shows the log of the average seconds per character for all of the books. The horizontal axis shows the log of the character frequencies for all of the Japanese Wikipedia articles. There is a weak negative correlation ($r = -0.311$, $p = 2.2e{-16} < 0.01$) between the per character CONCERT workload and the character familiarity. Although the correlation is not significant, this result indicates that if the candidate character that the OCR recognized is an unfamiliar character, the users naturally seem to need more time to correct or validate it.

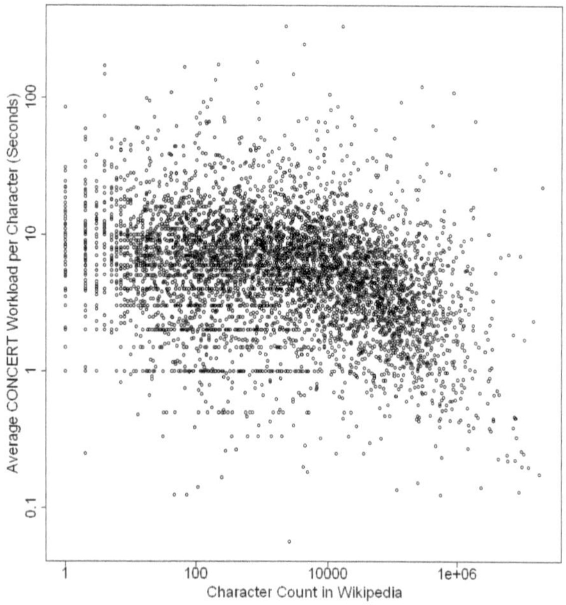

Figure 6. Relationship of Character Familiarity and CONCERT Processing Time

6.4 Estimating Structurization Workload

We also evaluated the structurization workload of each page for the different page types. In our prototype, the users need to add metadata for a page type for each page before its structurization. We defined five metadata labels for page types: Toc (a table of contents), Text (main text content), Title (title page of a book), Blank (page without text content), Other (other pages such as front or back matter).

Figure 7 shows the workloads for each page type. The vertical axis shows the log of the average seconds per page for all of the books. Repeated ANOVA analyses revealed significant differences between the average workloads for the five page types ($F(4,882) = 73.487$, $p < 0.010$). The Tukey HSD post-hoc test revealed that the average workload for table of contents pages was significantly larger than for any other page type ($p < 0.05$), and the average workload for blank pages was significantly smaller than for any other page type ($p < 0.05$).

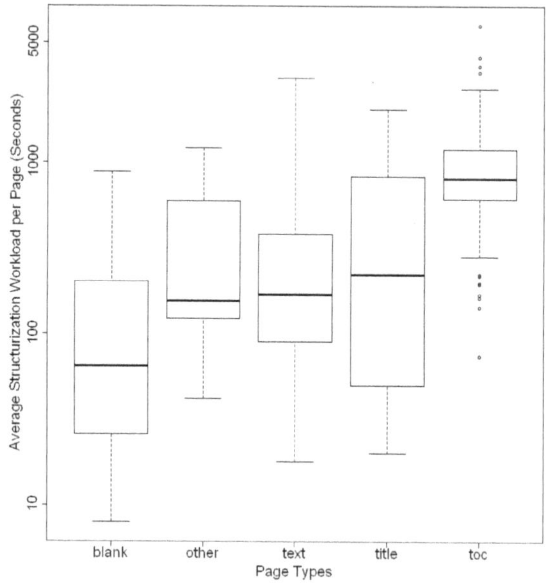

Figure 7. Time to add structure metadata for different types of pages

7. DISCUSSION

7.1 Workload Estimation for Entire Archive Digitization

The results showed us several factors that may strongly affect the workloads for digitization, but many factors remain uncertain. Therefore, in this section, we will discuss what we learned in the trial, and what should be done in the next phase to estimate the workload and reduce it.

The results in Section 6.2 showed a constant increase of workload according to the book's age. The result in Section 6.3 showed that the familiarity of characters affects the workload for OCR error correction. The results in Section 6.4 showed that the structurization workload differs for various page types.

These results are still statistically unreliable as the basis of a model to estimate the workload for the digitization of the entire archive. To reduce the error variance of the estimation model and to make the estimation results more consistent, we need to tackle two main areas.

Make the system more mature

The immaturity of the prototype system increased the variance of the results and limited the statistical significance. For example, the interface for Kanji-character searches could not be structured clearly because of a lack of base tools. The instructions were insufficient for many of the cases found in this broad range of historic books. Possible improvements appear in Section 7.2.

Parameterization of factors

The factors for analysis were limited because our parameterization was not sufficiently systematic. Such factors as paper quality, font faces, grammatical differences, and special layouts can all affect the workload, but we could not keep track of these factors for correlation in our analyses and could not attempt to define them with parameters. We will discuss this problem in Section 7.3.

7.2 Additional Workload Reduction

Inference Improvements

As our experimental results show, structurization requires a great deal of work, even though we evaluated only a limited set of structure information. Improving the function to automatically infer the structure of books could drastically reduce the workload for structurization. In our experiment, we used a rule-based approach and noticed several areas where major improvements can be possible.

Adaptive OCR

To reduce the workload for correcting the OCR results, improving the OCR recognition rate would have a direct positive effect. We are planning to investigate how we can improve the OCR recognition rates by adaptive training of the OCR. In addition, it may be possible to reduce the workload for OCR error correction by skipping past sufficiently similar errors, as described in [26].

Interface Improvements for OCR Error Correction

Another major improvement area is the exploration for the correct Kanji characters. As shown in Section 6.3, old books include rarely used characters that cannot be found without spending some time with the tools of our experiment. More efficient tools for character selection may effectively reduce the workload.

In English and other European languages, many OCR correction systems support word-level correction for higher efficiency. In some Asian Languages, such as Japanese and Chinese, words are not separated by spaces. As long as we have grammatically correct sentences, we can automatically separate the words with high precision by using natural language processing techniques. Unfortunately, such automatic word parsing does not work well if there are OCR errors. We want to study if automatic word separation combined with word-level correction could reduce the total workload for an improved system.

Improvements for Interface for Structurization

As shown in Section 6.4, the structurization of the table of contents required an especially large effort. In addition to improving automatic inference for structurization, we are considering ways to improve the effectiveness of the manual corrections for these pages. To add the structure for a table of contents, the operators need to move back and forth among the pages while adding links from the table of contents to the headings in other pages. Currently, our system provides an interface that views the structures on one page at a time. We believe that summarization or visualization techniques that can show the structures across different pages will help to reduce the workload.

Crowd-sourcing of Structurization

Our system provided two different levels of interface for the OCR error correction tasks (character-level and page-level). There were favorable comments about the simple and intuitive interface for the OCR error correction at the character level. In contrast, in our trial sessions we provided only a page-level interface for the structurization tasks and received feedback that the structure interface was too complex and had too many functions. Because most participants are not familiar with accessibility, they feel embarrassed at not knowing what they should do first.

We are investigating methods for crowd-source structurization work by utilizing inference engines. In the same way as CONCERT, it will be possible to create easy and small tasks by showing lists of structure information that were detected by an inference engine. If we can create such an interface, users will only have to accept or reject the automatically created structural metadata. To make this interface effective, we need to improve the performance of the inference engine. We are testing a new service using a crowd-sourcing interface for structurization, and we have received more favorable feedback.

Crowd-sourcing of Administrative Work

In our experimental results, the workload for the administrator was not included, but this workload is important in a large digitization project. Administrators prepare scanned images and check that the images were imported correctly. Also, an administrator should confirm the completion of each digitization step. We handled this work in these experiments, but we are considering how to crowd-source some of that work, too. Crowd-sourcing some of administrative tasks is done in other collaborative systems, such as Wikipedia. Ways to support the administrators' work should be considered in the future.

7.3 Methods for Further Parameterization

As mentioned in Section 7.1, in order to analyze the influence of various factors on the workload, several factors should be converted into measurable numerical parameters to develop a model for workload estimation. But we have following technical challenges to parameterize various factors.

Grammar

Written grammar tends to evolve over the years. The differences may affect automatic OCR error correction that uses grammar checks within the OCR engines. In addition, the difference from modern grammar can affect the human correction process, since additional time may be needed to understand the target text that was initially unclear. We need to develop technologies to detect such grammatical differences and their characteristics to parameterize this factor.

Paper Quality

The quality of paper clearly affected the accuracy of the OCR results, and this may be one of major factors that increased the workload for older books, as observed in Section 6.2. Statistical image quality metrics, such as [27] can measure this factor.

Font Faces

The text styles also directly affect the OCR accuracy, and [28] showed that OCR recognition is improved by considering style consistency over each text block. We think style consistency for entire books could help estimate the workload.

Uniqueness of Layouts

The layouts of books have evolved over time, and classic books include various types of layouts that are not seen in modern books. This affects the structurization workload, such as for the reading order compensation.

Text Direction

In Japanese, right to left, left to right, and top to bottom are all used in certain books. When alphanumeric characters are included in vertical layouts, these characters are rotated 90°. (See [18] for details.) OCR recognition rates are affected by such special layouts, and we have to consider this factor.

Skill of Operators

Variations in the skills of the operators affect the performance. For example, typing speed and knowledge of archaic characters directly affect the performance of OCR error correction. Even for the same operator, the performance of each step can change with experience.

7.4 Standardization for Asian Languages

To preserve the original images during the entire digitization process, our system used a metadata approach for structurization. We needed a standard file format for the OCR results in our system. There is no standard format that captures both the OCR results and original images for Japanese documents.

The main problems involve Japanese-specific layouts, such as vertical layouts, right-to-left horizontal layouts, and the placement of the ruby characters. The ALTO format is a widely used standard format, so we decided to extend the ALTO format so it can handle Japanese. That work will also be useful for supporting other Asian languages and we will report our results to the ALTO standards community.

There is an active discussion in the EPUB standards community about international language support. The latest release of EPUB enhanced the language support, especially for Asian languages such as Chinese, Japanese, and Korean. Since globalized digital book formats are still immature, there is no truly international OCR format. We believe that adding international language support to ALTO will help digitization projects all over the world.

7.5 Improving the Quality of Digital Books

Through the pilot service, we found that a lot of work is needed for high quality digitization. Even if the operators spend a long time looking for errors, it is difficult to find all of them. One of the key features of our system is that it can gradually improve the quality of digitized books. We are considering how to create a feedback system so that end users could report OCR errors or structure information problems from digital book readers or voice browsers. With such a model, the quality of digitization could be improved because more people could help check for problems.

We also found that an integrated discussion system helps discuss such topics as how to correct specific OCR errors and how to add structure metadata. Especially for the structurization interface, users are often afraid or unwilling to add structure metadata. For example, deciding on a heading level can be difficult. To create consistent metadata for all of the pages in a book, all of the users who are working on that book need to agree on the metadata. A discussion system can support consensus about how to add the structure metadata.

7.6 Lowering the Barriers to Participation

Reducing the cost and time for digitization has a higher priority than just reducing the total workload for digitization. The crowd-sourcing approach is promising for digitization because it can reduce both cost and time, even if the total workload with crowd-sourcing is larger than with another digitization approach. If large numbers of users can work effectively in parallel, then we can drastically reduce the time needed. Also, the crowd-sourcing approach can digitize books with significantly lower costs because recent research shows that people will actively participate in crowd-sourcing tasks for non-monetary reasons [29]. To make crowd-sourcing approach work effectively, we need to investigate ways to gather and motivate more participants.

To encourage more participation, a game-like interface is a promising approach. Gaming interfaces already worked well in different areas, such as OCR error correction and protein folding [30]. We are planning to study a game-like interface for structurization.

Simple interfaces also attract participants by making it easy for novices to join in the work. Such systems can also create job opportunities for older people who are not experts with computers. For digitizing historical texts, the special knowledge of older people can be especially valuable, since they may be more familiar with older styles of characters and expressions.

7.7 Evaluating Digital Book Quality

In this research, we evaluated the EBIS from the operators' perspective. But the value for the work should be evaluated by the output quality. Therefore, one of obvious next steps should be an evaluation of the effectiveness of the system from the readers' perspective. As discussed in Section 3.2, DAISY can be used as an accessible digital format for print-related disabilities. However, it is almost impossible to create an accessible and error-free digital book because humans are needed for the OCR error correction and structurization. For practical purposes, people with print-related disabilities can read digital books well enough even when those books include a few errors. Going forward, we need to study the quality level that these users find satisfactory. Also, the set of structure information that was used in our experiment was limited. We want to study what structure information is most essential for readers with print-related disabilities.

8. CONCLUSION

In this paper, we proposed a new approach to a collaborative digitization system. The page images and text overlays are preserved throughout the process to make the correction, structurization and enrichment process easier. Crowd-sourcing techniques were used in the text correction part. We reported on the experimental results of digitization with the NDL. Through this experiment, we confirmed that the proposed system allowed participants to digitize books, even classic books, with relatively low quality scans. The results shows that all digitization systems need more time to digitize older books and older Japanese books have special problems because of their numerous characters. The results also showed that some structure types need more time. We have plenty of room to improve the performance of the automatic metadata creation, and this is an area that could significantly reduce the total costs of digitization.

From these lessons we learned in the NDL trial session, we are testing crowd-sourcing structurization using automatic inference and have received favorable feedback.

Digitization will become a hot topic as many projects work on the full text digitization of all of the books of human history. One of our special foci is on insuring that these digitized results are as accessible as possible. Although we experimented with Japanese books, many parts of our approach will apply to other languages, because many of the problems in Japanese are similar to those found in other languages. The special demands of the complicated Japanese writing system will naturally produce robust tools. We hope our system will be used in other countries, and contribute to preserving the cultural heritages of people everywhere while making them accessible to everyone.

9. ACKNOWLEDGMENT

We thank the National Diet Library in Japan for giving us this valuable opportunity for experimental digitization.

10. REFERENCES

[1] ANSI/NISO Z39.86-2005; http://www.niso.org/workrooms/daisy/Z39-86-2005.html

[2] EPUB; http://idpf.org/epub/30

[3] Project Gutenberg; http://www.gutenberg.org/

[4] Newby, G. B. and Franks, C. 2003. Distributed proofreading. In *Proc. of the 3rd ACM/IEEE-CS Joint Conf. on Digital Llibraries.* JCDL '03, IEEE Computer Society, 361-363.

[5] Bookshare; http://www.bookshare.org/

[6] Balk, H. and Conteh, A. 2011. IMPACT: centre of competence in text digitisation. *In Proc. of the 2011 Workshop on Historical Document Imaging and Processing.* HIP '11, ACM, 155-160.

[7] Neudecker, C. and Tzadok, A. 2010. User Collaboration for Improving Access to Historical Texts. LIBER Quarterly, 20,1 (2010).

[8] Holley, R., Many Hands Make Light Work: Public Collaborative OCR Text Correction in Australian Historic Newspapers. National Library of Australia Staff Papers, ISBN 978-0-642-27694-0.

[9] von Ahn, L., Maurer, B., McMillen, C., Abraham, D., and Blum, M. 2008. reCAPTCHA: Human-Based Character Recognition via Web Security Measures. Science, Sep. 12, 2008, 1465-1468.

[10] Google Books; http://books.google.com/

[11] Chrons, O. and Sundell, S. 2011. Digitalkoot: Making old archives accessible using crowdsourcing. *In Proc. of the 3rd Human Computation Workshop.* HCOMP '11.

[12] Chaudhury, K., Jain, A., Thirthala, S., Sahasranaman, V., Saxena, S., and Mahalingam, S. 2009. Google Newspaper Search - Image Processing and Analysis Pipeline. *In Proc. of the 2009 10th Int. Conf. on Document Analysis and Recognition.* ICDAR '09, IEEE Computer Society, 621-625.

[13] Gao, L., Tang, Z., Lin, X., Liu, Y., Qiu, R., and Wang, Y. 2011. Structure extraction from PDF-based book documents. *In Proc. of the 11th Annual Int. ACM/IEEE Joint Conf. on Digital Libraries.* JCDL '11. ACM, 11-20.

[14] Tsonos, D., Xydas, G., and Kouroupetroglou, G. 2007. Auditory accessibility of metadata in books: a design for all approach. *In Proc. of the 4th Int. Conf. on Universal Access in Human-Computer Interaction.* UAHCI '07. 436-445.

[15] Doucet, A., Kazai, G. and Meunier, J. 2011. ICDAR 2011 Book Structure Extraction Competition. *In Proc. of the 2011 11th Int. Conf. on Document Analysis and Recognition.* ICDAR '11, IEEE Computer Society, 1501-1505.

[16] Uemura, K., Yamaguchi, M., Sakurai, S., Kashima, M. 2010. An empirical study on the cost of making text data of books : aiming to improve the reading environment for the visually impaired. Core ethics, Vol. 6, 2010, 37-49 (In Japanese).

[17] Techniques and Failures for Web Content Accessibility Guidelines 2.0, W3C Working Group Note 3 January 2012; http://www.w3.org/TR/WCAG-TECHS/

[18] Requirements for Japanese Text Layout, W3C Working Group Note 4 June 2009; http://www.w3.org/TR/jlreq/

[19] Structure Guidelines for DAISY 3; http://www.daisy.org/z3986/structure/SG-DAISY3/

[20] Leas, D., Persoon, E., Soiffer, N., and Zacherle, M. 2008. Daisy 3: A Standard for Accessible Multimedia Books. IEEE MultiMedia 15, 4, Oct. 08, 28-37.

[21] "Analyzed Layout and Text Object (ALTO) XML Schema", http://www.loc.gov/standards/alto/

[22] "CSS Writing Modes Module Level 3", http://www.w3.org/TR/css3-writing-modes/

[23] Kawanaka, S., Borodin, Y., Bigham, J. P., Lunn, D., Takagi, H., and Asakawa, C. 2008. Accessibility commons: a metadata infrastructure for web accessibility. *In Proc. of the 10th Int. ACM SIGACCESS Conf. on Computers and Accessibility.* Assets '08. ACM, 153-160.

[24] Takagi, H., Kawanaka, S., Kobayashi, M., Itoh, T., and Asakawa, C. 2008. Social accessibility: achieving accessibility through collaborative metadata authoring. *In Proc. of the 10th Int. ACM SIGACCESS Conf. on Computers and Accessibility.* Assets '08. ACM, 193-200.

[25] Sato, D., Kobayashi, M., Takagi, H., and Asakawa, C. 2009. What's Next? A Visual Editor for Correcting Reading Order. *In Proc. of the 12th IFIP TC13 Conf. in Human-Computer Interaction.* INTERACT '09, 364-377.

[26] Abdulkader, A. and Casey, M. R. 2009. Low Cost Correction of OCR Errors Using Learning in a Multi-Engine Environment. *In Proc. of the 10th Int. Conf. on Document Analysis and Recognition.* ICDAR '09, IEEE Computer Society, 576-580.

[27] Gao, X., Lu, W., Tao, D., and Li, X. 2009. Image quality assessment based on multiscale geometric analysis. IEEE Trans. Img. Proc. 18, 7, July 2009, 1409-1423.

[28] Veeramachaneni, S. and Nagy, G. 2005. Style Context with Second-Order Statistics. IEEE Trans. Pattern Anal. Mach. Intell. 27, 1, January 2005, 14-22.

[29] Malone, T.W., Laubacher, R., Dellarocas, C., Harnessing Crowds: Mapping the Genome of Collective Intelligence. Research Paper No. 4732-09, MIT, Sloan School of Management, Feb. 2009. Sloan Research Paper No. 4732-09.

[30] Cooper, S., Khatib, F., Treuille, A., Barbero, J., Lee, J., Beenen, M., Leaver-Fay, A., Baker, D., Popovic, Z.: Predicting protein structures with a multiplayer online game. Nature 466 (2010).

IPKB: A Digital Library for Invertebrate Paleontology

Yuanliang Meng[†], Junyan Li[†], Patrick Denton[†], Yuxin Chen[§],
Bo Luo[†], Paul Selden[‡], and Xue-wen Chen[†]

[†] Department of EECS, The University of Kansas, Lawrence, KS, 66045, USA
[‡] Department of Geology, The University of Kansas, Lawrence, KS, 66045, USA
[§] Department of Computer Science, Swiss Federal Institute of Technology, Zurich, Switzerland
{ymeng, j357l401, pdenton, bluo, selden, xwchen}@ku.edu, yuxin.chen@inf.ethz.ch

ABSTRACT

In this paper, we present the *Invertebrate Paleontology Knowledgebase* (IPKB), an effort to digitize and share the *Treatise on Invertebrate Paleontology*. The Treatise is the most authoritative compilation of invertebrate fossil records. Unfortunately, the PDF version is simply a clone of paper publications and the content is in no way organized to facilitate search and knowledge discovery. We extracted texts and images from the Treatise, stored them in a database, and built a system for efficient browsing and searching. For image processing in particular, we segmented fossil photos from figures, recognized the embedded labels, and linked the images to the corresponding data entries. The detailed information of each genus, including fossil images, is delivered to users through a web access module. Some external applications (e.g. Google Earth) are acquired through web services APIs to improve user experience. Given the rich information in the Treatise, analyzing, modeling and understanding paleontological data are significant in many areas, such as: understanding evolution; understanding climate change; finding fossil fuels, etc. IPKB builds a general framework that aims to facilitate knowledge discovery activities in invertebrate paleontology, and provides a solid foundation for future explorations. In this article, we report our initial accomplishments. The specific techniques we employed in the project, such as those involved in text parsing, image-label association and meta data extraction, can be insightful and serve as examples for other researchers.

Categories and Subject Descriptors

H.3.3 [**Information Storage and Retrieval**]: Information search and retrieval; E.2 [**Data Storage Representations**]: Linked representations

General Terms

Design, Documentation

Keywords

Digital library, Digitization, Paleontology

1. INTRODUCTION

The science of paleontology advances not only from discoveries of important new fossils but also through innovative ideas based on data accumulated over previous generations. The robustness of such studies depends on the quality of data. Paleontologists agree that the most authoritative compilation of data on invertebrate fossils is in the *Treatise on Invertebrate Paleontology*[1]. The *Treatise* was founded in 1948 and the first volume appeared in 1953. Since then, The Paleontological Institute of the University of Kansas has published 50 volumes, authored by more than 300 contributors worldwide. This encyclopedic work now occupies more than 1.3 meters of shelf space. For paleontologists (and geologists, biostratigraphers, etc.) the world over, the Treatise holds an almost biblical significance and is to be found in every good library.

Given the rich information in the Treatise, understanding and modeling paleontological data are significant in many areas, such as: understanding evolution; understanding climate change; finding fossil fuels, etc. The vast repository of paleontological data contained in the Treatise needs to be made available in electronic form for present and future workers to extract the greatest possible use from the work. In order to realize the maximum possible benefit from this landmark effort, there is a strong desire within the paleontological community to be able to readily access and use this data. However, it is non-trivial to convert large volumes of the Treatise into a structured, and easily accessible digital library. In particular, we face the following challenges: (1) the Treatise contains heterogeneous data objects that are not easy to be associated under a unified framework, in particular, linking text entries with fossil images; (2) although the editorial policies and procedures of the Treatise have always been of the highest standard, it consists of manuscripts from hundreds of paleontologists, which introduces significant inconsistency of styles, formats, and sometimes terminologies.

In this paper, we report *IPKB*, a first effort towards digitization, organization and integration of the rich information extracted from the Treatise. The ultimate goal is to provide scientists with a general framework that facilitates knowledge discovery activities in invertebrate paleontology. IPKB first extracts raw data from the Treatise, and processes textual and image data objects separately. We have designed an

[1]http://paleo.ku.edu/treatise/

ontology to capture fossil information, and explored ways to link fossil (genera) descriptions with images. Finally, a web interface is designed to present the information, and provide easy browsing and searching functions. With the help of our system, users can achieve some goals that are impossible with a PDF file alone. The following are examples of such scenarios:

Use case 1. A paleontologist wants to browse all genera of superfamily *Plectorthoidea* between geological times *Eifelian* and *Moscovian*.

Use case 2. In Japan, a geologist finds a brachiopod fossil which is subpentagonal and rectimarginate; and the foramen is permesothyrid. He wants to check the geological period it could correspond to.

In the following sections, readers will get to know how the system is designed and implementted. The rest of the paper is organized as follows: we introduce the general architecture of IPKB in Section 2, and present our text and image processing approaches in Sections 3 and 4. We then describe system integration, including accessing and searching components in Section 5. We summarize related works in Section 6, and finally conclude the paper in Section 7.

2. IPKB: SYSTEM OVERVIEW

The Treatise on Invertebrate Paleontology is a pandect of all invertebrate fossil genera, together with their taxonomic synonyms, stratigraphic ranges, geographic distributions, and illustrations of the type specimens. In the Treatise, tremendous amounts of data have been accumulated from different resources, and organized in old-fashioned ways. The Treatise is published in separate parts, *Part A* through *W*, and each part contains multiple volumes. Earlier volumes are scanned from printed books, while the newest volumes have PDF files from the publisher. We started from *Part H. Brachiopoda*, which has 6 volumes of paleontological data of brachiopods, a phylum of marine invertebrates with two valves (or "shells"). Fossils are classified in a hierarchical structure (from highest level to lowest): *orders* (e.g. *Lingulida*, *Orthida*); *suborders* (e.g. *Dalmanellidina*, *Orthidina*); *superfamilies* (e.g. *Plectorthoidea*, *Wellerelloidea*); *families* (e.g. *Allorhynchidae*, *Pontisiidae*); and finally *genera* (over 4,000 genera in Part H).

Although the recent volumes (e.g. all six volumes in Part H) are digitized [20], they are no more than electronic reprints of paper publications. As we know, the only way to search in a PDF file is using exact text matching. In our system, however, users are able to submit structured queries. As illustrated before, from a PDF file it is impossible to locate records of certain morphological features and/or geological distributions, across a variety of families. Our advanced search function, however, can find relevant records instantly and rank them according to relevancy. When reading a book, we often find it inconvenient to jump from one topic to a related one, not to mention some external sources. Our system provides a flexible interface for doing so, too. In addition, traditional publications do not sufficiently take users' experience into account. Modern systems like ours emphasize more on information layout and data presentation methods. Hopefully, information access turns out to be more enjoyable as well.

Figure 1 demonstrates the overall structure of the IPKB system. Please note that, for simplicity of the description,

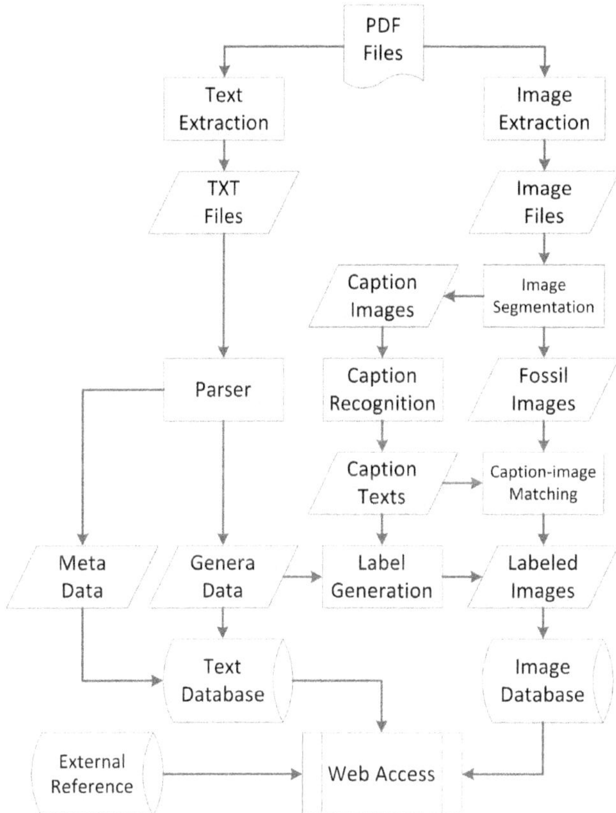

Figure 1: Overview of the IPKB system.

we omit the details in the *Web Access* component for now. As shown in the figure, we first extract text and image data from PDF files, and process them separately. Text data is parsed to obtain structured genus records and other meta data (e.g. phylum introduction, glossary, etc). Images are segmented and image captions are recognized and associated with the corresponding segment. Text descriptions of the genus records are then linked with the images. Finally, processed text and image data is provided to the web access module, which includes browsing, searching and genus display as three main components. In the rest of the paper, we use *Part H. Brachiopoda* as examples to describe each module in details. However, the methods are applied to all volumes.

3. TEXT PROCESSING

Part H of the treatise consists 6 volumes with 3,226 numbered pages in total. All volumes are available in PDF format, which was directly generated from the typesetting software. There are 1960 indexed figures. In most cases, a figure contains a number of fossil images, and each image has a label. In IPKB, text and images are extracted and processed separately. We will discuss text processing in this section, and image processing in next section.

In brachiopod paleontology literature, the basic taxon is usually a genus. In the Treatise, each genus record consists of a paragraph of text description, and a few corresponding images. According to the editorial requirements, genus de-

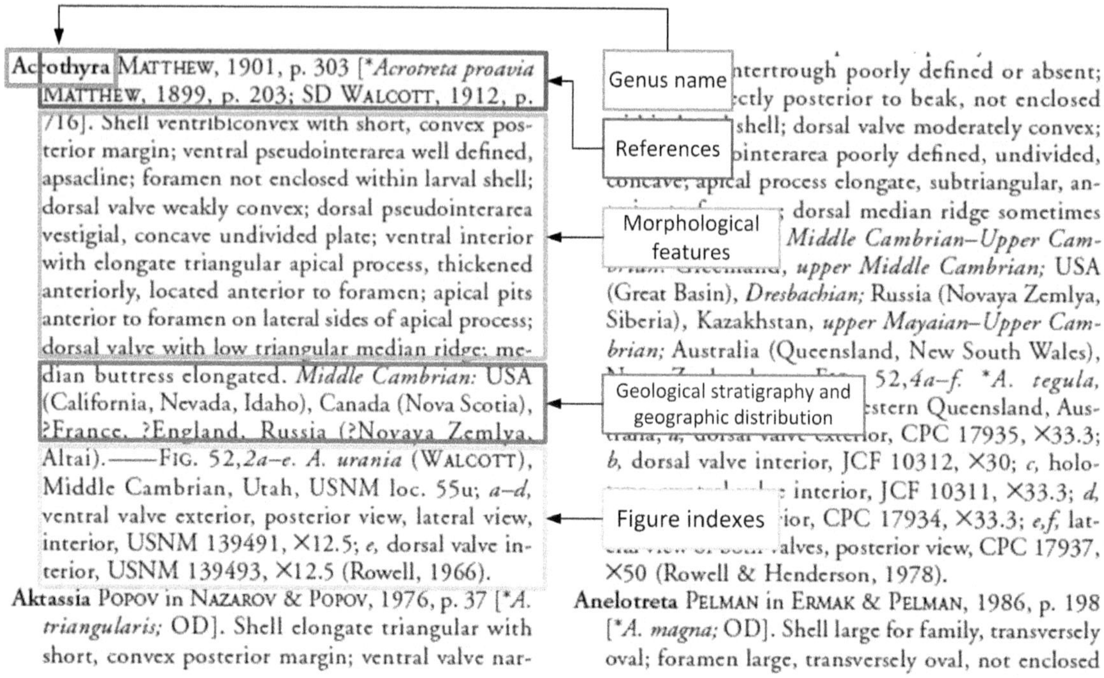

Figure 2: The description of individual genera in the treatise.

scription should provide the following pieces of information in a fixed order:

1. Genus name; e.g. *Acrothyra*.

2. References; linking to external publication(s), i.e. the original sources describing the genus.

3. Morphological features; e.g. "shell ventribiconvex with short, convex posterior margin; ventral ..." The editorial guidelines also requires the authors to describe features in a stated order, and use limited vocabulary. However, such guidelines are not strictly followed by all the contributors.

4. Geological stratigraphy and geographic distribution; e.g. "Middle Cambrian: USA (California, Nevada, Idaho), ..." Please note that fossils are usually found at multiple locations, and the locations are identified in highly inconsistent manner.

5. Figure indexes; e.g. "FIG. 52, 2a-e." Multiple images may be included for a genus.

Figure 2 shows an example of a genus record. In each paragraph of a genus, missing information is not uncommon and when something is absent, there is no explicit indicator. Currently, we are not exploiting the references, since all the related works are not digitally available, which prevents us from providing any hyperlink. All other pieces of information are crucial and are incorporated in the IPKB system. In addition, every genus is governed by some higher taxa as mentioned before. Names of the corresponding higher taxa are not given in the paragraphs, but they are found in the titles of corresponding chapters and their subordinate sections. These names are important information and are captured too.

We have implemented a Python program to extract the information and save the parsed text in an XML file. The algorithm is based on regular expression matching, which uses keywords and syntax of the text descriptions to split the text paragraph into structured data. Here the syntax does not refer to sentence structures, but merely indicates format patterns, including capital letters and punctuations and so on. Please note, other than pure textual data, we do not have any metadata (e.g. font, size, style, etc.), since we were unable to robustly extract typesetting data from the PDF (possibly due to the typesetting software used to produce the PDF file).

Genus names consist of a number of letters, with the first one capitalized. What follows is an author's name with all capital letters. This is a unique context and can be used in the extraction algorithm directly. The part of geological and geographical distributions starts with some reserved term for geological time, and ends with a long hyphen in the text. Therefore it can be obtained once a list of terms are provided. The beginning of the geological part is also the ending of the morphological description, so clear indicators of boundaries can be used in both ways, forward and backward. Such features also help us to identify and recover incorrectly formatted genus descriptions.

In order to get the names of higher taxa, we need to capture an order name first, and then assume all the genera belong to that particular order until a new order is captured. The same principle applies to suborders, super families, families, and subfamilies. Sometimes one or more taxon names are not available, and we just marked it as "UNKNOWN". Occasionally a taxon is "UNCERTAIN" because it is controversial in literature, and such cases are clearly indicated in the Treatise we work on.

We have designed an ontology to capture the genera data and meta data extracted in text processing. Genera data includes entries of genus records as described above, while meta data includes other descriptive information that is included in the volumes. For instance, volume information, the glossary, an introduction to the phylum, and so on. Structured textual data are then stored in XML format, which will be used not only in the IPKB project.

4. IMAGE PROCESSING

Image extraction is the most time-consuming task of data preparation. Currently what we have processed is photos of fossils, corresponding to the entries of the genus records. Figure 3 (a) shows an example of the original figures extracted from the PDF files.

As shown in Figure 3 (a), the fossil images in the Treatise are manually selected, grouped and placed in a single image canvas. Each figure in the PDF file is a flattened bitmap image, without any metadata to split individual fossil images, and we do not have access to individual fossil images either. Each figure typically contains images of a few fossils, all in grayscale. The images with the same numeric index belong to the same genus. For instance, Figure 3 (a) *1a – e* all belong to the genus *Overtonia*. Different letters a, b, c and so on usually refer to various views of the same fossil, but they could also be different specimen from the same genus. As a result, the label of an image is typically a number followed by a letter, and occasionally only a number (if the genus has only one fossil photo).

We first need to segment and extract all fossil images from the figures. In order to locate the images correctly, the label under each fossil (e.g. 1a) needs to be identified and recognized too. Moreover, we need to exploit the labels to match the images with the corresponding genus descriptions, hence link genus records with fossil images. Images are first extracted from PDF files using a function provided by Adobe Acrobat. The process is mostly automatic, while manual intervention is often necessary. Segmenting the images and recognizing the labels, however, are much more difficult. We implemented the algorithms with Matlab. The major steps are:

(1) Segment fossil images and label images;

(2) Detect contours of fossil images;

(3) Match fossil images with label images, using their mutual distances in the figure;

(4) Compare the label images with templates and determine the content;

(5) Name the fossil images with their label.

In the following we will describe the methods in more details.

4.1 Image segmentation

Part H of the Treatise documents Brachiopods, which are marine invertebrates with two shells, hence, the photos exhibit fossilized shells of various shapes. The vast majority of fossil images are presented with a blank background, such as those in Figure 3 (a). However, occasionally a fossil can been seen *in situ* i.e. in a rock, as Figure 4 demonstrates. Segmentation of such images is a hard computer vision problem, which is not handled at this stage of the project. In this case, we just treat the fossil with the rock as an entity and do not further segment.

We have implemented an approach that is similar to the

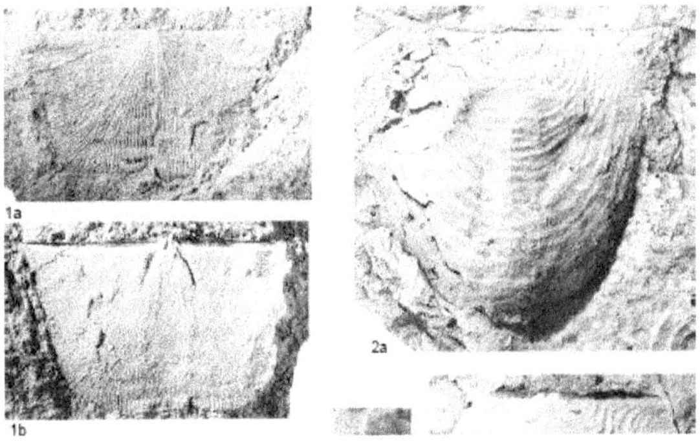

Figure 4: A figure from the Treatise. The fossils are embedded in rocks.

Marker-Controlled Watershed Segmentation method [10] to separate multiple fossil images in the same figure. First, we use the *opening-by-construction* approach to mark the objects i.e. fossil images as well as the background. This approach consists of an image erosion phase followed by an image reconstruction phase [32]. In image erosion, we choose a disk-like structuring element object with a diameter of 20 pixels. Anything smaller than 40 pixels in any dimension will be totally eroded. Since the labels and captions are usually about 30 pixels tall, such an operation can retain fossil photos and eliminate labels, markers, embedded captions and other noise. In the image reconstruction, the idea is to use the eroded image as the "seed", and use the original image as the mask. In our implementation, we reconstructed the background (which includes labels and captions), i.e. the reverse of the fossil photos. Figure 3 (b) shows the result of the reconstruction. The background is now bright (i.e. 1) and the fossil photos are dark (i.e. 0).

After the image fossils (i.e. large objects) are identified and the background is marked, we identify the labels (i.e. small objects) similarly. We first mask out the fossils from the original image, as Figure 3 (c) shows. Another image opening procedure is implemented to obtain the label blocks. In this case, we used an image erosion followed by an image dilation, and the size of the structuring element object is set to 10 pixels so that embedded text labels are kept. Among the identified text blocks, we retained the smaller ones since we are only interested in labels, not the captions (e.g. "Overtonia" in the figure). The identified labels are shown in Figure 3 (d).

Finally, we have employed the *watershed* approach to partition the fossil images in the figure, and later they are saved as separate JPG files. The watershed approach is to find local minima in an greyscale image, and cut them in pieces [17]. Assuming that pixel intensity values in a digital image represent the altitudes, we can draw an analogy between a grayscale image and a topographic relief. Therefore there are "peaks" with local maxima and "basins" with local minima. The idea of the watershed algorithm is to continuously add "water" into the basins to make them "flood". When the levels of water rise to the point where two water sources meet, a "barrier" is built. The resulting set of barriers are the watersheds, which separate the regions defined by basins. In our case, the fossils in the figure have been marked with dark pixels (i.e. basins), and the background has been marked with white pixels. The watershed method is used to determine

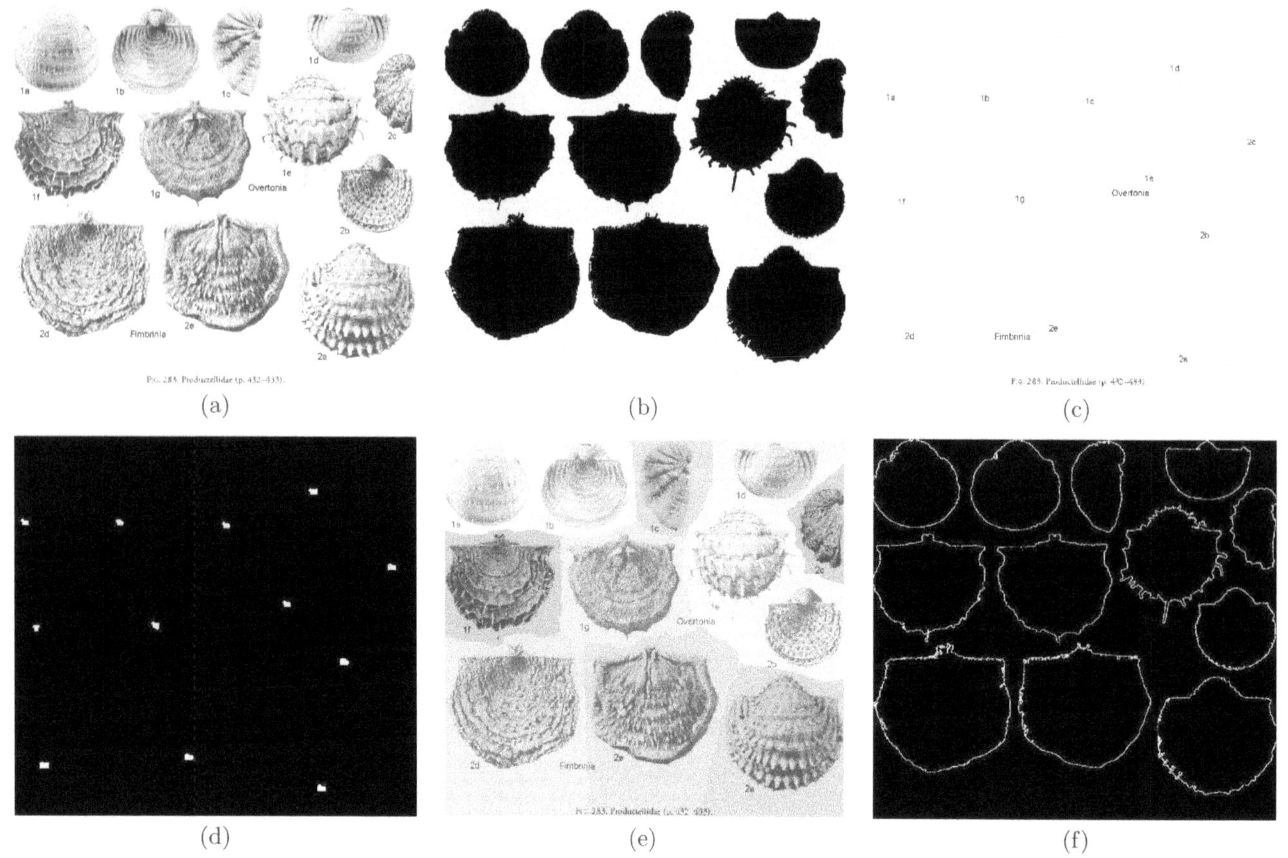

Figure 3: Image processing in IPKB: (a). the original figure extracted from from the Treatise; Images with the same numeric index belong to the same genus. (b). Opening-by-construction: fossils are masked. (c). Removing fossils from the figure, leaving only labels and captions. (d). Identified label blocks. (e). Using watershed method to split fossils. (f). Detected fossil contours.

the barrier between individual fossil images (i.e. basins), and hence split them from the figure. Figure 3 (e) shows the result of the watershed approach. After segmentation, each fossil image is padded to a square canvas and stored in separate JPG files.

The mathematic details are beyond the scope of our discussion, but interested readers may refer to [27].

4.2 Fossil contour detection

In the original figure, fossil labels are manually placed "near" the corresponding fossil image. They are supposed to be placed to the lower left corner of the fossil images, however, this rule is frequently violated. The amount of the images makes it impossible to manually fix such errors. Therefore, we have designed an automatic method to associated fossils and their labels.

Although fossils are segmented and extracted from the figures, we still need an accurate identification of the fossil contours to compute the minimum distance between labels and fossil images. Edge detection has been well studied in the image processing literature, among various methods [24, 10], we have employed the *sobel* edge detection approach. A sobel operator is a 3×3 kernel, which is applied to the image using 2-D convolution, to compute the (approximate) gradient of pixel intensity. For a 2D image, two kernels are used: one for the horizontal dimension and the other for the vertical dimension:

$$\mathbf{G}_x = \begin{bmatrix} -1 & 0 & 1 \\ -2 & 0 & 2 \\ -1 & 0 & 1 \end{bmatrix} * \mathbf{I} \text{ and } \mathbf{G}_y = \begin{bmatrix} 1 & 2 & 1 \\ 0 & 0 & 0 \\ -1 & -2 & -1 \end{bmatrix} * \mathbf{I} \quad (1)$$

The magnitude of the gradient can be obtained in the following way: one for the horizontal dimension and the other for the vertical dimension:

$$\mathbf{G} = \sqrt{\mathbf{G}_x{}^2 + \mathbf{G}_y{}^2} \quad (2)$$

The edge pixels are those with high values of **G**. If the image is masked, as in our algorithm, **G** is simply zero for all the non-edge pixels. Figure 3 (f) demonstrates the detected contours of the fossil photos.

4.3 Fossil label association

We link labels with fossils based on the distance between them. At high level, each label is associated with the nearest fossil. However, there could be confusion in some cases. For instance, in Figure 3, label `1d` is placed between two fossils, with similar distance to both of them. In this case, if we can first associate the lower fossil with label `1e`, we can confidently link `1d` to the upper fossil. Theoretically, this becomes a *bipartite graph matching* problem, i.e. to find a *perfect matching* with minimum distance.

Labels \ Fossils	1	2	3	4	5	6	7	8	9	10	11	12
1	17.493	47.043	100	100	100	100	100	100	100	100	100	100
2	100	19.235	64.498	100	100	100	100	100	100	100	100	100
3	100	100	21.19	100	100	100	100	100	100	100	100	100
4	76.217	45.706	100	18.028	68.622	100	100	100	100	100	100	100
5	100	100	76.968	100	21.587	74.465	100	100	100	100	100	100
6	100	100	100	100	100	17.464	100	100	100	100	100	100
7	100	100	100	88.482	100	100	16.971	98.732	100	100	100	100
8	100	100	100	100	100	100	100	23.77	100	100	100	100
9	100	100	100	100	100	100	100	25	100	16.971	100	100
10	100	100	100	100	100	100	100	100	17.493	100	100	100
11	100	100	100	100	100	100	100	100	31.385	100	18.385	100
12	100	100	100	100	100	100	100	69.318	100	100	50.537	16.031

Figure 5: The distance matrix. Each column represents a photo and each row represents a label. The value 100 is a dummy distance for those too far away.

First, we compute the Euclidean distance between the center pixel of the label block and all pixels of a fossil image contour. The minimum value is saved as the "distance" between the label and the fossil. After all labels loop over all fossils, we obtain a distance matrix. We have extracted the distance matrix for labels and fossils from Figure 3, and demonstrate the matrix in Figure 5. All distances greater than 100 are set to 100 (and ignored), while distances smaller than 100 are kept as candidates. We scan through the columns to identify the minimum distance between labels and images. We first identify columns with only one candidate (e.g. columns 7, 10, 12 in the figure), and eliminate the corresponding rows from the matrix. For instance, we link fossil 10 with label 9 (column 10) without confusion. Therefore, although label 9 is also close to fossil 8 (column 8), they cannot be associated. We repeat this process until all labels and fossils are linked.

4.4 Label image recognition

Since the labels have a limited scope of inventory and are small in size, it is adequate to use templates for recognition. We select some label images, binarize them and save them as templates.

The recognition task is to compute the distances between target images and templates, and the one with the minimum distance is the match. Since the label images are relatively small, we used the most intuitive method: computing the normalized pixel-wise sum of square error (SSE) between images (Equation 3). The pairs with the minimum SSE is a match. In reality, the target image and the template image do not often have the same size, so we need to try different positions. Again we used a pixel-by-pixel loop.

$$SSE = \frac{\sum_{(x,y)}(\mathbf{I}_{temp}(x,y) - \mathbf{I}_{targ}(x,y))^2}{\sum_{(x,y)}\mathbf{I}_{temp}(x,y)^2 + \sum_{(x,y)}\mathbf{I}_{targ}(x,y)^2} \quad (3)$$

Once we know what the label is, we name the associated fossil image with that label (and the figure index). Then the fossil images are properly named.

5. WEB ACCESS

An important goal of our project is to digitally deliver the Treatise to the research community and the general public. Therefore, we built a web interface to facilitate browsing and advanced searching functions. We have adopted the three-tier architecture, where the database server is powered by MySQL, the Web server is powered by Apache+PHP, and JavaScript is used on the client side. An schema shredding is enforced to convert the XML data generated in Section 3 into relational model to be handled in RDBMS, for its maturity and performance. Figure 6 shows the homepage of IPKB website. Since the Treatise is not an open-source product, subscribers need to login to view full volumes.

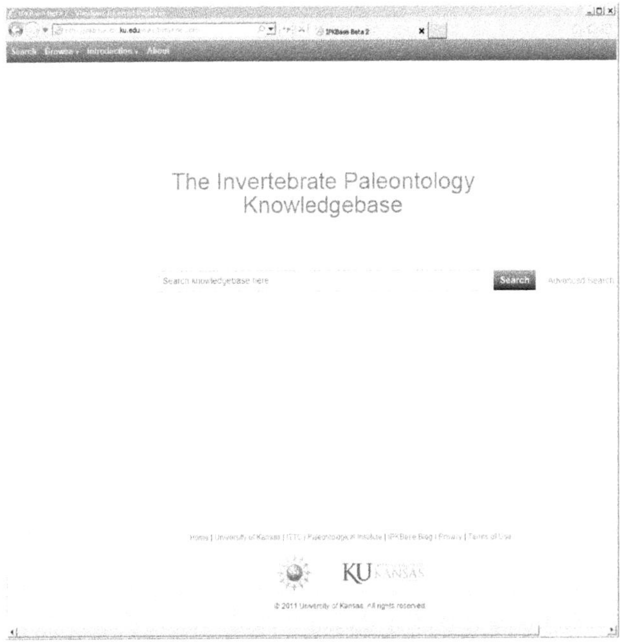

Figure 6: The homepage of the web interface.

5.1 Searching and browsing

A major function of the web access module is search. At present, we provide two search modes: quick search, which takes free text queries, and advanced search, which takes more complex predicates.

5.1.1 Quick search

Quick search accepts a free text query, which could be the name of a genus, or a family, or an order etc., and returns the records that match the name. Nomenclature in paleontology is often confusing even to professionals, hence, we support approximate matching. The algorithm runs int he following way:

(1) search for exact match of genus name;

(2) if no results are found, try a natural language full-text search over taxon names;

(3) if no results are found, try approximate search of genus name;

(4) if no results are found, ask the user to try another request.

The exact match function only returns entries which contain the exact keyword(s) in the query. The approximate search will allow partial matching. For instance, query "admi" will yield the genus records of "Adminiculoria" and "Adminixtella", as shown in Figure 8. When full-text search is implemented, the records are ranked according to relevance. For more details about relevance, please refer to the discussion on advanced search in next section.

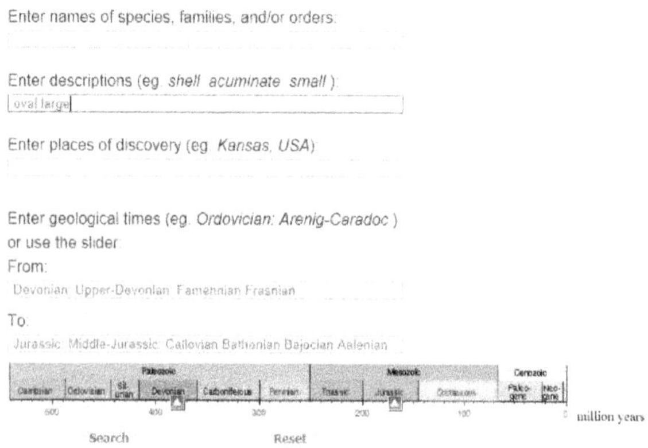

Figure 7: The webpage for advanced search.

5.1.2 Advanced search

Advanced search allows users to send structured queries to IPKB. Users could provide predicates on names, morphological features (descriptions), geological times, and/or geographic locations.

The fossils are dated from lower Cambrian (540 million years ago) to present. In order to help users select a geological time range, we designed a scrollbar with two pointers. In our database, the geological time of fossils are encoded into integers. For a user query, the provided starting and ending times are encoded in the same way, and sent to the database as predicates on a integer field. Moreover, we also send the corresponding geological *period* and *epochs* (if any) of the starting and ending points as keywords in the search query as well. This will yield records that contain geological period and epochs in their morphological descriptions (not in the geological stratigraphy field). This is also useful when people search in a small time range, and helps to provide better ranking.

We have employed the natural language full-text search function in MySQL to support full-text search and similarity-based ranking. In the database, the relevant columns are included in a FULLTEXT index. We have assigned different weights w to different columns to reflect the "importance" of the information in the search context (e.g. genus names are more important than descriptions): 3.0 for taxnon names, 1.5 for geological and geographical distribution, and 1.0 for morphological features.

MySQL implements a model similar to TF-IDF in the full-text search function. The *significance* of a term is calculated as:

$$s = \frac{log(dtf) + 1}{\sum dtf} \times \frac{U}{1 + 0.0115U} \times log(\frac{N - nf}{nf}) \qquad (4)$$

where dtf is the number of times the word appears in a document (i.e. a database record); $\sum dtf$ is the sum of $(log(dtf) + 1)$'s for all words in the same document. U is the number of unique words in the document (see [30] for more details). N is the total number of documents. nf is the number of documents that contain the term. The combined relevance of a term and a document is:

$$R = w \times s \times qf \qquad (5)$$

where qf is the frequency of the term in the query, and in most cases it is 1. It should also be mentioned that MySQL natural language full-text search ignores words shorter than 4 letters by default. In addition, there is a stopword list which excludes words with too high frequencies.

5.1.3 Browsing

The *Browse* function is *defacto* search by names, too. It provides a wizard for users to explore the hierarchical structure of fossil categories. Users see all the orders of brachiopods when the web page is loaded. When an order is clicked on, its subordinate suborders appear, and so on. In this manner, a user does not need to type in anything to locate the genus he wants to view. People can browse all the category names, even if they are not willing to view any specific record.

5.2 Genus record displaying

In designing the interface to show genus records, we consider the following factors: it must be easy to view and users should be able to perceive the relevant information immediately; there should be some links that allow users to check related information. The results of quick search and advanced search are essentially delivered in the same format. Up to 10 records (genera) are shown on each page. As shown in Figure 8, for each genus record, there are representative photos, if possible; and there are a few lines of textual information. On the top of the text, the name of the genus is shown. Under the genus name, there are names of higher taxa (i.e. family, order etc.) governing the genus. Users can click on a taxon name to view a general description for that taxon. Further down other information can be found, including morphological description, geological and geographic distribution.

In the results of advanced search, the keywords will be highlighted. This feature applies to keywords in geological and geographic distributions, as well as in morphological descriptions. For geological time in particular, the terms marking the beginning and the end of the searched time range will be highlighted. Many of the terms in geolog-

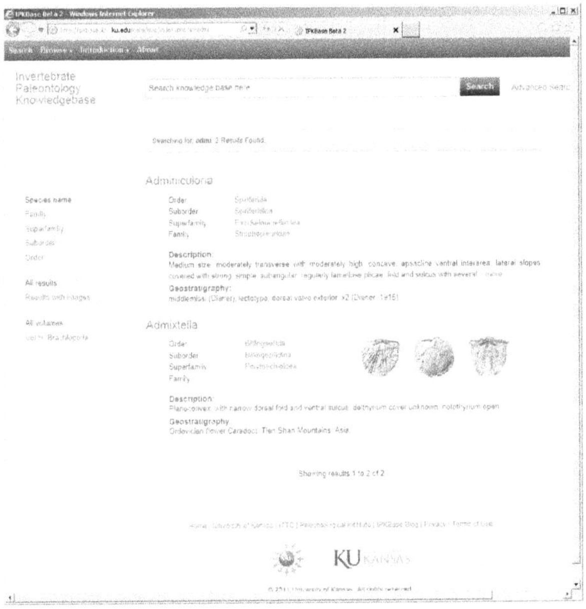

Figure 8: The result of quick search, using "admi" as keyword.

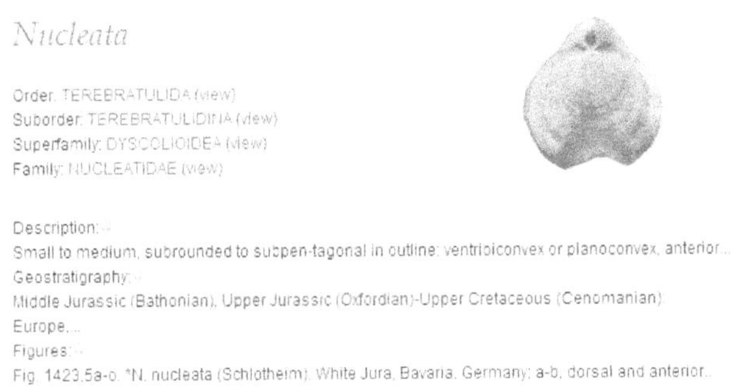

Figure 9: The result of advanced search.

ical time contain modifiers such as "upper", "middle" and "lower". When users are searching for "upper Jurassic", they certainly do not want to see records with a lot of "upper"s but no "Jurassic". At the same time, nevertheless, they do want the system to return and highlight records with "Jurassic" even though the modifier is absent. We took cautious treatments for this situation. As we can see from the result, when "Upper Jurassic" is searched for, the strings of "Upper Jurassic" or "Jurassic" are highlighted, but "Upper Cretaceous" and alike are not.

Once a user clicks on the genus name to view the details, a new page containing information of that specific genus is loaded. All the descriptions and photos of this genus display. Moreover, geographical distribution is crucial information in paleontology. Although it is nontrivial to visualize geological stratigraphy, we have employed Google Earth API [2] to visualize the sites of discovery of the fossils. The Google Earth API only accepts exact longitudes and latitudes to mark the locations. Therefore we first use the Google Map

[2]http://code.google.com/apis/earth/

Figure 10: View information of a genus. The photos are on the left side. Google Earth displays the geographical distribution.

API to convert the name of locations to coordinates, and then pass it to the Google Earth API. If a certain genus is found in more than one location, multiple markers will show up on Google Earth as well. We also employ the Google Image Search API [3] to embed results of Google Image Search in our system. Such plug-ins not only help with data interpretation, but also significantly improves user experiences.

6. RELATED WORK

In 1990s, digital libraries have been introduced to provide fast and flexible online access to digitalized information repositories (e.g. [7, 14, 6]). Traditional libraries, which house and provide access to collections of books, have made metadata (e.g. catalogs) available and searchable online (e.g. The Library of Congress online catalogs [4]). However, access to full content is usually not available over the web since most traditional media are yet to be digitized. Meanwhile, these projects only propose to provide digital access to traditional media, but do not make further explorations on the digitized contents.

We also have digital libraries that focus on a specialized area. For example, bibliographic databases (e.g. PsycINFO, PubMed, arXiv) are repositories for academic publications. On the other hand, Digital Himalaya [29] is an anthropology library to digitize, organize and publicize multimedia ethnographic materials from the Himalaya region. The goal is to preserve valuable information in digital format, and provide searchable access to the research community as well as general public.

A number of digital paleontological databases have sprung up over the last decade or so, the best known being the *Paleobiology Database* (PBDB) [5]. This NSF-funded database is the foremost online paleontological database. It differs from the *Treatise* and IPKB in a number of important ways. First, it is populated in a wiki-style process: large numbers of contributors, from a variety of backgrounds, input

[3]http://code.google.com/apis/imagesearch/
[4]http://catalog.loc.gov/
[5]PBDB: http://paleodb.org

data with varying degrees of accuracy. In many cases, it is student labor that inputs the data. As a consequence, the quality is highly variable. Second, the data is predominantly text-based, and thus similar to any other queryable dataset; there are few fossil images, and these are random additions by particular workers. In contrast, *Treatise* data is collected, peer-reviewed and verified by the experts in the field, and images of type specimens are an integral feature.

Meanwhile, numerous other paleontological databases can be found on the internet, with each one set up by generally a single worker to reflect their own interests. These vary greatly in scope and utility. For example, the Florissant Fossil Database [6] is essentially a collection of high-quality images of fossils from this National Park.

7. CONCLUSION AND FUTURE WORK

In this paper, we report our initial accomplishments in IPKB, a project aiming at digitalization, utilizing and sharing of the rich information from the *Treatise on Invertebrate Paleontology*, which is the most authoritative compilation of data on invertebrate fossils. In the project, we first extract raw data from the Treatise, and processes textual and image data objects separately. We have designed an ontology to capture fossil information, and explored ways to segment images, recognize labels, and link fossil (genera) descriptions with images. Finally, a web interface is designed to present the information, and provide easy browsing and searching functions. Google Earth and Google Image Search APIs are employed to help with presentation and improve user experiences.

IPKB provides a solid foundation for future discoveries based on the rich information repository of invertebrate paleontology data. Our next step is to extend the IPKB framework to provide the scientists with a knowledge discovery platform, which hosts complex data analysis, content-based retrieval, modeling, data mining, image processing and understanding, animation and visualization functions. We are also implementing a more illustrative and information-rich web portal for the general public. Meanwhile, to improve the accessibility and usability of IPKB, we are implementing a web services interface, and designing apps for mobile devices. For instance, paleontologists working in the field will be able to browse and search IPKB on hand-held devices, and submit their fossil images for identification and search.

8. ACKNOWLEDGMENTS

This work is supported by the US National Science Foundation Award CDI-1028098.

The authors would like to thank reviewers for their feedback, and thank Jill Hardesty from the Department of Geology, University of Kansas for her advice and help.

9. REFERENCES

[1] L. J. Barker. Science teachers' use of online resources and the digital library for earth system education. In *Proceedings of the 9th ACM/IEEE-CS joint conference on Digital libraries*, JCDL '09, pages 1–10, 2009.

[2] L. Bolelli, X. Lu, Y. Liu, A. Jaiswal, K. Bai, I. Councill, P. Mitra, J. Wang, K. Mueller, J. Kubicki, B. Garrison, B. J., and C. Giles. Chemxseer: A chemistry web portal for scientific literature and datasets. In *Open Repositories Conference*, 2007.

[3] J. Canny. A computational approach to edge detection. *IEEE Transactions on Pattern Analysis and Machine Intelligence*, PAMI-8(6):679–698, 1986.

[4] C.-c. Chen. Global memory net: New collaboration, new activities and new potentials. In Z. Chen, H. Chen, Q. Miao, Y. Fu, E. Fox, and E.-p. Lim, editors, *Digital Libraries: International Collaboration and Cross-Fertilization*, volume 3334 of *Lecture Notes in Computer Science*, pages 543–575. Springer Berlin / Heidelberg, 2005.

[5] H.-H. Chen, L. Gou, X. Zhang, and C. L. Giles. Collabseer: a search engine for collaboration discovery. In *Proceedings of the 11th annual international ACM/IEEE joint conference on Digital libraries*, JCDL '11, pages 231–240, 2011.

[6] Y. Choi and E. Rasmussen. What do digital librarians do. In *Proceedings of the 6th ACM/IEEE-CS joint conference on Digital libraries*, JCDL '06, pages 187–188, 2006.

[7] E. A. Fox, R. M. Akscyn, R. K. Furuta, and J. J. Leggett. Digital libraries. *Commun. ACM*, 38(4):22–28, 1995.

[8] C. L. Giles, K. D. Bollacker, and S. Lawrence. Citeseer: an automatic citation indexing system. In *Proceedings of the third ACM conference on Digital libraries*, DL '98, pages 89–98, 1998.

[9] C. L. Giles and I. G. Councill. Who gets acknowledged: Measuring scientific contributions through automatic acknowledgment indexing. *Proceedings of the National Academy of Sciences of the United States of America*, 101(51), 2004.

[10] R. Gonzalez, R. E. Woods, and S. L. Eddins. *Digital Image Processing Using MATLAB*. Gatesmark Publishing, 2009.

[11] H. Hsieh, B. Draxler, N. Dudley, J. Cremer, L. Haldeman, D. Nguyen, P. Likarish, and J. Winet. Facilitating content creation and content research in building the city of lit digital library. In *Proceedings of the 11th annual international ACM/IEEE joint conference on Digital libraries*, JCDL '11, pages 145–148, New York, NY, USA, 2011. ACM.

[12] M. Jones, E. Thom, D. Bainbridge, and D. Frohlich. Mobility, digital libraries and a rural indian village. In *Proceedings of the 9th ACM/IEEE-CS joint conference on Digital libraries*, JCDL '09, pages 309–312, 2009.

[13] D. J. Kennard, W. B. Lund, and B. S. Morse. Improving historical research by linking digital library information to a global genealogical database. In *Proceedings of the 9th ACM/IEEE-CS joint conference on Digital libraries*, JCDL '09, pages 255–258, 2009.

[14] D. M. Levy and C. C. Marshall. Going digital: a look at assumptions underlying digital libraries. *Commun. ACM*, 38:77–84, April 1995.

[15] H. Li, I. Councill, W.-C. Lee, and C. L. Giles. Citeseerx: an architecture and web service design for an academic document search engine. In *Proceedings of the 15th international conference on World Wide Web*, WWW '06, pages 883–884, 2006.

[16] N. Li, L. Zhu, P. Mitra, K. Mueller, E. Poweleit, and

[6]http://planning.nps.gov/flfo

C. L. Giles. orechem chemxseer: a semantic digital library for chemistry. In *Proceedings of the 10th annual joint conference on Digital libraries*, JCDL '10, pages 245–254, 2010.

[17] F. Meyer. Topographic distance and watershed lines. *Signal Processing*, pages 113–125, July 1994.

[18] A. Mikeal, J. Creel, A. Maslov, S. Phillips, J. Leggett, and M. McFarland. Large-scale etd repositories: a case study of a digital library application. In *Proceedings of the 9th ACM/IEEE-CS joint conference on Digital libraries*, JCDL '09, pages 135–144, New York, NY, USA, 2009. ACM.

[19] P. Mitra, C. L. Giles, B. Sun, and Y. Liu. Chemxseer: a digital library and data repository for chemical kinetics. In *Proceedings of the ACM first workshop on CyberInfrastructure: information management in eScience*, CIMS '07, pages 7–10, 2007.

[20] R. C. Moore and other editors. *Treatise on Invertebrate Paleontology: Part H.* Geological Society of America and the University of Kansas Press, http://www.ku.edu/ paleo/treatise.html, 1953-2006.

[21] F. Morchen, M. Dejori, D. Fradkin, J. Etienne, B. Wachmann, and M. Bundschus. Anticipating annotations and emerging trends in biomedical literature. In *Proceedings of the 14th ACM SIGKDD international conference on Knowledge discovery and data mining*, KDD '08, pages 954–962, 2008.

[22] T. Nagatsuka and C.-c. Chen. Global memory offers new innovative access to tsurumi's old japanese waka poems and tales, and maps. In E. Fox, E. Neuhold, P. Premsmit, and V. Wuwongse, editors, *Digital Libraries: Implementing Strategies and Sharing Experiences*, volume 3815 of *Lecture Notes in Computer Science*, pages 149–157. Springer Berlin / Heidelberg, 2005.

[23] C. Neuhaus and H. D. Daniel. Data sources for performing citation analysis: an overview. In *Journal of Documentation*, volume 64, 2008.

[24] J. R. Parker. *Algorithms for Image Processing and Computer Vision.* John Wiley & Sons, Inc., New York, 1997.

[25] Y. Petinot, P. B. Teregowda, H. Han, C. L. Giles, S. Lawrence, A. Rangaswamy, and N. Pal. ebizsearch: an oai-compliant digital library for ebusiness. In *Proceedings of the 3rd ACM/IEEE-CS joint conference on Digital libraries*, JCDL '03, pages 199–209, Washington, DC, USA, 2003. IEEE Computer Society.

[26] R. Sanderson, B. Albritton, R. Schwemmer, and H. Van de Sompel. Sharedcanvas: a collaborative model for medieval manuscript layout dissemination. In *Proceedings of the 11th annual international ACM/IEEE joint conference on Digital libraries*, JCDL '11, pages 175–184, 2011.

[27] J. Serra. *Analysis and Mathematical Morphology.* Academic Press, London, 1982.

[28] B. Shaparenko and T. Joachims. Information genealogy: uncovering the flow of ideas in non-hyperlinked document databases. In *Proceedings of the 13th ACM SIGKDD international conference on Knowledge discovery and data mining*, KDD '07, pages 619–628, 2007.

[29] S. Shneiderman, M. Turin, and the Digital Himalaya Project Team. Digital himalaya: an ethnographic archive in the digital age. *European Bulletin of Himalayan Research*, 20(1):136–141, 2002.

[30] A. Singhal, C. Buckley, and M. Mitra. Pivoted document length normalization. In *Proceedings of the 19th annual international ACM SIGIR conference on Research and development in information retrieval*, pages 21–29. ACM, 1996.

[31] M. Steyvers, P. Smyth, M. Rosen-Zvi, and T. Griffiths. Probabilistic author-topic models for information discovery. In *Proceedings of the tenth ACM SIGKDD international conference on Knowledge discovery and data mining*, KDD '04, pages 306–315, 2004.

[32] L. Vincent. Morphological grayscale reconstruction in image analysis: Applications and efficient algorithms. *IEEE Transactions on Image Processing*, 2(2):176–201, April 1993.

[33] J. Wang, J. Li, and G. Wiederhold. Simplicity: semantics-sensitive integrated matching for picture libraries. *IEEE Transactions on Pattern Analysis and Machine Intelligence*, 23(9):947 –963, sep 2001.

[34] C. Yang, B. Wei, J. Wu, Y. Zhang, and L. Zhang. Cares: a ranking-oriented cadal recommender system. In *Proceedings of the 9th ACM/IEEE-CS joint conference on Digital libraries*, JCDL '09, pages 203–212, 2009.

Descriptive Metadata, Iconclass, and Digitized Emblem Literature

Timothy W. Cole, Myung-Ja Han, Jordan Vannoy
Grainger Engineering Library Information Center
University of Illinois at Urbana-Champaign
1301 W. Springfield Avenue
Urbana, IL 61801
+1 (217) 244-7809
{t-cole3, mhan3, jvannoy}@illinois.edu

ABSTRACT
Early Modern emblems combined text and image. Though there were many variants, the archetypical emblem literary form (mid-sixteenth through mid-eighteenth centuries) consisted of an image (the *pictura*), a text inscription (the *inscriptio*), and a text epigram (the *subscriptio*), the last usually in verse. Digitized emblem literature poses interesting challenges as regards content and metadata granularity, the use of interdisciplinary controlled vocabularies, and the need to present digitized primary sources in a complex network of associated sources, derivatives, and contemporaneous context. In this paper, we describe a digital library Web application designed to better support the ways emblem scholars search for and use digitized emblem books, focusing on metadata design, issues of resource granularity and identification, and the use of Linked Data Web services for Iconclass, a multilingual classification system for cultural heritage art and images. Outcomes to date, achieved by emblem scholars and librarians working in collaboration, provide a case study for multi-faceted, interactive approaches to curating mixed text-image digital resources and the use of Linked Data vocabulary services. Lessons learned highlight the value of librarian-scholar collaboration and help to illustrate why digital libraries need to move beyond merely disseminating digitized book surrogates.

Categories and Subject Descriptors
H.3.7 [**Digital Libraries**]: Systems Issues

General Terms
Design, Management, Experimentation, Human Factors.

Keywords
emblem books, digital humanities, metadata, Iconclass

1. INTRODUCTION
Renaissance and Baroque emblem literature flourished throughout Europe as a popular genre from 1531, the publication date of the first emblem book, until about 1750. An emblem (e.g., Figure 1) is typically defined [11] as consisting of a symbolic and often enigmatic image (the *pictura*), a text motto or inscription (the *inscriptio*), and an epigram in verse (the *subscriptio*). Textual elements are sometimes written in Latin, but are more often written in the vernacular of the region where the book was published. Emblems are inherently a mixed format, integrating text and graphics. Emblems were often contextual, reflecting on cotemporaneous events such as the Reformation or the Thirty Years' War. Creators drew inspiration from such diverse sources as the Bible, Classical antiquity, fables, mythology, science or medicine. As objects of scholarship, Early Modern emblems straddle multiple domains, e.g., art and cultural history, literature, semiotics, political science and religious studies. Models and methods applied to emblem studies are relevant in the study of many other text-graphic forms, including even (for example) the study of modern advertising [7]. Similarly, approaches (such as described here) for organizing and facilitating access to digitized emblems can inform digital library designs for serving other mixed format content.

Figure 1. Example of a book-published emblem [18].

Since the mid-1990s, emblem scholars and librarians at the University of Illinois at Urbana-Champaign have been digitizing emblem books from Illinois collections and making surrogates of these books available via the Web [2]. In 2002 they joined forces with librarians at the Herzog August Bibliothek (HAB), Wolfenbüttel to undertake a collaborative project centered on the digitization of German language emblem books [22]. Over the course of these early projects, Illinois and HAB researchers and others involved in similar projects at the University of Glasgow, Utrecht University, the University of Munich, the Universidade da Coruña [4] and elsewhere, have made great strides in learning how best to digitize emblems. These projects have created a

JCDL'12, June 10–14, 2012, Washington, DC, USA.

foundation for further development [9]. By 2002, some 570 volumes, containing thousands of emblems, had been digitized ([8], p. 261).

The initial focus, understandably, was on the physical digitization process itself. Success was measured by the quality and quantity of page images digitized. Indeed, the availability of high-quality digital surrogates for emblem books has increased the reach of all emblem scholars, most especially faculty and students not located near major print collections of emblem books. However, by itself, the availability of emblem book digital surrogates is not sufficient to tap fully the potential for advances in modes of discovery, use, and cross-discipline emblem scholarship made possible by the Web. Peter Daly articulated this distinction in his 2002 census of European emblem digitization projects. "If increased accessibility is the goal, then simple digitizing is sufficient. . . . If **increased knowledge** is the goal, then we need to pause and ask ourselves what kinds of analysis the digitized emblem book is supposed to serve" ([8], p. 13; bold in the original). The desire to move beyond static online libraries of digital book reproductions is not unique to the emblem studies community. In their study of how humanities scholars more broadly use source materials, Neal Audenaert and Richard Furuta noted that digital libraries "hold the potential to move beyond merely disseminating resources toward creating environments that support the analysis required to understand them" ([1], p. 283). The question naturally arises, what do such environments look like?

In 2009, Illinois and HAB received a new grant from the U.S. National Endowment for the Humanities (NEH) and the German *Deutsche Forschungsgemeinschaft* (DFG) for *Emblematica Online*, a project designed in part to create a next generation emblem digital library. The Principal Investigator in the U.S. for the *Emblematica Online* grant is Mara Wade of the University of Illinois; her counterpart in Germany is Thomas Stäcker of the HAB. (It is noteworthy that Professor Wade is not a librarian, but rather an emblem scholar and past Head of the Germanic Languages and Literatures Department at Illinois.) While the *Emblematica Online* project has near-term practical ambitions, it is also a goal to explore, test and extend (relative to emblems) hypotheses about how to organize and provide access to digitized mixed format content. What metadata design best relates the taxonomy of emblem books to the requirements of their online presentation, e.g., simultaneously supports access to an emblem pictura, an individual emblem, and a book of emblems? What augmentations to generic post-digitization workflows are required to support access and use at multiple granularities? Given that emblem books were published in different languages, how best to facilitate multi-lingual subject access to digitized emblem content?

This paper describes innovative features of the *Emblematica Online* digital library prototype intended to better support the ways emblem scholars want to discover and use digitized emblem resources. We focus on collaboratively developed enhancements in descriptive metadata design to support the inherently multi-granular nature of emblem materials and on the integration into the portal of the multi-lingual, hierarchical Iconclass vocabulary. This latter feature exploits recently introduced Web services that disseminate Iconclass thesaurus entries as RDF and in accord with Linked Data principles.[1] Though systematic assessment remains to be done, initial response from the emblem studies community has been positive. In part this follows naturally from a project commitment to collaborate closely with emblem studies scholars, both in defining key features of the *Emblematica Online* portal, and in curating and enriching content accessed through the portal.

2. PROBLEM STATEMENT

In his survey of projects dedicated to the digitization of European emblems, Peter Daly differentiates between "Digitization as Preservation" and "Digitization as Enrichment" ([8], pp. 8-9). He defines the focus of the former to be on the scanning of pages, the processing of page images, and the long-term maintenance of digital copies; in other words, a focus on static digital surrogates for print emblem books. Conversely, the latter is about transcription, description, indexing, and other ways of adding scholarly value to make the surrogates contained in online emblem collections more discoverable and more useful for research and pedagogy. Though chronic underfunding of emblem digitization (as preservation) remains an issue, it is instructive to consider that the *Emblematica Online* project has digitized about 375 emblem books from the emblem book collections at Illinois in a short amount of time. This amounts to an order of magnitude increase over what was digitized at Illinois in the prior 15 years. Concrete progress on *digitization as enrichment* has been slower and entails a distinct set of challenges. In the context of emblem studies, *digitization for enrichment* entails addressing granularity and metadata issues and better use of controlled vocabularies, supported by rigorous adherence to identifier standards.

2.1 Granularity Issues

In a physical library of printed books, the volume-on-the-shelf is the dominant unit of granularity. While inescapable, this is not entirely propitious for emblem scholarship. Many individual emblem books contain more than 100 emblems; a few single volumes contain more than 1,000 emblems. While emblem books as a whole are studied by scholars, and while the bibliographic context of an emblem is important, individual emblems and components of individual emblems are also objects of scholarly inquiry in their own right. *Picturae*, the graphic elements of emblems, are important examples of Renaissance and Baroque imagery and symbolism. The textual components of emblems play specific roles in analyzing and interpreting emblems and can on their own be targets of research.

While book-level bibliographic metadata are essential, descriptions of emblem books must include fulsome descriptions of individual emblems and individual emblem components to fully support emblem scholars' preferred modes of discovery and use. Ideally, resources should be retrievable as well as citable at these sub-book levels of granularity, implying a need to mint identifiers at multiple levels of granularity. This in turn requires careful delineation of emblem boundaries and boundaries within each emblem. Done right, digitization can facilitate emblem-level description as well as more granular discovery, retrievability, and citation of individual emblems and emblem components. Once digitized, it is easier (not to mention less destructive) to disassemble an emblem book into its components, providing both a primary view (serving as a surrogate for the book as a whole) and complementary, citable secondary derivative views of individual emblems and emblem components. To achieve these goals, a flexible, albeit rigorous, approach to metadata design, the identification of emblems and emblem components, and the creation of derivatives is required.

[1] http://iconclass.org/help/lod

2.2 Metadata and Vocabulary Issues

Based on their survey and analysis of how humanities scholars use sources, Audenaert and Furuta proposed a model of information consumed by scholars that encompasses not only the central object of study (e.g., a digital surrogate, complete or partial, of a primary source), but also associated context surrounding the object and its creation, actors involved in the life cycle of the object, and object sources and derivatives ([1], pp. 290-91). This gestalt model of scholarly sources, which fits well with the way emblem scholars approach their research, has implications for how digital library architects must approach metadata design.

For example, emblems captured facets of contemporary culture and events. Emblem creators relied on allusions to well-known individuals and political figures, to then ubiquitous stories and parables and to dominant events of the time. The emblem format is often spare, meaning that such allusions are often implicit; they cannot be discovered by inspection of an emblem in isolation. Today many of these once obvious allusions are obscure. This suggests a need to accommodate in metadata and index design specialized controlled vocabularies that can capture such context. Similarly reliant on outside name authorities and other evidence (because bibliographic norms and standards were not yet fully established), the identities and roles of individuals involved in the creation of an emblem are equally important to describe.

Relationship metadata describing emblem antecedents and subsequent derivations also is valued by emblem scholars. This includes both emblem-to-emblem relationships and relationships to objects never published in emblem book form. Translation and reuse of emblem components, both textual and graphic, was frequent. Scholarship sometimes can determine that earlier emblems influenced subsequent emblems. As mentioned, emblem creators were influenced by popular culture. It is likely that the two *picturae* illustrated in Figure 12, published more than 100 years apart, were influenced by one or more of the ubiquitous (in Renaissance Europe) fables involving a fox and a bird. Whether the earlier emblem creator influenced the later Emblem artist is less certain, but also a possibility. Emblem derivatives appearing not in book form are frequent as well, e.g., in such diverse contexts as architecture [3] and porcelain [5]. Accordingly a metadata and identifier approach that supports linkages between heterogeneous Web resources is essential.

3. APPROACHES TESTED

To address some of these challenges, workflows for *Emblematica Online* (as compared to earlier emblem projects) were augmented, enhanced, and further automated in order to better support the anticipated needs of emblem studies scholars while still supporting requirements for scale. Descriptive metadata, both book-level and emblem-level, are serialized in Extensible Markup Language (XML) metadata records. Efficiency in metadata processing is accomplished by utilizing generic XML software applications and by manipulating components of metadata using stylesheets written in the Extensible Stylesheet Language for Transformations (XSLT). To provide metadata most germane to emblem studies use cases, *Emblematica Online* metadata records adhere to the Wolfenbüttel Emblem Schema,[2] created and maintained by HAB [20]. This schema, which has already been modified based on experience in the course of the *Emblematica Online* project, implements in large measure a 2004 emblem studies domain-based proposal for "A Spine of Information Headings for Emblem-Related Resources" [19]. Spine metadata records include a bibliographic description of a digitized emblem volume, a brief description identifying the print copy that was digitized (e.g., where located and by whom owned), and fulsome descriptions of each emblem contained in the volume. As described below, Iconclass descriptors are added to facilitate discovery based on emblem and image content. An emblem registry was implemented to facilitate the coining of identifiers. Post-digitization workflows also were augmented to generate more granular secondary digitization derivatives.

3.1 The Spine Metadata Schema

Records conforming to the Wolfenbüttel Emblem Schema (a partial example of such a record is shown in Figure 2) are dubbed "Spine" metadata records in acknowledgement of the inspiration for the metadata format. The Spine approach to emblem book description emerged from a collaboration between librarians and emblem studies scholars. While the Spine schema defines some new semantics, in accord with best practices for application profiles and project-specific metadata schemas, established standard semantics were imported when available. To express most book-level metadata, the Spine schema allows implementers to use either the <teiHeader> element from the Text Encoding Initiative namespace (P5 schema) or the <mods> element from the Metadata Object Description Schema (ver. 3.4). For other uses, Spine borrows semantics from the XML Linking Language (XLink), the Simple Knowledge Organization System (SKOS), and the Resource Description Framework (RDF). These particular semantic schemes were chosen in part to facilitate possible conversion to a Semantic Web version of the Spine schema at some date in the future.

The Spine schema also supports the inclusion of emblem-level metadata. A goal of the Spine proposal was to support scholars' access to and use of digitized emblems in a manner that could span emblem collections and institutional boundaries. To achieve this goal and be true to the schema's roots in the emblem studies community, the emblem descriptive elements integrated into the Spine schema align well with modes of scholarly discovery and use in that community. In other words, Spine metadata records capture and describe the structure and content of each digitized emblem using semantic elements that are recognizable to emblem scholars and simultaneously useful for generating indexes and creating links that facilitate the discovery of emblems and emblem relationships.

The approach used for emblem description is based on the *emblema triplex* [11, 15], i.e., the *pictura-inscriptio-subscriptio* model of book-published Early Modern emblems alluded to above. (The *inscriptio* is labeled as motto in Spine.) To introduce additional flexibility, the Spine schema allows for inclusion of an additional emblem component, the *commentatio* (a further gloss on themes of the emblem), a transcription of an emblem-specific dedication when present, any name metadata associated with the emblem and/or emblem *pictura*, and both free text and controlled vocabulary index terms (e.g., from authoritative linked data compliant vocabularies like Iconclass). Elements used in the Spine metadata record are repeatable. Links and identifiers are supported for emblems, index terms, and emblem components (e.g., *pictura*, *inscriptio*, *subscriptio*).

[2] http://diglib.hab.de/rules/schema/emblem/emblem-1-2.xsd

```
...
<mods:mods>
 <mods:titleInfo>
  <mods:title>XL [i.e. Quadraginta] emblemata miscella nova</mods:title>
  <mods:subTitle>Das ist : XL. underschiedliche Auszerlesene newradierte Kunststuck</mods:subTitle>
 </mods:titleInfo>
 <mods:name type="personal">
  <mods:namePart>Murer, Christoph</mods:namePart>
  <mods:namePart type="date">1558-1614</mods:namePart>
  <mods:role><mods:roleTerm authority="marcrelator" type="text">creator</mods:roleTerm></mods:role>
 </mods:name>
   ...
</mods:mods>
   ...
<emblem xml:id="E000944" citeNo="I." globalID="http://hdl.handle.net/10111/EmblemRegistry:E000944">
  <motto>
     <transcription xml:lang="de">Alchimisterey:
        <normalisation xml:lang="de">Alchemie:</normalisation></transcription>
     <transcription xml:lang="la">Alchimia.</transcription>
  </motto>
  <pictura xml:id="E000944_P1" xlink:href="http://djatoka.grainger.illinois.edu/adore...">
     <iconclass rdf:about="http://www.iconclass.org/rkd/31A247">
        <skos:notation>31A247</skos:notation>
        <skos:prefLabel>looking over the shoulder</skos:prefLabel>
     </iconclass>
       ...
  </pictura>
</emblem>
```

Figure 2. Portion of a Spine metadata record describing an emblem book and one of the emblems it contains [18].

Though recognized as a useful way to describe the structure of many emblems, as the basis for a metadata format for describing all emblems, the sufficiency of the *emblema triplex* view of structure is not a settled matter in the emblem studies community. To begin with, there is great variance in the layout, the functional role of emblem textual elements, and the overall structure of published emblems. Scholars working with different sub-genres of emblem books often disagree as to the elements that comprise the emblem archetype, both in number and in function. Researchers have made progress towards refining the *emblema triplex* and developing more comprehensive, function-based typographies of emblematic forms and structures (e.g., [11]). However, any systematic examination of structure and form over a general sampling of published emblems reveals that heterogeneity rather than homogeneity is the norm. Unresolved issues in emblem typographies and in dealing generally with the heterogeneity of emblems mean that delineating the boundaries of an emblem and labeling its components requires analysis and interpretation. This is not a task that most metadata librarians can do unilaterally; emblem description requires domain expertise and is best done by librarian and scholar collaboratively. Emblem-level components of metadata records included in the *Emblematica Online* project were created jointly by librarians and emblem studies scholars.

There is additionally the challenge of describing books containing forms closely related to emblems that do not map well to the *emblema triplex*. For example, many books of Italian *impresse*, though the form is closely related to emblems in other respects, have a prose-based structural framework which does not easily reduce in accord with the *emblema triplex* ([15], p. 172). Experimentation with approaches to reconcile such differences is ongoing, and presumably results will inform subsequent development of the Wolfenbüttel Emblem Schema and successor formats. Accordingly, the Spine descriptive approach should be considered a good starting point for better functionality and scholar support, but not necessarily the final end point.

3.2 The Emblem Registry

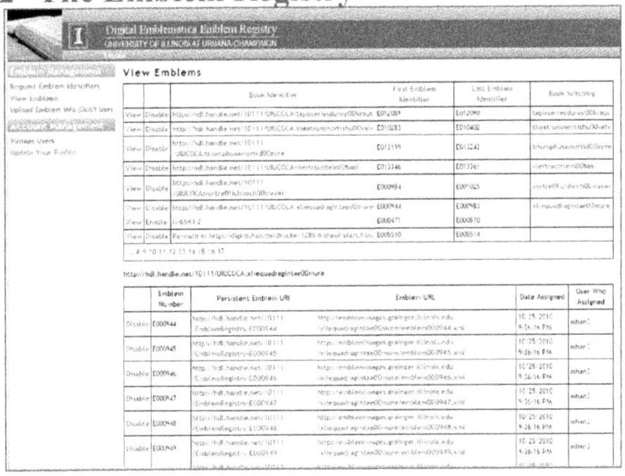

Figure 3. Screen shot of emblem registry

In developing the *Emblematica Online* project strategy for descriptive metadata and content management, the researchers at Illinois and HAB made a commitment to interoperability, community standards and best practices. The decision to utilize existing community-based descriptive metadata semantics when possible rather than to invent new, custom semantics illustrates this commitment. The Project's use of persistent, http-scheme global identifiers and metadata dissemination interoperability standards such as OAI-PMH is further illustration of this commitment. For example, to facilitate persistent global identification and retrieval of digitized emblems, the Illinois Library has created a prototype emblem registry (Figure 3). Through this Web-based application, Illinois and HAB librarians can associate a unique persistent Uniform Resource Identifier (URI) with each individual emblem contained in an emblem book digitized from their print collections. Identifiers can be minted emblem-by-emblem or created in batch for an entire volume of emblems. Presently, the identifiers assigned by the registry are handles based, i.e., as used in the Corporation for National

Research Initiatives (CNRI) Handle System [13]. When de-referenced, these URIs currently redirect to an online digital landing page for the identified emblem as maintained on the HAB or Illinois Library Website.

Though only a prototype, the emblem registry at Illinois is a partial blueprint for a potential community-wide emblem registry. Having persistent emblem URIs allows librarians and scholars to precisely reference individual emblems digitized from any specific print format emblem book. This facilitates citation and scholarly use of digitized emblems. It also allows scholars to assert relationships between digitized emblem surrogates and between digitized emblem surrogates and other kinds of resources found on the Web. Additional work to make emblem landing pages Linked Data friendly, e.g., in the way that handles-based CrossRef DOIs can now be used as Linked Data identifiers,[3] would better integrate these resources into the Semantic Web. Doing this will require (among other things) crosswalking elements of the Spine metadata into a scheme that better leverages RDF or RDFa and related Semantic Web technologies (e.g., schema.org). Currently the Illinois registry is used only for emblems, but discussions are ongoing to allow registration of emblem components (e.g., *pictura*) and/or to support minting and/or mapping of emblem book identifiers. (There are multiple book-level identifier schemes for Early Modern books; identifiers conforming to these schemes are included in Spine metadata records as available, but are not registered or mapped one to another in any systematic way.)

3.3 Additional Derivatives

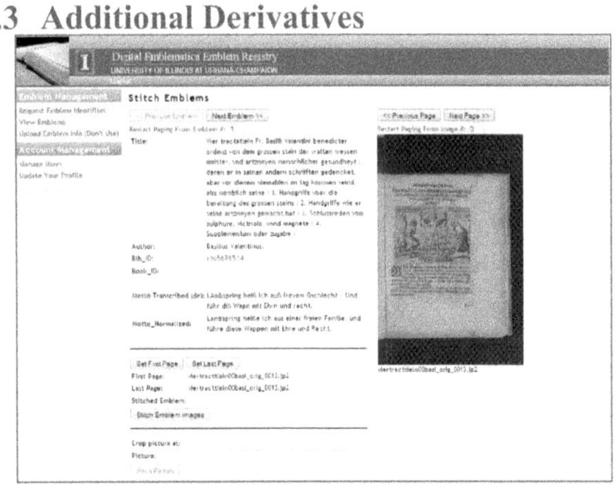

Figure 4. Screen shot of stitching application.

Many emblems span multiple pages in a print book. An Illinois-specific extension to the registry (Figure 4) allows Project participants at Illinois to identify the page images that comprise each emblem as well as the region of each emblem that is the *pictura*. During this process, the page images that comprise each emblem are stitched together by a background process (using ImageMagick[4]) and saved (in JPEG 2000 format) to an Illinois Webserver. A local instance of aDORe djatoka [6] is invoked to generate URLs (conformant to the OpenURL standard[5]) that return JPEG emblem and pictura views (Figure 5). URLs are then added to the Spine metadata record description of the emblem.

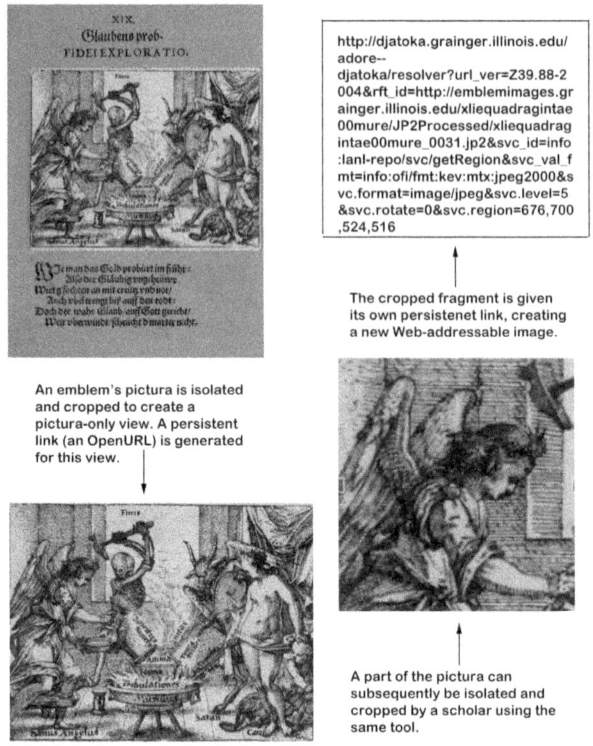

Figure 5. *Picturae* and segments of *picturae* can be isolated from an emblem view as secondary derivatives [18].

The boundaries of arbitrary emblem segments of interest to scholars at granularities finer than *pictura* cannot be anticipated and so neither URLs nor identifiers for such emblem segments can be pre-generated or pre-registered. Nonetheless, persistent URLs for such fine-grained emblem segments are desirable in order to facilitate scholarly citation and reference. To allow scholars to reference a specific segment of a digitized emblem pictura, Illinois created a JavaScript based application that uses the local implementation of the aDORe Djatoka Web service to generate a URL for any arbitrarily cropped segment of an emblem view (Figure 5). This allows scholars to define emblem segments of interest dynamically, creating a persistent URL by which they can reference that emblem segment of interest.

4. A SPINE-BASED PORTAL

Once digitization and metadata creation were underway, researchers at Illinois and HAB turned their attention to the design and execution of a shared portal to provide enhanced discovery and access over their combined digital emblem holdings. In the past Illinois has made do with generic, turnkey digital content management systems to provide access to digital representations of emblem books, e.g., CONTENTdm ([12], pp. 79–80) and the Internet Scout Collection Workflow Integration System ([22], p. 120). These systems are insufficiently tailored to meet the needs and increasingly more sophisticated expectations of emblem studies scholars today. Libraries need to organize and present digital content according to both the intrinsic nature of the content and how users interact with that content.

Accordingly the librarians at Illinois and HAB decided that the *Emblematica Online* project warranted a new, more customized

[3] http://www.crossref.org/crweblog/2011/04/crossref_and_international_doi.html;

[4] http://www.imagemagick.org/

[5] http://www.niso.org/apps/group_public/project/details.php?project_id=82

solution. This did not mean starting over entirely from scratch. The Web itself provides stable and well-understood infrastructure for portal development. Ubiquitous Web browsers such as Firefox, Google Chrome, Microsoft Internet Explorer, and Apple Safari provide a stable and robust client framework that can be employed to create robust digital resource discovery and use applications. Web services architectures and models for rapid prototyping of Web applications are now also relatively mature. The initial prototype of the Open Emblem Portal[6] created for the *Emblematica Online* project takes advantage of the free, widely available JQuery JavaScript software library.[7] This software library allows Web application developers to integrate tested user interface frameworks and features into their Web-based applications. In particular, JQuery supports both tabbed interface designs and the Asynchronous JavaScript And XML (AJAX) programming interface for leveraging Web Services.

Of course portal design in the context of an initiative like the *Emblematica Online* project must be viewed as an iterative process. As part of the *Emblematica Online* project, Illinois and HAB have implemented and are currently refining a functional prototype of a next generation Open Emblem Portal. This is not thought of yet as a final product. Additional testing with users will be required to refine, develop, and enlarge this prototype; the immediate goal is to create a working portal supporting functionality to which scholars can react and about which they can provide constructive feedback. Figures 6 through 9 are screen shots of the prototype Portal. As illustrated in these four screen shots, the design of this portal supports access to digitized content at multiple levels of granularity, i.e., at both the book and emblem level. A tabbed motif is used, for searching as well as browseing. Default search is by keyword, but options are provided to search for book metadata only, for emblem metadata only, or for both book and emblem metadata simultaneously (Figure 6).

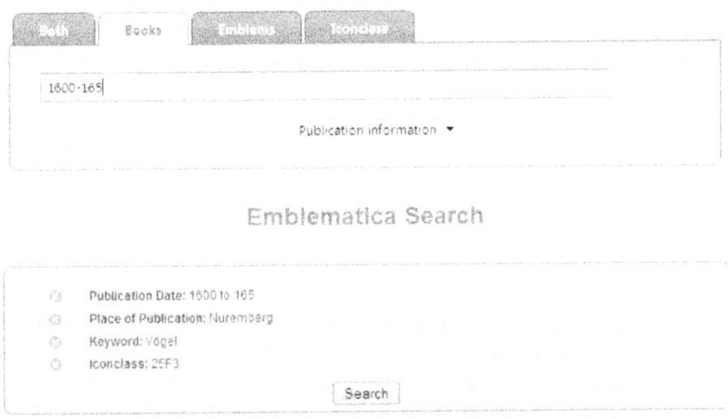

Figure 6. Open Emblem Portal prototype search page.

When displaying book-level search results, basic bibliographic metadata for matching titles are displayed in the first tab and this tab is labeled "Book Results." If an item from the search result list is selected, a complete display of all book-level metadata for that item is presented in this same tab, relabeled "Book Details" (Figure 7). This display includes a link to the digitized volume at Illinois or HAB, a link to the catalog record (at the owning institution) for the print volume digitized, and links to views of digital derivatives held at other locations when applicable.

[6] http://emblematica.grainger.illinois.edu/OEBP/UI/SearchForm

[7] http://jquery.com/

Figure 7. Presentation of book-level bibliographic description [18] as viewed in the prototype portal's "Book Details" tab.

When browsing search results, the second tab (Figure 8), labeled "Emblems," provides thumbnail representations of emblems (*pictura* and motto only) associated with a particular book or retrieved from a search (depending on context). Selecting an item from this display will activate a third tab (Figure 9), labeled "Emblem Detail," containing available metadata describing the emblem selected. The detailed display of emblem metadata includes a transcribed motto and potentially other transcribed or normalized text associated with the emblem (*subscriptio*, *commentatio*, etc.), a link to the description of the emblem book containing that emblem, the globally unique identifier of the emblem, links to the first page of the emblem on the HAB Website or to a single image complete view of the emblem on the Illinois Website, links to additional component views of the emblem when available (e.g., to the emblem's pictura), and links to Iconclass headings that have been assigned to the emblem.

Figure 8. The "Emblems" tab of the prototype displays *pictura* and motto for each emblem in the selected book [16].

The tabbed interface approach is designed to allow users to switch between granularity of emblem-related resources easily and quickly. A user can search for emblems by keyword, view detailed metadata for one of the emblems discovered, link to the detailed record for the book containing that emblem, see the *pictura* and motto for each of the other emblems contained in that book, select a different emblem to view in detail, and so on. The view associated with each tab is retrieved by the client Web browser using AJAX, which calls back to the portal server. Tab displays are coordinated and URLs generated persistent, allowing Web browser bookmarking of individual book and emblem descriptions (subject to updates of these descriptions in the underlying database). Searches can also be bookmarked;

however, when a bookmarked search result is retrieved the search will be re-executed (meaning additional results may be included if metadata records for new items have been added to the database), and the search result list will always be refreshed to the top.

Figure 9. The "Emblem Details" tab displays emblem-level description, including motto and Iconclass headings [16].

5. ICONCLASS INTEGRATION

As illustrated in Figure 2 above, an explicit provision is made in the Spine metadata format for including Iconclass controlled vocabulary headings in emblem *pictura* descriptions. As mentioned earlier, Iconclass is a multilingual classification system for cultural heritage art and images. It is a hierarchically ordered thesaurus consisting of more than 28,000 controlled vocabulary terms describing objects, people, events and abstract ideas. These terms can be used to describe what an image is about. Art historians, museum curators, emblem scholars, librarians, and others use Iconclass to describe and classify the content of images in a variety of formats, including paintings, emblems, drawings, and photographs [10]. Scholars use Iconclass to discover images of interest. Iconclass predates the Web. Henri van de Waal (University of Leiden) began work on what was to become Iconclass in the 1950's. After his death, the first complete edition of Iconclass was published over multiple years between 1973 and 1985. The current online edition of Iconclass[8] is maintained by the RKD (Rijksbureau voor Kunsthistorische Documentatie, Netherlands). Iconclass has two features that are especially relevant in the context of digitized emblem literature. First, Iconclass is multi-lingual (English, French, German, Italian) and intrinsically extensible. Second, core Iconclass notations have been assigned persistent http-scheme URIs. These URIs can be used to retrieve RDF descriptions of Iconclass headings via Web Services maintained by the RKD.

5.1 Multi-Lingual and Extensible

Each Iconclass heading is assigned an alphanumeric notation (aka classification code), a textual correlate (aka human readable label), and keywords. Textual correlates and keywords are available in four languages, with work-in-progress on translations into four additional languages. Iconclass notations begin with a digit (0-9) corresponding to the main divisions of Iconclass. The second character of the notation is also a digit, this time corresponding to the subdivision (maximum of nine subdivisions for any main division). Upper case letters are used to indicate the next level of hierarchy, with digits used for subsequent levels. Most emblem literature was published in contemporary vernacular, e.g., Renaissance variants of today's French, English, German, etc. Emblem scholars today often specialize in emblems of one language or another. The availability of a multi-lingual thesaurus facilitates searching and browsing a multi-lingual corpus. Figure 10 illustrates one way the multi-lingual features of Iconclass are exploited in the portal prototype.

Figure 10. A segment of the Iconclass hierarchy viewed in prototype portal in English (top) and in German (bottom).

Allusions and implicit references intended by emblem creators can be quite specific, i.e., to the level of specific individuals, events, locales, etc. Iconclass builds in extensibility mechanisms, called *Auxiliaries*, for dynamically creating more precise notations. This is helpful when classifying emblem *pictura*. Some Iconclass headings allow for *bracketed text*. The general Iconclass notation for literary proverbs, sayings, etc. is "86." A subdivision "86(...)" is provided to allow the inclusion of the specific text of a saying or proverb, e.g., "86(LIGHTLY COME, LIGHTLY GO)." Bracketed text is also used to assign headings for specific historical persons, places, and events, e.g., from the base notation "11H(...)," the notation for male saints (with NAME), "11H(FRANCIS)" is the notation for St. Francis of Assisi. (Iconclass Web services return parent headinga if the bracketed text has not previously been entered into the Iconclass database.) Constructs called *structural digits* are provided to create headings pertaining to a specific facet of an entity. Thus "11H(FRANCIS)2" is the notation for the early life of St. Francis of Assisi. *Keys* can be placed at the end of a notation to further refine meaning, e.g., the key "(+5245)" signifies an animal holding something. Thus "25F33(EAGLE)(+5245)" might be assigned to a pictura depicting an eagle, i.e., a predatory bird, holding something.

While the extensibility of Iconclass allows for precise assignments of index terms, it also is indicative of the level of expertise required to assign Iconclass terms to an emblem *pictura*. This further illustrates the need for collaboration between scholar and librarian in construction of emblem-level metadata. For the *Emblematica Online* project, Iconclass heading assignment is being done by researchers at Arkyves.org and the Bildarchiv Foto Marburg, the German documentation center for art history at the Philipps-University Marburg. Spine metadata records (sans Iconclass headings) prepared by librarians at Illinois and HAB are made available to Arkyves.org and the Foto Marburg using OAI-PMH. Iconclass headings (Iconclass notations) are assigned to each *pictura* and returned (Arkyves.org) or added to the Spine records and the records returned via OAI-PMH (Foto Marburg).

[8] http://www.iconclass.nl/

```
<rdf:RDF>
  <rdf:Description rdf:about="http://iconclass.org/25F33%28EAGLE%29">
    <rdf:type rdf:resource="http://www.w3.org/2004/02/skos/core#Concept"/>
        <skos:prefLabel xml:lang="fr">oiseaux de proie : aigle</skos:prefLabel>
        <skos:prefLabel xml:lang="en">predatory birds: eagle</skos:prefLabel>
        <skos:prefLabel xml:lang="de">Greifvögel: Adler</skos:prefLabel>
        <skos:prefLabel xml:lang="it">uccelli rapaci: aquila</skos:prefLabel>
        <skos:inScheme rdf:resource="http://iconclass.org/rdf/2011/09/"/>
        <skos:notation>25F33(EAGLE)</skos:notation>
        <skos:narrower rdf:resource="http://iconclass.org/25F33%28EAGLE%29%28%2B0%29"/>
        <skos:narrower rdf:resource="http://iconclass.org/25F33%28EAGLE%29%28%2B1%29"/>
        <skos:narrower rdf:resource="http://iconclass.org/25F33%28EAGLE%29%28%2B2%29"/>
        ...
        <skos:narrower rdf:resource="http://iconclass.org/25FF33%28EAGLE%29"/>
        <skos:related rdf:resource="http://iconclass.org/25Fk12"/>
        <skos:broader rdf:resource="http://iconclass.org/25F33%28...%29"/>
  </rdf:Description>
</rdf:RDF>
```

Figure 11. Iconclass heading 25F33(EAGLE) expressed in RDF/XML.

5.2 Reliance on Iconclass Web Services

Iconclass browsing and navigation functionality is built into the prototype portal. Users can browse the Iconclass hierarchy in their preferred language to discover digitized emblem content. This flexibility is accomplished without having to have a local copy of the complete thesaurus through JavaScript (AJAX) calls to Iconclass Web services. Figure 11 shows the RDF returned for the Iconclass Notation, "25F33(EAGLE)." RDF like this example was used to generate the multi-lingual display shown in Figure 10. For better performance and to avoid cross-domain scripting errors, a local short-term caching proxy service is used.

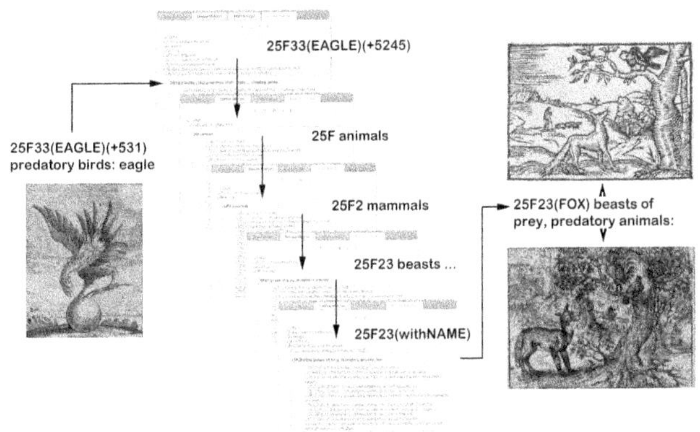

Fig. 12. Starting from a display of emblem details, scholars can link to and browse the Iconclass subject hierarchy to find other emblems with related Iconclass headings.

Figure 12 shows one way the prototype portal allows end-users to leverage Iconclass browsing to find emblems. In the scenario illustrated, a user has found emblem 24 (pp. 56-57, "Den Armen schafft man billich Rath.") from Johann Vogel's *Meditationes Emblematicae de Restaurata Pace Germaniae* [21]. One of the Iconclass headings assigned to the pictura of this emblem is 25F33(EAGLE)(+5245), "predatory birds: eagle (+ animal(s) holding something)." As illustrated in Figure 12, the user can move from the display of detailed emblem metadata to a view of the Iconclass hierarchy centered on this particular Iconclass heading (i.e., under another tab of the interface). The user may then browse up or down the hierarchy, and at any point selecting a heading for a new search in the portal. In this instance the user browses up the hierarchy to 25F, "animals," then down the hierarchy to search on 25F23(...), "beasts of prey, predatory animals (with NAME)." This search retrieves several *picturae* and associated emblems, including the ones shown in Figure 12 ([17], [18]). Iconclass headings assigned to emblem *picturae* are indexed locally in English and in the modern version of the language of the emblem. Notation codes are also indexed to take advantage of the hierarchical structure of Iconclass codes, so that searches retrieve *picturae* with exactly matched headings and any *picturae* with a heading below the requested heading in the Iconclass hierarchy.

6. DISCUSSION AND FUTURE PLANS

6.1 Expanding the Corpus

Peter Daly estimates the corpus of extant print emblem books (broadly defined) to be about 6,500 ([8], p. 261). This estimate includes atypical examples (e.g., *emblema nuda* -- emblems published without *pictura*) as well as some books that contain emblems in addition to non-emblem content. Still, 6,500 is a good starting estimate as to the size of the print emblem book corpus.

Assuming this estimate for the corpus size, the prototype Open Emblem Portal built as part of the *Emblematica Online* project currently contains emblem-level metadata, identifiers, and derivatives for at most two or three percent of this corpus, and book-level metadata and links for no more than ten percent of the corpus. (Given the collections involved, the DFG funding, and the interests of the project PIs, the percentage of German-language emblem books indexed by the Open Emblem Portal is of course much higher, possibly approaching forty percent of that sub-corpus.) A priority going forward is to substantially enlarge the number of books and emblems discoverable through the portal. This is not as difficult as it may seem.

Emblem book *digitization for access* has been ongoing for at least two decades. The pace has accelerated of late as a number of emblem books have been digitized in connection with the Google Book and Open Content Alliance mass book digitization projects -- e.g., about 250 emblem books from the Research Library of the Getty Research Institute have been digitized by the Open Content Alliance initiative. Inclusion of entries from the Universidade da Coruña's 2010 bibliography of Digital Emblem Books on the Web[9] would add another 1,000+ book-level metadata records to the Open Emblem portal. (This is currently being considered.)

Books with fully described emblems are fewer, but test records from two of the most important such collections, i.e., at the University of Glasgow and at Utrecht University have yielded

[9] http://www.bidiso.es/emblematica/CatalogoDEBOW.pdf

promising results. The inclusion of emblem-level metadata records from these digital libraries would immediately increase the number of emblem-level records in the portal substantially. These steps begin to create a digital library for emblem resources with sufficient scope and contextual mass to be useful. This in turn allows iterative development by working with users.

6.2 Support for Library Linked Open Data[10]

Beyond increases in size and scope, we also see the need to further develop our approach to relationship metadata -- e.g., to make digitized emblem books more useful in an increasingly Semantic Web and Linked Data world. This might entail converting the Spine metadata schema to be more Linked Data friendly (as mentioned above), adding RDFa to emblem landing pages, and/or linking with other authoritative data sets beyond Iconclass, e.g., name authorities, thesauri of geographic terms, and even indices of historic events or literatures pertinent to emblem resources. This will allow us to better support increasingly demanding expectations of digital humanities scholars, who have come to expect that technology should:

- facilitate discovery of and access to more and more richly described digital surrogates for primary sources;
- enable more scholars to more easily interact with content at the margins of their primary domain, bringing to bear as they do so broader and more diverse ranges of competencies;
- encourage broader collaboration and discourse over a wide range of content available in new and different ways.

This view recognizes that the lifeblood of humanities scholarship and pedagogy has been and continues to be engagement and discourse, underpinned by curated collections of well-described primary sources of verifiable provenance. The essential predicates for this emerging vision of Digital Humanities 2.0 are multilingual and transnational digital archives, ubiquitously available, collaboratively curated by librarians and scholars, and managed so as to support multi-modal discovery and access at multiple levels of granularity. In her paper, "Humanities 2.0: Promises, Perils, Predictions," Cathy Davidson outlines a broad, coherent vision of Digital Humanities 2.0 along these lines and describes its implications for scholarly practice. A prerequisite for her vision is increased access to and sharing of information. "Hybridity, exchange, flow, and cultural transaction are all explored more responsibly and adventurously when the resources of many nations, in many languages, have been digitized, made interoperable, and offered for research by scholars around the world, each of whom brings a local store of knowledge and experience to the theoretical, interpretive enterprise" ([9], p. 710).

The core long-term goal of the *Emblematica Online* project to enhance emblem literature access and sharing is well aligned with this vision. Illustrative of this view of Humanities 2.0 is recent work to support interoperable scholarly annotation of digital resources, e.g., the Open Annotation Collaboration.[11] This work in turn prompted an early experiment examining how an annotation facility might be added to a future iteration of the Open Emblem Portal. In this experiment, selected emblem metadata records (conforming to the Spine schema discussed above) were made available for annotation by a few scholars and graduate students using browser-based and desktop annotation tools. To avoid having to duplicate copies of Spine metadata records, the experiment was carried out by exploiting built-in Web server proxy features and using conditional stylesheet transformations based on whether an emblem description is being served directly or by proxy. Figure 13 illustrates one of the annotations created. The annotation tool interface was simplistic and constrained, and testing was not systematic. Nonetheless, the experiment generated enthusiasm on the part of the users involved and confirmed that our underlying use of identifiers and Spine metadata records is on the right track to support further annotation experiments. Consistently and openly available structured representations of annotation have the potential to facilitate interactivity with primary sources, discourse involving these resources, and collaborative curation of these resources.

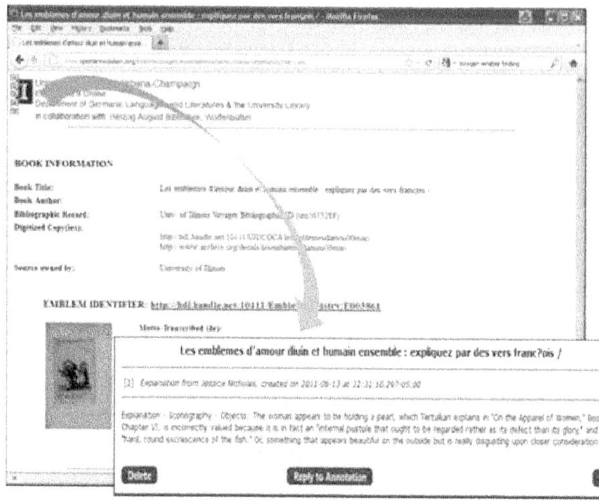

Fig. 13. Early experimentation with emblem annotation [14].

6.3 Collaboration is Key

Returning to Peter Daly's distinction between "Digitization as Preservation" and "Digitization as Enrichment," it is clear that the latter is much less determined by technology than the former. In the domain of emblem books, libraries now have the expertise, standards, and best practices in place to economically create and make accessible static digital surrogates of print emblem books. Providing services and creating environments in which users can more easily exploit these resources for analysis and to create new knowledge, *digitization as enrichment*, is more challenging.

Emblem scholars want access to thoroughly described and well-identified components within emblem books. They need access to and the ability to reliably cite individual emblems and emblem components. They need to be able to integrate these granular primary sources into a web of context and related sources and derivatives. Based on the lessons of the *Emblematica Online* project, it is clear that these objectives require collaboration between librarian and scholar. Any assumption that the construction of digital libraries and digital library services can be left solely in the hands of librarians and technologists is naïve, at least in the domain of digitized Early Modern emblem literature. As Peter Daly suggests, there is more to a digital library than hyperlinks; "We can have hyperlinks until we hyperventilate, but they will only be as useful as the information added by the emblem scholar. This is the rub" ([8], p. 10).

A recurring lesson of the *Emblematica Online* project has been the benefit and value of working with scholars to create metadata, to define how resources are sub-divided, identified and made

[10] http://www.w3.org/2005/Incubator/lld/wiki/Main_Page

[11] http://www.openannotation.org/

accessible, and to enrich indexing. We anticipate that as more interactivity with emblem resources is made possible through the Open Emblem Portal, opportunities to involve emblem scholars in ongoing curation will grow. As librarians, we see the need for collaborative curation as obvious. Fortunately this sentiment is shared by many in the emblem studies community.

7. ACKNOWLEDGMENTS

This material is based upon work supported by the National Endowment for the Humanities (NEH) and the *Deutsche Forschungsgemeinschaft* (DFG) under Digital Humanities Grant #A2763 HG-50004-09. Any opinions, findings, and conclusions or recommendations expressed are those of the authors and do not necessarily reflect the views of either the NEH or DFG. The authors wish to acknowledge the foundation for the metadata work described in this paper laid by Stephen Rawles, Honorary Senior Research Fellow, Humanities Advanced Technology and Information Institute, University of Glasgow, Thomas Stäcker, Deputy Director, Herzog August Bibliothek, Wolfenbüttel, and Hans Brandhorst of Arkyves.org. Emblem and *picturae* images used in this paper are courtesy of the Stirling Maxwell Collection, Glasgow University Library and the Rare Book and Manuscript Library at the University of Illinois at Urbana-Champaign.

8. REFERENCES

[1] N. Audenaert and R. Furuta. What humanists want: how scholars use source materials. In *Proceedings of the 10th annual joint conference on digital libraries*, pp. 283-292, New York, NY, USA, 2010. ACM.

[2] M. Billings. Digital Emblematica: The Scholarly Background of 'Digital Emblematica' and Its New Direction. In *Florilegio De Estudios Emblematicos. A Florilegium of Studies in Emblematics*, pp. 185-90, ed. B. Rafoth, Ferrol, España, 2004.

[3] H. Boker and P. M. Daly. *The Emblem and Architecture: Studies in Applied Emblematics from the Sixteenth to the Eighteenth Centuries*. Ed. by P. Daly and H. Boker. Turnhout, Brepols, 1999.

[4] N. R. Brisaboa, S. López Poza, M. R. Penabad, Á. S. Places, and F. J. Rodríguez. A System for the Integrated Access to three Digital Libraries of Spanish Golden Age Documents. In *Digital Collections and the Management of Knowledge: Renaissance Emblem Literature as a Case Study for the Digitization of Rare Texts and Images*, pp. 97-106, ed. M. Wade. Salzburg, 2004.

[5] M. Chilton. *Fired by passion: Vienna Baroque porcelain of Claudius Innocentius Du Pacquier*. 2009. Melinda and Paul Sullivan Foundation for the Decorative Arts, M. Chilton, editor-in-chief. Stuttgart: Arnoldsche Art Publishers: 388-95.

[6] R. Chute and H. Van de Sompel. Introducing djatoka. *D-Lib Magazine* 14: 9/10 (2008). Available at http://www.dlib.org/dlib/september08/chute/09chute.html.

[7] P. M. Daly. Modern Advertising and the Renaissance Emblem: Modes of Verbal and Visual Persuasion. In *Word and Visual Imagination: Studies in the Interaction of English Literature and the Visual Arts*, pp. 349-371, eds. K. J. Höltgen, P. M. Daly, and Wolfgang Lottes. Erlangen: Universitätsbund Erlangen-Nürnberg, 1988. Erlanger Forschungen. Reihe A, Geisteswissenschaften, Bd. 43.

[8] P. M. Daly. *Digitizing the European Emblem: Issues and Prospects*. AMS Press, New York, 2002.

[9] C. N. Davidson. Humanities 2.0: Promise, Perils, Predictions. *PMLA* 123(3): 707-717, 2008. Available at http://dx.doi.org/10.1632/pmla.2008.123.3.707.

[10] D. Graham. Three Phases of Emblem Digitization: the First Twenty Years, the Next Five. In *Digital Collections and the Management of Knowledge: Renaissance Emblem Literature as a Case Study for the Digitization of Rare Texts and Images*, pp. 13–18, ed. M. Wade. Salzburg, 2004.

[11] D. Graham. Emblema Multiplex: Towards a Typology of Emblematic Forms, Structures and Functions. In *Emblem Scholarship Directions and Developments: a Tribute to Gabriel Hornstein*, pp. 131–158, ed. P. M. Daly, Turnhout, Brepols, 2005.

[12] N. Koetter. Interoperability of Digital Emblematica Metadata Using the Open Archives Initiative Metadata Harvesting Protocol and Other Schemas. In *Digital Collections and the Management of Knowledge: Renaissance Emblem Literature as a Case Study for the Digitization of Rare Texts and Images*, pp. 79-87, ed. M. Wade. Salzburg, 2004.

[13] L. Lannom. In Brief : New Handle System Release and License. *D-Lib Magazine* 12(7/8), 2006. Available at http://www.dlib.org/dlib/july06/07inbrief.html.

[14] *Les Emblemes D'amour Diuin Et Humain Ensemble : Expliquez Par Des Vers François*. Chez Pierre Mariette ruë S Iacques a l Esperance, Paris, 164AD.

[15] D. Mansueto. From Page to Screen, from Screen to Page: Some Notes on Emblem Scholarship and Digitisation. In *Le livre demeure : studies in book history in honour of Alison Saunders*, pp. 157-179, ed. Alison Adams and Philip Ford; assisted by Stephen Rawles. Genève, 2011.

[16] S. Meinhard. *Geistliche emblemata oder Sinn-Bilder, aus den Sonntags-Evangelien* vom I. Advent biss auff Trinitatis. Druckts David-Fridrich Rhete, Dantzig, 1675.

[17] C. F. Menestrier. *L'art des emblemes*. Benoist Coral, Lyon, 1662.

[18] C. Murer. *XL [i.e. Quadraginta] emblemata miscella nova : Das ist : XL. underschiedliche Auszerlesene newradierte Kunststuck*. Gedruckt bey J. Rüdolff Wolffen, Zürych, 1622.

[19] S. Rawles. A Spine of Information Headings for Emblem-Related Electronic Resources. In *Digital Collections and the Management of Knowledge: Renaissance Emblem Literature as a Case Study for the Digitization of Rare Texts and Images*, pp. 19-28, ed. M. Wade. Salzburg, 2004.

[20] T. Stäcker. Practical Issues of the Wolfenbüttel Emblem Schema. In *Emblem Digitization: Conducting Digital Research with Renaissance Texts and Images*, ed. M. Wade. *Early Modern Literary Studies* Special Issue. 2012.

[21] J. Vogel. *Meditationes emblematicae de restaurata pace Germaniae*. Apud Joh. Dav. Zunnerum, Francofurti, [1649].

[22] M. R. Wade. Toward an Emblem Portal: Local and Global Portal Construction. In *Digital Collections and the Management of Knowledge: Renaissance Emblem Literature as a Case Study for the Digitization of Rare Texts and Images*, pp. 115-120, ed. M. Wade. Salzburg, 2004.

Categorization of Computing Education Resources with Utilization of Crowdsourcing

Yinlin Chen
Department of Computer Science
Virginia Tech
Blacksburg, VA
+1 540 808 9053
ylchen@vt.edu

Edward A. Fox
Department of Computer Science
Virginia Tech
Blacksburg, VA
+1 540 231 5113
fox@vt.edu

Paul Logasa Bogen II
Intelligent Computing Research Team
Computational Data Analytics Group
Oak Ridge National Laboratory
Oak Ridge, TN 37931
+1 865 241 0337
bogenpl@ornl.gov

Haowei Hsieh
School of Library and Information Science
University of Iowa
Iowa City, IA 52242
+1 319 335 5713
haowei-hsieh@uiowa.edu

Lillian N. Cassel
Department of Computing Sciences
Villanova University
Villanova PA 19085
+1 610 519 7341
lillian.cassel@villanova.edu

ABSTRACT

The Ensemble Portal harvests resources from multiple heterogeneous federated collections. Managing these dynamically increasing collections requires an automatic mechanism to categorize records in to corresponding topics. We propose an approach to use existing ACM DL metadata to build classifiers for harvested resources in the Ensemble project. We also present our experience with utilizing the Amazon Mechanical Turk platform to build ground truth training data sets from Ensemble collections.

Categories and Subject Descriptors

Copyright 2012 ACM 978-1-4503-1154-0/12/06...$10.00.H.3.7 [**Digital Libraries**]: *Collection.* I.5.2 [**Design Methodology**]: *Classifier design and evaluation.*

General Terms

Design, Experimentation.

Keywords

Digital libraries, machine learning, classification, Amazon Mechanical Turk.

1. INTRODUCTION

The Ensemble Project is a multi-university project funded by NSF to add a computing education portal to the NSDL family of STEM Pathways. Currently the Ensemble portal has 4432 metadata records harvested from 15 different content providers. These resources are harvested in the Dublin Core and NDSL_DC formats.

JCDL'12, June 10–14, 2012, Washington, DC, USA.

In order to help managers and users efficiently gather accurate information, resources need to be correctly classified. Correctly categorized resources help digital librarians to manage their collections and improve browsing as well as faceted searches.

We attempt to use the ACM Computing Classification System (CCS) as a source of categories for Ensemble resources. By using the CCS, we have a potential source of training data through the ACM DL for building classifiers that we believe will be able to classify Ensemble resources correctly. In this paper, we describe the building of our ground-truth test collection, our preliminary experiments with the ACML DL and our current results.

Section 2 describes related work about classification and other research using Amazon Mechanical Turk. Section 3 covers our procedure for training data preparation and ground truth selection. Section 4 describes our preliminary experiments. Section 5 summarizes our conclusions and future work.

2. RELATED WORK

Documents can be categorized manually, via an automatic technique (such as clustering), or semi-automatically using a classifier [1]. Manual categorization yields good results, but carries additional costs in terms of personnel. Automatic techniques are useful for finding patterns in data, but do not guarantee the classes found will correspond to pre-defined categories [2]. In many cases the difficulty in working with semi-automatic techniques is building adequate training data. Corpus analysis aims to mitigate this problem by using available document collections that have been pre-categorized as a source of training material. Large digital objects are ideal candidates for corpus-based training. Already this kind of technique has been used with Reuters's news archive to classify medical documents [3], and with Wikipedia articles to classify educational resources [4].

Amazon Mechanical Turk (MTurk) is a crowdsourcing service in which researchers can post tasks to be completed and give rewards to the workers who complete them [5-7]. These tasks are called Human Intelligence Tasks (HIT); researchers design HITs to conduct behavioral research [7], or to do annotation tasks for NLP [8]. In this paper, we designed and conducted two types of HITs in the MTurk and collected our ground truth records from the Ensemble project for evaluating classifiers we have built.

3. DATA SETS AND GROUND TRUTH

This section describes procedures to build training data sets from ACM metadata and a ground truth data set from Ensemble.

3.1 ACM Metadata Set

The ACM metadata set describes conference papers and journal articles from 1954 to 2011. There are 168,639 metadata records, classified according to the ACM Computing Classification System (CCS). The CCS is a hierarchical classification scheme with varying levels of specificity. To balance between specificity and ample numbers of documents for our test collection, we looked at CCS at the second-level of the hierarchy. There are 61 second-level categories. Because the Ensemble collection is relatively small compared to the ACM metadata set and we wanted at least 4 Ensemble records for each selected category in the testing data set, we selected 14 second-level categories from CCS for which we have a good number of entries in Ensemble.

The majority of the Ensemble records were published within the past ten years, thus we selected ACM DL metadata that was published after 2001 as our training data set.

For our selected categories, we extracted records from the ACM metadata set into a SQLite database to do facilitate feature extraction. We considered several factors when processing this metadata set. Since our purpose is to classify educational materials available through the Ensemble Portal, we focused on analogous metadata fields in both the ACM and Ensemble collections. This proved to be the title and abstract in ACM or description in Ensemble. Additionally, the documents in the ACM collection can be in multiple categories. Since no category is privileged over any other, we treat a document with multiple categories as multiple documents – each in a single category. For each such document we store the title, abstract, and a category. After the database was populated, we started building our ground truth set from the Ensemble collection. We asked two different user groups, information science students at University of Iowa and MTurk, to accomplish the ground truth selection tasks. The detailed procedures are described in the following two sections.

3.2 Iowa Ground Truth Selection

The ground truth selection task was planned as an in-class group exercise after a lecture about HCI research where Domain Experts and Human Intelligence Tasks (HITs) can be used.

3.2.1 Participants

The 25 participants were students taking the required Computing Foundation class at SLIS (School of Library and Information Science). In the class, they learn basic knowledge, terminology, and skills of computing and programming. Most of the students were also taking another SLIS required course, Conceptual Foundation, which covers "Theory, principles, and standards in organization of information; function of catalogs, indexes, bibliographic networks; introduction to meta-data descriptions, name and title access, subject analysis, controlled vocabularies, classification systems." The foundation classes should provide students with adequate background knowledge for the exercise.

3.2.2 Methodology

The 25 students in the computing foundation class were divided into 10 groups (5 2-person groups and 5 3-person groups). We chose 5 computing topics (Programming Techniques, Data Structures, Formal Languages, Discrete Mathematics, and Database Management) where each topic is assigned to two groups. Each group was asked to spend a little time to learn what that topic is about, a link to Wikipedia about that topic also was provided. We expected that students should be able to learn enough to categorize related resources and be able to identify records in the Ensemble collection related to their given topic. Each group was asked to find 20 items that belong to the given topic. For each record they found they were asked to include the URL to that record and a short explanation to justify their choice.

The exercise started in-class and continued two more days, allowing the students to finish typing the results. The reports were collected online through the course system. At the end, 9 student group reports were collected and 97 documents were categorized (one team did not finish the exercise in time).

3.3 Amazon Mechanical Turk (MTurk)

Additionally, we used MTurk to also build our ground truth set from the Ensemble portal to cover all 14 selected categories. We first employed a *Single assignment* strategy to gather records from Ensemble, and then we used a *Plurality* strategy to evaluate these records identified by both Iowa students and MTurk workers. Based on the majority vote result for these records, we selected our final ground truth records for testing our classifiers.

3.3.1 HIT design – Ground Truth

We used the same approach as in the Iowa class to collect these 14 selected categories records from Ensemble. We created a HIT for each category. In each HIT, we provided a short description of the category and a link to Wikipedia about that category. Workers were asked to use the Ensemble portal search interface to find 14 records that matched their assigned category. They also were instructed to not simply use the category as their search terms to find records. To ensure this, they had to document what search terms they used in this HIT and optionally provide reasons why they think this record is matched to this category. We estimated that each HIT required at least one hour to finish so we set the time allotted per HIT to 6 hours.

In order to get high quality results from workers, we set a high worker qualification on our HIT. Our qualification is a worker who has a HIT approval rate greater than or equal to 95%, has had greater than 50 HITs approved, and whose location is in the United States. We paid $1 for each approved assignment; this reward is rather high in the MTurk HIT pool.

We created another 9 HITs with the same rewards for Iowa students to have records covering all 14 categories. We announced these HITs to Iowa students twice during the experiment. However, no Iowa student accepted these HITs. One possible reason is that this experiment was hosted during the winter break and that was a bad time for students to do experiments. A second possible reason is that even though a $1 reward is high in MTurk, since the average hourly rate among campus workers is at least $5, the HIT reward is relatively low.

After three weeks, a total of 14 HITs were completed by at least one MTurk worker. We were able to get 263 records classified across 14 categories. The average completion time per HIT is one hour and 22 minutes. The effective hourly rate is $0.79. Workers had carefully answered each HIT. The workers not only gave the Ensemble record URL and search terms, but also detailed the reason why they chose this record for this category. Among these 263 records, 229 records have a reason provided.

In order to evaluate these records and compare the quality between Iowa students and MTurk workers, we used a *Plurality* strategy – majority vote to assess the records gathered from both user groups, as is described in the next section.

3.3.2 HIT design – Plurality

Our second MTurk experiment had two purposes: to find the ground truth records for testing our classifiers and to investigate whether MTurk workers can do the same work as students who have background knowledge in computing education materials.

To assess work quality for these groups, we used a plurality review strategy to design our second MTurk experiment. First, we reviewed the Iowa students' reports and identified 97 resources for evaluation. Second, we selected 236 resources for evaluation from our first MTurk experiment. For each resource we created a corresponding HIT. Inside each HIT, we listed the resource's title, description and category description. We asked workers to rate the decision from 1 to 5 based on the provided information. We assigned 5 workers to each HIT and accepted the categorization of that resource if the average score of the HIT is above 3.

We created a total of 485 assignments from the Iowa resources and 1180 assignments from the MTurk resources. The worker qualification was set to an overall hit approval rate of 70%. Since each HIT was relatively easy, and our estimated time requirement was 5 to 10 minutes for each HIT, we set our HIT reward to be 1 cent.

We used the time difference to detect suspicious cheating workers. We monitored worker's response time on each HIT. If a worker kept having the lowest completion time to answer HITs compared to other worker's completion time in the same HIT, we suspected that worker was cheating and rejected all the HITs answered by that worker. We found two workers who kept using the minimal time to answer HITs. Most of the HITs they answered used only 3 seconds, compared to other workers' completion time of 15 seconds. We rejected these two workers and republished HITs to the MTurk pool for other workers.

All of the HITs were completed by workers in three days. There were a total of 137 workers involved in our second experiment. We calculated each record's average score and selected records with score over 3 as our ground truth for that category.

3.4 Analysis

We compared the Iowa students' work with MTurk workers' work using the data from our second experiment. Our hypothesis was that MTurk workers could perform the same quality work as Iowa students. We used a t-test to verify whether our hypothesis is accepted or rejected. The t-test result shows that there is no significant difference between these two user groups at a confidence level of 0.95. To further verify our approach, we repeat our second experiment and conducted third MTurk experiment with worker qualification was set to an overall hit approval rate of 95%. The t-test shows that there is no significant difference between these two user groups at a confidence level of 0.95. Based on these results, we can conclude that workers can do the same categorization work as students.

We inspected the entries identified by Iowa students and MTurk workers. We found the resources selected by the two groups differed. Table 1 shows the number of common and total records identified by these two groups.

Table 1 - Results of ground truth set building.

ACM second-level category	*Records (Iowa)*	*Records (MTurk)*	*Records (Both)*
Programming Techniques	26	15	1
Data Structures	33	15	1
Formal Languages	9	15	3
Discrete Mathematics	10	15	3
Database Management	19	15	2

We can clearly see that the number of records for each category from Iowa varied, but they are consistent from MTurk. This is because not every document identified by Iowa was valid and some are duplicates. For example, some records were not Ensemble records. These invalid records were removed for our second experiment.

While both groups used the same interface, MTurk workers carefully followed instructions and used complex and different search terms to find documents. However, students in class often used one-search term and listed the top 20 records returned. There were only four Iowa students who gave us the detailed reason why they chose a document for a category. Other groups only gave us URLs without any explanation. Workers need to get HITs approved by the requester in order to get paid. A rejected HIT not only is a waste of the worker's time and effort, but can get them negative feedback, affecting their overall approval rate and reputation. We conducted a user study and gathered 8 students from Computer Science department at Virginia Tech to judge these entries identified by both groups. Both groups got average score 4 out of 5 based on students' judgment. Students found that some entries identified by both groups didn't belong to assigned category; 9 error entries identified by Iowa and 7 error entries identified by MTurk.

4. PILOT CLASSIFICATION STUDY

To move beyond manual-classification of documents in Ensemble collections, we experimented with classifiers trained on metadata from the ACM Digital Library. We extracted three distinct term vectors – one over titles, one over abstracts, and one over the combination of title and abstract. We remove stopwords using the Stanford stopword list, stemmed the remaining terms using Porter's Snowball algorithm, and removed terms present in less than 5% or over 95% of documents. Classifiers were validated first via 10-fold cross-validation on ACM metadata entries.

We found three techniques that performed well on training data – Nearest Neighbor, Random Trees, and Random Forest. Each archived an 85.697% accuracy for validation. However, when applied to hand-classified** Ensemble documents, performance dropped considerably. The best results (25% accuracy) obtained overall were by a locally weighted Multinomial Naïve Bayes classifier and the bagging extension of Multinomial Naïve Bayes.

Table 2 - Best techniques per category by F Score

Category	*Technique*	*F-Score*	*Precision*	*Recall*
B.3	J48 Graft Tree	0.190	0.333	0.133
B.7	Complement Naïve Bayes	0.200	0.400	0.133
C.1	Linear	0.316	0.750	0.200
C.2	LogitBoost	0.684	0.684	0.684
D.1	REP Tree	0.160	0.444	0.098
D.2	REP Tree	0.233	0.136	0.800
D.3	Decision Table	0.262	0.170	0.571
D.4	LogitBoost	0.491	0.464	0.520
E.1	Naïve Bayes Multinomial	0.222	1.000	0.125
F.4	Discriminative Multinomial Naïve Bayes	0.424	0.778	0.292
G.2	Random Committee of Random Trees	0.263	0.385	0.200
H.2	Discriminative Multinomial Naïve Bayes	0.286	0.364	0.235
K.4	Naïve Bayes Multinomial	0.300	0.185	0.800

When results are examined per class, some classes were better classified than others. Hyper Pipe classifiers obtained perfect recall on the B.3 category, albeit at the cost of very low precision (0.045). The Complement Naïve Bayes classifier obtained perfect precision at the cost of low recall (0.267) for C.1, high recall (0.789) and moderate precision (0.441) for C.2., and decent recall (0.643) and low precision (0.107) for D.3. The one rule classifier had perfect recall on D.2 but at the cost of low precision (0.048). The voting feature intervals classifier had perfect precision classifier for E.1 and F.4 but obtained poor recall on both (0.021 and 0.041 respectively). These results lead us to believe that our classifiers were overfit on training data and, thus, techniques, like improved feature selection, need to be adopted to mitigate this effect. The best techniques for each category by F Score are listed in table 2.

5. CONCLUSIONS & FUTURE WORK

We gained valuable experiences about conducting research with MTurk from this research:

- Experiments can be conducted on MTurk anytime with results obtained in a short period. On the other hand, it is difficult to engage students to participate in experiment during breaks even with participation rewards.
- Workers can quickly complete HITs with simple tasks; thus we need to have a validation technique to identify possible low quality results. An automatic approval and rejection workflow is needed.
- Workers cannot easily pretend they did a good job for HITs with complex tasks. It is easy to identify low quality work through completion times and result reports.
- Workers with higher approved rate are willing to spend time to participate in research even if the average hour rate is low.
- Worker skills and accuracy vary widely; thus it is important to find a group of trusted workers.
- We are working on an approach to automatically evaluate results from workers, approve qualifying HITs, reject low quality HITs and resubmit to the HIT pool.

Our preliminary experiments also provided us with valuable insight for moving forward. While our validation results were very good and test results in individual categories show promise, the poor test results in other categories continue to hold back the overall performance of our techniques. In order to better understand this issue, we intend to perform a more in depth examination of the Ensemble documents, expand the features sets used for analysis, and apply other ensemble learning techniques.

6. ACKNOWLEDGMENTS

This research is supported by NSF Grants DUE-0840713, 0840715, 0840719, 0840721, 0840668, 0840597, 0836940, and 0937863.

This document was prepared in part by Oak Ridge National Laboratory, P.O. Box 2008, Oak Ridge, Tennessee 37831-6285; managed by UT-Battelle, LLC, for the US Department of Energy under contract number DE-AC05-00OR22725.

This manuscript has been authored in part by UT-Battelle, LLC, under contract DE-AC05-00OR22725 with the U.S. Department of Energy. The United States Government retains and the publisher, by accepting the article for publication, acknowledges that the United States Government retains a non-exclusive, paid-up, irrevocable, world-wide license to publish or reproduce the published form of this manuscript, or allow others to do so, for United States Government purposes.

Our thanks go to ACM for providing us the ACM DL metadata to use in this research, to the Academy for Advanced Telecommunications and Learning Technologies at Texas A&M University for time on Brazos and to NICS/XSEDE/TeraGrid for the time on Nautilus.

7. REFERENCES

[1] Sebastiani, F. (2002). Machine learning in automated text categorization. *ACM Comput. Surv.*34, 1, 1-47.

[2] Jain, A.K., Murty, M.N., and Flynn, P.J. (1999). Data clustering: a review. *ACM Comput. Surv.* 31, 3, 264-323.

[3] Chen, G., Warren, J., and Riddle,P. (2010). Semantic Space models for classification of consumer webpages on metadata attributes. *J. of Biomedical Informatics* 43, 5, 725-735.

[4] Meyer, M., Rensing, C., and Steinmetz, R. (2008). Using community-generated contents as a substitute corpus for metadata generation. *Int. J. Adv. Media Comm.* 2, 1, 59-72.

[5] Kittur, A., Chi, E. H., & Suh, B. (2008). Crowdsourcing user studies with Mechanical Turk. *In Proc. of CHI 08.*

[6] Mason, W., & Suri, S. (2010). Conducting Behavioral Research on Amazon□s Mechanical Turk. Behavior Research Methods, 5(5), 1–23.

[7] Chen, J. J., Menezes, N. J., Bradley, A. D., & North, T. A. (2011). Opportunities for Crowdsourcing Research on Amazon Mechanical Turk. *Human Factors*, *5*, 3.

[8] Yetisgen-yildiz, M., Solti, I., Xia, F., & Halgrim, S. R. (2010). Preliminary Experiments with Amazon's Mechanical Turk for Annotating Medical Named Entities. Proceedings of the NAACL HLT 2010 Workshop on Creating Speech and Language Data with Amazon's Mechanical Turk, 180-183.

Re-ranking Bibliographic Records for Personalized Library Search

Tadashi Nomoto
National Institute of Japanese Literature
10-3 Midori Tachikawa,
Tokyo 190-0014, Japan
nomoto@acm.org

ABSTRACT

This work will introduce a new approach to ranking bibliographic records in library search, which is currently dominated by an OPAC style search paradigm, where results are typically not ranked by relevance. The approach we propose in the paper provides the user with the ability to access bibliographic records in a way responsive to his or her preferences, which is essentially done by looking at a community or a group of people who share interests with the user and making use of their publication records to re-rank search results. The experiment found that the present approach gives a clear edge over conventional search methods.

Categories and Subject Descriptors: H.3 [**Information Storage and Retrieval**]: Information Search and Retrieval // **General Terms**: Algorithms // **Keywords**: OPAC, Relevance Ranking

1. INTRODUCTION

WordCat, a global provider for online library records, states that their holding of bibliographic records reached 1,718,062,996 as of May 21, 2011, contributed from 170 countries and regions across the world,[1] while NDL-OPAC, Japanese National Library of Diet's online catalogue service, marked over 18 million search sessions in 2008.[2]

Despite a growing demand for online library services that these developments suggest, a cursory look at recent comments on online public access catalogues (OPACs) [5, 4] leaves one with a somewhat nagging feeling that little has changed since 1980s when they were first brought into service, which stands in a stark contrast to the rapid rise of Web search engines the last decade had witnessed. Another oft-cited criticism is that online library catalogues generally lack search by relevance, and do not go beyond a simple text match. Dellit et al [1] warns, however, that a straightforward implementation of relevance ranking in library catalogue could be harmful because of the way library cards are conceived: repetition in library cards for instance, does not always signal importance as it does in full-text documents, and argues against equating library cards with documents. Seen in this light, a relevance mechanism implemented in *Libraries Australia* search engine [1], with its emphasis on using structural features specific to catalogue data, e.g., subject, author, title fields, may represent an interesting (and perhaps significant) departure from the popular view that we should model OPAC on Web search engines such as Google and Yahoo!.

Amazon announced recently that its sale of ebooks surpassed the sale of print books for the first time since they started the business.[3] While we strongly expect that the number of digital books will continue to grow in years ahead, it is also true that there still remain tens of millions of books locked in print format, sitting in libraries across the world, and the only way to access them is by going through library cards, and visiting them in person.

This is the foremost issue that motivates the current work. In this paper, we will explore a new approach to re-arranging search results that the OPAC returns for a given query, a break from most OPACs today which produce a list of results in chronological or lexicographical order [4]. The approach builds on *author profiling* [6], a quantitative representation of an author's expertise or professional interests, and extends it to reorganize search results in a way more meaningful to the user.

2. THE APPROACH

We explore the use of library control codes (LCCs) to represent the user's preferences, such as those in the Dewey Decimal Classification scheme (DDC). In this paper, we work with NDC (Nippon Decimal Classification System), a particular rendition of DDC adopted by Japan's National Diet Library.

Broadly, NDC is a three-layered structure, with its topmost level consisting of 10 categories, general (000), philosophy (100), history (200), social science (300), natural science (400), technology (500), industry (600), art (700), language (800), and literature (900). Each book is assigned to a three-digit number indicating where it belongs in the NDC system: for instance, books about civil engineering will be assigned to 510, a subdivision of the industry category, and those about Chinese literature form a subclass of the literature division and are assigned to 920.

2.1 Author Profiling

Author profiling [6] aims to identify subjects of interest to an given author, say, X , by looking at LCCs of bibliographic records (BIBs) of books authored by X and those by X's coauthors. The reason why we look at X's coauthors is that if X works with Z, there is a good chance that Z's interests are also shared by X, and could serve as a useful indicator of what X is interested in. Furthermore, we say that people who have coauthored with X form a coauthor

[1] http://www.oclc.org

[2] http://www.ndl.go.jp/jp/publication/annual/h20/nen20.pdf#page=237

[3] http://www.nytimes.com/2011/05/20/technology/20amazon.html?_r=1& scp=2& sq=amazon&st=cse

JCDL'12, June 10–14, 2012, Washington, DC, USA.

Table 1: A bibliographic record

<record>
<title> Indignation </title>
<author> Philip Roth </author>
<publisher> Houghton Mifflin Harcourt </publisher>
<llc> 933 </llc>
<date> 2008.9 </date>
</record>

network of degree 1 if they had worked directly with X, and a coauthor network of degree 2 if they worked with someone who had worked directly with X, and so forth. We let $\mathcal{N}^k(X)$ represent a set of people who reside in a coauthor network of degree k with X as its root. We define

$$\mathsf{AP}(X, j) = \bigcup_{k=0}^{j} \bigcup_{Y \in \mathcal{N}^k(X)} \bigcup_{r \in \mathcal{B}(Y)} \mathsf{LCC}(r). \quad (1)$$

$\mathcal{B}(Y)$ denotes a set of books authored by Y,[4] $\mathsf{LCC}(r)$ represents an LCC of book r. $\mathsf{AP}(X, 2)$, for instance, stands for a set of LCCs of books produced by X and people who live in coauthor networks of up to 2 degrees. Note that $\mathcal{N}^0(X) = \{X\}$.

2.2 Pseudo User Profiles

In this paper, we work in a specific scenario where the user, a professional in some academic field, wishes to find books relevant to her area of study, using OPAC. The primary goal of this work is to rank BIBs in such a way that book records relevant to her specific domain appear higher on the list, a functionality generally in demand but absent in current library OPACs.[5] Meeting this goal could be considered a step toward personalizing OPAC search results.

We tackle this problem by making use of a list of publications she produced, rather than going over her search log or bookmarks to identify her interests, as the former is more readily available. We build a personal search profile by locating terms in the bibliography indicative of the user's area of interest and growing them into a set of LCCs. We do this by first searching OPAC, using a one- or two-word long term from each title in the bibliography as a query and examine a set of BIBs it returns: if a query term generates a set of BIBs, mostly of the same LCC, it would indicate the term's close connection to a particular field, which in turn suggests the author's association with that domain; if on the other hand, a term produces varying LCCs, it is not a good indicator of the user's academic leanings.

For the present work, we use the entropy to quantify the strength of term t as a topicality indicator. $H(t) = \sum_{j \in \mathcal{L}} -p(j|R) \log p(j|R)$ j stands for an LCC from the Decimal System $\mathcal{L}$, i.e., three-digit LCC codes ranging from 000 to 999. $p(j|R)$ represents the ratio of j in the search results R such that $\sum_{j \in \mathcal{L}} p(j|R) = 1$. Note that $H(t)$ gets smaller as R has fewer unique LCCs. In the experiments later described, we use 10 terms with the smallest entropy to retrieve BIBs from which we develop a personal profile.

We rank terms that appear in the user's bibliography in accordance to their entropy, choosing top k scoring terms (call it T) to

[4] In practice, we create $\mathcal{B}(Y)$ by querying OPAC with Y as an author name, and $\mathcal{N}^k(X)$ through repeated search over OPAC with names we find in $\mathcal{B}(X)$'s co-author fields.

[5] http://www.alatechsource.org/blog/2006/03/how-opacs-suck-part-1-relevance-rank-or-the-lack-of-it.html.

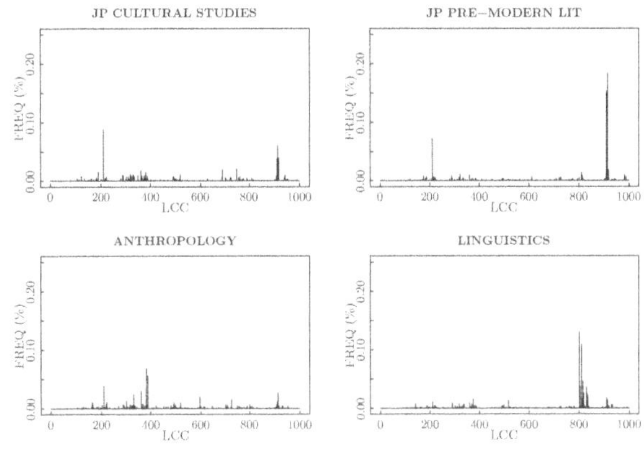

Figure 1: Community Profiles for Academic Societies in Japan

build a personal profile we call 'pseudo user profile' or PUP, which records the distribution of LCCs over a set of BIBs returned with terms in T (which we call $R(T)$). More formally, PUP could be expressed as: $\mathsf{PUP}(Z) = \bigcup_{r \in R(T)} \mathsf{LCC}(r)$, where Z denotes a set of publications in the user's bibliography and $T = \{q \mid q \text{ is a top scoring term in } Z\}$. Note that Z could be the entire bibliography or, any subset of it. One may choose Z in whatever way best suits her purposes: for instance, we may choose most recent publications so that PUP reflects the user's current interests. In what follows, we call Z a *focused bibliography*.

We also make use of a community level profile to make up for the possible lack of the breadth of PUP. Profiling communities involves three steps: (1) discover online communities with strong relevance to the user's interests, (2) locate their officers, staff, and members on a Web page and (3) collect their bibliographic data by querying OPAC with their names and build $\mathcal{N}^1$ for each of them. We create a community profile by running AP on each officer name found in a society's management web page, and lumping up individual profiles into one collective profile. We call the profile 'COP' as opposed to PUP, hereafter. We let $\mathsf{COP}(\mathbb{C}) = \bigcup_{u \in \mathbb{C}} \mathsf{AP}(u, j)$. In the experiments later discussed, we set j to 1.

Fig 1 illustrates what COPs would look like for some humanities societies in Japan. Each panel shows on the x-axis the library classification codes (LCC), and on the y-axis the ratio of the frequency of a given LCC. It is interesting that some of the profiles have multiple peaks, indicating that authors and their co-authors have publications that span across a number of different disciplines. A society dealing with Japanese cultural studies, depicted as 'JP CULTURAL STUDIES' in Fig. 1, has peaks around 200 and 900, which means that it is most active in areas of history and literature, whereas the anthropological society (ANTHROPOLOGY) has prominent spikes both at 400 (natural science) and 200 (history). In a literary society (JP PRE-MODERN LIT), book titles under 900 dominate the picture, with somewhat weaker peaks around 200. The linguistics society (LINGUISTICS) is a distinct case which has a uni-modal or single peak, indicating that people there do not work anywhere outside of their primary discipline.

2.3 Building Re-ranking Model

Our re-ranking model is guided by two types of information: (1) user preferences expressed in the form of PUP and (2) collective preferences that COP represents. The idea here is to re-order OPAC results in a way responsive to the communal as well as personal preferences. We do this by combining PUP and COP.

We define an author profile (both for a user and for a community) as a vector $\mathbf{y} = (c(y_1), \ldots, c(y_n))$, where $c(y_i)$ represents the count of LCC y_i in BIBs. For a given record r (returned by OPAC), we define a score $\mathcal{R}$ by

$$\mathcal{R}(r; \lambda, Z) = \lambda P(L(r)|\mathsf{COP}(\mathbb{C})) + (1-\lambda)P(L(r))|\mathsf{PUP}(Z)). \quad (2)$$

$L(r)$ denotes an LCC of r which ranges from 000 to 999. We let

$$P(x|\mathbf{y}) = \int f(x|\theta)g(\theta|\mathbf{y})d\theta. \quad (3)$$

$\theta = \theta_1, \ldots, \theta_n$ denotes a vector of probabilities for observing LCCs such that $\sum_i \theta_i = 1$. For a given LCC x, $f(x|\theta)$ represents the probability of x given θ, i.e., θ_x. g represents the Dirichlet density function. $P(x|\mathbf{y})$, which represents the probability of LCC x being chosen given a profile $\mathbf{y}$, is defined here as the expectation of the Dirichlet posterior at x given $\mathbf{y}$, namely, $(c(x_j) + \alpha(x_j))/(\sum_i c(y_i) + \alpha(y_i))$, where $c(x_j)$ and $\alpha(x_j)$ are the observed and prior count of x_j, respectively Finally, λ determines a mixing ratio of the two components in Eqn. 2. We note that the first part of the model, $P(L(r))|\mathsf{COP}(\mathbb{C}))$, could be viewed as a backoff model for $P(L(r)|\mathsf{PUP}(Z))$. Also of note is that Eqn. 2 has no parameter representing the query. This is because we intend to work on the result list OPAC returns for a query and regard items on the list as being already related to the query, one way or another.

2.4 Selecting Community on the Fly

We turn to a question of how we might choose a community whose COP we need to rank a record. There could be a number of research communities which might serve as a background model for PUP. In order to make a sensible choice, we need some measure by which to select a COP for a given PUP. In this work, we will focus on a kernel function and a language model.

We start off with a kernel function. Polynomial Kernel provides a convenient way to measure how similar two models are in a high dimensional space.

$$KER(q, r) = (\mathbf{q}^T\mathbf{r} + c)^d \quad (c \geq 0, d > 0), \quad (4)$$

where $\mathbf{q} = (q_{000}, \ldots, q_{999})$, $\mathbf{r} = (r_{000}, \ldots, r_{999})$, or multinomial distributions over LCCs. q_{000} represents the probability of LCC code '000' appearing in the user profile, and similarly for others.

Language modeling could also be retooled as a similarity measure.

$$LM(\mathbf{u}, \mathbf{c}) = \prod_{t \in \mathcal{L}} p(t \mid \mathbf{c})^{c(t,\mathbf{u})}, \quad (5)$$

where $c(t, \mathbf{u})$ represents the count of t in $\mathbf{u}$, a pseudo user profile and $p(t \mid \mathbf{c})$ the probability of t estimated with a community profile $\mathbf{c}$. LM selects a community whose model permits the highest probability for a pseudo user profile $\mathbf{u}$.

2.5 Explicit Semantic Analysis

Gabrilovich and Markovitch [2] discuss an interesting way to exploit external knowledge to grow a textual content. The approach, which they call ESA (Explicit Semantic Analysis), aims to gauge the similarity between two words based on the strength of associations the words have with Wikipedia pages. ESA works primarily by turning a query into a *concept* vector, where each element registers how strongly the query is associated with a particular Wikipedia page: each Wikipedia page is viewed as providing a unique semantic dimension along which to define a word. Given a pair of concept vectors, finding their similarity under ESA simply consists of computing their cosine measure.

Adopting ESA for a library search is fairly straightforward: apply ESA to a query and BIBs to expand them into concept vectors, and rank the BIBs based on how similar the associated concept vectors are to one that represents the query.

One caveat is that the ESA works on a word-by-word basis, so we break the query into a set of words, for each of which we create a corresponding concept vector. Obviously, this would leave us with a number of vectors, each corresponding to a word in the query. To represent the entire query, we make use of a centroid, or a geometric center of concept vectors built from individual words and let it act as a representative of component vectors.

Under ESA, the ranking model would look like the following.

$$\mathcal{R}(r, q) = \frac{\langle ESA(r), ESA(q)\rangle}{\sqrt{\langle ESA(r), ESA(r)\rangle}\sqrt{\langle ESA(q), ESA(q)\rangle}} \quad (6)$$

q represents a query which comes in the form of a title of book or a paper produced by the user and r a bibliographic record. $\langle \cdot, \cdot \rangle$ stands for an inner product. $ESA(x)$ represents the centroid of vectors created for x in the manner described above. In the experiments described below, we used 50 Wikipedia pages which scored highest by the cosine similarity (i.e., $\mathcal{R}$) with a query as features to build ESA, ignoring the rest.[6] We worked with the 2010-11-01 edition of Japanese Wikipedia.

3. EXPERIMENT SETUP

In the experiment, we primarily looked at whether our approach is effective in re-ordering OPAC results in a way that favors records of books dealing with a particular research area. To this end, we collected BIBs by querying an OPAC currently in service at Japan's National Library of Diet (NDL-OPAC), using frequent keywords extracted from query logs at the National Institute of Japanese Literature (NIJL).We hired four people, all experts on early Japanese literature and asked them to make a binary (yes/no) judgment on BIBs for their relevance to early Japanese literature. More specifically, we presented them with pools of BIBs returned by the NDL-OPAC with queries harvested from the NIJL's query logs and asked to judge each bibliographic record for its relevance to early Japanese literature.[7] (We refer to a list of bibliographic records OPAC returns for a given query as 'QURL' below). While at work, the participants were not allowed to talk to one another nor given any instruction other than to choose whatever titles they thought are relevant to the field. The idea here was to induce some variation among the individuals, as it could provide insights into how to make the search more in tune with personal interests.

Since our goal is to re-order search results in a way responsive to personal interests, we evaluate models on a user-by-user basis, that is, we look at how well they perform in mimicking choices of a particular user, and not those made collectively by the users. The following list the number of BIBs each judge worked, together with the number of QURLs assigned to them.

Judge	# QURLs (queries)	# BIBs in QURL
OO	84	13,021
YZ	85	13,284
SG	87	13,289
EZ	65	10,558

Among eight professional societies and institutions whose web sites we used to develop COPs are: the Linguistic Society of Japan (linguistics), Chusei-Bungaku-kai (Japanese medieval literature), National Museum of Ethnology, Japan (anthropology), the Association of Waka Poetry Studies (early Japanese poetry), International

[6] We retrieved data with Apache Lucene (http://lucene.apache.org).
[7] This means that queries are mostly about early Japanese literature.

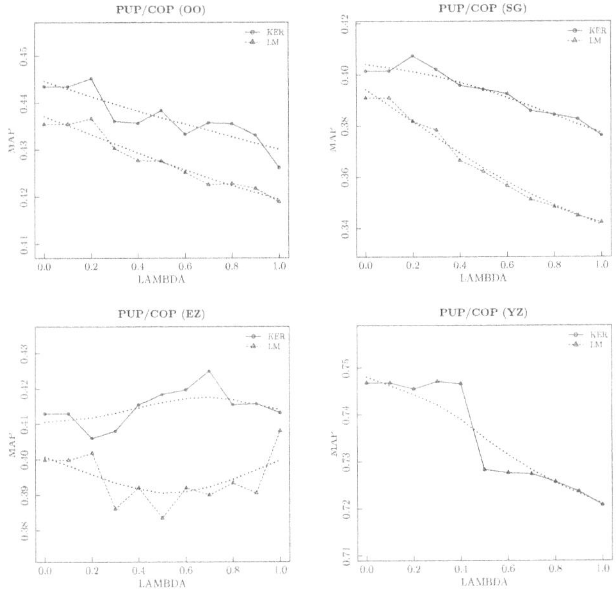

Figure 2: Effect of λ on performance.

Research Center for Japanese Studies (Japanese culture). For each name u we found in their sites, we ran $\mathsf{AP}(u, 1)$ to build community profiles (see Fig. 1 for some examples). We used publication lists of YZ, OO, SG, and EZ to create PUPs: YZ's publication list contained 2 items, while OO's had 10. SG had 9 items and EZ 2.

4. RESULTS AND SUMMARY

Figure 2 shows by-user performance of PUP/COP at a particular value of λ with either KER or LM engaged to select a community. We find that in case of OO, SG and YZ, the performance, whether with KER or LM, tends to peak at around 0 to 0.4, wheres on EZ, performance peaks much later at around 0.7 (KER), or at 1.0 (LM), indicating a significant variation in the optimal value of λ among the judges. In the experiment, we optimized the PUP/COP model, using part of the QURLs as development data: in particular, we ran a grid search over a $\mathcal{Z} \times \mathcal{L}$ parameter space [3] to find best values for $Z \in \mathcal{Z}$ and $\lambda \in \mathcal{L}$ in Eqn. 2, where $\mathcal{Z}$ represents a set of possible focused bibliographies and $\mathcal{L}$ the set of values of λ consisting of numbers from 0 to 1 at 0.1 intervals, i.e., $0, 0.1, 0.2, 0.3, \ldots, 1$. For the sake of simplicity, we restricted $\mathcal{Z}$ to having only singletons, i.e., $\{\{r_1\}, \{r_2\}, \ldots, \{r_n\}\}$, where r_i represents a single publication title. The testing was done by 10-fold cross validation, where we split the entire data into 10 blocks, set aside one block for testing and trained the model on the remaining blocks, estimating optimal values for Z and λ. As a comparison, we ran three baselines, NDL-OPAC (NDL, for short), COS, an approach based on the cosine between a publication title and that of a bibliographic record, and ESA (Explicit Semantic Analysis). We randomly chose Z for PUP when run in a solo mode.

Table 2 shows main results. Numbers represent MAP (Mean Average Precision) scores averaged over 10 folds. We find a consistent and significant superiority of PUP/COP over PUP and COP run independently and the three baselines, across all the judges. ESA and COS fare better than NDL, though their performance tends to vary among the judges and it is hard to tell which is better on the basis of what we found in Table 2.

Personalization in the context of information retrieval is generally about the re-ranking of search results in a way responsive to the user's particular interests. A key issue is where and how we get information about what interests the user. We argue that the title of a publication created by the user and terms that appear in it not only serves as sources we might usefully exploit to infer what the user is interested in, but they could also be viewed as social tags the user assigned to his or her own publications.

Our approach was guided by two kinds of information: a profile of the user and that of a professional community: the former was built from the user's own bibliography and the latter by profiling officers whose names appear in the community's web site. We conducted experiments with Japanese National Diet Library's OPAC to see the effectiveness of our approach. It turned out that it led to improving performance by nearly or more than two folds over NDL-OPAC. Still, we have yet to see how the results hold up in domains not covered in the present work, such as politics and economics, and whether it works for people at large. An interesting alternative to the present approach is a multi-stage generative model, which may offer a more streamlined view of how to rank bibliographic records. These are among questions we need to visit in the future.

Table 2: Results by Cross Validation on Per Annotator Performance in MAP (averaged over 10 folds).

	SG					
	PUP/COP	PUP	COP	NDL	COS	ESA
KER	**0.4377**	0.3950	0.3754	0.1919	0.1901	0.2602
LM	**0.4380**	0.3784	0.3355	0.1919	0.1901	0.2602

	EZ					
	PUP/COP	PUP	COP	NDL	COS	ESA
KER	**0.4432**	0.4060	0.4224	0.2512	0.2873	0.2745
LM	**0.4108**	0.4082	0.4066	0.2512	0.2873	0.2745

	OO					
	PUP/COP	PUP	COP	NDL	COS	ESA
KER	**0.5081**	0.4108	0.4279	0.1840	0.2324	0.1674
LM	**0.5051**	0.4216	0.4292	0.1840	0.2324	0.1674

	YZ					
	PUP/COP	PUP	COP	NDL	COS	ESA
KER	**0.7554**	0.7486	0.7263	0.4741	0.4780	0.4975
LM	**0.7554**	0.7490	0.7263	0.4741	0.4780	0.4975

5. REFERENCES

[1] A. Dellit and T. Boston. Relevance ranking of results from MARC-based catalogues. Technical report, National Library of Australia, 2007.

[2] E. Gabrilovich and S. Markovitch. Wikipedia-based semantic interpretation for natural language processing. *J. of Artificial Intelligence Research*, 34:443–498, 2009.

[3] C.-W. Hsu, C.-C. Chang, and C.-J. Li. A practical guide to support vector classification. http://www.csie.ntu.edu.tw/cjlin, 2010.

[4] D. Lewandowski. Ranking library materials. *Library Hi Tech*, 27, 2009.

[5] J. Mi and C. Weng. Revitallizing the Library OPAC: Interface, Searching, and Display Challenges. *Information Technology and Libraries*, 2008.

[6] T. Nomoto. Classifying library catalogue by author profiling. In Proc. of *SIGIR '09*, 2009.

Generating Ground Truth for Music Mood Classification Using Mechanical Turk

Jin Ha Lee
University of Washington
Mary Gates Hall, Suite 370
Seattle, WA 98195
+1 206.685.0153
jinhalee@uw.edu

Xiao Hu
University of Denver
1999 E. Evans Ave. Room 249
Denver, CO 80208
+1 303.871.3352
xiao.hu@du.edu

ABSTRACT
Mood is an important access point in music digital libraries and online music repositories, but generating ground truth for evaluating various music mood classification algorithms is a challenging problem. This is because collecting enough human judgments is time-consuming and costly due to the subjectivity of music mood. In this study, we explore the viability of crowdsourcing music mood classification judgments using Amazon Mechanical Turk (MTurk). Specifically, we compare the mood classification judgments collected for the annual Music Information Retrieval Evaluation eXchange (MIREX) with judgments collected using MTurk. Our data show that the overall distribution of mood clusters and agreement rates from MIREX and MTurk were comparable. However, Turkers tended to agree less with the pre-labeled mood clusters than MIREX evaluators. The system evaluation results generated using both sets of data were mostly the same except for detecting one statistically significant pair using Friedman's test. We conclude that MTurk can potentially serve as a viable alternative for ground truth collection, with some reservation with regards to particular mood clusters.

Categories and Subject Descriptors
H.3.4. [**Information Systems**]: Information Storage and Retrieval – Systems and Software – *Performance evaluation.* J.5 [**Arts and Humanities**]. *Music*

General Terms
Measurement, Human Factors, Performance

Keywords
Music Information Retrieval, Evaluation, Ground Truth, Gold Standard, Mood, Mechanical Turk, Crowdsourcing

1. INTRODUCTION
Generating ground truth for evaluating various music information retrieval (MIR) systems is an essential process for the improvement of MIR and music digital libraries (MDL) research, yet it often tends to be a challenging problem. This is especially true for generating ground truth based on human input since collecting human judgments tends to be expensive and time consuming [1]. In the MIR/MDL community, there are several evaluation tasks that use human input as the basis for evaluating the performance of algorithms, namely audio music similarity, symbolic music similarity, and audio music mood classification tasks. Getting enough people to verify evaluation results for these tasks is a tedious and long process since it can require tens of thousands of responses for a modest collection of several hundred songs [14], [22]. In order to alleviate the difficulty of collecting human responses, two studies [14], [24] have explored the viability of using Amazon Mechanical Turk (MTurk) for collecting human judgments on music similarity evaluation tasks. Both studies have compared the human music similarity judgments obtained from music experts in Music Information Retrieval Evaluation eXchange (MIREX)[2] with the ones obtained from MTurk. The authors from both studies suggest MTurk as a viable alternative for collecting human judgments rather than relying on music experts from the MIR community.

The motivation for our study is to explore if MTurk works well for the evaluation task of music mood classification. Mood has become an important access point for MDL and online music repositories [25] (e.g., allmusic.com, stereomood.com). A number of algorithms have been proposed to classify music by its mood in the MIR/MDL domain (e.g., [2], [8]). Since 2007, the MIREX has been hosting an Audio Mood Classification (AMC) task to evaluate and compare mood classification algorithms [9] (also see Section 2.1). However, generating ground truth for evaluating music mood classification remains a difficult problem [11]. In terms of collecting human judgments, the task of music mood classification differs from music similarity tasks such as Audio

[1] The authors recognize that the term "gold standard" may be more suitable for describing the data set generated by human judgments since "ground truth" is usually assumed to be the objective measure of reality. However, in order to maintain consistency with the terms that have been used in the MIREX domain, we use the term "ground truth" in this work.

[2] Music Information Retrieval Evaluation eXhange (MIREX) is the annual evaluation campaign for various music information retrieval algorithms hosted by the International Music Information Retrieval Systems Evaluation Lab (IMIRSEL) at the University of Illinois at Urbana-Champaign.

Music Similarity (AMS) and Symbolic Music Similarity (SMS) in MIREX in the following aspects:

1) Compared to music similarity, music mood is even more subjective as there is very little objective reference, if any, on how music carrying a particular mood should sound;

2) Assessment of music mood requires a human evaluator to select one mood label from a set of options whereas for judging music similarity, a human judge only needs to answer whether two music pieces are similar or not similar [14], or select one out of two variations that sound more similar to the original piece [24]. Therefore, the cognitive load for evaluators may be heavier for the task of assigning mood labels than judging music similarity.

3) There does not exist an authoritative taxonomy of music mood, meaning there is no formal agreement on what kinds of music moods exist and how to define them. This further complicates music mood judgment.

Due to these unique difficulties of labeling music mood, the results of previous studies on applying MTurk to music similarity tasks may not be applicable to the task of mood classification. Therefore, it is necessary to specifically study the viability of crowdsourcing music mood classification judgments using MTurk. In order to do this, we test the effectiveness of MTurk for Audio Music Mood Classification (AMC) task in MIREX. The findings from this study will also help us further our general understanding on the viability of relying on crowdsourcing for generating ground truth for music related evaluation tasks.

2. BACKGROUND

2.1 MIREX Audio Mood Classification

The annual MIREX is hosted by the International Music Information Retrieval Systems Evaluation Lab (IMIRSEL) where a variety of evaluation tasks are carried out in order to test the performance of different MIR algorithms. Some of these evaluation tasks, such as rating music similarity or classifying music mood, attempt to model human perception or understanding of music by relying on human judgments as the basis of the evaluation.

Audio Music Mood Classification (AMC) task first started in 2007 and has been run every year since then. The objective of this task is to test whether automatic algorithms can correctly predict mood labels for music clips based on their audio characteristics. The ground truth data set for this task requires a set of songs with mood labels that are agreed upon by multiple human evaluators. In other words, if song A were to be used as part of the ground truth for mood cluster 1 (see Table 1), then we want to make sure that multiple people agree that song A in fact carries "passionate, rousing, confident, boisterous, and rowdy" moods. This means that multiple human evaluators are needed to judge the mood of the songs in the test collection. The task organizers ended up using songs that received the same mood classification judgment from two or more people for generating the ground truth (more discussion in Section 4).

IMIRSEL built a web-based survey system called E6K in order to collect responses from human evaluators for the tasks that needed human input. The evaluators are mostly volunteers from the MIR community who have some background in music and/or music related research, thus considered music experts. Every year when new ground truth data are needed, IMIRSEL sends out a series of emails seeking volunteers and it often takes weeks to collect all the responses necessary [14].

2.2 Amazon Mechanical Turk

Amazon Mechanical Turk (MTurk)[3] is a crowdsourcing platform that provides 24/7, on-demand access to workers able to complete tasks requiring human-intervention. For task requesters, MTurk makes it possible to quickly collect human data in a cost-effective manner. The task requester can set up a "HIT" (Human Intelligence Task, the name for a task in MTurk) and set a fee for the completion of that HIT. The HITs are then worked on by human workers (called "Turkers" in MTurk) who are recruited by Amazon and may come from anywhere in the world. The task requester can also create a qualification test that needs to be passed before Turkers are able to work on particular tasks. When the HIT is completed and submitted, the requester can review the HITs and either approve or reject them.

3. RELATED WORK

3.1 MTurk used in Text IR Studies

Previous information retrieval (IR) literature proposed using MTurk for generating relevance judgments in TREC-like evaluations [1], [12], [23]. Alonso and Mizzaro [1] compared MTurk to TREC experts and found the results from MTurk to be comparable to TREC's ground truth generated by experts. Kitter et al. [12] applied MTurk to rating Wikipedia articles and found that the consistency of results provided by MTurk can be greatly improved by adding verifiable questions into the HITs and filtering out the bad results. An important lesson learned by Kitter et al. [12] is that some sort of verification questions are necessary to ensure the quality of answers gathered via Internet crowdsourcing platforms such as MTurk. In our study, we also employed multiple verification questions to filter out inconsistent answers [see Section 4.3].

With regards to affect, Snow et al. [23] used MTurk for generating ground truth data for Natural Language Processing tasks including determination of valence and emotion in text. They found that MTurk provided results on par with those obtained by domain experts. Determining the mood of music is potentially a more complicated task than determining the mood of text. As reported in Lee et al. [15], when people assess music mood, a range of factors come into consideration: lyrics, tempo, instrumentation, genre, delivery, and even cultural context. In addition, our study differs from Snow et al.'s [23] in that the mood space used in our study is a *categorical* model (five distinct mood clusters, Table 1) while Snow et al. [23] used a *dimensional* model where a continuous score was given to each of the seven dimensions of emotions (e.g., valence, joy, anger)[11].

3.2 MTurk used in MIR Studies

Previous MIR research has shown that MTurk can be used fairly successfully for rating music similarity [14], [24] and providing user tags [15], [17]. Lee [14] used MTurk for collecting human judgments for the past MIREX Audio Music Similarity task and found that the results from using MTurk were comparable to the ones from music experts. Urbano et al. [24] used MTurk to gather music preference judgments for the Symbolic Music Similarity

[3] http://www.mturk.com/mturk/welcome

task in MIREX. They reported that their results were very similar to the expert generated ones and recommended crowdsourcing as "a perfectly viable alternative to evaluate music systems without the need for experts" (p.9). Mandel et al. [17] used MTurk to collect user tags on different parts of the same songs and compared them to tags collected from a music tagging game. They found MTurk was a viable means to collect ground truth although the inter-rater agreement among the Turks was slightly lower than that of the gamers. It is noteworthy that the user tags collected in [17] were free terms that could be related to music genre, instrument, user's opinions or simply noisy text. This is different from our study in that we are asking users to select one of the five mood clusters that is most appropriate for the given music clip. More recently, Lee et al. [15] used MTurk to collect mood tags for various cover versions of the same song, with the purpose of investigating the factors affecting how end-users determine and describe music mood in their own terms. Although they also emphasized the mood aspect of music, their research focus was not on the viability of MTurk on generating ground truth for evaluation of mood classification algorithms, which is the main objective of our study.

4. RESEARCH QUESTIONS AND STUDY DESIGN

4.1 Research Questions

We explore the following two research questions in this paper:

I) How do music mood classification results obtained from Mechanical Turk compare to those collected from music experts in MIREX?

II) How different or similar are the evaluation outcomes for MIREX AMC task when based on ground truth collected from Mechanical Turk as compared to ground truth collected from E6K in MIREX?

In order to address these questions, we reproduced the human judgment collection measures like those in E6K for MIREX on MTurk. Specifically, we created an online survey, which asked Turkers to listen to the same music clips used in E6K and select appropriate mood clusters that reflect the mood of the songs. The results will inform us as to the viability of crowdsourcing mood classification judgments.

4.2 Test Collection

We used the same test collection that was used for collecting human judgments and generating ground truth in the MIREX 2007 AMC task[4] with the help of IMIRSEL. This test collection was created based on the APM (Associated Production Music)[5] collection [9], covering a variety of different music genres. This collection consists of 1250 tracks with 250 pieces from each of the five mood clusters. The mood clusters were derived from the 179 mood labels on allmusic.com, a major online music repository. These mood labels were generated by professional editors hired by allmusic.com. In order to identify a more general and clear way to describe the mood space, Hu and Downie [7] applied a hierarchical clustering algorithm to the most popular mood labels and their representative albums and songs on allmusic.com, which resulted in the five mood clusters as shown in Table 1. Further analysis revealed that the clusters had consistent relationships with more traditional music metadata types including genre and artist [7]. The five mood clusters have been used in the AMC task in MIREX as well as a number of other studies on music mood (e.g., [11], [13]).

Before presenting the music clips to human evaluators for mood judgment, each of the clips in the test collection was assigned an initial mood cluster based on the metadata and short descriptions of the songs provided by APM (part of the motivation for designing the AMC task in MIREX in this way was to have a balanced distribution of songs across mood clusters in the resultant ground truth data set). A 30-second clip was sampled from the middle of each of the tracks to be used in the classification task [9]. 30-second clips were used to reduce the burden on the human evaluators, as well as to minimize the potential for variation caused by changes in mood over the duration of a track (i.e., a song may start out with soft and sweet melody, but become loud and aggressive).

4.3 Task Design

In order to ensure that the task was similarly carried out as in MIREX, we included a qualification task that Turkers needed to pass in order to work on our HITs. The AMC task requires that the evaluators understand the meaning of the five mood clusters. In order to ensure that human evaluators can identify the kinds of songs that would fit into each cluster, in MIREX, they were asked to listen to three representative sample songs per cluster. In our qualification task on MTurk, we asked the Turkers to listen to the same sample songs for the clusters. After that, they had to provide answers to a short survey asking which mood clusters would be most appropriate for five given songs. We randomly selected one of the sample songs given for each cluster in order to set up this survey. If they provided the correct answers for all five questions, they were qualified to work on the HITs.

In the HIT, Turkers were instructed to select the most appropriate mood cluster that reflects the mood of each song out of the five given clusters [Table 1]. They were given an option to select the "other" cluster if they think the song does not fit into any of the five given mood clusters. Each HIT consisted of 25 different clips. The songs were randomly assigned in order to minimize the ordering bias. Instruction for the task was given as shown in Figure 1. When the link of "Song X" is clicked, the mp3 file of the clip is played by Yahoo! webplayer[6] embedded in the survey page so that the Turkers do not need to open an external player or download the mp3 file. We wanted to collect two responses for each of the 1250 music tracks in order to check the agreement rate, thus needing 2500 responses in total. We paid $0.55 for completing each of these HITs. As each HIT asked for 27 judgments (25 unique songs + 2 repeated songs for verification questions), the payment for each judgment was $0.02. In [14], $0.20 was paid for a HIT consisting of 13 query-candidate pairs (i.e., 13 similarity judgments), resulting in $0.015 paid for each

[4] http://www.music-ir.org/mirex/wiki/2007:Audio_Music_Mood_Classification; the same judgments were used for the AMC task in the following years.

[5] http://www.apmmusic.com/pages/aboutapm.html

[6] http://webplayer.yahoo.com/

judgment. Also in [24], each HIT contained one judgment on melody similarity and paid for $0.02. Therefore, the amount of payment in our study is in line with previous studies. The total cost for administering 100 HITs, including Amazon's fee was $60.50.

Table 1. Five Mood Clusters

Cluster1	passionate, rousing, confident, boisterous, rowdy
Cluster2	rollicking, cheerful, fun, sweet, amiable/good natured
Cluster3	literate, poignant, wistful, bittersweet, autumnal, brooding
Cluster4	humorous, silly, campy, quirky, whimsical, witty, wry
Cluster5	aggressive, fiery, tense/anxious, intense, volatile, visceral

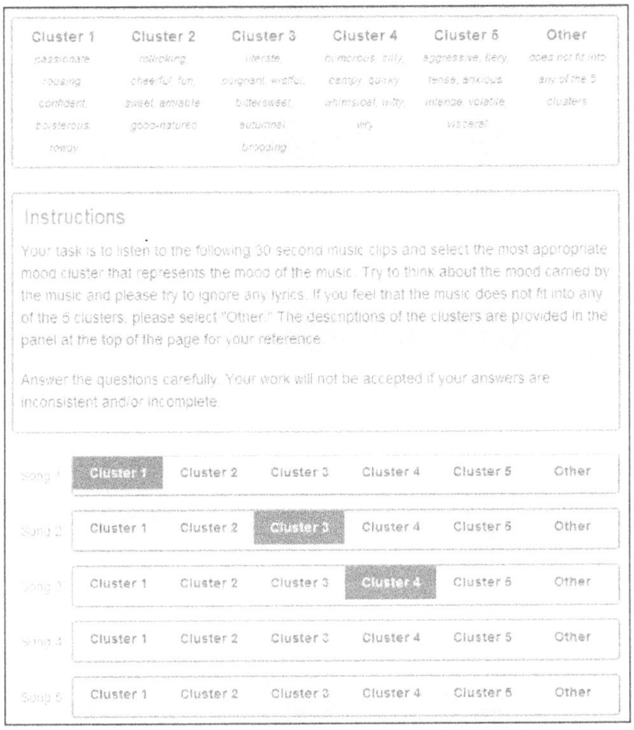

Figure 1. Screenshot of the MTurk HIT

As previously explained, on MTurk, task requesters are allowed to reject any responses that do not meet the requirements set by the requester. Previous studies have reported high proportions of bad responses in MTurk results [14], [15], [24]. Therefore having some kind of filtering mechanism is essential. Lee [14] used two different kinds of verification questions for the music similarity task: 1) inserting the same question twice to check the consistency of the answers, and 2) inserting a question in which they asked users to rate the similarity of the music clip compared to itself. In our study, we also employed a consistency check. We randomly selected two songs from the HIT and repeated them in the HIT. In other words, each Turker selected mood clusters for 27 songs, but there were only 25 unique songs in a single HIT. Our expectation was that the Turker should provide the same mood cluster to both instances of the same song. The submitted HITs which did not meet this consistency check were discarded. Among all the HITs submitted, 46.2% were rejected for inconsistent answers to the verification questions which is higher than [15] (26%), but comparable with [14] (44.3%).

5. DATA AND DISCUSSION

5.1 Comparison of E6K and MTurk Data

5.1.1 Number of Judgments and Distribution across Clusters

In E6K (for MIREX), each human evaluator was assigned 250 music clips. The initial plan was to have three different evaluators for each music clip, however, due to limited participation, only some clips received all three judgments, some received two or only one judgment. As a result, they were only able to collect 2468 judgments in total, with 1180 music clips that received at least one judgment.

On MTurk, we collected a total of 5022 mood classification judgments from 186 HITs that were submitted. Of 186 HITs that were submitted, we accepted 100 HITs (53.8%) and rejected 86 (46.2%) that did not pass the consistency check. After filtering out the rejected HITs and the consistency check judgments, we ended up with 2500 unique mood classification judgments. One benefit of using MTurk is that we do not have to rely on volunteers, which is an unknown variable. In E6K, there is no guarantee how many people will volunteer to provide classification judgments as there is no direct incentive for participation. Many volunteers started the task but never finished it, resulting in a large amount of incomplete data. This also resulted in complication for assignment of music clips; for example, one evaluator may take music clip 1 through 250 and only provide judgments on the first 100 clips which means that the evaluation task organizers have to ensure that clip 101 to 250 are reissued to another evaluator. On MTurk, this issue is non-existent due to the large number of available Turkers, who are compensated for completing tasks.

Table 2. Comparison of judgment distribution in E6K and MTurk

Cluster	E6K	MTurk	Diff. in % (E6K-MTurk)
Cluster1	405 (16.4%)	450 (18.0%)	-1.6%
Cluster2	472 (19.1%)	536 (21.4%)	-2.3%
Cluster3	542 (22.0%)	622 (24.9%)	-2.9%
Cluster4	412 (16.7%)	367 (14.7%)	2.0%
Cluster5	400 (16.2%)	403 (16.1%)	0.1%
Other	237 (9.6%)	122 (4.9%)	4.7%
Total	**2468**	**2500**	-

Table 2 shows the judgment distribution across the five mood clusters in E6K and MTurk. We can observe that Cluster 3 received most votes in both E6K and MTurk, followed by Cluster 2. E6K data contained a slightly larger proportion of votes for Cluster 4, and MTurk data had more votes in Cluster 1, 2, and 3. The proportions for Cluster 5 were almost the same. Since the total numbers of judgments are not equal, this is technically not an exact comparison. However, we can observe that overall proportions are fairly comparable when we take into account the difference in the total numbers (32, which counts for a difference of 1.3%).

5.1.2 Time for Collecting Judgments

On MTurk, the average time Turkers spent for completing a HIT (containing 27 songs) was 471.36 seconds, meaning they spent about an average of 17.46 seconds for listening to each music clip and making judgment. By comparison, the expert evaluators in E6K spent 21.54 seconds on each music clip on average. The 4 more seconds spent on each music clip on average may indicate a more serious attitude of the expert evaluators towards the task, and/or simply more interest in listening to music. It is also possible that Turkers did not spend a long time listening to the two repeated music clips for the verification questions. We were not able to test the statistical significance of the time difference as MTurk does not provide time spent on each question in a HIT. However, it is clear that both groups of evaluators tended not to finish listening to the entire clips available (i.e., 30 seconds).

In order to collect all the judgments needed, it took approximately 19 days on MTurk. On the other hand, for MIREX, it took about 38 days in order to collect all the judgments needed. Hu et al. [9] explain that their data were collected from 18 volunteers starting 1 Aug. until 19 Aug. In order to build the ground truth, they needed music clips with at least two agreed judgments. There were not enough responses from volunteers, however, and the IMIRSEL lab had to do additional in-house assessments on clips that only received one judgment. The whole process ended up taking 38 days.

The 19 days taken on MTurk, when compared to studies that tested music similarity tests ([14]: 12 hours, and [24]: a day and a half), is significantly longer. We suspect that this is due to the qualification task that the Turkers were asked to complete in order to work on our HITs, which was not required in the other studies. Still, it took half the time taken by MIREX, which is a significant improvement. In addition, using MTurk, we were able to obtain the complete data set. In other words, there was no need for additional in-house assessment.

5.1.3 *Inter-rater Reliability*

In MTurk, every two Turkers were assigned the same set of clips, and thus Cohen's Kappa (κ) [4] was calculated for the 50 pairs of Turkers who made judgments on the same set of 25 clips. The E6K data is more complex in that each expert evaluator judged different number of clips. As Hu et al. [9] reported, only 8 evaluators finished all 250 clips assigned to each of them while the remaining 10 evaluators completed 6 to 140 clips. In order to calculate the inter-rater reliability on the E6K data, we paired up the 18 assessors and the number of common clips judged by each pair ranging from 0 to 60. For comparison to the MTurk data, we calculated κ values on the E6K pairs sharing 25 or more clips. The results are shown in Table 3.

Table 3. Inter-rater reliability in E6K and MTurk

	E6K	MTurk
Pairs of assessors	28	50
Common clips each pair	26-60	25
κ : Maximum	0.68	0.71
κ : Minimum	0.31	0.03
κ : Mean	0.50	0.40
κ : Standard deviation	0.09	0.17

The average κ values of 0.50 and 0.40 are comparable to those reported by Schuller et al. [21] (κ values were 0.40 and 0.44 for music mood judgments with regard to *valence* and *arousal* respectively). According to [21], such agreement level is "moderate to good" (p.17) for the task of music mood assessment, although it seems lower than what is expected in text analysis [3]. Table 3 also shows that the experts (E6K) seemed to reach a slightly higher inter-rater agreement than the Turkers, and the Turkers had a larger standard deviation on κ values. However, such comparison is not conclusive as there were more comparable pairs among the Turkers (50) than the E6K experts (28).

5.1.4 *Agreement Rate*

Table 4 shows how the distributions of clips with agreed judgments compare between E6K and MTurk data. The number in each cell indicates the number of clips that received the same mood classification judgment from at least two evaluators. The overall agreement rate on the music clips was 57.7% (681/1180) in E6K compared to 52.4% (655/1250) in MTurk. A chi-square test was conducted on the frequency counts in Table 4 and the result showed the agreement distributions across E6K and MTurk were not identical (χ^2 = 19.67, df = 5, $p < 0.01$). In other words, there were disagreements among users in E6K and MTurk, as to how to classify the mood of these music clips. However, for both data sets, Cluster 3 had the highest number of agreed music clips whereas Cluster 1 and 4 were the least agreed clusters. Interestingly, the agreement among Turkers was much less than E6K evaluators for Cluster 1 and 4.

Table 4. Comparison of the agreed clips distribution in E6K and MTurk

Cluster	E6K	MTurk
Cluster1	121	89
Cluster2	130	131
Cluster3	163	216
Cluster4	121	85
Cluster5	126	121
Other	20	13
Total	**681**	**655**

Our data show that among the 2468 judgments in E6K, 1535 are the same in MTurk (1535/2468 = 62.20%). Among the 2500 judgments in MTurk, 1713 are the same in E6K (1713/2500 = 68.52%). The numbers are different because in E6K data, music clips can have a range of 1 to 3 judges while the in MTurk each clip has exactly 2 judges.

Table 5 shows the agreement between MTurk and E6K judgments across different clusters. The number in each cell indicates the number of judgments agreed by those in the other data set. For example, among the 1535 E6K judgments that are the same in MTurk, 196 have the value Cluster 1 and 457 have the value Cluster 3. Of the five clusters, Cluster 3 has the highest agreement and Cluster 1 has the lowest agreement. Overall, Cluster 3 seems to have the highest agreement: it had the highest agreement among the E6K evaluators, among the Turkers [Table 4], between the E6K evaluators and the Turkers [Table 5], between the E6K evaluators and the APM music experts [Table 8], and between the Turkers and APM music experts [Table 9].

Table 5. Agreement between E6K and MTurk judgments across clusters (percentages in parentheses)

			E6K			
C1	C2	C3	C4	C5	Other	Total
196 (12.8)	304 (19.8)	457 (29.8)	230 (15.0)	302 (19.7)	46 (3.0)	1535 (100)
			MTurk			
C1	C2	C3	C4	C5	Other	Total
242 (14.1)	321 (18.7)	485 (28.3)	280 (16.3)	338 (19.7)	47 (2.7)	1713 (100)

5.1.5 Confusions between the Clusters

We were also interested in knowing which cluster pairs are most confused by E6K evaluators and Turkers. Table 6 shows the distribution of disagreed judgments across different combinations of clusters sorted by the highest to the lowest number of clips receiving disagreements between the given clusters in the E6K data. In this data set, there were different number of judgments assigned for each clip (ranging from 1 to 3), thus there are more combinations than in the MTurk data [Table 7]. The sorted list in Table 6 indicates that Cluster 3 and Other were the mostly confused clusters followed by Cluster 2 and 4, and Cluster 4 and Other in E6K. Table 7 shows the distribution of disagreed judgments across different combinations of clusters in the MTurk data. Here we observe that Cluster 1 and 2 were the most confused clusters by the Turkers, followed by Cluster 2 and 4, and Cluster 1 and 5.

We can observe some similarities between the two lists: for example, Cluster 2 and 4, and Cluster 1 and 2 appear at the top of both lists, while Cluster 3 and 5, and Cluster 2 and 5 appear closer to the bottom of the lists (besides the confusion with the Other cluster). The results seem to suggest that the mood clusters may not be mutually exclusive, at least when they are perceived by real users. For instance, a song may perceived to be "cheerful" and "humorous" (Cluster 2 and 4) or "passionate" and "sweet" (Cluster 1 and 2) at the same time.

Table 6. Distribution of disagreed judgments across clusters (E6K)

Clusters	Disagreed judgments
Cluster 3 & Other	37
Cluster 2 & Cluster 4	31
Cluster 4 & Other	23
Cluster 1 & Cluster 2	20
Cluster 5 & Other	18
Cluster 2 & Other	17
Cluster 1 & Cluster 3	13
Cluster 1 & Cluster 5	13
Cluster 1 & Other	10
Cluster 2 & Cluster 3	9
Cluster 4 & Cluster 5	9
Cluster 1 & Cluster 2 & Cluster 4	7
Cluster 1 & Cluster 3 & Other	6
Cluster 1 & Cluster 4	6
Cluster 3 & Cluster 4	6
Cluster 1 & Cluster 2 & Cluster 3	5
Cluster 4 & Cluster 5 & Other	5
Cluster 1 & Cluster 2 & Other	4
Cluster 1 & Cluster 5 & Other	3
Cluster 2 & Cluster 4 & Other	3
Cluster 1 & Cluster 4 & Other	2
Cluster 1 & Cluster 2 & Cluster 5	1
Cluster 2 & Cluster 3 & Other	1
Cluster 2 & Cluster 4 & Cluster 5	1
Cluster 2 & Cluster 5	1
Cluster 3 & Cluster 5	1
Cluster 3 & Cluster 5 & Other	1
Total	**253**

Table 7. Distribution of disagreed judgments across clusters (MTurk)

Clusters	Disagreed judgments
Cluster 1 & Cluster 2	95
Cluster 2 & Cluster 4	86
Cluster 1 & Cluster 5	74
Cluster 2 & Cluster 3	61
Cluster 1 & Cluster 3	45
Cluster 1 & Cluster 4	41
Cluster 3 & Other	37
Cluster 4 & Cluster 5	28
Cluster 3 & Cluster 4	27
Cluster 2 & Cluster 5	22
Cluster 3 & Cluster 5	20
Cluster 1 & Other	17
Cluster 5 & Other	17
Cluster 4 & Other	15
Cluster 2 & Other	10
Total	**595**

Much of the previous research on music mood [5], [10], [16], [18], [19] confirmed the two dimensional model of valence and arousal for representing the mood space proposed by Russell [20] [Figure 2]. When we attempt to position the five mood clusters according to this two-dimensional model, both Clusters 2 (rollicking, cheerful, fun, sweet, amiable/good natured) and 4 (humorous, silly, campy, quirky, whimsical, witty, wry) seem to share positive valence. Additionally, Cluster 1 (passionate, rousing, confident, boisterous, rowdy) seems to consist of moods with positive valence as well. This may explain the reason for high confusion among these clusters by human evaluators. Then, it is interesting that Clusters 3 (literate, poignant, wistful, bittersweet, autumnal, brooding) and 5 (aggressive, fiery, tense/anxious, intense, volatile, visceral) are the least confused clusters, as they both consist of negative moods. We speculate that this may be because the difference between Clusters 3 and 5 in the arousal dimension is for some reason clearer, compared to Clusters 1, 2 and 4.

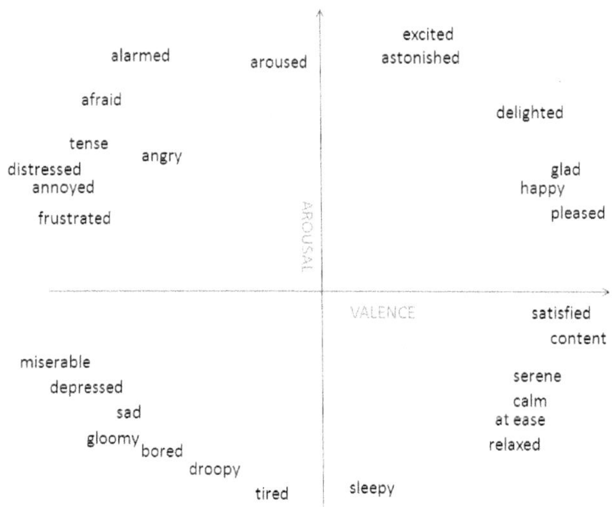

Figure 2. Russell's model of valence and arousal

The facts that these clusters in reality are not mutually exclusive and a song can carry multiple moods are good indications of why it is so challenging to evaluate music mood classification algorithms. Suppose there is a song that has a passionate mood as a dominant mood of the song, but it is delivered in a cheerful tone, can we really say it has to be classified in Cluster 1 and not 2? For the purpose of evaluation, there seems to be an underlying assumption that it is possible to classify songs into one type of mood cluster in MIREX. Based on this assumption, the songs that have agreed judgments are used for building the ground truth. Our data, however, suggest that maybe mood classification systems should be permitted to indicate multiple moods instead of classifying songs in to one particular "correct" mood cluster.

5.1.6 Reclassification

As previously explained, the AMC test collection had mood labels pre-assigned according to metadata provided by APM. We wanted to see to what extent human evaluators would agree with these pre-assigned labels in E6K and MTurk data sets. Table 8 and Table 9 show the numbers of clips that were reclassified according to the human judgments in EK6 and MTurk data set, respectively.

Table 8. Reclassification among all the judgments in E6K data (percentages in parentheses)

	Judgments						
Pre-label	C1	C2	C3	C4	C5	Other	Total
Cluster1	292 (54.0)	68 (12.6)	74 (13.7)	34 (6.3)	16 (3.0)	57 (10.5)	541 (100)
Cluster2	35 (7.6)	327 (70.8)	40 (8.7)	29 (6.3)	1 (0.2)	30 (6.5)	462 (100)
Cluster3	23 (4.6)	16 (3.2)	408 (81.6)	5 (1.0)	5 (1.0)	43 (8.6)	500 (100)
Cluster4	15 (10.2)	56 (11.6)	13 (2.7)	321 (66.3)	21 (4.3)	58 (12.0)	484 (100)
Cluster5	105 (21.0)	5 (1.0)	7 (1.5)	23 (4.8)	357 (74.2)	49 (10.2)	481 (100)
Total	450	472	542	412	400	237	2468

Table 9. Reclassification among all the judgments in MTurk data (percentages in parentheses)

	Judgments						
Pre-label	C1	C2	C3	C4	C5	Other	Total
Cluster1	160 (32.0)	130 (26.0)	119 (23.8)	43 (8.6)	27 (5.4)	21 (4.2)	500 (100)
Cluster2	87 (17.4)	235 (47.0)	68 (13.6)	84 (16.8)	4 (0.8)	22 (4.4)	500 (100)
Cluster3	47 (9.4)	21 (4.2)	368 (73.6)	10 (2.0)	23 (4.6)	31 (6.2)	500 (100)
Cluster4	51 (10.2)	125 (25.0)	48 (9.6)	208 (41.6)	40 (8.0)	28 (5.6)	500 (100)
Cluster5	105 (21.0)	25 (5.0)	19 (3.8)	22 (4.4)	309 (61.8)	20 (4.0)	500 (100)
Total	450	536	622	367	403	122	2500

By comparing this pair of tables, we can observe that overall the Turkers agreed less with pre-assigned labels than the E6K evaluators. Both data sets show that the pre-labeled mood cluster with the greatest agreement is Cluster 3, in fact, much more so than the other clusters. The cluster with least agreement is Cluster 4, meaning that many clips pre-labeled as Cluster 4 got controversial judgments in both data sets. Additionally, the Turkers seem to agree much less with the pre-assigned mood cluster 1 and 2 than E6K evaluators.

We also wanted to see the effect of reclassification among the music clips that had 2 or more agreed judgments. Table 10 and Table 11 show these results for the E6K and MTurk data in that order. In these two tables, we see lower percentages on reclassifications than those in Table 8 and 9 (i.e., higher percentages on the diagonal cells in Table 10 and 11). This observation indicates that for both E6K and MTurk data, agreed judgments were more in accordance with the pre-assigned labels than non-agreed judgments. However, while the reclassification rates were low for the E6K data [Table 10], for the MTurk data a larger number of music clips still needed to be reclassified with the exception of Cluster 3 [Table 11]. The pre-assigned labels were based on metadata and textual descriptions in the APM data set, which were written by music experts employed by APM. E6K judges are also expected to be music experts in the sense that they either have some background in music or music related research. Thus, we suspect this to be part of the reason for seeing this discrepancy. Perhaps the meanings of the mood clusters (except Cluster 3) are not as clear to lay people as they are to music experts. However, it is difficult to reach a solid conclusion based solely on these data, since we do not know how much music expertise the Turkers have. Future studies in a more controlled environment with two groups of evaluators, one consisting of music experts and the other, non-experts, will help us understand if there is significant difference between the two groups with regards to mood judgments.

Table 10. Reclassification among the clips with 2 or 3 agreed judgments in E6K data (percentages in parentheses)

	Reclassified Clips						
Pre-label	C1	C2	C3	C4	C5	Other	Total
Cluster1	111 (73.0)	12 (7.9)	18 (11.8)	7 (4.6)	0 (0.0)	4 (2.6)	152 (100)
Cluster2	1 (0.8)	109 (90.8)	6 (5.0)	1 (0.8)	0 (0.0)	3 (2.5)	120 (100)
Cluster3	3 (2.0)	2 (1.4)	136 (92.5)	1 (0.7)	1 (0.7)	4 (2.7)	147 (100)
Cluster4	0 (0.0)	7 (5.6)	1 (0.8)	110 (88.0)	2 (1.6)	5 (4.0)	125 (100)
Cluster5	6 (4.4)	0 (0.0)	2 (1.5)	2 (1.5)	123 (89.8)	4 (2.9)	137 (100)
Total	121	130	163	121	126	20	681

Table 11. Reclassification among the agreed clips in MTurk data (percentages in parentheses)

	Reclassified Clips						
Pre-label	C1	C2	C3	C4	C5	Other	Total
Cluster1	41 (34.7)	26 (22.0)	38 (32.2)	9 (7.6)	3 (2.5)	1 (0.8)	118 (100)
Cluster2	18 (13.8)	72 (55.4)	15 (11.5)	20 (15.4)	1 (0.8)	4 (3.1)	130 (100)
Cluster3	5 (3.1)	2 (1.2)	149 (92.5)	0 (0.0)	2 (1.2)	3 (1.9)	161 (100)
Cluster4	7 (6.3)	29 (26.1)	8 (7.2)	56 (50.5)	8 (7.2)	3 (2.7)	111 (100)
Cluster5	18 (13.3)	2 (1.5)	6 (4.4)	0 (0.0)	107 (79.3)	2 (1.5)	135 (100)
Total	89	131	216	85	121	13	655

5.2 Comparison of System Performances

5.2.1 Generating Ground Truth

In E6K, the ground truth data set was selected from the 681 music clips that received the same classification judgments from two or more human evaluators. 20 of the 681 music clips were classified in the "other" mood cluster, thus were not included in this process. Each cluster contained 120 music clips, thus resulting in 600 clips in total [Table 12].

Table 12. Composition of the ground truth data set from E6K

Cluster	Doubles w/2 judges	Doubles w/3 judges	Triples	Total
Cluster1	58	41	21	120
Cluster2	61	35	24	120
Cluster3	46	18	56	120
Cluster4	73	26	21	120
Cluster5	75	14	31	120
Total	**313**	**134**	**153**	**600**

In Table 12, each column indicates the number of music clips used for generating the ground truth based on the degree of agreement. The first column shows the music clips that only had 2 evaluators (judges) whom both agreed upon a mood cluster. The second column indicates the number of music clips that had 3 evaluators and 2 of them agreed upon a mood cluster. The third column shows the music clips that had 3 evaluators whom all agreed upon a mood cluster. When selecting music clips for the ground truth data set, triples (i.e., clips with 3 agreed judgments) were all included, since they had a higher level of agreement than other clips. Then the doubles (i.e., clips with 2 agreed judgments) were randomly selected to make the balanced data set of 120 clips in each cluster. The number of 120 clips in each cluster was decided by the MIR community via a poll on the AMC task audio collection in MIREX[7].

We also wanted to find out how much overlap exists between the ground truth data set generated from E6K and MTurk. We compared the ground truth data set from E6K with the MTurk data in order to find a common set of music clips that had agreed judgments. We were able to find a new ground truth set of 343 music clips as an intersection of MTurk agreements and E6K ground truth set [Table 13]. The system performance comparison in the next section is based on this new ground truth set. We were not able to compare system performance on all 655 clips with MTurk agreement because the systems were run against the E6K ground truth data set and thus IMIRSEL only has system classification results on the 600 clips of E6K ground truth set.

The fact that the intersection of MTurk agreements and the E6K ground truth only led to a set of 343 music clips (57.2% of the original E6K ground truth data set) further suggests that music mood classification is a challenging problems not only for machines, but for humans as well. By increasing the number of evaluators from 2/3 to 4/5 (i.e., E6K evaluators + Turkers), the number of music clips with agreement dropped to 270 (sum of numbers in the diagonal cells in Table 13), which is a significant loss of 55%. In future work, it would be interesting to see how the distribution of agreement changes with more evaluators.

Table 13. Intersection of E6K ground truth set and MTurk agreements

MTurk agreements	E6K ground truth set					
	C1	C2	C3	C4	C5	Total
Cluster1	29	4	0	2	7	42
Cluster2	17	44	0	14	0	75
Cluster3	5	5	91	1	1	103
Cluster4	0	13	0	42	0	55
Cluster5	4	0	0	0	64	68
Total	55	66	91	59	72	**343**

5.2.2 Cross-validation for Accuracies

Just like in the MIREX AMC task, we used 3-fold cross validation to test the accuracies of the algorithms that participated in the MIREX 2007 AMC task. Table 14 compares the order of those algorithms ranked by their accuracies based on E6K data and MTurk data.

Table 14. AMC algorithms ranked by accuracy (3-fold cross validation)[8]

E6K	Average accuracy	MTurk	Average accuracy
CL	0.65	GT	0.66
GT	0.64	CL	0.63
TL	0.64	TL	0.63
ME1	0.61	ME1	0.57
ME2	0.61	ME2	0.57
IM2	0.57	IM2	0.57
KL1	0.56	KL1	0.55
IM1	0.53	IM1	0.54
KL2	0.29	KL2	0.29

In comparing system (algorithm) performances, Friedman's ANOVA is applied to determine whether there are significant differences between the systems. Friedman's ANOVA is a non-parametric test which does not require the data to be normally distributed, and accuracy data are rarely distributed normally [9]. If Friedman's ANOVA indicates a significant difference exists among the systems (at $p < 0.05$), a follow up Tukey-Kramer Honestly Significantly Different (TK-HSD) analyses is then employed to determine which pairs of the systems are significantly different. These are the same tests done in the MIREX AMC task.

[7] http://www.music-ir.org/mirex/wiki/2007:Audio_Music_Mood_Classification#Audio_collection_poll

[8] In MIREX, algorithms are identified by the names of their developers. If multiple algorithms are submitted by the same developers, a number is attached to differentiate them: ME = Michael I. Mandel, Daniel P. W. Ellis; TL = Thomas Lidy, Andreas Rauber, Antonio Pertusa, José Manuel Iñesta; GT = George Tzanetakis; CL = Cyril Laurier, Perfecto Herrera; IM = IMIRSEL M2K; KL = Kyogu Lee

The order of the algorithms is almost the same for the two data sets except the first two, which are reversed (i.e., CL & GT). The results of the TK-HSD analysis indicate that there is no statistically significant difference between these two algorithms, however. The order of CL and GT algorithms was controversial within the E6K data set itself. Hu et al. [9] reported that "CL has the best ranks across all mood clusters despite its average accuracy being the second highest" (p. 465).

Figure 3 and Figure 4 show the TK-HSD evaluation results performed using the E6K and MTurk data, respectively. The X axes in both figures represent the mean column rank. As shown in Figure 3 [E6K data], the only pair that had statistically significant difference was CL and KL2. In Figure 4 [MTurk data], however, the only pair with statistically significant difference was GT and KL2. Therefore the E6K and MTurk data did produce different results with regards to that aspect. As previously discussed, however, CL and GT algorithms were indeed very close in their performance that one can hardly tell the difference even using the original E6K data set. No other pairs of algorithms were significantly different in either E6K or MTurk data set.

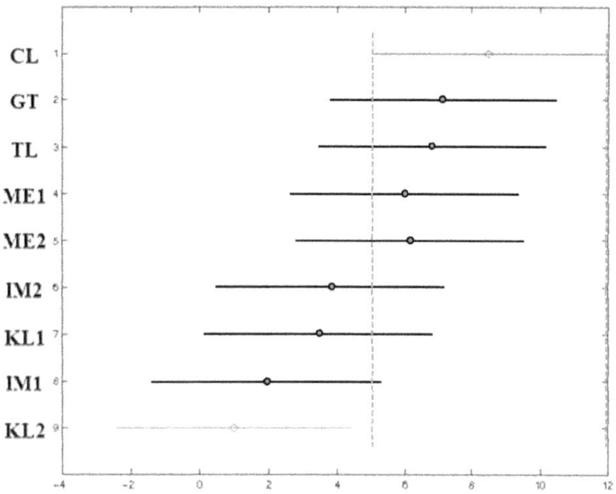

Figure 3. TK-HSD rank comparison for MIREX 2007 AMC based on judgments from E6K

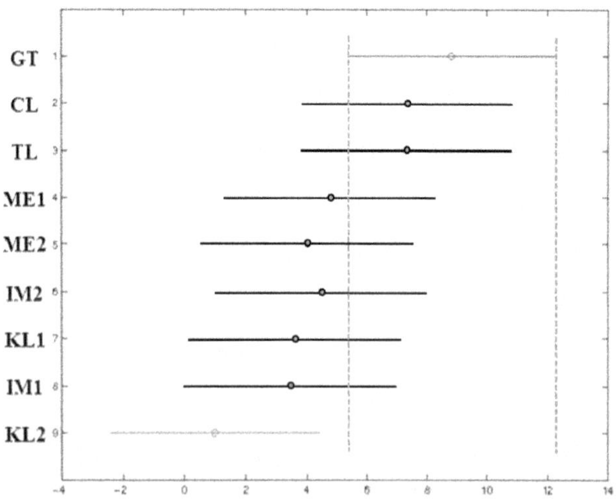

Figure 4. TK-HSD rank comparison for MIREX 2007 AMC based on judgments from MTurk

6. CONCLUSIONS AND FUTURE WORK

Overall the human judgments collected from E6K and MTurk showed similar distribution across the five mood clusters, and also comparable agreement rate overall. In general, Cluster 3 was the most agreed upon mood cluster among all user groups. We did observe some differences with the agreement between the E6K evaluators and APM music experts vs. Turkers and APM music experts for clusters, except for cluster 3. The comparison of confused mood clusters among E6K evaluators and among Turkers revealed a similar pattern. From the perspective of evaluating different algorithms, the results did slightly change the order of the ranked algorithms (i.e., the first and the second) although there was no statistical difference between these two algorithms. The rest of the order was preserved intact. This did change the statistically significant pair found in each data set, however.

Looking at the results, we would suggest using MTurk for Audio Music Mood Classification task with some reservation as there were data suggesting the differences between E6K evaluators and Turkers with regards to how they perceive certain mood clusters such as Cluster 1, in particular. Note that despite these differences, the evaluation outcome did not significantly change as the ranking of algorithms were mostly preserved. Additionally, MTurk does provide certain benefits over E6K, such as being able to collect the data much faster and in a more reliable way than having to continuously asking for help from volunteers from the MIR/MDL community. As a result, the MTurk data set was a lot easier to work with than the E6K data set, which contained music clips with different number of judgments.

More importantly, the confusion we observed among different mood clusters and the combined ground truth of 343 music clips which is only about 60% in size of the original E6K ground truth set all show how music mood is a challenging metadata to deal with. This is most likely due to the nature of music mood itself. Music mood is much more vague that other metadata such as artists, album/song titles [11], and even genre labels. As previously discussed, this is because music can carry multiple moods from mood clusters that are not mutually exclusive. Moreover, the mood can also change during the song [6]. We propose that better evaluation measures will have to take this into account permitting a song to be categorized in multiple mood clusters that perhaps can be weighted in some way.

One limitation of this study is that the E6K data were not as neat as the MTurk data due to the missing number of judgments, which inevitably made the comparison a bit challenging. We did, however, made our best effort to provide fair comparison of the results from E6K and MTurk. In future studies, we hope to conduct a more controlled study with different user groups (e.g., experts with music background, people who have no educational background in music) accompanied by in-depth interviews in order to find out more about how they perceive music mood and which factors play important role when they classify music clips in different mood clusters.

7. ACKOWLEDGEMENTS

We would like to thank the International Music Information Retrieval Systems Evaluation Lab (IMIRSEL) for providing us with access to the test collection for AMC task as well as past MIREX data. We also thank the anonymous reviewers for their helpful comments.

8. REFERENCES

[1] Alonso, O., and Mizzaro, S. 2009. Can we get rid of TREC assessors? Using Mechanical Turk for relevance assessment. In *Proceedings of the SIGIR 2009 Workshop on the Future of IR Evaluation*, 15-16.

[2] Bischoff, K., Firan, C. S., Nejdl, W., and Paiu, R. 2009. How do you feel about "Dancing Queen"? Deriving mood and theme annotations from user tags. In *Proceedings of THE 9th Joint Conference on Digital Libraries* (JCDL'09). ACM, New York, NY, USA, 285-294. DOI= http://doi.acm.org/10.1145/1555400.1555448

[3] Carletta, J. 1996. Assessing agreement on classification tasks: The kappa statistic. *Computational Linguistics*, 22, 2, 249–254.

[4] Cohen, J. 1960. A coefficient of agreement for nominal scales. *Educational and Psychological Measurement*, 20, 1, 37-46.

[5] Eerola, T, Lartillot, O., and Toivianen, P. 2009. Prediction of multidimensional emotional ratings in music from audio using multivariate regression models. In *Proceedings of the 10th ISMIR (International Society for Music Information Retrieval) Conference*, 621-626.

[6] Hu, X. 2010. Music and mood: Where theory and reality meet. In *Proceedings of 2010 iConference.*

[7] Hu, X. and Downie, S. J. 2007. Exploring mood metadata: Relationships with genre, artist and usage metadata. In *Proceedings of the 8th ISMIR (International Society for Music Information Retrieval) Conference*, 67-72.

[8] Hu, X. and Downie, S. J. 2010. Improving mood classification in music digital libraries by combining lyrics and audio. In *Proceedings of the 10th Joint Conference on Digital Libraries* (JCDL'10), ACM, New York, NY, USA, 159-168. DOI= http://doi.acm.org/10.1145/1816123. 1816146.

[9] Hu, X., Downie, S. J., Laurier, C., Bay, M., and Ehmann, A. F. 2008. The 2007 MIREX Audio Mood Classification task: Lessons learned. In *Proceedings of the 9th ISMIR (International Society for Music Information Retrieval) Conference*, 462-467.

[10] Kim, Y., Schmidt, E., and Emelle, L. 2008. Moodswings: A collaborative game for music mood label collection. In *Proceedings of the 9th ISMIR (International Society for Music Information Retrieval) Conference*, 231-236.

[11] Kim, Y., Schmidt, E., Migneco, R., Morton, B. G., Richardson, P., Scott, J., Speck, J. A. and Turnbull, D. 2010. Music emotion recognition: A state of the art review. In *Proceedings of the 11th ISMIR (International Society for Music Information Retrieval) Conference*, 255-266.

[12] Kitter, A., Chi, E. H., and Suh, B. 2008. Crowdsourcing user studies with Mechanical Turk. In *Proceedings of the 26th Annual SIGCHI Conference on Human Factors in Computing Systems* (CHI '08), ACM, New York, NY, USA, 453-456. DOI= http://doi.acm.org/10.1145/1357054.1357127

[13] Laurier, C., Sordo M., Serrà J., and Herrera P. 2009. Music mood representations from social tags. In *Proceedings of the 11th ISMIR (International Society for Music Information Retrieval) Conference*, 381-386.

[14] Lee, J. H. 2010. Crowdsourcing music similarity judgments using Mechanical Turk. In *Proceedings of the 11th ISMIR (International Society for Music Information Retrieval) Conference*, 183-188.

[15] Lee, J. H. , Hill, T., and Work, L. 2012. What does music mood mean for real users? In *Proceedings of the 2012 iConference*, ACM, New York, NY, USA, 112-119. DOI= http://doi.acm.org/10.1145/ 2132176.2132191

[16] Lu, L., Liu, D., and Zhang, H. 2006. Automatic mood detection and tracking of music audio signals. *IEEE Transactions on Audio, Speech, and Language Processing*, 14, 1, 5-18. DOI=10.1109/TSA.2005.860344

[17] Mandel, M., Eck, D, and Bengio, Y. 2010. Learning tags that vary within a song. In *Proceedings of the 11th ISMIR (International Society for Music Information Retrieval) Conference*, 399-404.

[18] Meharabian, A. and Russell, J. A. 1974. *An Approach to Environmental Psychology*. MIT Press.

[19] Mion, L., and Poli, G. D. 2008. Score-independent audio features for description of music expression. *IEEE Transactions on Audio, Speech and Language Processing*, 16, 2, 458-466. DOI=10.1109/TASL.2007.913743

[20] Russell, J. 1980. A Circumplex model of affect. *Journal of Personality and Social Psychology*, 39, 1161-1178.

[21] Schuller, B., Hage, C., Schuller, D., and Rigoll, G. 2010. Mister D.J., Cheer me up!: Musical and textual features for automatic mood classification. *Journal of New Music Research*, 39, 1, 13-34.

[22] Skowronek, J., McKinney, M.F., & van de Par, S. 2006. Ground truth for automatic music mood classification. In *Proceedings of the 7th ISMIR (International Society for Music Information Retrieval) Conference*, 395-396.

[23] Snow, R., O'Connor, B., Jurafsky, D., and Ng, A. Y. 2008. Cheap and fast – But is it good? Evaluating non-expert annotations for natural language tasks. In *Proceedings of the 2008 Conference on Empirical Methods in Natural Language Processing*, 254-263.

[24] Urbano, J. Morato, J., Marrero, M., and Martin, D. 2010. Crowdsourcing preference judgments for evaluation of music similarity tasks. In *Proceedings of the SIGIR 2010 Workshop on Crowdsourcing for Search Evaluation*, 9-16.

[25] Vignoli, F. 2004. Digital Music Interaction concepts: a user study. In *Proceedings of the 5th ISMIR (International Society for Music Information Retrieval) Conference,* 415-421.

Content-Based Layouts for Exploratory Metadata Search in Scientific Research Data

Jürgen Bernard
Fraunhofer Institute for
Computer Graphics Research
Fraunhoferstr. 5
D-64283 Darmstadt, Germany
juergen.bernard
@igd.fraunhofer.de

Tobias Ruppert
Fraunhofer Institute for
Computer Graphics Research
Fraunhoferstr. 5
D-64283 Darmstadt, Germany
tobias.ruppert
@igd.fraunhofer.de

Maximilian Scherer
TU Darmstadt
Fraunhoferstr. 5
D-64283 Darmstadt, Germany
maximilian.scherer
@gris.tu-darmstadt.de

Jörn Kohlhammer
Fraunhofer Institute for
Computer Graphics Research
Fraunhoferstr. 5
D-64283 Darmstadt, Germany
joern.kohlhammer
@igd.fraunhofer.de

Tobias Schreck
University of Konstanz
Universitätsstr. 10
D-78457 Konstanz, Germany
tobias.schreck
@uni-konstanz.de

ABSTRACT

Today's digital libraries (DLs) archive vast amounts of information in the form of text, videos, images, data measurements, etc. User access to DL content can rely on similarity between metadata elements, or similarity between the data itself (content-based similarity). We consider the problem of exploratory search in large DLs of time-oriented data. We propose a novel approach for overview-first exploration of data collections based on user-selected metadata properties. In a 2D layout representing entities of the selected property are laid out based on their similarity with respect to the underlying data content. The display is enhanced by compact summarizations of underlying data elements, and forms the basis for exploratory navigation of users in the data space. The approach is proposed as an interface for visual exploration, leading the user to discover interesting relationships between data items relying on content-based similarity between data items and their respective metadata labels. We apply the method on real data sets from the earth observation community, showing its applicability and usefulness.

Categories and Subject Descriptors

H.3 [**Information Storage and Retrieval**]: Information Search and Retrieval; H.3 [**Information Storage and Retrieval**]: Digital Libraries; J.2 [**Physical Sciences and Engineering**]: Earth and atmospheric sciences

Keywords

Information Visualization, Exploratory Search, Similarity Measures, Scientific Research Data, Visual Layouts

1. INTRODUCTION

Digital Libraries (DLs) organize, preserve, and make available to users all kinds of information. Often, textual and multimedia documents such as images, video, or audio are among the document types supported by DL systems. Recently, also *scientific research data* has come into focus as an important type of information that should be treated by DL efforts. New technologies for data collection are leading to data production at high rates, giving rise to large amounts of relevant data which users may be interested in. Examples, among many others, include the scientific domains of earth and space observation, where repositories such as PANGAEA [26] and SLOAN [31] host large amounts of relevant data, respectively. Jim Gray's *Fourth Paradigm* [15] suggests that the scientific discovery process as a whole could benefit tremendously if research data could be consistently collected, shared, and made available by means of a research data infrastructure.

To date, the data storage facilities in DLs have increased substantially, and the storage of large data becomes less an issue than appropriate forms of user access. Data in existing scientific data repositories are typically accessed by users according to metadata properties of the data items, e.g., time or location of observation, or the name of the creator of the respective data item. User access based on the actual *content* of the data, however, remains a difficult problem as the concept of data is very diverse, and appropriate search methods depend on the type of data and user intents.

The visual analysis has the goal to make big amounts of data and information processing transparent in a way that combines the strengths of humans *and* computers. Actual approaches unify automated data analysis with visual-interactive data exploration [18]. Exploratory search [38]

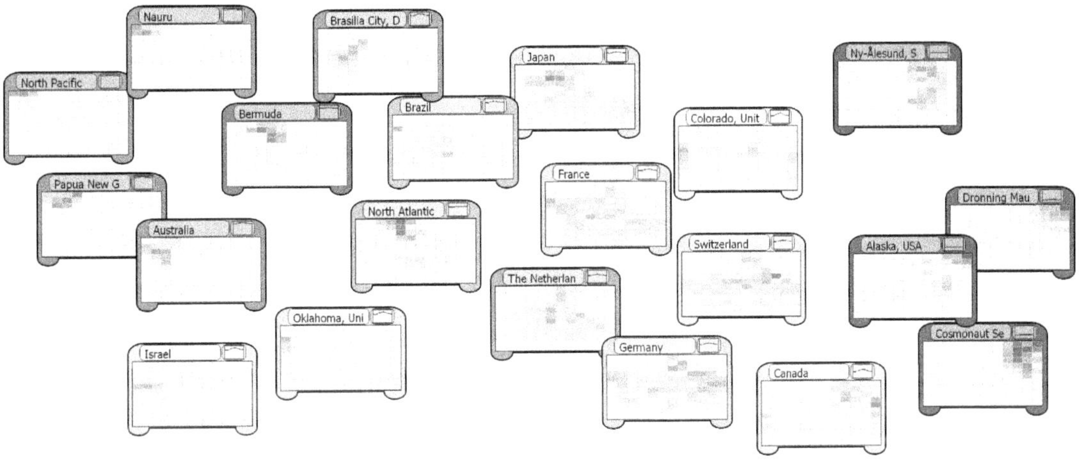

Figure 1: Graphical layout of metadata property 'Location' enriched by data content summaries based on temperature measurements. Hot temperature measurements to the left (red), measurements from polar regions to the right (blue), cluster of moderate temperatures at the center (yellow, green).

addresses the problem of users not having a well-defined information need that could be translated into a formal query. Appropriate overview and navigation facilities allow users to obtain a better understanding of the overall data space, before narrowing down the search to more specific queries. Facetted search approaches have proven to be very useful in the exploratory search process. They group documents according to categories of metadata, such as 'Author', 'Year', or 'Location'. The appropriate representation of relationships and patterns in data can lead to the discovery of expected and unexpected relationships [42] potentially relevant for the users' information need.

We propose a new approach for exploratory search in time-oriented research data. It reflects both metadata and the actual data content. A visual-interactive display is designed which allows users to navigate the metadata search space, discover relationships between data items, and access individual data records. Based on the notion of *metadata properties*, users are enabled to select a specific metadata field of interest. The similarity between instances of the selected metadata property (we call them *metadata entities*) is automatically computed based on the content of the underlying data items. A similarity-preserving 2D layout of the metadata entities, based on a force-directed network layout method, is then generated. This layout can be freely navigated by the user to explore interesting relationships between entities. The visual exploration is supported by showing, for each entity, a content summary of the represented data items based on the clusters within the data.

Our approach is applied to a repository of time-series data from the earth environment domain. We show the principal applicability of the method and recommend it as an approach for visual and exploratory search in this kind of data domain. Examples of the many useful application scenarios made possible by our approach include finding answers to questions such as "which data creator found the earth observation measurements most similar to mine?" or "which measurement stations produce the most similar measurement series?". In a case study, we show the practical applicability of our search and exploration display by incorporating scientific researchers from the earth observation field.

2. RELATED WORK

2.1 Scientific Research Data in the Digital Library Context

In modern information infrastructures, DLs are a key component. DLs provide and manage facilities for accessing information and data resource, and allow distributed access to large user communities. DL systems have developed over the years to a 'digital library universe' with a great variety of user roles, resources, technology and relationships, and yield many advantages in modern information infrastructure [22, 40]. Many DL systems provide mechanisms to search in well-defined metadata. Emerging nominatives for metadata properties are the Dublin Core standard [27]. Many other domain-focused metadata standards exist. For example, in research data, the DataCite metadata kernel [33] is proposed. Open data libraries cover a number of data and application domains like crystallography [13], earth observation [26], or chemistry [39]. A clear trend indicates that the number and size of public data repositories will continue to grow. Respective challenges in the DL area include the question how to integrate and access that data to support scholarly work flows.

DLs are fundamental components of E-science [15, 32], and the necessity of treating scientific research data by library services is generally recognized [17]. Moreover, significant challenges like handling complex data in the sense of (a) 'big data' and (b) heterogeneous data exist [19, 18]. Furthermore, a challenge with scientific research data retains: how to organize and access various kinds of scientific data content? In Section 2.3 we will identify the problem of creating content summary solutions in the scientific research data context. Hull et al. expect future DL tools with metadata and data content to be less isolated and rigid [17]. Based on our experience and a review of DL publications distributed among various scientific data domains, it is of invaluable importance to work closely together with researchers to appropriately meet the two-way requirements on target DL analysis systems. This need for multidisciplinary collaboration is stated in biological sciences [32], neuroscience [10],

E-Science [16] and other application areas [6, 13]. Making effective use of data sets based on a combined metadata-based and content-based approach is promising [3]. Like stated by Foster et al., understanding the scientific workflow and providing effective information tools has the potential to eventually realize massive benefit to science [17].

2.2 Similarity relations generated by metadata and content-based approaches

When are two entities related or similar? This is the driving question in related work about metadata-based and content-based approaches.

In *metadata*-based approaches, annotations primarily serve as a measure for similarity. If two annotations are similar, the annotated entities are considered similar [27]. Such metadata approaches rely heavily on the quality of the metadata – and accordingly on the curation process. Another metadata-based approach relies on usage statistics. Such approaches are most popular in collaborative filtering systems, where the assumed relatedness (or similarity) of two entities is increased, whenever they are being bought together, looked at the same time, have the same co-citation patterns etc. [5]. Hybrid algorithms employing both – content-based and collaborative filtering techniques – have also been successfully used [34]. A third approach comprises ontology-driven techniques and systems. Here, a strict ontology is imposed for a given domain. Under such constraints, retrieval with a focus on semantics becomes viable. Such approaches already started to enable new semantic applications in a wide span of areas such as bioinformatics, financial services, web services, business intelligence, DLs and national security [19]. Two of the most prominent examples include DBPedia [2], which enables semantic search of wikipedia knowledge, and Wolfram Alpha [41] which even allows for semantic searches with natural language querying.

Measuring *content*-based similarity is subject to research in many areas. These include multimedia information retrieval tasks [23], like 2D shape analysis, 3D object retrieval and content-based image retrieval [11], as well as information retrieval in time-series data [21]. This process usually involves (a) some kind of descriptor that represents data under concern, and (b) a distance measure between two descriptors that represent the dissimilarity of the data object. One prominent descriptor-scheme is the computation of feature vectors. For computing the distance between two feature vectors, a vast amount of distance functions is available [9]. Given a descriptor and a distance measure, users are allowed to search for data objects not only by similarity of the annotation, but also by similarity of content. Such queries often consist of query-by-example or query-by-sketch [14].

A key difference between content-based and metadata-based similarity notions is that the former can be computed fully automatically, but often suffer from limited discrimination capability and in general, the semantic gap problem [29]. Metadata-based approaches in the best case can provide better discrimination and semantic description, yet are often depending on manual annotation and quality control. Most retrieval and exploration systems consider either the content-based or the metadata-based similarity notions for supporting user queries or computing visual layouts for explorative search and browsing. Our work is novel in that we integrate both similarity notions in a joint approach. Specifically, we compute content-based similarity between data items, using it to visually map metadata properties of the data, for explorative analysis and correlation.

2.3 Visualization of Search and Exploration Spaces

There exist two classes of techniques for visualizing data entities on a 2D display reflecting their interdependencies and thereby generating a visual entity map. These are projection-based and graph-based layouts. The projection-based approaches map high-dimensional data spaces to spaces of lower dimensionality. In our case, the high-dimensional time-series data is projected to a space of lower dimensionality in order to visualize it in 2D. Examples for projection-based approaches include principal component analysis (PCA), multi-dimensional scaling (MDS) or self-organizing map (SOM) [12] layouts. All of these techniques are topology-preserving. Their goal is to preserve the pairwise distances between its entities, which is the main requirement for our 2D map. As a drawback of these projection-based layouts, their output is neglecting the overfitting problem on the display space. Entities of similar content will overlap in the visualization, which is a drawback for the user's exploration task.

As a second possibility, data entities and their pairwise similarities can be interpreted as complete graphs. Hence, the visual map can be generated via a graph-based layout. For the preservation of the edge lengths especially force-based graph layouts are suitable. An overview of graph layouts is given in [37]. In our approach, we apply the Weighted Edge-Repulsion LinLog model, an extension of the Edge-Repulsion LinLog model [24], to layout our metadata entity graph. Besides their topology-preserving characteristic, it addresses the overfitting problem by applying repulsive forces on overlapping entities.

There also exist metadata visualization approaches in the field of DL. In [35], powergraphs are used to visualize clustered co-author relationships from a bibliographical database. The experimental library software INVISQUE [42] uses an index card metaphor to realize a visual interactive exploration of library content. While approaches in providing 'content summary solutions' for generic data types like audio or image, or other multimedia data exist for years [28, 1], concepts for organizing scientific data by its content in the DL workflow are scarce. In [30], content summaries are provided via a k-means clustering approach. As another example, Bernard et al. [3] generate content summaries based on scientific research data via a self-organzing maps approach. A solution for visualizing icon-based cluster content summaries combined with graph layouts can be found in [8] from the information visualization research field.

In the information visualization field, mapping of data variables on the display space is often performed by means of visual attributes like color, transparency, object size, or object position. The use of color needs predefined color palettes, so called color maps. In our approach we apply color on the basis of a so called visual catalog to visually discriminate between distinct variations of data content. Therefore, a variety of two dimensional color maps can be applied [7]. We follow the idea of Vesanto et al. [36] where the output of the self-organizing map algorithm is color-coded.

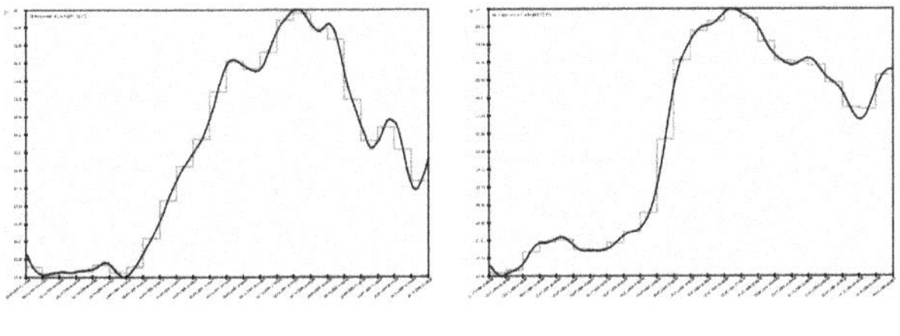

Figure 2: Visualization of time-oriented research data content. Daily temperature curves (black) with a similar visual appearance are shown, while absolute values differ (left: around 20°C, right: below -20°C). PAA descriptor of the curves (red) denotes the basis of our content-based similarity concept.

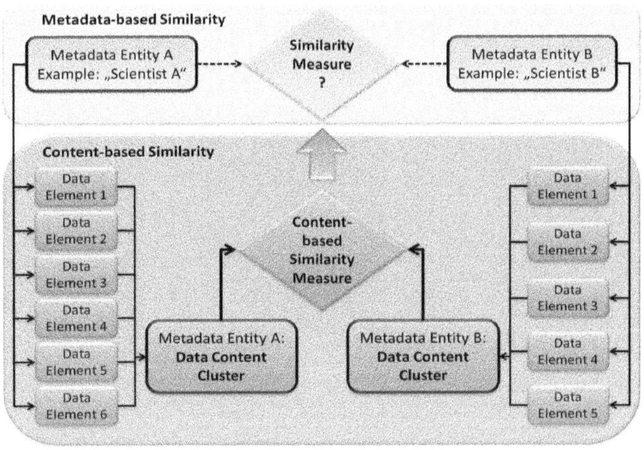

Figure 3: Content-based similarity for two given metadata entities: Measurement data of 'Scientist A' is compared with measurement data of 'Scientist B' to compute a content-based distance between these two (semantic) entities.

3. APPROACH

In this section we present our method for visual search and exploration of metadata properties. In current DL systems metadata often refers to nominal entities (authors, geo-annotation, sources, etc.) As a consequence, potential relations between different entities must be neglected in a metadata search: Only the library objects matching the name defined in the query can be considered as a valid result. For example, searching for a specific author will result in a list of all library objects composed by the author. Relations between different metadata entities (e.g., different authors) are neglected.

In the following Section 3.1 we propose a similarity measure in order to describe the relations between different metadata entities. This measure is computed based on the data content associated to the metadata property. In our use case, the content consists of time-oriented measurements taken by the author. The result of these content-based similarity computation is a distance matrix describing all pairwise similarities between the metadata entities. In Section 3.2, this distance matrix is visualized for a first comparison of different metadata entities regarding their content. In Section 3.3, we provide visual access to the metadata entity relations via a 2D layout. Here, authors that created similar measurements appear close to each other. In Section 3.4 we detail on our visual catalog which allows for a global overview of the data content. Moreover, we employ this visual catalog metaphor as a visual representation to enrich each of our metadata entity glyphs with associated data content information, see Section 3.5.

3.1 Content-based Metadata Similarity Measures

In our approach, we cluster entities based on similar metadata annotations like 'Author' or geo-spatial 'Location'. Given such a clustering, we wish to compute the content-based similarity between these semantic entities. In the application we consider here, the content of each entity consists of time-oriented climate measurements series.

A simple, yet powerful technique to describe sequential data is the so-called Piecewise Aggregate Approximation (PAA) [20] (see Figure 2). It is suitable for our purposes of describing time-series. The basic idea is to split a sequence of length n into m segments and compute the mean value of all data-points in each segment. Such a block-wise average can be computed extremely fast, only n (sequence length) additions and m (number of segments) divisions are required.

To measure content-based similarity we chose the Euclidean distance, because the PAA descriptor tries to approximate the original time-series as closely as possible. This avoids deviating any further from the true Euclidean distance of two given time-series.

However given two sets of descriptors and a distance measure, there are still several possibilties to assess the similarity. We can (a) compute the average of each pair-wise distance; (b) average the descriptors for each set and then compute the distance; (c) determine the median descriptor for each set and compute their distances.

We chose option (b), because we believe this to be the best trade-off between the discriminativeness of (a) and the outlier robustness of (c) (see Figure 3).

Please note that the choice of data descriptor and distance function is a user-parameter in general. As long as the descriptor computation result is a vector and the distance measure is a true metric, the particular concept of content-based similarity is interchangeable.

3.2 DistanceMatrixView: Visualizing Pairwise Distances of Metadata Entities

The similarity measures presented in Section 3.1 are used to identify relations between different metadata entities. A matrix consisting of all pairwise similarities between the metadata entities of a certain metadata property (e.g. 'Author') can be interpreted as a distance matrix. In Figure 4 we present a triangular distance matrix visualization, that supports the visual exploration of these similarities. Each diamond-shaped box represents the relation between two metadata entities. The color describes the similarity value from similar (white) to dissimilar (blue). We provide two possible scenarios for the user to interact with the visualization. First, similar or dissimilar metadata entities can be detected by clicking on bright or dark blue diamonds. The corresponding metadata entities are highlighted in the list (see Figure 4). With this interaction mode, extreme similarity values can be explored. Secondly, a user may want to

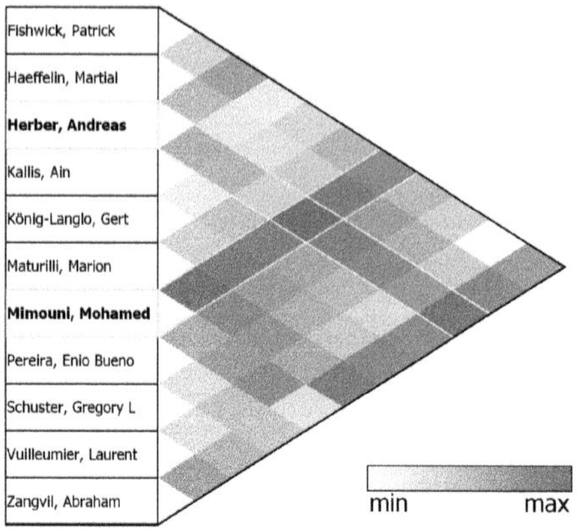

Figure 4: DistanceMatrixView: Visualization of a similarity matrix regarding metadata property 'Author'. Similarities are computed based on shortwave downward radiation measurements, which are prominent measures in climate research, especially for giving statements about cloud occurences. Highlighting of lowest similarity between the measurements of the two authors 'Andreas Herber' and 'Mohamed Mimouni'.

identify the similarities to one specific metadata entity. By selecting this entity in the list, the corresponding diamonds are highlighted. This helps the user to analyze the similarities of one specific metadata entity to the other entities (e.g, see Figure 7). The distance matrix visualization allows the user to visually explore the metadata space implying its inner relations regarding a specific metadata property (e.g. 'Author'). Please note, that the user can freely choose which metadata property to explore. Our concept can be applied to any metadata property provided in the data set. The properties only define the grouping of the data content.

3.3 MetaMap: Visual Mapping of Metadata Entities

Another method to support exploratory search in the metadata space is to display the metadata entities to be explored in a 2D map. One requirement to the resulting visualization is (a) that similar entities are depicted close to each other while dissimilar entities should have a greater visual distance. That way, the user can explore similar metadata entities in the vicinity of an entity of attention. Moreover, (b) the visualization has to arrange the icons representing the metadata entities with a minimum of overplotting, since the nearest neighbors of a metadata entity are most relevant for the exploration task.

From the visual mapping presented in the related work (see Section 2.3) the force-based graph layouts prove to fulfill both requirements for the visual mapping. Therefore, the metadata entities and their pairwise similarities are interpreted as nodes and edges respectively.

In our approach, we apply the Weighted Edge-repulsion LinLog model to layout our metadata entity graph. It is topology-preserving, and therefore, meeting requirement (a). Moreover, it addresses the overfitting problem, requirement (b).

In the following the metadata entity map is enriched by visual content summaries.

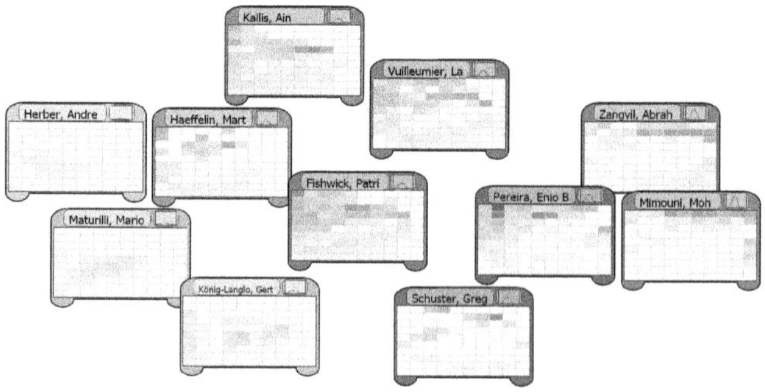

Figure 5: Visual layout of metadata entities represented by their content summary icons. Topology preservation (e.g., lowest similarity between authors 'Andreas Herber' and 'Mohamed Mimouni') and minimization of overlapping is shown.

3.4 Visual Catalog to Summarize the Data Content

So far, we introduced the computation of similarity measures for metadata entities based on their underlying data content, and two possible ways for visualizing the metadata entities and their similarity values. In both visualizations (presented in Section 3.2 and 3.3) the associated data content that is used to compute the metadata similarities is not visualized. Now, we present a visualization method for giving the user a 'global overview' of the underlying data content. In our use case, the data content consists of time-oriented measurement curves, each with the duration of one day. We make these daily patterns visually accessible via a visual catalog metaphor. This visual catalog has to (a) represent the underlying curve patterns, and (b) arrange them in an intuitive order showing similar curve patterns close to each other.

In our approach, we use a SOM algorithm to generate a visual catalog. The resulting visual catalog (see Figure 6 (left)) consists of a $n \times m$ grid of cells, each representing a cluster of curve patterns. Within each cell, a representative curve pattern and the number of curves contained in the cluster is depicted. The cells are automatically arranged in a way, that similar curve clusters appear close to each other. With these characteristics our visual catalog meets both requirements, visual overview and topology preservation. Please note, that the grid should not be interpreted as a coordinate system with a semantic meaning for both coordinate axes. The visual catalog is just a topology-preserving arrangement of clusters.

As a last step for generating our visual catalog, a color map is applied to the SOM grid. The purpose of this color map is to increase the recognition value of special areas, which is relevant for the content summaries in Section 3.5. Please note, that the color map does not depend on the data content. It is just applied to the grid structure of the visual catalog. This is important to visually discreminate different areas of the visual catalog. The color map can freely be chosen and adapted to specific use case scenarios. For example, in the application part of this paper (see Section 4), we choose a color map that supports the notion of warm (red) and cold (blue) temperatures.

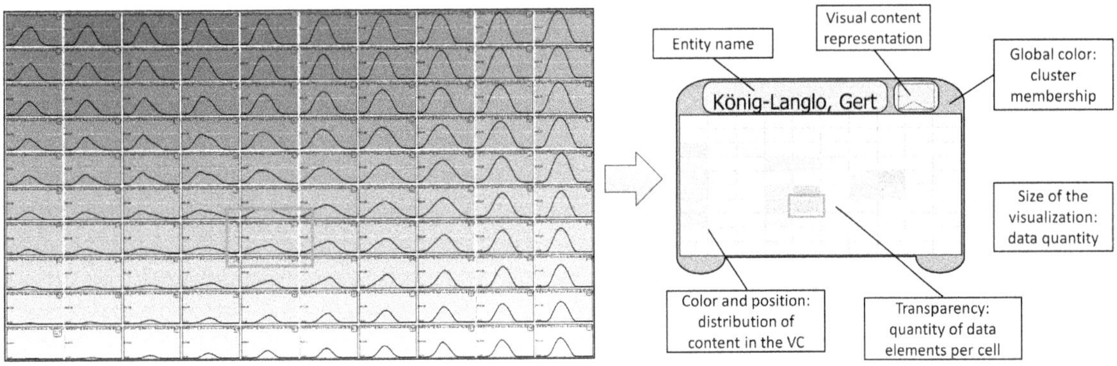

Figure 6: Left: Visual catalog of daily curve progressions generated by a SOM algorithm. Underlying data consists of shortwave downward global radiation measurements. Each cluster cell shows a representing curve pattern, the number of associated curves is depicted at the upper right, respectively. Independent of the actual data, a color map is applied to the 10×10 grid. Right: Content summary visualization representing the measurements of author 'Gert König-Langlo'. Transparency is applied to highlight associated measurements. Global color and visual content representation show the mean curve progression and cluster cell affiliation.

3.5 Enriching our Metadata Entity Glyphs with Visual Content Mappings

In the last section we introduced a visual catalog to give an overview of the data content, consisting of daily curve progressions. Now, we will combine the metadata map (see Section 3.3) with the visual catalog to obtain an integrated visualization depicting both metadata and content.

Therefore, each metadata entity in the metadata map is represented via visual content representations, we call them content summaries. A content summary consists of the visual catalog, presented in Section 3.4, with a color map adjusted to the corresponding metadata entity (see Figure 6 (right)). For example, each 'Author XY' has a certain number of associated measurement curves. These measurement curves are highlighted in the visual catalog to obtain a content summary for the respective author. That means that areas in the visual catalog with a low number of occurences regarding the associated measurement curves are visualized with a higher transparency on the color map.

With this method for each metadata entity a content summary represented by a visual catalog reflecting the occurences of measurement curves is calculated (see Figure 6 right). Now, these content summaries are visualized in the metadata map introduced in Section 3.3 (see Figure 5).

With this visualization the user can directly identify which metadata entities are similar and how their similarity can be interpreted regarding the data content. As an additional feature, the content summary border is depicted with the color most representative with respect to the visual catalog. With this method we provide a content summary solution that supports the user in the visual exploration task.

4. APPLICATION

In our case study we apply our visual search and exploration designs to a real-world example. On the basis of a scientific research data set, we aspire two aspects: (1) prove the functionality of our approach, and (2) explore interesting characteristics in the search space. The challenge in dealing with scientific research data in the DL context is on the one hand (a) to satisfy the expert user expectations and on the other hand (b) to come up with illustrative use cases to attract interested but non-expert user groups. In compliance with this need, we designed our case study in close collaboration with experts from the Alfred Wegener Institute (AWI) for Polar and Marine Research in Bremerhaven, Germany.

4.1 Data Set and Application Domain

Our incorporated data set [4] is acquired from the open data repository PANGAEA, operated by the AWI. PANGAEA archives and publishes georeferenced scientific earth observation data in the research areas of water, ice, sediment and atmosphere. Our data set focuses on atmospheric weather measurements, gathered in the scope of the Baseline Surface Radiation Network (BSRN)[25], a PANGAEA compartment. In general, data of BSRN concerns the development of radiation and meteorological measurements over time, expressed by up to 100 physical parameters, recorded up to a temporal resolution of one measurement per minute. Common physical units include atmospheric pressure, relative air humidity, temperature and a variety of radiation-based measurements like shortwave downward radiation and longwave upward radiation.

4.1.1 Definition of Data Content

We decided to use temperature neasurements as our data content for two reasons. Temperature measurements are especially qualified to satisfy the public interest of non expert users (see Section 4.2, case study A) and the critical examination view of expert users (see Section 4.3, case study B). In consultation with researchers from AWI, we decided to choose a temperature measurement set of 22 BSRN stations recorded within the year 2006. Considering temperature measurements of a whole year is especially important to get a complete impression of all thermal behaviors to be expected within the most typical climatic time period - one year. Another important time period in considering climatic examinations concerns the duration of single days. Different regions on earth evoke entirely different measurement curves within the duration of one day. Scientists call this the phenomena of diverse *diurnal variations*. To comply with this requirement, we define temperature measurements of a single day, taken at one distinct measurement station on earth

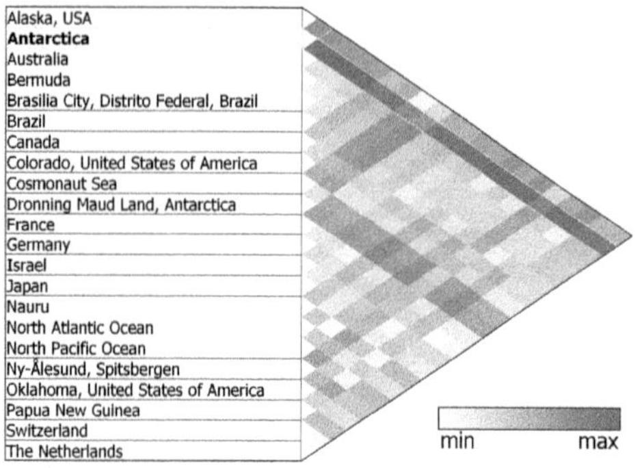

Figure 7: The DistanceMatrixView shows pairwise content-based distances of metadata property 'Location'. 'Antarctica' (selected) is dissimilar to all other metadata entities.

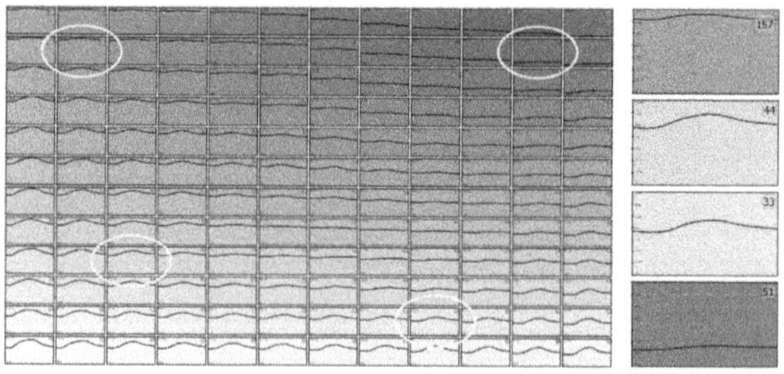

Figure 8: Left: Visual catalog of all daily temperature curves. Highest temperature values are discovered at the left (red, orange, brown), moderate values at the lower right (green, cyan), lowest temperatures at the upper right (blue). Right: Enlargements of four discriminative cells for closer examination.

as one data element (see Figure 2 for two exemplary daily curve progressions). In other words, the outcome of a daily temperature measurement is one 'pattern' that is applied as our content-based similarity modality and thus, the basis of our visual catalog that gives an overview of all (daily) temperature patterns measured in the data set (see Figures 8 and 9). Altogether we process 7677 daily patterns, since the 22 available BSRN stations produce 365 daily curve progressions each. About 400 patterns have been sorted out based on failed data consistency checks (e.g., missing values detection).

We want to point out that it only takes one mouse click to switch the entire data content to other available physical units. The same holds for the aggregation of measurement patterns, the similarity definition and the selection of metadata entities to be visually explored.

4.1.2 Selection of a Metadata Property

PANGAEA data files are divided in a clearly arranged metadata header and a data table with columns of measurements with distinct physical units. The interpretation of the metadata headers provides sufficiently enough metadata properties to comply the DataCite metadata standard we use in our platform. Besides mandatory DataCite attributes ('Identifier', 'Creator', 'Title', 'Publisher', 'Publication Year') and further optional DataCite metadata properties, we extract PANGAEA-specific metadata properties, like 'Location' or 'Coverage'. We decided to choose 'Location' as our focused metadata property, because the location of measurement stations on earth gives a good characterization of various climates to be expected. BSRN stations are distributed all over the world. Due to the heterogeneity of measured climates, we expect interesting exploration results within the defined search and exploration space.

4.2 Case Study A: Metadata Property 'Location' Explored by Absolute Temperature Measurements

Our first case study describes temperature measurements from 2006, taken from 22 BSRN stations all over the world. We choose the metadata property 'Location' as our metadata exploration space. Comparing *absolute* temperature values it can be expected that measurement stations geographically located close to each other score a high similarity. This scenario is qualified for expert and non-expert user groups in particular, since every user has a notion about temperature behavior of different locations on earth.

First, we will explore the result of our content-based similarity concept. The distance matrix (Figure 7) shows all metadata entities in alphabetical order. Remember that white diamonds denote high similarities, while blue diamonds show low similarities between two distinct metadata entities. We highlight 'Antarctica', which has considerably dissimilar temperature values to effectively all other locations in the data set, the highlighted row of 'Antarctica' comes along with the bluest color values in the entire exploration space. We record this statement and receive the validation of the researchers from AWI: Antarctica produces temperature measurements about 30°C colder than any other BSRN station. In contrast, the most similar metadata entities are 'Switzerland' and 'Germany', which is geographically comprehensible. Other similar entity pairs are the 'Cosmonaut Sea' and 'Alaska', or 'Papua New Guinea' and 'Australia'. Together with the researchers, we conclude that these pairs of locations are geographically grouped close together or rather on the same latitude. Due to the fact that 'Antarctica' is completely analyzed, we exclude this entity from the data set for more detailed exploration purposes.

Next, we calculate the visual catalog (see Figure 8) to get an overview over all daily measurement patterns of the data set. We choose our colormap in a way that red and orange color values denote high temperature measurements (left), moderate temperatures are color-coded in green and cyan (lower right) and coldest daily measurements are represented by blue cells (upper right). Furthermore, temperature progressions with higher peaks tend to be located at the lower half of the visual catalog (yellow, green, cyan). The overall temperature interval ranges from -29.2°C) to a maximum of 33°C.

With this obtained overview over the data content, we proceed our exploratory case study by examining the MetaMap (Figure 1). Together with the researchers, we discovered several groups of measurement stations with similar characteristics.

Result 1: At the upper left, the stations 'Papua New Guinea', 'North Pacific', 'Nauru' and 'Australia' are marked red. Most of these temperature measurements are located in

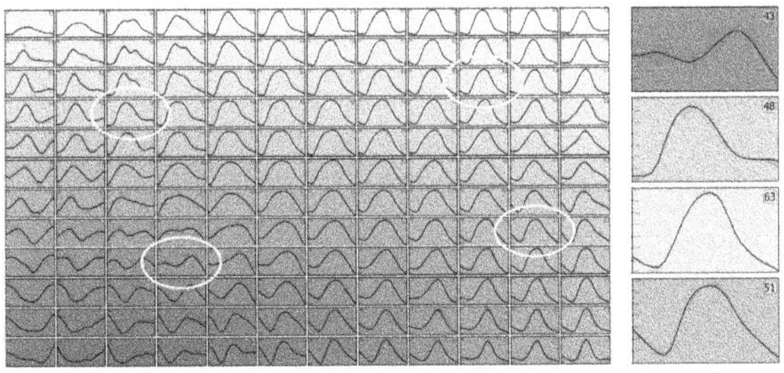

Figure 9: Visual catalog of all relative daily temperature curves. Progressions with an early maximum displayed at upper left (cyan), curves with daily maximum in the afternoon on the right (yellow, orange, red), diverse curve progressions with missing temperature peaks in the mid day at the lower left (blue).

the upper left of the visual catalog and also coded with red color values. This group of metadata entities comprises the hottest temperatures in the entire data set. We infer that these stations are located in tropical or desert-like climates.

Result 2: Another group of stations is located at the center of our layout, marked with yellow, green and cyan color. Most of the stations are located in moderate climates on earth like Europe ('Netherlands', 'Germany', 'Switzerland', 'France').

Result 3: Finally we want to explore the group at the upper right of our layout, denoted with blue and purple colors. This group comprises the coldest measurements in the data set, all content summaries of the entity glyphs contain measurements taken from the blue and purple region of the visual catalog (see Figure 8), denoting low temperatures (mostly below 0°C). On inspection, the locations 'NY-Ålesund', 'Alaska', 'Cosmonaut Sea' and 'Dronning Maud Land' provide the lowest temperature values in the data set, which is evidence for the validity of both our similarity concept and our topology-preserving MetaMap.

4.3 Case Study B: Metadata Property 'Location' Explored by Relative Temperature Measurements

With our second, more scientific case study, we follow a request of researchers at the AWI. We explore the metadata property 'Location', based on *relative* temperature curve progressions. Consider that the analysis of patterns can either be performed on absolute (temperature) values (like in case study A) or on relative curve progressions. The progression of each temperature curve within one day disregarding the absolute temperature values is of utmost importance for our present notion of similarity. To illustrate the benefit of relative curve analysis, the reader is referred to stock market analysis tasks, where stocks of similar branches often develop in a similar manner, even if their absolute values are entirely different. One reason might be that all concerning stocks are dependent on similar impacts.

Back to our case study, we firstly consider the visual catalog in Figure 9. We identify daily temperature progressions with a maximum before noon on the upper left (cyan) and curves with their peaks in the afternoon on the right (yellow, orange, red). In the upper left, the visual catalog shares curves with indefinite behavior (blue, purple). Many temperature progressions have maxima in the evening or even at night. Even though researchers from AWI describe this behavior as ordinary in arctic regions, we were surprised about this outcome of the visual catalog. Finally, we discover curves with clear daily maxima in the middle of the day to be located at the right of the visual catalog.

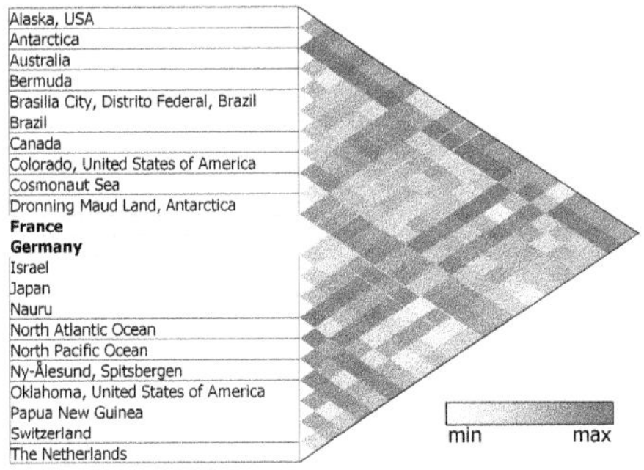

Figure 10: The DistanceMatrixView displays 'France' and 'Germany' as the most similar metadata entities in the data set (white diamond).

Next we investigate the DistanceMatrixView in Figure 10. We select the whitest diamond with the minimum pairwise distance and consider 'France' and 'Germany' as the most similar metadata entity pair in the data set. Furthermore we point out 'France' and 'Switzerland', 'North Pacific Ocean' and 'Bermuda', 'Switzerland' and 'Germany', as well as 'Switzerland' and 'Japan' to have above average degrees of similarity. A great many of the most dissimilar locations in the data set are addressed by the entities 'Antarctica' and 'North Atlantic Ocean'. We regard these findings as important and to deserve further exploration.

Together with the researchers from AWI, we explore our MetaMap of all locations in the data set based on the similarity measure of relative daily temperature curves. In the following, we detail the results of our explorations:

Result 1: The biggest group of locations is arranged at the lower right regions of the MetaMap (orange, brown). Measurements taken from the corresponding stations have sufficiently distinctive temperature peaks in the middle of the day, typically after noon. This attitude is obtained by moderate and continental climates. Locations from Central Europe and measurements taken from 'Oklahoma' and 'Canada' prove this hypothesis.

Result 2: A second cluster is found at the upper of the MetaMap (cyan). It is particularly noticeable that measurements within the distinct content summaries arise from the green and cyan colored regions of our visual catalog, where curves with a daily maximum before noon are discovered. The measurement stations are predominantly located at tropical, maritime places on earth - known to be influenced by gathering clouds at noon and rainstorms in the afternoon, which explains aggregated daily temperature maxima even before noon. The location 'Colorado' is depicted as an outlier. We inquired the researchers and found out that the measurement station is located on more than 1500 meters above sea level in a rainy climate region, which explains the cluster affiliation.

Result 3: A third group of metadata entities is recognized on the lower left (blue), all measurement stations are located at arctic regions. The crossover to the orange clus-

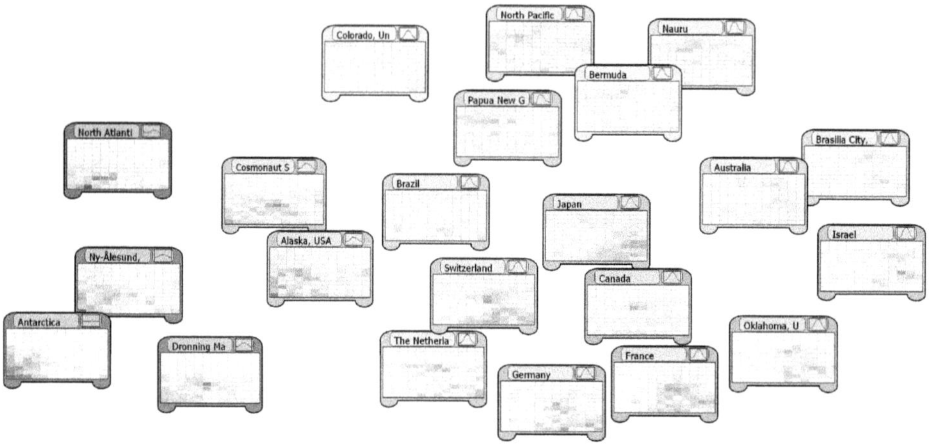

Figure 11: MetaMap of all 'Locations' in the data set. Predominantly maritime and tropical regions are arranged at the top (cyan), locations of moderate and continental climates are located at the bottom (orange, brown). At the lower left, a group of arctic locations is shown (blue).

ter is built by 'Cosmonaut Sea' and 'Alaska', which is also geographically comprehensible. Arctic climates are characterized by temperature behaviors apart from solar zenith angles, typically without a major temperature peak at noon. This behavior can be stated by the blue measurements in the content summaries denoting rather heterogeneous temperature progressions in the visual catalog. Note that the station 'Antarctica' even has no average temperature deviation within the whole day, which makes the station significantly dissimilar to all other locations in the data set.

5. CONCLUSIONS

We presented an approach for exploratory search in time-oriented research data. The approach is based on user-selectable metadata properties for which visual layouts are presented that reflect similarity of the underlying metadata entities. Our approach is novel in that it derives a notion of similarity from the content of the data, and allows exploration of the data based on metadata properties. It allows users to examine relevant relationships between entities and is a basis for subsequent drill-down queries. The approach is particularly useful for navigating in large data spaces for which users have no a-priori knowledge.

This work is only a first approach in our idea to provide users with a more encompassing access to research data both from the metadata and content perspectives. Future work includes extending the approach to further domain-specific similarity notions in time-series data, considering, e.g., similarity based on time-series motif analysis or correlation between measurements. Also, we currently neglect similarity between metadata properties themselves. For example, similarity between geospatial distance of measurement locations or similarity between authors according to their scientific institution could be considered. To this end, comparative exploration of groups of data according to content and metadata should be considered. The 2D layout could be enhanced by additional visual representations of data properties, such as the scientific methodology applied for obtaining measurements. Finally, validation of the approach by expanded domain user studies should be performed in the future.

Acknowledgments

We thank the Alfred Wegener Insitute (AWI) in Bremerhaven, particularly Rainer Sieger, Hannes Grobe and Gert König-Langlo, and everyone involved with PANGAEA for supporting this research effort. We are especially grateful to the many scientists that contributed the data available through BSRN and other research projects.

6. REFERENCES

[1] M. Agosti, S. Berretti, G. Brettlecker, A. D. Bimbo, N. Ferro, N. Fuhr, D. A. Keim, C.-P. Klas, T. Lidy, D. Milano, M. C. Norrie, P. Ranaldi, A. Rauber, H.-J. Schek, T. Schreck, H. Schuldt, B. Signer, and M. Springmann. Delosdlms - the integrated delos digital library management system. In *DELOS Conference*, pages 36–45, 2007.

[2] S. Auer, C. Bizer, G. Kobilarov, J. Lehmann, and Z. Ives. Dbpedia: A nucleus for a web of open data. In *Semantic Web Conf.*, pages 11–15. Springer, 2007.

[3] J. Bernard, J. Brase, D. Fellner, O. Koepler, J. Kohlhammer, T. Ruppert, T. Schreck, and I. Sens. A visual digital library approach for time-oriented scientific primary data. *Springer International Journal of Digital Libraries, ECDL 2010 Special Issue*, 2011.

[4] J. Bernard, T. Ruppert, M. Scherer, J. Kohlhammer, and T. Schreck. Reference list of 269 sources used for exploratory search. doi:10.1594/pangaea.778638, 2012.

[5] J. Bollen and H. Van de Sompel. An architecture for the aggregation and analysis of scholarly usage data. In *Proceedings of the 6th ACM/IEEE-CS joint conference on Digital libraries*, JCDL '06, pages 298–307, New York, NY, USA, 2006. ACM.

[6] C. L. Borgman, J. C. Wallis, and N. Enyedy. Little science confronts the data deluge: habitat ecology, embedded sensor networks, and digital libraries. *International Journal on Digital Libraries*, 7(1-2):17–30, 2007.

[7] S. Bremm, T. von Landesberger, J. Bernard, and T. Schreck. Assisted descriptor selection based on

visual comparative data analysis. *Comput. Graph. Forum*, 30(3):891–900, 2011.

[8] N. Cao, D. Gotz, J. Sun, and H. Qu. Dicon: Interactive visual analysis of multidimensional clusters. *IEEE Trans. Vis. Comput. Graph.*, 17(12):2581–2590, 2011.

[9] S. Cha. Comprehensive survey on distance/similarity measures between probability density functions. *International Journal of Mathematical Models and Methods in Applied Sciences*, 1(4):300–307, 2007.

[10] K.-H. Cheung, E. Lim, M. Samwald, H. Chen, L. N. Marenco, M. Holford, T. M. Morse, P. Mutalik, G. M. Shepherd, and P. L. Miller. Approaches to neuroscience data integration. *Briefings in Bioinformatics*, 10(4):345–353, 2009.

[11] T. Deselaers, D. Keysers, and H. Ney. Features for image retrieval: an experimental comparison. *Information Retrieval*, 11(2):77–107, 2008.

[12] R. Duda, P. Hart, and D. Stork. *Pattern Classification*. Wiley, 2001.

[13] M. Duke, M. Day, R. Heery, L. A. Carr, and S. J. Coles. Enhancing access to research data: the challenge of crystallography. In *JCDL*, pages 46–55. ACM, 2005.

[14] M. Eitz, K. Hildebrand, T. Boubekeur, and M. Alexa. A descriptor for large scale image retrieval based on sketched feature lines. In *Eurographics Symposium on Sketch-Based Interfaces and Modeling*, pages 29–36. ACM, 2009.

[15] T. Hey, S. Tansley, and K. Tolle, editors. *The Fourth Paradigm: Data-Intensive Scientific Discovery*. Microsoft Research, Redmond, Washington, 2009.

[16] T. Hey and A. Trefethen. Cyberinfrastructure for e-Science. *Science*, 308(5723):817–821, 2005.

[17] D. Hull, S. R. Pettifer, and D. B. Kell. Defrosting the Digital Library: Bibliographic Tools for the Next Generation Web, 2008.

[18] D. Keim, J. Kohlhammer, G. Ellis, and F. Mansmann. *Mastering the information age: solving problems with visual analytics*. Eurographics, 2011.

[19] D. Keim, F. Mansmann, J. Schneidewind, and H. Ziegler. Challenges in visual data analysis. In *Information Visualization*, pages 9 –16, 2006.

[20] E. Keogh, K. Chakrabarti, M. Pazzani, and S. Mehrotra. Dimensionality reduction for fast similarity search in large time series databases. *Knowledge and Inf. Systems*, 3(3):263–286, 2001.

[21] E. Keogh and S. Kasetty. On the need for time series data mining benchmarks: A survey and empirical demonstration. *Data Mining and Knowledge Discovery*, 7(4):349–371, 2003.

[22] C. Lagoze, S. Payette, E. Shin, and C. Wilper. Fedora: an architecture for complex objects and their relationships. *Int. J. Digit. Libr.*, 6(2):124–138, 2006.

[23] M. Lew, N. Sebe, C. Djeraba, and R. Jain. Content-based multimedia information retrieval: State of the art and challenges. *Transactions on Multimedia Computing, Communications, and Applications*, 2(1):1–19, 2006.

[24] A. Noack. An energy model for visual graph clustering. In *International Symposium on Graph Drawing*, pages 425–436. Springer-Verlag, 2003.

[25] A. Ohmura, E. G. Dutton, B. Forgan, C. Fröhlich, H. Gilgen, H. Hegner, A. Heimo, G. König-Langlo, B. mcarthur, G. Müller, R. Philipona, R. Pinker, C. H. Whitlock, K. Dehne, and M. Wild. Baseline surface radiation network (BSRN/WCRP): New precision radiometry for climate research. *Bull. Amer. Met. Soc.*, 79:2115–2136, 1998.

[26] PANGAEA Data Publisher for Earth & Environmental Science. `http://www.pangaea.de/`.

[27] A. Powell, M. Nilsson, A. Naeve, and P. Johnston. Dublin core metadata initiative - abstract model, 2005. White Paper.

[28] A. Rauber and M. Frühwirth. Automatically analyzing and organizing music archives. In *ECDL*, pages 402–414. Springer, 2001.

[29] S. Rueger. *Multimedia Information Retrieval*. Morgan and Claypool Publishers, 2010.

[30] M. Scherer, J. Bernard, and T. Schreck. Retrieval and exploratory search in multivariate research data repositories using regressional features. In *JCDL*, pages 363–372. ACM, 2011.

[31] Sloan Digital Sky Survey. `http://www.sdss.org/`.

[32] L. D. Stein. Towards a cyberinfrastructure for the biological sciences: progress, visions and challenges. *Nature Reviews Genetics*, 9(9):678–688, 2008.

[33] The DataCite consortium. DataCite: Helping you to find, access, and reuse data. `http://datacite.org/`.

[34] R. Torres, S. M. McNee, M. Abel, J. A. Konstan, and J. Riedl. Enhancing digital libraries with techlens+. In *Proceedings of the 4th ACM/IEEE-CS joint conference on Digital libraries*, JCDL '04, pages 228–236, New York, NY, USA, 2004. ACM.

[35] G. Tsatsaronis, I. Varlamis, S. Torge, M. Reimann, K. Nørvåg, M. Schroeder, and M. Zschunke. How to become a group leader? or modeling author types based on graph mining. *TPDL*, pages 15–26, 2011.

[36] J. Vesanto. SOM-based data visualization methods. *Intelligent Data Analysis*, 3(2):111–126, 1999.

[37] T. von Landesberger, A. Kuijper, T. Schreck, J. Kohlhammer, J. vanWijk, J.-D. Fekete, and D. Fellner. Visual analysis of large graphs: State-of-the-art and future research challenges. 2011.

[38] White and Roth. *Exploratory Search - Beyond the query-response paradigm*. Morgan and Claypool, 2009.

[39] A. J. Williams. A perspective of publicly accessible/open-access chemistry databases. *Drug discovery today*, 13(11-12):495–501, 2008.

[40] I. H. Witten, R. J. Mcnab, S. J. Boddie, and D. Bainbridge. Greenstone: A comprehensive open-source digital library software system. In *International Conference on Digital Libraries*. ACM, 2000.

[41] Wolfram Alpha. Wolfram|Alpha: Computational Knowledge Engine. `http://www.wolframalpha.com/`.

[42] B. Wong, S. Choudhury, C. Rooney, R. Chen, and K. Xu. Invisque: technology and methodologies for interactive information visualization and analytics in large library collections. *TPDL*, pages 227–235, 2011.

Refactoring HUBzero for Linked Data

Michael Witt
Purdue University Libraries
504 W. State Street
West Lafayette, IN 47907 USA
765-494-8703
mwitt@purdue.edu

Yongyang Yu
Dept. of Computer Science, Purdue University
305 N. University Street
West Lafayette, IN 47907 USA
765-494-6010
yu163@cs.purdue.edu

ABSTRACT

The HUBzero cyberinfrastructure provides a virtual research environment that includes a set of tools for web-based, scientific collaboration and a platform for publishing and using resources such as executable software, source code, images, learning modules, videos, documents, and datasets. Released as open source software in 2010, HUBzero has been implemented on a typical LAMP stack (Linux, Apache, MySQL, and PHP) and utilizes the Joomla! content management system. This paper describes the subsequent refactoring of HUBzero to produce and expose Linked Data from its backend, relational database, altering the external expression of the data without changing its internal structure. The Open Archives Initiative Object Reuse and Exchange (OAI-ORE) specification is applied to model the basic structural semantics of HUBzero resources as Nested Aggregations, and data and metadata are mapped to vocabularies such as Dublin Core and published within the web representations of the resources using RDFa. Resource Maps can be harvested using an RDF crawler or an Open Archives Initiative Protocol for Metadata Harvesting (OAI-PMH) data provider that were bundled for demonstration purposes. A visualization was produced to browse and navigate the relations among data and metadata from an example hub.

Categories and Subject Descriptors

H.3.7 [**Information Storage and Retrieval**]: Digital Libraries

General Terms

Experimentation, Standardization

Keywords

Linked Data, Object Reuse and Exchange (OAI-ORE), Open Archives Initiative, Resource Description Framework (RDF), Virtual Research Environments, HUBzero

1. BACKGROUND

The establishment of the Network for Computational Nanotechnology in 2002 by the National Science Foundation led to the development of nanoHUB.org, a unique cyberinfrastructure platform for developing and sharing nanoscience resources online, and in particular, an integrated development environment for creating and executing simulations within a web browser and that utilize backend grid resources. By 2007, nanoHUB.org was serving approximately 1,000 resources to over 56,000 users from 172 different countries [1]. Based on this success, the NSF supported the generalization of the platform so that it could be adapted and adopted by other scientific communities [2]. The result, HUBzero[1], was released as open source software in 2010 and is maintained by a non-profit consortium led by Purdue, Clemson, and Indiana Universities with the University of Wisconsin. Over twenty-five "hubs" have been deployed in a wide variety of communities such as pharmaceutical product development, energy, social change, high performance computing, earthquake engineering, ethics, and science, technology, engineering, and mathematics (STEM) education.

HUBzero functions much like an institutional repository system in which users can create and upload resources, which are organized by resource type. By default, HUBzero supports courses, seminars, tools, downloads, series, workshops, publications, and teaching materials. Descriptive metadata inputted by the submitter of the resource enables it to be searched and browsed in the system. HUBzero allows users to tag, rank, discuss, and annotate resources as well as integrate them into various social networking sites. Each type of resource offers its own manner of presentation (e.g., tools prompt for input and can be executed online, seminars can be streamed as video or audio, etc.) Usage statistics and citations are reported back to those who submit resources.

HUBzero utilizes the Joomla content management system, which provides a framework for managing users, content, and web-based functionality. Hub resources are instantiated using the Resource component, which is a Joomla extension. Joomla utilize a model-view-controller (MVC) architecture that separates the underlying data from the presentation and interaction of the component and its user. In practical terms, this allows multiple views and interactions with the same data model by modifying different PHP scripts. Data relating to hub resources are populated by SQL queries into variables that are parsed and presented differently depending on the context of the interaction.

[1] http://hubzero.org

2. DATA MODELING AND MAPPING

2.1 Lined Data

While the hub presents a robust interface and rich functionality for users, its resources are not presented in a way that user-agents (i.e., a user that is a machine) can understand and use. With this motivation, Linked Data was selected as the approach because of its simplicity and high rate of adoption in the digital library domain relative to other Semantic Web approaches. The four basic "rules" of Linked Data are to use Uniform Resource Identifiers (URI) to identify things; use HyperText Transfer Protocol (HTTP) URIs that can be linked and followed; provide useful metadata when URIs are dereferenced, such as Resource Description Framework (RDF); and link to other URIs to create relations to other information [3]. The goal of this work is to enable hubs to become a part of this "web of data" and to serve as a practical introduction of HUBzero and its communities to the Open Archives Initiative.

2.2 Object Reuse and Exchange (OAI-ORE)

The OAI-ORE specification defines a set of standards for describing and exchanging aggregations of web resources. In simple terms, OAI-ORE defines an Aggregation as a collection of web resources (Aggregated Resources), and each Aggregation includes a Resource Map that lists the contents of the Aggregation and additional metadata such as the relationship between an Aggregation and something else on the web. An Aggregation can include other Aggregations, resulting in a Nested Aggregation [4]. Applying this to HUBzero, its basic structural semantics can be captured by describing the entire hub as an Aggregation with hub resources grouped by type (e.g., seminars, tools, publications) as Nested Aggregations. Lastly, each individual hub resource is defined as its own Aggregation, nested within its respective Aggregation by resource type containing its own metadata and Aggregated Resources.

2.3 Dublin Core

HUBzero requires users who are submitting a resource to identify the type of resource and to describe it using a local, custom schema. Dublin Core[2] provides a convenient and generic descriptive vocabulary that was straight-forward to map. This information is stored natively in HUBzero's MySQL database in relational tables.

RDF triples are constituted using the URI of the hub resource Aggregation (using hash notation) as the subject, the URI to the Dublin Core term as the predicate, and a string literal as the object, which is parsed from variables returning data from Joomla from the database and environment. The example hub allows submitters to apply a Creative Commons license to their work; in these cases, the URI to the license is used for the object to `dc:rights`. The `dc:publisher` is assigned statically.

3. TOOLS

3.1 OAI-PMH Data Provider

The Open Archives Initiative Protocol for Metadata Harvesting defines a web service for data providers to expose metadata records serialized in eXtensible Markup Language (XML) for retrieval by service providers (i.e., harvesters) using a simple set of six verbs [Identify, ListSets, ListMetadataFormats, List Identifiers, ListRecords, and GetRecord], which are called as HTTP requests [5]. The OAI-PMH data provider created for HUBzero was written in PHP and implemented as a stand-alone component in Joomla. Each resource type in the hub is exposed as an OAI-PMH Set, and each resource in the hub minimally furnishes a descriptive metadata record in Dublin Core. The data provider also advertises OAI-ORE Resource Maps using the ListMetadataFormats verb and will furnish the Resource Maps of Aggregations that represent individual hub resources when the service provider specifies a metadataPrefix of "oai_ore". The Resource Map for a hub resource references the Set (`ore:isAggregatedBy`) to which it belongs as well as the data and metadata that it aggregates (`ore:aggregates`). Resource Maps are serialized as RDF/XML. The OAI-PMH data provider implements one of the batch discovery methods suggested by the OAI-ORE specification [6]. Because it was designed as a stand-alone component in the Joomla framework, the data provider could be easily modified to expose metadata from other content managed by Joomla outside or independent of HUBzero.

Table 1: Dublin Core Mapping to HUBzero

Dublin Core	HUBzero table
dc:title	jos_resources.title
dc:creator	jos_resources.created_by
dc:subject	jos_tags.raw_tag
dc:date	jos_resources.created
dc:identifier	jos_resources.id
dc:description	jos_resources.introtext
dc:type	jos_resources.type
dc:publisher	*(statically assigned)*
dc:rights	jos_resources.params

3.2 RDF Crawler

To demonstrate discovery and use of Linked Data from the web, a crawler was written in Python to traverse all the resource web pages in an example hub. The crawler begins from the top-level of the hub (the beginning splash page, which is the Aggregation that represents the entire hub) and dereferences URIs to the Aggregations and Resource Maps for resource types and individual resources. The task of the crawler is to parse the HTML source and extract div fragments that have a class property of "`ResourceMap`" or "`Aggregation`". The BeautifulSoup[3] parser was used to make the crawler resilient to ill-formed HTML fragments such as the incorrect embedding of `h2` tags within `span` tags.

Resources Maps are serialized in the RDFa+XHTML format such that metadata are embedded within div fragments in the HTML source. The `class` property of the div fragment indicates whether the fragment describes the Resource Map or the Aggregation based on its respective string value. The Dublin Core metadata are wrapped within `span` tags with `property="dc:title"`, etc. String literals are embedded in span tags, whereas URIs are embedded in `a` tags. The job of the crawler is to parse all the contents embedded

[2]http://dublincore.org

[3]http://www.crummy.com/software/BeautifulSoup/

in these tags and generate the triples with proper subjects, predicates, and objects.

The crawler traverses URIs to all the RDF triples and stores them in an N-Triples file. N-Triples is a line-based, plain text serialization format for RDF graphs. Each line of the file represents a single statement of information or a comment. Each statement consists of three parts, separated by whitespace – the subject, the predicate and the object – and is terminated with a full stop. Subjects take the form of URIs, which are delimited by angle brackets. Objects may be URIs or string literals, which are represented by a C-style string. The crawler builds a resource URI list by crawling and parsing URIs within each resource type of the hub. Whenever the crawler parses an a tag of the HTML with `rel` property of value of `ore:aggregates`, it will insert the URI contained in the tag in the list. By iterating all the resource types in the prototype, all the URIs of resources are inserted into the list. For each single URI in the list, the crawler parses the `div` fragments in the HTML source file and stores the RDF triples in the result file.

After all the triples have been harvested from the example hub, the N-Triples file is flushed to a TDB triplestore for permanent storage and retrieval within a Jena framework[4]. Jena implements APIs for dealing with Semantic Web building blocks such as RDF. TDB is a persistent graph storage layer for Jena. TDB works with the Jena SPARQL query engine to provide a SPARQL endpoint along with a number of extensions (e.g., property functions, aggregates, arbitrary length property paths).

3.3 Graph Browser

With the triples populated from the hub and stored in the native triplestore, a graph browser was developed to help us analyze the data quality and validate the metadata exposed as Linked Data (see Figure 1). JUNG[5], a Java based graph framework, was used to achieve the goal of visualization. JUNG is a software library that provides a common and extensible language for modeling, analysis, and visualization of data that can be represented as a graph or network. Our implementation of the graph browser has an interactive interface that enables one to click on individual nodes and navigates through the hub data and metadata.

The graph browser will first send a SPARQL query `"SELECT ?s ?p ?o WHERE ?s ?p ?o;"` to retrieve all the triples in the TDB triplestore. The graph browser will display the hub resources in different layers as the user clicks on various nodes in the browser. A circle node in the graph represents a URI or a plain string. A directed arrow with a URI above it denotes the predicates between the subject and the object. The circle node which the arrow points out is the subject of the triple and the circle node which the arrow points to is the object of the triple. There are three different colors of the circle nodes in all, i.e., blue, green, and grey. The blue circle nodes represent URIs of Aggregated Resources and Resource Maps. The green circle nodes represent plain strings appearing in the object field of the triple. The grey circle nodes are pointed to by dotted arrows from green circle nodes. These grey circle nodes indicate shared boundaries that connect to a larger graph outside of the immediate current scope.

The first page of the graph browser shows the aggregation of all the triples in the hub in a graphical form. One can click on any blue circle node to have a clear look at the details of this particular Aggregated Resource or Resource Map. If the blue node that one clicks on is a Resource Map, the browser will display the descriptive information of the Resource Map and the URI of the Aggregated Resource it describes. If the blue node that one clicks on is an Aggregated Resource, the browser will graph its Resource Map, all the Dublin Core metadata records about this Aggregated Resource, any resource it aggregates, and any Aggregation it belongs to. If a green circle node is clicked on, the browser will display all the triples with this string value in the object field.

With the help of the graph browser, we can debug the correctness of exposing the Dublin Core metadata records from the hub and validate the Resource Maps. This graph browser serves as a supplementary tool to navigate through RDF triples by introducing an interactive way between users and the data. It has also been a helpful tool for demonstrating to people the network power of Linked Data and to visualize the linkages that are being created between their data and metadata. Numerous classes and demonstrations of the visualization have been given in the campus Fakespace FLEX system Virtual Reality Theater.

4. FUTURE WORK

The combination of OAI-ORE and Dublin Core enables a base representation of HUBzero and its content.; however, richer and more specific vocabularies should be identified and incorporated. It would be useful to create more links to other, related information on the web, for example, to link to scientific workflows (e.g., MyExperiment) that are supported by hub tools and datasets. Another important, next step is to incorporate vocabularies on the front-end data ingest to produce more URIs and fewer string literals as objects in the RDF. For example, tags could be constructed as Library Congress Subject Headings or another linkable subject classification scheme.

Inspired by Tarrant et al.[7], a synchronization tool to replicate content and semantics from HUBzero to other repositories using OAI-ORE has been developed and described in a different paper that is currently under review.

Two new tools are under development now: one to enable users to create and publish their own collections (Aggregations) on the hub, and another to leverage Linked Data for semantic search.

The Linked Data implementation for HUBzero along with the OAI-PMH Joomla component, RDF Crawler, and Graph Browser are in the process of being incorporated into the HUBzero open source software distribution and should be available in the next major version release of HUBzero. An assessment is planned for 2013.

5. ACKNOWLEDGMENTS

This work was sponsored by a National Leadership Grant (LG- 05-10-0117-10) from the Institute of Museum and Library Services in collaboration with Clemson University and the National Parks Service. Contributions to software development were also made by Venkata Surya Srik Gandikota, Aswathy Siviram, Siddharth Kumar Singh, and Naveen Somasundaram.

[4] `http://incubator.apache.org/jena/documentation/tdb/index.html`

[5] `http://jung.sourceforge.net/`

6. REFERENCES

[1] G. Klimeck, M. McLennan, S.P. Brophy, G.B. Adams, and M.S. Lundstrom. Nanohub.org: advancing education and research in nanotechnology, *Computing in Science & Engineering* 10(5): 17–23, October 2008.

[2] M. McLennan, and R. Kennell. HUBzero: a platform for dissemination and collaboration in computational science and engineering, *Computing in Science & Engineering* 12(2):48–53, March 2010.

[3] C. Bizer, T. Heath, and T. Berners-Lee. Linked-Data - the story so far, *International Journal on Semantic Web and Information Systems* 5(3):1–22, 2009.

[4] C. Lagoze, H. Van de Sompel, M. Nelson, S. Warner, R. Sanderson, and P. Johnston. A web-based resource model for scholarship 2.0: Object Reuse & Exchange, *Concurrency and Computation: Practice and Experience*, June 2010.

[5] H. Van de Sompel, M.L. Nelson, C. Lagoze, and S. Warner. Resource harvesting within the OAI-PMH framework, *D-lib magazine* 10(12), December 2004.

[6] Open Archives Initiative Executive and Technical Committees. ORE User Guide - Resource Map Discovery, `http://www.openarchives.org/ore/1.0/discovery.html`, 2008.

[7] D. Tarrant, B. O'Steen, T. Brody, S. Hitchcock, N. Jefferies, and L. Carr. Using OAI-ORE to transform digital repositories into interoperable storage and services applications, `http://journal.code4lib.org/articles/1062`, March 2009.

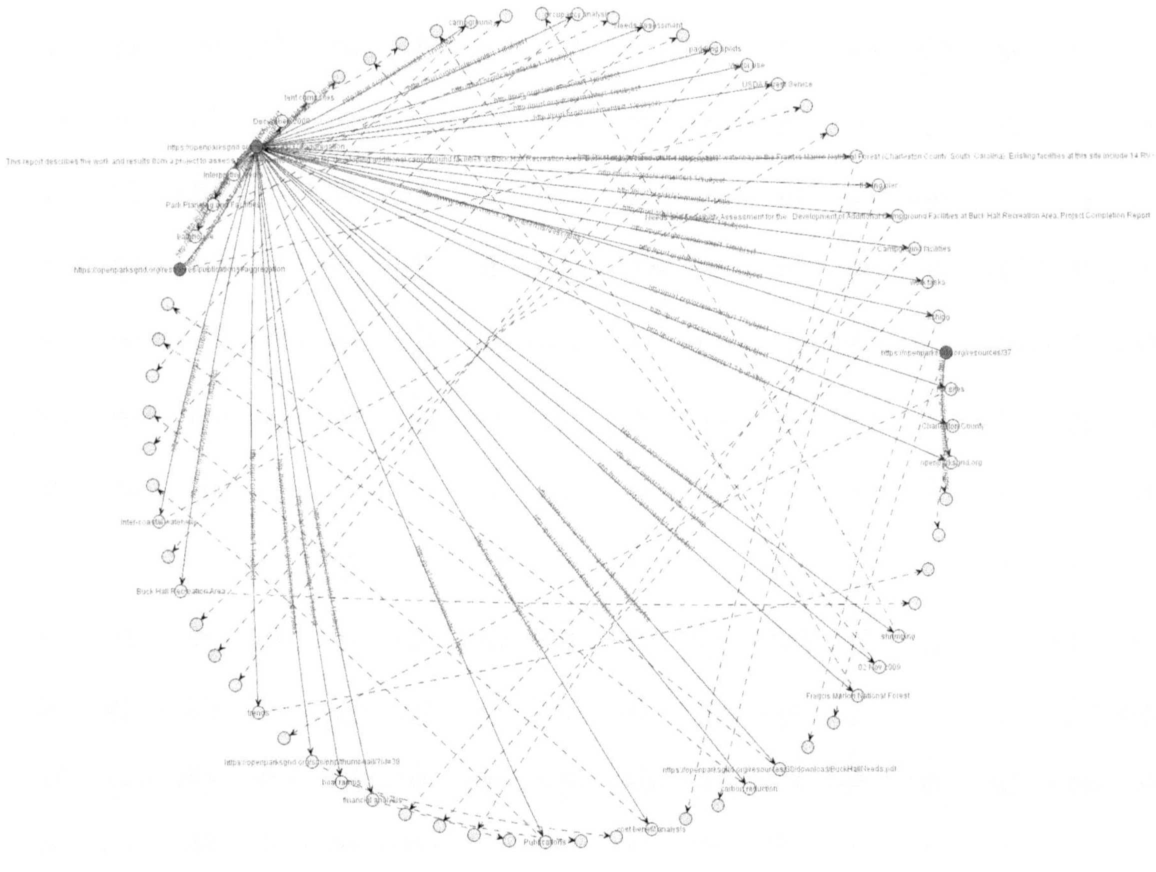

Figure 1: Connected Graph of Hub Resource Aggregation

Treating Data Like Software: A Case for Production Quality Data

Jennifer M. Schopf
Woods Hole Oceanographic Institution
Woods Hole, MA 02543
(Currently at the National Science Foundation, GEO/OAD)
jschopf@whoi.edu

ABSTRACT

In this short paper, we describe the production data approach to data curation. We argue that by treating data in a similar fashion to how we build production software, that data will be more readily accessible and available for broad re-use. We should be treating data as an ongoing process. This includes considering third-party contributions; planning for cyclical releases; bug fixes, tracking, and versioning; and issuing licensing and citation information with each release.

Categories and Subject Descriptors

E.5.3 [**Data**]: Files - *Organization, Structure*; E.4.3 [**Data**]: Coding and information theory - *Formal models of communication*; H.1 [Information Systems] - Models and principles

General Terms

Management, Documentation, Design, Verification

Keywords

Best practices, Cyclical development and release, Production data

1. INTRODUCTION

Collecting, organizing, distributing, and accessing digital data is a problem of growing concern. The amount of data generated by scientists is growing exponentially, and studies have shown [1] that un-archived data sets have a resource half-life that is only a fraction of those resources that are electronically archived. However, even when available digitally, the ability to find and access data is increasingly difficult.

In order to address the need for better data preservation and access, we propose that data sets should be managed in a similar fashion to how we maintain production quality software. These *production data sets* are not simply published once, but go through a cyclical process of development, verification, deployment, support, analysis, and then development again. Attention is given to ensuring the data is understandable, useful, and updated over time, the same way software products need updating over time, even if the core functionality does not change.

This short paper gives a brief definition of what is meant by data in this context. It then addresses at a high level standard factors that are part of the development of (academic) production software, and describes how similar processes can be applied to enable data sets to have extended lifecycles and improved usability. A key premise is that if this approach can be integrated into common practice, it will result in a higher level of preservation and usability of data.

2. DEFINITION OF DATA

There are many viewpoints, both political and technical, as to what can be included by term data. Different scientific communities may define data to include observations, data analysis results, modeling results, software, metadata, or other items, and possibly a different set depending where in the preservation cycle the data is.

For the purpose of this white paper, data refers to *everything needed to have reproducible science*. This is not dissimilar to the definition of data that must be shared in order to have an article considered for publication in the AAAS journal Science. Their definition states that an author must make available to all readers of Science "all data necessary to understand, assess, and extend the conclusions of the manuscript" [2]. The article that announced this change explicitly included computational codes and data descriptions in the materials to be made available.

It is important to our approach that we define a model for data preservation that will work for a variety of digital

Disclaimer: Any opinions, findings and conclusions or recommendations expressed in this material are those of the author and do not necessarily reflect the views of the National Science Foundation or Woods Hole Oceanographic Institution.

JCDL'12, June 10–14, 2012, Washington, DC, USA.

materials. One of the advantages of our approach is that by extending another common practice to include a broader set of materials we stay within an end-users comfort zone. In additions, lessons learned in one context can be applied to the other.

3. PRODUCTION SOFTWARE

Most groups still lack best practices and standard approaches to data archiving. Arguably, however, scientists know something about building software. A recent article in Nature [3] stated that 45% of research scientists spend more time now developing software than they did 5 years ago, and 38% spent at least 1/5th of their time developing software. In addition, Fox and Parson [4, 5] argue that a simple release of data is not the correct approach to data curation, and other metaphors instead of simple "publication" should be considered.

Our answer to this is to treat data in a similar way to how we work with software. Just as software is used in a wide variety of ways never initially envisioned by its developers, we're seeing this even to a greater extent with data sets. In addition, just as software has a long-term lifecycle, which can involve phases such as design, construction, test, release, and support, we believe that using this approach for data will result in more successful use and re-use of digital data.

Although there are many formalized approaches to developing software [6, 7, 8], it can be argued that most academic software does not follow a truly formal process. However, as software progresses from personal use, to the broader use of a prototype, to a formally released production software product, several elements remain consistent. Table 1 shows a summary of these elements and how we believe they compare to their data counterparts, as detailed in the following section.

4. PRODUCTION DATA

Just as software can develop from a prototype to production use, as we collect and archive data we should consider how its use may grow beyond our immediate approach and plan for future sharing. Data that is reliable and trust-worthy can expand a field through re-use and sharing, and the goal of this approach is to instill formalisms to enable this. Data is a process, not just a product.

An open question is when has a simple data set evolved to the point to consider the higher cost of treating it as a production data set. Just as software evolves from one-off private use to larger scale use, we would expect data to do this as well. As with anything, this must be a trade-off within the project. However, similar to software, keeping basic principles in mind from the beginning and cutting over to a production approach earlier than later will often pay off in the end.

Table 1. Comparison of production software and production data.

Production Software	Production Data
End-user considerations: off-label use, new features, need for documentation	End-user considerations: your noise is my signal, need for additional metadata
Multiple Coders: -Repository with check-in procedures -Coding conventions	Multiple producers or collectors: -Local archive with check-in procedure -Collection conventions
Formal testing	Formal testing
Bug tracking and fixes	Bug tracking and fixes, QA/QC
Documentation: code commenting, readme, installation guides	Documentation: metadata, acceptances by workflows
Formal Release Process	Formal release process to external archive
License	Citation/usage statement

Note that the consideration of when a data set should be considered for production quality data is subtly different from other data maturity metrics, such as NASA's data set processing levels [9]. The former has to do with how data is treated during its end-to-end life cycle management; the later has to do with how it is processed post-collection only.

4.1 End-user Considerations

Many pieces of production software grow in usefulness over time and may be used by additional end users, and in ways that are not strictly in adherence of the original vision of its functionality.

Similarly, many data sets get used by people other than the one who collected it and for uses not as envisioned. Arguably, even if the data is just to be used by the person collecting it, 6 months after collection if the data isn't properly tagged and archived, even that person won't remember enough of the details to be sure that the data meets whatever standard their current research requires.

In addition, with many data sets, one person's noise is another person's signal. For example, with observing data, in collecting a set of observations (for example, images of scallops from the ocean floor [10] to determine size and counts for harvesting policy use), can also be used for other biomass information or even identification of geological features. Because of this, there is often a strong interest in raw data as opposed to summarized data (in this example, the images themselves, not the simple count data), which should be taken into account.

Experienced data collectors often find that adding a small amount of additional information to a dataset can increase its usefulness and usability in the future. This is similar to developing software and keeping in mind likely additional future use cases.

4.2 Multiple Contributors

Approaches to building software grow and change as more coders and users are added to a development team. Often this will mean moving source code from a personal directory to a shared internal repository, establishing "check-in" procedures, and developing coding and naming standards (for example, set spacing and variable naming to increase readability).

In a data collection environment, this can be mapped to instances for example where instead of collecting data from a single instrument, the deployment is widened to a set of related instruments, or instead of collecting data just from one set of experiments several related sets of experimental data are archived together. Just as in software development collaborative coding is made easier by having unified approaches to naming of variables, in data collection having unified approaches to naming and tagging data will increase usability.

The corresponding functionality needed when multiple data contributions are combined are similar to those in the software space, namely shared repositories and well defined check-in standards. In this way, and users can be assured that the data will consistent (and usable). Similar to a software development environment, we recommend a separate internal archive from the external archive because at this stage often only preliminary checks are done.

4.3 Testing and Error Tracking

One of the main reasons that software development is formalized is to enable a developer a better way to track errors and to enable code testing. If the goal is to share a piece of software, this won't happen if it's got bugs in it or won't run. Similarly, data needs to be tested and checked in order for it to be trusted by third-party end users.

A formal test suite for data sets can include a variety of components, including checks that it falls within bounds, check for values in the expected dimensions, detection of unusual outliers, etc. This may be in the form of a quality assurance/quality control (QA/QC) loop or may be a one-off evaluation when data is initially gathered. Another way to do this would be to have a set of identified workflows which the data is meant to be used with, and to verify with every update that they are still consistent. Not ethat testing (and QA/QC) can also vary widely, and be indicted by its own scaling, such as using NASA's data set processing levels [9].

Regardless of what checks take place automatically, there should also be a way that erroneous data can be reported, or that the data owner can be notified of problems with the data set. This verification is critical for researchers and scientists to trust a data set. Just as an end user won't run software that throws exceptions or can't be easily installed, data sets with obvious errors will be rejected by end users.

There is a strong argument to be made for using multiple repositories to stage your data as it becomes closer to production quality. Several groups have found that having a 3 stage repository – initial, internal, and external – works well. Data can stored at first in an initial repository, then after basic testing moved to the internal repository where it may be combined or have additional QA/QC done on it by the group, and then eventually released publicly through an external repository. This mirrors the common software practice of having a personal development software branch, and internal shared development branch, and a released software package.

4.4 Documentation

Just as software has documentation, so should data sets. This is separate from metadata, and can include who produced the data, a detailed description of how the data was collected and what (if any) pre-processing has been performed. It can include not only notes on how to use the data, but on what the original intention for collecting the data was. This is also a place to include pointers to any of related data sets or related work in general. The documentation should include citation and sharing information.

Metadata is far too a complex a topic to adequately address here, and the issue of shared ontologies is one that will not be easily resolved in most settings. Suffice it to say that just as coding, documentation, and testing standards are needed to understand and use complex software, metadata standards are needed for shared data. The more that data is tagged during the collection, the more it will be able to be used in the future.

4.5 Release and Versioning

Versioning of data is a controversial issue, especially in communities who want to see data treated like publications where it is published once and set aside, as in a library. However, practice has shown that in many cases, data is a living growing entity. Additional tagging and analysis can create significant additional value for data sets, and should be strongly encouraged, not discouraged. If data is to be updated to address errors, then it is paramount that versioning be introduced so that analysis of different data sets can be tracked.

4.6 Citations and Licensing

Licensing is often a sensitive issue for software. The equivalent in the data space is two-fold: citation and licensing. Data citation is increasingly a way to provide a reference to a data set, and is a key practice underpinning the effort to have data resources recognized as a primary research output, as opposed to simply being a by-product [11, 12, 13]. All data should include a citation, and all data used in publications should be cited.

Licensing is a way to define allowable use policies, or to define allowable distribution of software or data data. Licensing is less common in the data world than with software, but the most commonly used approach is through use of a Creative Commons [14] license. Just as open source licenses [15] can be tailored to different end uses, reliability needs, flexibility, or access to commercialization, using Creative Commons licensing defines the expectations for the use of the data and when alterations are permitted. Licensing does not stop people from accessing software (or data), but clarifies when use is allowed and under what circumstances changes or commercialization is permitted, instead of leaving that important aspect of sharing undetermined.

5. CONCLUSIONS

Usable and accessible data sets are a first step toward reproducible science. By creating production quality data sets, we extend the potential of our data, both in terms of usability and usefulness to ourselves and other researchers. The more we treat data with formal processes and release cycles, the more relevant and useful it can be to the scientific community.

6. ACKNOLWEDGEMENTS

I would like to acknowledge the many helpful conversations that have made this work possible, including those with Stan Ahalt (RENCI), Amy Apon (Clemson), Neil Chue Hong (U Edinburgh), Peter Fox (RPI), William Gropp (UIUC), Robert Grossman (UC), and Andrew Maffei (WHOI), as well as the extremely useful comments of the reviewers, without whom this paper would not have been possible. Support for this work was made possible by the National Science Foundation Independent Research/Development program.

7. REFERENCES

[1] Koehler W., "A longitudinal study of Web pages continued: a consideration of document persistence", Information Research, 9 (2), January 2004. Also available at http://informationr.net/ir/9-2/paper174.html

[2] Science, "Information for Authors; Data Materials and Availability", 2011 http://www.sciencemag.org/site/feature/contribinfo/prep/gen_info.xhtml#dataavail

[3] Merali, Z., "Computational science: ...Error: ...why scientific programming does not compute", Nature 467, 775-777 (2010). doi:10.1038/467775a. Also available at http:// www.nature.com /news/2010/101013/full/467775a.html

[4] Fox, P., "Why the term 'data publication'?", http://tw.rpi.edu/weblog/2010/12/14/why-the-term-data-publication/

[5] Parsons, M.A., and Fox, P.A., "Is Data Publication the Right Metaphor", *submitted to the Data Science Journal*, January 2012, available online at http://mp-datamatters.blogspot.com/ 2011/12/seeking-open-review-of-provocative-data.html

[6] Abrahamsson, P., Salo, O., Ronkainen, J., & Warsta, J. "Agile Software Development Methods: Review and Analysis", VTT Publications 478, 2002.

[7] ISO/IEC 12207: Information Technology - Software life cycle processes, 1995.

[8] Royce, W., "Managing the Development of Large Software Systems", Proceedings of IEEE WESCON 26 (August): 1–9, 1970.

[9] Parkinson, C.L. and Greenstone, R, Eds, "EOS Data Products Handbook Volume 2", NASA Goddard Space Flight Center Publications, October 2000. Also available at http://eospso.gsfc.nasa.gov/ftp_docs/data_products_vol2.pdf

[10] HabCam, http://habcam.whoi.edu.

[11] Australian National Data Service, "Data Citation Awareness", http://www.ands.org.au/guides/data-citation-awareness.html

[12] Data Citation Principles Workshop, Harvard, Cambridge, Massachusetts, March 2011, http://projects.iq.harvard.edu/datacitation_workshop/

[13] CODATA: International Council for Science: Committee on Data for Science and Technology "Data Citation Standards and Practices", Approved by the CODATA 27th General Assembly in Cape Town 2010, http://www.codata.org/taskgroups/TGdatacitation/

[14] Creative Commons, http://creativecommons.org/

[15] Open Source Initiative, http://opensource.org/

A Quantitative Evaluation of Techniques for Detection of Abnormal Change Events in Blogs

Paul Logasa Bogen II
Intelligent Computing Research Team
Computational Data Analytics Group
Oak Ridge National Laboratory
Oak Ridge, Tennessee
bogenpl@ornl.gov

Frank Shipman, Richard Furuta
Center for the Study of Digital Libraries and
Dept. of Computer Science and Engineering
Texas A&M University
College Station, Texas 77843
dcm@csdl.tamu.edu

ABSTRACT

While most digital collections have limited forms of change—primarily creation and deletion of additional resources—there exists a class of digital collections that undergoes additional kinds of change. These collections are made up of resources that are distributed across the Internet and brought together into a collection via hyperlinking. Resources in these collections can be expected to change as time goes on. Part of the difficulty in maintaining these collections is determining if a changed page is still a valid member of the collection. Others have tried to address this problem by measuring change and defining a maximum allowed threshold of change, however, these methods treat all change as a potential problem and treat web content as a static document despite its intrinsically dynamic nature. Instead, we approach the significance of change on the web as a normal part of a web document's life-cycle and determine the difference between what a maintainer expects a page to do and what it actually does. In this work we evaluate the different options for extractors and analyzers in order to determine the best options from a suite of techniques. The evaluation used a human-generated ground-truth set of blog changes. The results of this work showed a statistically significant improvement over a range of traditional threshold techniques when applied to our collection of tagged blog changes.

Categories and Subject Descriptors

H.3.7 [**Digital Libraries**]: Collection, Systems issues, User issues; H.5.4 [**Hypertext/Hypermedia**]: User issues; I.5.2 [**Design Methodology**]: Feature evaluation and selection; I.5.4 [**Applications**]: Text Processing

General Terms

Management, Design, Experimentation, Human Factors

Keywords

Distributed Collection Manager, Pattern Recognition, Kalman Filters, Ensemble

1. INTRODUCTION

It is well known [19] that over time digital distributed collections age as their constituents change, become obsolete, or disappear. The result of collection aging has been a diminishing rate of return despite the significant effort required earlier in collection creation. If the lifespan of these collections can be extended, users may be more motivated to create them and thus decrease or prevent instances of rediscovery in the future.

It is this problem that the Distributed Collection Manager (DCM)—the successor to the Walden's Paths Project's PathManager path maintenance utility [8]—was designed to address. DCM is motivated not only by the observation that the fluidity of web pages leads to collections becoming stale, requiring revisions and updates [14], but also by observations that the web as a whole has changed and that assumptions we made in the past may no longer hold [7]. Unlike PathManager, which was used to maintain paths for Walden's Paths, DCM supports distributed collections of web sites in general.

To help inform the design of DCM, we performed two studies. The first study recruited users of social news sites and asked them about their habits regarding their personal collections including tools they use, kinds of sites they visit, and issues they face in managing their collections [9]. This study was followed with a series of interviews where we examined personal collections themselves, primarily bookmarks. Our studies affirmed the existence of personal collections of highly dynamic web sites, the inadequacies of existing tools to maintain these collections, and the importance of content over presentation and interactive features of a site for user re-evaluation of web pages.

Since 2006, we have been caching a collection of a wide variety of popular blogs [7]. From these caches, we observed patterns in the behavior of blogs [7]. We followed this with-qualitativeive evaluation of our Kalman Filter based modelling technique [8]. From these observations, we were able to subjectively match patterns in the filter's behavior to abnormal events in blogs. Given this subjective validation of our techniques we sought to objectively quantify our results. This paper follows up on our prior work by describing our work building a ground truth set for blog change that we

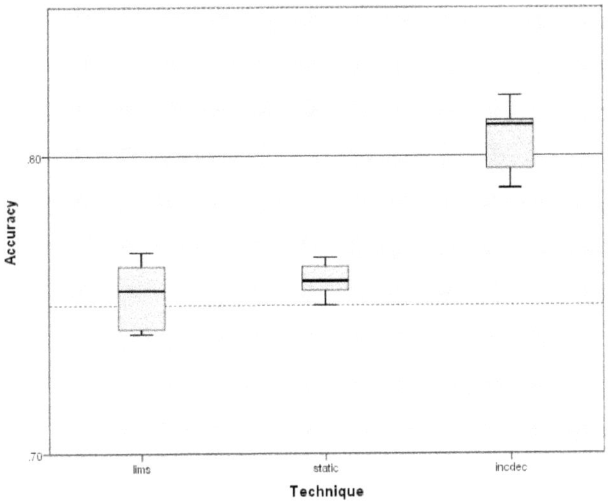

Figure 1: Accuracy Results for Heuristic Techniques.

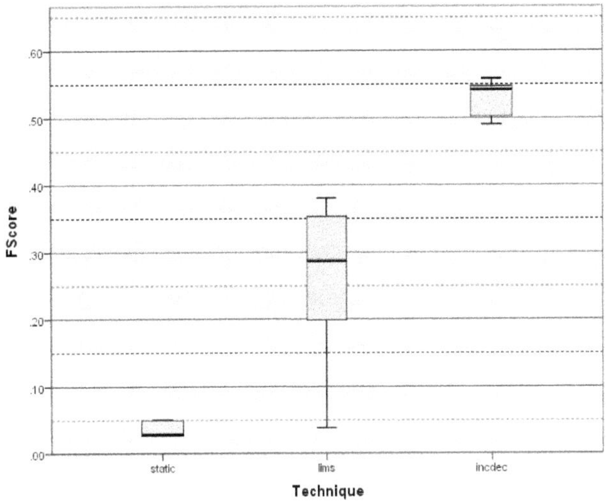

Figure 2: F-Score Results for Heuristic Techniques.

then use to evaluate a suite of Kalman filter based techniques to determine the best techniques in our suite. These best techniques are then compared totraditionall cosine similarity methods to show the improvement in performance over prior work.

The remainder of this paper will first discuss the problem of change management and some prior work surrounding change management and filter methods. This will be followed by a discussion of the construction of our ground truth set. Then we will discuss our selection of features. Next we will examine both the comparative evaluation between filter based techniques and cosine similarity based techniques. Finally we will discuss our conclusions and areas of future work.

2. PROBLEM

When a distributed collection of web resources is created, the curator has certain expectations to how the collection will or will not change. For instance, when a user creates a collection of news sites as a reference aid, she most likely expect the sites not to remain static. Not only would a change in behavior such as topic shift or abnormally frequent changes be considered problematic, but so would an abnormal lack of change, i.e., the page ceasing to change at all. Examples of this case include 9/11, when CNN's normal constant flow of articles halted while they were trying to sort out what was going on, and after Michael Jackson's death when entertainment news sites were rapidly posting every bit of information they received out of a concern that they would be perceived as disconnected from an unfolding event. As we will discuss in the next section, previous systems working on thresholds of change cannot distinguish between normal change and the abnormal activities associated with problematic behaviors or important but nonproblematic events. Additionally, these systems cannot recognize abnormally static behavior. The essential problem is these systems are not comparing change to expectation but to a pre-defined threshold amount.

Thus, our problem is defined as trying to identify changes that may be considered as abnormal in terms of what a user would expect when revisiting the page. Note that this is essentially the visceral reaction one would have when rechecking a site as part of a curator's maintenance task. The goal is to allow the first step of maintenance—re-visitation—to be done automatically either at a frequency more often than or to more resources than a curator normally would be able to. In order to better illustrate the issues with existing systems and the need for our approach, we will now discuss prior change management systems.

3. PRIOR WORK

Management of collections has been an important topic in many research communities even before the advent of information systems. In the past, change has been viewed from a perspective similar to that of a traditional library – new documents arrive and old documents are lost or are worn out, but the existing documents remain unchanged [26]. This perspective of change only contemplates types of change whose magnitude and frequency are very low since changes in the document contents are not possible except as a consequence of wear, damage, or annotation. As a result, the manual maintenance of the collection is possible in traditional libraries, even large ones.

This perspective of change has carried over to digital libraries. This is a reasonable approach not only in the traditional library, but in curated digital libraries, since they both share a fairly tight control over their collections; sometimes even more so in the digital library where wear is not as great of an issue. However, when the contents of the members of a collection are loosely controlled, like a collection of web resources, this approach does not apply. The source of this incompatibility is that many new types of change not only can occur, but often do. These changes are not only in membership to a category like in a curated collection, but can also be in what the individual documents contain or how they are presented. Additionally, the frequency of change can increase to unmanageable levels. Initially, the majority of responses from the community were to find ways to "deal with change" [2, 6, 15, 18, 21, 26]. These solutions essentially try to resist change. While more recently, the community has grown more aware that change is intrinsic to digital col-

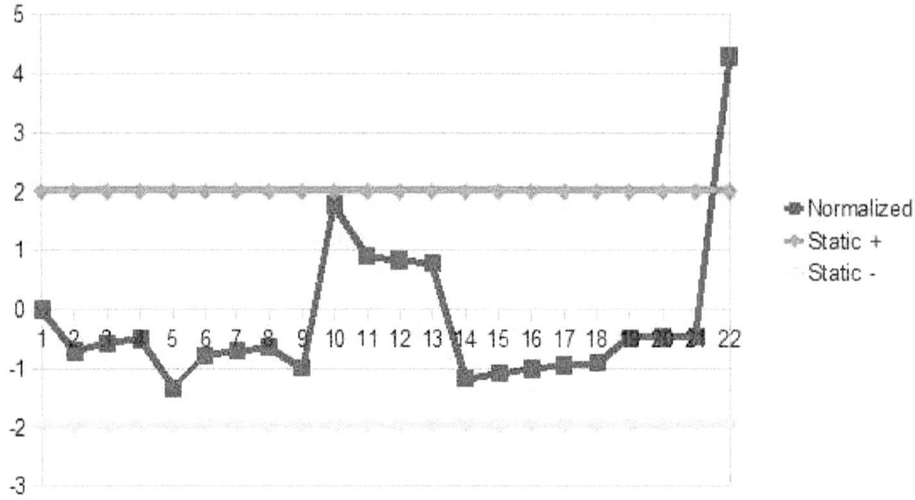

Figure 3: Static Technique Results on Outer Court Blog.

lections, it still seeks to only deal with change, as illustrated by existing work such as Askehave and Nielsen's work on digital genre where they saw change as a detrimental factor that could render their determination of characteristics of a genre invalid as time went on [3].

An early work to try and examine change on the web was the Do-I-Care Agent (DICA) [26]. DICA was primarily interested in finding new information for particular users. Changed documents were treated as if a new document had been entered in the user's collection. Later, Ashman described three classes of strategies for dealing with change on the web: preventative, corrective, and adaptive [2]. Preventative strategies are applied beforehand to avoid change from the beginning, such as caching. This makes the document static. Corrective strategies are applied after a problem occured and are designed to find replacements or equivalents. Adaptive methods are those that try to hedge the maintainer's bet by taking preventative actions that can then be used to form a corrective strategies. These classes still assume that change is a problem to be resolved and not the nature of the document. In 2001, the Walden's Paths project managed change by extending Johnson's approach for distance between page versions to determine how much a page had changed [15]. Further examples, can be seen in Koehler's change study [21], Boese and Howe's study that viewed change as a possible detriment to classification work [6], and Ivory and Megraw's study of Web Site Design Patterns [18]. In each of these cases the authors tried to factor out change in their collections. Their goal was either to find a underlying truth about the document without change getting in the way, or to restore the integrity of a collection *tainted by change*. While Askehave and Nielsen recognized change as an integral part of web documents, they admittedly did not fully account for their "view of web-mediated genres as dynamic documents" [3]. In fact, no change management systems have been built around the changing nature of web documents.

Results from the previously cited methods provide a two-point comparison, which in the past [6, 13, 14] was usually the extent of the comparison. However, when these comparisons continue over a large period of time, we found that patterns of magnitudes and frequencies of change emerge. These patterns provide a strong basis for identifying documents that may not be coherent with their original collection. After conducting a study of blogs from late 2006 to 2007 [7], we concluded that evidence of a commonality of change behavior across a given fine-grained genre, particularly blogs, indicates that associating a pattern of change to a genre enables pages to be grouped by observed change. This work was later confirmed by Saad and Gançarski's work on a collection of websites for French public television [4]. This better helps to determine an expectation of change. Despite the changing nature of web pages, existing genre-based approaches have treated them as a new class of *static* documents [6].

4. GROUND TRUTH BUILDING

In order to evaluate our methods, we created a corpus consisting of daily caches during the two month period surrounding the 2006 United States Congressional mid-term election. This period was picked both for its completeness, as there were no system or network outages, and since it was a political charged time, it was expected to produce more interesting results in many of the blogs in the collection. A total of 62 days of 66 blogs were first checked for static instances—days where no addition occurred—this reduced the blogs to 22 interesting days. These 1452 caches were then processed with an HTML differencing engine to produce an easier to scan display of what had changed. Each of these caches was shown to three evaluators who selected from a variety of classifications of change to tag the newer version. The options we provided were: no change, too slow change, too fast change, topic shift, abnormal content, and normal change. Due to the size of the collection, evaluators were given as much time as they wanted to spend to

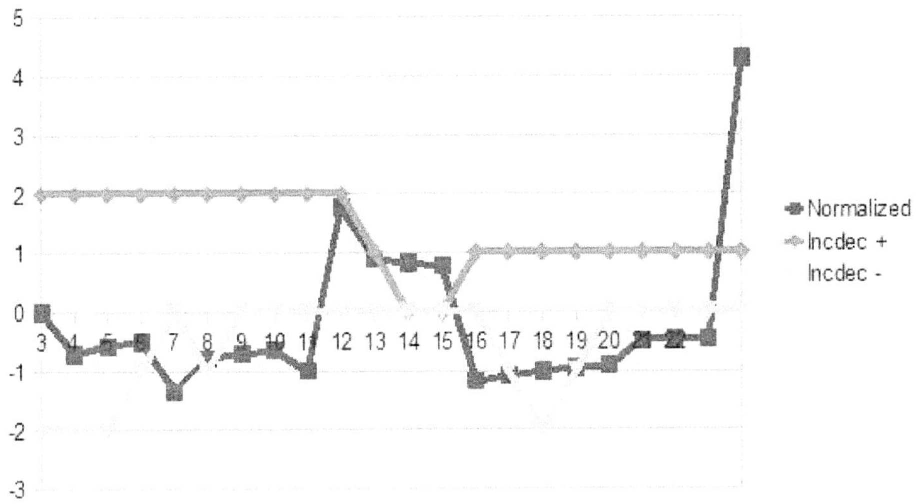

Figure 4: Constant Step Technique Results on Outer Court Blog.

tag as many as they could. While differences within a cache were shown consecutively in order of capture date, the order of sets of pages were randomly shuffled. Once a cache had been evaluated by three different judges, it was not shown to future judges. This corpus was then used to quantitatively compare different combinations of features, and analysis techniques.

5. FEATURE SELECTION

When revisiting a site, our surveyed social media users and interviewed graduate students indicated that their primary concerns when re-evaluating resources were in the areas of content, topic, target audience, and authorship. Because of these concerns we sought features that attempt to address these issues. For topic we included all 2-,3- grams in a document and the stemmed term vectors with stopwords removed. We used Porter's Snowball stemmer [24] for our stemming algorithm. For the target audience, we performed a Flesch-Kincaid readability index [20]. For authorship we included punctuation usage information and a structural analysis. Each of these features is used to create an ensemble feature vector that is then reduced using principal component analysis before being processed by our Kalman Filter.

Traditionally, feature selection is a fine-grained process that, due to the inherent computational complexity of calculating permutations, cannot be done exhaustively. Term vectors, in particular, have the potential to reach impractical running times even with small dictionaries. To avoid calculating every permutation, there are a variety of techniques to trim the decision space and test only options that are likely to provide an improvement. However, since DCM is built on coarse-grained feature extractors that each produce a number of features and because these features are reduced through principal components analysis, we chose to forgo the fine-grained analysis of each individual feature in preference of combinations of extractors. While better results may be found when selecting features individually, the results are more prone to overfitting [5] and don't help to provide insights into the usefulness of the coarse-grained extractors as a whole.

From these facts, we proceeded with a naive feature selection of all sixty-three combinations of the six features we currently have implemented. From the results of all feature combinations we performed an ANOVA on the F-Scores and the accuracies produced by each feature combination.

We determined that none of the features alone or any combination thereof provided a statistically significant improvement over any other. This most likely is explained by the application of principal component analysis performed by our analysis system before the Kalman filter is executed. Principal component analysis, by projecting the data into a lower dimensionality that maximizes the expression of the data's variance, would explain the wide variance we found for feature-wise analysis. This wide variance would result in a poor separation of feature-based classes thus resulting in needing to accept the null hypothesis (that the features are equivalent) in an ANOVA analysis.

6. ABNORMAL CHANGE DETECTION

The output of our Kalman Filter is a list of how far off each prediction made by the filter was compared to the actual observed results. These error measurements when standardized and manually inspected seemed to indicate a correlation between the standard score and the likelihood that they were abnormal pages. To quantify this observation we devised a number of candidate methods to pick out the abnormal pages. These methods can be divided into three categories—heuristic methods, classifiers, and statistical outlier detectors. Each of these categories has several alternate methods while sharing a common perspective on how to treat this data. The theory behind most of these techniques is that users can provide feedback to help improve future attempts to determine if an error measurement

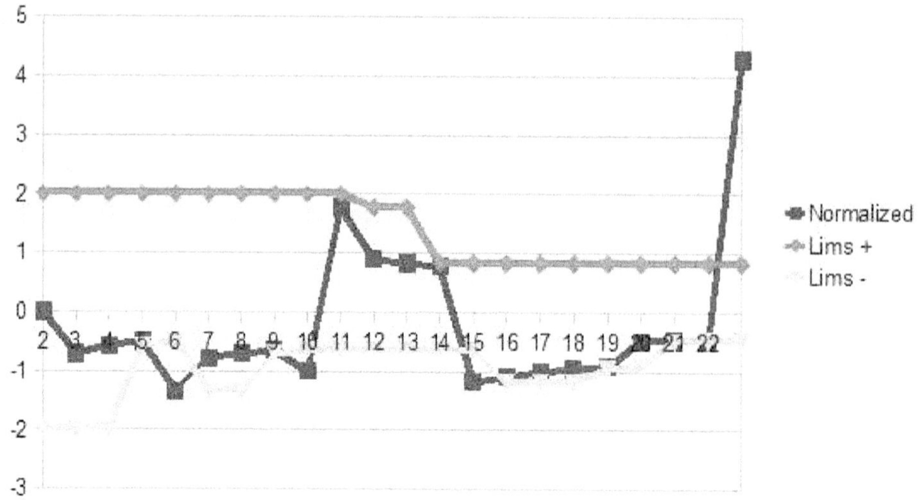

Figure 5: Limits Technique Results on Outer Court Blog.

is normal or abnormal. For the purpose of testing, we simulated the case where users always provide feedback. This is done by retraining the techniques by feeding the results of the ground truth study for each revision back into it after classification of a revision.

Due to the nature of results for machine learning type tasks, a single simple measure cannot capture the complexity of the data's results. For the remainder of this section we will present both the overall accuracy of the method and an F-Score, a commonly used technique that reports a balanced combination of precision and recall. Some techniques perform very well in terms of F-Score and some in terms in Accuracy. A few techniques perform well in both measures, albeit not as well as the maximal techniques for each measure independently. Many measures perform poorly on both and are clearly inappropriate for the task at hand. In particular, we have found Spectral Regression Discriminant Analysis [10] and nearest neighbor techniques [1] to be the most interesting for deployment.

6.1 Heuristic Methods

The heuristic methods are often the simplest and are informed by our observations of the data. Currently, we have tested three different heuristic methods. A summary of these results can be seen in Figures 2 and 1.

The first method and by far the simplest is a static error threshold placed at two standard deviations above and below the mean for past errors. If the new revision's prediction error is outside the range between the two thresholds then it is marked as abnormal, if it is between then it is normal. To provide an example of how the static technique behaves, please see Figure 3.

The purpose of a static error threshold was to provide a baseline to compare other heuristic techniques to, as the static threshold is the most naive means of analysis—one that does not change in response to feedback. The static technique provided one of the best of overall accuracies (75.86%) at the cost of one of the worst overall F-Scores (.035). This reflects the overall dominance of negative (normal behavior) results in our collection. The static method tended to err on the side of more negative items, thus having a good accuracy (mainly by chance) with such a poor F-Score.

The second method increases the complexity by allowing the bounds to grow and shrink using constant steps from a starting point (two standard deviations) in response to false positives and false negatives. In a production system this information would be obtained from user feedback. Thus in the case of no feedback it will perform like the previous method, while with perfect feedback it will perform as well as the algorithm can be expected to perform. One thing to note is the threshold above and below the mean change independently of each other. To provide an example of the results from the constant step technique, please see Figure 4.

Allowing constant steps has the effect of dampening the effect of highly abnormal results—a revision with error far outside other revisions, or an abnormal cache near the mean. This can be viewed as a conservative heuristic. Surprisingly, this conservative method obtained the best over all accuracy (80.67%) and a slightly better than a random classifier would be expected to perform on F-Score (.531). Unfortunately in cases where the misclassified cache is distant from the threshold, repeated distant caches may still be misclassified.

The third method takes a potentially more aggressive approach, that again could be informed by feedback. In this case, instead of steps in set increments, we expand or contract the limits so that the most recent false positive is just inside the limits and a false negative is just outside the limits. This ensures that a similar value with a similar classification in subsequent caches is not misclassified, however, if a misclassified cache has an error contained in normally correctly classified caches, the technique would then misclassify results it would otherwise classify correctly. To provide an example of how the limits technique behaves, please see Figure 5.

While the limits technique still maintained a decent ac-

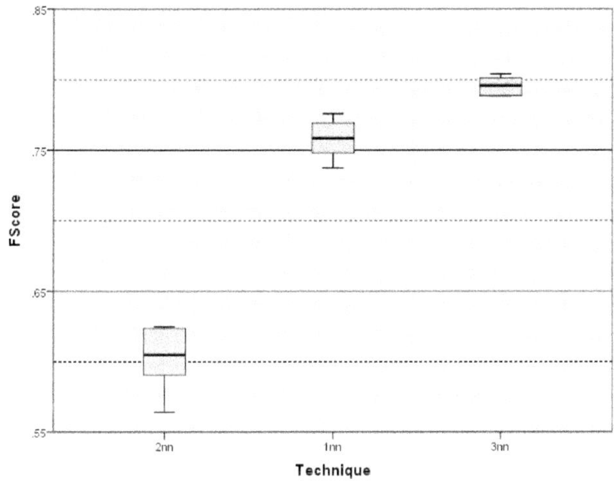

Figure 6: F-Score Results for kNN Techniques.

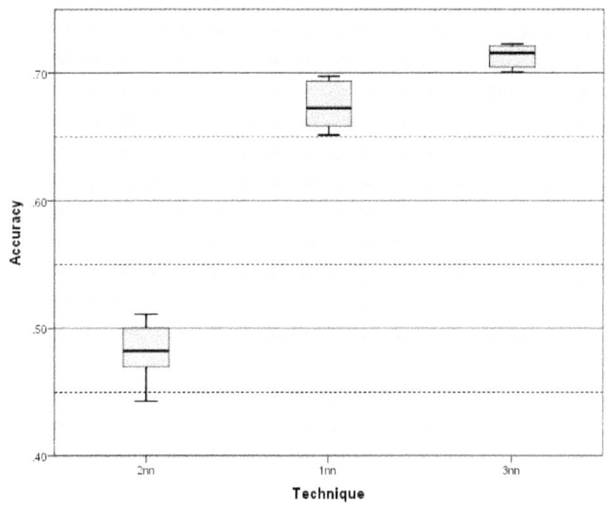

Figure 7: Accuracy Results for kNN Techniques.

curacy at 75.30%, this accuracy is worse than the static method. The results for F-Score did improve over static (.255) but not as well as either the expected random results or the constant step method.

6.2 Classifier Methods

Essentially, the problem of separating normal caches and abnormal caches using the error of prediction from a Kalman Filter is a binary classification task. As such, there are a wide variety of techniques that can be used. One difference from a traditional classification task where data is split into testing and training sets, data from an online predictive method should not be simply split. Every sample becomes a new piece of testing data using the prior data as a training set. After the new point is classified and a user provides feedback on the classification, the point can be folded into the training set to generate a new classifier. We tried a variety of supervised classifier methods which produced a variety of results. Some of these results provide a trade-off of overall accuracy with increased precision and recall when compared to the heuristic methods. The classifiers utilized were variations of three categories of binary classifiers—nearest-neighbor methods [1], support vector machine methods [12], and discriminant analysis methods [23].

Nearest-neighbor methods work by the assumption that the k nearest known samples to the test sample are likely to be of the same classification as the test sample [1]. In the case of mixed results, a majority vote of the neighbors is used to select the class. For the purposes of classifying errors, we tried 1-, 2-, and 3- nearest-neighbors variants. A summary of kNN results can be seen in Figures 6 and 7.

While for accuracy all methods perform worse than the static technique, two methods still perform better than random chance. 3NN is the most accurate (71.35%), followed by 1NN (67.49%), and finally 2NN is worse than random at 48.19%. Conversely, by F-Score, all methods perform better than random and the static technique for all cases. 2NN is again the worst method (.602), followed again by 1NN (.758), and finally 3NN performed the best at (.796). While the constant steps technique is still the most accurate technique, all three techniques improved on the F-Score from the heuristic methods.

Support vector machines are a broad set of techniques that can be used to find a hyperplane that maximally separates two classes of data by projecting the data in to a higher dimensionality [12]. The shape of the hyperplane is described by a kernel which can be easily replaced to provide separators of different complexities. For our tests, we tried four kernels – linear, Gaussian, terminated ramp, and the Tversky kernel. A summary of SVM results can be seen in Figures 8 and 9.

The linear kernel is the simplest kernel in that it uses a linear hyperplane to separate the two classes [12]. While it did perform better than random for accuracy, with an accuracy of 60.56%, the linear kernel did not out-perform a static measure. While the linear kernel does provide a better F-Score than heuristic methods and 2NN at .705, 1NN and 3NN still have better F-Scores.

The next kernel in order of complexity uses a Gaussian surface to separate the two classes [12]. Gaussian does provide an improvement for both accuracy (68.76%) and F-Score (.777) over the Linear kernel. However, it did not perform statistically better than 1NN, nor did it perform statistically worse than 3NN.

Terminated ramp uses a series of linear models to improve on linear separation for oppositely labelled points that lay close to the global separating hyperplane [22]. It does this by refining the seperation with local optimal linear hyperplanes between the opposing points. Terminated ramp, while proving a much better than random accuracy (71.36%), still is less accurate than heuristic techniques. However, the F-Score for terminated ramp is the best we obtained for any method (.802). Yet, it was not statistically better than 3NN and the Gaussian kernel.

The final kernel method we used is unique from the others in that it is a non-geometric asymmetrical technique devised by Amos Tversky to match his observations of human behavior when classifying objects [28]. Despite the method being designed to better model how humans perform classification tasks, Tversky's method was the worst performing SVM method for both accuracy (69.49%) and F-Score

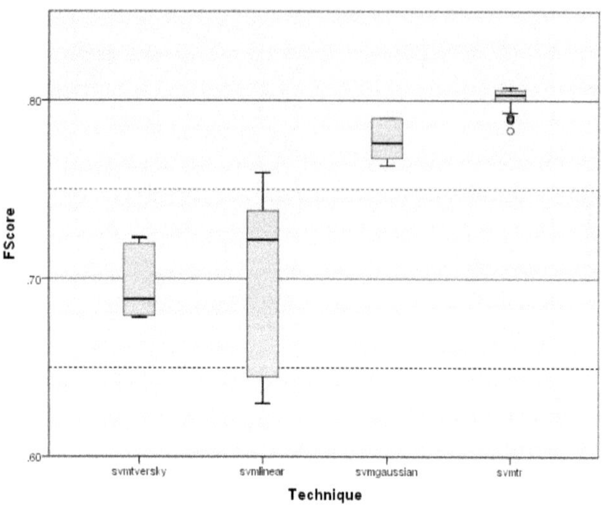

Figure 8: F-Score Results for SVM Techniques.

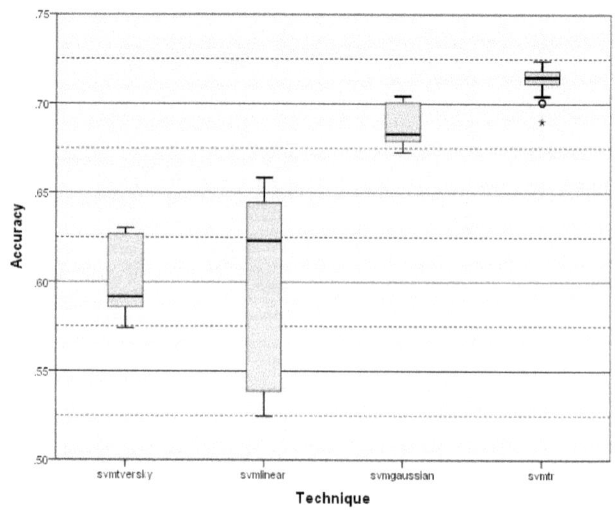

Figure 9: Accuracy Results for SVM Techniques.

(.599), albeit still better than random selection and 2NN for both measures in addition to having an F-Score better than all of the heuristic methods. This is most likely due to Tversky's dependence on feature vectors with different keys. However, the preprocessing steps taken before the application of the Kalman Filter eliminate keys with a low document frequency thus homogenizing the key set.

Discriminant analysis is similar to support vector machines in that the goal is to separate two classes of data. However, discriminant analysis reduces the dimensionality of data to a single dimension with a maximal separation between the class means. While SVM methods have been shown to be more powerful, adaptable, and generally usable for binary classification tasks, they incur a complexity penalty that makes their advantages only preferable when discriminant analysis cannot provide sufficiently accurate results. For this reason we decided to evaluate the use of discriminant analysis techniques for the classification of errors. The versions of discriminant analysis we tested were Fisher Discriminant Analysis [23], Spectral Regression Discriminant Analysis [10], Penalized Discriminant Analysis [16], and Diagonal Linear Discriminant Analysis [25]. Each version uses a different discriminant function to find the maximized separator between classes. A summary of discriminant analysis results can be seen in Figures 10 and 11.

Fisher's Discriminant (FDA) measures the ratio of the variance between classes to the variance within classes [23]. The results in terms of accuracy for FDA were better than random chance (51.60%), but not as good as heuristic methods, SVM-based methods, 1NN, or 3NN.

The second discriminant, Spectral Regression Discriminant Analysis (SRDA) [10] takes advantage of spectral analysis to reduce the complexity of the calculation of the discriminant in addition to improving overall accuracy. SRDA proved to be the best discriminant analysis technique with an accuracy of 67.41% and an F-Score of .777. While for accuracy, several methods, most notably the constant step heuristic and the static heuristic out-perform SRDA. The F-Score was statistically equivalent to 3NN and terminated ramp, the best overall methods.

The Penalized Discriminant (PDA) [16], is a modification to Fisher's that regularizes covariance matrices to overcome deficiencies when the covariance matrix is degenerate. This can be used to overcome overfitting in large numbers of highly correlated variables or to prevent underfitting for nonlinear or complex class separations. Unfortunately, PDA not only proved to be the absolute worst method, but it managed to get 0% accuracy and a 0 F-Score. Most likely this is caused by having a covariance matrix that is not degenerate.

The Diagonal Linear Discriminant Analysis (DLDA) [25], is a simplified case of Fisher's where the covariance matrix is found to be diagonal. This allows assumptions to be made that enable a less complex algorithm to be used to find a discriminant. While DLDA proved to be more accurate (51.63%) and have a better F-Score (.588) than FDA, it was not a statistically significant improvement.

6.3 Statistical Outlier Detection

In previous sections we viewed the problem in terms of, first, threshold tuning, and, second, as binary classification, in this section, instead, we cast the problem as detecting statistical outliers. Outlier detection is an important area of study for mathematical statistics. Undetected outliers can skew data and in some cases can help statisticians identify a multimodal distribution in an assumed unimodal one. To address this, statisticians have sought algorithms and heuristics to identify outliers for centuries. Each method has its own drawbacks and caveats. Usually these warnings are concerning the results of overly liberal data point elimination. In our case since we are not aiming to eliminate these points, but to simply identify them for human inspection, we can proceed without fear of negative repercussions. For this class, we tested two outlier detection techniques—Chauvenet's criterion and Grubbs' test. A summary of outlier detection results can be seen in Figures 12 and 13.

One of the earliest techniques created was Chauvenet's criterion [11] for detecting outliers. This method rejects values where the probability of normalized data is multiplied by the number of data points. This value is rejected as an outlier if the result is less than 0.5. The results of our application of Chauvenet's criterion produced results that were

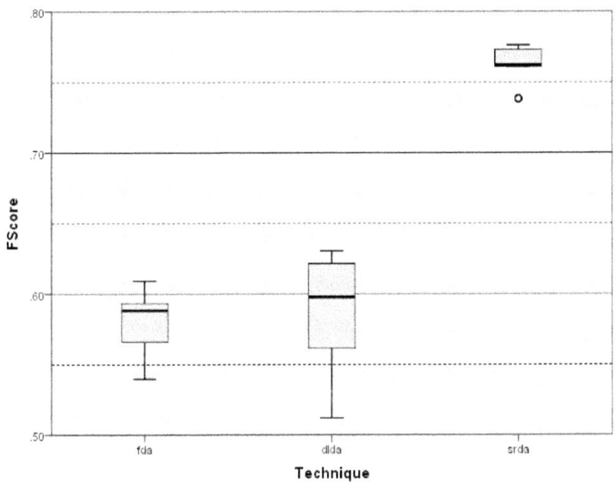

Figure 10: F-Score Results for Discriminant Analysis Techniques.

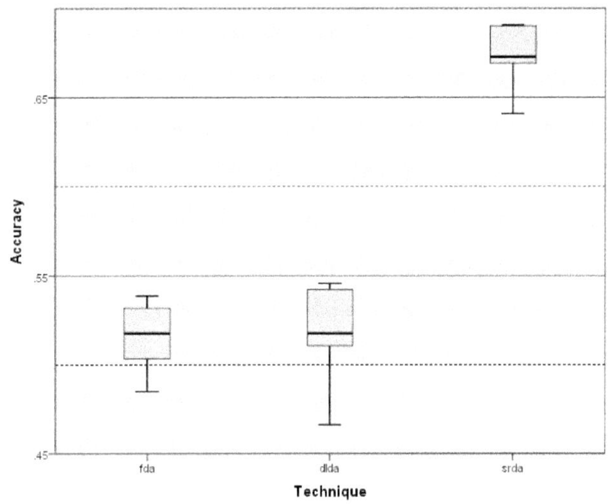

Figure 11: Accuracy Results for Discriminant Analysis Techniques.

not significantly different than the static method for both accuracy (75.75%) and F-Score (.578).

Grubbs' test [17] is a more recent method for outlier detection. The test relies on a variation of the t-statistic compared to the absolute value of the standardized minimum and maximum scores in a set and runs iteratively until neither maximum nor minimum is greater than the critical region.

While Grubbs' test performed the second best by accuracy (76.63%), it had the second worse F-Score (.010) which was not significantly any better than PDA. Additionally, Grubbs' accuracy was not significantly any better than the static heuristic.

6.4 Ensemble Method

Finally we selected the methods with the best accuracy and F-scores and used them as votes for each cache where a majority classification ruled. The methods we used for our votes were 3NN, SVM with the Terminated Ramp kernel, SVM with the Gaussian Kernel, the constant step heuristic and Grubbs' outlier detection method. Unfortunately we were not able to improve performance and only obtained a 75.32% accuracy and an F-Score of .229. We suspect that a deeper analysis of results and a weighted ensemble method could yield better results.

6.5 Versus Cosine Similarity

From the combined results of feature selection and technique selection, we identified two pairs of feature set and technique that can be objectively called the best for each of our vital methods of importance—accuracy and F-Score. For optimal accuracy we selected the static step technique using the structural change algorithm with an accuracy of 82.02%. While many other combinations of features performed equivalently to this, this single feature represented the simplest of the best accuracy techniques. For F-Score, we picked the SVM technique using the terminated ramp kernel and a feature set consisting of structural changes and punctuation counts. This combination achieved and F-Score of .807. However, one portion of our analysis has not been objectively measured – the effectiveness of the Kalman filter technique over traditional threshold techniques. In order to address this issue, we performed cosine similarity tests both between the first and each subsequent revision and between each pair of adjacent revisions. These results are then evaluated at a variety of threshold levels to determine if the Kalman technique is better or worse than traditional techniques for every combination of feature set. Similarity is defined depending on the dimensionality of the data. If the data is one-dimensional, we use a linear distance between revisions, if it is multi-dimensional, we use the standard cosine similarity metric defined for term vectors.

Given the usage of both absolute and relative measures to calculate threshold, the first question is—are these different measures different and if so which one is better? we performed an ANOVA with a post-hoc Tukey's Test [27] to determine if any pair of absolute and relative measures for each threshold level were significantly different. We found no statistically significant difference between measures at any threshold level for accuracy. For the F-Scores, we found that only at the 0.1 and 0.0 threshold levels was there a significant difference between measures. In both cases the absolute measure out-performed the relative one.

We did find that different threshold levels provided an advantage over others. For accuracy, the level for the relative measure provided the best results (71.77%), while it was not statistically better than those obtained from levels at or above 0.5, it did out perform all of the levels below 0.5. For F-Score, however, the results were the opposite with the absolute method at a threshold level of 0.0 obtaining a better F-Score (.307) than all other threshold levels.

The final step in our analysis is the comparison between threshold methods and our Kalman filter based method. As stated before, we selected the best results for each measure—SVM with a truncated ramp kernel for F-Score and the constant step heuristic for accuracy—as a point of comparison to threshold methods. In both cases, the optimal Kalman-filter based methods outperformed all of the threshold options. Just as with the comparisons between threshold options, we again used ANOVA with a post-hoc Tukey's

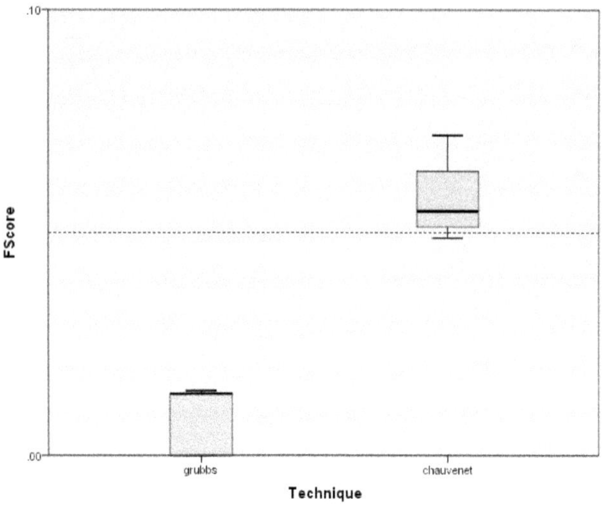

Figure 12: F-Score Results for Outlier Detection Techniques.

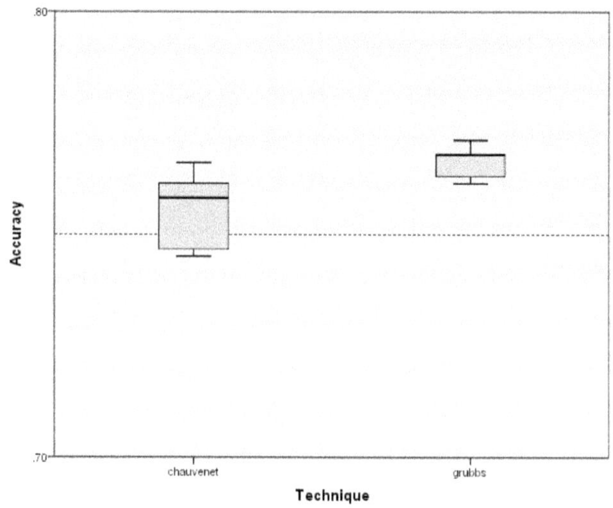

Figure 13: Accuracy Results for Outlier Detection Techniques.

Test to make the comparison. For accuracy, the constant step heuristic statistically outperformed the best threshold method— with a relative measure ($p = .001$). For F-Score, the SVM method with the terminated ramp kernel statistically outperformed the best threshold method—0.0 with the absolute measure ($p = .000$). What was more surprising was that while the SVM method with the terminated ramp kernel was statistically equivalent on accuracy to the most accurate threshold method ($p = 1.000$), the constant step heuristic did statistically out perform all of the threshold tests for F-Score also ($p = .000$).

7. CONCLUSIONS

From these results we are able tquantitativelyly select the best options for classification of blog changes for accuracy and F-Score. For accuracy our constant step heuristic usinstructuralal change features alone provided the best accuracy (82.02%) over all other Kalman filter based techniques and statistically outperformed all of the threshold based techniques. For F-Score, our SVM with the truncated ramp kernel using both structural change and punctuation count features provided the best F-Score (.807). This technique also statistically outperformed all threshold methods.

This shows that the Kalman-based technique is capable of outperforming threshold based techniques for finding unexpected change in blogs. For practical considerations, while accuracy is theoretically interesting, since the collection is dominated by expected changes, it is not of high concern for designing systems to help collection managers. Instead the manager is more concerned with the precision and recall of the unexpected changes. Thus, F-Score is the preferred measure to optimize for. Therefore we can suggest the usage of SVM with Terminated Ramp as the preferred technique.

While our work has shown good results with the blog collection, there are four areas in which further inquiry can be done. First, our feature set could be expanded upon to include more sophisticated techniques, perhaps from topic tracking and sentiment analysis work. Second, the substitution of other filters, such as particle filters, instead of the Kalman filter may provide better results. Third, while we conducted classification of Kalman filter results with a broad set of techniques, there are still more classification techniques that we could experiment with, such as self-organizing maps and fuzzy clustering techniques. And fourth, moving to a more general ground-truth set would provide us with the ability to compare results based on genre and potentially infer generalized strategies.

8. ACKNOWLEDGEMENTS

The Distributed Collection Manager is being developed as part of the Ensemble Computing Pathways Project. This work has been funded in part by the National Science Foundation under grants DUE-0840715 and DUE-1044212.

This document was prepared by Oak Ridge National Laboratory, P.O. Box 2008, Oak Ridge, Tennessee 37831-6285; managed by UT-Battelle, LLC, for the US Department of Energy under contract number DE AC05-00OR22725.

This manuscript has been authored by UT-Battelle, LLC, under contract DE-AC05-00OR22725 with the U.S. Department of Energy. The United States Government retains and the publisher, by accepting the article for publication, acknowledges that the United States Government retains a non-exclusive, paid-up, irrevocable, world-wide license to publish or reproduce the published form of this manuscript, or allow others to do so, for United States Government purposes.

9. REFERENCES

[1] Cover, T. and Hart, P. Nearest Neighbor Pattern Classification. *IEEE Transactions on Information Theory*, 13(1), 1967.

[2] Ashman, H. Electronic Document Addressing: Dealing with Change. *ACM Comp. Surv.*, 32(3), 2000.

[3] Askehave, I and Nielsen, A. E. What are the Characteristics of Digital Genres? - Genre Theory from a Multi-Modal Perspective. In *Proc. of HICSS 2005*, 2005.

[4] M. Ben Saad and S. Gançarski. Archiving the web

using page changes patterns: a case study. In *Proc. of 11th JCDL*, JCDL '11, pages 113–122, 2011.

[5] Bishop, C. M. *Pattern Recognition and Machine Learning*, volume 4. Springer, 2006.

[6] Boese, E. S. and Howe, A. E. Effects of Web Document Evolution on Genre Classification. In *Proc. of 14th ACM Int. Conf. on Information and Knowledge Management*, 2005.

[7] Bogen, P. L., Francisco-Revilla, L., Furuta, R., Hubbard, T., Karadkar, U. P. and Shipman, F. Longitudinal Study of Changes in Blogs. In *Proc. of JCDL 2007*.

[8] Bogen, P. L., Johnston, J., Karadkar, U. P., Furuta, R. and Shipman, F. Application of Kalman Filters to Identify Unexpected Change in Blogs. In *Proc. of JCDL 2008*.

[9] Bogen, P. L., Shipman, F. M. and Furuta, R. An analysis of personal collections among users of social media. In *Proc. of JCDL 2011*.

[10] Cai, D., He, X. and Han, J. SRDA: An Efficient Algorithm for Large-Scale Discriminant Analysis. *IEEE Transactions on Knowledge and Data Engineering*, 20, 2008.

[11] Chavuenet, W. *A Manual of Spherical and Practical Astronomy*. Lippincott, 1871.

[12] Cristianini, N. and Shawe-Taylor, J. *An Introduction to Support Vector Machines: and Other Kernel-Based Learning Methods*. Cambridge UP, 2000.

[13] Dalal, Z., Dash, S., Dave, P., Francisco-Revilla, L., Furuta, R. and Karadkar, U. and Shipman, F. Managing Distributed Collections: Evaluating Web Page Changes, Movement, and Replacement. In *Proc. of 4th ACM/IEEE-CS Joint Conference on Digital Libraries*, 2004.

[14] Francisco-Revilla, L., Shipman, F., Furuta, R., Karadkar, U., Arora, A. Managing Change on the Web. In *Proc. of JCSDL 2001*.

[15] Furuta, R., Shipman, F. M., Marshall, C. C., Brenner, D. and Hsieh, H.-W. Hypertext Paths and the World-Wide Web: Experiences with Walden's Paths. In *Proc. of 8th ACM Conference on Hypertext*, 1997.

[16] Ghosh, D. Penalized Discriminant Methods for the Classification of Tumors from Gene Expression Data. *Biometrics*, 59(4), 2003.

[17] Grubbs, F. E. Procedures for Detecting Outlying Observations in Samples. *Technometrics*, 11(1), 1969.

[18] Ivory, M. Y. and Megraw, R. Evolution of Web Site Design Patterns. *ACM Transactions on Information Systems*, 23(4), 2005.

[19] Jones, W., Bruce, H. and Dumais, S. Keeping Found Things Found on the Web. In *Proc. of 10th Int. Conf. on Information and Knowledge Management*, 2001.

[20] Kincaid, J., Fishburne, R., Rodgers, R. and Chissom, B. Derivation of New Readability Formulas for Navy Enlisted Personnel. Technical Report 8-75, National Technical Information Service, 1975.

[21] Koehler, W. Web Page Change and Persistence—a Four-Year Longitudinal Study. *Journal of the American Society for Information Science and Technology*, 53(2), 2002.

[22] Merler, S. and Jurman, G. Terminated Ramp-Support Vector Machines: A Nonparametric Data Dependent Kernel. *Neural Networks*, 19, December 2006.

[23] Mika, S., Smola, A. J. and Schölkopf, B. An Improved Training Algorithm for Kernel Fisher Discriminants. In *Proc. of Eighth International Workshop on Artificial Intelligence and Statistics*, volume 2001, 2001.

[24] Porter, M. Snowball Stemmers and Resources Page. On line http://www.snowball.tartarus.org. [Visited 8/22/2011].

[25] Simon, R. Supervised Analysis When the Number of Candidate Features (p) Greatly Exceeds the Number of Cases (n). *ACM SIGKDD Explorations Newsletter*, 5, December 2003.

[26] Starr, B., Ackerman, M. S. and Pazzani, M. Do-I-Care: A Collaborative Web Agent. In *Conference Companion on Human Factors in Computing Systems*, 1996.

[27] Tukey, J. W. *Exploratory Data Analysis*, volume xvi of *Behavioral Science*. Addison-Wesley, 1977.

[28] Tversky, A. Features of Similarity. *Psychological Review*, 84(4), 1977.

‘Similar Researcher Search’ in Academic Environments

Sujatha Das G.
Computer Science and Engineering
The Pennsylvania State University
University Park, PA 16802 USA
gsdas@cse.psu.edu

Prasenjit Mitra, C. Lee Giles
Information Sciences and Technology
Computer Science and Engineering
The Pennsylvania State University
University Park, PA 16802 USA
{pmitra,giles}@ist.psu.edu

ABSTRACT

Entity search is an emerging IR and NLP task that involves the retrieval of entities of a specific type in response to a query. We address the “similar researcher search” or the “researcher recommendation” problem, an instance of “similar entity search” for the academic domain. In response to a ‘researcher name’ query, the goal of a researcher recommender system is to output the list of researchers that have similar expertise as that of the queried researcher. We propose models for computing similarity between researchers based on expertise profiles extracted from their publications and academic homepages. We provide results of our models for the recommendation task on two publicly-available datasets. To the best of our knowledge, we are the first to address content-based researcher recommendation in an academic setting and demonstrate it for Computer Science via our system, `ScholarSearch`.

Categories and Subject Descriptors

H.3.3 [**Information Search and Retrieval**]: Retrieval Models

General Terms

Algorithms

Keywords

Similar-entity Search, Recommendation

1. INTRODUCTION

Entity search and retrieval where the goal is to retrieve “objects” (such as cars, books, people) in response to user queries is an emerging research interest in the Information Retrieval community. The recent systems submitted to the entity tracks of INEX[1] and TREC[2] illustrate some approaches for facilitating entity retrieval in the general domain. In this paper, we focus on enabling entity retrieval in the academic domain where the entities of interest are researchers. We use the terms entity, expert, and researcher interchangeably in this paper. Entity retrieval has been studied in form of the “expertise search” problem in the academic domain and has been implemented in systems such as ArnetMiner[3] and Microsoft Academic Search[4]. However, to the best of our knowledge, “similar researcher search” has not been addressed via content-based approaches in the academic domain although previous work exists on predicting collaborators based on co-authorship networks [8]. Researcher recommendation differs from expertise search in that the input to the system is not a “topic query” but instead a “researcher name”, and the goal is to find researchers who are similar to the queried researcher in their expertise areas. In contrast with co-author prediction, we wish to retrieve researchers who work on similar areas even if they are far apart in the co-authorship network.

As a motivating application, consider the panel selection process for a conference where the program chair wants to select a panel of reviewers for the “information extraction” track. Given an expert search system, the chair can obtain a list of “expert” recommendations for forming a panel in response to the topic query, “information extraction”. On the other hand, she could use an exemplar entity in a “similar researcher search” system and search for researchers similar to “Andrew McCallum”. Note that the retrieved entities in both the cases need not be the same because “Andrew McCallum” can be associated with several other expertise areas apart from “information extraction” and our recommender system seeks to retrieve researchers whose profiles are most similar to that of “Andrew McCallum” but at the same time need not be close collaborators of McCallum.

Researcher expertise profiles could be modeled using various representations. Some representations explored for the expertise search task include term vectors based on the documents authored by the researcher, probability distribution of topics s/he worked on or structural attributes describing the researcher [13, 19, 11, 3]. Irrespective of the underlying representation, for enabling “similar researcher search”, we require that there exists a function that acts on two profiles and outputs a real value, ($\exists f(s_1, s_2) \rightarrow R$), that can be used to compare the closeness between two profiles. Therefore, given the set of researchers, $E = \{e_1, e_2, \dots e_n\}$ with profiles ($S = \{s_{e_1}, s_{e_2}, \dots s_{e_n}\}$), an input researcher name, e_q, and a parameter k, our recommender system retrieves $E_q \subseteq E$,

[1] https://inex.mmci.uni-saarland.de/about.html
[2] http://trec.nist.gov
[3] http://arnetminer.org
[4] http://academic.research.microsoft.com

JCDL'12, June 10–14, 2012, Washington, DC, USA.

ranks them using f and outputs the top-k researchers with profiles most similar to s_{e_q}.

Contributions and Organization: We have just formally defined "researcher recommendation", an instance of "similar entity search" for the academic domain. Next, we propose models for representating researcher profiles and computing similarity with these representations (Section 2). We provide experimental evaluation for the recommendation task on two publicly-available datasets: ArnetMiner and the UvT collection[5] in Section 3. We demonstrate ScholarSearch (Figure 1), that implements researcher recommendation for the Computer Science domain using the data from the digital library portal, CiteSeer^{X}[6]. Finally, we summarize previous research that is closely related to our problem in Section 4 before concluding in Section 5.

2. OBTAINING SIMILAR RESEARCHERS

In Section 1, we defined the "similar researcher search" problem. Note that measuring similarity between expertise profiles presumes that we have evidence that can be used to compute similarities. For the academic domain, it is typical to measure expertise in an area in terms of a researcher's publications, descriptions of projects he or she has previously worked on, course contributions, citation information, the academic network involving a researcher, etc. This information is not easily available for all disciplines. For instance, it is more common to find research literature online for disciplines like Computer Science rather than Chemistry. Needless to say, expertise modeling depends on what evidence is available for a given discipline and various techniques are possible for extracting the same [15, 4, 20]. In the following discussion, we assume the availability of such evidence in terms of a representative document collection or at least academic homepages that concisely summarize a researcher's activities and publication information. Even if the former is not available for a discipline, previous research has illustrated techniques for obtaining researcher homepages from the web [9].

Given the set of expertise profiles for researchers, we explore the following techniques for computing similarity between two researcher profiles:

1. **Okapi BM25** (OKAPI): A researcher profile is represented using a vector corresponding to terms in a vocabulary derived based on the content associated with the researcher. Treating one profile as the query and the second as a document, ranking functions employed in IR can be used to obtain the similarity between them. Consider for instance, the Okapi BM25 ranking function widely used in various IR systems and across text collections. The similarity between two profiles is computed using the BM25 formula as follows:
$$\sum_{w \in s_1} IDF(w) * \frac{tf(w, s_2) * (k_1 + 1)}{tf(w, s_2) + k_1 * (1 - b + b.\frac{|D|}{avgdl}}$$
In the above formula, $IDF(w)$ refers to the inverse document frequency of the word, a measure of rareness of the word computed as:
$$IDF(w) = log\frac{N - N(w) + 0.5}{N(w) + 0.5}.$$
N is the total number of profiles in the collection, $N(w)$, the number of profiles containing w and $tf(w, s_2)$, the number of times, the term w appears in the profile of e_2. The parameter k_1 is typically set to a value between $[1.2, 2]$ whereas b is typically set to 0.75 in this formula in absence of other information. Additional details on this formula and parameter settings can be found in Jones, et al. [16].

2. **KL Divergence** (KLD): In this representation, a researcher profile is represented in terms of a probability distribution. For instance, given a set of documents associated with a researcher, a multinomial distribution can be fit to model the term counts in these documents and Kullback–Leibler divergence used to quantify the similarity between two probability distributions. Given θ_{s_1} and θ_{s_2}, the multinomial probability distributions associated with the profiles of researchers, e_1 and e_2 respectively, KL divergence [6] between them is given by
$$KL(\theta_{s_1}||\theta_{s_2}) = \sum_{w \in s_1} p(w|\theta_{s_1})log\frac{p(w|\theta_{s_1})}{p(w|\theta_{s_2})}$$

3. **Probablistic Modeling** (PM): Researchers tend to work on multiple related areas and it might be more more appropriate to model their profiles as topic mixtures instead of a single multinomial distribution. Latent Dirichlet Allocation is a commonly-used topic modeling tool for unsupervised clustering of data and exploratory analysis [7]. We model the set of expertise profiles using T topics and obtain the topic distribution corresponding to each profile. The similarity between two profiles, s_1 and s_2 can now be measured in terms of the conditional probability of generating the profile s_2, from the profile $s_1, P(s_2|s_1)$. Assuming conditional independence between s_1 and s_2 given a topic and a uniform distribution on topics and entities this can be evaluated as follows
$$p(s_2|s_1) \propto \sum_{t \in T} p(s_2 \cap s_1|t) * p(t) \propto$$
$$\sum_{t \in T} p(s_2|t)p(s_1|t) \propto \sum_{t \in T} p(t|s_2)p(t|s_1)$$
The above formulae only show terms that affect the relative ranking of profiles with respect to s_1.

4. **Trace-based Similarity** (REL): He, et al. extended van Rijsbergen's proposal to use Gleason's theorem in IR by modeling concepts as vector subspaces that are represented using density matrices (A density matrix is a symmetric, positive semi-definite matrix whose trace is 1) [18, 14]. In their formulation the density matrix for a document d, in terms of concepts c_i, $i = 1 \dots k$ can be written as $T_d = \frac{1}{k}\sum_{i=1}^{k} c_i c_i'$ and the probability that a concept c is relevant to a document d is computed as $p_d(c) = Tr(c'T_d c)$. Based on the derivations worked out by these authors, a relevance score between two researcher profiles, s_1 and s_2 can be computed using the corresponding density matrices using the formula
$$Rel(s_1, s_2) = \frac{1}{k_1 k_2}\sum_{i=1}^{k_1}\sum_{j=1}^{k_2}(c_i.b_j)^2$$
where $T_{s_1} = \frac{1}{k_1}\sum_{i=1}^{k_1} c_i c_i'$ and $T_{s_2} = \frac{1}{k_2}\sum_{i=1}^{k_2} b_i b_i'$. In our experiments, we computed the density matrices as

[5]http://ilk.uvt.nl/uvt-expert-collection/
[6]http://citeseerx.ist.psu.edu

Figure 1: Demo: The ScholarSearch System

$T_s = ss'$ where s is the one-dimensional unit TFIDF vector representing a researcher's profile. More complicated techniques for setting the density matrices are possible but are a subject of future study.

3. EXPERIMENTS

To the best of our knowledge, no standard datasets exist for evaluating the academic researcher recommendation task. However, the UvT Expert collection and the datasets used in ArnetMiner [20] are publicly available for evaluating Expertise Search. These datasets contain 'topic' queries and associated with each query are manually-identified lists of researchers with expertise on the specific topic. We created datasets for evaluating the recommendation task as follows: for a given topic query, from the set of experts listed with the query, we randomly choose one of the experts as the "researcher name query". The other experts in the set comprise the similar researchers (or the 'gold' list) for this query. The lists of researchers recommended by our techniques are compared against these gold lists during evaluation. Considering only topic queries for which five or more researchers are listed with the query, we obtained a list of 163 queries for the UvT collection and 16 for ArnetMiner. The UvT collection was collected using the Webwijs system developed at Tilburg University (UvT) and contains information on UvT employees who are involved in research or teaching. The homepages, research profiles, publications and course pages of employees are included in this collection when available. Content from these sources was used to model the profiles for researchers in this dataset. For ArnetMiner, we use the document collection of CiteSeerX for modeling the expertise profiles of researchers. That is, for both the datasets, all documents associated with a given researcher are used as an aggregate document while forming the expertise profile representations (of Section 2) for that researcher.

We measure the performance of the models proposed in Section 2 on the UvT and the ArnetMiner datasets for the researcher recommendation task using average recall and Mean Reciprocal Rank (MRR) scores as a function of K (the number of retrieved results examined). Recall measures the overlap between the 'gold' lists and the retrieved lists whereas MRR indicates the rank at which the first "correct" researcher was found. As indicated in Table 1, for both the datasets, simpler models based on term vectors such as OKAPI and REL performed better than the more involved models, KLD and PM. Note that these results are indicative but an error analysis including a user study is required for a precise performance evaluation. This is because the researchers recommended by various methods may still be relevant despite not being marked as 'correct' in the 'gold' lists of our datasets. Retrieval measures that are sensitive to incomplete relevance judgements need to be studied for evaluation [1].

ScholarSearch Demo[7]: Figure 1 illustrates two modes of operation of ScholarSearch on a small subset of 15,000 authors in CiteSeer^X. Snapshot (a) denotes the results of topic-based querying for "query optimization" whereas snapshot (b) shows the results of similar-researcher search with the researcher name, "Jayant Haritsa". In this system, topic-based expertise search was implemented using the models proposed in Demartini, et al. [12]. ScholarSearch also provides the "homepage search" functionality (not shown in the

[7]will be publicly-available soon from the first author's homepage

	ArnetMiner			UvT		
	K=10	K=30	K=100	K=10	K=30	K=100
OKAPI	**0.0266, 0.2569**	**0.0461, 0.2662**	**0.0965, 0.2682**	0.1175, 0.2857	0.1828, 0.2945	0.3069, 0.2979
KLD	0.0034, 0.0625	0.0034, 0.0625	0.0119, 0.0665	0.0701, 0.1555	0.1128, 0.1605	0.2169, 0.1654
PM	0.0062, 0.1063	0.0130, 0.1104	0.0224, 0.1125	0.0907, 0.1591	0.2177, 0.1746	0.4239, 0.1782
REL	0.0203, 0.2188	0.0360, 0.2267	0.0892, 0.2303	**0.1787, 0.3006**	**0.2997, 0.3112**	**0.4774, 0.3131**

Table 1: Average Recall and MRR values on the ArnetMiner and UvT datasets

figure) using the ranking function previously proposed by us [10]. The "Find Similar Experts" option implements the researcher recommendation task described in this paper, using the **REL** (Section 2) model. We provide the top-5 recommendations retrieved by our system in response to a few researcher names in Table 2. As the anecdotal evidence indicates ScholarSearch predictions for "similar researchers" in response to the queried researcher's name are quite reasonable.

Q1. Andrew McCallum	**Q2. Avi Wigderson**
James Allan	Frederic Green
Lise Getoor	Vikraman Arvind
Fernando C. N. Pereira	Eric Allender
Dan Roth	Sanjeev Arora
Thomas G. Dietterich	Umesh V. Vazirani
Q3. Christopher Manning	**Q4. W. Bruce Croft**
Eugene Charniak	Omar Alonso
Amy Weinberg	Dawn J. Lawrie
Kathleen McKeown	Dell Zhang
Nicholas Bambos	Michael S. Lew
Mark Liberman	Jesus Vilares Ferro

Table 2: Top-5 recommendations by ScholarSearch for sample queries, Q1-Q4.

4. RELATED WORK

The list-completion tasks in TREC and INEX address the similar-entity finding task in the general domain. The proceedings of these competitions discuss various systems that were designed to handle this task. In contrast to our problem, the input queries in these systems, include a query topic description with examples of entities. The participating systems need to extract the relation between the example entities and the topic description and propose entities that hold a similar relation with the topic description, as part of the answer. Similar expert finding was addressed by Balog, et al. on the TREC data using the relations a candidate expert has with other experts, documents and terms [5]. Hofmann, et al. considered the contextual factors such as organizational setup and combined them with content-based retrieval scores to find similar experts within an organization [15]. Although we could not find previous work on content-based similar-entity finding in academic disciplines, previous work exists for predicting researchers to collaborate with. Chen, et al. presented CollabSeer that uses the structure of the co-author network to predict research collaborators [8]. Xu, et al [21] use a two-layer network model that combines co-author network and researcher-concept network for making researcher recommendations. However, our approach targets the prediction of researchers with similar expertise profiles based on content they generate and not on their distance in the co-authorship graph. Several models also address the closely-related task of expert search/ranking given a topic query both in academic domains and enterprises. Typically, a document collection available in a domain is used to infer the expertise of an author based on the authorship information [2, 17, 13]. In some cases, the underlying connections between documents, researchers and other entities can be explored via graph-based models [19, 11].

5. CONCLUSIONS AND FUTURE WORK

In this paper, we formulated the researcher recommendation problem in academic environments. We discussed several techniques for representing expertise profiles based on the available evidence and proposed models for computing similarity between two profiles. We evaluated our proposed techniques on two publicly-available datasets and showed the viability and usability of researcher recommendation via our demo system, `ScholarSearch`. We are currently focusing on improving the accuracy as well as the response time of our recommendation system. To this end, we are exploring techniques for a more accurate representation for researcher profiles, not just in terms of the documents but including also the underlying academic network between researchers and metadata information such as university affiliations.

Acknowledgments: We acknowledge support from NSF (Grant Nos. 0845487, 0949891 and 0958143) and DTRA (Grant No. HDTRA1-09-1-0054) for this work.

6. REFERENCES

[1] P. Ahlgren and L. Grönqvist. Evaluation of retrieval effectiveness with incomplete relevance data: Theoretical and experimental comparison of three measures. *Inf. Process. Manage.*, 2008.

[2] K. Balog, L. Azzopardi, and M. de Rijke. Formal models for expert finding in enterprise corpora. In *SIGIR*, 2006.

[3] K. Balog, T. Bogers, L. Azzopardi, M. de Rijke, and A. van den Bosch. Broad expertise retrieval in sparse data environments. In *SIGIR*, 2007.

[4] K. Balog and M. de Rijke. Determining expert profiles (with an application to expert finding). In *IJCAI*, 2007.

[5] K. Balog and M. de Rijke. Finding similar experts. In *SIGIR*, 2007.

[6] C. M. Bishop. *Pattern Recognition and Machine Learning (Information Science and Statistics)*. 2007.

[7] D. M. Blei, A. Y. Ng, and M. I. Jordan. Latent dirichlet allocation. *J. Mach. Learn. Res.*, 2003.

[8] H.-H. Chen, L. Gou, X. Zhang, and C. L. Giles. Collabseer: a search engine for collaboration discovery. In *JCDL*, 2011.

[9] S. Das, C. L. Giles, P. Mitra, and C. Caragea. On identifying academic homepages for digital libraries. In *JCDL*, 2011.

[10] S. Das, P. Mitra, and C. L. Giles. Learning to rank homepages for researcher name queries. In *EOS Workshop at SIGIR*, 2011.

[11] S. Das, P. Mitra, and C. L. Giles. Ranking authors in digital libraries. In *JCDL*, 2011.

[12] G. Demartini, J. Gaugaz, and W. Nejdl. A vector space model for ranking entities and its application to expert search. In *ECIR*, 2009.

[13] H. Deng, I. King, and M. R. Lyu. Formal models for expert finding on dblp bibliography data. In *ICDM*, 2008.

[14] Q. He, J. Pei. D. Kifer, P. Mitra, and C. L. Giles. Context-aware citation recommendation. In *WWW*, 2010.

[15] K. Hofmann, K. Balog, T. Bogers, and M. de Rijke. Contextual factors for finding similar experts. *JASIST*, 2010.

[16] K. S. Jones, S. Walker, and S. E. Robertson. A probabilistic model of information retrieval: development and comparative experiments. *Inf. Process. Manage.*, 2000.

[17] D. Mimno and A. McCallum. Mining a digital library for influential authors. In *JCDL*, 2007.

[18] C. J. v. Rijsbergen. *The Geometry of Information Retrieval*. 2004.

[19] P. Serdyukov, H. Rode, and D. Hiemstra. Modeling multi-step relevance propagation for expert finding. In *CIKM*, 2008.

[20] J. Tang, J. Zhang, L. Yao, J. Li, L. Zhang, and Z. Su. Arnetminer: extraction and mining of academic social networks. In *KDD*, 2008.

[21] Y. Xu, J. Hao, R. Y. Lau, J. Ma, W. Xu, and D. Zhao. A personalized researcher recommendation approach in academic contexts: Combining social networks and semantic concepts analysis. In *PACIS*, 2010.

An Analysis of the Named Entity Recognition Problem in Digital Library Metadata

Nuno Freire[1,2], José Borbinha[1] and Pável Calado[1]
[1]IST/INESC-ID, Portugal
[2]The European Library, National Library of the Netherlands, Netherlands
{nuno.freire,jlb,pavel.calado}@ist.utl.pt

ABSTRACT

Information resources in digital libraries are usually described, along with their context, by structured data records, commonly referred as *metadata*. Those records often contain unstructured information in natural language text, since they typically follow a data model which defines generic semantics for its data elements, or includes data elements modeled to contain free text. The information contained in these data elements, although machine readable, resides in unstructured natural language texts that are difficult to process by computers. This paper addresses a particular task of information extraction, typically called named entity recognition, which deals with the references to entities made by names occurring in the texts. This paper presents the results of a study of how the named entity recognition problem manifests itself in digital library metadata. In particular, we present the main differences between performing named entity recognition in natural language and in the text within metadata. The paper finalizes with a novel approach for named entity recognition in metadata.

Categories and Subject Descriptors

E.1 [Data] Data Structures – Records; H.3.7. [Digital Libraries]; I.2.7 [Artificial Intelligence]: Natural Language Processing - Text analysis; I.7.m [Document and Text Processing]:[Miscellaneous]

Keywords

Information extraction, entity recognition, metadata, digital libraries.

1. INTRODUCTION

A wide range of potentially usable business information exists in unstructured forms. Although this information is machine readable, it consists of natural language texts (it was estimated that 80% to 90% of business information may exist in those unstructured forms[1]).

As businesses become more data oriented, much interest has arisen in these unstructured sources of information. This interest gave origin to the research field of *information extraction*, which looks for automatic ways to create structured data from unstructured data sources [1]. An information extraction process can be characterized by an intention of selectively structure and combine data that is found in text, either explicitly stated or implied. The final output of the process will vary according to the purpose, but typically it consists in semantically richer data, which follows a structured data model, and on which more effective computation methods can be applied.

Information resources in digital libraries are usually described, along with their context, by structured data records. These data, which is commonly referred in the digital library community as *metadata*, may serve many purposes, and the most relevant being resource discovery. Those records often contain unstructured information in natural language text, which might be useful to judge about the relevance of the resource. The natural hypothesis is if that information can be represented with finer grained semantics, then the quality of the digital libraries is expected to improve.

This paper addresses a particular task of information extraction, typically called named entity recognition (NER), which deals with the textual references to entities, that is, when they are referred to by means of names occurring in natural language expressions, instead of structured data. This task deals with the particular problem of how to locate these references in the data set and how to classify them according their entity type [2].

In previous work, we have observed that current entity recognition and resolution techniques underperform in text within metadata [4][5]. In this paper we present a study on how named entities appear in metadata records, and on how structured metadata can be exploited to support the NER task, in order to improve the quality of the results.

The paper will follow with an introduction to NER and related work in Section 2. The data sets, which were the object of this study, are presented in Section 3, and the main results of the study are described in Section 4. The final section presents the conclusions of the study, proposes a novel approach for NER in metadata, and presents the future work.

2. PROBLEM AND RELATED WORK

The NER task refers to locating atomic elements in text and classifying them into predefined categories such as the names of persons, organizations, locations, expressions of time, quantities, etc. [2].

Initial approaches were based on manually constructed finite state patterns and/or collections of entity names [2]. However, named entity recognition soon was considered as a typical scenario for the application of machine learning algorithms, because of the potential availability of many types of evidence, which form the algorithm's input variables [3]. Current solutions can reach an F-measure accuracy around 90% in well-formed text, thus a near-human performance [2].

[1]http://clarabridge.com/default.aspx?tabid=137&ModuleID=635&ArticleID=551

JCDL'12, June 10–14, 2012, Washington, DC, USA.

However, previous work suggested that current NER techniques underperform when applied to unstructured texts existing within digital library metadata records [4][5]. Most research on NER has focused mainly on natural language processing, involving text tokenization, part-of-speech classification, word sequence analysis, etc. These techniques are, therefore, language specific and dependent of the lexical evidence given by the natural language text.

We are not aware of any studies specifically addressing the NER task in digital library metadata. The most similar scenarios, we are aware of, have researched information extraction techniques within relational database management systems, in order to improve the use of unstructured text inside relational databases [6]. This approach also was followed in [7], which addresses information extraction in a similar type of data with lack of lexical evidence, but applies simultaneously named entity recognition and entity resolution (the recognized names are resolved in a data set of known entities). The contribution of this work for advancing in NER techniques in this type of data is somewhat limited, since it was mainly focused on the recognition of entities that are present in the source data set.

3. STUDIED DATA SETS

Our study was performed on the data sets from Europeana[2], which consist in descriptions of digital resources of cultural interest. These data sets follow a data model using mainly Dublin Core elements, and named entities appear in data elements such as titles, textual descriptions, tables of contents, subjects, contributors and publication.

These data sets originate from several European data providers from the cultural sector, such as libraries, museums and archives. Several European languages are present, even within the description of the same resource. For example when the resource being described is of a different language than the one used to create its description. The data providers follow different practices for describing the digital resources. This environment makes the data sets to be highly heterogeneous in terms of data structure.[3]

We have studied two subsets of metadata from Europeana. The first subset is focused on the entity type location, which has been the focus of our previous work [5] on the recognition and resolution of this particular entity type. In this data set all references to locations have been manually annotated.

A second subset of the Europeana data sets has been manually annotated specifically for studying the general problem of NER in metadata. In this subset, we studied the three entity types on which most NER research has been focused, and which are commonly known as *enamex* [8]: person, location and organization.

4. STUDY RESULTS

Our main observation from the study of the data sets is that this kind of data typically presents different characteristics from well-formed text, which has been the focus of previous research in information extraction.

When applied to metadata without adaptations, the results of applying NER techniques designed for well-formed text will be negatively affected by three main limiting factors:

- The text within metadata may not contain enough lexical evidence to support the recognition of entities.
- The NER techniques designed for well-formed text can only be applied to metadata by first extracting the text, and then process it without taking in consideration the semantic context provided by the metadata record structure.
- If NER techniques use only the evidence available within the text, they will not take in consideration relevant evidence available in other structured data elements within the metadata record.

In the rest of this section we will present the results of our study that support our observations on each of these three limiting factors.

4.1 Availability of Lexical Evidence

In order to measure the extent to which the lack of lexical evidence influences the results of recognizing entities in digital libraries' metadata records, we have setup a small experiment on the recognition of the entity type *location*. We compared the results of two techniques that use lexical evidence for recognizing the location names, against a simple NER technique based on look ups of names in a geographical gazetteer.

The first technique tested was the implementation, provided by the OpenNLP package, of conditional maximum entropy models [9]. The second technique was the Stanford Named Entity Recognizer based on conditional random fields [10]. For both cases, we used the respective predictive models trained on the CoNLL 2003 training data [11]. The geographic gazetteer look up technique was developed by us for the purposes of this study. It was designed to perform a simple matching of the location names in the texts without using any lexical evidence, so that we could analyse to what extent the lack of lexical evidence affects the quality of the NER results.

The experiment was conducted by processing, with the three techniques, a collection of records from the Europeana data sets. The techniques were evaluated according to the *exact-match* method, which has been used in several named entity recognition evaluation tasks [11]. In the *exact-match* method, a named entity is only considered correctly recognized if it is exactly located as in the manual annotation. Recognition of only part of the name, or with words that are not part of the name, is not considered correct. In combination with the *exact-match* method, we used the metrics of precision[4], recall[5] and F_1-measure[6].

This collection is a subset of the evaluation collection described in [5], which contains 752 metadata records with a total of 2823 annotated location names. For this study, we only used records in the languages supported by the NER techniques we tested. Therefore, it was restricted to 372 records in English, Spanish, Dutch and German.

The results are presented in Table 1. Both techniques that used lexical evidence achieved higher precision than the gazetteer look up technique, but performed much lower in terms of recall, resulting in considerably lower F_1-measure, with less 0.20 for the Maximum Entropy ($P<0.001$), and less 0.12 for the CRF ($P<0.01$).

[2] http://www.europeana.eu/

[3] http://dublincore.org/

[4] The percentage of correctly identified named entities in all named entities found

[5] The percentage of named entities found compared to all existing named entities

[6] The weighted harmonic mean of precision and recall (equal weights for recall and precision)

Table 1. Location recognition results on a collection of 372 metadata records

Technique	Precision	Recall	F1-measure
Conditional Maximum Entropy	0.95	0.29	0.45
Conditional Random Fields	0.95	0.38	0.53
Geographic Gazetteer Lookup	0.92	0.53	0.65

These results support our hypothesis that the lack of lexical evidence in the text of metadata elements negatively affects the results of NER techniques. It can also be observed that it mainly affects recall.

4.2 Semantic Context of the Metadata Elements

Each metadata element provides its own semantic context to the text contained within, and this context influences the types of entities that are referenced.

To investigate this aspect we have analysed the occurrence of referenced entity types found in the Europeana data sets. These data sets contain several different data elements with different associated semantics, allowing us to study the extent to which the semantic context influences the entity types of named entities. In this study we addressed the three entity types on which most NER research has been focused: person, location and organization.

This collection was created by randomly selecting records in the English language. The selection process was done in two steps: first, all records in the English language were selected from all Europeana data providers; and second, a random selection of records was performed, balancing the number of records chosen across different providers.

The evaluation data set was manually annotated. In very few cases, the manual annotation was uncertain, because the metadata records may not contain enough information to support a correct annotation. For example, some sentences with named entities were too small and no other information was available in the record to support a decision on the annotation of the named entities to their entity type. Annotation was performed as follows:

- Named entities were annotated with their entity type: *person*, *location* or *organization*;
- If the annotator was unsure of the entity type of a named entity, he would annotate it as *unknown*. These annotations were not considered for our study.

In total, the evaluation data set consisted in 120 records containing in its elements 584 references to persons, 457 to locations and 153 to organizations.

For each element, the distribution of references to different entity types was calculated, and the results can be visualized in Table 2. We can observe that the elements *title* and *description* have a similar distribution of entity types, and notice that persons were the most frequently found entity type. The element *subject* and *table of contents* also share a similar distribution, but with a higher frequency for locations. All other elements presented distinct distributions. In the *creator* element, only persons and organizations were found, in the element *coverage* exclusively locations were found, and in element *publisher* mostly organizations and locations were found. Such difference in distributions of entity types, if made available as evidence to the NER algorithm, can support the recognition of a name, and the disambiguation of the entity type. For example, if the name

Table 2. Distribution of textual references to entities by entity type across data elements of the Europeana data set

Element	Locations	Persons	Organiz.	Total
Title	86 (34%)	142 (56%)	26 (10%)	254
Creator/Contributor	0 (0%)	156 (85%)	27 (15%)	183
Subject	136 (64%)	60 (28%)	16 (8%)	212
Coverage	79 (100%)	0 (0%)	0 (0%)	79
Publisher	52 (44%)	17 (15%)	48 (41%)	117
Table of Contents	29 (69%)	10 (24%)	3 (7%)	42
Description	75 (24%)	199 (65%)	33 (11%)	307
Total	**457**	**584**	**153**	**1194**

Washington is found, although it can be of type *person* of *place*, if found in a *coverage* element it likely refers to a place, while if found in a *creator* element, it likely refers to a *person*.

4.3 Evidence from Structured Data within the Metadata Records

Application of the NER techniques designed for well-formed text in metadata, does not take advantage of the semantic context provided by the metadata record structure.

Metadata records however, have available not only the text of the data elements, but also other data elements which may be structured. These structured elements may be exploited during the NER process, allowing the use of semantic information to support a correct recognition of the named entities.

An example of one such case was observed in our study of the named entities of the entity type *location* within the Europeana data sets (in the data sets described in Section 4.1). In these data sets, a structured data element contained structured data about the provenance of the metadata: the country code of the institution from where the data record originated.

In order to study the possible influence of making the country of provenance available to the NER algorithms, we have analysed the relationship between the country of provenance of the data and the correct resolution for the names of locations. In this data set, the named locations are annotated also with their correct resolution in a geographic gazetteer, allowing us know the country corresponding to each named location.

In the data sets, we encountered 54% of the references that matched the country of origin of the data, 9% matched a neighbour country, and 37% were from the rest of the world. We tested the hypothesis that the probability of a named location to be from the country of provenance of the data, is higher that the probability of being located in the rest of the world. The differences in the percentages were found to be statistically significant, with $P<0.01$.

Several different metadata models are used in digital libraries, therefore the availability of structured data for use in NER will vary in each case. But these results support that the structured data may be used to improve the NER results.

Table 3. **Relationship statistics between named locations and the country of provenance of the metadata in the Europeana data set**

Total named locations	In the same country	In a neighbour country	Rest of the World
2823	1524 (54%)	255 (9%)	1044 (37%)

5. CONCLUSIONS AND FUTURE WORK

Based on the results of the study presented in the previous Section, we believe that an approach for NER on digital libraries' metadata should follow the following general guidelines:

- The data record should be available throughout the entire NER process. If the processing exploits the data record, instead of just the text within, more evidence will be available, allowing better recognition of the named entities.
- The approach must capture lexical and non-lexical evidence from the text. This would allow process to handle cases of data containing well-formed text, as well as simple textual expressions.
- The approach must be adaptable. Different data sets will present different textual patterns and languages, therefore the evidence to support the recognition and resolution of entities will vary considerably in different data sets. Supervised machine learning based approaches are the state of the art in both entity recognition and resolution in well formed, and the adaptability of these algorithms is just as relevant for the large variety of metadata models in use.

Based on this analysis, we believe that improvements for NER in metadata can be achieved over using NER algorithms for well-formed text. The results of this study provide evidence which motivate the investigation of adaptations to the state of the art NER techniques, and in the methods of their application in metadata.

Our proposal for a general NER process for metadata is depicted in **Error! Reference source not found.**. The first design decision of this process is to start by having as input a metadata record, instead of a data element or the text previously extracted from a data element or record. This allows the process to have the structured record available throughout the entire process, for providing evidence.

The first task of the process consists in selecting the target data elements where entity names are to be recognized and resolved. It is then followed by a task of basic text processing, in order to transform the text within the data elements into a sequence of tokens (words, punctuation marks, numbers, etc.).

In the third task, the text tokens are analyzed in order to extract any possible evidence that may support the recognition of the entities names. Typically, this task includes lexical analysis of sentences (e.g. part-of-speech tagging), analysis of words features (e.g. capitalization), checking the existence of the tokens in collections of entity names, textual patterns detection, etc. The data element itself may provide evidence as well, since it provides a semantic context for the interpretation of the text. Also extra evidence can be extracted from other structured elements on the same record.

The following, and final task, is the recognition of names of entities. It consists in reasoning on the sequence of tokens and the associated evidence gathered in the previous task. Its outcome consists in the recognized names and their respective positions in the source text. We advocate that this task needs to be performed by machine learning based techniques, in order to have an approach that is adaptable to different data sets and data elements with different evidences and textual patterns.

In future work we will conduct experiments with implementations of this proposed NER process. These experiments will be designed to allow the analysis of the performance of state of the art techniques in metadata, and evaluate the use of alternative methods that may provide improvements.

6. REFERENCES

[1] S. Sarawagi, "Information Extraction", Found. Trends databases, vol. 1, pp. 261-377, Now Publishers Inc., 2008.

[2] D. Nadeau, S. Sekine, "A survey of named entity recognition and classification", Linguisticae Investigationes, volume. 30, number 1, pp. 3-26, John Benjamins Publishing Company, 2007.

[3] A. McCallum, D. Freitag, and F. C. N. Pereira, "Maximum Entropy Markov Models for Information Extraction and Segmentation", 17th International Conference on Machine Learning, pp. 591-598, 2000.

[4] B. Martins, J. Borbinha, G. Pedrosa, J. Gil, N. Freire, "Geographically-aware information retrieval for collections of digitized historical maps". 4th ACM Workshop on Geographical information Retrieval, 2007.

[5] N. Freire, J. Borbinha, P. Calado, B. Martins, "A Metadata Geoparsing System for Place Name Recognition and Resolution in Metadata Records", ACM/IEEE Joint Conference on Digital Libraries, 2011.

[6] P. King, A. Poulovassilis, "Enhancing database technology to better manage and exploit Partially Structured Data". Research Report pjhk/ap,11/2000, University of London, 2000. Available at http://www.dcs.bbk.ac.uk/research/techreps/2000/bbkcs-00-14.pdf.

[7] D. Williams: Combining Data Integration and Information Extraction. PhD thesis, University of London (2008)

[8] R. Grishman, B. Sundheim, "Message Understanding Conference - 6: A Brief History", International Conference on Computational Linguistics, 1996.

[9] J. Goodman, "Sequential Conditional Generalized Iterative Scaling", 40th Annual Meeting of the Association for Computational Linguistics, pp. 9-16, 2002.

[10] J. R. Finkel, T. Grenager, C. Manning, "Incorporating Non-local Information into Information Extraction Systems by Gibbs Sampling", 43nd Annual Meeting of the Association for Computational Linguistics (ACL 2005), pp. 363-370, 2005.

[11] E. Sang, F. Meulder, "Introduction to the CoNLL-2003 shared task: language-independent named entity recognition," seventh conference on Natural language learning at HLT-NAACL 2003 - Volume 4, pp. 142-147, 2003.

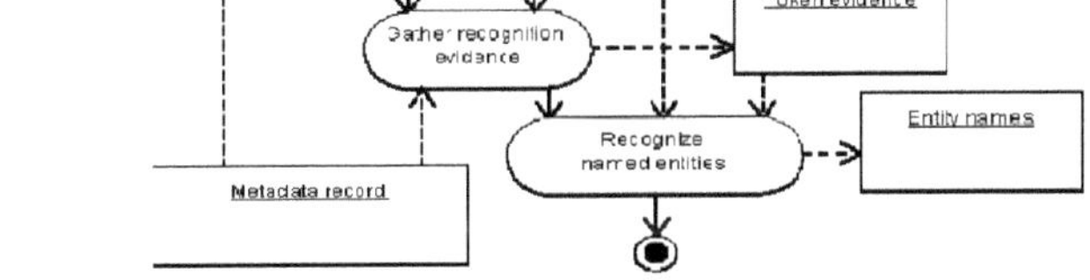

Figure 1. A general process for named entity recognition in metadata

Active Associative Sampling for Author Name Disambiguation

Anderson A. Ferreira[1,2] Rodrigo Silva[1] Marcos André Gonçalves[1]
Adriano Veloso[1] Alberto H. F. Laender[1]

[1]Departamento de Ciência da Computação
Universidade Federal de Minas Gerais
31270-901 Belo Horizonte, Brazil

[2]Departamento de Computação
Universidade Federal de Ouro Preto
35400-000 Ouro Preto, Brazil

{ferreira, rmsilva, mgoncalv, adrianov, laender}@dcc.ufmg.br

ABSTRACT

One of the hardest problems faced by current scholarly digital libraries is author name ambiguity. This problem occurs when, in a set of citation records, there are records of a same author under distinct names, or citation records belonging to distinct authors with similar names. Among the several proposed methods, the most effective ones seem to be based on the direct assignment of the records to their respective authors by means of the application of supervised machine learning techniques. The effectiveness of such methods is usually directly correlated with the amount of supervised training data available. However, the acquisition of training examples requires skilled human annotators to manually label references. Aiming to reduce the set of examples needed to produce the training data, in this paper we propose a new active sampling strategy based on association rules for the author name disambiguation task. We compare our strategy with state-of-the-art supervised baselines that use the complete labeled training dataset and other active methods and show that very competitive results in terms of disambiguation effectiveness can be obtained with reductions in the training set of up to 71%.

Categories and Subject Descriptors

H.3.3 [**Information Search and Retrieval**]: Information Retrieval; I.5.2 [**Pattern Recognition**]: Classifier design and evaluation

General Terms

Algorithms, Experimentation

Keywords

Name Disambiguation, Bibliographic Citations, Active Sampling

1. INTRODUCTION

Author name ambiguity is a problem which occurs when a set of citation records[1] contains ambiguous author names, i.e., the same author may appear under distinct names, or distinct authors may have similar names. This is one of the hardest problems faced by current scholarly digital libraries (DLs), such as DBLP[2], CiteSeer[3], MEDLINE[4] and BDBComp[5]. The content of such DLs may list millions of bibliographic citation records and have become an important source of information for academic communities since they allow the search and discovery of relevant publications in a centralized way. Moreover, studies about the DL content can lead to interesting results such as coverage of topics, tendencies, quality and impact of publications of a specific sub-community or individuals, patterns of collaboration in social networks, etc. These types of analysis and information, which are used, for example, by funding agencies for decisions on grants and for individual's promotions, presuppose *high quality content* [22, 23]. Obviously, author name ambiguity decreases such quality and the reliability on the information that can be extracted from those repositories. Not to mention the decrease in effectiveness of information services such as searching and browsing.

To resolve such problem in a scalable and automated way, an automatic *author name disambiguation* procedure may be applied to the DL content. More formally, the author name disambiguation procedure may be formulated as follows. Let $C = \{c_1, c_2, ..., c_k\}$ be a collection of *citation records*. Each citation record c_i has a list of *attributes* which includes at least author names, work title and publication venue title. With each attribute in a citation is associated a specific value, which may be composed of several *elements*. In case of the attribute "author names", an element corresponds to the name of a single unique author. Each author name element is a *reference* r_j to an author. In case of the other attributes, an element corresponds to a word/term. The objective of the disambiguation task is to produce a disambiguation function that is used to partition the set of references to authors $\{r_1, r_2, \ldots, r_m\}$ into n sets $\{a_1, a_2, \ldots, a_n\}$, so that each partition a_i contains (all and ideally only all) the references to a same author. We consider that each reference r to an author extracted from a citation record c contains

[1]Here understood as a set of bibliographic attributes, such as author names, work title and publication venue title, of a particular publication.
[2]http://dblp.uni-trier.de
[3]http://citeseer.ist.psu.edu
[4]http://medline.cos.com/
[5]http://www.lbd.dcc.ufmg.br/bdbcomp

at least the following attributes: author name, coauthor names that contain the other references extracted from the record c, work title and publication venue title of the citation c.

Several automatic disambiguation methods have been proposed in the last years [15, 16, 17, 38, 2, 18, 28, 6, 3, 19, 34, 35, 45, 21, 30, 32, 40, 5, 12, 24, 11, 36, 25, 41]. These existing methods usually attempt to either group references to the same author using some type of similarity between them or try to directly assign the references to their respective authors. Among all those methods the most effective ones seem to be based on direct assignment by means of the application of supervised machine learning techniques. These methods receive as input a data set called the *training data* (denoted as $\mathcal{D}$) which consists of examples or, more specifically, references for which the correct authorship is known. Each example is composed of a set of m features $\{f_1, f_2, \ldots, f_m\}$ along with a special variable called the *author*. This *author* variable draws its value from a discrete set of labels $\{a_1, a_2, \ldots, a_n\}$, where each label uniquely identifies an author. The training data is used to produce a learned disambiguation function that relates the features in the training data to the correct author. The *test set* (denoted as $\mathcal{T}$) for the disambiguation problem consists of a set of references for which the features are known while the correct author is unknown. The learned disambiguation function, which is a function from $\{f_1, f_2, \ldots, f_m\}$ to $\{a_1, a_2, \ldots, a_n\}$, is used to predict the correct author of references in a new unseen test set.

The effectiveness of the learned disambiguation functions is usually directly correlated with the amount of supervised training data available. However, the acquisition of training examples requires skilled human annotators to manually label references. Annotators may face hard-to-label references with highly ambiguous author names. The cost associated with this labeling process thus may render vast amounts of examples unfeasible. Not considering the fact that new entries with new ambiguous authors are always being inserted into the DL repositories. This leads to the need for a continuous labeling process in order to guarantee the effectiveness of the method.

Active learning techniques have been given much attention lately to help with the labeling effort problem [9, 33]. Such techniques are used to actively sample an unlabeled dataset to select instances that maximize the effectiveness of learned functions. By carefully selecting and labeling examples, it may be possible to use a small training set and yet achieve highly effective learned functions minimizing the labeling effort. The intuition behind active learning is that the selected examples are representative of the collection and more informative to the learning algorithm. By using only a highly informative examples, there may be a reduction of noise and uncertainty in the learning process. Moreover, in the specific case of continuous update of the DL, an active method may also help to indicate which new examples need to be labeled, reducing even further the effort.

In this paper, we propose a new active sampling strategy based on association rules for the author name disambiguation task. In a previous work [12, 41], we have shown that disambiguating author names using demand-driven association rules has been shown to provide state-of-the-art results. Our proposed strategy uses association rules to actively select references from an unlabeled dataset based on how many inference rules are generated for each reference. At each step, a new reference is chosen for labeling as the most dissimilar with respect to the already selected references, with the goal of increasing the diversity and representativeness. Our strategy chooses from the unlabeled dataset the reference r_i that generates the smallest number of rules when considering the "projection" (i.e., the selection of examples from the training set that have feature-values in common with r_i) of the current selected training set with respect to the features of r_i. The more dissimilar the candidate reference, fewer the rules generated for it, meaning that few already labeled examples in the projected training set share common feature-values with the candidate. This process is repeated until the algorithm converges, which happens when an already selected reference is selected again, i.e., there is no more information useful for generating rules from any other reference in the unlabeled dataset.

To demonstrate the effectiveness of our strategy, we compare it with supervised baselines that use the complete labeled training dataset based on support vector machines (SVMs), naïves Bayes, as well as a state-of-the-art associative disambiguator [41]. We also compare our proposed method with another SVM-based active learning method. Experimental results show that very competitive results in terms of disambiguation effectiveness can be obtained in all cases with reductions in the training set of up to 71%.

The remaining sections of this article are organized as follows. In Section 2 we discuss related work. In Section 3 we present our strategy to actively select examples to learn a disambiguation function as well as our main disambiguation method. In Section 4 we evaluate our strategy. Finally, in Section 5 we present our conclusions and future work.

2. RELATED WORK

2.1 Author Name Disambiguation

Automatic name disambiguation methods proposed in the literature adopt solutions that may be classified according to the main type of exploited approach: *author grouping* [17, 38, 18, 28, 3, 6, 19, 21, 29, 34, 35, 45, 30, 39, 40, 5, 12, 11], which tries to group the references to the same author using some type of similarity among reference attributes, or *author assignment* [15, 16, 2, 12, 36, 41], which aims at directly assigning the references to their respective authors.

Author grouping methods apply a similarity function to the attributes of the references to authors (or group of references) in order to decide whether to group the corresponding references using a clustering technique. The similarity function may be predefined (based on existing ones and depending on the type of the attribute) [17, 3, 29, 34, 5], learned using a supervised machine learning technique [38, 18, 6, 39, 40, 25], or extracted from the relationships among authors and coauthors, usually represented as a graph [28, 24, 11]. The defined similarity function is then used along with some clustering technique to group references of a same author, trying to maximize intra and minimize inter-cluster similarities, respectively.

Author assignment methods directly assign each reference to a given author by constructing a model that represents the author (for instance, the probabilities of an author publishing an article with other (co-)authors, in a given publication venue and using a list of specific terms in the work title) using either a supervised classification technique [15, 12, 41] or a model-based clustering technique [16, 2, 36].

In this work, we exploit an associative technique that actively samples an unlabeled dataset to select examples to compose the training data. These examples are used by an author assignment method [41] that produces rules associating features to individual authors, being also able to detecting novel authors and exploit reliable predictions for self-training. In experiments performed in [41], this technique was able to outperform all baselines delivering state-of-the-art performance in the disambiguation task.

2.2 Active Learning

Active Learning strategies have been largely used mainly in classification tasks such as document classification [37] and learning to rank [46, 8, 9, 26] but to the best of our knowledge it has never been applied to author name disambiguation with the explicit goal of reducing the need for training.

The closest work to ours are [18] and [44]. In [18], Huang et al. present a framework for solving the name ambiguity problem in which a blocking method is first applied to create blocks of references to authors with similar names. Next DBSCAN, a density-based clustering method [10], is used for clustering references by author. For each block, the distance metric between pairs of citations used by DBSCAN is calculated by a trained online active support vector machine algorithm (LaSVM), which yields, according to the authors, a simpler and faster model than the standard support vector machines (SVMs). Although an online active SVM is used, the goal in that work is not to reduce the training set, but to improve the scalability of the method proposed by the authors. In fact, they use all of the training data in their experiments. In any case, we compare our solution to the one described in that work.

The second work that has somewhat exploited active selection, again with a very different goal, aims at improving the disambiguation performance by maximizing the utility of the user's corrections [44]. It works in a interactive mode actively choosing only a few potentially erroneous disambiguated results, *after a disambiguation process has been run*, in order to ask the user for corrections, instead of passively waiting for user inputs. The active selection aims to minimize the number of interactions needed to maximize effectiveness. Notice that in order to obtain good results, the authors make use of additional information such as affiliation, references, etc., that is usually not available in many cases when we have only the minimal information of a citation (i.e., author and coauthor names, publication and venue titles).

A related effort, which does not rely in active sampling, but tries to reduce the need for training data using self-training techniques is presented in [12]. It presents superior results when compared to unsupervised methods, but it still not able to completely beat the best supervised methods. As we shall see in our experimental evaluation, our proposed active selection method along with the associative disambiguator is able to produce results competitive with the state-of-the-art, while producing significant reductions in labeling effort.

Finally, when compared to other active learning strategies our solution has interesting properties not exhibited by many similar solutions. Among them, we do not need an initial labeled set as many methods need and select all samples from the unlabeled set. Furthermore, there is no need to empirically determine (using the validation or test sets) how many iterations are required to obtain competitive results, since the selection process naturally converges (see Section 3).

3. ACTIVE SAMPLING FOR NAME DISAMBIGUATION

In this section, we describe our selective sampling strategy in order to deal with the high cost of labeling large amounts of examples to produce the training data (referred to as $\mathcal{D}$). $\mathcal{D}$ is used by the associative name disambiguator to produce a learned disambiguation function to disambiguate the references. In the following, we describe SLAND (Self-training Lazy Associative Name Disambiguator) [12, 41], our lazy associative author name disambiguation method, and next our selective sampling strategy to produce the reduced training data.

3.1 Associative Author Name Disambiguation

SLAND receives as input the *training data* $\mathcal{D}$, which consists of a set of records of the form <r,a>, where r is a reference to an author (represented as a list of m feature-values or $\{f_1, f_2, \ldots, f_m\}$) and a is a label that identifies the correct author of r. It exploits the fact that, frequently, there are strong associations between features $\{f_1, f_2, \ldots, f_m\}$ and specific authors $\{a_1, a_2, \ldots, a_n\}$. Such associations are uncovered from $\mathcal{D}$, producing a disambiguation function $\{f_1, f_2, \ldots, f_m\} \rightarrow \{a_1, a_2, \ldots, a_n\}$ [43]. Typically, these associations are expressed using rules[6] of the form $\mathcal{X} \rightarrow a_1$, $\mathcal{X} \rightarrow a_2$, ..., $\mathcal{X} \rightarrow a_n$, where $\mathcal{X} \subseteq \{f_1, f_2, \ldots, f_m\}$. In the following discussion, we denote as $\mathcal{R}$ an arbitrary rule set. Similarly, we denote as $\mathcal{R}_{a_i}$ a subset of $\mathcal{R}$ that is composed of rules of the form $\mathcal{X} \rightarrow a_i$ (i.e., rules predicting author a_i). A rule $\mathcal{X} \rightarrow a_i$ is said to match a record x if $\mathcal{X} \subseteq x$ (i.e., x contains all features in $\mathcal{X}$) and this rule is included in $\mathcal{R}^x_{a_i}$. That is, $\mathcal{R}^x_{a_i}$ is composed of rules predicting author a_i and matching record x. Obviously, $\mathcal{R}^x_{a_i} \subseteq \mathcal{R}_{a_i} \subseteq \mathcal{R}$. The *test set* (referred to as $\mathcal{T}$) consists of records <r,?> for which only the feature-values of the reference r to an author are known, while the author of r is unknown. Disambiguation functions obtained from $\mathcal{D}$ are used to estimate the correct authors of such records in $\mathcal{T}$.

Demand-Driven Rule Extraction

Rule extraction is a major issue for associative name disambiguation, since the number of extracted rules may increase exponentially with the number of features in the training data. Our method, on the other hand, extracts rules from the training data on a demand-driven fashion [42], at disambiguation time. The method projects the search space for rules according to information in records in $\mathcal{T}$, allowing rule extraction with efficiency. In other words, our method projects/filters the training data according to the features in record $x \in \mathcal{T}$, and extracts rules from this projected training data, which is denoted as $\mathcal{D}^x$. This ensures that only rules that carry information about record x are extracted from the training data, drastically bounding the number of possible rules.

Prediction

Naturally, there is a total ordering among rules, in the sense that some rules show stronger associations than others. A widely used statistic, called confidence [1] (denoted as $\theta(\mathcal{X} \rightarrow a_i)$), measures the strength of the association between $\mathcal{X}$ and a_i. Put simple, the confidence of the rule $\mathcal{X} \rightarrow a_i$ is given by the conditional probability of a_i being the author of record x, given that $\mathcal{X} \subseteq x$.

Using a single rule to predict the correct author may be prone to error. Instead, the probability (or likelihood) of a_i being the author of record x is estimated by combining rules in $\mathcal{R}^x_{a_i}$. More specifically, $\mathcal{R}^x_{a_i}$ is interpreted as a poll, in which each rule $\mathcal{X} \rightarrow a_i \in \mathcal{R}^x_{a_i}$ is a vote given by features in $\mathcal{X}$ for author a_i. The weight of a vote $\mathcal{X} \rightarrow a_i$ depends on the strength of the association between $\mathcal{X}$ and a_i, which is given by $\theta(\mathcal{X} \rightarrow a_i)$. The process of estimating the probability of a_i being the author of record x starts by summing weighted votes for a_i and then averaging the obtained value by the total number of votes for a_i, as expressed by the score function $s(a_i, x)$ shown in Equation 1 (where $r_j \subseteq \mathcal{R}^x_{a_i}$ and $|\mathcal{R}^x_{a_i}|$ is the number of rules in $\mathcal{R}^x_{a_i}$). Thus, $s(a_i, x)$ gives the average confidence of the rules in $\mathcal{R}^x_{a_i}$ (obviously, the higher the confidence, the stronger the evidence of authorship).

[6]These rules can be efficiently extracted from $\mathcal{D}$ using the strategy proposed in [43].

$$s(a_i, x) = \frac{\sum_{j=1}^{|\mathcal{R}^x_{a_i}|} \theta(r_j)}{|\mathcal{R}^x_{a_i}|} \quad (1)$$

The estimated probability of a_i being the author of record x, denoted as $\hat{p}(a_i|x)$, is simply obtained by normalizing $s(a_i, x)$, as shown in Equation (2). A higher value of $\hat{p}(a_i|x)$ indicates a higher likelihood of a_i being the author of x. The author associated with the highest likelihood is finally predicted as the author of record x.

$$\hat{p}(a_i|x) = \frac{s(a_i, x)}{\sum_{j=1}^{n} s(a_j, x)} \quad (2)$$

Exploiting Reliable Predictions

Additional examples may be obtained from the predictions performed using the disambiguation function. In this case, reliable predictions are regarded as correct ones and, thus, they can be safely included in the training examples. Next we define the *reliability* of a prediction.

Given an arbitrary record $x \in \mathcal{T}$, and the two most likely authors for x, a_i and a_j, we denote as $\Delta(x)$ the reliability of predicting a_i, as shown in Equation 3.

$$\Delta(x) = \frac{\hat{p}(a_i|x)}{\hat{p}(a_j|x)} \quad (3)$$

The idea is to only predict a_i if $\Delta(x) \geq \Delta_{min}$, where Δ_{min} is a threshold that indicates the minimum reliability necessary to regard the corresponding prediction as correct, and, therefore, to include it into the training data $\mathcal{D}$. An appropriate value for Δ_{min} can be obtained by performing cross-validation [14], which is a way to predict the fit of a disambiguation function to a hypothetical validation set.

Naturally, some predictions are not enough reliable for certain values of Δ_{min}. An alternative is to abstain from such doubtful predictions. As new examples are included into $\mathcal{D}$ (i.e., the reliable predictions), new evidence may be exploited, hopefully increasing the reliability of the predictions that were previously abstained. To optimize the usage of reliable predictions, we place records in a queue, so that records associated with reliable predictions are considered first. The process works as follows. Initially, records in the test set are randomly placed in the queue. If the author of the record that is located in the beginning of the queue can be reliably predicted, then the prediction is performed, the record is removed from the queue and included into $\mathcal{D}$ as a new example. Otherwise, if the prediction is not reliable, the corresponding record is simply placed in the end of the queue and will be only processed after all other records. The process continues performing more reliable predictions first, until no more reliable predictions are possible. The remaining records in $\mathcal{T}$ (for which only doubtful predictions are possible) are then processed normally, but the corresponding predictions are not included into $\mathcal{D}$. The process stops after all records in $\mathcal{T}$ are processed.

Detecting Novel Authors

We use the lack of rules supporting any already seen author (i.e., authors that are present in some record in $\mathcal{D}$) as evidence indicating the appearance of an unseen author. The number of rules that is necessary to consider an author as an already seen one is controlled by a parameter, γ_{min}. Specifically, for a record $x \in \mathcal{T}$, if the number of rules extracted from $\mathcal{D}^x$ (which is denoted as $\gamma(x)$) is smaller than γ_{min} (i.e., $\gamma(x) < \gamma_{min}$), then the author of x is considered as a new/unseen author and a new label a_k is created to identify such author. Further, this prediction is considered as a new example and included into $\mathcal{D}$. An appropriate value for γ_{min} can be obtained by performing cross-validation.

3.2 Rule-Based Active Sampling

In this section we present a novel algorithm referred to as SSAND (Selective Sampling for Author Name Disambiguation), which relies on an effective selective sampling strategy in order to deal with the high cost of labeling large amounts of examples. The key idea of SSAND is that it may provide results as effective as SLAND by carefully choosing a much smaller set of training examples from which it learns the disambiguation functions. As we will see in detail below, SSAND takes each unlabeled reference in turn, obtaining its projection from the current reduced training set and generating the rules that would be used to predict the author of such reference. After it has the rules for all unlabeled references, it chooses the one that generated the fewest rules, obtaining its label and inserting it into the current selected and labeled training set. The goal is to label as few instances as possible, while providing equal or even improved ranking performance.

Sampling Function

Consider a large set of unlabeled references $\mathcal{U} = \{u_1, u_2, \ldots, u_n\}$. The problem we investigate in this section is how to select a small subset of references in $\mathcal{U}$, such that the selected references carry almost the same information of all references in $\mathcal{U}$. These highly informative references will compose the training data $\mathcal{D}$, and, ideally, $|\mathcal{D}| \ll |\mathcal{U}|$. Particularly, SSAND exploits the redundancy in feature-space that exists between different references in $\mathcal{U}$. That is, many references in $\mathcal{U}$ may share some of their feature-values and SSAND uses this fact to perform an effective selective sampling strategy.

Intuitively, if a reference $u_i \in \mathcal{U}$ is inserted into $\mathcal{D}$, then the number of useful rules for references in $\mathcal{U}$ that share feature-values with u_i will possibly increase. In contrast, the number of useful rules for those references in $\mathcal{U}$ that do not share any feature-value with u_i will clearly remain unchanged. Therefore, the number of rules extracted for each reference in $\mathcal{U}$ can be used as an approximation of the amount of redundant information between references already in $\mathcal{D}$ and references in $\mathcal{U}$. The sampling function employed by SSAND exploits this key idea, by selecting references that contribute primarily with non-redundant information, and these informative references are those likely to demand the fewer number of rules from $\mathcal{D}$. More specifically, the sampling function $\gamma(\mathcal{U})$ returns a reference in $\mathcal{U}$ according to Equation 4.

$$\gamma(\mathcal{U}) = \{u_i \text{ such that } \forall u_j : |\mathcal{R}_{u_i}| \leq |\mathcal{R}_{u_j}|\} \quad (4)$$

The reference returned by the sampling function is inserted into $\mathcal{D}$, but it also remains in $\mathcal{U}$. In the next round of SSAND, the sampling function is executed again, but the number of rules extracted from $\mathcal{D}$ for each reference in $\mathcal{U}$ is likely to change due to the reference recently inserted into $\mathcal{D}$. The intuition behind choosing the reference which demands the fewest rules is that such reference should share less feature-values with references that were already inserted into $\mathcal{D}$. That is, if only few rules are extracted for a reference u_i, then this is evidence that $\mathcal{D}$ does not contain references that are similar to u_i and, thus, the information provided by reference u_i is not redundant and u_i is a highly informative reference. This simple heuristic works in a fine-grained level of feature-values trying to maximize the diversity in the training set. The extracted

Algorithm 1 Selective Sampling for Author Name Disambiguation

Input: Unlabeled data $\mathcal{U}$, and σ_{min} (≈ 0)
Output: The training data $\mathcal{D}$

continue
  for all reference $u_i \in \mathcal{U}$ **do**
    $\mathcal{D}_{u_i} \Leftarrow \mathcal{D}$ projected according to u_i
    $\mathcal{R}_{u_i} \Leftarrow$ rules extracted from $\mathcal{D}_{u_i} \mid \sigma \geq \sigma_{min}$
  end for
  if $\mathcal{D} = \emptyset$ **then**
    $\gamma_i(\mathcal{U}) \Leftarrow u_i$ such that $\forall u_j : |\mathcal{U}_{u_i}| \geq |\mathcal{U}_{u_j}|\}$
  else
    $\gamma_i(\mathcal{U}) \Leftarrow u_i$ such that $\forall u_j : |\mathcal{R}_{u_i}| \leq |\mathcal{R}_{u_j}|\}$
  end if
  if $\gamma_i(\mathcal{U}) \in \mathcal{D}$ **then break**
  else append $\gamma_i(\mathcal{U})$ **to** $\mathcal{D}$

rules capture the co-occurrence of feature-values, helping in our goal of increasing diversity, since in this case, the reference which demands the fewest rules is exactly the one which shares the least possible number of feature-values with references already in the training data. In the case of a tie, the algorithm selects the reference based on the size of the projection.

Notice that initially $\mathcal{D}$ is empty and, thus, SSAND cannot extract any rules from $\mathcal{D}$. The first reference to be labeled and inserted into $\mathcal{D}$ is selected from the set of available references $\mathcal{U}$. In order to maximize the initial coverage of $\mathcal{D}$, the selected reference is the one that maximizes the size of the projected data in $\mathcal{U}$, that is, it is the reference d for which $\mathcal{U}_d$ is the largest. This is the reference that shares more feature-values with the other references of the collection and can be considered as the best representative of it. After the first reference is selected and labeled, the algorithm proceeds using the fewest rules heuristic, as described above.

Natural Stop Condition

After selecting the first reference and at each posterior round, SSAND executes the sampling function and a new example is inserted into $\mathcal{D}$. At iteration i, the selected reference is denoted as $\gamma_i(\mathcal{U})$ and it is likely to be as dissimilar as possible from the references already in $\mathcal{D}$=$\{\gamma_{i-1}(\mathcal{U}), \gamma_{i-2}(\mathcal{U}), \ldots, \gamma_1(\mathcal{U})\}$. The algorithm keeps inserting references into the training data, until the stop criterion is achieved.

Lemma 2:. If $\gamma_i(\mathcal{U}) \in \mathcal{D}$ then $\gamma_i(\mathcal{U})$=$\gamma_j(\mathcal{U})$ $\forall j>i$.

Proof:. If $\gamma_i(\mathcal{U}) \in \mathcal{D}$, then the inclusion of $\gamma_i(\mathcal{U})$ does not change $\mathcal{D}$. As a result, any further execution of the sampling function must return the same reference returned by $\gamma_i(\mathcal{U})$, and $\mathcal{D}$ will never change. ■

The algorithm stops when all available references in $\mathcal{U}$ are less informative than any reference already inserted into $\mathcal{D}$. This occurs exactly when SSAND selects a reference which is already in $\mathcal{D}$. According to Lemma 2, when this condition is reached, SSAND will keep selecting the same reference over and over again. At this point, the training data $\mathcal{D}$ contains the most informative references and SLAND can be applied to estimate the relevance of references in $\mathcal{T}$. All steps of SSAND are shown in Algorithm 1.

4. EXPERIMENTAL EVALUATION

In this section we present experimental results that demonstrate the effectiveness of our selective sampling strategy. We first describe the collections, the baselines and the evaluation metric. Then, we discuss the effectiveness of our strategy in comparison with the baselines.

4.1 Collections

To evaluate our selective sampling strategy, we use two collections of references derived from DBLP[7]. These collections contain several ambiguous groups (i.e., groups of references with ambiguous author names).

The first collection, hereafter referred to as DBLP, contains references extracted from DBLP. It sums up 4,287 references associated with 220 distinct authors, which means an average of approximately 20 references per author. Small variations of this collection have been used in several other works [12, 15, 17, 16, 30, 45]. Its original version was created by Han et al. [15] and they manually labeled the references. For this, they used the author's publication home page, affiliation name, e-mail and coauthor names in a complete name format, and also sent emails to some authors to confirm their authorship. The references for which they had insufficient information to be judged were eliminated. Han et al. [15] also replaced the abbreviated publication venue titles by their complete version obtained from DBLP. We used 11 ambiguous groups extracted by Han et al. [15] with some corrections[8].

The second collection, hereafter referred to as KISTI, was built by the Korea Institute of Science and Technology Information [20] for English homonyms author name disambiguation. The top 1000 most frequent author names from late-2007 DBLP citation records were obtained jointly with their citation records. Afterwards, for each author name in each citation record, a reference was built. To disambiguate this collection, the authors submitted a query composed of the surname of the author and the work title of each reference to the Google search engine, aiming at finding personal publication pages. The first 20 web pages retrieved for each query were manually checked to identify the correct personal publication page for each authorship record. This identified page was then used to disambiguate the record. This collection has 37,613 citation records, 881 groups of same-name persons and 6,921 authors[9]. Due to the very large number of experiments and comparisons we perform, in our evaluation we use the top 40 most frequent ambiguous groups, i.e., the groups with the largest number of ambiguous authors. These groups are potentially the most difficult ones to disambiguate. In this subset, there are 7,841 citation records, 40 groups of same-name persons and 1,132 authors, with an average of 28.3 different ambiguous authors per group (with a maximum of 59).

4.2 Baselines

In this subsection, we give some details of the name disambiguation methods used as baselines in our experiments.

We used five baselines in our experiments: SLAND that was discussed in Section 3.1, the two supervised methods proposed by Han et al. in [15], the active method proposed by Huang et al. [18] and a strategy of randomly selecting samples to build the training set with the same size of that selected by our method.

The first method proposed by Han et al. [15], referred to as NB, uses a naïve Bayes model, a generative statistical model frequently used in word sense disambiguation tasks, to capture all writing patterns in the authors' citations. The second method, referred to as SVM, is based on Support Vector Machines, which are discriminative models basically used as a classifier [27]. An important

[7]http://www.informatik.uni-trier.de/~ley/db/

[8]It is available at *http://www.lbd.dcc.ufmg.br/lbd/collections/disambiguation*

[9]It is available at *http://www.kisti.re.kr*

difference between the two techniques is that a naïve Bayes model requires only positive examples to learn about the writing patterns whereas SVMs require both positive and negative examples to learn how to identify the author.

The method proposed by Huang et al. [18], referred to as LaSVM-DBSCAN, as discussed in Section 2.2, uses DBSCAN, a density-based clustering method [10], for clustering references by author. The distance metric between pairs of references used by DBSCAN is calculated by a trained online active support vector machine algorithm (LaSVM). The authors use different functions for each different attribute, such as the edit distance for emails and URLs, Jaccard similarity for addresses and affiliations and soft-TFIDF for names. Notice that in that work the online active method is not targeted towards reducing the training cost, but we decided to include a comparison with it in order to determine its potential in disambiguation under the same experimental design.

Finally, the last baseline, referred to as Random, randomly selects samples from an unlabeled set to build the training data. For comparison purposes, we randomly select the same number of examples selected by SSAND to construct the training data and use SLAND to learn the disambiguation functions.

4.3 Evaluation Metrics

In order to evaluate the effectiveness of our selective sampling strategy, we used two evaluation metrics: Accuracy and F_1 macro-averaging. Below, we describe these metrics.

Accuracy

We calculate the accuracy of the methods as the proportion of correctly disambiguated references (i.e., references for which the corresponding author was correctly predicted by the method). Accuracy estimation was based on the availability of a gold standard for these collections.

F_1 macro-averaging

For F_1 macro-averaging (Macro-F_1), the disambiguation performances were first computed for individual authors and then averaged over all authors. In this case, we need to assess the precision, recall and F_1 values for each author, and then average the F_1 values over all authors. Precision p is defined as the proportion of correctly disambiguated references. Recall r is defined as the proportion of correctly disambiguated references out of all the references having the target author. F_1 is defined as the harmonic mean of precision and recall (i.e., $\frac{2pr}{p+r}$).

4.4 Experimental setup

In our experimental evaluation, we used a 5-fold cross-validation and the performance of LaSVM-DBSCAN corresponds to the performance only in test set (one fold). Experiments were conducted with each ambiguous group, considering list of coauthor names, work title and publication venue title as attributes. We preprocessed all references by removing punctuations and stopwords of work and publication venue titles, and stemming work titles using Porter's algorithm [31]. Additionally, all coauthor names were standardized by considering only the initial letter of the first name along with the full last name.

For SSAND, the training set for the selection process is initially empty and grows one example at a time as they are selected from the large set of unlabeled references and then labeled. The algorithm eventually converges when it selects an example that has already been selected before. Once that happens, the selected examples can be used as a reduced training set to learn disambiguation functions. The results presented here by SLAND, SVM and NB use the whole four folds as training data, while SSAND uses the selected examples. So, for SSAND, the labeling effort is restricted to the examples selected by the algorithm directly from the unlabeled set[10].

We also evaluated SSAND with another set of selected examples that was obtained as follows: we first select examples as discussed above and, in a next iteration, we remove such set of examples from the set of unlabeled references and select a new set of examples. These two selected set of examples are considered jointly as the training set to SSAND. In this case, we will refer to it as SSAND-Round2.

For SVM, we used the implementation provided by the LibSVM-2.84 package [11], with RBF (Radial Basis Function) as the kernel function, where the best γ and cost values were obtained from the *Grid* program, available with the LibSVM package. LibSVM uses the "one-against-one" and voting for multi-class classification. In our experiments, we used TFIDF as feature weight scheme. We used this weighting scheme since it is the most commonly used for the comparison of textual attributes. Other schemes, such as Gain, could be used in future work. We used a non-parametric implementation for Naive Bayes [7].

For LaSVM-DBSCAN, we used the LaSVM package [4][12] with RBF as the kernel function using the default values for cost and γ, respectively, and the DBSCAN version available from Weka[13] with the values of 1.5 and 2 for ϵ and the minimum number of points, respectively. We should stress that parameter tuning with cross-validation in the training was also performed for LaSVM but results produced by the default parameters turned out to be the best.

We also used soft-TFIDF for determining the similarity between coauthor names and the token-based Jaccard[14] coefficient as the similarity measure for work and publication venue titles when constructing the similarity vectors. In addition, we used the similarity vectors of "A Kumar", "D Johnson" and "M Jones" ambiguous groups as training sets for the LaSVM classifier, as done in [18].

The values for Δ_{min} and γ_{min}, used by SLAND, SSAND and Random, were set automatically by performing 5-fold cross-validation using the training data. Specifically in the case of SSAND, the training data corresponds to the set actively chosen by the method. The results are compared using statistical significance tests (t-test) with a 99% confidence interval.

For Random, references to authors in the training set are randomly selected from the set of unlabeled data. We construct 10 randomly selected training sets with the same number of references selected by SSAND and SSAND-Round2 in each training set.

4.5 Results

How effective is our strategy for sampling examples compared with the use of whole unlabeled set as training data? And how much can we reduce the training set with the proposed active method without significant losses in disambiguation effectiveness?

As can been seen in Tables 1 and 2, the results of SSAND and SSAND-Round2 are competitive with the results of SLAND, mainly the later, reminding that SLAND produces state-of-the-art results

[10]In our experiments, the presence of the user who would provide the correct author of each reference is simulated by using the original authors available in the collections.

[11]http://www.csie.ntu.edu.tw/~cjlin/libsvm

[12]Available at *http://leon.bottou.org/research/lasvm*

[13]*http://www.cs.waikato.ac.nz/ml/weka/*

[14]The implementation of the Jaccard coefficient in our work is the one available at *http://www.dcs.shef.ac.uk/~sam/simmetrics.html*

Table 1: Results (with their standard deviations) obtained by SLAND, SSAND and SSAND-Round2 in each ambiguous group in the DBLP collection.

	SLAND		SSAND			SSAND-Round2		
Ambiguous Group	Accuracy	Macro-F_1	Accuracy	Macro-F_1	% Selected	Accuracy	Macro-F_1	% Selected
A. Gupta	0.920 (0.026)	0.891 (0.032)	0.835 (0.049)	0.744 (0.059)	27%	0.906 (0.035)	0.855 (0.060)	53%
A. Kumar	0.918 (0.039)	0.826 (0.099)	0.720 (0.103)	0.568 (0.177)	20%	0.901 (0.022)	0.789 (0.099)	58%
C. Chen	0.851 (0.028)	0.778 (0.055)	0.632 (0.048)	0.493 (0.074)	23%	0.771 (0.046)	0.638 (0.081)	47%
D. Johnson	0.940 (0.039)	0.856 (0.042)	0.856 (0.046)	0.745 (0.074)	33%	0.919 (0.056)	0.835 (0.102)	61%
J. Martin	0.875 (0.048)	0.848 (0.111)	0.759 (0.051)	0.680 (0.066)	48%	0.857 (0.057)	0.811 (0.116)	81%
J. Robinson	0.948 (0.052)	0.950 (0.046)	0.907 (0.090)	0.883 (0.097)	46%	0.936 (0.064)	0.949 (0.051)	73%
J. Smith	0.936 (0.018)	0.807 (0.044)	0.836 (0.039)	0.614 (0.084)	22%	0.914 (0.026)	0.784 (0.053)	45%
K. Tanaka	0.950 (0.015)	0.815 (0.094)	0.946 (0.022)	0.825 (0.102)	47%	0.950 (0.008)	0.816 (0.092)	73%
M. Brown	0.934 (0.034)	0.892 (0.072)	0.915 (0.038)	0.877 (0.089)	49%	0.941 (0.028)	0.907 (0.081)	86%
M. Jones	0.885 (0.041)	0.758 (0.070)	0.777 (0.057)	0.626 (0.099)	28%	0.877 (0.026)	0.788 (0.082)	63%
M. Miller	0.963 (0.035)	0.839 (0.080)	0.965 (0.022)	0.903 (0.046)	30%	0.960 (0.034)	0.878 (0.084)	65%
Average	0.920 (0.010)	0.842 (0.008)	0.832 (0.016)	0.723 (0.013)	34%	0.903 (0.010)	0.823 (0.009)	64%

Table 2: Results (with their standard deviations) obtained by SLAND, SSAND and SSAND-Round2 in each ambiguous group in the KISTI collection.

	SLAND		SSAND			SSAND-Round2		
Ambiguous Group	Accuracy	Macro-F_1	Accuracy	Macro-F_1	% Selected	Accuracy	Macro-F_1	% Selected
A. Achoudhary	1.000 (0.000)	1.000 (0.000)	1.000 (0.000)	1.000 (0.000)	48%	1.000 (0.000)	1.000 (0.000)	80%
A. Gupta	0.820 (0.102)	0.654 (0.131)	0.808 (0.081)	0.670 (0.119)	57%	0.843 (0.094)	0.695 (0.104)	91%
D. Eppstein	0.995 (0.011)	0.997 (0.006)	0.995 (0.011)	0.997 (0.006)	46%	0.995 (0.011)	0.997 (0.006)	79%
D. Lee	0.882 (0.055)	0.763 (0.113)	0.866 (0.059)	0.766 (0.118)	48%	0.892 (0.043)	0.749 (0.118)	86%
H. Chen	0.773 (0.064)	0.659 (0.105)	0.733 (0.085)	0.666 (0.099)	53%	0.767 (0.062)	0.671 (0.075)	87%
H. Wang	0.855 (0.048)	0.753 (0.106)	0.780 (0.097)	0.694 (0.174)	35%	0.814 (0.070)	0.676 (0.123)	64%
J. Chen	0.746 (0.089)	0.528 (0.072)	0.762 (0.084)	0.592 (0.069)	53%	0.754 (0.087)	0.548 (0.076)	79%
J. Dongarra	1.000 (0.000)	1.000 (0.000)	1.000 (0.000)	1.000 (0.000)	37%	1.000 (0.000)	1.000 (0.000)	72%
J. Halpern	0.932 (0.035)	0.629 (0.142)	0.928 (0.023)	0.554 (0.163)	34%	0.936 (0.037)	0.682 (0.138)	65%
J. Kim	0.670 (0.081)	0.583 (0.070)	0.637 (0.119)	0.606 (0.091)	72%	0.683 (0.127)	0.607 (0.139)	98%
J. Lee	0.740 (0.095)	0.661 (0.100)	0.576 (0.123)	0.516 (0.081)	49%	0.730 (0.095)	0.680 (0.085)	85%
J. Li	0.811 (0.043)	0.698 (0.084)	0.777 (0.074)	0.690 (0.114)	61%	0.771 (0.067)	0.642 (0.103)	88%
J. Liu	0.794 (0.083)	0.643 (0.141)	0.724 (0.105)	0.557 (0.174)	53%	0.729 (0.096)	0.533 (0.156)	89%
J. Mitchell	0.965 (0.013)	0.912 (0.143)	0.965 (0.025)	0.909 (0.143)	43%	0.965 (0.013)	0.912 (0.143)	78%
J. Smith	0.696 (0.070)	0.503 (0.088)	0.715 (0.088)	0.593 (0.080)	49%	0.765 (0.068)	0.596 (0.115)	86%
J. Wang	0.825 (0.047)	0.710 (0.036)	0.714 (0.042)	0.575 (0.066)	45%	0.788 (0.025)	0.688 (0.040)	77%
J. Wu	0.927 (0.028)	0.651 (0.112)	0.916 (0.046)	0.625 (0.148)	41%	0.937 (0.029)	0.666 (0.121)	72%
J. Zhang	0.822 (0.058)	0.678 (0.111)	0.792 (0.090)	0.689 (0.129)	55%	0.842 (0.053)	0.736 (0.102)	88%
L. Zhang	0.904 (0.055)	0.803 (0.132)	0.850 (0.041)	0.747 (0.087)	50%	0.893 (0.037)	0.777 (0.081)	89%
M. Chen	0.867 (0.032)	0.657 (0.077)	0.878 (0.014)	0.698 (0.116)	51%	0.894 (0.042)	0.753 (0.112)	89%
M. Pedram	1.000 (0.000)	1.000 (0.000)	1.000 (0.000)	1.000 (0.000)	69%	1.000 (0.000)	1.000 (0.000)	97%
M. Vardi	0.989 (0.016)	0.797 (0.278)	1.000 (0.000)	1.000 (0.000)	46%	1.000 (0.000)	1.000 (0.000)	79%
N. Jennings	1.000 (0.000)	1.000 (0.000)	1.000 (0.000)	1.000 (0.000)	34%	1.000 (0.000)	1.000 (0.000)	76%
N. Jha	1.000 (0.000)	1.000 (0.000)	1.000 (0.000)	1.000 (0.000)	31%	1.000 (0.000)	1.000 (0.000)	57%
N. Lynch	1.000 (0.000)	1.000 (0.000)	1.000 (0.000)	1.000 (0.000)	44%	1.000 (0.000)	1.000 (0.000)	84%
P. Yu	0.988 (0.016)	0.848 (0.227)	0.988 (0.016)	0.848 (0.227)	53%	0.988 (0.016)	0.848 (0.227)	86%
Q. Yang	0.925 (0.035)	0.654 (0.211)	0.919 (0.035)	0.666 (0.215)	67%	0.912 (0.040)	0.644 (0.212)	96%
S. Jajodia	0.977 (0.016)	0.863 (0.101)	0.968 (0.013)	0.822 (0.055)	46%	0.977 (0.016)	0.863 (0.101)	86%
S. Kim	0.776 (0.077)	0.701 (0.074)	0.743 (0.121)	0.675 (0.130)	68%	0.757 (0.089)	0.684 (0.080)	96%
S. Lee	0.715 (0.066)	0.596 (0.121)	0.670 (0.034)	0.579 (0.064)	59%	0.693 (0.056)	0.598 (0.073)	88%
T. Henzinger	0.988 (0.016)	0.994 (0.008)	0.988 (0.016)	0.994 (0.008)	54%	0.988 (0.016)	0.994 (0.008)	88%
W. Wang	0.883 (0.053)	0.762 (0.057)	0.843 (0.064)	0.688 (0.089)	61%	0.827 (0.111)	0.650 (0.156)	93%
X. Li	0.730 (0.099)	0.620 (0.121)	0.651 (0.074)	0.544 (0.077)	47%	0.720 (0.101)	0.643 (0.155)	78%
X. Zhou	0.960 (0.043)	0.869 (0.127)	0.926 (0.037)	0.796 (0.091)	54%	0.953 (0.050)	0.861 (0.137)	89%
Y. Chen	0.748 (0.074)	0.599 (0.083)	0.665 (0.070)	0.582 (0.103)	45%	0.751 (0.043)	0.608 (0.056)	79%
Y. Liu	0.801 (0.024)	0.682 (0.064)	0.698 (0.053)	0.598 (0.060)	39%	0.766 (0.021)	0.638 (0.026)	77%
Y. Wang	0.774 (0.065)	0.661 (0.117)	0.669 (0.075)	0.556 (0.152)	41%	0.724 (0.077)	0.625 (0.122)	75%
Y. Yang	0.830 (0.051)	0.677 (0.127)	0.812 (0.072)	0.698 (0.113)	64%	0.855 (0.050)	0.700 (0.137)	95%
Y. Zhang	0.765 (0.038)	0.654 (0.039)	0.745 (0.049)	0.695 (0.076)	58%	0.735 (0.041)	0.635 (0.057)	87%
Z. Zhang	0.776 (0.059)	0.591 (0.066)	0.805 (0.087)	0.654 (0.125)	60%	0.786 (0.073)	0.594 (0.086)	91%
Average	0.849 (0.010)	0.724 (0.022)	0.811 (0.017)	0.699 (0.018)	50%	0.839 (0.006)	0.723 (0.017)	83%

for name disambiguation. In more details, considering SSAND, reductions in terms of the amount of training used by the method for DBLP and KISTI collections are significant: up to 71% and 43% respectively, while the loss in disambiguation effectiveness is, on average, around 14% in terms of Macro-F_1 (and 9.5% in accuracy) for DBLP and only 4.4% in Macro-F_1 for KISTI (3.4% in accuracy). Considering SSAND-Round 2, reductions in the training sets are obviously smaller but still considerable: we used only 50% of the whole training set for DBLP and reduced KISTI by 18%. These results correspond to reductions in labeling considering the whole collection not the average of the ambiguous groups as shown in the Tables. Moreover, there were basically no losses in disambiguation effectiveness in terms of both, accuracy and Macro-F_1, as the results are statistically tied according to a t-test with 99% of confidence in both collection, with the exception of Macro-F_1 in DBLP with a very small loss of about 2%. Notice, particularly, that the improvements of SSAND-Round2 over SSAND in KISTI is smaller and the use of additional training provided by the second selection performed by the active strategy may not be worth due to the cost of labeling.

How effective is our strategy compared with the SVM and NB methods using the whole training data?

Results for this question can be obtained from Tables 3 and 4. We can see that in DBLP (Table 3), SSAND is very close to SVM in terms of accuracy and ties with it in terms of Macro-F_1. Recall that Macro-F_1 considers the average effectiveness in all ambiguous groups while accuracy may be dominated by the effectiveness in few larger groups. Thus, it is a more important metric for this problem. SSAND is also superior to NB for both metrics. Moreover, in this collection the reduction in the training set achieves more than 70%. Regarding SSAND-Round2, it is superior to both supervised methods, achieving gains in terms of Macro-F_1 of about 14% and 30% against SVM e NB, respectively.

Table 3: Average results (with their standard deviations) obtained by SSAND, SSAND-Round2, SVM and NB in the DBLP collection.

Method	Accuracy	Macro-F_1
SSAND	0.832 (0.016)	0.723 (0.013)
SSAND-Round2	0.903 (0.010)	0.823 (0.009)
SVM	0.869 (0.013)	0.721 (0.016)
NB	0.821 (0.004)	0.630 (0.019)

When considering the KISTI collection (Table 4), both SSAND e SSAND-Round2 are always superior than SVM and NB for both evaluation metrics, with a maximum gain of 31.5% in Macro-F_1 over SVM for SSAND-Round2 and 27% for SSAND. Recall that in case of SSAND we use only half of the training set.

Table 4: Average results (with their standard deviations) obtained by SSAND, SSAND-Round2, SVM and NB in the KISTI collection.

Method	Accuracy	Macro-F_1
SSAND	0.811 (0.017)	0.699 (0.018)
SSAND-Round2	0.839 (0.006)	0.723 (0.017)
SVM	0.726 (0.012)	0.550 (0.018)
NB	0.762 (0.003)	0.584 (0.015)

How effective is SSAND when compared to Random?

Tables 5 and 6 show that, for all cases, the selections made by our active samplers are better than a random choice of the same number of examples to label[15]. The differences are higher for the DBLP collection in terms of Macro-F_1, which, as we discussed before, is a better metric for evaluating the overall performance of the disambiguation methods over all ambiguous groups. Results show a degradation of about 9% in effectiveness when random choices of the same size of that chosen by SSAND in DBLP (corresponding to 29% of the training data available) are used.

In general, the differences in effectiveness are also higher when less training is chosen for labeling, i.e., the case of SSAND. The smaller differences between SSAND-Round2 and Random-Round2, mainly in KISTI, may be explained by the size of the training data. SSAND-Round2 and Random-Round2 use on average 83% of the training data available. Moreover, it is worth mentioning that these methods are self-training, that is, they are capable of identifying new authors and to add reliable references from the test set into the training data. This fact may help reduce the differences between both methods. To test this hypothesis, we performed Random without the self-training capacity, obtaining 0.763 (0.007) of accuracy and 0.599 (0.009) of Macro-F_1. These values correspond to a degradation of 4% and 11% in accuracy and Macro-F_1, respectively, with respect to the use of self-training, meaning that, in fact, new entries are being successfully incorporated to the training set during the disambiguation process. However, to start with a better initial set actively selected helps the overall process as we have seen. Moreover, SSAND is able to indicate us a good size for this initial set.

Table 5: Average results (with their standard deviations) obtained by SSAND, SSAND-Round2, Random and Random-Round2 in the DBLP collection.

Method	Accuracy	Macro-F_1
SSAND	0.832 (0.016)	0.723 (0.013)
Random	0.807 (0.005)	0.660 (0.011)
SSAND-Round2	0.903 (0.010)	0.823 (0.009)
Random-Round2	0.880 (0.009)	0.754 (0.007)

Table 6: Average results (with their standard deviations) obtained by SSAND, SSAND-Round2, Random and Random-Round2 in the KISTI collection.

Method	Accuracy	Macro-F_1
SSAND	0.811 (0.017)	0.699 (0.018)
Random	0.793 (0.003)	0.676 (0.004)
SSSAND-Round2	0.839 (0.006)	0.723 (0.017)
Random-Round2	0.833 (0.006)	0.707 (0.014)

How effective is SSAND compared with another active method?

To calculate the accuracy and Macro-F_1, we assigned each cluster generated by LaSVM-DBSCAN to the most popular author in that cluster. If the most popular author of a cluster was already assigned to another cluster, we assign it to the second most popular author and so on. Tables 7 and 8 show the results obtained by LaSVM-BDSCAN as well as SSAND and SSAND-Round2 in DBLP and

[15]Random-Round2 corresponds to the evaluation of random with the same number of references selected by SSAND-Round2.

KISTI. SSAND and SSAND-Round2 largely outperform LaSVM-DBSCAN in both collections, mainly in terms of accuracy, being SSAND only statistically tied with LaSVM-DBSCAN in terms of Macro-F_1 in KISTI, according to a t-test with 99% of confidence.

Table 7: Average results (with their standard deviations) obtained by SSAND, SSAND-Round2 and LaSVM-DBSCAN in the DBLP collection.

Method	Accuracy	Macro-F_1
SSAND	0.832 (0.016)	0.723 (0.013)
SSAND-Round2	0.903 (0.010)	0.823 (0.009)
LaSVM-DBSCAN	0.535 (0.011)	0.681 (0.011)

Table 8: Average results (with their standard deviations) obtained by SSAND, SSAND-Round2 and LaSVM-DBSCAN in the KISTI collection.

Method	Accuracy	Macro-F_1
SSAND	0.811 (0.017)	0.699 (0.018)
SSAND-Round2	0.839 (0.006)	0.723 (0.017)
LaSVM-DBSCAN	0.645 (0.021)	0.682 (0.034)

5. CONCLUSIONS

In this paper, we presented a new active associative strategy to select the most informative examples from an unlabeled dataset to be used to learn low-cost effective disambiguation functions that assign ambiguous authors to their respective records. The main goal is to reduce the size and cost of the training set to be labeled without significant losses in disambiguation effectiveness. We evaluated our strategy using two collections and five baselines, including an active method. Our strategy shows that very competitive effectiveness can be obtained in all cases, including against state-of-the-art methods that use the whole training set, while being able to reduce labeling costs in more than 70%.

In future work, we intend to extend our strategy to incorporate relevance feedback in order the help actively selecting the most probable erroneously assignments and correct them, as well as to work to reduce even further the need for training with the help of other techniques such as query-by-committee [13] and distant supervision [25].

Acknowledgments

This research is partially funded by InWeb - The Brazilian National Institute of Science and Technology for the Web (MCT/CNPq/FAPEMIG grant number 573871/2008-6), and by the authors's individual research grants from CAPES, CNPq, and FAPEMIG.

6. REFERENCES

[1] R. Agrawal, T. Imielinski, and A. Swami. Mining association rules between sets of items in large databases. In *Proceedings of the 1993 ACM SIGMOD International Conference on Management of Data*, pages 207–216, Washington, USA, 1993.

[2] I. Bhattacharya and L. Getoor. A latent dirichlet model for unsupervised entity resolution. In *Proceedings of the Sixth SIAM International Conference on Data Mining*, Bethesda, MD, USA, 2006.

[3] I. Bhattacharya and L. Getoor. Collective entity resolution in relational data. *ACM Transactions on Knowledge Discovery from Data*, 1(1), 2007.

[4] A. Bordes, S. Ertekin, J. Weston, and L. Bottou. Fast kernel classifiers with online and active learning. *Journal of Machine Learning Research*, 6:1579–1619, 2005.

[5] R. G. Cota, A. A. Ferreira, M. A. Gonçalves, A. H. F. Laender, and C. Nascimento. An unsupervised heuristic-based hierarchical method for name disambiguation in bibliographic citations. *Journal of the American Society for Information Science and Technology*, 61(9):1853–1870, 2010.

[6] A. Culotta, P. Kanani, R. Hall, M. Wick, and A. McCallum. Author disambiguation using error-driven machine learning with a ranking loss function. In *Proceedings of the International Workshop on Information Integration on the Web*, Vancouver, Canada, 2007.

[7] P. Domingos and M. Pazzani. On the optimality of the simple Bayesian classifier under zero-one loss. *Machine Learning*, 29:103–137, 1997.

[8] P. Donmez and J. G. Carbonell. Optimizing estimated loss reduction for active sampling in rank learning. In *Proceedings of the Twenty-Fifth International Conference on Machine Learning*, pages 248–255, Helsinki, Finland, 2008.

[9] P. Donmez and J. G. Carbonell. Active sampling for rank learning via optimizing the area under the roc curve. In *Proceedings of the 31th European Conference on IR Research*, pages 78–89, Toulouse, France, 2009.

[10] M. Ester, H.-P. Kriegel, J. Sander, and X. Xu. A density-based algorithm for discovering clusters in large spatial databases with noise. In *Proceedings of the 2nd International Conference on Knowledge Discovery and Data Mining*, pages 226–231, Portland, Oregon, 1996.

[11] X. Fan, J. Wang, X. Pu, L. Zhou, and B. Lv. On graph-based name disambiguation. *ACM Journal of Data and Information Quality*, 2:10:1–10:23, February 2011.

[12] A. A. Ferreira, A. Veloso, M. A. Gonçalves, and A. H. F. Laender. Effective self-training author name disambiguation in scholarly digital libraries. In *Proceedings of the 2010 ACM/IEEE Joint Conference on Digital Libraries*, pages 39–48, Gold Coast, Queensland, Australia, 2010.

[13] Y. Freund, H. S. Seung, E. Shamir, and N. Tishby. Selective sampling using the query by committee algorithm. *Machine Learning*, 28:133–168, September 1997.

[14] S. Geisser. *Predictive Inference: An Introduction*. Chapman & Hall, New York, 1993.

[15] H. Han, C. L. Giles, H. Zha, C. Li, and K. Tsioutsiouliklis. Two supervised learning approaches for name disambiguation in author citations. In *Proceedings of the 4th ACM/IEEE-CS Joint Conference on Digital Libraries*, pages 296–305, Tuscon, USA, 2004.

[16] H. Han, W. Xu, H. Zha, and C. L. Giles. A hierarchical naive Bayes mixture model for name disambiguation in author citations. In *Proceedings of the 2005 ACM Symposium on Applied Computing*, pages 1065–1069, Santa Fe, New Mexico, USA, 2005.

[17] H. Han, H. Zha, and C. L. Giles. Name disambiguation in author citations using a k-way spectral clustering method. In *Proceedings of the 5th ACM/IEEE Joint Conference on Digital Libraries*, pages 334–343, Denver, CO, USA, 2005.

[18] J. Huang, S. Ertekin, and C. L. Giles. Efficient name disambiguation for large-scale databases. In *Proceedings of*

the European Conference on Principles and Practice of Knowledge Discovery in Databases, pages 536–544, Berlin, Germany, 2006.

[19] P. Kanani, A. McCallum, and C. Pal. Improving author coreference by resource-bounded information gathering from the web. In *Proceedings of the 20th International Joint Conference on Artificial Intelligence*, pages 429–434, Hyderabad, India, 2007.

[20] I.-S. Kang, P. Kim, S. Lee, H. Jung, and B.-J. You. Construction of a large-scale test set for author disambiguation. *Information Processing & Management*, 47:452–465, May 2011.

[21] I.-S. Kang, S.-H. Na, S. Lee, H. Jung, P. Kim, W.-K. Sung, and J.-H. Lee. On co-authorship for author disambiguation. *Information Processing & Management*, 45(1):84–97, 2009.

[22] A. H. F. Laender, M. A. Gonçalves, R. G. Cota, A. A. Ferreira, R. L. T. Santos, and A. J. C. Silva. Keeping a digital library clean: new solutions to old problems. In *Proceedings of the ACM Symposium on Document Engineering*, pages 257–262, 2008.

[23] D. Lee, J. Kang, P. Mitra, C. L. Giles, and B.-W. On. Are your citations clean? *Communications of the ACM*, 50(12):33–38, 2007.

[24] F. H. Levin and C. A. Heuser. Evaluating the use of social networks in author name disambiguation in digital libraries. *Journal of Information and Data Management*, 1(2):183–197, 2010.

[25] M. Levin, S. Krawzyk, S. Bethard, and D. Jurafsky. Citation-based bootstrapping for large-scale author disambiguation. *Journal of the American Society for Information Science and Technology*, 2012.

[26] B. Long, O. Chapelle, Y. Zhang, Y. Chang, Z. Zheng, and B. Tseng. Active learning for ranking through expected loss optimization. In *Proceeding of the 33rd international ACM SIGIR conference on Research and development in information retrieval*, pages 267–274, Geneva, Switzerland, 2010.

[27] T. M. Mitchell. *Machine Learning*. McGraw-Hill, New York, NY, USA, 1997.

[28] B.-W. On, E. Elmacioglu, D. Lee, J. Kang, and J. Pei. Improving grouped-entity resolution using quasi-cliques. In *Proceedings of the 6th IEEE International Conference on Data Mining*, pages 1008–015, Hong Kong, China, 2006. IEEE Computer Society.

[29] B.-W. On and D. Lee. Scalable name disambiguation using multi-level graph partition. In *Proceedings of the 7th SIAM International Conference on Data Mining*, pages 575–580, Minneapolis, Minnesota, USA, 2007.

[30] D. A. Pereira, B. A. Ribeiro-Neto, N. Ziviani, A. H. F. Laender, M. A. Gonçalves, and A. A. Ferreira. Using web information for author name disambiguation. In *Proceedings of the 2009 ACM/IEEE Joint Conference on Digital Libraries*, pages 49–58, Austin, TX, USA, 2009.

[31] M. F. Porter. An algorithm for suffix stripping. *Program*, 14(3):130–137, 1980.

[32] L. Shu, B. Long, and W. Meng. A latent topic model for complete entity resolution. In *Proceedings of the 2009 IEEE International Conference on Data Engineering*, pages 880–891, Shanghai, China, 2009. IEEE Computer Society.

[33] R. Silva, M. A. Gonçalves, and A. Veloso. Rule-based active sampling for learning to rank. In *Proceedings of Machine Learning and Knowledge Discovery in Databases - European Conference (3)*, pages 240–255, Athens, Greece, 2011.

[34] J. M. Soler. Separating the articles of authors with the same name. *Scientometrics*, 72(2):281–290, 2007.

[35] Y. Song, J. Huang, I. G. Councill, J. Li, and C. L. Giles. Efficient topic-based unsupervised name disambiguation. In *Proceedings of the 7th ACM/IEEE Joint Conference on Digital Libraries*, pages 342–351, Vancouver, BC, Canada, 2007.

[36] J. Tang, A. C. M. Fong, B. Wang, and J. Zhang. A unified probabilistic framework for name disambiguation in digital library. *IEEE Transactions on Knowledge and Data Engineering*, 99, 2011.

[37] S. Tong and D. Koller. Support vector machine active learning with applications to text classification. *Journal of Machine Learning Research*, 2:45–66, 2002.

[38] V. I. Torvik , M. Weeber, D. R. Swanson, and N. R. Smalheiser. A probabilistic similarity metric for Medline records: A model for author name disambiguation. *Journal of the American Society for Information Science and Technology*, 56(2):140–158, 2005.

[39] V. I. Torvik and N. R. Smalheiser. Author name disambiguation in medline. *ACM Transactions on Knowledge Discovery from Data*, 3(3):1–29, 2009.

[40] P. Treeratpituk and C. L. Giles. Disambiguating authors in academic publications using random forests. In *Proceedings of the 2009 ACM/IEEE Joint Conference on Digital Libraries*, pages 39–48, Austin, TX, USA, 2009.

[41] A. Veloso, A. A. Ferreira, M. A. Gonçalves, A. H. F. Laender, and W. Meira Jr. Cost-effective on-demand associative author name disambiguation. *Information Processing & Management*, 2012. (to appear).

[42] A. Veloso, W. Meira Jr., M. Cristo, M. Gonçalves, and M. Zaki. Multi-evidence, multi-criteria, lazy associative document classification. In *Proceedings of the 2006 ACM International Conference on Information and Knowledge Management*, pages 218–227, Arlington, USA, 2006.

[43] A. Veloso, W. Meira Jr., and M. J. Zaki. Lazy associative classification. In *Proceedings of the International Conference on Data Mining*, pages 645–654, Washington, DC, USA, 2006.

[44] X. Wang, J. Tang, H. Cheng, and P. S. Yu. ADANA: Active name disambiguation. In *Proceedings of the 11th IEEE International Conference on Data Mining*, pages 794–803, Vancouver, Canada, 2011.

[45] K.-H. Yang, H.-T. Peng, J.-Y. Jiang, H.-M. Lee, and J.-M. Ho. Author name disambiguation for citations using topic and web correlation. In *Proceedings of the European Conference on Research and Advanced Technology for Digital Libraries*, pages 185–196, Aarhus, Denmark, 2008. Springer-Verlag.

[46] H. Yu. SVM selective sampling for ranking with application to data retrieval. In *Proceedings of the eleventh ACM SIGKDD International Conference on Knowledge Discovery in Data Mining*, pages 354–363, Chicago, Illinois, USA, 2005.

AckSeer: A Repository and Search Engine for Automatically Extracted Acknowledgments from Digital Libraries

Madian Khabsa
Computer Science and Engineering
The Pennsylvania State University
University Park, PA 16802
madian@psu.edu

Pucktada Treeratpituk
Information Sciences and Technology
The Pennsylvania State University
University Park, PA 16802
pxt162@ist.psu.edu

C. Lee Giles
Information Sciences and Technology
Computer Science and Engineering
The Pennsylvania State University
University Park, PA 16802
giles@ist.psu.edu

ABSTRACT

Acknowledgments are widely used in scientific articles to express gratitude and credit collaborators. Despite suggestions that indexing acknowledgments automatically will give interesting insights [9], there is currently, to the best of our knowledge, no such system to track acknowledgments and index them [1]. In this paper we introduce *AckSeer*[2], a search engine and a repository for automatically extracted acknowledgments in digital libraries. *AckSeer* is a fully automated system that scans items in digital libraries including conference papers, journals, and books extracting acknowledgment sections and identifying acknowledged entities mentioned within.

We describe the architecture of *AckSeer* and discuss the extraction algorithms that achieve a F1 measure above 83%. We use multiple Named Entity Recognition (NER) tools and propose a method for merging the outcome from different recognizers. The resulting entities are stored in a database then made searchable by adding them to the *AckSeer* index along with the metadata of the containing paper/book. We build *AckSeer* on top of the documents in CiteSeerx digital library yielding more than 500,000 acknowledgments and more than 4 million mentioned entities.

Categories and Subject Descriptors

I.2.7 [**Artificial Intelligence**]: Natural Language Processing—*Text analysis*; H.3.1 [**Information Storage and Retrieval**]: Content Analysis and Indexing—*Linguistic processing*; H.3.1 [**Information Storage and Retrieval**]: Digital Libraries—*Collection*

General Terms

Algorithms, Search engines

Keywords

Acknowledgments, Information Extraction, Disambiguation

[1]An early acknowledgement indexing system was built in CiteSeer but was not refactored into the new CiteSeerX
[2]`http://ackseer.ist.psu.edu`

JCDL'12, June 10–14, 2012, Washington, DC, USA.

1. INTRODUCTION

While author information and affiliation are considered to be sufficient metadata to describe the creators of items in digital libraries, there is still plenty of information available from acknowledgment sections of papers and books, much of which is not readily accessible. Acknowledgments are rich with information about indirect contributors and collaborators of the work which lead one researcher to call acknowledgments "Super Citations" [13]. Cronin went further and argued that the first acknowledged person might have contributed to the work more than the last author[9]. Acknowledged contributors maybe who funded the work.

An early study dissected the different types of acknowledgments found in scholarly work, and found that the most common types were:"

- Moral support
- Financial support
- Access (facilities, data ..etc.)
- Clerical support
- Technical support (programming, statistics.. etc)
- Peer interactive communication " [10, 12]

These categories of acknowledgments may indicate significant contribution to the published work, given that such an entity was mentioned in the acknowledgments. While the promotion and tenure process in academic institutions is mostly affected by citations and authorship, acknowledgments can be argued to have enough credit that could possibly affect promotion and tenure decisions [9]. In fact, the previously mentioned work argues that the the most significant reason keeping acknowledgments out of consideration for promotion and tenure can be traced back to the lack of a central repository that keeps track of acknowledged entities in scientific articles. Such a repository, which would be similar to the Institute for Scientific Information (ISI), would be imperative for studying acknowledgments on a larger scale, and could possibly contribute to the measuring academic influence.

Acknowledgments are domain dependent, in the sense that different communities tend to have different forms and structure of constructing the list of acknowledged entities. The venue plays a significant role in determining what should be acknowledged and what should not. For example, a PhD dissertation would probably have larger section for acknowledgments than a journal article or a conference paper. In the medical domain, studies can be a result of multicentral clinical trials where the number of authors can go beyond double digits as a result of collaboration. In this case, a significant number of contributors cannot be listed as authors, and hence their contribution is credited in the acknowledgments section. Another trend in medical papers is to list the primary investigators as authors with the name of the study group as a co-author and the members of the study group are listed in the acknowledgments section. In 1991, *The New England Journal of Medicine* published an editorial to describe the guidelines of acknowledgments and authorships after accepting a manuscript in which five pages of the article's twelve were acknowledgments [18].

To the best of our knowledge, there is no active system that keeps track of acknowledgments in digital libraries. Therefore, our work is an important step towards making acknowledgments more accessible for researchers, academic evaluators, and economists for many uses such as promotion decisions and the effectiveness of funded research[15]. The *AckSeer* architecture is built with domain independence in mind and can therefore be used to index acknowledgments from various domains even though our experiments are limited to documents primarily in computer and information science.

In addition, analyzing and understanding the the co-authorship network would benefit a great deal by incorporating acknowledgment information within the graph, since persons and organizations being acknowledged have interacted with the authors and contributed their share to the published work. Hence, a bigger graph comprising both authors and acknowledged entities would be very interesting to study, providing an additional feature to a co-authorship network that has already been extensively studied.

Our contributions are several. We design and describe the architecture of acknowledgments repository and search engine. We introduce methods for extracting acknowledgment sections as well as the entities mentioned within, and list the top acknowledged entities in computer and information science. We use a novel approach to cluster entities based on search engine results. Finally, we introduce different ranking functions that can be used in an acknowledgments search engine.

The remainder of this paper is organized as follows. In section two we survey related work. Section three describes the architecture of *AckSeer* and the system components. The extraction method along with the disambiguation algorithm and ranking functions are described in section four. In section five we discuss the experiments and the statistics obtained. We conclude in section six and identify directions for future work.

2. RELATED WORK

The related work can be categorized into two different components, first studying acknowledgments in scientific publications whether it has been extracted manually or automatically. The second component is concerned with building repositories and search engines for sub-objects of information in digital libraries such as tables, figures and acknowledgments that can be found inside articles and books.

Acknowledgments have received a fair amount of interest from sociologists, information scientists, and to some level from computer scientists. The attention given to acknowledgments has not been comparable to that given to citations and authorship. However, it was suggested far before automatic citation indexing became feasible (i.e. Google Scholar[3], CiteSeer[14]).

Early work on acknowledgments was carried out manually. Cronin et al. [9] examined prominent journals of sociology for 10 years period manually extracting acknowledgments. As part of their work they conducted the same study but on psychology and philosophy journals for a 100 years span [11]. Other fields received attention as well including history [26] , information sciences [7], and humanities [8].

Recent work [6, 15] proposed extracting acknowledgments automatically and indexing them using the CiteSeer digital library as an example. That work is most similar to ours as they extract acknowledgments along with their entities and make them searchable. However, our work builds a standalone repository and search engine for acknowledgments, using improved entity extraction techniques. Furthermore, our passage extraction algorithm achieves a higher F1 measure due to much better recall score of our algorithm (90% on average) while they achieved a recall around 67% [4]. As mentioned, we use multiple state-of-the-art Named Entity Recognition (NER) tools to identify entities in the acknowledgments section. We introduce a method to utilize results from multiple NER instances and merge them. This is very useful as some NERs are better in extracting person names while others are superior in identifying organizations. Their NER was based on hand written rules that are only capable of extracting certain organization names but not person names. In both cases we are able to outperform their work and also propose a novel approach for entity merging and clustering.

Extracting acknowledgments from digital libraries can be considered another variation of information and metadata extraction where multiple approaches have been proposed including regular expressions, rule based extractors, and machine learning methods. Regular expressions and rule-based systems can perform well in certain problems as long as the data does not change but are tedious to maintain when new data becomes available. As in that work [6, 15] we use regular expressions to identify acknowledgment passages since this extraction can be robust. But in the case of NERs, those

[3]http://scholar.google.com

[4]The values were achieved on different datasets because the data they used in experiments was lost along with the code. Hence, we used a different dataset that includes the top cited papers of all time which is more likely to be in their dataset

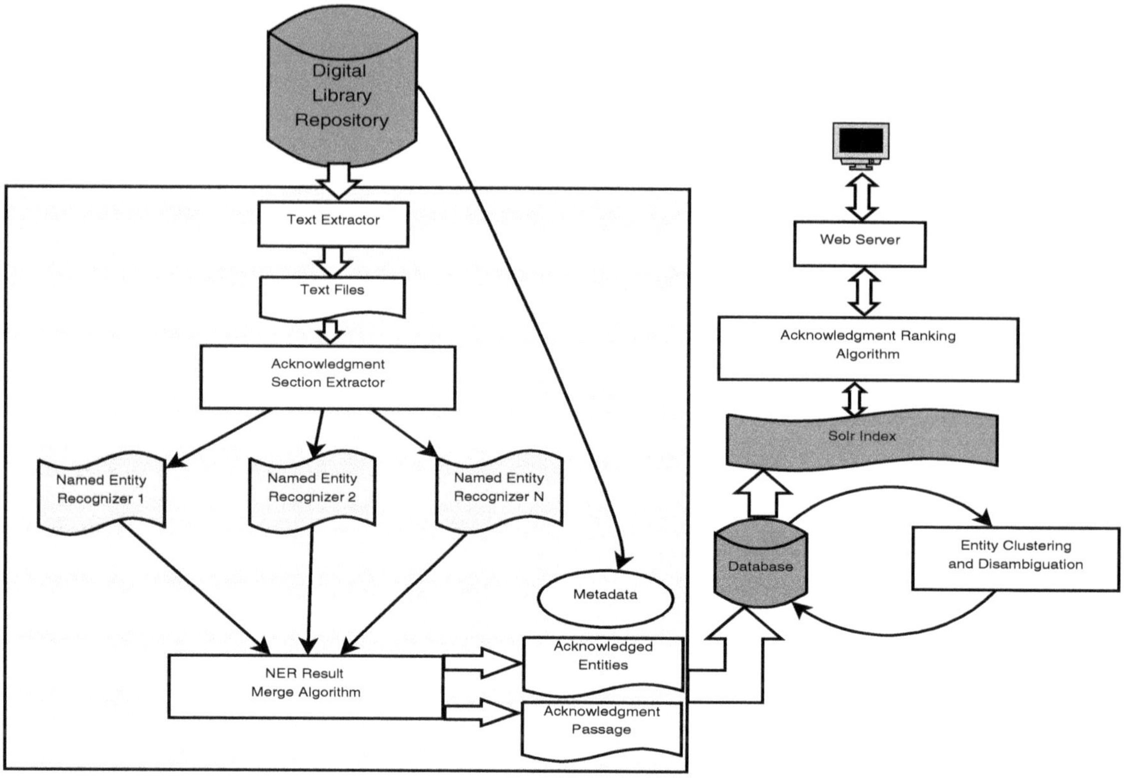

Figure 1: The Architecture of AckSeer

based on machine learning methods such as Hidden Markov Models (HMM)[32] and Conditional Random Fields (CRF) [27] have been applied successfully to multiple domains reducing the need to hand-craft rules and to manually extract entities. Other machine learning techniques like Support Vector Machines (SVM) are very popular in classifying high dimensional data , and information extraction can be cast as a classification problem [5]. Han et al. [16] used SVMs to automatically extract metadata in building digital libraries, while others have applied SVM for chunk identification [22] and named entity recognition [17, 28].

Repositories of sub-objects are gaining popularity due to the need to browse and search these sub-objects independently of their parent-objects (i.e. paper, book) and since they might represent summaries of the work discussed within the article. Searching for figures, tables, algorithms and chemical formulas are examples of sub-object repositories made possible. Tables have been extracted from digital libraries and repository was built that indexs tables and ranks them with a novel ranking algorithm [24, 23]. Along with tables, plots and figures are often used to provide measures, comparisons and results of experiments, which has led to an interest in extracting these plots and associated data [19, 25]. While summaries are usually reported in tables and figures, computer scientists and software developers are also interested in algorithms and pseudo code. Bhatia et al. [3, 4] built a search engine for extracting and indexing algorithms found in the computer science literature.

3. ARCHITECTURE

3.1 System Overview

Figure 1 shows the architecture of *AckSeer*. The system can be built for any digital library that can provide documents in PDF format along with their metadata. These files are then converted to text using a converter such as PDFbox and the output is passed to the section extraction algorithm which is discussed in section 4.1. If acknowledgments are found within the documents, the extracted passage would be passed to multiple NERs to extract the entities mentioned. Currently, we use OpenCalais[2] and AlchemyAPI[1] as NERs but there is no limit on the number of NERs that can be used simultaneously. The results from the NERs are aggregated and merged together removing duplicates and ignoring entities that are contained in other NERs results. The resulting acknowledgment passage along with the entities and the metadata generated by NERs and given by the digital library are stored in the database. The entity clustering and disambiguation process is run in batches on the entities within the database to merge variations of the same entity. For example, NSF and National Science Foundation are merged into the same cluster. The entities are then indexed with Solr/Lucene along with metadata of the containing document and the acknowledgment passage and become searchable through the web interface.

3.2 User Interface

The user interface resembles most standard search engines in order to keep the system familiar and easy to use. Figure 2 shows different screenshots from the user interface. The

(a) The landing page of AckSeer

(b) The results page for a specific query

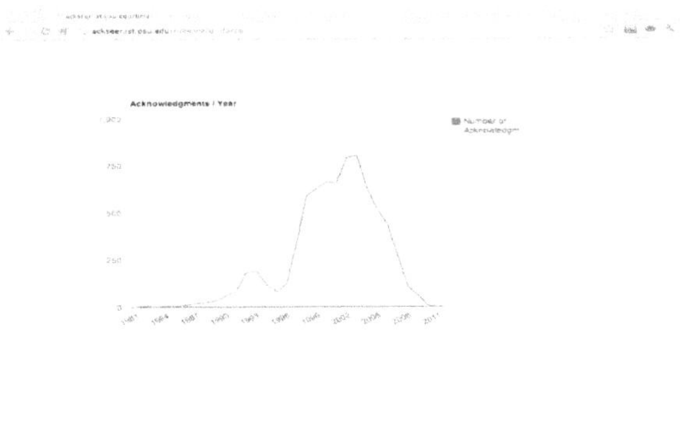

(c) Timeline view for the query DARPA.

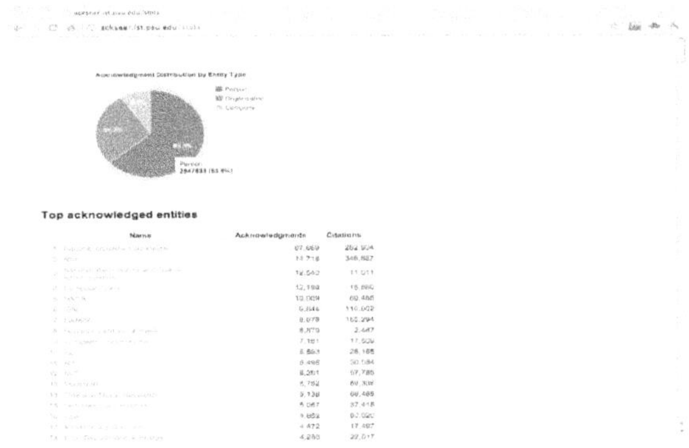

(d) The statistics page of Ackseer

Figure 2: Screenshots of AckSeer

landing page shown in figure 2(a) [5] is where a query can be submitted to the system. There are multiple types of queries which the system is capable of handling. The default query mode would try to match the terms of the query against the words of the acknowledgment passage in a digital document. Alternatively, the user may specify the field against which the query is matched by preceding the query terms with the field name followed by colon. Available fields are *entities* and *title*. The query "entities:NSF"would search for NSF in the list of extracted entities of each acknowledgment passage, while the query "title:Google" would search for acknowledgments appearing in documents that have the word Google in its title. The results page for a query is shown in figure 2(b). For each matching acknowledgment the metadata shown includes the title of the containing paper, the number of citations the paper received, the list of extracted entities, and the acknowledgment passage itself.

For a specific query q it is possible to view the timeline of papers that contain q in the acknowledgements section. The timeline is a plot where the x axis represents the year and the y axis represents the number of papers published in that year where q appeared in the acknowledgments. Figure 2(c) shows the timeline for the query *DARPA*. The last interface of *AckSeer* is the statistics page which shows a pie chart of the distribution of entity types in the repository. Further, we maintain four lists showing the top acknowledged entities, persons, companies, and organizations where each list presents the entities along with the number of times they have been acknowledged and the number of citations these papers acknowledging them have received.

[5]The image on AckSeer homepage is courtesy of PhD Comics `http://www.phdcomics.com/comics/archive.php?comicid=870`

4. ACKNOWLEDGMENT EXTRACTION

In this section we describe the methods deployed in extracting acknowledgment passages and entities. After that we introduce a novel approach to cluster and disambiguate entities appearing in acknowledgments. Eventually we propose ranking functions that can be used while searching for acknowledgments.

4.1 Passage Extraction

Identifying acknowledgment sections is a crucial part of *AckSeer* and is the first step towards building the repository. Errors encountered during the extraction would carry through the indexing pipeline; therefore, we try to mitigate the effect of accumulated errors by building robust passage extractors. Previous work on acknowledgments extraction used regular expressions achieving a high precision , 99%, but relatively moderate recall, 67% [6, 15]. Inspired by that work we devised an algorithm to identify the different sections and chapters of digital documents mainly though regular expressions, since most of documents in digital libraries including papers and books are semi-structured.

To evaluate an extraction algorithm we need a tagged dataset or gold standard on which we can measure the performance of different extraction methods. To the best of our knowledge, there is no tagged dataset for acknowledgments extraction. Our constructed dataset contains the top 200 cited papers/books in the CiteSeerX[6] digital library. Highly cited papers were chosen so that the performance of the extractors would be biased towards higher quality papers and books, assuming that the number of citations is correlated with the quality of the work. Among the 200 papers that we manually examined, 130 of them had an acknowledgments section accounting for about 65% of the dataset. We use the following tags to identify objects appearing in the acknowledgment passage, while of course others could be considered:

- Acknowledgment: the acknowledgments section
- Person: indicates a person being acknowledged
- Entity: indicate an agency or company being acknowledged
- Scholarship: acknowledging a scholarship
- Project: acknowledging a project
- GrantNum: grant number
- ContractNum: contract number

Listing 1: Example of a tagged acknowledgment

```
<acknowledgment>
ACKNOWLEDGEMENTS W.M. and Z.Z. are
supported by grant <grantNum> LM05110
</grantNum> from the <entity>National
Library of Medicine </entity>. We thank
Dr <person> Warren Gish</person> for
helpful conversations , Dr <person> Eugene
 Koonin</person> for assistance with the
examples , and Dr <person> Gregory Schuler
</person> for producing several of the
figures . </acknowledgment>
```

After examining numerous papers and books in the CiteseerX digital library to understand how and where authors tend to write the acknowledgments section, we devised an algorithm that utilized regular expressions to segment each paper/book into sections (chapters for books). The header or the title of each section is then filtered, and headers referring to acknowledgments are stored. This is a modified version of the section identification method used in [31]. Algorithm 1 shows the pseudocode of the section extraction process. Briefly, the algorithm checks each line in the document against a predefined set of regular expressions that detect section headers. If the line is considered a match, a new section is detected and all the lines following the header are considered section content. A new section is started whenever a content line matches the header regular expressions. Eventually, all identified section headers are examined and if acknowledgments were to be found between them, the content is extracted. The algorithm is linear in both time and space making it quite scalable on large numbers of documents.

The regular expression based extraction algorithm yields hard precision and hard recall values at 83.7% and 83.8% respectively. The hard precision and hard recall is defined such that an extracted acknowledgment is only correct if it

[6]http://citeseerx.ist.psu.edu

Algorithm 1: Section extraction algorithm

```
input  : A text document D
output: Acknowledgment section
Sections ⟵ HashTable;
header ⟵ read line ;
content ⟵ ∅;
while not at end of D do
    read line l;
    if l matches new section regex then
        Add header and content to Sections;
        header ⟵ l;
    else
        Append l to content;
    end
end
for header, content ∈ Sections do
    if header matches acknowledgment regex then
        return header, content;
    end
end
```

Table 1: Performance of the acknowledgment extractor on the training dataset of 200 papers

Measure	Value
Hard Precision	83.7%
Hard Recall	83.8%
Hard F1 score	83.7%
Precision	92.3%
Recall	91.6%
F1 score	91.9%
Precision without books	98.3%
Recall without books	97.6%
F1 score without books	97.9%

is a verbatim match of the manually tagged one. So if the extractor extracted an extra dot or semicolon, the acknowledgment is not considered to be successfully extracted. We found that the extractor sometimes extracted an extra line such as the title of the journal article along with the issue that sometimes appears at the header or footer of the page. This small line doesn't make the extracted acknowledgment necessarily incorrect, as the original acknowledgment is extracted completely but with an extra line. A similar scenario can occur when journal articles list the date on which the paper was received. Based on our definition above, when there is more than one extra line beyond the original acknowledgment, the extracted passage is considered incorrect. We relaxed this restriction and now consider such a passage to be a correctly extracted acknowledgment. Under this relaxed assumption, the value of precision and recall are 92.3% and 91.6% respectively. It's worth noting that our dataset comprises both books and papers, and the errors which our extractor makes are mostly on books, which is expected since books have more variation in their acknowledgement format than papers. If we exclude books, our precision and recall jumps to 98.3% and 97.6% respectively. Table 1 summarizes the performance of the section extractor on the top 200 cited papers in computer science in CiteSeerX digital library.

4.2 Entity Extraction

The next phase in building the acknowledgments repository is to extract the entities inside the acknowledgment section. Named Entity Recognition (NER) has been studied extensively in the literature, and systems have been able to achieve 90% accuracy in many competitions. Instead of building our own NER system, we decided to leverage what is available in open source and free web services. We have examined many open source tools: OpenNLP, NLTK, Apache UIMA, Illinois Named Entity Tagger, OpenCalais[2] and AlchemyAPI[1]. Upon examining the different NERs it became clear that certain extractors perform better on specific types of entities and poorly on other types. For example, some NERs are more suited to extract celebrity names and organizational entities, while they fail to recognize normal person names. Others, however, might do a better job on person names due to their large dictionary of names, but perform poorly on organizations and company entities.

Guided by this, we designed a name extraction module that is capable of consuming results from different NERs and allowing them to work in parallel. The outputs from all the NERs are collected and merged together to generate a single list of entities. The merger is performed as follows: for an acknowledgment passage p, a set of NERs $N_1...N_k$ is ran on p, with each N_i generating a list of entities E_i. Then, all the lists $E_1...E_k$ are concatenated into single list L. For each entity $e_i \in L$ we remove all verbatim duplicates e_j such that $e_i = e_j$ and $i \neq j$ from the list L. After that, we find and remove all entities e_k such that $e_k \in e_i$ and e_i starts with e_k. In other words we eliminate all substrings of the entity e_i that share the same prefix. This step helps remove sub-identified entities that are not extracted in full form. The problem occurred quite often in our experiments and the suggested solution helped mitigate the issue. For example, while extracting *National Research Council Canada* extractor A successfully identified the entity, while extractor B would only extract *National Research Council*.

In *AckSeer* we chose to use OpenCalais and AlchemyAPI because they provide a web service that can be easily called and provide quality extraction and disambiguation results. OpenCalais is a web service developed by Reuters that provides many knowledge extraction services, but we only use the entity extraction part. AlchemyAPI is another system which provides a plethora of text extraction services including text stripping, language detection, and last but not least Named Entity Extraction. Similar to OpenCalais, we only use the NER part of AlchemyAPI.

In our experiments with both OpenCalais, and AlchemyAPI we found OpenCalais to be superior to AlchemyAPI in identifying and extracting organizations and companies, while AlchemyAPI is better at extracting names of persons. As such, we use both systems to extract the entities and then merge them based on the name of the entity (as it appears in the text). If the entities are well known, OpenCalais and AlchemyAPI would provide disambiguated canonical names, along with links to dbpedia[7] and freebase[8]. However, our experiments with the disambiguation results of both APIs showed clearly that the results are not accurate enough and a standalone disambiguation method is needed. The above mentioned section identification method is similar to what was used in our previous work[20].

[7]http://dbpedia.org/

[8]http://www.freebase.com/

4.3 Instance Merging and Disambiguation

OpenCalais and AlchemyAPI tag the extracted entities into three categories: person, company, and organization. In the following sections we propose methods to disambiguate and merge instances of the same entity.

4.3.1 Entity Names

Authors have different ways of writing their acknowledged entities; some prefer to use the full name of the entity while others tend to use abbreviations and acronyms. For example, *National Science Foundation*, the most acknowledged entity in our dataset, is frequently written in full form but the acronym *NSF* is also as frequent but never in lower case. To have accurate statistics about each entity we should handle all naming variations and cluster them together. The variations are not only acronyms v.s. full form; sometimes entities are written with a shorter name than the full form. For example, *"Natural Sciences and Engineering Research Council of Canada"* and *"Engineering Research Council"* appear to refer to the same entity, and both are frequently used in acknowledgments. Similar examples include: *"Stanford"* and *"Stanford University"*; *"U.S Federal Reserve"*, *"The Federal Reserve"*, *"United States Federal Reserve"*. Therefore, disambiguating entities is far more complicated than just using a dictionary of acronyms along with their long form. Even popular acronym databases are ineffective in disambiguating acknowledged entities because they are built by matching a letter from the acronym with the beginning of a word in the full form. These methods would fail to recognize many acronyms especially if the acronym stems from languages other than English. For example *German Research Foundation*, which is the German NSF equivalent, is acknowledged in three different formats: 1) *DFG* , 2) *Deutsche Forschungsgemeinschaft*, 3) *German Research Foundation*. Predefined acronym databases fail to recognize that all the three forms refer to the same entity.

Earlier work on acknowledgment indexing used manually crafted dictionaries to match and merge instances of the same entity [6]. Building a dictionary is a very labor intensive task, and simply not feasible because our repository contains more than 4 million mentioned entities. Given the aforementioned challenges in disambiguating entities we explored other approaches that utilize outside world information for clustering, and at the same time scale to the size of our data. Hence, we propose an approach that relies on search engine results to cluster entities. The basic idea is that variations of the same entity should have similar search results when querying a search engine like Google or Bing. For example, searching Bing for "NSF" or "National Science Foundation" returns *www.nsf.gov* in both queries. Search engines invest a lot of resources in disambiguating queries and clustering them to return the best results. Using a search engine API would allow us to access this information and use it for clustering. In this work Bing API[9] is used to create a profile for each entity, where the profile contains the top ten results returned by Bing when querying for that entity. A similar approach [29] to our work uses search engine results to disambiguate authors of research papers. We differ in how these results are used.

[9]http://www.bing.com/toolbox/bingdeveloper/

For each entity e_i in our repository where $i \in 1..n$, we create a list l_i containing the top ten urls returned by Bing API when querying for e_i. For each domain d appearing as the first result on l_i we create a new cluster d and add e_i to it. If that cluster already exists, we just add e_i to it. The resulting cluster d contains all the entities whose first search result is on on the domain d. Algorithm 2 shows the pseudo-code of our approach. The variable k in algorithm 2 controls the number of clusters that e_i get assigned to. Currently we use $k = 1$ to use the first search result only.

Algorithm 2: Entity Disambiguation Algorithm

```
input : Set of entities Entities and list of domains L_e
Clusters ⟵ HashTable;
for e ∈ Entities do
    u ⟵ L_e[0];
    if u ∈ Clusters then
        Add e to Clusters[u];
    else
        Create new cluster Clusters[u];
        Add e to Clusters[u];
    end
end
for e ∈ Entities do
    for i ← 1 to k do
        if L_e[i] ∈ Clusters then
            Add e to Clusters[L_e[i]];
        end
    end
end
return Clusters;
```

Our search engine driven disambiguation method showed promising results, and is very fast since it only needs to scan the list of entities once, yielding linear run time, assuming the search results are available. We generate the list of url results in a separate batch job before running the disambiguation method. This linearity allows us to process the entire repository of more than 4 million entities in few minutes.

Future work could explore the number of URLs that can be used for each entity (the variable k in the algorithm). Currently, we only use the first search result for efficiency, but in many cases we found that the correct cluster for the url is not the first one. Our estimate suggests that using the first url increases the precision but decreases the recall. Other potential future work is to consider the results as features in a high dimension space and apply a hierarchical clustering algorithm.

4.3.2 Person Names

Person disambiguation in the case of acknowledgments can be considered a form of author disambiguation. The assumption is reasonable given the patterns of acknowledgments described in the introduction. As of now we do not perform any person specific disambiguation however one could treat acknowledged persons as coauthors and use random forest based author disambiguation [30]. Errors here do occur and *John Wiley* is classified as a person.

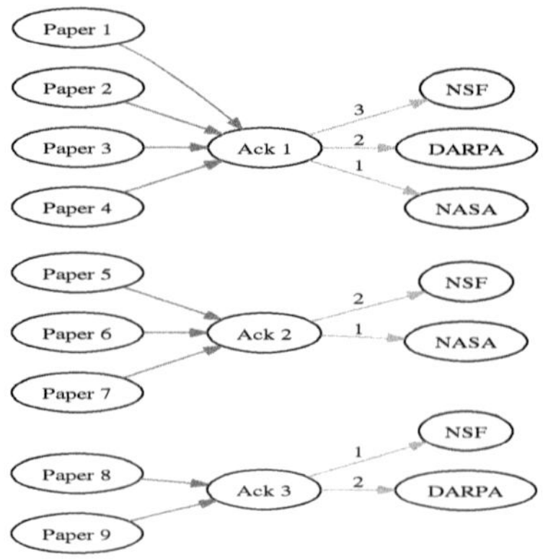

Figure 3: Graph of citations and acknowledgments used for ranking

4.4 Searching and Ranking

AckSeer provides a search interface to access millions of acknowledged entities that were extracted from more than 500,000 papers and books. An effective ranking algorithm is required to navigate through the hundred of thousands of acknowledgments. Traditional ranking methods based on term frequency and inverse document frequency are not effective here because an entity appears only once inside the acknowledgment passage. TF-IDF based ranking would be no different than a database query returning all matching records in no specific order. We propose an approach to rank acknowledgments which takes advantage of the number of citations received by the document containing the acknowledgment. The intuition is that citations can be considered as incoming credit to the paper, while acknowledgments are outgoing credit. By distributing the incoming credit to the outgoing credit, we would be able to rank the important acknowledgment passages. This method is inspired by the HITS algorithm [21] and earlier rankings of acknowledgements in CiteSeer. Figure 3 shows three acknowledgment passages receiving citations from papers 1 through 9 and acknowledging the entities NSF, DARPA and NASA. The blue edges denote citations while red edges denote acknowledgment. The number on the red edges denotes the order of appearance in the acknowledgment passage.

4.4.1 Citations

Given a query Q, a list of matching acknowledgments L is retrieved from the inverted index and the returned result is ranked by the inverse order of the citations count. With this method citations are distributed evenly on all acknowledged entities. In the example shown in figure 3, given the query NSF the returned result will be $[Ack1, Ack2, Ack3]$.

4.4.2 Citations Inverse Entity Count Boost

The Citations Inverse Entity Count Boost ($CIECB$) ranks acknowledgments by citations by first boosting the matching entities with the reciprocal of the entities count in the acknowledgment. So for a given query Q and matching acknowledgment passage A, the similarity score is computed:

$$Sim(Q, A) = Citations(A) * \frac{1}{|entities \in A|}$$

In the same example of figure 3 and the query NSF, the resulting order would be $[Ack2, Ack1, Ack3]$

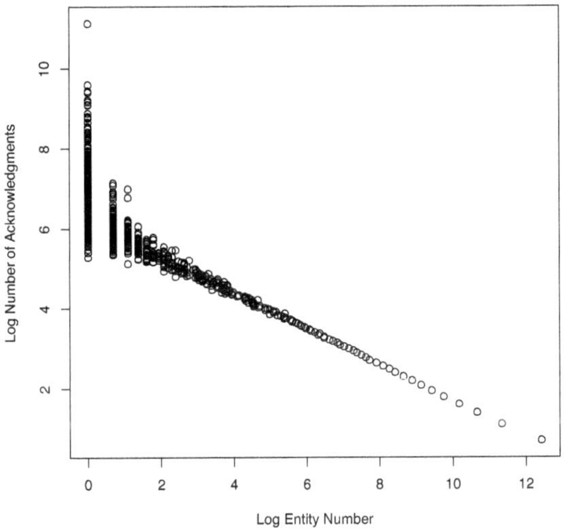

Figure 4: A scatter plot in log log scale for number of acknowledgments against the number of entities

4.4.3 Citations Inverse Entity Count with Order Boost

The Citations Inverse Entity Count with Order Boost ($CIECOB$) assumes that acknowledged entities are similar to authors, hence the order of appearance matters. The first acknowledged entity should receive higher credit than the subsequent entities, just like in the case of authorship. The similarity function from $CIECB$ is augmented as follows: $Sim(Q, A) = Citations(A) * \frac{1}{|entities \in A|} * \frac{1}{Order(Q) in A}$

Going back to our example in figure 3 and the query NSF, the result in this case would be $[Ack3, Ack2, Ack1]$. Using $CIECOB$ we are able to capture the importance of order, count, and citations in a single ranking scheme.

5. EXPERIMENTS AND ANALYSIS

5.1 Repository

In our experiments of *AckSeer* we use the repository of CiteSeerX digital library which for this work contained more than 1.5 million documents in computer science, math and statistics. The section extractor identified acknowledgments in 526,930 of the papers in the repository. From the extracted acknowledgments we extracted 4,486,134 entity mentions, 1,648,013 of which were unique textually. The distribution of entity types was as follows: 2,847,893 persons, 1,225,947 organizations, and 412,294 companies. We ranked the top acknowledged entities, and our results are similar to [15, 6] in showing that National Science Foundation is the top acknowledged entity. Table 2 shows the top acknowledged entities with manual disambiguation of top results. It also shows the number of citations received from by the papers that acknowledge these entities. The last column is the result of dividing the citations by the acknowledgments. These statistics are an extension of what we found in our previous work [20].

As noted in table 2, the top acknowledged entities are all organizations and companies. We extracted the top acknowledged persons in our dataset, and noticed that there

Table 2: Top acknowledged entities in CiteSeerX

Entity	# Acks	# Cites	Cites/Acks
NSF	67659	282904	4.18
NASA	12540	11011	0.88
European Union	12199	15660	1.28
IBM	9644	110902	11.50
DARPA	8976	155294	17.30
NIH	8879	2487	0.28
European Commission	7181	17509	2.44
MIT	6291	57785	9.19
Microsoft	5752	58336	10.14
Office of Naval Research	5138	66465	12.94

Table 3: Top acknowledged persons in CiteSeerX

Entity	Number of Acks	H-Index
Oded Goldreich	471	37
Olivier Danvy	350	24
Avi Wigderson	325	29
Vern Paxson	325	36
David Wagner	313	32
Jim Gray	309	21
Paul Taylor	292	14
Sally Floyd	288	40
Jon Crowcroft	270	25

is a relation between the h-index[10] of the person and the number of time she/he has been acknowledged. We use the h-index values computed by CiteSeerX. We leave further analysis of this observation to future work.

5.2 Disambiguation

We evaluate our disambiguation algorithm by constructing a dataset that consists of the top 500 acknowledged entities in *AckSeer*. As our baseline, we implement the longest common subsequence algorithm (LCS). The LCS algorithm is a common method for sequence alignment. It uses dynamic programming to compute optimal alignment between two sequences of characters. We use simple heuristics to separate acronyms from non-acronym entity names. For each non-acronym name we generate its potential acronym, by taking the first letter of each word in the name. To determine if an acronym name s matches a target name t, which can be either another acronym or a full name, we compute the longest common subsequence between s and t (or the potential acronym of t, if t is a full name). If the length of the longest common subsequence is greater than 0.7 of the length of the longer acronym, they are considered to match, , for instance, between 'USAF' and 'US Air Force.' On the other hand, for two non-acronym names to match, one has to be a substring of the other, e.g. 'US Department of Energy' and 'Department of Energy.' We compute the pairwise LCS score between all the elements in our dataset. The clusters are created such that all the entities in cluster c have pairwise LCS score > 0.7. A cluster c is considered correct if all the entities inside that cluster refer to the same entity. In our evaluation we only consider clusters that have more

[10]An author would have h-index = X if he has X papers each of which has been cited at least X times

than one entity. LCS generates 89 clusters that have *support*[11] > 1. We manually inspected these clusters and found out that 49 of them are correct resulting in 55% accuracy.

Next we evaluate the accuracy of our search engine based algorithm. The search results are retrieved for entities in the dataset and we run algorithm 2 with default parameter values. We manually examine the generated clusters for accuracy, that is the purity within the cluster. Overall, the algorithm detects 345 clusters with 70 of them having *support* > 1. Among the 70 clusters, 65 of them were correct resulting in an accuracy of 92.8%. That is a significant improvement over the base line.

The following list shows some of the correctly detected clusters:

- **www.bmbf.de**: {BMBF , German Federal Ministry of Education and Research, German Ministry of Education}
- **www.defense.gov**: { Department of Defense, U.S. Department of Defense, DoD}
- **www.usa.gov**: {U.S. government, United States Government, US Government, federal government }

Some of the mistakes that the algorithm makes can be traced back to the generality of the entity. For example our algorithm clusters the entity **"Department of Electrical Engineering"** with the *princeton.edu* cluster because their department of electrical engineering appears as the first result on Bing, and the url of the result is on the princeton domain (not a subdomain). Future work would research the trade-off between using domain name and full URL in building the clusters.

5.3 Acknowledgments Social Graph

In our previous work we have studied a small graph [20] of the acknowledgment network where the nodes are authors and acknowledged entities. The edges are created between an author a whose paper p acknowledges entity e. Our experiment was conducted on the graph resulting from the top 1000 cited papers in CiteSeerX. We examined a few social network measures on the small graph such as degree distribution, centrality and clustering coefficients where we found out that the in-degree and out-degree follow a power law distribution.

6. CONCLUSIONS AND FUTURE WORK

In this paper we introduced *AckSeer*, the repository and search engine for automatically extracted acknowledgments. We described the architecture of an acknowledgment search engine that is domain independent and repository independent. Our section extraction algorithm is based on regular expressions but it is robust enough with average F1 score 85%. We extract entities from the acknowledgments using multiple NERs and introduce a method to merge their results. In addition, we disambiguate and merge instances of the same entity using a novel search engine based disambiguation algorithm. The nature of acknowledgments and entity frequencies lead us to devise new ranking functions that utilize the importance of the paper and its citations. *AckSeer* was built on top of CiteSeerX digital library with more than 500,000 acknowledgments and 4 million entities. Future work could take many directions, i.e. exploration of the semantics of acknowledgments in order to understand the reasoning behind mentioned entities. Other disambiguation and NER techniques could be investigated due to current limitations in accuracy and disambiguation. Better entity clustering could explored and large heterogeneous acknowledgement graphs might give social insights.

[11]The support of the cluster denotes the number of elements in it

7. ACKNOWLEDGMENTS

We thank Pradeep Teregowda and Sharon Koppman for the useful discussions and suggestions. We gratefully acknowledge AlchemyAPI for increasing our requests limit, and partial funding from NSF.

8. REFERENCES

[1] AlchemyAPI. `http://www.alchemyapi.com/`.

[2] OpenCalais. `http://www.opencalais.com/`.

[3] S. Bhatia, P. Mitra, and C. L. Giles. Finding algorithms in scientific articles. In *Proceedings of the 19th international conference on World wide web*, WWW '10, pages 1061–1062. ACM, 2010.

[4] S. Bhatia, S. Tuarob, P. Mitra, and C. L. Giles. An algorithm search engine for software developers. In *Proceedings of the 3rd International Workshop on Search-Driven Development: Users, Infrastructure, Tools, and Evaluation*, SUITE '11, pages 13–16, 2011.

[5] H. Chieu and H. Ng. A maximum entropy approach to information extraction from semi-structured and free text. In *Proceedings of the National Conference on Artificial Intelligence*, pages 786–791. Menlo Park, CA; Cambridge, MA; London; AAAI Press; MIT Press; 1999, 2002.

[6] I. Councill, C. Giles, H. Han, and E. Manavoglu. Automatic acknowledgement indexing: expanding the semantics of contribution in the citeseer digital library. In *Proceedings of the 3rd international conference on Knowledge capture*, pages 19–26. ACM, 2005.

[7] B. Cronin. Acknowledgement trends in the research literature of information science. *Journal of Documentation*, 57(3):427–433, 2001.

[8] B. Cronin, G. McKenzie, and L. Rubio. The norms of acknowledgement in four humanities and social sciences disciplines. *Journal of Documentation*, 49(1):29–43, 1993.

[9] B. Cronin, G. McKenzie, L. Rubio, and S. Weaver-Wozniak. Accounting for influence: Acknowledgments in contemporary sociology. *Journal of the American Society for Information Science*, 44(7):406–412, 1993.

[10] B. Cronin, G. McKenzie, and M. Stiffler. Patterns of acknowledgement. *Journal of Documentation*, 48(2):107–122, 1992.

[11] B. Cronin, D. Shaw, and K. La Barre. A cast of thousands: Coauthorship and subauthorship collaboration in the 20th century as manifested in the scholarly journal literature of psychology and philosophy. *Journal of the American Society for Information Science and Technology*, 54(9):855–871, 2003.

[12] C. Davis and B. Cronin. Acknowledgments and intellectual indebtedness: A bibliometric conjecture. *Journal of the American Society for Information Science*, 44(10):590–592, 1993.

[13] D. Edge. Quantitative measures of communication in science: A critical review. *History of Science*, 17:102–134, 1979.

[14] C. Giles, K. Bollacker, and S. Lawrence. Citeseer: An automatic citation indexing system. In *Proceedings of the third ACM conference on Digital libraries*, pages 89–98. ACM, 1998.

[15] C. Giles and I. Councill. Who gets acknowledged: Measuring scientific contributions through automatic acknowledgment indexing. *Proceedings of the National Academy of Sciences of the United States of America*, 101(51):17599, 2004.

[16] H. Han, C. L. Giles, E. Manavoglu, H. Zha, Z. Zhang, and E. A. Fox. Automatic document metadata extraction using support vector machines. In *Proceedings of the 3rd ACM/IEEE-CS joint conference on Digital libraries*, JCDL '03, pages 37–48, Washington, DC, USA, 2003. IEEE Computer Society.

[17] H. Isozaki and H. Kazawa. Efficient support vector classifiers for named entity recognition. In *Proceedings of the 19th international conference on Computational linguistics - Volume 1*, COLING '02, pages 1–7, Stroudsburg, PA, USA, 2002. Association for Computational Linguistics.

[18] J. Kassirer and M. Angell. On authorship and acknowledgments. *New England Journal of Medicine*, 325(21):1510–1512, 1991.

[19] S. Kataria, W. Browuer, P. Mitra, and C. L. Giles. Automatic extraction of data points and text blocks from 2-dimensional plots in digital documents. In *Proceedings of the 23rd national conference on Artificial intelligence - Volume 2*, AAAI'08, pages 1169–1174. AAAI Press, 2008.

[20] M. Khabsa, S. Koppman, and C. Giles. Towards building and analyzing a social network of acknowledgments in scientific and academic documents. *Social Computing, Behavioral-Cultural Modeling and Prediction*, pages 357–364, 2012.

[21] J. Kleinberg. Authoritative sources in a hyperlinked environment. *Journal of the ACM (JACM)*, 46(5):604–632, 1999.

[22] T. Kudoh and Y. Matsumoto. Use of support vector learning for chunk identification. In *Proceedings of the 2nd workshop on Learning language in logic and the 4th conference on Computational natural language learning-Volume 7*, pages 142–144. Association for Computational Linguistics, 2000.

[23] Y. Liu, K. Bai, P. Mitra, and C. Giles. Tablerank: A ranking algorithm for table search and retrieval. In *Proceeding Of The National Conference On Artificial Intelligence*, volume 22, page 317. Menlo Park, CA; Cambridge, MA; London; AAAI Press; MIT Press; 1999, 2007.

[24] Y. Liu, K. Bai, P. Mitra, and C. L. Giles. Tableseer: automatic table metadata extraction and searching in digital libraries. In *Proceedings of the 7th ACM/IEEE-CS joint conference on Digital libraries*, JCDL '07, pages 91–100, New York, NY, USA, 2007. ACM.

[25] X. Lu, J. Wang, P. Mitra, and C. Giles. Automatic extraction of data from 2-d plots in documents. In *Document Analysis and Recognition, 2007. ICDAR 2007. Ninth International Conference on*, volume 1, pages 188 -192, sept. 2007.

[26] L. Scrivener. An exploratory analysis of history students' dissertation acknowledgments. *The Journal of Academic Librarianship*, 35(3):241–251, 2009.

[27] B. Settles. Biomedical named entity recognition using conditional random fields and rich feature sets. In *Proceedings of the International Joint Workshop on Natural Language Processing in Biomedicine and its Applications*, pages 104–107. Association for Computational Linguistics, 2004.

[28] K. Takeuchi and N. Collier. Use of support vector machines in extended named entity recognition. In *proceedings of the 6th conference on Natural language learning-Volume 20*, pages 1–7. Association for Computational Linguistics, 2002.

[29] Y. F. Tan, M. Y. Kan, and D. Lee. Search engine driven author disambiguation. In *Proceedings of the 6th ACM/IEEE-CS joint conference on Digital libraries*, JCDL '06, pages 314–315. ACM, 2006.

[30] P. Treeratpituk and C. Giles. Disambiguating authors in academic publications using random forests. In *Proceedings of the 9th ACM/IEEE-CS joint conference on Digital libraries*, pages 39–48. ACM, 2009.

[31] P. Treeratpituk, P. Teregowda, J. Huang, and C. Giles. Seerlab: A system for extracting key phrases from scholarly documents. In *Proceedings of the 5th International Workshop on Semantic Evaluation*, pages 182–185. Association for Computational Linguistics, 2010.

[32] G. Zhou and J. Su. Named entity recognition using an hmm-based chunk tagger. In *Proceedings of the 40th Annual Meeting on Association for Computational Linguistics*, pages 473–480. Association for Computational Linguistics, 2002.

Learning Topics and Related Passages in Books

David Newman
Computer Science
Univ. California, Irvine
newman@uci.edu

Youn Noh
Office of Digital Assets and Infrastructure
Yale University
youn.noh@yale.edu

Kat Hagedorn
University Libraries
University of Michigan
khage@umich.edu

Arun Balagopalan
Computer Science
Univ. California, Irvine
abalagop@ics.uci.edu

ABSTRACT

The number of books available online is increasing, but user interfaces may not be taking full advantage of advances in machine learning techniques that could help users navigate, explore, discover and understand interesting and useful content in books. Using a group of ten students and over one thousand crowdsourced judgments, we conducted multiple user studies to evaluate topics and related passages in books, all learned by topic modeling. Using ten books, selected from humanities (e.g. Plato's *Republic*), social sciences (e.g. Marx's *Capital*) and sciences (e.g. Einstein's *Relativity*), and four different evaluation experiments, we show that users agree that the learned topics are coherent and important to the book, and related to the automatically generated passages. We show how crowdsourced evaluations are useful, and can complement more focused evaluations using students who have studied the texts. This work provides a framework for (1) learning topics and related passages in books, and (2) evaluating those learned topics and passages, and moves one step toward automatic annotation to support topic navigation of books.

Categories and Subject Descriptors
H.4.0 [**Information Systems**]: *General*

Keywords:
topic modeling, book navigation, text mining

INTRODUCTION

In Plato's *Republic*, what place does justice have in virtue? In Marx's *Capital*, in what sense can we say that nature does not produce value; only labor produces value?[1] These are typical questions asked of students studying these texts. To answer these questions a student may page through a copy of the text, looking for relevant passages. The student may also make use of the book's index or table of contents.

With electronic books, students can conduct searches for key terms or phrases, and possibly find key passages to help them answer these types of essay questions. But the searching the *Republic* for 'justice' produces over 700 hits. A list of 700+ search results, or even a visualization of these hits within the book, barely scratches the surface of what could be done to provide effective navigation.

In this work we investigate whether topic modeling can automatically learn useful topics and related passages in books. Topic modeling is a technique for automatically extracting semantic themes from document collections, and has been shown to produce highly coherent and relevant topics. Here we focus on the value and utility of these learned topics. Since "useful" depends on the need or task, we use students studying the texts as a context for our evaluation.

METHODOLOGY

We present users with topics learned by the topic model, and related passages. In addition to exploring the degree to which users approved of topics produced by the topic model, we wanted to find out if there were important topics that the topic model missed. To provide implicit context for the identification of topics, we worked with students from the University of Michigan who had been enrolled in courses in which the texts used in the study were taught. To gain insight into the degree to which user characteristics inform approval ratings, we broadened the study to include crowdsourced workers.

Selection of Texts: Our criteria for selecting texts were that they be widely taught and that they be long enough to benefit from topic navigation. Additionally, for easier access, we required all texts to be out-of-copyright. We identified a list of ten authors/books in the sciences, social sciences, and humanities. Table 1 shows the ten authors, separated into the three used for the evaluation conducted with University of Michigan students, and then using the set of ten books for our study with crowdsourced workers.

Author (Book-of-Interest)	Evaluators
Plato (Republic)	6 students / crowdsourced
Marx (Capital – Part 1)	2 students / crowdsourced
Weber (The Protestant Ethic and the Spirit of Capitalism)	2 students / crowdsourced
Plato, Marx, Weber, Darwin, Keynes, Mendel, Newton, Malthus, Einstein, Wollstonecraft	crowdsourced

Table 1. Books used in the student evaluation.

[1] Questions taken from
http://www.lawrence.edu/dept/freshman_studies/resource/fsplato.html
http://www.marxists.org/archive/marx/works/1867-c1/guide/index.htm

JCDL'12, June 10–14, 2012, Washington, DC, USA.

Topic Modeling

We used standard LDA topic modeling [1], learning 20 topics in every case. Each book was split into 1-page segments and modeled as part of a collection of similar texts by the same author or as a collection itself. We used the conventional approach of representing a topic with its top-10 terms. Table 2 shows one selected example topic from each of the ten books.

Author	Example Topic
Plato	just justice man good injustice unjust friend ...
Marx	money gold price circulation commodities silver ...
Weber	life asceticism puritan spirit rational ethical self worldly ascetic ...
Darwin	species varieties distinct genus difference genera ...
Keynes	export percent goods import trade million raw ...
Mendel	white colour red dominant recessive type coloured
Newton	moon tide sea hour force after water height ...
Malthus	population country increase food number birth mortality age ...
Einstein	ordinate space continuum system four dimensional point event ...
Wollstonecraft	woman man behaviour kind men reputation respect

Table 2. Example topic from 20 topics learned from each of the ten books used in the crowdsourced evaluation.

In the above topics, the words are listed in order of importance to the topic. The topics learned by the topic model, while being relatively coherent, sometimes take some interpretation. For example, the topic from Mendel's *Principles of Heredity* "white colour red dominant recessive type coloured" relates to the idea of Mendelian genetics and the transmission of characteristics (e.g. experiments crossing flowers of different colors). Likewise, the Einstein *Relativity* topic of "ordinate space continuum system four dimensional etc." relates to Einstein's four-dimensional formulation of space-time, one of several topics discussed in *Relativity*. Assuming some familiarity of these books, one could suggest that these topics have an instant face validity of being both relevant and important to the book. Our next step was to evaluate this suggestion.

EXPERIMENTAL DESIGN

The experiments used the ten books from Table 1, and two groups of evaluators (students and crowdsourced workers). The students had studied one book from Plato, Marx and Weber, and crowdsourced workers came from Amazon Mechanical Turk (AMT). The experiments were as follows:

Student-Eval-1: What topics are in this book? (Students -- Plato/Marx/Weber)

Student-Eval-2: Evaluate learned topics/passage for book (Students -- Plato/Marx/Weber)

Crowd-Eval-1: Evaluate learned topics/passage for book (Crowd -- Plato/Marx/Weber)

Crowd-Eval-2: Select which topic better relates to passage (Crowd -- Ten books)

Student-Eval-1: What topics are in this book?

Participants were assigned to one of three texts by Plato, Marx, and Weber that they had previously studied in a course. They were then asked to identify ten or more major topics, ideas, or themes discussed in the text.

Student-Eval-2: Evaluate learned topics for book

Participants were asked to complete a questionnaire on topics produced by the topic model for the text they had been assigned in Student-Eval-1. We took the fifteen or so topics that most related to the book of interest, and conducted the evaluation on those topics. For each of these topics, participants were presented with the top-10 words in the topic and a sample passage identified by the model as being about the topic. Students were then asked to rate their agreement with the following statements using a 5-point scale, ranging from *Strongly Agree* to *Strongly Disagree*.

1. The topic represents a coherent concept.
2. The topic is important in the book.
3. The topic accurately describes the passage.

Crowd-Eval-1: Same as Student-Eval-2 run on AMT

This task was identical to Student-Eval-2, with the following exceptions: (1) each item was presented individually to workers as a separate Human Intelligence Task (HIT); and (2) the second question on the importance of the topic in the book was omitted given that we could not assume AMT workers had read the book in question.

Crowd-Eval-2: Which topic better relates to passage?

The Crowd-Eval-2 task was designed to evaluate the topics and passages automatically learned for our set of ten books. While our long-term goal is to create and evaluate topic segmentation and topic navigation of books, this task addresses the smaller question of evaluating the coherence of topics, and the relevance of automatically learned topics to automatically selected matching passages. For the mini-collections, we needed to first identify topics that related to the book-of-interest. Here, with just the single book, we performed our evaluation over all twenty learned topics (and matching passages) for each of the ten books, with the entire evaluation generated in a fully-automated fashion. This comprehensive approach reduces potential bias in the evaluation, and gives a realistic evaluation of the range of quality one could expect from topic modeling.

EXPERIMENTAL RESULTS

Student-Eval-1: What topics are in this book?

Ten students from the University of Michigan participated in the student evaluations. Participants were selected on the basis of having previously studied one of the texts used in the study (Plato, Weber, Marx) and worked with the same text in Student-Eval-1 and Student-Eval-2.

In Student-Eval-1, participants were asked to identify major topics discussed in the text and give a representative passage about each topic. Participants were asked to use a short phrase to describe each topic. Because the students had previously studied the texts in a course, we expected some agreement on important themes but also some variation in emphasis and expression. We used the sample passages to help identify overlapping topics.

We assembled responses from the six students studying Plato, and the learned topics. While there was broad agreement among participants on several general topics, there was also considerable variation in how students described their version of the topic. For example, two of the six students suggested there was a topic relating to *City*; however, one provided the more specific *Just City*. For this general topic, the topic model had three potentially matching topics, each emphasizing a distinct aspect of cities (law and justice, war and security, economy and trade). We see broad overlap in the learned topics and topics suggested by students that echo some of the major themes emphasized in the teaching of *The Republic* (the theory of forms, the immortality of the soul, the notion of philosopher-kings). It is also interesting to note that in some cases the topic model learned topics that were not identified by any of the students (e.g., Pleasure/Pain) and vice versa (e.g., Specialization).

We observed similar results for Marx and Weber, with the topic model learning approximately 80% of the topics suggested by the students (for all of Plato, Marx and Weber), based on there being semantic overlap in key terms or phrases.

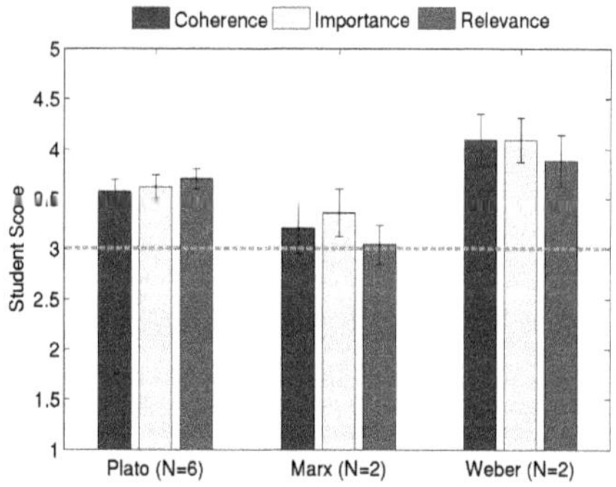

Figure 1. Average student evaluations of Plato/Marx/Weber (Student-Eval-2). Red line is neutral, above that is better.

Student-Eval-2 / Crowd-Eval-1: Evaluation of topic / passage for Plato/Marx/Weber

Student-Eval-2 was conducted with the same set of students that had participated in Student-Eval-1. For the crowdsourced task Crowd-Eval-1, a total of 199 usable responses were obtained after removal of responses from spamming workers with each HIT being performed by 3-5 workers. Note that for both Student-Eval-2 and Crowd-Eval-1, the same set of passage-topic pairs from the three books were presented, to allow direct comparison of student and worker responses.

The bar graphs in Figure 1 show mean student scores for the three questions relating to coherence, importance-to-book, and relevance-to-passage. Note that Marx and Weber only have N=2 students. The error-bars show standard error (when making comparisons, one could consider a difference significant if the respective error bars do not overlap). Our first observation is that the students on average agree that the learned topics and passages are coherent / important / relevant (the red dashed line at Score=3 indicates a neutral judgment). The results indicate that students found the topics for Weber slightly better than those for Plato, which in turn were better than the Marx topics.

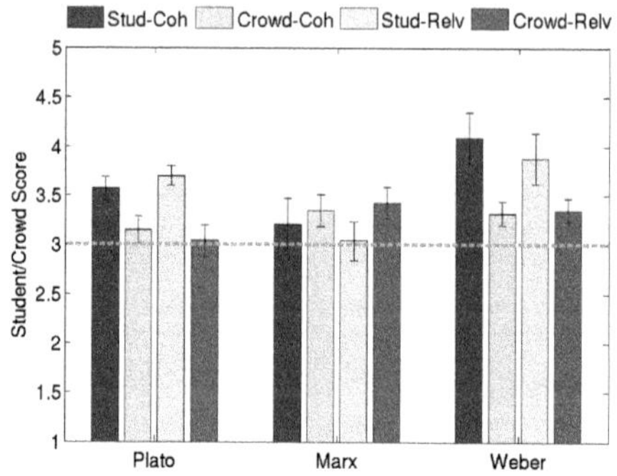

Figure 2. Comparison of student and worker evaluations of Plato/Marx/Weber (Student-Eval-2 / Crowd-Eval-1). Red line is neutral, above that is better.

Figure 2 gives a comparison of evaluations from students and crowdsourced workers. For Marx, there is no significant difference between students and workers in their evaluations. However, for both Plato and Weber, we see that the students scored both coherence and relevance higher than the workers. One possible explanation is that some of the words in a topic make sense only in the overall context of the passage in the book. Thus a worker who has not read the book might not infer as much meaning from just the passage, and therefore give lower ratings to the topic. While there are some difference in the results from students and workers, this could possibly be more of a calibration issue, particularly given that the students have studied the texts in a classroom setting.

Crowd-Eval-2: Evaluation of topic/passage for ten books

We crowdsourced judgments of 200 topics and passages (20 topics for each of the ten books). After omitting responses from spammers and other sub-standard workers who failed too many traps, we obtained a total of 1020 non-spam accepted responses, averaging five judgments per topic.

Our first result from Crowd-Eval-2 is shown in Figure 3. This Figure shows the accuracy or proportion of the time that workers selected the topic model topic in preference to the random list of words (given the choice between the two). We see this accuracy (of correctly identifying the topic) range from 64% for Einstein, up to 98% for Darwin, and approximately 80% averaged over all the ten books. This result is quite promising: It says that 4 out of 5 times the automatically learned topics are identified as being more related to the passage than a set of ten words taken from the passage. Or -- said more strongly -- that workers do indeed think that the topics coherently relate to the passage.

But how difficult was this task? On average, the learned topic has anywhere from 6-8 out of the 10 words appearing in the passage (with an average of 6.7 matches). But the random topic, by design, always has all 10 words appearing in the passage, making this task more cognitively involved than simply counting word matches.

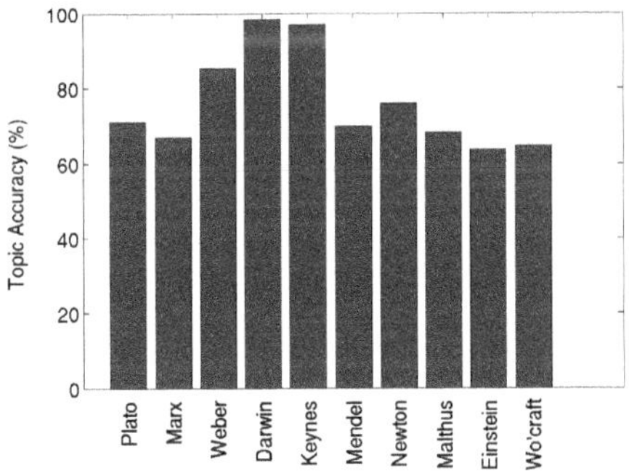

Figure 3. Percent of time worker selected learned topic over random list of words (N=1020).

We also asked workers to score (on a 1 to 5 scale) how well their selected topic relates to the passage. On average, workers scored the learned topics 17% better than the random list of words, showing that workers think the learned topic better relates to the passage than the random list of words.

Looking forward: Illustration of how topics could be used for user navigation in books

While these experiments laid groundwork for topic navigation, we can illustrate how the topic modeling approach might be used in a topic navigation tool in an appropriate user interface (e.g. compare to [2]). Figure 4 shows topic trends from Plato's Republic and Darwin's Origin of Species. The figure shows the relative importance of selected topics throughout the course of the book. Not only do we see that the topic model provides page ranges that are relevant to a particular topic, using Origin of Species we see validation with existing chapter boundaries, in this case the "struggle" topic clearly matching up with Chapter 3: Struggle for Existence. One can imagine a user interface where the user has this type of graphical display and moves a slider to quickly flip to pages of interest, relating to some selected topic.

DISCUSSION AND CONCLUSION

We performed a series of experiments and evaluations of topics learned by a topic model of books, both using a group of ten knowledgeable students, and using more than one thousand judgments from crowdsourced workers. In conclusion, this work has shown that (1) topic modeling is able to learn sensible and usable topics and related passages in books, suitably granular for within-document navigation of longer texts; (2) user evaluation is important and should be incorporated early, possibly even before applications are developed, and (3) crowdsourced evaluations can enable inexpensive and rapid evaluation and prototyping.

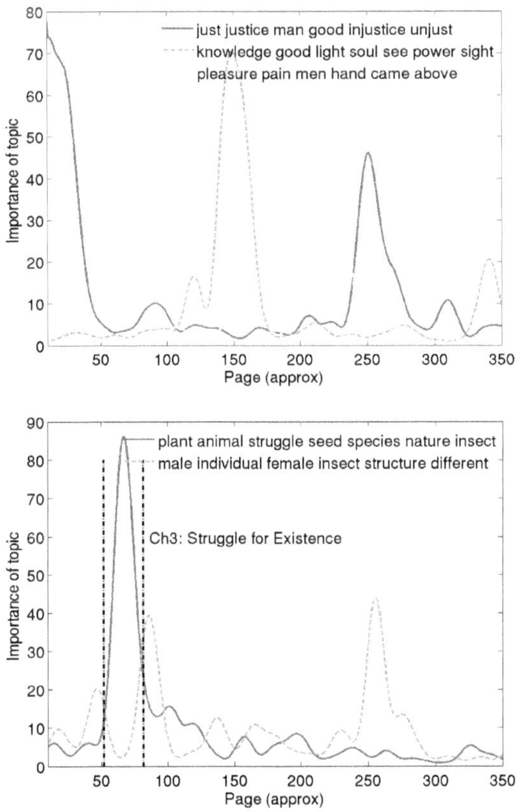

Figure 4. Topic vs. page for selected topics in Plato's Republic (top), and Darwin's *Origin of Species* (bottom).

ACKNOWLEDGMENTS

This study was funded by a National Leadership Grant (LG-06-08-0057-08) from the Institute of Museum and Library Services.

REFERENCES

[1] Blei, D. M., Ng, A. Y., & Jordan, M. I. (2003). Latent Dirichlet Allocation. *The Journal of Machine Learning Research*, *3*, 993–1022.

[2] Hearst, M. A. (1997). TextTiling: Segmenting text into multi-paragraph subtopic passages. *Computational linguistics*, *23*(1), 33–6

Emphasis on Examining Results in Fiction Searches Contributes to Finding Good Novels

Suvi Oksanen
School of Information Sciences
University of Tampere
33014 University of Tampere, Finland
Suvi.Oksanen@uta.fi

Pertti Vakkari
School of Information Sciences
University of Tampere
33014 University of Tampere, Finland
Pertti.Vakkari@uta.fi

ABSTRACT

We studied how an enriched public library catalogue is used to access novels. 58 users searched for interesting novels to read in a simulated situation where they had only a vague idea of what they would like to read. Data consist of search logs, pre and post search questionnaires and observations. Results show, that investing effort on examining results improves search success, i.e. finding interesting novels, whereas effort in querying has no bearing on it. In designing systems for fiction retrieval, enriching result presentation with detailed book information would benefit users.

Categories and Subject Descriptors

H.3.7. [**Digital Libraries**]: User Issues

General Terms

Human Factors

Keywords

Fiction Retrieval, Novels, Readers, Public Libraries, Search Tactics, Search Effort, Search Success

1. INTRODUCTION

Reading novels is a popular leisure time interest. Fiction was read at least once a year by 50 % of Americans in 2008 [9] and by 80 % of Finns in 2010 [12]. Public libraries are major channels of getting access to novels [8]. Studies on the outcomes of public libraries show that the major benefit derived from their use is the pleasure of reading fiction [5, 14]. Despite this fact, there has not been much interest in studying and developing systems for fiction retrieval since the 1980s [1]. The effort in developing search systems has been focused on retrieving non-fiction [2, 3].

Traditionally library catalogs have supported accessing novels if the reader knows the name of the author or the title of the novel. It is know that about half of the fiction borrowed is found by browsing, half by known item search [13]. This indicates a need to develop systems supporting other fiction search tactics than known item search. There are signs of enriching public library catalogs to include features supporting fiction retrieval like extended book descriptions or indexing [1, 11]. However, the utility of these tools for accessing novels is not studied. Our aim is to analyze how tools provided by an enriched public library catalogue are used to access interesting novels to read.

JCDL'12, June 10–14, 2012, Washington, D.C., USA.

2. RELATED RESEARCH

Next we introduce studies on how readers access fiction in libraries and on evaluation of fiction search systems The literature in this field is scarce [1]. As far as we know, there have been no published studies on fiction searching in commercial sites like Amazon.

Goodall [4] differentiates two stages in the book search process in the library. Readers identify first attributes in the books, which trigger their interest, and after that focus on attributes, which generate the decision to borrow the book. In the filtering stage, external attributes of the book like its cover or title are perceived as important, whereas in the selection stage, internal attributes of the book like text on the back of the cover or passages of the text in the book are considered as useful. Ross [10] has made a roughly similar distinction based on interviewing 194 committed readers. She distinguished between the clues in the book and elements in the book as indicators of an interesting book.

Pejtersen [7] has defined three strategies for accessing fiction, which match to our research goals. Analytical search strategy is used when readers wish to find novels about some topic like the Second World War. Search by analogy is generated when readers want something similar to novel X, e.g. a novel they had previously read. Browsing strategy is applied in situations when readers have only a vague idea of what they would like to read. They are simply browsing for finding a good novel.

Based on observing user-librarian negotiations for finding fiction, Pejtersen [7] has designed a fiction search system called the Book House. It consisted of facets representing various attributes of novels as perceived by library users. These facets were access points to novels. The evaluation showed that the system was useful and pleasurable to use [7] All the available system functionalities were used and the fiction classification system fully accepted. The users found it useful in finding novels.

3. RESEARCH DESIGN

The aim of this study is to analyze how an online catalog in a public library is used for finding novels to read. We focused on a situation when the readers have only a vague idea of what they would like to read. This corresponds to the browsing strategy in Pejtersen [7]. In addition to known item search, browsing is the second major strategy for accessing fiction [7, 13]. Therefore, it is important to study how users access fiction in an open-ended search situation. The specific research questions are:

- What kind of search moves were used for accessing novels?
- Was there an association between moves and search success?

PIKI library system serves several municipalities in Tampere region in Finland. It includes a database containing metadata about the books in the networked libraries, and an interface to interact with that information and search books. The metadata for fiction contains typical bibliographic information added with keywords from the fiction thesaurus "Kaunokki" [11] and tags assigned by users. The metadata includes also images of book covers, recommendations by users and librarians, and availability information. The object of a default search is the whole database. Search results are ranked by relevance, but they can be ordered also alphabetically by author or title, and by publication year. Search results can be limited by category, i.e. fiction vs. non-fiction, by the type of material like book, video, etc., by keyword, by language, or by library. Clicking the book title on the result list reveals the metadata of the book with availability information.

In addition to author, title, free term or keyword search, users may start from recommendation pages. They include various lists of books and recommendations by users and librarians. Users can also search for similar books based on keywords.

For the study 58 participants were recruited in May 2011 on the spot in three public libraries of various sizes in PIKI area. Of the study subjects, 26 were recruited in a big main library, 22 in a medium sized main library and 10 in a small branch library. They participated without compensation. 36 were females and 22 males. Their age varied between 14 and 70 years, the average age being 34 years. They were relatively highly educated, 39 % had a university degree, and 23 % had a high school education, and the rest had a lower education. They read on average 24 novels per year ranging from 0 to 120 novels.

The search task was as follows: You are in a library in a situation when you do not have a clear idea of what you would like to read. Please use the PIKI catalog to search for a novel of interest to you, which you would like to read. Do not search for a particular author or novel, although you may use this as a point of departure for your search. Thus, we simulated a typical browsing situation [4, 10] when readers have only a vague idea of what they would like to read [7]. The search was ended when an interesting novel was found, or when the searcher gave up the search task as unsuccessful. Each participant made one search.

The search screen was recoded. The researcher observed the search sessions and made notes. The searchers filled in a pre-search questionnaire eliciting demographic information, information about reading orientation, the use of the library and search tactics for books in the library. After the search they filled in a post-search questionnaire including a pattern of questions for assessing various features of PIKI interface, ranking of the novel found and open questions concerning the criteria of selecting the novel and the difficulty of the search task.

Search moves were observed from the search logs. 29 move types were identified. A move is an identified use of a system feature like a keyword search, an author search, inspecting result list, limiting it, or exploring book metadata. The number of the moves varied from 2 to 21. The distribution of the moves was very scattered. For the economy of analysis we collapsed similar move categories like field search (by publication date, library, language, category, material) or limiting result list (by keyword, language, etc). We also recorded the time used for the search.

The indicator of the success of search was an interesting novel found. The searchers rated the novel in a three-point scale from one to three (least to most interesting). If the searcher could not find an interesting novel, the scoring was zero.

4. RESULTS

When starting a search, readers could select either a quick search, an advanced search or a recommendation page as their point of departure. Quick search consists of a search box with a drop down menu suggesting a keyword with information about its type like author when keying in search terms. In an advanced search it is possible to formulate a query by selecting several fields to search. Recommendation pages include various lists of books and recommendations with links.

Advanced search was the most popular search mode (72.4 %) followed by quick search (19 %) and recommendations (17.5 %) (Table 1). Readers made on average 7.9 moves when attempting to find a good novel. Of these moves on average 3 were advanced searches, 0.4 quick searches and 0.5 recommendation moves. Users retrieved on average 1.6 result lists, and limited these result lists 0.6 times. On the result lists they clicked 1.6 books, but read only 0.2 book descriptions containing more than bibliographic data. The average interest score of the book accepted was 2.4. The average search time was 215 seconds.

Table 1. Basic statistics of the main study variables (n=58)

Variable	Mean	Stddev	Min	Max	% using
Quick search	0.4	1.1	0	6	19.0
Advanced search	3.0	2.9	0	12	72.4
Result list	1.6	1.4	0	6	86.2
Result list limit.	0.6	1.3	0	6	27.6
Book info	1.6	1.3	0	7	95.1
Book description	0.2	0.6	0	3	10.3
Recommendatio n	0.5	1.3	0	7	17.5
All moves	7.9	4.3	2	21	100
Book scores	2.4	0.9	0	3	100
Search time	215	118	76	593	100

As table 2 indicates, the most popular search tactic was field search (63.8 %) followed by free term search (44.8 %). Known item search and keyword search were equally popular.

An average search was relatively short consisting of about eight moves and lasting about 3.5 minutes. A typical search consisted of advanced searches including mostly field searches or searches with terms from controlled or free text vocabulary. Searchers seldom limited the result list, but immediately assessed novels by examining bibliographic book information. They explored very seldom more detailed book descriptions for assessing novels' value. The searches can be considered as successful. Only five searchers out of 55 could not find a novel, which they considered as interesting. Evaluation scores in three cases were missing. Thus, 50 searchers had a successful result, i.e. a novel rated at least with value one. Of the searchers only one rated the novel with value one, nineteen with value two, and the rest thirty with value three. Thus, about 55 % of the searchers retrieved a novel with the highest interest rank.

Table 2. Basic statistics of the search tactics variables (n=58)

Search Variable	Mean	Stddev	Min	Max	% using
Known item	0.6	1.1	0	5	32.8
Free term	0.8	1.3	0	6	44.8
Keyword	05	1.0	0	5	32.8
Field search	1.4	1.4	0	5	63.8

We were curious to know whether the search process variables were associated to the success of search measured by the interest rate of the novel found. We analyzed the association between search moves and search success by calculating Pearson correlation coefficients. The results indicated that none of the search process variables in tables 1 and 2 excluding the result list was significantly associated with the perceived value of the novel. The number of result lists visited correlated significantly with the success (r=.28; p=.04). Thus, it seems that search success was not associated with the search moves or their combinations used excluding the number of visits in the result list.

Success was neither associated with search effort measured as time used in searching (r=-.14; p=.31) or the total number of moves (r=.23; p=.10). We found that effort invested in exploring the search results and in querying were significantly associated with the search success. Correlation between the time invested on an average move and the interest rating of a novel found was -.45 (p=.001) (Table 3). Thus, quick shifts from move to move predict finding an interesting novel. The correlations show also that the greater proportion of the moves devoted to looking at the result list (r=.34; p=.013) or examining novels more in detail found on the result list (r=.31; p=.022), the more likely searchers found an interesting novel. Deviating from this finding, the proportion of quick and advanced (Q&A) searches of all moves was negatively associated with the ratings of the novels selected (r=-.27; p=.045). Thus, the greater the proportion of quick or advanced search moves of all moves, the less interesting novels were found.

Table 3. Correlations between the average time per move, search effort and the interest grade of a novel (n=58)

Variables	Book scores	Time/ moves	Results/ moves	Results, book/mo
Time/moves (mo)	-.45**			
Results/mo	.34*	-.19		
Results, book/mo	.31*	-.24	.70***	
Q&A searches/mo	-.27*	.16	-.03	-.54***

Legend: *= p<.05; **=p<.01; ***=p<.001

In all, these findings hint, that search formulation variables, i.e. querying, were not associated with finding an interesting novel to read, and their great proportion of all moves contributed to an unsuccessful search result. The proportion of moves devoted to exploring result lists and book information, however, helped searchers to find interesting novels. Thus, the more swiftly the searchers proceeded from move to move, but the more effort they invested in exploring results list and book information, and the less effort in search formulation moves, the more interesting novels they found. The findings imply, that search formulations are less important than examination of search results as conditions for finding an interesting novel to read.

The correlation analyses suggest that the following variables were associated with search success: the average time per move, result lists per move, results and book information per move, Q&A searches per move. We use these variables for predicting search success, i.e. the rating of the novel found. Because the two variables measuring the proportion of result list exploration of all moves were conceptually correlated, we removed the variable measuring only visits in result lists, and kept that one which included also exploring book information. The latter one reflects more validly the effort put in exploring the search results.

The model building aims at analyzing the direct and intermediated effects of each independent variable to dependent variable. The model indicates the relative effect of each variable to other variables, i.e. it indicates the effects other variables controlled [6]. Path analysis was used for testing the model. In the path analysis standard regression coefficient are used [6]. The model (Figure 1) was significant (F=7.14; p=.000) indicating a good fit with the data. The multiple correlation (R) of the model was .548, R squared was .300, and adjusted R squared .258. Thus, the model explains about 26 % of the variance in the scores of the novels.

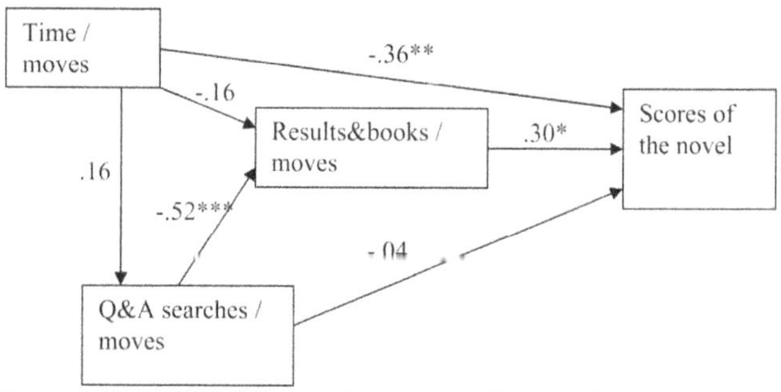

Legend: * = p<.05; ** = p<.01; ***=p<.001 (n=58)

Figure 1. A path model for predicting the scores of the novel

The path analysis indicates that time used per move has a significant direct effect on the scores of the novel found (ß=-.36). Also the proportion of search result exploration of all moves has a significant effect on novel scores (ß=.30), whereas the proportion of Q&A searches of all moves has no effect on the interest rating of the novel (ß=-.04). The average time per move has a significant effect neither on the proportion of results exploration (ß=.-.16) nor on Q&A searches of all searches (ß=.16). Interestingly, the proportion of Q&A searches has a very large significant effect on the variation in the proportion of result exploration (ß=-.52).

In all, the model indicates, that the less time the searcher used per move, the more interesting novel was found. The average time used per move did not have a significant influence on the proportion of moves devoted either to search formulation or the results exploration. Although these beta coefficients were not significant, their directions hint, that the less time used per move, the more effort was invested in examining the result lists and books information, and the less effort in search formulations. In addition, the more effort put in querying, the less effort allocated in examining results. Thus, it seems that there was a bifurcation of search strategies emphasizing either querying or result list examination. These two strategies had very different effects on finding an interesting novel. Investing effort on examining the result list and book information has a significant positive effect on finding an interesting novel, whereas emphasis on search formulations has no bearing on finding an interesting novel.

5. DISCUSSION AND CONCLUSIONS

As far we know, this is the first study since Pejtersen [7] to analyze the search tactics used by readers for accessing fiction in enriched public library catalogs. We observed how readers searched for an interesting novel in a situation where they had only a vague idea of what they would like to read [7]. We found out that the use of various moves for searching novels was scattered. The most common moves were advanced search, browsing result list and examining book information. The use of various moves was not associated with the success of the search, with finding an interesting novel. However, it turned out that the less time used per move, and the greater the proportion of moves for examining the result list and book information, the more interesting the novel found. The proportion of search formulation moves was not associated to the search success. The model build hints that readers used two alternative strategies with differing success for accessing good novels. The strategy emphasizing search formulations was not associated with finding an interesting novel, whereas the more effort invested in examining results in the search, the more interesting novel was found.

Effort invested in exploring search results instead of querying is an essential factor for finding interesting novels in a situation when readers do not have a clear idea of what they wish to read. Although readers have only a vague idea of the object of interest, they know genres, authors and titles, and have attributes of good novels in their mind [10]. They use this information when selecting books to read. It is likely that what is considered as an interesting novel varies a lot in the sense that the substitutability of novels is great in this situation. Several alternatives may do, not only one. Therefore, effort put on exploring the result list is more productive than querying in the search for good novels to read.

Our search task simulated a situation when searchers know only vaguely what they would like to read. This situation resembles exploratory search, when actors are not familiar with a topic and have difficulties in articulating what they should look for. It may be that our finding that emphasis on examining search results compared to querying contributes more to finding useful documents, applies also to exploratory search. This hypothesis should be tested empirically.

Our results suggest that in designing systems for fiction retrieval, it is important to enrich result list presentation. Readers need more clues about where to infer that the novel could be of interest, and also more options to be informed about the content of the novel [4, 10]. The latter include e.g. recommendations by fellow readers and librarians, texts on the back of the books and links to critics of the novels and to author information like in some e-bookshops.

It can be supposed that the more readers know about literature, the more effectively they can identify interesting fiction [10]. In the studies to come, we analyze whether readers' literary competence is connected to fiction search process and output. Also experimental studies on evaluating new tools like fiction indexing or recommender systems for supporting fiction retrieval are needed.

6. REFERENCES

[1] Adkins, D. & Bossaller, J. E. 2007. Fiction access points across computer-mediated book information sources: a comparison of online bookstores, reader advisory databases, and public library catalogs. *Library & Information Science Research* 29(3), 354-368.

[2] Case, D. 2007. *Looking for information. A survey of research on information needs, seeking and behavior*. 2nd ed. Academic Press.

[3] Elsweiler, D., Wilson, M.L. & Lunn, B.K. 2011. Understanding casual leisure information behavior. In: Spink, A & Heinström, J.. (Eds). *Future directions in information behaviour*. Emerald, 211-241.

[4] Goodall, D. 1989. *Browsing in the public libraries*. LISU Occasional paper No 1. Loughborough: Library and Information Statistics Unit.

[5] Lance, K.C., Steffen, N.O., Logan, R., Rodney, M.J., & Kaller, S. 2001. *Counting on results: new tools for outcome-based evaluation of public libraries*. Aurora, CO: Bibliographical Center for Research. Retrieved in December 20, 2009 from http://www. lrs. org/documents/cor/CoRFin. Pdf.

[6] Pedhazur E. 1982. *Multiple regression in behavioral research*. 2nd ed. New York: Holt, Rinehart & Winston.

[7] Pejtersen, A.M. 1989. *The Book House. Modeling user's needs and search strategies as a basis for systems design*. Roskilde: Risö National Laboratory.

[8] *Perceptions of Libraries, 2010: Context and Community*. (2010). OCLC. Retrieved August 10, 2011 from http://www.oclc.org/reports/2010perceptions.htm.

[9] *Reading on the Rise* (2008). National Endowment for the Arts. Retrieved November 27, 2011 from www.nea.gov/research/Readingonrise.pdf

[10] Ross, C.S. 2001. Making choices: What readers say about choosing books to read for pleasure. *The Acquisition Librarian* 13(25): 5-21.

[11] Saarti, J. & Hypén, K. 2010. From thesaurus to ontology: the development of the *Kaunokki* Finnish fiction thesaurus. *The Indexer* 28(2): 50-58.

[12] Serola, S. & Vakkari, P. 2011. *The public library in the activities of people*. In Finnish. Publications of the Ministry of Culture and Education 2011/21. MCE: Helsinki.

[13] Spiller, D. 1980. The provision of fiction for public libraries. *Journal of Librarianship* 12(4): 238-266.

[14] Vakkari P. & Serola, S. 2012. Perceived outcomes of public libraries. *Library & Information Science Research* 34(1): 37-44. doi:10.1016/j.lisr.2011.07.005

The "City of Lit" Digital Library – A Case Study of Interdisciplinary Research and Collaboration

Haowei Hsieh[1], Bridget Draxler[2], Nicole J. Dudley[1], Jon Winet[3]

School of Library & Information Science[1], Intermedia Program[3]
The University of Iowa
Iowa City, Iowa, USA, 319-335-5713
{haowei-hsieh, jon-winet}@uiowa.edu

Department of English[2]
Monmouth College
Monmouth, Illinois, USA
bdraxler@monmouthcollege.edu

ABSTRACT

In 2008, Iowa City was designated as one of only five "Cities of Literature" worldwide by UNESCO. To take advantage of our rich local literary history, an interdisciplinary research team from the University of Iowa collaborated to develop a digital library featuring Iowa City authors and locations. The UNESCO City of Literature digital library (referred to internally as "City of Lit") consists of a mobile application for the general public to access the database and a set of web-based interfaces for researcher and content creators to contribute to the database. Members of the research team have developed undergraduate literature courses to study the feasibility of using young scholars for digital content creation, and the pedagogical effect of including digital research in traditional literary courses. Students in the courses were trained to conduct scholarly research and generate a variety of digital resources to be included in the digital collection. This paper reports our experience building the City of Lit digital library and the results from evaluations and studies of the students in the courses. We also outline the implementation and development of the digital library, its framework, and the client-side mobile application.

Categories and Subject Descriptors

H.3.7 [**Information Storage and Retrieval**]: Digital Libraries – *Collection.* K.3.1 [**Computers and Education**]: Computer Uses in Education – *Collaborative learning.*

General Terms

Design, Experimentation, Human Factors.

Keywords

Digital libraries, mobile application, iPhone app, mobile devices, digital humanities, literary research.

1. INTRODUCTION

Building upon a rich literary tradition and community of writers in Iowa City, our interdisciplinary team of faculty, researchers, graduate and undergraduate students ("The University of Iowa UNESCO City of Literature Mobile App Development Team", or "UCOL") has developed a digital library accessible to the public via a mobile app – "City of Lit" [14].

The UCOL team is committed to engaged, interdisciplinary digital scholarship and hopes to take advantage of the popularity of mobile devices and location-aware services to provide the general population with easy access to the rich writing heritage of Iowa City. The team launched its first-phase product in Fall 2010: "City of Lit," an app for Apple mobile devices [1] (Figure 1) to access the digital collection.

In linked undergraduate classes, we provide a research and learning environment for undergraduate researchers to create authentic, original content for a digital library – one intended for active and interactive public consumption, with opportunities for students to review each other's work. We believe that this model not only facilitates student learning but also enhances humanities research.

"City of Lit" promotes a thoughtful redefinition of community and text. Intergenerational, multi-organizational participants work collectively to create multimedia hypertext documents for the digital collection. The project encourages undergraduate and graduate research, with an emphasis on interdisciplinary and collaborative practice, while recognizing the unique potential of mobile devices for public scholarship and civic engagement. The UCOL project provides opportunities for researchers, teachers, and students to experience the interdisciplinary research process and develop innovative approaches for research and learning.

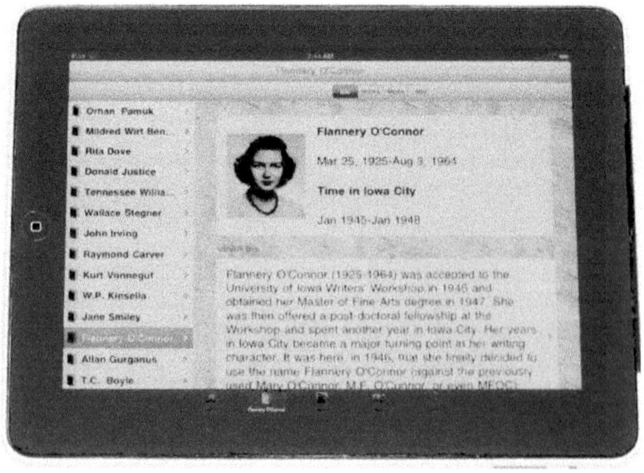

Figure 1: "City of Lit" app running on an Apple iPad.

We hope that the "City of Lit" project can encourage new forms of humanities research and publication, and a new way to teach the humanities to undergraduate students, in its application of intercollegiate collaboration to digital humanities research.

2. RELATED WORK

Traditional humanities research is costly in terms of time and resources. Many modes of publication are not flexible enough to fully accommodate the anecdotal research UCOL uncovers. As one example, how many people outside Iowa City know of the infamous Dave's Fox Head Tavern, a literary meeting place for generations of writers that has produced an untold number of anecdotes concerning local authors? In addition, traditional humanities scholarship doesn't tend to include contributions from community members, though these "citizen scholars" often have unique insights and privileged knowledge about local culture. The "City of Lit" app addresses these issues, reinventing both the production and publication of humanities research. By crowdsourcing the research task (while experienced scholars serve as curators) – inviting students, writers and community members to add their narratives and insight – we can supplement current sources for literary research with New Media, including interviews, readings, maps, and personal histories.

Digital libraries have been used in classroom environments for many purposes. Zhou and Stahl discuss how elementary and high school students use a digital library to study math within a collaborative platform where they can share information and ask each other questions [26]. Yaron, on the other hand, focuses on collection content and how a digital library can help students see connections among different science disciplines [25]. On the opposite side from the end-user experience of digital libraries, Nichols et al. examine technical complications encountered by Library and Information Science students constructing digital libraries with existing content [20]. Stewart also documents information students' digitization and curation of media content for a university collection [24]. In these projects, digital libraries are constructed as students do research and then learn how to convert traditional contents into digital form.

There is also a precedent of students producing original digital content. For instance, in a study done by Bos, high school students contributed reviews of web resources about pollution to a school webpage [7]. There have been a variety of projects to promote student content creation, from the building of student websites and wikis [7][13] to the production and sharing of podcasts [6][11][16]. Other projects, such as Buckner's work involving undergraduates in the building of a genetics database [9], the Atterbury Files project to encourage middle school students to conduct and publish local history research [19], and a number of undergraduate-only research journals, such as ReInvent and the McGill Journal of Medicine [18], that bring non-graduate student work into the public eye. It is widely accepted that the perception of an audience and the feeling that assignments are an authentic means of production, rather than contrived for the classroom, motivates students to write work that is more accurate and communicative [8][9][13]. However, according to Guth, many of these projects are private or semi-private and not intended for public consumption [13].

Recently, scholars have begun to explore specific ways that mobile technology can serve as a platform for participatory, problem-based pedagogy. Radosevich and Kahn have showed the impact of using tablet technology and recording software to increase student engagement in their learning process. [21] Cochrane and Bateman have published a model and rubric for "m-learning" (mobile learning projects), which emphasizes the use of interactive technology projects for students in online courses who do not identify themselves as tech-savvy [10]. In a study of mobile-based games, Matthews discusses a Neighborhood Game Design Project that creates a virtual reality simulation [17]. However, scholarship on mobile technology has not yet considered student publication on mobile devices, in which students create content rather than simply using mobile apps.

Educators are also making efforts to integrate new media and digital technology in K-12 and higher education. MIDEA (Marcus Institute for Digital Education in the Arts) [2] at NMC (New Media Consortium) [3] and CNMTL (Columbia Center for New Media Teaching and Learning) [1] host many digital collections and projects that distribute digital content and use new media and technology to enhance teaching and learning. For example, the Portable Podcasting Studio project created the Visiting Artists Journal that documents the visits and teaching moments of selected artists and distributes the content through a variety of new media spaces [4] [1]. Most of these projects provide content that is professionally-created, either by teachers, artists, or authors.

The "City of Lit" project differentiates itself from these projects by including undergraduate students, who are usually the consumers in a classroom environment, as content creators. Students are actively involved in the research process and contribute to the collection, learning traditional literary research skills alongside technical and multimedia skills.

Our work seeks to promote a 'trialogic' approach in learning, in which students learn not only through consuming and communicating with peers but also creating original content [21].

The following section describes the implementation and development process of the "City of Lit" digital library, the functionality of the "City of Lit" app, and the potential contributions to the scholarly community. Finally, we discuss our study from one semester of training undergraduate students in content research and creation.

3. "CITY OF LIT" DIGITAL LIBRARY

The digital library utilizes database systems to manage the collection. We have created a variety of web-based interfaces for users of different roles to use or administer the databases. The three different roles for the City of Lit digital library are (1) information consumers – representing general users, (2) information creators – representing researchers or students in the planned literature class, and (3) content experts – the editorial staff in the research team.

For the information consumers, we provide a native iOS app that runs on iPad, iPhone and iPod Touch devices. The app contains basic navigational items (a list of authors, maps, news events) and stores recently accessed data in the cache of the mobile device. Maps and news information will be streamed from the Internet to ensure they are up-to-date. The Android version of the mobile app is at its final testing stage. We have also worked on a mobile web application (interactive web pages optimized for mobile devices) for those mobile devices not supported natively. Using the mobile device as an information delivery tool provides convenient access and allows us to take advantage of the ever-growing availability of location-aware services.

For information creators and content experts, we have implemented web-based interfaces for data entry, content review, and ad-

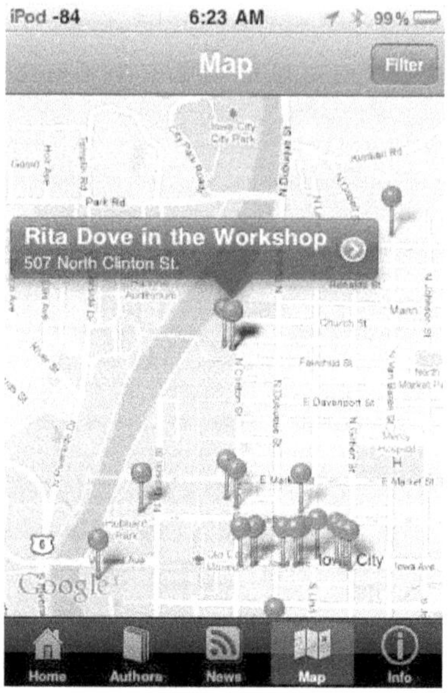

Figure 2: A map of Iowa City with locations marked with pins. Touching the pin will reveal its caption, address, and an option to view more.

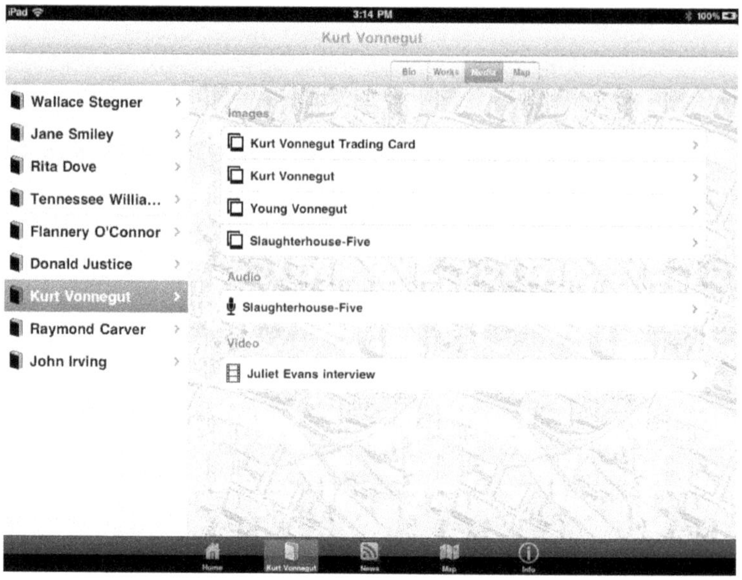

Figure 4: Multimedia content of an author is grouped together in the "Media" tab for each author. In the example here, there are images, audio, and video recordings for Kurt Vonnegut.

Figure 3: The "City of Lit" app can present video and audio created by users, allowing community members to contribute their knowledge to our project.

ministration duties. Users of the web-interface login via a university-administered authentication system. The UCOL team authorizes each user with a pre-determined role and presents appropriate interfaces.

One goal of the UCOL project is to construct a framework for content creators and researchers to easily contribute to the content of the digital library. The framework, in addition to serving content to the mobile application, also (1) allows content creators to easily work with the collection, and (2) provides tools for editorial staff and researchers to moderate and maintain the collection. The framework consists of a set of databases and web-based interfaces, a collection of online repositories that hosts full-length original content for a selection of authors, and an application server to communicate between the database and the mobile application.

While local and university libraries already housed existing digital archives for many of the featured authors, most of these materials were scattered around different sources, including traditional and digital archives in the University library's Special Collections (http://www.lib.uiowa.edu/spec-coll/), the Virtual Writing University (http://www.writinguniversity.org/), and the Iowa Writer's Workshop (http://www.uiowa.edu/~iww/). Centralizing these resources in a single collection simplifies mobile access. This translates to a more responsive interactive system and more satisfying user experience. The centrally managed database servers are also essential for the consistency of data.

In this section, we describe the mobile app, the databases, the database model, and the web-based interface for content creators and editors.

3.1 The "City of Lit" App

We have released a mobile app for users to easily access and explore the digital library. When the app is started, the user is presented with a "quote of the day" immediately following the UNESCO City of Literature splash screen. The quote of the day is determined by the server, and it will not change during the day in order to encourage viewers to come back the next day.

A tap on the screen will bring the users to a list of available authors (such as in Figure 1). Other options for navigating the app can be accessed at the bottom of the screen (Figure 2 and 4). Users can choose either "News" or "Map" to explore the collection. The map will use the device's location service to determine the user's proximity and show a map (Figure 2) with pins to identify interesting nearby locations available in the digital library.

Multi-media elements are central to the app. Users can access a constantly growing collection of audio and video recordings of readings and interviews (see Figure 3), along with photography and graphics related to the authors (Figure 4). Other constantly updated features of the app include "News" (reports on Iowa City and the literary world) and "Events" (local readings, book launches, films and lectures), information dynamically fed from the Virtual Writing University website. These features improve university/community relations by sharing information about both community and on campus events.

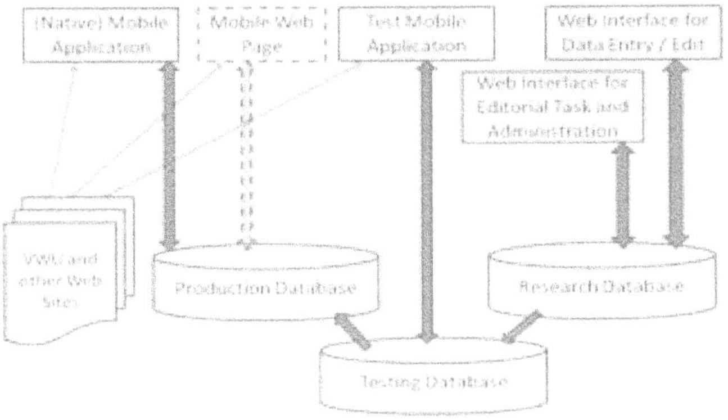

Figure 5: System Architecture of the UCOL digital library. The dash-lines represent soon-to-be-released components.

3.2 The Databases

This project utilizes three databases configured slightly differently but with similar internal data schema. The Research Database is for initial data entry, updating, and content moderation. The Production Database is for serving published material. An intermediate Testing Database is used to verify the data transfer process and to test pre-released mobile applications. The system architecture is shown in Figure 5.

Content providers and scholars use the web interface to enter data into the Research Database. The editorial staff review and revise entered material before approving for publication. If the material is approved, data is then copied to the Testing Database for the development team to test its compatibility with the app. The development team and editorial staff also use the Testing Database to double check that the data transfer process is working properly. Additionally, the Testing Database provides the development team a sandbox to experiment with new features available in any pre-released version of the mobile application. Data is copied to the Production Database when both teams are satisfied. The use of the Research Database for data entry and the approval process ensure that content not intended for publication is secluded. This is important for a research environment, especially when we are training the content providers as part of the research process.

The server is hosted by The University of Iowa's Digital Studio for Public Humanities. The decision to store content separately from the mobile application allows frequent updates to the content by our many contributors. The server side applications are implemented in PHP, and the database engine is MySQL. The server-side application responds to the mobile application's request by querying the MySQL database to provide up-to-date information.

With the limited display space on mobile devices, care has been taken to prepare an abbreviated version of the information for a more comfortable viewing experience. The database mainly stores abridged versions; most full-length content or source materials are housed within their original sources, such as the Virtual Writing University Web servers. Users can read or view condensed versions, then choose to follow the links and read the full content within the mobile application.

3.3 The Database Model

In the database, there are a variety of artifacts stored in the collection, including authors, locations, transcripts, media, literary works, events, etc. Most artifacts are represented by a corresponding entity in the database model. A few categories of artifacts share a database entity, because they have similar attribute sets and will be grouped logically in the application. For example, the metadata for audio and video materials are stored in a single media table.

The database model was designed to be flexible in anticipation of possible expansion. Even though the current display interface uses authors as the starting point to navigate the collection, it is possible that any single artifact can be connected structurally with any number of other artifacts. For this reason, we have created a general purpose "relationship" table in the database to maintain connections between any two artifacts, regardless of type.

In order to ensure data consistency and integrity, we have also implemented a "*Proxy*" table to map universal UCOL_IDs to corresponding IDs in their specific entity group. Figure 6 demonstrates how Author A in the *Author* table can be associated with Location L in the *Location* table by way of the *Proxy* table and the *Relationship* table. In the example, Author A is assigned with an A_ID of '00015' (in the *Author* table) and location L is assigned with an L_ID of '00015' (in the *Location* table). Notice that even though both IDs are the same number, they represent different artifacts because they are from different database tables. From the proxy table, we can obtain the universal UCOL_IDs for each item. In this case, we have UCOL_ID '0000252' for A_ID 00015 and

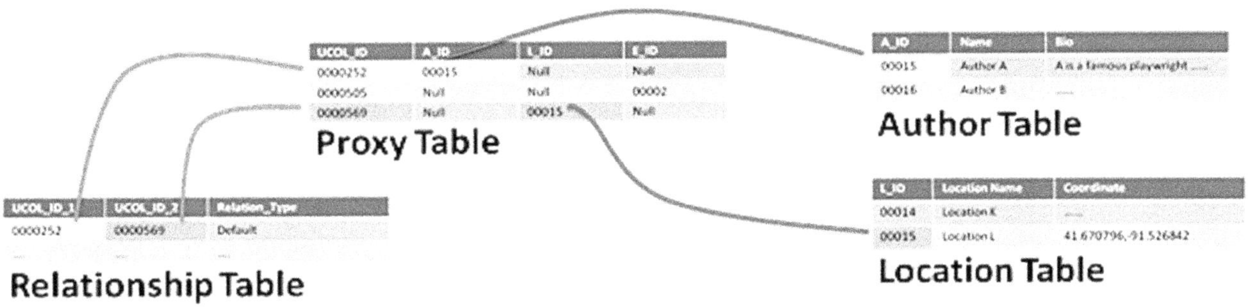

Figure 6: An example of the database structure shows how different entities (Author, Location) are associated together in the Relationship Table by an indirect reference through the Proxy Table.

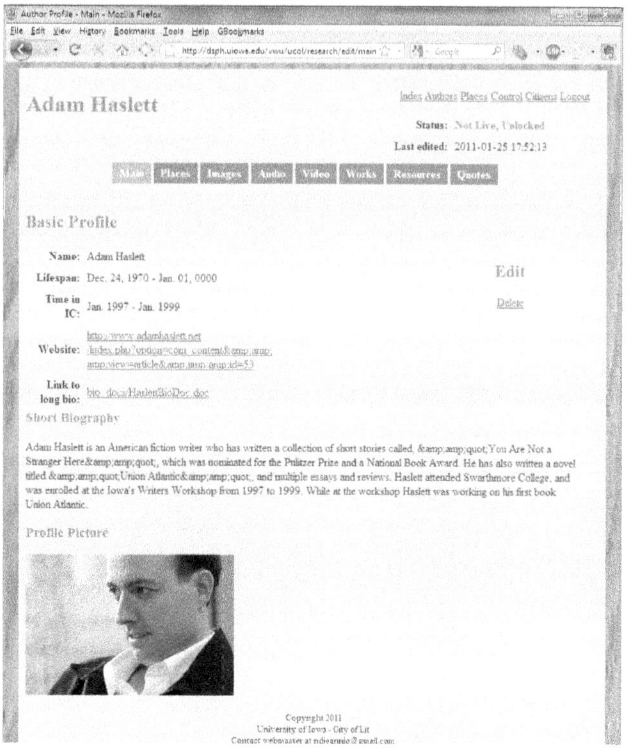

Figure 7: Web-based interface for data-entry and update. Different aspects of information related to an author can be accessed from the tabbed interface.

UCOL_ID '0000569' for L_ID 00015. Thus, if we want to associate Author A with Location L in the database, we need to associate author 00015 to location 00015, which in turn will be translated into a relationship that links UCOL_ID 0000252 to UCOL_ID 0000569 in the *Relationship* table.

The indirectness of this proxy table ensures the simplicity and flexibility of the *Relationship* table. The *Relationship* table does not need to know which two entity types are to be associated, and it requires no changes if there are new types of entities added to the database. If new entities are added to the database, the required change to the existing database schema involves only the *Proxy* table, and it is as simple as appending an additional column to account for the new entity type. The use of this *Proxy* table trades a bit of space (the null values used in the table) for more robust database integrity by asserting that each row in the table contains one and only one entity ID (e.g., an author ID, a location ID, or an event ID, etc) in addition to the UCOL_ID. All other fields in the same row must be of the value "null". The design of the *Proxy* table also allows specification for foreign keys in the *Proxy* table to their associated entity tables, which helps avoid deletion anomaly for better database integrity. With the proposed data model, it is possible to form arbitrary[1] interconnections between any entities in the database. However, we chose to use "Author" and "Location/Map" as the main portals for users to explore the digital library since we anticipate that most users will be interested in a particular writer or place.

Figure 8: A web interface for authoring a Geo-tagged event.

3.4 The Data-Entry Interface

A set of web-based interfaces allow distributed data entry and content administration. Authorized scholars and researchers can contribute to the collection in remote locations. Editors on the research team review and approve content in these interfaces for public release.

The data-entry web interface (Figure 7) was tested by staff researchers and undergraduate students in the experimental general education literature class. The interface consists of multiple tabbed panels structured to represent different aspect of information about an author, rearranged and relabeled slightly from the structure of the database to reflect the syllabus and students' understanding of the project. This design logically connects essential information so that it can be formalized and stored in the proper location within the database. The interconnection of different pieces of information allows the digital library to form hypertext structures for the incoming information. This hypertext structure becomes the underlying navigational structure for the mobile application. For inexperienced content creators and scholars, the structured interface creates a logical sequence to assist students as they navigate the information structure.

The multi-tabbed interface allows users to create content and organize the numerous small, multimedia components of the research assignment in one place to be submitted to the instructor. By using a single, multi-faceted, web-based interface, we hope to avoid issues of information fragmentation and provide a simplified system in the spirit of Reimer's 'Global Information Gatherer' [23].

A major component of the app is the geographically-aware map. This map can acquire the user's position via GPS and display geo-

[1] Arbitrary in this sense is referring to the idea that the system will allow us to make a connection between any two objects, since the connection capability is not limited by entity type. For instance there's nothing to stop users from connecting two books together should s/he chooses to do so.

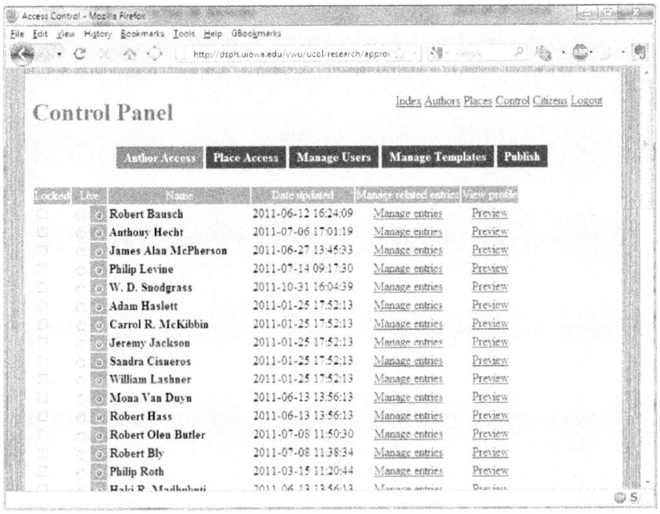

Figure 9: A Web interface for editorial staff and researchers to review and approve content to be published. 'Live' status approves content to the app, and 'locked' status prevents content from being edited.

tagged "events" from the app. In Larson's research about placing biographies in the context of events and places, he argues that the content is made more useful and interesting when put in geographic and event-related context [15]. By connecting the research materials that student researchers find with real places in Iowa City, they contribute to a more in-depth, community-relevant body of work for the digital library. Examples of geo-tagged events include locations of local readings, former dwellings of resident writers, and real or imagined Iowa City locations referenced in literature. This information can be used to take a literary stroll through Iowa City or to visit sites relevant to a specific author. Of course, as the amount of information included in the app increases, we can feature geo-locations anywhere in the world (Figure 2).

Geo-tagged events (called Places) can be associated with different types of records, such as images. GPS coordinates are stored within Places so associated records (such as images) are accessible through the map view in the application. Records associated with Places can also be associated with authors so they can be reached through authors list. Figure 8 shows how the web interface can be used to create a geo-tagged event.

3.5 The Administrative Interface

Since all content is reviewed by UCOL staff before publication, a set of web-based administrative interfaces are provided for editing. The administrative interfaces include a main interface (Figure 9) that shows a list of the authors, each with a last-updated date. Editors can review all uploaded material and control whether an author's content should be published (go live) or not. Editors can also lock a selection of authors to prevent other editors or content creators from making changes while the editor is reviewing or updating these authors.

The administrative interface also allows a finer granularity of management over which related artifacts are published. An individual artifact-management interface (Figure 10) displays all artifacts associated with the selected author and groups them by category. Staff editors proofread and preview each entry to decide

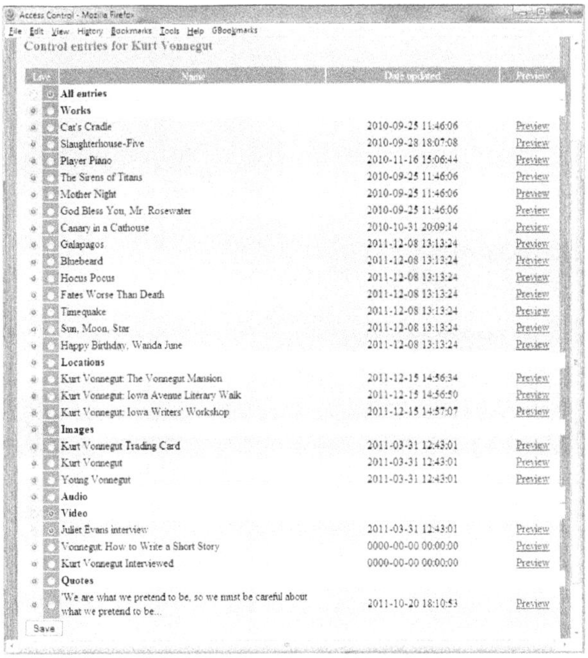

Figure 10: Individual artifacts related to an author can be approved by the editorial staff by checking the "live" button on the left column. Artifacts are grouped by categories and can be approved as a group or individually.

which entries should be published with the author or edit as necessary before publication. The approved database records can be published by copying from the Research Database to the Testing Database for further testing, and eventually to the Production Database.

4. STUDENT CONTENT CREATION AND COURSE EVALUATION SETUP

Transferring content into a digital library and keeping it updated is a challenge for many digital libraries. A small set of the initial collection was converted and migrated by our editorial staff from the Virtual Writing University website, where much of the original content is available. We also trained undergraduate researchers to perform basic research while contributing to the collection. We have since conducted one pilot session in Fall 2010, one formal evaluation in Spring 2011, and are finishing up another session of data analysis from Fall 2011. The first two studies were for a general education course taught by Bridget Draxler, and the third was for an elective course cross-listed in English and Art and Art History, co-taught by Raquel Baker and Jon Winet.

UCOL team members worked closely with the undergraduate students by providing technical support and training in multimedia authoring for the class. Tutorials were presented in class to clarify conceptual issues and address technical questions for the content creation process (Figure 11). At the same time, student feedback helped the UCOL team to improve the data-entry interface. After this iteration, much of the content for the digital library has been generated by undergraduate student researchers and vetted by a professional scholar and biography author.

After this pilot study in 2010, the research team worked with Draxler in 2011 to implement an updated student assignment and conduct a more formal study, including surveys on students' per-

Figure 11: The UCOL research team provides tutorial sessions for the content creation process. Here is a sample illustration used in the tutorial to demonstrate how the data-entry interface maps to the mobile app display.

ception of personal growth in research skills and collaborative scholarship[2]. We also evaluated the data-entry interface, the design of the project, and collected students' feedback and reflections about the course.

The participants of the study are the 38 students enrolled in the undergraduate "Interpretation of Literature" course. There are 28 freshman, 6 sophomores, 2 juniors, and 2 seniors in the class. They came from variety of majors, ranging from Art, Anthropology, Elementary Education, to Nursing, Math, Computer Science, etc. These majors are categorized by the team into 7 categories, including humanities (7), business and finance (6), sciences (5), social sciences (5), education (4), health studies (4), and undeclared (7).

Student reflections and evaluations, along with a formal survey designed by the UCOL team, were collected at the end of the semester. Students were informed by the research team that the results would not be available to the instructor before the grades were finalized.

Survey results suggest that involving undergraduate researchers in the project not only helped build content, but also broadened the students' research experience. The following two sections discuss the feedback we obtained from the Spring 2011 classes and the benefits of training undergraduate students to conduct scholarly research with digital library and new media technologies.

5. RESULT AND DISCUSSION

In this paper, we present results related to student learning, the data-entry interface, and students' content creation experience. On the question concerning assignment goals, students were asked to answer [agree/disagree] on a set of sub-questions (see Table 1). According to our survey, the structure of the research assignment allows enough flexibility and creativity (73.7% agreement), gave students ideas in directing and presenting their research (76.3%),

[2] You can view the course syllabus for Spring 2011 at the following link: https://docs.google.com/document/d/1uxtXjgB4OiSlogb7Px_zVu6jASpfA9HRsA6OHnyQPEQ/edit

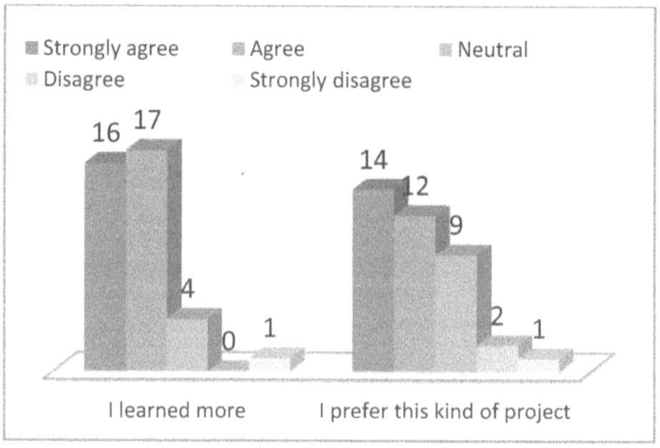

Figure 12: On questions "I learned more by doing this type of assignment than a traditional research paper" and "I prefer this kind of assignment to a traditional research paper"

and taught useful skills to students (71.1%). The assignment, however, did not give students enough opportunity to explore personal interests (34.2%). A handful of students (13.2%) also commented that the structure of the interface interfered with their ability to organize and present their research.

Table 1: Results and sub-questions to the question "The structure of the assignment: (please select all that are true)"

Sub-questions	Agree
(a) Gave me enough room for flexibility and creativity	73.7%
(b) Gave me ideas in directing and presenting my research	76.3%
(c) Prevented me from fully realizing my ideas for my research	13.2%
(d) Allowed me to explore issues of personal interest to me	34.2%
(e) Taught me skills that I think are useful	71.1%

Students overwhelmingly agreed that they learned more by doing this type of assignment than a traditional research paper (Figure 12) and prefer this kind of project than a traditional paper.

In a following question where students were asked to recommend changes for multimedia training, students suggested that we provide future students with online tutorials to follow-up in-class demonstrations, to make the rather technical process of creating multimedia content easier. Students wanted these additional materials, like the project itself, to be published digitally for easy access.

In addition to identifying their development in digital literacies, the students also noted perceived improvement in several categories based on their self assessment. The assessments were collected though a set of questions (Q14 ~ 19 in our survey, listed in the next page) where they answer each item with either [little or no improvement | some improvement | significant improvement].

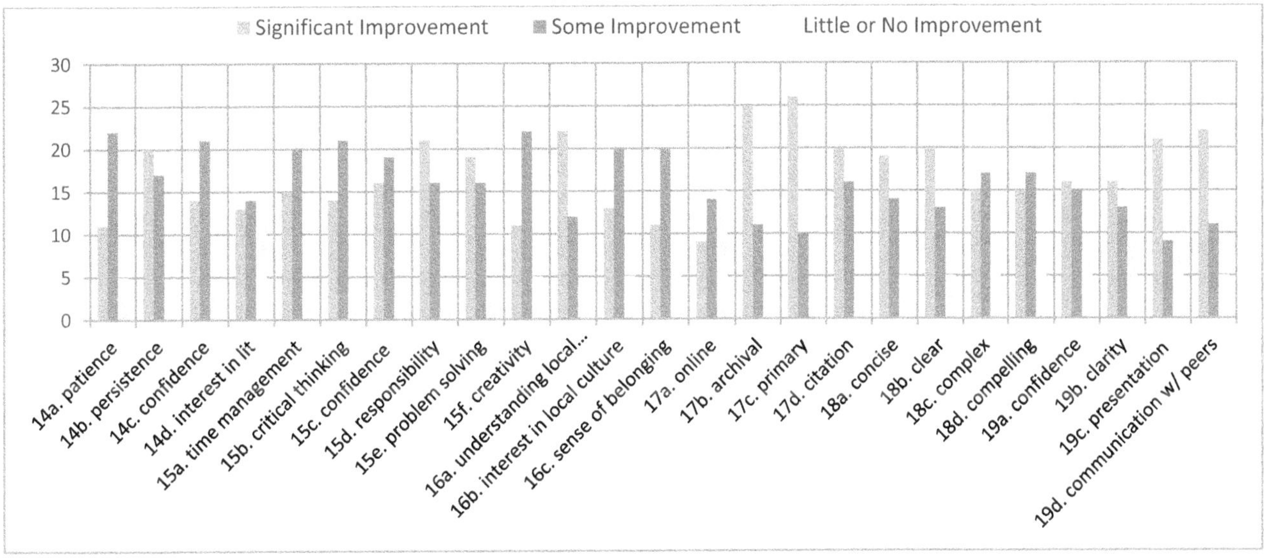

Figure 13 Result for students' self assessment on personal improvement in different areas.

In general, students perceived stronger improvements in Academic Growth (Q15) and Research Methods (Q17). Results from Figure 13 shows that students felt more positively that they become more persistent (14b), more responsible (15d), more capable solving problems (15e), and better at conducting research (17).

Most interesting for this study is question 17 (Research Methods), which recorded students' self-perceived improvement in collecting and creating content for the digital library. While students reported the least improvement in online research, they reported significant improvement in archival and primary research methods. In fact, online research skill (17a) was the least improved category among the 25 surveyed, while traditional research skills (17b-d) were the most improved. While the assignment asked students to create a digital product, they made greater improvements in more traditional research skills.

The 6 categories and their sub items are listed below.

14. Personal growth:
    (a) patience, (b) persistence, (c) confidence in personal abilities, and (d) interest in literature.
15. Academic Growth:
    (a) Time management, (b) Critical thinking, (c) Confidence in academic abilities, (d) Personal responsibility for learning, (e) Problem solving, and (f) creativity.
16. Civic Engagement:
    (a) Understanding of local culture, (b) Interest in local culture, and (c) Sense of belonging in the local community.
17. Research Methods:
    (a) Online Research (i.e., Google), (b) Archival Research (i.e., special collections), (c) Primary Research (i.e., interviews), and (d) Citation/reference/bibliographic skills
18. Writing Skills:
    (a) Concise writing, (b) Clear writing, (c) Complex writing, and (d) Compelling writing.
19. Speaking Skills:
    (a) Confidence, (b) Clarity, (c) Presentation style, and (d) Communication with peers.

We evaluated data-entry interfaces and the training students received on using the interface to determine where and how we can improve future students' experience. The questions are listed in Table 2 and the results are presented in Figure 14. In general, students responded positively to the experience of contributing to

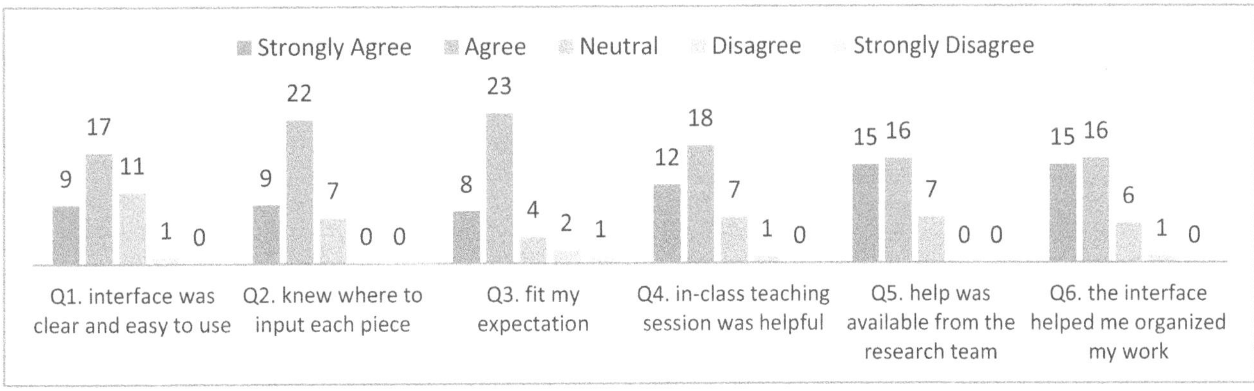

Figure 14: Results of Interface and Training related questions (Table 2).

the digital library. We have noticed slightly more disagreement in question 3, indicating a possible mismatch between students' conceptual model and the data model. The UCOL research team has since integrated new preview functions to help students understand what is to be expected. Revised tutorial for the training session may be necessary to address this problem.

Table 2: Questions related to the data-entry interface and support for the interface and the percentage of agreement (Strongly Agree + Agree).

	Question	agree
1	The interface was clear and easy to use	68.4%
2	I knew where to input each piece of my research into the interface	81.6%
3	The interface fit my expectations based on how I understood the assignment.	81.6%
4	The in-class teaching session on the how to use the interface was informative and helpful.	78.9%
5	Help was available from the research team when I had questions about the interface	81.6%
6	Putting my research into an online interface helped me organized my work	81.6%

One thing we changed from the pilot study was to make the research assignment a team assignment. Feedbacks from the pilot study indicated that students could benefit from workload sharing and peer support when the assignment requires unfamiliar skills, such as the assigned literary research, data entry, and multimedia authoring.

Data from the formal survey noted a high perceived impact on student learning. When asked "Did working in a group improve the quality of your project?" 73.69% (31.58% + 42.11%) of students agreed, and 7.89% (2.63% + 5.26%) disagreed (Table 4).

Table 3: Responses to the question "Working in a group improved the quality of the project."

	Count	Percentage
Strongly Agree	12	31.58%
Agree	16	42.11%
Neutral	7	18.42%
Disagree	1	2.63%
Strongly Disagree	2	5.26%
Total	38	100.00%

The semester concluded with public presentations of the students' work. Rather than presenting their research findings, students described their research process. These presentations, which are published online with students' permission, offer further evidence of students' perceived learning within the digital library assignment.

One group emphasized that the project is student-guided <video at http://www.youtube.com/watch?v=P7yzva7L-YU>. "What that means to us," they said, speaking as *we* rather than *I* throughout, "is that we find the resources, search for the interviews, and then conduct the formal interview; then, we take all of our information and enter it into the interface" (0:25). While the students remarked that the project challenged them to do research beyond a Google search, they admitted that the abundance of archival resources available on their author made their process easier than their peers' (1:21).

6. CONCLUSION AND FUTURE WORK

We have developed a framework for young scholars to learn and contribute their research into the digital collection. A model of integrating this framework with literary research component was designed and studied in an undergraduate literature course. Student feedback suggests that the integration of literary research and analysis, new media and technology, and local community engagement provided valuable learning outcomes. Overall, our research shows that this project positively impacted students' perceived learning and motivation. We plan to keep improving the framework by working with course instructors and collecting more student feedback.

The database and the data-entry interface were used extensively and evaluated by students and editors. The implementation of the framework has gone through a few iterations to accommodate new requirements and feedback from users, and will continue to improve. An iOS app for the digital library was released a year ago, and the development team is actively working on supporting more platforms. An updated iOS app, along with an Android mobile application, and a mobile web app (a web version of the digital library optimized for mobile users) will be released soon.

In the next phase of mobile application development, users will be able to move from a more passive role of consumers to an active role of producing citizen-scholars, able to contribute personal text, photo, video and audio commentaries by calling, texting, or uploading via the app. This multimedia content will vary from scholarly contributions to anecdotal video or audio recordings of important literary moments to personal experiences with and responses to local literature.

We have obtained positive feedback from the participating group of users, but one thing we wish we had time to complete is a detailed analysis or a comparison study to determine whether the use of such a digital library and its authoring environment affect the quality of generated content and of students' achievements. This research is planned for the forthcoming semesters. In addition to the classes at the University of Iowa, we are working with Monmouth College and Drew University to offer similar classes, to expand the student population involved in the project, and to investigate a proper collaboration model to share our digital library framework in other interdisciplinary environment.

As a team, UCOL recognizes the importance of collaboration and communication in interdisciplinary research. Diversified expertise from collaborating members is important, but having a matched vision and enthusiasm for the project is essential. The UCOL team's success depends on the willingness of participating members not only to contribute their own knowledge, but also to pursue shared goals.

The University of Iowa has made a commitment to the digital humanities. Working with the newly established Digital Studio for Public Humanities, the City of Lit project can serve as an exemplar at the University of Iowa and in the field of digital humanities and new media, illustrating how both traditional and young scholars can participate in engaged digital humanities research, facilitating intercollegiate collaboration at the highest levels of creative research and practice.

7. ACKNOWLEDGMENTS

We would like to thank UCOL team members, including Jim Cremer and Dat Nguyen (Department of Comuter Science, University of Iowa), Lauren Haldeman (Virtual Writing University, University of Iowa), Peter Likarish (Department of Mathematics and Computer Science, Drew University), Kelly Thompson (School of Library and Information Science),Raquel Baker (Department of English, University of Iowa), and Xiaoxing Liu (Interdisciplinary Graduate Program in Informatics, University of Iowa). We would also like to thank Iowa City's literary community, the Graduate College, the College of Liberal Arts & Science, and Information Technology Services at the University of Iowa for their support.

8. REFERENCES

[1] Columbian Center for New Media Teaching and Learning, http://ccnmtl.columbia.edu/

[2] Marcus Institute for Digital Education in the Arts, http://midea.nmc.org/

[3] New Media Consortium, http://www.nmc.org/

[4] Portable Podcasting Studio project ant MIDEA, http://midea.nmc.org/proj/minigrant2011ssapodcast/

[5] UCOL "City of Lit" iPhone application. http://itunes.apple.com/us/app/the-iowa-city-unesco-city/id396516495.

[6] Armstrong, G.R., Tucker, J.M., Massad, V.J. and Kutztown, P. Interviewing the experts: Student produced podcast. Journal of Information Technology Education, 8(2009), pp 79-90.

[7] Bos, N. Student Publishing of Value-Added Contributions to a Digital Library. *Annual Meeting of the American Educational Research Association* (Chicago, Illinois, 1997).

[8] Berland, L. K. and Forte, A. When Students Speak, Who Listens?: Constructing Audience in Classroom Argumentation. In *Proceedings of the 9th International Conference of the Learning Science* (Chicago, Illinois, 2010), pp 428-435.

[9] Buckner, B., Beck, J., Browning, K., Fritz, A., Grantham, L., Hoxha, E., Kamvar, Z., Lough, A., Nikolova, O. and Schnable, P. S. Involving undergraduates in the annotation and analysis of global gene expression studies: creation of a maize shoot apical meristem expression database. *Genetics*, 176, 2 (2007), 741.

[10] Cochrane, Thomas and Roger Bateman. "Smartphones Give You Wings: Pedagogical Affordances of Mobile Web 2.0." The Australian Journal of Educational Technology 26.1 (2010): pp. 1-14.

[11] Evans, L. Using student podcasts in literature classes. Academic Commons, *Center for Teaching and Learning*, (2006), pp. 123-136.

[12] Forte, A. and Bruckman, A. From Wikipedia to the Classroom: Exploring Online Publication and Learning. In *Proceedings of the 7th International Conference On Learning Sciences* (Bloomington, Indiana, 2006), pp 182-188.

[13] Guth, S. Wikis in education: is public better?, In *Proceedings of the 2007 International Symposium on Wikis* (2007, Montreal, Quebec, Canada), pp 61-68.

[14] Hsieh, H., Draxler, B., Dudley, N., Cremer, J., Haldeman, L., Nguyen, D., Likarish, P., Winet, J., Facilitating Content Creation and Content Research in Building the "City of Lit" Digital Library, In *Proceedings of Joint Conference on Digital Libraries* (JCDL 11, Ottawa, Canada), pp 145-148.

[15] Larson, R.R., and Shaw, R., 2009, Mapping Life Events: Temporal and Geographic Context for Biographical "Information, In *Proceedings of Joint Conference on Digital Libraries* (JCDL 09, Austin, Texas, USA), p 471.

[16] Lee, M. J. W. and McLoughlin, C. Teaching and learning in the Web 2.0 era: Empowering students through learner-generated content. *International Journal of Instructional Technology and Distance Learning*, 4, 10 (2007), pp. 21-34.

[17] Matthews, J. M. , Using a Studio-Based Pedagogy to Engage Students in the Design of Mobile-Based Media, *English Teaching: Practice and Critique* 9.1 (2010): pp. 87-102.

[18] Metcalfe,D. The launch of an undergraduate research journal. Reinvention: a *Journal of Undergraduate Research*, (2007).

[19] Morris, R.V. The Atterbury Files: An Extracurricular Inquiry Project Illustrating Local History. *Gifted Child Today*, 27, 3 (06/01 2004), pp. 28-35.

[20] Nichols, D.M., Bainbridge, D., Downie, J.S., and Twidale, M.B., 2006, Learning by Building Digital Libraries, In *Proceedings of Joint Conference on Digital Libraries* (JCDL 06, Chapel Hill, North Carolina, USA), pp 185-186.

[21] Paavola, S. and Hakkarainen, K. The knowledge creation metaphor–An emergent epistemological approach to learning. *Science & Education*, 14, 6 (2005), pp. 535-557.

[22] Radosevich, D. J. and Kahn, P., Using Tablet Technology and Recording Software to Enhance Pedagogy. *Innovate: The Journal of Online Education* 2.6 (2006).

[23] Reimer, Y. J., Bubnash, M., Hagedal, M. and Wolf, P. Helping Students with Information Fragmentation, Assimilation and Notetaking. In *Proceedings of the 9th ACM/IEEE-CS Joint Conference on Digital libraries* (JCDL 09, Austin, Texas, 2009) pp 15-18.

[24] Stewart, Q., and Todd, D.,2009, Using University Collections in Digital Library Education, In *Proceedings of Joint Conference on Digital Libraries* (JCDL 09, Austin, Texas, USA), p 477.

[25] Yaron, D.J., Davenport, J.L., Karabinos, M., Leinhardt, G.L., Bartolo, L.M., Portman, J.J., Lowe, C.S., Sadoway, D.R., Carter, and W.C., Ashe,C., 2008, Cross-Disciplinary Molecular Science Education in Introductory Science Courses: An NSDL MatDL Collection, In *Proceedings of Joint Conference on Digital Libraries* (JCDL 08, Pittsburgh, Pennsylvania, USA), pp 70-73.

[26] Zhou, N., and Stahl, G., 2007, Information Behavior of Small Groups: Implications for Design of Digital Libraries, , In *Proceedings of Joint Conference on Digital Libraries* (JCDL 07, Vancouver, British Columbia, Canada), pp 183-184.

Student Researchers, Citizen Scholars and the Trillion Word Library

Gregory Crane, Bridget Almas, Alison Babeu, Lisa Cerrato Matthew Harrington
Tufts University
Perseus Project
{gregory.crane,bridget.almas, alison.babeu,lisa.cerrato, matthew.harrington}@tufts.edu

David Bamman
Carnegie Mellon University
School of Computer Science
Language Technologies Inst.
dbamman@cs.cmu.edu

Harry Diakoff
Alpheios Project
Alpheios.net
Harry.Diakoff@gmail.com

ABSTRACT
The surviving corpora of Greek and Latin are relatively compact but the shift from books and written objects to digitized texts has already challenged students of these languages to move away from books as organizing metaphors and to ask, instead, what do you do with a billion, or even a trillion, words? We need a new culture of intellectual production in which student researchers and citizen scholars play a central role. And we need as a consequence to reorganize the education that we provide in the humanities, stressing participatory learning, and supporting a virtuous cycle where students contribute data as they learn and learn in order to contribute knowledge. We report on five strategies that we have implemented to further this virtuous cycle: (1) reading environments by which learners can work with languages that they have not studied, (2) feedback for those who choose to internalize knowledge about a particular language, (3) methods whereby those with knowledge of different languages can collaborate to develop interpretations and to produce new annotations, (4) dynamic reading lists that allow learners to assess and to document what they have mastered, and (5) general e-portfolios in which learners can track what they have accomplished and document what they have contributed and learned to the public or to particular groups.

Categories and Subject Descriptors
H.3.7. [Information Systems]: Information Storage and Retrieval: digital libraries.

General Terms
Documentation, Design, Human Factors,

Keywords
Automatic linking, collection development, document design, reading, browsing.

1. INTRODUCTION
Even deeply traditional disciplines such as the study of Greek and Latin language and literature have begun to shift the infrastructure upon which they depend from a focus primarily upon books and written artifacts to one that includes the words that these artifacts preserve. Every preserved word (or fragment) in every edition, manuscript, inscription, and papyrus,—in every surviving document produced in Greek or Latin—is now an object of interest that must possess a unique identifier. Each word then becomes the object for annotations that are multiple in the present (e.g., morphology, dictionary entry, link from transcription of region of written object) and that will increase in number as automated systems and human annotators identify an increasing range of phenomena. Even a few thousand books generate datasets with billions of objects. Traditional library systems, focused upon books and catalogue records, are inadequate, if not wholly irrelevant, to current, emerging research and instruction.

This shift to words and data demands not only a transformation in the infrastructure of earlier humanities work but has already begun to provoke a more general change in the culture of intellectual production and scholarship [13, 27]. Advanced researchers and library professionals must enlist student researchers and citizen scholars as key partners if they are to manage the quantity and range of historical sources already available under open licenses to the net public. Academic institutions must also develop correspondingly new collaborative and participatory models of education, where students contribute new knowledge as they learn and then learn so that they can contribute more new knowledge.

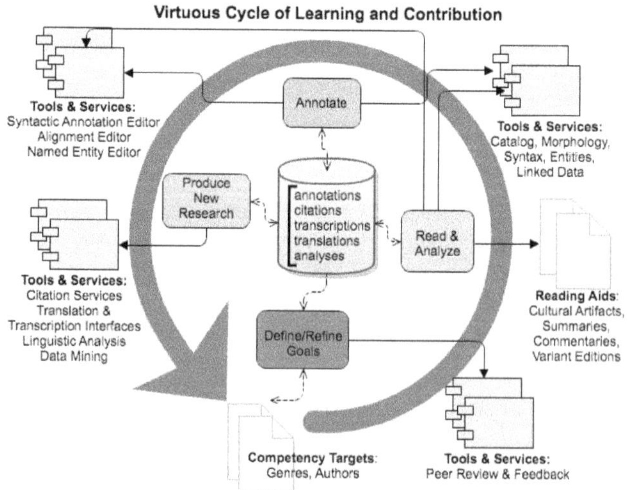

Figure 1: Virtuous cycle of contributing and learning

We focus upon how the production of annotations and internalization of linguistic knowledge can reinforce each other creating a virtuous cycle of contribution and learning (Figure 1).

Students produce data as they learn and they learn by producing useful data of increasing complexity. Figure 2 illustrates an implementation of the Son of Suda Online (SoSOL) editing environment [4], customized to support distributed editing for the TEI XML sources available from Perseus, with editorial workflows and mechanisms for contributors to document what they have contributed.

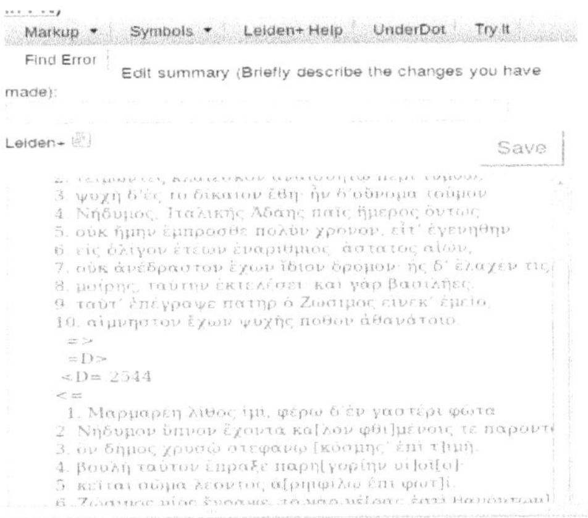

Figure 2: Editorial workflow for corrections, XML markup

Learners can thus know that they receive named credit for contributions to historical corpora that have been studied for many years—and in some cases for millennia—and will be the object of analysis for generations to come. At the same time, some categories of annotation—and often precisely those categories for which automated methods are least effective—not only depend upon, but also develop, linguistic mastery.

In the following section this paper provides background about the shift from books and written objects to words and associated annotations as the primary objects upon which infrastructure must focus. In section 3, we describe implementations of the five strategies of the aforementioned virtuous cycle. The final three sections cover related work, future development and the conclusions.

2. FROM BOOKS TO WORDS

Historical languages such as Classical Greek and Latin represent relatively finite corpora—language analysis determined that 22,000 of the first 1.2 million books extracted from the Internet Archive were primarily in Latin and contained 2.7 billion words [6]. The default OCR output for Classical Greek is too noisy to support such analysis but the Hathi Trust reports that only 8,600 of the 10 million books already in the collection are in Classical Greek.[1] For most students of these languages, however, the books are not the objects of primary interest. The words in the texts—if not the morpho-graphemic components—are the primary objects of interest. A collection with 30,000 books is small in conventional terms but even this modest collection represents a dataset of more than 3 billion words, each of which is the object of multiple annotations. Information infrastructures that focus on the books rather than upon the words that they contain cannot support either the research or pedagogy already taking shape.

As more of the human record becomes available in digital form,—representing not only Greek and Latin, but also Classical Arabic, Sanskrit, Chinese, Persian, the Cuneiform languages of the Middle East, Egyptian from hieroglyphics through Coptic, and the medieval dialects of Europe,—that figure will grow into the hundreds of billions. If we focus on the period before sound recording, for which only written sources preserve textual and linguistic data, then the figure may exceed one trillion words.

Table 1: Overview of open data for Classical Greek and Latin

	Classical Greek	*Latin*
MS pages, papyri, inscriptions	10,000	5,000
MSS metadata	720 MSS	340 MSS
Page Images	170,000	6,600,000
OCR output	50 million	2.7 billion
Transcribed Words	10 million	7 million
TEI XML tags	860,000	787,000
FRBR Authors	841	536
FRBR Works	2,186	1,042
Citations into	733,000	512,000
Citations within	265,000	185,000
Part of speech	39 million	2.1 billion
Morphology	40 million	2.2 billion
Dictionary words	125,000	62,000
Word senses	162,000	102,000
Treebank words	300,000	50,000
Grammatical categories	3,300	650
Named entities	580,000	352,000
Textual variants	24,000	51,000
Aligned English words	5 million	3 million

Table 1 provides some general figures about currently available open content Greek and Latin sources (primarily from Perseus, Papyri.info, and the Homer Multitext Project). The table contains a number of figures that may not be immediately clear (e.g., "*citations into*" describes citations from secondary sources to primary sources, "*citations within*" describes primary sources quoting each other, "*dictionary words*" and "*word senses*" enumerate categories while "*OCR output*" enumerates running words) but the point of the table is to demonstrate that the shift from books to words is not a future abstraction but a pressing reality with which students of historical languages are already grappling (and for which conventional library infrastructures are largely irrelevant). Collections such as those listed in Table 1 demand services that respond to at least six basic features.

(1) **Granularity**: Ultimately, we may need to focus upon the morpho-graphemic units out of which words are composed rather than on the words themselves, but a shift from cataloging books to annotating words provides an adequate—and dramatic—first step.

(2) **Scale**: once we move from cataloging physical artifacts to tracking the words within those artifacts, our objects of interest immediately increase by a factor of at least four orders of magnitude—from millions of books to tens of billions of words. At the same time, any arbitrary combination of these words can constitute an object of interest that must be recorded. Objects in the opening words of Vergil's *Aeneid* (arma virumque cano, "arms and the man I sing") include not only (1) *Arma,* (2) *virumque,* and (3) *cano*, but also (4) *virum* and (5) *-que* (a word that comprises two separable dictionary entries), and combinations of words such as (6) *arma virumque*, (7) *arma ... cano*, (8) *virum ... cano*. These combinations are fundamental to the way we talk about texts and thus the number of objects that we must be able to address is closer in scale to the set of sentences that we can generate from a language.

(3) **Inter-textuality**: The billions of words from the human record already available in digital form are not simply a stream of sources that were produced independently and in sequence over

[1] http://www.hathitrust.org/visualizations_languages.

time (where in fact we know the sequence, which we often do not). We have multiple versions of the same source—sometimes thousands of versions, when we consider every quotation of the Bible or Shakespeare as a separate version with its own context. We need to be able to track textual sources as they evolve, in some cases over thousands of years [31]. Large collections may have hundreds or thousands of versions of *Hamlet* and hundreds of thousands of passages that quote sections of the Bible.

(4) **Hyper-linguality**: Human beings can be multilingual and converse fluently in various languages. Traditional research problems are challenging enough. For instance, Aristotle's works circulated in Greek, Syriac translation, Arabic translation from the Syriac, Latin translation from the Arabic. Then, Aristotle (and Euclid) re-entered Europe and helped spark a process that led to the Renaissance and the formulation of the modern western world. With collections such as Google Books that contain more than 400 languages and with nearly 7,000 languages spoken today, we live in a hyper-lingual digital space where we cannot hope to study, much less master more than a tiny fraction of the languages that surround us. Our infrastructure must relentlessly provide increasingly accurate and increasingly sophisticated services whereby we can trace ideas across the full linguistic breadth of the human record [26].

(5) **Dimensionality**: the words in our collections have multiple features, each of which can depend upon the particular context in which a particular word appears. Some of these features—such as dictionary entry and word sense, morphological features, syntactic function, name class (Washington as place vs. person) and identification (Washington State vs. Washington, DC)—are familiar from print but researchers in corpus linguistics and other fields have developed new and growing sets of features, each of which can affect the potential dimensionality of any word—and the relationship between subsets of words—in our collections. Each of the rows in Table 1 constitutes a separate class of annotation, each of which can have multiple components of data.

(6) **Materiality**: each written word preserved from the analog record reflects an interpretation, generated by human or machine, from a written object. Where those objects exist, they may be represented in multiple digital formats, including 2D and 3D and multiple spectra and resolutions (as is the case for carefully studied inscriptions and manuscripts) [3]. In each case our infrastructures need to map particular—and in some cases conflicting—transcriptions of the words or characters on subsets of preserved written objects.

Automated systems can provide many of the annotations to manage the six features outlined above but these systems in at least some cases produce too many errors for at least some activities. Advanced researchers and library professionals must engage a generation of student researchers and citizen scholars who can participate as critical partners, making credited contributions of tangible value that grow increasingly sophisticated, with advanced expertise representing space on a continuum that many can traverse given time and determination, whether or not they belong to formal academic programs.

3. ANNOTATION AS FOUNDATIONAL DATA STRUCTURE

Every element listed in Table 1 is an annotation, i.e., a labeled link from one object to another. Text generated by OCR or transcribed by humans constitutes a stream of annotations on regions of a written object. Translations consist of annotations upon subsets of the source texts, as do morphological and syntactic analyses, links from words to dictionary entries and word senses pertaining to a particular context, textual notes on variants and conjectures, the classification of named entities and the association of those named entities with external authority lists, and representations of inter-textual re-use/allusion. Nor are these annotations simple assertions of fact. Figure 3 shows two competing interpretations of the same sentence, originally produced decades ago but now represented as machine actionable annotations [8]. We need to manage not only multiple classes of annotation but multiple interpretations as well. Annotations thus are a foundational data structure for historical corpora and provide a common thread for the work described below.

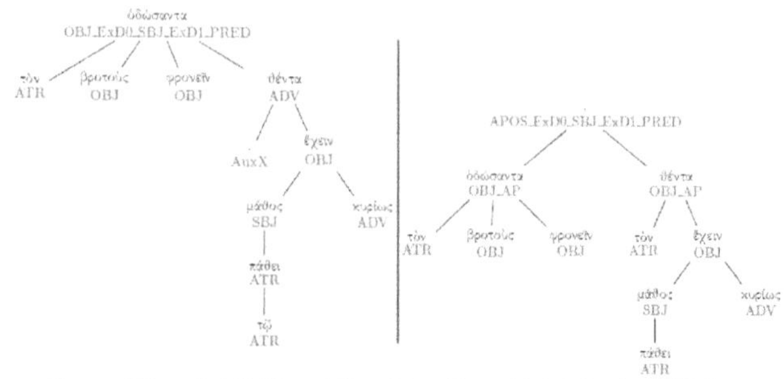

Trees of Fraenkel (left) and Denniston-Page (right) for *Ag.* 176-8.

Figure 3: Machine actionable interpretations

3.1 Annotations and Reading Environments

When the right kinds of annotations accumulate for particular texts, the realizable value of those texts can change radically. **First**, on the macro-level, automated systems can perform new operations and generate new services—much of the multilingual software now in use, for example, depends upon links between aligned source texts and translations. Corpus linguists have begun to transform our understanding of language by studying annotated corpora and these methods are—or must be—foundational to any modern philology: all students of historical languages are conducting corpus linguistics.

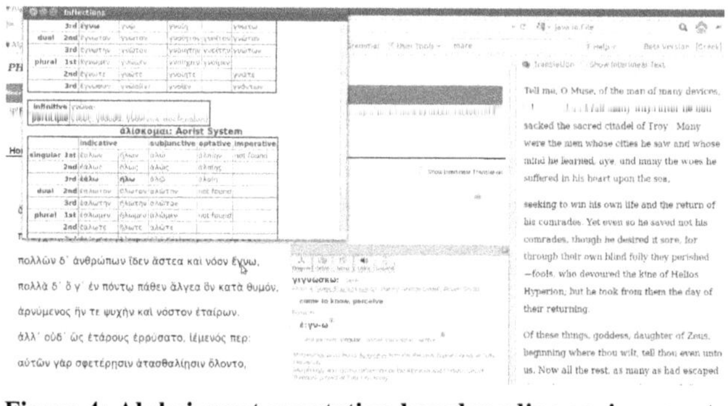

Figure 4: Alpheios.net annotation-based reading environment

Second, Figures 4 and 5 illustrate an environment developed by Alpheios.net, that integrates morphological analyses and syntactic analyses, automated dictionary lookups, and translations aligned to the source text to provide intensive reading support. In this environment, readers can quickly begin to make direct use of sources in languages that they have not studied—a substantive and tangible transformation in intellectual reach. Such intensive reading support has been studied in Chinese [2] and is established practice in languages such as Classical Greek and Latin for which collections, services, and annotations have evolved over decades.

Reading by looking up morphology, syntax, and translation equivalents for every word and corresponding section of a translation is, of course, not the same as interacting directly with a language one has mastered. It is, however, a quantum leap beyond staring at inert symbols that convey no meaning at all. We can never again just shrug and say, "it's Greek to me," if we confront a source in an unknown language, certainly not if that source is in Classical Greek.

We can, however, only provide dense, curated annotations for subsets of the human record, with ever richer annotation covering progressively smaller subsets of available corpora. Thus, we have very large sets of text generated by OCR software (e.g.. 2.8 billion words of Greek and Latin), subsets that have been manually corrected or keyed in (e.g., 17 million words of Greek and Latin with TEI XML structural markup), and intensively analyzed corpora (e.g., the 350,000 words with curated morphological and syntactic analyses in the Perseus Greek and Latin Treebanks).

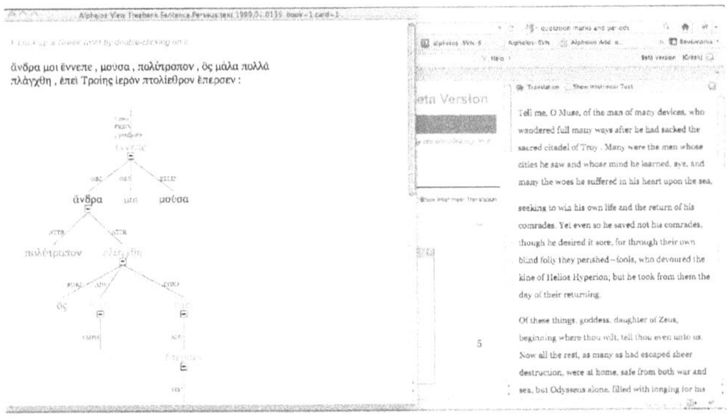

Figure 5: A treebank view in Alpheios.net

The interlinear visualization of aligned Greek and English versions of the Homeric *Odyssey* (figure 6), illustrates how readers can annotate English translations with structural markup or named entity identifiers (e.g., "Washington" in a given context is George Washington), then have these annotations applied to the original language source text [7]. Figure 2 illustrates an environment where introductory Greek students can not only fix typos but also help analyze and annotate the structure of complex manuscripts [12].

3.2 Annotation and Language Learning

Annotation is not only an essential chore as we organize historical sources. The act of annotation also provides new opportunities for learning the historical languages in which those sources are preserved, addressing in a fundamentally novel way the critical need for rapid and on-going feedback.

Unlike those learning modern languages, students of historical languages such as Classical Greek and Latin cannot receive immediate feedback by interacting with native speakers in a classroom or by visiting a foreign country. This presents a major barrier. Several experienced teachers of Greek and Latin in one recent departmental discussion, for example, went so far as to argue that independent reading of source texts was bad for students because they did not receive immediate feedback to call their mistakes and bad habits to their attention. While not all agree that the net result of independent reading was negative, there is virtually complete agreement that students reading source material require more and faster feedback.

For historical languages, access to pre-existing linguistic data thus opens up a major opportunity, because curated linguistic annotations provide training data not only for automated systems but for human learners as well. The same annotations by which we provide intensive reading support can, however, provide exhaustive questions by which learners can practice recognizing and generating morphology, syntax and (where parallel corpora are available) vocabulary in authentic source materials.

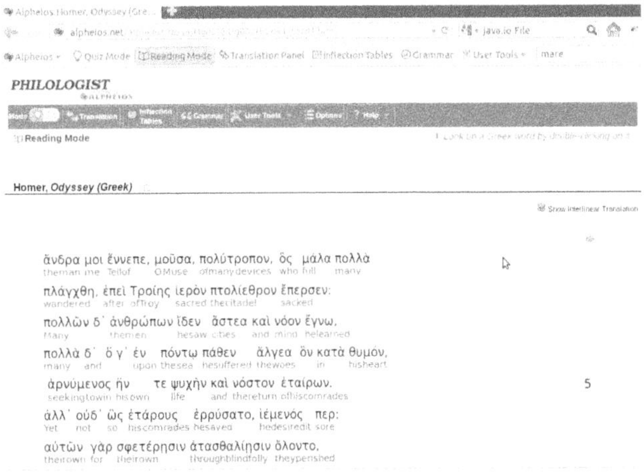

Figure 6: Interlinear view of aligned Greek/English texts

In first and second year language curricula students intensively study relatively small subsets of a language (e.g., corpora of c. 10,000 words and 2,000 vocabulary entries). Thus relatively small treebanks and/or aligned corpora can provide learners with enough curated training data to practice their ability to recognize and (by not showing selected forms) to generate the morphology and the syntax of a language. We can measure the fluency (which demands both the accuracy and the speed) with which learners can analyze and produce authentic language materials.

We then enable teams of learners to annotate new materials, comparing their independent analyses against each other and resolve differences by discussion or by a course instructor. Both processes provide far more accurate data than any morphological or syntactic analyzers.

Figure 7 illustrates differing interpretations of the same sentence from the *Res Gestae*[2] by two third semester students of Latin at Tufts University in the fall of 2011. Students in this class produced machine actionable interpretations of the morphological and syntactic functions of words from this text, adding to the machine actionable data by which researchers can fundamentally rebuild their understanding of these ancient languages.[3]

There are various methods whereby we can review contributions and reconcile differences where no canonical analyses are available. We can calculate the probability that students independently make the same errors and thus model the reliability of those instances where they agree. The two students can review their work together. A third student can annotate independently and then enter the discussion. The class can review the annotations. The instructor can review the annotations. Students then receive feedback on their performance. Or these methods can be combined, with students assigned the task of analyzing sentences and reviewing analyses by their peers before the

[2] The *Res Gestae* is official history published by the Emperor Augustus to celebrate his accomplishments and a major source for our understanding both of what happened and how Augustus wished posterity to understand what happened.

[3] Classes at Tufts and Holy Cross have already contributed to data for Homer and Petronius now published in the Greek and Latin Treebanks.

instructor then reviews the aggregate work. In this case, feedback is rapid, with students interacting with each other and the instructor entering to review overall results and to focus upon particularly difficult questions.

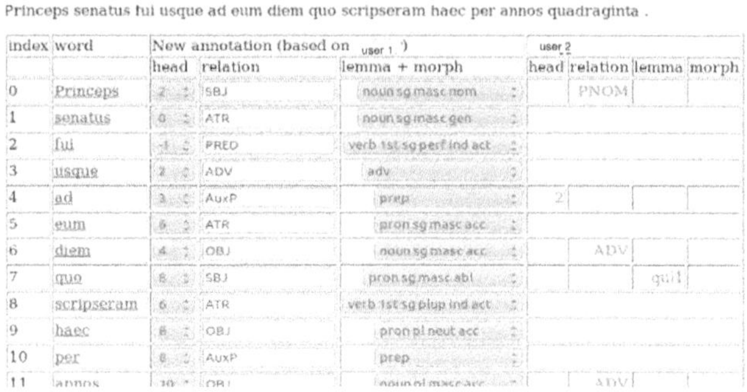
Princeps senatus fui usque ad eum diem quo scripseram haec per annos quadraginta .

index	word	New annotation (based on user 1)			user 2			
		head	relation	lemma + morph	head	relation	lemma	morph
0	Princeps	2	SBJ	noun sg masc nom		PNOM		
1	senatus	0	ATR	noun sg masc gen				
2	fui	-1	PRED	verb 1st sg perf ind act				
3	usque	2	ADV	adv				
4	ad	3	AuxP	prep	2			
5	eum	6	ATR	pron sg masc acc				
6	diem	4	OBJ	noun sg masc acc		ADV		
7	quo	8	SBJ	pron sg masc abl			qui	
8	scripseram	6	ATR	verb 1st sg plup ind act				
9	haec	8	OBJ	pron pl neut acc				
10	per	8	AuxP	prep				
11	annos	10	OBJ	noun pl masc acc		ADV		

Figure 7: Two student interpretations of a source text

Results can then be presented in percentages. The list below illustrates the performance of selected annotators within the Greek Treebank on syntactical and morphological analyses.

```
<annotator n="10215" Syntax=".999" Morph=".889"/>
<annotator n="10090" Syntax=".959" Morph=".885"/>
<annotator n="10085" Syntax=".918" Morph=".885"/>
<annotator n="10079" Syntax=".918" Morph=".885"/>
<annotator n="10078" Syntax=".89"  Morph=".882"/>
```

As students contribute more data, their differing strengths and weaknesses begin to emerge. Figure 8, presented in two graphs, visualizes the overall performance of each student set against their ability to analyze particular phenomena. Most students are quite successful associating adjectives with nouns (the second graph: "attributive modifiers") but student ability to analyze the function of verbal participles (the first graph: "participial attachment") varies widely (user 12 has no idea how to perform this operation). Individual learners, their instructors, and automated tools can use such data to personalize subsequent questions and to reinforce phenomena that particularly challenge individual learners.

As students of the language become proficient, they can analyze new materials on their own, both to improve their understanding of the language and to contribute to human knowledge. We can solicit multiple analyses of the same sentence (or even the same word or phrase) from multiple contributors until shared agreements produce results of any realistic statistical reliability. If divergent answers suggest genuine ambiguity, we can flag that instance for manual review.

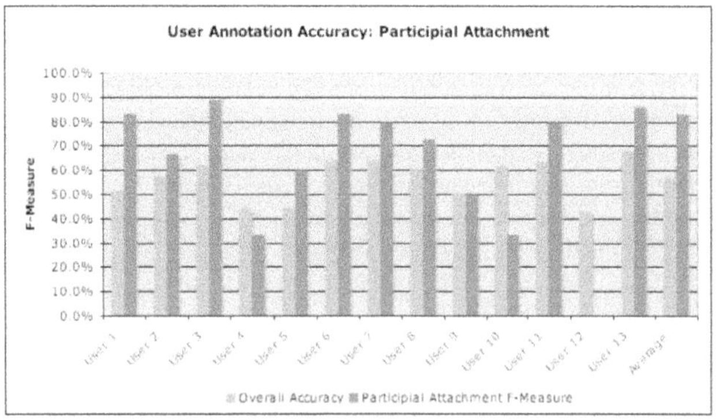

Figure 8a: Varying performance by students on two tasks

For Greek and Latin, the language communities remain substantial. Of the 1.2 million unique users who visited the Perseus Digital Library alone in Q4 of 2011, 120,000 worked directly with the Greek and Latin sources.

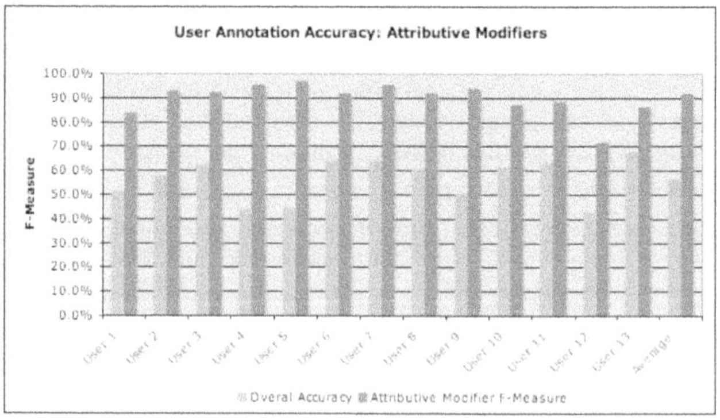

Figure 8b: Varying performance by students on two tasks

Contributions of this type are essential. Because no native speakers survive, annotating historical languages takes, in our experience, twice as long as the annotation of modern Chinese and with higher error rates—more than $1 per curated word when we pay for annotators and editors. Even if we can reduce these costs, we cannot expect to pay with external funding for a treebank representing 2000 years of Latin. The more learners practice, the more feedback they receive and the more proficient they become and the more they contribute. The act of learning, in this environment, expands and improves the scholarly data with which the learning began. Learners can thus receive the psychological benefits of contributing to something larger than themselves and of long term value—annotations to a historical source such as the *Res Gestae* will be used for years, if not generations. By combining two problems—the need to generate more linguistic data than we can fund and the need to provide better feedback for students of historical languages—we provided new methods by which to address both challenges at once.

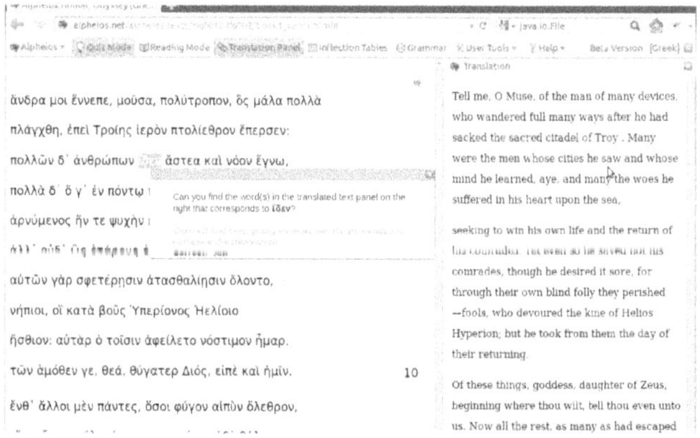

Figure 9: Aligned text as source for interactive quizzing

Access to structured data opens up a range of opportunities both to refine the results of automatic analyses and to use refined results as training data for human and machine learning alike. Figure 9 illustrates an exercise that builds upon aligned corpora. In this illustration, learners match words in the Greek to words in the English (the system is prompting the learner to match not only "saw" but "he saw"). Learners can go from English to Greek. We can also hide the corresponding Greek or English so that learners can practice generating language. Here we draw upon semantic analysis to allow for synonyms (e.g., student suggests "rock" and the translation contains "stone") to allow for multiple answers. The parallel text analysis not only allows learners new ways to reinforce their active and passive command of vocabulary, morphology and syntax but also enables new kinds of collaborative work, an example of which follows.

3.3 Annotations and Multilingual Learning

Various, emerging ways now permit students working together first, to explore problems that were intellectually inaccessible, not only to them but to most professional researchers, and then, to produce new data of lasting value as a by-product of their activities in a formal class.

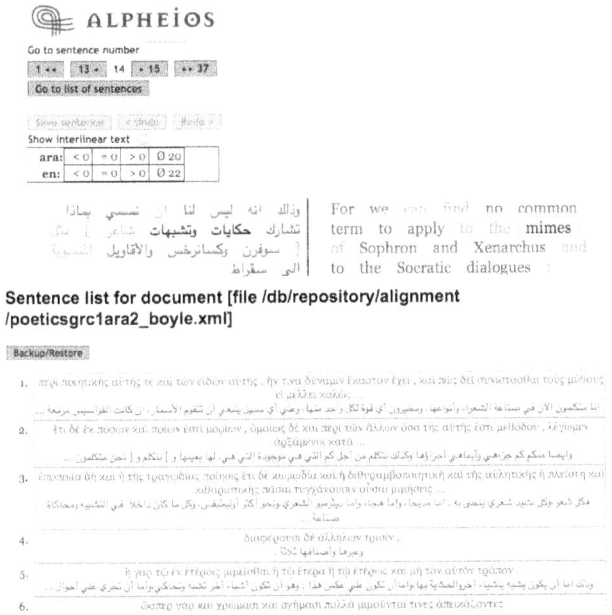

Figure 10: Collaborative alignment of Greek and Arabic

Students in a fall 2011 course at Tufts University, for example, studied the circulation of ideas from Greek sources, through Arabic translation and then back to Western Europe, via translation from Arabic into Latin, with a particular focus on Greek, Arabic, and Latin versions of Aristotle's *Poetics*. Three of the students had studied Greek and Latin, three were in third year Arabic, and one had studied both languages. In a take-home midterm exam, each group first used the Alpheios parallel text editor to align the words of the source text in the language with which they were most familiar (Greek or Arabic) with the words in an English translation. They then shifted from English to the language that, in most cases, they had not studied, using manual annotation and the morphological + dictionary lookup tools to explore the meaning of each word in the unfamiliar language.

There were two outcomes from this exercise. First, all the students were able to analyze, at a fine-grained level, the relationship between the Greek and the Arabic versions of Aristotle by using the aligned English (Figure 10) and the reading tools—an intellectual activity that would have been otherwise impractical and which allowed them to think about the circulation of ideas at a much greater level of precision than would have previously been possible. The Greek and Arabic sources were both immediately and directly accessible. Second, the students produced refined alignments from the Greek source to the Arabic translation, alignments that are stored as machine-actionable annotations that can support readers (who wish to see which words in the Greek correspond to the Arabic) and that contribute to a larger corpus of automatically aligned Greek and Arabic being developed by a project supported by the Mellon Foundation at Harvard and Tufts.

3.4 Annotations and Dynamic Reading Lists

We have developed a Dynamic Reading Lists service to expand the use and the value of reading lists at all levels. Dynamic Reading Lists support several functions that can generate annotations between citations and texts and between words and grammatical categories.

First, we need to measure the actual size of traditional reading lists. Such measurement is difficult when reading lists are static lists—we had to calculate the word counts for the Harvard undergraduate and Berkeley PhD reading lists. Another major PhD program estimated its new PhD reading lists in Greek and Latin at 1700 pages each—a very rough metric, since the content pages varies widely from publication series and genre. The reading list probably contains between 300,000 and 400,000 words for each language.

Support from the Google Digital Humanities program has allowed us to augment our holdings in Greek and Latin sources. We now can offer more than 95% of the sources covered in the published reading lists that we have analyzed.[4] These texts are encoded as TEI XML and, equally important, the structural markup represents the canonical citations—the chapter and verse style coordinate systems—whereby classicists have referenced and annotated their source texts for generations.

Second, we need to be able to convert citations that describe subsets of texts into machine actionable queries by which we can extract that section of a text that a citation describes. Because we have digitized versions of Classical Greek and Latin source texts in PhD reading lists, we can automatically calculate how many words are in books 1 and 6 of the *Iliad* or the *Medea* of Euripides. Identifying how many words are in particular subsets of a work (such as Herodotus' *Histories*, book 3, chapters 76-138), is also possible if we extract that particular chunk. The Dynamic Reading List service builds upon the Canonical Text Services protocol to resolve machine actionable citations such as "Herodotus 3.76-138" into a chunk of source text, extracting the precise citation.

Third, we need to be able to generate links between words and as many grammatical categories as possible so that learners understand what they need to know to comprehend a particular text or textual genre.

At present we can measure some general linguistic phenomena in corpora. Because we can generate links between inflected forms and their morphological features, we can, for example, detect that the optative mood—and with it, a long list of verbal conjugations—only occurs in a single form in the New Testament and thus help learners prioritize what they do and do not need to master for the corpora in which they are interested.

Where we have curated morpho-syntactic annotations in the Greek and Latin Treebanks we can provide far more precise analysis of the grammatical structures that learners will encounter. By using parallel texts (e.g., source texts in one language with translations into English), we can also begin to identify differing word senses (e.g., not only how often do forms of the Latin word *oratio* appear but how often do they correspond to a "speech" in a court room or political context and how often do they correspond to a "prayer" [5]). Learners can, as described above, refine automatic annotations of morphology, syntax, word sense and other features, providing (and receiving recognition for) more refined data for others to use.

---

[4] We have focused on the very large source texts that no individual or small group could digitize. The remaining sources are small texts, often fragmentary sources that survive only as scattered quotations in other authors and require special attention for proper digital publication [10].

Table 2: Cumulative words and vocabulary in a Dynamic Reading List, automatically calculated

Author	*Work*	*Cit.*	*Words*	*Vcb.*	*New Vcb.*
Homer	*Iliad*	bk 1	4519	**1172**	**1172** (25%)
Homer	*Iliad*	bk 9	5093	**1937**	**765** (15%)
Homer	*Odyssey*	bks 9-12	15973	**3585**	**1648** (10%)
Hesiod	*Theog.*	1-109	756	**3678**	**93** (12%)
Euripides	*Medea*	all	8105	**4642**	**964** (11%)
Thucydides	*Pel. War*	1.1-23	3522	**5045**	**403** (11%)
Thucydides	*Pel. War*	2.35-47	1933	**5200**	**155** (8%)
Plato	*Euthyph.*	all	5405	**5413**	**213** (3%)
Plato	*Apology*	all	8749	**5763**	**350** (4%)
Total			**54313**	**5763**	

We can also calculate one critical feature of a reading list, the number of distinct vocabulary entries in a given source text. Table 2 illustrates a Dynamic Reading List for a particular pathway through a Greek reading list. It calculates the number of words and vocabulary entries in a given reading and then calculates aggregate summaries for both. The total number of words covered increases linearly. But because readers encounter an increasing number of vocabulary items more than once, the total vocabulary increases more slowly. Readers who start by mastering the first book of the *Iliad* will actually have seen, on the average 75% (3,347) of the words they encounter as they work through the 4,519 words in this text, with a new vocabulary word appearing 25% of the time. As they move on to book 9 of the *Iliad* (the embassy to Achilles), new vocabulary drops to 15%, then to 10% when they move on to *Odyssey* books 9-12 (where Odysseus travels through the world of gods and monsters). Shifting to other authors introduces learners to different sets of vocabulary and the new vocabulary rate remains a bit higher (12%, 11%, 11%) until declining as the reader works through Greek prose—with only 4% of the words in Plato's *Apology* unseen.

We can recalculate these figures depending upon the paths that learners take. Thus, if a learner goes directly from Books 1 and 9 of the *Iliad* to Thucydides 1.1-23, 589 of the vocabulary items (16%) will be unseen as opposed to 403 (11%) for the learner who has worked through the path in Table 2.

We can also identify which vocabulary items will occur in a corpus. Table 3 shows what percentage of the vocabulary items in the Dynamic Reading List of Table 2 occur 5 or more times, 4 or more times etc. Learners (and, where formal course work is involved, their instructors) can prioritize vocabulary items based upon how often these words will occur in the particular sources that each learner chooses to explore—allowing the student of Greek philosophy to generate a list that differs from that of a student of Classical Greek historians or of the Homeric epics. Learners can review where they have encountered terms that they have forgotten.

We can also use this vocabulary data to retrieve unseen sentences that (1) reinforce new vocabulary items and (2) contain as many previously seen vocabulary items as possible (thus allowing the learning to reinforce both the new term and other known words), while automatically identifying, glossing and prioritizing any new words in the retrieved sentence. This service addresses a long-standing problem for assessment. We want to understand how well learners can recognize and use what they have encountered in the past in novel contexts, but it is impossible to determine with any precision what vocabulary items in a new passage are unseen and how often and when in the past learners have encountered those passages which they have seen. We now have the data so that learners can test themselves on new passages and so that we can generate smart exams that personalize themselves to the backgrounds of particular learners.

Table 3: Running words covered by vocabulary words

Frequency	*Cumulative*	*Words Covered*
5+	1,375	46,780 (86.4%)
4	1,694	48,056 (88.8%)
3	2,218	49,628 (91.7%)
2	3,180	51,552 (95.2%)
1	5,763	54,313 (100%)

Simple calculation of vocabulary items is not by itself a perfect measure of linguistic difficulty. The syntax of Thucydides is famous for its complexity—the Greek author Dionysius of Halicarnassus himself complained that he could not understand some passages from Thucydides—but the Thucydides' vocabulary is smaller than that of Homer or Plato. A student working through 75,000 words in each of these authors will encounter 3,966 vocabulary items in Thucydides, 4363 in Plato and 5,024 in Homer, even though Homeric Greek is commonly judged to be far easier to read than that of either Thucydides or Plato. We need additional metrics to capture other features of linguistic complexity when evaluate the difficulty of a corpus.

Nevertheless, even simple Dynamic Reading Lists such as that presented in Table 2 have immense potential. For the first time, we can immediately measure the absolute words and the number of vocabulary items in an arbitrary reading list, allowing us to compare the size and (by using other available metadata) chronological or genre coverage of various published reading lists.

More importantly, learners can establish their own dynamic reading lists, customized to help them learn the linguistic knowledge they need to pursue their own needs and interests. Learners can then publish these reading lists as a part of their e-portfolios. At present, a particularly ambitious student at a small program must depend upon their grades and upon the letters of their instructors to establish what he or she has accomplished. The independent learner has virtually no way to document what they have accomplished. Learners can, however, publish their dynamic reading lists as a part of their e-portfolios. They can also include any formal evaluation that they have received. Third parties can then use these dynamic reading lists to generate examination materials with which to evaluate the degree to which individual students have mastered their published lists.

The potential of published Dynamic Reading Lists is substantial. Learners are not so dependent upon the reputations of their home institutions and the grades that they have received if they can document what they have actually done. The Dynamic Reading Lists thus reward merit and provide concrete encouragement for ambitious learners, who have much better instruments whereby to establish their own accomplishments.

3.5 E-Portfolios, Linguistic Annotation, and the Shift from Authority to Achievement

Dynamic Reading Lists provide one particularly important feature for the e-portfolios of those who work with historical languages. To document what students have contributed and the linguistic skills that they have acquired, we need to support the data structures by which we store this information. We have developed methods with which to manage both.

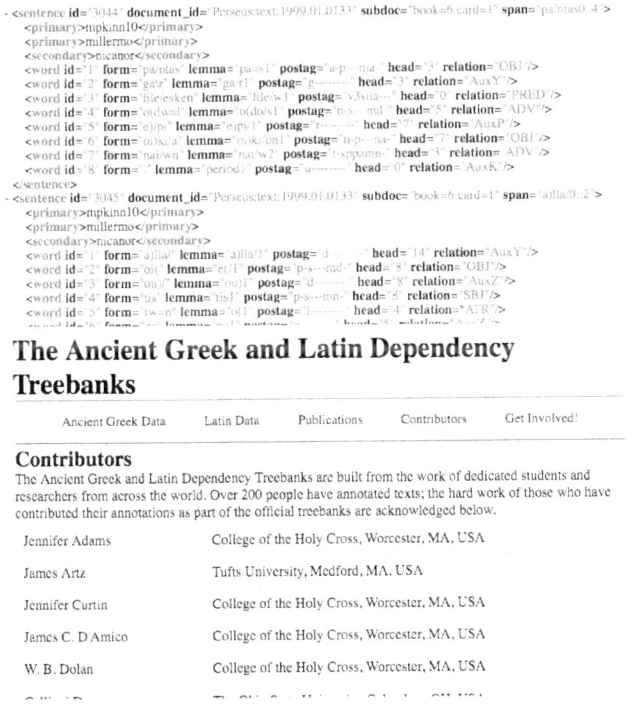

Figure 11: E-portfolios for Treebank contributions

We have created an environment with which users can develop and publish e-portfolios with a wide range of their *contributions*. These include not only morpho-syntactic analyses but varied curation and editorial tasks such as adding corrections to data entry errors, adding TEI XML structural markup, marking textual variants, disambiguating names or word senses, and creating parallel text alignments. Figure 11 illustrates how unique user IDs are stored as core elements to annotations within the Greek and Latin Treebanks in Perseus where two independent annotators analyzed each sentence *and* an expert reviewed instances where those annotators differed, producing a final shared analysis. Learners may choose to publish their own individual analyses for public review to demonstrate what they can accomplish on their own (or with less intensive supervision, such as statistical sampling of their work). This data allows us to provide e-portfolios either as stand-alone products or in a structured format for integration into Learning Management Systems (LMS) such as Sakai and Moodle, alongside more conventional materials such as papers or presentations.

E-portfolios also allow students of historical languages to re-invent one of the most traditional metrics of success: mastery of extensive reading lists that challenge learners to familiarize themselves with a cumulative network of sources building upon each other over time (e.g., as Vergil's *Aeneid* builds upon the Homeric *Iliad*). Such reading lists are demanding for independent learners—the Harvard Department of the Classics first reduced its undergraduate reading lists to c. 160,000 words of Greek and of Latin each and then finally abolished the reading lists altogether. Even at a competitive school such as Harvard, too few students had the linguistic training to cover a reading list of that size, much, if not most, of which students traditionally have had to tackle on their own. Nevertheless, extensive reading lists were, along with undergraduate theses, key elements for undergraduate education. The passage of language exams on reading lists for Greek and Latin remain an established rite of passage for PhD students of Classics, with demanding programs such as Berkeley posting reading lists of 500,000 for Classical Greek.

4. RELATED WORK

The study of annotations and their use in both digital libraries and online reading environments has an extensive amount of literature. One early and frequently cited web-based annotation system is Annotea [22] that made use of an RDF based model. A large body of work on the nature of scholarly annotation, hypertext and digital reading has also been presented by [24, 25]. Work by [1] has presented a formal model of the different types of annotations, and ongoing research by the Open Annotation Consortium (OAC) seeks to develop an "interoperable data model for scholarly annotation" based on the principles of Linked Data [11] and utilizing the technologies of the Semantic Web [16]. Recent work by [30] has experimented with the OAC model for providing persistent web annotations and also provides an excellent summary of the most significant recent work on the topic of annotation. [33] has also made use of the OAC model to develop the open source YUMA Media Annotation Framework.

Europeana and the **Europeana Data Model (EDM)** have addressed the larger shift from books to data to which the work presented here seeks to contribute. Europeana is best known for the millions of objects and images for which it has aggregated metadata but its long-term significance may lie in the fact that Europeana has moved beyond older metaphors of library and catalogue, and is currently experimenting with making all of its metadata available as Linked Open Data [20]. Thus, the EDM is designed to provide a single space in which words and physical objects of all kinds can be addressed [18]. For the Perseus Digital Library the CIDOC CRM, FRBR, and TEI XML have provided separate—and largely disconnected—spaces within which to organize information about art and archaeological objects, authors and their works, and textual data. The EDM provides the first space in which all of the Perseus collections can be fully represented. Every annotation to which this paper alludes can be represented in the EDM.

In terms of expanding contributions to digital cultural heritage, humanities projects have begun encouraging citizen scholars to contribute to digital history [32] and exploring crowd-sourcing tools such as Amazon's MechanicalTurk [23] and wikis [28] to support large scale user manuscript transcription (e.g., the Transcribe Bentham Project) as well as creating games to encourage users to assist in correcting OCR errors in historical text [15].

Additionally, a survey of potential technologies to be used in the assessment of student learning in intelligent language learning systems such as the one described in this paper has been offered by [29] and [14] has also provided a promising initial examination into the use of NLP in language learning assessment.

Another related field of work is that of e-portfolios and language learning. An e-portfolio augments traditional forms of assessment and it typically includes a variety of materials that document student capabilities in a given language. The research presented in [17] provides a through overview of two potential portfolio models, while [21] has offered an initial exploration in terms of the success of e-portfolios in helping students to successfully assess their own skills.

In terms of machine translation, the Chinese Room: Machine Translation Visualization Project has created [2] visualization for diverse types of linguistic information to allow greater comprehension of machine translations by users with little or no fluency in the source language of the translation. They were able to develop an interface that exploits linguistic resources to allow these users to understand and to measurably improve broken machine translations.

The Homer Multitext Project [34], the first of its kind in Homeric studies, seeks to present the textual transmission of the *Iliad* and *Odyssey* in a historical framework [19]. It is particularly relevant to the work described here because undergraduate student researchers at Furman, Holy Cross, and the University of Houston collaborate to analyze, document, transcribe, markup, explicate, and translate not only the Homeric text but also the extensive Greek annotations on each manuscript. Students in first semester Greek can analyze page layout of manuscripts and then assume increasingly challenging tasks as their knowledge of the language and experience grows.

The Hestia Project [9] created for the Greek Historian Herodotus an Encoded Space-Text Archive, where each reference to a place in the text was geo-coded and aligned to an authority list with data such as longitude and latitude. The Hestia team was then able to use that data to explore ways in which Herodotus' *History* potentially represents a decentered or multi-centered understanding of the Mediterranean world based on relational flow and connectivity. Because an automatically geocoded English translation of Herodotus was available, project members used this as their data source, correcting and augmenting the annotations on the English rather than the Greek. They thus documented how annotation on an English translation could generate data that would advance expert knowledge about the underlying ancient source texts.

5. FURTHER WORK

A great deal remains to be done on each of the functions described above. Our larger goal is, however, to integrate these services from Perseus and Alpheios.net into Philologist (Figure 12), an open environment for annotating and learning historical languages.

The work presented above has been tested primarily with student researchers in formal academic programs. We recognize the need to generalize these results by working with independent learners who may emerge as citizen scholars. More generally, we need to globalize the tools that we have presented, reducing their dependence upon English. The annotations that we are collecting are largely independent of the annotator's native language—it does not matter if your first language is Arabic or English if you are publishing syntactic analyses for sentences in Plato. Such globalization is critical if we are to work with sources in multiple languages and to understand global cultural heritage as a network of cultures, each interacting with the other. The 2009 MLA "Enrollments in Languages other than English survey" cites 35,000 students of Modern Standard Arabic (p. 19) but only 306 students of the Classical and Quranic Arabic (p. 29), 202 students of Classical Chinese (p. 29), and 499 students of Sanskrit (p. 32). Every major cultural system from the Atlantic to the Pacific interacted over thousands of years but established North American and European centers of academic learning have produced enough experts in the relevant languages. We must develop new scholarly relationships in which colleagues from India, China, the Middle East and elsewhere play a fundamental, tangible and immediate role. Much critical work involves digital editing and annotation, the products of which do not necessarily depend upon the native language of the producer.

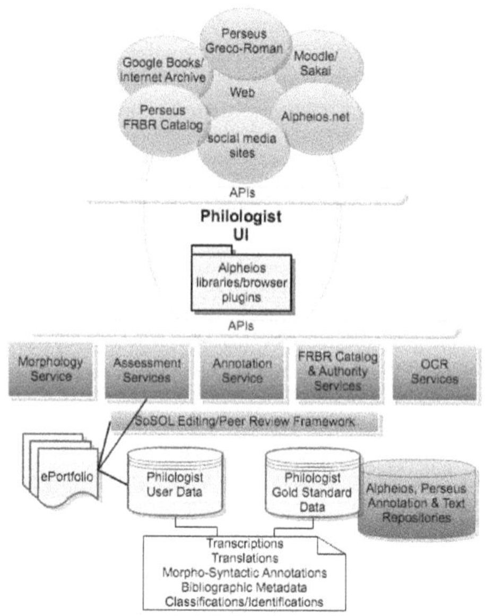

Figure 12: Philologist

6. CONCLUSIONS

We have shown that (1) billions of words with an open set of annotations, rather than tens of thousands of books, have already emerged as the objects which emerging digital infrastructure must manage; (2) that a participatory culture, combining features of laboratory and library, has begun to emerge in formal education, as student researchers (and ultimately citizen scholars) collaborate with library professionals and student researchers to manage this explosion of data; (3) that learners can track and document the annotations that they contribute, thus reaping the psychological rewards of making credited contributions to an intellectual enterprise that extends thousands of years into the past and forward into the future; (4) that the contribution of some annotations also advances core tasks of language learning, developing skills from introductory through advanced mastery of the language; (5) that learners can, by working with and adding to annotations, conduct more sophisticated research, working with a wider range of linguistic sources than was feasible with book-oriented print infrastructures; (6) that learners can document both what they have contributed and what they have mastered, publishing their own personalized reading lists and much more tangible, quantifiable and ultimately verifiable data about what they have accomplished than summary grades or institutional reputations alone can convey. We have thus created working elements of a larger infrastructure for the study, at all levels, of textual sources from the human record.

7. ACKNOWLEDGEMENTS

This work has been supported by grants from the NEH [Dynamic Lexicon (PR-50013-08), Digging into Data (HJ-50013-10), Hellespont Project (HG-50020-10)], NSF [Mining a Million Books (091065)], Mellon Foundation (Cybereditions, Bamboo, Greco-Arabic), the Cantus Foundation, and the Google Digital Humanities Program.

8. REFERENCES

[1] Agosti, M. and Ferro, N. 2007. A formal model of annotations of digital content. *ACM Trans. Inf. Syst.* 26 (Nov. 2007): 3+. DOI= http://dx.doi.org/10.1145/1292591.1292594

[2] Albrecht, J., Hwa, R., and Marai, G.E. 2009. The Chinese room: visualization and interaction to understand and correct

ambiguous machine translation. *Comput Graph Forum*, 28 (June 2009), 1047-1054.
[3] Babeu, A. 2011. "*Rome Wasn't Digitized in a Day": Building a Cyberinfrastructure for Digital Classicists.* Technical Report. CLIR.
[4] Bagnall, R. 2010. Integrating digital papyrology. In *Online Humanities Scholarship: The Shape of Things to Come.* http://hdl.handle.net/2451/29592.
[5] Bamman, D, and Crane, G. 2011. Measuring historical word sense variation. In *Proceedings of the 11th annual international ACM/IEEE joint conference on Digital libraries* (JCDL '11). ACM, New York, NY, USA, 1-10. DOI=http://doi.acm.org/10.1145/1998076.1998078.
[6] Bamman, D. and Smith, D. To appear. Extracting two thousand years of Latin from a million book library. *JOCCH.*
[7] Bamman, D., Babeu, A., Crane, G. 2010. Transferring structural markup across translations using multilingual alignment and projection. In *Proceedings of the 10th annual joint conference on Digital libraries (JCDL '10).* ACM, New York, NY, USA, 11-20. DOI= http://dx.doi.org/10.1145/1816123.1816126
[8] Bamman, D., Mambrini, F., and Crane, G. 2009. An ownership model of annotation: the Ancient Greek Dependency Treebank. In *TLT 2009: Proceedings of the Eighth International Workshop on Treebanks and Linguistic Theories Conference.*
[9] Barker, E., Bouzarovski, S., Pelling, C., Isaksen, L. 2010. Mapping an ancient historian in a digital age: the Herodotus Encoded Space-Text-Image Archive (HESTIA). *Leeds International Classical Studies*, 9 (March 2010). http://www.leeds.ac.uk/classics/lics/2010/201001.pdf
[10] Berti, M., Romanello, M., Babeu, A., and Crane, G. 2009. Collecting fragmentary authors in a digital library. In *Proceedings of the 9th ACM/IEEE-CS joint conference on Digital libraries (JCDL '09). ACM, New York, NY, USA,* 259-262. DOI=http://dx.doi.org/10.1145/1555400.1555442.
[11] Bizer, C. Cyganiak, R. and Heath, T. 2007. How to publish linked data on the Web. Available at: http://sites.wiwiss.fu-berlin.de/bizer/pub/LinkedDataTutorial/
[12] Blackwell, C., and Martin, T. 2009. Technology, collaboration, and undergraduate research. *Digital Humanities Quarterly*, 3, 1 (Jan. 2009).
[13] Bulger, M., Meyer, E.T., and de la Flor, G. 2011. *Reinventing Research? Information Practices in the Humanities.* Technical Report. Research Information Network.
[14] Chapelle, C.A., and Chung, Y.R. 2010. The promise of NLP and speech processing technologies in language assessment. *Language Testing*, 27 (July 2010), 301-315.
[15] Chrons, O., and Sundell, S. 2011. Digitalkoot: Making old archives accessible using crowdsourcing. In *HCOMP 2011: 3rd Human Computation Workshop.*
[16] Cole, T., and Han, M. 2011. The Open Annotation Collaboration Phase I: Towards a shared, interoperable data model for scholarly annotation. *Journal of the Chicago Colloquium on Digital Humanities and Computer Science*, 1 (3), July 2011.
[17] Cummins, P. W. and Davesne, C. 2009. Using electronic portfolios for second language assessment. *The Modern Language Journal*, 93 (2009), 848-867.
[18] Doerr, M., et al. 2010. The Europeana Data Model (EDM). In *World Library and Information Congress: 76th IFLA General Conference and Assembly*, 10-15 Aug. 2010, Gothenberg, Sweden.
[19] Dué, C., and Ebbott, M. 2009. Digital criticism: editorial standards for the Homer Multitext. *Digital Humanities Quarterly*, 3 (Jan. 2009).
[20] Haslhofer, B. and Isaac, A. 2011. data.europeana.eu - The Europeana Linked Open Data pilot. In *Proc. Int'l Conf. on Dublin Core and Metadata Applications 2011*, 94-104
[21] Hung, S. T. 2009. Promoting self-assessment strategies: an electronic portfolio approach. *The Asian EFL Journal Quarterly*, 11, 2 (June 2009), 129-146.
[22] Kahan, J. and Koivunen, M.R. 2002. Annotea: an open RDF infrastructure for shared Web annotations. In *Proceedings of the 10th international conference on World Wide Web* (WWW '01). ACM, New York, NY, USA, 623-632. DOI=http://dx.doi.org/10.1145/371920.372166
[23] Lang, A., and Rio-Ross, J. 2011. Using Amazon Mechanical Turk to transcribe historical handwritten documents. *The Code4Lib Journal* (Oct. 2011).
[24] Marshall, C. C. 1998. Toward an ecology of hypertext annotation. In *Proceedings of the ninth ACM conference on Hypertext and hypermedia:* (HYPERTEXT '98). ACM, New York, NY, USA, 40-49. DOI=http://doi.acm.org/10.1145/276627.276632.
[25] Marshall, C.C. and Brush, A.J. 2004. Exploring the relationship between personal and public annotations. In *Proceedings of the 4th ACM/IEEE-CS joint conference on Digital libraries* (JCDL '04). ACM, New York, NY, USA, 349-357. DOI=http://dx.doi.org/10.1145/996350.996432.
[26] Michel, J. B., Shen, Y.K., and Aiden, A.P. 2011. Quantitative analysis of culture using millions of digitized books. *Science*, 331, 6014, (Jan. 2011), 176-182. DOI=http://dx.doi.org/10.1126/science.1199644
[27] Molin, C., Nyhan, J., Ciula, A, et al. 2011. *Research Infrastructures in the Digital Humanities.* Technical Report. European Science Foundation.
[28] Moyle, M., Tonra, J., and Wallace, V. 2011. Manuscript transcription by crowdsourcing: Transcribe Bentham. *Liber Quarterly - The Journal of European Research Libraries* 20 (Sept. 2011).
[29] Ockey, G. J. 2009. Developments and challenges in the use of computer-based testing for assessing second language ability. *The Modern Language Journal*, 93 (2009): 836-847.
[30] Sanderson, R. and Van de Sompel, H. 2010. Making web annotations persistent over time. *Proceedings of the 10th annual joint conference on Digital libraries* (JCDL '10). ACM, New York, NY, USA, 1-10. DOI=http://dx.doi.org/10.1145/1816123.1816125
[31] Schmidt, D. and Colomb, R. 2009. A data structure for representing multi-version texts online. *Int. J. Hum.-Comput. Stud.*, 67, 6 (June 2009), 497-514.
[32] Sikarskie, A.G. 2011. Citizen scholars: Facebook and the co-creation of knowledge. In Jack Dougherty and Kristen Nawrotzki, eds. *Writing History in the Digital Age.* Under contract with the University of Michigan Press. Web-book edition, Trinity College (CT), Fall 2011.
[33] Simon, R., J. Jung, and B. Haslhofer. 2011. The YUMA media annotation framework. *Proceedings of the 15th international conference on Theory and practice of digital libraries: research and advanced technology for digital libraries.* Berlin, Heidelberg: Springer-Verlag, 2011, 434-437.
[34] Smith, Neel. 2010. Digital infrastructure and the Homer Multitext Project. *Digital Research in the Study of Classical Antiquity.* Eds. Gabriel Bodard and Simon Mahony. Burlington, VT: Ashgate Publishing, 121-137.

Event-centric Search and Exploration in Document Collections

Jannik Strötgen
Institute of Computer Science
Heidelberg University
Heidelberg, Germany
stroetgen@uni-hd.de

Michael Gertz
Institute of Computer Science
Heidelberg University
Heidelberg, Germany
gertz@uni-hd.de

ABSTRACT

Textual data ranging from corpora of digitized historic documents to large collections of news feeds provide a rich source for temporal and geographic information. Such types of information have recently gained a lot of interest in support of different search and exploration tasks, e.g., by organizing news along a timeline or placing the origin of documents on a map. However, for this, temporal and geographic information embedded in documents is often considered in isolation. We claim that through combining such information into (chronologically ordered) event-like features interesting and meaningful search and exploration tasks are possible.

In this paper, we present a framework for the extraction, exploration, and visualization of event information in document collections. For this, one has to identify and combine temporal and geographic expressions from documents, thus enriching a document collection by a *set of normalized events*. Traditional search queries then can be enriched by conditions on the events relevant to the search subject. Most important for our event-centric approach is that a search result consists of a sequence of events relevant to the search terms and not just a document hit-list. Such events can originate from different documents and can be further explored, in particular events relevant to a search query can be ordered chronologically. We demonstrate the utility of our framework by different (multilingual) search and exploration scenarios using a Wikipedia corpus.

Categories and Subject Descriptors

H.3.3 [**Information Systems**]: Information Search and Retrieval—*Query formulation, Search process*; I.2.7 [**Artificial Intelligence**]: Natural Language Processing—*Text analysis*

Keywords

event extraction, temporal information, geographic information, querying, corpora exploration

1. INTRODUCTION

Driven by the dramatic increase of textual data generated through social media such as blogs and news feeds or simply through the digitalization of (historic) paper-based documents, a rich resource for spatial and spatio-temporal information has become available. While models, techniques, and system architectures are well established for traditional sources of spatial and spatio-temporal data, typically obtained from observations and experiments, the processing and exploration of such information embedded in textual documents is much more challenging.

In the information retrieval community, on the other hand, there have been advances to utilize temporal and geographic information embedded in documents. Existing approaches, however, mostly deal only with either temporal or geographic information in isolation (see, e.g., [3, 22]). There are a few approaches combining temporal and geographic information [15, 21], and recently, we also presented a system called TimeTrails for exploring geographic and temporal information in documents [26]. We claim that especially combinations of geographic and temporal information in documents play an important role for exploration tasks. This is because combinations of such information often correspond to descriptions of events that take place at some specific location and at some point or duration in time.

As we will show in this paper, once expressions referring to geographic locations and points or durations in time have been identified they can be (1) normalized to a standard format and (2) combined to describe event-like features. Temporal information can be placed on a timeline and geographic information can be represented as latitude/longitude information, possibly with some region information.

Our particular interest in this paper is on event-centric search and exploration tasks. Given a document corpus, a traditional search query would "simply" return all documents relevant to the search terms. Having a large set of events extracted from a corpus, however, in our approach, a sequence of events relevant to the search terms is retrieved. To tailor the search to geographic regions or points in time of interest, constraints on the geographic and temporal components of events can be added to the search terms. Thus, our approach allows to retrieve constrained events (and underlying documents) related to one or more subjects described by the search terms. Most importantly events can be ordered chronologically to form a sequence of events that are relevant to the search subject. Especially the latter feature provides a very intuitive event-based summary of a search subject. Therefore, in our event-centric search, different exploration tasks can be supported, e.g., a simple comparison of event sequences retrieved in the context of two search queries. It is even possible, to make statements about the similarity of documents based on events [29].

The above tasks can effectively be realized using a map on which retrieved events for queries are placed based on the geographic component of each event. It should be noted that the source documents from which events have been extracted could be retrieved as well. Through this, for a search query one also can get information about the distribution of events among the documents relevant to a query subject.

The realization of such a framework poses several challenges. First, temporal and geographic expressions in documents must be identified as such, normalized to some standard format, and then be combined into events. Such events can be of different temporal and geographic granularity as the underlying expressions can be of different granularities (e.g., "March 2011" versus "First of March 2011", or "Germany" versus "Berlin"). For forming events, we adopt a simple yet very effective approach. If a geographic and a temporal expression occur in close proximity in a document, they describe an event. Second, events related to a constrained search query need to be efficiently retrieved and presented to the user. Third, it should be possible to group and/or order events retrieved in the context of queries.

In summary, the main contributions of this paper are:

- We describe in detail how events are determined by extracting temporal and geographic expressions from documents, combining this information into event descriptions, and organizing them as *event sequences*.
- We present an *event-centric approach* for querying document corpora. For this, we combine a textual search query with geographic and temporal constraints on (relevant) events by defining simple yet expressive query language constructs.
- We illustrate how different event-centric search and exploration tasks can be used in a *language-independent* way. For this, we employ multilingual corpora of Wikipedia documents.

The remainder of the paper is structured as follows: After a review of related work, in Section 3, we present the extraction and organization of events. In Section 4, we introduce our multi-dimensional query approach, and in Section 5, we discuss several exploration scenarios based on events, adding extensive functionality to systems that aim at supporting an event-centric exploration of document corpora. To demonstrate the usefulness of events for search and exploration tasks, we present a multilingual evaluation in Section 6.

2. RELATED WORK

There is some research on extracting and exploring temporal and geographic information, although there is much less work combining both types of information. An exception is some work in the area of natural language processing (NLP) and information extraction (IE) in particular [1, 5, 10]. However, the focus there is on linguistic aspects and not extensions to traditional IR tasks that focus on querying and exploring event-like features in document collections.

The value of temporal information for information retrieval is discussed in [2]. In addition, temporal information plays an important role in areas that rely on richer natural language processing, e.g., question answering and summarization. A good overview is given in [13]. To be able to exploit the temporal information mentioned in documents, one has to extract and normalize temporal expressions, one task of temporal information extraction. The most recent standard for temporal annotating documents is TimeML [23] including TIMEX3 tags for temporal expressions.

Similar to temporal information retrieval, there is a lot of research on geographic information retrieval. Again, the first step is to extract and disambiguate geographic expressions, a task solved by so-called geo-taggers. Tools provided by companies, such as MetaCarta [18] and Yahoo! Placemaker [33], as well as various research systems are usually based on gazetteers. Context information, heuristics, and linguistic rules are used to disambiguate between alternatives [8, 9]. There are several applications that exploit geographic information extracted from documents, e.g., the spatial textual search engine STEWARD [11] and determining the spatial reader scope [24].

Only some work exists on combining temporal and geographic information for IR-style querying and exploring documents. One of the first works is GeoTracker, which uses the document creation time of RSS feeds and extracts geographic expressions mentioned in them to visualize the feeds on a map [4]. Note that in contrast to our work, they only associate one time point and location with a document. Martins et al. extract both temporal and geographic expressions from RSS feeds to visualize them using a map and time slider [15]. Furthermore, the CITER project combines temporal, geographic, and thematic metadata to search within historic text books of different languages [21]. However, both GeoTracker and CITER do not explicitly combine the temporal and geographic dimensions into events. Petras et al. associate time and place information to period names, which can then be used to search spatio-temporal metadata of digital libraries [20]. Recently, the NTCIR-GeoTime, a geographic and temporal information retrieval challenge, was organized [6]. In comparison to our work, the focus was on querying for temporal and geographic answers, i.e., answering queries of the form "when and where did something happen". The same kind of queries were addressed in [16] based on a semi-automatically built reference ontology in which the thematic, temporal, and geographic information of interest is organized. Thus, the search is based on a matching between query terms and ontology concepts. In [31] a method has been proposed to utilize spatio-temporal information extracted from text to construct trajectories of individuals but without rich search and exploration support. Similarly, in [34] historic events are extracted and a system is presented to geographically navigate through them.

In [26], we outlined a prototype system called TimeTrails to explore events related to a hit-list of documents, containing those documents that are relevant to a simple search query. In this paper, we extend the idea of event-centric search of documents by exploring the *set of events* relevant to a search query and not just the relevant list of documents. For this, we provide a multi-dimensional query approach to specify geographic and temporal conditions when querying a corpus and several ways for exploring the events extracted from a corpus of documents.

3. EXTRACTING NORMALIZED EVENTS

Temporal and geographic information is characteristic for many documents that textually describe events such as historic documents or biographies. In this section, we first outline key characteristics of temporal and geographic information that make it valuable for many search and exploration tasks. Then, we describe how expressions carrying temporal or geographic information occur in documents and how they can be extracted and normalized. Finally, we define how to combine temporal and geographic information extracted from documents resulting in a set of event descriptions for a document corpus. These provide the basis for the querying and exploration scenarios described in Sections 4 and 5.

3.1 Key Characteristics of Temporal and Geographic Information

Temporal and geographic information is very similar with respect to the key characteristics, making them valuable for search and exploration tasks:

- The information is well-defined: Assuming two points or intervals in time or two location points or regions, the relationship between them can be identified, e.g., the temporal relationship can be of the types *before*, *after*, or *overlap*, and the geographic one of the types *inside*, *overlap*, or *disjoint*.
- The information can be normalized: Regardless of the language or the used terms, two temporal or geographic expressions referring to the same point in time or location, respectively, can be normalized to the same value in some standard format. Thus, both types of information are language-independent.
- The information can be organized hierarchically: Temporal and geographic information can be of different granularity, e.g., of the type day and month, or city and country, respectively. Thus, a temporal or geographic expression of a fine granularity can be mapped to a coarser granularity based on the hierarchy of temporal and geographic information.

These key characteristics make it possible to extract temporal and geographic expressions from documents of different languages, normalize them to some standard format, and compare entities independently of their granularities. These characteristics also build the basis of the concept of event sequences introduced in Section 3.4.

3.2 Temporal and Geographic Information in Documents

Only when temporal and geographic information in documents is identified as such, it can be normalized and is thus accessible in a standardized format. Otherwise, temporal and geographic expressions are just dealt with as usual terms and the latent temporal and geographic information cannot be used for any subsequent task. For example, when querying a document collection, a document is only found if exact expressions that occur in the document are used instead of the semantics that the expressions in the document are carrying.

It is a challenging task to extract and normalize both types of expressions since one is faced with the ambiguity problems of synonymy and polysemy, i.e., that more than one expression may refer to the same referent and that one expression may refer to more than one referent, respectively. For example, in the sentence, "the battle began on September 4th in Springfield", one wants to extract *September 4th* and *Springfield*. However, normalization is difficult due to the polysemy of these expressions. Without context information, one cannot decide on which "September 4th" and in which "Springfield" the battle began since the year is unknown and there are many cities – more than 30 in the US alone – called "Springfield". In addition, one has to recognize that several expressions may refer to the same location or point in time, e.g., "New York", "NYC", and "Big Apple" refer to the same city, and "Independence Day 2011" and "July 4th, 2011" refer to the same point in time. Solving these problems is one of the tasks of so-called *temporal taggers* and *geo-taggers* as described in the next section.

3.3 Extraction of Temporal and Geographic Expressions

The extraction and normalization of temporal and geographic information are typical named entity recognition and normalization tasks. Systems performing these tasks are so-called temporal taggers, e.g., GUTime [7] and HeidelTime [25], and industry-based geo-taggers such as MetaCarta [18] and Yahoo! Placemaker [33].

There are different approaches for the extraction of temporal expressions, rule-based and machine learning ones, but normalization is done in a rule-based fashion by almost all systems. While the normalization is straightforward for explicit expressions (e.g., "March 11, 2011"), normalizing relative expressions is a challenging task. To normalize relative expressions such as "Monday", "last year", or "today", a temporal tagger has to identify the reference time and the relation to this reference time. Once this information is known, the value of such expressions can be calculated.

For the annotation of temporal expressions, the current standard is TimeML [23], a markup language for rich temporal annotation including TIMEX3 tags for temporal expressions and tags for events and temporal relationships. In TIMEX3, for expressions of the type *date*, the most important attribute *value* is set according to the ISO 8601 standard, i.e, using YYYY-MM-DD. For example, the date "January 22, 2011" is represented as "2011-01-22". Note that no matter what language or what kind of expression is used to refer to a date, the normalized value will be the same.

Definition 1. Given a document d, an *extracted temporal expression* te_i is a three tuple $te_i = \langle t_i, v(t)_i, p(t)_i \rangle$, with t_i being the temporal expression, $v(t)_i$ the normalized value of t_i, and $p(t)_i$ the offset, i.e., start and end position in d.

As mentioned above, geographic expressions are extracted and normalized using geo-taggers. These are usually based on gazetteers, which contain names of locations and different types of additional information associated with the locations, e.g., their standardized name and containment and population information. While the names are used for the extraction, there are several key concepts used to disambiguate the location names if they refer to more than one location. These concepts include that one assumes that only one referent is used per discourse, that locations mentioned in one document are related to each other, and that the more populated a location is the higher is the probability that an expression refers to it [9]. For example, if "Stuttgart" occurs several times in the same document, one assumes that all "Stuttgart" refer to the same location called Stuttgart. The popularity information would indicate that "Stuttgart" refers to "Stuttgart (Baden-Württemberg)" in Germany since this city is the most populated one. However, if a document contains several location names that refer to locations in the US state Arkansas, it may be likely that "Stuttgart" refers to "Stuttgart, Arkansas". As normalized information, geo-taggers assign latitude/longitude information to an extracted location. This is done, however, often only in a point and not a polygon format. Thus, no matter how large a location is, it is represented as a point. For this, as the geographic dimension of an event, we use not only the latitude/longitude information but the containment information associated with a location, e.g., for Stuttgart, this would be "Stuttgart, Baden-Württemberg, Germany, Europe". Thus, similar to an extracted temporal expression, we have the following.

Definition 2. Given a document d, an *extracted geographic expression* ge_j is a three tuple $ge_j = \langle g_j, v(g)_j, p(g)_j \rangle$ with g_j being the geographic expression, $v(g)_j$ the normalized containment value of the expression, and $p(g)_j$ the expression's offset in d.

As already pointed out, we regard co-occurring geographic and temporal expressions as two dimensions of an event since these usually occur at some specific point at some specific time. As combining all temporal expressions with all geographic expressions of a document would result in many combinations that do not describe an event, we apply the following restriction.

Definition 3. Given a document d and extracted temporal and geographic expressions te_i and ge_j, respectively. The two expressions form an *event* if they co-occur in the same sentence in d.

Although this is a rather simple approach compared to deep language understanding techniques, using co-occurrences has the advantage that it is language-independent. Furthermore, we can show in our evaluation that despite its simplicity this approach works well in many cases. To determine whether te_i and ge_j co-occur in a sentence, sentence boundaries have to be detected and the offset information $p(t)_i$ and $p(g)_j$ is used. All extracted events of a document can be organized in a document event set, defined as follows.

Definition 4. An *event set* for a document d, denoted $des(d)$, is a set of tuples $\langle te_i, ge_j \rangle$ describing co-occurring temporal and geographic expressions in d.

To be able to consider event sets of a collection of documents, we add the origin of an event, i.e., its document id, to the offsets $p(t)_i$ and $p(g)_j$. Thus every event in an event set is unique. However, in the following, events with identical temporal and geographic information are considered as same events. Next, we describe how document event sets can be mapped into event sequences, an important concept for representing the result of (constrained) search queries.

3.4 From Event Sets to Event Sequences

As discussed above, a document event set is just a set of events. Based on their geographic component, in general, events can easily be visualized on a map. However, if there are many events, e.g., those relevant to a search subject, such a map can become cluttered and it might be hard to see relationships among events. Given the temporal component of an event, it seems natural to organize events chronologically and to choose another form of representation for a set of events. For this, in our approach we use the concept of *event sequences*. Conceptually, an event sequence corresponding to an event set $\{\langle te_1, ge_1\rangle, \ldots, \langle te_l, ge_l\rangle\}$ is a chronologically sorted sequence of events. Analogous to trajectories of moving objects extensively studied in the area of moving object databases, such a sequence can be considered a path a subject is taking over time. In the case of an event sequence, such a path is based on the locations corresponding to where the events extracted from an event set "happen" and is sorted chronologically. This is an intuitive approach even for several types of documents such as biographies or historical documents where in a document events are described, but not necessarily in a chronological order.

Now, given an event set (from a single document or collection of documents), how can an event sequence be constructed? For this, we have to distinguish different cases that depend on the granularity of the normalized values $v(t)_i$ of the temporal expressions $E = \{te_1, \ldots, te_l\}$.

The most simple case is when all normalized values have the same granularity. Then, based on these values, a complete order can be determined among the events. What still can happen is that for two expressions te_i and te_j the normalized values $v(t)_i$ and $v(t)_j$ are identical. In the case where the two event have been extracted from the same document, we assume that the event with the smaller offset $p(t)$ precedes the other event. For example, for the two events ⟨2011-01-15, Berlin⟩ and ⟨2011-01-15, Hamburg⟩, if the expression corresponding to the first event occurs after the expression for the second event in the document, then the event with location "Hamburg" would precede the event with location 'Berlin" in the event sequence. If the two events have been extracted from different documents, using the offsets of the events is not meaningful. In such a case, we assume that there is an order among the documents (as it will be the case in our query framework) and the order among the events then follows that document order.

The more difficult case is when the normalized temporal values of the events are of different granularity. Assume, for example, the four events e_1 = ⟨2011-02-10, Hamburg⟩, e_2 = ⟨2010-12-12, Vienna⟩, e_3 = ⟨2011-02, Munich⟩, and e_4 = ⟨2011-02, Heidelberg⟩. Clearly, one cannot immediately establish a total order among these events. Our approach to handle such cases is as follows. First, we build groups of ambiguous events. In the above example, such a group comprises e_1, e_3 and e_4. For each group, we map the normalized values to the coarsest temporal granularity in that group (here the type month) and then establish an order among these events based on the document order as described above. For example, assume a list of documents d_1, d_2, and d_3 with event sets $\{e_4\}, \{e_1, e_3\}$, and $\{e_2\}$, respectively, where in d_2, e_1 occurs before e_3. We then obtain the following order among the events: e_2, e_4, e_1, e_3.

An event set and its corresponding event sequence can thus easily be determined for a document or set of documents and thus is accessible to event-centric query and exploration tasks, which are described next.

4. MULTI-DIMENSIONAL QUERYING

Our main goal is to add functionality to existing information retrieval applications that deal with a large amount of textual documents in which events play an important role, e.g., biographies, travel reports, and historic documents. Due to the importance of events in such documents, our search result is not a hit list of documents but a list of events extracted from different documents. As described in Section 5, using deep exploration functionality provides a lot of information about the events, e.g., where they were extracted.

Usually when querying large document collections, one is limited to standard text search as known from search engines like Google or Yahoo!. If further features for querying are provided, they are often limited to the metadata of the documents like the date and location of the publication. As shown in the previous section, we extract directly from the documents' texts combinations of temporal and geographic information that form events. In this section, we show how this information can be utilized to query document collections with respect to events by introducing our multi-dimensional query model consisting of a textual, a geographic, and a temporal dimension. While for the textual dimension of the query model we rely on an existing method, namely Lucene [12], we present our methods for the temporal and geographic dimensions in Section 4.1 and Section 4.2, respectively. The full multi-dimensional query model is described in Section 4.3, describing how the dimensions can be combined in a meaningful way.

4.1 The Temporal Dimension

The temporal dimension of a query is used to search for documents containing events that take place at some specific point in time or during a specific time interval. For the formulation of the temporal dimension of a query, we use the ISO standard for temporal information, which is used in the value attribute of TIMEX3 to represent the semantics of an expression (see Section 3.3). Although one can imagine a formulation of the temporal query in natural language, using the standard format is language-independent and can directly be interpreted so that no temporal tagger has to be used. Thus, an error source, i.e., the misinterpretation of the query, can be eliminated.

As elementary queries, we want to be able to query for time points and time intervals. In addition, combinations of elementary queries shall be expressible, namely the operations of the boolean algebra: conjunction, disjunction, and negation, as well as an arbitrary combination of them. Formally, the temporal query language can be written in Extended Backus-Naur-Form (EBNF) in the following way, with *value* in lines (5) and (6) describing the standard format of a temporal expression, e.g., "2002-01" for "January 2002", "1999-12-31" for "December 31, 1999", and "2010-H1" for "the first half of 2010".

$$
\begin{aligned}
\text{<query}_{temp}\text{>} &::= \text{<conjunction>} \mid \text{<disjunction>} \\
&\mid \text{<negation>} \mid \text{<point>} \\
&\mid \text{<interval>} && (1)\\
\text{<conjunction>} &::= \underline{(}\text{<query}_{temp}\text{>}\underline{\wedge}\text{<query}_{temp}\text{>}\underline{)} && (2)\\
\text{<disjunction>} &::= \underline{(}\text{<query}_{temp}\text{>}\underline{\vee}\text{<query}_{temp}\text{>}\underline{)} && (3)\\
\text{<negation>} &::= \underline{\neg(}\text{<query}_{temp}\text{>}\underline{)} && (4)\\
\text{<point>} &::= \mathit{value} && (5)\\
\text{<interval>} &::= \underline{[}(\mathit{value}\mid\underline{\text{-INF}})\underline{,}(\mathit{value}\mid\underline{\text{INF}})\underline{]} && (6)
\end{aligned}
$$

Note that although a <point> is a single expression according to the standard format, it may represent an interval, due to the different granularities of temporal expressions. For example, the value "2002-01" contains all the days, hours, minutes, and seconds of "January 2002". Thus, if <point> is used as the only part of the temporal query, it is handled as an interval with a starting and ending point. For the given example, these are "2002-01-01T00:00:00" and "2002-01-31T23:59:59", respectively. According to this, if a <point> is set as the lower bound or as the upper bound of an interval, the starting point or the ending point of <point> are used, respectively.

Technically, the processing of a temporal query is done as follows: all normalized values of the temporal components of the events in the document collection are indexed using a B-tree in a PostGIS database. In addition, for all references to these normalized values, an inverted index is created, a concept widely used in standard information retrieval (see, e.g., [14]). For every normalized temporal value in the corpus, an entry is created and associated with a postings list. This list contains all the identifiers of the documents in which a temporal expression occurs referring to the corresponding normalized temporal value. Using the B-tree and the inverted index allows to efficiently identify all normalized values that match a temporal query and to retrieve all documents containing a reference to these normalized values. When additionally adding to the inverted index the number of how often a temporal value occurs in a document, it is possible to quickly calculate which documents fit a temporal query best, as will be outlined in Section 4.3.

4.2 The Geographic Dimension

The geographic dimension of a query is used to search for documents containing events that take place at a specific location. To allow querying regions that do not have a specific name, and for the same reasons as for a temporal query, i.e., to provide language independence of the query and to avoid misinterpretations, we do not use a query formulated in natural language. To formulate the geographic query, we use a map-based approach that allows the user to draw regions on a map, in which she is particularly interested in.

Then, all documents in the document collection are checked for extracted events whose geographic extent is contained in the specified region. Similar to the temporal query language, one can describe boolean combinations of regions in EBNF, for example, to exclude a part of a selected region. The regions that are drawn on a map and combined using boolean operators are translated into EBNF, which is formally described below. Although other shapes of regions are possible, only rectangles can be drawn on the map. Thus, in lines (11) and (12), rectangles are used as terminal symbols of the formal language.

$$
\begin{aligned}
\text{<query}_{geo}\text{>} &::= \text{<conjunction>} \mid \text{<disjunction>} \\
&\mid \text{<negation>} \mid \text{<region>} && (7)\\
\text{<conjunction>} &::= \underline{(}\text{<query}_{geo}\text{>}\underline{\wedge}\text{<query}_{geo}\text{>}\underline{)} && (8)\\
\text{<disjunction>} &::= \underline{(}\text{<query}_{geo}\text{>}\underline{\vee}\text{<query}_{geo}\text{>}\underline{)} && (9)\\
\text{<negation>} &::= \underline{\neg(}\text{<query}_{geo}\text{>}\underline{)} && (10)\\
\text{<region>} &::= \mathit{rectangle} && (11)\\
\text{<region>} &::= \mathit{rectangle}\underline{\setminus}\mathit{rectangle} && (12)
\end{aligned}
$$

In addition to the boolean operators for conjunction ($\wedge$), disjunction ($\vee$), and negation ($\neg$), we define a *without* operator ($\setminus$) to be able to describe regions with holes. Assuming a user wants to select a region R1 containing a hole R2, one cannot use the negation operator ("R1 $\wedge$ $\neg$ R2") since this query would not return documents that contain places of events in R1 if the document contains one or more places of events in R2. Compared to the negation operator that defines regions where no events of a document are allowed, the *without* operator defines a rectangle as a region that is not to be considered. Thus, to query for a region R1 containing a hole R2, one uses the query "R1 \ R2".

For all map-based geographic queries that can be formulated according to equations (7) to (12), the normalized latitude/longitude information of the extracted events is used by checking whether a location is within the query region. Thus, the technical processing of the geographic query is done in a similar way as for the temporal query except using an R-Tree instead of a B-tree index in the PostGIS database for the geospatial information. This allows to efficiently determine all geographic entities whose positions are contained in a query rectangle. As for the temporal query, the inverted index is used to return all ids of the documents containing events with the geographic component referring to these geographic entities, i.e., satisfying the geographic query. Finally, since the text search results in a postings list as well, the postings lists of the textual, temporal, and geographic query can be combined to determine all documents satisfying all three query constraints.

4.3 The Multi-dimensional Query Approach

Combining the query dimensions text, time, and space into one query processing strategy is a challenging task and several aspects need to be taken into account. As already pointed out, the event-centric search does not result in a hit list of documents, but in a set (or sequence) of events that are extracted from several documents. For the selection of events that are to be shown in the result, we employ the following two strategies, depending on which parts of a search query are given. In the following, assume a search query composed of a text component q_{text}, a temporal component q_{temp}, and a geographic component q_{geo}. All events have already been extracted from a given document collection D.

Case 1: q_{text} is not empty.

1. rank documents of D according to q_{text}, using Lucene's ranking functionality.
2. select top-k documents that have at least 1 event satisfying q_{temp} and q_{geo}. As for each document an event set has already been extracted, this can be done efficiently.
3. combine all events from the top-k documents' event sets that satisfy q_{temp} and q_{geo}.

In this case, the assumption is that the most relevant documents with respect to q_{text} contain the most relevant events, too. In the presence of the two components q_{temp} and q_{geo}, the events (and their corresponding document ids) to be retrieved are further constrained.

Case 2: q_{text} is empty, i.e., no text query has been specified. In this case, relevant events are solely retrieved based on the conditions q_{temp} and q_{geo} (assuming at least one of them has been specified).

1. rank documents of D according to the number of events satisfying q_{temp} and q_{geo}. This again can be done efficiently based on the index structures on the event components outlined in Section 3.
2. select top-k documents from the ranked list.
3. combine the event sets of these k documents, considering only events that satisfy q_{temp} and q_{geo}.

By using only the top-k relevant documents for creating the event sets, only the events of those documents are taken into account that are most relevant to a specific subject defined by q_{text} or that are most relevant for the specified temporal and geographic constraints, respectively. Thus, we avoid events being part of an event set that only occur in irrelevant documents. It should also be noted that in both cases above, a document order is established, which can be used to transform the resulting event set into an event sequence, as discussed in Section 3.4.

The resulting events, in the following called *query event set*, can then be used for several search and exploration scenarios as described in the next section.

5. EXPLORATION AND VISUALIZATION

After a description of the document processing pipeline (Section 5.1), we perform an event-centric analysis of different document types (Section 5.2). Then, in Section 5.3, we describe several examples for the event-centric exploration and visualization of document collections based on query event sets that are realized in our prototype.

5.1 Document Processing Pipeline

All documents of the corpus that is to be analyzed are processed with our document processing pipeline. For sentence splitting, temporal tagging, and geo tagging, we use the OpenNLP Sentence Splitter [19], our temporal tagger HeidelTime [25], and Yahoo! Placemaker [33], respectively. Then, co-occurrences of temporal and geographic expressions in the same sentence are identified and all events are stored in a PostGIS database. Finally, the inverted indexes are created as described in Section 4.1 and Section 4.2. Note that the only requirement for a document collection to be utilizable with our approach is that for the documents' language a temporal tagger and a geo-tagger have to be available. While Yahoo! Placemaker can process several languages, HeidelTime is currently limited to English, German, and Dutch but there are temporal taggers for other languages and, furthermore, HeidelTime's architecture allows the easy integration of more languages [28].

5.2 Document Type Analysis

We analyzed for which types of documents using temporal and geographic information is particularly suitable. For this, we created a corpus consisting of the English Wikipedia featured articles [32] and the German articles linked to the English ones through cross-language links. Besides their high quality, we chose the featured articles since they are grouped into 30 categories and 13 biography sub-categories. As depicted in Table 1, our analysis shows that documents of categories such as history, geography, and biographies contain many events and are thus most suitable for event-centric search and exploration scenarios, while documents of categories such as computing and physics contain only a few events. Note that the German documents are much shorter.

5.3 Exploration and Visualization

While the TimeTrails system, which we described in [26], returns a hit list of documents along with information about the events in the documents, our new prototype directly returns an event set with events extracted from several documents. This allows for a better event-centric exploration of document collections as we will outline next.

Category	English Documents	Events	German Documents	Events
geography, places	178 (-/-)	198	114 (15/26)	31
history	115 (-/2)	186	57 (8/16)	30
sport, recreation	151 (-/3)	138	65 (7/16)	38
warfare	254 (-/3)	119	147 (14/51)	20
all biographies	717 (2/11)	105	496 (47/81)	23
...				
video gaming	128 (12/32)	21	81 (24/33)	9
computing	18 (2/3)	17	15 (8/11)	2
physics, astronomy	92 (11/24)	14	81 (38/54)	2

Table 1: Statistics of the featured articles corpus grouped by category showing the average number of events per document. In parentheses are the numbers of documents with no/less than 3 events.

5.3.1 *Multi-dimensional Querying*

Our system realizes the multi-dimensional query approach as described in Section 4. This allows to formulate region queries and temporal restrictions to search for relevant events in a document collection. Figure 1(a) shows the user interface with a temporal and a geographic query. The multi-dimensional querying results in an event-centric visualization as described next.

5.3.2 *Visualization*

For a user query, a query event set is calculated based on the strategies described in Section 4.3. The visualization of the result is realized with the following components: (i) a list of events with all events that are contained in the top-k documents and satisfy the temporal and geographic query constraints, and (ii) a map-based view of the event sequence directly providing information on the temporal and geographic relations of the events. An example of this visualization is shown in Figure 1(b).

5.3.3 *Event Sequences*

The event list does not only consist of the events that are contained in the query event set in isolation. Additionally, some information about the top-k documents from which the events are extracted is given. On the one hand, one can directly see how many events of each document are part of the event set, and, on the other hand, the origins of the listed events is given, i.e., from which document(s) a specific event was extracted. This provides information on the importance of the extracted events and also on the importance of the documents that contribute to the query event set.

5.3.4 *Event Sequence Map*

Grounding the events on a map provides information about the geographic distribution of the events in the query event set. However, as described in Section 3.4, visualizing the event sequence on a map combines the temporal and the geographic dimensions by linking events chronologically and geographically. The user can select between showing all events of the query event set or only those events that are extracted from more than one document. This results in a clearer representation of the most important events.

5.3.5 *Event Snippets*

To directly get more detailed information about result events shown on a map, so called *event snippets* are created. These contain the geographic and the temporal information of the event, the document's title and the sentence containing the event description. In the case of the same event being extracted from more than one document, a snippet containing this information for all top-k ranked documents is created as shown in Figure 1(b). If a document contains more than one sentence describing the same event, a simple heuristics about the event information is used to rank the sentences and only the top ranked sentence is shown by default. Of course, the user can decide to visualize and explore the events extracted from the other sentences as well.

5.3.6 *Prototypical Realization*

For our prototypical implementation, we used a subset of Wikipedia containing 100,000 English documents. In our example shown in Figure 1(a), we queried the document collection for events about "crisis" with the temporal constraint set to the interval 1950 to 1970 and the region of interest set to the Caribbean area. As shown in Figure 1(b), the query event set contains several events extracted from the top-k documents, with k set to 5. Most events were extracted from the article about Che Guevara, but there are also several events extracted from multiple documents. For events with the temporal granularity $v(t) \leq$ day, the event sequence is presented in Figure 1(b) as well. Using the feature of event snippets, one can further explore the single events, as shown for the event ⟨1959-01-01, Dominican Republic⟩.

6. EVALUATION

The main goals of our evaluation are (i) to demonstrate the usefulness of event-centric search and exploration with events being combinations of temporal and geographic information and (ii) to show that the chronology of event sequences makes sense. For this, after giving some details on the corpus we selected for the evaluation in Section 6.1, we divide the evaluation into sub-items. To get an impression of the quality of the temporal and geographic dimensions of events, we evaluate the temporal and the geographic named entity recognition tasks in Section 6.2 and Section 6.3, respectively. Then, in Section 6.4, we verify the idea of events as combinations of temporal and geographic information and investigate the correctness and informative value of a query event set and event sequences.

6.1 Evaluation Corpus

To perform an evaluation of temporal expressions, geographic expressions, and events, the following requirements can be formulated for the evaluation corpus: Annotations of temporal expressions (a), geographic expressions (b), and events as combinations of temporal and geographic information (c) should be available. Furthermore, the documents of the corpus should be applicable for event-centric search and exploration (d), i.e., contain documents of categories such as "history", "biographies", and "warfare" since these are rich in events as we showed in Section 5.2. Finally, we want to demonstrate that the proposed event-centric methods can be applied in a language-independent manner. Thus, a multilingual corpus is desirable (e).

To demonstrate the usefulness of events as defined in our approach, (c) is the most important requirement. However, there is no corpus containing annotations of events as combination of temporal and geographic information. Furthermore, there is no corpus satisfying all remaining requirements, so that we decided to use the WikiWars [17] and WikiWarsDE [27] corpora, which contain parts of 22 English and the corresponding German Wikipedia documents

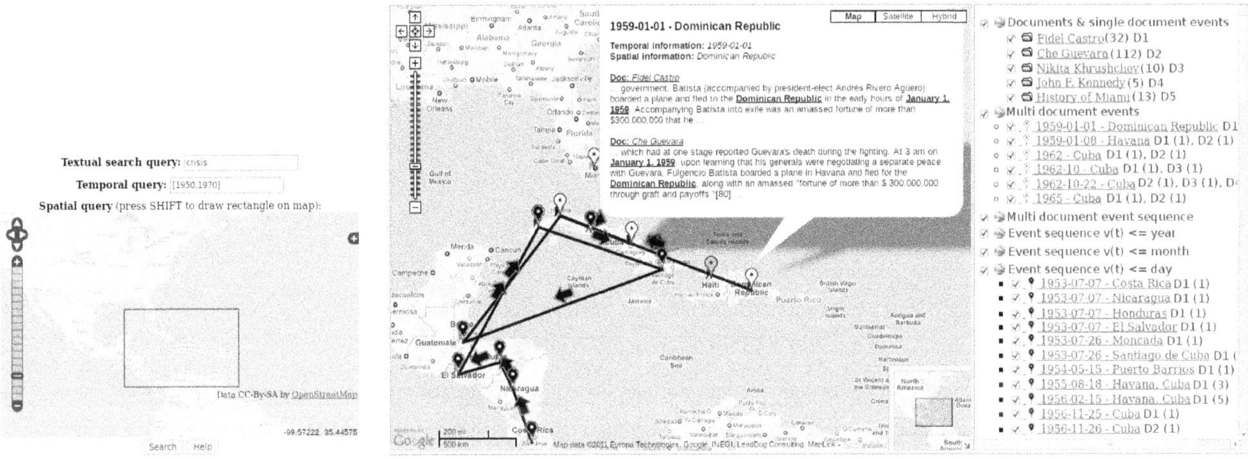

(a) Query interface. (b) Map-based visualization of event sequence with v(t) $\leq$ day for query in (a).

Figure 1: Query interface showing a combination of textual, temporal (interval), and geographic (single rectangle) constraints (a), and visualization of event information retrieved for this query using the concepts of event sequences and event snippets (b).

about famous wars in history. By combining these two corpora, requirements (a), (d), and (e) are satisfied. Although the number of documents for the evaluation corpora is quite low, Table 2(a) shows that the documents are very long and contain many temporal expressions. Details on how we will handle the evaluation of geographic expressions and event information are given in Sections 6.3 and 6.4, respectively.

6.2 Temporal Evaluation

As described in Section 5.1, we use our temporal tagger HeidelTime, which was developed for the TempEval-2 challenge where it achieved the best results among all participating systems for the extraction and normalization of English temporal expressions [30]. Since the documents of TempEval-2 are news documents and due to the different challenges in normalizing temporal expressions on news and on narrative-style documents, we extended HeidelTime to be able to deal with both document types. Furthermore, HeidelTime was extended to further languages, currently supporting English, German, and Dutch [28].

We evaluate HeidelTime on WikiWars and WikiWarsDE using the well-known measures of precision, recall, and f-score. For the extraction task, we distinguish between strict (exact match) and lenient (overlapping match) measures. For the normalization, usually the *value* attribute of a temporal expression is evaluated. We present the normalization results for all expressions that were correctly extracted by the system (value), as well as for all expressions in the corpus (lenient+value and strict+value). In Table 2(b), HeidelTime's evaluation results on WikiWars and WikiWarsDE are presented. With f-scores of 87.9% and 91.3% for English and German extraction (lenient) and 78.7% and 79.4% for English and German normalization (lenient+value), HeidelTime achieves high quality results. This indicates that the temporal dimension of events as defined in our approach is of high quality.

6.3 Geographic Evaluation

As for the temporal dimension, we want to investigate the quality of the geographic dimension of events. Since WikiWars and WikiWarsDE are not annotated with geographic information, we manually annotated one third of the corpora (7 documents of each corpus) with geographic expressions. Note that we rely on an external tool for geo-tagging (Yahoo! Placemaker) that could be replaced by any other/better geo-tagger returning the information needed by our model (e.g., the containment information). Thus, and due to the large annotation effort, we only evaluate the extraction and not the normalization of geographic expressions.

Overall, the manual evaluation resulted in 1.047 and 825 geographic expressions in WikiWars and WikiWarsDE, respectively. Table 2(c) shows the extraction results of Yahoo! Placemaker. While the precision is high for both, English and German, the recall is much lower for German. However, when performing event-centric search and exploration of document collections, precision is more important since incorrect events are more confusing than missing events. In summary, although many events might be missed due to the low recall of the geo-tagger on German documents, the geographic dimension of the events is of high precision.

6.4 Event and Event Sequence Evaluation

In this section, we evaluate the quality of the extracted events. Note that we focus on precision since the recall of our event extraction approach only depends on the recall of the temporal tagger and geo-tagger, which were evaluated in the previous sections. The quality of the extracted events directly influences the quality of the event sequences, i.e., whether the chronological ordering of the extracted events makes sense. Unfortunately, to judge whether an extracted event as a time/location pair is correct is a challenging task and the reasons for judging an extracted time/location pair to not be an event may be manifold. In addition, these reasons may influence the value of the concept of event sequences. Thus, we manually analyze the extracted events and keep track of the following information for every event:
(1) the temporal and geographic granularities
(2) correct extraction of temporal & geographic dimensions
(3) do temporal & geographic information belong together?
(4) is the extracted event correct?
(5) reason for an extracted event to be incorrect

(a) Corpus statistics.

	WikiWars	WikiWarsDE
language	English	German
documents	22	22
token	119,468	95,605
timex	2,671	2,240
timex / doc	121.41	101.82

(b) Temporal evaluation.

	WikiWars			WikiWarsDE		
	P	R	F	P	R	F
lenient	93.9	82.6	87.9	98.5	85.0	91.3
strict	86.0	75.7	80.5	92.6	79.9	85.8
value	89.5	90.1	89.8	87.0	87.0	87.0
lenient+value	84.1	73.9	78.7	85.7	74.0	79.4
strict+value	79.6	70.0	74.5	82.5	71.2	76.5

(c) Geographic evaluation.

WikiWars	P	R	F
lenient	86.1	77.3	81.4
strict	79.6	71.4	75.3

WikiWarsDE	P	R	F
lenient	91.3	52.0	66.3
strict	89.4	50.9	64.9

Table 2: Statistics on the WikiWars and WikiWarsDE corpora (a), the temporal evaluation results using HeidelTime (b), and the geographic evaluation results for Yahoo! Placemaker (c).

For (4), according to the definition given in Section 3.3, we define an event (te_i, ge_j) to be correct if something happens at time te_i and at location ge_j. Due to the immense annotation effort needed to judge the extracted events, we evaluated one third of WikiWars and WikiWarsDE (7 documents of each corpus).

Table 3 shows the annotation results, with the overall results given in Table 3(a). For every combination of temporal and geographic granularities, the number of extracted events, the percentage of how often the temporal and the geographic information of events belong together syntactically, and the percentage of how often events are correct are given in Table 3(b) for English and in Table 3(c) for German.

For 81% (English) and 83% (German) of all events, the temporal and the geographic components of an event belong syntactically together. Thus, although our model of using co-occurrences of temporal and geographic expressions is simple, it is very effective. However, only 63% and 64% of all extracted English and German events, respectively, were annotated as being correct. At a first look, these results are relatively low, especially since only 7% and 3% of the events contain wrongly extracted temporal or geographic components. However, our error analysis showed that there are two reasons for these low values.

The first error source is due to the simplicity of using co-occurrences as events, especially if there are several temporal and geographic expressions in one sentence. Then, using the cross-product to create events often results in many incorrect events. For example, in cases such as "*Tarragona* fell on *14 January*, followed by *Barcelona* on *26 January* and *Girona* on *5 February*", only three of the extracted nine events are correct. A possible solution to tackle this problem is to group the expressions, i.e., to cut sentences with many temporal and geographic expressions after each identified event. Another idea is to only extract the closest time/location pairs in such sentences as events. Furthermore, identifying sub-clauses could improve event extraction in long sentences.

The second error source is due to the fact that not always when the temporal and geographic components belong together, they form an event. As can be seen in Table 3(b) and Table 3(c), this occurs mainly for events with the geographic component being of the granularity "country". An error analysis showed that in most of these cases, the geographic expressions do not refer to the location but to a country as an agent. For example, in the sentence "The *Soviet Union* and *Germany* entered a trade pact in *February of 1940* ...", both extracted events (1940-02,'Soviet Union') and (1940-02,'Germany') are evaluated as not being events since the geographic expressions do not refer to a location but to the countries as agents. However, one may argue that the event of "entering a trade pact" took place in both these countries. Regarding such events as correct results in even 81% and 83% correct events. Furthermore, geographic expressions referring to countries as agents is typical in documents about wars since wars are usually between different countries as agents. When analyzing documents of other event-rich categories (e.g., biographies), geographic expressions with this behavior are rare and thus the event sets and event sequences contain much less incorrect events.

All correctly extracted events make sense in the event list of a query result. However, for the visualization on a map, using fine-grained events to form event sequences may result in a clearer visualization of events. In addition, these events tend to be of higher quality, with 82% and 81% correct events for English and German, respectively. In summary, the accuracy of the extracted events demonstrates the high quality of our approach despite its simplicity.

7. CONCLUSIONS AND ONGOING WORK

In this paper, we introduced an event-centric approach to search and exploration of document collections. Event sets and event sequences as results of user queries are based on extracted temporal and geographic information from documents. We detailed a multi-dimensional query model for querying documents with textual, temporal, and geographic constraints. In addition, we demonstrated the usefulness of the concept of event sets and sequences by presenting several techniques for their exploration and visualization as well as a multilingual evaluation. Both, the query model and the exploration and visualization techniques add significant advancements to existing information retrieval techniques that thus far have not considered event-centric search scenarios.

Currently, we are working on different ranking techniques for the events in a result set when querying with more than one constraint. When a query contains a textual part in addition to a temporal and/or geographic part, there are many aspects that can be taken into account for ranking the events in the hit list. For example, how close the event information and the textual information occur in the document. This information may additionally be valuable to rank the sentences for the event snippets if more than one sentence contains the same event that is to be visualized.

8. REFERENCES

[1] D. Ahn. The Stages of Event Extraction. In *Proc. of the Workshop on Annotating and Reasoning about Time and Events*, pages 1–8, 2006.

[2] O. Alonso, M. Gertz, and R. Baeza-Yates. On the Value of Temporal Information in Information Retrieval. *SIGIR Forum*, 41(2):35–41, 2007.

[3] O. Alonso, J. Strötgen, R. Baeza-Yates, and M. Gertz. Temporal Information Retrieval: Challenges and Opportunities. In *Proceedings of the 1st International Temporal Web Analytics Workshop*, pages 1–8, 2011.

(a) Event evaluation results with error analysis.

	WikiWars	WikiWarsDE
total number of events	648	415
events with correct time/space	603	402
wrong time or space	7%	3%
time, space belong together	81%	83%
fully correct (fc)	63%	64%
country is agent	20%	19%
fc, country as agent correct	81%	83%
events,$v(t) \leq$ month,$v(g) \leq$ state	219	184
fc, $v(t) \leq$ month, $v(g) \leq$ state	82%	81%

(b) English granularity matrix.

	city	state	country
day	81	17	78
belong	72%	76%	81%
correct	72%	76%	41%
month	102	19	258
belong	94%	79%	89%
correct	92%	79%	62%
year	6	4	38
belong	100%	100%	100%
correct	100%	100%	61%

(c) German granularity matrix.

	city	state	country
day	153	19	118
belong	81%	68%	82%
correct	81%	68%	49%
month	12	0	56
belong	100%	-	89%
correct	100%	-	41%
year	13	4	27
belong	69%	100%	93%
correct	69%	100%	85%

Table 3: The event evaluation results and a detailed error analysis are given in (a). Event granularity matrices for English (b) and German (c) with number of extracted events, percentage of events where space and time belong together, and percentage where space and time form a correct event.

[4] Y.-F. R. Chen, G. Di Fabbrizio, D. Gibbon, S. Jora, B. Renger, and B. Wei. GeoTracker: Geospatial and Temporal RSS Navigation. In *WWW '07*, pages 41–50, 2007.

[5] H. L. Chieu and Y. K. Lee. Query based Event Extraction along a Timeline. In *SIGIR '04*, pages 425–432, 2004.

[6] F. Gey, R. Larson, N. Kando, J. Machado, and T. Sakai. NTCIR-GeoTime Overview: Evaluating Geographic and Temporal Search. In *Proceedings of NTCIR-8*, 2010.

[7] GuTime. http://timeml.org/site/tarsqi/modules/gutime.

[8] J. L. Leidner, G. Sinclair, and B. Webber. Grounding Spatial Named Entities for Information Extraction and Question Answering. In *Proceedings of the HLT-NAACL 2003 Workshop on Analysis of Geographic References*, pages 31–38, 2003.

[9] H. Li, R. K. Srihari, C. Niu, and W. Li. Location Normalization for Information Extraction. In *COLING'02*, pages 1–7, 2002.

[10] S. Liao and R. Grishman. Using Document Level Cross-Event Inference to Improve Event Extraction. In *ACL'10*, pages 789–797, 2010.

[11] M. D. Lieberman, H. Samet, J. Sankaranarayanan, and J. Sperling. STEWARD: Architecture of a Spatio-textual Search Engine. In *GIS '07*, pages 186–193, 2007.

[12] Lucene. http://lucene.apache.org/.

[13] I. Mani, J. Pustejovsky, and R. Gaizauskas, editors. *The Language of Time*. Oxford University Press, 2005.

[14] C. D. Manning, P. Raghavan, and H. Schütze. *Introduction to Information Retrieval*. Cambridge University Press, 2008.

[15] B. Martins, H. Manguinhas, and J. Borbinha. Extracting and Exploring the Geo-Temporal Semantics of Textual Resources. In *ICSC'08*, 2008.

[16] F. Mata and C. Claramunt. GeoST: Geographic, Thematic and Temporal Information Retrieval from Heterogeneous Web Data Sources. In *W2GIS'11*, pages 5–20, 2011.

[17] P. Mazur and R. Dale. WikiWars: A New Corpus for Research on Temporal Expressions. In *EMNLP'10*, pages 913–922, 2010.

[18] MetaCarta. http://www.metacarta.com/.

[19] OpenNLP. http://opennlp.sourceforge.net/.

[20] V. Petras, R. R. Larson, and M. Buckland. Time Period Directories: A Metadata Infrastructure for Placing Events in Temporal and Geographic Context. In *JCDL'06*, pages 151–160, 2006.

[21] D. Pfoser, A. Efentakis, T. Hadzilacos, S. Karagiorgou, and G. Vasiliou. Providing Universal Access to History Textbooks: A Modified GIS Case. In *W2GIS'11*, pages 87–102, 2009.

[22] R. Purves, P. Clough, and C. Jones, editors. *GIR '10: Proceedings of the 6th Workshop on Geographic Information Retrieval*, Zurich, Switzerland, 2010.

[23] J. Pustejovsky, R. Knippen, J. Littman, and R. Sauri. Temporal and Event Information in Natural Language Text. *Language Resources and Evaluation*, 39(2-3):123–164, 2005.

[24] G. Quercini, H. Samet, J. Sankaranarayanan, and M. D. Lieberman. Determining the Spatial Reader Scopes of News Sources using Local Lexicons. In *GIS'10*, pages 43–52, 2010.

[25] J. Strötgen and M. Gertz. HeidelTime: High Quality Rule-Based Extraction and Normalization of Temporal Expressions. In *SemEval'10*, pages 321–324, 2010.

[26] J. Strötgen and M. Gertz. TimeTrails: A System for Exploring Spatio-Temporal Information in Documents. In *VLDB'10*, pages 1569–1572, 2010.

[27] J. Strötgen and M. Gertz. WikiWarsDE: A German Corpus of Narratives Annotated with Temporal Expressions. In *GSCL'11*, pages 129–134, 2011.

[28] J. Strötgen and M. Gertz. Multilingual and Cross-domain Temporal Tagging. *Language Resources and Evaluation*, accepted for journal publication, 2012.

[29] J. Strötgen, M. Gertz, and C. Junghans. An Event-centric Model for Multilingual Document Similarity. In *SIGIR'11*, pages 953–962, 2011.

[30] M. Verhagen, R. Sauri, T. Caselli, and J. Pustejovsky. SemEval-2010 Task 13: TempEval-2. In *SemEval'10*, pages 57–62, 2010.

[31] Y. Wang, B. Yang, S. Zoupanos, M. Spaniol, and G. Weikum. Scalable Spatio-temporal Knowledge Harvesting. In *WWW'11*, pages 143–144, 2011.

[32] Wikipedia Featured Articles. http://en.wikipedia.org/wiki/Wikipedia:FA.

[33] Yahoo! Placemaker. http://developer.yahoo.com/geo/placemaker/.

[34] M. Yamamoto, Y. Takahashi, H. Iwasaki, S. Oyama, H. Ohshima, and K. Tanaka. Extraction and Geographical Navigation of Important Historical Events in the Web. In *W2GIS'11*, pages 21–35, 2011.

Dynamic Online Views of Meta-Indexes

Michael Huggett and Edie Rasmussen
University of British Columbia
Suite 470, 1961 East Mall
Vancouver, BC V6T 1Z1
(1-604) 827-5486
{m.huggett, edie.rasmussen}@ubc.ca

ABSTRACT

For a collection of digitized monographs in a subject domain, a domain meta-index provides a summary of domain concepts, and a structured vocabulary to support a scholar's navigation and search. We present a prototype of a Meta-index User Interface (MUI) that provides views of a domain at three levels: summarizing and comparing domains, exposing the regularities of a domain's vocabulary, and displaying book information and page content related both to objectively-representative books, and to specific user searches.

Categories and Subject Descriptors

H.3.7 [**Information Systems**]: Information Storage and Retrieval – *Digital libraries*

General Terms

Algorithms, Design, Human Factors.

Keywords

Digital libraries, digital books, digital collections, index, meta-indexes.

1. INTRODUCTION

Although the back-of-book index (BoBI) is a traditional knowledge structure to support browsing and search in the print domain [1], it has been largely neglected in the digital environment, with only a few studies examining user access to a single document [2,3,4,5]. Millions of books are now available in digital form due to mass digitization projects such as the Gutenberg Project, the Million Books Project, the Open Content Alliance, and Google Books [6], as well as many localized projects. Recent surveys show that scholars are increasingly using digital monographs, while expressing concern about the ability of these digital works to support scholarly research [7,8].

Very little attention has been paid to the knowledge in back-of-book indexes as an information resource. When digital books are considered as a subject-specific collection, the indexes in aggregate could be used for multiple purposes: to classify books based on summarized content [9], to generate vocabulary that can describe a domain, to structure the knowledge within the collection, and to navigate within the collection—all of which we are investigating in the Indexer's Legacy project. The concept of a *meta-index* that acts as an integrated guide to all works within a digital domain (as defined by a subject area or theme) is central to our project. In this paper we describe how the index information is extracted and the meta-index constructed. We also describe how the meta-index can provide different views on texts within the digital domain to aid users in browsing, search, and navigation.

JCDL'12, June 10–14, 2012, Washington, DC, USA.

2. BUILDING META-INDEXES

To build a test collection, we have assembed domain corpora in the Arts (Art History, Music), Humanities (Economics, Cooking), and Sciences (Geology, Anatomy, Darwin). Each domain contains at least 100 books. All books are in the public domain, to avoid problems with licensing and copyright, and to ensure that the resulting test collection can be shared with other researchers. Most of the books were acquired through search and download from the Internet Archive [10].

Most of the books are in PDF format, which is the most reliable way to collect large numbers of texts in a particular domain quickly, as there are many online sources available [11]. These are supplemented as necessary by books in plain text format (ASCII and UTF-8), downloaded from online book sites that carry public-domain materials [12].

PDF and plain-text files each have their advantages and disadvantages. The PDF format is a *de facto* standard for sharing immutable text and as such there are many books are available in PDF format. Another key advantage is that the pages of the book are often shown as images, so that all the beauty and nuance of the original text is preserved for reading on digital devices. Also, many PDFs provide an invisible *text layer* that contains the content of the book, allowing easy copy-and-paste of text into a much smaller plain-text file suitable for sharing with team members and for processing by our software suite.

The disadvantage of PDFs is that if the book is not *native digital* (i.e. written as a digital manuscript) then it relies on optical character recognition (OCR) to generate the PDF's text layer. OCR is notoriously difficult to do well for older materials [13], and as a result books of average length can contain thousands of misspelled words and corrupted characters. Indexes from earlier published works can require considerable cleanup prior to processing, and perhaps 10 percent of all books that we work with are abandoned due to badly corrupted and incomplete text layers. In contrast, more recently-published materials with clear print and good-quality OCR are good candidates for highly-automated processing. Books in plain-text digital format could also be used, but there are relatively few of them available when compared to PDFs (particularly in the public domain), they often lose their pagination during digitization from paper, and lacking an image of the original book, it is often impossible to correct ambiguous spelling or formatting errors that arise (though such errors are far less common than in OCR text).

2.1 From Digital Text to Meta-Index

The meta-index for each domain is built following the same multi-step process. First, plain text is 'extracted' from the source material, and the book's index is separated from its content. Then the index is 'cleaned' manually to join broken lines and fix typos and OCR errors. Then all sub-entries of the index are 'expanded' to include all parent entries up to the *anchor* (i.e. main entry). When the indexes of an entire domain have been expanded

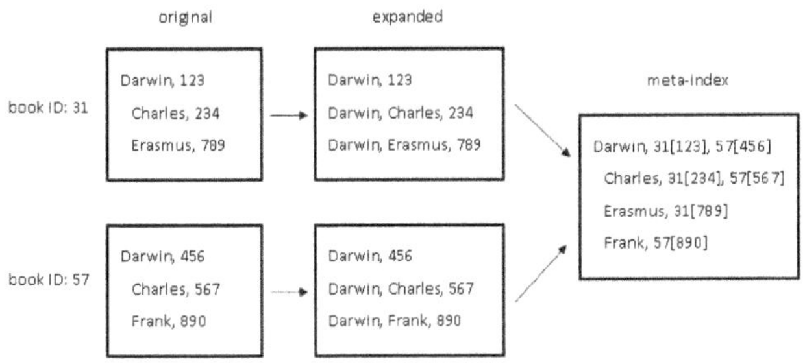

Figure 1: Expansion and aggregation into a meta-index

correctly, the expanded indexes are then aggregated into a single monolithic alphabetic index. The aggregated index is then 'compressed', both removing redundancies and grouping references to produce the meta-index (Figure 1).

All steps (extraction, cleaning, expansion, aggregation, and compression) are done using the tools of our Meta-Dex software suite. At each step, data is collected that characterizes the domain: the number of words, lines, and pages of book content (i.e. the chapters of the book), and the attributes unique to the index, such as the number of main entries and sub-entries. These raw numbers are then used to compute various metrics.

All of these results are available through our online meta-index user interface (MUI) [14].

3. THE META-INDEX USER INTERFACE

The Meta-index User Interface (MUI) provides tabular and graphical representations of the domain meta-indexes at domain, vocabulary, and book levels. Each of these levels provides a different way of searching or browsing the digital domain.

MUI pages are grouped according to their level. Each page contains its own data view specific to that page. On most pages, the page-specific view also contains links that open *utility views* that display entry or book details, wherever these are relevant.

Two utility views are provided, the *Entry View* and the *Book View*. The Entry View (Figure 2) displays a complete entry as it appears in the domain meta-index. Main and sub-elements of the entry are displayed, including all of the collated book and page references. The book and page references are themselves links to the *Book View* (Figure 3), which is comprised of two parts. The top part shows the selected book's meta-data: its author, title, year of publication, domain, where it was obtained, etc. The bottom part displays page content, with search terms highlighted; a text box lets users jump directly to specific pages, and prev/next buttons let users scroll through the book a page at a time. Utility views are available as appropriate at all three levels of pages: domain, vocabulary, and book.

3.1 Domain pages

Domain pages display the meta-index at its most general level, characterizing each domain by its statistics (thereby allowing direct quantitative comparison between domains), showing the distribution of years of publications, and displaying the domain's meta-index. There are three domain-view pages:

• *Domain Summaries.* For comparing completed domains side-by-side, the Domain Summaries page shows a tabular view with raw bibliometric counts and calculated measures. The table summarizes data collected during the steps of meta-index generation. Raw counts include the total number of words, lines, anchors, and sub-entries per domain, as well as average-median-min-max values for main entries, sub-entries, lines, and words per book in the domain. Additional calculated domain-summary measures describe:

- *shared entries*, which represents the proportion of meta-index entries that appear in at least one book (versus unique 'singleton' entries).
- *coherence factor*, which represents the degree to which the books of the domain contain the same entries. A coherence factor of 0 indicates that none of the books share any entries; a coherence factor of 1 indicates that all of the entries are shared by all of the books.
- *expansion ratio*, which represents the average proportion by which the indexes grew when expanded.
- *compression ratio*, which represents the proportion by which the meta-index shrank when redundancies in the aggregated monolithic index were resolved.
- *sub-entry coefficient*, which represents the proportion of sub-entries to main entries.

The remaining two domain pages are interactive.

• *Domain Years.* An interactive graphical view shows the distribution of years of publication in all domains for which raw texts have been collected. This view is particularly important to us as we gather books, since one of our research goals is to determine how indexes have evolved over the years. Due to our requirement that our test collection be in the public domain, the distribution is heavily weighted toward materials of the late 19th and early 20th centuries.

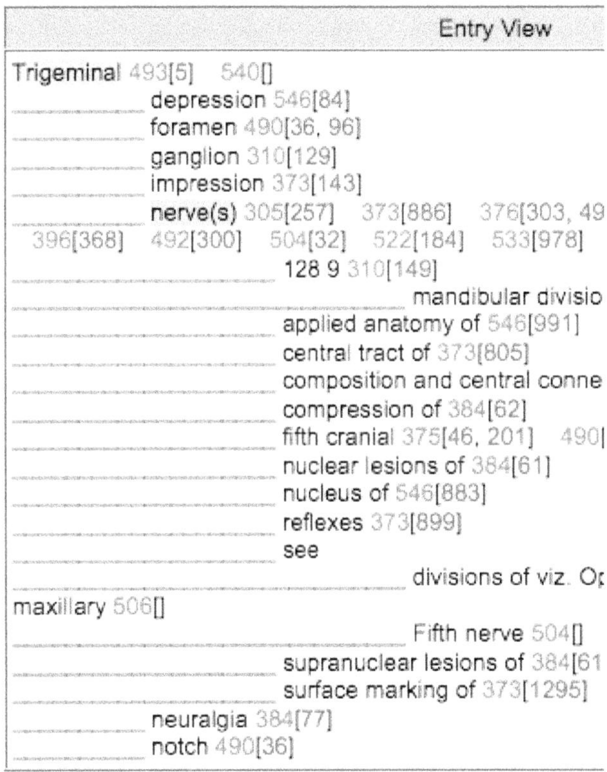

Figure 2: Entry view (detail) of the meta-index for the Anatomy domain. The terms of the user query "trigeminal nerve" are highlighted. Leading numbers are book IDs, the numbers in brackets that follow are the page references. Clicking on either number opens the Book View (Figure 3). Empty brackets occur for see-also references.

The view displays a histogram of book frequencies per year across the two centuries in which all of the books of the corpus domains were published, from 1800 to 2010. A mouse-over of any of the frequency bars displays a pop-up of the year, the number of books from that year, and the list of authors of those books.

• *Search Meta-Index*. For finding meta-index entries that contain terms of interest to the user, the Search Meta-Index page provides a search engine that allows users to drill down on search results through three views. This UI component is the main tool for accessing the content of the meta-index, and through its familiar index structure, the domain as a whole.

The page's initial *Search View* gives standard search options, such as using search terms as whole or partial (i.e. implicitly wildcarded) words and the choice of returning results using all versus any of the terms. Results in the *Search View* show main entries that contain the term(s), ranked by the proportion of book indexes in the domain that contain the entry. Clicking on any of the entry names opens the utility Entry View, which displays the entry as it appears in the meta-index (Figure 2). Clicking on book IDs in the Entry View opens the utility Book View, displaying the book's meta-data. Clicking on a page number in the Entry View opens both the meta-data, and displays the page text with search terms highlighted (Figure 3).

3.2 Vocabulary pages

Since indexes are compiled by human domain experts, one of our research goals is to determine the extent to which the indexer's choice of vocabulary is consistent across a domain, and the degree to which it matches the author's use of vocabulary in the book's content. In support of these analyses *Vocabulary Pages* show the words and phrases that are most important to the domain's indexers. There are two interactive vocabulary-view pages:

• *Anchor Frequencies* suggests key topics in a domain by showing main entries of the meta-index, ranked by the proportion of books in the domain that contain them. The entry names displayed in the table are themselves links; clicking on them opens an *Entry View* to display the full entry as it appears in the meta-index.

• *Term Frequencies* shows the most common terms across all indexes in the selected domain. The terms displayed in the table are themselves links to an *Entry View* that shows the largest, most representative main entry that contains the term(s). To see other important meta-index entries that contain the term, users would use the *Search Meta-Index* page described above.

As with the other pages, clicking on book-ID and page-number links in the Entry View will open the Book View.

3.3 Book pages

Book pages show information on individual books, to help the user determine which books are most appropriate to their needs. There are three pages, all of which are interactive:

• *Book Anchors* shows a tabular view of books in the selected domain, ranked simply by the number of index entries that they contain. In blunt terms, these are the books of the domain that contain the most information.

• *Book Information Gain* shows a tabular view of books ranked by their effect on domain coherence. Books with the greatest positive effect bind the domain together (make it more 'coherent') by sharing their entries with multiple other books. Books with the greatest negative effect are actually detrimental to domain coherence, since they have few or no entries in common with other books.

• *Book Representativeness* shows a tabular view of books ranked by how many of the domain's entries they contain. Highest-ranked books may contain up to a third of the entries in the meta-index. Not surprisingly, there appears to be a correlation between this measure and those of the other two Book pages above.

In the tabular view of each page, each book is listed by its unique ID number, which is displayed as a link. Clicking on a book's unique ID number opens a Book View that displays the book's meta-data.

• *Search Content* provides search within the domain's content (i.e. the chapter text of books). Unlike the *Search Meta-Index* page, which returns a list of meta-index entries, Search Content returns a list of books, ranked in standard information-retrieval fashion to reflect the term frequency within documents and across the corpus.

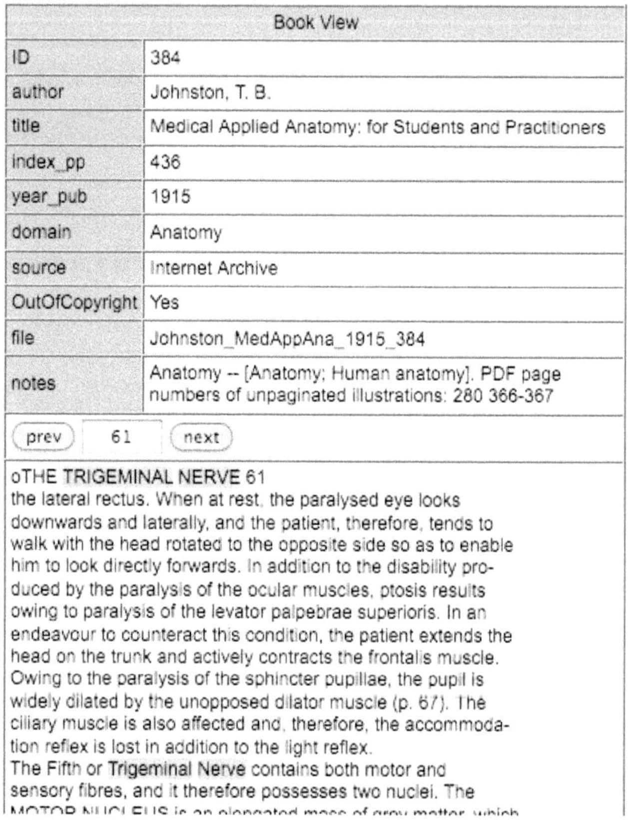

Book View	
ID	384
author	Johnston, T. B.
title	Medical Applied Anatomy: for Students and Practitioners
index_pp	436
year_pub	1915
domain	Anatomy
source	Internet Archive
OutOfCopyright	Yes
file	Johnston_MedAppAna_1915_384
notes	Anatomy -- [Anatomy; Human anatomy]. PDF page numbers of unpaginated illustrations: 280 366-367

prev 61 next

oTHE TRIGEMINAL NERVE 61
the lateral rectus. When at rest, the paralysed eye looks downwards and laterally, and the patient, therefore, tends to walk with the head rotated to the opposite side so as to enable him to look directly forwards. In addition to the disability produced by the paralysis of the ocular muscles, ptosis results owing to paralysis of the levator palpebrae superioris. In an endeavour to counteract this condition, the patient extends the head on the trunk and actively contracts the frontalis muscle. Owing to the paralysis of the sphincter pupillae, the pupil is widely dilated by the unopposed dilator muscle (p. 67). The ciliary muscle is also affected and, therefore, the accommodation reflex is lost in addition to the light reflex.
The Fifth or Trigeminal Nerve contains both motor and sensory fibres, and it therefore possesses two nuclei. The

Figure 3: Book View (detail) showing meta-data (top) and page text of the reference 384[61], opened if clicked on in the Entry View (Figure 2). The search terms "trigeminal" and "nerve" are highlighted as they occur in the page text.

4. DISCUSSION

Our goal is to facilitate access to the rich content of digital books within a domain, through use of the back-of-book indexes they contain. At this point, we have successfully completed several of our key objectives.

First, we have built a test collection of digital scholarly works with back-of-book indexes, divided into a number of subject domains. This collection contains the full text of each book, with structure (pages, chapters, etc.) identified, and fully-corrected indexes with headings, subheadings, and page locators extracted for further processing.

Second, using this test collection, we have developed a set of book utility metrics that allow comparisons of books within a domain, to determine the extent to which the books reinforce or extend domain knowledge.

Third, we have developed a software suite allowing us to analyze, extract and process back-of-book indexes. The ultimate goal of the suite is to aggregate the indexes and create an omnibus meta-index of the entire domain.

Finally, we have developed an interface which facilitates access to book collections at several levels: to the domain as a whole, to the vocabulary characterizing the domain, and to content of individual books.

5. FURTHER WORK

The meta-index and the accompanying domain metrics are designed to aid scholars to search and browse large and growing collections of digital materials. In our current work, we are investigating how scholars interact with digital works and how effective the meta-index can be in creating a logical structure within a scholarly collection. We recognize that our initial formulation of the user interface is information-rich and expect that users will require a simplified view of the data. Our initial user-centered work involves interviews and focus groups with candidate user groups.

We are also designing a more formal experiment to test the MUI in user studies, which will involve two types of study:

- A single-session user study will test the MUI's ability to help non-experts find topical information in a large corpus, compared against a standard text-based search engine.
- A longitudinal study will provide the MUI to domain experts over the course of a month or more, to answer questions such as what domain-summarization tools, and what sort of interfaces (textual, versus graphical), can best assist domain experts in their research. We hope to clarify how domain experts prefer to interact with large-scale domain summaries.

Currently we are presenting the meta-index in a traditional text index format, but we are also exploring the potential of a visual presentation. Search visualization of meta-indexes is an interesting problem, due to the very large size of the domain meta-indexes (on the order of 100,000 lines of text) .

In the near term, our visualizations will include online interactive graphs and charts. Since our project generates a large amount of tabular data, we feel it would be instructive to be able to select data source, axis, and scale for a more direct and intuitive comparison of data trends. Online interactive graphing would be a useful tool for exploring data, and would give any interested user an opportunity to participate in data exploration and discovery.

In the longer term, we intend to expand this "graphing on demand" approach to 3D visualizations. For example, our Domain Years view, currently a 2D histogram of a domain's years of publication, could be exploded orthogonally to display the prevalence of additional properties, say the size of the book's content, or the presence and attributes of bibliography, notes, plates, appendices, and so forth.

Since much of our data reflects relationships *between* data, such as domain coherence and the co-existence of terms and anchors, we are also interested in visualizing navigable network displays that connect related items and allow users to move quickly between them.

Also, as the amount of data and number of views grows, we will need to create an "index of indexes" that will direct users to data of different types, and to particular appropriate visualizations.

Finally, availability has been the primary determining factor in adding books to our collection. We should increase the relevance and utility of our meta-index by purposely incorporating books that domain experts consider most central to their domains. These would be the ideal texts from which to start a domain meta-index, after which more peripheral books could be added to expand breadth, without sacrificing accuracy of the domain vocabulary.

6. ACKNOWLEDGMENTS

Funding from the UBC Hampton Fund and the Social Science and Humanities Research Council is gratefully acknowledged. We also thank our Graduate Research Assistants who have sourced and pre-processed the many books for our test collections.

7. REFERENCES

[1] Jörgensen, C. and Liddy, E.D. 1996. Information access or information anxiety?—an exploratory evaluation of book index features. *The Indexer* 20, 64-68.

[2] Abdullah, N. and Gibb, F. 2008. Using a task-based approach in evaluating the usability of BoBIs in an E-book environment. *ECDL 2008, LNCS* 4956, 246-257.

[3] Egan, D.E., Remde, J.R., Gomez, L.M., Landauer, T.K., Eberhardt, J. and Lochbaum, C.C. 1989. Formative design evaluation of Superbook. *ACM Transactions on Information Systems* 7(1), 30-57.

[4] Liesaputra, V., Witten, I.H., and Bainbridge, D. 2009. Searching in a book. *ECDL 2009, LNCS* 5714, 442-446.

[5] Chi, E. H., Hong, L., Heiser, J., Card, S. K. 2006. ScentIndex: Conceptually reorganizing subject indexes for reading. *VAST 2006*, 159-166.

[6] Coyle, K. 2006. Mass digitization of books. *Journal of Academic Librarianship* 32(6), 641-645.

[7] University of California Libraries. (2011). *UC Libraries Academic e-Book Usage Survey*. May 2011. http://www.cdlib.org/services/uxdesign/docs/2011/academic_ebook_usage_survey.pdf

[8] Gielen, N. (2010). *Handheld E-Book Readers and Scholarship: Report and Reader Survey*. ACLS Humanities E-Book White Paper No. 3. August 18, 2010. http://www.acls.org/uploadedFiles/Publications/Programs/HEBWhitePaper3.pdf

[9] Enser, P.G.B. 1985. Automatic classification of book material represented by back-of-the-book index. *Journal of Documentation* 41(3), 135-155.

[10] *The Internet Archive*, http://www.archive.org/

[11] Roe, M. 2011. Problems of provenance for digital libraries. *Security Protocols 2008, LNCS* 6615: 126-133.

[12] *UC Press E-Books Collection, 1982-2004*, http://publishing.cdlib.org/ucpressebooks/

[13] Tanner, S., Munoz, T. and Ros, P.H. 2009. Measuring mass text digitization quality and usefulness. *D-Lib Magazine* 15(7/8), July/August 2009. http://www.dlib.org/dlib/july09/munoz/07munoz.html

[14] Meta-Dex Research Site, http://meta-dex.no-ip.org

Topic Models for Taxonomies

Anton Bakalov, Andrew McCallum,
Hanna Wallach
Dept. of Computer Science
University of Massachusetts
Amherst, MA 01003
{abakalov,mccallum,wallach}@cs.umass.edu

David Mimno
Dept. of Computer Science
Princeton University
Princeton, NJ 08540
mimno@cs.princeton.edu

ABSTRACT

Concept taxonomies such as MeSH, the ACM Computing Classification System, and the NY Times Subject Headings are frequently used to help organize data. They typically consist of a set of concept names organized in a hierarchy. However, these names and structure are often not sufficient to fully capture the intended meaning of a taxonomy node, and particularly non-experts may have difficulty navigating and placing data into the taxonomy. This paper introduces two semi-supervised topic models that automatically augment a given taxonomy with many additional keywords by leveraging a corpus of multi-labeled documents. Our experiments show that users find the topics beneficial for taxonomy interpretation, substantially increasing their cataloging accuracy. Furthermore, the models provide a better information rate compared to Labeled LDA [7].

Categories and Subject Descriptors

I.2.7 [**Artificial Intelligence**]: Natural Language Processing—*Text analysis*; H.3.7 [**Information Systems**]: Digital Libraries; G.3 [**Mathematics of Computing**]: Probability and Statistics—*Statistical computing*

Keywords

Topic modeling, Taxonomy annotation, Taxonomy browsing

1. INTRODUCTION

Many organizations such as the Association of Computing Machinery (ACM) use taxonomies of classes as structured metadata to facilitate browsing of their document libraries. Users browse and search these libraries by navigating a hierarchy of named concept nodes. When new documents are added to the library they must also be assigned one or more concept names. This task is often performed by the document authors themselves, not trained catalogers.

Unfortunately, the concept node names often do not describe the concept in sufficient detail for unfamiliar users to fully understand the topics a node is intended to capture. We present a user study (Section 4.3) confirming that substantial inaccuracies arise when asking computer science graduate students to assign a research paper to nodes of the ACM taxonomy when given its node names and hierarchical structure. Users could gain better understanding by reading titles of papers that have previously been accurately assigned, but this would be time consuming. Taxonomy builders could augment each concept name with a list of keywords that delineate the concept. But this task would be burdensome to perform manually for large taxonomies, and furthermore would need to be redone frequently since new ideas and topics within a concept arise over time.

This paper presents two semi-supervised topic models that automatically discover lists of relevant keywords for taxonomic concepts. The models, termed Labeled Pachinko Allocation (LPAM) and LPAM-List, take as input an existing taxonomy as well as documents with their concept assignments. Then they run inference in a latent-Dirichlet-allocation-like manner in which there is one topic per concept node, and the set of topics allowable in the document is restricted by its taxonomic concept labels, augmented with their ancestors in the hierarchy. Document terms are assigned to the topics, and the highest weighted words in each topic become the concept keywords. Notably, even though most documents are labeled with multiple concepts and all concepts pull in their ancestors, the model is able to partition the keywords into their appropriate concepts. Furthermore, incorporating ancestor nodes enables our models (a) to discover keywords for more abstract concepts located close to the root of the taxonomy, and (b) to separate more generic words out of the taxonomy leaves.

Multiple previous papers have focused on learning topic hierarchies (*e.g.*, [2, 4]). We are addressing the complementary problem—leveraging a given human-defined hierarchy such as ACM's Computing Classification System. Like our work, some other methods sample paths to nodes in a given taxonomy (*e.g.*, Hierarchical Concept Topic Model (HCTM) [9], Hierarchical Pachinko Allocation (HPAM) [5], Multilingual Supervised LDA (ML-SLDA) [3]). However, LPAM leverages available labels to select a subtree of the taxonomy to generate a given document. Furthermore, LPAM differs from HCTM in that each node has a distribution over the whole vocabulary, not over a pre-specified subset.

The second model we propose, LPAM-List, represents a document as a mixture of the same topic nodes as LPAM's, but does not use the tree structure in its generative process. This makes it more similar to Labeled LDA [7] which also

JCDL'12, June 10–14, 2012, Washington, DC, USA.

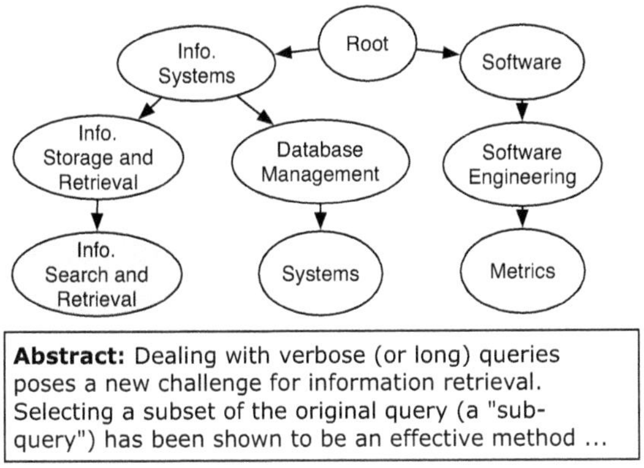

Figure 1: The first two sentences from the abstract of a paper about information retrieval [11]. The publication is labeled with the shaded node from the ACM taxonomy. Some of the neighboring nodes are also displayed.

constrains the choice of topics to those associated with the document's assigned concepts. However, LPAM-List additionally incorporates the taxonomic ancestors of the assigned nodes. This simple change enables it to learn about both leaves and interior nodes of the taxonomy. Similarly to Labeled LDA, Newman et. al. [6] also uses a non-hierarchical set of concept labels, but rather than discovering a distribution of words for each concept, they instead estimate a distribution of topics for each concept; this is accomplished by using document labels as authors in the author-topic model [8].

Our experiments show that leveraging the internal structure of taxonomies imparts our methods with two advantages. First, we obtain a better information rate compared to Labeled LDA (Section 4.2), indicating that our models more precisely capture characteristics of the data. Second, we obtain a list of keywords for each concept in the taxonomy, including the high-level interior concepts that do not usually appear as labels. Our user study shows that our concept description keywords help people interpret a taxonomy as measured by the accuracy of concept label assignments (Section 4.3).

2. MODELS

2.1 Labeled Pachinko Allocation

LPAM is a semi-supervised topic model for documents labeled with nodes from a taxonomy. It builds on latent Dirichlet allocation (LDA) [1] and hierarchical pachinko allocation [5] by leveraging additional structure, as described in this section. For each document d, it considers a restricted set of taxonomy nodes C_d consisting of the document labels, augmented with their ancestors in the hierarchy. For example, the document in Figure 1 is a mixture of the nodes Info. Search and Retrieval, Info. Storage and Retrieval, Info. Systems, and Root. Each node $c \in C_d$ defines a multinomial distribution $\boldsymbol{\theta}^{(d,c)}$ over child nodes in C_d plus an additional one termed the *exit*. Also, each node r in the taxonomy is associated with a multinomial distribution $\boldsymbol{\phi}^{(r)}$ over the vocabulary. Like some other models such as HPAM, LPAM represents a distribution over paths using multinomials over child nodes; however, LPAM additionally enforces path constraints based on labels.

LPAM's generative process operates as follows:
1. For each node r draw $\boldsymbol{\phi}^{(r)} \sim \text{Dir}(\boldsymbol{\beta})$
2. For each document d:
(a) For each node $c \in C_d$, draw $\boldsymbol{\theta}^{(d,c)} \sim \text{Dir}(\boldsymbol{\alpha}^{(d,c)})$.
(b) For each word w:
- Draw $r \sim \text{Mult}(\boldsymbol{\theta}^{(d,root)})$
- While r is not an *exit*, draw $r \sim \text{Mult}(\boldsymbol{\theta}^{(d,r)})$
- Draw $w \sim \text{Mult}(\boldsymbol{\phi}^{(a)})$ where a is r's parent

We train the models by Gibbs sampling. The probability of choosing node c as the topic of the i'th token (w_i) given the remaining topic assignments ($\mathbf{z}_{\setminus i}$) and all words ($\mathbf{w}$) is:

$$P(z_i = c|\mathbf{z}_{\setminus i}, \mathbf{w}, \mathbf{U}) \propto$$
$$\left(\prod_{j=2}^{k} \frac{n^{(d)}_{c_{j-1},c_j} + \alpha^{(d,c_{j-1})}_{c_j}}{\sum_r (n^{(d)}_{c_{j-1},r} + \alpha^{(d,c_{j-1})}_r)}\right) \frac{n^{(w)}_c + \beta_w}{\sum_m (n^{(m)}_c + \beta_m)}$$

where $\mathbf{U}$ is the set of hyperparameters; $n^{(d)}_{c_{j-1},c_j}$ is the number of times node c_j is visited from its parent c_{j-1} for document d; $n^{(w)}_c$ is the number of times word w is assigned to node c; k is the level at which the *exit* is located, *i.e.*, c_{k-1} is the node generating the word. The contribution of the token being sampled is removed from these counts.

The first term of the right-hand side expression above is the probability of traversing the path to node c and choosing to emit from it. The second term is the probability of generating word w from the word distribution associated with concept c.

2.2 Labeled Pachinko Allocation - List

LPAM-List considers the same restricted set of topics C_d as LPAM's but sampling a path is not part of the generative process. If $\boldsymbol{\psi}^{(d)}$ is a multinomial distribution over the nodes in C_d, then the generative storyline is:
1. For each node r draw $\boldsymbol{\phi}^{(r)} \sim \text{Dir}(\boldsymbol{\beta})$
2. For each document d:
(a) Draw $\boldsymbol{\psi}^{(d)} \sim \text{Dir}(\boldsymbol{\alpha}^{(d)})$
(b) For each word w draw $c \sim \text{Mult}(\boldsymbol{\psi}^{(d)})$ and $w \sim \text{Mult}(\boldsymbol{\phi}^{(c)})$

In contrast, Labeled LDA [7] constrains the topics only to those associated with the document labels. LPAM-List's sampling equation is:

$$P(z_i = c|\mathbf{z}_{\setminus i}, \mathbf{w}, \boldsymbol{\alpha}^{(d)}, \boldsymbol{\beta}) \propto (n^{(d)}_c + \alpha^{(d)}_c) \frac{n^{(w)}_c + \beta_w}{\sum_m (n^{(m)}_c + \beta_m)}$$

where z_i is the topic of the i'th token w_i; $\mathbf{z}_{\setminus i}$ are the topic assignments of the remaining tokens; $c \in C_d$; $n^{(d)}_c$ is the number of times node c is sampled in document d; $n^{(w)}_c$ is the number of times word w was assigned to node c. Similarly to LPAM's sampling equation, the contribution of the token being sampled is removed from these counts.

3. DATASETS AND PREPROCESSING

We perform experiments on two datasets: (1) abstracts of scientific publications from the ACM digital library, and (2) the first 300 tokens of articles from the New York Times (NYT) dataset. We remove stopwords and tokens that appear fewer than five times in the corresponding corpus.

Statistics	ACM	NYT
Taxonomy size	268	580
Taxonomy depth	4	6
Labels/doc	3.13	5.98
Nodes/doc	8.2	8.94
Branching nodes/doc	1.65	2.11
Number of docs	20,527	15,493
Vocabulary size	13,906	27,544
Num tokens	1,499,878	3,323,851
Tokens/doc	73.07	214.54

Table 1: Dataset statistics. *Taxonomy size* is the number of nodes in the taxonomy. (We exclude nodes that are not used to label any document in our dataset and are not ancestors of label nodes. These concepts do not affect sampling and it is impossible to discover keywords for them.) *Labels/doc* is the average number of document tags. *Nodes/doc* is the average number of restricted nodes, i.e., label nodes and their ancestors. *Branching nodes/doc* - a branching node is a restricted node that has at least 2 child nodes. *Tokens/doc* - number of tokens per document after removing stopwords.

Documents from each dataset are labeled with node(s) from a dataset-specific taxonomy. These taxonomies have tree structures. However, our models can be trivially extended to handle directed acyclic graphs as well. ACM documents are tagged with at least one leaf node. We ignore the additional descriptors beyond the leaf-node labels. If a document is tagged with a node called "General", that implies the paper is relevant to most of the nodes in that subtree. The models we propose and Labeled LDA require a specific set of document labels. For this reason we discard papers tagged with "General." These documents constitute only 4% of the dataset and our goal of attaining concept keywords can be achieved without them.

NYT articles can be tagged with multiple leaf or internal nodes. For 98% of the documents, an ancestor of a document label is also used to tag the article. However, in merely 0.6% of the documents all the ancestors are labels. Table 1 contains more statistics.

4. EXPERIMENTAL RESULTS

Let $\mathbf{1}^{(N)}$ be a vector of size N containing 1's. The parameters $\boldsymbol{\beta}$, $\boldsymbol{\alpha}^{(d)}$, and $\boldsymbol{\alpha}^{(d,c)}$ are set, respectively, to $0.01 \times \mathbf{1}^{(V)}$, $\mathbf{1}^{(|C_d|)}$, and $\mathbf{1}^{(K)}$, where V is the vocabulary size, C_d is the set of restricted nodes for document d, and K is the number of c's child nodes that are in C_d plus 1 (because of the *exit*).

4.1 Topic examples

Figure 2 shows the topics that LPAM and LPAM-List learn for a few ACM nodes—Database Applications and its ancestors. Labeled LDA considers only labels, so it produces topics only for leaf nodes such as Database Applications. We can see that the higher in the taxonomy the concepts are located, the more general the corresponding keywords are. The reason is that those concepts take part in the generation of many documents, so domain-specific stopwords (*e.g.*, "paper" and "based" highlighted in bold in Figure 2) common to all these documents are driven higher up the tree. Labeled LDA does not use internal nodes. As a result, general words

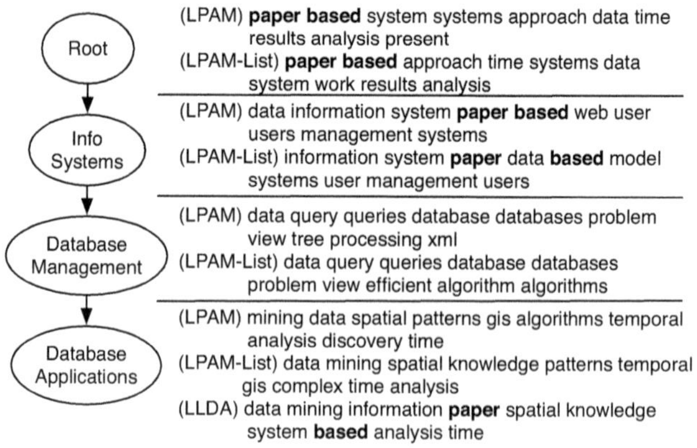

Figure 2: Four taxonomy nodes along with the corresponding top 10 words learned by LPAM, LPAM-List and Labeled LDA (LLDA). Note that LLDA provides no keywords for the internal nodes and that the new models successfully pull domain-specific words to the top of the hierarchy (see the examples shown in **bold**).

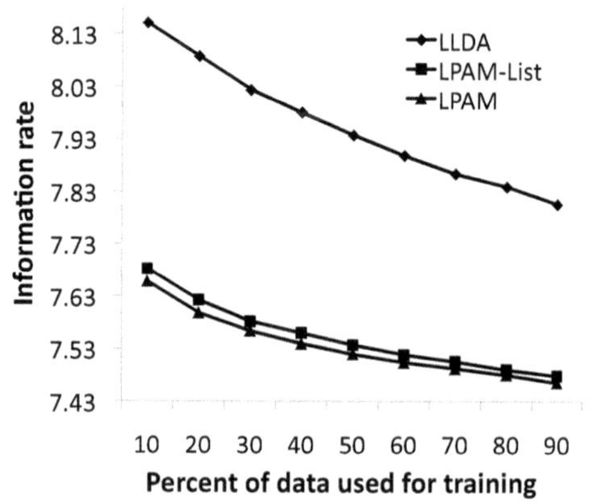

Figure 3: Information rate calculated on the ACM dataset. Note that lower is better. The difference between the models is statistically significant ($p < 0.001$).

are prominent in the distributions corresponding to the leaf nodes.

4.2 Information rate

We set aside 10% of the data for testing ($\mathbf{w}^{test}$) and 90% of the data for training ($\mathbf{w}^{train}$). We use the "left-to-right" algorithm [10] to compute $P(\mathbf{w_d}^{test}|\mathbf{w}^{train}, \mathbf{z}^{train}, \mathbf{U})$ where $\mathbf{U}$ is the set of hyperparameters and $\mathbf{w}_d^{test}$ denotes the words in the d'th test document. This probability is averaged across 5 runs to calculate the estimate $\tilde{P}_d$ and the information rate $-\frac{\ln \tilde{P}_d}{N_d}$, where N_d is the number of tokens in the test document.

Because of limited space, we present in Figure 3 the average information rate obtained using one of the datasets, the ACM corpus. We compare the models using a two-tailed paired t-test. LPAM consistently outperforms LPAM-List, which in turn is better than Labeled LDA. The differences between the models is statistically highly significant ($p < 0.001$) for varying amounts of training data. In the NYT

Action	Correct	Approx.	Incorrect
Addition	10	5	2
Deletion	21	-	5

Figure 4: User study results - actions taken after viewing discovered keywords

dataset LPAM achieves a slightly worse information rate compared to LPAM-List. However, both of these models outperform LLDA. As we point out in Section 3, if a NYT document is labeled with a given concept, then in many cases some of the ancestor nodes are also among the document tags. As a result, the margin between Labeled LDA and the other two models is smaller compared to the results we obtain with the ACM dataset. In future work, we plan to examine the differences between LPAM and LPAM-List.

4.3 Dataset navigation

We would like to know whether the concept keywords help taxonomy interpretation. We focus on the ACM dataset and use the keywords discovered by LPAM-List.

To address this question we designed and issued a survey to 15 graduate student volunteers at the Computer Science Department at University of Massachusetts Amherst. In our survey each participant is presented with a randomized list of abstracts and has to complete the following four tasks:
Step 1: Select four ACM abstracts that are about topics with which they are not significantly familiar. Since we have 15 participants, the total number of labeled abstracts is 60.
Step 2: For a given abstract, we present the user the subtrees rooted at the second level (the level under the top node) that contain the document's labels. In this way, we save the survey participants from needing to browse subtrees that are obviously irrelevant. The users are asked to label each abstract with at least one relevant tag among the leaves of the presented subtrees. The keywords that our models discovered are not presented.
Step 3: The users are shown the top 20 keywords associated with each concept and are asked to classify the same four abstracts they select in *Step 1*. If the users change any of the tags, they have to explain what prompted the change.
Step 4: The users comment whether they find it useful to have the LPAM-List's topic keywords at their disposal.

Note that although all participants are experts in computer science, they are not experts in the particular research sub-areas of the test documents. We analyze the node additions and deletions the participants made in *Step 3*. An addition can be *correct* (the added label is in the set of true labels), *approximate* (the added label shares a parent with a true label), or *incorrect* (none of the previous two cases). A deletion can be *correct* (the removed label is not in the set of true labels) or *incorrect* (the removed label is correct).

The results are summarized in Figure 4. The majority of the actions (36 out of 43) are beneficial. More specifically, the fraction of correctly removed labels is significantly greater than the fraction of incorrectly removed ones. This result indicates that keywords are helpful for identifying errors. Similarly, the fraction of correct and approximate additions is greater than the fraction of incorrect ones which leads us to the conclusion that concept keywords help users interpret taxonomies. Furthermore, in their responses in *Step 4* all but one of the surveyed students say that the keywords are helpful. We conclude that LPAM-List can play an important role in document classification.

5. CONCLUSIONS AND FUTURE WORK

We present two topic models that automatically build lists of clarifying keywords for each node in a given taxonomy. Our user study shows that presenting a few of the highest weighted keywords as concept summaries is beneficial for taxonomy interpretation. Also, the information rate produced by LPAM and LPAM-List is significantly better compared to Labeled LDA's performance.

In future work, we plan to extend LPAM, so that it can suggest edits to taxonomies. This is an important problem because new ideas emerge over time and the accompanying taxonomies should be adjusted accordingly. In fact, the output of LPAM was provided to the committee that edited the ACM Computing Classification System in 2011. We also plan to apply LPAM and LPAM-List to the problem of taxonomy alignment.

6. ACKNOWLEDGMENTS

The authors would like to thank Laura Dietz for useful discussions and ACM for providing metadata from their digital library. This work was supported in part by the Center for Intelligent Information Retrieval, in part by NIH award #HHSN271201000758P and in part by NSF grant #CNS-0958392.

7. REFERENCES

[1] D. Blei, A. Ng, and M. Jordan. Latent Dirichlet allocation. In *JMLR*, 2003.
[2] D. M. Blei, T. Griffiths, M. Jordan, and J. Tenenbaum. Hierarchical topic models and the nested Chinese restaurant process. In *NIPS*, 2003.
[3] J. Boyd-Graber and P. Resnik. Holistic sentiment analysis across languages: Multilingual supervised latent Dirichlet allocation. In *EMNLP*, 2010.
[4] W. Li, D. Blei, and A. McCallum. Nonparametric Bayes pachinko allocation. In *UAI*, 2007.
[5] D. Mimno, W. Li, and A. McCallum. Mixtures of hierarchical topics with pachinko allocation. In *ICML*, 2007.
[6] D. Newman, S. Karimi, and L. Cavedon. Using topic models to interpret MEDLINE's medical subject headings. In *Advances in Artificial Intelligence*, 2009.
[7] D. Ramage, D. Hall, R. Nallapati, and C. D. Manning. Labeled LDA: A supervised topic model for credit attribution in multi-labeled corpora. In *EMNLP*, 2009.
[8] M. Rosen-Zvi, T. Griffiths, M. Steyvers, and P. Smyth. The author-topic model for authors and documents. In *UAI*, 2004.
[9] M. Steyvers, P. Smyth, and C. Chemudugunta. Combining background knowledge and learned topics. In *Topics in Cognitive Science*, 2010.
[10] H. Wallach, I. Murray, R. Salakhutdinov, and D. Mimno. Evaluation methods for topic models. In *ICML*, 2009.
[11] X. Xue, S. Huston, and W. B. Croft. Improving verbose queries using subset distribution. In *CIKM*, 2010.

Concept Chaining Utilizing Meronyms in Text Characterization

Lori Watrous-deVersterre
Information Systems
New Jersey Institute of Technology
Newark, NJ 07003, USA
llw2@njit.edu

Chong Wang
Information Systems
New Jersey Institute of Technology
Newark, NJ 07003, USA
cs87@njit.edu

Min Song
Information Systems
New Jersey Institute of Technology
Newark, NJ 07003, USA
min.song@njit.edu

ABSTRACT
For most, the web is the first source to answer a question formulated by curiosity, need, or research reasons. This phenomenon is due to the internet's ubiquitous access, ease of use, and the extensive and ever expanding content. The problem is no longer the need to acquire content to encourage use, but to provide organizational tools to support content categorization that will facilitate improved access methods. This paper presents the results of a new text characterization algorithm that combines semantic and linguistic techniques utilizing domain-based ontology background knowledge. It explores the combination of meronym, synonym, and hypernym linguistic relationships to create a set of concept chains used to represent concepts found in a document. The experiments show improved accuracy over bag-of-words based term weighting methods and reveal characteristics of the meronym contribution to document representation.

Categories and Subject Descriptors
H.3.1 **[Information Storage and Retrieval]:** Content Analysis and Indexing – *dictionaries, indexing methods, linguistic processing;* H.3.7 [**Digital Libraries**]: Miscellaneous

General Terms
Algorithms, Performance, Reliability, Experimentation

Keywords
Concept extraction, text characterization, clustering, digital libraries, machine learning, natural language processing, ontology

1. INTRODUCTION
For most, the web is the first source to answer a question formulated by curiosity, need, or research reasons. This phenomenon is due to the internet's ubiquitous access, ease of use and the extensive amount of content. Internet access is available at home, work and via mobile connections just about everywhere else. Ease of use is due to the extensive indexing of content used by search engines. Finally, authoritative, amateur, or simply voyeurs into content generation provide a steady stream of new material for digestion. With this explosive growth in digital content comes the frustration of "weeding through" useless content that matches terms used in indexing. We need better text characterization representation to improve management and access methods used for digital content.

Current management tools use indexing and cataloging techniques based on age-old methods used by libraries, museums, and archives. The structured information captured by these tools is accessed by end-users to find content but these predefined classifications may not capture user's information needs. Users of catalogues often spend time examining the digital content retrieved to determine the correct terminology to use. This translation process from what the user wants and how it is indexed is manual and time consuming. In recent years, the need for information access systems that can capture the cultural diversity of its users while providing structural information to support effective retrieval has been identified [1].

Cultural diversity influences the concepts of a document and the indexing/cataloguing of a document in a digital library. Ontologies capture some of this cultural diversity. In this paper, we use the background knowledge provided by ontologies to extract and chain together a document's major concepts. We also capture how much of a document is devoted to each concept chain, creating a representative concept signature.

While current research explores the incorporation of ontologies for concept generation, most only utilize synonyms to identify concepts and hypernyms to calculate their frequencies ([2], [5]). In this paper, we present a novel algorithm that uses the linguistic meronym relationship to chain together concepts that would otherwise show no relationship. This additional information about a document can improve text characterization and the quality (accuracy) of indexes in a digital library. Additionally, we explore a pruning technique to the final document representation that leaves the significant concepts and removes noise. The experiments show improved accuracy with meronyms included and reveal characteristics of the meronym contribution to document representation.

In this paper we provide a summary of related work (Section 2), followed by a description of the concept chain algorithm (Section 3). Section 4 describes the experimental results obtained with comments on the methods and limitations. We conclude in Section 5 with suggested future directions for our research.

2. BACKGROUND AND RELATED WORK
The explosive growth in digital content emphasizes the need to develop automated management (organizational) and access (discovery) tools to support the processing of digital content for information access systems. Organization of this generally unstructured content requires one to identify the scope, concepts, and purpose of the resource and then analyze the relationships of

the concepts to provide an overall understanding of the document [7]. A concept is a set of words that have semantic relationships [2]. Representing a document as a set of concepts provides a richer representation which, when used with clustering techniques, makes the resulting index scheme more useful [2]. This paper suggests a content analysis method for the storage and retrieval of textual documents utilizing a set of concepts to represent a document. The novelty in this approach is in the set of relationships used to associate the concepts and the resulting concept signature created to represent the document.

In the concept chain algorithm, we use an ontology to provide the concepts and relationships. An ontology contains a shared, controlled vocabulary which models a specific domain with the definition of concepts and their properties and relations [8]. WordNet is an ontology popularly used in natural language processing. Using WordNet's background knowledge, text documents are analyzed for concepts based on relationships between terms. Common linguistic relationships are antonyms (opposite meaning), synonyms (similar meaning), hypernyms ("IS-A" generalization of a term), hyponyms (more specific meaning of a term), holonyms ("PART-OF" relationship), and meronyms ("HAS-A" relationship). These relationships are diagramed as a concept map and shown in Figure 1:

Figure 1. Concept map using natural language relationships

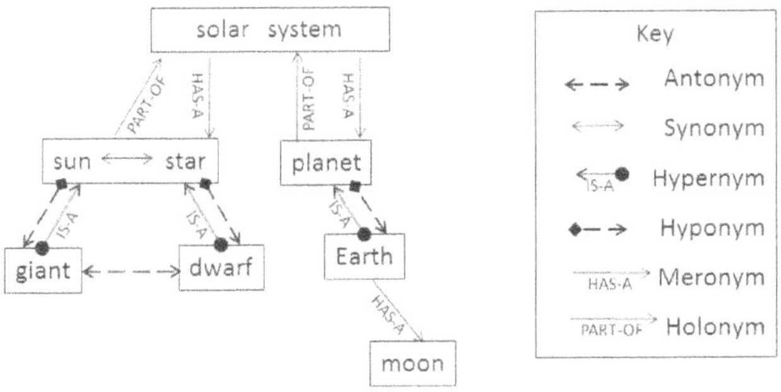

Our study examines hypernym, synonym, and meronym relationships. Hypernym relationships form a directional "IS-A" connection between two terms that moves from a specific meaning to a more generalized one ("Earth IS-A planet"). Many studies have been performed to automatically extract these relationships from unstructured text, such as in Snow et al. [4]. Unlike hypernyms, terms which are synonyms can replace each other and still hold a similar meaning. For example, "sunshine" and "sunlight" terms may be used interchangeably in a sentence without significant loss of meaning. Meronyms are a bit more complex. Girju et al. [9] defined six types of meronyms which WordNet consolidates three categories; *member-of* (faculty HAS-A professor), *stuff-of* (tree HAS-A wood), and *part-of* (solar system HAS-A sun). Additionally, Girju et al identifies the *part-of* category as the most prominently used while Miller [10] indicates meronym transitivity may be optional as one moves away from the original relationship. For example, "Earth HAS-A moon" but the "plant HAS-A moon" relationship is optional (not all planets have moons).

WordNet has been used in numerous document-clustering experiments. Some of the earliest uses of WordNet in text categorization supported techniques to address effectively the classification of low frequency categories [11]. Green, in [12], used WordNet's hypernym and hyponym links to build lexical chains to analyze the similarity between information in different paragraphs. Hotho et al. in [5] showed utilizing background knowledge (i.e., relationships) between terms improved document-clustering. Hung and Wermter in [13] present three text vector representations, two of which used hypernym as concepts to improve classification accuracy. Recupero in [14] builds on past research using WordNet's hypernym relationship to improve on vector representation and clustering. In [2], Zheng et al. used WordNet relationships with noun phrases to analyze clustering improvements. Wang and Taylor [15] used WordNet to capture hypernym relations in short text documents creating clusters of concepts called concept forests to represent a document. In [6], Elberrichi et al, used WordNet to create a concept vector format they compared to traditional bag-of-word vector representation.

Except for [2], all these methods use single term analysis (using synonyms) and calculate term frequency from hypernyms. In fact, many of the papers listed suggest using more than one relationship as a future area research.

Accurately identifying concepts for categorization purposes is fraught with time-consuming manual analysis by content experts and librarians. A digital library catalog/index must represent the digital content and reflect the expectations of its users. Automating this process requires new techniques in concept extraction to analyze any size document and capture main concepts based on the appropriate domain. This paper describes extension to existing natural language and machine-learning techniques to improve the accuracy of extracting concepts from small text based resources and grouping them appropriately.

The selection of terms is a critical first step in concept generation. Terms with multiple meanings (polysemy) create ambiguity, while a term that is similar (synonyms) to others or have a degree of generalization (hypernym) can strengthen the importance of a concept. For these reasons, term frequency calculations often use hypernym and synonym information once ambiguity is resolved [7]. We also use this approach in our algorithm but the novelty of our approach is the inclusion of meronyms. The choice of meronyms stems from the idea of finding mechanisms to improve frequency measures for significant terms in short text documents without over constraining larger documents.

Some meronyms studies have been conducted as outlined by Yang and Callan [16]. Basu et al. in [17] developed a set of measures for different lexical relationships, including meronyms to identify the average semantic difference (i.e., the weight of an edge between two terms). Meronyms were given the same weight as hypernyms in this study. Berland and Charniak in [18] and Girju et al. in [9] suggest techniques for identifying meronyms for the specific use of incorporating them into taxonomies so they may be used in concept extraction. In [2], Zheng et al., used meronyms as the relationship to support clustering and found it to be not as good as hypernyms and holonyms. The novelty of our study examines the effects of weighing meronyms differently than synonyms or hypernyms when incorporating them into a frequency count for text characterization.

3. CONCEPT CHAIN ALGORITHM

The main steps in our concept chain algorithm include document preprocessing, concept/synset extraction, concept chain construction, and concept purification. Document data preprocessing is discussed in section 3.1. Section 3.2 discusses concept extraction based on WordNet's synsets. The last step that forms concept chains is described in section 3.3. Table 1 shows the complete concept chain algorithm.

Table 1. Concept Chain Algorithm.

Input: Text based digital resource

Output: Set of weighted concepts

Method:

Given a text based digital resource,

1. Identify Parts of Speech, retain nouns
2. Tokenize text and remove stopwords
3. Stem words (terms) and count frequencies
4. Choose the first synset of each word and discard others
   For each word A and its first synset S_A,
   Let P → S_A
   Do
   1. For each word B, other than A, and its first synset S_B,
      Do
      If S_B and all synsets in P are in the same hypernym (same branch), then do
      Add S_B into P
      Else if S_B and one synset in P are in the same synonym, then do
      Add S_B into P
      Else if S_B and all synsets in P are in the same meronym, then do
      Add S_B into P
   2. Add P into final concept chains
5. Compute SCR for each concept chain and rule out the concept chains whose SCR are lower than 3%

3.1 Data Preprocessing

The first step of our algorithm performs part-of-speech (POS) tagging for a given document and only retains nouns. After tokenizing each sentence, we convert all words to lowercase and filter stopwords. In our experiment, we use the NLTK stopwords corpus [19]. Finally, WordNet's morphology function stems the remaining words to find a possible base form for the given word. Using the given POS, the algorithm recursively strips affixes until a form in WordNet is found. As the text is processed, we record the frequencies of stemmed words in the document.

3.2 Concept/Synset Extraction

WordNet [10] groups English words into sets of synonyms called synsets. Synset words can be used interchangeably without significant change to the meaning or concept discussed in the document. In WordNet, synonyms are included in multiple synsets to represents the different meanings or concepts. Through a word's context, its meaning is derived but there may be ambiguity. For instance, the sentence "How much dough do you have?" has two meanings: a quantity of material used in cooking or the slang version to represent the concept "money". Identifying the correct meaning is the challenge of word sense disambiguation (WSD). In selecting a synset to represent a word's concept, we reduce complexity by eliminating the other word senses but in doing so we may sacrifice accuracy by selecting the wrong sense. In building the document's concept chains, we have to decide which synset represents the proper meaning of the word. Assigning a proper synset to each word is a form of WSD.

In [15], if a term has multiple senses, Wang et al. added only those senses that paired with other terms, making them candidate concept chains. This slightly reduced complexity while maintaining accuracy but we found this solution introduced noise preventing the capture of a concept signature for each document.

For example, the word "unit" has six senses in WordNet. It is used most frequently to mean a unit of measurement. This sense usually does not add uniqueness to a document's representation but "unit's" third sense defines an organization regarded as part of a larger social group. In this sense, a "team" and "crew" can create many IS-A relationships creating a more unique document signature by capturing the concept that discusses an organizational unit. But, if a document contains a high occurrence of "unit" as its first sense as well as many words that form IS-A relationships with the third sense, such as "team" and "crew", the merging result, {'unit', 'team'} and {'unit', 'crew'} are misleading and become noise.

Moreover, too many irrelevant candidate concept chains such as the two just described may dilute or over constrain the significant concepts. As discussed in the next section, the pruning of "noisy" concept chains may result in only a few or, worse, no concept chains remaining to represent the document. In our experiments when using all possible senses of a term we discovered about 20% of the documents processed became too constrained. This prevented the final generation of a unique set of concept chains to form a concept signature for each document.

To address this issue, we adopted the first synset of a word which are ordered by popularity in WordNet [10]. Adopting only the first sense reduces noise and total semantic content weight in the purification phase but it also reduces the potential accuracy of the correct word sense selected. In future plans, we will explore other WSD algorithms to improve accuracy.

3.3 Concept Chain Construction

Once synsets are determined, they are used to discover semantic relationships among words with the help of the WordNet ontology. Every pair of words in the document is checked to determine if their synsets in WordNet have a hypernym, synonym or meronym relationship. The set of concept chains and their proportionate contribution to the document is based on a weighted term frequency contained in a concept chain. The output of this phase is a set of candidate concept chains.

We define *a group of words are in same hypernym relationship (IS-A relationship), only when every pair of words in the group is in same hypernym branch in WordNet. They must form a chain without bifurcation.* Words in one hypernym branch are merged into a hypernym chain if they have the same relationship. Words with no hypernym relationships or are not directly connected, stay in distinct hypernym chains.

Let's consider the two scenarios shown in Figures 2 and 3. The line above "vehicle" indicates this is only a subset of an entire WordNet hypernym tree. In WordNet, "vehicle" and its several hyponyms follow the hierarchy shown. Each word represents the synset it contains.

Figure 2. IS-A relationship Scenario 1

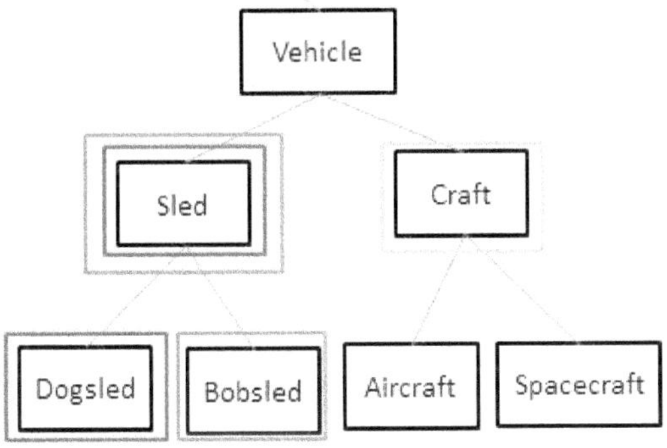

Figure 3. IS-A Relationship Scenario 2

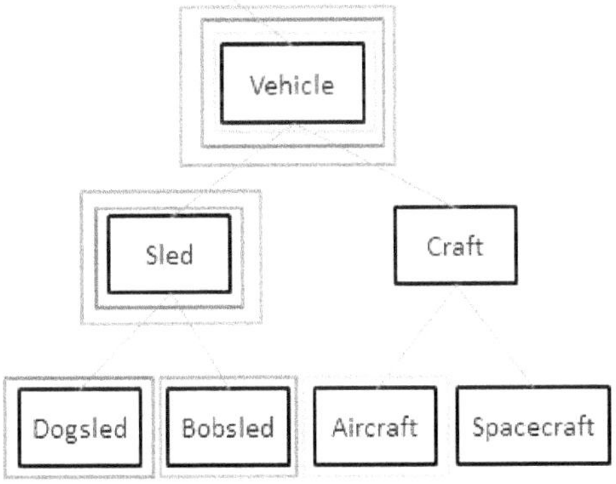

Figure 2 assumes a document contains "sled", "craft", "dogsled", and "bobsled". "Sled" and "dogsled" are grouped due to the IS-A relationship. Then "sled" and "bobsled" are grouped separately because of same reason but note that {'sled', 'dogsled'} and {'sled', 'bobsled'} are in different concept chains and that "dogsled" and "bobsled" are not in same hypernym branch due to our definition of a hypernym relationship. In this same figure, "craft" has no hypernym in the document so it is in a concept chain by itself. Thus, the output of concept chain construction will be {'craft'}, {'sled', 'dogsled'}, and {'sled', 'bobsled'}.

In Figure 3, a different document contains "dogsled", "vehicle", "aircraft", "sled" and "bobsled". After forming three concept chains: {'sled', 'dogsled'}, {'sled', 'bobsled'}, and {'aircraft'}, "vehicle" is detected. This is added into all three concept chains. Therefore, the output is {'sled', 'dogsled', 'vehicle'}, {'sled', 'bobsled', 'vehicle'}, and {'aircraft', 'vehicle'}. Note that {'aircraft', 'vehicle'} is valid even if "craft" is not in the document. We can set a distance threshold to limit the allowed maximum distance of two words in a branch. If this distance threshold is 1, then "vehicle" and "aircraft" will not be grouped because the distance between them is 2. In our project, we set the distance threshold to infinity so all concepts will be included. With this approach, we are able to capture multiple chains without over constraining the document.

In addition, we check synonyms to determine if they should be included in a concept chain. If two words in WordNet have the same first synset number, then they are synonyms. The concept chain algorithm examines a word's first synset. If it matches an existing word's first synset in a concept chain, then we add the word to the same concept chain. Note, a word may match multiple concept chains. When this happens, the concepts in these chains become more significant and reflect the major concepts in a document.

During concept chain construction we also include the three kinds of meronym relationships found in WordNet but we do not consider if a meronym relation is optional or mandatory – we include both. Simply, if several words are in same meronym tree in WordNet, they are added to one concept chain. For instance, a 'solar system' must have a 'sun' but 'planets' are optional. If 'solar system' and 'planet' are found in a document they will be added to the same concept chain.

3.4 Purification

The output of last step is a set of candidate concept chains for each document. However, as stated in the previous section, some concepts may appear as noise and misrepresent the significant semantic meaning of the document. These irrelevant candidate chains must be filtered. In order to do this we must quantify the relevancy of each concept chain and then provide a threshold for pruning.

Using Wang et al.'s [3] terminology, the semantic content weight (SCW) of a concept chain is the sum of the frequencies of all the words found in that specific concept chain. As indicated in earlier sections, *wordfreq* is a combination of synonym, hypernym, and meronym relationships. So, if the ith concept chain has j words then,

$$SCW_i = C \cdot \sum_{j=1}^{j} wordfreq_j$$

Therefore, the sum of all SCWs is the total weight for the document. While calculating the SCW of a concept chain, a coefficient, C, is applied to the frequency from 0 and 1, where 0 excludes meronyms in the relationship, while a 1 provide a full weight equivalent to a IS-A relationship.

With this information we can represent each concept chain's SCW as a fraction or rate of the total document. Given n concept chains in a document, the semantic content rate (SCR) of the ith concept chain can be described as:

$$SCR_i = \frac{SCW_i}{\sum_{n=1}^{n} SCW_n}$$

Once the SCR's for all concept chains have been established, a concept chain can be ruled out or kept depending on whether the quotient of its SCR and total SCR of the document is larger than a SCR threshold. In our experiment, we set SCR threshold to 3%.

Wang et al.'s work mapped stemmed words to particular synsetIDs. If several stemmed words mapped to the same synsetID, the word frequency value of this synsetID became the sum of the word frequency values of these associated words. This became the *wordfreq* used to compute SCW [15]. Although this approach recognizes synonyms and can support WSD it also loses specific information about a document which can lead to incorrectly cataloging a document.

For instance, 'Java' has multiple meanings ('island', 'coffee', 'programming language'). The " island" synset is the most popular usage of the word sense. Since our algorithm picks the most frequently used concept as part of the WSD process a document about 'Java programming' would be misclassified. Using just the synsetID in the final representation of the document would further exacerbate the problem. Instead, we maintain the more specific information, which is the document term, to support clustering or classification methods to catalog/index it more accurately.

4. EVALUATION

To evaluate the accuracy of the representation of a document produced by the concept chain algorithm, we compared it to two common text classification techniques: vector space model (VSM) and term frequency-inverse document frequency (TF-IDF). For each classification technique, we converted the documents in a dataset to the appropriate representation. In VSM and TF-IDF, stopwords were removed but the rest of the words were not stemmed by WordNet's morphology function. We then performed a clustering algorithm to group the documents. The results were analyzed against the categories specified in the collection to determine accuracy. Accuracy is a measure of how many documents correctly clustered over the entire number of documents in the test set:

$$Accuracy = \frac{Total\ number\ of\ docs\ correctly\ clustered}{Total\ number\ of\ documents}$$

4.1 Similarity Computations

To compare the concept chain algorithm, we need to develop semantic vectors based on concept chains to represent semantic features of these documents. A document vector consists of attributes, each of which represents a stemmed word. The values of these attributes are the word frequencies. Taking Figure 2 as an example, its output of concept chain construction is {{'craft'}, {'sled', 'dogsled'}, {'sled', 'bobsled'}}. Making up the word frequencies, the semantic vector of this document is:

craft, sled, dogsled, bobsled
{3, 2, 3, 4}

Note, the word frequency of 'sled' can potentially be higher than the count in the document since it is found in two sub-chains; {'sled', 'dogsled'}, {'sled', 'bobsled'}. We use this vector to compute similarity between this document and others. Similarity measures are used to group similar document together into distinct clusters based on feature that is being measured against. This is a common means in text processing used to classify documents. Cosine similarity is a measure of similarity between two vectors by measuring the cosine of the angle between them. The closer the similarity value reaches 1, the more similar the documents:

$$\text{Similarity} = \cos\theta = \frac{A \cdot B}{||A||\ ||B||}$$

We use this same measure when computing the similarity between the text representations used by VSM and TF-IDF. VSM is an algebraic model to represent text documents. It treats a document as "a bag of word" and represents it as a vector [20]. TF-IDF measures the importance of a word in a document based on the number of times the word appears in the document but is offset by the frequency of the word in the corpus [21]. Since VSM and TF-IDF are very common and widely accepted models to represent documents, we choose them as baseline techniques in our experiment.

4.2 Clustering Algorithm

We use an agglomerative clustering algorithm to cluster documents. This hierarchical, clustering algorithm takes a document as input and assigns it to a cluster. Then, all pairwise similarities of all clusters are computed and sorted from largest to smallest. The two clusters having the largest similarity (i.e., most similar) are merged to form a new cluster. The similarities between this new cluster and all other clusters are then computed. This process repeats until one of two conditions is triggered:

1. The number of clusters decreases to a predefine number.
2. The similarity between all clusters is 0, i.e., there is no similarity between any current pairwise clusters. This stopping condition may cause the number of output clusters to be larger than the predefined number.

A third condition prevents the "over-merging" of clusters by estimating a threshold difference, *Est.Diff*, between the sizes of input categories. Using 0.5 as a constant works only when the estimated differences among the sizes of document categories are not large:

$$Est.Diff = \frac{(total\ number\ of\ doc)}{(number\ of\ predefined\ clusters)} * 0.5$$

3. If the sizes of both clusters are larger than *Est. Diff.* value then the agglomerative algorithm will not merge them but will continue with the next pair of clusters.

The following example explains how the stopping conditions work. Assume there are 40 documents and a predefined cluster number of 2. If we only have conditions 1 and 2, then after iteration *n*, the following shows the new clusters formed:

Iteration *n*:
Cluster 1: {'coffee': 1, 'sugar': 1}
Cluster 2: {'coffee': 4, 'sugar': 1}
Cluster 3: {'coffee': 0, 'sugar': 18}
Cluster 4: {'coffee': 15, 'sugar': 0}

Since a cluster change occurred, the *n+1* iteration results are:

Iteration *n+1*:
Cluster 1: {'coffee': 1, 'sugar': 1}
Cluster 2: {'coffee': 4, 'sugar': 1}
Cluster 3: {'coffee': 15, 'sugar': 18}

This iteration "over merges" clusters 4 and 5 due to the influence of outliers. If no changes are made in the next iteration, the accuracy of this clustering is (4+18)/40=55%. Using condition 3 resolves this improper merge. Using the third condition, the calculated estimated difference in sizes is 10 and in iteration *n+1*, condition 3 prevents the merger of clusters 4 and 5 since they both have sizes greater than 10. With no other merges found, condition 2 triggers ends clustering with an accuracy of (15+18)/40=82.5%.

4.3 Datasets

We chose to use the document collection used by [15]. This is from Reuters-21578 Text Categorization Collection in UCI KDD archive [22]. This collection contains newswire documents from 1987. The sizes of the documents range from 12 to 900 words. In [15] size was important. For us, it was not a consideration in document selection. The Reuters-21578 Collection categorizes each of the 21,500 files into 132 categories. A document can contain multiple categories. For instance, a document with two topic tags, "oilseed" and "veg-oil" means it can be classified into either "oilseed" or "veg-oil" category. Document selection randomly collected documents with single and multiple categories. The process avoided any category combinations that did not provide a sufficient set of documents with either single or multiple categories. In Table 2 we've listed the characteristics of six datasets we used in the study.

Table 2. Document Datasets Used in Study

Dataset Number	Categories used	Number of documents
T-1	gnp, trade	100 docs/category
T-2	dlr, earn, money-supply	50 docs/category
T-6	money-fx, trade	50 docs/category
T-8	wheat, sugar, cpi, trade	80 docs/category
T-10	sugar, coffee	80 docs/category
T-12	ship, interest, gold	50 docs/category

Datasets T-1, T-6, and T-10 identified documents in the Reuters-21578 Collection that contain two categories. Categories selected have some type of association. For instance, the categories 'coffee' and 'sugar' in T-10 included articles that contained both terms when describing how people drink coffee. We also varied the number of documents to see any impact on accuracy or performance.

Datasets T-2 and T-12 used three associated categories with 150 documents evenly distributed in the datasets. We also created one dataset, T8, containing 320 documents that identified four different categories. We collected other datasets but have not completed analysis.

To ensure the distribution of meronyms in each dataset would not influence the accuracy calculation, we used a 5-fold cross-validation process for all cases. Since these are stratified cross-validations where each category had an equal number of documents, we are able to use an average of the runs to compute accuracy [23]. This is the value displayed in Tables 3 through 5.

4.4 Clustering Results Comparison

Comparison without Meronyms

First, we established a baseline similar to other experiments ([5], [3]). Only synonyms and IS-A (hypernym) relationships were used to represent the document. As in previous work, the results in Table 3 show that background knowledge increases accuracy with additional useful information when compared to VSM and TF-IDF methods.

Table 3. Baseline without Meronyms

Dataset Number	VSM	TF-IDF	Concept Chain without Meronyms
T-1	51.5%	69.5%	**76.4%**
T-2	57.3%	78.7%	**83.2%**
T-6	51.0%	51.0%	**73.5%**
T-8	31.3%	51.6%	**69.3%**
T-10	73.0%	75.0%	**88.8%**
T-12	46.7%	56.0%	**69.3%**

Comparison with Meronyms

Next, we examined the impact of including meronyms into our concept chains. If a meronym relationship was discovered, its word frequency was incremented by one (1), carrying the equivalent weight of a synonym. As seen in table 4, all datasets found the inclusion of meronyms to produce more accurate results than VSM or TF-IDF.

Further examination shows half the datasets (T-6, T-10 and T-12) produced poorer accuracy when compared to the concept chain algorithm that excluded meronyms. Table 4 results support previous conclusions that a meronym relationship influences accuracy in a weaker, less reliable manner than synonym and hypernym relationships ([24], [2]). The following two sentences show how a meronym could add noise into the accuracy:

"A car has a window." verses "A car has a windshield."

Both sentences specify a meronym but in the second sentence, the word 'windshield' has a closer relationship to 'car'. This implies it is a more significant noun than the word 'window'.

Additionally the word 'window' is not synonymous with 'windshield' in WordNet. Therefore, we do not capture any meronym. If term frequency of 'window' is high enough to create a concept chain, it never merges with the chain about cars and can potentially add noise to the text characterization, reducing accuracy.

Table 4. Added Meronyms at full weight

Dataset Number	VSM	TF-IDF	Concept Chain with Meronyms
T-1	51.5%	69.5%	**78.8%**
T-2	57.3%	78.7%	**83.3%**
T-6	51.0%	51.0%	**72.0%**
T-8	31.3%	51.6%	**73.3%**
T-10	73.0%	75.0%	**85.8%**
T-12	46.7%	56.0%	**66.2%**

Comparison with weighted meronyms

Most studies consider hypernym and synonym relationships to have stronger or more reliable relationships [2]. With this premise, we decided to explore fractional weights for meronym relationships to see if incremental increases could reduce noise and constraints to document characterization while adding useful information.

We re-ran the same datasets but altered the weight associated with the frequency count of a meronym relationship. The weights used to calculate the contribution of a meronym to the concept chain were 0.25, 0.5, and 0.75. Table 5 shows the results of all weights of meronyms including concept chains with no meronyms (column titled Concept Chain 0) and placing meronyms on equal footing to synonyms and hypernyms (column titled Concept Chain 1).

Table 5. Weighted Meronyms

Dataset	Concept Chain (0)	Concept Chain (0.25)	Concept Chain (0.5)	Concept Chain (0.75)	Concept Chain (1)
T-1	76.4%	72.9%	**82.6%**	79.4%	78.8%
T-2	83.2%	**85.3%**	82.5%	83.3%	83.3%
T-6	73.5%	70.8%	68.3%	**73.8%**	72.0%
T-8	69.3%	70.0%	**74.6%**	71.5%	73.3%
T-10	88.8%	88.6%	90.04%	**91.0%**	85.8%
T-12	69.3%	69.3%	**69.8%**	67.5%	66.2%

The results show meronyms provide additive information to the characterization of documents. All accuracy values show improvement with the meronym contribution if we use a constant less than 1 in calculating the frequency count of a meronym, but the degree of improvement varies with the weighted value used. We speculate this is due to the different types of meronyms contained in each document and suggest further experiments to analyze the influence of the 3-types of meronyms classified in WordNet. Our assumption is the different types of meronyms provide different levels of useful information for document characterization. The more informative meronyms contribute to improve accuracy but the less informative may add noise. This can over constrain text characterization, making it difficult to identify the major concepts found in a document.

4.5 Runtime Comparison

In addition to analyzing accuracy of utilizing meronyms with concepts, we captured runtime performance information shown in Figure 4. From the graphs, we see that combined vector construction and clustering time of VSM and TF-IDF is longer than concept chain (CC) performance. We notice clustering time takes a much longer time in VSM and TF-IDF. This is most likely due to the longer vectors lengths in this representation verses the concept chain sizes due to the purification phase.

In VSM and TF-IDF, a vector will contain many low frequency term counts that need to be analyzed during the clustering process. In the concept chain algorithm, these low frequency terms are pruned out during the purification phase based on the specified threshold as described in section 3.4. Fewer terms in any algorithm will mean a shorter clustering phase. However, the concept chain construction and purification steps in the concept chain algorithm increase vector construction time.

Additionally, TF-IDF and VSM vectors include all non-stopwords which were not stemmed by WordNet's morphology function. This lengthens the vectors of VSM and TF-IDF and thus increasing the cluster time.

It is also easy to see that datasets that contained larger numbers of documents will also have longer clustering times. T-1 has 200 documents (100 for each category) and T-8 has 320 documents Since TF-IDF and VSM will have longer vectors due to the previous reasons stated, the clustering times will also increase as is shown in Figure 4.

Figure 4. Time perfomance analysis

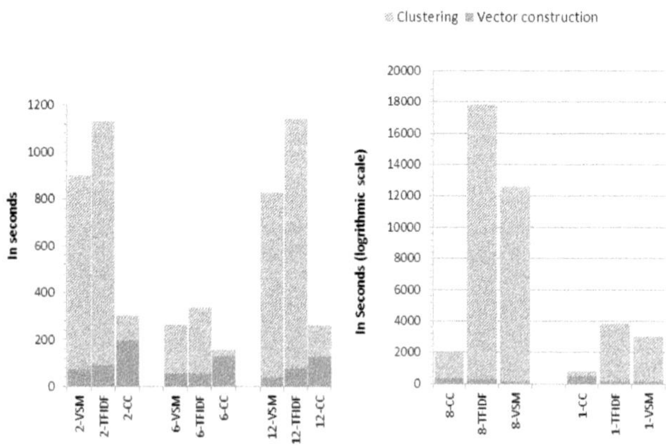

5. CONCLUSION AND FUTURE WORK

Text categorization in concept extraction has employed synonym and hypernym linguistic relationships to improve accuracy in document representation but with the explosion of digital content we need more accurate methods. In this study, we propose a method to capture concepts as a set of chains to represent the significant concepts in a document. This novel algorithm incorporates meronym relationships to provide new information for better text characterization.

The results show meronyms provide additive information to the characterization of documents. We also confirm meronyms provide different levels of useful information for document characterization that is not as strong as synonyms and hypernyms. We speculate the more informative meronyms contribute to improve accuracy but the less informative may add noise. This can over constrain text characterization, making it difficult to identify the major concepts found in a document.

We recognize there are limitations to this study that future work will investigate. A replacement to the current WSD method to provide better context analysis in the decision-making will eliminate noise and provide useful information to the concept chain. We also will investigate WordNet's characterization of meronym types to improve accuracy. Additionally, we will examine other similarity measures to understand their impact on accuracy. Finally, we plan to use the concept chain algorithm in an educational domain to confirm it is not a domain-specific algorithm.

Our intent with this future work is to utilize the concept chain algorithm to characterize digital resources in the support of cataloging efforts. We also see the potential of this algorithm in information retrieval applications to support user needs.

6. ACKNOWLEDGMENTS

Partial support for this research was provided by the National Science Foundation under grant DUE-1043647 and by the New Jersey Institute of Technology.

7. REFERENCES

1. Boast, R., Bravo, M. and Srinivasan, R. Return to Babel: Emergent Diversity, Digital Resources, and Local Knowledge. *The Information Society*, 23, 5 2007), 395-403.
2. Zheng, H.-T., Kang, B.-Y. and Kim, H.-G. Exploiting noun phrases and semantic relationships for text document clustering. *Inf. Sci.*, 179, 13 2009), 2249-2262.
3. Wang, J. Z. and Taylor, W. Concept Forest: A New Ontology-assisted Text Document Similarity Measurement Method. In *Proceedings of the IEEE/WIC/ACM International Conference on Web Intelligence (WI '07)* (Washington, DC, USA, 2007). IEEE Computer Society.
4. Snow, R., Jurafsky, D. and Ng, A. Y. *Learning syntactic patterns for automatic hypernym discovery*. City, 2004.
5. Hotho, A., Staab, S. and Stumme, G. *Wordnet improves Text Document Clustering*. City, 2003.
6. Elberrichi, Z., Rahmoun, A. and Bentaalah, M. A. Using WordNet for Text Categorization. *The International Arab Journal of Information Technology*, 5, 1 2008), 16-24.
7. Tseng, Y.-H., Lin, C.-J. and Lin, Y.-I. Text mining techniques for patent analysis. *Inf. Process. Manage.*, 43, 5 2007), 1216-1247.
8. Arvidsson, F. and Flycht-Eriksson, A. *Ontologies I*. City, 2002.
9. Girju, R., Badulescu, A. and Moldovan, D. Automatic Discovery of Part-Whole Relations. *Comput. Linguist.*, 32, 1 2006), 83-135.

10. Miller, G. A., Beckwith, R., Fellbaum, C., Gross, D. and Miller, K. WordNet: An on-line lexical database. *International Journal of Lexicography*, 3, 4 1990), 235-244.
11. Rodriguez, M. D. B., Hidalgo, J. M. G. and Agudo, B. D. Using WordNet to Complement Training Information in Text Categorization. In *Proceedings of the Second International Conference on Recent Advances in Natural Language Processing (RANLP)* (Stanford CA USA, 1997). John Benjamins Publishing.
12. Green, S. J. Building Hypertext Links By Computing Semantic Similarity. *IEEE Trans. on Knowl. and Data Eng.*, 11, 5 1999), 713-730.
13. Hung, C. and Wermter, S. Neural Network Based Document Clustering Using WordNet Ontologies. *Int. J. Hybrid Intell. Syst.*, 1, 3,4 2004), 127-142.
14. Reforgiato Recupero, D. A new unsupervised method for document clustering by using WordNet lexical and conceptual relations. *Information Retrieval*, 10, 6 2007), 563-579.
15. Wang, J. Z. and Taylor, W. Concept Forest: A New Ontology-assisted Text Document Similarity Measurement Method. In *Proceedings of the IEEE/WIC/ACM International Conference on Web Intelligence* (2007). IEEE Computer Society.
16. Yang, H. and Callan, J. A metric-based framework for automatic taxonomy induction. In *Proceedings of the Joint Conference of the 47th Annual Meeting of the ACL and the 4th International Joint Conference on Natural Language Processing of the AFNLP: Volume 1* (Suntec, Singapore, 2009). Association for Computational Linguistics.
17. Basu, S., Mooney, R. J., Pasupuleti, K. V. and Ghosh, J. Evaluating the novelty of text-mined rules using lexical knowledge. In *Proceedings of the seventh ACM SIGKDD international conference on Knowledge discovery and data mining* (San Francisco, California, 2001). ACM.
18. Berland, M. and Charniak, E. Finding parts in very large corpora. In *Proceedings of the 37th annual meeting of the Association for Computational Linguistics on Computational Linguistics* (College Park, Maryland, 1999). Association for Computational Linguistics.
19. *Natural Language Toolkit (NLTK)*. Bird, Steven (site is maintained by), City, 2011.
20. Salton, G., Wong, A. and Yang, C. S. A Vector Space Model for Automatic Indexing. *Communications of the ACM*, 8, 11 1975), 613-620.
21. Spärck Jones, K. A statistical interpretation of term specificity and its application in retrieval. *Journal of Documentation*, 28, 1 1972), 11-21.
22. Collection, R.-T. C., City.
23. Forman, G. and Scholz, M. *Apples-to-Apples in Cross-Validation Studies: Pitfalls in Classifier Performance Measurement*. City, 2010.
24. Yang, H. and Callan, J. *A metric-based framework for automatic taxonomy induction*. Association for Computational Linguistics, City, 2009.

Improving Multi-Faceted Book Search by Incorporating Sparse Latent Semantic Analysis of Click-Through Logs

Deng Yi
College of Computer Science, Zhejiang University, Hangzhou, China
yideng@zju.edu.cn

Yin Zhang
College of Computer Science, Zhejiang University, Hangzhou, China
zhangyin98@zju.edu.cn

Haihan Yu
College of Computer Science, Zhejiang University, Hangzhou, China
yuhaihan@zju.edu.cn

Yanfei Yin
College of Computer Science, Zhejiang University, Hangzhou, China
yanfei_yin@live.cn

Jing Pan
College of Computer Science, Zhejiang University, Hangzhou, China
panjing0525@zju.edu.cn

Baogang Wei
College of Computer Science, Zhejiang University, Hangzhou, China
wbg@zju.edu.cn

ABSTRACT

Multi-faceted book search engine presents diverse category-style options to allow users to refine search results without re-entering a query. In this paper, we propose a novel multi-faceted book search engine that utilizes users' query-related latent intents mined from click-through logs as multiple facets for books. The latent query intents can be effectively and efficiently discovered by applying the Sparse Latent Semantic Analysis (LSA) model to users' query and clicking behaviors in the click-through logs. This paper presents the details to improve the multi-faceted book search by incorporating the compact representation of query-intent-book relationships generated by Sparse LSA into the off-line and online processing procedures. The specificity of latent query intents can be flexibly changed by adjusting the sparsity level of projection matrix in the Sparse LSA model. We evaluated our approach on CADAL click-through logs containing 45,892 queries and 164,822 books. The experimental results show the Sparse LSA model with more sparse projection matrix tends to discover the more specific latent query intents. The latent query intents suggested by our approach usually gain the high user satisfaction ratio.

Categories and Subject Descriptors

H.2.8 [**Database Management**]: Database Applications—*data mining*; H.3.3 [**Information Storage and Retrieval**]: Information Search and Retrieval—*information filtering, search process*; H.3.7 [**Information Storage and Retrieval**]: Digital Libraries —*systems issues*

General Terms

Algorithms, Design, Experimentation

Keywords

Multi-Faceted Search, Query Intent, Sparse LSA

1. INTRODUCTION

Faceted search has become the prevailing user interaction mechanism in e-commerce search engines, particularly for online retailers and libraries. Faceted search can provide flexible access to information by one or more facets which represents dimensions of information (e.g. category, time and location)[21]. Many works on the faceted search focus on the faceted metadata[7, 29], category-based interface design[20]and information organization[21]. The existing faceted classification schemes are solely made from the perspective of items. However, the original objective of multi facets is to help users efficiently explore the information space. It is straightforward that user query intents should be taken into account when building multiple facets.

For example, if a user wants to search for a book on the web, he then raises a query into the search engine, traditional multi-faceted search engine will return a list of books based on the faceted metadata. We can find that facets based on metadata are always fixed, which may be totally unrelated with the user's original query. If we could provide the related latent query intent suggestions in a multi-faceted search style, the searching efficiency will be greatly promoted. We believe providing multi-faceted query intent suggestions will be helpful for the information search process.

Several authors have studied mining query logs to explore the issue of identifying and discovering user intent in web information search. But most of these studies just place each query into one or two fixed dimensions [3, 25]. In [4], the author analyzed and characterized a wide range of facets or dimensions that may be useful for user's intents identification when searching for information on the Web. But the suggested facets are still pre-determined and independent of users' queries in the information search process. Though presenting a small number of fixed facets for each user's query is useful to some extent, it would be appreciated that a new search engine can identify as many facets as possible by mining users' query-book bipartite graph in the click-through logs and flexibly suggest latent query intent facets highly relevant to the user's original query.

In this paper, we propose a novel multi-faceted book search engine that provides multi-faceted latent query intents to the user. Figure 1 shows the framework of our multi-faceted book search engine, which consists of two major procedures: the off-line processing procedure and the on-line search procedure.

Completing off-line processing consists of four steps: (1) Indexing the metadata of million books in CADAL digital library [30]. (2) Preprocessing click-through logs to obtain a query-book matrix X. (3) Appending queries for each book in X into the index file of books metadata. (4) Applying Sparse Latent Semantic Analysis (LSA) [5] upon the query-book matrix X to discover D orthogonal users' latent query intents and identify two latent factor matrices (i.e., query-intent relationship matrix and intent-book relationship matrix).

Completing online search consists of five steps: (I) A user raises a query. (II) Generating the candidate book results based on the index file of book metadata. (III) Obtaining the queries associated to each candidate book. (IV) Identifying the latent intents to be suggested based on query-book matrix, intent-book latent factor matrix and queries in the former step. (V) Displaying query intents and associated queries on the multi-faceted search interface.

The main contributions of this paper are as follows:

First, the common multi-faceted book search engine focuses on the faceted metadata and categories of books whose expressive abilities are limited and don't reflect the users' in-depth query intents. Our novel multi-faceted book search engine provides a multi-faceted search interface based on the latent query intents embedded in the click-through logs, which can reflect actual query intents of all users of book search engines.

Second, facets of user's intents in related works are often manually pre-defined and the number of facets are often small. We utilize a method called Sparse LSA [5] to model users' query and clicking behaviors in the click-through logs and obtain the latent query intents. As our approach belongs to unsupervised analysis of click-through logs, a large number of latent query intents can be automatically discovered as candidate facets.

Third, Due to properties of Sparse LSA model, compact and interpretable representations for the latent query intents can be discovered. Moreover, by adjusting sparsity level of projection matrix in sparse LSA model, we can flexibly change the specificity or uniqueness of latent query intents to be discovered. The sparse projection matrix also makes us save the computation and storage cost, which greatly boosts the efficiency of our multi-faceted book search engine.

The rest of this paper is as follows. In Section 2, we present some related works of discovering the latent query intents. We introduce the off-line procedure of our multi-faceted book search engine in Section 3. The online procedure will be introduced in Section 4. We present our experimental evaluations upon the Sparse LSA model and our multi-faceted book search engine in Section 5. We conclude the paper in Section 6.

2. RELATED WORK

Defining and discovering the user's query intents behind a query is considered to be a great challenge for the modern internet search engines. In practice, the query that the user provides is often of limited length and is usually less than

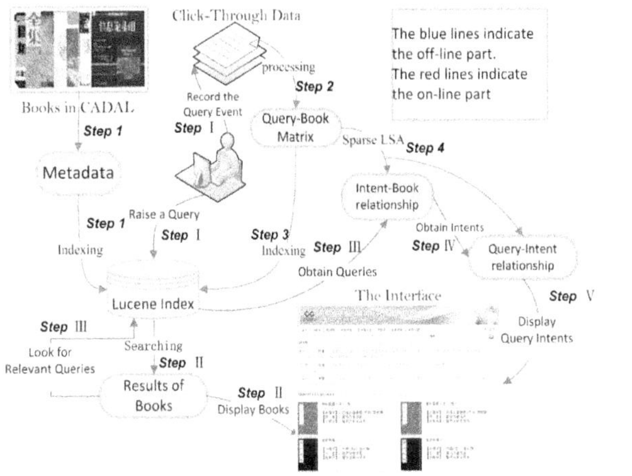

Figure 1: Our framework of multi-faceted book search engine for CADAL digital library.

two on average according to [24]. Hence, it is difficult to discover the query intents after a user raises a query.

Recently, most commercial search engines such as Google, Yahoo!, Bing and Baidu provide query suggestions to suggest queries which may better reflect the user's query intent. A common query suggestion method [1, 2, 24] is to find similar queries in click-through data and use those queries as suggestions for query intents. Another method [8, 13, 17] mines pairs of adjacent queries co-occurring in the same query sessions. The mined query pairs were then used as query suggestions for each other.

Another method called query expansion expands the query terms with similar keywords for refining search results and guessing the user's query intents [2, 11, 27, 28]. The basic idea is to use the click-through logs, which record the interactions between users and a search engine, as the feedback to learn the similarity between the query words [31].

The above two kinds of methods discover the user's query intents based on the similarity between query words. Hence, suggestions for a query are still similar queries. Though query suggestion and query expansion can better reflect the user's query intents to some extent, these forms of suggesting queries are too straightforward and lack the novel suggestions, compared to the multi-faceted search interface.

Several works have studied to characterize some possible dimensions for the user query intents, and utilized those dimensions to identify the query intent. Broder [3] classified web queries into three categories: informational, transactional, and navigational. Then, several works have researched the automatic classification and characterization of the user query intents [15, 19, 22]. the author in [4] analyzed and characterized a wide range of facets or dimensions that may be useful for user's query intents.

Although previous works characterize some useful dimensions or facets for the user's query intent and utilize these facets to identify the user's query intent, these dimensions or facets are pre-defined and the number of facets is often small. From a machine learning perspective, we think that those dimensions or facets of the users' intents could be automatically learned from users' query and clicking behaviors in the click-through log, which can well reflect all kinds of the users' query intents.

Table 1: A click-through log as a stream of query and book click events.

User IP	Time Stamp	Event Type	Event Value
49.52.19.38	23/Nov/2011:00:00:15 -0800	QuickSearch	management
203.208.60.186	23/Nov/2011:00:00:16 -0800	GET book	15017395
49.52.19.38	23/Nov/2011:00:00:16 -0800	GET book	08003254
49.52.19.38	23/Nov/2011:00:00:17 -0800	GET book	32006455

3. OFF-LINE PROCESSING PROCEDURE

In this section, we first introduce the method of processing the historical click-through logs corresponding to Step 2 in Figure 1. we then introduce how to utilize the Sparse LSA model to discover the users' latent query intents and their relationships with queries and books corresponding to Step 4 in Figure 1. Finally, we introduce the details of the off-line processing workflow.

3.1 Query-Book Bipartite Graph

In order to utilize the Spares LSA model to discover the users' query intents from our historical click-through logs, we first need to obtain a query-book bipartite graph from the click-through logs. In our book search engine, when a user raises a query into the book search engine, a set of related books will be returned as the search results. If the user is interested in some returned books, he or she will be glad to click that book and read its content. So each book clicked by that user can be seen as the information that describes the query he raises. Intuitively, the set of clicked books can be used as the features of that query.

A click-through log can be seen as a sequence of query and book events generated by users. Table 1 shows an sample piece of the click-through log. In order to obtain a *query-book bipartite graph*, we distill every unique query in the click-through log and add a corresponding *query node* into the bipartite graph for each unique query. Similarly, we also add each unique *book node* into the bipartite graph. An *edge* e_{ij} is then created between *query node* q_i and *book node* b_j if the book b_j was clicked by the user after he raised the query q_i. The *weight* w_{ij} of *edge* e_{ij} is the total number of times of when book b_j is clicked after query q_i over the whole click-through logs. Figure 2 shows an example of the query-book bipartite graph.

After obtaining the query-book bipartite graph, we can easily transform it into a matrix. Suppose the query-book bipartite graph obtained from the click-through logs has M unique queries and N unique books. Then a query-book matrix $X \in \mathbb{R}^{M\times N}$ can be created according to the following rules:

$$X_{ij} = \begin{cases} w_{ij}, & \text{if edge } e_{ij} \text{ exists;} \\ 0, & \text{otherwise.} \end{cases}$$

We then remove rows or columns which are all zeros to alleviate the sparsity of this matrix. Finally, we normalize the matrix X as follows:

$$X^*_{ij} = \frac{X_{ij}}{\|X_j\|_\infty},$$

where X_j is the j-th column of the matrix X and $\|\cdot\|_\infty$ denotes the l_∞-norm of a vector. Following the aforementioned steps, we can obtain a normalized query-book matrix X^* from the click-through logs.

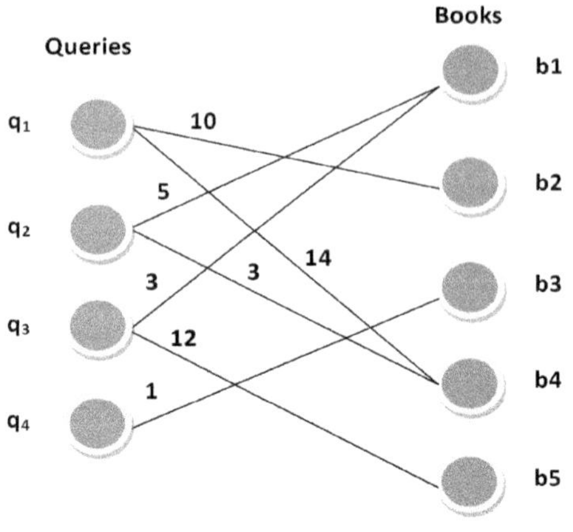

Figure 2: An example of query-book bipartite graph

3.2 Latent Query Intents Discovery

Different from many previous works that pre-defined a small number of useful dimensions or facets for query intents, we propose to automatically discover a large number of facets for users' latent query intents by applying sparse LSA models to the book-query bipartite graph matrix distilled from users' query and clicking behaviors in the click-through logs. The sparse LSA model introduces a latent query intent variable to decouple the query-book relationship, see Figure 3 for an example of the query-intent-book relationship.

We find that one discovered query intent typically corresponds to only a small number of queries and books, though the number of unique queries M and books N are often very huge. There also exists some noise entries in the query-book matrix, which may be generated by the wrong queries or the casual book clicking behaviors. So the method to discover the latent query intents should be robust to a portion of outliers and have a precise interpretability.

3.2.1 Latent Semantic Analysis

Latent Semantic Analysis (LSA) [6] is often used to estimate latent semantic structure in the data, which has widely been used for dimension reduction and information retrieval. Hence, we can utilize the LSA model to discover latent query intents from the query-book matrix. The typical technique used for latent semantic analysis is the singular-value decomposition.

Suppose we have a query-book matrix $X \in \mathbb{R}^{M\times N}$, where M is the number of queries and N is the number of books. We also assume the dimensionality of the latent space (i.e., the number of latent topics) is D ($D \leqslant \min\{N, M\}$). After applying singular-value decomposition on the matrix X, a rank D approximation of matrix X is $X \approx USV^T$, where U is $M \times D$, and V is $N \times D$. Both matrix U and matrix V are

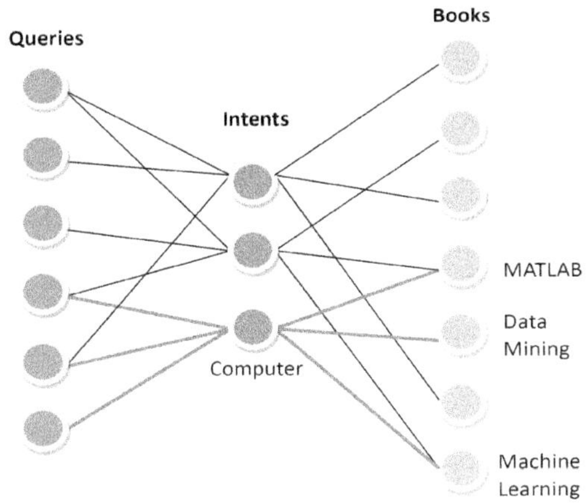

Figure 3: An example of the query-intent-book relationship

column orthogonal, which can be described as $U^TU = I$ and $V^TV = I$, where I is an identity matrix. S is a diagonal matrix with D singular values of X on its diagonal in a descending order. In traditional LSA, the first few topics with largest singular values are often too general to have specific meanings. As singular values decrease, the topics become more and more specific[5]. Furthermore, the matrix defined as $A = SV^T$ is called the projection matrix, which provides a transformation of query representation from the book space to the latent topic space.

The LSA model also can be formulated as an optimization problem [5]. We can denote the query-book matrix X as $X = [X_1, \ldots, X_N] \in \mathbb{R}^{M\times N}$, where $X_j \in \mathbb{R}^M$ is the feature vector for the j-th book. Our purpose is to project the high-dimensional feature space into a D-dimensional latent space where D is smaller than N. Inspired by the latent factor analysis [10], we assume that D latent variables are uncorrelated. We can express the latent variables as a matrix U, where $U = [U_1, \ldots, U_D] \in \mathbb{R}^{M\times D}$. Because the latent variables are uncorrelated, we have $U^TU = I$, where I is the identity matrix. So each feature vector X_j in matrix X can be expressed as a linear combination of these D latent variables in matrix U:

$$X_j = \sum_{d=1}^{D} a_{dj}U_d + \varepsilon_j. \tag{1}$$

the matrix form of (1) is expressed as $X = UA + \varepsilon$, where ε is the zero mean noise [5], and the matrix $A \in \mathbb{R}^{D\times N}$ is the projection matrix. Our goal is to compute the so-called projection matrix A.

We can solve the following optimization problem which minimizes the rank-D approximation error subject to the orthogonality constraint of U:

$$\begin{aligned} &\min_{U,A} \frac{1}{2}\|X - UA\|_F^2 \\ &subject\ to: U^TU = I, \end{aligned} \tag{2}$$

Where $\|\cdot\|_F$ denotes the matrix Frobenius norm, and $U^TU = I$ is the orthogonality constraint. After solving the optimization problem (2), we will get a rank D approximation of matrix $X \approx UA$. Here we complete the optimization formulation of the LSA model. In general, the larger D is, the better the reconstruction performance is. However, the larger value of D requires more computational cost and bigger memory for storing the projection matrix A [5].

Though LSA model can discover latent query intents from the query-book matrix, we find that each latent intent in traditional LSA model is represented by all book features. Hence it is sensitive to the casual clicked books, and difficult to precisely describe relationships between an intent and actual related books.

Moreover, in the LSA model, the latent intent corresponding to the larger singular value will cover a broader range of concepts. On the other hand, the latent intent corresponding to the smaller singular value will describe the concept more specifically. Hence, in order to obtain more specific latent query intents, we often need to obtain rather a large number of latent query intents.

But a large number of latent intents would greatly increase the cost of mapping queries from book space to the latent intent space. If we control the sparsity of projection matrix A, we could significantly reduce the mapping computation cost and the memory size storing projection matrix. Hence, the large number of latent intents can be obtained efficiently and ensure the uniqueness of most of latent intents. The uniqueness of the latent intent can also promote the understanding of latent intent itself.

3.2.2 The Sparse LSA Model

In order to solve the aforementioned problems to a large extent, we utilize a novel model called sparse Latent Semantic Analysis [5], which enforces the sparsity on the projection matrix A. Compared to the traditional LSA model, the sparse LSA model selects only a small number of relevant books for each latent intent and hence provides a compact representation of intent-book relationships. With the adjustment of the sparsity degree of projection matrix, sparse LSA could control the specificity or uniqueness of most of the latent intents. Compared to traditional LSA model, we think this model is more suitable for discovering the latent query intents from the query-book bipartite graph matrix.

In order to obtain a sparse projection matrix, we add an entry-wise l_1-norm of the projection matrix [5] as in the lasso model [26] into the formulation of traditional LSA model.

The formulation of sparse LSA is shown as follows:

$$\begin{aligned} &\min_{U,A} \frac{1}{2}\|X - UA\|_F^2 + \lambda\|A\|_1 \\ &subject\ to: U^TU = I, \end{aligned} \tag{3}$$

where $\|A\|_1 = \sum_{d=1}^{D}\sum_{j=1}^{N}|a_{dj}|$ is the entry-wise l_1-norm of A and λ is the positive regularization parameter which controls the density (the number of nonzero entries) of A [5]. X is the query-book matrix obtained from the click-through logs and U is the latent variables matrix.

If we increase λ into a larger value, the projection matrix A will have more zeros entries (more sparse), which results in obtaining the more specific and compact intent-book relationships. Therefore, in practice we change the specificity of the query intents (or the uniqueness of the intents) by adjusting the value of λ according to our needs. We will show the impact of λ in our experiments.

As mentioned in [5], a natural approach to solving (3) is the alternating approach. When matrix U is fixed, we can let A_j denote the j-th column of the projection matrix A. The optimization problem with respect to A_j is shown as follows:

$$\min_{A_j} \frac{1}{2}\|X_j - UA_j\|_2^2 + \lambda\|A_j\|_1; \quad j = 1, \ldots, N. \qquad (4)$$

We find that there are N standard lasso problems in (4), where N is the column number of matrix A. So the state-of-the-art lasso solver [14] which is essentially a coordinate descent approach can be directly applied here. It is straightforward that those standard lasso problems in (4) are independent to each other. So in our implementation, these lasso problems are solved in parallel using multiple cpu cores, which achieves great speedups of solving N lasso problems.

When the projection matrix A is fixed, the optimization problem (3) is equivalent to:

$$\min_{U} \frac{1}{2}\|X - UA\|_F^2 \quad subject\ to: U^T U = I. \qquad (5)$$

After transformation, (5) can be further rewritten as:

$$\max_{U}\ tr(U^T X A^T) \quad subject\ to: U^T U = I. \qquad (6)$$

To solve the optimization problem in (6), we use a matrix V and let $V = XA^T$. In fact, V represents the query-intent relationships, i.e., there is a D-dimensional intents vector for each query. Suppose the singular value decomposition (SVD) of V is $V = P\Delta Q$, then the optimal solution to (6) is $U = PQ$[5]. So the solving strategy to (6) is to conduct singular value decomposition of matrix $V : V = P\Delta Q$ and then let $U = PQ$.

We find that if we enforce the sparsity on the projection matrix A, the matrix $V = XA^T$ will also be a sparse matrix. To speedup the computation of singular value decomposition of sparse matrix V, we utilize an efficient sparse SVD algorithm proposed in [18].

Different from SVD algorithms based on the symmetric Lanczos algorithm [9, 16, 23], the proposed sparse SVD algorithm utilizes a partial reorthogonalization procedure (BPRO) for maintaining semi-orthogonality among the left and right Lanczos vectors in the Lanczos bidiagonalization (LBD). The proposed sparse SVD algorithm is both computationally efficient and capable of computing the singular values with good relative accuracy [18].

As for the starting point, the writer in [5] suggests a very simple initialization strategy as follows:

$$U^0 = \begin{pmatrix} I_D \\ 0 \end{pmatrix}, \qquad (7)$$

where I_D is the $D \times D$ identity matrix. It is intuitive to find $(U^0)^T U^0 = I$.

The alternating approach first utilize the U^0 as the starting point, then fixes the U^0 to obtain the projection matrix A, and then fixes the A to obtain another U which will be used in the next iteration. The iteration will not stop until the convergence of matrix U and A.

The criterion to judge the convergence of matrix U and A is defined as follows: we calculate the maximum change in matrix U and A respectively for two consecutive iterations t and $t+1$, which can be computed as $\|U^{(t+1)} - U^t\|_\infty$ and $\|A^{(t+1)} - A^t\|_\infty$, where $\|\cdot\|_\infty$ denotes the matrix entry-wise l_∞-norm. If both the maximum change in matrix U and A is smaller than prefixed constant γ, we break the iteration and obtain the latent variables matrix U and the projection matrix A. The value of γ we set in our system is 0.1.

3.3 Off-line Processing Workflow

In this section, we introduce the off-line processing workflow of our multi-faceted approach. We first utilize Lucene [12] to create the index for the metadata of books in CADAL digital library (*Step 1 in Figure 1*). Then, we process the historical click-through logs in CADAL book search engine as described in Section 3.1 to obtain the query-book matrix (*Step 2 in Figure 1*). The time span of click-through logs are from 1st. May 2011 to 12th. Dec 2011.

The obtained query-book matrix contains 45,892 queries and 164,822 books. We grouped the clicked books by the number of unique queries associated with them, and counted the total number of books in each group. Table 2 shows the histogram distribution of the books in terms of the number of unique queries associated to them. We find that about 95% of books in the obtained query-book matrix are clicked after less than 3 queries, which makes a big challenge for the sparse LSA model. We also add the query-book matrix into the index of books metadata. Each query in the query-book matrix is added as a tag into the index of its corresponding books (*Step 3 in Figure 1*).

Next, we utilize the Sparse LSA model to dicover the query intents from the query-book matrix (*Step 4 in Figure 1*). As mentioned in section 3.2.2, the N lasso problems can be solved in parallel. So we employ the Parallel Computing Toolbox in Matlab to accelerate our calculation. The toolbox makes it possible to execute applications up to twelve parallel workers on multi-core workstations, which greatly boost the efficiency of solving those lasso problems. The workstation we utilized contains two 8-cores 2.4GHz Xeon CPUs and 16GB of memory. The number of query intents we want to discover in the experiments is 500, and the value of λ impacting the specificity of query intents is set to 0.3.

After executing the sparse LSA on the query-book matrix, we obtain a projection matrix which represents the relationship between intents and books. Next, we will introduce how to utilize this projection matrix and index to suggest multi-faceted query intents in our book search engine.

4. THE ON-LINE SEARCH PROCEDURE

In the on-line search procedure, we utilize the index of book metadata and the query intents obtained in the off-line processing procedure to generate book search results and suggest multiple query intents in our book search engine.

When a user raises a query into the book search box, the search engine begins to record this query into the click-through log (*Step I in Figure 1*). A list of books will be returned as the search results according to the Lucene index, our engine then displays those returned books in two columns to the user. (*Step II in Figure 1*).

We denote those IDs of returned books as a vector $B \in \mathbb{R}^m$, where m is the number of returned books. As mentioned above, each query in the query-book matrix is added as a tag into the metadata index of its corresponding books. Hence, we can obtain a query ID vector $Q \in \mathbb{R}^n$ (n is the number of query ID) according to the metadata index of $B_i (i \in m)$(*Step III in Figure 1*).

We defined the query-book matrix obtained from the click-

Table 2: The distribution of the clicked books in terms of the number of unique queries associated to them.

Number of associated queries	1	2	3	4	5	6	7	≥8
Number of books	135879	21371	5129	1459	546	198	95	145

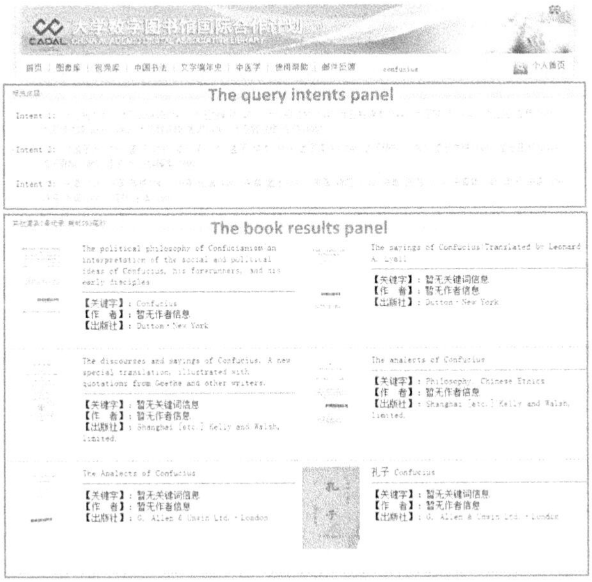

Figure 4: An example of the result obtained by our multi-faceted book search engine.

through logs as $X \in \mathbb{R}^{45892\times164822}$. Then each query in the query ID vector Q can be represented as a vector $X_{q_i} \in \mathbb{R}^{1\times164822}$ according to the query-book matrix X. In order to obtain the most relevant query intent, we calculate the score obtained by each query intent as follows:

$$d_i = AX_{q_i}^T, \quad i = 1, 2, \ldots, n,$$

where $A \in \mathbb{R}^{500\times164822}$ is the projection matrix learnt by the sparse LSA model in the off-line processing part, n is the number of query ID, d_i is the 500-dimensional vector representing query intents. The sparse projection matrix A here can reduce the computation and memory cost of the projection operation that classifies the query into different query intents.

We then add up those d_i vectors to obtain the final query intent vector D as follows:

$$D = \sum_{i=1}^{n} d_i.$$

After obtaining the final query intent vector D, we use the 3 largest entries in it. Those 3 entries are the query intents most relevant to the query given by the user of our search engine (*Step IV in Figure 1*).

For each query intent, we further display its most relevant queries according to the intent-query relationship which can be obtained by AX^T(*Step V in Figure 1*). Hence, our multi-faceted book search engine presents the most relevant three query intents as facets to allow the user to refine the book search results.

An example of the search result by our multi-faceted book search engine is shown in Figure 4. We raised a query *"Confucius"* into our book search engine. *Confucius* was a thinker, educator, and founder of the Confucianism of Chinese traditional culture. The books matching the query *"Confucius"* were displayed in the book results panel at the bottom. The query intents panel is at the top of book results, displaying 3 query intents most relevant to the original query *"Confucius"*. The first query intent is about the Thirteen Confucian Classics. The second one is about *Mencius* who was also a famous Confucianism member and lived about the same time as Confucius. The last one is about *ZhuXi* who has been the most famous Confucianism member since the Song Dynasty.

All three query intents presented in Figure 4 are all relevant to the *"Confucius"* and his thought. The user can further click any label in each query intent to refine the book search results, e.g., the books related to Mencius. Hence, our novel multi-faceted book search engine provides a multi-faceted search by regarding the latent query intents as orthogonal facets. The suggested query intent corresponding to each facet is relevant to the query word raised by the user. We believe this kind of multi-faceted book search engine will greatly boost the efficiency and accuracy of the book search.

5. EXPERIMENTAL EVALUATION

In this section, we first evaluate the effectiveness of the Sparse LSA model based on CADAL click-through logs. Then, we present the experimental results of evaluating our multi-faceted book search engine.

5.1 Evaluating the Sparse LSA model

We first obtained the raw query-book matrix via the off-line processing procedure, and then create a validation matrix by picking up books that were clicked after more than 3 unique queries in the raw query-book matrix for evaluation. The validation query-book matrix contains 14,552 unique queries and 7,572 unique books.

We then applied the Sparse LSA algorithm to this validation query-book matrix in Matlab to obtain the latent query intents. The number of query intents we set in the experiments is 300 and the minimum λ value that impacts the specificity of the query intents is 0.1.

After executing the Sparse LSA program, we obtain a projection matrix A whose size is 300×7572 dimensions. In fact, this projection matrix A is also the compact query intents representations of books. So we can list the top 10 relevant books in each row of A (i.e., each query intent). Via the sparse projection matrix A, the D-dimensional query intents vector for each query can be precisely computed. In matrix form, the intent-query relationship is $V = AX^T$, where V is also a sparse matrix of 300×14552 dimensions. Hence we can also list the top 10 relevant queries for each query intent according to the matrix V.

Finally, for each query intent, we listed its most 10 relevant queries and books to evaluate the effectiveness of the Sparse LSA model. Figure 5 shows an example of queries and books belonging to one query intent. If most of those

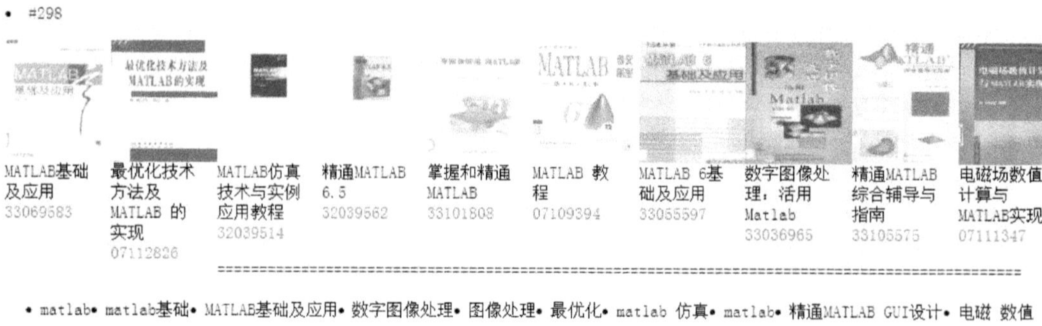

Figure 5: An example of queries and books belonging to one query intent.

Table 3: The Accuracy Results obtained by three strategies.

Strategy	Accuracy
Traditional LSA	50.25%
Sparse LSA ($\lambda = 0.1$)	58.416%
Sparse LSA ($\lambda = 0.7$)	74.415%

Table 4: The number of intents that contain less than 5 queries and books.

Strategy	The number
Sparse LSA ($\lambda = 0.1$)	23
Sparse LSA ($\lambda = 0.7$)	159

10 queries and 10 books which belong to each query intent could clearly indicate an obvious intent or topic, we think that the sparse LSA model is effective in obtaining the latent query intent. We also evaluate the results of traditional LSA as a baseline to compare with those of Sparse LSA model.

We chose 10 people from different specialized fields (i.e., computer science, physics, Chinese literature, finance) to judge the experiment results. The judging rule we adopted is the following: Suppose we have D query intents obtained by one strategy, then 10 queries and 10 books corresponding to each intent will be shown as in Figure 5 to each judge. If the judge thinks these queries and books can clearly indicate an specific topic, the judge then add 1-point to that strategy. Suppose each strategy gets M_k points from the k-th judge. To compare different strategies, we then calculate the accuracy of clearly indicating specific intents as follows:

$$ACC = \frac{\sum_{k=1}^{10} M_k}{10 \times D} \tag{8}$$

Table 3 shows the accuracy results obtained by three strategies. We can find that the sparse LSA model with $\lambda = 0.1$ has an relative improvement of about 16.25% over the traditional LSA model. It is clear that sparse LSA has a more compact and precise representation of query-intent-book relationships.

We also set the λ value which controls the specificity of intents to 0.7. A bigger λ value leads to a more sparse projection matrix, and results in much more specific query intents. We assume that the more specific one intent is, the smaller the number of corresponding queries and books are. So we counted the number of intents whose number of queries and books is less than 5. The result is shown in Table 4, we find that the result obtained by a larger lambda value has more specific query intents than that obtained by the smaller one. Hence, we can flexibly change the specificity or uniqueness of the query intents by changing the λ value in the Sparse LSA formulation.

We also calculate the accuracy of mining intents for the Sparse LSA with $\lambda = 0.7$, the result is also shown in Table 3. We find that the result obtained by the Sparse LSA with $\lambda = 0.7$ has a relative improvement of about 48.092% over the traditional LSA model and 27.389% over the Sparse LSA with $\lambda = 0.1$. Hence, as the sparsity degree of projection matrix increases, the Sparse LSA model will obtain much more specific intents, which improves the interpretability to precisely describe the query-intent-book relationship. However, using a larger λ value will lead to the loss of many general query intents. Hence, the choice of λ value in practice should meet the needs of the book search engine.

Finally, we report the density, storage and projection time of the projection matrix A obtained by the above three strategies. The density of projection matrix A is defined as the percentage of nonzero entries in it. For testing the projection time, we randomly chose 3,000 queries in the validation query-book matrix. Notice that each query can be expressed as a vector $q \in \mathbb{R}^{7572}$ and its representation in the lower dimensional latent space can be computed as: $\hat{q} = Aq$.

We calculated the average time of this projection operation executing in the Matlab. The result is shown in Table 5, we can find that the sparse LSA model saves a lot of storage for keeping the projection matrix. Obviously, the projection time of the sparse LSA with $\lambda = 0.7$ has a huge improvement over the traditional LSA model. When the number of query intents is huge, projecting queries from book space to latent intent space via a highly sparse projection matrix will be computationally much more efficient.

5.2 Evaluating Multi-Faceted Book Search

To evaluate our multi-faceted book search engine based on the Sparse LSA model, we adopted the following judgement rule. As mentioned above, we also find 10 people from the different specialized fields to manually judge our book search engine. Those people judge the quality of query intents suggested by our book search engine from two aspects: relevance and novelty.

The relevance depends on whether the queries of the query intents is very relevant to the query word. The novelty de-

Table 5: Computational Efficiency and Storage of each Strategy.

Strategy	Storage(KB)	Density(%)	Proj. Time(ms)
Traditional LSA	36405	99.998	84.126
Sparse LSA ($\lambda = 0.1$)	6714	18.308	13.863
Sparse LSA ($\lambda = 0.7$)	230	0.466	0.378

Table 6: The statistics of manual evaluation of multiple intents suggested by our book search engine.

Relevance(%)	67.5
Novelty(%)	62.5

pends on whether query intents suggested by our search engine can provide something new or unusual for the user.

we randomly chose 100 query words from the field of Chinese ancient books, education and famous people in ancient China for judging the quality of suggested intents. Each judger should evaluate the relevance and novelty of the suggested three query intents for each query by our search engine. If he think the suggested query intents is helpful to him, he can add 1 point to the relevance or the novelty aspects.

The percentage of relevant and novel query intents suggested by our book search engine is shown in Table 6. We find that about 67.5% query intents suggested by our book search engine is relevant to the query word and about 62.5% query intents can provide novel information to the user. We think this ratio has been able to suggest the appropriate query intents to the user and achieve good user experience in our multi-faceted book search engine.

6. CONCLUSION

In this paper, we propose a novel multi-faceted book search engine that uses multiple query intents learnt from the click-through logs as the facets to allow the user to refine the book search results. The latent query intents can be effectively and efficiently discovered by applying the Sparse LSA model to users' query and clicking behaviors in the click-through logs. The Sparse LSA model can provide a rather compact representation of query-intent-book relationships by adjusting the sparsity level of projection matrix in terms of search application requirements. The more sparse the projection matrix is, the more specific the learnt query intents are. Due to the significantly reduced computation and memory cost when using the sparse projection matrix, a large number of latent intents can be efficiently calculated in the off-line processing procedure and applied in the online search procedure. Experimental results show that the Sparse LSA model with more sparse projection matrix achieves the better performance. The query intents suggested by our multi-faceted book search engine often gain a high user satisfaction ratio.

7. ACKNOWLEDGMENTS

This work was supported by the China Academic Digital Associative Library Project, the Special Funds for Key Program of National Science and Technology (Grant No. 2010ZX01042-002-003), the Program for Key Innovative Research Team of Zhejiang Province (Grant No.2009R50009), the China Postdoctoral Science Foundation, the Fundamental Research Funds for the Central Universities.

8. REFERENCES

[1] R. Baeza-yates, C. Hurtado, and M. Mendoza. Query recommendation using query logs in search engines. *In EDBT*, 2004.

[2] D. Beeferman and A. Berger. Agglomerative clustering of a search engine query log. *In KDD*, 2000.

[3] A. Z. Broder. A taxonomy of web search. *SIGIR Forum*, 36(2):3–10, 2002.

[4] L. Calderon-Benavides, C. Gonzalez-Caro, and R. Baeza-Yates. Towards a deeper understanding of the user's query intent. *SIGIR*, 2010.

[5] X. Chen, Y. Qi, B. Bai, Q. Lin, and J. Carbonell. Sparse latent semantic analysis. *SIAM 2011 International Conference on Data Mining*, 2011.

[6] S. Deerwester, S. T. Dumais, G. W. Furnas, T. Landauer, and R. Harshman. Indexing by latent semantic analysis. *Journal of the American Society for Information Science*, 41, 1990.

[7] J. English, M. Hearst, R. Sinha, K. Swearingen, and K.-P. Yee. Hierarchical faceted metadata in site search interfaces. *CHI '02 extended abstracts on Human factors in computing systems*, 2002.

[8] B. M. Fonseca, P. Golgher, and et al. Concept-based interactive query expansion. *Proceedings of the 14th ACM international conference on Information and knowledge management*, 2005.

[9] G.H.Golub, F.T.Luk, and M.L.Overton. A block lanczos method for computing the singular values and corresponding vectors of a matrix. *ACM Trans. Math. Software*, 7:149 169, 1981.

[10] T. Hastie, R. Tibshirani, and J. Friedman. *The Elements of Statistical Learning*. Springer, 2001.

[11] H.Cui, J.-R.Wen, J.-Y.Nie, and W.-Y.Ma. Probabilistic query expansion using query logs. *In Proceedings of International World Wide Web Conference*, pages 325–332, 2002.

[12] http://lucene.apache.org/.

[13] C. K. Huang, L. F. Chien, and Y. J. Oyang. Relevant term suggestion in interactive web search based on contextual information in query session logs. *Journal of the American Society for Information Science and Technology*, 54(7):638–649, May 2003.

[14] T. H. J. Friedman and R. Tibshirani. Regularized paths for generalized linear models via coordinate descent. *Journal of Statistical Software*, 33(1), 2010.

[15] B. J. Jansen, D. L. Booth, and A. Spink. Determining the informational, navigational,and transactional intent of web queries. *Information Processing and Management*, 44(3):1251–1266, 2008.

[16] J.K.Cullum, R.A.Willoughby, and M.Lake. A lanczos algorithm for computing singular values and vectors of large matrices. *SIAM J. Sci.Statist.Comput*, 4(2):197 215, 1983.

[17] R. Jones, B. Rey, and O. Madani. Generating query substitutions. *In WWW*, 2006.

[18] R. M. Larsen. Lanczos bidiagonalization with partial reorthogonalization. *Department of Computer Science, Aarhus University, Technical report, DAIMI PB-357, code available at http://soi.stanford.edu/~rmunk/PROPACK/ (1998).*

[19] U. Lee, Z. Liu, and J. Cho. Automatic identification of user goals in web search. *In Proc. of the WWW '05,*, pages 391–400, 2005.

[20] K. W.-T. Leung, D. L. Lee, and W.-C. Lee. Personalized web search with location preferences. *2010 IEEE 26th International Conference on Data Engineering (ICDE)*, pages 701–712, March 2010.

[21] Z. Liao, J. Yang, C. Fu, and G. Zhang. Integrating web videos for faceted search based on duplicates, contexts and rules. *Intelligent Information Processing'10*, pages 203–212, 2010.

[22] Y. Liu, M. Zhang, L. Ru, and S. Ma. Automatic query type identification based on click through information. *In Proc. of the AIRS '06,*, pages 593–600, 2006.

[23] M.W.Berry. Large-scale sparse singular value computations. *International Journal of Supercomputer Applications*, 1992.

[24] J. rong Wen, J.-Y. Nie, and H.-H. Zhang. Clustering user queries of a search engine. *In Proceedings of the International World Wide Web Conference*, pages 162–168, 2001.

[25] D. E. Rose and D. Levinson. Understanding user goals in web search. *In Proc. of the WWW '04*, pages 13–19, 2004.

[26] R. Tibshirani. Regression shrinkage and selection via the lasso. *Journal of the Royal Statistical Society*, Series B(58):267–288, 1996.

[27] J. Xu and W. B. Croft. Improving the effectiveness of information retrieval with local context analysis. *ACM Transactions on Information System*, 18(1):79–112, 2000.

[28] G.-R. Xue, H.-J. Zeng, Z. Chen, Y. Yu, W.-Y. Ma, W. Xi, and W. Fan. Optimizing web search using web click-through data. *In Proceedings of ACM CIKM Conference*, pages 118–126, 2004.

[29] K.-P. Yee, K. Swearingen, K. Li, and M. Hearst. Faceted metadata for image search and browsing. *Proceedings of the SIGCHI conference on Human factors in computing systems*, 2003.

[30] Y. Zhang, X. Wang, H. Yu, R. Li, B. Wei, and J. Pan. When personalization meets socialization: an icadal approach. *JCDL 2011*, pages 459–460, 2011.

[31] Q. Zhao, S. C. H. Hoi, T.-Y. Liu, S. S. Bhowmick, M. R. Lyu, and W.-Y. Ma. Time-dependent semantic similarity measure of queries using historical click-through data. *WWW*, pages 543–552, 2006.

Personalized Query Expansion in the QIC System

Prat Tanapaisankit
Information Systems
New Jersey Institute of Technology
Newark, NJ 07003, USA
pt26@njit.edu

Lori Watrous-deVersterre
Information Systems
New Jersey Institute of Technology
Newark, NJ 07003, USA
llw2@njit.edu

Min Song
Information Systems
New Jersey Institute of Technology
Newark, NJ 07003, USA
min.song@njit.edu

ABSTRACT
Query In Context (QIC) is a personalized search system that enhances individual search by incorporating user preferences in query expansion, capturing meanings embedded in documents, and ranking search results with context-enriched features. In this paper, we propose a new technique for QIC's Query Expansion module, which reformulates user queries by using novel statistical-based and knowledge-based query expansion techniques to improve the returned results. The promising preliminary results analyzed through precision and recall metrics show better alignment between the user's interests and the results retrieved.

Categories and Subject Descriptors
H3.3 [**Information Search and Retrieval]:** ***Query formulation***

General Terms
Algorithms, Human Factors.

Keywords
Query Expansion. Semantic Query Analysis, Personalized Search

1. INTRODUCTION
Searching is a part of our online lives. Unfortunately, current search tools are unable to satisfy a diverse range of users with their unique search goals. Queries are usually short and inherently ambiguous [1]. Moreover, users may have completely different intentions for the same query [2]. Traditional search systems employ content-based approaches without incorporating personal and contextual information. Consequently, these systems yield cookie-cutter results for all users regardless of context. While internet search engines have tried to address this problem and improved personalized search for individual users, digital libraries are typically still oriented towards a generic user.

Our goal is to reduce the number of contextually inaccurate search results displayed during in order to improve digital library search performance for the individual. We accomplish this by leveraging user contextual information when analyzing a search request. Query terms having multiple meanings are weighted towards contexts more frequently referenced by an individual.

JCDL'12, June 10–14, 2012, Washington, DC, USA.

We determine additional query terms to augment the appropriate context by utilizing information mined from CiteSeer's query logs [3], an individual's profile information, and online dictionaries supporting domain-specific and linguistic information. Our novel approach combines underutilized statistical-based techniques to discover relationships between user preferences and query terms.

This paper is structured as follows: we begin with a discussion of related work in section 2. Then, a detailed description of our approach is presented in section 3. In section 4, we discuss our experiment and the result. We conclude in section 5.

2. RELATED WORK AND BACKGROUND
Query expansion has two approaches; the traditional statistical and knowledge based approaches and the methods focused on capturing individual preferences. This section explores both.

2.1 Individual Preference Expansion
Personalized search focuses on the user. This is a shift from consensus relevancy to personal relevancy. In consensus relevancy, the population is presumed relevant to each user, while personal relevancy is computed based on each individual within the context of their interactions [4]. For more than a decade, information retrieval researchers have been interested in the use of context. In 2000, Lawrence surveyed many early works related to the use of context in web search[5]. He suggested the use of context in web search may increase competition, diversity, functionality, and help mitigate any negative effects of biases in access to information on the web. In 2002, Pitkow et al. proposed a contextual computing approach to improve personalized search efficiency [4]. They identified two ways to personalize a search through query augmentation and search result ranking.

Cui et al. utilized user logs to extract correlations between query terms and document terms [6]. This approach outperforms many other query expansion techniques. However, user logs may contain query sessions from multiple users so the term correlations may not reflect the preference of a particular user. Chirita et al. proposed an adaptive personalized query expansion which analyzes user data at increasing granularity levels [7]. However, their technique employs data aggregated over a long period of time so it cannot adapt to the user needs which may change over time or abruptly.

The simplest approach utilizes the information a user provides in their user profile associated with a login to a digital library. In 2002, Zeng et al. developed PASS, a system that employs a user profile to filter the content by computing the similarity of probabilistic distributions between documents and user profiles [8]. Another system, InfoWeb, provides adaptive content-based retrieval of documents [9]. It employs a stereotype knowledge base to model a user.

2.2 Statistical and Knowledge-based Expansion Approaches

Data-driven statistical-based techniques try to discover word relationships based on term co-occurrence analysis and feature selection. Traditional IR models assume terms are independent and treat queries and documents as bags-of-words. Recently, this assumption was challenged by researchers who acknowledge dependencies exist between terms which improve retrieval performance [10]. The dependencies could occur between terms within a query or document, as well as between query and document terms. In query expansion frameworks, these dependencies are observed as co-occurrences frequency [11, 12] or the distance between terms [10, 13].

In statistical approaches, linguistic analysis often does not fully utilize the syntactic property of a query during the expansion process and ignores the semantic meanings of terms. We propose an approach incorporating linguistic analysis and utilizing the semantic property of terms to improve expansion performance.

The knowledge-based approach uses external sources to provide background knowledge. These sources include ontologies, dictionaries, and web corpora such as Wikipedia. Ontologies provide richer information than dictionaries and are easier to use than web corpora. Ontologies can be domain specific or general [14]. General ontologies, such as WordNet, are suitable for broad queries [15].

3. SYSTEM DESCRIPTION

We built the query expansion algorithm, described in this paper, on QIC, a new information retrieval system. The steps outlined in Figure 1 describe the process to expand a query within QIC's query expansion (QE) Module. An offline pre-processing phase builds a user profile model based on user-defined preferences. Next, the query phase uses the model to produce a custom result for the user. During the query phase, knowledge resources, such as, WordNet and CiteSeer, further help to fine-tune the query. The following subsections describe these phases in more detail.

Figure 1. Query Expansion Process.

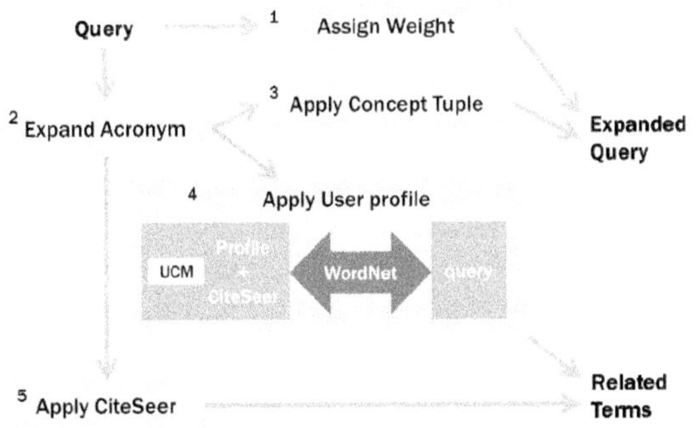

3.1 Pre-processing Phase

The pre-processing phase builds the user context model (UCM) which is a representative model of a user's behavior. Key in this phase is the capture of user information. The phase employs two methods to gather representative data. The first comes directly from the user's input to an online registration form. The second is a data-driven method based on user logs captured by CiteSeer's online public search engine and digital library.

Before using QIC, a user fills out a user profile form. The required information includes first and last name, age, and one or more subject terms. Subject terms are common search terms employed by the user. This information is stored in a database and retrieved during a user's search activity. Currently, our system only utilizes subject terms while capturing the remaining fields for future algorithm extensions.

The second method to collect UCM information utilizes search terms recorded by CiteSeer's user query logs. These logs were obtained from http://proc2.ist.psu.edu:90/data/ and include 8 compressed files totaling ~1.2 GB. We extracted user queries, grouping them by session id, to find terms that occurred within the same session. Next, we counted the frequency occurrence of a pair of terms and saved it along with the pair in QIC's CiteSeer co-occurrence database. The number of pairs of co-occurred terms is 27042. Table 1 shows the partial results of terms typed in queries containing the term 'java'.

Table 1. Sample data in QIC's CiteSeer co-occurrence table

Term 1	Term2	frequency
java	simulation	8
java	class	6
java	classes	6
java	code	6
java	development	5

We selected the CiteSeer logs because of the similarity between CiteSeer's document domain (computer science and information systems) and the document domain of the digital library we used in our experiment.

3.2 Query Phase

The query phase enables users to find personalized answers to a user's information needs by utilizing the UCM information. QIC's search components include query expansion, search and result ranking. In this paper, we focus on the query expansion module.

Query expansion incorporates relevant information from a user's context into an expanded query. As seen in Figure 1 there are five steps. The first four steps add terms based on extracted new information. A parallel step generates new terms returned to the user as suggestions. The details of these steps are as follows:

Step 1: Assign weight

The assign weight step breaks a user's query into its terms and examines two features, domain-specificity and Part-of-Speech (POS).

We assume words related to the domain of a digital library are the most useful to include in a search. For instance, if a query searching a library of computer science related resources uses the term 'database', the search engine should find documents containing this term and ignore documents that are missing it. Therefore, this step requires a domain-specific dictionary used to filter out words in the query not found in the dictionary.

The second feature analyzes a term's linguistic meaning, i.e., noun, verb, adjective, etc. Using parts-of-speech processing available in WordNet, we extract this information to determine a term weight. For instance, we give nouns a higher weight than adjectives, and we give no additional weight to verbs. The higher the weight given a term, the more significant it becomes when using QIC's results ranking module.

We set weights by trial and error. The left-most computing term found in the user query is assigned the highest weight of 2. Other computing nouns are set at 1.25. Adjectives found in the computing dictionary are set at 1.2. Any adjectives or nouns not found in the domain-specific dictionary are set at 1.15. Additional terms added during query expansion process are given a weight of 1. For instance, we assign weights to terms in the query "intro to functional programming with Scheme" as follows:

"intro"^1.15 "functional"^1.2 "programming"^2 "Scheme"^1.25

The first computer related term, 'programming', is given a weight of 2. 'intro' is not in the domain-specific dictionary so it is set to 1.15. Computer related terms 'functional' (an adjective) and 'scheme' (a noun) are set to 1.2 and 1.25, respectively.

Step 2: Expand Acronym

Next, we examined terms for acronyms. We replaced any acronyms found with the fully expanded term phrase. We utilized AcroMine for this task. It is an abbreviation dictionary that can be accessed through a web service interface [16]. For example, we expand 'SQL' to 'structured query language'. Other technical abbreviations include CPU (Central Processing Unit) and DBMS (DataBase Management System). Note, weights for abbreviations are always set to 1. We do not favor automatically added terms over explicitly specified user terms.

Step 3: Apply Concept Tuple

In this step, the system detects the query's named entities and uses this to build the best concept tuple for each named entity by Language Model based weighting [17]. A concept tuple contains three components, the concept, a description, and a class. The algorithm is as follows:

Input: user query
Output: expanded query
Method:
Given a query,
1. Tag the query with Conditional Random Field (CRF)-based Named Entity Recognizer (NER) tagger [18].
2. Break the query into chunks
3. For each chunk,
   Do
      If (the chunk contains a named entity), then do
         1. Extract named entity
         2. Search concept tuple index based on the name entity
         3. Rank search results based on Language Model based ranking algorithm
         4. Add the highest rank concept tuple to the expanded query
4. Return the expanded query.

Step 4: Apply User Profile

Next, the system enhances the user's profile database with the highest frequency term from the prebuilt CiteSeer database. It compares the enhanced profile with user's query to find the profile terms related to the current query using a semantic similarity score based on Jiang and Conrath's algorithm [19]. Our algorithm uses the noun portion of WordNet to compute the similarity. We add the term with a similarity score higher than our threshold to a list that is returned to the user as suggestions. Jiang and Conrath's algorithm was shown to have superior precision and the best overall in the performance of five proposed measures of semantic relatedness (Hirst and St-Onge, Leacock and Chodorow, Resnik, Jiang and Conrath and Lin) [20]. The algorithm combines a lexical taxonomy structure with corpus statistical information. It combines an edge-counting scheme with an information content scheme so the information content of the two nodes and their most specific subsumer (parent node) play a part in the calculation. The formula of the algorithm is as follows:

$$dist(c_1,c_2) = 2\log(p(lso(c_1,c_2)))-(\log(p(c_1)) + \log(p(c_2)))$$

where *lso* is the most specific common subsumer.

After calculating the similarity score, we present the profile term with the score higher than our threshold to the user as a suggested term. We set the threshold by trial and error to 0.11. This is the point that excludes irrelevant terms into the expand query.

Step 5: Apply CiteSeer

This step is retrieves the term in the CiteSeer database (described in the Pre-processing Phase) that occurs most frequently with the user query terms. For example, if the user query is 'java', then 'simulation' is included since it occurs the most frequently with 'java' as shown in Table 1. The search screen displays the terms added by this step to help the user refine their search.

Lastly, the results from steps 1, 3, and 4 are merged. During this process, we remove duplicated terms, display the new query to the user, and send it to QIC's search module for processing.

4. EVALUATION

In the initial experiments to evaluate QIC, we recruited 42 participants to compare the performance of QIC with the Ensemble Computing Pathway (ECP) [21], our baseline. ECP is a computer and information systems digital library used for educational purposes. The ECP dataset was obtained from the Ensemble OAI provider at http://figo.cc.vt.edu:8080/fedora3/oai. The collection contains 9901 documents although only 1918 documents provide an abstract (description). We indexed all documents using QIC. The fields used for search are title and abstract. We separated participants into two groups. The first group was asked to find documents related to 'java' while the second group was asked to find documents related to 'database'. We recorded users' queries in log files which we used to calculate precision and recall for the ECP system (baseline), the original semantic query expansion module for QIC (QIC) and our enhance version described in this paper (QIC with QE). Table 2 shows the precision and recall results for both tasks in the 3 systems.

Table 2. Precision and recall task results.

	JAVA Task		Database Task	
	Precision	**Recall**	**Precisio n**	**Recall**
QIC	0.029	0.128	0.122	0.355
QIC with QE	0.083	0.574	0.202	0.547
Baseline	0.049	0.287	0.006	0.160

Table 2 shows QIC with QE performs better than our baseline and the original QIC system for both tasks. Our query expansion enhancements show significantly higher precision and recall at statistical significance level of 0.01.

To gain a deeper understanding of which enhancements provided the greatest improvement in performance to QIC's query expansion module, we created two additional configurations of the Query Expansion module that were different from the original QIC system but did not contain all the features of the enhanced QIC with QE system. We chose to investigate the Apply User Profile step and Apply Concept Tuple step, which focus solely on personalization. The first configuration, QIC_QE_woap, is built without the Apply User Profile step (step 4). In the second configuration, QIC_QE_woct, we removed the Apply Concept Tuple step (step 3).

We reran the experiment using the same log files as the previous experiment. Figure 2 compares the new configurations to QIC with QE. We found the configuration without the Concept Tuples step performs the best. We suspect step 3 places unrelated terms into the expanded queries, decreasing precision and recall. This may be due to word sense ambiguity or limitations in the concept tuples set. Nevertheless, we plan to study this anomaly in the future. The precision and recall of the configuration without the Apply User Profile step is not much different from the QIC with QE because the terms from step 4 are not included in the query but presented to the user as suggestions.

Figure 2. QIC with QE vs. QIC with QE without the Apply Concept Tuples vs. QIC with QE without Apply Profile.

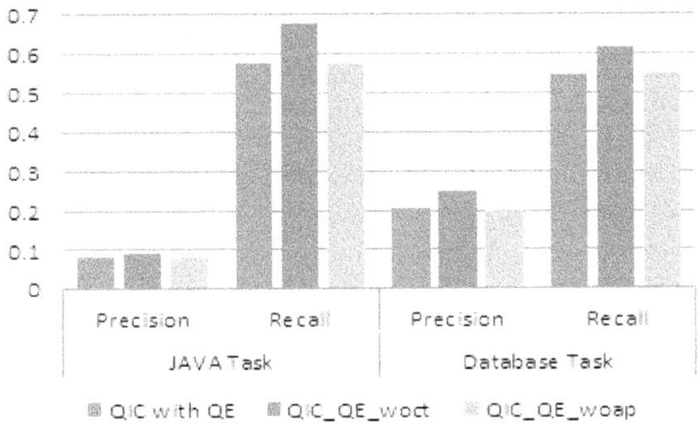

5. CONCLUSION

In this paper, we present a query expansion technique that improves individual search by utilizing contextual information. It incorporates user context to make an expanded query more relevant. We utilize users' interest indicated in their profile and semantically add related terms from CiteSeer logs. In addition, we analyze query terms based on their part-of-speech, position in the query and semantic. Our preliminary study shows that precision and recall of the system improve after integrating the new query expansion module.

Future work is planned to understand what user provided information influences search results. We also intend to explore other techniques to incorporate the semantic properties of terms in user queries. In addition, we plan to continue our investigation of the impact of applying concept tuples to improve search results.

6. ACKNOWLEDGEMENTS

Partial support for this research was provided by the National Science Foundation under grant DUE-1043647 and by the New Jersey Institute of Technology.

7. REFERENCES

[1] Jansen, B. J., Spink, A. and Saracevic, T. Real life, real users, and real needs: a study and analysis of user queries on the web. *Inf. Process. Manage.*, 36, 2 (2000), 207-227.

[2] Krovetz, R. and Croft, W. B. Lexical ambiguity and information retrieval. *ACM Trans. Inf. Syst.*, 10, 2, 115-141.

[3] Giles, C. L., Bollacker, K. D. and Lawrence, S. CiteSeer: an automatic citation indexing system. In *Proceedings of the third ACM conference on Digital libraries* (United States, 1998). ACM.

[4] Pitkow, J., Schütze, H., Cass, T., Cooley, R., Turnbull, D., Edmonds, A., Adar, E. and Breuel, T. Personalized Search. *Communications of the ACM*, 45, 9 (2002), 50-55.

[5] Lawrence, S. Context inWeb Search. *IEEE Data Engineering Bulletin*, 23, 3 (2000), 25-32.

[6] Cui, H., Wen, J.-R., Nie, J.-Y. and Ma, W.-Y. Query Expansion by Mining User Logs. *IEEE Transactions on Knowledge and Data Engineering*, 15, 4 (2003), 829-839.

[7] Chirita, P.-A., Firan, C. S. and Nejdl, W. Personalized Query Expansion for the Web. In *Proceedings of the SIGIR'07* (Amsterdam, The Netherlands, 2007). ACM.

[8] Zeng, C., Zheng, X., Xing, C. and Zhou, L. *Personalized Services for Digital Library*. Springer, 2002.

[9] Gentili, G., Micarelli, A. and Sciarrone, F. Infoweb: An Adaptive Information Filtering System for the Cultural Heritage Domain. *Applied Artificial Intelligence*, 17 (2003).

[10] Song, R., Wen, J.-R. and Ma, W.-Y. Viewing Term Proximity from a Different Perspective. In *Proceedings of the European Conference on IR Research* (Scotland, UK, 2008).

[11] Metzler, D. and Croft, W. B. A markov random field model for term dependencies. In *Proceedings of the SIGIR'05* (Salvador, Brazil, 2005).

[12] Metzler, D. and Croft, W. B. Latent concept expansion using markov random fields. In *Proceedings of the SIGIR'07* (Amsterdam, The Netherland, 2007). ACM.

[13] Gao, J., Nie, J.-Y., Wu, G. and Cao, G. Dependence language model for information retrieval. In *Proceedings of the SIGIR'04* (Sheffield, UK, 2004). ACM.

[14] Mena, E., Kashyap, V., Illarramendi, A. and Sheth, A. P. Imprecise answers in distributed environments: Estimation of information loss for multi-ontology based query processing. *International Journal of Cooperative Information Systems*, 9, 4 2000), 403-425.

[15] Bhogal, J., Macfarlane, A. and Smith, P. A review of ontology based query expansion. *Information Processing & Management*, 43, 4 2006), 866-886.

[16] Okazaki, N. and Ananiadou, S. Building an abbreviation dictionary using a term recognition approach. *Bioinformatics*, 22, 24 2006), 3089-3095.

[17] Ponte, J. M. and Croft, W. B. A language modeling approach to information retrieval. In *Proceedings of the 21st annual international ACM SIGIR* (Melbourne, Australia, 1998). ACM.

[18] McCallum, A. and Li, W. Early results for named entity recognition with conditional random fields, feature induction and web-enhanced lexicons. In *Proceedings of the seventh conference on Natural language learning at HLT-NAACL 2003 - Volume 4* (Edmonton, Canada, 2003).

[19] Jiang, J. J. and Conrath, D. W. Semantic Similarity Based on Corpus Statistics and Lexical Taxonomy. In *Proceedings of the International Conference Research on Computational Linguistics* (Taiwan, 1997).

[20] Budanitsky, A. and Hirst, G. Evaluating WordNet-based Measures of Lexical Semantic Relatedness. *Comput. Linguist.*, 32, 1 2006), 13-47.

[21] Hislop, G. W., Cassel, L., Delcambre, L., Fox, E., Furuta, R. and Brusilovsky, P. Ensemble: creating a national digital library for computing education. In *Proceedings of the Proceedings of the 10th ACM conference on SIG-information technology education* (Fairfax, Virginia, USA, 2009). ACM.

Investigating Keyphrase Indexing with Text Denoising

Rushdi Shams
rshams@csd.uwo.ca

Robert E. Mercer
mercer@csd.uwo.ca

Department of Computer Science
University of Western Ontario
London, ON N6A 5B7, Canada

ABSTRACT

In this paper, we report on indexing performance by a state-of-the-art keyphrase indexer, Maui, when paired with a text extraction procedure called *text denoising*. Text denoising is a method that extracts the denoised text, comprising the content-rich sentences, from full texts. The performance of the keyphrase indexer is demonstrated on three standard corpora collected from three domains, namely food and agriculture, high energy physics, and biomedical science. Maui is trained using the full texts and denoised texts. The indexer, using its trained models, then extracts keyphrases from test sets comprising full texts, and their denoised and noise parts (i.e., the part of texts that remains after denoising). Experimental findings show that against a gold standard, the denoised-text-trained indexer indexing full texts, performs either better than or as good as its benchmark performance produced by a full-text-trained indexer indexing full texts.

Categories and Subject Descriptors

H.3.1 [**Information Storage and Retrieval**]: Content Analysis and Indexing—*Indexing method*

General Terms

Experimentation, Performance.

Keywords

Keyphrase indexing, text denoising, Maui, fog index.

1. INTRODUCTION

Today, most of the automatic indexers use supervised full-text classifiers to extract keyphrases from full texts [2][5][7][10]. Maui [5] is the final successor of a legacy of keyphrase indexers and inherits from and builds upon both of its predecessors KEA [10] and KEA++ [7]. To extract keyphrases from test documents, Maui uses 13 features to develop its supervised classifier. However, a revealing experiment by Witten *et al.* [10] demonstrates that indexer performances depend not only on the set of features but also on document size. As they apply their full-text trained KEA on paper abstracts and compare against a gold standard, they find its performance on these reduced texts somewhat inferior and not competitive to that on full texts. Although Maui outperforms its predecessors to extract full-text keyphrases from food and agriculture, nuclear physics, and biomedical science texts [5], it has not been tested with a reduced set of texts till date.

Text Denoising is a method proposed by Shams and Mercer [9] which reduces the amount of text in biomedical papers to 30% of the original. The authors suggested that the describing of biomedical relations lengthens sentences and increases the use of polysyllabic words. Some readability indexes, the Fog Index [3] in particular, are based on these two factors. They proceeded to use Fog Index to measure sentence readability and showed experimentally that the 30% of the sentences which had the lowest-readability, the denoised part of a text, contained the relations of interest. The rest is termed as *noise text* that are not as content-rich as denoised text.

In this paper, we report on the performance of a state-of-the-art keyphrase indexer named Maui [5] when paired with text denoising. We use three standard full-text corpora from the food and agriculture, nuclear physics, and biomedical science domains. From each corpus, we develop training sets comprising full texts and their denoised parts. The test sets are composed of full texts, and their denoised and noise parts. For training and testing each dataset, we use a standard 10-fold cross validation. We show experimentally that a 70% text denoising improves Maui's indexing performance. To evaluate Maui, we use quantitative measures like precision, recall and F-score, as well as qualitative measures like inter-indexer agreements. Experimental results show that Maui, trained with denoised texts, performs either better or comparably to its benchmark performance—those with full-text trained models to extract keyphrases from full-text test sets. Further details about this paper can be found in its full version at `arXiv:1204.2231v1 [cs.DL]`.

The remainder of this paper discusses the methods for training and testing the indexer (Section 2), an analysis of the results (Section 3), and ends with some concluding remarks (Section 4).

2. METHODOLOGY

In this section, we describe the datasets, training and testing procedure, performance measures, and the means to find

JCDL'12, June 10–14, 2012, Washington, DC, USA.

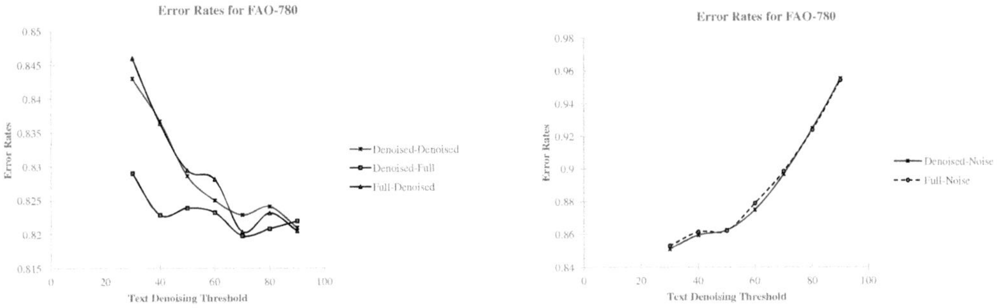

(a) (b)

Figure 1: Error rates for different denoising thresholds with FAO-780 (a) denoised texts and (b) noise texts

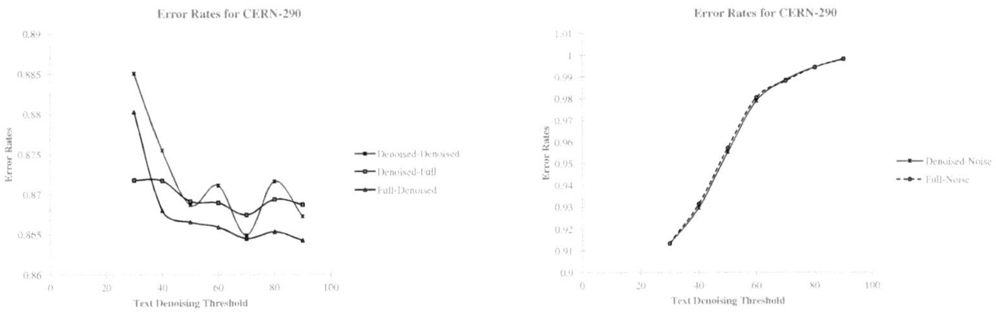

(a) (b)

Figure 2: Error rates for different denoising thresholds with CERN-290 (a) denoised texts and (b) noise texts

the appropriate text denoising threshold for keyphrase indexing.

2.1 Datasets

To train and test Maui, we use three standard corpora of full texts and keyphrases associated with them. Among the datasets are FAO-780 which comprises 780 full texts from food and agriculture; CERN-290 which is composed of 290 high energy physics documents; and NLM-500 which has 500 biomedical research articles. The details about these datasets can be found in the doctoral thesis by Medelyan [5].

2.2 Training and Testing

In this experiment, we use a conventional stratified k-fold experimental approach set by Medelyan [5] except that we train Maui not only on full texts but also on their denoised parts and test it on full texts as well as their denoised and noise parts. We consider the full texts along with their denoised and noise parts from each dataset and divide them randomly into 10 equal-sized folds without overlap. We train Maui on the training sets comprising full texts and denoised texts from each fold. The models that the indexers develop from full texts are called *full-text trained models* and those that are developed from denoised texts are called *denoised-text trained models*. The indexer then applies these models, k-th full-text trained model and k-th denoised text trained model, to extract keyphrases from the k-th test set composed of full texts, and their denoised and noise parts. According to the average number of keyphrases in every document, we had the indexers extract 8 keyphrases, 7 keyphrases, and 15 keyphrases for each document in the FAO-780, CERN-290, and NLM-500 test sets, respectively. The extracted keyphrases are then compared against a gold standard which are the author-assigned keyphrases associated with the test documents.

2.3 Performance Measures

In this experiment, as well as conventional quantitative performance measures like precision, recall and F-score, we use three inter-indexing agreement measures popularly used for qualitative indexing assessment [6], namely Hooper's (H) [4], Rolling's (R) [8] and Cosine (C) inter-indexing agreements. The closer the agreement measures are to 1, the more the indexers agree on extracted keyphrases. We also calculate the error rates for each cross validation to find a text denoising threshold described in Section 2.4 and measure a *10-fold cross validated paired t-test* [1] to report statistical significance of Maui's indexing when paired with denoised texts. For any two given sets of results, we consider their error rates to calculate a paired t-value. If this calculated t-value lies outside ± 2.26 with a degree of freedom 9, then the difference between the set whose results have the lower error rate and the other set is said to be statistically significant at significance level $\alpha = 0.05$.

2.4 Text Denoising Threshold

To find the appropriate text denoising threshold for keyphrase indexing, we evaluate Maui's performance on each dataset by increasing the text denoising threshold in increments of 10% from 30% to 90%. As we vary the threshold, we plot the error rates of Maui on different test sets. Being a supervised indexer, Maui's best-fit model should be where the test error has its global minimum. That point eventually will also be the denoising threshold.

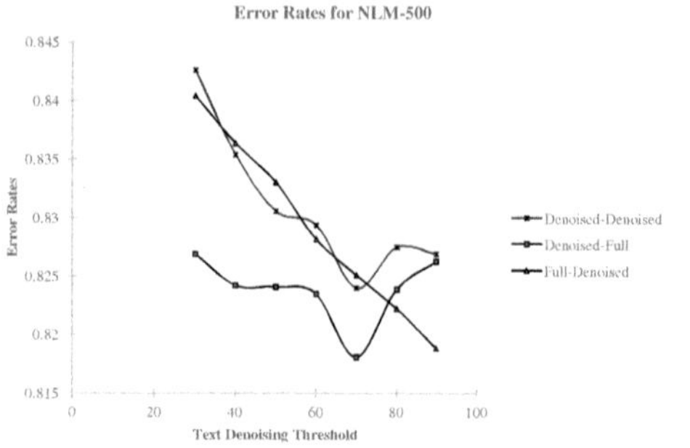

(a)

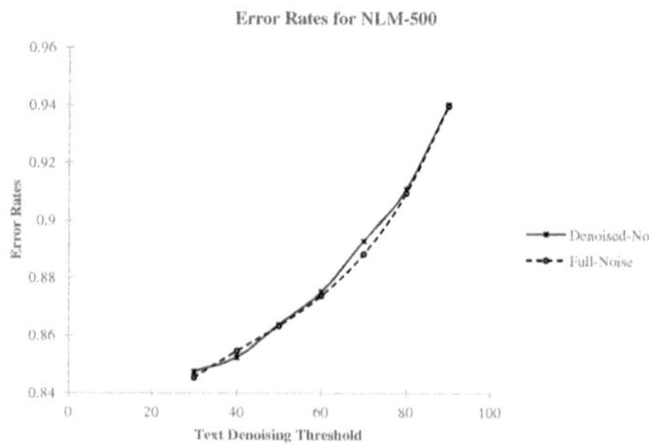

(b)

Figure 3: Error rates for different denoising thresholds with NLM-500 (a) denoised texts and (b) noise texts

					Benchmark Performance			
Trained Model	Test Set	Precision	Recall	F-score	Precision	Recall	F-score	t value
Denoised Text	Denoised Text	30.02	32.92	31.36	30.56	33.47	31.86	2.23
Denoised Text	**Full Text**	**30.49**	**33.50**	**31.87**				**2.76**
Full Text	Denoised Text	30.48	32.96	31.63				1.81

(a) Maui's performance on FAO-780 dataset with denoising level of 70% of each text

					Benchmark Performance			
Trained Model	Test Set	Precision	Recall	F-score	Precision	Recall	F-score	t value
Denoised Text	Denoised Text	24.38	25.33	24.79	24.58	25.56	24.99	2.16
Denoised Text	Full Text	23.99	24.95	24.42				2.26
Full Text	Denoised Text	24.38	25.40	24.82				1.31

(b) Maui's performance on CERN-290 dataset with denoising level of 70% of each text

					Benchmark Performance			
Trained Model	Test Set	Precision	Recall	F-score	Precision	Recall	F-score	t value
Denoised Text	Denoised Text	29.14	32.36	30.66	29.69	32.74	31.13	2.01
Denoised Text	**Full Text**	**29.96**	**33.22**	**31.50**				**3.52**
Full Text	Denoised Text	28.99	32.00	30.40				1.85

(c) Maui's performance on NLM-500 dataset with denoising level of 70% of each text

Table 1: Precision, recall and F-score of Maui with text denoising

The error rates for different denoising thresholds for FAO-780 are plotted in Figure 1. It is notable that for both trained models, Maui has its global minimum at 70% denoising (Figure 1a). From this point on, the error rate increases and thus indicates an overfitting in Maui's models. Figure 1 shows that Maui's best performing pair is *Denoised-Full*—those models that are trained with denoised texts for keyphrase extraction from full texts. Similarly, Maui's best-fitted models with denoised texts for CERN-290 and NLM-500 are also at the 70% threshold (Figure 2a and 3a). Figure 1b, 2b, and 3b, on the other hand, show that the error rate for the noise test sets increases. This indicates that noise texts are less content-rich as Maui fails to extract a substantial number of keyphrases from them. These observations lead us to set the denoising threshold at 70%. At this threshold, Maui predicts keyphrases from unseen test examples most accurately.

3. RESULTS AND DISCUSSIONS

In this section, we discuss the performance of Maui with text denoising and compare this with its benchmark performance—full-text trained model on full texts.

Table 1a compares the precision, recall and F-score of Maui with denoised texts and its benchmark performance on the FAO-780 dataset. Maui, using its denoised-text and full-text trained models on denoised text test sets, achieves F-scores of 31.36 and 31.63, respectively, compared to its benchmark F-score of 31.86. We see that for these two cases, the t-values are 2.23 and 1.81, respectively, which means that the differences between the F-scores are not statistically significant. In other words, the benchmark performance of Maui cannot be said to be different than that with text denoising. On the other hand, Maui's F-score with its denoised text trained model on full-text keyphrase extraction is 31.87 with a t-value of 2.76. So, with 98% confidence we can say that the result is better than the benchmark performance. In addition, from Table 2a, we can see that Maui's agreements with the gold standards are as good as the benchmark agreements. This demonstrates that the indexing quality of Maui has not been compromised with text denoising.

For the CERN-290 dataset, although Maui could not outperform its benchmark F-score of 24.99, none of the t-values are significant at $\alpha = 0.05$. In other words, its performance with denoised texts cannot be said to be different than its benchmark performance with a 95% confidence level (Table 1b). Interestingly enough, although Maui agrees less with the gold standard for the CERN-290 dataset than that for FAO-780, its agreements on keyphrases with denoised texts are as good as its benchmark performance (Table 2b).

					Benchmark Performance		
Trained Model	Test Set	Hooper	Rolling	Cosine	Hooper	Rolling	Cosine
Denoised Text	Denoised Text	0.18	0.29	0.30	0.18	0.30	0.31
Denoised Text	**Full Text**	**0.18**	**0.30**	**0.31**			
Full Text	Denoised Text	0.18	0.30	0.30			

(a) Maui's indexing agreements on FAO-780 dataset with denoising level of 70% of each text

					Benchmark Performance		
Trained Model	Test Set	Hooper	Rolling	Cosine	Hooper	Rolling	Cosine
Denoised Text	Denoised Text	0.14	0.24	0.24	0.14	0.24	0.24
Denoised Text	Full Text	0.14	0.24	0.24			
Full Text	Denoised Text	0.14	0.24	0.24			

(b) Maui's indexing agreements on CERN-290 dataset with denoising level of 70% of each text

					Benchmark Performance		
Trained Model	Test Set	Hooper	Rolling	Cosine	Hooper	Rolling	Cosine
Denoised Text	Denoised Text	0.18	0.30	0.30	0.18	0.30	0.31
Denoised Text	**Full Text**	**0.19**	**0.31**	**0.31**			
Full Text	Denoised Text	0.18	0.30	0.30			

(c) Maui's indexing agreements on NLM-500 dataset with denoising level of 70% of each text

Table 2: Inter-indexing agreements of Maui with text denoising

Maui's best performance for the NLM-500 corpus is with a denoised text trained model on full texts. Its F-score of 31.50 outperforms the benchmark F-score of 31.13 at the significance level of $\alpha = 0.05$. However, although its other two F-scores with denoised texts is somewhat lower than its benchmark F-score, they are not statistically significant with t-values of 2.01 and 1.85 (Table 1c). Maui's inter-indexing agreement on NLM-500 is somewhat similar to that on FAO-780 except that it agrees more with NLM-500 gold standards than its benchmark performance (Table 2c).

4. CONCLUSIONS

In this paper, we show that a 70% text denoising improves Maui's performance for the biomedical science texts, or it allows Maui to perform as good as its benchmark performance on the food and agriculture, and the physics texts. Although there are some cases where Maui, when paired with text denoising, experiences marginally lower F-score than its benchmark, indexing agreement measures show that its indexing quality has never been compromised; it extracts even better quality keyphrases from biomedical texts than its benchmark. From the experimental findings, we also can conclude that document size, per se, does not have the suggested effect on keyphrase indexing, rather it is the content richness that plays the key role in indexing. We leave the investigation on the effect of text denoising paired with other indexers as future work.

5. ACKNOWLEDGMENTS

This work was partially funded through a Natural Sciences and Engineering Research Council of Canada (NSERC) Discovery Grant to Robert E. Mercer. Thanks are due to Olena Medelyan and Ian H. Witten for providing the datasets and Maui, and their remarks on experiment setup and results.

6. REFERENCES

[1] E. Alpaydin. Assessing and comparing classification algorithms. In *Introduction to Machine Learning*, pages 342–343. The MIT Press, Cambridge, UK, 2004.

[2] K. Frantzi, S. Ananiadou, and J. Tsujii. The c-value/nc-value method of automatic recognition for multi-word terms. In *Proceedings of the 2nd European Conference on Research and Advanced Technology for Digital Libraries (ECDL'98)*, pages 585–604, London, UK, 1998.

[3] R. Gunning. Fog index after twenty years. *Journal of Business Communication*, 6:3–13, 1969.

[4] R. S. Hooper. Indexer consistency tests: Origin, measurements, results and utilization. *IBM, Bethesda*, 1965.

[5] O. Medelyan. *Human-competitive automatic topic indexing*. PhD thesis, University of Waikato, New Zealand, 2009.

[6] O. Medelyan and I. Witten. Measuring inter-indexer consistency using a thesaurus. In *Proceedings of the 6th ACM/IEEE-CS Joint Conference on Digital libraries (JCDL-2006)*, pages 274–275, NC, USA, 2006. ACM Press.

[7] O. Medelyan and I. Witten. Domain-independent automatic keyphrase indexing with small training sets. *Journal of the American Society for Information Science and Technology (JASIST)*, 59:1026–1040, 2008.

[8] L. Rolling. Indexing consistency, quality and efficiency. *Information Processing and Management*, 17:69–76, 1981.

[9] R. Shams and R. E. Mercer. Extracting connected concepts from biomedical texts using fog index. *Procedia - Social and Behavioral Sciences*, 27:70 – 76, 2011. Elsevier Science.

[10] I. Witten, G. Paynter, E. Frank, C. Gutwin, and C. Nevill-Manning. Kea: Practical automatic keyphrase extraction. In *Proceedings of the 4th ACM conference on Digital Libraries*, pages 254–255. ACM Press, 1999.

Exploiting Real-Time Information Retrieval in the Microblogosphere

Feng Liang
liangfeng@pku.edu.cn

Runwei Qiang
qiangrw@gmail.com

Jianwu Yang*
yangjw@pku.edu.cn

Institute of Computer Science and Technology
Peking University,Beijing 100871,China

ABSTRACT

Information seeking behavior in microblogging environments such as Twitter differs from traditional web search. The best performing microblog retrieval techniques attempt to utilize both semantic and temporal aspects of documents. In this paper, we present an effective approach, including the query modeling, the document modeling and the temporal re-ranking, to discover the most recent but relevant information to the query. For the query modeling, we introduce a two-stage pseudo-relevance feedback query expansion to overcome the severe vocabulary-mismatch problem of short message retrieval in microblog. For the document modeling, we propose two ways to expand document with the help of the shortened URL. For the temporal re-ranking, we suggest several methods to evaluate the temporal aspects of documents. Experimental results demonstrate that our approach obtains significant improvements compared with baseline systems. Specifically, the proposed system gives 26.37% and 9.94% further increases in P@30 and MAP over the best performing result on *highrel* in the TREC'11 Real-Time Search Task.

Categories and Subject Descriptors

H.3.3 [**Information Search and Retrieval**]: Information Search and Retrieval—*Retrieval models*

General Terms

Algorithms, Experimentation, Performance

Keywords

Real-Time Search, Query Expansion, Language Model, Temporal Search

*Corresponding author.

1. INTRODUCTION

Microblog is a light-weight, easy form of communication that enables users to broadcast and share information about their activities, opinions and statuses [10]. Microblog is provided by several internet services such as Twitter[1], Facebook[2] and Tumblr[3]. One of the most popular microblogging platforms is Twitter [18]. A microblog consists of individual posts and in Twitter, particularly, a user's post is called tweet. In Twitter, text is strictly under the length limitation of 140 characters. To enrich the information in Twitter, users usually post a shortened URL within a tweet. Besides, a tweet includes a group of well-defined symbols: RT denotes retweet, '@' followed by a user's screen name stands for mentioning or replying to the specific user, '#' symbol (i.e. hashtag) is used for organizing tweets into a particular topic.

User's information need for microblog is expressed in semantic and temporal aspects. For the semantic aspect, user specifies a small number of keywords as a query to search tweets, saying from this perspective, user wants to obtain a list of relevant tweets. However, for the temporal aspect,the same query with different timestamps may result in different retrieval results. For instance, when a user issued the query "Kubica crash" at the very beginning of a high-speed rally crash in Italy, he may just want to check whether this news is true. As time passes by, a burst of tweets were posted, and user entered the same query to keep informed of this accident, e.g. how badly Kubica was injured. Finally, as the number of tweets about this accident decreased, user typed the same query to review the whole story of this incident. This implies that temporal profile may be helpful for expressing user's information need in the microblogosphere. From this perspective, user would like to seek the most recent tweets.

To explore the information seeking behavior in microblogging environments, TREC introduced a novel pilot task named Real-Time Search Task (RTST) at the TREC'11 Microblog Track, aiming to "find the most recent but relevant information to the query" [17]. The real-time search task can be summarized as "*At time t, find tweets about topic X*". This task is akin to ad-hoc search on Twitter, where a user's information need is represented by a query at a specific time.

Some new characteristics keep RTST distinctive from previous ad-hoc tasks such as Web Ad-hoc Search. First, we

[1]http://twitter.com
[2]http://www.facebook.com
[3]http://www.tumblr.com/

are supposed not to use all the data in the corpus but only to take advantage of information available at the time the query is issued. Therefore, systems for RTST should build a dynamic dataset for each query. Second, RTST is confronted with the difficulties posed by the severe vocabulary-mismatch problem rooted in the sparsity of documents (i.e. tweets). For this reason, expansion techniques should be applied to enrich the representation of query and document. Third, participants are required to rank the returned tweets by timestamp instead of by relevance score. Hence, we should make a trade off between relevance and recentness, otherwise, re-ranking by time will sharply decrease the search effectiveness.

To solve these challenges,we present an effective approach that can improve the performance of the proposed system for RTST. The main contributions of this paper are: (1) we describe a two-stage pseudo-relevance feedback query expansion to estimate a query language model. (2) we propose two ways to expand document with the help of shortened URL to enrich the representation of document. (3) we suggest several temporal re-ranking functions and two representations of temporal profile to evaluate the temporal aspects of documents. In a set of experiments performed over TREC'11 Real-Time Search Task test collection, we compare the proposed system against both the baseline systems and the best performing systems in the TREC'11 RTST, and the experimental results demonstrate that the proposed approach delivers a significant retrieval performance.

The remainder of paper is organized as follows: In Section 2, we give an overview of related work. In Section 3, we introduce the framework of our system, and the proposed methods to search information in the microblogosphere in detail. In Section 4, we conduct a series of experiments and evaluate the performance of the proposed methods. Finally, in Section 5, we conclude the paper and outline our future work.

2. RELATED WORK

As a new pilot task, RTST aims to retrieve information in real-time environment, and to provide a ranked list of tweets from the latest timestamp to the earliest timestamp. There are few research findings for ad-hoc search in the microblogosphere. Three most relevant research topics to our work are pseudo-relevance feedback query expansion, sentence retrieval and temporal aspects analysis in IR and TDT.

Pseudo-relevance feedback technique has been widely used in various retrieval models [21, 19, 22, 2, 20, 11, 25]. In the past few years, several attempts have been made in developing pseudo-relevance feedback in language model framework [11, 25, 14, 23]. In the mixture-model feedback [25], words in feedback documents were supposed to be sampled from two models: (1) background language model and (2) to-be-discovered topic model. The mixture-model feedback revealed that background language model is reasonable of irrelevant information in feedback document while topic model is responsible for generating topically related words. The expanded query was then updated by incorporating original query model with topic model. Relevance model [11] improved query language model by first computing the joint probability of observing a word together with words in original query in a single feedback document and then summing the evidence over all the document set. Finally, documents were weighted by query likelihood $P(Q|D)$ and probability of word given by each document language model.

Both Sentence Retrieval (SR) and RTST suffer severely from the vocabulary-mismatch problem [8] because there is little overlap between the query and document terms. There was some previous work that exploits local context to enrich the representation of document (i.e. sentence) [8, 16, 13]. Losada and Fernándz's work [13] informally introduced the local context of a sentence into the computation of sentence similarity. Essentially, terms that have high frequency in the associated documents were assigned an extra weight. Murdock [16] estimated sentence language model by utilizing some local context and combing them with evidence from the sentence and document level.

Previous work has shown that temporal evidence can be incorporated into IR techniques [5, 7], particularly in the language model framework [12]. Li and Croft proposed taking advantage of the publish date of news articles under an exponential distribution to estimate the document prior [12]. Dakka, Gravano and Iperirotis suggested that the standard query likelihood framework should take time into consideration [5]. They divided a given document into two components: (1) lexical terms in document and (2) timestamp of document. Moreover, temporal evidence was also used in New Event Detection Task in TDT [3, 4]. Chen et al proposed an aging theory to improve the performance for event detection [3]. Chen et al also used the aging theory combined with a sentence modeling to extract hot topics from news articles [4].

To our knowledge, (1) two-stage pseudo-relevance feedback query expansion using different estimations of query model in each stage has not been previously seen; (2) document expansion by refining the representation of tweet with the shortened URLs has not been described previously; (3) the two representations of temporal profile described in this paper is novel but effective to estimate the temporal aspects of documents in the microblogosphere.

3. REAL-TIME TWEET RANKING MODEL

To mine valuable information in the microblogosphere, we rank tweets by evaluating their importance to the given query at a specific timestamp. We conclude several criteria to estimate the importance of a tweet as follows:

- **Accuracy** Tweets that are accurate to feed user's information need are important.
- **Abundance** A high-quality URL within the tweet can enrich the representation of tweet, thus to improve the importance.
- **Timeliness** Tweets that were posted an hour ago are often more worthy than those that were updated a day before even though the former are not as much accurate as the latter.
- **Significance** A tweet that has been re-tweeted a lot of times or shared by some key users in the social network would spread fast in the microblogosphere, as a result, its importance would be increased.
- **Trend** People mentioned via '@' symbol and topics that tweets are organized into through '#' symbol also affect the importance of tweets.

Considering the lack of some crucial metadata such as user's profile in the HTML version of Tweet11 Corpus [17], we determine to adopt the first three criteria to measure the importance of a tweet. We assume that a tweet satisfies the criteria well when it occurs near the query timestamp and, at the same time, receives a high relevance score with respect to the query.

Motivated by our assumption, we propose our real-time tweet ranking model under the language model framework which is widely used in various IR tasks. Given the RTST problem, the proposed approach is to estimate the probability of generating a query Q given the content D and timestamp t of the tweet as follows:

$$P(Q|D,t) = \frac{P(t|Q,D) \cdot P(Q|D)}{P(t|D)} \tag{1}$$

Assuming that $P(Q|D) \propto Score(Q,D)$ which can be calculated using KL-divergence retrieval model [24], and that $P(t|D)$ can be assumed as a constant because it is query-independent, we rewrite the ranking formula as follows:

$$\begin{aligned} P(Q|D,t) &\propto P(t|Q,D) \cdot P(Q|D) \\ &\propto P(t|Q,D) \cdot Score(Q,D) \\ &= P(t|Q,D) \cdot \sum_{w \in V} P(w|\hat{\theta}_Q) \cdot \log P(w|\hat{\theta}_D) \end{aligned} \tag{2}$$

With the ranking formula, the retrieval task is reduced to three subtasks, i.e. the estimation of query model $\hat{\theta}_Q$, the estimation of document model $\hat{\theta}_D$ and the temporal re-ranking component $P(t|Q,D)$, respectively.

3.1 The Estimation of Query Model

Thanks to the flexibility that KL-divergence retrieval model offers, we can reformulate query model $\hat{\theta}_Q$ by taking pseudo-relevance feedback information into account. Much like most of pseudo-relevance feedback (PRF) approaches do, we consider the top-ranked document, which we call the support tweet, to expand the original query. However, the main difference between previous PRF methods and our approach derives that we employ a two-stage PRF query expansion with the help of the support tweet to estimate different feedback models in each stage. The motivations of our two-stage PRF query expansion can be concluded as follows:

- User tends to express a single topic in one document(i.e. tweet), due to the 140-character length limitation in Twitter. Hence, a single tweet can be utilized to generate accurate topical words to expand the original query.
- Top-ranked document set can enrich the feedback information, but may include noisy topics due to the severe vocabulary-mismatch problem in the initial retrieval. Therefore, relevant information should be discriminated from the irrelevant one in the pseudo-relevant document set.

Inspired by the motivations, we employ our two-stage PRF query expansion in the following steps: (1) In the first stage, we pick up a single support tweet to generate accurate topical words, helping to mitigate the vocabulary-mismatch problem for better initial retrieval results. (2) In the second stage, we obtain top-ranked documents as support tweet set and distill the relevant content of the support tweet set by implementing the model-based approach [25].

Technically, we employ the two-stage PRF query expansion under the language model framework. Specially, let $\hat{\theta}_Q$ be the original query model, $\hat{\theta}_{PRF_1}$ be the first-stage feedback model estimated based on the single support tweet. Then, we define our first-stage updated query model $\hat{\theta}_{Q'}$ after the first-stage query expansion as follows:

$$P(w|\hat{\theta}_{Q'}) = (1-\alpha) \cdot P(w|\hat{\theta}_Q) + \alpha \cdot P(w|\hat{\theta}_{PRF_1}) \tag{3}$$

where $\alpha \in [0,1]$ is a parameter to control the amount of first-stage feedback.

To select the single support tweet for the first-stage query expansion, we first obtain ζ top-ranked tweets (we set ζ as 10 in our experiments) retrieved by the original query, then pick the single support tweet from ζ tweets with the following three strategies: (1) the tweet with the earliest timestamp(**ET**). (2) the tweet with the latest timestamp(**LT**). (3) the tweet assigned with the highest score according to its similarity with respect to the query(**HS**).

After selecting the single support tweet T_s, we can estimate $\hat{\theta}_{Q'}$ with the combination of $\hat{\theta}_Q$ and $\hat{\theta}_{PRF_1}$ linearly. Adopting the unigram language model, we intuitively estimate the $\hat{\theta}_Q$ according to the maximum likelihood estimator. Recall that T_s is assumed to generate accurate topical words, and that first-stage feedback aims at improving the initial ranking quality thus to produce reliable support tweet set for second-stage feedback, we estimate the $\hat{\theta}_{PRF_1}$ using the same distribution that $\hat{\theta}_Q$ follows. Thus, we have:

$$P(w|\hat{\theta}_Q) = \frac{c(w,Q)}{\sum_{w' \in V} c(w',Q)} = \frac{c(w,Q)}{|Q|} \tag{4}$$

$$P(w|\hat{\theta}_{PRF_1}) = \frac{c(w,T_s)}{\sum_{w' \in V} c(w',T_s)} = \frac{c(w,T_s)}{|T_s|} \tag{5}$$

where $c(w,Q)$, $c(w,T_s)$ mean the count of term w in Q and T_s, respectively, $|Q|$ and $|T_s|$ is the length of query and the single support tweet.

Then, the modified query $\hat{\theta}_{Q'}$ can be further updated in the second-stage PRF query expansion. Let $F = \{t_1, t_2, ..., t_k\}$ be the pseudo-relevant document set, k is the size of the F which is set as 5 in our experiments, $\hat{\theta}_{PRF_{set}}$ be a feedback model based on F, and $P(\cdot|C)$ be the collection model. Finally, the query model $\hat{\theta}_{Q''}$ after the second-stage PRF query expansion is estimated as follows:

$$P(w|\hat{\theta}_{Q''}) = (1-\beta) \cdot P(w|\hat{\theta}_{Q'}) + \beta \cdot P(w|\hat{\theta}_{PRF_{set}}) \tag{6}$$

where $\beta \in [0,1]$ is a weighting parameter to control the amount of second-stage feedback.

To estimate $\hat{\theta}_{PRF_{set}}$, we implement the model-based feedback approach [25]. The model-based feedback approach helps to purify the document by eliminating some background noise and concentrates on words that are common in the support tweet set. In the approach, the log-likelihood function for the support tweet set is:

$$\begin{aligned} \log P(F|\hat{\theta}_{PRFset}) = \sum_i \sum_w c(w,t_i) \cdot \\ \log((1-\lambda) \cdot P(w|\hat{\theta}_{PRFset}) + \lambda \cdot P(w|C)) \end{aligned} \tag{7}$$

where $c(w,t_i)$ is the count of word w in tweet t_i. Then we implement the EM algorithm [6] with the fixed smoothing parameter $\lambda = 0.5$ as follows:

$$P^{(n)}(z_w = 1) = \frac{(1-\lambda)P^{(n)}(w|\hat{\theta}_{PRF_{set}})}{(1-\lambda)P^{(n)}(w|\hat{\theta}_{PRF_{set}}) + \lambda p(w|C)} \quad (8)$$

$$P^{(n+1)}(w|\hat{\theta}_{PRF_{set}}) = \frac{\sum_{i=1}^{k} c(w, t_i)P^{(n)}(z_w = 1)}{\sum_u \sum_{i=1}^{k} c(u, t_i)P^{(n)}(z_u = 1)} \quad (9)$$

Overall, we have our query model with two-stage PRF query expansion as follows:

$$P(w|\hat{\theta}_{Q''}) = (1-\beta)\cdot\{(1-\alpha)\cdot P(w|\hat{\theta}_Q) + \alpha\cdot P(w|\hat{\theta}_{PRF_1})\} + \beta\cdot P(w|\hat{\theta}_{PRF_{set}}) \quad (10)$$

3.2 The Estimation of Document Model

The 140-character length limitation in Twitter makes shortened links popular when users update their statuses. URLs within tweets always aim at tracking breaking news stories, recommending interesting video clips and brand marketing [9]. Through clicking a high-quality external link, users can browse a topic-related web page to learn more details about the issues talked in the tweet. Thus, expanding tweets by leveraging external links can enrich the representation of the to-be-retrieved document.

Effective information of the web page that the external link directs to should be extracted to help expand the original tweet. Considering that web information extraction is a challenging task and it is usually domain-dependent, we employ a quick but effective method to extract the topic information from the given URL as follows: (1) we convert the shortened URL to the original long URL through the LongURL web service[4]. (2) we identify the substantive part of domain name in the original URL as the URL keyword (e.g. *cnn* in *www.cnn.com*). (3) we extract text embedded in the <*TITLE*> tag from the raw HTML markup. (4) we split the extracted text by common separator (e.g. '_', '|','-') and discard the substring that contains the URL keyword. For instance, we obtain "BBC News - Egypt blames Gaza group for Alexandria church bombing" from the URL *http://www.bbc.co.uk/news/world-middle-east-12261668* after step (3), then we divide it into two parts: "Egypt blames Gaza group for Alexandria church bombing" and "BBC News", finally we omit the second part which contains the URL keyword "bbc" and take "Egypt blames Gaza group for Alexandria church bombing" as the topic information of the web page that the corresponding URL directs to.

To estimate the document model, we propose two methods under the language model framework by incorporating topic information of the corresponding URL into the original tweet.

3.2.1 Topic Information as Local Context

In the first method, we consider the topic information as the local context of the tweet to estimate a new document model (i.e. LocCtxt document model). Specially, for a tweet T with a URL L, we posit that the topic information I of the corresponding L is supposed to be posted next to T but actually, it is not due to the length limitation in Twitter. Through "translating" L to I, we can include the context of T and refine the representation of T consequently. To summarize, we merge T and I to form a new document D and estimate the document language model using Dirichlet Smoothing [24] with collection language model $P(\cdot|C)$:

$$P(w|\hat{\theta}_D) = \frac{c(w, D) + \mu P(w|C)}{|D| + \mu} \quad (11)$$

where $|D| = |T \bigcup I|$ is the text length of the new document, $c(w, D)$ means the number of term w appearing in the new document D, μ is a smoothing parameter to control the amount of $P(\cdot|C)$.

3.2.2 Topic Information as External Resource

Except for considering the topic information I as the local context of the tweet T, we also utilize the topic information extracted from web pages as external resources. We first collect all URLs in the Tweet11 corpus and then obtain the corresponding topic information to generate a so-called **TopicInfo** corpus. Therefore, the original document model $\hat{\theta}_T$ is smoothed using linear incorporation with the topic information model $\hat{\theta}_I$ estimated based on TopicInfo corpus. The ExRes document model $\hat{\theta}_D$ is estimated as follows:

$$P(w|\hat{\theta}_D) = (1-\eta)\cdot P(w|\hat{\theta}_T) + \eta\cdot P(w|\hat{\theta}_I) \quad (12)$$

where $\eta \in [0, 1]$ is the smoothing parameter. Note that only the tweet which has URL(s) can receive an additional smoothing value from the topic information model while the tweet with pure text is assigned with a zero probability in the topic information model.

Also, we estimate the original document model $\hat{\theta}_T$ and the topic information model $\hat{\theta}_I$ under the language model using Dirichlet Smoothing with collection language model $P(\cdot|C_T)$ and $P(\cdot|C_I)$, respectively.

$$P(w|\hat{\theta}_T) = \frac{c(w, T) + \mu_T P(w|C_T)}{|T| + \mu_T} \quad (13)$$

$$P(w|\hat{\theta}_I) = \frac{c(w, I) + \mu_I P(w|C_I)}{|I| + \mu_I} \quad (14)$$

where μ_T and μ_I is the Dirichlet smoothing parameter, $|T|$,$|I|$ is the length of the original tweet and topic information, $c(w, T), c(w, I)$ mean the count of term w in T and I, respectively.

3.3 Temporal Re-Ranking Component

In the microblogosphere, documents to be retrieved should not only be topically related with the given query, but also be posted in the recent past. Therefore, to some extent, the retrieval system is supposed to favor the newer document while penalizing the older one. In this section, we introduce three temporal re-ranking functions to estimate the importance of temporal evidence, and suggest two ways to represent temporal profile.

3.3.1 The Estimation of Temporal Importance

To evaluate the impact of temporal profile, we suggest several temporal re-ranking functions.

Exponential function

Taking advantage of an exponential distribution to combine temporal profile and language model has been shown effective in previous work [12], thus we employ our first approach by letting $P(t|Q, D)$ follow an exponential distribution as follows:

$$P(t|Q, D) = e^{-\frac{\aleph}{k}} \quad (15)$$

[4]http://longurl.org

where $\aleph$ denotes the temporal profile, and k is an exponential rate parameter.

Gaussian function

With the approximation method proposed in [15], the following estimation of $P(t|Q,D)$ is obtained by using Gaussian function:

$$P(t|Q,D) = e^{-\frac{\aleph^2}{2\sigma^2}} \quad (16)$$

where $\aleph$ denotes the temporal profile, and σ is a parameter to control the width of Gaussian function.

Cosine function

Following [15], we define our temporal weighting function using the Cosine function as follows:

$$P(t|Q,D) = \begin{cases} cos(\frac{\pi \cdot \aleph}{2a}) & \aleph < a \\ 0 & \aleph \geq a \end{cases} \quad (17)$$

where $\aleph$ denotes the temporal profile, and a is a parameter to control the width of the Cosine function.

3.3.2 *Representation of Temporal Profile*

We define temporal profile associated with a document in two different ways: (1) positional information in the recency ranking list and (2) time difference between query timestamp and document timestamp.

Ranking Position as Temporal Profile

Motivated by the positional information used in [15], we re-rank the initial relevance ranking list by document timestamp,from latest to earliest, to obtain a recency ranking list. For each document D, we have the ranking position P_r, and then set temporal profile $\aleph = P_r$. By taking ranking position into consideration, we assign the newer document with a higher probability while penalizing the older one with an appropriate discount.

Time Difference as Temporal Profile

Time difference between the query timestamp and the document timestamp can be used to measure the recentness of document with respect to the given query. We define t_D as the timestamp associated with a document D and let t^* denote the time when the query is issued. Thus we have the time difference as follows:

$$\triangle t_D = (t^* - t_D)/H \quad (18)$$

where H is an interval factor which helps normalize the time difference into a specific interval (we set H as 2 hour in our experiments).

After aggregating documents into intervals according to their time difference, we do an intuitive filtering work for every interval to omit some documents whose relevant score is lower than an interval-specific threshold $\tau_{interval}$ shown in Eq.19

$$\tau_{interval} = \varphi \cdot \frac{1}{N} \sum_{i=1}^{N} Score(Q, D_i) \quad (19)$$

where φ is a scale factor which we set as 0.2 in our experiments, N is the count of documents in the interval, $Score(Q, D_i)$ is the relevance score calculated by KL-divergence retrieval model.

Finally, for every document D, we set temporal profile $\aleph = \triangle t_D$ and then estimate $P(t|Q,D)$ according to Eq.15-17.

Table 1: Summary statistics of Tweet11 corpus

HTML Code	Status	# of Tweet
200	OK	13,839,083
302	Found	1,106,999
403	Forbidden	284,225
404	Not Found	844,494
Null	Null	67,011
Searchable		14,946,082

Table 2: Summary statistics of TopicInfo corpus

HTML Code	Status	# of URLs
200	OK	1,225,947
302	Found	688
403	Forbidden	5,050
404	Not Found	92,378
Other	Unavailable	265,468
Searchable		1,226,635

4. EXPERIMENTS

Several experiments are conducted to evaluate each component of our proposed system for RTST. We first evaluate the effect of the two-stage PRF query expansion. Second, we investigate the impact of the document expansion using external URLs. Third, we measure the performance of our temporal re-ranking component. Finally,we compare the integrated systems against the best performing systems in the TREC'11 RTST.

4.1 Setup

In this section, we describe the experimental dataset and evaluation method which are also adopted in TREC'11 Microblog Track [17]. In addition, baseline systems are set up to estimate the effect of the proposed methods.

4.1.1 *Data set*

Tweet11 corpus was obtained using a donation of the unique identifiers of a sample of tweets from Twitter [17]. We crawled the HTML version copy of the corpus with the provided tools[5]. The Tweet11 corpus was created by sampling 16 million tweets from January 24, 2011 to February 8, 2011, covering the time period of great events all around world, e.g. Egyptian revolution. Besides, different types of tweets are provided, including replies and retweets in the Tweet11 corpus. Table 1 shows basic statistics of our HTML version acquisition on June 23, 2011. In addition, we collect all the external URLs (i.e. TopicInfo corpus) contained in Tweet11 corpus and extract their topic information for our document expansion process in early December, 2011. Note that web pages might be deleted as time elapsed, we have only crawled a portion of the external URL set. Each piece of topic information in TopicInfo corpus is processed by Porter stemming algorithm and word elimination. Summary statistics of TopicInfo corpus is presented in Table 2.

For every query, we built a dynamic dataset consisting of a set of tweets whose timestamps are smaller than the query timestamp. We discarded the non-English tweets through analyzing the encoding of tweets and removed simple retweets beginning with 'RT'. Then, each tweet was processed by

[5]https://github.com/lintool/twitter-corpus-tools

stemming using the Porter stemmer and word elimination using the INQUERY words stoplist [1].

4.1.2 Evaluation Method

Tweets were judged on the basis of the defined information need using a three-point scale [17]:

- **Not relevant** The content of the tweet does not provide any useful information on the topic, or is either written in a language other than English, or it is a retweet.
- **Minimally Relevant** The tweet provides some information on the topic, but it is not sufficiently informative.
- **Highly Relevant** A highly relevant tweet will either contain highly informative content, or link to highly informative content.

The top-ranked documents which are strictly ranked by timestamp for all runs were evaluated in terms of their precision at rank 30 (P@30) and mean average precision (MAP).

We carried out all experiments based on two standard topic sets used in the TREC'11 RTST. The first topic set which we call **allrel** considers both minimally relevant and highly relevant tweets as relevant over 49 topics. The second topic set that considers only highly relevant tweets over 33 topics is called **highrel**.

4.1.3 Baseline System

In section 4.2, we discuss the performance of our proposed system. To contextualize our methods, we used the Lemur toolkit[6] (version 4.12) to implement two baseline systems for comparison.

The baseline retrieval model labeled as "KLNoFB" is the KL-divergence retrieval model [24] as follows:

$$Score(Q, D) = \sum_{w \in V} P(w|\hat{\theta}_Q) \cdot \log P(w|\hat{\theta}_D) \qquad (20)$$

where both $\hat{\theta}_Q$ and $\hat{\theta}_D$ are estimated using empirical word distribution, and we choose the Dirichlet smoothing method for document model estimation with the smoothing parameter μ set as 100. This baseline is set up for evaluation of the performance of the proposed query model and document model.

To measure the usefulness of temporal re-ranking component, we set up KL2SFBExR as another baseline based on KL-divergence retrieval model where we estimate query model using the proposed two-stage PRF query expansion (we set α=0.4, β=0.6), and utilize topic information as external resource to generate the document model (we set η=0.6).

Note that both in baseline systems and the proposed system, we obtain the top-ranked 30 tweets from the relevant ranking list achieved by the Real-Time Tweet Ranking Model described in Section 3, and then re-rank them according to their timestamps as an experimental run.

4.2 Experimental Results

In this section, we report the results of experiments carried out to evaluate the effectiveness of each component compared with the baseline systems, and the performance of the integrated systems compared with the best performing systems in the TREC'11 RTST. In addition, to explain the numerous acronyms for the various methods, we summarize the Table 8 which contains a brief description for each acronym.

4.2.1 The Evaluation of Query Model

We conducted several experiments to measure the effect of our two-stage PRF query expansion for RTST. These experiments aim at evaluating (1) how different support tweet selection strategies in the first-stage feedback affect the performance of the proposed query expansion; and (2) how each stage feedback boosts the effectiveness of retrieval results.

We first examined the three strategies we adopted to obtain the single support tweet. In this group of experiments, we only employed the first-stage feedback by setting the parameter β in Eq.10 as 0 to update the original query model, and we estimated the document model in a way as KLNoFB does. With the three selection methods described in Section 3.1, we labeled three variations of first-stage feedback approach as "KLFSFBET", "KLFSFBLT" and "KLFSFBHS", respectively. We compared the results of KLFSFBET, KLFSFBLT and KLFSFBHS in terms of P@30 in Table 3. From the table, it suggests that support tweet in the first-stage feedback can enhance the retrieval performance with varied improvements. Specifically, KLFSFBET hardly improves the search effectiveness while KLFSFBLT achieves a much better search performance, indicating that the latest tweet from the candidate feedback set is more effective than the earliest one to generate the feedback words; however, selecting the tweet according to the highest relevance score as the single support tweet can improve the system performance significantly, showing that semantic aspects of document outperform the temporal aspects in the first-stage feedback modeling.

We then evaluated the retrieval precision of the proposed PRF query expansion step by step. The results are summarized in Table 4. Note that all the methods listed in the table adopt the same document model as KLNoFB does. As we can see, by only employing the second stage of feedback, the method labeled as "KLSSFB" can improve both P@30 and MAP on two topic sets, though not significantly. However, the relative improvements of KLFSFBHS over KLNoFB on allrel and highrel are 12.92% and 18.52% in terms of P@30 respectively; while the corresponding MAP improvements of KLFSFBHS over KLNoFB on allrel and highrel are 27.18% and 50.21%, respectively, which may suggest that the first-stage feedback is more effective than the second-stage feedback. Moreover, the "KL2SFB" method that combines two stages of feedback can further enhance the effectiveness of retrieval results.

4.2.2 The Evaluation of Document Model

We investigated two methods to estimate the document model by incorporating topic information with the original tweet text. We experimentally evaluated the effectiveness of the proposed estimation of the document model. Let KLLocCtxt and KLExRes be the methods regarding topic information as local context and external resource, respectively. To compare with KLNoFB, we estimated the query model without further expanding the original query. Furthermore, we set the Dirichlet smoothing parameter μ as 100 in the KLLocCtxt while in the KLExRes, the Dirichlet

[6]http://www.lemurproject.org/lemur.php

Table 3: P@30 comparasion of three support tweet selection strategies using first-stage PRF query expansion

Topic Set	KLNoFB	KLFSFBET	KLFSFBLT	KLFSFBHS
allrel	0.3422	0.3442(+0.58%)	0.3748(+9.53%)	**0.3864(+12.92%)**
highrel	0.1253	0.1253(0%)	0.1445(+15.32%)	**0.1485(+18.52%)**

Table 4: The performance comparison of two-stage PRF query expansion, not using document expansion

Topic Set	Metric	KLNoFB	KLFSFBHS	Improv.	KLSSFB	Improv.	KL2SFB	Improv.
allrel	P@30	0.3422	0.3864	+12.92%	0.3653	+6.75%	**0.4082**	+19.29%
	MAP	0.1810	0.2302	+27.18%	0.1969	+8.78%	**0.2401**	+32.65%
highrel	P@30	0.1253	0.1485	+18.52%	0.1283	+2.39%	**0.1515**	+20.91%
	MAP	0.1657	0.2489	+50.21%	0.1749	+5.55%	**0.2514**	+51.72%

Table 5: The performance comparison of LocCtxt document model and ExRes document model, not using query expansion

Topic Set	Metric	KLNoFB	KLExRes	Improv.	KLLocCtxt	Improv.
allrel	P@30	0.3422	0.3422	-	**0.3973**	+16.10%
	MAP	0.1810	0.1830	+1.10%	**0.2139**	+18.18%
highrel	P@30	0.1253	**0.1626**	+29.77%	0.1596	+27.37%
	MAP	0.1657	0.1957	+18.11%	**0.2068**	+24.80%

Table 6: The performance comparison of three temporal re-ranking functions, and two temporal profile representations based on KL2SFBExR

Topic Set	Metric	KL2SFB ExR	KL2SFB ExRPE	KL2SFB ExRPG	KL2SFB ExRPC	KL2SFB ExTDE	KL2SFB ExTDG	KL2SFB ExTDC
allrel	P@30	0.4116	0.4177	**0.4177**	0.4170	0.4177	0.4156	0.4156
	MAP	**0.2380**	0.2378	0.2365	0.2359	0.2377	0.2374	0.2374
highrel	P@30	0.1889	0.1950	**0.1979**	0.1970	0.1960	0.1960	0.1960
	MAP	0.2680	0.2713	**0.2722**	0.2714	0.2665	0.2713	0.2713

smoothing parameters μ_T, μ_I are set as 100, 50 for original tweet language model and topic information language model, respectively.

Table 5 shows the performance of two document modeling approaches. Comparing the performance of proposed methods on two topic sets, we can conclude that KLLocCtxt outperforms KLNoFB significantly and consistently on both allrel and highrel; however, it is interesting to observe that KLExRes behaves quite differently on two topic sets: it improves P@30 and MAP on highrel strikingly compared with the KLNoFB baseline while it only slightly increase the MAP score over the baseline KLNoFB by 1.10% when running on allrel topic set. Besides, when comparing the performance of two methods running on a particular topic set in terms of P@30, we can figure out that KLLocCtxt outperforms KLExRes on allrel while KLExRes obtains better retrieval results than the corresponding one achieved by KLLocCtxt on highrel.

4.2.3 Temporal Re-Ranking Component

We suggest three temporal re-ranking functions to estimate the importance of the temporal aspects of documents and investigate two representations of temporal profile. To evaluate the usefulness of temporal re-ranking component, we combined three functions with two different types of temporal profile based on the KL2SFBExR baseline to form six methods: KL2SFBExRPE, KL2SFBExRPG, KL2SFBExRPC, KL2SFBExTDE, KL2SFBExTDG and KL2SFBExTDC. The retrieval results are summarized in Table 6, where we highlight the best result for each row. From Table 6, we observe that, compared with the KL2SFBExR baseline, all six temporal re-ranking functions achieve better search performances in terms of P@30. For a particular representation of temporal profile (e.g. ranking position), different temporal re-ranking functions can achieve the similar improvements when we tune their parameters to make the value of function at argument r_{max} (i.e. the max ranking position) is around 0.6. Besides, for a particular temporal re-ranking function, two different representations work similarly, which may indicate that any rational representation of temporal profile can obtain a reliable retrieval performance.

4.2.4 Integration of Query Model, Document Model and Temporal Re-Ranking Component

Finally, we measured the performance of the proposed system that integrates the query expansion component, document expansion component and temporal re-ranking component. For the query expansion component, we adopt two-stage PRF query expansion with HS selection strategy. For the document expansion component, we employ both LocCtxt document model and ExRes document model based on the observation that the two document models behave differently on different topic sets. For the temporal re-ranking component, we employ Gaussian function with ranking position as temporal profile. Overall, we have two runs labeled as KL2SFBLocRPG and KL2SFBExRPG .

Table 7 demonstrates the performance of our systems. In addition, we also report the best three performing results of the TREC'11 Real-Time Search Task [17] for comparison purpose. This result suggests that both of our systems outperform the best performance of TREC'11 RTST on the highrel topic set significantly, specifically, KL2SFBExRPG achieves 26.37% and 9.94% further increases in P@30 and MAP, respectively. On the other hand, the performances of

Table 7: The performances of systems integrating query expansion (we set $\alpha = 0.4$, $\beta = 0.6$), document expansion (we set η=0.6 when using ExRes document model) and temporal re-ranking components (we set σ=120 in Gaussian function). isi, FUB, CLARITY_DCU are the best three performances in TREC'11 Real-Time Search Task on highrel and allrel. The best performances are shown in bold. †, ‡, ¶ mean the corresponding improvements over isi, FUB and CLARITY_DCU are significant respectively.

Topic Set	Metric	isi	FUB	CLARITY_DCU	KL2SFBExRPG	KL2SFBLocRPG
allrel	P@30	**0.4551**	0.4401	0.4211	0.4177	0.4490
	MAP	0.1923	0.2348	0.2139	0.2365†¶	**0.2552**†‡¶
highrel	P@30	0.1566	0.1495	0.1434	**0.1979**†‡¶	0.1727†‡¶
	MAP	0.2476	0.2286	0.2065	**0.2722**†‡¶	0.2606‡¶

Table 8: Summary of mentioned acronyms

Acronyms	Description
KLNoFB	KL-divergence retrieval model without any expansion technique
KLFSFBET	KL-divergence retrieval model, only using first stage query expansion(support tweet with Earliest Timestamp)
KLFSFBLT	KL-divergence retrieval model, only using first stage query expansion(support tweet with Latest Timestamp)
KLFSFBHS	KL-divergence retrieval model, only using first stage query expansion(support tweet with Highest Score)
KLSSFB	KL-divergence retrieval model, only using second stage query expansion
KL2SFB	KL-divergence retrieval model, using two-stage query expansion(support tweet with Highest Score for first stage)
KLExRes	KL-divergence retrieval model, only using document expansion(topic infomation as external resource)
KLLocCtxt	KL-divergence retrieval model, only using document expansion(topic infomation as local context)
KL2SFBExR	KL-divergence retrieval model, using two-stage query expansion(support tweet with Highest Score for first stage) and document expansion(topic infomation as external resource)
KL2SFBLoc	KL-divergence retrieval model, using two-stage query extension(support tweet with Highest Score for first stage) and document expansion(topic infomation as local context)
KL2SFBExRP*	Using Temporal re-ranking (ranking position as temporal profile, * can be G(aussian),E(xponential),C(osine)) based on KL2SFBExR
KL2SFBExTD*	Using Temporal re-ranking (time difference as temporal profile, * can be G(aussian),E(xponential),C(osine)) based on KL2SFBExR
KLNoFBRPG, KL2SFBRPG, KL2SFBLocRPG	Using Temporal re-ranking (ranking position as temporal profile in gaussian function) based on KLNoFB,KL2SFB, KL2SFBLoc , respectively

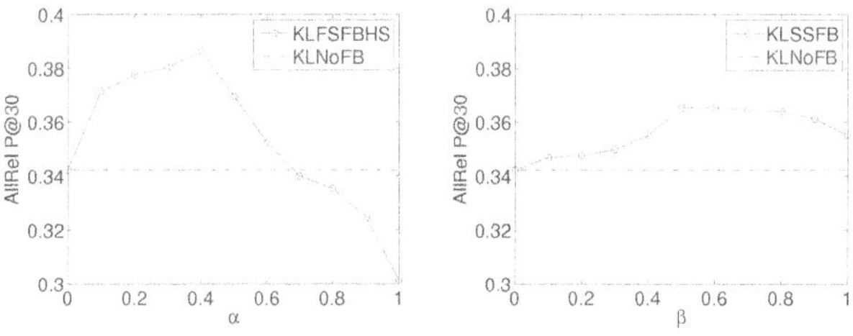

Figure 1: Sensitivity to the first-stage feedback interpolation coefficient α (left) and second-stage feedback interpolation coefficient β (right) of PRF query expansion.

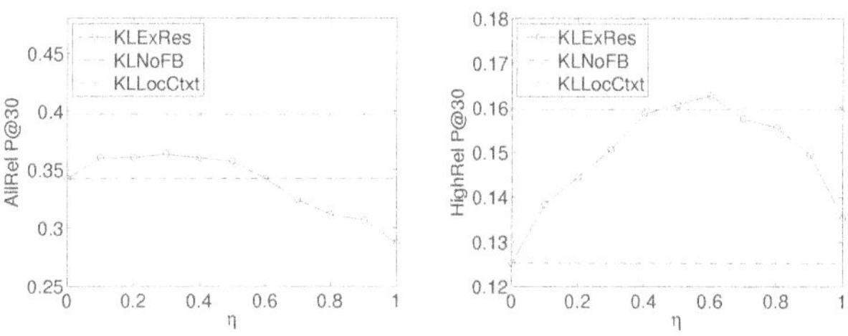

Figure 2: Sensitivity to the ExRes document model interpolation coefficient η on allrel (left) and highrel (right).

our systems on allrel are very competitive compared with the top 3 performances of TREC'11 RTST, though not better than the best one. Besides, it is not surprisingly to observe that KL2SFBLocRPG beats KL2SFBExRPG on the allrel topic set while losing to KL2SFBExRPG on the highrel topic set, because we have seen the different behaviors between ExRes document model and LocCtxt document model in section 4.2.2.

4.3 Discussion

Many parameters in our proposed approach can affect the behavior of the system performance. In this section, we analyze the robustness to the parameter setting in query expansion component, document expansion component and temporal re-ranking component.

In the two-stage PRF query expansion, there are parameters α and β to control the amount of first-stage feedback and second-stage feedback. Specifically, when $\alpha = 0$ (i.e. we ignore the effect of first-stage feedback), and let β range from 0 to 1.0, we can see how second-stage feedback affect the retrieval results; when $\beta = 0$, and let α vary from 0 to

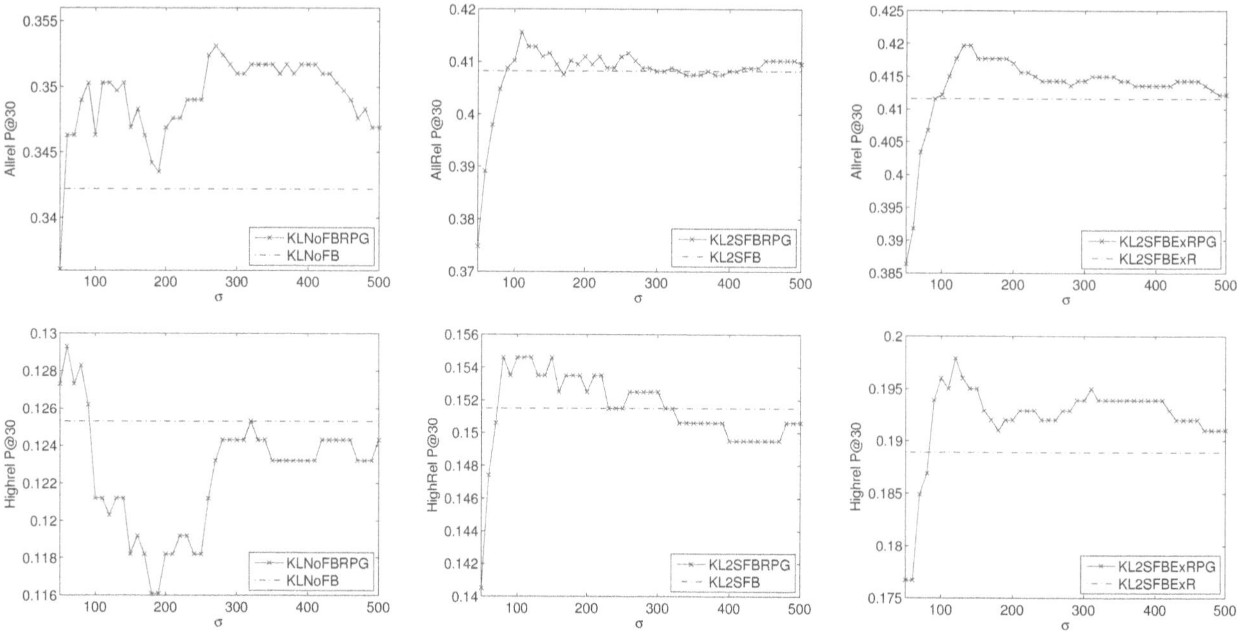

Figure 3: Sensitivity to the Gaussian function parameter σ over KLNoFB (left), KL2SFB (middle) and KL2SFBExR (right) on alrel(top) and highrel (down).

1.0, we can see the behavior of the first-stage feedback. The effects of first-stage feedback and second-stage feedback are shown in Figure 1. The experimental results indicate that when α is around 0.4 and β is around 0.6, each stage of query expansion can achieve their own best performances, which outperform the KLNoFB baseline. Besides, first-stage feedback can receive a better performance than second-stage does when they are assigned with their optimal parameters (i.e. $\alpha = 0.4, \beta = 0.6$). However, second-stage feedback seems to be more robust.

Recall that we build KLExRes document model by interpolating the topic information model with the original document model. The interpolation is controlled by a coefficient η. When $\eta = 0$, we only use the original document model (i.e. no topic information), while if $\eta = 1$, we completely ignore the original document model and only take advantage of topic information model. We demonstrate in Figure 2 how the score of P@30 changes according to the value of η along with the performance of KLNoFB and KLLocCtxt. From Figure 2, it is worthy to point out that KLExRes works differently on the two topic sets: when running on allrel topic set, topic information seems not to be effective, resulting in that KLExRes loses to KLLocCtxt consistently and only defeats KLNoFB when $\eta < 0.6$; however, when running on highrel topic set, the pure topic information model ($\eta = 1$) result is much better than the original document model ($\eta = 0$), which may indicate that topic information is very effective for retrieving highly relevant document in the microblogosphere, as a result, KLExRes consistently outperforms KLNoFB and can achieve a better result than KLLocCtxt when η is around 0.6. A rational reason for this interesting phenomenon may be that a highly relevant tweet tends to include a high-quality URL, thus topic information within the URL can boost the effectiveness of retrieval results.

According to the results shown in section 4.2, both query expansion component and document expansion component can boost the retrieval effectiveness, so we employ the temporal re-ranking component over KLNoFB, KL2SFB and KL2SFBExR, to further compare the robustness of temporal re-ranking component with respect to the different initial retrieval results. Note that all the temporal re-ranking functions and both representations of temporal profile perform similarly, we only take Gaussian function and ranking postion representation for example. From Figure 3 we can see that temporal re-ranking component improves the KL2SFBExR's performance in most cases when σ ranges from 50 to 500, however, it seems to be unstable when running over worse initial retrieval results (i.e. KLNoFB and KL2SFB) with parameter σ at the same range. Thus, based on the observation, we can conclude that temporal re-ranking component performs much better and more robust when running over better initial retrieval results. In addition, when tuning σ around 120, we obtain the best retrieval performance on allrel and highrel.

5. CONCLUSION AND FUTURE WORK

In this study, we propose an effective approach to improve the performance of our system to mine valuable information in the microblogosphere. Our system consists of three important components: query modeling, document modeling and temporal re-ranking. To estimate the query model, we introduce a two-stage pseudo-relevance feedback query expansion based on language model framework. For the document modeling, we present LocCtxt document model and ExRes document model which refine the representation of document with the topic information in different ways. For the temporal re-ranking component, we suggest several functions as well as different representations of temporal profile.

Experiments on Tweet11 corpus indicate the usefulness

of each component, as we obtain significant improvements over the baseline systems. Besides, the proposed system for RTST which integrates all the components increases the best performing system of TREC'11 RTST on the highrel topic set by 26.37% and 9.94% in P@30 and MAP, respectively.

Many studies remain for the future work. One of the most interesting directions is to explore the users' connection in social network for a further analysis on user's information need in the microblogosphere. Moreover, another interesting direction is to classify the type of URLs for more accurate document expansion (e.g. detect the news articles and extract the main content as topic information). Furthermore, we are also interested in how to incorporate the temporal profile into the language model to obtain better retrieval results.

6. ACKNOWLEDGMENTS

The work reported in this paper was supported by the National Natural science Foundation of China Grant 60875033.

7. REFERENCES

[1] J. Allan, M. E. Connell, W. B. Croft, F. Feng, D. Fisher, and X. Li. Inquery and trec-9. In *TREC*, 2000.

[2] C. Buckley, G. Salton, J. Allan, and A. Singhal. Automatic query expansion using SMART: TREC 3. In D. K. Harman, editor, *Overview of the 3th Text REtrieval Conference TREC-3*, pages 69–80, Gaithersburg, 1995. NIST.

[3] C. C. Chen, Y.-T. Chen, Y. S. Sun, and M. C. Chen. Life cycle modeling of news events using aging theory. In N. Lavrac, D. Gamberger, L. Todorovski, and H. Blockeel, editors, *ECML*, volume 2837 of *Lecture Notes in Computer Science*, pages 47–59. Springer, 2003.

[4] K.-Y. Chen, L. Luesukprasert, and S. cho Timothy Chou. Hot topic extraction based on timeline analysis and multidimensional sentence modeling. *IEEE Trans. Knowl. Data Eng.*, 19(8):1016–1025, 2007.

[5] W. Dakka, L. Gravano, and P. G. Ipeirotis. Answering general time sensitive queries. In J. G. Shanahan, S. Amer-Yahia, I. Manolescu, Y. Zhang, D. A. Evans, A. Kolcz, K.-S. Choi, and A. Chowdhury, editors, *CIKM*, pages 1437–1438. ACM, 2008.

[6] A. P. Dempster, N. M. Laird, and D. B. Rubin. Maximum likelihood from incomplete data via the EM algorithm. *Journal of the Royal Statistical Society, B*, 39, 1977.

[7] A. Dong, R. Zhang, P. Kolari, J. Bai, F. Diaz, Y. Chang, Z. Zheng, and H. Zha. Time is of the essence: improving recency ranking using twitter data. In M. Rappa, P. Jones, J. Freire, and S. Chakrabarti, editors, *WWW*, pages 331–340. ACM, 2010.

[8] R. T. Fernández, D. E. Losada, and L. Azzopardi. Extending the language modeling framework for sentence retrieval to include local context. *Inf Retr.*, 14(4):355–389, 2011.

[9] B. J. Jansen, M. Zhang, K. Sobel, and A. Chowdury. Micro-blogging as online word of mouth branding. In D. R. O. Jr., R. B. Arthur, K. Hinckley, M. R. Morris, S. E. Hudson, and S. Greenberg, editors, *CHI Extended Abstracts*, pages 3859–3864. ACM, 2009.

[10] A. Java, X. Song, T. Finin, and B. Tseng. Why we twitter: understanding microblogging usage and communities. In *Proceedings of the 9th WebKDD and 1st SNA-KDD 2007 workshop on Web mining and social network analysis*, pages 56–65. ACM, 2007.

[11] V. Lavrenko and W. B. Croft. Relevance-based language models. In *Proceedings of SIGIR*, pages 120–127, 2001.

[12] X. Li and W. B. Croft. Time-based language models. In *CIKM*, pages 469–475. ACM, 2003.

[13] D. E. Losada and R. T. Fernández. Highly frequent terms and sentence retrieval. In N. Ziviani and R. A. Baeza-Yates, editors, *SPIRE*, volume 4726 of *Lecture Notes in Computer Science*, pages 217–228. Springer, 2007.

[14] Y. Lv and C. Zhai. A comparative study of methods for estimating query language models with pseudo feedback. In D. W.-L. Cheung, I.-Y. Song, W. W. Chu, X. Hu, and J. J. Lin, editors, *CIKM*, pages 1895–1898. ACM, 2009.

[15] Y. Lv and C. Zhai. Positional relevance model for pseudo-relevance feedback. In F. Crestani, S. Marchand-Maillet, H.-H. Chen, E. N. Efthimiadis, and J. Savoy, editors, *SIGIR*, pages 579–586. ACM, 2010.

[16] V. Murdock. Aspects of sentence retrieval. *SIGIR Forum*, 41(2):127, 2007.

[17] I. Ounis, C. Macdonald, J. Lin, and I. Soboroff. Overview of the TREC-2011 Microblog Track. In *Proceedings of TREC 2011*, 2012.

[18] J. Pontin. From many tweets, one loud voice on the Internet. *New York Times Online [web site]. Retrieved May*, 8:2006, 2007.

[19] S. E. Robertson and K. S. Jones. Relevance weighting of search terms. *Journal of the American Society for Information Science*, 27:129–146, 1976.

[20] S. E. Robertson, S. Walker, S. Jones, M. Hancock-Beaulieu, and M. Gatford. Okapi at trec-3. In *TREC'94*, pages 109–126, 1994.

[21] J. Rocchio. Relevance feedback in information retrieval. In *The SMART Retrieval System: experiments in automatic document processing*, pages 313–323. Prentice Hall, 1971.

[22] G. Salton and C. Buckley. Improving retrieval performance by relevance feedback. *Journal of the American Society for Information Science*, 41:288–297, 1990.

[23] T. Tao and C. Zhai. Regularized estimation of mixture models for robust pseudo-relevance feedback. In E. N. Efthimiadis, S. T. Dumais, D. Hawking, and K. Jarvelin, editors, *SIGIR*, pages 162–169. ACM, 2006.

[24] C. Zhai and J. Lafferty. A study of smoothing methods for language models applied to information retrieval. *ACM Trans. Inf. Syst.*, 22(2):179–214, 2004.

[25] C. Zhai and J. D. Lafferty. Model-based feedback in the language modeling approach to information retrieval. In *CIKM*, pages 403–410. ACM, 2001.

Improving Algorithm Search Using the Algorithm Co-Citation Network

Suppawong Tuarob†, Prasenjit Mitra†‡ and C. Lee Giles†‡
† Computer Science and Engineering, ‡ Information Sciences and Technology
The Pennsylvania State University
University Park, PA 16802
suppawong@psu.edu, {pmitra, giles}@ist.psu.edu

ABSTRACT

Algorithms are an essential part of computational science. An algorithm search engine, which extracts pseudo-codes and their metadata from documents, and makes it searchable, has recently been developed as part of the Citeseer^X suite [3, 4]. However, this algorithm search engine only retrieves and ranks relevant algorithms solely on textual similarity. Here, we propose a method for using the algorithm co-citation network to infer the similarity between algorithms. We apply a graph clustering algorithm on the network for algorithm recommendation and make suggestions on how to improve the current Citeseer^X algorithm search engine.

Categories and Subject Descriptors

H.3.3 [**Information Search and Retrieval**]

Keywords

Algorithms, Clustering, Algorithm Co-Citation Network

1. INTRODUCTION

Computer science is often about algorithms. Searching for the right algorithms for a specific problem can be a challenging task, as there has not been a way for automatically interpreting the semantics of algorithms. Methods for searching for algorithms have been implemented by applying traditional search engine techniques on algorithm metadata. Bhatia et al.[3] developed an algorithm extractor which extracts pseudo-codes along with their metadata such as captions, reference sentences and synopses [1, 2]. Indexing such algorithm metadata makes it searchable. However, the search is done by text based matching of user queries with the metadata.

The ability to infer the similarity of algorithms could also be beneficial when searching for algorithms. One may want to know if there are other available algorithms which address the same problem as a known algorithm. For example, one might want to know if there are other algorithms that find shortest paths in a graph such as Dijkstra's algorithm. Researchers often would want to search for existing algorithms so that they can develop a better algorithm or use these algorithms as baselines for their experiments. Detection of the similarity of algorithms could also lead to the discovery of newly emerging algorithms which are not yet well known.

We hypothesize that the similarity between algorithms can be captured using an algorithm co-citation network. We generate the algorithm co-citation network from scientific documents in the Citeseer^X[1] repository. We apply a clustering algorithm on a sample subset of the algorithm co-citation network which gives groups of relevant algorithm-proposing documents. We evaluate the clustering results by varying the clustering granularity levels and measure the meaningfulness of each cluster.

2. OBSERVATIONS AND MOTIVATIONS

In an algorithm-proposing document, there is usually a paragraph (in the introduction or the related work sections) devoting to addressing past work. In this case, we are interested in algorithms used in previous documents. From reading multiple documents throughout our own research, we find that if multiple algorithms are mentioned in a paper, then it is likely that these algorithms address similar problems. From these observations, we hypothesize that, if two algorithms are co-cited multiple times, then there could exist a relationship between them which can be used to infer their similarity. Such a relationship could be represented using the algorithm co-citation graph, which is explained in a later section.

3. RELATED WORK

Even though the document co-citation has been extensively studied, to the best of our knowledge, there has not been any work on algorithm co-citation analysis. Hence, the related work that we present here are mostly related to the current Citeseer^X algorithm search engine.

The current Citeseer^X algorithm search engine uses an automated algorithm extractor to extract pseudo-code which appears as document-elements with captions in scientific documents. The automated algorithm extractor extracts related information of each pseudo-code such as its caption, reference sentences, and year of publication (if available). A pseudo-code reference sentence is a sentence in the document which mentions the pseudo-code. A synopsis is also generated as part of the metadata to provide an overview

[1] http://citeseerx.ist.psu.edu

JCDL'12, June 10–14, 2012, Washington, DC, USA.

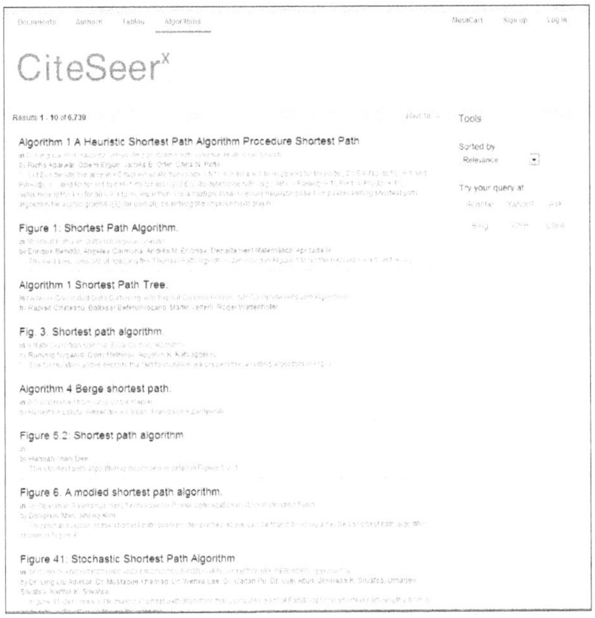

Figure 1: Citeseer^X algorithm search engine.

for each pseudo-code extracted[1]. A synopsis of a pseudo-code is generated from the set of its reference sentences, constructed by heuristics and machine learning techniques. All the extracted metadata information is then fed to the indexer. When a user inputs a query, TF-IDF based cosine similarity scores are computed to retrieve and rank the relevant pseudo-codes. Each search result gives a pointer to the document where the pseudo-code resides. Figure 1 shows the results returned by the Citeseer^X algorithm search engine using query "shortest path." The current Citeseer^X algorithm search engine only retrieves pseudo-codes based on textual similarities between user queries and pseudo-codes. This method is effective if the user uses the right keywords. However, there are some cases where the desired algorithms are proposed in different fields of studies, resulting in a different set of context that might not be familiar to the user. The current search engine would treat these algorithms as unrelated to the search query.

4. ALGORITHM CO-CITATION NETWORK

The algorithm co-citation network is an undirected, weighted graph where each node is a document that proposes some algorithms, and each edge weight is the frequency of algorithm co-citation. Formally, for the set of all documents D, the algorithm co-citation network G is defined as follows:

G= <V,E>
V={d | d ∈ D, d proposes one or more algorithms}
E={(a,b) | a,b ∈ V}
Weight((a,b))=|{d | d ∈ D,d cites algorithms in both a and b,(a,b)∈E}|

An algorithm co-citation network is different from a document co-citation network defined in [7] in the sense that each node in the network is a document which proposes algorithms, and one or more of the algorithms are cited in the document. The weight of each link represents the frequency that the algorithms in at least two documents are co-cited. We describe how we detect algorithm citations and construct the algorithm co-citation network in the next sub-sections.

4.1 Algorithm Citation Detection

Given an input document, the algorithm citation detection returns the cited documents whose algorithms are mentioned in the input document. A document is treated as an ordered set of sentences. Briefly, the algorithm citation detector first extracts the set of algorithm-citation sentences in a document. An algorithm citation sentence is defined as a sentence which contains at least one or more algorithm keywords (i.e. 'algorithm', 'method', and 'procedure'), and at least a citation symbol. An example of a sentence where an algorithm is cited is:

> Optimization methods for ECG compression were developed, such as the cardinality constrained shortest path (CCSP) ***algorithm*** presented in [1], [8], [24], [25].

We make an assumption that if both an algorithm keyword and one or more citations appear in a sentence, then it is likely that the citing document mentions the algorithms proposed in the cited documents. After obtaining the set of algorithm-citation sentences, the detector extracts the set of documents cited in such sentences. We use document IDs to represent documents.

4.2 Constructing Algorithm Co-Citation Network

The algorithm co-citation network is constructed by taking the algorithm citations from each document, finding the corresponding document ID for each citation, and creating for each pair of the cited documents an edge of weight 1. If the edge already exists, the weight is incremented by 1. Algorithm 4.1 describes the network construction process. D is the set of input documents from which we extract algorithm citations and construct the algorithm co-citation network. We generate the algorithm co-citation network from roughly 1,370,000 documents in the Citeseer^X repository. The network created contained 9,409,433 edges and roughly 1 million nodes.

Algorithm 4.1: AlgoCoCiteNetworkConstruct(D)

```
Initialization :
V = {}
E = {}
G = <V,E>

Begin :
  for each document d in D:
    N ← list of algorithm-proposing documents cited in d
    For each (a, b) where a, b∈V,a ≠ b:
      if edge (a, b) ∈E:
        Increase weight of edge (a, b) by 1
      Else :
        Add edge (a, b) to E, and set the weight to 1
      End If
  Rerurn G
End.
```

4.3 Clustering the Algorithm Co-Citation Network

The algorithm co-citation network captures the similarity between two algorithm-proposing documents, based on the assumption that if two algorithms are cited together, then they are likely to be used for similar problems. Such similarity is reflected by the weight of the edge linking the two

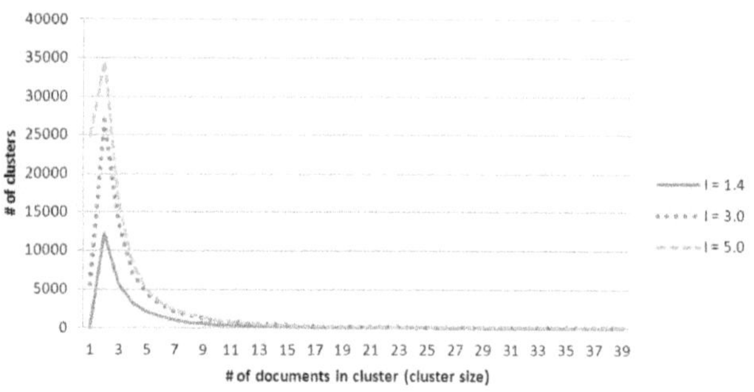

Figure 2: Distribution of cluster sizes with granularity parameters of 1.4, 3.0, and 5.0.

Granularity Level	# clusters	Avg. # documents/cluster
1.4	30,862	14.89
3.0	73,779	6.23
5.0	105,329	4.36

Table 1: Output cluster and average cluster sizes generated using different granularity parameters.

documents in which the co-cited algorithms are mentioned. Based on such a relationship, the network is clustered to produce groups of similar algorithm-proposing documents. A number of clustering tools can be considered; however, the MCL[2] tool worked well for this task. The MCL clustering tool implements the Markov Cluster Algorithm. The algorithm is unsupervised and is based on the simulation of network flow. MCL is designed to specifically cluster large and preferably undirected weighted networks [5].

The other clustering tools that we have considered include Weka[3], Gephi[4], GraphClust[5], and Graclus[6]. Weka [6] supports datasets where all the data points have the same set of attributes. Such data points are different from nodes in the algorithm co-citation network where the only information associated with a node is the similarities between the node and its neighbors. GraphClust is also a network clustering tool; however, it only supports undirected graphs with uniform edge weights. Gephi and Graclus presented problems for large datasets such as ours. For our experiments, they all crashed on an input network of 600,000 edges and 33,601 nodes.

5. EXPERIMENT AND EVALUATION ON CLUSTERING RESULTS

The MCL tool was the most suitable tool we found for clustering large graphs. However, the complete algorithm co-citation network generated from the whole Citeseer^X repository was still too large for the tool to handle. As such, for experimental purposes, we generated a subgraph by randomly selecting 3,000,000 edges from the complete network. The selected subgraph contains 459,585 nodes. Figure 2 shows the distributions of the cluster sizes with different

[2]http://micans.org/mcl/man/mcl.html
[3]http://www.cs.waikato.ac.nz/ml/weka/
[4]http://gephi.org/
[5]http://cs.nyu.edu/shasha/papers/GraphClust.html
[6]http://www.cs.utexas.edu/users/dml/Software/graclus.html

C#	Keywords	#D	#RD	Pr(%)
1	integration, structural, analysis, dynamic, time	41	29	70.73
2	walking, biped, control, robot, locomotion	60	49	81.67
3	technology, programmable, error, cmos, performance	41	20	48.78
4	geometric, constraint, rigidity, graph, system	45	30	66.67
5	mammogram,detection,microcalcification,digital,clustering	43	30	69.77
6	requirement, diagram, model, object-oriented, statechart	46	23	50.00
7	knowledge, ontology, system, design, management	40	31	77.50
8	neural, parallel, network, mapping, architecture	41	32	78.05
9	scheduling, crew, system, transport, driver, transit	43	34	79.07
10	reduction, eigenvalue, power, dominant, system	46	35	76.09
Avg		**44.6**	**31.3**	**70.73**

Table 2: Precision calculated from the sample clusters using granularity parameter 1.4.

clustering granularity levels. With granularity parameter of 1.4 (I = 1.4), the clustering results tend to be coarse-grained, leading to the smallest number of clusters, but highest average number of documents per cluster. At the other extreme where the granularity parameter is 5.0 (I = 5.0), the clustering results tend to be fine-grained, resulting in the largest number of output clusters, and smallest average number of documents per cluster. The granularity parameter of 3.0 (I = 3.0) results in values somewhere in between. Table 1 lists the numbers of output clusters and average cluster sizes for each granularity parameter.

This experiment aims to measure the meaningfulness of the clustering results. The experiment and evaluation use the following steps:

1. Run the MCL clustering algorithm with granularity parameters of 1.4, 3.0, and 5.0 on the sample network with 3,000,000 edges and 459,585 nodes.
2. Randomly choose 10 clusters from each clustering result.
3. For each cluster:
   (a) Retrieve the paper titles of all the documents in the cluster.
   (b) From all the document titles, run the term frequency count to determine top 5 keywords. We use these keywords to describe the cluster.
   (c) Examine each document (manually) and determine the number of documents in the cluster which are related to these 5 keywords.
   (d) Calculate the precision of the cluster, where the precision is the ratio of the number of related documents to the number of all the documents in the cluster.
4. Calculate the average precision of all the 10 clusters.
5. Compare the average precisions of the results from the three granularity levels.

Table 2, 3, and 4 lists the results of the precision measurement of a sample of 10 clusters selected from each of the clustering results generated with different granularity parameters. **C#** is the cluster number, **#D** is the number of documents in the cluster, **#RD** is the number of documents relevant to the 5 chosen keywords, and **Pr(%)** is the precision in percent.

It is worth noting that the highest average precision is achieved in the clustering result using the granularity parameter of 1.4. This granularity level produces the most coarse-grained clustering among all the three parameters. It is also interesting to see that the average precision tends to decrease as the clustering results are more fine-grained.

C#	Keywords	#D	#RD	Pr(%)
1	reduction, model, eigenvalue, power, system	40	13	32.50
2	element, finite, superconvergence, analysis, recovery	52	46	88.46
3	recovery, distribute, rollback, synthesis, system	54	28	51.85
4	java, program, analysis, compiler, object-oriented	58	38	65.52
5	programming,approximation,problem,algorithm,application	48	30	62.50
6	algorithm, system, stability, matrix, linear	52	42	80.77
7	spectral, system, analysis, estimation, identification	46	25	54.35
8	partition, parallel, architecture, language, dataflow	40	30	75.00
9	distributed, signal, sparse, linear, sensor	49	30	61.22
10	feature, selection, analysis, learn, approach	56	26	46.43
Avg		**49.5**	**30.8**	**61.86**

Table 3: Precision calculated from the sample clusters using granularity parameter 3.0.

C#	Keywords	#D	#RD	Pr(%)
1	clustering, data, algorithm, sampling, spatial	47	30	63.83
2	nonlinear, equation, dynamic, solution, schrodinger	41	21	51.22
3	animation, method, simulation, model, realistic	52	32	61.54
4	convex, version, enumeration, facet, version	48	26	54.17
5	match, recognition, contour, object, shape	56	32	57.14
6	waveguide, microwave, multiplexer, design, analysis	51	31	60.78
7	language, entropy, maximum, model, statistical	55	32	58.18
8	testing, protocol, conformance, generation, machine	41	34	82.93
9	learning,reinforcement,stochastic,markov,approximation	43	22	51.16
10	motion, estimation, image, structure, optical	58	33	56.90
Avg		**49.2**	**29.3**	**59.78**

Table 4: Precision calculated from the sample clusters using granularity parameter 5.0.

6. SUGGESTED APPLICATIONS

The clustering on the algorithm co-citation network provides us with groups of related algorithm-proposing documents. We can create clusters of similar algorithms by grouping together pseudo-codes extracted from the documents in the same clusters. There are a number of applications that can be employed from such algorithm clustering. Here, we propose two possible applications which can potentially be used to improve the Citeseer^X algorithm search engine or any similar full text digital library.

6.1 Algorithm Recommendation

Suppose every algorithm in each cluster addresses similar problems. When the algorithm search engine retrieves an algorithm, the algorithms in the same cluster can be displayed as recommended algorithms.

6.2 Improving Ranking

Assuming that algorithms in the same cluster are similar in the sense that they address similar problems, then when an algorithm is textually matched with the search query, the algorithms in the same cluster could receive extra scores so they can be ranked higher. To do this, we propose a technique similar to query expansion:

1. First, the search engine pre-generates a list of keywords that represent each cluster. The keywords may be chosen from the documents which propose the algorithms in the cluster, or they may be chosen from the information (i.e. captions, reference sentences, and synopses) of the algorithms in the clusters.

2. When a user inputs a query, the query engine modifies the original query such that if the original query contains at least one word that belong to the list of keywords of a cluster, then some or all of the keywords that represents such cluster are added to the original query. Adding cluster keywords to an original query would make sure that when at least an algorithm matches the original search query, ranking scores are also given to the rest of the algorithms in the same cluster.

7. CONCLUSIONS AND FUTURE WORK

The algorithm co-citation network captures the similarity between algorithm-proposing documents. The similarity comes from the observation that if two algorithms are cited together, then it is likely that these algorithms address similar problems. Based on this assumption, clustering the network would result in groups of similar algorithm-proposing documents. The clustering results could be applied in many applications to improve the current Citeseer^X or any algorithm search engine, such as improving the ranking and recommending related algorithms. There are several aspects of the methodology that could be improved. For example content analysis techniques can be used to identify additional features which would infer similarity between two algorithm proposing documents. This will generate a different type of algorithm graph. It would be useful to implement clustering algorithms which can handle large networks such as our dataset making it possible to perform experiments on the complete algorithm co-citation network generated from the whole Citeseer^X repository. Using the methods proposed here, many algorithm recommendation systems should be feasible.

8. ACKNOWLEDGMENTS

We gratefully acknowledge useful suggestions from S. Bhatia and S. Das, plus partial support from the NSF and DTRA.

9. REFERENCES

[1] S. Bhatia, S. Lahiri, and P. Mitra. Generating synopses for document-element search. *Proceeding of the 18th ACM conference on Information and knowledge management - CIKM '09*, page 2003, 2009.

[2] S. Bhatia and P. Mitra. Summarizing Figures , Tables and Algorithms in Scientific Publications to Augment Search Results. *ACM Transactions on Information Systems (TOIS)*, pages 1–24, 2010.

[3] S. Bhatia, P. Mitra, and C. L. Giles. Finding algorithms in scientific articles. *Proceedings of the 19th international conference on World wide web - WWW '10*, page 1061, 2010.

[4] S. Bhatia, S. Tuarob, P. Mitra, and C. L. Giles. An Algorithm Search Engine for Software Developers. *SUITE '11: Proceedings of 2011 ICSE Workshop on Search-driven Development: Users, Infrastructure, Tools and Evaluation, 2011*, 2011.

[5] S. Dongen. Graph clustering by flow simulation [Ph.D. dissertation]. *Centers for Mathematics and Computer Science University of Utrecht*, 2000.

[6] M. Hall, H. National, E. Frank, G. Holmes, B. Pfahringer, P. Reutemann, and I. H. Witten. The WEKA data mining software: an update. *SIGKDD Explorations*, 11(1):10–18, 2009.

[7] H. SMALL. Co-citation in the Scientific Literature : A New Measure of the Relationship Between Two Documents. *Journal of the American Society for Information Science*, pages 265–269, 1973.

Evaluating and Ranking Patents Using Weighted Citations

Sooyoung Oh
Computer Science and Engineering
The Pennsylvania State University
University Park, PA 16802
sooh@cse.psu.edu

Zhen Lei
Energy and Mineral Engineering
The Pennsylvania State University
University Park, PA 16802
zlei@psu.edu

Prasenjit Mitra John Yen
Information Sciences and Technology
The Pennsylvania State University
University Park, PA 16802
{pmitra, jyen}@ist.psu.edu

ABSTRACT
Citation counts have been widely used in a digital library for purposes such as ranking scientific publications and evaluating patents. This paper demonstrates that distinguishing different types of citations could rank better for these purposes. We differentiate patent citations along two dimensions (assignees and technologies) into four types, and propose a weighted citation approach for assessing and ranking patents. We investigate five weight learning methods and compare their performance. Our weighted citation method performs consistently better than simple citation counts, in terms of rank correlations with patent renewal status. The estimated weights on different citations are consistent with economic insights on patent citations. Our study points to an interesting and promising research line on patent citation and network analysis that has not been explored.

Categories and Subject Descriptors
H.3.3 [**Information Systems**]: Information Search and Retrieval

General Terms
Algorithms

Keywords
patent ranking, patent citation, weighted citation, patent renewal.

1. INTRODUCTION
Evaluating and ranking patents, such as identifying influential patents in a field or assessing the value of a patent or a patent portfolio, are important yet challenging problems. Patent citation counts, i.e. the number of citations that a patent receives, have been one of the most important and widely used indicator for patent value and importance [1,4,5,6]. Analogous to journal article citations that can help identify particularly seminal discoveries, patent citations suggest that the cited patents the relatively important precursor that defines the state of the art. The broader and more important the shoulder, the more likely it is to be cited. Furthermore, patent citations are referenced more parsimoniously than journal article citations as they define the scope of the citing patents and thus have significant legal and economic implications.

Previous studies have focused on the total number of patent citations a patent receives, paying little attention to a distinction among citing patents, a distinction that could have important implications for the value of the cited patent. Specifically, citing patents (and patent citations) can be distinguished among two dimensions: (1) whether a citing patent is owned by the same assignee (owner) as the cited patent (i.e. self-citations); and (2) whether a citing patent is the same technology class as the citied one. Patent self-citations suggest that a firm invests in further developing an innovation disclosed in the cited patent and thus presumably signify the economic value of the cited patent. With regard to technology classes, if a patent receives citations from other technology domains, it is likely that the patent is more valuable as it has impacts on subsequent innovations in other classes [4].

In this study, we classify patent citations along the two dimensions (assignees and technologies) into four groups: self-cited in the same class, self-cited from different class, other-cited in the same class, and other-cited from different class. We show that these four types of citations have different implications for patent value, and therefore, weighted patent citations are a better indicator for patent evaluation and patent ranking than a simple citation count that puts equal weights on different types of citations.

More specifically, we use patent renewal status as a reference to evaluate our weighted citation based measurement for patent value. U.S. patents are required to be renewed at the 4th, 8th and 12th year after patent grant by paying maintenance fees, and it is no surprise that patent renewal status are indicative of patent value. We assume that the ranking of patents based on our weighted citations method correlates closely with the ranking pattern based on patent renewal status, and we measure this correlation by the Spearman's rank correlation coefficient [11].

We first apply an unconstrained nonlinear optimization method to estimate optimal weights on the four types of patent citations, by maximizing the Spearman's rank correlation coefficient. However, this numerical optimization approach is quite an expensive operation which sometimes even does not guarantee convergence. We then investigate other simpler regression-based approaches for estimation of weights and compare their performance with the performance of the optimal weights obtained from the nonlinear optimization approach, as an effort to find good methods for learning the weights.

According to our experimental results, our new weighted citation approach consistently shows a better performance, in terms of rank correlations with patent renewal status, than the simple unweighted citation approach, with around 20% improvement. The estimated weights for the four types of patent citations also shed interesting insights on economic implications of patent citations.

2. RELATED WORK
The literature on patent citation and patent evaluation has been exclusively on simple patent citation counts. Lanjourw and Schankerman [7] found a positive statistical relationship between measurements such as patent citations, the number of claims, patent renewal and litigation. Bessen [1] used patent renewal data to assess the value of patents and found that citations received are

JCDL'12, June 10–14, 2012, Washington D.C., USA.

positively and significantly associated with renewal. Harhoff et al. [6] showed that patent citations are correlated with patent value obtained from a survey of German patent holders on the price at which they would have been willing to sell the patent right three years after filing. Hall et al. [5] found that a firm's market value is larger when its patents cite more of its older patents, suggesting that the firm has been doing accumulative and follow-on research in its specialized area. This study is somewhat related to our proposed distinction of patent citations between self-cited vs. other-cited, but in the context of firm evaluation rather than patent evaluation.

There is also a large literature on journal article citation analysis. In bibliometrics, citations received by a paper are a very popular measure of paper quality. Walker et al. [12] proposed a CiteRank algorithm that incorporates two parameters, the inverse of the average citation depth and a time constant that is biased toward more recent publications. Bollen et al. [2] used a weighted PageRank algorithm to measure journal prestige, and Radicchi et al. [9] proposed a weighted PageRank algorithm on a directed weighted author citation network for ranking scientists by considering the diffusion of their scientific credits.

3. WEIGHTED CITATIONS

We classify patent citations using information on patent assignees and patent technology classes. On the dimension of assignees, if a patent is cited by patents filed by the same assignee (e.g. patents owned by the same company), we classify these citations as *Self-cited*. *Other-cited* refers to citations made by patents filed by different assignees. On the dimension of technology domains, if a patent is cited by patents from the same technology domain, we classify these citations as *Same-class*; otherwise, as *Diff-class*. Therefore, each citation belongs to one of four types. Table 1 listed the types of patent citations and their distribution for patent citations to patents granted between 1981 and 2000.

Table 1. Type of Citations

Type of citations	By Assignee		By Technology Category		Ratio in the total citations
	Same assignee	Different assignee	Same category	Different category	
C_1. Self-cited in the Same-class	O		O		10.74%
C_2. Self-cited from the Diff-class	O			O	2.67%
C_3. Other-cited in the Same-class		O	O		66.38%
C_4. Other-cited from the Diff-class		O		O	20.21%

Our approach is to put different weights on each type of citations, to improve patent citation based measurement for patent evaluation and rankings. Let $Wcited_i$ be the weighted citation of a patent i and C_{ij} is the aggregated number of the type j citations received by a patent i. Then the weighted citation is defined as follows:

$$Wcited_i = \sum_{j=1}^{4} w_j C_{ij}$$

Patent Renewal Data

Patent holders have to pay maintenance fee to renew their patents. In the United States, maintenance fees on utility patents are due 3.5, 7.5, and 11.5 years from the date of the original patent grant. Table 2 lists the maintenance schedule and fees. For small entities, including for-profit companies with 500 or fewer employees, non-profit organizations or individual inventors, the fees are reduced by 50%.

Patent renewal status is a strong indicator for patent importance and value. When a patent owner pays a renewal fee, it implies that the patent is worth more than the fee required to keep it in force. Hence, we learn the weights on four types of patent citations by evaluating the correlation between a patent's renewal status and its weighted citations. In future work, we shall use the maintenance fees as another indicator to measure the value of patents.

Table 2. Maintenance Schedule and Fee

Renewal	Maintenance fee* (Large entity)	Maintenance fee* (Small entity)	Patents Expired	Ratio of Expired
No renewal	0	0	4th year	12.13%
4th-year renewal	$1,130	$565	8th year	20.45%
8th-year renewal	$2,850	$1,425	12th year	19.16%
12th-year renewal	$4,730	$2,365	20th year	48.26%

(*http://www.uspto.gov/web/offices/ac/qs/ope/fee092611.htm)

Spearman's Rank Correlation Coefficient

We use each patent's renewal status as the reference to learn the weights on different types of citations. We posit that the rank of patents by weighted citations is highly correlated with the rank by their renewal stages. Therefore, it seems appropriate to use Spearman's rank correlation coefficient [11] to measure the correlation between weighted citations and renewal stage. The Spearman's rank correlation coefficient is calculated using the Pearson correlation coefficient between the ranked variables. For a sample of size n, the n raw scores X_i, Y_i are converted to ranks x_i, y_i and the rank correlation coefficient, ρ, is computed from these:

$$\rho = \frac{\sum_i (x_i - \bar{x})(y_i - \bar{y})}{\sqrt{\sum_i (x_i - \bar{x})^2 \sum_i (y_i - \bar{y})^2}}$$

Learning the Weights

To learn the weights on different types of patent citations, we first use an unconstrained nonlinear optimization method [8] to maximize the Spearman's correlation coefficient between weighted citations and patent renewal status, which gives us the optimal results if the rank correlation is our objective function. Let X be the patent citation data set and Y is the renewal status of patents. The row of X is patent citations that are classified into the four types shown in Table 1: self-cited in the same class, self-cited from different class, other-cited in the same class, and other-cited from different class. Each feature represents the number of citations received for each type. The renewal status of each patent is presented by ordered numbers such as 0 (expired at 4th-year), 1 (renewed at 4th-year but expired at 8th-year), 2 (renewed at 4th-year and 8th-year but expired at 12th-year), or 3 (full-term renewal). The nonlinear optimization will search for the optimal weights on different types of patent citations to maximize Spearman's correlation coefficient between patent weighted citations and patent renewal status, as described as follows:

$$\max_{w} \rho(Xw, Y)$$

However, it is expensive to use a numerical optimization method. Sometimes it does not even converge with an inappropriate initial condition. Hence, we turn to regression-based and simpler methods to learn the weights. First we use a linear regression to learn the weights, where the dependent variable is ordered patent renewal status (0,1,2,3).

Table 3. Rank Correlation Results of Patents Granted in 1990 with 10 Years Citations

Weight learning methods	C_1. Self-cited in the same-class	C_2. Self-cited from the diff-class	C_3. Other-cited in the same class	C_4. Other-cited from the diff-class	Constant	Spearman's rank correlation coefficient	Improvements
Not weighted	1	1	1	1	-	0.2037	(baseline)
1. Nonlinear optimization	2.1060 (14.79)	2.2610 (15.88)	0.2298 (1.61)	0.1424 (1.00)		0.2466	21.02%
2. Linear regression	0.0530 (4.57)	0.0593 (5.11)	0.0141 (1.22)	0.0116 (1.00)	1.7905	0.2393	17.46%
3. Exponential-scaled linear regression	0.3902 (4.41)	0.4648 (5.26)	0.1046 (1.18)	0.0884 (1.00)	10.1430	0.2392	17.42%
4. Linear regression on log-scaled features	0.3054 (4.82)	0.2460 (3.88)	0.1526 (2.41)	0.0634 (1.00)	1.5513	0.2453	20.38%
5. Nonlinear regression	0.9537 (8.63)	1.1064 (10.01)	0.1647 (1.49)	0.1105 (1.00)	4.2464	0.2451	20.31%

Table 4. Rank Correlation Results of Patents Granted from 1985 to 1989 with 10 Years Citations

Patents granted year (# of patents)	Not weighted (baseline)	1. Nonlinear optimization	2. Linear regression	3. Exponential-scaled linear regression	4. Linear regression on log-scaled features	5. Nonlinear regression
1985 (50,293)	0.1779	0.2169 (21.89%)	0.2049 (15.15%)	0.2038 (14.53%)	0.2151 (20.91%)	0.2149 (20.81%)
1986 (50,172)	0.1867	0.2257 (20.89%)	0.2186 (17.13%)	0.2180 (16.77%)	0.2239 (19.97%)	0.2245 (20.24%)
1987 (59,868)	0.1946	0.2309 (18.69%)	0.2241 (15.16%)	0.2237 (14.99%)	0.2294 (17.91%)	0.2295 (17.95%)
1988 (56,687)	0.1993	0.2377 (19.28%)	0.2075 (4.12%)	0.2072 (3.98%)	0.2335 (17.17%)	0.2364 (18.60%)
1989 (69,439)	0.2002	0.2430 (21.37%)	0.2347 (17.24%)	0.2341 (16.95%)	0.2410 (20.36%)	0.2419 (20.81%)

Table 5. Rank Correlation Results of Patents Granted in 1990 with Truncated Citations

Truncated year (# of patents)	Not weighted (baseline)	1. Nonlinear optimization	2. Linear regression	3. Exponential-scaled linear regression	4. Linear regression on log-scaled features	5. Nonlinear regression
1991 (17,507)	0.0718	0.0894 (24.47%)	0.0883 (23.00%)	0.0882 (22.90%)	0.0874 (21.72%)	0.0885 (23.21%)
1992 (35,509)	0.1031	0.1280 (24.11%)	0.1241 (20.31%)	0.1227 (18.97%)	0.1270 (23.17%)	0.1280 (24.09%)
1993 (46,298)	0.1243	0.1539 (23.80%)	0.1517 (22.09%)	0.1519 (22.19%)	0.1531 (23.18%)	0.1529 (23.02%)
1994 (52,845)	0.1464	0.1781 (21.68%)	0.1745 (19.17%)	0.1743 (19.08%)	0.1761 (20.29%)	0.1775 (21.22%)
1995 (56,867)	0.1640	0.1963 (19.72%)	0.1924 (17.35%)	0.1922 (17.24%)	0.1950 (18.91%)	0.1956 (19.31%)
1996 (59,566)	0.1757	0.2122 (20.74%)	0.2067 (17.61%)	0.2066 (17.55%)	0.2101 (19.56%)	0.2107 (19.90%)
1997 (61,485)	0.1821	0.2206 (21.16%)	0.2151 (18.14%)	0.2148 (17.94%)	0.2189 (20.19%)	0.2190 (20.27%)
1998 (63,259)	0.1914	0.2318 (21.10%)	0.2255 (17.80%)	0.2254 (17.76%)	0.2301 (20.20%)	0.2303 (20.27%)
1999 (64,548)	0.1976	0.2391 (21.04%)	0.2323 (17.58%)	0.2323 (17.56%)	0.2377 (20.30%)	0.2377 (20.34%)

Now, X also includes all 1's constant feature column.

$$Y = Xw$$

Given that the distribution of citations is more skewed than the distribution of ordered patent renewal status, we also try another linear regression where we use exponentials of Y as dependent variables, as specified below:

$$e^Y = Xw$$

We also try the nonlinear regression as follows:

$$Y = \log(Xw + 1)$$

Our last approach is a linear regression on logarithms of each type of citations, as shown below:

$$Y = w_0 + \sum_{i=1}^{4} w_i \log(x_i + 1)$$

4. EXPERIMENTS AND RESULTS

Patent Data Set

We use the U.S. utility patent citation data from the National Bureau of Economic Research (NBER) patent data project [10]. It includes information on patent citation between 1976 through 2006, patent assignees and technology categories. To classify technology domain for each patent, we use the HJT 6-class fields suggested by Hall, Jaffe, and Trajtenberg [4], which consist of six technology categories: Chemical, Computers and communications, Drugs and medical, Electrical and electronic, Mechanical, and Others. We also tested the HJT 36-class category which is a more refined system, and the results are similar.

For the patent renewal data, we use Patent Maintenance Fee event data set downloaded from Google USPTO Bulk download site [3]. This data set provides maintenance fee events from 1981 to present. We parse maintenance fee events to get the renewal stage for each patent.

Comparison of Learning Methods

To test our five weight learning methods, we investigate patent citations within a window of 10 years after patent grant for each of the patents granted in 1990. For evaluation, we use 10-fold cross validation and average the results from 10 10-fold cross validations.

The results in Table 3 show that using weighted citations improves the Spearman's rank correlation between patent citations and patent renewal status by more than 20%. The nonlinear optimization method leads to the optimal weights for the four types of patent citations and the highest rank correlation. Among the four regression methods, performance with the linear regression using log-scaled features and the nonlinear regression is quite close to the optimal performance.

Weights on Different Types of Citations

The weights on each type of citations, shown in Table 3, confirm that self-citations get much more weights than citations made by other assignees. While self-citations suggest that a firm has further developed innovations based on the cited patent, other-citations might indicate that competitors have entered the market and ruined the value of the cited patent. Thus we observe a stark difference between the weights for self-cited and for other-cited.

Moreover, when a self-citation is from different technology domains, it gets more weights than a self-citation from the same technology field, suggesting that, other things equal, a patent that get utilized in other domains within the firm is more valuable. However, if a patent becomes the shoulder for innovations and products in other domains by the competitors, then it is least valuable to the patent owner, as suggested by the weight on other-cited from different classes.

Results with Other Patent Sets

We confirm these results with other patent test sets. Table 4 presents the rank correlation results for five different sets of patents that were granted at different years. All of the five test sets show consistent results, including around 20% improvements in the performance of each of the five weight learning methods.

Even though the nonlinear optimization method and the nonlinear regression method show the best outcomes, but they are computationally expensive compared to linear regressions. It is interesting that the linear regression with log-scaled features shows promising results, which essentially takes the product (rather than the sum) of weight powered citations. We will explore this interesting finding more in future studies.

Truncated Citation Window

Table 5 shows the rank correlation results for patents granted in 1990 with truncated citations. It is a more difficult problem to estimate the value of patents with some shortage in citation information, for example, when a patent was granted not long ago. However, it might be more useful to predict a patent's importance as early as possible as the patent owner can decide more strategically what to do with the patent. At each truncation year, we conduct experiments for the subset of patents that had received at least one citation up to that year. The result shows that the weighted citation performs even better when patent citations are further truncated.

Table 6 shows the changes in weights for the four types of citations if citations are truncated. The test set is patents granted in 1990 and the weights are learned using the nonlinear optimization method. The weights in the table are relative to the weight on other-cited from different classes. The results show that the weights on self-citation continuously increased when the citation window becomes larger, whereas the changes in weights for other-cited are modest. One possible reason for why self-citations are much more sensitive than other-citations is that the proportion of self-citations among all citations is decreasing with more citation years, dropping from about 20% in a three year window to 10% in an eleven year window.

Table 6. The Ratio of Weights by Truncated Years

Citation Window	C_1. Self-cited in the same class	C_2. Self-cited from the diff-class	C_3. Other-cited in the same class	C_4. Other-cited from the diff-class
3-year	2.13 (17.46%)	2.31 (3.48%)	1.03 (62.44%)	1.00 (16.62%)
4-year	7.73 (15.69%)	8.42 (3.27%)	2.01 (63.66%)	1.00 (17.38%)
5-year	8.06 (14.38%)	9.14 (3.14%)	1.79 (64.46%)	1.00 (18.02%)
8-year	12.73 (11.54%)	12.84 (2.82%)	1.49 (65.73%)	1.00 (19.91%)
11-year	15.51 (9.71%)	15.02 (2.52%)	1.44 (66.43%)	1.00 (21.34%)

5. CONCLUSIONS

To our best knowledge, this is the first paper that distinguishes the different types of patent citations and proposes weighted citation based indicators for patent evaluation and ranking. We compare various methods for learning the weights for different citations. We find that the linear regression with log-scaled features leads to results as good as the optimal solutions obtained from the nonlinear optimization method. Our weighted citation approach shows consistent improvements on rank correlation with the renewal data. These results point to a promising approach to better ranking scientific literature and patents in digital libraries that has not been explored before.

6. REFERENCES

[1] Bessen, J. 2008. The value of us patents by owner and patent characteristics. *Research Policy*, 37(5), 932-945.

[2] Bollen, J., Rodriguez, M.A., and Van de Sompel, H. 2006. Journal status. *Scientometrics*, 69(3), 669-687.

[3] Google Patents: USPTO Bulk Downloads: Patent Maintenance Fees. http://www.google.com/googlebooks/uspto-patents-maintenance-fees.html

[4] Hall, B.H., Jaffe, A.B., and Trajtenberg, M. 2001. The NBER Patent Citations Data File: Lessons, Insights and Methodological Tools. *NBER Working Paper*. No. 8498.

[5] Hall, B.H., Jaffe, A.B., and Trajtenberg, M. 2005. Market value and patent citations. *The RAND Journal of Economics*, 36(1), 16-38.

[6] Harhoff, D., Narin, F., Scherer, F.M., and Vopel, K. 1999. Citation frequency and the value of patented inventions. *Review of Economics and Statistics*, 81(3), 511-515.

[7] Lanjouw, J.O. and Schankerman, M. 2004. Patent quality and research productivity: Measuring innovation with multiple indicators. *The Economic Journal*, 114(495), 441-465.

[8] Nocedal, J. and Wright., S. J. 1999. *Numerical Optimization*. Springer-Verlag.

[9] Radicchi, F., Fortunato, S., Makines, B., and Vespignani, A. 2009. Diffusion of scientific credits and the ranking of scientists. *Physical Review E.*, 80(5).

[10] The New NBER Patent Data Project. https://sites.google.com/site/patentdataproject/

[11] Wackerly, D. D., Mendenhall, W., and Scheaffer, R. L. 2002. *Mathematical Statistics with Applications*. Duxbury Advanced Series.

[12] Walker, D., Xie, H., Yan, K.K., and Maslov, S. 2007. Ranking scientific publications using a model of network traffic. *Journal of Statistical Mechanics: Theory and Experiment*, 7, P06010.

A Hybrid Two-Stage Approach for Discipline-Independent Canonical Representation Extraction from References

Sung Hee Park
Digital Library Research Laboratory
Department of Computer Science
Virginia Tech
Blacksburg, Virginia, 24061
shpark@vt.edu

Roger W. Ehrich
Center for Human Computer Interaction
Department of Computer Science
Virginia Tech
Blacksburg, Virginia, 24061
rehrich@vt.edu

Edward A. Fox
Digital Library Research Laboratory
Department of Computer Science
Virginia Tech
Blacksburg, VA, 24061
fox@vt.edu

ABSTRACT

In education and research, references play a key role. However, extracting and parsing references are difficult problems. One concern is that there are many styles of references; hence, given a surface form, identifying what style was employed is problematic, especially in heterogeneous collections of theses and dissertations, which cover many fields and disciplines, and where different styles may be used even in the same publication. We address these problems by drawing upon suitable knowledge found in the WWW. In particular, we research a two-stage classifier approach, involving multi-class classification with respect to reference styles, and partially solve the problem of parsing surface representations of references. We describe empirical evidence for the effectiveness of our approach and plans for improvement of our methods.

Categories and Subject Descriptors

H.3.7 [**Information storage and retrieval**]: Digital Libraries—*systems issues*; I.5 [**Pattern Recognition**]: Design Methodology—*classifier design and evaluation*

General Terms

Algorithm, Performance, Design, Experimentation

Keywords

Canonical Representation Extraction, Knowledge Acquisition, Reverse-Engineering, Style-Free Reference Metadata Extraction

1. INTRODUCTION

In scholarly digital libraries, citation/reference analysis can support patrons if it leads to suitable services. Citation relations between digital objects in collections can be identified. Examples of citation analysis include: metadata extraction [1, 4, 5, 6, 12, 14, 29], citation matching/entity resolution [2, 23, 27], and citation/co-authorship network construction/analysis [7]. These studies are important, since scholars use citations to support their discussion and argumentation, and since collections of references aid in identifying relationships among works.

Garfield and others have used citation indexes to aid bibliometric studies [10]. Further, as research papers have become readily available on the WWW, *automated* citation indexing systems, such as CiteSeer [18], have been developed. Accurate citation metadata extraction now plays a critical role in research evaluation [25].

Some work on digital libraries aims to aggregate publications across groups and disciplines. For instance, consider Virginia Tech's ETD-db digital library, which is an instantiation of the ETD-db system originally developed at Virginia Tech. It contains over 18,000 electronic theses and dissertations from 8 colleges and 79 departments[1]. Another example is arXiv, with 662,023 e-prints from 7 large disciplines, covering 148 sub-categories[2] as of March 2011.

Extracting references from such collections is difficult since those references have a variety of different forms depending on disciplines. Currently, a number of reference extraction and analysis approaches and systems have been making use of domain knowledge, and have been specialized to an area, such as computing or chemistry. However, in order for a citation analysis algorithm to be scalable, it should be able to extract information from heterogeneous collections, putting results into suitable canonical forms. It should operate across disciplines and reference styles, and handle a broad range of reference surface forms [25].

Due to the success of machine learning, natural language processing, and web mining, some researchers envision Machine Reading [22], which goes beyond domain-independent and unsupervised text understanding.

We aim to help move toward the vision of Machine Reading by using knowledge derived from web mining, along with machine learning techniques such as support vector machines (SVM) and conditional random fields (CRF). This

[1] http://www.vt.edu/academics/academic-departments.html

[2] Physics (45), Mathematics (35), Nonlinear Science (5), Computer Science (40), Quantitative Biology (10), Quantitative Finance (7), Statistics (6)

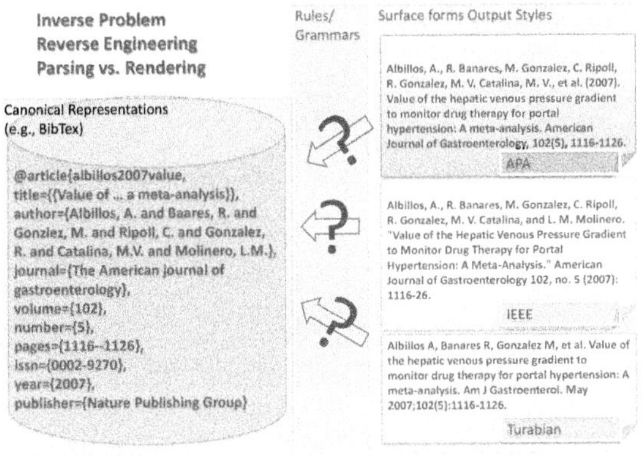

Figure 1: Overview of Canonical Representation Extraction Problem

will overcome limitations of current citation information extraction techniques, which work in a domain-specific and supervised manner. Further, we can learn from analysis of collections of references that appear in large documents, as opposed to only working on individual references.

This paper is logically structured as follows: In Section 2, challenging problems that we will deal with will be defined. In Section 3, related work will be reviewed in terms of classification methods and features in classification. Our novel and elaborated methodology to tackle the challenging problems will be described in Section 4. Evaluation to examine the performance and effectiveness will be discussed in Section 5. At the end of this paper, conclusions & future work will be described.

2. PROBLEM STATEMENT

Our problem, as illustrated intuitively in Figure 1, can be considered as an inverse problem to mathematicians, as well as a reverse engineering problem for software engineering researchers, and a parsing vs. rendering problem for compiler and linguistics experts.

More formally speaking, problems that we are dealing with include: 1) the surface & semantics mapping problem, 2) the disciplines & styles problem, and 3) the implicit background knowledge acquisition problem.

The surface & semantics mapping problem is a *semantic tagging* problem / *sequence labeling* problem in natural language processing and bioinformatics, which is the association of a sequence of reference tokens with their semantic labels, where the input sequence is a reference surface form. This can be formalized as follows. Let a reference surface form be *a sequence of tokens* $T(t_1, t_2, .., t_n)$ and let its meaning (semantics) be *a sequence of semantic labels* $L(l_1, l_2, .., l_m)$. A sequence labeling is a mapping $f : T \rightarrow L$. The sequence labeling problem from the conditional probabilistic perspective is to find a mapping f that maximizes the conditional probability $P(L|T)$ which means that given a sequence of tokens T, how often a sequence of labels T occur.

The disciplines & styles problem concerns the scalability of the surface and semantics mapping problem. For the many specific disciplines found, reference styles must be interpreted so references can be analyzed. For this reason, two terms, *style-free* and *discipline-independent*, will be used in this paper interchangeably. Thus, solving this problem will provide a discipline-independent & style-independent surface & semantics mapping solution for users. This research involves knowledge acquisition from the Web. When humans interpret the semantics of the surface form of references, they use implicit background knowledge in terms of a variety of reference styles.

Table 1: Comparison of Previous Approaches

Approach	Author&Year	Uns/Su
Rule-based	Day et al. (2006) [6]	S
	Cortez et al. (2007) [4]	U
	Afzal et al. (2010) [1]	U
Machine learning	Councill et al. (2008) [5]	S
	Hong et al. (2009) [14]	S
	Hetzner (2008) [12]	S

Citation analysis is a challenging problem because of: 1) the wide variety of citation styles [20], 2) different document types [26], 3) domain dependent properties [20], 4) lexical ambiguities (e.g., acronyms, homonyms of acronyms), 5) missing information (e.g., pages or venues), 6) inconsistency, and 7) errors in typing and other inaccuracies. The large number of reference styles (e.g., APA, IEEE) makes it difficult to fit a machine learning model to each specific reference style. Different document types, sometimes referred to as genres (e.g., books, book chapters, journal articles, and web pages), also complicate the task of citation metadata extraction.

In particular, it is worth noting that different domains (e.g., Computer Science, Health Science, and Social Science) tend to generate different terminals (e.g., different journal titles and conference titles) in the references, and these effect the output. This dependency property reduces the generality of existing solutions, and complicates the problem of developing scalable approaches that can operate across the myriad domains found in large heterogeneous collections.

Our problems raise the following research questions:

1. What features should be selected for training?

2. What methods give the best performance and greatest effectiveness?

3. LITERATURE REVIEW

In this section, we review prior work regarding canonical representation extraction in terms of 1) sequence labeling methods and 2) features used in sequence labeling.

3.1 Sequence Labeling Methods

Many efforts have been made to improve canonical representation extraction performance. Those can be categorized into two large types of approaches: 1) Rule & knowledge-based approaches [6, 4, 1] and 2) machine learning approaches [5, 14, 12, 29]. Table 1 shows a summary of labeling methods in terms of the classification method.

3.1.1 Rule/Knowledge-Based Approaches

Rule-based approaches to canonical reference representation extraction, basically, are classification methods that exploit rules to mark tokens in the questioned sequence with proper semantic labels, where, generally, one or more human experts in the specific areas would consult rules.

Some prior successful research has been done using rule-based approaches to reference metadata extraction, in a limited problem space (e.g., less than ten reference styles, two or three disciplines). Day et al. [6] adopted a rule-based approach using a knowledge representation frame, which is called INFOMAP, with respect to six styles. This knowledge describes layout appearances of semantic labels such as *author*, *title*, *publisher*, and *year*. Ding et al. [8] used different templates designed to deal with the specific citations from digital contents.

Cortez et al. [4] proposed a knowledge-based approach for extracting citation metadata in a flexible way called FLUX-CiM, which consists of blocking, matching, binding, and joining processes. Unlike other knowledge/ontology based approaches such as [4, 6], this approach used a knowledge base to gather frequencies of terms that occur in each field like authors, titles, journals, etc. To evaluate the effectiveness of the method on reference style-free extraction, it used two or three disciplines (e.g., health science and social science). However, the feature, term frequency, that they have used as a primary feature is likely to be dependent on discipline. In addition, Embley et al. [9] used a conceptual model like Ding's template based approach not only in citation parsing but also in general information extraction.

A general disadvantage of rule-based approaches is that it is not easy to extract rules. Although previous research has shown that they are effective in the case of limited reference styles and disciplines [4, 6], they are not easily adapted to our problem, which involves extending the problem space so that there almost certainly is a requirement for solutions that are discipline-independent and style-free.

3.1.2 Machine Learning Approaches

The surface and semantics mapping problem can be framed as the sequence labeling problem in a natural language processing context.

Machine learning approaches have led to sequence labeling machine learning techniques involving hidden Markov models (HMMs) [12], conditional random fields (CRFs) [14, 5, 21], prediction by partial matching (PPM) [28], and support vector machines (SVMs) [11].

Machine learning approaches can generally be categorized into two main categories: *kernel function based* such as support vector machine and *probabilistic graphical models* such as CRF, HMM, and Maximum Entropy Markov Model (MEMM). Originally, SVM was a binary classifier, but it has been extended to solve the sequence labeling problem. SVM^{struct} is one of the support vector machine implementations for sequence labeling [16]. Probabilistic graphical models can further be grouped into *generative models* and *discriminative models*. A *generative model* is a probabilistic graphical model in which an input sequence generates an output sequence. Generally, generative models calculate a joint probability $P(X, Y)$, whereas a *discriminative model* directly calculates a conditional probability of $P(Y|X)$, where X is an input sequence and Y is an output label sequence. An example classifier for a single classification involves a naïve Bayesian network. HMM [24] is a typical generative model for a sequence data segmenter and labeler, while a *discriminative model*, for example, CRF, directly calculates the conditional probability $P(Y|X)$, where X is an input sequence and Y is an output label sequence.

Supervised learning techniques learn from a training set, labeled by human effort. This is time consuming and expensive. To alleviate this burden in supervised learning methods, some efficient methods called semi (weak)-supervised learning have been proposed and evaluated [15, 19].

In this paper, we describe how these machine learning approaches can be applied to our research problems.

Table 2: Features for Canonical Representation Extraction

Features	Description	Literature
Local features	Non-lexical information about the token	[5, 14, 21, 29, 30]
Lexical features	Information about the meaning of the words within the token	[5, 14, 21, 29, 30]
Contextual features	Lexical or local features of a token's neighbours	[5, 14]
Layout features	Relative position of a word in the entire reference string	[5, 14, 21, 29]

3.2 Features

In general, with classification methods, features are considered to play a critical role so that it is possible to discriminate the data belonging to a class from data belonging to other classes. Novel and effective features have been proposed and utilized.

Councill et al. [5] used 23 features grouped as: Token identity (3 features), N-gram prefix/suffix (9 features), Orthographic case (1 feature), Punctuation (1 feature), Number (1 feature), Dictionary (6 features), Location (1 feature), and Possible editor (1 feature), in an open source reference parsing tool, *ParsCit*. It is currently used in CiteSeerX. Hong et al. [14] used a set of ten features, which are categorized into lexical (dictionary) features, local features, contextual features, and layout features, in the lightweight real-time reference string extraction & parsing system called *FireCite*.

Similarly, Zou et al. [30] used 14 binary features consisting of three dictionary features (Author Name, Article Title, and Journal Title) and an additional 11 binary features describing local and orthographic information (e.g., pagination pattern, name initial pattern, four digit year pattern, etc.). Yu and Fan [29] used 15 features, including nine local features (ALLCHINESE, CONTDIGITS, ALLDIGITS, SIXDIGITS, CONTDOTS, CONTAINS@, SINGLECHAR, NAME, EMAIL), three layout features (LINE_START, LINE_IN, LINE_END), and three lexicon features (FAMILYNAME, AFFILIATION, ADDRESS) for metadata extraction from Chinese research papers. Peng et al. [21] investigated state transition features, unsupported vs. supported, local features, layout features, and lexicon features.

Recognizing the properties of features, automatic reference metadata labeling methods have used the following four classes of features which we arbitrarily categorize: 1) local features, 2) lexical features (dictionaries), 3) contextual features, and 4) layout features. Comparisons of classes of features are given in Table 2.

4. METHODOLOGY

In this study, we consider a hybrid method of knowledge-based approaches and machine learning methods to solve the style-free reference metadata extraction problem. One

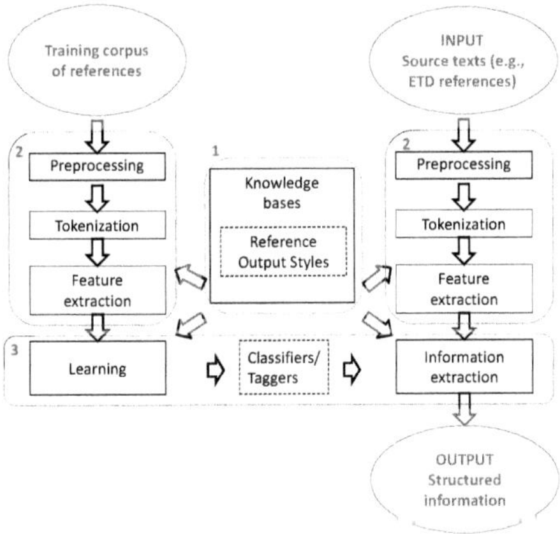

Figure 2: A Flow of the Hybrid Information Extraction Process

of the key features in our proposed method is that knowledge bases from web mining of tagging tokens are obtained to make reference metadata extraction more accurate. In addition to the knowledge bases, datasets consisting of concepts and instances for training also are crawled from the Web. Once knowledge bases and training datasets are built, machine learning methods capture the rules for labeling a sequence of input reference strings. Our methodology (see Figure 2) can be largely divided into three parts: 1) Building knowledge bases through web mining, 2) feature extraction including preprocessing and tokenization, and 3) two-stage classification and sequence labeling as highlighted with labels 1, 2, and 3 in Figure 2.

4.1 Building Knowledge Bases from Mining the Web

4.1.1 Knowledge Bases

Recently, Cortez et al. [4] defined a knowledge base as a set of pairs of objects and instances like a dictionary. Here, we also will borrow their definition of knowledge base. A *knowledge base* is defined as a set of pairs $K = \{(o_1, i_1), (o_2, i_2), \ldots, (o_n, i_n)\}$ where o_i is a bibliographical field like *author*, *title*, *journal*, or *years*, and i_i is its corresponding instance or value. For example, examples of entries in the knowledge base might be (‘*AUTHOR*’, ‘John Smith’), (‘*JOURNAL*’, ‘ACM Transactions on Information System’), and (‘*YEAR*’, ‘2011’). We also find other formats for knowledge bases than as $(object, instance)$ pairs; thus, a so called compound object is a set of objects, that can describe a canonical representation of references (e.g., (‘IEEE styles’, ‘A. Albillos, et al.,“Value of the hepatic venous pressure gradient to monitor drug therapy for portal hypertension: A meta-analysis,” American Journal of Gastroenterology, vol. 102, pp.1116-1126, May 2007.’))

4.1.2 Reference Styles

Sources: *EndNoteWeb*[3] is a private web resource that can be accessed by subscription. It provides a service of generating more than 3,000 reference styles from an imported canonical representation (e.g., BibTex, RIS, EndNote format).

Pipelines: Figure 3 illustrates a knowledge acquisition process for reference styles by reverse-engineering a reference management tool. Input data are randomly sampled data crawled from the Web. The input data are imported to a reference management tool such as EndNote or Zotero, which exports a large number of styles of references (see Algorithm 1). This knowledge is used as a training corpus of references for training our reference style classifiers and sequence labelers.

[3]http://www.myendnoteweb.com

Algorithm 1 Acquiring training data for reference style from the Web

1: Extract all style names from the bibliographical reference generation interface.
2: Import a reference set into the EndNoteWeb.
3: Crawl all styled references.
4: Convert HTML files to text files.
5: Convert raw files to training sets.

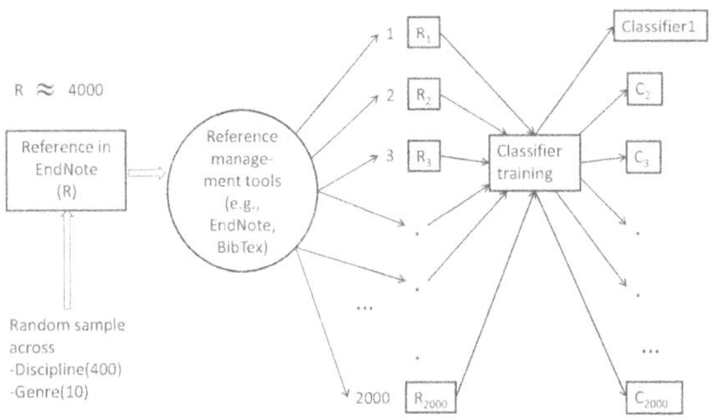

Figure 3: Our Proposed Reference Style Knowledge Acquisition Method

Knowledge instances: Instances of the more than 3000 reference styles [4] are shown in Figure 4. The second frame is illustrative of the 3,338 style entries. Reference surface forms are listed in the third frame.

4.2 Feature Extraction

4.2.1 Tokenization

Generally, in natural language processing, tokenization is a step in which an input string is segmented into a set of tokens. This utilizes non-alphanumeric letters, such as commas (,), parentheses (()), spaces (‘ ’), or tabs (‘\t’), etc., as delimiters; thereafter, the delimiters are usually ignored. However, we exploit these delimiters as significant features for discriminating among fields even after the tokenization step since our input reference strings are closely associated with the delimiters in the surface form.

4.2.2 Feature Types

We consider two types of features: local features and contextual features.

Local features: Local features provide orthographic information for a token. Local features shown in Table 3 will be investigated as used in both reference style classification (stage 1) and sequence labeling (stage 2).

Contextual features: Contextual features are features that can capture state transitions. In our problem, these fea-

[4]http://parsifal.dlib.vt.edu/kbstyles

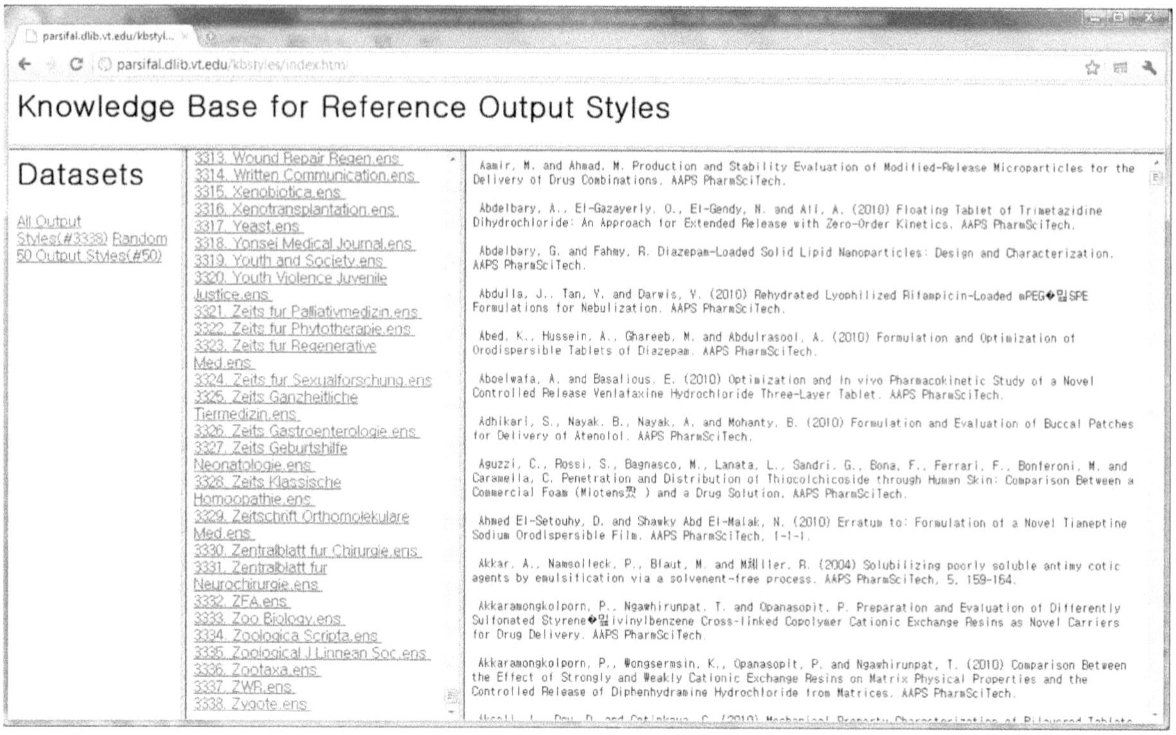

Figure 4: Knowledge Base for Reference Styles Acquired from EndNote

Table 3: Local Features

Categories	Names	Descriptions	Examples
Letters Patterns	INITCAP	Starts with a capitalized letter	Computer Science
	ALLCAP	All letters are capitalized	COMPUTER
	ACRO	Acronyms	WWW
	LONELYINITIAL	One single capitalized letter	S.
	CAPLETTER	Contains capital letters	arXiv
	SINGLECHAR	One single character	p
Special Character Patterns	CONTAINSDOTS	Contains at least one dot	S., C4.5
	CONTAINSDASH	Contains at least one dash	123-124
	PUNC	Punctuation	dot ("."), comma (",")
	URL	Regular expression for URLs	http://www.acm.org
	ENDEDWITHDOT	Regular expression for ending with a dot	A.
Special Patterns	EMAIL	Regular expression for e-addresses	smith@gmail.com
	WORD	Word	references
	PAGINATION	Regular expression for pagination formats	200-5, H100-H105
Numeric Patterns	FOURDIGITYEAR	Regular expression for four-digit year pattern	2005
	SIXDIGIT	Regular expression for six-digit patterns	2005
	CONTAINSDIGITS	Contains at least one digit	1, F1, A1*
	ALLDIGITS/DIGITONLY	All letters are numeric	111
	DIGITANDLETTERONLY	Contains digits and letters only	H1N1
	DIGITANDLETTER	Contains both digits and letters	2-3-4 tree
	PHONEORZIP	Phone number or zip	231-3615
Length Patterns	FIELDLENGTH	# of characters the token has	fieldLength(style)=5

tures will measure possibilities of orderings of tokens. The contextual features reviewed in Table 2 are being investigated.

4.3 Style-Free Canonical Representation Extraction through Two-Stage Method

To solve our challenging problem, discipline-independent and style-free canonical representation extraction, we propose a hybrid combination of machine learning based and knowledge-based approaches. Figure 5 illustrates the proposed method.

Our solution for discipline-independent citation metadata extraction uses reference style information, built from mining the Web, as a critical aid. The Web is a resource abundant in structured knowledge.

Our method is broadly divided into two stages. The first stage is reference style classification while the second is sequence labeling.

4.3.1 Two-stage SVM/CRF Sequence Classifier

We adopt a two-stage SVM/CRF sequence classifier. The reason we choose this structure is because the references dealt with have a characteristic that the identical citation style has the same rules to generate references. A two-stage classifier has been used in several tasks [13]. Hoefel et al. [13] exploited a two-stage SVM/CRF sequence classifier on the task of handwritten word recognition. Our style classification is illustrated by labels 1-7 in Figure 5 and our sequence labeling is shown by labels 5-14. The following sections describe more details.

4.3.2 Reference Style Classification

Reference style classification is a general *multi-class clas-*

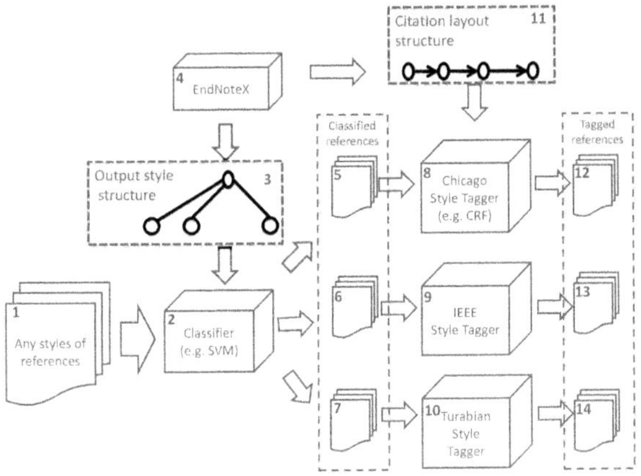

Figure 5: Our proposed extraction method

sification problem. It is convenient to convert a multi-class problem into multiple *binary classification problems*. In this work, we will use one of the machine learning techniques, support vector machine (SVM) [3], which was first proposed by Vapnik. This SVM technique classifies two classes in a way to maximize margins between one class and the other. For a complex dataset, sometimes, a function called a *kernel function* transforms the dataset into a high dimension space in which a dataset can be linearly separable and later mapped back to the original space.

In Figure 5, input data (see the part labeled 1) is a styled *reference string* S. After input data are preprocessed and tokenized involving a set of m *delimiters* $D = \{d_1, d_2, ..., d_m\}$, they are segmented into a set of n tokens $T = \{t_1, t_2, ..., t_n\}$. Next, a set of m features $F = \{f_{i,1}, f_{i,2}, ..., f_{i,j}\}$ are extracted per each token t_i. Once features have been extracted, they comprise a reference feature vector $\vec{r} = (f_{1,1}, f_{1,2}, ..., f_{p,q})$ where $f_{i,j}$ is the jth feature of the ith token, similar to a *document vector* in information retrieval. A set of reference feature vectors are fed into the SVM classifier mentioned above (see part 2 in Figure 5). This SVM has learned from a training corpus of references (part 3 in Figure 5), resulting from collecting important general world knowledge from the Web (e.g., EndNoteWeb reference management tool of part 4). As a result of reference style classification, a reference string, transformed into a feature vector, has been classified into one of the reference styles (parts 5-7 in Figure 5). The next steps are concerned with the sequence labeling problem, described in the next section.

4.3.3 Sequence Labeling

A reference string (e.g., reference 5 out of classified references 5-7 in Figure 5), already classified into a specific reference style (e.g., Chicago style tagger, style tagger 8 out of style taggers 8-10 in Figure 5), is input into a sequence labeler that is dedicated to the specific reference style. Style taggers are trained by knowledge from the Web (a web resource 11, labeled citations from EndNoteWeb, in Figure 5). These sequence labelers (style taggers) tag each field corresponding to the tokens. The output of sequence labeling is a tagged reference string (canonical form), e.g., tagged references 12-14 in Figure 5.

For the sequence labeling problem, we will use one of the machine learning methods based on probabilistic graphical models. Conditional random fields (CRFs), first proposed by Lafferty et al. [17], involve a discriminative probabilistic graphical model; they can help label sequence data. This method has been reported to outperform techniques such as hidden Markov model. Our goal is to find parameters maximizing $argmax_Y P(Y|X; W)$ instead of $argmax_Y P(Y, X)$ where Y is a permutation of a set of labels $L = \{l_1, l_2, ..., l_k\}$, X is an input reference string, transformed into a set of tokens $T = \{t_1, t_2, .., t_n\}$, and W is a set of weights for feature functions $W = \{w_1, w_2, .., w_m\}$.

Table 4: Different Styles and Surface Forms of Dataset 1

Styles	Surface forms
AAG	Albillos, A., R. Banares, M. Gonzalez, C. Ripoll, R. Gonzalez, M. V. Catalina & L. M. Molinero (2007) Value of the hepatic venous pressure gradient to monitor drug therapy for portal hypertension: A meta-analysis. *American Journal of Gastroenterology*, 102, 1116-1126.
Turabian	Albillos, A., R. Banares, M. Gonzalez, C. Ripoll, R. Gonzalez, M. V. Catalina, and L. M. Molinero. "Value of the Hepatic Venous Pressure Gradient to Monitor Drug Therapy for Portal Hypertension: A Meta-Analysis." American Journal of Gastroenterology 102, no. 5 (2007): 1116-1126.
AIP	A. Albillos, R. Banares, M. Gonzalez, C. Ripoll, R. Gonzalez, M. V. Catalina and L. M. Molinero, Am J Gastroenterol 102 (5), 1116-1126 (2007).
APA	Albillos, A., Banares, R., Gonzalez, M., Ripoll, C., Gonzalez, R., Catalina, M. V., et al. (2007). Value of the hepatic venous pressure gradient to monitor drug therapy for portal hypertension: A meta-analysis. American Journal of Gastroenterology, 102(5), 1116-1126.
Chicago15A	Albillos, A., R. Banares, M. Gonzalez, C. Ripoll, R. Gonzalez, M. V. Catalina, and L. M. Molinero. "Value of the Hepatic Venous Pressure Gradient to Monitor Drug Therapy for Portal Hypertension: A Meta-Analysis." American Journal of Gastroenterology 102, no. 5 (2007): 1116-26.
IEEE	A. Albillos, et al.,"Value of the hepatic venous pressure gradient to monitor drug therapy for portal hypertension: A meta-analysis," American Journal of Gastroenterology, vol. 102, pp. 1116-1126, May 2007.
JAMA	Albillos A, Banares R, Gonzalez M, et al. Value of the hepatic venous pressure gradient to monitor drug therapy for portal hypertension: A meta-analysis. Am J Gastroenterol. May 2007;102(5):1116-1126.
MLA	Albillos, A., et al. "Value of the Hepatic Venous Pressure Gradient to Monitor Drug Therapy for Portal Hypertension: A Meta-Analysis." American Journal of Gastroenterology 102 5 (2007): 1116-26. Print.
NLM	Albillos A, Banares R, Gonzalez M, Ripoll C, Gonzalez R, Catalina MV, Molinero LM. Value of the hepatic venous pressure gradient to monitor drug therapy for portal hypertension: A meta-analysis. Am J Gastroenterol2007 May;102(5):1116-26.

5. EVALUATION

5.1 Reference Style Classification

5.1.1 Experimental Design

Objectives: The objective of this experiment is to investigate what methods give the best performance and greatest effectiveness in improving canonical reference extraction.

Datasets:

We use three large and heterogeneously styled reference datasets. These datasets are randomly selected from a knowlege base for the reference styles described in Section 4.1. Datasets 1 and 2 are described in Table 4 and Table 5, respectively. As we can see in the **styles** column, the reference styles include ones used in a variety of disciplines.

Tokenization and Features Extraction: Tokenization is also one of the critical processes to determine accuracy of style classification. Tokenization involves delimiters. A *nor-*

Table 5: Different Styles and Surface Forms of Dataset 2

No.	Styles	Surface forms
1	396. Behavioral Cognitive Psycho	BONFERONI, M., ROSSI, S., FERRARI, F., STAVIK, E., PENA-ROMERO, A., & CARAMELLA, C. (2000). Factorial analysis of the influence of dissolution medium on drug release from carrageenan-diltiazem complexes. AAPS PharmSciTech, 1 (2), 72-79.
2	186. Anal Soc Issues Pub Policy	Bonferoni, M., Rossi, S., Ferrari, F., Stavik, E., Pena-Romero, A., & Caramella, C. (2000). Factorial analysis of the influence of dissolution medium on drug release from carrageenan-diltiazem complexes. AAPS PharmSciTech, 1 (2), 72-79.
3	2143. J Phytopathology	Bonferoni, M., Rossi, S., Ferrari, F., Stavik, E., Pena-Romero, A. & Caramella, C. (2000) Factorial analysis of the influence of dissolution medium on drug release from carrageenan-diltiazem complexes. AAPS PharmSciTech, 1: 72-79.
4	721. Circulation	58. Bonferoni M, Rossi S, Ferrari F, Stavik E, Pena-Romero A, Caramella C. Factorial analysis of the influence of dissolution medium on drug release from carrageenan-diltiazem complexes. AAPS PharmSciTech . 2000;1:72-79
5	2815. Proc Amer Thoracic Soc.ens	58. Bonferoni M, Rossi S, Ferrari F, Stavik E, Pena-Romero A, Caramella C. Factorial analysis of the influence of dissolution medium on drug release from carrageenan-diltiazem complexes. AAPS PharmSciTech 2000;1(2):72-79.
6	17. ACS	58. Bonferoni, M.; Rossi, S.; Ferrari, F.; Stavik, E.; Pena-Romero, A.; Caramella, C., Factorial analysis of the influence of dissolution medium on drug release from carrageenan-diltiazem complexes. AAPS PharmSciTech 2000, 1 (2), 72-79.
7	1047. Entomologia Exp et App	A. Bonferoni M, Rossi S, Ferrari F, Stavik E, Pena-Romero A & Caramella C (2000) Factorial analysis of the influence of dissolution medium on drug release from carrageenan-diltiazem complexes. AAPS PharmSciTech 1: 72-79. doi:citeulike-article-id:6447037.
8	1721. J Biogeography	Bonferoni, M., Rossi, S., Ferrari, F., Stavik, E., Pena-Romero, A. & Caramella, C. (2000) Factorial analysis of the influence of dissolution medium on drug release from carrageenan-diltiazem complexes. AAPS PharmSciTech , 1 , 72-79
9	2326. Law Probability Risk	BONFERONI, M., ROSSI, S., FERRARI, F., STAVIK, E., PENA-ROMERO, A. and CARAMELLA, C. 2000 Factorial analysis of the influence of dissolution medium on drug release from carrageenan-diltiazem complexes. AAPS PharmSciTech 1 , 72-79.
10	2866. Public Finance Review	Bonferoni, Maria, Silvia Rossi, Franca Ferrari, Evy Stavik, Angelina Pena-Romero, and Carla Caramella. "Factorial Analysis of the Influence of Dissolution Medium on Drug Release from Carrageenan-Diltiazem Complexes." AAPS PharmSciTech 1, no. 2 (2000): 72-79.

Table 6: Three Datasets Used in Experiments

Item	dataset 1	dataset 2	dataset 3
# of Styles	9	10	10
# of instances	2,250	4,290	4,290
# of features (normal tokenizer)	3,880	8,022	5,014
# of features (simple tokenizer)	6,801	10,887	7,927

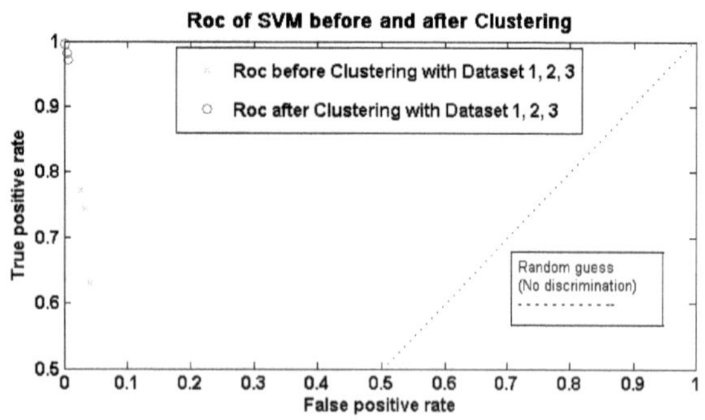

Figure 6: ROC of SVM before and after Clustering with Datasets 1, 2, and 3

mal tokenizer that we used in this evaluation uses delimiters as follows: *carriage return, tab, blank, period, comma, semicolon, colon, single quotes, double quotes, round parentheses, question mark*, and *exclamation mark*. Sometimes the delimiters are noise. However, some delimiters in the normal tokenizer are also the cues for distinguishing the reference styles, such as a period (.), a comma (,), a semicolon (;), a colon (:), double quotes (") as well as parentheses (*()*). So, some delimiters should be included as critical features along with word features, (e.g., *A.*, and *"A Hybrid*). Thus, in addition to experimenting with the normal tokenizer, we also test a *Simple tokenizer* which includes just *carriage return, tab, blank, single quotes, question mark*, and *exclamation mark*.

Methods: We compare several multi-class classification methods: 1) decision tree, 2) naïve Bayes, and 3) support vector machine. In addition, to answer the concern about the difficulty of classifying similar reference styles, we investigate if a clustering before classification helps classifiers to select the reference styles effectively and to enhance the sequence labeling accuracy. The methods that we choose are decision tree, naïve Bayes, support vector machine, clustering + decision tree, clustering + naïve Bayes, and clustering + support vector machine. To implement the reference style classification, we used the WEKA toolkit.

Metrics: To assess classification ability, we use accurary, receiver operating characteristic (ROC), precision, and recall as performance and effectiveness metrics. Each metric can be formalized as follows using true positives (A), true negatives (B), false positives (C), and false negatives (D).

$$Accuracy = \frac{A+B}{A+B+C+D},$$
$$True\ positive\ rate\ (TP\ rate) = \frac{A}{A+D},$$
$$False\ positive\ rate\ (FP\ rate) = \frac{C}{C+B},$$
$$Receiver\ Operating\ Characteristic\ (ROC) = \frac{TP\ rate}{FP\ rate},$$
$$Precision = \frac{A}{A+C},\ Recall = \frac{A}{A+D}$$

5.1.2 Results

We conducted 10-fold cross-validation with each dataset. First, Figure 6 illustrates a receiver operating characteristic (ROC), which shows the true positive rate vs. false positive rate. Figures 7, 8, and 9 display the precision and recall before and after clustering with Datasets 1, 2, and 3, respectively.

5.1.3 Discussion

Table 7 lists the accuracy and F1-score in terms of the variants of classification methods with Datasets 1, 2, and 3. Figure 6 shows the result of classification before and after clustering with all data, which are located in the upper part on the non-discrimination line. Classifiers above a discrimination line are generally regarded as better classifiers. Using a complete randomized design, we have conducted an ANOVA test. In terms of clustering vs. non-clustering, the p-value is less than 0.0001 (< 0.05). Thus, the null hypothesis that there is no significant difference between the variation of clustering, which is likely to affect the variation of feature types, is rejected. In other words, it can be said that the variation of clustering method significantly affects the variation of accuracy. In addition, with respect to a simple tokenization method vs. a normal one, the p-value is 0.0004 (< 0.05), so we also can reject the next null hypothesis that there is no significant difference between the variation of

Table 7: Accuracies of Different Classifiers with the Preprocessing Combinations

Clustering	Tokenization	Classifier	Dataset1 F1	Dataset1 Acc.	Dataset2 F1	Dataset2 Acc.	Dataset3 F1	Dataset3 Acc.	Avg. Acc.
Individual classes	Normal tokenizer	Decision Tree	0.73	74.0	0.49	50.2	0.31	32.1	52.1
		Naïve Bayes	0.58	58.6	0.44	43.8	0.21	21.1	41.1
		SVM	0.71	71.2	0.50	47.9	0.24	23.2	47.4
	Simple tokenizer	Decision Tree	0.75	74.7	0.75	73.7	0.67	67.5	72.0
		Naïve Bayes	0.66	65.8	0.72	72.5	0.61	61.2	66.5
		SVM	0.74	74.4	0.76	77.2	0.63	62.9	71.5
Clustered classes	Normal tokenizer	Decision Tree	0.94	93.7	0.82	83.1	0.60	63.6	80.1
		Naïve Bayes	0.94	94.3	0.82	81.8	0.55	55.4	77.2
		SVM	0.98	98.4	0.86	85.9	0.59	60.1	81.5
	Simple tokenizer	Decision Tree	0.96	95.8	0.95	95.4	0.94	94.3	95.2
		Naïve Bayes	0.98	97.8	0.94	93.6	0.96	95.7	95.7
		SVM	**1.00**	**99.6**	**0.98**	**98.1**	**0.97**	**97.1**	**98.2**

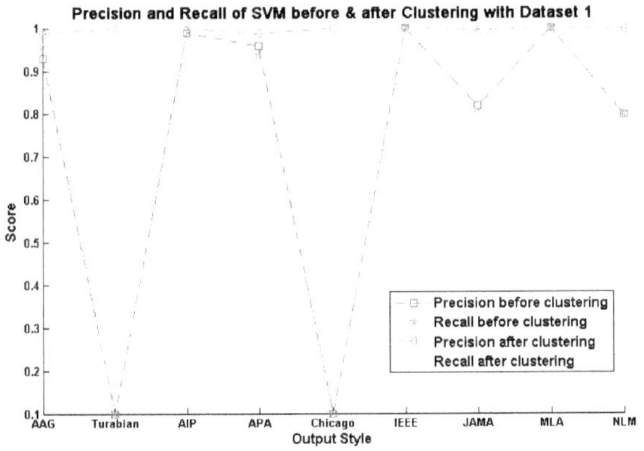

Figure 7: Precision and Recall of SVM before & after Clustering with Dataset 1

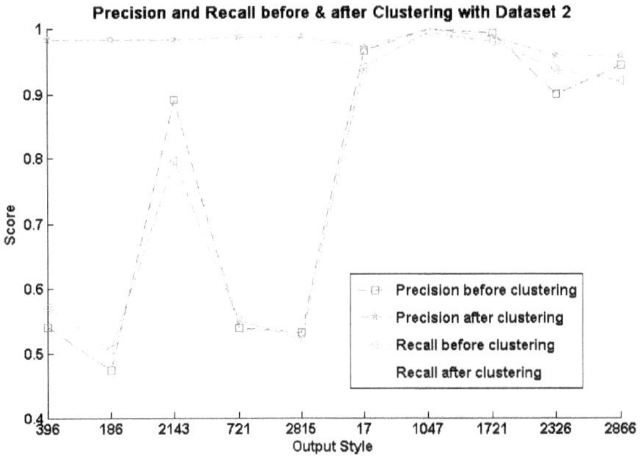

Figure 8: Precision and Recall of SVM before & after Clustering with Dataset 2

feature types by means of the different tokenization methods. Similarly, the use of simplified delimiters in the simple tokenization method can be said to affect the improvement of accuracy. The use of different classifiers (decision tree, naïve Bayes, and SVM) shows 0.3892 as the p-value, which means that the corresponding null hypothesis is accepted, that is, there was no significant difference between the use of different classifiers. However, since SVM showed the best accuracy with all three datasets, we used only the classification outcomes by the SVM method in the sequence labeling stage.

As a result of classification, there were a few misclassified references even after clustering. For example, in Table 5, for Dataset 2, 7 references out of 858 from class 9 (*2326. Law Probability Risk*) clustered with class 10 (*2866. Public Finance Review*) were mis-assigned to class 1. We looked into one of them, an instance *3471* of Dataset 2: *"BARAKAT, N. In Vitro and In Vivo Characteristics of a Thermogelling Rectal Delivery System of Etodolac. AAPS PharmSciTech."* from class 1 and *"BARAKAT, N. In Vitro and In Vivo Characteristics of a Thermogelling Rectal Delivery System of Etodolac. AAPS PharmSciTech."* from class 9. In these cases, the year was missing so the two references became identical. Originally, instances in the two classes 1 and 9, as you can see from Dataset 2 in Table 5, except only the year part, are almost the same. Clearly, identical references should yield the same result regardless of *before* or *after* reference style classification.

5.2 Sequence labeling

5.2.1 Experimental Design

Objectives: The objective of this experiment is to check the dependency of styles on reference metadata extraction accuracy and to ascertain the effectiveness of the two-stage method for improving canonical representation extraction performance. Accordingly, we compare the performance of a tagger for a single style to that of the tagger for a combination of styles.

Datasets: We used 2,250 references of Dataset 1, described in Table 4. This dataset consists of nine different surface forms and 250 reference entries per reference style. We searched 250 reference entries from EndNote under 'citation' and 'analysis' keywords and generated references in nine different reference styles. The reference styles used in this experiment are 1) AAG, 2) Turabian, 3) API, 4) APA, 5) Chicago15A, 6) IEEE, 7) JAMA, 8) MLA, and 9) NLM. Additionally, we used the **CORA** dataset to evaluate the effectiveness of our approach.

Methods: We used a machine learning method, conditional random fields (CRFs). We used an open source implementation in Java, CRF[5], coded by Sarawagi et al. Methods to be compared to are one-stage CRF and two-stage CRF with the same dataset and features.

[5]http://crf.sourceforge.net

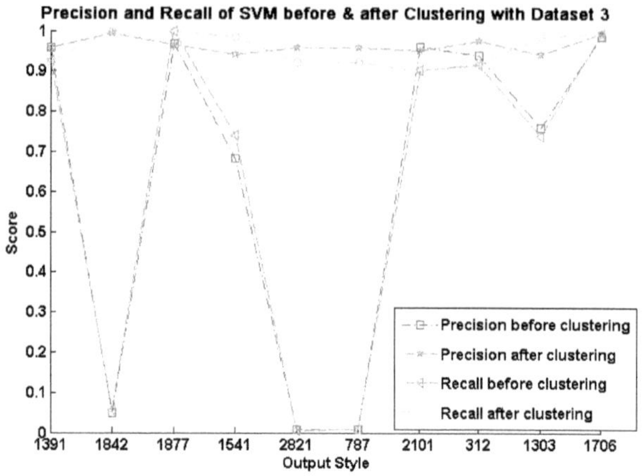

Figure 9: Precision and Recall of SVM before & after Clustering with Dataset 3

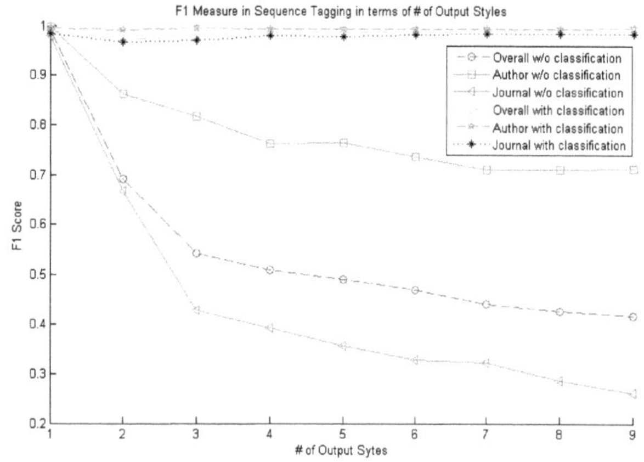

Figure 10: Performance of Reference Labeling with Regard to the Number of Reference Styles

Metrics: We used F1, in the reference style classification stage, as effectiveness metric.

5.2.2 Results

Figure 10 shows the performance comparison of sequence labeler methods with respect to the AUTHOR field, JOURNAL field, and overall over the number of reference styles 1 to 9. In the graph, the result shows that the performance of methods without reference style classification is decreasing as the number of reference styles increase. Surprisingly, in contrast to one stage sequence labelers, two-stage sequence labelers keep their F1-scores close to 1 as they seem to be dealing with one reference styled references. Table 8 compares the results of sequence labeling of the **CORA** dataset using our approach versus existing methods.

5.2.3 Discussion

We conducted an experiment about the dependency between the sequence labeling ability of CRF and the number of reference styles without style classification. We obtained some results before classification, as illustrated in Figure 10, that show that the performance is decreasing as the number of reference styles increases. We cautiously inferred that the smaller the number of reference styles observed in a collection, the better the performance. Notice that the performance when a single style is used is close to 100. This observation has inspired our approach, a hybrid two-stage methodology. We apply machine learning and knowledge-based techniques to the discipline-independent canonical representation extraction problem. The sequence tagging after classification approach results in high F1-score regardless of reference style. In other words, our two-stage method appears to be independent of reference styles.

Table 8: Sequence labeling result of CORA dataset with respect to different methods

	Hybrid			ParsCit	Peng
	Precision	Recall	F1	F1	F1
Author	0.98	0.99	0.98	0.99	0.99
Booktitle	0.91	0.88	0.89	0.93	0.94
Date	0.98	0.96	0.97	0.99	0.99
Editor	1.00	0.47	0.63	0.86	0.88
Institution	0.89	0.81	0.83	0.89	0.94
Journal	0.88	0.95	0.91	0.91	0.91
Location	0.87	0.89	0.88	0.93	0.87
Note	0.95	0.62	0.69	0.65	0.81
Pages	0.96	0.98	0.97	0.98	0.99
Publisher	0.86	0.87	0.86	0.92	0.76
Tech	0.86	0.80	0.82	0.86	0.87
Title	0.95	0.98	0.97	0.97	0.98
Volume	0.91	0.97	0.94	0.96	0.98
Average	0.94	0.94	0.94	0.95	0.91

6. CONCLUSIONS

In this paper, we proposed a hybrid two-stage method for canonical representation extraction from heterogeneously styled references. To go beyond domain-specific and specialized reference style citation analysis methods, we built up a reference style knowledge base. Based on our hybrid methods, combining the general background knowledge and machine learning, we have conducted several experiments. We showed that our hybrid two stage approach along with preclustered classes is effective regarding our challenging problem: discipline-independent and style-free canonical representation extraction.

In future work, we plan to compare our CRF sequence tagger with additional machine learning approaches to sequence labeling, such as HMM, structured SVM, and MEMM.

7. ACKNOWLEDGMENTS

This material is based upon work supported by Digital Library and Archives, Virginia Tech and the National Science Foundation under Grant No. IIS-0916733.

8. REFERENCES

[1] M. Afzal, H. Maurer, W. Balke, and N. Kulathuramaiyer. Rule based Autonomous Citation Mining With TIERL. *Journal of Digital Information Management*, 8(3), 2010.

[2] I. Bhattacharya and L. Getoor. Collective entity resolution in relational data. *ACM Trans. Knowl. Discov. Data*, 1, March 2007.

[3] C. Cortes and V. Vapnik. Support-vector networks. *Machine learning*, 20(3): 273–297, 1995.

[4] E. Cortez, A. da Silva, M. Gonçalves, F. Mesquita, and E. de Moura. FLUX-CIM: flexible unsupervised extraction of citation metadata. In *Proceedings of the 7th ACM/IEEE-CS joint conference on Digital libraries*, page 224. ACM, 2007.

[5] I. Councill, C. Giles, and M. Kan. Parscit: An open-source CRF reference string parsing package. In *Proceedings of the 6th international Conference on Language Resources and Evaluation (2008)*, volume 2008. European Language Resources Association (ELRA), 2008.

[6] M. Day, R. Tsai, C. Sung, C. Hsieh, C. Lee, S. Wu, K. Wu, C. Ong, and W. Hsu. Reference metadata extraction using a hierarchical knowledge representation framework. *Decision Support Systems*, 43(1): 152–167, 2007.

[7] Y. Ding. Applying weighted pagerank to author citation networks. *Journal of the American Society for Information Science and Technology*, 62(2): 236–245, 2011.

[8] Y. Ding, G. Chowdhury, and S. Foo. Template mining for the extraction of citation from digital documents. In *Proceedings of the Second Asian Digital Library Conference, Taiwan*, pages 47–62, 1999.

[9] D. Embley, D. Campbell, Y. Jiang, S. Liddle, D. Lonsdale, Y. Ng, and R. Smith. Conceptual-model-based data extraction from multiple-record Web pages. *Data & Knowledge Engineering*, 31(3): 227–251, 1999.

[10] E. Garfield and R. Merton. *Citation indexing: Its theory and application in science, technology, and humanities.* Wiley, New York, 1979.

[11] H. Han, C. Giles, E. Manavoglu, H. Zha, Z. Zhang, and E. Fox. Automatic document metadata extraction using support vector machines. In *International Conference on Digital Libraries: Proceedings of the 3rd ACM/IEEE-CS joint conference on Digital libraries*, pages 37–48. IEEE, 2003.

[12] E. Hetzner. A simple method for citation metadata extraction using hidden Markov models. In *Proceedings of the 8th ACM/IEEE-CS joint conference on Digital libraries*, pages 280–284. ACM, 2008.

[13] G. Hoefel and C. Elkan. Learning a two-stage SVM/CRF sequence classifier. In *Proceeding of the 17th ACM conference on Information and knowledge management*, pages 271–278. ACM, 2008.

[14] C. Hong, J. Gozali, and M. Kan. FireCite: Lightweight real-time reference string extraction from webpages. In *Proceedings of the 2009 Workshop on Text and Citation Analysis for Scholarly Digital Libraries*, pages 71–79. Association for Computational Linguistics, 2009.

[15] F. Jiao, S. Wang, C. Lee, R. Greiner, and D. Schuurmans. Semi-supervised conditional random fields for improved sequence segmentation and labeling. In *Proceedings of the 21st International Conference on Computational Linguistics and the 44th annual meeting of the Association for Computational Linguistics*, pages 209–216. Association for Computational Linguistics, 2006.

[16] T. Joachims, T. Hofmann, Y. Yue, and C. Yu. Predicting structured objects with support vector machines. *Communications of the ACM*, 52(11): 97–104, 2009.

[17] J. Lafferty, A. McCallum, and F. Pereira. Conditional random fields: Probabilistic models for segmenting and labeling sequence data. In *Machine Learning-International Workshop and Conference*, pages 282–289, 2001.

[18] S. Lawrence, L. Giles, and K. Bollacker. Digital libraries and autonomous citation indexing. *Computer*, 32(6): 67–71, 2002.

[19] G. Mann and A. McCallum. Simple, robust, scalable semi-supervised learning via expectation regularization. In *Proceedings of the 24th international conference on Machine learning*, pages 593–600. ACM, 2007.

[20] K. Nagao and K. Hasida. Automatic text summarization based on the Global Document Annotation. In *Proceedings of the 17th international conference on Computational linguistics-Volume 2*, pages 917–921. Association for Computational Linguistics, 1998.

[21] F. Peng and A. McCallum. Information extraction from research papers using conditional random fields. *Information Processing & Management*, 42(4): 963–979, 2006.

[22] H. Poon, J. Christensen, P. Domingos, O. Etzioni, R. Hoffmann, S. Soderland, D. Weld, F. Wu, and C. Zhang. Machine Reading at the University of Washington. In *First International Workshop on Formalisms and Methodology for Learning by Reading (FAM-LbR)*, page 87, 2010.

[23] H. Poon and P. Domingos. Joint inference in information extraction. In *Proceedings of the National Conference on Artificial Intelligence*, volume 22, page 913. Menlo Park, CA; Cambridge, MA; London; AAAI Press; MIT Press; 1999, 2007.

[24] L. Rabiner and B. Juang. An introduction to hidden Markov models. *ASSP Magazine, IEEE*, 3(1): 4–16, 1986.

[25] A. Strotmann and D. Zhao. Combining commercial citation indexes and open-access bibliographic databases to delimit highly interdisciplinary research fields for citation analysis. *Journal of Informetrics*, 4(2): 194–200, 2010.

[26] A. Stubbe, C. Ringlstetter, and K. Schulz. Genre as noise: Noise in genre. *International Journal on Document Analysis and Recognition*, 10(3): 199–209, 2007.

[27] M. Wick, A. Culotta, K. Rohanimanesh, and A. McCallum. An entity based model for coreference resolution. In *SIAM International Conference on Data Mining (SDM)*, 2009.

[28] S. Yeates, I. Witten, and D. Bainbridge. Tag insertion complexity. In *Data Compression Conference, 2001. Proceedings. DCC 2001*, pages 243–252. IEEE, 2001.

[29] J. Yu and X. Fan. Metadata Extraction from Chinese Research Papers Based on Conditional Random Fields. In *FSKD 2007*, volume 1, pages 497–501, 2007.

[30] J. Zou, D. Le, and G. Thoma. Locating and parsing bibliographic references in HTML medical articles. *International journal on document analysis and recognition*, 13(2): 107–119, 2010.

Web-based Citation Parsing, Correction and Augmentation

Liangcai Gao
ICST, Peking University, Beijing
China
glc@pku.edu.cn

Xixi Qi
ICST, Peking University, Beijing
China
qixixi@pku.edu.cn

Zhi Tang
State Key Laboratory of Digital Publishing Technology, Beijing, China
tangzhi@founder.com

Xiaofan Lin
A9.com
130 Lytton Ave, Palo Alto, CA
USA
xiaofanl@a9.com

Ying Liu
Department of Knowledge Service Engineering,
Korea Advanced Institute of Science and Technology
Daejeon, Republic of Korea
yingliu@kaist.ac.kr

ABSTRACT

Considering the tremendous value of citation metadata, many methods have been proposed to automate Citation Metadata Extraction (CME). The existing methods primarily rely on the content analysis of citation text. However, the results from such content-based methods are often unreliable. Moreover, the extracted citation metadata is only a small part of the relevant metadata that spreads across the Internet. As opposed to the content-based CME methods, this paper proposes a Web-based CME approach and a citation enriching system, called as BibAll, which is capable of correcting the parsing results of content-based CME methods and augmenting citation metadata by leveraging relevant bibliographic data from digital repositories and cited-by publications on the Web. BibAll consists of four main components: citation parsing, Web-based bibliographic data retrieval, irrelevant bibliographic data filtering, and relevant bibliographic data integration. The system has been tested on the publicly available FLUX-CIM dataset. Experimental results show that BibAll significantly improves the citation parsing accuracy and augments the metadata of the original citation.

Categories and Subject Descriptors

H.3.3 [**Information Systems**]: Information Search and Retrieval

Keywords

Citation Extraction and Augmentation, Automatic Metadata Generation, Web-based Extraction, Digital Libraries

1. INTRODUCTION

A citation in an academic text provides the reader with exact and structured publication information to uniquely identify and locate a scholarly resource [24]. Such structured information is called citation metadata, which is essential for many digital library applications, such as citation analysis, academic search and topic discovery. Citation metadata can be extracted both manually and automatically. However, the manual way is usually time-consuming and costly. Furthermore, a manual qualification on the Web scale seems impractical because the number of documents is far too large. Thus, automatic approaches are conceivable and have attracted much attention from researchers.

JCDL'12, June 10–14, 2012, Washington, DC, USA.

A number of automatic Citation Metadata Extraction (CME) approaches have been reported in recent years. These approaches can be classified into three types: rule-based, learning-based, and template-based [4]. Rule-based methods usually are simple and effective, and have been widely used in real-world applications. For example, CiteSeer [3] uses heuristic rules to extract bibliographic attributes and has become a well-known academic search engine. Wei et al. [23] also proposed a rule-based method for bibliographic attribute extraction with layer-upon-layer tagging. The method proposed by Besagni et al. [2] can be considered as a rule-based method as well. It segments bibliographic references by tagging contextual field. Among the learning-based methods, Hidden Markov Model (HMM) [11, 21, 22] is the first one used for the task, and has enjoyed great success. Support Vector Machine (SVM) [10] is also applied to the task and has achieved a better result in handling dependent features through loosening the relationship between state transformation and observation sequence. Conditional Random Fields (CRF) combines the advantages of both HMM and SVM by allowing use of arbitrary and dependent features and joint inference over entire sequences, and it has achieved the best overall word accuracy on the Cora reference dataset [18]. A popular implementation of CME using CRF is ParsCit[1] [5]. It is worth noting that the new version of CiteSeer, called CiteSeerX, seems to have switched to the ParsCit for extracting citation metadata. Template-based methods use template databases with various styles of citation templates. M. Y. Day et al. [6] considered six major citation templates in computer science literature and constructed a hierarchical knowledge representation framework (INFOMAP) to extract citation metadata. Huang [13] and Chen [4] used protein sequence to represent citations and applied the Basic Local Alignment Search Tool (BLAST) to find similar templates. Eli Cortez [7] proposed an unsupervised citation metadata extraction method to automatically generate templates from the training data set. ParaCite [12] is also a widely used system that parses citation data based on templates.

From the aforementioned CME methods, we can see that they only utilize the information from the processed citation and primarily rely on content analysis of the citation. On this point, we call them as content-based methods. Although the best content-based CME method has achieved accuracy as high as 95.37% on the Cora reference dataset [18], they often suffer from unreliable extraction results for reasons such as: a large variety of citation formats, lack of standards, high similarity between different

[1] ParsCit: http://aye.comp.nus.edu.sg/parsCit/

attributes (e.g., 'title' and 'book title', 'volume' and 'issue', even 'page number' and 'date'), ambiguity in author names, and abbreviations for publication venues [14]. Furthermore, citation strings sometimes contain spelling errors probably introduced by Optical Character Recognition (OCR) software or even by mistyping of authors. For example, the page number of one publication, '24-37', might be incorrectly recognized as '24-31' by OCR. Obviously, such errors are very difficult to process using content-based methods.

In addition, content-based CME methods cannot acquire metadata, which are not physically present in the full citation text, so the extracted metadata from such methods only contains a small portion of the existing bibliographic data related to a publication. In practice, finding the missing metadata of a citation, namely citation metadata enrichment, is essential in many applications. For example, when preparing the reference section of a manuscript, we usually have to search multiple digital libraries storing the publications cited in the manuscript, check the full text of those publications, and even check the publications (called 'cited-by' publications) that also cite the same publications, in order to collect the required citation metadata of the manuscript. Thus, just like the extraction process, the enrichment of citation metadata with additional relevant bibliographic data is time-consuming when performed manually.

On the other hand, citations are commonly found not only in the bibliography section of academic publications, but also on the researchers' personal websites, or on the on-line digital libraries like DBLP, ACM, CiteSeerX. Moreover, the bibliographic data of a part of those digital libraries are authored manually and so tend to be reliable. It is common that the publication referred by a citation has multiple copies of bibliographic data on the Web. Naturally, those copies are information-redundant and can validate and complement each other. For one citation, a relationship network can be built according to citation metadata similarity among its copies from different bibliographic data sources. Then we can utilize the network to harvest citation metadata to validate, correct, and augment the results of content-based CME methods. This is the central idea of our Web-based CME method.

Actually, such Web-based ideas have been utilized in other information search and retrieval applications. PageRank algorithm [16] is the best example, where the link structure of one page, instead of the content of the page, is analyzed to assess the page's significance. In metadata generation, Rodriguez et al. [20] proposed an automatic associative network-based metadata generation system by leveraging resource relationships generated from existing metadata as a medium for propagation from metadata-rich to metadata-poor resources. In their system, occurrence and co-occurrence algorithms are first used to generate an associative network of repository resources based on existing repository metadata. Second, using the associative network as a substrate, metadata associated with metadata-rich resources is propagated to metadata-poor resources by spreading activation algorithms. Claverie et al. [19] also proposed a semi-automatic method for propagating metadata. In the first step, homogeneous corpus is extracted through clustering, which uses a similarity measure based on the co-citation frequency between pages. Given the cluster hierarchy, the second step selects a reduced number of documents to be manually qualified, and then propagates the given metadata values to the other documents belonging to the same cluster. Wenneker [24] did a similar research with ours in his master thesis, which demonstrated the good role of online digital libraries for citation metadata extraction and enrichment. Aumüller and Rahm [1] presented a tool called PDFMeat to automatically assign publication metadata for the PDF files of scholarly papers. PDFMeat matches local full texts of a PDF file to an on-line repository, and it then propagates the retrieved metadata to the file. Marinai [15] described a package to extract basic metadata from PDF papers with document analysis techniques. Furthermore, he utilized the information gathered from a widely known citation database (DBLP) to assist the tool in the task of author and title identification.

In the context of metadata propagation used in the aforementioned metadata generation methods, our Web-based CME method can be considered as metadata propagation from Web sources to citations. It attempts to address the two main problems with content-based CME methods: the unreliability of the extraction results and the incompleteness of the extracted citation metadata. This paper focuses on how the results from content-based CME methods can be corrected and augmented through collecting and integrating additional relevant bibliographic data. And a complete system, called BibAll[2], is implemented.

The following sections will introduce the proposed method and system in more details. Section 2 describes the workflow of the proposed approach. Sections 3-6 elaborate on the technical details of various steps in BibAll: citation parsing, searching, filtering, and integration. Section 7 discusses the experimental results. Conclusions are drawn in Section 8.

2. METHOD OVERVIEW

As mentioned earlier, our goal is to correct and augment the parsing results of content-based CME methods using relevant bibliographic data spreading across the Web. In order to accomplish this, we introduce a pipeline consisting of four independent phases: parsing, searching, filtering, and integration. Figure 1 provides an overview of the pipeline. The input is a free-form citation text string. The parsing phase is responsible for CME from the input string and representing the extracted metadata as an input reference of the next phase. During the searching phase additional bibliographic data from several heterogeneous data sources are collected through executing a query with the input reference on external digital libraries and parsing the bibliography sections of relevant publications on the Web. Then the collected bibliographic data are passed to the filtering step to filter out the irrelevant bibliographic data. The collected bibliographic data that differ significantly from the input reference are removed. The remaining data are passed on to the integration step where the bibliographic data are integrated with the input reference. The end result of the pipeline is a BibTeX modeled reference containing citation metadata integrated with bibliographic data from the Web sources. Simultaneously, the errors in the input reference are corrected. In addition, BibAll also contains validation modules to assess the results from the individual phases. The various phases and the validation modules between them are described in the following sections.

3. CITATION PARSING

The parsing phase starts by passing the citation to a CME module. Two questions need to be answered first: How many candidate CME methods should be included? And which one should be selected to parse a particular citation? As mentioned in Section 1, there are many contented-based CME methods, each of which

[2] BibAll: http://www.icst.pku.edu.cn/cpdp/BibAll

excels at specific types of citations. For example, if the format of a citation fully matches with a predefined template, the template-based method would be the best solution. Specially, the citations using different languages usually need different CME modules to achieve satisfactory parsing results. Thus, a validation step is included in BibAll to select the CME module to parse a particular citation. In BibAll, one template-based CME method and three learning CME methods have been implemented. And ParsCit is also employed in the system. The CME methods are first selected according to the character Unicode which could be used to determine the language type of citations. Then the template-based CME method is used to parse a citation. If no template matches with the citation, the learning CME methods are executed.

For example, if the input reference is in Chinese, a learning-based method [8] will be selected to parse it. It is worth noting that BibAll works independently from the adopted CME component. Since the CME phase is not the emphasis of this paper, the details of CME components would not be elaborated. Instead, we only give an example to illustrate the CME function. The second column of Table 1 is the ParsCit result for the citation shown in Figure 2. Obviously, ParsCit incorrectly recognizes the publisher as the title, thus the publisher attribute is not present in the extracted metadata.

The resulting 'structured citation metadata' from the selected CME component is then transformed into a BibTeX reference model (see the result in the second column of Table 1). We select BibTex reference model [17] as the common data structure shared by the BibAll components. This decision is based on two facts. First, the BibTeX file is the most popular format among bibliographic modeling methods and major digital libraries. Second, almost all scholarly search engines support importing and exporting citations in the BibTeX format now. As listed in Table 3, the most common twenty two fields in the BibTex reference model are targeted in BibAll. After the transformation the reference is passed on to the searching phase.

[10] Han, H., Giles, C.L., Manavoglu, E., Zha, H., Zhang, Z., and Fox, E.A. 2003. Automatic document metadata extraction using Support Vector Machines. Proceedings of the 3rd ACM/IEEE-CS joint conference on digital libraries. IEEE Computer Society, Washington, DC, USA. 37-48.

Figure 2. A citation as shown in a fragment of a bibliography section

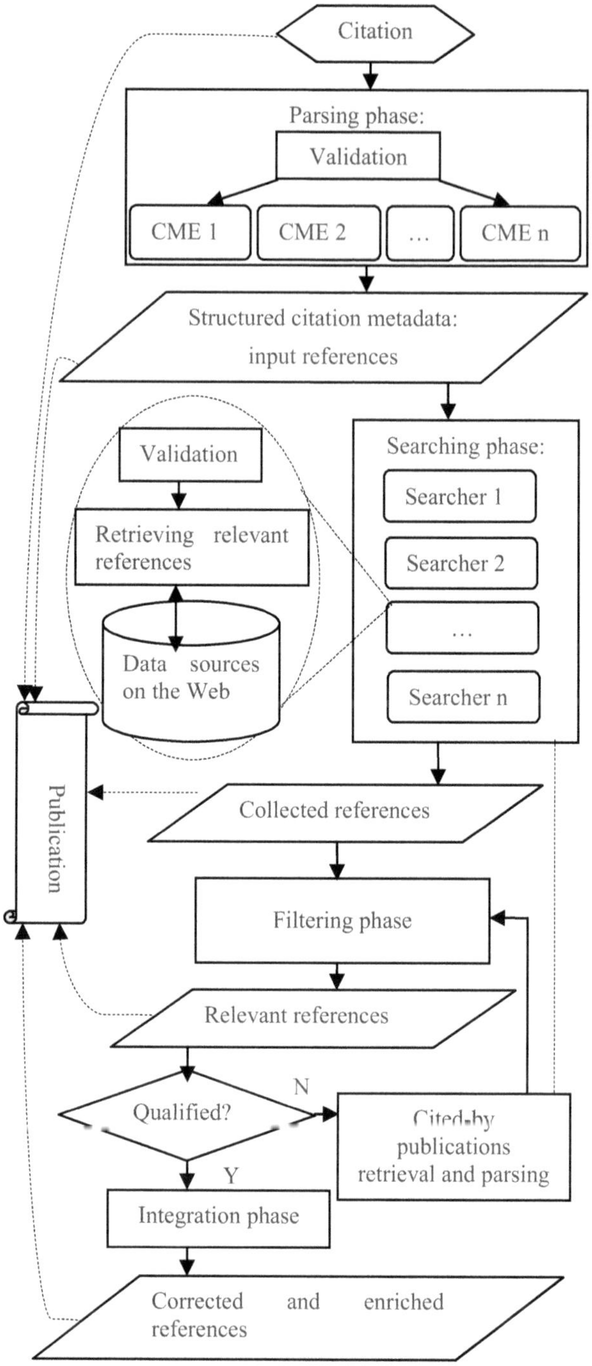

Figure 1. An overview of the BibAll pipeline

Table 1. The metadata extracted from ParsCit and BibAll for the citation shown in Figure 2

BibTeX record fields	Metadata from ParsCit (input reference)	Metadata from BibAll
Address	Washington, DC, USA	Washington, DC, USA
Author	Han, H., Giles, C.L., Manavoglu, E., Zha, H., Zhang, Z., and Fox, E.A.	Han, H., Giles, C.L., Manavoglu, E., Zha, H., Zhang, Z., and Fox, E.A.
Booktitle	Proceedings of the 3rd ACM/IEEE-CS joint conference on digital libraries. IEEE Computer Society	Proceedings of the 3rd ACM/IEEE-CS joint conference on digital libraries.
Editor		Marshall, C.C., Henry, G. and Delcambre, L.
Month		May
Pages	37-48	37-48
Publisher		IEEE Computer Society
Series		JCDL '03
Title	Automatic document metadata extraction using Support Vector Machines	Automatic document metadata extraction using Support Vector Machines
Year	2003	2003

4. SEARCHING BIBLIOGRAPHIC INFORMATION ON THE WEB

4.1 Data Sources

Citation metadata, namely the metadata of a publication present in a citation, can be commonly found in the bibliography sections of academic publications, and is also hosted on the researchers' personal websites or on-line digital libraries. Those data sources can be divided into two categories according to the manner of obtaining citation metadata from the sources. In the first category, the citation metadata can be directly collected from well-defined and edited metadata through metadata harvesting [9]. Most of on-line digital libraries belong to this category because the metadata provided by them is produced by human operators or semi-automatic processes utilizing software tools, and thus can be harvested directly. Academic publications and most of personal websites, on the other hand, belong to the second category, where citation metadata cannot be obtained through simple metadata harvesting but be extracted from a resource's content. For completeness, both categories of citation metadata sources are utilized in BibAll.

In BibAll, each data source is automatically retrieved by a searching handler, called searcher, which is responsible for retrieving bibliographic information from the source. The key is to intelligently decide which data source to target based on the characteristics of the input reference. For example, if the "booktitle" or "journal" attributes contain the word "ACM", the ACM searcher should be used to look for relevant bibliographic data in the ACM Digital Library. The data sources are selected in the following validation step.

Table 2. The data source configurations of two examples

Items	Source 1	Source 2
Name	Google Scholar	CiteSeerX
Address	http://scholar.google .com	http://citeseerx.ist.psu. edu
Flag	true	false
Weight	20	40
Domain	general	computer science
Format	BibTex	BibTex
Language	general	English
Cited-by	true	true

Name: the name of a data source. Address: the URL of a data source. Flag: the controlling parameter to determine whether a data source is queried. Weight: the creditability of a data source. Domain: the topic domain of the resources in the data source. Format: the data structure of the citation metadata present in the source. Language: the language which the resources of a source adopt. Cited-by: denoting whether the source contains the information of cited-by resources.

4.2 Validation

The validation step of the searching phase ensures that the input reference contains at least some bibliographic information, which is necessary in later steps. When the validation fails, the searcher step is skipped and the input reference is given to the next searcher. Otherwise, if the reference does contain the required query information, the reference is passed along to the retrieval step. The other task of the validation step is to select the searchers according to the characteristics of the input reference. For example, if the input reference is in Chinese, BibAll only executes the searchers corresponding to data sources with 'general' or 'Chinese' in the language field of Table 2. If the input reference is about computer science domain, only the sources with 'general' or 'computer science' in the domain field of Table 2 are retrieved later. If a data source is selected in this step, its "Flag" attribute in Table 2 is assigned true.

4.3 Retrieval

The implementation of the searching phase of BibAll comprises of a predefined and configurable sequence of searchers. In order to implement those searchers of BibAll, the configuration information is assigned first, as shown in Table 2. After configuration, BibAll executes the searcher sequence as below.

4.3.1 Digital library retrieval

BibAll harvests bibliographic data from multiple digital libraries through their corresponding searchers. For different searchers, the differences are the way to query, the way to collect bibliographic data, the criteria of reference similarity, besides the targeted digital libraries. Due to the page limitation, this paper only illustrates the digital library retrieval steps using Google Scholar. The main principles can be applied to other digital libraries.

a) Selecting the attributes used in a query: In the searcher responsible for Google Scholar, BibAll formulates a query based on the title and the first author of the input reference. These two attributes are selected to query relevant literature because they are present in nearly every reference and their combination is usually unique. For the publication shown in Figure 2, the query string is formulated as "Han, H. Automatic document metadata extraction using Support

Vector Machines" (see Figure 3(a)) based on the parsing result shown in the second column of Table 1. The Google Scholar search engine is then queried using the composed query string. The returned web page containing a list of articles is shown in Figure 3(b).

b) Parsing the returned web page: The returned web page contains links to pages where BibTeX formatted metadata can be found. As shown in Figure 3(b), the links are denoted in the ellipse-surrounded parts. And one of the linked pages is shown in Figure 3(c). Then, the linked pages are scraped and the BibTeX formatted data are parsed.

c) Matching relevant articles: The top *n* (e.g., 10) articles returned by Google Scholar are selected to match with the input reference using an open source record linkage tool called FRIL[3] (Fine-grained Records Integration and Linkage tool). FRIL provides a rich set of tools for comparing records, or references in our case. After configuring the compared attributes, distance metrics and corresponding weights, FRIL compares two references by returning their similarity (*RefSimilarity*) defined in Formula 1. For example, when comparing the first article in Figure 3(b) and the input reference, the BibTex data shown in Figure 3(c) and the parsing result shown in the second column of Table 1 are sent to FRIL.

$$\text{RefSimilarity}=\sum W_i \times \text{Dist}_i\left(\text{Attr}_i(r_1),\text{Attr}_i(r_2)\right) /100 \quad (1)$$

Where, $Attr_i$ is one of the k attributes selected to compare two references, r_1 and r_2. $Dist_i()$ is the function calculating the distance on $Attr_i$, and W_i is the corresponding weight.

BibAll chooses not to compare references based on all attributes, but on just five attributes (e.g. title, author, year, pages, booktitle/journal). This is because these five attributes generally are sufficient for a human being to distinguish the targets from all references. On the other hand, if all attributes are compared, the relevant references with just a few attributes will be ignored because of low similarity and thus will be ignored. Furthermore, the "title" is weighted the highest among all the attributes in the similarity calculation for the fact that it is present in practically every reference and it is the attribute that is unique in most of the times.

In addition, the comparison of author names is difficult because the order in which the authors are listed and the number of listed authors may differ in different sources. Furthermore, author names may be abbreviated or not. So BibAll first separates the first and last names of the first authors from the two compared references. Then it remains the last names changeless and abbreviates the first names using their first characters in order to compare the names in the common format. For example, the authors "C. Lee Giles, and Isaac G. Councill" in a reference are formulated as "C. L. Giles".

There also exist some special cases in the content of booktitle/journal, which might cause difficulty comparing the attributes. For example, the booktitle/journal names may be abbreviated or not, and the common words such as 'proceeding', 'international', 'conference', 'journal' may be abbreviated or not. And even the word order of their name might be various in different sources. For example, the booktitle "*In Proc. of the 5th Inter. Conf. on Document Analysis and Recognition. ICDAR '99*" in the input reference is presented as "*Document Analysis and Recognition, 1999. ICDAR '99. Proceedings of the Fifth International Conference on*" in Google Scholar and IEEE Xplore Digital Library. Therefore, in order to reduce the impact of various formats, BibAll normalizes the common words using their abbreviation and filters out the characters on punctuations, articles, prepositions and conjunctions. At the same time, we also implement and add a distance metric to FRIL for the comparison on sets. With the metric, two sets are considered the same, when they contain the same words in spite of the different word orders. As expected, the distance metric performs better than the common edition distance in processing the attribute, booktitle/journal, where the word order is usually different in different references.

d) Collecting bibliographic data: After the top *n* listed articles are compared with the input reference in Step c), the article with the highest *RefSimilarity* is selected as the reference to harvest bibliographic data. As shown in Figure 3(b), the first article has the same author name, title, year, pages with the input reference and has the highest *RefSimilarity*, so it is chosen for bibliographic data harvest. And its BibTex formatted metadata shown in Figure 3(c) is collected to pass on to the filtering phase.

After all the selected searchers are executed, their output references are collected and transformed into BibTex format. Then the references are passed on to the filtering phase.

4.3.2 Cited-by publication retrieval

Bibliography sections of cited-by publications are an important bibliographic data source for old publications because they tend to have very few duplicates in digital repositories and their metadata is less in the repositories compared to the newer publications. At the same time, the early publications are usually cited in the newer publications (namely cited-by publications), whose reference sections contain the bibliographic information of the cited literatures. Thus the bibliographic information can be extracted from the reference sections using the content-based CME methods and the extracted metadata could be selected as a metadata source for the early publications. Moreover, cited-by publication retrieval is quite feasible because many on-line digital libraries and searching engines provide the cited-by publications. For example, Google Scholar has already provided the information in the search result page to link the cited-by publications, as shown in the diamonds of Figure 3(b). Therefore, BibAll utilizes the links to find the cited-by publications. The implementation is described below on the example of using Google Scholar.

a) In the above section, the publication with the highest *RefSimilarity* is determined as the reference to harvest bibliographic data. We name the publication '*BasePub*'. In the searching result page, Google Scholar lists the cited-by publications' URLs in the item 'cited-by' for each collected resource, as shown in the diamonds in Figure 3(b). In this step, BibAll downloads the cited-by publications with the URL addresses stored in 'cited by' item of *BasePub* entry. Only the PDF files of the cited-by publications are downloaded. Please note that some of these PDF files are unusable. The reasons can be that the text is represented as image only, enabled read restrictions, or unknown document encoding issues. For the sake of the speed, we set 10 as the maximal number of the downloaded usable PDF files of the cited-by publications.

[3] FRIL: http://fril.sourceforge.net

b) The bibliography section of each downloaded publication in Step is identified and segmented into multiple citation strings. According to our experiments, ParsCit performs well in extracting citation metadata from a citation string, while it often makes mistakes in bibliography section segmentation. In BibAll, we use the detection and segmentation method proposed in our previous paper [8] instead of the corresponding component of ParsCit to locate the bibliography section of a publication and to segment the section into individual citation string which represents an individual literature.

c) Each citation string obtained in Step b) is given to a content-based CME component to extract citation metadata. And the parsed metadata is collected to compose a reference.

d) Each reference obtained in Step c) is compared with the input reference using FRIL. And the references with the *RefSimilarity* above a threshold are selected and are passed on to filtering phase after they are transformed into BibTex format.

5. FILTERING AND ASSESSING THE COLLECTED REFERENCES

The references collected from the digital library retrieval step (see Section 4.3.1) sometimes return bibliographic data representing irrelevant publications. To filter them out, the filtering step will be triggered. The filtering step first compares each of the collected references with the input reference. The comparison is also done by FRIL to look for syntactic similarities between attributes of both references. The collected references that differ significantly from the input reference are removed. The remaining references are called as relevant references, and are passed on to the assessment step where the references are checked if they are enough for correction and augmentation. If they pass the assessment, the remaining relevant references are passed on to the integration step. Otherwise, BibAll would execute another searching phase for retrieving the publications that cite the literature present in the input reference, namely the cited-by publications. The assessment step is introduced to make a better balance between the speed and accuracy. On the one hand, searching, downloading and parsing the cited-by publications can be time-consuming. On the other hand, their reference sections can provide abundant and well-formed bibliographic information and might potentially improve the accuracy. Thus, when the collected references from online digital libraries are enough for correcting and augmenting the input reference and pass the assessment, the step on cited-by publication retrieval (see Section 4.3.2) is skipped to improve the efficiency of BibAll. Otherwise, the step is executed to find the cited-by publications from which the citation metadata are extracted to integrate with the input reference and potentially improve the accuracy of BibAll.

In the assessment step, BibAll first counts two numbers: *DiffAttr*, *SameAttr*.

DiffAttr is the number of the attributes that are present in the relevant references but not in the input reference.

SameAttr is the number of the attributes that are present both in the relevant references and the input reference and are not similar in the content.

(a) An example query string

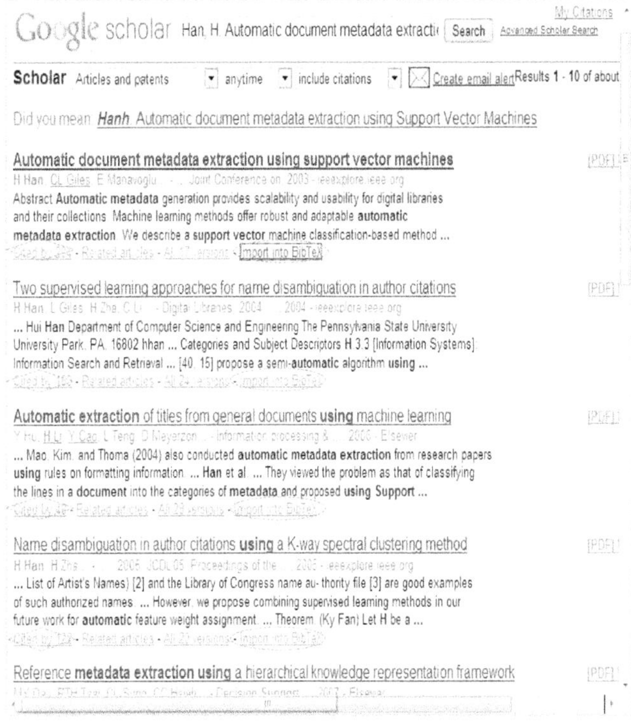

(b) The returned page after the query of (a)

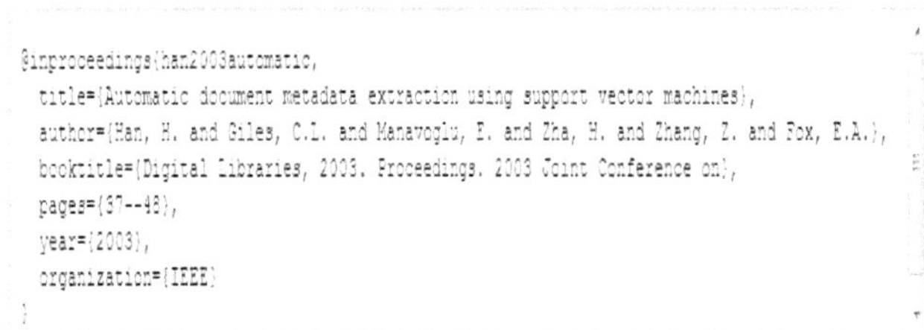

(c) The BibTex of the first article listed in (b)

Figure 3. An example of digital library retrieval of BibAll using Google Scholar

AugmAttr = DiffAttr + SameAttr, where AugmAttr reflects the number of attributes that can enrich the input reference potentially.

If *AugmAttr* is above a predefined proportion (called *AugmProp*) of the number of the attributes contained in the input reference, BibAll considers that the relevant references pass the assessment step. Otherwise, the step described in the Section 4.3.2 is executed to retrieve the cited-by publications. As a case in point, the *AugmAttr* is usually low when the input reference presents a literature published early. This reason is illustrated in Section 4.3.2. Thus, the step for cited-by publication retrieval is included in BibAll.

6. INTEGRATION OF THE RELEVANT REFERENCES

The reference integration phase produces an enriched reference, with the bibliographic data from the Web sources. Obviously, the citation parsing errors are also corrected by integrating the right bibliographic information from the Web in the enriched reference. In the integration phase, an integration conflict occurs when the input reference and the relevant references have different values for the same attribute. Thus, the integration needs to decide how the bibliographic data is integrated. In addition, it also decides how integration conflicts can be resolved. The details are described as follows.

a) Denote the references fed into the integration phase as a set of references R:

$R = \{r_0, r_1, r_2, \ldots, r_i, \ldots, r_m\}$,

$r_i = \{atrr_1, atrr_2, \ldots, atrr_j, \ldots atrr_k\}$

where m is the number of the relevant references filtered from the filtering phase, r_0 represents the input reference, namely the parsing result of a given citation, r_i is the ith of the m relevant references and consists of a set of metadata attributes. $atrr_j$, namely $r_i(j)$ is the jth one of the k attributes in r_i. k is the number of attributes contained in a reference, and k is set to 22, the number of attributes supported by the BibTex reference model in BibAll. The name of $atrr_j$ is the same for each reference in R, and corresponds to the jth field of the BibTex reference model.

b) Establish a resulting reference (*objectRef*) with 22 attributes just like a reference in R, and each of its attributes is assigned a value one by one. For example, the jth attribute of *objectRef*, *objectRef* (j), is assigned a value in the following way:

For the references in R, their values in $atrr_j$ are listed in a set $V=\{v_0, v_1, \ldots, v_i, \ldots, v_p\}$. p is usually below m because some references in R have no value in $atrr_j$ or have the same value in the attribute. There are a number of possibilities of the generated V:

i. if p is equal to 0, namely, all the references in R have no value in their j^{th} attribute, then the resulting reference, *objectRef*, also remains empty in the attribute.

ii. if p is equal to 1, namely all the references with a value in $atrr_j$ share the same value, then the value is assigned to *objectRef* (j).

iii. if p is larger than 1, *objectRef* (j) is assigned through weighted voting of v_i. For example, the value, v_i is voted by the data sources of the references which provide a value equal to v_i in $atrr_j$. The weight of a data source reflects its creditability degree (see Table 2). For example, BibAll gives a high weight to DBLP because it is a large bibliography database and is manually authored and examined. In addition, a vote number (w_0) is also specified for the input reference. When the input reference has the same value with v_i in $atrr_j$, the vote of v_i is added with w_0. Finally, the value in V with the highest vote is determined as the value of *objectRef* (j). An example is shown in Figure 4 to illustrate this step.

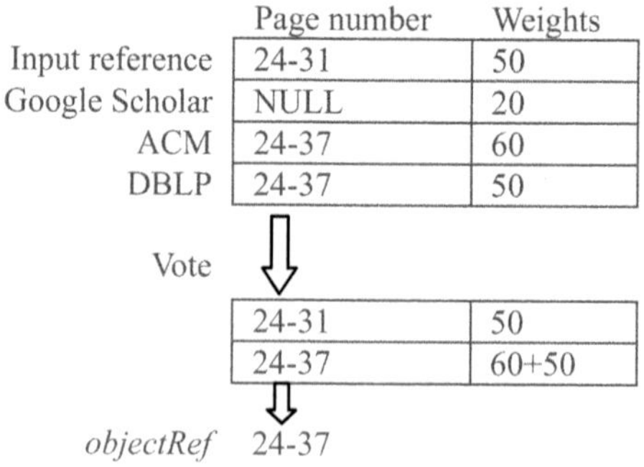

Figure 4. An example of integration conflict processing

After the integration phase, the end result is a BibTeX modeled reference which contains citation metadata enriched with bibliographic data from sources on the web. The enriched reference is richer than the input reference. Furthermore, the errors of the citation parsing phase are also corrected in the enriched reference. As shown in Table 1, during the integration step, the mistake with the booktitle and publisher attributes is fixed. Moreover, the editor, series and month attribute are also added in the enriched reference, which are not present in the original citation.

7. EXPERIMENTS

We have implemented a prototype of BibAll, which can be accessed on-line to provide the services of citation parsing, correction, and argumentation. The input and output pages are shown in Figure 7.

Since the goal of this paper is to address two main problems with content-based CME methods, the unreliability and incompleteness of the extracted citation metadata, we perform two different evaluations of BibAll. The first evaluates the performance of correcting the errors of the extracted citation metadata, while the second evaluates the performance of augmenting additional citation metadata absent in the original citation.

7.1 Evaluation Dataset, Tools, Data Sources, and Parameters

The evaluation is conducted in the computer science domain largely because there are a number of high-quality data sources publicly available on the Web. We use FLUX-CIM[4] [7] dataset to evaluate BibAll, which consists of 300 references from several computer science conferences and journals.

In order to compare BibAll with content-based CME methods, we choose an existing CME tool, ParsCit as the CME component of BibAll. ParsCit is selected because it shows a state-of-the-art performance and it is under active development. Furthermore, it is open-source software and is freely available. The ParsCit Version 110505B is used in BibAll. In addition, the FRIL Version 2.1.5 is integrated in BibAll to compare two references.

In our evaluation experiment, BibAll executes retrieval on five digital libraries: Google Scholar[5], CiteSeerX[6], Engineering IndexCompendexWeb[7] (EI), ACM[8], and DBLP[9]. Please note that

[4] FLUX-CIM: http://www.dcc.ufam.edu.br/~eccv/flux-cim

[5] Google Scolar: http://scholar.google.com/

[6] CiteSeerX: http://citeseerx.ist.psu.edu

[7] EI: http://www.engineeringvillage.com

[8] ACM Digital Library: http://dl.acm.org/

[9] DBLP: http://www.informatik.uni-trier.de/~ley/db/

the data sources of BibAll could be expanded if necessary. We also establish an assessment mechanism of data sources. Their weights defined in Table 2 are dynamically updated along with the decision of the values of *objectRef*. The weight of a data source will be increased when the metadata from the source is accepted in *objectRef*, and vice versa. The minimum and maximum of the weights of data sources are set as 0 and 100. The initial weights of the five sources above are set as 20, 40, 55, 60, 50 respectively.

The other parameters used in the system are set manually through experiments. For example, the parameter referred in Section 5, *AugmProp*, is set to 0.3 based on the observation and experience.

7.2 Correction Performance Evaluation

It is common to measure the performance of the CME in terms of precision and recall. We can do the same for the evaluation of the correction performance. The precision and recall rates are defined as follows:

$$\text{precision}=\frac{|\text{correctly extracted attributes}|}{|\text{extracted attributes}|} \quad (2)$$

$$\text{recall}=\frac{|\text{correctly extracted attributes}|}{|\text{current attributes}|} \quad (3)$$

The precision is the percentage of extracted attributes that are correctly extracted. An example of incorrect CME is shown in Table 1. The publisher "IEEE Computer Society" is mistaken as the booktitle by ParsCit. Fortunately, BibAll corrects this result by tagging "IEEE Computer Society" as the publisher, and modifying the value of booktitle attribute as "Proceedings of the 3rd ACM/IEEE-CS joint conference on digital libraries".

The recall rate indicates the probability that BibAll extracts a value that is actually present in the citation. For example, the citation shown in Figure 2 contains the publisher, but the publisher attribute is not extracted from ParsCit. In the end, BibAll assigns the publisher attribute to "IEEE Computer Society".

As always, the precision and recall rates are inversely correlated. Therefore we introduce a third metric, namely F1. The F1 measure is the harmonic mean of precision and recall, and it serves as a better overall performance indicator than recall or precision alone.

$$F1=\frac{2\times\text{precision}\times\text{recall}}{\text{precision}+\text{recall}} \quad (4)$$

The results are displayed in Figure 5. Please note that only the performance of the attributes present in the citations is shown.

Figure 5 clearly shows that BibAll outperforms ParsCit in every metadata type through the correction by bibliographic data from the Web. Several metadata types, such as address, pages, and volume, have low performance for ParsCit, while BibAll dramatically improves the results on those fields.

More specifically, we also measure the correction precision of BibAll, namely the percentage of modified attributes that are correctly modified. For the results of ParsCit on FLUX-CIM dataset, BibAll has modified 46 attributes, and 44 of them are correctly modified attributes. Thus the correction precision of BibAll on FLUX-CIM dataset is 96%. Based on the results shown in Figure 5 and the correction precision, we can conclude that the bibliographic data from the Web have positive effects on correcting citation parsing results, and our Web-based CME approach is very effective.

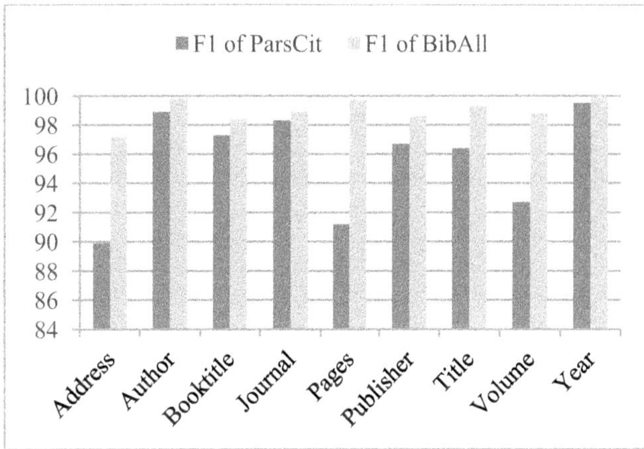

Figure 5. F1 of ParsCit and BibAll on citation metadata extraction

7.3 Augmentation Performance Evaluation

To measure the performance of BibAll on citation metadata augmentation, we count the augmentations in two granularities, namely references and attributes. For the 300 references in the FLUX-CIM dataset, the test results are shown in Table 3.

Table 3. The result of BibAll on augmenting citation metadata

Items	The number of augmented items	The number of correctly augmented items
Reference	277	264
Address	95	91
Annote	0	0
Author	1	1
Booktitle	10	9
Chapter	3	3
Edition	0	0
Editor	68	66
Howpublished	0	0
Institution	4	4
Journal	25	22
Month	33	31
Note	4	4
Number	93	90
Organization	13	13
Pages	51	50
Publisher	144	142
School	0	0
Series	140	139
Title	1	1
Type	0	0
Volume	92	89
Year	14	13

We consider that a reference is augmented correctly when all the augmented attributes in the reference are right. From the second row of Table 3, we can see that most of the references in dataset are augmented, and the augmentation precision is high, nearly 96%. Among the 23 references that are not augmented, 9 references contain much spelling errors so that no relevant bibliographic data are found in the Web sources. Due to the errors in citation parsing phase, two references are not augmented. The other 12 references are not augmented because no additional bibliographic data that are not present in the references are collected. For the thirteen references that are augmented incorrectly, one is augmented by mistake because an irrelevant article is selected to enrich the reference. The other twelve references are augmented by mistake because of the inherited errors from the on-line digital libraries.

It can be also seen from Table 3 that BibAll augments citation metadata on most attributes and most of the augmentation precisions are above 90%. Furthermore, the commonly occurring attributes in citation strings, such as author, year and title, are enriched less than other uncommon attributes, such as editor, series and publisher which are usually edited and stored in digital libraries and seldom appear in citations.

We also measure the role of cited-by publication retrieval (see Section 4.3.2) for citation metadata correction and augmentation. In the correction performance evaluation of BibAll, the bibliographic data from cited-by publications modify seven attributes, and all of them are correctly modified attributes. Among the 791 augmented attributes in the augmentation performance evaluation of BibAll, the cited-by publications contribute 83 attributes, and 81 of them are correctly augmented attributes. Thus, cited-by publication retrieval is included in BibAll as an important complement of digital library retrieval in order to collect more bibliographic data.

We implemented the whole system in C++ and conducted the experiments with a standard PC (dual-core 1.4GHz, 2GBRAM, Windows Server 2008). The processing time is about 15 seconds without executing the 'cited-by publication retrieval' step. The time of the 'cited-by publication retrieval' step depends on the speed of downloading and parsing PDF files, which can vary a lot.

7.4 Error Analysis

Although BibAll generally exhibits excellent performance, it does make occasional mistakes. Based on an extensive observation, we summarize the major error patterns reasons as follows:

Errors in citation parsing: For example, as shown in the second column of Table 1, the booktitle in the parsing result contains the text of the publisher. When the booktitle is used to query a data source, the source might return incorrect bibliographic data.

Errors in citation strings: For example, the title of the second citation in FLUX-CIM dataset is 'Type inclusion constraints and type ıatexence', but the real title is actually 'Type inclusion constraints and type inference'. The incorrect data might cause no relevant bibliographic data to be collected or might be integrated into the final result.

Data sources providing incorrect data: In some cases, the data sources provide inconsistent bibliographic data. For example, the CiteSeerX returns the year '1961' for the publication shown in Figure 6, while the ACM Digital Library returns the year '1995', and the parsing results of the citations shown in the figure respectively return the year '1961' and '1963'. This inconsistence is usually caused by the different editions of the same publication. The other common error from data sources is that a citation represents a conference article while the data source regards it as a journal article. A case in point is that Google Scholar stores the real booktitle name of the publication shown in Figure 6(a) in the 'journal' attribute.

(a) Minsky, M. (1961). Steps toward artificial intelligence. Proc. Inst. Radio Engr. *49*, 8–30.

(b) Minsky, M., Steps towards Artificial Intelligence, in: E.A. Feigenbaum and J.A. Feldman (Eds.), *Computers and Thought* (McGraw-Hill, New York, 1963) 442.

Figure 6. An example of a publication with multiple versions

8. CONCLUSIONS

In order to solve the two main problems with content-based CME methods, namely the unreliability of the extraction results and the incompleteness of the extracted citation metadata, this paper proposes a Web-based CME approach and a complete system ("BibAll") by combining the information from three sources: input citation, relevant bibliographic data from on-line digital repositories, and cited-by publications on the Web. The approach incorporates a pipeline consisting of four phases: parsing, searching, filtering, and integration. The parsing phase is responsible for CME from the input citation. During the searching phase additional bibliographic data are collected from several heterogeneous data sources. Then the collected bibliographic data are given to the filtering step to filter out the irrelevant bibliographic data of the input citation. Finally, the integration step integrates the relevant bibliographic data together after reconciling conflicts. The experiments demonstrate that BibAll achieved outstanding performance on correcting the parsing results of content-based CME methods and enriching citation metadata for most of input references.

Although BibAll is currently only tested in the computer science domain, it is quite straightforward to apply it to other domains, as it does not require any analysis on the actual content. Extending BibAll to support the other domains is one of our next tasks in the near future. We are also interested in establishing a database storing the complete metadata of publications enriched by BibAll and then providing public metadata query service using the database.

9. ACKNOWLEDGMENTS

This research is financially supported by the Ministry of Science and Technology of PRC (No. 152101650032). The FLUX-CIM test dataset is created by Eli Cortez Custódio Vilarinho's group of Federal University of Amazonas. The integrated FRIL is developed by Pawel Jurczyk's group of Emory University and Centers for Disease Control and Prevention. ParsCit, an open-source CRF reference string and logical document structure parsing package, is integrated in our system. In addition, Xiaoyan Lin, Xuan Hu, and Chengying Lv have contributed to the implementation of BibAll.

10. REFERENCES

[1] Aumuller, D., Rahm, E. 2011. PDFMeat: Managing Publications on the Semantic Desktop. In *Proceedings of the 20th ACM Int. Conf. on Information and Knowledge Management* (Glasgow, Scotland, UK, October 24 - 28, 2011). ACM Press, New York, NY, 2565-2568.

[2] Besagni, D., Belaid, A., and Benet, N. 2003. A segmentation method for bibliographic references by contextual tagging of fields. In *Proceeding of the ICDAR '03* (Edinburgh, Scotland, August 3 - 6, 2003). IEEE Computer Society Press, 384-388.

[3] Bollacker, K. D., Lawrence, S., and Giles, C. L. 1998. CiteSeer: an autonomous web agent for automatic retrieval and identification of interesting publications. In *Proceeding of the Agents '98* (Minneapolis, MN, USA, May 10 - 13, 1998). ACM Press, New York, NY, 116-123.

[4] Chen, C. C., Yang, K.H., Kao, H. Y., and Ho, J. M. 2008. BibPro: A citation parser based on sequence alignment techniques. In *Proceeding of the IEEE AINA '08* (Okinawa, Japan, March 25 -28, 2008). 1175-1180.

[5] Councill, C. L. G. I. and M.-Y. Kan. 2008. ParsCit: an open-source CRF reference string parsing package. In *Proceedings*

of the Sixth International Language Resources and Evaluation (Marrakech, Morocco, May 38 - 30, 2008). LREC '08. European Language Resources Association (ELRA). 661-667.

[6] Day, M. Y., et al. 2007. Reference metadata extraction using a hierarchical knowledge representation framework. *Decision Support Systems*. 41, 1 (Feb. 2007), 152 - 167.

[7] Eli, C., Altigran S. da Silva, Marcos A. G., Filipe M., and Edleno S. de Moura. 2007. FLUX-CIM: flexible unsupervised extraction of citation metadata. In *Proceedings of the JCDL '07* (Vancouver, BC, Canada, June 17-23, 2007). ACM Press, New York, NY, 215-224.

[8] Gao, L., Tang, Z. and Lin, X. 2009. CEBBIP: A parser of bibliographic information in Chinese electronic books. In *Proceeding of the JCDL '09* (Austin, TX, USA, June 15-19, 2009). IEEE Computer Society, Washington, DC, 73-76.

[9] Greenberg, J. 2003. Metadata extraction and harvesting: A comparison of two automatic metadata generation applications. *Journal of Internet Cataloging*. 6, 4 (2003), 59-82.

[10] Han, H., Giles, C.L., Manavoglu, E., Zha, H., Zhang, Z., and Fox, E.A. 2003. Automatic document metadata extraction using Support Vector Machines. In *Proceeding of the JCDL '03* (Houston,TX, USA, May 27-31, 2003). IEEE Computer Society, Washington, DC, 37 - 48.

[11] Hetzner, E. 2008. A simple method for citation metadata extraction using Hidden Markov Models. In *Proceeding of the JCDL '08* (Pittsburgh, Pennsylvania, June 16 - 20, 2008). ACM Press, New York, NY, 280-284.

[12] http://paracite.eprints.org/.

[13] Huang, A., Ho, J. M., Kao, H. Y., and Lin, S. H. 2004. Extracting citation metadata from online publication lists using BLAST. In *Proceedings of the PAKDD '04* (Sydney, Australia, May 26-28, 2004). Springer, Berlin, vol. 3056, 539-548.

[14] Lee, D., J. Kang, P. Mitra, C. L. Giles, and B.-W. 2007. Are your citations clean?. *Communications of the ACM*. 50, 12 (2007), 33-38.

[15] Marinai, S. 2009. Metadata Extraction from PDF Papers for Digital Library Ingest. In *Proceeding of the ICDAR '09* (Barcelona, Spain, July 26-29, 2009). IEEE Computer Society Press, 251-255.

[16] Page, L.; Brin, S.; Motwani, R.; and Winograd, T. 1998. The PageRank citation ranking: Bringing order to the web. Stanford Digital Library Technologies Project, 1998.

[17] Patashnik, O. 1988. Bibtexing. In *Proceedings of the IEEE 77 Hidden Markov Models and Selected Applications in Speech Recognition*. 257–286.

[18] Peng, F., and McCallum, A. 2004. Accurate information extraction from research papers using conditional random fields. In *Proceeding of the HLTNAACL '04* (Boston, MA, USA, May 2 -7, 2004). 329-336.

[19] Prime-Claverie, C. and Beigbeder, M. and Lafouge, T. 2005. Metadata propagation in the web using co-citations. In *Proceedings of the 2005 IEEE/ACM In-ternational Conference on Web Intelligence* (Compiegne University of Technology, France, September 19-22, 2005). IEEE Computer Society. 602-605.

[20] Rodriguez, M. A.; Bollen, J.; and Van de Sompel, H. 2009. Automatic metadata generation using associative networks. *ACM Trans. On Information Syst*. 27, 2 (Feb. 2009), 1-20.

[21] Seymore, K., McCallum, A., and Rosenfeld, R. 1999. Learning Hidden Markov Model structure for information extraction. In *Proceeding of the AAAI '99* (Orlando, FL, USA, July 18 - 22, 1999). 37-42.

[22] Takasu, A. 2003. Bibliographic attribute extraction from erroneous references based on a statistical model. In *Proceeding of the JCDL '03* (Houston, TX, USA, May 27-31, 2003). IEEE Computer Society, Washington, DC, 49-60.

[23] Wei, W., King, I., and Lee, J.H.-M. 2007. Bibliographic attributes extraction with layer-upon-layer tagging. In *Proceeding of the ICDAR '07*. (Curitiba, Paraná, Brazil, September 23 - 26, 2007). IEEE Computer Society Press, 804-808.

[24] Wenneker, B. 2010. BibMix: Enrichment of citation metadata based on integration of bibliographic data. Master's Thesis. Delf University of Technology.

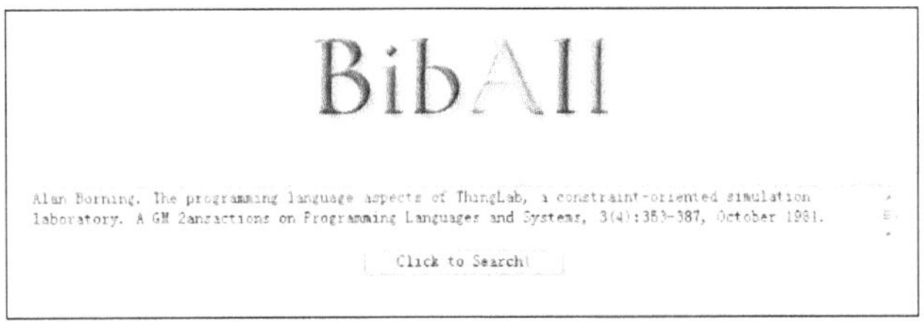

(a) The input page, where a citation string can be input

(b) The output page, where lists all the citation metadata in BibTex format collected from different source

Figure 7. The input and output pages of BibAll

Book Selection Behavior in the Physical Library: Implications for eBook Collections

Annika Hinze
Computer Science Department
University of Waikato
Hamilton, New Zealand
hinze@cs.waikato.ac.nz

Dana McKay
Library, The Swinburne Institute for Social Research
Swinburne University of Technology
Melbourne, Australia
dmckay@swin.edu.au

Nicholas Vanderschantz, Claire Timpany, Sally Jo Cunningham
University of Waikato
vtwoz, ctimpany, sallyjo@cs.waikato.ac.nz

ABSTRACT
Little is known about how readers select books, whether they be print books or ebooks. In this paper we present a study of how people select physical books from academic library shelves. We use the insights gained into book selection behavior to make suggestions for the design of ebook-based digital libraries in order to better facilitate book selection behavior.

Categories and Subject Descriptors
H3.7. Digital Libraries: User issues;
H5.4. Hypermedia: User Issues

Keywords
Digital libraries, ebooks, human-computer interaction, information seeking behavior.

1. INTRODUCTION
Rowlands, *et al.* noted in 2007 that there is surprisingly little data on how readers select books; a data deficit that remains true today [33]. This dearth of data on how readers select books makes it difficult to design interfaces that adequately support book selection, an activity that has been shown to rely heavily on serendipity in physical environments [26, 35]; unfortunately, this strategy simply doesn't work online [27].

Using information seeker behavior in physical environments to inform DL design is a well established technique: [14] uses music shopping behavior to inform DL design; and [13] uses ethnographic observation to determine the limitations of a digital library for technical support workers. Closer to our work, [11] considers DL design with respect to the reference interview, [8] uses observations of book shoppers to further understanding of book seeking, and [31] reflects on e-reader design with respect to print reading behavior. In this vein, we seek to use book selection behavior in libraries to better inform the design of ebook-based DLs.

Getting a library book is typically a four step process:

(1) identifying books of interest (e.g. via the catalogue),
(2) physically retrieving the books from the shelves,
(3) choosing among the available options, and
(4) accessing and reading the book for the desired content.

JCDL'12, June 10–14, 2012, Washington, DC, USA.

The first step, searching for books (or indeed any kind of information) is a well understood behavior. There are numerous studies of information search processes (e.g., [17, 22]) and similarly plentiful studies of how users search for books in the catalogue (e.g., [10, 18, 37]). Previous literature also exists on how readers identify interesting fiction books [30], the types of questions they ask librarians [11, 29], and the kinds of queries posed in bookshops [8].

While the fourth step, reading, is the subject of less research, nonetheless that research is relevant here. Some facets of reading, such as the ability to easily annotate or flip through a text [1] may affect the reader's preference of reading medium [31]. There are a number of studies (e.g., [31]) on the use of e-readers, but little work on the physical act of reading books, perhaps because this activity is difficult to study without being 'creepy' [23]. As reading behavior is relatively unlikely to impact book selection (outside of the medium), it will not be further considered here.

The third step, choosing among available resources, is poorly studied for books, particularly in physical environments [33]. While there is considerable literature on document triage for journal articles (see Section 2.3), this literature does not translate well to book selection because it shows readers using article-specific features (e.g., the abstract) to make decisions [2, 3, 9]. Book selection is largely ignored in the literature on scholarly information seeking, though there have been some studies in artificial environments of decision making over both print books [36] and ebooks [19]. Natural behavior, however, is often very different from that observed in experimental settings [15]; for example, book selection literature does not reflect the shelf-based serendipitous discovery academics value in libraries [35]. Finally, the second step, retrieving a book from the shelves, has been overlooked as not being of significance to the book selection process. We argue, however, that at this point the reader is typically verifying whether or not the potentially useful book is actually relevant to their information needs. Further, during physical retrieval of the book, a reader typically also browses the adjoining shelf space for other books of interest and, again, uses physical cues to decide which books to take home. Surprisingly, which cues readers use to determine whether or not books are useful at the shelves has not been formally investigated.

The work reported in this paper seeks to understand what factors contribute to decision making when selecting books by observing readers selecting books in physical libraries and interviewing them about their behavior. Section 2 of this paper outlines related work, Section 3 describes our methodology, and Section 4 gives our results. In Section 5 we discuss the implications of our work for digital libraries, and in Section 6 we draw conclusions and outline future work.

2. RELATED WORK

Our study has three areas of related work: literature on interacting with library shelves (Section 2.1), book selection (Section 2.2), and document triage (Section 2.3).

2.1 Interacting with library shelves

Surprisingly little literature exists on how readers interact with library shelves, and the majority of this work focuses on children. One such study is Moore's work that examines children's information search processes by observing children interacting with library shelves [28]. Moore noted that the children often selected the first book they found with a Dewey number related to their query rather than comparing all the books on their topic for usefulness. She also noted that the majority of children could not effectively use the library shelves.

Reutzel and Gali's ethnographic observation of children investigated how children select books from the library shelves [32]. For their study, they developed a *classification of observable book selection behavior*, which we adopt for our study. The observed children were strongly biased toward books on shelves at eye level (60% of selected books), and tended to select books that were in some way eye-catching to them. They were also very aware of the geographical layout of the library and could successfully locate the section, shelf and position of books they were looking for.

Borgman, *et al.* [7] extensively studied the use of the shelf metaphor in a children's DL. The observed children were largely effective at using a DL interface based on the shelf metaphor. This efficacy is in keeping with observations [28, 32] that children seemed to prefer approaching the shelves directly or asking a librarian as opposed to using the catalogue in physical libraries.

Studies of adults' use of library shelves are limited: McKay and Conyers observed that users struggle with every aspect of locating library books on shelves, but provide little insight into how readers select books at the shelves [26]. Stelmaszewska and Blandford's ethnographic study of computer scientists using the physical library noted the occurrence of serendipitous discoveries at the library shelves [35]. This work also showed how participants make judgments about the utility of books based on visual cues such as their apparent age and whether or not they were dusty (a reflection of recent use). In contrast, [8] found that purchasers in bookshops first turned to shop assistants for help, then for the most part engaged in a 'grab and go' strategy, with little browsing or serendipitous discovery.

In summary, the literature on how adults interact with bookshelves to select books is decidedly scant; to our knowledge our study is the first examining this behavior specifically.

2.2 Book selection

There is limited work on how people select books, though some of this work is quite detailed and thus provides significant insight.

Flipping behavior (particularly flipping linearly through books) was reported in a study of readers' engagement with ebooks [25]. [28] and [32] both reported children flipping through books to make decisions, however, similarities end there. Reutzel and Gali observed children selecting and rejecting books based on the presence or absence of images within the book, value statements about the content of the book, and external limitations such as the number of books they were allowed to have out of the library at a time. Moore observed children using textual features such as the table of contents, index and headings. These differences may result from the different nature of the studies; in [32] children selected books freely, in [28] children selected books to meet a pre-defined information need. The table of contents (TOC) was observed to be used by college students when comparing similar books with the intention of meeting a specific information need [36]. This dependence on TOC—and, to a lesser extent, index—was also noted in a number of studies on how searchers find information within books [6, 19, 21, 35], an activity likely to influence book selection. Ooi [30] found evidence that recommendations from popular media and, to a lesser extent, peer recommendations influenced book selections. Similarly, [8] observed that many customers in bookshops used references to non-bibliographic cues to describe the book they needed: for example, popular cultural relationships (such television tie-ins), cover information, reviews in mainstream media, and book appearance.

In summary, the literature shows a range of information being used in book selection. Behaviors used to leverage this data include flipping, skim-reading, reading the TOC, seeking recommendations, and examining the outer book covers. What is little studied is how readers integrate these behaviors with their interactions with library shelves. While [35] reports work on this with computer scientists, no broader study has been conducted.

2.3 Document triage

While there is little information regarding how readers choose between available books, choosing between journal articles has been well studied. This process is referred to in the literature as 'document triage'. [24] and [35] studied document triage in physical journals where readers use the TOC, article titles and authors as well as images and figures (assessed while flipping though the document) to select reading material. Online articles are evaluated in similar ways, with readers using title, author, abstract, introduction and conclusion to evaluate works of interest, and to a lesser extent images and emphasized text [3, 9, 20]. Readers accessed this information by scrolling rapidly through documents [20] (sometimes through and back), the digital equivalent of flipping (though much more prone to leaving users feeling lost [19]). This strong correlation between on- and offline behavior suggests that selection strategies translate well between physical and digital formats, at least for journal articles.

3. METHODOLOGY

Here we describe our methodology for understanding the book selection process in academic libraries. Section 3.1 outlines our observation and interview technique, Section 3.2 describes the target libraries, and Section 3.3 gives participant demographics.

3.1 Observation and interviews

All studies took place in academic or government libraries. We visited libraries individually or in pairs and observed readers' book selection behavior, paying careful attention to the location of sampled books and book sampling behavior. We typically observed interaction with two to five books before briefly interviewing readers about their book selection and motivations in book choice.

We coded observational data using the framework introduced in [32], however we cut the original six criteria down to three objectively observable phenomena: how readers located a desired book within the library, which parts of a book users examined to determine its usefulness, and where in the library participants looked.

Interviews were executed in situ, and explored how readers made the decision whether to use a book, how they searched for the book, where they would use the book, what they were looking for, what notes they had taken, whether they had considered an ebook, and any other interesting behavior. We also collected demographic information. Due to the low frequency of in-person use for the government library we studied, we typically did not conduct observations in this library, though we interviewed a number of researchers.

The ability to generalize from these results is of course limited by the location of the study: our findings are unlikely to be applicable in a fiction or public general library context.

3.1 Target libraries

All three libraries in this study were academic or government research libraries. At the University of Waikato, New Zealand (UoW), conducted our study in the main library. At the Freie Universitaet Berlin (FUB) Germany, we conducted our study mostly in the Philological library, but also in the Library for Psychology and Education. Our final study location was Bundesamt fuer Materialforschung and -pruefung Berlin (BAM). BAM is the Federal Institute for Materials Research and Testing, and its library functions are those of a specialized research library, and as such we treated it slightly differently (see Section 3.1). Each of these libraries holds specialist non-fiction books (such as reference books, technical books and textbooks). By selecting these libraries, we restricted our study to information access in educational and scholarly contexts (not recreational).

3.3 Participant demographics

We interviewed 65 readers (20 at UoW, 25 at FUB and 20 at BAM), 51 of whom were also directly observed interacting with books in the stacks. Because the labyrinthine layout at BAM made it difficult to track patrons though the stacks, some participants at BAM were interviewed but not directly observed in their interactions. Of the interviewed readers 33 were male and 32 female (22 and 29, respectively, for observed readers). The age distribution is in keeping with expectations for university and government libraries (see Fig. 1).

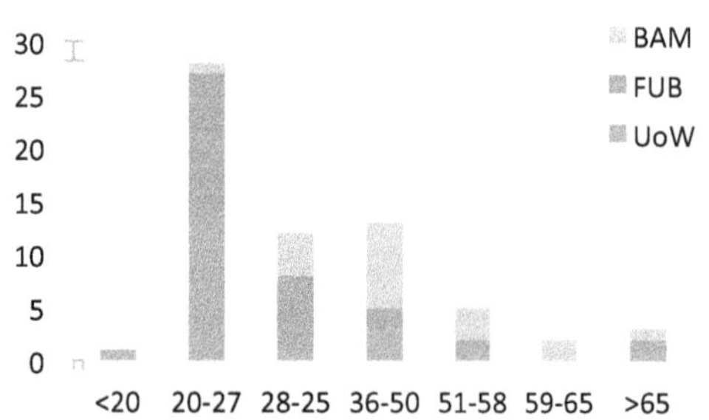

Figure 1. Age distribution of study participants

As would be expected of university libraries, approximately half of the readers interviewed were engaged in research (31) while the other half were conducting their tertiary studies (30). Only two readers were searching for teaching-related material and one patron was visiting the library for recreational purposes, while one declined to respond to that question. Names of participants were neither asked nor recorded; in the remainder of this paper, individual participants are identified by the three letter acronym for the library in which they were observed or interviewed (BAM, FUB, UoW) appended to a numeric identifier (e.g., UoW07).

Searches covered a wide range of topics, including materials science, anthropology, management, education, and accounting; these topics accord with the research and teaching strengths at the institutions studied. Subjects naturally mirror the specializations of the libraries in which searches were conducted (e.g., German in the philological library at FUB, explosives at BAM).

4. RESULTS

This section summarizes the patterns of behavior observed from our study of participants in the three physical libraries and the results of the brief interviews.

4.1 Physical and digital books

Even in the face of the bias introduced by doing this study, nearly half of all participants (30/65) had considered using an ebook instead of a pint book, and 25 of those expressed a preference for ebooks. Some participants, however, had not considered using an ebook until our questioning suggested it.

Most participants suggested a reason (sometimes quite forcefully) for their preference of one format over another (see Fig.2). 20 participants stated a strong preference for physical books, of whom 13 wanted "real" books, and 7 preferred the "physicality" of paper books (UoW06: "[ebooks] seem so impersonal", UoW04: "print books are easier for research").

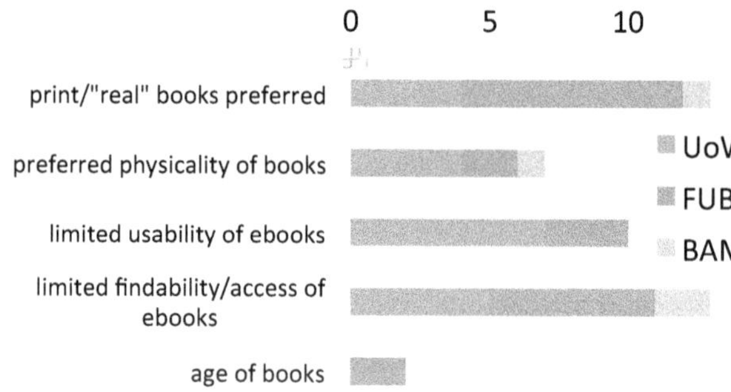

Figure 2. Reasons given for preference for physical books

Ten participants criticized the usability of ebooks in terms of screen access (UoW13: "I get headaches when reading on the screen, Kindle is better"; UoW19: "...gives me a really bad headache"; FUB12: "...strenuous for the eyes") but also in terms of possible interactions (FUB24: "I need to translate [it] and [with a paper copy] I can write the translation into the text"; BAM19: "physical books are better for sharing"). BAM19 felt that physical books enforced "proper reading": "it is important to read everything, not just what comes marked in yellow when you search...the students have to learn that again, to really look at things".

The age of a book was frequently mentioned with respect to both physical and digital books: some participants claimed they could not or would not be able to find an ebook to meet their needs because "only new books are ebooks" (FUB24). Conversely, some participants complained about the age of physical books available in the library FUB02: "I'm annoyed by how old all the books are".

While most readers were aware of the availability of electronic resources (only four participants were not aware of the availability of ebooks), the electronic nature of the materials did not seem to affect the understanding and interaction of some participants. One participant asked, "can you access [ebooks] at home?" (UoW11), and a number of BAM users liked the idea of "books in PDF so you can print them for reading" (BAM13). In both these examples the electronic nature of ebooks is poorly understood at best, and ignored at worst.

It is clear from our questioning about ebooks that physical books are both clearly understood by readers, and hold a real draw for readers. Some of the reasons for this preference became evident on observing readers' interactions with the library as a physical space. We observed several library users sleeping or sprawling, and we saw repeated evidence of the influence of the physical nature of the library on information seeking.

Several readers explicitly named serendipity as a reason for coming to a physical library (FUB14: "I prefer to go to the library and look for books on the shelf to see what you can find serendipitously").

Figure 3: Reading and sorting books on the floor

Some people took chairs into the shelves to read there or to look at the books (3 of 51). A number of readers were found crouching, kneeling or sitting on the floor (13 of the 51 observed readers, see Fig. 3). In part readers did this to reach the books on the lowest shelves, but also to sort selected books on the floor. Readers typically had several books in their hands, not all of which they planned to take out. People sitting on the floor often made piles of books (definitely borrow, maybe borrow) and also moved books around on the floor while making decisions. This behavior mirrors the observations in [32] of children selecting four or five books which they would line up for deeper consideration, deciding which to check out among this smaller subset.

The physical layout was not without its problems, however: if readers did not write down adequate information they would have to leave the stack to repeat their searches (BAM01:"I will have to go back to the catalogue and look again"). Sometimes they forgot to check whether the book was available in the library or out on loan. Some users were confused by local cataloguing systems, rather than finding they supported serendipity ("they [the books] are all in the wrong order - I am completely lost" (UoW10); "I do not understand the system they use here" (FUB 05)). These experiences represent the negative sides of the physical library reported in previous literature (for example [26, 35]).

4.2 Searching the catalogue

34 of the 51 interviewed participants had searched the catalogue before entering the stack; 16 had searched the online catalogue using a library computer (see Fig. 4). Nine participants did not search the catalogue, saying they were familiar enough with the layout of the library that they could go straight to the shelves or sections where books they wished to use were found.

Participants at BAM used the library almost exclusively remotely, searching the catalogue from their offices and then ordering any useful books to be sent over. Many BAM participants claimed, in fact, not to use the library because "everything is on the intranet" (BAM 15)—unaware that this electronic access via the intranet or online is in fact a service provided by the library.

A number of people reported difficulty with the catalogue and the library layout. It seemed that often they expected the catalogue to work similarly to Google (UoW09: "Why does it not work like Google?"), and were disappointed to find it much harder to use.

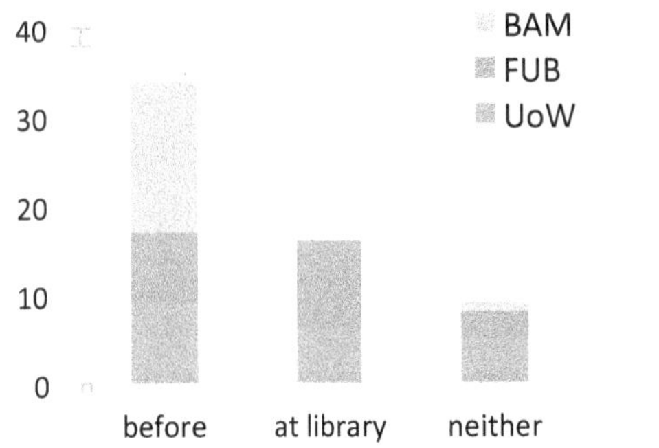

Figure 4: Catalogue use

27 participants reported keyword searching in the catalogue, 22 title searching, 13 authors, and 8 BAM participants used specialist standard identification numbers. 4 participants used other details, including publication date and recommendations from colleagues.

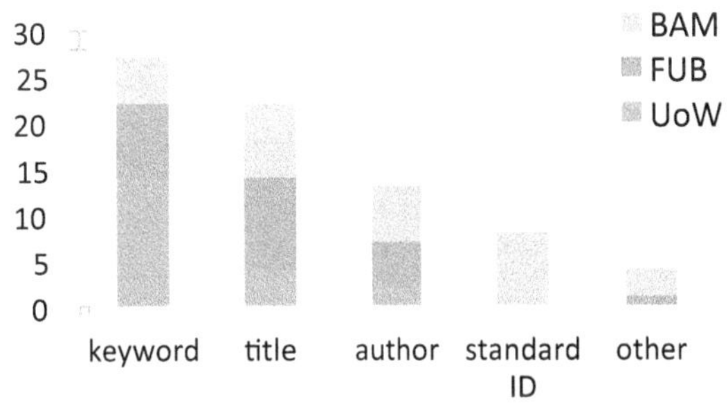

Figure 5. Catalogue search strategies

There were differences between institutions as to the search strategy used (see Fig. 5): UoW participants searched mostly by keyword (only 6 of 20 used title or author), whereas FUB participants mostly (20 of 24) used title or author. These differences may be due to local variations in catalogue software, or they may reflect the different participant groups seen at FUB and UoW: UoW participants were younger and more likely to be studying (as opposed to conducting research) than those at FUB. BAM participants, like FUB participants typically did not search by byword (only 5 of 22 did). BAM researchers are typically experienced in their field, and reported using the library only when they had identified a resource that they wished to access.

4.3 Artifacts used as finding aids

Participants who searched the catalogue before entering the library stacks often had notes to assist in locating books. 24 participants permitted the researchers to photograph their notes (3 refused). Few BAM notes were recorded as the participants had largely discarded the notes before being interviewed, demonstrating that these notes are used to store information only temporarily while readers navigate to desired information resources on the shelves.

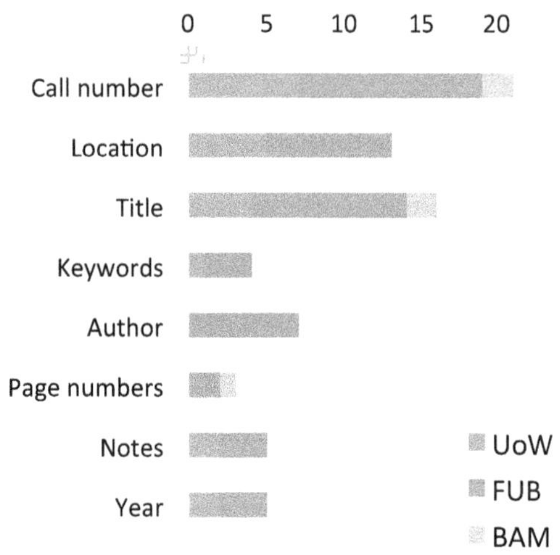

Figure 6. Details included on notes created to assist in locating books

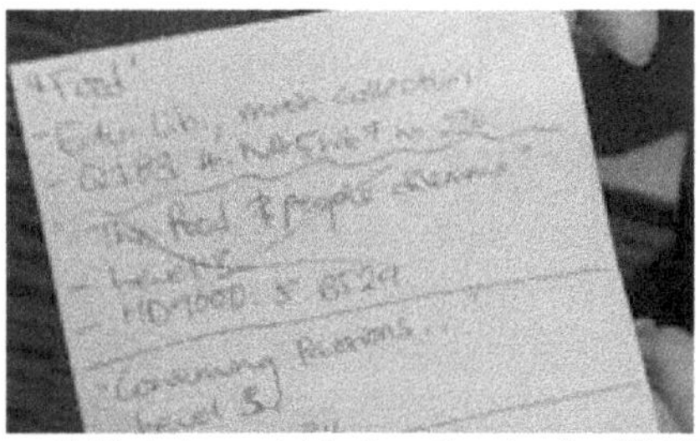

Figure 7. Note to assist in locating books (UoW19)

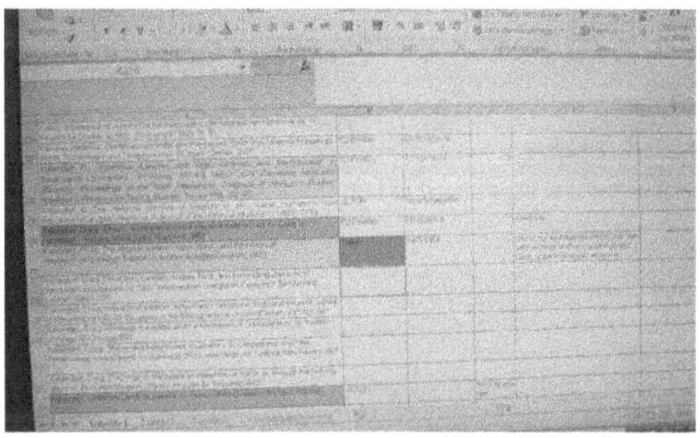

Figure 8. Electronic notes (FUB19)

Of the 24 photographed notes, 21 were handwritten, two were printed and one participant had brought a laptop to the library. Notes included call numbers, location, and titles (see Fig. 6). Figure 7 (UoW19) shows a typical example of a note. The participant had crossed out books they had checked but rejected as not suitable.

One participant (FUB19) used an electronic spreadsheet to keep track of their research material. The list included both printed books and electronic material (see Fig. 8); color-coding was used to indicate importance and to keep track of what had been read or examined.

4.4 Looking at the shelves

Readers located potentially interesting books on the shelves in one of four ways (see Fig. 9). The first strategy was "scanning a section" by looking along several shelves belonging to the same topic, the second was "sampling the shelf" in a more concentrated view (sometimes moving in an orderly top-to-bottom and left-to-right pattern, sometimes taking a more scattershot approach such as for display books), and the third was standing in one place close to the shelf and examining the shelf above, at or below eye level. Finally, some readers found books on display shelves of newly acquired or other promoted books (called "display books" hereafter). The relatively infrequent use of display books is commensurate with the small proportion of any library's collection on display at any time.

While three readers discovered books on display shelves, they were not the only readers to discover books in passing. One reader walked past a shelf and noticed a book's cover, which could be seen at the end of the shelf (it turned out to not be relevant to the topic of interest). Three of the four people who "found" books in passing were on their way to/from the washroom. In addition to these four, several participants found books by scanning the shelves adjacent to those containing a book of interest. This finding supports participants' assertions that the physical library facilitates serendipitous discovery of books.

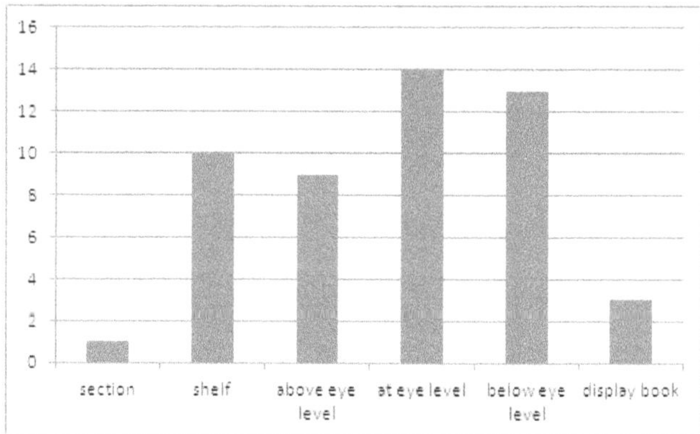

Figure 9. Sampled book geography

4.5 Choosing books from the shelves

51 readers were observed choosing books from the shelves. Their actions in doing so are described in Figure 10. Readers touched books (without pulling them out), tilted them (typically to look at the cover), pulled or half pulled books (and put them back). Only 31 out of the 51 took books completely off the shelves for further examination. When examining books on the shelf, readers cocked their heads to read what was on the spine, and two mumbled as they were looking for specific books. The use of the spine refers to readers who were observed to explicitly read the spine; only 10 of 51 readers did this. As described in Section 4.4, four readers chanced upon books displayed in such a way that their covers were already visible. All other readers had to base their decision to investigate further on the spine of the book.

Tilt, pull and half pull were interpreted as an intention to glimpse the cover when this could not be examined directly. "Pull" refers to the action of lifting the book off the shelf to examine the front cover without opening the book, whereas 'take off shelf' refers to removing a book and then opening it to investigate further.

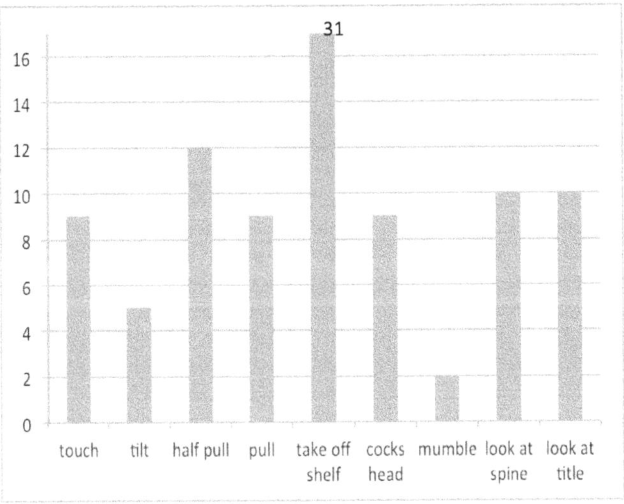

Figure 10. Book search behavior

4.6 Evaluating books

31 readers examined books more closely than just looking at the shelves in their decision making; some examined books in the stacks, while some removed their selections to a nearby table to make a decision. We observed more than half of all readers looking at the TOC, many of these followed up by reading sections of pertinent chapters and/or flipping through the book (see Fig. 11, blue). A number of readers were observed flipping *backwards* through books. Overall four main strategies were used for sampling the content of books: examination of the front cover, flipping backwards or forwards through the book reading part of the book, and examining the TOC.

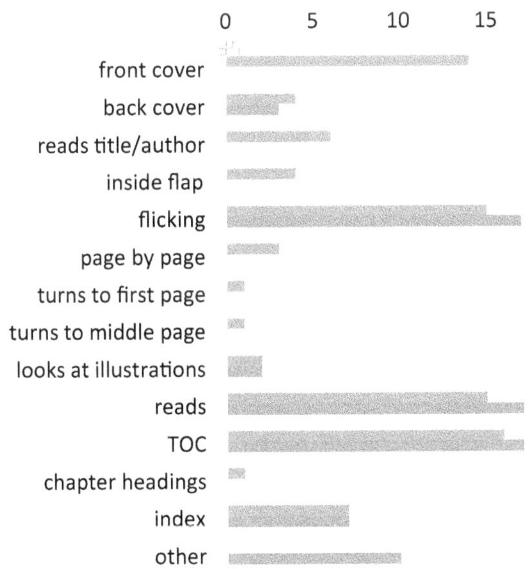

Figure 11. In-book browsing behavior (blue) and reported decision-making behavior (red)

Only one visitor carried out a "grab and go" behavior— he had returned for the very same book that he had used that morning. This is in stark contrast to Buchanan's bookshop observation where over half of the observed bookshop readers showed a "grab and go" strategy [8]. Buchanan's study, however, reports behaviors of those who had already asked a question of a bookseller and who were often purchasing for others, where our participants did not report talking to a librarian and were looking for books for their own use.

Readers' self-reported decision making (triage) behavior was largely in accordance with observed book sampling behavior (see Figure 11, red). Participants reported placing importance on the TOC and reading pertinent parts of a book as influencing their decision making behavior. Many of them also believed that flicking through the book was important. Participants who looked at the index and at illustrations reported using them for decision making. Participants used the back of the book to determine content and target audience. 'Other' facets mentioned were references and edition. Two readers needed to check whether the book was mentioned by their lecturer. One person said they wanted to spend time with a book (about 10min) to see if it "felt like" the right text.

4.7 Using books

Participants planned to access books in three ways (see Fig. 12): using the books in the library (15), checking the books out of the library to use at home or in the office (25), or copying all or part of the book to use later (20). Readers' choices were naturally strongly influenced by the options on offer at each library. All three libraries offered reading desks; however, the ones at BAM were more geared towards brief interactions with the books close to the shelves, whereas FUB and UoW offered work areas (partially equipped with computers and LAN connections for laptops). BAM and UoW had copy machines that allowed hardcopy as well as electronic copy into PDF documents. Copy machines at FUB only allowed hardcopy.

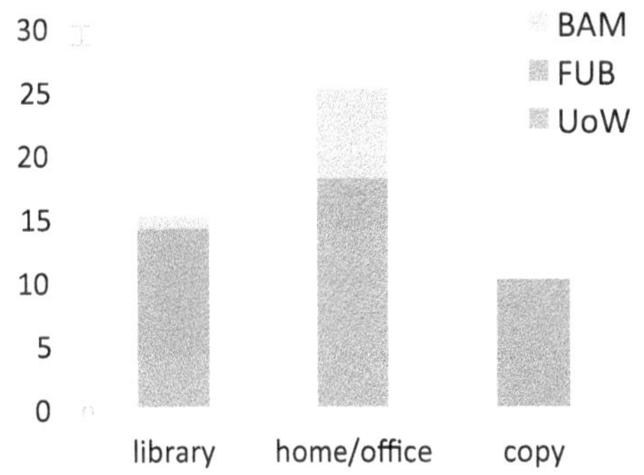

Figure 12. Planned interaction with selected books

Researchers at BAM reported that they visit the library to confirm the validity of citations: upon finding the relevant books they immediately turned to the pages given in the citations, to check the text they expected was present in the books, and if it was indeed present then they made copies to read later in their offices. The FUB philological library is predominantly a reference library (that is, most books cannot be taken out of the library) and so it provides desks and computing facilities in the library. Consequently, readers either used books in the library or copied out the parts they were interested in. In contrast, UoW offers a relatively small number of workspaces, and so UoW patrons check books out or copy them and take copies home (though explicit warnings about copyright infringement over photocopy machines and the cost of copying may influence preferences in this behavior).

5. Discussion

Drawing on summaries of observations and interviews (Section 4), and in reference to previous studies, we here explore interface and interaction design implications for ebook collections.

5.1 Finding books on the shelves.

Physical bookshelves are awkward to browse: only the tallest patrons are able to easily scan the top-most shelves, and for all but the shortest, viewing the lowest shelves involves bending or kneeling on the floor (Section 4.1). In our study these physical limitations are reflected in the participants' shelf scanning patterns: shelves above eye level were scanned less frequently (Section 4.3) than shelves at eye level or lower. This pattern of behavior is even more pronounced in children [32].

We might expect the digital display of ebooks to ease the tyranny of height imposed by shelves in the physical library; however, the conventional list-based display of digital library documents introduces similar difficulties. In digital library, ebooks are no longer less accessible due to the physical limitations of readers and shelves; instead, the digital library interface typically limits the collection view to a one-dimensional list, with only a few (often 10 to 25) ebooks visible at a time. The facility to scan hundreds of books on a physical shelf in seconds has been reduced to slowly limping from one keyhole view to another in a digital library – suggesting the need for further research into more quickly and more easily browsable DL displays. For example, Shneiderman suggested presenting digital library results as color-coded dots in a 2D-space [34]. Another option is to show ebooks in a two-dimensional space representing search similarity (as typically done in catalogues and DLs) and category surroundings (as on a library shelf), one example of which is seen in [7]. The link between searching and browsing could be strengthened by presenting search results with the hits highlighted within their category.

Physical books are typically grouped on shelves by subject classification (e.g., Dewey, Library of Congress). Readers arrive at relevant books either through searching the online catalogue (See Section 4.2), or browsing the shelves of a relevant subject (where that subject and its physical location in the library may have been identified in a previous online catalogue search). Browsing and searching are thus interleaved, though somewhat awkwardly, in the physical collection and online catalogue. While we might expect that this interleaving would be easier in a purely digital library, this may not be the case. In the popular Greenstone digital library system, for example, it is not possible to search within a subject classification, and not easy to switch to browsing the subject classification of a document identified by a search [27]. The DL users are thus less likely then physical library users to arrive at an ebook within a subject display, and so an ebook is most frequently viewed as part of the search term list (book among other books matching that search term) rather than the physical library view of a book in context with other books in the same subject category. At the same time, participants in our study reported valuing browsing by subject context (Section 4.1) and generally seemed to have a sound understanding of how the shelf classification worked.

The presentation of books in a physical library remains largely constant. The extent to which readers rely on this stability is documented by the observed nine library visitors who approached the shelves directly because they "know where things are" (FUB03). The layout allows visitors to build a mental map of "their" part of the library. This is not possible when ebooks are viewed primarily as elements within search results; search result displays are transient and it is notoriously difficult to recall previous search terms. Stronger support for subject-related access may help readers to grow familiar with an ebook collection.

Physical bookshelves let humans do what we do well: quickly scan and identify what might interest us from a herd of similar objects [5]. Our study confirms that people scan shelves, or sections or parts thereof; rarely did a reader look only at the book they wanted. Serendipitous finds of books were observed (Section 4.4) and valued by participants (Section 4.1); they typically happen when readers physically encounter books as they move though the library [26, 35]. In ebook collections, limited serendipity can be achieved by adding more stable displays (e.g., by using the 2D category references discussed earlier), however, there is further scope for offering additional ebook browsing to online users. Currently there are two documented ways to offer serendipity in digital libraries: the highlighting of a single, featured document, and streaming collage display [4]. The use of a single featured document does not meet the need for serendipity described by participants in this and other studies, as it shows only a single document as opposed to groups of related documents. Streaming collage displays have been demonstrated to be highly effective for collection understanding, which suggests they may also be effective for serendipitous discovery [12].

5.2 Selecting books from the shelves

Adult readers were observed to predominantly judge books by sight (Section 4.5), not needing to run fingers along the spines as was common for children [32]. The tilt and look (pull and half pull) mechanism was prevalent in our results as was the sampling act of opening, flicking through and reading (Section 4.6), whereas children tend not to read or skim within books. The prevalence of physical interaction with books during the selection process would suggest that it is worthwhile investigating interfaces that enable people to quickly, easily, and intuitively 'touch' a book. 'Touching' ebooks is increasingly possible with tablet technologies, and could result in the display of metadata, a selection of images, or other document navigation devices. It is clear from our study that touch is a common and useful way to interact with objects, and being able to do that in a digital space could bring people closer to "get a feel" for the documents (Section 4.4).

All observed participants at some point interacted with books to discover more information than was visible from the spine. The large number of readers considering the covers of books in the physical library suggests that information and metadata contained on this artifact is germane to the book selection process and thus also of significance to the presentation of books in a digital library. Metadata found on the covers of books within academic libraries commonly includes titles, authors, book synopses or book reviews. Thus a quick pull or half-pull can reveal information about the tone and target audience of a book. DL and catalogue interfaces do not offer the same visual cues (often no cover image is provided); presenting this type of visual data in DLs is likely to benefit information seekers.

Several studies [8, 26, 35] observed the use of non-conventional cues such as book age, size and dustiness, cover image, and popular cultural associations in book decision-making. Our study corroborates these findings, as participants used age, cover, and images for decision making (Section 4.2). These types of cues are typically absent from ebook collections, and as such represent a significant opportunity to develop more usable DLs.

5. 3 Evaluating and comparing books

Participants quickly scanned significant portions of books by flicking through the pages (Section 4.6). Flicking can give an overview of the contents of a book and an indication of a book's style. Flicking and quick reading as decision making behavior may not translate directly into current ebook environments. The act of opening an ebook often constitutes 'lending' of the book. This distinction may not matter for libraries that buy bundles of ebooks, but for libraries that have a pay-per-view system or use-strategy for buying an ebook once a number of readers have downloaded the book, flicking behavior could have serious budgetary consequences. An alternative approach to linear digital flicking could be the provision of a field of thumbnails for all the pages of the book. Additionally one interviewed reader commented that he "rather flips than scrolls" (BAM09)–even though his comment was meant to justify a preference for physical books over ebooks. One possible implementation may be a swiping motion across pages as in [19] instead of scrolling though ebook—shown in to be more effective for many users in the aforementioned study.

Readers in the physical library were observed stacking, ordering and closely inspecting books at various stages in their decision making process, often on the floor, or by re-purposing an empty shelf or ledge (Section 4.1). There is no analogue for this in DLs, and as mentioned above budgetary constraints may even act as a constraint on this behavior. Offering readers a lightweight way to compare ebooks side-by-side in DLs would likely significantly improve users experience significantly, and as such is a ripe avenue for future work.

5.4 Keeping track of books

Participants planned to read at the library, copy or take books out of the library (Section 4.5). The problem of how to keep track of what has been evaluated, read or identified to be read is encountered for physical and digital books alike. A physical book checked out of a library is a physical reminder that the book is relevant. However, once the book is returned, the reminder is lost, and any records about books that have been read or remain to be read must be kept by readers themselves. Some participants used written notes to cross out books that they had evaluated and dismissed. These notes were typically discarded in the library; only one patron was observed to keep track of books they wanted to read in future (keeping an electronic reference, Section 4.7). This lack of a personal book interaction history can waste readers' time: several participants reported mistakenly re-evaluating books they had previously examined and discarded as irrelevant.

Often readers found several books of interest during the information seeking process that they want to set aside for later reading (a discovery also seen in [35]); how readers manage this bears further investigation. This is an area where DLs and electronic books have an advantage. Though currently not a main feature of available e-readers and DLs, it would be a simple extension to highlight books a reader has accessed, read or plans to read—or has rejected as not relevant.

The physical library helps people keep track of books during the selection process by providing context: readers often elected to triage books within the shelves rather than moving to a more comfortable location (Section 4.1). This context allows readers to readily scan possibly useful books, and cycle rapidly between examining individual books and scanning shelves. This facility for context is an advantage of physical libraries not seen in DLs; the ability to provide stronger contextual information is an avenue for future DL design work.

In physical libraries we have several cues when books are added to the collection: for example, frequently acquisitions will first appear in a 'new books' display. A reader familiar with a particular section of a library can tell at a glance when new and unfamiliar volumes are added to 'their' shelf. Identification of new results to prior searches can be implemented in ebook collections with relative ease by alerting services, resulting in personalized recommendations to readers [16].

6. Conclusions and future work

The study presented here is a pioneering look at the book selection process as it occurs at the library shelves. Our findings are based on a combination of observation and interviews with library users. Our discoveries have a variety of implications for DLs, particularly in terms of lightweight interaction, browsing, and decision-making metadata. This study also provides considerable scope for future work.

Even though it appeared that sorting books and document triage would be more comfortable at a near-by desk, participants largely preferred to work proximate to the shelves even if that meant they had to sit on the floor (Section 4.10). Here proximity retains context in the process of looking through a book shelf or section. Ebook collections can allow the capturing of richer contexts than is possible in the physical library. Context in a physical library can only reflect current interaction history, whereas DLs can potentially maintain records of previous interactions with the collection.

It is evident that many of the physical features of library space support users in their book decision making. The escalation from a glance to reading the spine of a book to examining the cover to flipping through the pages is simple and intuitive to readers, as is the ability to compare books side by side. Conversely, the physicality of library spaces also cause difficulties for users: most shelves are too high or too low for most users and none of the libraries in question provided adequate sorting space, meaning users often sorted books on the floor. There is a real opportunity for DLs to replicate the positive aspects of physicality by allowing users to 'touch' books in lightweight ways and to compare books side by side without imposing the burdens of physical space.

Related to the issue of physical space, though not dependent on it, is the way in which physical libraries facilitate browsing. Many users in our study deliberately used the co-location of related books to assist their information seeking, and for others it facilitated serendipitous discovery of useful resources. Browsing as an activity is poorly supported in DLs, but 'co-locating' works which are in some way related to facilitate serendipity is possible. Again, DLs have an advantage over physical environments in that it is possible in a DL to 'rearrange the shelves' according to an information seeker's interests.

Finally, we noted that information seekers used a wide range of criteria to make decisions about books. Some of these were the type of bibliographic metadata typically available in DLs (such as author and title), but some were less widely available, such as cover image, usage history, images within the book, and table of contents. To best facilitate decision making, DLs must seamlessly provide this information to readers at the point of need.

This work also raises a number of questions for future examination. Our work shows considerable differences from earlier work with respect to the number of books examined from above and below eye-level; eye tracking studies would help us to understand what drives these behaviors. Our work also raises the question of which decision-making criteria are already used when choosing ebooks. A careful analysis of log data would explore this issue.

Our work, while raising many questions, is an examination of a largely unstudied part of the information seeking process: the act of selecting among books at the shelves. This work has considerable implications not just in the physical realm, but also for digital libraries. Based on our work, the three main challenges for DLs in this area are supporting serendipitous discovery and browsing, providing a lightweight means of investigation and comparison of books, and supplying the information users actually want to use to choose between books. Meeting these challenges would be a significant step to replicating the advantages of physical libraries in the online sphere and providing the usable, useful DLs that readers so clearly desire.

9.References

[1] Adler, A., Gujar, A., Harrison, B. L., O'Hara, K. and Sellen, A. A diary study of work-related reading: design implications for digital reading devices. In *Proceedings of CHI '98* Los Angeles, California, United States. ACM Press/Addison-Wesley Publishing Co., New York, NY USA,1998. 241-248.

[2] Bae, S., Hsieh, H., Kim, D., Marshall, C. C., Meintanis, K., Moore, J. M., Zacchi, A. and Shipman, F. M. Supporting document triage via annotation-based visualizations. *ASIST Proceedings*, 45, 1, 1-16.

[3] Bae, S., Marshall, C. C., Meintanis, K., Zacchi, A., Hsieh, H., Moore, J. M. and Shipman, F. M. Patterns of reading and organizing information in document triage. *ASIST Proceedings*, 43, 1, 1-27.

[4] Bainbridge, D., Cunningham, S. J. and Downie, J. S. Visual Collaging of Music in a Digital Library. In *Proceedings of ISMIR* Barcelona, Spain, October 10-14, ,2004. 397-402.

[5] Bates, M. J. The design of browsing and berrypicking techniques for the online search interface. *Online Information Review*, 13, 5, 407-424.

[6] Berg, S. A., Hoffmann, K. and Dawson, D. Not on the Same Page: Undergraduates' Information Retrieval in Electronic and Print Books. *The Journal of Academic Librarianship*, 36, 6, 518-525.

[7] Borgman, C. L., Hirsh, S. G., Walter, V. A. and Gallagher, A. L. Children's searching behavior on browsing and keyword online catalogs: The Science Library Catalog project. *JASIS*, 46, 9, 663-684.

[8] Buchanan, G. and McKay, D. In the Bookshop: Examining Popular Search Strategies. In *Proceedings of JCDL 2011* Ottawa, Canada, June 14-17. ACM, New York, NY, USA, 2011.

[9] Buchanan, G. and Owen, T. Improving skim reading for document triage. In *Proceedings of IIiX '08* London, United Kingdom. ACM, New York, NY USA, 2008. 83-88.

[10] Cousins, S. A. In their own words: an examination of catalogue users' subject queries. *J. Inf. Sci.*, 18, 5, 329-341.

[11] Crabtree, A., Twidale, M. B., O'Brien, J. and Nichols, D. M. Talking in the Library: Implications for the Design of Digital Libraries. In *Proceedings of DL 97* Philadelphia, PA, USA. ACM Press, New York, NY USA, 1997. 221-228.

[12] Cunningham, S. and Bennett, E. Understanding Collection Understanding with Collage. In *Proceedings of ICADL* Bali, Indonesia, December 2-5. Springer Berlin / Heidelberg, 2008. 367-370.

[13] Cunningham, S. J., Knowles, C. and Reeves, N. An ethnographic study of technical support workers: why we didn't build a tech support digital library. In *Proceedings of JCDL 01* Roanoke, Virginia, United States, June 24-28. ACM, New York, NY USA,2001.

[14] Cunningham, S. J., Reeves, N. and Britland, M. An ethnographic study of music information seeking: implications for the design of a music digital library. In *Proceedings of JCDL 03* Houston, Texas. IEEE Computer Society, Washington, DC, USA ,2003. 5-16.

[15] Greifeneder, E. The Impact of Distraction in Natural Environments on User Experience Research In *Proceedings of TPDL '11* Berlin, Germany, 26-28 September. Springer, Berlin/Heidelberg ,2011.

[16] Hinze, A., Schweer, A. and Buchanan, G. An Integrated Alerting Service for Open Digital Libraries: Design and Implementation In *Proceedings CoopIS 05* Agia Napa, Cypris. Springer Berlin / Heidelberg, 2005.

[17] Kuhlthau, C. C. Inside the Search Process: Information Seeking from the User's Perspective. *JASIST*, 42, 5, 361-371.

[18] Lau, E. P. and Goh, D. H.-L. In search of query patterns: A case study of a university OPAC. *Information Processing & Management*, 42, 5, 1316-1329.

[19] Liesaputra, V. and Witten, I. H. Seeking information in realistic books: a user study. In *Proceedings of JCDL '08* Pittsburgh PA, PA, USA. ACM, New York, NY USA,2008. 29-38.

[20] Loizides, F. Investigating Document Triage on Paper and Electronic Media. In *Proceedings of ECDL 2007*. Springer Berlin / Heidelberg,2007. 416-427.

[21] Malama, C., Landoni, M. and Wilson, R. Fiction Electronic Books: A Usability Study. In *Proceedings of ECDL '04*. Springer Berlin / Heidelberg, ,2004. 69-79.

[22] Marchionini, G. *Information Seeking in Electronic Environments*. Cambridge University Press, Cambridge, UK, 1995.

[23] Marshall, C. C. *Reading and Writing the Electronic Book*. Morgan & Claypool, Chapel Hill, NC USA, 2010.

[24] Marshall, C. C. and Bly, S. Turning the page on navigation. In *Proceedings of JCDL'05* Denver, CO, USA. ACM, New York, NY USA, 2005. 225-234.

[25] McKay, D. A jump to the left (and then a step to the right): reading practices within academic ebooks. In *Proceedings of OZCHI 2011* Canberra, Australia. ACM, New York, NY USA ,2011. 202-210.

[26] McKay, D. and Conyers, B. Where the streets have no name: how library users get lost in the stacks. In *Proceedings of CHINZ 2010* Auckland, New Zealand, 8 July. ACM, New York, NY USA ,2010. in press.

[27] McKay, D., Shukla, P., Hunt, R. and Cunningham, S. J. Enhanced browsing in digital libraries: three new approaches to browsing in Greenstone. *JoDL*, 4, 4, 283-297.

[28] Moore, P. Information Problem Solving: A Wider View of Library Skills. *Contemporary Educational Psychology*, 20, 1, 1-31.

[29] Nordlie, R. "User Revealment"— A Comparison of Initial Queries and Ensuing Question Development in Online Searching and in Human Reference Interactions. In *Proceedings of IR 99* Berkeley, CA, USA, August 15-19. ACM Press, New York, NY USA ,1999. 11-18.

[30] Ooi, K. How Adult Fiction Readers Select Fiction Books in Public Libraries: A Study of Information Seeking in Context. Masters, Victoria University of Wellington, Wellington, New Zealand, 2008.

[31] Pearson, J., Buchanan, G. and Thimbleby, H. HCI design principles for ereaders. In *Proceedings of Booksonline '10* Toronto, ON, Canada. ACM, New York, NY USA, 2010.

[32] Reutzel, D. R. and Gali, K. The Art of Children's Book Selection: A Labyrinth Unexplored. *Reading Psychology*, 19, 1, 3-50.

[33] Rowlands, I., Nicholas, D., Jamali, H. R. and Huntington, P. What do faculty and students really think about e-books? *Aslib Proceedings*, 59, 6, 489-511.

[34] Shneiderman, B., Feldman, D., Rose, A. and Ferre Grau, X. Visualizing digital library search results with categorical and hierarchical axes. In *Proceedings of DL '00* San Antonio, Texas, United States. ACM, New York, NY USA,2000. 57-66.

[35] Stelmaszewska, H. and Blandford, A. From physical to digital: a case study of computer scientists' behavior in physical libraries. *JoDL*, 4, 2, 82-92.

[36] Stieve, T. and Schoen, D. Undergraduate Students' Book Selection: A Study of Factors in the Decision-Making Process. *The Journal of Academic Librarianship*, 32, 6, 599-608.

[37] Wallace, P. M. How do patrons search the online catalog when no one's looking? Transaction log analysis and implications for bibliographic instruction and system design. *RQ*, 33, 2, 239-253.

How Do People Organize Their Photos in Each Event and How Does It Affect Storytelling, Searching and Interpretation Tasks?

Jesse Prabawa Gozali[1] Min-Yen Kan[1] Hari Sundaram[2]
[1]Department of Computer Science, National University of Singapore, Singapore
[2]Arts Media & Engineering, Arizona State University, USA
{jprabawa, kanmy}@comp.nus.edu.sg hari.sundaram@asu.edu

ABSTRACT

This paper explores photo organization within an *event photo stream*, *i.e.* the chronological sequence of photos from a single event. The problem is important: with the advent of inexpensive, easy-to-use photo capture devices, people can take a large number of photos per event. A family trip, for example, may include hundreds of photos. In this work, we have developed a photo browser that uses automatically segmented groups of photos—referred to as chapters—to organize such photos. The photo browser also affords users with a drag-and-drop interface to refine the chapter groupings.

We conducted an exploratory study of 23 college students with their 8096 personal photos from 92 events, to understand the role of different spatial organization strategies in our chapter-based photo browser, in performing storytelling, photo search and photo set interpretation tasks. We also report novel insights on how the subjects organized their photos into chapters. We tested three layout strategies: bi-level, grid-stacking and space-filling, against a baseline plain grid layout. We found that subjects value the chronological order of the chapters more than maximizing screen space usage and that they value chapter consistency more than the chronological order of the photos. For automatic chapter groupings, having low chapter boundary misses is more important than having low chapter boundary false alarms; the choice of chapter criteria and granularity for chapter groupings are very subjective; and subjects found that chapter-based photo organization helps in all three tasks of the user study. Users preferred the chapter-based layout strategies to the baseline at a statistically significant level, with the grid-stacking strategy preferred the most.

Categories and Subject Descriptors

H.5.2 [**Information Interfaces and Presentation**]: User Interfaces

General Terms

Design, Human Factors.

Keywords

Photo browser, photo digital library, photo layouts, event photo stream segmentation

1. INTRODUCTION

Today, people take more photos with the help of inexpensive, easy-to-use and portable photo capture devices—in contrast to an earlier era of film rolls and analog cameras [17]. Not surprisingly, large photo collections are becoming more common. People with large collections are everyday photographers, interested in simply capturing the moment, in contrast to the serious amateur or professional photographer of the analog era. Most personal photos are commonly associated with an event: a holiday trip, picnic, dinner or walk in the park. Many academic and commercial photo browsers, like iPhoto[1] and Picasa[2], advocate event-based photo organization. With the ease of photo-capture however, a family trip can contain hundreds of photos—sifting through these event photos is still cumbersome.

To complement event-based photo organization and help make photos of each event more manageable, we propose to organize photos in each event into smaller groups of photos, *i.e.* all of the groups belong to *the same event.* Figure 1 shows an example *event photo stream*, where the chronological sequence of photos from a single event is segmented to produce groups of photos, each corresponding to a photo-worthy moment in the event. This paper explores photo organization within such an event photo stream. We want to answer the following question: *How do people organize their photos in each event and how does it affect storytelling, searching and interpretation tasks?*

We have developed a photo browser called *Chaptrs* that helps users organize their event photos by automatically grouping photos in each event into smaller groups of photos we call chapters. *Chaptrs* builds upon our prior work to segment an event photo stream [?]. The *Chaptrs* photo browser also affords users with a drag-and-drop interface to refine the chapter groupings.

With *Chaptrs*, we conducted an exploratory study involving 23 college students with a total of 8096 personal photos

[1]http://www.apple.com/ilife/iphoto
[2]http://picasa.google.com

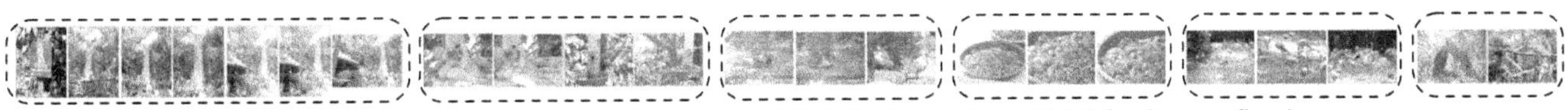

Figure 1: Part of an event photo stream is segmented into smaller groups of photos. We refer to each group as a chapter of the event. The chapters are labelled in this example.

from 92 events. To facilitate the study, we implemented four photo layouts in *Chaptrs* (see Figures 2, 3, 4, and 5). The first is our baseline, a plain grid layout commonly used by commercial photo browsers and offers no chapter-based photo organization. The other three layouts present chapter-based photo organizations but each emphasizes on a different key aspect. The **bi-level layout** emphasizes an overview of the event photos afforded by presenting chapter thumbnails. The **grid-stacking layout** emphasizes the chronological order of the chapters. Lastly, the **space-filling layout** maximizes screen space usage.

The three chapter-based layouts were chosen because they emphasize and represent distinct key layout aspects. As such, they facilitated our study to explore which key aspects are important for chapter-based photo organization. To our knowledge, our study is the first to explore chapter-based photo organization and its photo layouts.

The key research contributions in this paper are as follows:

- *Novel insights on how users group their event photos into chapters.* The main insights are as follows: users value chapter consistency more than the chronological order of the photos; criteria for chapters include moment, object, location, photography type, and intention; and that the choice of criteria and granularity for segmentation are very subjective.
- *Explore how chapter-based photo organization affects three key photo-related tasks.* We found several statistically significant results, among them: subjects found grouping event photos by chapter helps present the event's story, helps to find a photo, and helps to interpret unfamiliar photos. In contrast, the plain grid layout without chapter-based photo organization was preferred the least for all three tasks.
- *Explore key photo layout aspects for chapter-based photo organization.* Most subjects value the chronological order of the chapters more than maximizing screen space usage. Subjects also appreciate having an overview of the event photos afforded by chapter thumbnails.

In the next section, we review related works on photo organization and photo layouts in personal digital photo libraries. Section 3 describes the photo layouts. We present the user study and its results in Sections 4 and 5. Finally, we conclude in Section 6.

2. RELATED WORK

2.1 Photo Organization

Over the past decade, there have been a number of studies on how people manage—including organization and sharing—their personal photo collections. Rodden [24, 25] has studied how people manage their photo collections, printed or otherwise. Some findings from his study include: printed photo albums are mostly classified by event, with one album for each event. Searching a printed photo collection is typically done for a photo album of a specific event. Even if the search was for a specific photo, people will try to locate the album containing the photo first before starting the search. For personal digital photo libraries, people regard the ability to organize photos into folders as very useful and would arrange them according to events in a chronological order. People prefer to browse their photos by event rather than querying. Similar findings were also found by Cunningham and Masoodian [7]. They conclude that browsing, rather than searching, is a more practical tool for locating photos.

Other studies go beyond how the photos are organized. Kirk *et al.* [17] coined the term "photowork", *i.e.* activities done after photo capture but before sharing. These include reviewing, downloading, organizing, editing, sorting, as well as filing of photos. Frohlich *et al.* [10] conducted a study to establish requirements for photo sharing technologies. A recent article by Sandhaus and Boll [27] presents a good overview of research in this field of personal photo collections. To our knowledge, however, our study is the first to explore chapter-based photo organization.

2.2 Photo Layouts in Personal Digital Photo Libraries

An effective photo layout is one that presents photos in a way that supports users in one or more photo-related tasks. Here, we review existing works on photo layouts for personal digital photo libraries to gather the key aspects they emphasize and the tasks they support effectively.

While there has been prior work to study event-based photo organization, the absence of work on photo layouts for chapter-based photo organization, *i.e.* layouts to present groups of photos with all groups belonging to *the same event* is notable. In event-based photo organization, the groups of photos belong to *different events*. The closest work we found was by Graham *et al.* [15]. They proposed a hierarchical photo browser to better support search tasks by presenting a 25 photo summary at various levels of hierarchy of the user's photo collection: year, month, event, and also for groups of photos within an event. The user navigates through the view hierarchy using a tree view in the sidebar.

For event-based photo organization, the most common photo layout is a 2D grid: photos are ordered chronologically row by row on a grid. Many photo browsers [18, 20, 8, 19] including commercial ones like Picasa and iPhoto adopt this layout to display photos of an event. A plain grid layout is a simple layout that maximizes use of the available screen space. Having many photos visible at once allows users familiar with the photos to scan them very quickly [25].

Photo browsers typically display one event (one grid) at a time, but some photo browsers relieve users from having to select individual events from the view hierarchy by displaying all the events at once: the grids are stacked on top of each other in chronological order, *e.g.* Picasa. The layout remains uniform as the grids have the same number of columns. With this layout, users can browse their events by simply scrolling. To demarcate the events, each grid has a title bar on top with the event information. Alternatively, in the timeline view of [20], each grid is labeled hierarchically on its left margin by month and year. In [4], all the photos in the collection are displayed as one massive grid and event titles are displayed as grid elements to demarcate the events.

Time Quilt[16], a zoomable photo browser designed to enhance search tasks, also displays photos from all events at once. Its layout trades-off screen space usage for better presentation of the chronological order of the photos. Photos from each event are displayed in their own grid. The grids are then displayed chronologically column by column. The number of rows and columns of each grid follows the aspect ratio of the corresponding thumbnail of the event. Each grid is replaced with the event thumbnail of the same size and the grid only becomes visible when the user zooms in.

Some photo browsers do not use a grid layout. TreeBrowser[5] is a photo browser for multiple photo collections. The collections are displayed chronologically at the top of the photo browser as a single scrollable row of thumbnails. The main part of the photo browser displays events from the selected collection as a tree of depth one. The tree root is the collection thumbnail. Each leaf corresponds to an event in the collection and is displayed as a single row of photos.

The photo browsers we have reviewed so far have layouts that emphasize one or more of the following key aspects: use of view hierarchy, chronological order of event photos, and maximization of screen space usage. We emphasize on similar key aspects in the three layouts used for the user study: the bi-level, grid-stacking and space-filling layouts.

The works we have reviewed have also weaved the chronological order of the photos into two dimensions (*e.g.* row-by-row) to make better use of screen space. However, in interfaces where visualizing the timeline is more important, chronological order is commonly conveyed as a single dimension in the layout [23, 9, 1]. Photo storytelling interfaces exhibit similar linear structures in their layouts. Here, we highlight three notable interfaces: the first two are well cited and the third is a recent contribution to the field. First is the story-editing environment in FotoFile[18]. Here, users can select photos from an *Image Tape* at the top of the photo browser and place them into one of the row of *Scraplets* in the main part of the photo browser. Each scraplet displays its photos as a single column. Balabanović *et al.* [2] developed a portable device for sharing and authoring stories. In its interface, the navigation area consists of rows of photo thumbnails. Photos in the rows are shown in groups of alternating backgrounds to distinguish separate photo rolls. Recently, Raconteur[6] is a story editing system that helps users assemble stories from annotated media files. The media files are arranged in chronological order in a single row.

Some photo browsers were designed with the key aspect of effectively conveying inter-photo similarity, *e.g.* in terms of visual appearance, location, or tag. These photo browsers generally present more visually interesting and novel layouts. However, the chronological order of the photos often suffers as a result. For example, PhotoMesa[3] employs quantum treemaps and bubblemaps to display labelled photo clusters in a grid layout to maximize screen space usage. More recently, MediaGlow[12] uses a spring layout algorithm to help users stack and retrieve similar photos. PHOTOLAND[26] presents a layout that places photos on a 2D grid based on an inter-photo similarity measure computed from temporal and spatial information. The result is a layout that presents photos from an event as an island of thumbnails.

Figure 2: Plain grid layout

Following the motivation behind event-based photo organization, we suspect that similarly, users will create chapters corresponding to moments in the event. As such, the chapter-based layouts in *Chaptrs* present the chronological order of the chapters in different ways. Following the works we have reviewed here, another aspect to explore is the issue of screen space usage maximization. As such, the chapter-based layouts in *Chaptrs* have varying degrees of screen space utilization. Lastly, the bi-level layout presents a two-level view hierarchy to provide an overview of all the event photos using a horizontal film strip of chapter thumbnails.

3. PHOTO LAYOUTS USED FOR STUDY

In *Chaptrs*, we implemented four layouts for displaying photos from a single event (see Figures 2, 3, 4, and 5):

1. **Plain grid layout** is our baseline layout and it consists of a single grid of row-by-row chronologically-ordered photos. No chapter information is presented in this layout.
2. **Bi-level layout** consists of a split view where the bottom view displays a film strip of chronologically-ordered chapter thumbnails for selection and the top view displays photos of the selected chapter in a grid layout, in chronological order row-by-row.
3. **Grid-stacking layout** consists of chronologically-ordered vertically-stacked grids, each corresponding to a chapter. Photos in each grid are ordered chronologically row-by-row.
4. **Space-filling layout** consists of a single grid of row-by-row chronologically-ordered event photos with an outline surrounding each span of photos that are part of the same chapter.

Chaptrs also affords users with a drag-and-drop interface to edit the chapter groupings in the bi-level layout. By default, our event photo stream segmentation algorithm automatically groups event photos into chapters so users only

Figure 3: Bi-level layout

Figure 4: Grid-stacking layout

need to adjust the chapter groupings instead of starting from scratch. To combine adjacent chapters, users simply drag one chapter thumbnail onto another from the film strip. When users have a chapter selected in the film strip, its photos are shown in the top view. To move photos into a new chapter, users can select a span of photos at the beginning or end of the chapter and then drag the photos onto the film strip. Other kinds of selections are not valid to ensure that the chronological order of the photos in the stream is not violated. The four layouts take inspiration from our review of existing photo layouts for personal digital photo libraries. We adapt them to organize chapters, instead of other group types (*e.g.* events, similar photos). The bi-level layout takes inspiration from photo storytelling interfaces which present the chronological order unweaved in a single horizontal dimension. The space-filling layout takes inspiration from the bubblemap layout in PhotoMesa and maximizes screen space usage. The grid-stacking layout is similar to how Picasa displays photos from all events at once with a separate grid for each event. Screen space is still wasted but not as much as in the bi-level layout. We now discuss each of the chapter-based layouts in more detail.

3.1 Bi-Level Layout

The bi-level layout consists of a split view where the bottom view provides an overview of all the photos by displaying a scrollable film strip of chapter thumbnails. The top view displays photos from the selected chapter in a grid layout.

Chapter thumbnails are displayed in chronological order. Each thumbnail is labelled with the timestamp of the first photo in the corresponding chapter and optionally, labelled with a user-defined title. The film strip provides users with an overview of all the photos. It acts as an index into the event photos, allowing users to glean over moments in the event through the chapter thumbnails without having to sift through individual photos. The chapter groupings allow users to collapse the timeline in a meaningful way and present chapter thumbnails in a linear structure that effectively conveys their chronological order.

3.2 Grid-Stacking Layout

The grid-stacking layout displays all photos from the event with photos of each chapter in its own grid. Photos in each grid are ordered chronologically row-by-row. All grids have the same number of columns and are displayed in chronological order separated by a horizontal line and chapter title.

Compared to the bi-level layout, the grid-stacking layout makes better use of screen space. While the grids may not be fully occupied with photos, the grids are stacked one after another, leaving no room between adjacent grids. The chronological order of the chapters are also presented in a linear structure by stacking the grids in one dimension.

3.3 Space-Filling Layout

The space-filling layout displays all photos from the event in a single grid. Photos are ordered chronologically row-by-row. In addition, an outline is drawn around photos of the same chapter. To keep photos contiguous within each chapter outline, some grid elements may be left empty (see Figure 5). This layout is similar to the bubblemap layout in PhotoMesa but maintains a row-by-row chronological order. As such, the space-filling layout is not as densely packed and may still waste some screen space.

Of the three chapter-based layouts, the space-filling layout is the one that wastes the least amount of screen space and displays the most number of thumbnails at once while still presenting the chapter groupings. These space savings are however, at the expense of the chronological order of the chapters. Unlike the grid-stacking layout, the chronological order of the chapters is weaved into two dimensions row-by-row, instead of linearly top-down.

4. USER STUDY

The goal of our user study is to explore three questions:

1. How do people organize their photos in each event?
2. How does chapter-based photo organization affect photo-related tasks such as storytelling, searching, and interpretation tasks?
3. What photo layout aspects are important for chapter-based photo organization?

We recruited 23 college students. One subject is a professional photographer who often participates in photography trips at public events or at leisure. Another subject maintains an active food blog and always has a digital camera

Figure 5: Space-filling layout: Event photos are displayed in a grid layout, in chronological order row-by-row, with an outline surrounding photos of the same chapter. The bottom figure illustrates how some grid elements may be left empty in order to keep photos contiguous within each chapter outline.

at hand. Some are enthusiastic amateur photographers who carry their digital cameras for social events. Others only carry their digital cameras during holiday trips. Most subjects use Windows Explorer or Windows Live Photo Gallery as their primary photo browser. Some use Picasa, two subjects use iPhoto, and one subject uses Aperture.

Following Institutional Review Board exemption guidelines, photos were immediately discarded at the end of each study session and all collected data was anonymized.

4.1 Photo Sets

Subjects were asked to bring four sets of personal photos, each from a different event. While most events are associated with holiday trips, others span a variety of event types: a public cosplay event, a college orientation camp, talks at a conference, a stage performance, visit to the museum, etc. The total number of photos in the study is 8096 photos from 92 photo sets. We asked the subjects to bring at least one set with more than 100 photos and at least one with 40-60 photos. This allowed us to ask the subjects to reflect on sets with many photos or few photos. Before we imported the subject's photo sets into *Chaptrs*, we asked the subject to choose four different favorite photos from the set with the most photos, using the default file explorer application. These photos were later used in the searching task.

After the photo sets have been imported, we asked the subject to *"group the photos into chapters according to their preference and liking"*. Additionally, we randomly selected two photo sets from the subject for s/he to group into chapters *without help* from our event photo stream segmentation algorithm, *i.e.* the subject started with *no initial chapter groupings*. For his/her photo sets, we asked the subject to group the photos to his/her satisfaction; the subject's final organization for the photo sets is used for the study tasks. This protocol allowed us to analyze the effects of initializing the chapter groupings on how the subjects group their photos into chapters.

4.2 Study Tasks

Subjects were asked to complete three tasks. Subjects were also asked to fill a questionnaire after each task, and another overall questionnaire after all three tasks. All questionnaires use a standard 5-point Likert scale from 1 (strongly disagree) to 5 (strongly agree). Finally, each study session ended with a semi-structured interview[3]. The audio from the interview session was recorded for note-taking purposes.

In our study, we focused on common photo-related tasks for users – tasks that fit the STU (Situations, Tasks, and Users) context [22]. In particular, the first two tasks have been used in the related works we reviewed in Section 2. We describe each task in more detail next, followed by more details on how we eliminated confounding variables.

4.2.1 Task 1: Storytelling from familiar event photos

In this task, subjects were asked to tell the story of each event from their personal photo sets. We asked subjects to imagine sharing about the event and its photos, as they normally would, to their friends. We used a within-subject design where each subject carries out the task four times, each with a different layout. To avoid learning effect on the story told, each layout was used with a different photo set.

4.2.2 Task 2: Finding a given photo from familiar event photos

In this task, subjects were asked to find the favorite photos they chose at the beginning of the study. We used a within-subject design where each subject carries out the task four times, each for a different favorite photo and with a different layout. At each iteration, the target favorite photo was clearly displayed on an adjacent external monitor. The four favorite photos were chosen from the same photo set to make the iterations comparable. There is no learning effect between iterations on the photo set because the subject – who also owns the photo set – has been through the photos at least twice from the storytelling task and from grouping the photos into chapters at the beginning of the study.

4.2.3 Task 3: Interpreting unfamiliar event photos

In this task, subjects were shown and asked to interpret unfamiliar event photos. We asked the subjects: *"Tell me about the event. What do you think was happening?"*. For this task, we prepared four sets of event photos that were not used in any other part of the study. The photo sets

[3]Questionnaires and interview questions available in [14]

were titled, grouped into chapters, but chapters were left untitled. We used a within-subject design where each subject carries out the task four times, each with a different layout. To avoid any learning effects, each layout was used with a different photo set. This task is the most synthetic of the three tasks in our user study. While subjects are unlikely to find themselves having to interpret event photos without any context other than the photos themselves and the event title, our goal was simply to create a scenario where the subjects have very little knowledge of the event, similar to how they would find themselves when faced with an old set of event photos but not remembering any details of the event [10].

4.3 Internal Validity

We chose a within-subject design, *i.e.* repeated measurements per subject, to have better internal validity, as is common for user studies with few subjects. The personal nature of the photos and the length of the study per subject made recruiting hundreds of subjects impractical.

As mentioned in Section 4.2, we have tried to eliminate any learning effects. In addition, we eliminated learning effects on the four layouts by demonstrating *Chaptrs*, its four layouts, and all their features at the beginning of the study, prior to any of the tasks. We prepared five sets of photos, grouped into chapters, exclusively for this purpose. The subjects were also asked to spend five minutes to familiarize themselves with the four layouts and ask any questions.

To eliminate ordering effects from the four layouts, we balanced the user study for each task, *i.e* the order in which subjects used the four layouts was systematically varied for each task; each subject used a different order from the other subjects for each task[4]. Subjects were also asked to revisit all four layouts with all photo sets when they answer each questionnaire.

5. RESULTS

5.1 How Do People Organize Their Photos in Each Event?

At the beginning of the user study, we asked subjects to *"group the photos into chapters according to their preference and liking"*. This allowed us to first observe and later inquire on the criteria they used to decide the chapter groupings. We have gathered three insights into this process:

First, **users value chapter consistency more than the chronological order of the photos.** While past findings have shown that people want their photos displayed in chronological order [25], all but one of the subjects in our study requested that they be allowed to combine non-adjacent chapters in the timeline, effectively displaying the photos out of their chronological order.

Almost all subjects had at least one photo set where in the midst of photos capturing one moment in the event, *e.g.* a performance on stage, there were a handful of photos that did not belong, *e.g.* photos of the audience. Another example is where in the midst of scenic photos of a nearby landscape, there were photos of friends and/or family. In these cases, subjects wanted to keep all but the handful of photos in one chapter. This observation is similar to how people keep printed photos in albums in chronological order, but with small adjustments done for aesthetic reasons [24].

By allowing the subjects to create meaningful chapters as the organizational unit for their photos, what becomes important to them is the consistency of the photos within each chapter. In explaining why they wanted certain photos taken out of a chapter, subjects said that the photos *"do not belong there"*. This importance supercedes displaying the photos in chronological order. Some subjects mentioned that they *"don't really care"* if the photos are not in chronological order, that *"sometimes [it] is not that important"*.

Secondly, **criteria for chapters include moment, object, location, photography type,** and **intention.** These criteria pertain to the kind of consistency discussed in the first point. From our study, we observed that the subjects commonly adopted one of the following five criteria for their chapters:

1. **Moment** – This criteria is the most common and refers to chapters that correspond to moments in the event. Several subjects refer to photo sets whose chapters followed this criteria as being *"according to time"*.

2. **Object** – Subjects wished to group photos of the same object or object type in the same chapter. For example, in a photo set of a trip to a defunct railroad, the subject wanted all photos depicting the track in its own chapter, regardless of when the photos were taken.

3. **Location** – Subjects also commonly organized their photos with a chapter for each location, for example, in holiday photos where photos were captured from a variety of different locations (*e.g.* tourist spots).

4. **Photography type** – For example, subjects wished to group photos of their friends in the same chapter. Another example is to have a chapter for all the scenic photos.

5. **Intention** – On several occasions, subjects wished to have a different chapter for photos of different groups of individuals, *e.g.* one chapter for photos with friends and another chapter for photos with colleagues. Another example is where one subject has several *"silly shots"* taken at very different times during the event but would like to have them all in the same chapter.

Lastly, **choice of criteria and granularity for segmentation are very subjective**. We found that deciding a criteria for the chapters is a very subjective process. For example, in a photo set of performances on stage, the subject *separated visually similar photos* into several chapters to have one chapter for each performance. On the other hand, another subject wanted to *combine visually similar photos* of different speakers into the same chapter to create a summary of the event in a single chapter. Several subjects noted that they would group photos of the same location, even if taken at different times, *e.g.* night and day, into the same chapter. However, they will separate portrait photos of their friends/family into a different chapter, separate from the chapter with scenic photos of the same location.

Subjects also had different notions of granularity for their chapters. One subject wanted to create a chapter with many photos to depict *"photos of the path [he] took from the entrance to the mountain"*. Photos taken near the path would

[4]There are 24 distinct permutations in ordering the four layouts.

Initialized?	Num Photo Sets	Average Pr_{miss}	Average Pr_{fa}	Average Pr_{error}
No	30	0.193	0.508	0.350
Yes	47	0.118	0.290	0.204
Improvement		38.7%	43.0%	41.8%

Table 1: Comparison between the chapter groupings by our algorithm with the ground truth by the subjects as measured by miss rate, Pr_{miss}, false alarm rate, Pr_{fa}, and error rate, Pr_{error}. A smaller number indicates better agreement. One group of photo sets were initialized by our algorithm and further organized by the subjects. The other was done by the subjects without help.

be grouped into separate chapters. Another subject mentioned that he would like to group his photos *"by visual similarity"* unless *"[the photo set] is for a big event because there will be too many chapters"*. Many subjects disliked having a chapter with just one or two photos and would combine the chapter with an adjacent one simply because s/he *"want[s] to combine it with something else"*.

While deciding the chapter grouping is a subjective process, subjects agree that *"grouping [their] photos by chapter makes sense"* (μ=4.3, δ=0.6). In response to the subjectivity, more subjects found it *"easy to decide the correct chapter groupings"* (μ=3.7, δ=1.0). These subjects said that they will know what to do when they see the photos.

To assess how automatically grouping photos into chapters affected their final organization by subjects, at the beginning of the study we randomly selected two photo sets from each subject for s/he to group without the help of our event photo stream segmentation algorithm. The other two photo sets of each subject were initialized with a chapter organization given by our algorithm. This allows us to compare the chapter groupings from our algorithm with those by the subjects (as ground truth) for two kinds of photo sets: 1) photo sets that were organized by the subjects without help[5], and 2) photo sets that were initialized by our algorithm and further organized by the subjects.

Some photo sets were from older generation cameras that did not embed photo metadata[6] in the image files. Since the metadata is necessary for our event photo stream segmentation algorithm, we could not run our algorithm on these photo sets. For this initialization analysis, we have a total of 7073 photos in 77 sets.

To perform the comparisons, we used the error rate metric, Pr_{error}, proposed by Georgescul *et al.* [11]. This metric improves on *WindowDiff*, previously used by Naaman *et al.* [21] to evaluate their photo stream segmentation method. A lower Pr_{error} indicates better agreement with the ground truth by the subjects; a score of 0 indicates perfect agreement. Pr_{error} is an average of the miss and false alarm rates. As such, a method that proposes no chapter boundaries or proposes chapter boundaries everywhere will have an error rate of about 0.5.

In our previous work [13], we noted that our event photo stream segmentation algorithm has a tendency to propose more fine-grained segmentations. We can see this in Table 1 where the false alarm rate, Pr_{fa}, is markedly smaller – a 43% improvement from a high rate of 0.508 – for the initialized photo sets. With initialization, subjects were provided with the opportunity to explicitly agree or disagree with our fine-grained results. The effect is that subjects found meaningful chapter boundaries among the many proposed. Without initialization, subjects had to find meaningful chapter boundaries for themselves, resulting in higher false alarm rates for our algorithm in comparison.

While the error rate values we report in Table 1 were computed by penalizing misses and false alarms equally, we found through our user study that in practice, having a high miss rate is more detrimental to the user experience than having a high false alarm rate. Many subjects in our study mentioned during the interview that it was easier to decide if two chapters should be combined than to decide how to split up a chapter. To correct a false alarm is a one-step process of combining the two chapters. But to correct a miss, the user must first realize that there is a miss, then figure out the best position to split the chapter.

5.2 How Does Chapter-based Photo Organization Affect The Study Tasks?

In this section, we present quantitative and qualitative results from each task of the study. We also present the level of statistical significance of the quantitative results, *i.e.* the p-value from a two-tailed paired student's t-test in comparison with the plain grid layout. While our findings have different levels of significance, we note that most are significant at $p<0.005$. We present the subjects' mean response values from the questionnaire in Table 2 for easy reference. Values that are statistically significantly in comparison with the plain grid layout are shown with their p-values in subscript. We elaborate on the tabulated results in the following subsections, but defer comparisons between the three chapter-based layouts to Section 5.3.

5.2.1 Task 1: Story-telling from familiar event photos

Subjects agree that *"having chapters helps present the event's story for sets with many photos"* (μ=4.3, $p<0.001$). We obtained similar results for sets with few photos (μ=3.9, $p<0.05$), but less statistically significant. When asked for each layout specifically however, subjects agree that each of the chapter-based layouts helps present the event's story for sets with many or few photos, all with $p<0.005$.

We also asked the subjects whether having chapters helps them remember what to say about the event. One subject said that the chapters *"help give focus"* in remembering. Subjects agree that *"having chapters helps [them] remember the event's story"* for sets with many or few photos (μ=4.7, μ=4.1; both $p<0.005$). When asked for each layout specifically, subjects agree that each of the chapter-based layouts helps them remember the event's story for sets with many photos ($p<0.001$). We obtained similar results for sets with few photos, but only the grid-stacking and space-filling layouts are statistically significant at $p<0.001$; the bi-level layout is less statistically significant at $p<0.05$.

Chapters can guide users with their storytelling. In the plain grid layout where no chapter information is presented, one subject said that s/he was *"scrolling, scrolling, scrolling"*

[5]We ran our algorithm on these photo sets but the results were neither used nor shown to the subjects.
[6]Exchangeable Image File Format (EXIF) data; http://exif.org

Questionnaire Statement	Bi-Level	Grid-Stacking	Space-Filling	Plain Grid
The layout helps present the event's story for sets with many photos	$4.2_{0.005}$	$4.2_{0.005}$	$3.7_{0.005}$	2.4
The layout helps present the event's story for sets with few photos	$4.1_{0.005}$	$4.3_{0.005}$	$4.1_{0.005}$	3.2
The layout helps them remember the event's story for sets with many photos	$4.0_{0.001}$	$4.3_{0.001}$	$3.9_{0.001}$	2.6
The layout helps them remember the event's story for sets with few photos	$4.0_{0.05}$	$4.4_{0.001}$	$4.1_{0.001}$	3.2
The layout helps to find a photo in a set with many photos	$3.6_{0.01}$	$4.4_{0.001}$	$3.7_{0.001}$	2.7
The layout helps to find a photo in a set with few photos	3.6	$4.4_{0.001}$	$4.0_{0.001}$	3.1
The layout helps to interpret photos of an event with many photos	$3.9_{0.005}$	$4.6_{0.005}$	$4.0_{0.005}$	2.9
The layout helps to interpret photos of an event with few photos	$3.7_{0.05}$	$4.4_{0.001}$	$3.9_{0.001}$	3.1

Table 2: Mean response values from the subjects to various questionnaire statements for each layout. The values follow a standard 5-point Likert scale from 1 (strongly disagree) to 5 (strongly agree). Values that are statistically significant in comparison with the plain grid layout are shown with their p-values in subscript.

and did *"not know where to stop and say something more"*. In contrast, subjects use the chapter information presented in the other chapter-based layouts to pace their story. Subjects would refer to a particular chapter and start a part of their story with, *e.g.* *"this chapter is about..."*. Subjects also gesture around chapter outlines with their forefingers or cursors in the space-filling layout to highlight the photos relevant to their stories at the time. One subject however, adopted a purely photo-driven storytelling method [2] where s/he would double-click to maximize the photo and subsequently use the navigation keys on the keyboard to go to the next or previous photos.

On average, the grid-stacking layout is most preferred, followed by the bi-level, space-filling and plain grid layouts. The difference in preference between each of the chapter-based layouts with the plain grid layout is statistically significant ($p<0.001$).

5.2.2 *Task 2: Find a given photo from familiar event photos*

From the measured completion times, we determined the layout that allowed subjects to complete the task the fastest. On average, the space-filling layout was the fastest (7.0s), followed by the plain grid (7.8s), grid-stacking (11.2s), and bi-level (14.2s) layouts. The difference between the grid-stacking and bi-level layouts ($p<0.005$); and the plain grid and bi-level layouts ($p<0.05$) are statistically significant. We note that this ranking aligns closely with how well the layouts make use of screen space, making our results consistent with past findings that propose displaying many thumbnails at once to help users with their visual search tasks [25].

While the plain grid layout ranks second for the fastest completion time, subjects actually preferred the plain grid layout the least for this task. On average, the most preferred layout for this task is the grid-stacking layout, followed by the space-filling, bi-level, and plain grid layouts. The difference in preference between each of the chapter-based layouts with the plain grid layout is statistically significant ($p<0.001$).

We note that subjects were not informed on how fast they performed with each layout. This was done so that their layout preference for this task was not affected by the completion time rankings. The contrast between the layout preference and the completion time rankings suggests that for the task of finding a photo within a familar set, where the fastest and slowest times only differ by several seconds, completion time does not play a major role for their preference.

One subject noted that for tasks like this, *"they like to find the chapter first"*. Subjects agree that *"having chapters helps [them] find a photo in a set with many photos"* (μ=4.4, $p<0.001$). We obtained similar results for sets with few photos (μ=4.0, $p<0.05$), but with less statistical significance. Subjects also agree that each of the chapter-based layouts helps them find a photo in a set with many photos ($p<0.001$, except the bi-level layout with $p<0.01$). For sets with few photos, only the grid-stacking and space-filling layouts are with statistical significance ($p<0.001$).

While the subjects' layout preference contradicts with the completion time rankings, the behavior to find chapters first before finding the photo is similar to past findings. The same study we quoted above [25] found that when users want to search for a particular photo, they will first attempt to remember the event at which it was taken. In our case, we observed that subjects use the chapter groupings to skip chapters that they know will not contain the photo, and look deeper into chapters that might. This process is easiest to perform with the grid-stacking layout, which is the most preferred layout for this task.

5.2.3 *Task 3: Interpreting unfamiliar event photos*

Subjects agree that *"having chapters helps [them] interpret photos of an event with many photos"* (μ=4.6, $p<0.001$) as well as those with few photos (μ=4.0, $p<0.001$). When asked for each layout specifically, subjects agree that each of the chapter-based layouts helps them interpret photos of an event with many photos ($p<0.005$). For sets with few photos, only the grid-stacking and space-filling layout are statistically significant at $p<0.001$; the bi-level layout is less statistically significant at $p<0.05$.

We observed that generally, the subjects fall into two groups, each with a different approach to the task. Subjects in the first group rely on gathering a visual overview of all the photos to interpret the event. They would scroll up and down fairly quickly to gather a general idea of the event. For this group, a layout that displays many thumbnails at once is most preferred and not having chapter information presented in the layout is not a loss. One subject disliked the bi-level layout for this reason: *"I can't grasp what's happening because it [displays] one chapter at a time"*. Subjects would give a very general interpretation of the event and only comment for every other chapter.

Subjects in the second group rely on chapter information to guide them through the event photos. Some would still gather a visual overview from all the event photos, but they would describe each chapter in chronological order: *"Here they went to... and then to..."*. With the plain grid layout where no chapter information is presented, these subjects are at a loss and *"can't tell if the photos are apart or together"* and the photos were *"hard to describe"*. In contrast, the layouts with chapter groupings *"look very organized"*.

There were more subjects in the second group. As such, the most preferred layout for this task is the grid-stacking layout, followed by the bi-level, space-filling, plain grid layouts. The difference in preference between each of the chapter-based layouts with the plain grid layout is statistically significant ($p<0.001$).

5.3 What Layout Aspects are Important for Chapter-based Photo Organization?

Among the chapter-based layouts, the grid-stacking layout was the only layout that outperformed some others with statistical significance; and it does so for each task. For helping to present the event's story for sets with many photos, subjects agree more with the grid-stacking layout than with the space-filling layout ($p<0.01$). For helping to find a photo in a set with many or few photos, subjects agree more with the grid-stacking layout than with the bi-level layout ($p<0.01$). For helping to interpret photos of an event with many or few photos, subjects agree more with the grid-stacking layout than with all the other layouts ($p<0.01$).

Regarding the methods used by the chapter-based layouts to present the chapters, subjects like the grid-stacking layout (μ=4.6) statistically significantly more ($p<0.005$) than the bi-level (μ=3.9) and space-filling layouts (μ=3.6). They liked how the layout shows the *"chapter groupings each in a separate grid"*. In all tasks and in overall ranking, most subjects indicated the grid-stacking layout as their top preference. All this suggests that subjects value the strength of the grid-spacing layout – a clear top-down presentation of the chronological order of the chapters – more than the strengths of the bi-level and space-filling layouts.

The bi-level layout features an overview of all the event photos afforded by the film strip of chapter thumbnails. Subjects like the film strip (μ=4.4, δ=0.7) as it shows *"the flow of the event"*. Subjects also found it is easy to navigate the user interface (μ=4.2, δ=0.8). On the other hand, for the statement *"I do NOT like the wasted screen space"*, subjects only somewhat disagree (μ=2.7[7], δ=1.0). This contrast suggests that while subjects like and appreciate having the overview, they prefer not to waste much screen space imposed by the restricting view hierarchy, even if its easy to navigate.

The space-filling layout maximizes screen space usage; minimal screen space is wasted while still presenting the chapter groupings. A number of subjects do value maximizing screen space usage more than the chronological order of the chapters; five subjects chose this layout as their most preferred layout overall. Most subjects however, prefer the grid-stacking layout. These subjects found the space-filling layout to be *"confusing"*.

6. CONCLUSION

This paper explores chapter-based photo organization and reports results – qualitative and quantitative with statistical significance – that advocates its use for personal digital photo libraries.

We developed a photo browser, *Chaptrs*, and integrated the event photo stream segmentation algorithm from our previous work to explore how people organize their photos in each event. Our algorithm helps users by automatically grouping event photos into smaller groups of chapters. We implemented a baseline plain grid layout and three chapter-based photo organization layouts in *Chaptrs* to explore how chapter-based photo organization affects storytelling, searching and interpretation tasks; and what photo layout aspects are important for such tasks.

Our subjects found chapter-based photo organization to be helpful in all three tasks. Our study also revealed how the subjects employed chapters in these tasks. The grid-stacking layout was preferred the most in all three tasks and the baseline plain grid layout was preferred the least. Among the results, the following are our primary findings from the study:

1. Users value chapter consistency more than the chronological order of the photos in grouping photos into chapters
2. Choice of chapter criteria and granularity for chapter groupings are very subjective
3. Having low misses is more important than having low false alarms for automatic event photo stream segmentation
4. Users value chronological order of the chapters more than maximizing screen space usage in photo layouts

While we discovered that the preference for criteria and granularity of our subjects were very subjective, our study also shows that our algorithm helps subjects discover chapter groupings. In future work, our algorithm can be coupled with photo clustering algorithms based on intra-photo similarity measures to help users achieve their preferred criteria for organization. In the current state, our algorithm has a characteristic of producing smaller chapter groupings that users can use as building blocks to form an organization of their criteria or to build up into a more coarse grained organization. Additionally, our algorithm currently assumes that photos in the user's personal digital photo library are not part of any overlapping events. Integrating a photo stream alignment algorithm [29] as a pre-processing step for our algorithm would be beneficial for users with such photos.

With our findings on the key layout aspects, we plan to integrate the film strip overview into the grid-stacking layout in the next design iteration of *Chaptrs*. With this next iteration, we will conduct a longitudinal study that will provide us with long-term usage data to support the findings and conclusions we have made in this paper. In addition, we can couple this with a qualitative study that focuses on exploratory divergent cognitive tasks [28].

7. REFERENCES

[1] P. André, M. L. Wilson, A. Russell, D. A. Smith, A. Owens, and m. schraefel. Continuum: designing timelines for hierarchies, relationships and scale. In *Proc. of ACM Symposium on User Interface Software and Technology*, pages 101–110, 2007.

[2] M. Balabanović, L. L. Chu, and G. J. Wolff. Storytelling with digital photographs. In *Proc. of*

[7] 2 – Disagree, 3 – Neither agree nor disagree

ACM SIGCHI Conference on Human Factors in Computing Systems, pages 564–571, 2000.

[3] B. B. Bederson. Photomesa: a zoomable image browser using quantum treemaps and bubblemaps. In *Proc. of ACM Symposium on User Interface Software and Technology*, pages 71–80, 2001.

[4] C. Chen, M. Oakes, and J. Tait. Browsing personal images using episodic memory (time + location). In *Proc. of European Conference on Information Retrieval*, pages 362–372, 2006.

[5] Y.-X. Chen, M. Reiter, and A. Butz. Photomagnets: supporting flexible browsing and searching in photo collections. In *Proc. of International Conference on Multimodal Interfaces and Workshop on Machine Learning for Multimodal Interaction*, pages 25:1–25:8, 2010.

[6] P.-Y. Chi and H. Lieberman. Raconteur: from intent to stories. In *Proc. of International Conference on Intelligent User Interfaces*, pages 301–304, 2010.

[7] S. J. Cunningham and M. Masoodian. Metadata and organizational structures in personal photograph digital libraries. In *Proc. of International Conference on Asian Digital Libraries*, 2007.

[8] S. M. Drucker, C. Wong, A. Roseway, S. Glenner, and S. De Mar. Mediabrowser: reclaiming the shoebox. In *Proc. of International Working Conference on Advanced Visual Interfaces*, pages 433–436, 2004.

[9] S. Fertig, E. Freeman, and D. Gelernter. Lifestreams: an alternative to the desktop metaphor. In *Proc. of ACM SIGCHI Conference on Human Factors in Computing Systems*, pages 410–411, 1996.

[10] D. Frohlich, A. Kuchinsky, C. Pering, A. Don, and S. Ariss. Requirements for photoware. In *Proc. of ACM conference on Computer Supported Cooperative Work*, pages 166–175, 2002.

[11] M. Georgescul, A. Clark, and S. Armstrong. An analysis of quantitative aspects in the evaluation of thematic segmentation algorithms. In *Proc. of SIGdial Workshop on Discourse and Dialogue*, pages 144–151, 2006.

[12] A. Girgensohn, F. Shipman, T. Turner, and L. Wilcox. Flexible access to photo libraries via time, place, tags, and visual features. In *Proc. of ACM/IEEE Joint Conference on Digital Libraries*, pages 187–196, 2010.

[13] J. P. Gozali, M.-Y. Kan, and H. Sundaram. Hidden Markov Model for event photo stream segmentation. In *Proc. of ICME 2012 Workshop on Human-Focused Communications in the 3D Continuum (HFC3D)*, 2012.

[14] J. P. Gozali, M.-Y. Kan, and H. Sundaram. How do people organize their photos in each event and how does it affect storytelling, searching and interpretation tasks? Technical Report TRC4/12, National University of Singapore Department of Computer Science, April 2012.

[15] A. Graham, H. Garcia-Molina, A. Paepcke, and T. Winograd. Time as essence for photo browsing through personal digital libraries. In *Proc. of ACM/IEEE Joint Conference on Digital Libraries*, pages 326–335, 2002.

[16] D. Huynh, S. Drucker, P. Baudisch, and C. Wong. Time quilt: scaling up zoomable photo browsers for large, unstructured photo collections. In *Proc. of ACM SIGCHI Conference on Human Factors in Computing Systems*, pages 1937–1940, 2005.

[17] D. Kirk, A. Sellen, C. Rother, and K. Wood. Understanding photowork. In *Proc. of ACM SIGCHI Conference on Human Factors in Computing Systems*, pages 761–770, 2006.

[18] A. Kuchinsky, C. Pering, M. L. Creech, D. Freeze, B. Serra, and J. Gwizdka. Fotofile: a consumer multimedia organization and retrieval system. In *Proc. of ACM SIGCHI Conference on Human Factors in Computing Systems*, pages 496–503, 1999.

[19] T. Mei, B. Wang, X.-S. Hua, H.-Q. Zhou, and S. Li. Probabilistic multimodality fusion for event based home photo clustering. In *Proc. of IEEE International Conference on Multimedia and Expo*, pages 1757–1760, 2006.

[20] T. J. Mills, D. Pye, D. Sinclair, and K. R. Wood. Shoebox: A digital photo management system. Technical Report 2000.10, AT&T Research, 2000.

[21] M. Naaman, Y. J. Song, A. Paepcke, and H. Garcia-Molina. Automatic organization for digital photographs with geographic coordinates. In *Proc. of ACM/IEEE Joint Conference on Digital Libraries*, pages 53–62, 2004.

[22] D. R. Olsen, Jr. Evaluating user interface systems research. In *Proc. of ACM symposium on User interface software and technology*, pages 251–258, 2007.

[23] C. Plaisant, B. Milash, A. Rose, S. Widoff, and B. Shneiderman. Lifelines: visualizing personal histories. In *Proc. of SIGCHI Conference on Human Factors in Computing Systems*, pages 221–227, 1996.

[24] K. Rodden. How do people organize their photographs? In *Proc. of BCS IRSG 21st Annual Colloquium on Information Retrieval Research*, 1999.

[25] K. Rodden and K. R. Wood. How do people manage their digital photographs? In *Proc. of ACM SIGCHI Conference on Human Factors in Computing Systems*, pages 409–416, 2003.

[26] D.-S. Ryu, W.-K. Chung, and H.-G. Cho. Photoland: a new image layout system using spatio-temporal information in digital photos. In *Proc. of SAC*, pages 1884–1891, 2010.

[27] P. Sandhaus and S. Boll. Semantic analysis and retrieval in personal and social photo collections. *Multimedia Tools Appl.*, 51:5–33, 2011.

[28] A. M. Webb and A. Kerne. Integrating implicit structure visualization with authoring promotes ideation. In *Proc. of ACM/IEEE joint conference on Digital libraries*, pages 203–212, 2011.

[29] J. Yang, J. Luo, J. Yu, and T. S. Huang. Photo stream alignment for collaborative photo collection and sharing in social media. In *Proc. of the 3rd ACM SIGMM international workshop on Social media*, pages 41–46, 2011.

Co-Reading: Investigating Collaborative Group Reading

Jennifer Pearson[1], Tom Owen[1], Harold Thimbleby[1], George Buchanan[2]
[1] FIT Lab, Swansea University
csjen, cstomo, csharold@swan.ac.uk
[2] Centre for HCI Design, City University, London
george.buchanan.1@city.ac.uk

ABSTRACT

Collaborative reading, or *co-reading* as we call it, is ubiquitous—it occurs, for instance, in classrooms, book-clubs, and in less coordinated ways through mass media. While individual digital reading has been the subject of much investigation, research into co-reading is scarce. We report a two-phase field study of group reading to identify an initial set of user requirements. A co-reading interface is then designed that facilitates the coordination of group reading by providing temporary 'Point-out' markers to indicate specific locations within documents. A user study compared this new system with collaborative reading on paper, with a positive outcome; the differences in user behavior between paper and the new interface reveal intriguing insights into user needs and the potential benefits of digital media for co-reading.

Keywords

Co-reading, Documents, Collaboration, Slate PCs

Categories and Subject Descriptors

H.3.7 [**Digital Libraries**]: User Issues

General Terms

Design, Experimentation, Human Factors

1. INTRODUCTION

The commonplace act of reading is often portrayed as a solitary activity. Looking deeper, however, it becomes apparent that reading in groups is actually surprisingly common [20]. For example, children are encouraged to read in a variety of collaborative forms for much of their school careers (i.e., reading novels, reciting plays, or studying for exams). Many adults also unwittingly read together on a daily basis, whether it be looking at posters, web-pages or even television screens. There are also many examples of more structured collaborative reading sessions such as research groups and book clubs. Reading in groups is both pervasive and important, yet to date there has been surprisingly little research into the topic of *collaborative reading*, or *co-reading*.

JCDL'12, June 10–14, 2012, Washington, DC, USA.

Jack, Jill, Wendy and Peter are sitting around a desk reading a research paper in an attempt to understand its relevance and impact on their work. They each have an individual paper copy of the article which they annotate independently. As the group is small, they sit near each other and can point out areas of interest using hand gestures coupled with spoken directions. Despite this, they have problems co-ordinating at specific areas of a document: half way through the session, Jack notices a useful quote near the end of the paper. He says "look here, on page 10, column two, paragraph three—that quote is useful". Wendy quickly navigates to the correct page but struggles to locate the exact quote Jack is referring to.

Figure 1: A typical co-reading scenario.

Co-reading has many facets, and in some cases books have been written or printed with special structures to help readers share understandings of the text. One established case is in religious texts, such as the Bible, where standardized structuring of books, chapters and verses allow two (or more) people to identify the same words, even in different editions with different paginations. The use of chapter-and-verse references allows particularity without verbose quotations, and in the context of a shared reading in worship or study, a familiar and rehearsed form of identifying locations can be exchanged due to a common document markup.

However, such structured documents are not always used during collaborative reading, which can lead to challenges for both the group as a whole and the individuals within. Figure 1 provides an example where four co-readers are using multiple paper copies of a single document. A challenge for each member is to accurately point-out specific point in the text to the other members; in this case, a useful quote. Upon locating the quote, each member may make their own notes, creating four distinct artefacts. This scenario demonstrates how users need to coordinate their reading within a group environment: a challenge we term *mutual navigation*.

These variations suggest that co-reading is not a single activity but, rather, a range of different tasks that have varying requirements and goals. In this paper we focus on the specific needs of a peer group that reads together, in the same place, at the same time, using individual media. We investigate user needs by two fieldwork studies, develop a system to support the identified requirements, and evaluate its interaction and use in a laboratory test.

2. BACKGROUND AND MOTIVATION

We will now briefly recap some recent related work of particular and direct relevance to our work. Further literature will be discussed in later in Section 7.

Digital reading and hypertext have been the subject of a vast amount of research since the early days of PCs. Performance has been studied through measures such as reading speed and comprehension, often with particular consideration of screen size and display technology. The wide-scale adoption of mobile devices and the popularization of commercial reading appliances such as the Kindle have sustained an interest in the topic of digital reading and have given rise to numerous research projects in the area.

As Cathy Marshall has noted ([20], Chapter 4), the predominant focus of this long tradition of research has, however, been on *individual reading*. This is despite good evidence that reading in groups is an important aspect of information work [1]. Furthermore, contemporary innovations in technology have started to provoke questions about the appropriate technological configurations for supporting reading in groups [22].

In contrast, collaborative writing has been a subject of extensive research (e.g., [13]). It has long been established that reading is closely connected to writing [1], and research in collaborative writing has considered reading within a group of co-authors. However, within this collaborative context of group writing, reading has still been seen as a primarily solitary activity.

Just as group writing and personal reading are connected, group reading and individual reading are also related. Marshall et al. [21] undertook an early investigation into co-reading, introducing a reading appliance, XLibris, into a reading group. XLibris was used individually, prior to a group meeting, not in the meeting itself. During the group discussion, further reading was done on paper. While most of their paper focusses on individual reading, the interaction between members during the group meeting is reported, if only briefly. Nonetheless, this insight does show the value of having an individual copy of the text when reading as a group: each person can make their own notes and interleave discussion with independent reading. That work, and Marshall's later re-analysis of the same material [20] also suggests that the coordination between group members of their shared reading is a complex activity that occurs alongside brief individual phases of reading.

Our own recent research on information work added further confirmation of the value of individual copies in the context of group reading. Observations of study groups in a university library [7] concluded that groups often had multiple copies of the same book or notes, frequently one copy per person. Notes taken during that work suggested that coordination and sharing of reading was a complex activity. However, as with the work of Marshall et al, our primary focus was elsewhere.

We also mirrored Marshall's observation that coordinating group reading is a complex activity. This reminded us strongly of an emerging theme in the understanding of reading as an interactive activity: specifically, the role of cognitive attention. Research on reading has started to suggest that during attentive reading, the vital cognitive state of flow [9] is particularly vulnerable to disruption by the attention demanded by secondary tasks [28, 26]. Unfortunately, the insights we presently have reveal only a little detail of the appropriate management of attention in the context of collaborative reading. Given the social complexity of this reading activity, it is likely that cognitive attention is handled very differently than the processes used when reading alone. It is therefore vital to understand how readers coordinate with each other and read together.

The best existing research has not directly focussed on co-reading as its primary interest. This suggests that an important literate activity is under-researched. We have taken a formulative approach to discovering collaborative reading practices by studying group work first on paper. We then designed, implemented and evaluated an interactive system to aid coordination within group reading sessions.

		Time	
		Same	Different
Location	Same	Book Club	Notice Board
	Remote	Tele-Conference	Article Reviews

Table 1: Different types of collaborative reading

By probing co-reading in this way, we were able to discover several notable differences between the two media as well as the potential benefits of digital implementations for group reading.

3. OBSERVING GROUP READING

Reading in groups can take many forms: for example, reading individually in the context of a wider group task, reading for recitation or performance, or reading at the same time in different places. In undertaking an investigation into reading, we first narrowed our focus to a specific form.

One classification of collaborative work is the two-dimensional CSCW matrix of time and space [15]. In terms of time, work may occur at the same moment (synchronous) or at different times (asynchronous). Similarly, space, or location, may be either be co-located or remote. With the four different combinations that this matrix creates, different user needs will emerge (see Table 1).

Group structures can also vary: a group of peers (e.g., a leisure reading "book group" discussing a novel); or a hierarchical group led by an authority figure (e.g., a teacher leading a group of junior school students). Similarly, there is a question as to whether the medium being read is shared (e.g., a large single display), or if each person has an individual copy.

In selecting a focus for our research, we first considered the practicalities of observation and experimentation. Studying groups that read at different times seemed problematic: a realistic setting would require many individual reading sessions and extensive coordination. Reading at the same time appeared to be much more viable. Remote, synchronous reading would require a number of experimental observers, and consistency would become a problem, or logging could be used (with a loss of detailed insight). Researching co-located, simultaneous reading would allow one set of observations and minimize the challenge of coordinating groups.

We also considered the extent of exisiting research. We already possessed observational data on co-located, contemporary group reading [7]. Marshall [21] had reported individuals' personal reading activity within a group context (remote, asynchronous mode), with some additional information on co-located, synchronous reading. It was these two modes where the existing material gave us the greatest volume of information on readers' needs.

The two possible focii were thus synchronous, co-located; and remote, asynchronous reading. The first was more achievable logistically, and we also had more direct primary data of our own upon which to build. As a result, we targetted studying collaborative reading in the same place, at the same time.

3.1 Method

To pursue our interest in collaborative reading, we ran two sets of observations to gather requirements. The first extended our previous observations [7] of reading groups in libraries. Our aim here was to confirm or eliminate a number of potentially interesting research areas from our earlier work. In particular, we aimed to identify an initial set of activities within collaborative reading from which a wider body of knowledge can later be derived.

Following the first phase of observing groups in the library, we undertook a second phase to add detail to the initial set of co-reading tasks. We adopted an autoethnographic approach [10], and one of the authors joined two active research reading groups. In total we participated in seven sessions with one group (on multimedia); and five with the other (on cultural studies). Our researcher was already a regular member of one other reading group, but did not participate in it for the purposes of investigation. The groups and their members were informed of the purpose of participation, and both topics were areas of research where our researcher already had an active interest. While this may have created some artificial behavior, disclosure was deemed necessary for ethical reasons. The aim at this stage was to better understand the needs of group reading from the 'inside'. Rather than diversify our research goals, we decided not to investigate new issues, as basing any requirements on a single user's needs or experiences is clearly poor practice.

3.2 Observation Results

Most of the group members pre-read material, but in every group reading, at least one member had not pre-read the material. In either of the groups, the unprepared readers were not consistently the same person. The texts were, nonetheless had typically already been read by half or more of the reading group. This contrasted with the library groups, where most group members, and on approximately half the occasions, all, had apparently not encountered the text before. We now synthesize the main patterns discovered in the two complementary observations:

Loose coordination Reading was only periodically closely synchronized on a particular page by the whole group; all groups demonstrated periods where individual reading occurred before shared reading was resumed.

Localised synchronization Within loose coordination, there were periods where the reading of the group appeared to focus on the same part of the text, before the reading de-synchronized again. This pattern was found in all the observation sessions.

The difficulty of identifying the 'end' of more coordinated periods of reading became evident during our participation in the two reading groups. While there were occasions where groups did wait for everyone to complete a part of a paper, this was exceptional (only three instances per group, in a total period of five hours or more). More typically, after some individual reading, one person would respond to part or all of the text, and this would occur in parallel with others continuing their reading (perhaps paying selective attention). Others would participate in discussion before returning to their own reading. Though the 'start' of a synchronization was not perfectly co-ordinated, there was always some utterance by one of the group members that signalled a call for others to join them in reading a particular part: e.g., 'Ah, this bit seems interesting' (followed by guidance to the content).

View competition Where two or more readers had to share a copy of the book, there was some conflict over the resource. This occurred in seven groups in the library setting, and when the group read as a 'whole', the text could be shared, but this regularly broke out into swapping between the sharing readers for individual study. In contrast to the library situation, the reading groups had individual copies of text. On three total occasions (of eleven sessions) one person did not bring their own copy; two of which were resolved by printing or copying another individual text. When members were reading with content in their lap, there was a similar conflict between documents or pages for visibility.

Mutual navigation When the loose coordination of a group synchronized more closely to attend to the same point in the text, considerable time and effort was made for everyone to arrive at that point. This involved the use of page numbers, geometry of the page and reference to content (e.g., "below the big diagram", or "The paragraph that starts 'The European Free Trade Agreement'"), plus turning the document to other members and physically pointing at the desired location.

During the participatory phase, further detail emerged. During mutual navigation, where one participant was endeavouring to direct the attention of others onto a point in the text, all but one case commenced with spoken instructions. These sometimes (10%+ of cases) started with a description of the content, in those and all other cases proceeded to identifying the page (more easily where page numbers were present), and then the point on the page. The latter was described in one or both of two ways: first, the starting words of the paragraph (70%+); second, the sequence of the text in a page or column (e.g., 'third paragraph down') was given (< 40%). Occasionally, other approaches were used - e.g., landmarks like large diagrams were used as waypoints towards the content.

If spoken instructions failed, pointing out of the content was used. One participant regularly used the pointing method by default, but this was exceptional. Requests for the repetition of details occurred in almost all cases too. Communication seemed to be more effective among regular group members, but due to our small sample, full conclusions cannot be drawn.

Negotiated navigation On three occasions during the library sessions, mutual navigation involved conflicting interest in two different locations at once, which the groups had to negotiate.

The order of reading was regularly discussed by the research reading groups, but we saw minimal evidence of any use of note-taking or other explicit action to direct the planned reading. In all cases, the group appeared to rely on at least one member remembering what the agreed plan was, evidenced in comments like "what part was it we're going to read next?".

Parallel reading In seven groups one or more members were seen to read two or more documents at the same time, or very quickly interleaved. In six of these groups, this occurred alongside synchronized group reading - i.e. the individual was apparently working with the 'shared' view of the moment, and alongside that undertaking a separate, individual reading. This was also observed in periods when the group reading was not synchronized.

During our participatory phase, we encountered three sessions where the group read more than one text; twice this was due to a member bringing a new text that they thought might be relevant. This suggests some planning, following Marshall et al. [21]; but it also increased the frequency of parallel reading. Personal notes and papers were more involved as parallel texts, with note-taking (on separate paper) being observed in seven sessions, and other personal papers being used in six sessions.

3.3 Prioritisation and Requirements

Examining these findings, we were able to reduce the scope of our research. We first eliminated each action that appeared too complex to support in software or that was better conducted as a discussion between users, and where, consequently, designing new digital tools is unlikely to be beneficial.

Negotiated navigation and localised synchronization both involved considerable social negotiation between participants in the group. It did not appear likely that technology could assist a conversation between the group, and further intervention would probably only add to the work of the members.

View competition appears to be a consequence of limited resources, and while it will be a key aspect where views are shared, individual copies vastly reduce its occurrence. While designing within constraints can be useful, we concluded that any viable solution revisited a topic that we had previously researched [6], and this overlap reduced the scope for adding to the scientific literature. Parallel reading is a complicated issue, particularly if content is displayed on a single device. However, solutions are not too complex to imagine (e.g., two rapidly switchable views, each of which preserves their state), and more complex solutions would require closer understanding again of the dynamics of group reading. Again, previous research seems to suggest some early directions, such as different combinations of display hardware [22]. Furthermore, we should as there are more critical actions among this set, these less frequent interactions should be set aside for now.

In contrast, mutual navigation appeared to be tractable, as much work was spent articulating where content was. These indications often had to be restated due to loose coordination: momentary inattention by one or more members meant that such repetition was commonplace. One further point that we observed from the participation in these groups was a regular return to points in the text that had been read – and discussed – together. However, informal interviews with group participants, including a discussion of their annotation practices, revealed that these locations were seldom explicitly recorded, and had little role outside of the group reading. Mutual navigation also is closely connected to the overall pattern of local synchronization. Mutual navigation also seemed to more readily suggest effective tool support, as synchronizing reading speeds between users, whilst viable, was predicted to cause irritation as, in fact, individuals read at different speeds, and previous research has shown that reading is not, in truth, a linear activity [1]. We thus arrived on a primary focus on mutual navigation.

The requirements for mutual navigation are teasingly simple. While coordination can be done using page numbers, describing paragraphs or diagrams, often the most effective method we observed was the simple gesture of turning your own copy of the document towards the other members of the group, and pointing to the desired place with your finger. The inconsistent presence of page numbers (and their variable location), variable discriminability of paragraphs (e.g., due to similar beginning phrases) and other factors make other methods less effective. However the person making the gesture cannot then see the content, and continuing to talk about it becomes cognitively demanding. The transience of gestures also appears to be valuable. Across a session, mutual navigation occurs many times, and few of these instances appear to be, in retrospect, of particular long-term value. Thus, an 'idealized' mutual navigation tool would be indicative, transient and automatically place the reader on the right page. However, as noted above, other group members join the synchronous reading phase in a loosely coordinated fashion, after completing their own localised reading. This further suggests that the receiving group members should be able to engage in mutual navigation after a short time delay of their choosing. In any interaction design, a degree of speculation is inevitable – as here – but we will examine, and re-validate, these insights later through a laboratory experiment.

4. SUPPORTING CO-READING

Before designing our system, we first reviewed the literature to identify potential solutions to the question of mutual navigation. We did not identify any full solutions to mutual navigation in an extensive review of existing digital library, hypertext, CSCW and human-computer-interaction research.

4.1 Mutual Navigation

One partial solution to the challenge of mutual navigation could be Telepointers [17]—representations on the display of one group member of the pointer locations indicated by another, which provide real-time gestural foci and enable mutual coordination on a group workspace during discussions. Typically, telepointers are used to indicate a focus of attention to other participants. This has some potential for group reading. It is known that when reading at home, adult and child reading pairs can point to a position in a document using a finger, or some technological counterpart [29]. However, it is important to analyse these interactions with care.

Telepointers were envisioned for remote working between two or more collaborating groups. One group can indicate a point of interest on a shared view to the participants in other locations. While indicating location, telepointers are transient and 'real-time'. There is no record of the gesture: the pointer behaves just like a laser-pen on a shared display, or a mouse pointer being used to gesture onscreen content to a colleague. Replaying the gesture requires the original performer of it to repeat the indication again, or, alternatively, it demands the immediate attention of all group members.

Demanding continuous attention from a group of readers is, unfortunately, likely to prove problematic. In the context of co-reading, which includes many elements of 'active reading' [2], users need to manage their cognitive attention with great care [9]. Marshall alludes to [21] and Buchanan confirms [7], that there are tensions between the need to collaborate and the individual's need to maintain attention to complete their reading: e.g., oral directions to a location in the text had to be restated when a member's own reading distracted them from the discussion, or when the discussion was interrupted so others could complete their reading. Extending the underlying principle of the telepointer, there is a need for a shared pointer that can be individually reproduced at will.

As noted in Section 3.2, within a group's collaborative reading, individuals will frequently indicate items and locations to other group members, e.g., "look at this figure on page 45." When working on a single document or machine, this process is straightforward: the user can simply point out the section they are looking at with their finger. Assuming all members of the group have visible access to the shared document or screen, they will easily see the required information. When collaboration occurs over multiple copies of the same document however, this process becomes more troublesome as there is no single shared view.

4.2 Collaborative Reading

As we noted in Section 1, reading has been a consistent topic within digital-library research for some years. The primary focus of research on digital reading has been on the individual [20]. However, the existing literature on reading and information does indicate that collaborative work is valuable in its own regard, and collaboration is frequently a key element of the context within which individual work sits [1].

We approach reading as an interactive process. DL research on collaborative reading as interaction is relatively rare. One good example is Liu et a [18] which studies the provision of children's picture books on a digital table. The main focus of the paper is on providing interactions for both an electronic bookshelf and a set of digital books that are consistent with the physical originals. Though the reading is among a group of peers, and is co-located at the same time, comparison is tenuous given the differences between our focus on novel interaction during reading rather than the completeness of digital metaphors with the physical world.

5. DESIGN AND IMPLEMENTATION

To reify the requirements gathered in the previous section we implemented BuddyBooks—a collaborative reading interface that we deploy on multiple iPads. The slate PC form factor allows users to sit around the same desk while providing them with a personal document view as well as instant updates of all mark-ups (e.g., annotations, bookmarks and highlights) made by other members of the group. The key feature of the BuddyBooks interface is the 'Point-out' tool which facilitates the coordination of group members via direct pointers to specific parts of the document. Creating this interface later allowed us to compare group reading practices using paper documents against our prototype.

In this section, we first report the conceptual design, followed by the system architecture, before describing the interaction design and, specifically our support for mutual navigation, annotation. Following this, we describe how we envisage the system in use, demonstrated by a scenario. In the following section, we then report a laboratory study of BuddyBooks in use.

5.1 Conceptual Design

One key initial design decision was which hardware platform to develop an application on. Our own observations had highlighted the value of having individual documents, and this led us to consider an individual display. Marshall et al's work on XLibris demonstrated the benefits of the 'reading appliance' form factor [21]. Our observations of library reading, and participation in reading groups, also both underlined the same point and, comparatively, the disadvantages of desktop and laptop PCs which create a more marked constraint on the seating – and hence communication – of each group.

An alternative form of collaborative reading occurs in classroom or brainstorming situations where large physical displays are used. Large computerized screens now offer multi-touch capabilities; for example interactive white boards and touch-screen table tops [14, 23, 31] which can promote simultaneous collaboration. Although this approach makes it easy for everyone to see the material, it does sometimes lead to the situation where there is one "leader" doing all the writing and can hinder collaboration [20]. Such concerns led us to adopt a reading appliance approach instead.

Our work coincided with the launch of Apple's iPad device, and this provided an opportunity to develop a system without the tethering cables that the original XLibris had been forced to use. In contrast to Amazon's Kindle and other electronic ink e-Book readers, the iPad was not a closed software environment, and developing bespoke applications was straightforward. In our recent work on reading support, a continuous reservation has been the need to use laptop and desktop PCs, and embracing a form factor that appears to be of increasing importance as a reading device seems to be timely. Given that recent research has indicated the slate or tablet device form-factor has many advantages for active reading by individuals, this seemed to be a judicious starting point [22].

In designing the system, we generated a number of usage senarios to envisage its use. Figure 2 illustrates one example of a possible co-reading session. The real-time aspect of the system ensures that each member of the group has immediate access to all notes made by other users as well as facilitating an easy method of referencing specific sections to support mutual navigation.

5.2 System Architecture

BuddyBooks uses a central server to connect each iPad with others in the group. The server allocates each user a unique color and nickname which is used to distinguish between the activity of different readers, and IP addresses are currently used as a simple means of identifying a specific iPad. The server receives notifications of any mark-up that a user adds to their document, and then forwards that information to all the other devices in the group. BuddyBooks allows users to collaboratively *read* a common document; it is not, therefore, concerned with the collective *editing* of a document, but

Kris, Joe, Laura and Hannah are studying for an exam. They each have a copy of the course text on their individual iPads and are discussing the material around a table. Joe notices that there is a section within one of the chapters that is not fully explained. He read a web article on this topic earlier today and decides to make a note clarifying the information for the benefit of his friends. Immediately after he makes the note, it automatically appears on the others' iPads. Later in the session, the group are discussing a past exam question and decide to look up the answer within the document. Kris finds the appropriate page and paragraph and 'points it out' to the other three via the system's Point-out tool. Joe, Laura and Hannah's iPads instantly recognize that Kris is indicating a place and offer them the chance to automatically jump to the appropriate page and view the exact location Kris chose.

Figure 2: BuddyBooks Usage Scenario

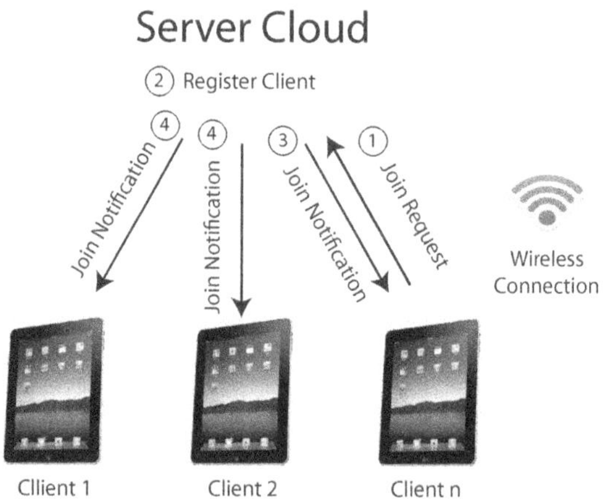

Figure 3: The BuddyBooks Cloud Architecture

rather is an aid to mark-up and coordination of content where the original text remains unchanged.

The basic architecture of BuddyBooks is shown in Figure 3. To join the working group, a client iPad must first send an XML join request ① to the server passing it its IP address and a user defined nickname. The server, after receiving a join request from a new client, creates a new thread to deal with any more incoming messages and adds it to its active client list. The server then uses the clients position in the clients array to allocate it a unique color which completes the client registration ②. Following a successful join, the server then distributes a join confirmation back to the client ③ and join notifications to all other active clients within the working group ④.

Once an iPad is connected to the group, any annotations made are encoded into an XML format and sent to the cloud service, before being forwarded instantly to any other connected devices. The other iPads receive the XML message, decode it, and display the annotation accordingly. The server retains a log of all messages with a timestamp, and a device that connects to an existing group will be updated with the stream of previous messages.

5.3 Supporting Mutual Navigation

BuddyBooks includes a 'Look-at-this' queue that allows users to point out specific areas of the original document to other members of the group – a key requirement to support mutual navigation. The

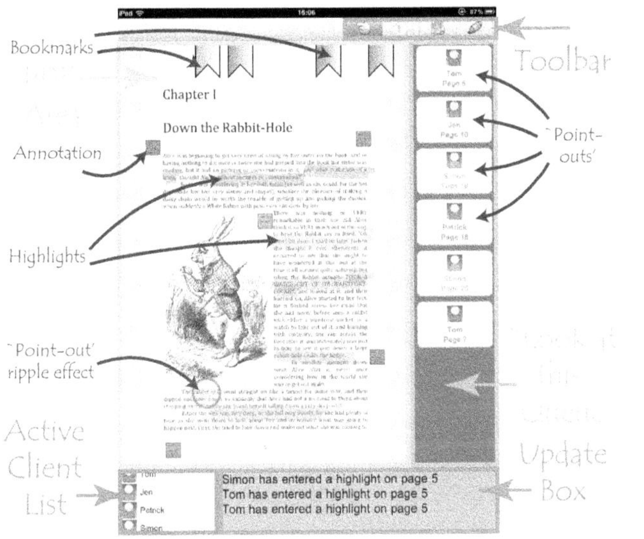

Figure 4: Screen shot from BuddyBooks.

Look-at-this queue is designed to hold a list of temporary placeholders made by members of a working group to allow them to quickly and easily navigate to the exact area of the document indicated by the original creator.

When a 'Point-out' is made by a member of a group, it is subsequently added to the top of every member's Look-at-this queue along with the color and nickname of its creator. Receiving a Point-out from another member of the group does not automatically navigate every user to the point in the text at which the point-out was made, however. Rather, each entry in the Look-at-this queue is hyper-linked, so users can choose a convenient time to access the information. This allows the users to complete personal reading before choosing to follow an indication from another group member. This avoids immediate disruption of their reading, and also means they can 'catch-up' without having to ask the group to repeat the directions to the current point of attention. For all group members, we are therefore reducing the number of interruptions that they must cope with. A 'point-out' has no associated annotation - it simply indicates location.

Figure 4 shows an example of BuddyBooks in use. Clicking on an entry in the "Look-at-this queue" (on the right) navigates the user to the correct document page and animates a ripple effect (a circle outline that pulses in and out around the coordinate point for several seconds – see lower left) to indicate to the user the exact location at which the Point-out was made. The user can select any item from the look-at-this-queue at any time.

5.4 Basic Annotation Tools

The BuddyBooks interface includes several basic mark-up tools which we incorporated to provide a fully functioning reading prototype for use in a comparative study. We noted in our preliminary studies that participants did undertake personal annotation within the context of collaborative reading. Omitting fundamental support for annotation would have multiple undesirable effects on a study: it may force participants to either co-opt our support for mutual navigation for traditional annotation purposes, or, alternatively, to reject the system outright due to the absence of vital features.

BuddyBooks therefore includes a range of traditional annotation tools. The text tool supports written comments, each note being represented by a small marker on the page, that interacts as a pop-up once the note is written. Pressing on the mark reveals the comment, and touching away from the expanded text closes it again. The small marker minimizes the visual impact of the note, and improves visibility of the main text. There is a highlighter tool, which when selected leaves a permanent colored trace on the page, like a real-world highlighter. Finally we provided a simple bookmarking function; tapping the bookmark created a bookmark for the current page that could then be selected later in the session, and return the reader to the chosen page. Each of these mark-ups will appear in real-time on every group member's iPad, and can be distinguished by each user's unique color.

Figure 5: BuddyBooks running on four iPads

A screen shot of BuddyBooks is shown in Figure 4. The toolbar containing the annotation tools appears on the top-right corner, with example highlights, bookmarks and annotations shown on screen. This is a demonstration document that is intended to show all the potential features – it does not represent a display from 'real' use.

6. EVALUATION

To investigate how co-reading is performed on paper and how it could benefit from a digitized solution, we conducted a comparative study of BuddyBooks against paper-based co-reading. We recruited 18 participants (10F, 8M) aged between 22 and 61 to take part in the study. All participants were educated to Bachelor's degree level or above, in a range of academic subjects. To mimic collaborative working sessions, we recruited participants in sets of four, which, due to two potential participants not attending, led to groups of 3 and 4 (3 groups of 4 and 2 groups of 3). Each group was asked to perform a reading task together. Group sessions took on average 1 1/2 hours to complete and participants were given a £10 gift voucher for their time.

Before the study, participants completed a short questionnaire to gather information on their experience of reading in groups, including how often they read in a group, and the purposes for which the reading was done. The media and software that they use for group work was also elicited, in order to provide a backdrop against which any main results could be interpreted.

Each study began with the group performing a comprehension-style reading task on a paper document, with individual particpants starting with their own unmarked personal copy. A range of writing implements was given for personal markup purposes (highlighters, pens, etc.). This style of reading reflected the activity that we had observed and participated in while investigating co-reading. After completing their work on paper, the group undertook a similar task on a different document using BuddyBooks.

The two documents were of the same length and overall format, and of similar complexity. The topics were different (to avoid learning effects from the material being read); one being on an envi-

	Paper		BuddyBooks		Mann-
	Avg	SD	Avg	SD	Whitney
Q1: How *easily* could you point out bits of information to one another?	5.06	2.29	8.17	1.62	p<0.0005 U=281.5
Q2: How *quickly* could you point out bits of information to one another?	5.22	2.62	8.61	1.29	p<0.0005 U=281.5
Q3: What score would you give each system overall for co-reading?	5.67	2.25	8.56	1.34	p<0.0005 U=283

Table 2: Average subjective ratings (out of 10).

ronmental issue, and the other on a social concern, and were taken from a current affairs periodical. The goal of the group reading was to identify weaknesses and errors in the paper, and to mark these on the document. To ensure an unbiased experimental design, we alternated the order these documents were presented to each group. Both documents were unseen, as requiring prior reading from participants was unlikely to be consistently complied with, and reading the documents individually only moments before the group reading would not match any behaviors we observed in natural settings. After the study was complete, each participant was asked to fill out an in-depth questionnaire probing their thoughts on the major aspects of each method of collaboration.

The experiment was conducted in a quiet, naturally well-lit room. The iPads used were connected to a local WiFi hub to which the BuddyBooks server was directly wired, so as to minimize network latency effects. During the study, the users' annotations using BuddyBooks were logged, and the paper documents gathered for comparison. Observational notes were taken throughout.

Through the experiment, we wished to identify: first, if the point-outs would be adopted by the participants; second, if the transient point-outs would be used in preference to other shared, permanent annotations; thirdly, what the impacts on the BuddyBook system were on the collaboration between the group members.

6.1 Results

The pre-study questionnaire revealed that 11 of the 18 participants regularly participated in group reading for work, with a mean reported group size of 3.56 people. The main purposes reported included: to assist writing (10 participants); studying (9); reviewing (6) and proofreading (4). The media used included paper (15 participants) and digital (11 participants), with only 4 using computers as their primary medium. Taking collaboration more generally, Google docs were used by two users, while six participants used Word's annotation and change tracking tools.

Taking the post-study responses, the first part of the questionnaire asked participants to rate each co-reading method (paper and BuddyBooks) out of 10 (1=low, 10=high) for a range of attributes. To test the statistical significance of these subjective ratings, we conducted a two-tailed Mann-Whitney test. Table 2 shows a selection of the ratings most relevant to this paper.

This evaluation indicated a strong preference for our interface (Q3), producing highly significant ($p < 0.0005$) average ratings of 5.67 (paper) and 8.56 (BuddyBooks). Preference for our implementation was also detected during later discussion; one user from group 2 stated under Additional Comments, "*I really like it, it's ace*" and one from group 4 commented "*I would love to adopt this over the reams of paper*".

These subjective ratings also showed a distinct fondness for the Point-out tool with users ranking it both *easier* (Q1) and *quicker* (Q2) to point out bits of information in BuddyBooks than on paper ($p < 0.0005$ in both cases). This was backed up by subjective responses from participants, with a member of group 1 stating "*I preferred BuddyBooks to paper because the group work could be much more interactive and dynamic, I was able to say 'look at this now' by using the pointer, whereas on paper I would have to say 'go to page 9, 2nd paragraph down 3rd word from the left'*," one from group 3 stating "*the pointer made it easy to get everyone to look at the same thing at the same time*" and another from group 1 saying "*the point out thing is great! You can just say here and there it is*". Conversely, difficulties were reported with using paper: "*takes too long to explain where you are pointing at*". Our observations taken during the studies suggested similar differences. Groups scarcely discussed where to look, with only the occasional cue being used to attract attention when someone wanted to discuss another point in the text (e.g., "look here").

The use of the different tools also bears some attention. Point-outs were used regularly by the groups, typically every 2-3 minutes (just over 17% of all marks used), while highlighting was used extensively (just under 75% of all marks), and annotations and bookmarks only minimally (5% and 3% respectively). For example, group 1 used 13 point-outs, 66 highlights, 5 annotations and 2 bookmarks. For the three established tools (highlights, annotations and bookmarks) this pattern generally reflects their relative frequency in previous research on digital annotation [28].

One possible response of our participants could have been to use familiar tools such as bookmarks to indicate positions to each other, as these were shared with other participants. However, in practice they were used much less frequently than point-outs, and discussions amongst the groups never suggested their use for mutual navigation. Similarly, highlights could potentially be used to indicate position for navigational purposes, but this was not observed during the five group sessions. The 'point-outs' were adopted by the groups for mutual navigation while traditional annotation tools continued in their established roles.

During our observation of the groups, we uncovered several notable differences in behavior between paper and the BuddyBooks system. Perhaps the most interesting difference was the apparent difficulties group members experienced while attempting to coordinate each other's mark-ups when using paper. Comments made by participants included: "*Did someone already say this?*"; "*I suggest we adopt a new strategy where we don't move on to a new page until we are all ready because I'm really lost*" and "*I need more information than that—what page are you on?*"

This evidence suggests that participants found it difficult to keep up with mark-ups made on paper. In contrast, there were no such comments made when using BuddyBooks: group members successfully used the Point-out tool to indicate to others where they were in a document.

The pattern of communication observed during the BuddyBooks portion of the study was distinct from that seen when using paper. Specifically, using paper led to repeated discussions about the *location* of parts of the document (e.g., "*over here on page 10, half way down paragraph 2*")) whereas these directions were absent when using BuddyBooks. Speech was still used to attract the attention of the group members when moving along the document (e.g., "*I think there's a problem here*", the participant then used a point-out).

Our co-reading support enabled participants to see others mark-ups, and to co-ordinate their reading through the temporary Point-out markers. Participant responses in the post-study interviews established this point: "*There was no need to communicate verbally with BuddyBooks. You can basically just look at the screen and that is it!*"; "*It's very useful to be able to mark specific places and have a tab to instantly reach that spot unlike trying to find some-*

thing from people's descriptions" and "*pointing things out...is much better than explaining where you're looking—like on paper*".

Our observation data and interview feedback suggests that the absence of navigational directions resulted in an increased focus on the content of the document itself. One participant commented: "*I would use this out of choice, as it encourages discussion of the [mark-ups] being made as opposed to where they exist*", while another reported "*I preferred BuddyBooks ... the group work could be much more interactive and dynamic*" It may be that BuddyBooks actually promotes effective group discussion—an extremely desirable situation that greatly supports collaboration.

Returning to the findings of our preliminary research (see Section 3.2), we were able to validate our earlier insights. The patterns of location description mirrored what we had observed earlier, and it was notable that the participants' responses in the post-study interview also reported these strategies. For example, one participant commented about how "*On a paper document you have to explain first which page/section/line etc.*" and another seven participants described ways of indicating locations to others.

7. DISCUSSION

Having investigated the activity of co-reading, we built a system that provided a number of common annotation tools. To that familiar set, we added support for one aspect of collaborative reading – mutual navigation – in small, co-located groups. Subjective feedback, observational data, and logging of the participants' activity all suggested that the specific support of mutual navigation via the point-out tool was beneficial to the groups' reading. The adoption of point-outs *reduced the frequency and length of discussion about navigation dramatically*. The temporary, transient nature of point-outs was positively received, and participants appeared to select permanent or temporary place indicators with minimal distraction.

We have noted the importance of managing, or supporting, the user's attention during reading tasks (Section 2). Marshall has reflected that switching tasks (or tools) undermines reader attention to a text [20], and our work on individual reading concurs [28]. Our observations of real-world use suggested that this is also a key problem in collaborative reading. Mutual navigation was a specific issue (Section 3) that motivated our idea of the 'point-out'. When using BuddyBooks' collaborative tools, less discussion was needed for mutual navigation, and participants reported a lower level of interruption, compared to traditional paper. Using print caused repeated descriptions of the location of specific text in the document.

In the field work phase of our research, mutual navigation seemed to consume a lot of effort for work that was not central to the groups' task. The observations during the experiment, and participant responses both suggested that attention to reading was better supported when the secondary task of mutual navigation was reduced in complexity through the point-out tool. This in turn encourages more exclusive focus and a state of Flow [9] with the primary task of discussing the document.

Returning to the wider view of collaborative reading with which we started the paper, there are other circumstances in which collaborative reading occurs. For groups that read together at the same time, but in different locations, we believe that it is likely that support for mutual navigation will still be of value, and give similar benefits to groups reading in the same place. The common methods for supporting such groups at present are variations on teleconferencing. When using such technology, it is likely that the practices for mutual navigation will be similar, but identifying specific locations by physically pointing would be less effective when using remote cameras rather than being in the same room.

The case of reading at different times (asynchronously) seems to be a poorer fit for the point-out tool. Our field studies suggest that mutual navigation is tied to contemporaneous interaction, and traditional, enduring annotations may prove more effective when interactions are diffused across time. The design of effective support for reading at different times needs further primary field research to identify the frequency, operation and requirements of that work style. We set this topic aside in the the course of our own research, because of the challenges of data capture. If 'permanent' markers are more useful, then one caution is that Marshall [19] has noted the difficulty of an individual understanding their own mark-up from reading a text. One area, therefore, for initial research would be the interpretation of marks and comments in asynchronous reading.

In Section 2 we drew attention to earlier work that had touched on group reading. Our observational work produced a set of six behaviours within this context. A return to the existing literature allows us to further triangulate our results. Marshall et al. [21] noted the use of two different documents by individuals: an example of *parallel reading*. Furthermore, Marshall's recent return to the same material [20] identifies the difficulties of "shared focus" – a compound of our *localised synchronization*, *mutual navigation* and *negotiated interaction*. We can also identify instances of *localised synchronization* and *view competition* in our own previous data [7]. Our current work provides a more thorough underpinning of what appeared to be promising glimpses snatched during earlier research, and allows us to disentangle and separate phenomena that were previously conflated. Further work can separate and better define these different strands. One further point is that there will likely be different behaviours depending on whether many or no group members have previously read the document - an issue we have only reported briefly here.

The XLibris project identified the value of digital annotation, and provides the fundamental research on the interaction of reading upon which all subsequent work has been built [21]. In the years since, the focus of most research – including our own – has been on improving and developing on the touchstone of XLibris. Novel forms of annotation and placeholding have been rare: highlighting, notes and drawing have remained as constants ever since. BuddyBooks has added a new type of mark to this existing repertoire: a transient, shared placeholder that can be replayed at will, but relies on social context and user selection to be used.

We will now consider the impact of our work on a wider range of DL research, and the issues and factors that require further study.

7.1 Reading and Collaboration

In Section 4.2 we reviewed some of the existing literature on collaborative reading. We noted then the paucity of work on the topic. Recently, Golovchinsky, who played a major role in XLibris, has returned to the issue of reading, now including a greater collaboration with his new ARA tool [11]. Though that work is at an early stage, it demonstrates the timeliness of our own research.

One area where collaboration in the context of reading has been regularly researched is around the activity of annotation. An early example of this is the work of the DEBORA project [25], and this was followed a stream of increasingly mature and insightful work from Agosti and others [3, 16]. The technical infrastructure that underpins BuddyBooks bears a close relationship to the architectural elements of such research. However, our main emphasis is on the interactive properties of the system, rather than a complete system for a wide range of annotation. A common motivation for collaboration support, and associated features such as social filtering, is typically for remote users working together at different points in time – a stark contrast to our own interest on co-located, contemporary reading. Furthermore, the purpose of the point-out tool is to support transient information marking for navigation, or 'placeholding', rather than more permanent interpretative annotation [8].

The recent emergence of social tagging and social bookmarking sites has led to them taking a role in reading. Nelson et al. [24] investigated one such tool – SpartTag.us – in the context of group sense-making and reading. Like similar research, they investigated the impact of social markup on individual activity (specifically, learning), but did not pursue an understanding of group work within the wider community. In contrast, we focussed on groups that meet together. It would be intriguing to investigate how such groups would interact with wider social material and other teams in different locations, or who read at different times.

The social selection of books for book groups has also been addressed [27]. In this popular form of reading, book choice was also a social activity, including an extended range of friends and family. While this work addresses another part of the reading process, it serves to demonstrate the ubiquity of collaboration as a context for reading. The specifics of book groups seems to be a potential focus for understanding group reading in detail, and the interaction between book choosing and reading may be one valuable angle.

7.2 Collaborative Information Seeking

Information seeking is a major focus of research in digital libraries. Across the last decade, collaborative information seeking – particularly interactive retrieval – has received increasing attention from researchers [12], and is becoming an active and fertile field for research. However, it is premature to expect a substantial theorized understanding of collaborative information work in general, and so it is difficult to find appropriate material against which our findings can be directly compared.

Reddy and Jansen examine the reasons for moving from individual to collaborative information seeking. Tget suggest that lack of domain expertise plays a key role [30]. Our previous and current observations partially confirm this, with student reading groups seeming to form in a context of uncertainty. However, while understanding the motivation for group work tells us *why* collaboration occurs, it is less helpful in telling us *how* to provide good support.

In contrast, Golovchinsky et al. examine different group structures such as peer groups, novice/expert groups etc. [12]. This provides useful contextual categorisation to understand potential group dynamics, but does not directly provide guidance in terms of interaction design. Our focus on peer groups is a limitation to our work that can be addressed through adopting Golovchinsky's classification of group structure.

CoSearch [5] provides support for co-located collaborative search, and raises a number of issues in common with our task. The problems of varying reader pace, pointing and loose co-ordination all are indentified as key concerns. However, there are profound differences. For one, their use of pointers is a very close mirroring of traditional telepointers, albeit providing one per user. There is no provision for replay, in contrast with our point-outs. Furthermore, CoSearch emphasizes negotiated search sequences (a parallel to our negotiated navigation from Section 3.2), and annotation capture was through an emailed set of notes, due to the dynamic nature of web search content. As a result, an annotation is necessarily separated from the material it refers to.

7.3 CSCW and Placeholding

Another relevant domain is, of course Computer-Supported Collaborative Work (CSCW). We introduced telepointers in Section 4. Telepointers are a key technique to compare against our own approach. As we noted earlier, telepointers, are like the mouse position on a GUI interface, and cannot be replayed without external software support such as a screen recorder. Furthermore, telepointers are usually used in the context of remote working, and where displays are often shared by more than one person. In contrast, point-outs are readily replayed by individual users on their personal device after they occur.

7.4 Annotation and 'The Cloud'

The use of cloud–based storage to coordinate reading has recently been introduced commercially. The most common example is, perhaps, Apple's iBook application for the iPad. In iBooks, the bookmarks made by a user can be transferred via the cloud between different iPads registered as the same user. Our method here is similar in that we use "cloud" technology to coordinate bookmarks and annotations. However, we differ from Apple's technology in a number of ways. First, our cloud supports a collaborative, multi-user context, which is private to the group, while iBooks collates private, personal annotations to identify commonly annotated spans of text to *all* users, as well as the user's own personal bookmarks. Second, our "point-out" marks are transient and pinpoint specific locations in the text, and are specifically intended for group work, whereas iBook's "bookmarks" specify a whole *page* and are private only. In addition to point-outs, we do provide the classic bookmark and annotation tools that are offered both by iBooks and established DL annotations services such as DiLAS [4]. In other words, we offer a clear superset of existing annotation functionality, and support collaboration between a known group through reading tools specifically for group work. Furthermore, there is no current available information on the usability issues surrounding iBook's design. Had iBooks Cloud technology been available during this research, we would have been able to undertake such a comparison.

8. CONCLUSIONS & FUTURE WORK

The experience of shared reading remains a popular activity in many social and working environments. Some technological responses of this can be identified in popular devices. Systems like Amazon's Kindle support collaborative highlighting, but in rather modest way: there is no substantial communication between readers, and little shared critical engagement with the text. Some of the techniques provided – e.g., showing the popular parts of a text – have a limited semantic value. Arriving at a rigorous scientific understanding of collaborative reading would help us better critique our current approaches and identify new methods to enhance it.

We have reported an investigation into the practice of co-located, contemporary reading. We identified six practices that support this activity, and outlined some requirements of each. One practice – mutual navigation – was chosen as our initial focus, and we demonstrated the effectiveness of a novel interaction to support mutual navigation through a laboratory evaluation. Through this, we have shown both the need for tools to support co-reading, and the potential value that such tools can bring to social reading. The use of a device with a similar form factor to paper, and that allows users to sit near to each other has a great potential to open new shared interactions around reading.

As we noted at the start of this paper, we have focussed on one particular form of collaborative reading: at the same time, in the same place, among a group of peers. By adopting individual devices, we allowed for independent personal views of the document. There are a host of different styles and contexts of collaborative reading, and there is plentiful scope to embark on further research. One route would be to explore the tactical activities we observed. One intriguing topic we did not explore is the issue of parallel reading. While there are possible methods for supporting this already

[6], it is a need that is poorly understood even with individual reading, and the current work is limited in scope.

Alternatively, one could approach a different context, and address remote or asynchronous reading. While researching remote collaboration is challenging, it is a problem commonly faced by CSCW researchers. There seems ample scope for ambitious research to address this topic, and the growing use of digital reading devices would make an investigation highly timely.

9. ACKNOWLEDGEMENTS

We would like the participants of both our observational work and laboratory experiment for their generous gift of their time. This work was generously supported by Microsoft Research Lab Cambridge and EPSRC grants EP/F041217 and EP/G003971/1.

10. REFERENCES

[1] A. Adler, A. Gujar, B. L. Harrison, K. O'Hara, and A. Sellen. A Diary Study of Work-Related Reading: Design Implications for Digital Reading Devices. In *Proc. CHI '98*, pages 241–248. ACM, 1998.

[2] M. J. Adler and C. Doren. *How to Read a Book*. Simon and Schuster, 1972.

[3] M. Agosti, N. Ferro, I. Frommholz, and U. Thiel. Annotations in Digital Libraries and Collaboratories: Facets, Models and Usage. In *Procs. 8th European Conf, on Digital Libraries*, pages 244–255. Springer, 2004.

[4] M. Agosti, N. Ferro, E. Panizzi, and R. Trinchese. Annotation as a support to user interaction for content enhancement in digital libraries. In *AVI '06: Procs. Conf. on Advanced Visual Interfaces*, pages 151–154. ACM, 2006.

[5] S. Amershi and M. R. Morris. Cosearch: a system for co-located collaborative web search. In *Procs. ACM SIGCHI*, pages 1647–1656. ACM, 2008.

[6] G. Buchanan. Rapid document navigation for information triage support. In *Pros. ACM/IEEE Joint Conf. on Digital libraries*, JCDL '07, pages 503–503. ACM, 2007.

[7] G. Buchanan. The fused library: integrating digital and physical libraries with location-aware sensors. In *Proc. JCDL '10*, pages 273–282. ACM, 2010.

[8] G. Buchanan and J. Pearson. Improving placeholders in digital documents. In *Procs. European Conf. on Digital Libraries (ECDL)*, pages 1–12. Springer, 2008.

[9] M. Csikszentmihihalyi. *Flow: The Psychology of Optimal Experience*. Harper and Row, 1990.

[10] S. J. Cunningham and M. Jones. Autoethnography: a tool for practice and education. In *Procs. ACM SIGCHI New Zealand Int. Conf.*, pages 1–8, New York, NY, USA, 2005. ACM.

[11] G. Golovchinsky, S. Carter, and A. Dunnigan. Ara: the active reading application. In *Procs. 19th ACM Int. Conf. on Multimedia*, MM '11, pages 799–800. ACM, 2011.

[12] G. Golovchinsky, P. Quarfordt, and J. Pickens. Collaborative information seeking. *Computer*, 42(3):47–51, 2009.

[13] C. Gutwin, S. Greenberg, R. Blum, J. Dyck, K. Tee, and G. McEwan. Supporting informal collaboration in shared-workspace groupware. *Journal of Universal Computer Science*, 14(9):1411–1434, 2008.

[14] P. Isenberg and D. Fisher. Collaborative brushing and linking for co-located visual analytics of document collections. *Comput. Graph. Forum*, 28(3):1031–1038, 2009.

[15] R. Johansen. *GroupWare: Computer Support for Business Teams*. The Free Press, New York, NY, USA, 1988.

[16] J.-K. Kim, R. Farzan, and P. Brusilovsky. Social navigation and annotation for electronic books. In *BooksOnline '08: Procs. 2008 ACM Workshop on Research advances in large digital book repositories*, pages 25–28. ACM, 2008.

[17] J. Lauwers and K. Lantz. Collaboration awareness in support of collaboration transparency: requirements for the next generation of shared window systems. In *Proc. CHI '90*, pages 303–311. ACM, 1990.

[18] J. Liu, K. Sato, M. Nakashima, and T. Ito. Browseread picture books in a group on a digital table. In G. Buchanan, M. Masoodian, and S. Cunningham, editors, *Digital Libraries: Universal and Ubiquitous Access to Information*, volume 5362 of *LNCS*, pages 309–312. Springer, 2008.

[19] C. C. Marshall. Annotation: From Paper Books to the Digital Library. In *DL '97: Proceedings of the 2nd ACM International Conference on Digital libraries*, pages 131–140, New York, NY, USA, 1997. ACM.

[20] C. C. Marshall. *Reading and Writing the Electronic Book*. Synthesis Lectures on Information Concepts, Retrieval, and Services. Morgan & Claypool Publishers, 2009.

[21] C. C. Marshall, M. N. Price, G. Golovchinsky, and B. N. Schilit. Introducing a digital library reading appliance into a reading group. In *Proc. DL '99*, pages 77–84. ACM, 1999.

[22] M. R. Morris, A. J. B. Brush, and B. Meyers. Reading revisited: Evaluating the usability of digital display surfaces for active reading tasks. In *Tabletop*, pages 79–86, 2007.

[23] M. R. Morris, J. Lombardo, and D. Wigdor. Wesearch: supporting collaborative search and sensemaking on a tabletop display. In *Proc. ACM Conf. on Computer supported cooperative work*, pages 401–410. ACM, 2010.

[24] L. Nelson, C. Held, P. Pirolli, L. Hong, D. Schiano, and E. H. Chi. With a little help from my friends: examining the impact of social annotations in sensemaking tasks. In *Procs. ACM SIGCHI*, CHI '09, pages 1795–1798. ACM, 2009.

[25] D. M. Nichols, D. Pemberton, S. Dalhoumi, O. Larouk, C. Belisle, and M. Twidale. Debora: Developing an interface to support collaboration in a digital library. In *Procs. European Conf. on Digital Libraries*, pages 239–248. Springer, 2000.

[26] K. O'Hara and A. Sellen. A Comparison of Reading Paper and on-line Documents. In *Procs. SIGCHI Conf. on Human Factors in Computing Systems*, pages 335–342. ACM, 1997.

[27] K. Ooi and C. L. Liew. Selecting fiction as part of everyday life information seeking. *Journal of Documentation*, 67(5):748–772, 2011.

[28] J. Pearson, G. Buchanan, and H. Thimbleby. The reading desk: Applying physical interactions to digital documents. In *Procs. SIGCHI Conference on Human Factors in Computing Systems*, pages 3199–3202. ACM, 2011.

[29] H. Raffle, R. Ballagas, G. Revelle, H. Horii, S. Follmer, J. Go, E. Reardon, K. Mori, J. Kaye, and M. Spasojevic. Family story play: reading with young children (and elmo) over a distance. In *Proc. ACM SIGCHI Conf. '10*, pages 1583–1592. ACM, 2010.

[30] M. C. Reddy and B. J. Jansen. A model for understanding collaborative information behavior in context: A study of two healthcare teams. *Information Processing and Management*, 44(1):256–273, 2008.

[31] P. Tuddenham, I. Davies, and P. Robinson. Websurface: an interface for co-located collaborative information gathering. In *ITS '09: Procs. ACM Int. Conf. on Interactive Tabletops and Surfaces*, pages 181–188. ACM, 2009.

A Digital Library for Water Main Break Identification and Visualization

Sunshin Lee
Digital Library Research Laboratory
Department of Computer Science
Virginia Tech, Blacksburg, VA 24061
sslee777@vt.edu

Noha Elsherbiny
Digital Library Research Laboratory
Department of Computer Science
Virginia Tech, Blacksburg, VA 24061
noha@vt.edu

Edward A. Fox
Digital Library Research Laboratory
Department of Computer Science
Virginia Tech, Blacksburg, VA 24061
fox@vt.edu

ABSTRACT

This paper describes a prototype of a digital library for water main break identification and visualization. Many utilities rely on an emergency call to detect water main breaks, because breaks are difficult to predict. Collecting the information by call requires time consuming human effort. Furthermore, it is not archived and not shared with others. Collecting and archiving the information by tweets, news, and web resources helps users to identify relevant water main breaks efficiently. In developing this prototype, we extracted location information from text instead of using GPS data. We also describe the importance of tweet visualization by location, and how we visualize tweets on a map.

Categories and Subject Descriptors

H.3.7 [**Information Storage and Retrieval**]: Digital Libraries

General Terms

Management, Design

Keywords

Digital library, water main break, tweet, map, location

1. INTRODUCTION, RELATED WORK

The detection and archiving of water main breaks can be useful to utility workers, as well as researchers who analyze and design the infrastructure of cities and towns. There is no automated technique for the collection or identification of water-related events. Current collections are maintained by manual entry of events, which is cumbersome and requires extensive work.

We prototyped a digital library for water main break identification and visualization, which automatically collects data about water-related events from tweets, news, and other web sources; identifies the event location and time; locates each events on a map; and provides a notification system.

In related work, researchers have used Twitter as a human sensor [6]; others have used Twitter to classify text messages and to deliver relevant information to the appropriate personnel during the recovery from the Haiti Earthquake [3]. Another method for extracting detailed location information from tweets is studied in [4], and a different approach to extracting location information using USGS data has been presented in [5].

Section 2 describes our proposed digital library followed by its prototype development in Section 3.

2. PROPOSED DIGITAL LIBRARY

Figure 1. An outline of the digital library

Figure 1 shows an outline of the digital library for water main break identification and visualization. It involves a 3-step process: collecting data about water-related events, identifying key information about the event, and finally visualizing the information.

The digital library holds a collection of data about various water main breaks; this data is collected from tweets, news articles, and various web sources. Keywords such as "water main break" are used as search terms in yourTwapperKeeper [2], to capture water-related events. The data collected from these sources is cleaned up and stored in the digital library for the identification process.

The identification process involves extracting three main pieces of information about every water event: Where, When, and Who. Where has the event occurred? When did the event occur? Who reported it and any information related to it?

In order to identify *where* the event occurred, a Named Entity Recognizer can be used to identify location information. Identifying *when* an event occurred can be determined by searching for words or number combinations that identify a date or time. In order to identify *who* reported it, machine learning tools can be used. After the identification of where, when, and who, the event is stored in the digital library for visualization.

The visualization and dissemination of the information about a water-related event is an important feature of the digital library. The events are categorized by location and are visualized on Google Maps using Google Fusion Table and geocoding.

JCDL'12, June 10–14, 2012, Washington, DC, USA.
ACM 978-1-4503-1154-0/12/06.

In order to visualize relevant tweets within a specific time period, the "Time Window" concept can be applied. For example, "Most recent", "A week", "One month", "One year" or "5 years" time windows can be created to cover all recent and historical data.

The digital library also can be used to provide a notification system. Users can get information about water-related events that have occurred near them and may affect them. Notifications can be sent by email or directly to a smartphone.

Figure 1 shows the proposed DL; solid lines indicate parts completed in the prototype. In the collecting phase our prototype uses tweet messages, in the identification phase the location information is identified to answer "where", and in the visualization phase the events are plotted on maps.

3. PROTOTYPE

3.1 Collecting

To collect data from Twitter.com, *yourTwapperKeeper* is used, which is an open source tool for collecting tweets [2]. The program is installed on Red Hat Fedora 15 Linux, and a LAMP (Linux, Apache, MySQL and PHP) server was installed to provide a user interface to manage the program.

The tool collects tweets using a *Search API* and a *Stream API*, which are provided by Twitter.com. The *Search API* is used in the archiving process where the tweets that match certain keywords are retrieved and stored in the database. The archive is updated every 5 minutes, where the new relevant tweets are added using the *Stream API*, and the database is updated.

We have been collecting 17 different water-related events using keywords such as water main break, water pipe leak, sewage spill, etc. For our prototype, we selected the most appropriate dataset (keyword: water main break), that has less noise.

Table 1. A sample dataset

Dataset Keyword	Total tweets	# of tweets which have GPS information (percentage)
water main break	13382	156 (1.17%)
water pipe leak	967	1 (0.10%)

Table 1 shows that at most 1.17 percent of tweet messages have GPS location information (longitude, latitude); this is a very small percentage, justifying the need to use another method for location extraction along with the GPS location. All datasets were collected between 10/24/2011 and 1/30/2012.

3.2 Identification

In order to automatically extract location information from tweets, a Named Entity Recognizer (NER) is applied. It can identify people, organizations, and locations from a text. The Stanford NER [1] is a widely used implementation.

The twitter data needs to be cleaned before the location or other detailed information can be extracted from it. Removing special characters, such as '#' and '@', and removing URLs, help the SNER to find location information more accurately.

SNER extracts location information from each tweet message, and then it returns a set of geonames as location information. The selected dataset has 3333 tweets. Table 2 shows that we get 1,473 relevant tweets by extracting location information from text. In contrast, we only get 36 tweets using GPS data.

Table 2. A comparison of # of tweets between GPS data and extracted location data from text

Location information type	# of tweets
GPS data (longitude, latitude)	36 (1.08%)
Location information extracted from text	1,473 (44.19%)

3.3 Visualization

The categorization of tweets by location may facilitate the search for relevant information. For example, a Blacksburg utility worker usually monitors water main break events that occurr within the town of Blacksburg.

To visualize tweets on a map, locations (longitude, latitude) are required. Google Fusion Table, which enables gathering, visualizing, and sharing data online, provides a geo-coding function to visualize tweets according to Google Maps locations.

Figure 2 shows an example of the visualized tweets on a map of the New York area, USA. On the Google Maps, each dot represents a tweet event. When a dot is clicked, a pop-up displays a tweet message, location, and created time.

Figure 2. An example of the visualized tweets on Google Maps

4. ACKNOWLEDGEMENTS

This material is based upon work supported by the National Science Foundation under Grant No. IIS-0916733

5. REFERENCES

[1] The Stanford NLP group, Stanford NER, accessed Jan 2012 http://nlp.stanford.edu/software/CRF-NER.shtml

[2] Jobrieniii , yourTwapperKeeper, accessed Jan 2012 https://github.com/jobrieniii/yourTwapperKeeper.

[3] C. Caragea, M. McNeese, A. Jaiswal, G. Traylor, H. Kim, P. Mitra, D. Wu, A. Tapia, C. Giles, J. Jansen, and J. Yen. Classifying text messages for the Haiti earthquake. In *8th International Conference on Information Systems for Crisis Response and Management (ISCRAM)*, pages 1-10, Lisbon, Portugal, May 8-11, 2011.

[4] W. J. Corvey, S. Vieweg, T. Rood, and M. Palmer. Twitter in mass emergency: what NLP techniques can contribute. In *Proceedings of the NAACL HLT 2010 Workshop on Computational Linguistics in a World of Social Media*, WSA '10, pages 23–24, Stroudsburg, PA, USA, 2010.

[5] S. M. Paradesi. Geotagging tweets using their content. In *R. C. Murray and P. M. McCarthy, editors, FLAIRS Conference*. pages 355-356, AAAI Press, 2011.

[6] T. Sakaki, M. Okazaki, and Y. Matsuo. Earthquake shakes twitter users: real-time event detection by social sensors. In M. Rappa, P. Jones, J. Freire, and S. Chakrabarti, editors, WWW, pages 851–860. ACM, 2010

A Preliminary Analysis of FRBR's Bibliographic Relationships for Path Based Associative Rules

Ya-Ning Chen[1, 2,]
[1]Graduate Institute of Library and Information Studies, National Taiwan Normal University, Taipei 10610, Taiwan
arthur@gate.sincia.edu.tw

Hui-Pin Chen[2,]
[2]Computing Center
Academia Sinica
Taipei 11529, Taiwan
winefast@gate.sinica.edu.tw

Fei-Yen Tu[3]
[3]Research Center for Information Technology Innovation
Academia Sinica
Taipei11529, Taiwan
clairtu@iis.sinica.edu.tw

ABSTRACT
The Functional Requirements for Bibliographic Records (hereafter FRBR) has been adopted to address the relationships for bibliographic records and the related aggregate works. However, an approach to transform FRBR-based bibliographic relationships and their patterns into path-based rules for retrieval, navigation, display and data mining in the bibliographic space is still lacking. This study used the FRBR as a basis to analyze bibliographic relationships and their path-based rules. The novel "Harry Potter and the Philosopher's Stone" was used as a case study. Up until now, 87 unique records were retrieved from OCLC's Open WorldCat for analysis. Two specialists in library and information science familiar with FRBR conducted in-depth analysis to achieve inter-reliability agreement. This study generalizes several patterns of path-based rules for associating bibliographic records and outlines related issues for future study.

Categories and Subject Descriptors
H.3.7 [Information storage and retrieval]: Digital Libraries

General Terms
Documentation, Design, Standardization.

Keywords
FRBR, Bibliographic Relationship, Association Rule, WorldCat

1. INTRODUCTION
With the advancement and implementation of Functional Requirements for Bibliographic Records (hereafter FRBR) [4], the employment of FRBR's bibliographic relationships for aggregating related works in the digital library domain has become an issue. In the case study of OCLC's WorldCat [2] generalized works into elemental, simple and complex work, and complex works further categorized into augmented works, revised works, collected/selected works, multiple translation works, multiple forms of expression, and multiple translations, multiple forms of expression. Although the percentage of complex works in OCLC's WorldCat is small, they are significant in associating expressions, manifestations and items [2]. In other words, complex works can collocate related four FRBR Group-1 entities and their bibliographic records. In their study on alignment of MARC with FRBR, [1] also proposed an approach to analyze the bibliographic relationships for transforming MARC records into FRBR centric records. In practice, the concept of FRBR-based bibliographic relationships has been employed to aggregate related bibliographic records and their works. However, there is still no approach which transforms FRBR-based bibliographic relationships and their patterns into path-based rules for retrieval, navigation, display and data mining in the bibliographic space.

2. Methodology
The purpose of this study was to adopt FRBR as a basis to analyze bibliographic relationships for path-based rules on aggregating related bibliographic records. The "Harry Potter" series of novels was selected as a case study. This series of novels written by J.K. Rowling has been translated into different languages and published by different publishers around the world. Owing to their wide popularity, these novels have also been adapted into movies and distributed in different languages around the globe. In this study, the Harry Porter works were, therefore, regarded as target subject suitable for in-depth analysis.

In this preliminary study, only the first volume of Harry Potter published on 30 June 1997 by Bloomsbury in London was selected for analysis. "Harry Potter and the Philosopher's Stone" was used as a keyword query on Open WorldCat (http://www.worldcat.org/) to retrieve 483 bibliographic records in total as target subject between 15 November, 2011 and 12 January, 2012. The reason Open WorldCat was selected rather than FirstSearch WorldCat was because our study intended to examine how bibliographic relationships are beneficial to users by facilitating resource discovery to find relevant works. Due to the difficulty in identifying brief bibliographic information about some of the targeted records, book retail websites such as Amazon (http://www.amazon.com) and Barnes and Noble (http://www.barnesandnoble.com) were utilized for verification. In addition to book retail websites, IMDB (http://www.imdb.com/) and Wikipedia (http://www.wikipedia.org/) were used to get more detailed background information about the Harry Potter novel series. When contents of the targeted records were found in a language other than English, "Google Translate" was employed to translate the content into English for identification.

Up until now, 88 unique bibliographic WorldCat records for the first volume of the Harry Potter series were analyzed; one record was hard to be recognized in analysis, therefore, a total of 87 records were used in this preliminary study; 58 records belonged to the novel, and 29 were related to the movie. Key elements of the bibliographic records (Author, Publisher, Edition/Format, Summary, Genre/Form, Material Type, All Authors/Contributors, Notes, Description, Details, Other Titles, and Responsibility) were picked to identify the bibliographic relationships between works. Two library and information science specialists with an understanding of FRBR then performed the in-depth analysis. If there was any difference in scoring, a meeting was convened to discuss and achieve agreement for inter-rater reliability. In order

JCDL'12, June 10-14, 2012, Washington, DC, USA.
ACM 978-1-4503-1154-0/12/06.

to delineate the bibliographic relationships clearly, this study adopted the RDF data model. Based on expression in the RDF data model, it was also useful to generalize the path-based patterns for bibliographic relationships and then transform them into a semantic web representation.

3. Findings

The English novel "Harry Potter and the Philosopher's Stone" has basic type FRBR bibliographic relationships, one Work to one Expression and Manifestation. The path can be described as "W1→E1→M1". Other relationship types were derived from this basic type. This study proposes five types of bibliographic relationships for "Harry Potter and the Philosopher's Stone" as follows:

- Translated Versions: the original English version has been translated into different languages and published by various publishers in different countries. Paths for this pattern can be described as: W1→E1→E2-4→M2-4.
- Adapted and Translated Versions: the original English version has been adapted into an American version, and then the American version has been translated into different languages by various publishers. Paths for this pattern can be described as: W1→E1→E2→M2, and W1→E1→E2→E5-7 →M5-7.
- Reproduction Manifestations: the original English version has been reprinted or re-published by various publishers at different times. The path can be described as follows: W1→ E1→M1→M1.1-1.2.
- Binding Manifestations: existing manifestations of original English works from volume 1 to 7 have been bounded as a set of series by publishers. Sometimes the binding volume ranges from 3 to 5. The result of this type echoes the finding of [3][5]. It means that one manifestation has more than two works and is contradictory to FRBR's definition. The path can be illustrated as follows: W1-7→E1-7→M8.
- Adapted Works and Alternative Format Manifestations: in addition to computer games, learning materials and illustrations, Movies (i.e., W1→W2→EM1) are the most popular derivations for original English work. The film can be manifested into various formats such as 32mm film, VCD, DVD and blue ray disc (i.e., MM1-4), and further subtitle texts and language tracks can be translated into different languages, such as French, Germany, and Chinese (i.e., EL1-4).This type is consistent with result of [5]. The path can be described as: W1→W2→EM1→MM1-4, and W1→W2→EM1→EL1-4→MM5-8.

In additional to all of six types of bibliographic relationships can be used to aggregate related bibliographic records and their works, they can be turned into path-based associative rules for semantic query. Take the "reproduction manifestations" path-based type as example. In terms of RDF data model, each entity of path (e.g., W1), the relationship (i.e., object property) between entities, and data properties of each entity can be defined in the following:

- Each entity is regarded as class.
- Relationships between M1 and M1.1-1.2 classes can be defined as "has a reproduction".
- Data properties for M1.1 can be further labeled as reprinted by Bloomsbury in 2011in London, and M1.2 can be labeled as re-published by Petersen in 2000 in Hamburg of German.

According to the above definition, user can perform semantic queries as follows: Apart from the original English version published by Bloomsbury, how many manifestations have been reprinted by Bloomsbury and when? How many manifestations have been published by other publishers, rather than Bloomsbury? Furthermore, each relationship between classes can be indexed, queries and navigated by ontology editing tools (e.g., Protégé).

4. Conclusion and Future Work

Although this study has generalized various paths and their patterns for the bibliographic relationships of "Harry Potter and the Philosopher's Stone", some tasks still remain for the future. First, these paths and their semantic relationships must be transformed into RDF triples with ontology editing tools (e.g., Protégé) for completion of RDFization. Next, fields and their MARC's tags of corresponding bibliographic records must be verified for the above paths as a matching basis to build up path-based rules for distinguishing and associating records automatically. Finally, in the future we will select a classic or popular Chinese work as subject to conduct a similar analysis for comparing English and Chinese works, and examining the feasibility of the proposed paths and their patterns.

5. ACKNOWLEDGMENTS

We are grateful for the helpful comments of the reviewers. The work described in this paper was partially supported by the Taiwan E-learning and Digital Archives Program (TELDAP) sponsored by the National Science Council of Taiwan under NSC Grants: NSC 101-2631-H-001-005, 101-2631-H-001-006, & 101-2631-H-001-014.

6. REFERENCES

[1] Aalberg, T., Merčun, T., & Žumer, M. 2011.Coding FRBR-structured bibliographic information in MARC. Lecture Notes in Computer Science, 7008(2011), 128-137.

[2] Bennett, R., Lavoie, B.F., & O'Neill, E.T. 2003. The concept of a work in WorldCat: An application of FRBR. Library Collections, Acquisition, & Technical Service, 27, 1(2003), 45-59.

[3] Buchanan, G., Gow, J., & Rimmer, J. 2007. Representing aggregate works in the digital library. In Proceedings of the 7th ACM/IEEE-CS Joint Conference on Digital Libraries(pp. 247-256).

[4] FRBR. 1998. Functional requirements for bibliographic records: Final report. München: KG Saur.

[5] O'Neill, E., Cato, A., Murtomaa, E., Tillett, B., Thurston, P., & Žumer, M. 2011. Final report of the Working Group on aggregates. 1 April 2012, from http://www.ifla.org/files/cataloguing/frbrrg/AggregatesFinalReport.pdf

A Qualitative Analysis of Information Dissemination through Twitter in a Digital Library

Hae Min Kim
College of Information Science and Technology
Drexel University
3141 Chestnut Street, Philadelphia, PA 19104
haemin.kim@drexel.edu

Christopher C. Yang
College of Information Science and Technology
Drexel University
3141 Chestnut Street, Philadelphia, PA 19104
chris.yang@drexel.edu

Eileen G. Abels
College of Information Science and Technology
Drexel University
3141 Chestnut Street, Philadelphia, PA 19104
eabels@drexel.edu

Mi Zhang
College of Information Science and Technology
Drexel University
3141 Chestnut Street, Philadelphia, PA 19104
mi.zhang@drexel.edu

ABSTRACT
This study examines the use of Twitter in a digital library, the Internet Public Library (ipl2), to understand the content and dissemination patterns of Twitter messages posted by the ipl2. We conducted a content analysis on ipl2's messages on Twitter to develop a categorization of the type of tweets, and examined retweets and the active users who retweeted ipl2 tweets. We present our analysis of four areas related to the tweets: motivation, content, audience, and sources. Active users are categorized into eight groups. The research findings contribute to a further understanding of the actual use of Twitter in a digital library.

Categories and Subject Descriptors
H3.5 [**Online Information Services**]: Web-based services

General Terms
Management, Measurement, Performance

Keywords
Twitter, microblogging, ipl2, digital library, retweet, information dissemination

1. INTRODUCTION
Twitter is a social networking and micro-blogging service that allows registered users to post 140-character messages and to follow others' updates without confirmation. Messages, called tweets, are searchable and can be posted through various routes and devices, and users can relay any tweets to share them with their followers. Through these features, Twitter emerged as an information network having the power of information dissemination.

Many libraries have established Twitter accounts, mostly since 2009 [12], and have tried to find possible ways to use Twitter as an effective medium for their users. Libraries have posted tweets primarily as a means of outreach to their users. Previous studies focused on the growing need to use Twitter and categories of tweets posted by academic and public libraries [1, 7, 9, 11]. However, little research has been conducted to analyze tweets and retweet activities of digital libraries from multiple perspectives. We address this gap by analyzing data from the ipl2's Twitter account as a case study.

This study presents a content analysis of ipl2[1]'s Twitter usage to determine the categories of messages and to explore how those messages are disseminated through Twitter. Our research questions are:

1) What categories of information does the ipl2 share through Twitter?
2) What type of information are disseminated and by whom?

The results will contribute to understanding how one digital library has embraced Twitter, and what kind of information is distributed. These findings may help other digital libraries study their use of Twitter and to identify and implement the appropriate uses of Twitter.

2. METHODOLOGY
2.1 Data Collection
The ipl2, hosted by the iSchool at Drexel University since 2007, opened a Twitter account on July 29, 2010. The ipl2 Twitter account is run primarily by volunteers, including students in library and information science (LIS) programs and ipl2 staff; there is no staff designated to post on Twitter. Between July 29, 2009 and September 30, 2011, the ipl2 had posted 463 tweets, and has more than 1,000 followers who receive tweets posted by the ipl2.

We collected data from the ipl2's public timeline [2] on Twitter.com. Among 463 tweets, we deleted redundant tweets and 455 total tweets were used for the content analysis. The data contains tweets, user IDs, dates, numbers of retweet, and the user IDs of those who retweeted.

Retweet data for the 455 tweets were collected from December 1 through 5, 2011. One hundred twenty-eight ipl2 tweets were retweeted. These were retweeted 217 times; 113 users retweeted tweets. We collected those users' public profiles on their Twitter accounts to analyze their characteristics and categorize them by groups. Most users contained profiles; four users who didn't have any information on their profiles were assigned to "other" group.

JCDL'12, June 10–14, 2012, Washington, DC, USA.
ACM 978-1-4503-1154-0/12/06.

[1] http://ipl.org

[2] https://twitter.com/#!/theipl

2.2 Data Analysis

The data set of 455 tweets was coded using an open coding process [11]. First, we generated initial concepts by analyzing 100 randomly selected tweets, and found different aspects needed to be analyzed. Second, we organized those aspects into four themes: motivation, content, audience, and source domains. *Motivation* explains why the ipl2 posted a tweet; *content* describes the "aboutness" of a tweet; *audience* defines who the target users of a tweet are; and *source* identifies links provided within a tweet for further information. Third, we extracted categories for each theme as they emerged and also referred to related studies [1, 3, 4, 5, 8, 9, 11]; seven categories emerged for motivation, ten for content, seven for audience, and seven for source.

The categories for the 455 tweets were assigned manually by the first author. Multiple codes were allowed for motivation and audience as needed. A coding manual was developed for use by a second coder to analyze the same data set. Using Cohen's kappa to measure inter-coder reliability, there was 78.6% agreement for motivation, 85.5% for content, 88.4% for audience, and 99.5% for source domain. Discrepancies were discussed, and codes were revised yielding a final coding result.

We used retweet data to analyze information dissemination, based on the assumption that retweets indicate users' common interests and yield information flow to their followers [13]. We borrowed the concept of 'audience activity' from the communication research area [2, 6], and considered 'using' status after exposure to communication as 'retweeting' of tweets which they read and shared with their followers. We defined 'active users' as any user who retweeted at least one ipl2 tweet. After filtering, there were 113 active users in our sample, who revealed the characteristics of diffusing the ipl2's information. Based on user public profiles information, we categorized active users into 8 groups according to institutions or individuals, and their roles and jobs: Librarians, Libraries, LIS students, Professional associations, Other professionals, Educators, Publishers, and Others.

3. RESULTS AND DISCUSSION

The analysis revealed that the ipl2 utilized Twitter to share various types of information, including information about their own services, for members of the general public and for librarians with ipl2-generated resources. As the ipl2's mission is to provide learning experiences for LIS students, research forums for professionals, to serve the public with authoritative digital collections, and to provide a question answering service [5], the study result indicated that Twitter was used to achieve the goal of the ipl2. It is an information channel in itself by providing a variety of topics, and not a peripheral library service.

The division of tweet categories into four topics improves our understanding of the characteristics of tweets which is hard to achieve by analyzing tweets based on only one aspect or mixed categories. There are tweets which cannot be explained by one category; for instance, tweets asking followers for their opinions about a new IT device with a link to ipl2's web blog, and providing children's book information with an external link to guidance for parents. The most prevalent categories are 'Providing information' (42.4%) for motivation; 'ipl2' (27.5%) for content; 'General audience' (57.1%) and 'No source' (29.5%).

Active users relayed tweets to their followers by retweeting. We found that the most active retweeting group was 'Librarians' (34.5%). 'Library' (16.8%) and 'LIS student' (15.0%) were also active retweeters showing that these three specific groups played a key role in the dissemination of ipl2's information on the Twitter network.

4. CONCLUSION

The ipl2 provides information through Twitter, and some of that information is disseminated on the Twitter network. To understand the phenomenon, this study conducted a qualitative analysis of Twitter data by analyzing characteristics of information posted by the ipl2 and examining groups of active users who disseminated information.

We will proceed with a more detailed interpretation of the results to reveal cross relations among categories of the four themes, what type of tweets are retweeted, and associations between audience categories and active user groups.

5. REFERENCES

[1] Aharony, N. 2011. Twitter use in libraries: an exploratory analysis. *Journal of Web Librarianship*. 4, 4, 333-350.

[2] Cha, M., Haddadi, H., Benevenuto, F., and Gummadi, K. P. 2010. Measuring user influence in Twitter: the million follower fallacy. In *Proceedings of 4th International Conference on Weblogs and Social Media*. (Washington, USA, 2010). AAAI Press, Menlo Park, California, 10-17.

[3] Dann, S. 2010. Twitter content classification. *First Monday*, 15 (Dec. 2010).

[4] Honeycutt, C., and Herring, S. C. 2009. Beyond microblogging: conversation and collaboration via Twitter. In *Proceedings of the 42th Hawai'i International Conference on System Sciences*. Los Alamitos, CA: IEEE Press.

[5] Ipl2, The Mission and Vision Statements of ipl2. 2008. Retrieved Jan 10, 2011, from ipl2: http://ipl2.org/div/about/mission_and_vision.html

[6] Java, A., Song, X., Finin, T., and Tseng, B. 2007. Why we Twitter: understanding microblogging usage and communities. In *Proceedings of the 9th WEBKDD and 1st SNA-KDD Workshop on Web Mining and Social Network Analysis*, 56–65.

[7] Levy, M. R., and Windahl, S. 1984. Audience activity and gratifications: a conceptual clarification and exploration. *Communication Research*. 11, 1, 51-78.

[8] Milstein, S. 2009. Twitter for libraries (and librarians). *Computers in Libraries*. 29, 5, 17-18.

[9] Naaman, B., Boase, J., and Lai, C.-H. 2010. Is it really about me? Message content in social awareness streams. In *Proceedings of the 2010 ACM conference on CSCW*, Feb 6–10, 2010, Savannah, Georgia.

[10] Phillips, N. K. 2011. Academic library use of Facebook: building relationships with students. *The journal of Academic Librarianship*. 37, 6, 512-522.

[11] Strauss, A., and Corbin, J. 1998. *Basics of qualitative research techniques and procedures for developing grounded theory*. Sage Publications, London.

[12] Stuart, D. 2010. What are libraries doing on Twitter?. *Online*, Jan/Feb, 45-47.

[13] Suh, B., Hong, L., Pirolli, P., and Chi, E. H. 2010. Want to be retweeted? Large scale analytics on factors impacting retweet in Twitter network. In Proceedings of 2nd *IEEE International Conference on Social Computing*, Aug 20-22, 2010, Minneapolis, MN. Los Alamitos CA, 177-184.

A Study of Automation from Seed URL Generation to Focused Web Archive Development: The CTRnet Context

Seungwon Yang, Kiran Chitturi, Gregory Wilson, Mohamed Magdy Gharib Farag, and Edward A. Fox

Digital Library Research Laboratory
Department of Computer Science, Virginia Tech
114 McBryde Hall, Blacksburg, VA 24061, U.S.A
+1-540-231-6256
{seungwon, kiranch, mrwilson, mmagdy, fox}@vt.edu

ABSTRACT
In the event of emergencies and disasters, massive amounts of web resources are generated and shared. Due to the rapidly changing nature of those resources, it is important to start archiving them as soon as a disaster occurs. This led us to develop a prototype system for constructing archives with minimum human intervention using the seed URLs extracted from tweet collections. We present the details of our prototype system. We applied it to five tweet collections that had been developed in advance, for evaluation. We also identify five categories of non-relevant files and conclude with a discussion of findings from the evaluation.

Categories and Subject Descriptors
H.3.7 [**Information Storage and Retrieval**]: Digital Libraries – *Collections*.

Keywords
Archiving, crawling, Crisis Tragedy and Recovery Network, digital library, seed URL generation, tweet.

1. INTRODUCTION
The Crisis, Tragedy, and Recovery Network project (www.ctrnet.net) group has been archiving various disaster-related webpages and tweets in collaboration with the Internet Archive [1]. The scope of the archives spans from the U.S. to international disaster events both in the natural (e.g., earthquakes, floods, hurricanes, volcanic eruptions) and man-made (e.g., shootings, transportation crashes, terrorism, political turmoil) disaster domains.

The usual steps to develop an archive of webpages are:

1. Prepare a list of seed URLs to crawl data from
2. Provide those seed URLs to the Heritrix crawler [2]
3. Fetch the webpages (e.g., HTML, image on the page) and store them as compressed files (i.e., in WARC format)
4. Extract textual resources from the compressed files
5. Index extracted resources for search/browse services

The procedure above requires much human labor and time, especially for steps 1, 2, and 4. Also it is difficult for a human archivist to keep up with the speed of newly generated webpages in the events of massive scale disasters such as the Japan Earthquake of 2011.

This study presents our approach to further automate the steps above. Section 2 describes related studies. Following are details of our prototype system, in Section 3. Section 4 explains an evaluation of our approach. Conclusions and future plans are discussed in Section 5.

2. RELATED STUDIES
The LiWA project aims to provide a framework for building archives appearing identical to the online version [5]. Two application scenarios are supported. One is the Streaming Archive application, which preserves audio and video Web information. The other is the Social Web application that captures the dynamics of user interactions in the social web. Similar to LiWA, our goal is to develop archives of textual documents in an efficient manner using automation, which allows us to construct archives for massive scale disasters.

Kandylas and Dasdan discuss that search engine researchers are becoming more interested in adding Twitter posts to their search results [6]. The main problem with tweets is assessing quality. The authors discuss the characteristics of the shortened URLs in the post, showing that most URLs fall into two categories: high quality or spam. We attempt to overcome the URL quality issues through our planned integration of a component for document filtering. Hughes and Palen show how the URLs in tweets play an important role in emergency events as a Web information broker and a means for distributing information resources on the Web [7]. Their study presents why it is important to use URLs found in tweets as seeds for crawls, and also shows the need for automation because there is a higher percentage of URLs in tweets during emergency events.

3. PROTOTYPE SYSTEM

3.1 System Components
Figure 1 shows components of the prototype system and the data used as inputs and outputs.

- Input data comes from (1) Tweet Archive DB, built from [3].
- URL Extractor (A) periodically identifies URLs embedded in tweets from (1) and stores them into Extracted URL DB (2).
- The Heritrix crawler (B) visits each URL in (2) and retrieves webpages.
- Crawled data are stored in Web ARChive (WARC) (3) format.

JCDL'12, June 10–14, 2012, Washington, DC, USA.
ACM 978-1-4503-1154-0/12/06.

- Data Extractor (C) retrieves resource types such as HTML pages, PDFs, images, etc. (4) from multiple WARC files.

(A) and (C) have been implemented using Python. We used an open source version of Heritrix for (B). Current prototyping has integrated all the components in the Django framework [4] except for (A). We soon will have it connected to the UI.

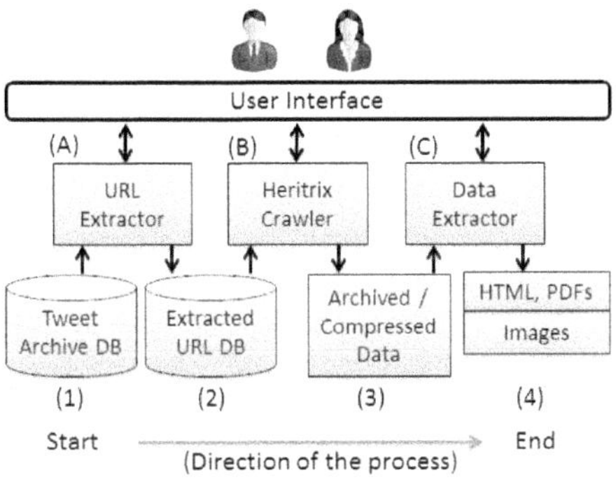

Figure 1. An overview of the prototype system. (A)-(C) are processing components. (1)-(4) are components for the produced data and its management.

3.2 UI Design and Using the System

Figure 2 presents a list of Extracted URL DB tables, each of which contains seed URLs from its corresponding Tweet Archive DB table. Users identify an archive ID of interest in the Database List tab. Then they start URL extraction at the URL Extractor tab.

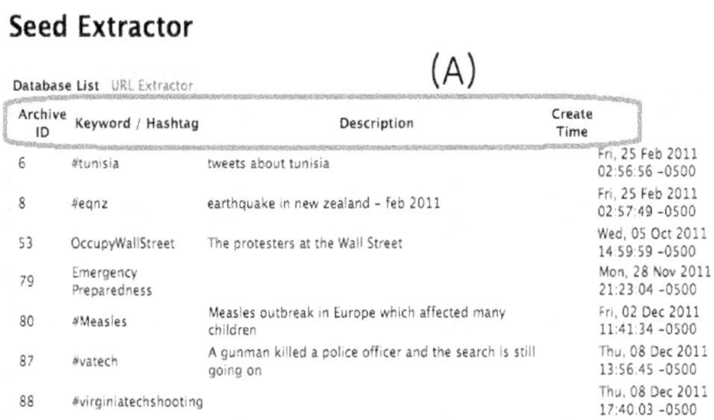

Figure 2. A list of Extracted URL DB tables with keywords, hashtags, descriptions, and the creation times of the original tweet archives.

4. EVALUATION

4.1 Analysis for Relevance

Table 1 presents five tweet archives that we selected for this study. The number of HTML files extracted was less than the number of seed URLs for all the archives, since in some cases the website's robots.txt policy blocked the site from being crawled. The archive, *Cagayan de oro*, named after one of the typhoon-hit cities in Philippines, had a low precision of 31.2%. We used the keyword 'cagayan de oro' as a keyword to collect tweets. As a result, many tweets about travel, job advertisements, and other issues in the city of Cagayan De Oro also were captured, and their URLs were extracted for crawling. However, due to the use of 'violence' along with 'South Sudan', we had theobserved a high precision of 84.0% in the *Violence South Sudan* archive.

Table 1. Details of the tweet archives used in the analysis. The highest and lowest precision scores are marked gray.

Keywords, Hashtags	Tweets	Seed URLs	HTML files	Precision (%)
#virginiatech shooting	456	149	43	48.8
#measles	761	174	155	54.4
Cagayan de oro	1,132	262	237	31.2
Violence South Sudan	1,118	434	431	84.0
Emergency preparedness	7,427	641	386	41.2

4.2 Analysis for Non-Relevant Content

We also classified the non-relevant HTML pages into five categories: too short; empty-error pages; non-English pages; blocked pages; and off-topic. Detailed results will be presented on our poster.

5. CONCLUSION AND FUTURE PLANS

We presented how our prototype system integrated multiple components, and showed how these components work together to construct archives with minimal human intervention. Prototype capabilities were clarified as we applied it to five selected tweet archives. To ensure high quality in the archives, a de-duplication process, which is based on a content comparison instead of a URL strings comparison, is necessary. Another necessity is a sophisticated filtering component. Updating the UI and fine-tuning of the parameters in the Heritrix configuration file are planned, too.

6. ACKNOWLEDGMENTS

We thank NSF for support (IIS-0916733) and the Internet Archive for collaboration. Thanks also go to the CTRnet project team and the members of the DLRL for their feedback.

7. REFERENCES

[1] The Internet Archive. URL http://www.archive.org accessed Jan. 21, 2012.

[2] The open source Heritrix crawler from the Internet Archive at https://webarchive.jira.com/wiki/display/Heritrix/Heritrix accessed Jan. 21, 2012.

[3] yourTwapperKeeper, an open source tweet collection tool at https://github.com/jobrieniii/yourTwapperKeeper accessed Jan. 21, 2012.

[4] Django Web Framework at https://www.djangoproject.com/ accessed Jan. 21, 2012.

[5] T. Risse, J. Masanes, A. A. Benczur, and M. Spaniol, "Turning pure Web Page Storages into Living Web Archives," in "Proc. Cultural Heritage on line. Empowering users: an active role for user communities," Florence, Italy, pp. 151-155, Dec. 15-16, 2009.

[6] V. Kandylas and A. Dasdan, "The utility of tweeted URLs for web search," in Proceedings of the 19th international conference on World Wide Web, Raleigh, North Carolina, USA, 2010, 1127-1128.

[7] A. L. Hughes and L. Palen, "Twitter adoption and use in mass convergence and emergency events," International Journal of Emergency Management, vol. 6, pp. 248-260, 2009.

A System for Indexing Tables, Algorithms and Figures

Pradeep Teregowda
Computer Science and Engineering
The Pennsylvania State University
University Park, PA 16802
pbt105@cse.psu.edu

Madian Khabsa
Computer Science and Engineering
The Pennsylvania State University
University Park, PA 16802
mkhabsa@psu.edu

C. Lee Giles
Information Sciences and Technology
The Pennsylvania State University
University Park, PA 16802
giles@ist.psu.edu

ABSTRACT

Indexing objects such as documents, figures, tables and algorithms in a single system presents challenges in schema mapping, detecting overlapping objects in documents, presenting results from such an system to users. We propose a federated approach to indexing and retrieving such objects in academic papers.

Categories and Subject Descriptors

H.3.3 [**Information Search and Retrieval**]: Retrieval models; H.3.1 [**Content Analysis and Indexing**]: Indexing methods

Keywords

Indexing, Embedded Objects, Information Retrieval Systems

1. INTRODUCTION

Objects embedded in academic documents such as figures, tables, equations and algorithms provide valuable metadata in the form of results, data, pseudocode and relationships. Extraction and indexing of such objects has been studied in the context of [4] and algorithms [1]. In these cases, the indexing and ranking are specific to particular objects and features specific to the objects. CiteSeer^x [6] [1] provides an example, allowing search for such objects using multiple independent indices and interfaces.

Such an approach is highly inefficient to the user, and information relevant to a particular topic could be distributed across several indices. Many approaches to solving this exist and have been studied as problems of diversity in retrieving documents [5] and subtopic retrieval [7]. We propose a system built by indexing diverse objects obtained from academic documents into a single index which can be queried by the user. The interactive query interface enables users to drill down into particular object types.

2. PROPOSED SYSTEM

The architecture of the proposed system is show in Figure 1. It includes extractors, overlap detection coupled with an index and an user interface.

[1]`http://citeseerx.ist.psu.edu`

JCDL'12, June 10–14, 2012, Washington, DC, USA.
ACM 978-1-4503-1154-0/12/06.

Figure 1: System Architecture

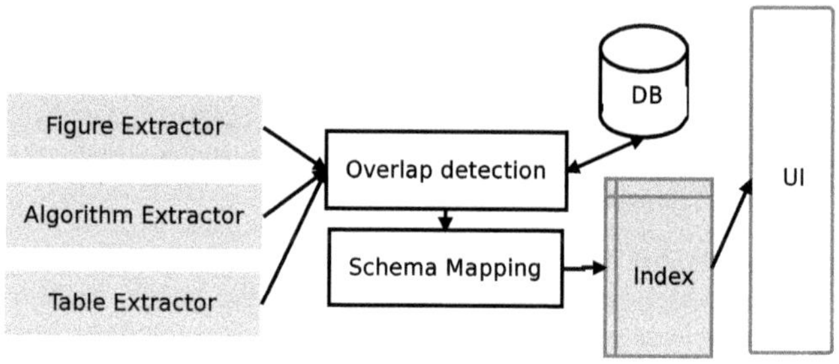

We utilized previously existing extractors for tables [4] and algorithms [1]. For figure mention extraction we built a extractor using PDFBox with a rule based system (derived from a CART model). We link objects to documents utilizing a checksum or a processing id. The metadata available from these extractors are shown in table 1. We choose document metadata (title, citations, id), object type and the most common elements (in bold in table 1) for indexing. In case of missing fields, equivalent fields were identified for the object type. Objects extracted from a document might be labeled as algorithms and as figures or tables. We built a detection system for detecting such overlaps with noisy metadata using near duplicate detection methods. It uses a similarity measure for object content of two objects, selected by blocking using document id and object id.

Empirically, utilizing a threshold of 0.66 for similarity with the Jaccard similarity measure for captions produced good results.

3. INDEXING AND RANKING

In comparison to building individual index and customized ranking for each object, building a single index is more complex. One of the prominent challenges, is to infer the object type from an user query to effectively satisfy user needs. In this context we identify the relevant object type for queries by utilizing existing query logs and keywords relevant to particular object types and finally the object content itself [3, 2].

We make use of Apache Solr [2] an open source search server, for indexing objects. Using citation based ranking methods is the probably the first choice such a method would not be able to rank all objects due to limitations in the ci-

[2]`http://lucene.apache.org/solr/`

Field	Tables	Figures	Algorithms
Page number	×	×	×
Caption	×	×	×
Contents	×		
Footnote	×		
Reference text	×	×	×

Table 1: Object Schema

tation graph coverage. For example only 32% of the documents in the collection are cited in CiteSeer^x.

Instead we modify user queries by adding weights to queries based on identified keywords. Keywords for boosting for indexing tables were were obtained after cleaning the existing table index in CiteSeer^x. In the case of algorithms, we made use of keywords extracted from a list of algorithms from Wikipedia and text books on data structures and algorithms.

For cases where a keyword occurs in both lists of previous query terms from logs and keywords, we weight both object types equally.

4. RETRIEVAL

A query submitted to the user interface is processed by the application to identify keywords, the query is then weighed and submitted to the index. Results returned are displayed in the web interface. The interface allows users to view results from each object type by selecting the object type tab. Each search result includes the caption, reference text and document title. The particular document page on which the embedded object is placed can be viewed by clicking on the search result. The query interface allows the user to choose whether to make use of the query weighing by the application.

Figure 2: User Search Interface

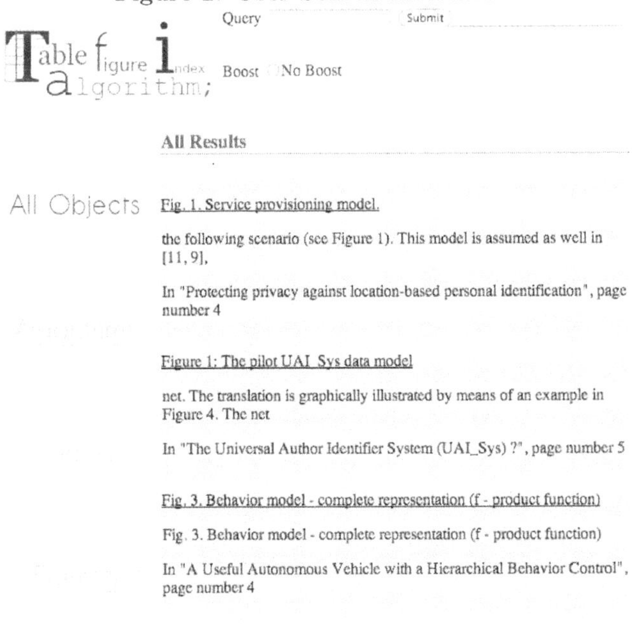

4.1 Evaluation

A set of 32 queries consisting of common computer science keywords and phrases were utilized to evaluate the retrieval system built with 5076 objects (1274 algorithms, 1746 tables, 2056 figures). The distributed cumulative gain metric was used for each query, with a resulting combination. Weighing maintained or improved the quality of results obtained for 90.32% of the queries with significant improvement for 19.35% of queries.

5. CONCLUSIONS

We briefly discussed the implementation of a system for indexing multiple embedded object types within a single index. We adopt a common schema, overlap detection and query weighing mechanisms to satisfy user information needs.

The implementation discussed in this article provides a good starting point for further research and development. We hope that this inspires a more detailed and extensive effort to indexing and retrieving diverse objects and an implementation as a stand alone system or part of other digital library systems such as SeerSuite.

6. ACKNOWLEDGMENTS

We would like to acknowledge Anurag Acharya and Pucktada Treeratpituk for useful suggestions.

7. REFERENCES

[1] S. Bhatia, P. Mitra, and C. L. Giles. Finding algorithms in scientific articles. In *WWW*, pages 1061–1062, 2010.

[2] R. Bodner and F. Song. Knowledge-based approaches to query expansion in information retrieval. *Advances in Artifical Intelligence*, pages 146–158, 1996.

[3] H. Cui, J. Wen, J. Nie, and W. Ma. Probabilistic query expansion using query logs. In *WWW*, pages 325–332. ACM, 2002.

[4] Y. Liu, K. Bai, P. Mitra, and C. Giles. Tableseer: automatic table metadata extraction and searching in digital libraries. In *JCDL*, pages 91–100. ACM, 2007.

[5] R. Santos and I. Ounis. Diversifying for multiple information needs. In *ECIR, DDR Workshop*, pages 37–41, 2011.

[6] P. Teregowda, I. Councill, R. Fernández, M. Khabsa, S. Zheng, and C. Giles. Seersuite: Developing a scalable and reliable application framework for building digital libraries by crawling the web. In *USENIX WebApps*. USENIX Association, 2010.

[7] C. Zhai, W. Cohen, and J. Lafferty. Beyond independent relevance: methods and evaluation metrics for subtopic retrieval. In *ACM SIGIR*, pages 10–17. ACM, 2003.

A Technique for Suggesting Related Wikipedia Articles using Link Analysis

Christopher Markson
New Jersey Institute of Technology
University Heights
Newark, NJ 07102
crm23@njit.edu

Min Song
New Jersey Institute of Technology
University Heights
Newark, NJ 07102
min.song@njit.edu

ABSTRACT

With more than 3.7 million articles, Wikipedia has become an important social medium for sharing knowledge. However, with this enormous repository of information, it can often be difficult to locate fundamental topics that support lower-level articles. By exploiting the information stored in the links between articles, we propose that related companion articles can be automatically generated to help further the reader's understanding of a given topic. This approach to a recommendation system uses tested link analysis techniques to present users with a clear path to related high-level articles, furthering the understanding of low-level topics.

Categories and Subject Descriptors

H.0 [Information Systems]: General

Keywords

Link Analysis, Recommendation System, Social Media Mining, Wikipedia

1. INTRODUCTION

Wikipedia has continued to grow as an important source of information in both the formal and informal learning environment [4]. However, the mass collection of information stored in Wikipedia does not present a clear path to readers looking to use the database as an educational tool. Also, the crowdsourcing model of Wikipedia's articles does not allow for intelligent assignment of categories within each page. We propose that recommended related articles can be automatically generated using link analysis techniques.

The collaboration of experts authoring Wikipedia articles narrowly focuses topic contribution to a detailed level. Similarly, these experts are the users responsible for electing category assignments for each article submission. Because of the detailed focus of each expert author, many articles have uninformative categories assignments. This presents a clear problem for users navigating the site seeking a direct path to articles higher in the hierarchical tree of topics.

To address the aforementioned issue, this paper proposes a new approach to generating category information for articles using the inter-article connections manually generated by authors when providing keyword links. Preliminary experimental results indicate that this approach successfully recommends related articles using this technique.

JCDL'12, June 10–14, 2012, Washington, DC, USA.
ACM 978-1-4503-1154-0/12/06.

2. RECOMMENDATION APPROACH

2.1 Data Set

Wikipedia is rich with millions of manually verified intra-Wikipedia links [1,2]. Intra-Wikipedia links typically follow a downward flow in the hierarchy of topics [5]. As users click author-tagged keywords, the linked Wikipedia articles generally suggest more detailed information on a topic (see Figure 1). These interconnections between articles generate the hierarchical path mimicking the model used in traditional educational institutions. Also, many fundamental articles arise as hubs of information with a high ratio of inward connecting links compared to outward connections. A sample visualization of the data collected clearly demonstrates the emergence of fundamental hub articles (seen in Figure 2). This figure begins with an outlying article entitled *Alumna,* and by visualization the intra-Wikipedia connections, three strong related categories emerge, namely: *Education, College, and Alumni.* This principle is the basis for the approach in recommending suggested related articles.

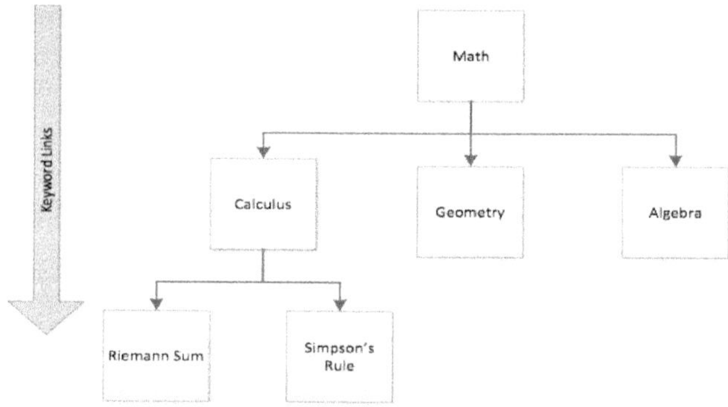

Figure 1. Sample keyword downward movement in hierarchical tree of information stored in Wikipedia

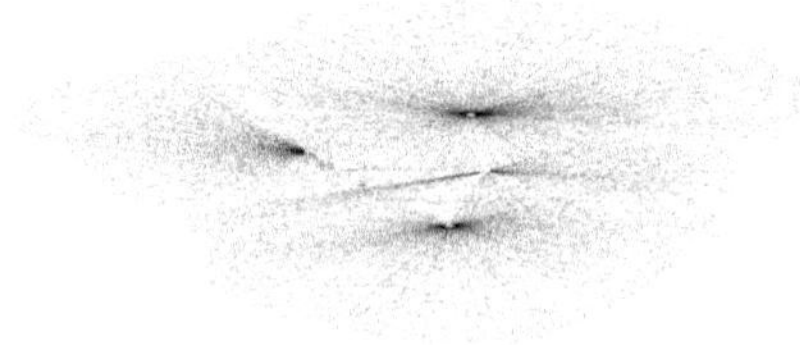

Figure 2. Visualization of Intra-Wikipedia Links

2.2 Generating Recommendations

In the approach of recommendation generation, there are two factors influencing the convergence on a recommended article, namely the frequency count of inward links and the overall rank of the article.

First, the starting article is analyzed to locate any neighboring articles with any downward connections into that starting article. A frequency count of these downward links is calculated and stored in a matrix. This establishes the nearest neighboring article with the most amount of downward links into the starting article. However, it was found that many neighboring articles have equivalent or almost equivalent frequency counts into a given article. This is a direct result of authors generating single downward links once within each article written. Conversely, some articles provide many inward links into starting articles. For this reason, we have chosen frequency counts as one of the convergence criterion for recommending a related article. After selecting a higher-level article based on frequency counts, this approach then reevaluates the selected article for its inward links. This is necessary because directly connected articles with the highest frequency count are not always the best recommendation for related articles. It sometimes requires several steps away from the initial article to make the most compelling recommendation. Frequency counts are summed across each step of the algorithm to help decide on the most related recommendation. In the case of Figure 3-First Iteration, the directly connected starting article accumulates only three frequency counts. Stepping outward to the next directly connected article (Figure 3 Second Iteration) provides an additional three downward links, thus strengthening the recommendation.

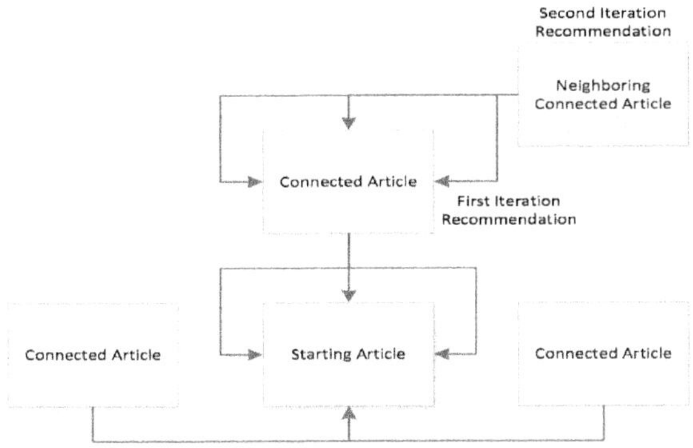

Figure 3. Visualization of multi-step article frequency count

Because the sum of outward frequency counts often will not provide enough discriminating evidence for converging on a specific article, we must establish a second form of evaluation for calculating a recommendation. Visualizing the links between articles (see Figure 1) presents a clear solution to this problem. Articles with many inward links from random articles are established as hubs of information. By calculating not only the frequency counts into the starting article, but also analyzing the total sum of links into a potential recommendation, we can easily converge on the most fundamental of articles as our choice for recommendation. For each iteration, we must calculate the number of outward links and also, equally as important, the sum of inward links. As evident in Figure 1, articles with many inward links become reasonable recommendations for fundamental articles.

Using these two criteria to converge on a recommendation, users can adjust convergence thresholds to be provided with nearer or more distant recommendations. We found the larger the step size, allowing recommendations to be made further from the initial article, the more likely a user is to converge on a hub of information. The smaller the step size, the more likely the user is to converge on an article only slightly less high-level than the starting article.

3. EVALUATION

To validate the accuracy of the recommendation system, thirteen experts were recruited for evaluation. Expert authors on low-level topics, qualified to assess the accuracy of the results of the recommendation system, scored results on a scale of 0-10. Evaluators were asked to submit starting articles to the system that was within their area of expertise. Based on the result of the recommendation, evaluators used a 0-10 scale to assess the relevancy of the recommendation as being a high-level article describing the low-level starting article. On average, experts rated the results of the recommendation system at 7.2 with a standard deviation of 1.9936. Sample recommendations provided by the recommendation system can be seen in Table 1. These results are encouraging and also demonstrate the opportunity to further tune the recommendations given by the system.

Table 1. Sample Recommendations

Starting Article	Recommendation	Convergence Type
Discretization	Applied Discrete Mathematics	Outward Frequency Count
Cat	Felidae	Inward Frequency Count
Riemann Sum	Calculus	Outward Frequency Count

4. CONCLUSION

It has been shown that elementary link analysis techniques, primarily frequency arrays, can be applied to the Wikipedia dataset to intelligently construct related article recommendations. Using multiple iterations of this approach, one can converge on hub articles containing fundamental high-level topical information. These results have been evaluated and scored by a set of external experts, rating the recommendations on average a 7.2 out of 10. We expect that the application of additional web mining techniques will increase the accuracy of this recommendation system. We anticipate the primary potential of this work will be the automatic generation of ontologies based on information stored in Wikipedia's links.

5. REFERENCES

[1] Nie, Tiezheng, Zhenhua Wang, Yue Kou, and Rui Zhang. "Crawling Result Pages for Data Extraction Based on URL Classification." *IEEE Computer Society* (2010): 79-84. Print.

[2] Milne, David, and Ian Witten. "Learning to Link with Wikipedia." *ACM* (2010). Print.

[3] Huang, Decai, Huachun Qi, Yuan Yuan, and Yue-feng Zheng. "TC-PageRank Algorithm Based on Topic Correlation." *IEEE Computer Society* (2006). Print.

[4] Zhao, Haifeng, William Kallander, Tometi Gbedema, Henric Johnson, and Felix Wu. "Read What You Trust: An Open Wiki Model Enhanced by Social Context." *IEEE International Conference on Privacy, Security, Risk, and Trust, and IEEE International Conference on Social Computing* (2011). Print.

[5] Milne, D., and Witten, I.H. (2008) An effective, low-cost measure of semantic relatedness obtained from Wikipedia links. In *Proceedings of the AAAI 2008 Workshop on Wikipedia and Artificial Intelligence (WIKIAI 2008)*, Chicago, IL.

An Exploration of the Research Trends in the Digital Library Evaluation Domain

Giannis Tsakonas, Angelos Mitrelis, Leonidas Papachristopoulos, Christos Papatheodorou
Department of Archives and Library Sciences, Ionian University
72 Theotoki Str.,
Corfu, 491 00, Greece
{gtsak, l11mitr, l11papa, papatheodor}@ionio.gr

ABSTRACT
Evaluation is a vital research area in the digital library domain, demonstrating a growing literature in conference and journal papers. In this poster we present the research trends that governed the field within the decade 2001–2010 in the JCDL and ECDL conferences. The DL evaluation literature was annotated using the domain ontology DiLEO, which defines explicitly the main concepts of the digital library evaluation field and their correlations. Several findings from this study underline the persistent character of quantitative research in evaluation initiatives.

Categories and Subject Descriptors
H.3 [**Information Storage and Retrieval**]: H.3.7 Digital Libraries

General Terms
Measurement, Documentation, Performance.

Keywords
Digital library evaluation, ontologies, literature analysis, research trends.

1. INTRODUCTION
Evaluation is one of the most critical areas of the digital library (DL) domain and is virtually omnipresent in the scholarly communication of the domain. Evaluation often reflects the complexity of the systems and the contexts to which it is conducted. It also requires a wide view and a deep understanding of high-level concepts for supporting epistemological orientation, as well as low-level information to practice it. DL evaluation has progressed and evolved as much as the systems and these contexts have, requiring analytical tools for reasons of historical research as well as for effective experimental planning. In this poster we present the preliminary findings of an analytical work that includes the use of ontological schemas, as a vocabulary to facilitate semantic annotation, and network analysis techniques to construct first level research maps.

2. DiLEO
DiLEO [1] is an ontological representation of the DL evaluation domain. DiLEO is not the only attempt to use conceptual constructs to represent the DL domain. The DL universe is represented as ontology in [2], while [3] uses a formalistic way to express the most critical DL constructs and workflows. However, the use of ontologies to explore the scientific literature is not wide-spread. Despite the immense interest in the analysis of research patterns in conferences [4], topics [5] and communities [6], the employment of ontologies seems to be a promising enhancement. Figure 1 presents the two layered structure of DiLEO, with the upper layer, the strategic level, to designate the decisions regarding the direction and the scope of an evaluation initiative and the lower layer, the procedural level, to conceptualize the implementation process. The classes are associated by a set of properties that reveal reasoning paths for designing evaluation experiments.

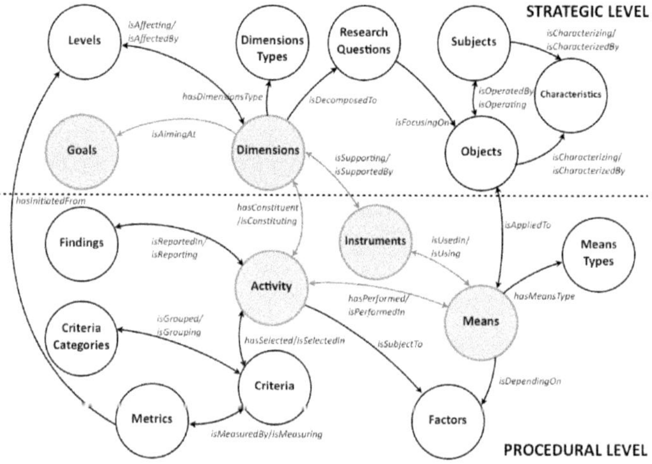

Figure 1. The two layered organization of DiLEO.

3. SETTING
The dataset we explored was selected from the papers presented in two major DL conferences, namely the Joint Conference on Digital Libraries and the European Conference on Digital Libraries (now Theory and Practice of Digital Libraries). Data represent evaluation studies that were presented during the decade 2001–2010 and were based only on short and full papers. To identify the papers with DL evaluation interest, two domain experts worked independently. Their decisions were based on a triple of common descriptive fields, namely the papers' (a) title, (b) abstracts and (c) author keywords. Disputes between the experts were resolved with the intervention of a third researcher who provided additional ratings. If the ambiguity about a paper persisted, then its inclusion in the corpus was decided after discussion among the three researchers. Finally, 79 papers out of 569 were identified for JCDL (13.88%) and 118 out of 400 for

JCDL'12, June 10–14, 2012, Washington, DC, USA.
ACM 978-1-4503-1154-0/12/06.

ECDL (29.5%). The researchers proceeded with the study and annotation of the selected literature items with the DiLEO classes. During the annotation, random entries were cross-checked for consistent annotating and disagreements were resolved through discussion.

4. RESULTS

A weighted undirected graph (Figure 2) was constructed to highlight the significance of concepts and their in-between associations. The nodes of the graph correspond to DiLEO subclasses, while the edges refer to the properties associating them. The betweenness centrality (C_B) of the graph nodes reflects the DiLEO subclasses significance [7]. The square shapes denote *Dimensions (D)*, the diamonds denote *Means (M)*, the circles *Activity (A)* and the discs denote *Instruments (I)* subclasses.

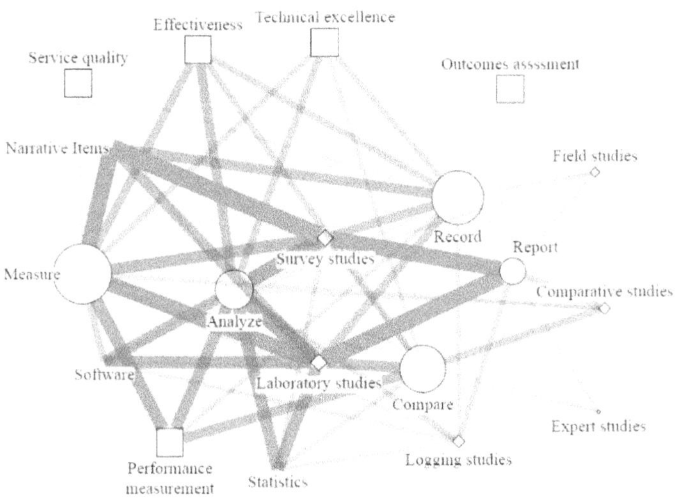

Figure 2. Betweenness centrality of DiLEO classes and property frequencies.

In general, the most central subclasses are those of the class *Activity*, followed by the ones of *Dimensions* and *Means*. This ranking shows the importance of the upper level decisions, though evaluation studies present mainly methodological steps and tools. In detail, the subclasses *A/measure* (C_B=28.55) and *A/record* (C_B=25.46) hold a central position in the research processes of scholars, followed by the *A/compare* (C_B=22.55) and *A/analyze* (C_B=18.96) subclasses. Concerning the *Dimensions* class, it should be that its subclasses share the same centrality (C_B=13.71 for each of the effectiveness, performance measurement, service quality, outcome assessment and technical excellence subclasses).

Regarding the evaluation means, the most popular methods are *M/laboratory studies* and *M/survey studies* (both holding C_B value equal to 8.69). These two *Means* are followed by the *M/comparison studies* (C_B=6.44) and *M/logging studies* (C_B=6.82). The most important associations found are between the classes *M/survey studies –isUsing– I/narrative items*, *A/report – isPerformedIn– M/laboratory studies*, *A/measure – isSupportedBy– I/narrative items*, *A/analyze –isPerformedIn– M/laboratory studies*, *A/report – isPerformedIn– M/Survey studies*, *A/analyze –isPerformedIn– M/survey studies*, *A/measure – isPerformedIn– M/laboratory studies*. These patterns reflect the methodological details of the DL evaluation experiments.

On the other side, the most significant properties involving *Dimensions* are recorded between *D/performance measurement – hasConstituent– A/report* and *D/performance measurement – hasConstituent– A/measure*. The most frequent paths that designate the general trends of the high level evaluation decisions are (a) from *G/design* to *D/performance measurement* and then to *A/report*, (b) from *G/document* to *D/effectiveness* and then to *A/report* and (c) from *G/design* to *D/technical excellence* and then to *A/measure*. The first path implies that the evaluation initiatives aiming to improve the *design* of a DL are strongly motivated by the need to *report* its *performance*. Furthermore, the trend to measure performance indices and analyze them through relevant criteria is also evident by the betweenness centrality values of the nodes *D/performance measurement*, *A/measure* and *A/analyze*, as well as the weight values of their in between edges.

5. CONCLUSIONS

In this poster we exhibited the use of an ontological schema to annotate the literature of DL evaluation as published in two major conferences of the domain. Our analysis highlights the governing practices of the field in the decade 2001–2010 as far as experimental design and practices regards. Several of the findings indicate the strong presence of quantitative research in DL evaluation. Future work includes the slicing of that period in temporal segments according to the concepts of DiLEO and the in-parallel analysis of the field evolution in the two conferences.

6. REFERENCES

[1] Tsakonas, G. and Papatheodorou, C. An ontological representation of the digital library evaluation domain. *Journal of the American Society for Information Science and Technology* 62(8): 1577–1593, 2011.

[2] Athanasopoulos, G., Candela, L., Castelli, D., Innocenti, P., Ioannidis, Y., Katifori, A., and Ross, S. et al. (2010). The Digital Library Reference Model. Retrieved from *http://www.dlorg.eu/uploads/DL%20Reference%20Models/The%20Digital%20Library%20Reference%20Model_v1.0.pdf*

[3] Goncalves, M.A., Fox, E.A., and Watson, L.T. Towards a digital library theory: a formal digital library ontology. *International Journal on Digital Libraries 8*(2): 91–114, 2008.

[4] Smeaton, A.F., Keogh, G., Gurrin, C., McDonald, K. and Sodring, T. Content analysis of SIGIR conference papers. *ACM SIGIR Forum 37*(1): 49–53, 2003.

[5] Sugimoto, C.R. and McCain, K.W. Visualizing changes over time: a history of information retrieval through the lens of descriptor tri-occurrence mapping. *Journal of Information Science 36*(4): 481–493, 2010.

[6] Reitz, F. and Hoffmann, O. An analysis of the evolving coverage of Computer Science sub-fields in the DBLP Digital Library. In *Proceedings of the 14th European Conference on Digital Libraries*, pages 216–227. Springer, Berlin, 2010.

[7] Freeman L.C. A set of measures of centrality based on betweenness. *Sociometry 40*(1): 35–41, 1977.

An Iterative Reliability Measure for Semi-anonymous Annotators

Peter Organisciak
University of Illinois at Urbana-Champaign
501 E. Daniel Daniel Street, MC-492
Champaign, IL
organis2@illinois.edu

ABSTRACT

This study addresses problems of reliability in the creation of tagged corpora by self-selected semi-anonymous raters. In order to account for both strong and weak raters, this paper contributes a recursive technique for scoring rater reliability. By assigning raters trust scores in the proposed method, candidate labels can be weighted by a confidence score and low-confidence ratings can be routed to an expert rater or additional amateur raters for further action.

Categories and Subject Descriptors

H.1.2 [**Models and Principles**]: User/Machine Systems—*Human factors*

Keywords

crowdsourcing, annotation, reliability

1. INTRODUCTION

One of the challenges in annotating digital work is reconciling the breadth of the undertaking with the human resources required for high-quality data. Such tasks can be arduous and do not automate effectively. In recent years, an alternative has emerged in the concept of crowdsourcing: the large-scale collaboration of online users on a task. Crowdsourcing is being used for perception-based tasks such as classification and encoding, using multiple independent annotations to balance out the trade-off in quality from expert raters.

Whether crowdsourcing with interested volunteers, such as OCR correction for the Australian Newspaper Digitization Project[3], or paid workers, the inexperience of the raters may result in problematic data and the act of opening tasks to the public may attract malicious raters. When compensation is involved, as is done with more tedious tasks, it introduces an additional incentive to hurried or careless tagging. For both volunteers and paid workers, systems need to account for problem users.

This study looks at the reliability of online raters in the generation of a tagged corpus. Specifically, raters are self-selected and semi-anonymous paid workers, resulting in unknown trustworthiness and reliability. To account for this uncertainty, the primary contribution of this poster is a recursive algorithm that develops a trust score for users and adjusts certainty in their ratings accordingly.

JCDL'12, June 10–14, 2012, Washington, DC, USA.
ACM 978-1-4503-1154-0/12/06.

2. COLLECTING RAW ANNOTATIONS

The impetus for this study was a practical need: a gold standard tagged corpus where one did not exist. In the author's research on sentiment analysis of microblogging messages, a parallel corpus was required in order to build a classifier. A set of microblogging messages were needed with their sentiment classified, and the classifications needed to be clean. Since the identification of an opinion's sentiment is a low-difficulty task, the primary challenge to clean data was expected to be carelessness in providing ratings.

To collect the raw data, the documents requiring classification were placed on Mechanical Turk.[1] Mechanical Turk is an online paid crowdsourcing service from Amazon that emphasizes micro-payments for piecemeal tasks. Past studies on Turk have found that only a few redundant annotations are required to reach expert quality [5] and that increasing redundant labor offers diminishing returns [4].

From a large corpus of microblogging messages, random selections were uploaded to Mechanical Turk for tagging. Each tagging task included six messages asking for the opinion expressed (e.g. "What is the opinion of 'Obama' in the following tweet..."). The reason for including six messages per task was threefold: to reduce page loads for high volume taggers, to discourage skipping of individual tasks and lower selection bias, and to collect enough data to build a trust profile for even a one-time tagger. There were five possible ratings, three for classification—*negative*, *neutral*, *positive*—and two for flagging—*spam* and *incoherent*.

To evaluate the quality of the Turk ratings, a parallel set of classifications was tagged by the study author. Since identifying opinions is presumed to be a low-expertise task, the assumption being made is that the threat to clean data is not in a rater's lack of expertise but in carelessness. Since a system does not know who the contributing raters are until ratings are made, there is a risk of what Bernstein et al. [1] characterize as Lazy Turkers – workers that do the bare minimum. For this reason the evaluation standard was whether the ratings agreed with a careful classification by the study author.

2.1 Evaluating Annotators

In building a clean set of annotated data, this study explores the possibility of algorithmically ranking document

[1]http://www.mturk.com

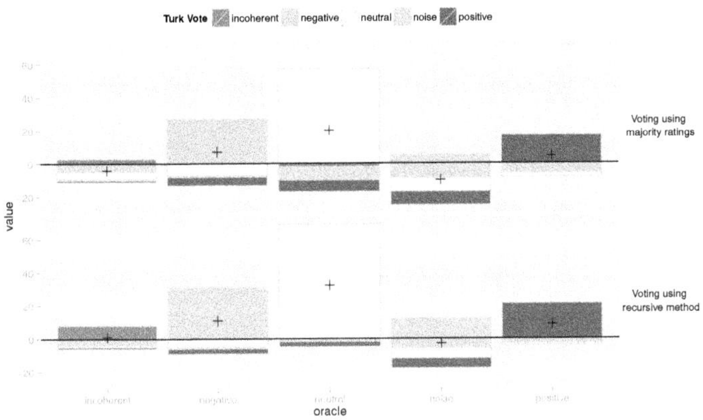

Figure 1: Distribution of Rater Classifications Relative to Evaluation Set

sentiment confidence and user reliability. Traditionally in problems of inter-annotator agreement, one assumes equally competent raters and tries measure their agreement on possibly divisive observations. Unlike agreement measures like Fleiss' kappa [2], however, this study makes an assumption of unevenly reliable raters that rise beyond chance to be systematically strong or weak raters.

The proposed technique weighs classification certainty by employing a recursive technique. A confidence score C_{ij} is calculated for each classification category i of each document j. Then, for every rater l in the system, a trust score U_m is calculated based on the confidences in that user's ratings. The confidence is calculated in the following way:

$$C_{ij} = ln(1 + r_{ij} R^k * \prod_{i=1} (R + r_i)^{-1}) \tag{1}$$

Where r_{ij} is the number of votes that rating option i received for document j, k is the total number of classification possibilities and R is the total number of classifications, weighted to user reliability scores. R is calculated as $\sum_{i=1}^{k} r_i * \sum_{m=1}^{n} \frac{1}{n} u_m$, which is the number of ratings given for all rating categories multiplied by the average of the user scores for the raters. User scores are 1 by default, meaning that initially, R is simply the number of raters that are participating.

Though users rate in isolation, a user score derived from that rating is not, as the unknown *true rating* means that the accuracy needs to be estimated based on agreement. In order to isolate a user's reliability, the calculation of confidence scores C_{ij} is iterated, taking into account the trust score of the raters, which are subsequently recalculated. Both the user and confidence scores iterate until eventually arriving at a stable value. Through the iterations, the trust in the raters becomes less dependent on who rated documents alongside them. In other words, if a good rater is unlucky enough to disagree with two bad raters, they will not be punished because the system will consider them more reliable than the bad raters.

Equation 1 was designed to satisfy a number of intuitively derived characteristics. Consensus among raters is not uniform, meaning that 5/5 raters agreeing on a classification is considered more confident than 3/3 agreements. However, each new rater added to the classification task add a diminishing increase in confidence i.e. adding a 100th rater has less of an effect over the ratings than adding a fifth rater.

After the confidence rating are calculated, user ratings are set as the average of all confidence ratings plus a normalizing modifier κ. For this study, 0.35 has been effective as a modifier, though more study into an ideal κ modifier is required. Once user scores are calculated, confidence ratings are recalculated, with the user score modifiers reflecting the average user scores for a given rating option.

Only ratings with a final confidence score above 0.8 are accepted, while others are queued for additional ratings. When comparing this set of more reliable raters to the evaluation set, the error rate fall noticable. Figure 2.1 shows the distribution of final rating votes in two plots – the top plot shows votes made through majority agreement, while the bottom plot shows the distribution of votes made using the algorithm presented in this paper. Bars are grouped by the 'true' oracle rating and stacked according to the vote that was made by the raters. In this way, the correct classifications are shown with a positive value, while the distribution of incorrect classications stacks as negative values.

It should be noted that despite improvements in each category, the accuracy of 'incoherent' and 'noisy' ratings is still quite low. This suggests a flaw in the task design. These two classification categories were identified with near-perfect recall when using the iterative algorithm, but raters also mislabelled many other items with the same categories.

3. CONCLUSIONS

This study outlines an iterative scoring algorithm for evaluating ratings of semi-anonymous users by the confidence of their ratings. This algorithm appears to be robust, and continued work in this area will further evaluate the technique against alternate approaches.

4. ACKNOWLEDGMENTS

The author would like to thank Miles Efron and Catherine Blake for their valuable comments and input.

5. REFERENCES

[1] M. S. Bernstein, G. Little, R. C. Miller, B. Hartmann, M. S. Ackerman, D. R. Karger, D. Crowell, and K. Panovich. Soylent: a word processor with a crowd inside. In *ACM symposium on User interface software and technology*, New York, NY, 2010. ACM Press.

[2] J. L. Fleiss. Measuring nominal scale agreement among many raters. *Psychological Bulletin*, 76(5), 1971.

[3] R. Holley. Tagging full text searchable articles. *D-Lib Magazine*, 16(1/2), Jan. 2010.

[4] S. Novotney and C. Callison-Burch. Cheap, fast and good enough: Automatic speech recognition with non-expert transcription. In *The 2010 Annual Conference of the North American Chapter of the Association for Computational Linguistics*, Stroudsburg, PA, USA, 2010.

[5] R. Snow, B. O'Connor, D. Jurafsky, and A. Ng. Cheap and fast-but is it good?: evaluating non-expert annotations for natural language tasks. In *Proceedings of the Conference on Empirical Methods in Natural Language Processing*, 2008.

An Unsupervised Technical Difficulty Ranking Model Based on Conceptual Terrain in the Latent Space*

Shoaib Jameel Wai Lam Xiaojun Qian
Department of Systems Engineering and Engineering Management
The Chinese University of Hong Kong
{msjameel,wlam,xjqian}@se.cuhk.edu.hk

Ching-man Au Yeung
ASTRI
3/F, Bio-Informatics Centre, Science Park
Hong Kong
albertauyeung@astri.org

ABSTRACT

Search results of the existing general-purpose search engines usually do not satisfy domain-specific information retrieval tasks as there is a mis-match between the technical expertise of a user and the results returned by the search engine. In this paper, we investigate the problem of ranking domain-specific documents based on the technical difficulty. We propose an unsupervised conceptual terrain model using Latent Semantic Indexing (LSI) for re-ranking search results obtained from a similarity based search system. We connect the sequences of terms under the latent space by the semantic distance between the terms and compute the traversal cost for a document indicating the technical difficulty. Our experiments on a domain-specific corpus demonstrate the efficacy of our method.

Categories and Subject Descriptors

H.3.3 [**Information Search and Retrieval**]: Information Filtering, Retrieval Models, Search Process, Selection Process; H.3.7 [**Digital libraries**]

General Terms

Algorithms, Experimentation

Keywords

LSI, Terrain, Conceptual Difficulty, Ranking

1. INTRODUCTION

When it comes to searching for domain-specific content on the web, people with diverse background query search engines to locate the text which is both relevant and can fit the level of understanding. General web search engines are too broad in terms of topical coverage. Simply using the link structure such as PageRank [4] or simple cosine similarity [7] based measure to retrieve and rank documents will not achieve the goal of matching conceptual difficulty. Technical expertise varies from one person to another and it is difficult to cater for such needs without building a user model [8] for every user and reflect results accordingly.

We present an unsupervised method for re-ranking domain-specific documents given a query based on the technical difficulty of documents. We first obtain search results for a query from an IR system. After that the retrieved documents are re-ranked automatically based on the conceptual difficulty using our proposed model.

*The work is supported by a grant from the Research Grant Council of the Hong Kong Special Administrative Region, China (Project Code: CUHK413510). This work is also affiliated with the Microsoft-CUHK Joint Laboratory for Human-centric Computing and Interface Technologies.

JCDL'12, June 10–14, 2012, Washington, DC, USA.
ACM 978-1-4503-1154-0/12/06.

2. THE CONCEPTUAL TERRAIN MODEL

We use LSI for our task because it exploits the co-occurrence matrix to bring out new structural relationships between the terms and documents in the latent space. Terms which contribute with more synergy in one context will be *close* to that context in the latent space [1]. In the LSI latent space, our model considers *hop* from one term to another in sequence to determine the conceptual cohesion between the terms in the document.

2.1 Inter-term Cohesion

For the smoothness of conceptual comprehensibility, connections between terms with the surrounding parts in the text are necessary. It is because the interpretation of elements in a discourse is dependent on how the reader is able to semantically relate with other elements in the discourse [2, 3]. In a document d, the inter-term cohesion distance between the term t_n and the term t_{n+1} is denoted by $\hat{s}(t_n, t_{n+1})$ which is computed using Euclidean distance formula in the LSI latent space. We normalize the semantic distance between the two consecutive terms t_n and t_{n+1} by computing the distance between t_n and each term τ which follows t_n in the entire corpus.

$$s(t_n, t_{n+1}) = \frac{\hat{s}(t_n, t_{n+1})}{\sum_{\tau} \hat{s}(t_n, \tau)} \tag{1}$$

2.2 Term Difficulty

The term difficulty score $\hat{F}(t_n, d)$ for every term t_n in the document d is formulated as:

$$\hat{F}(t_n, d) = idf_{t_n} \times \frac{1}{r(t_n, d) + \epsilon} \tag{2}$$

idf_{t_n} is the Inverse Document Frequency as in [5]. The Euclidean distance between the term and document vectors in the LSI latent space is denoted by $r(t_n, d)$. ϵ is a very small constant added to accommodate the case when $r(t_n, d) = 0$ and in general $\epsilon << \min(r(t_n, d))$. We normalize $\hat{F}(t_n, d)$ such that its global sum is 1. Let D represent the total number of documents in the corpus. We adopt the following normalization formula:

$$F(t_n, d) = \frac{\hat{F}(t_n, d)}{\sum_{i=1}^{D} \hat{F}(t_n, d_i)} \quad (3)$$

2.3 Traversal Cost in the Conceptual Terrain

The conceptual difficulty is directly proportional to the term difficulty and also inter-term cohesion i.e., inter-term semantic distance. It means that the more the term difficulty and the greater the semantic distance, the more will be the technical difficulty of the sequence of terms. Assume a reader begins from the term t_n in the document d with term difficulty denoted by $F(t_n, d)$ and hops to the next term t_{n+1} in sequence whose term difficulty score is denoted by $F(t_{n+1}, d)$ and covers a semantic distance of $s(t_n, t_{n+1})$ in between the two terms in the latent space. We then compute the traversal cost, $C_d(t_n, t_{n+1})$ for each sequential term bigram in document d, which is expressed as:

$$C_d(t_n, t_{n+1}) = \beta\Big[F(t_n, d) + F(t_{n+1}, d)\Big] + (1-\beta)s(t_n, t_{n+1}) \quad (4)$$

where $0 \leq \beta \leq 1$ is a parameter indicating the role that each of the components plays in determining the technical expertise of a document.

Ranking: Our approach focuses on the relative "technical difficulty" of a document when traversing through the text sequentially, where the difficulty of terms are measured by both the scores in the latent space that represent the deviation from common terms and the cost of transitions from term to term. We aggregated the term difficulties and inter-term cohesion scores to come up with the document's conceptual difficulty score normalized by the document length and then re-ranked the results from simple documents to advanced.

3. EXPERIMENTS AND RESULTS

Existing standard IR test collections do not fulfill our purpose of evaluation as we need domain-specific documents and technical difficulty judgment for the documents. We chose Psychology domain to conduct our experiments and crawled about 170,000 documents from Psychology websites. No term stemming was performed and stop words were not removed. We obtained 110 queries (related to Psychology domain) from AOL query logs. We used Zettair[1] to conduct retrieval and obtained a ranked list using the Okapi BM25 [6] ranking function. We then selected the top ten documents retrieved from the ranked list. We refer our model as "Terrain". The number of latent concepts was 200. The parameter β in Equation 4 was set to 0.5 so that the two components viz. the term difficulty and inter-term cohesion could equally contribute in determining the overall document's conceptual difficulty.

To obtain a ground truth of the technical difficulty of the documents for evaluation purpose, human annotators who were undergraduate students having varied background were invited. They had basic knowledge about Psychology. The annotators were fluent in reading English passages. The standard deviations of judgments among the annotators were 1.23. We compared our method with popular ranking methods and also re-ranked documents using readability formulae. We used NDCG as our evaluation metric.

[1]http://www.seg.rmit.edu.au/zettair/index.html

Table 1: NDCG@10 results. "Terrain" is our proposed model.

Terrain	Cosine	BM25	ARI	Coleman	Flesch	Fog	Kincaid	LIX	SMOG
0.552	0.302	0.347	0.390	0.376	0.365	0.413	0.402	0.390	0.369

Table 1 shows that our terrain model has performed better than the traditional readability formulae and popular ranking functions such as Okapi BM25 and cosine. According to a single-tailed student's t-test our results are statistically significant ($p < 0.05$). What makes our model superior when compared with other models is that we are able to effectively capture term difficulties of domain-specific terms based on their contextual information. It means that in one technical discourse, if a term is used as a general term, its difficulty will be low. However the same term in a more technical thematic discourse will have a high technical difficulty score. Our model also captures conceptual leaps during terrain traversal. The leaps are captured locally with respect to the terms in the vicinity rather than in a global perspective as done by many other models. Thus our terrain model effectively captures inter-term cohesion better.

4. CONCLUSIONS

We have presented our terrain based document re-ranking model based on conceptual difficulty which has outperformed comparative methods. Our approach considers two components in determining the document's technical difficulty which are term difficulty and inter-term cohesion. Traditional readability formulae cannot capture domain-specific jargon, for example, *"star"*, *"shock"* and hence perform poorly on such documents.

5. REFERENCES

[1] J. Bellegarda. A multispan language modeling framework for large vocabulary speech recognition. *IEEE Transactions on Speech and Audio Processing*, 6(5):456–467, sep 1998.

[2] P. Freebody and R. C. Anderson. Effects of vocabulary difficulty, text cohesion, and schema availability on reading comprehension. *Reading Research Quarterly*, 18(3):pp. 277–294, 1983.

[3] W. Kintsch. The role of knowledge in discourse comprehension: A construction-integration model. *Psychological Review*, 95:163–182, 1988.

[4] L. Page, S. Brin, R. Motwani, and T. Winograd. The pagerank citation ranking: Bringing order to the web. *World Wide Web Internet And Web Information Systems*, (1999-66):1–17, 1998.

[5] S. Robertson. Understanding inverse document frequency: on theoretical arguments for idf. *Journal of Documentation*, 60(5):503–520, 2004.

[6] S. E. Robertson, S. Walker, S. Jones, M. Hancock-Beaulieu, and M. Gatford. Okapi at trec-3. In *TREC*, 1994.

[7] G. Salton, A. Wong, and C. S. Yang. A vector space model for automatic indexing. *Commun. ACM*, 18:613–620, November 1975.

[8] X. Shen, B. Tan, and C. Zhai. Implicit user modeling for personalized search. In *Proc. of 14th CIKM*, pages 824–831, 2005.

Longitudinal Analysis of Historical Texts' Readability

Adam Jatowt[1,2] and Katsumi Tanaka[1]

[1]Kyoto University
Yoshida-Honmachi, Sakyo-ku
606-8501 Kyoto, Japan

[2]Japan Science and Technology Agency
4-1-8, Honcho, Kawaguchi-shi, Saitama
332-0012 Tokyo, Japan

{adam, tanaka}@dl.kuis.kyoto-u.ac.jp

ABSTRACT

Digital libraries often contain historical documents of varying age. The degree to which users can understand their content depends much on their reading difficulty. In this poster paper we report the results of our studies on the readability of historical documents from the viewpoint of present users. We investigate the correlation between the outcomes of different readability measurements and publication dates of prose texts on the basis of two datasets, the *Victorian Women's Writers Project* and the *Corpus of Late Modern English Texts*.

Categories and Subject Descriptors

H.3.0 [**Information Storage and Retrieval**]: General

General Terms

Algorithms, Measurement, Experimentation

Keywords

readability, historical documents, language evolution

1. INTRODUCTION

Readability indices have been employed to measure complexity of various document types ranging from scientific papers, clinical reports, legal documents, textbooks to, more recently, web pages. However, little work has been devoted to approaching the readability of historical documents as seen from the viewpoint of present users. In recent years we have witnessed massive digitalization of historical text sources that are being preserved by libraries, museums and other institutions. This joint digitalization effort has resulted already in a large body of content that can be effectively measured, compared and described using computers.

Document readability is a key aspect of information accessibility and to ensure the access to information in historical documents their readability levels should be quantified. They could then serve as an indicator of the ease of reading of resources and should be made clear to users while browsing and searching old documents. Perhaps, also specialized tools such as ones using statistical translation models could be offered for readers to support understanding of old documents. Readability measure could be also used as a feature for automatically dating documents.

In this paper we investigate the correlation between readability of English prose and its age using two well-known datasets, *Victorian Women's Writers Project* (VWWPC) and the *Corpus of Late Modern English Texts* (CLMETEV) spanning different sub-periods within the last three centuries. Both the VWWPC and CLMETEV corpora have been created by professional linguists with the aim of being used for linguistic analysis.

JCDL'12, June 10–14, 2012, Washington, DC, USA.
ACM 978-1-4503-1154-0/12/06.

Sherman [2] first observed that the lengths of sentences decreased over time and written language become closer to spoken one. However, his work lacked quantitative analysis and was limited to the study of the sentence length effect on the readability. Danielson and Lasorsa [1] investigated whether prose can be dated using stylistic markers of sentence length, word length, rare punctuation, and word shortening or informality. They found positive correlation between the document age and these markers.

2. DATASETS AND METRICS

The first dataset, Victorian Women's Writers Project Corpus[1] (VWWPC) contains 200 original texts written by female writers from the 1820s to the 1920s. The corpus includes balanced samples of different genres such as poetry, novels, children's books, political pamphlets, religious tracts, histories etc.

The second dataset, *Corpus of Late Modern English Texts*[2] (CLMETEV), incorporates texts written by British native speakers with the constraint that no author contributes more than 200,000 words of text. Although the corpus texts vary in terms of genre, ranging from personal letters to literary fiction to scientific writing, its main part contains prose. The texts were written by both men and women of varying social class within the period of the 1720s to the 1920s. Table 1 shows the summary of the key statistics of both the datasets.

Table 1 Summary of key statistics of the datasets.

Dataset	#Resources	#Sentences	#Words	Period
VWWPC	200	319K	7mln	1830s-1920s
CLMETEV	176	665K	14,9mln	1720s-1920s

As readability measures we have used *Flesch Reading Ease* (FRE), *Coleman Liau Index* (CLI) which are common readability metrics and own readability measure based on the analysis of part-of-speech distributions. FRE is defined as $206.876 - 1.015ASL - 84.6ASW$ where ASL is the average number of syllables per word and ASW is the average number of words per sentence. Higher FRE values indicate more readable text. On the other hand, CLI approximates the U.S. grade level thought to be necessary for comprehending any text. It is defined as $0.0588L - 0.296S - 15.8$ where L stands for the average number of letters per 100 words and S denotes the average number of sentences per 100 words. High values of CLI indicate difficult texts.

We have also created own measure of grammatical complexity, called *POSR*, based on the analysis of category sections of Encyclopedia Britannica[3] treated as a training set. We have taken

[1] http://webapp1.dlib.indiana.edu/vwwp/welcome.do

[2] https://perswww.kuleuven.be/~u0044428/clmetev.htm

[3] http://www.britannica.com

98K Britannica's articles in the three categories: introductory, intermediate and standard (Encyclopedia) and subject them to part-of-speech (POS) analysis. We have then determined significant differences between average numbers of POS tags across different categories (see Figure 1). We have also noticed higher number of verb phrases (VP) than prepositional phrases (PP) in easier article categories. Equation 1 shows the way to calculate POSR. High values point to easy texts.

$$\text{POSR} = \text{POS-Score} * \text{Chunk-Score}$$
$$\text{POS-Score} = (\#NNS + \#JJS + \#NNPS + \#VB + \#VBD + \#VBP + \#VBZ) / (\#NN + \#VBG + \#VBN) \quad (1)$$
$$\text{Chunk-Score} = \#VP / \#PP$$

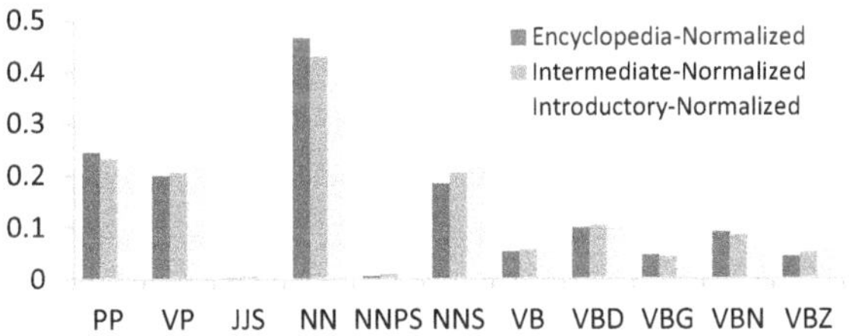

Figure 1 Average distribution of POS tags used in POSR measure across different categories of Britannica.

3. EXPERIMENTS AND CONCLUSIONS

Figures 2 and 3 demonstrate the outcomes of the tree readability measures in different decades for both the datasets. Fitted linear functions with R^2 values are overlaid on the figures. For the VWWPC dataset we can observe the steady increase in the ease of reading over time as measured by FRE (51% change) and by the tag-based POSR measure shown at the bottom of Figure 2 (57% change). The CRI index decreases along time, which again indicates improving ease of reading (-39% change). These results point to the apparent simplification of written language over time. The analysis of CLMETEV dataset (see Figure 3) confirms the results obtained for VWWPC; although the change seems to be less dramatic, especially for the POSR metric. This may be due to more diverse nature of this dataset.

Based on the results we conclude that recent texts are more readable to the current users in terms of the readability metric based on sentence and word lengths than the older texts on the basis of CLMETEV and VWWPC datasets. We have quantified the correlation of the two readability measures, FRE and CLI, and the text age. However, the readability metric using POS distribution gives a mixed picture. We have also observed varying levels of difficulty of texts written by different authors and published at the same decade. This justifies the need for multiple studies of readability using diverse corpora. We plan also to conduct detailed studies on the effect of language evolution on the comprehensibility of documents.

4. ACKNOWLEDGMENTS

This research was supported by MEXT Grant-in-Aid for Young Scientists B (#22700096) and JST research promotion program Sakigake: "Analyzing Collective Memory and Developing Methods for Knowledge Extraction from Historical Documents".

5. REFERENCES

[1] Danielson, W. A and Lasorsa, D. L. A New Readability Formula Based on the Stylistic Age of Novels. Journal of Reading, 33(3), 194-197, 1989

[2] Sherman, L.A., Analytics of Literature: *A Manual for the Objective Study of English Prose and Poetry*, Boston-Ginn, 1893.

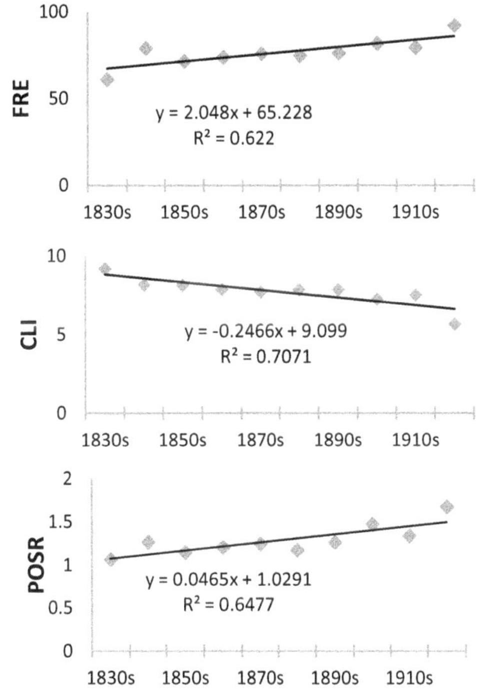

Figure 2 FRE, CLI and POSR readability measures of VWWPC dataset (σ = 3.39, σ = 1.05 and σ = 0.57, respectively).

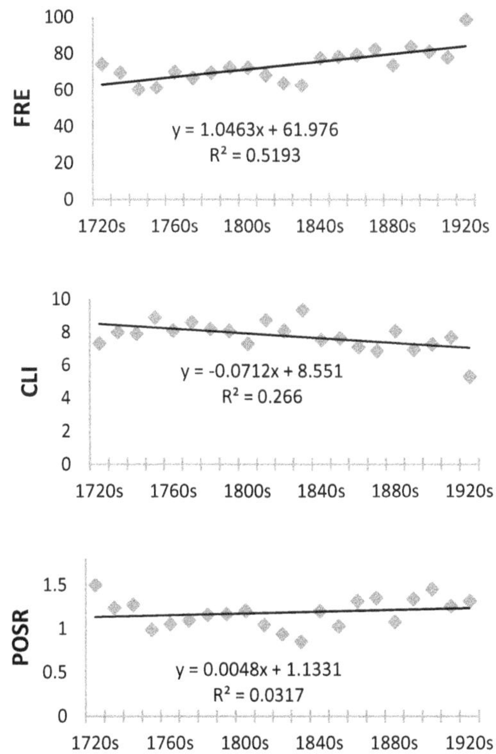

Figure 3 FRE, CLI and POSR readability measures of VWWPC dataset (σ = 3.15, σ = 1.07 and σ = 0.54, respectively).

Bi^{2}SoN – A Digital Library for Supporting Biomedical Research

Benjamin Köhncke
L3S Research Center
Appelstrasse 9a
30167 Hannover
Germany
koehncke@l3s.de

Sascha Tönnies
L3S Research Center
Appelstrasse 9a
30167 Hannover
Germany
toennies@l3s.de

Wolf-Tilo Balke
IFIS TU Braunschweig
Mühlenpfordtstrasse 23
38106 Braunschweig
Germany
balke@ifis.cs.tu-bs.de

ABSTRACT

In the domain of biology a huge amount of different data sources is available. Therefore, information gathering and searching are challenging tasks. To avoid a manual assessment of all relevant data sources, their knowledge has to be integrated. The presented system focuses on all aspects needed for suitable data integration and retrieval for domain experts from the field of biology. The knowledge from different data sources is combined and further used for, e.g. synonym enrichment of the query term. The resulting prototype was presented to a group of domain experts who confirmed that the system delivers suitable results supporting the scientists by their literature search.

Categories and Subject Descriptors

H.3.3 [**Information Systems**]: Information Storage and Retrieval – *Information Search and Retrieval.*

General Terms

Management, Design, Human Factors

Keywords

Architecture, Biology, Personalization, Digital Library

1. INTRODUCTION AND BACKGROUND

Nowadays, the directed information search is usually performed via the Internet. Independent of the field of interest a huge amount of online accessible information is available. Especially in the field of biology searching for relevant data is a challenging task. Biology is a wide domain with many different working areas. Each area has special data sources where the required knowledge is stored. In total there are more than 1000 different data sources storing biological knowledge.

Today the search for information in biology is performed by manually requesting all required data sources and manually combining the retrieved information. The combined information is subsequently used for a literature search in specialized digital libraries. The most widely-used library for the field of biomedical and life sciences information is MEDLINE (Medical Literature Analysis and Retrieval System Online) covering more than 21 million articles from around 4500 different journals. It is compiled by the United States National Library of Medicine (NLM) and freely accessible via the PubMed interface.

JCDL'12, June 10–14, 2012, Washington, DC, USA.
ACM 978-1-4503-1154-0/12/06.

The strength and weaknesses of commonly used search portals for biomedical information retrieval are compared in [1], namely PubMed, Web of Science, Scopus, and Google Scholar. The authors compared the content coverage and practical utility of these sources. They used example keyword searches to evaluate the usefulness and specific published articles to evaluate their utility in performing citation analysis. Whereas PubMed and Google Scholar offer free access to their search platform, Scopus and Web of Science are commercial products requiring access fees. The evaluation showed that PubMed is up-to-date due to frequent updates, reliable and easy to use. With GoPubMed [2] it exists a portal allowing users to explore PubMed search results with a hierarchically structured vocabulary for molecular biology, the Gene Ontology [3]. In GoPubMed an overview of the document abstracts according to the Gene Ontology is given. Therefore, the user is able to navigate through the abstracts by category. Furthermore, also more general ontology terms are shown, related to the original query that do not occur directly in the abstracts.

However, all approaches have in common that they only index the terms directly occurring in the documents. But most of the query terms have several synonyms frequently used in different documents. In [4] it was mentioned that for many proteins also different names were used even within the same article. Without taking these synonyms into account a huge amount of relevant literature is not included in the result set. Another aspect is that PubMed does not support a suitable ranking. Usually the result set is ordered by showing the newest documents first. Most of the queries deliver huge results sets making it impossible for the user to find the most important documents without a suitable ranking.

Furthermore, the user's relevance sensation is usually not only query dependent, but also related to his implicit background knowledge and the task he is currently working on. This knowledge cannot be expressed in the query. To summarize, the following additional aspects have to be considered in a retrieval system for biological literature:

- Query expansion using synonyms
- Suitable ranking functions
- Personalized access to information sources

In the course of the Bi^{2}SoN project we will focus on these aspects to build an architecture supporting biomedical researchers with their literature search. Our aim is to support the scientist by offering a portal with direct access to all required data sources. Beside the literature research this also includes an analysis of the required data sources for query expansion. We did a survey with domain experts from the field of infection research and found out that depending on the task the scientist is working on the different knowledgebases for query enrichment differ. We will introduce a framework integrating the knowledge from the required data sources by taking the search task and implicit knowledge of each individual user into account.

2. Bi²SoN ARCHITECTURE

During the project we work together with experts from the Helmholtz Centre for Infection Research (HZI). For the area of infection research it is important to understand bio-chemical reactions in cells. Therefore, a lot of mass-spectrometric experiments are accomplished leading to huge amounts of experimental data. In a first step, this data is analyzed using statistical approaches. An even more important step is the comparison of these results with other approaches known in literature. For example, it is possible that the same reactions are also known from other organisms. Hence, after the relevant entities have been determined from the experimental data, they are further used for literature search. Figure 1 gives an over view of our architecture.

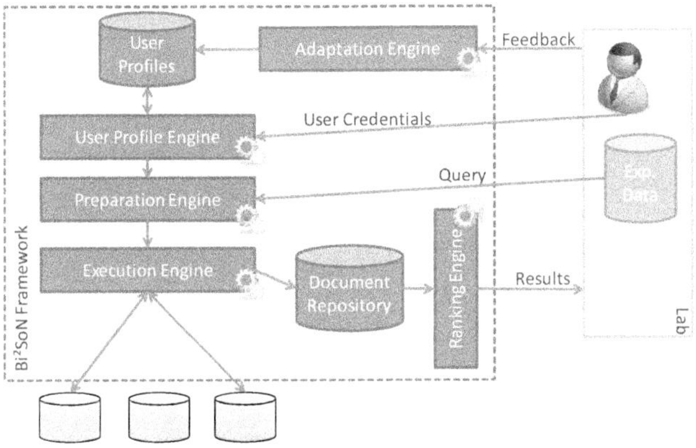

Figure 1. Bi²SoN architecture

The scientist analyzes the experimental data and determines the interesting entities. He identifies himself to the Bi2SoN system and submits a query term out of these entities. For each user a user profile is stored in our repository including information about preferred data sources and working tasks. The user profile engine is responsible for managing the user profiles. The profile and the query is analyzed by the preparation engine which is responsible for choosing adequate data sources. The resulting service set is transmitted to the execution engine which requests the included data sources. Each data source delivers information related to the query entity. The execution engine analyzes and merges the data from each data source and finally transmits the enriched query to the document repository. In a last step a suitable ranking function is chosen taking the user preferences defined in the profile into account. The ranked result set is delivered to the user who has the choice to give a relevance feedback to the system. The user feedback is used to adapt information in the profile, e.g. if the precision of the top-x documents is low another ranking function has to be used for this user.

We implemented the introduced architecture in a first prototype. Our document repository includes around 220000 documents from the PubMed Central corpus. Furthermore, we used external knowledgebases to extract all genes and pathways included in each document. We combined the information from several sources, e.g. UniProt and KEGG, to allow for automatic synonym retrieval. Figure 2 shows a screenshot of our system which we presented to the domain experts from the HZI. The feedback was very positive since the system already retrieves good search results due to the integration of different data sources and synonym enrichment.

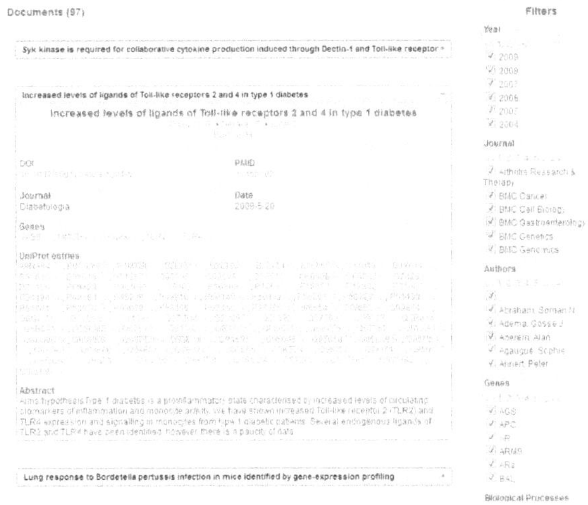

Figure 2. Bi²SoN portal screenshot

The user has the ability to filter the result set using bibliographic and semantic facets. The description of each document includes, among others, all genes and UniProt entries.

3. CONCLUSION

In the field of biology a huge amount of different data sources is available. To allow for high quality document retrieval an integration of this knowledge is essential. We have shown in a first prototype that the integration of different sources for synonym enrichment already leads to pleasant retrieval results. For future work we plan to further investigate the definition of the user profile. Beside the already included information about preferred data sources and working tasks, it would be interesting to model the implicit knowledge of a biologist. Usually he has an exact perception of what he is interested in which cannot be expressed in a query. Moreover, it is important to invent personalized ranking functions to further improve the user's search experience.

4. REFERENCES

[1] M. E. Falagas et al., "Comparison of PubMed, Scopus, Web of Science, and Google Scholar: strengths and weaknesses.," The FASEB journal, vol. 22, no 2, 2008.

[2] A. Doms, M. Schroeder, "GoPubMed: exploring PubMed with the Gene Ontology.," Nucleic acids research, vol. 33, no Web service issue, 2005.

[3] M. a Harris et al., "The Gene Ontology (GO) database and informatics resource.," Nucleic acids research, vol. 32, no Database issue, 2004.

[4] L. Hirschman et al., "Accomplishments and challenges in literature data mining for biology.," Bioinformatics (Oxford, England), vol. 18, no. 12, 2002.

CADAL Digital Calligraphy System

Gao Pengcheng
College of Computer Science
Zhejiang University
Hangzhou, China
gaopengcheng@zju.edu.cn

Wu Jiangqin*
College of Computer Science
Zhejiang University
Hangzhou, China
wujq@zju.edu.cn

Xia Yang
College of Computer Science
Zhejiang University
Hangzhou, China
332371503@qq.com

Lin Yuan
College of Computer Science
Zhejiang University
Hangzhou, China
simple_ivy@yahoo.cn

ABSTRACT

CADAL(China Academic Digital Associate Library) plays a primary role in Universal Digital Library. By the end of 2011, CADAL has digitized 1.85 million books. Chinese calligraphy occupies an important place in Chinese culture, and the collection of digitized Chinese calligraphy is the large part of CADAL resources. So, the services of making full use of the collections are required for diverse users, such as art historians, students and the public. Here we propose a CADAL Digital Calligraphy System, in which over 1,100 works and 100,000 characters are included, the services of multi-level metadata-based search(metadata-based books search, works search and characters search) and multi-grain calligraphic character search(content-based search and radical-based search) are provided. In the end, some search-related applications of CADAL Digital Calligraphy System are discussed.

Categories and Subject Descriptors

J.5 [**Computer Application**]: Arts and Humanities – *Arts and Humanities*

General Terms

Performance, Design.

Keywords

CADAL, calligraphy, radical-based search, content-based search

1. INTRODUCTION

Chinese calligraphy is the art of Chinese characters written with a hairy brush, which has been popular for 3000 years and illustrates the art culture. Large collections of ancient Chinese manuscripts and rubbings, especially the four great schools of calligraphy '*Yan*', '*Liu*', '*Ou*', '*Zhao*' are models for Chinese calligraphy learning. With the development of technology, it is a good and possible job to scan Chinese historical calligraphy works and books, and make them universally accessible on internet so that users can appreciate Chinese calligraphy on line. Many famous ancient calligraphic works, such as LanTingXu(**Figure 1.(a)**) written by Wang Xizhi, a famous calligrapher of Jin dynasty and DuoBaoTaBei(**Figure 1.(b)**) written by Yan Zhenqing, a famous calligrapher of Tang dynasty, have been digitized and stored in CADAL[1]. CADAL, which has the amount of 1.85 billion digitized books, plays a primary role in universal digital library[2]. Based on the digitized books and information technologies, we implemented a digital Chinese calligraphy system, which is called CADAL Digital Calligraphy System. In the CADAL Digital Calligraphy System we provide many services for diverse users, like multi-level metadata-based search, multi-grain calligraphic character search and some other search-related services.

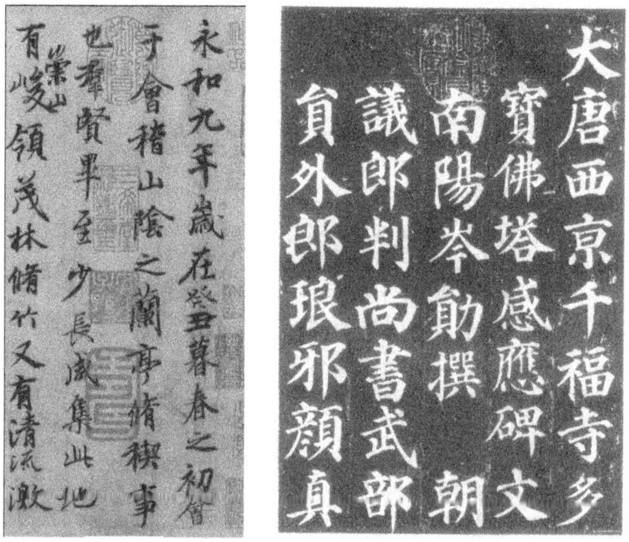

(a) (b)

Figure 1. (a)*LanTingXu* by Wang Xizhi (b) *DuoBaoTaBei* by Yan Zhenqing

2. ARCHITECTURE

As shown in **Figure 2**, the CADAL Digital Calligraphy System is composed of three parts: Database building, Searching and Application. In the first part, original works are obtained from digitized books, works are decomposed into single characters by the page segmentation system, and the characters are decomposed into radicals. The books, works, characters and radicals are annotated for further search. In the second part, multi-level search(metadata-based books, works, and characters searching) and multi-grain calligraphic character search(character-based and radical-based character search) are provided. In the third part, tablet generation and some other search-related services are presented.

JCDL'12, June 10–14, 2012, Washington, DC, USA.
ACM 978-1-4503-1154-0/12/06.

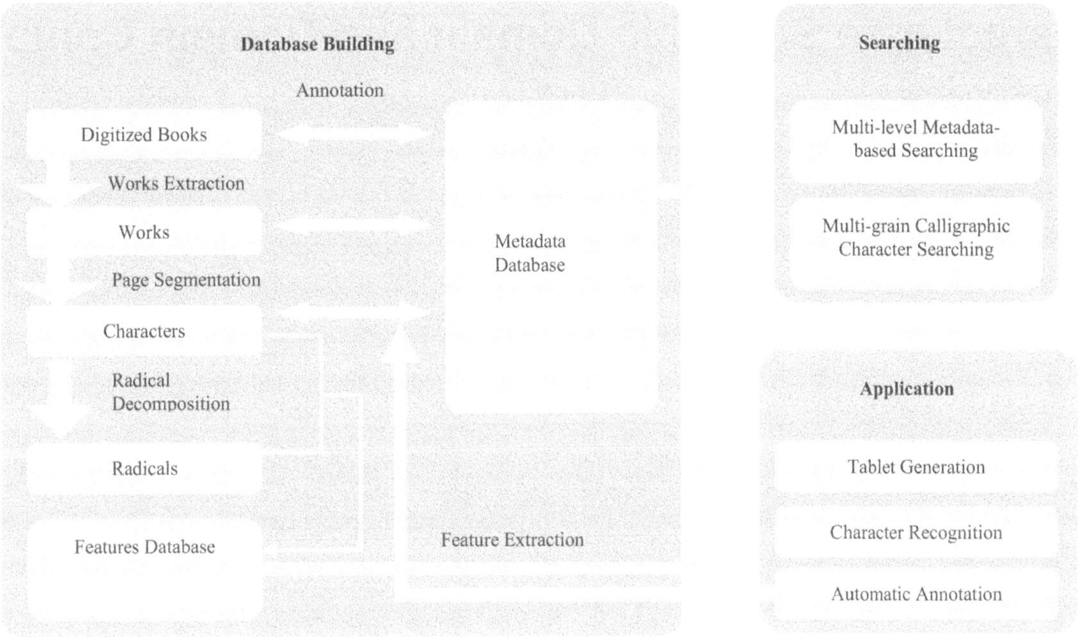

Figure 2. Architecture of CADAL Digital Calligraphy System

3. DATABASE BUILDING

Most source data of CADAL Digital Calligraphy System comes from digitized books of CADAL digital library, which are the reproductions of original calligraphic works(usually stone rubbings or inked scrolls). A set of over 100,000 calligraphic characters were segmented and labeled, which are all extracted from 61 digitized books. The database contains over 1,100 works, some from over 1,000 years ago.

4. SEARCHING

The key part of CADAL Digital Calligraphy System is searching, which is the basic and most important part. Here we provide multi-level, multi-grain services of searching, not only providing multi-level metadata-based calligraphy searching, such as the metadata-based books search, metadata-based works search and metadata-based character search, but also providing multi-grain services of character searching, such as, content-based and radical-based calligraphic character search.

5. APPLICATION

CADAL Digital Calligraphy System is very useful in many domains. For example, we can use the metadata-based calligraphic character search to generate tablet of some famous historical calligrapher(**Figure 3**). In addition, unlike the printed character, Chinese calligraphic character is not easy to be recognized, content-based Chinese calligraphic character search method can help users to recognize the characters they don't know. Furthermore, the technique of recognition can also be used to perform auto annotation.

Figure 3. Tablet Generated(*Yan Style*)

6. CONCLUSION

In this paper, we described the CADAL Digital Calligraphy System, in which over 1,100 works and 100,000 characters are included. The services of multi-level metadata-based search(metadata-based books search, works search and characters search) and multi-grain calligraphic character search(content-based search and radical-based search) are provided. In the end, some search-related applications of CADAL Digital Calligraphy System like tablet generation and calligraphic character recognition are discussed.

7. ACKNOWLEDGMENTS

This work is supported by National Natural Science Foundation of China (No. 61070066), the CADAL Project and Research Center, Zhejiang University. We sincerely thank Yu Kai and Zhang Xiafeng for their advices and help during the work.

8. REFERENCES

[1] CADAL web site: http://www.cadal.zju.edu.cn.

[2] Universal Digital Library web site: http://www.ulib.org.

Characterize Scientific Domain and Domain Context

Jinsong Zhang
College of Transportation Management
Dalian Maritime University
Dalian, China, 116026
zhangjinsong85@163.com

Chun Guo
School of Library and Information Science
Indiana University
Bloomington, IN, USA, 47405
chunguo@indiana.edu

Xiaozhong Liu
School of Library and Information Science
Indiana University
Bloomington, IN, USA, 47405
liu237@indiana.edu

ABSTRACT

Domain knowledge map construction as an important method can describe the significant characters of a selected domain. In this research, we will address three problems for knowledge graph generation. Firstly, this paper will construct domain (core journals and conference proceedings) knowledge and domain context (domain citation) knowledge graphs, and propose a novel method to integrate those graphs. Secondly, two different methods will be investigated to associate keywords on the graph: Co-occur Domain Distance and Citation Probability Distribution Distance. Last but not least, the paper will propose an innovative method to evaluate the accuracy and coverage of knowledge graphs based on training keyword oriented Labeled-LDA model and validate different domain or domain context graphs.

Categories and Subject Descriptors

H.3.7 [**Digital Libraries**]: Digital Libraries

Keywords

Domain; Domain Context; Co-occur Domain Distance; Citation Probability Distribution Distance; Labeled LDA; Evaluation.

1. INTRODUCTION

Domain knowledge graph modeling is one of the most important methods to describe the significant characters of a selected domain, which is essential for domain information visualization, information retrieval, and bibliometric analysis. The constructed domain knowledge graph represents not only the important components, i.e. authors, keywords, publications, or journals, of the domain, but also the illustration of the social network relatedness between them, i.e. publication relatedness, co-authorship, or keyword co-occur probability. Most of the existing efforts of domain characterization are based on a selected domain publication corpus, such as the particular core journals or conference proceedings, and this sampling strategy can be biased. Especially when a large number of domain literatures are not available, it is difficult to generate or estimate comprehensive and accurate domain knowledge.

Fortunately, utilizing "domain context" publications, i.e. closely related journals or domain cited publications, can be able to solve the disconnection problem between the domain and its context. While more vertices and edges are imported in the domain context map, more noise notes will be emerged, which will threaten the precision of the graph. As a result, we will propose some rules to combine the domain and domain context graphs into a, hopefully, more accurate domain knowledge map.

As another contribution, we will propose a new method to evaluate and validate different graphs. For each graph, the cost of the shortest path between two random vertexes is validated by using the real-world keyword topical distribution divergence. For each keyword topic, the unigram probability language model is trained via Labeled LDA (LLDA) algorithm [1].

2. LITERATURE REVIEW

Domain characterization researches were popularized since 1960s, and have been studied in terms of co-author and citation based bibliometric analysis. Recent developments in metadata and text mining make it possible to harvest rich knowledge by leveraging word and keyword distributions across large number of publications by means of keyword co-occurrence likelihood. For example, Ding et al. [2] mapped information retrieval literatures by using co-word analysis on papers collected from the Science Citation Index (SCI) and Social Science Citation Index (SSCI). Tian et al. [3] used the Institute for Scientific Information (ISI) database to measure the field of Geographic Information System (GIS) using keyword analysis. More recent work by Su and Lee [4] visualized the two-dimensional knowledge map by utilizing keyword co-occurrence network for Technology Foresight related papers from different perspectives. But there are few researches about comparison of domain modeling and domain context modeling.

On the other hand, generally, it is difficult to evaluate a graph, and the most common method is to compute the amount of vertices and edges or the connectivity and density. For example, Molloy et al. [5] introduced a method for judging the size of the giant component of a random graph using by a given vertices of degree sequence. Havel et al. [6] presented the basic theorems of distance geometry in Euclidean space and gave formal proofs of the correctness, as well as discussed the implications of distance geometry for the energy minimization of macromolecules.

3. DOMAIN AND DOMAIN CONTEXT

In this section, we will describe the approaches we have taken to characterize the domain and domain context by using four different keyword based graphs. And provide the details of how to construct 4 different kinds of graph: Domain co-occur graph; Domain context co-occur graph; Domain citation graph; Domain context citation graph. After that, two new graphs are generated by combining domain and domain context graphs based on rules.

JCDL'12, June 10–14, 2012, Washington, DC, USA.
ACM 978-1-4503-1154-0/12/06.

Table 1. Graphs generated in this paper

	Co-occur approach	Citation approach
Doman knowledge	Domain co-occur graph	Domain citation graph
Domain Context knowledge	Domain context co-occur graph	Domain context citation graph
Domain and Domain Context	Combine co-occur graph	Combine citation graph

For co-occur approach, we will utilize Normalized Domain Distance (NDD), stemmed from Normalized Google Distance [7], which weight the normalized domain based keyword distance by using the likelihood that two keywords co-occur in the same publications.

$$NDD(key_1, key_2) = \frac{\max\{\log f(key_1), \log f(key_2)\} - \log f(key_1, key_2)}{\log M - \min\{\log f(key_1), \log f(key_2)\}}$$

where M is the total number of keywords; $f(key_1)$ and $f(key_2)$ are the number of key_1 and key_2 in the search result, respectively; and $f(key_1, key_2)$ is the number of two keywords co-occur in the same publications.

For citation approach, we first compute the probability of keyword and citation, according to:

$$P(C_i \mid Key_i) = \frac{count(C_i, Key_i)}{count(Key_i)}$$

Then, the relatedness between keywords is calculated by KL-Divergence between the citation distributions.

In order to get a combine the domain graph and domain context graph, we used the following rules. Please note, domain context is a much larger and nosier graph compared with domain graph.

a. Re-weight edges (by using linear combination)

$$Edge\ weight = \alpha \cdot Edgeweight(domain) + (1-\alpha) \cdot Edgeweight(domaincontext)$$

b. Integrate additional edges from domain context

Any two nodes (domain) do not have edge:
If (Edge exist in (domain context) && weight > threshold1)
Create Edge.

c. Integrate additional vertexes from domain context

For each vertex in (domain context):
If (vertex connect number to node in (domain)> threshold2 && vertex not exist in (domain))
Integrate vertex && edges.

4. CONNECTIVITY EVALUATION

In this section, a list of essential keywords for IR domain will be sampled, and the connectivity of those keywords will be compared by using 6 different graphs (in table 1).

First, we trained the LLDA [1] topic model for each keyword based topic (the keyword is assumed as the topical label for each publication) by using publication abstract, and generate a probability distribution for each keyword $P(word_x|keyword_y)$.

Then, we calculated the cosine similarity for each two keywords pair, and using the similarity between two keywords as the real-world topical distance. To validate the accuracy of a specific keyword based knowledge graph, we assume if, on the graph, two keywords are directly connected, the cosine similarity (with LLDA model) score should be high. Otherwise, if they are not directly connected, the similarity score should be low. Based on this assumption, we calculated the graph precision, number of edges LLDA similarity > 0.9 (on graph) / number of edges on graph, and recall, number of edges LLDA similarity > 0.9 (on graph) / number of all keyword pairs LLDA similarity > 0.9. Finally, we compared the graph quality by using the F measure.

In the preliminary experiment, we find the new constructed graph by integrating domain and domain context graphs can enhance the F score, which result is presented in Table 2.

Table 2 F1-Score for 6 graphs

Graph name	precision	Recall	F-Score
Domain co-occur	0.765	0.317	0.224
Context co-occur	0.167	0.761	0.137
Combine co-occur	0.497	0.426	0.229
Domain citation	0.935	0.126	0.111
Context citation	0.291	0.37	0.162
Combine citation	0.813	0.313	0.226

5. CONCLUSION

In this paper, we make the following contributions: (1) Generated 4 graphs based on domain and domain context with the methods of Co-occur Distance and Citation Probability Distribution Distance. (2) Used 3 rules to combine domain and domain context graphs. (3) For each keyword, the unigram probability model is trained via LLDA algorithm and seen as the real-world distribution, and then presented an evaluation method to compare the precision, recall and F1-score for the 6 graphs.

6. REFERENCES

[1] Ramage, D., Hall, D., Nallapati, R., and Manning, C. D. 2009. Labeled LDA: a supervised topic model for credit attribution in multi-labeled corpora. In *Proceedings of the 2009 Conference on Empirical Methods in Natural Language Processing* (Singapore, August 06 - 07, 2009). EMNLP '09. ACM, New York, NY, 248-256.

[2] Ding, Y., Chowdhury, G. G., and Foo, S. 2001. Bibliometric cartography of information retrieval research by using co-word analysis. *Information Processing & Management*, 37, 6 (Nov. 2001), 817-842. DOI= http://dx.doi.org/10.1016/S0306-4573(00)00051-0.

[3] Tian, Y., Wen, C., and Hong, S. 2008. Global scientific production on GIS research by bibliometric analysis from 1997 to 2006. *J. Informetrics*. 2, 1 (Jan. 2008), 65-74. DOI= http://dx.doi.org/10.1016/j.joi.2007.10.001.

[4] Su, H. and Lee, P. 2010. Mapping knowledge structure by keyword co-occurrence: a first look at journal papers in Technology Foresight. *Scientometrics*. 85, 1 (Jun. 2010), 65-79. DOI= 10.1007/s11192-010-0259-8.

[5] Molloy, M. and Reed, B. 1998. The Size of the Giant Component of a Random Graph with a Given Degree Sequence. *Combinatorics, Probability and Computing*. 7 (1998), 295-305.

[6] Harary, F. 1962. The Maximum Connectivity of a Graph. *Proc Natl Acad Sci U S A*. 48, 7 (July 1962),1142-1146.

[7] Cilibrasi, R. L. and Vitanyi, P.M.B. 2004. The Google Similarity Distance, *IEEE Trans. Knowledge and Data Engineering*. 19, 3 (2007), 370-383.DOI= 10.1109/TKDE.2007.48.

Collaboration and Communication Tools used by the Biodiversity Heritage Library: Refining Strategies for Success

Trish Rose-Sandler
Center for Biodiversity Informatics
Missouri Botanical Garden 4344
Shaw Blvd. St. Louis, MO 63110
1 314-577-9473 x6396
Trish.rose-sandler@mobot.org

Constance Rinaldo
Ernst Mayr Library of the Museum of Comparative Zoology, Harvard
University 26 Oxford St.
Cambridge, MA 02138
1 617-495-4576
crinaldo@oeb.harvard.edu

William Ulate
Center for Biodiversity Informatics
Missouri Botanical Garden 4344
Shaw Blvd. St. Louis, MO 63110
1 314-577-9473 x6398
William.Ulate@mobot.org

Keri Thompson
Smithsonian Institution Libraries
NMNH, 10th and Constitution Ave
NW Washington, DC 20560
1 202-633-1716
thompsonk@si.edu

Martin Kalfatovic
Smithsonian Institution Libraries
NMNH, 10th and Constitution Ave
NW Washington, DC 20560
1 202-633-1705
kalfatovicm@si.edu

ABSTRACT

Through the application of multiple strategies and tools, the Biodiversity Heritage Library has created an effective and collaborative multi-institutional virtual organization. The purpose of this paper is to explore the communication and collaboration strategies used by the BHL to create, maintain, and provide open access to its corpus of biodiversity literature. BHL, in its seventh year, is a mature service and no longer a pilot project. Largely driven from the ground up, and without any institutional mandate, the BHL has successfully and organically fostered an organizational model that has encouraged innovation, user engagement, and global expansion.

Categories and Subject Descriptors

H.3.7 [**Digital Libraries**]:User Issues

Keywords

Communication, collaboration, digital library, biodiversity, libraries, biodiversity heritage library, social media, subject repository

1. Communication and Collaboration in the Biodiversity Heritage Library

The purpose of this poster is to explore the communication and collaboration strategies used by the Biodiversity Heritage Library (BHL)[1]to create, maintain, and provide open access to its corpus of biodiversity literature. We will review how, through the application of multiple strategies and tools, BHL has created an effective and collaborative multi-institutional virtual organization. We will also discuss the tools and strategies employed by BHL to communicate with users in order to leverage their experiences and feedback to improve and maintain the content and functionality of the digital library.

[1] http://www.biodiversitylibrary.org/

JCDL '12, June 10–14, 2012, Washington, DC, USA.
ACM 978-1-4503-1154-0/12/06.

The Biodiversity Heritage Library is a global initiative of collaborating projects and activities that seeks to digitize, preserve and make available to the world the legacy literature of biodiversity. What started as a consortium of 10 natural history, research and botanical libraries in the United States and the United Kingdom in 2005 has now grown to 14 members as of January 2012. Additionally, BHL now includes collaborating projects in Europe, Australia, China, Brazil, and Egypt with over 40 individual institutions as members. The BHL portal1 is the primary access point through which the BHL resources are served and the content now encompasses more than 37 million pages from around 53,000 titles.

The idea was then, and still remains, to support biodiversity related sciences by providing free and open access to biodiversity science publications such as Linnaeus's *Systema naturae*[2] and Darwin's *Origin of Species*[3] along with hundreds of thousands of other works describing the biodiversity of species. BHL has received strong support both in the library and the biodiversity science communities. After seven years, the BHL is no longer a pilot project but a mature service which researchers in systematic biology rely on for their daily work. Reaching this important milestone provides an opportunity to reflect on how collaboration and communication amongst its members as well as with its users has played a key role in the growth and continued enhancement of this digital repository.

The BHL has employed multiple collaboration and communication strategies over its seven-year existence. Its loosely coupled operational structure allows for nimbleness of decision- making (i.e. recommendations do not necessarily need to go through multiple hierarchical levels of decision making in order to be turned into action items). As a result, BHL has been able to respond to its users and the needs of the biodiversity community much more quickly.

Adoption of collaboration tools among BHL partners, both freely available and commercial and employment of those tools in sometimes non-traditional ways, has enabled a virtual

[2] http://biodiversitylibrary.org/page/6981741

[3] http://biodiversitylibrary.org/item/18405

organization to perform as effectively as a non-virtual organization. Varying time zones became less important as BHL found ways to communicate with its members in both synchronous and asynchronous ways. In recognition of its outstanding collaborative partnerships, the BHL received the Outstanding Collaboration Citation Award in 2010 from the Association for Library Collections & Technical Services, a division of the American Library Association.

Experimenting with multiple social media platforms simultaneously has allowed BHL to reach diverse audiences, receive user input through multiple channels, and engage with users in a way that simulates in-person interactions. User input is given equal weight as input from BHL staff and oftentimes users suggestions result in newly available content or user interface changes within days or weeks rather than months or years. In this way users feel they are active contributors to the BHL rather than just passive users of its content and become much more invested in its success and longevity.

Not satisfied with just building a silo of biodiversity content, BHL pushes content out into the biodiversity commons to allow it to be recontextualized and built upon by others working in similar domains. This openness of data has been well received by the community and users have done commendable work giving it new life beyond its original form of publication. To be a part of the global "biodiversity commons" means going beyond merely providing a portal for 37 million plus and counting pages of historic texts to users. One key goal is to expose data for reuse. Many BHL users requested machine and human harvestable data. This allows data which was created for a specific purpose and audience (e.g. historic texts, nomenclatural services, encyclopedias) to interact with other data and serve new, previously unimagined, roles.

BHL is a massive dataset: not only of bibliographic data but also page images (often extraordinarily beautiful illustrations), text that has been run through optical character recognition (OCR) software, and of particular note, scientific names that are useful in multidisciplinary research (e.g. systematics, natural language processing, humanities).Scientific names found in the historic literature demonstrate the power of open data because they are an important access point for researchers in biodiversity. . Each page in BHL has been OCR'd and that text is run against a webservice available via UBio's Taxonfinder[4] resulting so far, in the identification of 80 million scientific names in our corpus. Not only is access to the literature important but making use of the data elements embedded within the text is critical to connecting the dots throughout the cycle of research. Applications such as this "taxonomic intelligence" expose the occurrences of scientific names within the OCR'd text and this rich dataset is made available for re-use via standard protocols.

Numerous projects have taken advantage of BHL's "open data" and some have even developed applications that re-contexualize BHL data such as the Encyclopedia of Life[5], BioStor[6], and Synynyms[7].

BHL is now looking to bring some of that enhanced content, for example articles derived from BHL journals, back into the portal to further enrich its services. In this way the crowdsourced data completes an object's "digital content life cycle" whose primary processes include: creation, management, discovery, use and reuse. [6]

We acknowledge there are potential weaknesses in our organizational model such as redundancy and duplication of effort. But in considering them within the model, by making intentional choices to accept these overlaps in order to achieve cost efficiency and not derail timelines, we have turned these issues into strengths that provide resilience. BHL members will continue to investigate new collaboration and communication strategies, abandon those it feels no longer serve its mission and adopt and develop new tools as needed for the community we serve.

ACKNOWLEDGMENTS

The authors would like to thank all of our BHL colleagues for sharing their expertise so freely in all venues. Funding for the BHL has been generously provided by the MacArthur, Sloan, Moore, and Lounsbery Foundations along with the Institute for Museum and Library Services, the Smithsonian Institution and the Museum of Comparative Zoology at Harvard University.

REFERENCES

[1] Waibel, Gunter. 2010. Collaboration Contexts: Framing Local, Group and Global Solutions. Report produced by OCLC Research.http://www.oclc.org/research/publications/library/2010/2010-09.pdf

[2] Gwinn, N.E. & C. Rinaldo. The Biodiversity Heritage Library: sharing biodiversity literature with the world. *IFLA Journal* 35(1): 25-34 (2009).

[3] Pilsk, Suzanne C., Person, Matthew A., DeVeer, Joseph M., Furfey, John F. and Kalfatovic, Martin R. 2010. The Biodiversity Heritage Library: Advancing Metadata Practices in a Collaborative Digital Library. *Journal of Library Metadata*, 10: 136-155. DOI:10.1080/19386389.2010.506400

[4] Costantino, G. , B. Crowley, R. Morin, and E. Thomas. 2011. Heeding the call: user feedback management and the digital library. *66th IFLA Council and General Conference*, San Juan, Puerto Rico.

[5] Schrier, Robert A. 2011. Digital Librarianship & Social Media: the Digital Library as Conversation Facilitator *D-Lib Magazine*, July/August 2011 Volume 17, Number 7/8. DOI:10.1045/july2011-schrier

[6] Ooman, Johan and Lora Aroyo. 2011. Crowdsourcing in the Cultural Heritage Domain: Opportunities and Challenge

[4] http://www.ubio.org

[5] http://eol.org

[6] http://biostor.org

[7] http://synynyms.no.de/

Data Determination, Disambiguation, and Referencing in Molecular Biology

Shuheng Wu Besiki Stvilia Dong Joon Lee
College of Communication and Information, Florida State University, PO Box 3062100, Tallahassee, FL 32306-2100
sw09f@my.fsu.edu bstvilia@fsu.edu dl10e@my.fsu.edu

ABSTRACT
Entity and instance determination, disambiguation, and referencing, referred to as authority control in libraries, are essential for scientific research. This study examines the authority control practices and issues in molecular biology using literature and scenario analyses. The analyses imply that the concept of authority control in molecular biology is associated with three tasks: named entity recognition, disambiguation, and unification. The identified authority control issues were conceptualized as quality problems caused by four sources: inconsistent or incomplete mapping, context changes, entity changes, and changes in entity metadata. This study can inform librarians and repository curators of the needs and issues of authority control in molecular biology and other related disciplines.

Categories and Subject Descriptors
H.3.7 [Information Storage And Retrieval] Digital Libraries - *standards*

Keywords
Entity determination, entity disambiguation, entity referencing, authority control, metadata, molecular biology.

1. INTRODUCTION
With advances in computational technologies, scientific research is increasingly data driven. There are growing needs to share, reuse, and aggregate data from different contxts. To maintain data in a (re)usable state for ongoing research, it is necessary to assure the quality of entity metadata. Effective management of entity metadata and the ability to determine and disambiguate entities and instances are essential for scientific research. In biology, taxonomists may need to determine whether a species belongs to an established taxon or represents a new taxon. Biomedical researchers may need to identify gene variants and their locus in the genome by comparing their sequences to the reference sequences in nucleotide databases. There have been distinct, domain specific approaches to entity metadata management. Different communities have proposed different conceptual models, metadata schemas, and controlled vocabularies for building entity profiles. Understanding the needs for entity determination and disambiguation across different domains can help the development of more effective data management systems, and enable interoperability of these systems.

Entity and instance determination, disambiguation, and referencing, referred to as authority control in libraries, are essential for data management in any domain. With advances in sequencing technologies, the large amount of quantitative data generated from high-throughput experiments poses challenges for organizing, retrieving, analyzing, and curating biological data. This study examines the authority control practices and issues in molecular biology, which can inform librarians and repository curators of the needs of and approaches to authority control in molecular biology, biomedicine, and biochemistry.

2. RESEARCH QUESTIONS
This study uses literature review and scenario based task analysis [4] to answer the following research questions:

- What are the needs and requirements for authority control in molecular biology?
- How is authority control currently implemented in molecular biology? What entities and attributes are controlled? What are some of the issues of the current practices of authority control?

3. AUTHORITY CONTROL PRACTICES
Molecular biology is a branch of biology dealing with the structure, function, and interaction of the most important macromolecules of living matter, primarily nucleic acids (i.e., DNA, RNA) and proteins [8]. Biological scientists usually report newly found entities in the literature, and deposit their information to related databases as required by journals or affiliated institutions. They also use these databases to retrieve information about these entities using their names and alternates, which are usually incomplete with respect to those found in the literature [2]. The concept of authority control in molecular biology is associated with three tasks: *named entity recognition, disambiguation*, and *unification*. Named entity recognition identifies all the instances of a name for a specific type of biological entity within the literature. Name entity disambiguation links a recognized named entity to a concept in a controlled vocabulary or an ontology [1]. Named entity unification is a process to aggregate and conceptualize all the biological entities shared among communities, standardize the nomenclature and use of these entities, and enable interoperability of biological databases [3]. Literature analysis indicates the primary entities controlled in molecular biology are RNA, DNA, proteins, cells, tissues, species, organisms, drugs, and diseases [6].

4. AUTHORITY CONTROL ISSUES
The issues of authority control in molecular biology can be analyzed within four categories of quality problem sources: inconsistent or incomplete mapping, context changes, entity changes, and changes in entity metadata [7]. The last three categories can be generalized as dynamic quality problems.

4.1 Dynamic Quality Problems

Genes and proteins are recommended to be named according to their functions [5]. However, scientists are still learning about protein functions. They may claim different names for proteins to indicate their findings of protein functions. As a result, several synonymous names are in use for the same genes and proteins across databases and the literature. Researchers will risk missing information, if they do not consider all available gene or protein names when doing database or literature searches.

Scenario 1: Biological researchers are interested in the function of a protein named FAM20C in humans. They want to know about previous research on this protein by doing database and literature searches. This protein might have various names if different scientists have identified different functions over time. Researchers use the current protein name FAM20C to find related articles from databases, and analyze the reference list of these articles to know about other names (e.g., dentin matrix protein 4) of this protein. They then use these names to find more related articles.

4.2 Inconsistent Mapping

Biological researchers may need to collect data from multiple sources to do experiments, interpret results, and make predictions. Even though many biological databases have cross-references to related databases, each of them has its own identifier system and metadata schema. Most of the time, users have to manually convert an identifier from one database to another.

Scenario 2: Biomedical researchers are studying proteins in Androgen-repressed human prostate cancer cells. They have the names and International Protein Index (IPI) accession numbers (identifiers) of these proteins, and want to identify their cellular locations and functions by searching the National Center for Biotechnology Information (NCBI) databases. However, these databases do not use the IPI accession numbers as identifiers. Since these protein names are long and complicated (e.g., ABCF1 Isoform 1 of ATP-binding cassette sub-family F member 1) and various names are in use for the same proteins in the databases, researchers have to use X-REF Converter (i.e., an identifier converter) to convert the IPI accession numbers to the GenBank and UniProt protein accession numbers that are recognized in these databases.

4.3 Incomplete Mapping

Biologists may have difficulty finding and reusing data underlying published research due to incomplete metadata in existing biological databases [5]. For example, contextual metadata, which is essential to understand the function of genes and proteins, is missing in sequence databases. Missing the metadata necessary for discovering, (re)using, and interpreting existing data may hamper the research process.

Scenario 3: A graduate student is doing a bioinformatics course project to determine the taxonomy of the giant panda. The student wants to collect the ND2 gene sequence of the giant panda and six different kinds of bears from the GenBank to do phylogenetic analysis. In particular, the student is trying to determine whether the giant panda belongs to Ursidae as true bears or is an independent species. To answer this question, the student wants to collect the ND2 gene sequence from multiple individuals within a species. However, several records retrieved from the GenBank are repetitive or redundant, representing the same sequence. As no identify information about the specimen is provided in the GenBank, the student has to find and read the publications that discuss the data to determine if the sequence was collected from the same individual or not.

5. DISCUSSION

The analyses imply that entity metadata in molecular biology is dynamic in that biological entities can change or mutate with time and space (e.g., mutated genes). Due to the semantic ambiguities in entity names and symbols, the biological community makes use of natural language processing techniques (e.g., text-mining) to perform entity recognition and disambiguation in the literature. Furthermore, the complexity of biological entities and their attributes leads to the development and adoption of bio-ontologies to represent, disambiguate, and unify entities, and manage biological knowledge. Future research will examine entities and relationships, knowledge organization systems, and authority control practices in other scientific disciplines.

6. REFERENCES

[1] Ananiadou, S., Friedman, C., and Tsujii, J. 2004. Introduction: Named entity recognition in biomedicine. *Biomedical Informatics.* 37, 6 (Dec. 2004), 393-395. DOI=http://dx.doi.org/10.1016/j.jbi.2004.08.011

[2] Cohen, A. M. and Hersh, W. R. 2005. A survey of current work in biomedical text mining. *Briefings in Bioinformatics.* 6, 1, 57-71. DOI=http://dx.doi.org/10.1093/bib/6.1.57

[3] Gene Ontology Consortium. 2000. Gene Ontology: Tool for the unification of biology. *Nature Genetics.* 25, 25-29. DOI=http://dx.doi.org/10.1038/75556

[4] Go, K. and Carroll, J. M. 2004. In *The handbook of task analysis for human-computer interaction,* D. Diaper and N. Stanton, Eds. Lawrence Erlbaum Associates, Mahwah, NJ, 117-133.

[5] Greenberg, J. 2009. Theoretical considerations of lifecycle modeling: An analysis of the Dryad Repository demonstrating automatic metadata propagation, inheritance, and value system adoption. *Cataloging & Classification Quarterly.* 47, 3-4, 380-402. DOI=http://dx.doi.org/10.1080/01639370902737547

[6] Krallinger, M., Valencia, A., and Hirschman, L. (2008). Linking genes to literature: Text mining, information extraction, and retrieval applications for biology. *Genome Biology, 9*(Suppl. 2), S8-S8.14. DOI=http://dx.doi.org/10.1186/gb-2008-9-S2-S8

[7] Stvilia, B., Gasser, L., Twidale M., and Smith, L. C. 2007. A framework for information quality assessment. *Journal of the American Society for Information Science and Technology.* 58, 12 (Oct. 2007), 1720-1733. DOI=http://dx.doi.org/10.1002/asi.20652

[8] Turner, P., McLennan, A., Bates, A., and White, M. 2005. *Molecular biology* (3rd ed.). Taylor & Francis, New York, NY.

[9] Wain, H. M., Bruford, E. A., Lovering, R. C., Lush, M. J., Wright, M. W., and Povey, S. (2002). Guidelines for Human Gene Nomenclature. *Genomics, 79*, 464-470. DOI=http://dx.doi.org/10.1006/geno.2002.6748

Digital Libraries for Computational Journalism

Luis Francisco-Revilla
School of Information
1 University Station D7000
Austin, TX, 78715-0390
1+512-471-3821
revilla@ischool.utexas.edu

ABSTRACT

Computational journalism is driving the evolution of news media, devising new ways for collecting and analyzing large numbers of digital artifacts such as tweets and memes. This paper presents Breadcrumbs PDL, a specialized Personal Digital Library system that helps readers and journalists to access and use a collection of user-detected memes. PDL is part of Project Breadcrumbs, which aims to capitalize on public participation in the news media cycle. PDL supports browsing and exploration, and supports recommendations services that suggest alternative memes to read and ways to organize the users' personal workspace. Based on the users' clipping and organizational behaviors and textual similarities between clips, PDL can infer relationships between memes that computers alone cannot easily detect.

Categories and Subject Descriptors

H.3.7 [**Information Storage and Retrieval**]: Digital Libraries – *systems issues, user issues.*

General Terms

Measurement, Experimentation, Human Factors.

Keywords

Computational journalism, human computation, spatial hypertext.

1. INTRODUCTION

Computational journalism is an emergent interdisciplinary field that brings together computation and journalism. While in the past computation has been blamed for disrupting the traditional models and processes of news media, journalism now recognizes computation as a driving force for lowering costs, increasing effectiveness, and encouraging participation [2].

An interesting aspect of computational journalism is that it has two foci: one is data-centric, focusing on handling and analyzing large collections, and on the other is human-centric, focusing on gathering, producing and distributing the right information to the right people. The key to the success of computational journalism is to create and support a collaborative enterprise that balances the computation with human participation. To achieve this, the work presented here follows a human computation approach that aims at taking advantage of the brainpower of people to solve problems that computers cannot. This work is based on the idea that readers and journalists can detect important text segments in news media, and identify relationships between them, which computers cannot.

JCDL'12, June 10–14, 2012, Washington, DC, USA.
ACM 978-1-4503-1154-0/12/06.

2. MOTIVATION

Computational journalism is profoundly changing the processes of production, distribution, and consumption, providing insights in areas such as *coverage bias* (assessing if different cultural or ethnic groups have similar new coverage), *saga construction* (identifying a series of related stories and events), and *meme tracking* (tracking how specific phrases travel over the Web) [4].

Memes are broadly defined as "*signatures* of topics and events that propagate and diffuse over the Web" and they are often operationalized as short distinctive text segments that appear in documents with relatively little variation [4]. Meme tracking is particularly useful for journalists because they can use it for identifying "what's hot" (news stories that spread the furthest over the Web), and for studying how their own stories are disseminated. However, in order to track memes, it is first necessary to detect text segments that are relevant memes. *Meme detection* can be accomplished by using machine-based or human-based approaches. Machine-based approaches for meme detection rely on explicit textual cues such as titles or bolded text [4]. This type of approach can be automated and scale up easily but, it is worth noting that it is the writers (not the readers) who chose the words that make the title or bolded text. In contrast, human-based approaches for meme detection are based on user actions (e.g., highlighting or sharing). This type of approach is it provides a high accuracy from the reader perspective.

The success of human-based approaches for meme detection depends on a proper interaction design, making it extremely easy and natural to create and gather the memes. The Breadcrumbs Project [1] aims to capitalize on public participation in the global news cycle by supporting *human-based meme detection* in order to enhance and facilitate the work of journalists [1]. Breadcrumbs provides an interface that enhances newspaper Web sites, allowing readers to select memes (here on referred as *clips*) and store them online. This behavior is similar to sharing of reading activities in iCADAL [5], or clipping text in Amazon's Kindle. The resulting collection of clips provides the opportunity to infer relationships between uses and clips. Humans can participate in this process provided that they have proper interaction mechanisms for accessing and manipulating the collection. This work introduces a Personal Digital Library interface designed that allows readers and journalist to interact with their clip collection.

3. BREADCRUMBS PDL

PDL is a specialized personal digital library interface built upon WARP [3] that connects with the Breadcrumbs project. It presents users with a workspace that allows them to read, manipulate and organize their clips, making it easier to find and express relationships between clips. Figure 2 shows the initial interface for

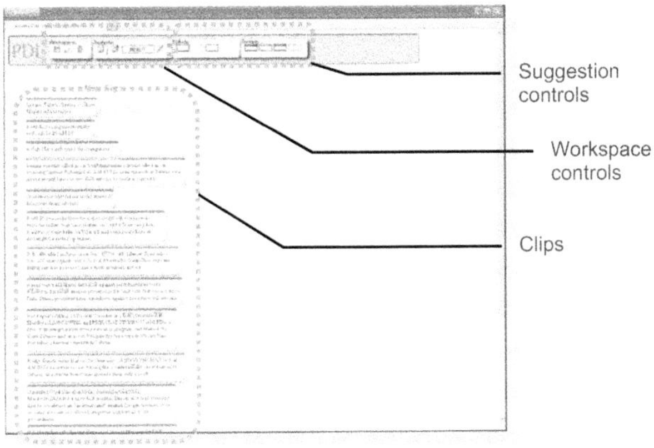

Figure 2. Initial Workspace in PDL

a user. All new clips (previously created with the Clipper) appear in the "New Clips" section Breadcrumbs can suggest a workspace organization automatically. Figure 3 shows an organization of clips divided into 12 clusters. Each cluster is given a heading. Users can accept or decline the organization, and then proceed organizing manually by moving and arranging clips, classifying them with labels and groups.

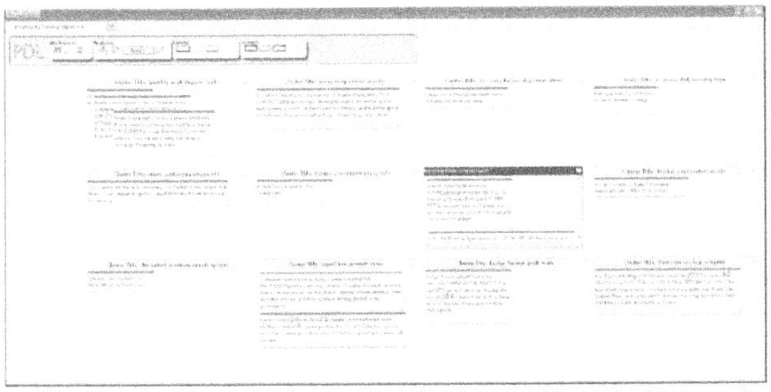

Figure 3. Alternative Workspace Organization

As users organize the clips, PDL infers the visual relationships between them (see Figure 5). These actions express relationships that are difficult to detect using automatic mechanisms. For example, users who are bilingual can easily organize their clips in different languages into topical groups.

As PDL detects spatial relationships between groups of clips, it also starts analyzing and aggregating their content and metadata. This allows PDL to produce aggregate digital artifacts such as tag clouds and meme clusters. PDL informs Breadcrumbs to access the inferred groups, tag clouds, and meme clusters to provide more targeted suggestions, and learn which user communities select which memes. In addition, PDL combines the spatial parser inferences with content analysis algorithms that analyze the clips' text and metadata in order to suggest relevant clips from other users, and suggest proper places for new clips in the workspace.

4. CONCLUSION

A key problem in computational journalism is to create and a collaborative enterprise that integrates human and machine computation. PDL encourages human computation and combines it with algorithmic approaches. PDL helps readers to discover and

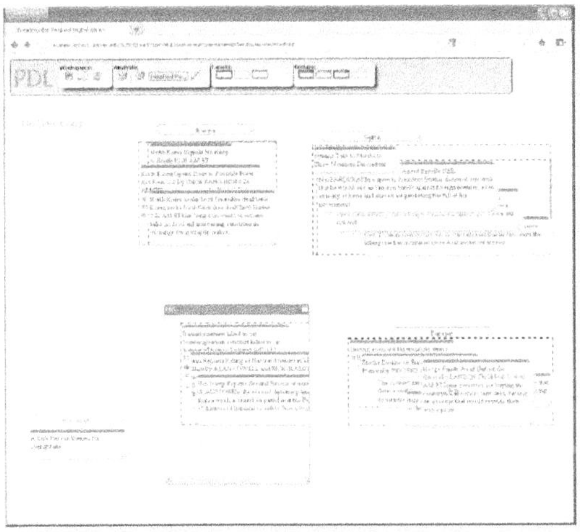

Figure 5. Visual Relationships in Workspace

express relationships between, explore clips and workspaces authored by other people, and understand better their clip collection as a whole. PDL helps journalists to learn which user communities select which memes, discover hidden relationships between clips, and understand better their readers' perspective.

PDL contributes to the field of computational journalism by showing how to create a collaborative enterprise that balances human and machine computation. PDL uses a spatial hypermedia to support the activities of readers and journalists by providing services that help them interact with their collections.

5. ACKNOWLEDGMENTS

This work is financed by the European Regional Development Fund through the COMPETE Programme (operational programme for competitiveness) and by National Funds through the FCT – Fundação para a Ciência e a Tecnologia (Portuguese Foundation for Science and Technology), project UTA-Est/MAI/0007/2009.

6. REFERENCES

[1] Figueira, A. 2011. A Social Network Built from Clips of Online News. In *Proc. of the International Conference on Internet Technologies & Society (ITS 2011)*. Shanghai, China. December, 2011.

[2] Essa, I., Computation + journalism: A study of computation and journalism and how they impact each other [online]. Available: http://www.computation-and-journalism.com/

[3] Francisco-Revilla, L., and Shipman, F.M. 2004. WARP: a web-based dynamic spatial hypertext. In *Proc. of the fifteenth ACM conference on Hypertext and hypermedia* (HT '04). ACM, New York, NY, USA, 235-236.

[4] Leskovec, J., Backstrom, L., and Kleinberg, J. 2009. Meme-tracking and the dynamics of the news cycle. In *Proc. of the 15th ACM SIGKDD international conference on Knowledge discovery and data mining* (KDD '09). ACM, New York, NY, USA, 497-506.

[5] Zhang, Y., Wang, A., Yu, H., Li, R., Wei, B., and Pan, J. 2011. When personalization meets socialization: an iCADAL approach. In *Proc. of the 11th annual international ACM/IEEE joint conference on Digital libraries* (JCDL '11). ACM, New York, NY, USA, 459-460.

Comparison of Three Digital Library Interfaces: Open Library, Google Books, and Hathi Trust

Matthew Miller
Pratt Institute
144 West 14th Street
New York, NY 10011
thisismattmiller@gmail.com

Gilok Choi
Pratt Institute
144 West 14th Street
New York, NY 10011
gchoi58@pratt.edu

Lindsay Chell
Pratt Institute
144 West 14th Street
New York, NY 10011
lindsay.chell@gmail.com

ABSTRACT

Digital libraries often require very specialized interfaces in order to present various types of digital content. It is therefore critical to create interfaces that improve presentation of digital information and maximize user experience with digital collections. In this respect, this research aims to examine interfaces of three digital libraries that provide collections of digital text. The three digital libraries include Open Library, Google Books, and Hathi Trust. An evaluation matrix was developed to measure usability, aesthetics and interface components.

The overall findings of the study showed that the majority of the participants preferred the Open Library interface followed by Google Books. The statistical analysis indicated that Open Library is significantly better than Google Books and Hathi Trust in terms of usability, aesthetics, and interface components. The preference for the Open Library stemmed largely from aesthetic choices. Participants also appreciated the use of elements that are analogous to their physical counterparts.

Categories and Subject Descriptors

H.5.2 [**Information Interfaces and Presentation**]: User Interfaces – *User-centered design; Screen design (e.g., text, graphics, color); Evaluation/methodology*

Keywords

Interface, design, usability, aesthetics, Open Library, Google Books, Hathi Trust

1. INTRODUCTION

Over the last decade, technology has made possible the development and deployment of very large digital collections. These online depositories provide instant access to thousands of formerly analog materials to anyone connected through the Internet. The primary goal of a digital library is to provide an easy and rich interaction with information [2]. Digital libraries offer a means to improve the presentation of information by expanding technological capabilities. The integration of analog information with the digital interface enriches the user's experience of the information. Also, a digital library allows users to access digital collections in a more efficient and faster way by reducing large amounts of textual information into visual formats [1]. This conversion of textual data into a visual pattern is one of the major strengths of a digital library.

JCDL'12, June 10–14, 2012, Washington, DC, USA.
ACM 978-1-4503-1154-0/12/06.

Digital libraries often require very specialized interfaces in order to present various types of digital content. These interfaces take traditionally analog materials and create a digital means of interaction. For this reason, it is critical to create interfaces that improve the presentation of digital information and maximize user experience with digital collections. In this respect, this research aims to examine interfaces of digital libraries in terms of usability, aesthetics and interface components.

2. METHODOLOGY

Twenty participants were recruited and participated in an experiment-like usability evaluation of three digital library interfaces. Participants included 13 males and 7 females, ranging in age from their 20s and 30s. All participants had a prior experience with digital libraries, and spent 20-30 minutes to complete this experiment. Three digital libraries were chosen based on their size, years of operation, and prominence in the community. They included:

- **Open Library** (www.openlibrary.org)

Open Library is a division of the non-profit Internet Archive organization. It provides a digital version of public domain and free texts.

- **Google Books** (www.books.google.com)

Google Books provides full versions of public domain and free texts as well as selections from non-public domain monographs.

- **Hathi Trust** (www.hathitrust.org)

Hathi Trust is a non-profit partnership of major research institutions and libraries concerning cultural records. It provides public domain texts.

The evaluation was conducted using a within-participant factorial design to identify differences between three digital library interfaces in terms of aesthetics, usability, and interface components.

First, respondents were asked to indicate their perceptions of aesthetics with four items. These items were proposed by Lavie and Tractinsky [3] and are used to measure classic dimensions of aesthetics (aesthetic, pleasant, clear, and clean).

Second, usability was evaluated with ten items based on McGee, Rich and Dumas [4] and Flanagin [5]. Respondents assessed the extent to which interfaces were consistent and efficient, organized, easy and intuitive, effective, useful, controllable, complete and sophisticated, professional, trustworthy, and reliable.

Finally, interface components were tested with seven items including collection browse, collection search, viewer navigation, viewer options, output options, accessibility and help features.

Responses to all three measures were recorded on a 1-to-7 Likert-type scale for which the higher score indicated greater perception of aesthetics, usability, and interface components.

Analysis of Variance (ANOVA) repeated measure was performed to identify the differences among three digital library interfaces in terms of usability and aesthetics. Qualitative data were also collected from the open-ended questionnaires to look at specific thoughts and ideas participants had in comparing three library interfaces.

3. RESULTS

ANOVA repeated measure revealed significant differences among three digital libraries in terms of usability ($F(2, 59) = 3.36$, $p<.05$), aesthetics ($F(2, 59) = 5.80$, $p<.001$), and interface components ($F(2, 59) = 4.89$, $p<.05$).

The subsequent pairwise comparisons showed Open Library and Google Books received significantly higher scores than Hathi Trust in terms of usability at the .05 level. However, there was no robust difference between Open Library and Google Books. With regard to aesthetics, Open Library showed significantly higher scores compared to Google Books and Hathi Trust at the .01 level. However, Google Books and Hathi Trust did not show any robust differences. Finally, there were statistically significant differences between Open Library and Hathi Trust in terms of interface components at the .05 level. Table 1 summarizes the results from pairwise comparisons.

	Libraries	Mean Diff.	SD	P
Usability	Hathi Trust vs. Open Library	4.95	2.14	.05
	Hathi Trust vs. Google Books	4.65	2.14	.05
Aesthetics	Open Library vs. Hathi Trust	2.90	1.07	.01
	Open Library vs. Google Books	3.35	1.07	.01
Interface Components	Open Library vs. Hathi Trust	6.05	1.94	.05

Table 1: Pairwise comparisons of three digital library interfaces in terms of usability, aesthetics, and interface components

4. CONCLUSION

This research showed that the majority of participants preferred the Open Library interface followed by Google Books. The preference for the Open Library stemmed mainly from aesthetic reasons such as the color scheme and large interface elements. Also, participants appreciated the use of elements that are analogous to their physical counterparts. For example, using book covers as item records reminded users of physical library environments.

The preference for Google Books was caused by the participant's familiarity with the general Google interface. With the ubiquitous presence of Google products, users felt familiar with a Google-based interface.

Finally, the least preferred digital library was the Hathi Trust digital library. It was found that the interface of Hathi Trust was overly complicated with too many options.

5. REFERENCES

- Börner, K., Chaomei C. (2001). Visual interfaces to digital libraries. ACM SIGIR Forum. vol. 35, no. 12.
- Rao, R., Pedersen, J. O., Hearst, M. A., Mackinlay, J. D., Card, S. K., Masinter, L., Halvorsen, P. K., Robertson, G. G. (1995). Rich interaction in the digital library. Communications of the ACM, vol. 38, no. 4, pp. 29-39.
- Lavie, T. Tractinsky, N. (2004).Assessing dimensions of perceived and visual aesthetics of web sites. International Journal of Human Computer Studies, vol. 26, no. 3, pp. 269-298.
- McGee, M., Rich, A., Dumans, J. (2004). Understanding the usability construct: User-perceived usability. In Proceedings of the Human Factors and Ergonomics Society, pp. 912-916.
- Flanagin, A. J., Metzger, M. J. (2003). The perceived credibility of personal Web page information as influenced by the sex of the source. Computers in Human Behavior, vol. 19, pp. 683-701.

Digital Preservation in a Box: Outreach Resources for Digital Stewardship

Butch Lazorchak
Library of Congress
101 Independence Ave. SE
Washington, DC 20540
wlaz@loc.gov

Susan Manus
Library of Congress
101 Independence Ave. SE
Washington, DC 20540
sman@loc.gov

Dever Powell
National Library of Medicine
8600 Rockville Pike
Bethesda, MD 20894-3819
powellem@mail.nih.gov

Jane Zhang
School of Library & Information Science
Catholic University of America
Washington, DC 20064
zhangj@cua.edu

ABSTRACT
"Digital Preservation in a Box" is a major activity of the National Digital Stewardship Alliance (NDSA) Outreach Working Group. This toolkit of digital stewardship outreach resources can be utilized by diverse communities as a gentle introduction to the concepts of preserving digital information.

Categories and Subject Descriptors
H.3.7 [**Information Storage and Retrieval**]: Digital Libraries–*user issues*.

General Terms
Documentation

Keywords
National Digital Stewardship Alliance, NDSA, outreach, personal archiving, digital stewardship, digital preservation, digital curation.

1. INTRODUCTION
The National Digital Stewardship Alliance is a collaboration of over 100 organizations from academia, science, government, and professional associations working together to find solutions for many of today's digital preservation challenges. The NDSA has several working groups; the Outreach Working Group [1] focuses on building relationships with stakeholder communities and preparing and sharing digital preservation information resources.

One activity of the group has been the creation of a toolkit of digital stewardship outreach resources that can be used by a variety of user communities. "Digital Preservation in a Box" is designed as a gentle introduction to the concepts and tools of preserving digital information.

JCDL'12, June 10–14, 2012, Washington, DC, USA.
ACM 978-1-4503-1154-0/12/06.

This poster presents an overview of the "Box" concept and describes the methodologies used by the NDSA and its member organizations to get resources into the "Box" and to disseminate the materials in support of Library and Information Science (LIS) education and professional outreach.

2. DIGITAL PRESERVATION IN A BOX - CONTENTS
The box of resources can be used to provide introductory-level education for those with little or no knowledge of digital preservation and digital curation issues. The "Box" includes a "Digital Preservation 101" guide, a glossary of terms, resources for educators, marketing and outreach guidance, slides, videos, and handouts. The resources are designed to be modular so that users can choose items that support a particular purpose. The "Box" is also designed to help users steward personal digital information, including photographs, audio, video, electronic mail, personal documents and web archives.

3. DIGITAL PRESERVATION IN A BOX - AUDIENCE
The materials are geared towards two potential audiences: those who create or manage digital information and need a working knowledge of digital preservation concepts on the job (professional development); and library and archives educators and those who teach or train others to preserve digital resources (curriculum development).

4. THE NDSA AND DIGITAL CURATION EDUCATION AT CATHOLIC UNIVERSITY
The School of Library and Information Science (SLIS) at the Catholic University of America (CUA) is an ALA-accredited LIS school located in Washington, DC [2]. In recent years, the School has launched a new Cultural Heritage Information Management (CHIM) course of study designed to provide 21st century LIS professionals with the knowledge and skills needed to help cultural heritage institutions address challenges posed by the evolving information environment [3].

New courses have been added to the CHIM curriculum, among them LSC617, *Digital Curation*, a course first offered in spring 2012 to 17 enrolled students. The course was developed at the same time CUA joined the NDSA in 2011. Two SLIS faculty, Interim Dean Ingrid Hsieh-Yee and Assistant Professor Jane

Zhang, joined the Outreach Working Group of the NDSA. The collaboration between SLIS and NDSA has been instrumental in the pedagogical design and implementation of digital curation education at CUA.

5. USE OF THE BOX AS A CURRICULUM DEVELOPMENT PROJECT

One important activity incorporated in the SLIS course is a digital preservation outreach project built around "Digital Preservation in a Box." Realizing the potential of the "Box" as a general education tool for digital preservation, NDSA Outreach Working Group members from multiple institutions – the Library of Congress (LC), National Library of Medicine (NLM), and CUA – worked together to implement a semester-long digital preservation outreach project for the class.

5.1. Design of the Project

The project design is based on a fundamental understanding of the role of LIS professionals in curating and preserving cultural heritage digital materials as well as the need to reach out and educate the public on the basic concepts and practices of digital preservation. The "Box," a central component of the project, introduces the concepts of preserving and curating digital information through a suite of resources that are available to anyone planning an outreach event or presentation, or teaching introductory digital preservation and curation concepts [4]. The project required students to evaluate the "Box" resources, conduct literature reviews, contribute content, and design, promote, and hold a public digital preservation and curation awareness workshop for college and university students.

The SLIS students worked in groups on a series of topics generated from the existing "Box" resources to address the needs of a targeted audience (college and university students) for preserving personal digital information. The goal was for the SLIS students to both discover new resources to recommend as additional materials for incorporation into to the Box, and to play a role in promoting a digital preservation and stewardship as part of a national effort.

5.2 Implementation of the Project

Two NDSA Outreach Working Group members visited the class in January and introduced the SLIS students to the NDSA and the rich potential of the "Box" [5]. Outreach Working Group members also hosted individual mentoring meetings for some students during the semester.

The outreach component of the project was integrated into the course as a major assignment. The students were divided into four groups. Each group selected four topics to address the digital preservation needs of college and university students and developed a series of questions to guide discussions at a public worshop: Why preserve personal digital information? What digital content should be selected to keep? How should personal digital content be organized and managed? How should they organize and manage their materials? What are appropriate long-term storage media and methods?

With the support of the CUA Mullen Library, the workshop was scheduled on a class day during the ALA Preservation Week (April 22-28, 2012) [6] in a special event room of the Library. In addition to the workshop and the submission of additional resources to be added to the "Box," each student kept a weekly journal documenting their participation in the project and reflecting their learning experiences. The SLIS students are also developing a project poster proposal for the 2012 NDIIPP/NDSA Partners Meeting.

6. FUTURE USES OF THE BOX

The NDSA/CUA collaboration on this project has resulted in the further development of "Box" content by providing researchers with a unique testbed for vetting the value of the "Box" concept and materials. This engagement with SLIS students represents the first stage of building a national learning community around the "Box." The success of this effort provides a template for engaging not only students in other LIS programs but the general public as well. The next phase of the development of the "Box" is the roll-out of a publically-accessible website and outreach to library and information professionals and the general public to build community engagement and communicate the value of the "Box."

7. ACKNOWLEDGMENTS

Thanks to the National Digital Stewardship Alliance, the National Library of Medicine and the School of Library and Information Science at the Catholic University of America for their support.

8. REFERENCES

[1]http://www.digitalpreservation.gov/ndsa/working_groups/outreach.html

[2] http://slis.cua.edu/

[3] http://slis.cua.edu/MSinLS/coursesStudy/CHIM.cfm

[4]http://www.digitalpreservation.gov/meetings/documents/ndiipp11/7Outreach.pdf

[5]http://blogs.loc.gov/digitalpreservation/2012/02/box-out-taking-digital-preservation-outreach-resources-to-the-classroom/

[6] http://www.ala.org/alcts/confevents/preswk

Distinguishing Venues by Writing Styles

Zaihan Yang Brian D. Davison
Department of Computer Science and Engineering
Lehigh University
Bethlehem, PA, 18015 USA
{zay206|davison}@cse.lehigh.edu

ABSTRACT

A principal goal for most research scientists is to publish. There are different kinds of publications covering different topics and requiring different writing formats. While authors tend to have unique personal writing styles, no work has been carried out to find out whether publication venues are distinguishable by their writing styles. Our work takes the first step into exploring this problem. Using the traditional classification approach and carrying out experiments on real data from the CiteSeer digital library, we demonstrate that venues are also distinguished by their writing styles.

Categories and Subject Descriptors: H.3.3 [Information Storage and Retrieval]: Information Search and Retrieval

General Terms: Algorithms, Performance

Keywords: classification, features

1. INTRODUCTION

For research scientists, a fundamental task is to publish their work. There are many different kinds of publications requiring different writing formats. In this paper, we regard the publishing venues of all kinds of publications as venues. We have different venues for different research domains; for example, the 'SIGIR' conference for Information Retrieval (IR) research, and the 'VLDB' conference for database research. Moreover, even in one research domain, we also have multiple venues. To take the 'IR' research domain as an example, we have journal publications such as J.ASIST, as well as conferences, such as SIGIR, JCDL, WWW, CIKM, WSDM, etc. With so many different kinds of venues provided, a straightforward question may arise: how can they be distinguished from each other? Besides their topic-related differences, are they also distinguishable in writing styles?

A writing style, according to Karlgren [5], is a consistent and distinguishable tendency in making some linguistic choices. Compared to the content of a paper, writing style more reflects the preferences of authors in organizing sentences and choosing words. It has long been recognized in author attribution (verification or identification) that writing styles are one of the key features in distinguishing among authors. The earliest work was conducted by Mendenhall [6] in the nineteenth century who studied authorship attribution among Bacon, Marlowe and Shakespeare. Much subsequent work has demonstrated that authors tend to have personal writing styles [7, 8].

However, no work has been carried out, to the best of our knowledge, investigating whether *venues* are also distinguishable by their writing styles. This task is actually equivalent to the question as to whether the papers published in one specific venue share common characteristics in writing styles, and how are they distinguishable from papers published in other venues. We approach this problem by using classification, in which a set of papers with known venue information are used for training, and the ultimate goal is to automatically determine the corresponding publishing venue of a paper whose venue information is missing. Specifically, we are interested in determining the extent to which venues can be distinguished from each other in terms of writing styles and what features are valuable for that purpose.

JCDL'12, June 10–14, 2012, Washington, DC, USA.
ACM 978-1-4503-1154-0/12/06.

2. FEATURES

Since we focus on writing-style based venue classification, one of the main concerns is to extract features that are unrelated to topic and context-free. Based on the review of previous studies in the task of author attribution, we incorporate three types of features: lexical features, syntactic features and structural features. The entire set of features are listed in Table 1.

Lexical Features: Lexical features can be further divided into character-based or word-based features. It reflects a paper's preference for particular types of characters or words. In our work, we include features like number of terms, number of distinct terms, vocabulary richness [3], Hapax terms, etc., resulting in a total of 66 lexical features.

Syntactic Features: The discriminating power of syntactic features is derived from different formats and patterns in which sentences of a paper are organized. One of the most important syntactic features is the short yet all purpose words, which are often referred to as the function words [4], such as 'the', 'a', 'and', 'to' etc. Another example syntactic feature is punctuation which is considered as the graphical correlation of intonation that is the phonetic correlation of syntactic structure [2]. We adopt a set of 298 function words, and compute the count of eight predefined punctuation symbols that appear in the paper.

Structural Features: Structural features represent the layout of a piece of writing. De Vel [1] introduced several structural features specifically for email. We adopt five structural features specifically for scientific papers: the number of sections, figures, equations, tables, and bibliographic references. Since the original paper content

Table 1: Features

Type	Features		
Lexical	TokenNum SentenceNum ShortWordNum ValidCharNum UpperCaseNum TabSpaceNum	TypeNum AvgSenLen HapaxVSToken AlphaCharNum WhiteSpaceNum VocabularyRichness	CharNum AvgWordLen HapaxVSType DigitalCharNum SpaceNum
Syntactic	FuncWordNum	PunctuationNum	FuncWordFreq
Structural	SectionNum TableNum	FigureNum ReferenceNum	EquationNum

available is in raw text format, we approximate the values by counting the number of times the word 'figure' or 'Figure' appears in the paper. We do the same for number of sections, number of tables and number of equations.

In summary, we have collected a total of 371 features.

3. EXPERIMENTS

3.1 Data Corpus

We carried out experiments on the CiteSeer digital library of scientific literature, which was distributed by the 2011 HCIR challenge workshop[1]. The corpus is divided into two parts. Meta-data about a paper, such as its title, publishing venue, publishing year, abstract, citation references are kept in XML format; the full content of that paper is in pure text format. We extract 119,727 papers published between 1949 and 2010, which have abstract, full content and venue information, and 48,797 venues that have at least one paper with full content provided.

3.2 Overall Performance

We are firstly interested in finding out whether venues are distinguishable by their writing styles in general. For multi-venue classification testing, we randomly choose K venues (where K varies among 2, 5, 10, 30, 50, 100 and 150) that have at least 50 papers in the CiteSeer data set. We collect all the papers published in those chosen venues to construct the training/testing set. The same process is repeated ten times for each particular K, and the result is the average of the ten iterations.

Three state-of-the-art classifiers (SVM, Naive Bayes, RandomForest) provided by WEKA were constructed for classifying, and 10-fold cross validation was used for evaluation. We adopt two traditional IR evaluation metrics, Accuracy and F-1 Score to measure the classification performance.

We compared performance among several classifiers. The **Baseline Classifier** randomly guesses the venue label for each paper instance in the testing set. We extract stylometric features from either the abstract or the full content of papers to construct the **Stylometric (A) Classifier** and **Stylometric (F) Classifier** respectively. Moreover, working on paper full content, we compare the performance under RandomForest, Naive Bayes and SVM classifiers.

As shown in Figure 1, several observations can be found. 1) The classification performance continues to drop as the number of venues considered is increased. However, under all circumstances, our stylometric classifier can retrieve better performance than the baseline classifier. A student's t test indicates that the improvement is statistically significant, which confirms that venues are also distinguishable by their writing styles. 2) There exists a tendency to achieve greater improvement over random guessing as the number of venues tested increased. Working on paper full content with RandomForest, there is a 70.25% improvement for 2-venue classification, and the performance is 7.37 times over random guessing for 10-venue and 8.83 times for 150-venue respectively. 3) We can achieve better performance when working on papers' full content than working only with abstracts. It is reasonable since more signs of writing styles can be presented when more paper content is included. 4) All three classifiers achieve consistent classification results. RandomForest works the best with small number of venues considered, however, SVM outperforms it when the number of venues exceeds 50.

3.3 Importance of Features

To determine the different contributions of lexical, syntactic, and structural groups of features, we first test performance on each individual group, and then add them one by one to determine the

[1]http://hcir.info/hcir-2011

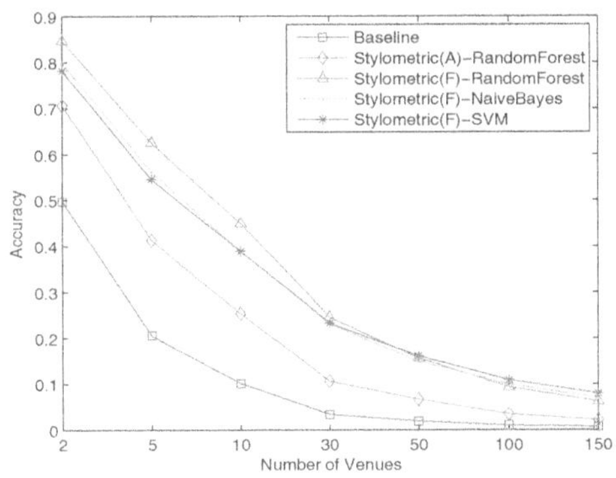

Figure 1: Classification Result: Accuracy

Table 2: CiteSeer Data Set: Feature Contribution

	Accuracy	F-1 Score
Lexical Only	0.4348	0.3822
Syntactic Only	0.4164	0.3543
Structural Only	0.2938	0.2468
Lexi+Syn	0.4474	0.3889
Lexi+Str	0.4405	0.3756
Syn+Str	0.4355	0.3731
Lexi+Syn+Str	0.4502	0.3906

changes in performance. Table 2 shows the results when considering on 10 Venues using RandomForest classifier.

We can see that lexical features still play the most important role in venue classification, while structural features are least useful. However, we can also find out that each group of features contributes positively to the overall performance, since when we add them together, the performance is better than each individually. We further investigate the importance of each individual feature by comparing the classification results based on the feature set that leaves out the tested target feature. Working on 5-venue set with RandomForest Classifier, we can find out that the three best features are: FuncWordFreq, TypeNum and TokenNum.

Acknowledgments

This work was supported in part by a grant from the National Science Foundation under award IIS-0545875.

4. REFERENCES

[1] O. de Vel. Mining Email authorship. In *Text Mining Workshop. KDD*, 2000.

[2] O. de Vel, A. Anderson, M. Corney, and G. Mohay. Mining e-mail content for author identification forensics. *SIGMOD Record*, 30(4):55–64, 2001.

[3] G.Zipf. *Human Behaviour and the principle of least effort. An introduction to human ecology*. Oxford, England: Addison-Wesley Press, 1949.

[4] D. Holmes and R. Forsyth. The Federalist revisited: New Directions in author attribution. In *Library and Linguistic Computing*, pages 111–127, 1995.

[5] J. Karlgren. The wheres and whyfores for studying text genre computationally. In *Workshop on Style and Meaning in Larguange, Art, Music and Design. National Conference on Artificial Intelligence*, 2004.

[6] T. Mendenhall. The characteristics curves of composition. *Science*, 11(11):237–249, 1887.

[7] F. Mosteller and D. Wallace. *Inference and Disputed Authorship: The Federalist*. Addison-Wesleym Reading, Mass., 1964.

[8] E. Stamatatos, N. Fakotakis, and G. Kokkinakis. Automatic text categorization in terms of genres and author. *Comp. Ling*, 26(4):471–495, 2001.

Do Public Library Websites Consider the Disabled or Senior Citizens?

Yong Jeong Yi
School of Library & Information Studies
College of Communication & Information
Florida State University
142 Collegiate Loop
Tallahassee, FL 32306-2100, USA
850-491-3180
yjy4617@my.fsu.edu

Ji Hei Kang
School of Library & Information Studies
College of Communication & Information
Florida State University
142 Collegiate Loop
Tallahassee, FL 32306-2100, USA
443-235-4026
jk11e@my.fsu.edu

ABSTRACT
The issues of mobility and sight impairment with respect to virtual accessibility are as important as physical accessibility when it comes to using public library services. However, few studies have discussed public library website accessibility from the perspective of underrepresented user groups. The purpose of this study is to evaluate the accessibility of websites of public libraries and further identify the association between accessibility and public libraries' budgets. The study selected 20 public library systems that have the highest percentages of the disabled or senior citizen patrons. The study employed the Pearson correlation test in order to investigate the correlation between the accessibility and the budgets of public libraries. Preliminary findings show that most current public library websites do not comply with the Section 508. The findings indicate that public libraries did not consider their users or potential users with physical disabilities when designing their websites. Therefore, the findings suggest that public library websites are not suited to deliver effective information services for underrepresented user populations who need special assistance. Furthermore, this study finds that there is no significant association between the public library websites' accessibility and the budgets.

Categories and Subject Descriptors
C.4 [**Performance of Systems**]:Design studies; H.5.2 [**User Interfaces**]: User-centered design

General Terms
Design, Standardization

Keywords
Accessibility, Information Services, Evaluation of Websites, Disability, Senior, Public libraries

1. INTRODUCTION
Previous studies indicate that the disabled and senior citizens are special populations for information services [1]. They are also identified as underrepresented in the venue of public libraries. Due to the issue of mobility and sight impairment, virtual accessibility is as important as physical accessibility for the disabled and seniors in using public library services. Previous studies have discussed the accessibility issue on websites in general [2][3], or on government websites [4]. However, little attention has been paid to the accessibility of public library websites that have high rates of these underrepresented groups as their users or potential users. Previous studies discussed that public libraries meet the information needs of a community by relying on information and communication technologies that the libraries provide [5][6]. Public library websites are often the first entrance to the use of information and communication technologies. Further, public library services are closely related to funding issues allocated by government [5]. In sum, public library websites deliver online information services as part of their duties and budgets. Developing websites that include technologies (e.g., screen readers, braille translator, text-to-speech and speech-to-text) to support virtual accessibility takes considerable cost, which can be affected by public library budgets. In order to bridge the research gap, the current study aims to evaluate the accessibility of public library websites and determine whether or not library funding affects public library website accessibility. Accordingly, this study addresses the following research questions:

- Do public library websites support the disabled or senior citizens, allowing them to overcome physical difficulty accessing the public libraries? Do the websites comply with Section 508?
- Is there any association between public library website accessibility and budgets?

2. SECTION 508
World Wide Web Consortium (W3C)(2008) defines Web accessibility as "Web accessibility means that people with disabilities can perceive, understand, navigate, and interact with the Web, and that they can contribute to the Web" [7]. Website accessibility is evaluated according to standards of Section 508 of the Rehabilitation Act. Along with Section 504 of the Rehabilitation Act of 1973 which declares equal opportunity for individuals with a disability in having the benefits and participating in public services, Congress revised Section 508 in 1998 [2]. It requires any federally funded agencies to make electronic and information technology accessible to everyone. This revision served as a momentum for public libraries to facilitate use of their websites and electronic resources.

JCDL'12, June 10–14, 2012, Washington, DC, USA.
ACM 978-1-4503-1154-0/12/06.

More specifically, section 508 subpart B, 'Technical Standards' has 17 items which are the basic requirements for Web accessibility [8]. These items are very important to disabled users but frequently overlooked by non-disabled users. These requirements include use of alternative text for images, color changing functions, and client side image maps.

3. METHODS

This study employs purposive sampling to select public library websites. According to the U.S Census (2010) [9], the current research chose 10 public library websites administered by the cities with highest percentage of disabled and 10 Websites in the cities with 10 largest percentage of the senior citizens (older than 65 years old) [10]. The study used HiSoftware [11] to test for Section 508 compliance. HiSoftware is one of the most reliable automated software solutions that provide accessibility testing of websites [11]. The scope of this study limited evaluation of accessibility only to Section 508 standards. Among 17 items, in particular, the study focused on 10 standards (A, B, E, F, G, H, I, L, M and N) which can be tested automatically. From each library system the researchers selected 7 Web pages which are likely to be most frequently visited by the disabled or senior users. The study tested general sites, such as main page, search, my account, reference services including ASK-A-Librarian, online resources, databases, catalog, location/hour, and contact. Furthermore, the test included some specialized sites such as senior, accessibility, and health information services. With regard to data analysis, the study used descriptive statistics to identify the status of overall accessibility of public libraries. For preliminary findings, the study selected 8 libraries with the highest and lowest results of accessibility and conducted the Pearson correlation test to investigate whether or not there was any association between accessibility and library funding. To ensure inter-reliability, the researchers tested 10 websites respectively, and then conducted cross-checks.

4. FINDINGS & IMPLICATIONS

Key preliminary findings show that most of the current websites of public libraries in this study did not comply with the Section 508. Overall compliance percentage of the Website accessibility was considerably low with the average of 15.4%. Ten public libraries with the largest percentage of the senior citizens had an average of 15.6% compliance of the legal requirements. The public library websites with the highest test results met compliance of 27.1%, while the websites with the lowest results got 10%. Another 10 public libraries with the highest percentage of disabled patrons met the average of 15.3% of the requirement of the accessibility standards. The public library websites with the highest results attained compliance at 20% while the websites with the lowest had 10%.

The results of the accessibility evaluation raised critical issues that neither public libraries comply with the legal standards, nor consider their users or potential users with physical difficulty when designing their Websites. Therefore, the findings suggest that the public library websites in this study are not suited to deliver effective information services for these underrepresented user populations who need special assistance. Furthermore, the study finds that there is no association between public library website accessibility and budgets (sig. p=.709).

5. FUTURE RESEARCH

Considering that budget limitation is not a significant factor affecting accessibility public library websites, further research needs to investigate why the public libraries in the study did not take into account the legal requirements of Section 508. Future research needs to interview public library directors and ask what kinds of support they need to enhance their websites.

6. REFERENCES

[1] Kars, M., Baker, L., and Wilson, F. 2008. The Medical Library Association guide to health literacy (Eds.). Neal-Schuman, New York, NY.

[2] Brobst, J. 2009. Evaluating the accessibility of Florida's public library home pages. *Libri*, 59, 2, 88-103.

[3] Yu, Y. T. and Lau, M. F. 2006. A comparison of MC/DC, MUMCUT and several other coverage criteria for logical decisions. *J. Syst. Softw*, 79, 5 (May. 2006), 577-590. DOI= http://dx.doi.org/10.1016/j.jss.2005.05.030.

[4] Jaeger, P. 2006. Assessing Section 508 compliance on federal e-government websites: A multi-method, user-centered evaluation of accessibility for persons with disabilities. *Government Information Quarterly*, 23, 2, 169-190.

[5] Gould, E. and Gomez, R. 2010. New challenges for libraries in the information age: a comparative study of ICT in public libraries in 25 countries. *Information Development*, 26, 166-176. doi:10.1177/0266666910367739

[6] Pact. 2008. Public access to information & ICTs: Kazakhstan. Public Access Landscape Study final report, presented to University of Washington Center for Information & Society (CIS), Seattle.

[7] World Wide Web Consortium (W3C). 2008. *Introduction to Web Accessibility, What is Web Accessibility*. URL: http://www.w3.org/WAI/.

[8] Section 508.gov. (2012). *Section 508 Standards Guide*. URL: http://www.section508.gov/index.cfm?fuseAction=stdsdoc

[9] U. S. Census. 2010a. *The Older Population: 2010* (2011. C2010BR-09.). U.S. Census Bureau, Washington, DC. URL: http://www.census.gov/prod/cen2010/briefs/c2010br-09.pdf.

[10] U.S. Census. 2010b. *American Community Survey*, U.S. Census Bureau, American Community Survey Office, URL: http://www.census.gov/acs/www/.

[11] HiSoftware Inc. 2003-2012. *Welcome to the HiSoftware® Cynthia Says™ Portal*. URL: http://www.cynthiasays.com.

Electronic Records Processing: It's a CINCH!

Amy Rudersdorf
State Library of North Carolina
109 East Jones Street
Raleigh, North Carolina 27601
919-807-7446
amy.rudersdorf@ncdcr.gov

Dean Farrell
State Library of North Carolina
109 East Jones Street
Raleigh, North Carolina 27601
919-807-7438
dean.farrell@ncdcr.gov

Lisa Gregory
State Library of North Carolina
109 East Jones Street
Raleigh, North Carolina 27601
919-807-7468
lisa.gregory@ncdcr.gov

ABSTRACT
In August 2011, five project partners (the State Library of North Carolina, the North Carolina State Archives, North Carolina Libraries for Virtual Education, Elon University, and the University of North Carolina at Charlotte) began a collaboration to develop a computer application that collects, ingests, and authenticates the electronic records that libraries and archives are often mandated to maintain. The application, called "CINCH," incorporates existing digital curation technologies, but adds to their functionality by creating a pull-down (or capture) utility to gather content available from the Internet. The final product will be a lightweight, open-source software tool that institutions required to collect and authenticate records on ingest can employ to retrieve and process their digital content.

Categories and Subject Descriptors
J.1 [**Administrative Data Processing**]: Government; E.1 [**Data Structures**]: Records; H.3.6 [Library Automation]: Large text archives; H.3.7 [**Information Storage and Retrieval**]: Digital Libraries – *collection*; K.5.2 [Governmental Issues]: Regulation; K.6.4 [System Management]: Centralization/decentralization.

General Terms
Management, Documentation, Experimentation.

Keywords
Records retrieval, file transfer, file sharing, ingest, hash, checksum, authentication, digital preservation, digital curation, collaboration, state publications, electronic records, OAIS reference model, DCC curation lifecycle, open-source software, REST (representational state transfer).

1. INTRODUCTION
Since August 2011, thanks to an Institute of Museum and Library Services (IMLS) Sparks! Ignition grant [1], staff from the State Library of North Carolina (a division of the Department of Cultural Resources, or Cultural Resources) in conjunction with staff from the North Carolina Libraries for Virtual Education (NCLIVE) have been developing an application that captures, ingests, and checksums records that they are legislatively mandated to maintain[1]. The "Capture, Ingest, and Checksum" tool (CINCH), is designed to address the need to automate the transfer of online content between creators/providers to repository managers using appropriate ingest methodologies, such as running checksums, virus checking, and authentication. The tool can be used by institutions of various sizes, although the intention is to support small and medium organizations that may not have access to this type of technology.

JCDL'12, June 10–14, 2012, Washington, DC, USA.
ACM 978-1-4503-1154-0/12/06.

2. WHAT MAKES CINCH DIFFERENT?
Many current ingest systems rely on the creator to initiate submission activities when material is ready for deposit. For example, Harvard University's Batch Builder tool [2] incorporates several ingest tasks – virus and fixity checks, metadata extraction – but relies on the creator to first upload their content through an ftp interface. This is no easy task for many content creators, as many repository managers have expressed vocally and often.[2] CINCH, on the other hand, "grabs" content from its location online, authenticates it, and packages it into a simple submission information package (SIP) for manual ingest into a repository.

CINCH is valuable for smaller and mid-sized organizations that would have difficulty developing tools of this nature to ensure authenticity of their digital content. It is a free, repository-neutral, open-source tool that requires modest IT expertise for installation. Once installed [3], repository managers access CINCH through a

[1] Three statutes (N.C. Gen. State § 132, *North Carolina Public Records Laws*; N.C. Gen. Stat. § 121, *Archives and History*; and N.C. Gen. Stat. § 125, *State Library Agency*) provide the mandate for the Cultural Resources digital preservation program.

[2] For examples of repository managers struggling to get content for ingest into institutional repositories, which have found minimal success with voluntary deposit, see: Thomas, Chuck, and Robert H. McDonald. 2007. Measuring and Comparing Participation Patterns in Digital Repositories. *D-Lib Magazine* 13, no. 9 (9). URL: http://www.dlib.org/dlib/september07/mcdonald/09mcdonald.html. AND Davis, Philip M., and Matthew J. L. Connolly. 2007. Institutional Repositories: Evaluating the Reasons for Non-use of Cornell University's Installation of DSpace. *D-Lib Magazine* 13, no. 3 (April). URL: http://www.dlib.org/dlib/march07/davis/03davis.html. AND Foster, Nancy Fried, and Susan Gibbons. 2005. Understanding Faculty to Improve Content Recruitment for Institutional Repositories. *D-Lib Magazine* 11, no. 01 (1). URL: http://www.dlib.org/dlib/january05/foster/01foster.html.

web-based user interface. CINCH moves these institutions beyond the one-off file deposit or "drop-box" ideas, which are becoming less and less feasible for institutions experiencing budget and staffing cuts, or who have distributed content that falls into their collecting scope but is hard to acquire through voluntary submission. Minimizing the effort required by content creators and automating the submission process should greatly increase content creator participation in digital preservation efforts.

3. HOW DOES CINCH WORK?

After ingest, the foremost goal of CINCH is ease of use. A simple manifest file (.csv format) points CINCH at the digital content to be downloaded from content creators' file servers. This manifest includes URLs of the files to be gathered. CINCH can accommodate .csv, .doc, .docx, .gif, .pdf, .png, .ppt, .pptx, .txt, .xls, and .xlsx. A fixity check is performed on the files identified in the manifest and then the objects are downloaded. Upon download, CINCH checks each file for viruses, deletes those that are corrupted, and adds the file names and URLs to an error manifest. A hash value comparison is run to ensure that no corruption occurred during the download and virus check. The tool then creates unique filenames for all files to ensure that files will not be overwritten in subsequent downloads. CINCH stores the original file names in a metadata manifest (along with hash values, the audit trail for all activity performed on each file, the new filename, the date retrieved, and the location from which the file was retrieved). [image 1.]

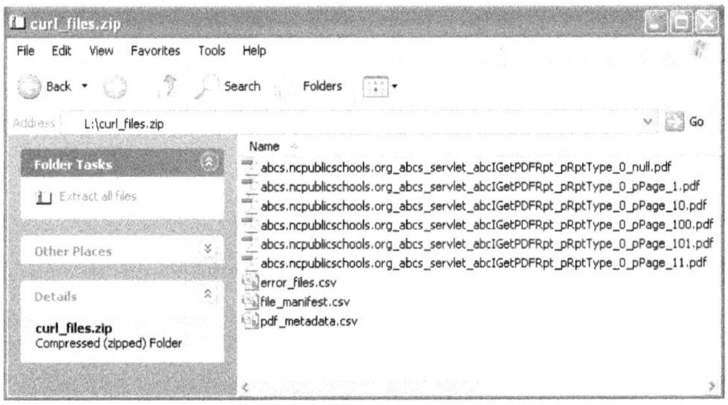

Image 1. Contents of ingest package. PDFs are harvested files; .csv files contain notes on errors encountered, a list of the files downloaded, and the files' metadata.

Using the hash values, CINCH identifies any duplicate files from this and previous downloads and separates them out for manual review.

Once these processes have been run, CINCH validates the files, extracts any metadata from the files' properties, and, for text-based files, does some basic natural language processing to determine additional possible metadata. All results are added to the metadata manifest. Data is described according to the PREMIS 2.0 data dictionary entities of object, event, and agent [4]. Descriptive data that falls outside the PREMIS specifications is captured using Qualified Dublin Core.

4. DEVELOPMENT STATUS

The development of CINCH began in full force in August of 2011 and has proceeded according to the schedule proposed in the IMLS grant application. Alpha tests have involved Cultural Resources staff testing CINCH using their own data. In June, staff at Elon University and the University of North Carolina at Charlotte will begin beta tests.

The intention is for the tool to be made freely available under the MIT License [5] by August of 2012. In addition, a hosted version of CINCH will be available free of charge to institutions in North Carolina through the support of NCLIVE.

5. SUMMARY

CINCH addresses the need to ingest digital content properly to ensure authenticity. Its greatest impact will be on small and mid-sized institutions and organizations, from a single academic archive to a statewide public library consortium. Two key advantages of the tool are that it will be (1) free and easy to implement, requiring no programming expertise, and (2) allow repository managers to collect content from locations that are already part of the creators' existing workflows. It represents the best case scenario for many institutions: a win for content creators, a win for digital repository managers, and a win for those who will need to access the content in the future.

6. ACKNOWLEDGEMENTS

The work of the Digital Information Management Program of the State Library of North Carolina is supported, in part, by a Statewide Leadership Grant funded through the Institute of Museum and Library Services' (IMLS) Library Services and Technology Act. The development of the CINCH grant is made possible through an IMLS Sparks! Ignition grant.

7. REFERENCES

[1] Institute of Museum and Library Services Sparks! Ignition grants for Libraries and Museums. URL: http://www.imls.gov/applicants/detail.aspx?GrantId=19.

[2] Harvard University Library Digital Repository Service Batch Builder tool. URL: http://hul.harvard.edu/ois/systems/drs/bb.html.

[3] CINCH code. URL: https://github.com/lfarrell/Cinch and CINCH about. URL: http://digitalpreservation.ncdcr.gov/cinch

[4] PREMIS Data Dictionary for Preservation Metadata. URL: http://www.loc.gov/standards/premis/

[5] Open Source Initiative: MIT License. URL: http://www.opensource.org/licenses/MIT

Exploiting Canonical Structures to Transmit Complex Objects from a Digital Library to a Portal

Scott Britell[1], Lois M. L. Delcambre[1], Lillian N. Cassel[2], Edward A. Fox[3] and Richard Furuta[4]

[1]Computer Science Department
Portland State University
Portland, OR
{britell,lmd}@cs.pdx.edu

[2]Dept. of Computing Sciences
Villanova University
Villanova, PA
lillian.cassel@villanova.edu

[3]Dept. of Computer Science
Virginia Tech
Blacksburg, VA
fox@vt.edu

[4]Dept. of Computer Science and Engineering
Texas A&M University
College Station, TX
furuta@cse.tamu.edu

Categories and Subject Descriptors
H.3.7 [**Digital Libraries**]: Systems issues; Standards

General Terms Management; Standardization.

Keywords Data models; Schema mapping.

1. INTRODUCTION

When a digital resource is composed of other digital resources, how should we describe it in a digital library or portal? As a simple example, should we represent a collection of books with the book as the first-class object? Or should we represent each book as a collection of individual chapters? What about the list of questions at the end of a chapter of a textbook; are they of interest? We believe that showing fine-grained resources within the context of larger-grained resources that they may be contained within is valuable. Thus, we want to enable viewing of structured resources (e.g., books, chapters, and questions) both independently and as part of complex object(s).

Our work has three goals: (1) describe the structure of complex resources explicitly so that we can implement new browsing and other widgets in a digital library and portal generically, (2) transfer individual resources and the structure of the complex objects from one source (e.g., a digital library) to another (e.g., a digital library portal), and (3) transfer the generic structure so that generic widgets can be used in the receiving site.

To meet the first goal, we define what we call *canonical structures*: data model fragments with associated navigational access. Canonical structures can represent a wide range of local structures. Once mapped, the digital library can use our generic navigational widgets that exploit the canonical structures. We have implemented canonical structures in an educational repository of curricula with a variety of simple and complex structures and we have implemented a generic navigation widget that shows the context of the currently viewed resource as well as the other context(s), if any, in which this resource is used.

To transfer the complex structures of digital resources, our second goal, we have implemented and evaluated the use of the Open Archives Initiative (OAI) Protocol for Metadata Harvesting (OAI-PMH) [6] and the OAI Object Reuse and Exchange (OAI-ORE) [4] standards. We also defined a custom namespace for use with these two approaches to describe the composition of complex objects as well as the mapping to canonical structures. The custom namespace and the generic navigation widget have been implemented in the Ensemble [3] portal for computing education, thus meeting our third goal.

JCDL'12, June 10–14, 2012, Washington, DC, USA.
ACM 978-1-4503-1154-0/12/06.

2. THE PORTAL AND REPOSITORY

The Ensemble project has built and is hosting a portal that provides access to independent collections of resources that support education in computing. As one part of the Ensemble effort, we have built and are hosting a new collection, called STEMRobotics [8], comprised of robotics curricula developed by our collaborators who teach at the middle and high school levels. The STEMRobotics site was designed to: (1) host various curricula for teaching robotics, (2) allow individual resources (such as a video) to be used in multiple curricula, (3) support community feedback on all aspects of the curricula, and (4) allow teachers to select portions of and download courses for use at local schools.

Our collaborators are providing courses for STEMRobotics in a variety of structures. Given the variation in structure across these courses while recognizing that they have structural patterns in common, we are defining canonical structures and mapping various structures to the canonical structures. Each canonical structure is a schema fragment, represented in an entity-relationship diagram [1] commonly used to represent data models.

To exploit the canonical structures along with the associated mappings from local structure, we built a general, hierarchical navigation widget that provides an easy-to-use browser for all of the courses found in STEMRobotics.

3. ARCHITECTURE

Figure 1 shows our architecture in a digital library (on the left) and a digital library portal (on the right), separated by a vertical dotted line. The next two subsections address these two parts.

3.1 Implementation in STEMRobotics

STEMRobotics is implemented using the Drupal[1] content management system. Drupal allows developers to create a number of different content types within the system. The content in a Drupal site is stored in a database and accessed, formatted, and displayed through a number of PHP scripts. We created a content type for each entity type. A content type contains a set of fields,

[1] http://drupal.org

such as title, author, description, etc. A field may hold a simple value or a list of links to other content types. For example, a unit may have a field specifying an ordered list of its lessons.

Extra database tables have been created for the canonical structures and a mapping is defined between each of the content types and the appropriate canonical structure.

Drupal is easily extended by implementing new modules; we have implemented a module that handles the canonical structures and one that implements the new navigation widget.

3.2 Transmission of Structure from a Drupal Repository to a Portal

We describe here the mechanisms we used to transport the description of complex objects from a digital library to a portal.

3.2.1 OAI-PMH

OAI-PMH is a protocol that enables the exchange of metadata records between digital libraries. For the most part, content metadata in STEMRobotics maps directly to the Dublin Core Metadata Initiative (DCMI) [2] terms and the National Science Digital Library (NSDL) [5] vocabularies. One exception is the "Type" element. Multiple content types in STEMRobotics can map to the same term in the NSDL type vocabulary.

In order to export a more meaningful description of the structure than that provided by the DCMI standard, we have defined our own namespace, the "cs" namespace. While a lesson may be used in multiple units in the STEMRobotics site, the ordering of those lessons is unique to each unit. We transmit structure looking down (using hasPart) rather than looking up (using PartOf) to simplify the representation of the ordinal position of components.

By serializing the canonical structures into the OAI-PMH feed, we transmit the detailed complex structures in STEMRobotics to any portal that can recognize our namespace. Since OAI-PMH allows harvesters to request their desired metadata prefix, we pass structure through the partOf relation in DCMI terms, to portals that request only DCMI terms, and we pass the complete structure to portals requesting our "cs" metadata prefix.

3.2.2 OAI-ORE

OAI-ORE represents a resource as an aggregation of its various parts and its metadata. OAI-ORE uses the Resource Description Framework (RDF) [7] to create machine readable resource maps that describe the metadata of a complex object as well as its components. Each aggregation is described by a resource map consisting of RDF triples from the OAI-ORE namespace. Resource maps also can contain RDF triples representing the standard DCMI elements as well as any other RDF triples.

Since an OAI-ORE resource map can also contain arbitrary RDF, we express our canonical structures using our namespace and add triples that express the ordering of materials within our site. Using OAI-ORE, anyone requesting a given resource map will be presented with all of the RDF triples for that resource. Typically, a requestor will ignore triples it does not understand; any requestor unfamiliar with our namespace would ignore triples representing our canonical structures.

3.3 Implementation in the Ensemble Portal

From our serialization of the canonical structures in either the OAI-PMH or OAI-ORE records we can materialize the canonical structures in the portal. There are two differences between the canonical structures in the repository and portal. First, since we want to use these canonical structures with the metadata records in the repository, we map the original content identifiers to the identifiers used in the portal. Second, since we cannot easily reference the original content records in order to retrieve local names and ordering, we store this information in canonical structures in the portal. Using the canonical structures in the portal, we can build a detailed navigation hierarchy with ordering and relationship type information using our widget.

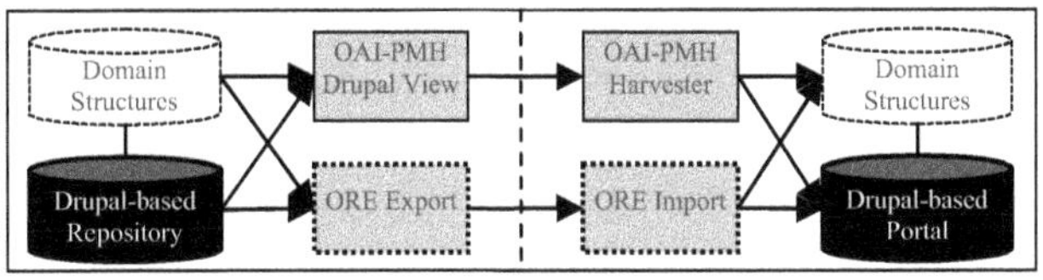

Figure 1. Architecture of the use of canonical structures and their transmission from repositories to portals.

4. CONCLUSIONS

As repositories of user-generated materials become a larger part of the digital landscape, we have the opportunity to represent and make use of additional semantics that users add to these materials. In fact, the heterogeneity of structure in the STEMRobotics site motivated our interest in providing generic support for complex data models. By working within an application domain, we seek to identify and exploit commonly occurring structures by mapping them to our canonical structures. This work reports on our investigation into the use of canonical structures in a digital library and portal context. By mapping from canonical structures to standards such as OAI-PMH and OAI-ORE we may facilitate the adoption of standards and their associated tools.

5. ACKNOWLEDGMENTS

This work was supported in part by the National Science Foundation (Project 0840668).

6. REFERENCES

[1] Chen, P.P.-S. 1976. The entity-relationship model---toward a unified view of data. *ACM Transactions on Database Systems*. 1, 1 (Mar. 1976), 9-36.

[2] Dublin Core Metadata Initiative: *http://dublincore.org/*. Accessed: 2012-01-05.

[3] Ensemble: *http://www.computingportal.org*. Accessed: 2012-01-12.

[4] Lagoze, C. et al. 2008. Object Re-Use & Exchange: A Resource-Centric Approach. *CoRR*. abs/0804.2, (Apr. 2008).

[5] National Science Digital Library: *http://nsdl.org*. Accessed: 2012-04-05.

[6] Open Archives Initiative Protocol for Metadata Harvesting: *http://www.openarchives.org/pmh/*. Accessed: 2012-01-03.

[7] RDF - Semantic Web Standards: *http://www.w3.org/RDF/*. Accessed: 2011-12-16.

[8] STEMRobotics: *http://stemrobotics.cs.pdx.edu*. Accessed: 2012-01-12.

Global Web Archive Integration with Memento

Robert Sanderson
Los Alamos National Laboratory
Los Alamos
NM 87544, USA
+1 (505) 665-5804
rsanderson@lanl.gov

ABSTRACT

In this poster, we describe the approach taken to designing and implementing a tera-scale multi-repository index of archived web resources using massively parallel processing.

Categories and Subject Descriptors

H.5.4 [**Information Interfaces and Presentation**]: Hypertext/ Hypermedia – *Architectures, Navigation.*

General Terms

Performance, Design, Experimentation.

Keywords

Digital Preservation, High Performance Computing, Memento

1. INTRODUCTION

The World Wide Web is in a constant state of change with resources being modified every second. While it is impossible to capture every change, there are many institutions that crawl the web looking for new and modified resources to archive. While the Internet Archive[1] is probably the most well known and accessible, the International Internet Preservation Consortium[2] (IIPC) currently has 42 member institutions, all committed to this task. Each institution has its own archive of resources, their own user interfaces, and their own country's legal frameworks to abide by. However, a user's information needs may not be able to be satisfied by resources from a single archive, as other institutions may hold more relevant ones.

The majority of the archives use the same software, written and maintained by the Internet Archive, for both crawling the web (Heretrix) and making the archived content accessible (Wayback). A Wayback repository keeps track of the time the resource was retrieved and its URL, amongst other information, which is then used to discover the closest archived copy of a given resource. The Memento framework[9] uses this information to provide cross-archive discovery from the web browser, but without a single access point, Memento clients must use distributed search techniques across the archives to discover the closest matching copy, termed a Memento.

In this poster we describe the centralized Aggregator platform that is being built to enable the Memento framework to have instant access to all of the archives holding information without resorting to distributed, real-time queries for each of the URLs needed to construct the representation of a web page.

JCDL'12, June 10-14, 2012, Washington, DC, USA.
ACM 978-1-4503-1154-0/12/06.

2. REQUIREMENTS

For the first phase of the current project, ten of the IIPC member institutions, including the Internet Archive, Library of Congress, British Library, Bibliothèque Nationale de France, and the Koninklijke Bibliotheek of the Netherlands, contributed their archives' indexes of URLs and crawl times. These were made available in the Wayback's CDX format from the majority of the participating institutions, and the data totals 5.25 terabytes (Tb) when compressed with the highest GZip compression, expanding to over 40Tb when decompressed. Each line of the each CDX file contains the metadata for a single archived resource.

The Aggregator platform must have sub-second access to the complete set of archived copies of a resource with a given URL, and thus these indexes must be merged into a single global index. To process 40Tb of uncompressed data within the time-frame of the project required access to supercomputing facilities, which were made available at Los Alamos National Laboratory. The Data Intesive Super Computer (DISC) has 165 nodes available, each with 2Tb of disk space, 8 Gigabytes of RAM, and dual 2.4 Ghz processors.

A real-time access to the super-computer from the web is not feasible, the results of the processing must be able to be exported and run on a single high-end web-connected machine. This requirement shaped the architecture and implementation of the platform. The access will be via a Memento TimeGate (G in Figure 1) that redirects the browser to the temporally closest copy, based on time preferences conveyed in an HTTP request header.

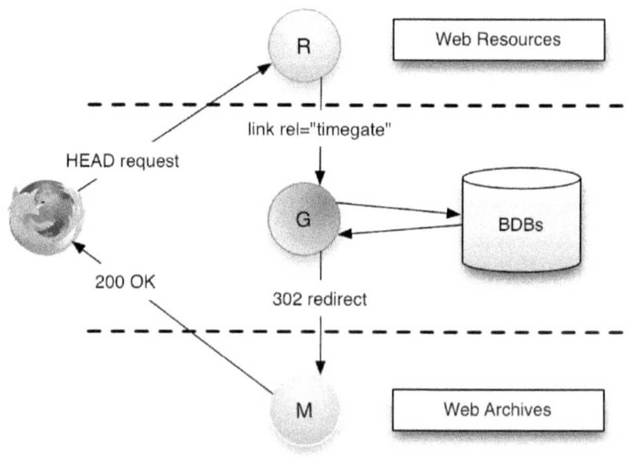

Figure 1. Memento TimeGate Architecture

3. BACKGROUND RESEARCH

The indexing software for the platform was researched, with five products being evaluated directly, and several more carefully considered but not tested. The requirement to be able to move the data off the supercomputer after processing severely limited the number of choices, with Berkeley DB[3], Tokyo Cabinet and Kyoto Cabinet[4] being the most carefully evaluated. MongoDB[5] and Casssandra[6] implementations were used as benchmarks for distributed storage solutions, but are tied to the cluster. Discarded products included Redis (the database must fit in the memory of the cluster), LevelDB (only allows a single client at once, and the codebase is not yet stable), CouchDB (HTTP interface would be too slow), and Hadoop's HDFS (tied tightly to the cluster).

In the final evaluation, BerkeleyDB outperformed KyotoCabinet for very large-scale implementations. While KyotoCabinet was superior for individual databases up to a million keys, the performance then degraded beyond the point of usability.

4. ARCHITECTURE

The Aggregator only has one task: given a URL discover the locations of Mementos of that URL and the time they were archived. As such, it does not need to have a single ordered list of URLs to walk through, nor does it have to perform pattern-based queries. Given this single task, a hash table is sufficient where the key is the URL and the value the list of Mementos and their datestamps. This hash table must be built in parallel across all of the machines in the DISC cluster.

The data was transferred to the cluster and divided amongst 25 of the nodes. The remaining 140 nodes each maintain 25 BerkeleyDBs for a total of 3500 slices of the complete database. The appropriate database slice for each URL is determined by hashing the canonicalized version of the URL to a long integer, and then finding the modulus of the total number of slices. At query time, the query URL is canonicalized and then hashed using the same, machine-independent algorithm to determine which database slice the information is held in.

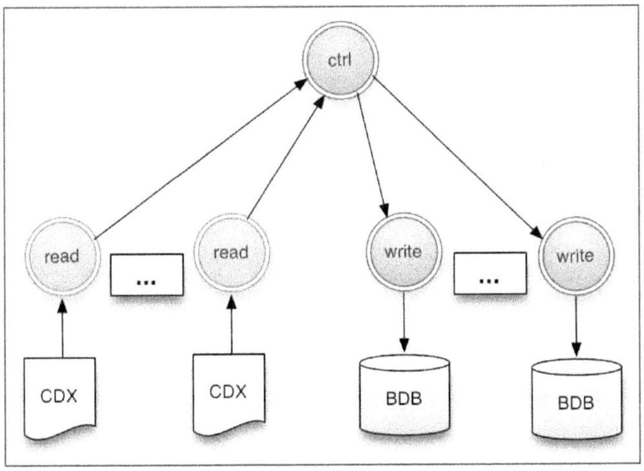

Figure 2. Distributed Processing Architecture

A simple master-slave architecture was adopted as the easiest and most efficient. One node in the cluster (ctrl in Figure 2) acts as a controller through which all messages pass. It instructs the 25 data nodes to read the CDX files and send the information to the appropriate write task on one of the 140 other nodes, with caching in place to avoid network overload in the message passing interface. After experimentation, 500 URLs per message seemed to be optimal. These URLs are returned to the control task to send to the write task. If the write task is still busy from another set of URLs, the controller queues the message. In this way all of the read and write tasks are constantly active.

An alternative strategy was explored where the read tasks could communicate directly with the write tasks, however the network overhead of so many messages at unpredictable intervals resulted in an overall less performant system. Thus, the apparent bottleneck of the controller node does not appear to be significant.

5. IMPLEMENTATION

The system was implemented using Python and OpenMPI for the message passing, based on the grid processing module for Cheshire3[8]. As each node has a large amount of RAM, in memory caches for the BerkeleyDBs were set to minimize disk access and allow the caching and synchronization systems to function at their full potential. The hardware speed at which the nodes could read and write to disk is the limiting factor in the implementation, as the computational requirements to perform the hashing are trivial.

The primary challenge to overcome in the implementation was also hardware related. The network switch over which the messages are routed would crash at random, approximately once per week, and require a physical reset. Thus it was necessary to include checkpointing code to enable a restart from save points throughout the processing.

6. FUTURE WORK

The data was transferred to Los Alamos via physically shipping hard disks. This is currently the only convenient method for a bulk load of multiple terabytes, however it is important to remain synchronized with the archives new crawls. Work is ongoing in the ResourceSync[7] project to determine the best method for achieving this synchronization on a large scale.

7. ACKNOWLEDGMENTS

This research was funded by the Library of Congress, and supported by the members Access Working Group of the International Internet Preservation Consortium, and the Los Alamos National Laboratory, especially Herbert Van de Sompel, C. Rees Baird, and Katherine Nystrom.

8. REFERENCES

[1] http://web.archive.org/

[2] http://www.netpreserve.org/

[3] http://www.oracle.com/technetwork/database/berkeleydb/

[4] http://fallabs.com/kyotocabinet/

[5] http://www.mongodb.org/

[6] http://cassandra.apache.org/

[7] http://www.niso.org/publications/newsline/2011/newslinedec2011.html#report5

[8] Sanderson, R. Larson, R. "Indexing and Searching Tera-scale Grid-based Digital Libraries" Procs. of First International Conference on Scalable Information Systems, Hong Kong, 2006, ISBN 1-59593-428-6

[9] Van de Sompel, H. Sanderson, R. et al. "An HTTP-based Versioning Mechanism for Linked Data", Procs. of Linked Data on the Web Workshop, Raleigh, USA, April 2010

GROTOAP: GROund Truth for Open Access Publications

Dominika Tkaczyk
d.tkaczyk@icm.edu.pl

Artur Czeczko
a.czeczko@icm.edu.pl

Krzysztof Rusek
kr292291@students.mimuw.edu.pl

Łukasz Bolikowski
l.bolikowski@icm.edu.pl

Roman Bogacewicz
r.bogacewicz@icm.edu.pl

Centre for Open Science, Interdisciplinary Centre for Mathematical and Computational Modelling, Univ. of Warsaw
ul. Prosta 69, 00-838 Warszawa, Poland

ABSTRACT

The field of digital document content analysis includes many important tasks, for example page segmentation or zone classification. It is impossible to build effective solutions for such problems and evaluate their performance without a reliable test set, that contains both input documents and expected results of segmentation and classification. In this paper we present GROTOAP — a test set useful for training and performance evaluation of page segmentation and zone classification tasks. The test set contains input articles in a digital form and corresponding ground truth files. All input documents included in the test set have been selected from DOAJ database, which indexes articles published under CC-BY license. The whole test set is available under the same license.

Categories and Subject Descriptors

D.2.10 [**Software Engineering**]: Design—*Quality analysis and evaluation*; I.7.5 [**Document and Text Processing**]: Document Capture—*Document analysis*

General Terms

Performance

Keywords

document analysis, page segmentation, zone classification, system evaluation, ground truth

1. INTRODUCTION

Page segmentation and zone classification tasks play very important role in document analysis. The goal of page segmentation is to build a geometric hierarchical structure of the document by dividing the document's pages into zones, lines and words. Classifying zones means finding their function in the document and assigning corresponding labels (eg. title, authors, affiliation) to them. An efficient page segmentation or zone classification solution needs to be carefully evaluated, which requires a reliable test set containing multiple examples of input documents and expected results of segmentation and classification.

JCDL'12, June 10–14, 2012, Washington, DC, USA.
ACM 978-1-4503-1154-0/12/06.

In this paper we present GROTOAP — a test set useful for adapting, training and performance evaluation of document analysis-related solutions, such as page segmentation and zone classification. The test set is built upon a group of scientific articles from Directory of Open Access Journals (DOAJ) database [1] and contains original publications in PDF format, ground truth files holding hierarchical structure and zone labels extracted from publications, and finally the SegmEdit tool useful for editing the ground truth files. The whole set is distributed under the CC-BY license in the Open Access model and can be downloaded from *http://ceon.pl/en/research/solutions/*.

Existing test sets containing ground truth data useful for page segmentation or zone classification are usually based on scanned document images instead of born-digital documents. For example UW-III [4] contains various document images along with structure-related ground truth information. Unfortunately UW-III is not free and difficult to purchase. MARG [2] is a data set containing scanned pages from biomedical journals. The main problem is that it contains only the first pages of documents and only a small subset of zones is included, and as a result its usability is very limited. Other data sets built upon scanned document images of various layouts and corresponding ground truth data are: PRImA [5], MediaTeam Oulu Document Database [7], UvA [3] and Tobacco800 [6].

GROTOAP test set was built as part of the implementation of the metadata extraction process [8] for born-digital documents and has been successfully used for training and performance evaluation of the process and its individual steps.

2. GROTOAP TEST SET

GROTOAP test set consists of three parts:

- input documents in PDF format, that contain scientific articles from DOAJ database,
- ground truth files in XML format, that contain the geometric hierarchical structure of input documents along with their zone labels,
- SegmEdit tool, useful for editing ground truth files.

To make the test set useful for performance evaluation of page segmentation and zone classification tasks, the ground truth files store their typical output: the hierarchical structure holding all the pages, zones, lines, words and characters of the document, and also zone labels. We have used TrueViz format for storing all ground truth data.

The process of creating the test set required a manual phase of correcting the structure of the documents stored in ground truth files. To make this as easy as possible, we have created SegmEdit, a tool for editing TrueViz files. SegmEdit consists of two parts: SegmEditGUI and SegmServer. SegmEditGUI is a desktop program that allows to view, edit and save TrueViz files. It may be used as a standalone application, in such case PDFs and ground truth files are stored and saved locally. An alternative is to use SegmServer, a HTTP server that is able to store all files and serve them to SegmEditGUI. In such case the server communicates with multiple SegmEditGUI instances over the network sending files and receiving them partly or completely processed, which makes editing ground truth files by multiple users very easy.

The input documents and ground truth files are published in Open Access model under the CC-BY license. The source code of SegmEdit tool is published under the GPL v3 license.

3. BUILDING THE TEST SET

The process of creating GROTOAP test set was semi-automatic. It consisted of three main phases (the second and third phase were performed twice):

1. selecting and downloading a set of publications based on metadata from DOAJ database,
2. automatic extraction of hierarchical structure using metadata extraction tools,
3. manual correction of the results of automatic structure extraction with the use of SegmEdit tool.

All the publications in the test set have been taken from journals distinguished with SPARC Europe Seal for Open Access Journals. We have harvested Directory of Open Access Journals for basic metadata of all articles from said journals, including links to full texts. Next, we have pseudo-randomly selected articles to be downloaded and included in two test groups. The first group contains one article from each four journals published by the same publisher, 113 articles in total. Articles published by the same publisher have usually very similar layout, and as a result the layout distribution in the first test group is similar to the layout distribution in the entire DOAJ database. The second group consists of 115 articles and has been compiled by randomly choosing one article from each publisher, as a result it contains most layouts that appear in the DOAJ database. Currently only the first group is included in the test set. The second group will be processed and added to the test set in the near future.

To minimize the time needed for manual correction, first we processed selected publications using tools implemented in our metadata extraction process [8] in order to automatically extract their structure. Currently the process requires a document in PDF format on the input. First individual characters and their bounding boxes were extracted using iText library, then a modified Docstrum algorithm was used to segment pages. Finally, a classifier based on Hidden Markov Models found labels for all zones of the document.

During the last phase TrueViz files created automatically were corrected by a group of people with the use of SegmEdit tool. We used one SegmServer instance to store and serve PDF and ground truth files to multiple SegmEditGUI instances run on client computers. As a result of choosing this architecture we did not have to manually distribute files to a group of people and gather the results together. The correction phase included verifying words, lines and zones generated by metadata extraction tools, splitting incorrectly merged objects and merging incorrectly split ones, verifying and correcting labels assigned to zones. To minimize human errors we performed an additional checking phase, which included an inspection and approval by an independent judge.

4. CONCLUSIONS

We have presented GROTOAP — a test set useful for training and evaluation of content analysis tasks like page segmentation and zone classification. We have described in details the contents of the test set and the process of creating it. Two main features distinguishing GROTOAP from earlier efforts are:

- usefulness in testing algorithms optimized for processing born-digital content,
- and reliance on Open Access publications which guarantees easy distribution of both original material and derived ground truth data.

5. ACKNOWLEDGMENTS

The work is supported by the National Centre for Research and Development (NCBiR) under Grant No. SP/I/1/77065/10 by the Strategic scientific research and experimental development program: "Interdisciplinary System for Interactive Scientific and Scientific-Technical Information".

We would like to thank a number of people involved in the process of manual correction of the ground truth files. We would also like to thank Klaudia Grabowska for her help in preparing information about publishing documents in the Open Access model.

6. REFERENCES

[1] DOAJ. http://www.doaj.org/.

[2] MARG. http://marg.nlm.nih.gov/.

[3] UvA. http://www.science.uva.nl/UvA-CDD/.

[4] UW-III. http://www.science.uva.nl/research/dlia/datasets/uwash3.html.

[5] A. Antonacopoulos, D. Bridson, C. Papadopoulos, and S. Pletschacher. A Realistic Dataset for Performance Evaluation of Document Layout Analysis. *2009 10th International Conference on Document Analysis and Recognition*, pages 296–300, 2009.

[6] D. Lewis, G. Agam, S. Argamon, O. Frieder, D. Grossman, and J. Heard. Building a Test Collection for Complex Document Information Processing. In *Proc. 29th Annual Int. ACM SIGIR Conference*, pages 665–666, 2006.

[7] J. Sauvola and H. Kauniskangas. MediaTeam Document Database II, a CD-ROM collection of document images, 1999.

[8] D. Tkaczyk, L. Bolikowski, A. Czeczko, and K. Rusek. A modular metadata extraction system for born-digital articles. In *Proceedings of the 10th IAPR International Workshop on Document Analysis Systems*, 2012.

Has it Been Already Digitized? How to Find Information about Digitized Documents.

Tomas Foltyn
National Library of Czech Republic
Klementinum 190, Prague 1
110 00, Czech Republic
+420 281 013 314
Tomas.Foltyn@nkp.cz

Martin Lhotak
Academy of Sciences Library
Narodni 3, Prague 1
110 00, Czech Republic
+420 281 013 314
Lhotak@knav.cz

Pavel Kocourek
INCAD, spol. s r. o.
U Krcskeho nadrazi
38a/2062,Prague4
140 00, Czech Republic
+ 420 241 721 059
pavel.kocourek@incad.cz

ABSTRACT

The Digitization Registry of the Czech Republic is a research project the aim of which is to create a national registry of digitized documents to avoid unwanted duplications in the digitization as well as to share digitization results throughout the Czech Republic. This could make the digitization more effective and also economize financial resources of participating institutions.

Categories and Subject Descriptors

H.3.5 [**Information storage and retrieval**]: On-line Information Services

General Terms

Algorithms, Management, Verification.

Keywords

digitization registry, digitization, metadata, records, duplicities.

1. INTRODUCTION

The Digitization Registry of the Czech Republic is a national project which has been developed through the close cooperation of the National Library of Czech Republic, Academy of Sciences Library and the private IT company INCAD. The aim of the project is to create a national registry of digitized documents, which could help librarians avoid unwanted duplications and to facilitate sharing the results of digitization throughout the Czech Republic. It is designed especially for libraries or other memory institutions that digitize their collections. Because the system helps avoid unwanted duplications, it can economize financial resources used for scanning and subsequent processing and make the digitization more effective.

2. THE DIGITIZATION REGISTRY INTRODUCES ITSELF

2.1 Project Background

The initiative connected with the establishment of the Digitization Registry project arose from the needs of two libraries – the National Library of the Czech Republic and Academy of Sciences Library. The National Library increased its production of digitized documents with funds furnished by Norway funds that allowed it to digitize and process more than 2 400 000 pages of monographs, the age of the paper having been endangered by degradation. This greatly increased the digital content of its collections because in a parallel way, the National Library and Academy of Sciences Library had already been digitizing their collections of contemporary periodicals.

As of April 2012, more than 10 000 000 pages have been digitized and are available through digital libraries. During the production of monographs, the National Library announced a need to coordinate original document preparation with other heritage institutions in the Czech Republic.

A special need for an adequate digitization workflow was the second parallel issue. A nearly identical need was also announced by Academy of Sciences Library (due digitization at its workplace). This purposed joint research project was submitted and subsequently approved and funded by the Czech Ministry of Culture. Research activities were underway from 2008 to 2011. The Registry web service was established during the project development and it has been in use from the beginning by many libraries in the Czech Republic.

2.2 Interfaces and Technical Description

There are two user interfaces in the system. Public interface is available on the website www.registrdigitalizace.cz, both in Czech and English language mutation. It can provide information about the location of the original document, its location in the digital library and library catalogues (including direct links to both systems), the status of the process, etc. This information is very useful, because through this system anyone can find immediately whether a book is already digitized or is in processing of digitization, or if any institution has selected the document for digitization and plans to process it.

In this way, a user can readily contact the owner of the digital document and, where possible, to arrange conditions for replication and thereby reduce the cost of digital form. We believe this solution welcomed from a user´s perspective, especially from those who desire information about all digitized documents. To simplify browsing, a multicolored semaphore was added to the front webpage. The green color indicates the "Document was digitized," yellow that the "Document is in process of digitization" and red signifies that "Document will be digitized soon."

From a workflow management perspective, the system is developed so as to record the different working processes and various types of documents. For workflow evidence, the second

JCDL'12, June 10–14, 2012, Washington, DC, USA.
ACM 978-1-4503-1154-0/12/06.

interface is used. It is accessible only after user registration. Registered users can access and insert information about microfilming, scanning, post-processing, OCR processing, metadata creation or publishing procedures.

The system is based on the Relief III application framework (J2EE) and all data are stored in the relational database Oracle. For user search and retrieval, Microsoft FAST is used. All user access is implemented via web application. The Digitization Registry is independent of the operation system and can be adapted to a number of languages. The implementation team is currently working on a new version which should be freely available as an open source application based on FEDORA commons, Grails and Jasper.

2.3 Connection to Other Library Systems Used in the Czech Republic

The first of the main subsystems is digitization workflow, where all metadata related to images are created. Bibliographic metadata, which are used in this workflow, are downloaded directly from the library catalogue Aleph in the MARCXML format and transformed to MODS. That is why the library catalogue is the second important pillar of the mentioned dataflow. The third subsystem is the digital library called Kramerius. A unique identification of digital documents is necessary as well as the persistent URL. This keeps the connection between the digital library and final user alive in the sphere of linking, references and citations. The Digitization Registry is the subsystem which holds connections to other systems. It serves as register of all digitized documents in the Czech Republic. It should avoid duplications and to monitor the lifecycle of digitized documents from stage of planning to the final archiving and dissemination.

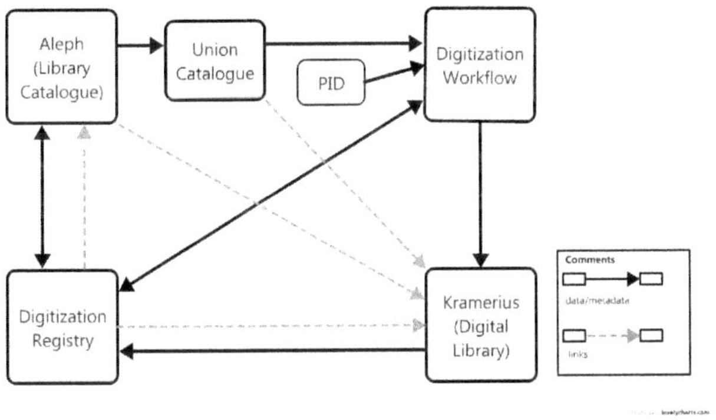

Figure 1. The Digitization Registry and relations with other library systems

2.4 How to Submit Records?

As of April 2012, there are nearly 60 000 records in the web application coming mainly from collections of researchers and from the largest project partners – the Moravian State Library, Municipal Library in Prague or National Technical Library. But of course included as well are many more libraries with specific collections or with regional importance. The National Medicine Library or Research Library in Usti nad Labem could be mentioned as typical examples. The essential fact is that the Digitization Registry is open to foreign libraries holding Bohemical collections as well. The owners of published documents also include other institutions. Any institution which would like to enter and insert its records may have a brief look to the webpage in the section *"Do you want to join us?"* read the conditions and user guide and in that way initiate cooperation.

Users desiring to cooperate properly should also learn how to browse the records. There are many ways to do so on the web. Of course, it is possible to a use simple question in the "Google box" or advance searching based on the knowledge of the metadata. Anyone may also search via the list of involved libraries (if he/she knows their collections and digitization activities) consulting a list of digital libraries or via types of documents. The first page offers also timeline searching. When the requested document is found, it is possible to open a whole record on it. The basic bibliographic information is available here as well as the information about the size, location and owner of the original document, URLs to the digital library and library catalogue and some other information.

3. THE IMPORTANCE OF THE PROJECT

3.1 International Scope

Since the described project is unique in the European context, a project proposal for the creation of a Coordinating Registry of the Central European countries was submitted in April 2010. In addition to the Czech partners, important institutions from Slovakia, Slovenia, Poland, Hungary, Germany and Austria were invited. But unfortunately the project was not approved by Central Europe Program Review Committee despite the fact it reached the final round of the competition. Now the Czech researchers are waiting for another EU program to which the project of the Central European countries digitization registry could be submitted. If appropriate funding emerges, the research team will ensure the creation of registries at national levels and their harvesting to the central registry.

3.2 National Value and Current Development

During May 2011, the Digitization Registry project was fully accepted and approved by the Central Librarian Council, which is advisory body of the Ministry of Culture. The Council was in full agreement on the importance of the system and recommended the National Library of Czech Republic as the guarantor of the system responsible for the content of the registry and for cooperation among Czech cultural heritage institutions. That was a very important step for the Registry because that would enable the research team ask the Ministry to support future development.

Since mass digitization has started at the National Library and at main regional libraries in the Czech Republic, thanks to funding from the Integrated Operational program of the European Union in 2012, the team will be waiting for the first mass digitization inputs to determine where potential problems could arise and solve them immediately. The beginning of the mass digitization increases the importance of the Registry as such a tool.

4. CONCLUSION

For libraries looking for a good, sophisticated system for their digital documents monitoring, which is also user friendly, the Digitization Registry could be the right solution. The credibility of the system has already been proved by its wide use in the Czech Republic of millions of digitized pages and it is available for all interested institutions and digitization projects. The most widespread cooperation, especially in the case of mass digitization activities, could save a considerable amount of money, time and personal resources.

How can spreaders affect the indirect influence on Twitter?

Xin Shuai
School of Informatics and Computing
Indiana University
Bloomington
IN, USA
xshuai@indiana.edu

Ying Ding
School of Library and Information Science
Indiana University
Bloomington
IN, USA
dingying@indiana.edu

Jerome Busemeyer
Dept. of Psychological and Brain Science
Indiana University
Bloomington
IN, USA
jbusemey@indiana.edu

ABSTRACT

Most studies on social influence have focused on direct influence, while another interesting question can be raised as *whether indirect influence exists between two users who're not directly connected in the network and what affects such influence*. In addition, the theory of *complex contagion* tells us that more spreaders will enhance the indirect influence between two users. Our observation of intensity of indirect influence, propagated by n parallel spreaders and quantified by retweeting probability on Twitter , shows that complex contagion is validated globally but is violated locally. In other words, the retweeting probability increases non-monotonically with some local drops.

Categories and Subject Descriptors

J.4 [**Social and Behavioral Science**]: Psychology

Keywords

Twitter, social influence, complex contagion

1. INTRODUCTION

Social influence has been studied by many researchers. However, most relevant studies focused on direct influence [4, 5] while few touched indirect influence [2]. Normally, multiple intermediate persons called spreaders are involved in the indirect communication between two persons, i.e., the sender and the receiver. Those spreaders may have a combinational effect on the indirect influence propagated from the sender to the receiver.

A concept closely related to parallel indirect influence is *complex contagion*, a phenomenon where repeated exposures of an individual to an idea recommended by his/her multiple neighbors positively affect the probability he/she will eventually follow that idea [1]. Romero et al. [3] studied the spread of hashtags in Twitter and quantified the probability of a user adopting a new hashtag as the function of the number of his/her neighbors who have already adopted it. They found that the spread of political hashtags validates the complex contagion, where the adoption probability increases monotonically as the number of neighbors who have already adopted the same hashtags increases, until a plateau is finally reached.

JCDL'12, June 10–14, 2012, Washington, DC, USA.
ACM 978-1-4503-1154-0/12/06.

The problem we are studying is similar to [3], but we focus on message spread behavior and indirect influence on Twitter. A concrete example of this is shown in Figure 1, where Alice sends out original messages, Charlie and Carol

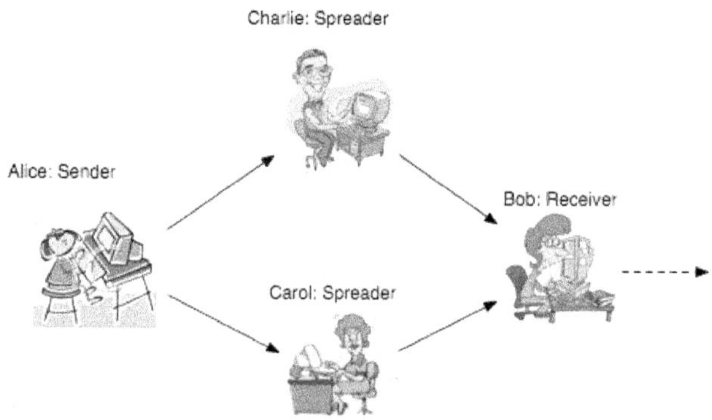

Figure 1: Typical information spread in a social network

further spread Alice's messages (i.e., by retweeting) and Bob finally receives them. After that, Bob may choose to further spread Alice's messages to others, just like his two neighbors Charlie and Carol have done, or not. Here, the intent of Bob to further spread Alice's messages would reflect the intensity of the indirect influence of Alice on Bob, which can be measured as the probability that Bob will further spread Alice's messages, given that Charlie and Carol have already spread these messages. If complex contagion takes effect, the influence intensity will be higher when both Charlie and Carol spread Alice's messages than when either or none of the two spread them.

In this paper, we examine the intensity of indirect influence as the function of the number of parallel spreaders, between two users on Twitter, who don't have direct following relations. We found that *complex contagion* is observed globally but is violated locally. Especially, when the number of spreaders increases from one to two, there's an obvious drop in the intensity.

2. PROBLEM DEFINITION

Twitter user can read another user's messages by following them and re-send their messages via retweeting. A retweeting message starts with the identifier "*RT @username*". Given a collection of tweets $C = \{t\}$, V represens all Twitter users while $E = \{(u, v) \, |u, v \in V\}$ represents all following relations where u follows v. We provide several formal definitions as follows:

- DEFINITION 1. [Following Triple] $\forall t$ starting with "*RT @y: RT @x*" posted by z, we build a following triple $T_{xyz} = (x, y, z), x, y, z \in V$ and claim that $(z, y) \in E$ and $(y, x) \in E$. We also define $C(T_{xyz})$ as the total count of tweets that belongs to T_{xyz} and $C(v), v \in V$ as the total count of tweets v posted.
- DEFINITION 2. [Spreaders] $\forall a, b \in V$, we define spreaders between a and b as $S_{ab} = \{y | T_{ayb} \neq NULL, y \in V\}$.
- DEFINITION 3. [N-spreader Retweeting Pattern] $\forall a, b \in V$ we define a retweeting pattern $P_{ab} = \{T_{ayb} | y \in S_{ab}\}$ and $|S_{ab}| = n$. Consequently, we define a n-spreader retweeting pattern as $P_n = \{P_{ab} || S_{ab}| = n\}$, and P_{ab} is an *instance* of P_n.
- DEFINITION 4. [Retweeting Probability] $\forall P_{ab} \neq \emptyset$, we define the probability of b retweeting from a as $Pr(b|a; S_{ab}) = \sum_{y \in S_{ab}} C(T_{ayb})/C(a)$. Consequently, we define the retweeting probability of n-spreader retweeting pattern as $Pr(n) = \sum_{P_{ab} \in P_n} Pr\{b|a; S_{ab}\}/|P_n|$.
- DEFINITION 5. [Indirect Influence] $\forall x, z \in V \cap P_{xz} \neq \emptyset$, we think x exerts indirect influence on z. $Pr(n)$ indicates the average intensity of indirect influence in n-spreader retweeting pattern.

Our research question can be formulated as: *Given n spreaders, how does the curve $Pr(n)$ change with n?*

3. DISCUSSION AND CONCLUSION

The dataset[1] contains 467 million tweets from 20 million Twitter users from June to December 2009 , which covers 20%-30% of total public tweets during this period. Figure 2 shows the global trend of $Pr(n)$ is increasing as n increases. That is to say, overall, the intensity of indirect influence tends to become higher, or at least persists, as more spreaders are included, which validates the phenomenon of complex contagion in the global level. However, there are two drops spotted in $Pr(n)$, i.e. from n =1 to 2 and 8 to 9. We use t-test of *difference between two means* to examine the two hypothesis: $Pr(1) > Pr(2)$ and $Pr(8) > Pr(9)$. Both p-values turn out to be close to zero, implying that the decrease is statistically significant and complex contagion is violated locally.

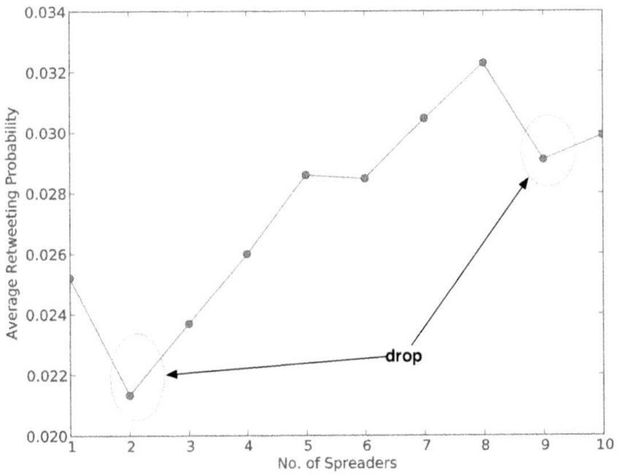

Figure 2: The curve of $Pr(n)$

[1]http://snap.stanford.edu/data/twitter7.html

The emerging field of *quantum cognition* might be able to provide a potential interpretation for the decreased influence phenomenon. Notably, in the process of decision making where a decision depends on multiple factors, quantum cognition assumes that these factors are not independent but have quantum-like interference effects on the final decision in a manner similar to the explanation for results from double-slit experiments [6]. In Figure 1, we assume that initially only Charlie spreads Alice's messages while Carol does not. Bob receives Alice's messages through Charlie and further spreads them because Bob thinks Alice's messages are relevant. Later on, Carol also begins to spread Alice's messages but they largely overlap with those already spread by Charlie. Bob therefore becomes less interested in Alice's messages because he's overwhelmed with redundant information. Thus Bob's intent to further spread Alice's messages (i.e., the indirect influence of Alice on Bob) decreases. Here, the interference between two spreaders leads to destructive effects on the indirect influence from the sender to the receiver.

In conclusion, we investigated the propagation of parallel indirect influence on Twitter with a focus on how the intensity of influence changes with the number of spreaders. We quantified the intensity of indirect influence with the retweeting probability, and plotted the curve of retweeting probability against the number of spreads. We found that the phenomenon of complex contagion is validated globally but violated locally since the retweeting probability increases non-monotonically with some local drops. We finally proposed quantum cognition hypothesis in an attempt to interpret the local anomaly yet further verification is needed.

4. REFERENCES

[1] D. Centola and M. Macy. Complex contagion and the weakness of long ties. Technical report, 2005.

[2] Y. Ding. Scientific collaboration and endorsement: Network analysis of coauthorship and citation networks. *Journal of Informetrics*, 5:187–203, 2011.

[3] D. M. Romero, B. Meeder, and J. Kleinberg. Differences in the mechanics of information diffusion across topics: idioms, political hashtags, and complex contagion on twitter. In *WWW '11*, pages 695–704, Hyderabad, India, 2011.

[4] J. Tang, J. Sun, C. Wang, and Z. Yang. Social influence analysis in large-scale networks. In *KDD '09*, pages 807–816, Paris, France, 2009.

[5] R. Xiang, J. Neville, and M. Rogati. Modeling relationship strength in online social networks. In *WWW '10*, pages 981–990, Hong Kong, China, 2010.

[6] V. I. Yukalov and D. Sornette. Decision theory with prospect interference and entanglement. *Theory and Decision*, 70:283–328, 2011.

Improving a Hybrid Literary Book Recommendation System through Author Ranking

Paula Cristina Vaz
INESC-ID/IST-Portugal
paula.vaz@inesc-id.pt

Bruno Martins
IST/INESC-ID-Portugal
bruno.martins@ist.utl.pt

David Martins de Matos
INESC-ID/IST-Portugal
david.matos@inesc-id.pt

Pavel Calado
IST/INESC-ID-Portugal
pavel.calado@ist.utl.pt

ABSTRACT

Literary reading is an important activity for individuals and can be a long term commitment, making book choice an important task for book lovers and public library users. In this paper, we present a hybrid recommendation system to help readers decide which book to read next. We study book and author recommendations in a hybrid recommendation setting and test our algorithm on the LitRec data set. Our hybrid method combines two item-based collaborative filtering algorithms to predict books and authors that the user will like. Author predictions are expanded into a booklist that is subsequently aggregated with the former book predictions. Finally, the resulting booklist is used to yield the top-n book recommendations. By means of various experiments, we demonstrate that author recommendation can improve overall book recommendation.

Categories and Subject Descriptors

H.3.3 [**Information Storage and Retrieval**]: Information filtering; H.3.7 [**Digital Libraries**]: System issues

General Terms

Algorithms, Experimentation

Keywords

Hybrid Recommender, Book Recommendation, Author Recommendation

1. INTRODUCTION

Literary reading is an important activity for individuals and public libraries enable users to participate in this activity free of charge by allowing them to borrow books for short periods. As a consequence, good recommendations in a public library can improve a reader's usability of the library.

Libraries have limited shelf space, but still have enough books to make book selection difficult and time consuming. However, the number of books and users is not enough to successfully use the traditional collaborative techniques that rely on large amounts of data to detect patterns.

JCDL'12, June 10–14, 2012, Washington, DC, USA.
ACM 978-1-4503-1154-0/12/06.

In this paper, we aim to (*i*) assess whether item-based collaborative filtering (CF) can be used to make good recommendations in a public library, and (*ii*) assess whether selecting books by author preferences can improve recommendations. We also propose HyBook: a weighted hybrid approach to recommend literary books. Our approach combines two item-based CF algorithms to improve recommendations, where one recommends books and the other recommends authors. Author recommendation is used to improve the book top-n recommendations through a fusion approach.

2. RELATED WORK

Literature on recommendation systems typically classifies systems such as collaborative-, content-, demographic-, and/or knowledge-based. Moreover, hybrid systems combine two or more algorithms to improve recommendations, overcoming limitations of the individual approaches [2].

There are several book recommendation sites that can be found on the Internet. We highlight: *gnooks*[1], a CF book and author recommender through a literature map; and *Similar authors*[2] a CF author recommender. In [4], the author investigates the effectiveness of author rankings in a library catalog to improve book retrieval. However, to the best of our knowledge, this is the first study attempting to improve book recommenders through author recommendation.

3. PROPOSED METHOD

HyBook algorithm uses two matrices: the $book \times user$ matrix, where $cell_{i,j}$ contains the rating that $user_j$ gave to $book_i$; and the $author \times user$ matrix, where $cell_{i,j}$ contains the average of ratings that $user_j$ gave to books of $author_i$. These matrices are used to calculate both $book \times book$ and $author \times author$ matrices where the $cell_{i,j}$ contains similarity between items i and j. Similarity is calculated using item co-occurrences.

HyBook uses the active user preference vector and the $book \times book / author \times author$ matrix to yield the book/author rank vector. Position i of the rank vector contains the rank predicted for $book_i / author_i$ according to the active user preferences. The author rank vector is then expanded into a book rank vector by assigning to each book its author predicted rank. Rank vectors are calculated by aggregating

[1]http://www.gnooks.com
[2]http://www.similarauthors.com

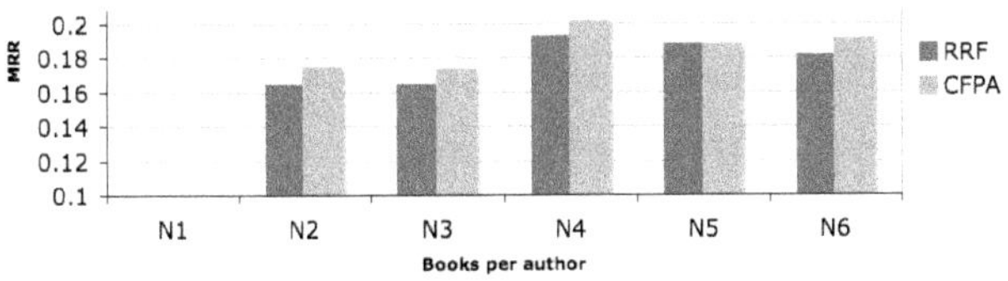

Figure 1: MRR per author neighborhood size.

the columns of the similarity matrices corresponding to the items preferred by the active user. We tested our CF predictions with two aggregation functions: the reciprocal rank fusion (RRF) [3]; and the traditional collaborative filtering preference aggregation (CFPA) [1].

Finally, book rank vectors are aggregated and sorted, generating the top-n book list for the active user. Rank vectors are aggregated using a weighted arithmetic mean (WAM) as shown in Equation 1.

$$WAM(u) = \frac{\alpha\ CF_{author}(u) + (1-\alpha)\ CF_{book}(u)}{2} \tag{1}$$

4. EXPERIMENTS

This section describes the LitRec data set and discusses experiments with HyBook. To evaluate the quality of top-n lists generated by HyBook, we used the mean reciprocal rank (MRR). In Equation 2, p_i is the position, at the top_i, of the first relevant document.

$$MRR = \frac{\sum_{i=1}^{number\ of\ tops} \frac{1}{p_i}}{number\ of\ tops} \tag{2}$$

4.1 LitRec data set

LitRec is a data set built by the authors for recommendation purposes. It combines documents from Project Gutenberg[3] with ratings from *Goodreads*[4] and contains 38,591 ratings from 1,927 users and 3,710 documents. The data set also contains book authors (1,627 different authors) and the review date among others. The review date was used to sort and divide ratings in a train-test set of 90%-10%.

4.2 CF Aggregating function

We used RRF and CFPA to aggregate book and author predictions. Results showed that the best predictions were achieved using CFPA for books (MRR = 0.28) and RRF for authors (MRR = 0.22).

4.3 Author neighborhood

The author neighborhood is the number of books written by the author and used in predictions. Experiments have shown that if the number of books per author is not restricted, the expanded book rank vector will be saturated by authors with more books, leading to less accurate predictions. As shown in figure 1, predictions improve when the book neighborhood varies from 1 to 4 and decreases after 4. Based on this experiment, we set author neighborhood to 4 books.

[3]http://www.gutenberg.org
[4]http://www.goodreads.com

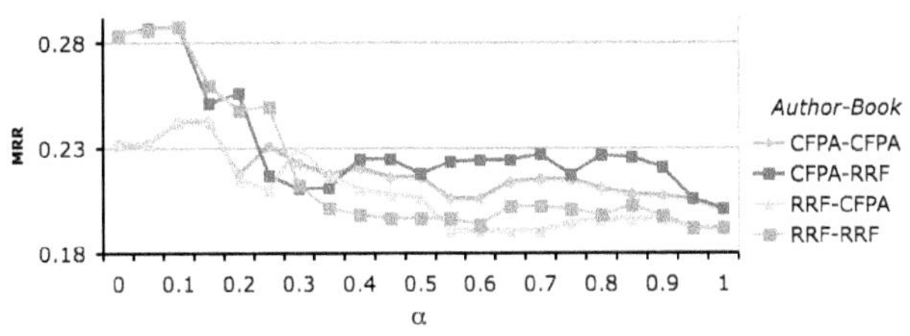

Figure 2: HyBook MRR for all combinations of author-book rank aggregation.

4.4 Aggregating book ranks

HyBook aggregates rank vectors yield by book and author predictions using WAM (Equation 1). We also experimented with RRF, but results were not promising. We varied the α parameter between 0 and 1 in order to assess the importance of the author in final recommendations. As shown in figure 2, HyBook yields the best predictions when ranks have the combination of 10% author and 90% book.

The graphic also outlines the evolution of all combinations of score aggregations. As expected from results obtained in the previous experiments, when author predictions use CFPA and books predictions use RRF, overall results are better. However, at the 10%-90% author-book combination the RRF-RRF combination can achieve the same results.

5. CONCLUSIONS & FUTURE WORK

In this paper we describe a HyBook: a hybrid book recommendation algorithm. HyBook combines author and book predictions to yield the top-n book recommendations.

Regarding the first of the initial goals presented in Section 1, experiments led us to conclude that the common CF approaches yield poor predictions due to limitations of this version of LitRec. Regarding the second goal experiments in LitRec have shown that overall predictions can be improved using author prediction. However, a maximum number of books per author must be established, otherwise authors with more books will appear to have an advantage over less productive authors.

We also observed that for the LitRec data set, the contribution of choosing books by author must be smaller than that of choosing books by their popularity.

This paper describes exploratory work in LitRec data set that opens a path for further research. We intend to continue exploring LitRec. We will try to assess if book choice is related to content, user location, and the month in which the book was read. Finally, the use of feature augmentation and dimensionality reduction techniques will also be considered.

6. REFERENCES

[1] G. Beliakov, T. Calvo, and S. James. Aggregation of preferences in recommender systems. In *Recommender Systems Handbook*, pages 705–734. Springer, 2011.

[2] D. Burke. Hybrid web recommender systems. In *The Adaptive Web*, pages 377–408, 2007.

[3] G. Cormack, C. Clarke, and S. Buettcher. Reciprocal rank fusion outperforms condorcet and individual rank learning methods. In *SIGIR '09: Proceedings of the 32nd international ACM SIGIR conference on Research and development in information retrieval*, pages 758–759, New York, NY, USA, 2009.

[4] J. Kamps. The impact of author ranking in a library catalogue. In *Proceedings of the 4th ACM workshop on Online books, complementary social media and crowdsourcing*, BooksOnline '11, pages 35–40, New York, NY, USA, 2011. ACM.

Introducing High Performance Computing in Digital Library Processing Workflows

Bill Barth
Texas Advanced Computing Center
bbarth@tacc.utexas.edu

Maria Esteva
Texas Advanced Computing Center
maria@tacc.utexas.edu

Jon Gibson
University of Texas Libraries
jongibson@austin.utexas.edu

Ladd Hanson
University of Texas Libraries
ladd@austin.utexas.edu

Christopher Jordan
Texas Advanced Computing Center
ctjordan@tacc.utexas.edu

ABSTRACT
As larger collections need to be processed for digital library projects, libraries have to adopt technologies of scale. We present a case that involved creating image derivatives using High Performance Computing (HPC) resources. This experience opens up possibilities to conduct various processing tasks effectively and in reasonable time frames. Most importantly, it enables library IT staff access to cyberinfrastructure that can address the computing challenges of large-scale digital library projects.

Categories and Subject Descriptors
D.1.3 [**Programming Techniques**]: Concurrent Programming – *parallel programming.* H.3.7 [**Information Storage and Retrieval**]: Digital Libraries.

Keywords
Digitization, High Performance Computing, Digital Libraries.

1. INTRODUCTION
Post-processing operations in digitization workflows, such as the creation of derivative images for web access, are generally conducted on individual digitization workstations or on shared servers. As the number of files increases, post-processing tasks become computationally intensive, time consuming, and prone to errors, creating the need to consider the use of distributed compute systems [1].

As part of an international collaboration to preserve and give access to the collection of digitized police records from the Guatemalan National Police Historical Archive, the University of Texas Libraries has made the collection web accessible (https://ahpn.lib.utexas.edu/). The project encompasses 80 million pages that are being digitized on an ongoing basis at the Guatemalan Archives. Hard-drives containing millions of images are brought to Texas and processed for web access. This project represents an example of a task that is orders of magnitude larger than previous digital library projects undertaken by the UT Libraries.

To address the scale of the project efficiently and to meet the deadline of the first web deliverable, the Library Systems staff consulted with the Texas Advanced Computing Center (TACC).

JCDL'12, June 10–14, 2012, Washington, DC, USA.
ACM 978-1-4503-1154-0/12/06.

Using the Ranger cluster, a first batch of 10+ million TIFF images (5TB) was converted into JPEG format. A process that would take an estimated 2 to 4 months of continuous compute time using the systems that the library currently could assign to the task, took five days using TACC resources.

HPC is traditionally used to run large-scale simulations and data intensive computing analyses. This case introduces parallel computing into digital libraries workflows. We describe the methods, resources and the results of this project, and discuss its potential for future use.

2. WORKFLOW AND METHODOLOGY

2.1 Data
A first batch of 10.1+ million pages was scanned in Guatemala at 300 DPI. The original images are a mixture of grayscale and black and white TIFF files. Most of the black and white images are compressed with Lossless CCITT h.6 TIFF compression and the remainder images are uncompressed. Files range in sizes from 563 bytes to 13MB, with a mean size of 499KB and a median size of 75.8KB. This distribution of file sizes is skewed towards the smaller side with over 70% of the images being less than 125KB and over 80% being less than 500KB.

2.2 Parallel Processing
To create the derivatives we used TACC's Ranger system, a large-scale NSF-funded parallel computing resource for open science research. Ranger consists of 3936 tightly-integrated computing servers with 62,976 AMD "Barcelona" computing cores, 123TB of aggregate memory, and 1.73PB of raw disk storage capacity all interconnected with InfiniBand [2]. Ranger uses the Oracle Grid Engine (OGE) batch job scheduling system to coordinate usage of the system among hundreds of active users.

This project used the TACC Parametric Job Launcher to aggregate the task of converting the original TIFF images to JPEG formatted images using the ImageMagick open source program [3]. Additional metadata files were also produced. The launcher collects sequential tasks into a single parallel job suitable for use on large-scale parallel machines like Ranger. It is a straightforward aggregation script that runs a given UNIX command over a sequence of specified input parameters. It takes a divide-and-conquer approach to parallelizing the tasks by distributing them to the available compute resources in a job, running groups of them in parallel, and starting new individual tasks as prior ones complete until all the tasks are done. Each assigned processor works on a subset of the overall workload.

This image-processing project converted the original TIFF image files to 1000-pixel-wide primary JPEG files and 180-pixel-wide thumbnail JPEG files while keeping the aspect ratio constant. This was done using the ImageMagick "convert" program through the launcher. The ImageMagick "identify" program was used to write a separate text file containing the width and height information for the original TIFF images. A text file containing a list of conversion errors was also output.

The original 10.1 million images were processed in batches of approximately 200,000. Each batch was processed sequentially. The batches of input TIFF images were copied to Ranger using *scp* from the UT Libraries' storage servers. OGE job control scripts and TACC Job Launcher inputs were created using a bash shell script. The OGE job control script was submitted to the Ranger OGE scheduling system. Once the job had completed successfully, the resulting image files were copied back to the UT Libraries' servers.

3. RESULTS

3.1 Time and Error

The 10.1 million TIFF images were processed in 106 hours on Ranger (0.036 second per image). 5TB of original data was transformed into 5.6TB of output products. The overall transfers between systems required 667 hours.

During processing a total of 7403 images failed to be converted. The most common cause of these failures (>95%) was that the original images were multi-page TIFF images and the processing scripts were not written to handle them. The remainder of the issues were images that were either corrupt or of 0KB size. These errors were handled on an individual basis after the data was transferred back to the libraries.

Table 1. Time and Error During Workflow

Upload Time (hr:min:sec)	Processing Time (hr:min:sec)	Download Time (hr:min:sec)	Error Rate
113:32:31	106:29:42	554:03:38	0.07%

As seen in Table 1, there was an asymmetric result between uploads and download times from TACC. In both cases, the amount of data transferred was similar but the resulting data contained approximately 2x the number of files due to the creation of two derivatives for each original image. The use of other protocols, such as bbcp or GridFTP for bulk transfer may have improved these times.

3.2 Lessons

As shown in Table 1, the majority of time-cost relates to transferring the data between the library and TACC systems. Reduction of this cost will be one of the top priorities for the library's future work with TACC. It is possible that there are better transfer protocols than *scp* that can help reduce this cost. Storing the library's original image files on TACC's storage resources would remove the upload time.

An important gain from this increased processing speed is workflow flexibility. During processing, a total of 7403 images failed to be converted by ImageMagick. While that rate may change from batch to batch, the fast processing allowed detection of problems and mitigation on a much quicker time frame.

The fast turn-around time allows for iteration and multiple solutions can be tried in quick succession. The workflow used on this project centered on a fairly simple operation: images were converted in format and the size of the image standardized to a uniform pixel width. Other than basic error handling, no attempt was made to ascertain the correctness of the resulting derivatives. Given that visual validation, manually comparing each derivative to its original, is not feasible due to the sheer number of images, faster processing times will make automated methods of quality control possible. In future workflows we plan to use image metadata such as average hue and alpha transparency to compare originals to derivatives.

Lastly, the library learned that no specialized training was required for the IT staff to use TACC systems. The UNIX development environment is familiar and similar to the existing library environment.

4. CONCLUSIONS

As the use of HPC for long-term storage and delivery of massive digital library materials is becoming more common [4], its potential for large scale processing tasks is beginning to be exploited. This experience has given us the confidence to tackle future large-scale digital collections in more complex and efficient ways. To date only 10 million of the estimated 80 million images encompassed in this project had been digitized. Recently the library has received another 1 million images and expects to receive approximately 2 million additional images annually. Future batches using HPC processing workflows will include error recovery and quality control workflows. Moreover, the experience as described in this paper opens up new opportunities for the libraries to use HPC to conduct massive digital preservation tasks such as metadata extraction and file migration.

5. ACKNOWLEDGEMENTS

The authors acknowledge the Texas Advanced Computing Center (TACC) at The University of Texas at Austin for providing HPC resources that have contributed to the research results reported within this paper. URL: http://www.tacc.utexas.edu

6. REFERENCES

[1] Henrik Johansson, Per-erik Svedlund, Eric Siira, Hamid Sarve, (2010). A cost-efficient and automatic digitization workflow using commodity hardware and image analysis. In Proceedings of the IS&T Archiving Conference, June 1- 4 2010. Den Haag, The Netherlands. pp 101 – 107.

[2] Texas Advanced Computing Center. Ranger User Guide. Retrieved 01/30/2012 from, http://www.tacc.utexas.edu/user-services/user-guides/ranger-user-guide

[3] ImageMagick 6.7.5-0. Retrieved 01/30/2012 from, http://www.imagemagick.org/script/index.php

[4] Robert McDonald, Chris Jordan, et al. (2011). An iRODS Based Data Replication Service for Institutional Data Curation. Poster presentation at the 6th International Conference on Digital Curation, December 6-8, 2011. Chicago, USA.

Investigating User Perceptions of Engagement and Information Quality in Mobile Human Computation Games

Dion H. Goh, Khasfariyati Razikin, Chei Sian Lee, Alton Y. K. Chua
Wee Kim Wee School of Communication and Information
Nanyang Technological University
{ashlgoh, khasfariyati, leecs, altonchua}@ntu.edu.sg

ABSTRACT

We investigate user perceptions of engagement and information quality of a mobile human computation game (HCG) by comparing it against a non-game-based application. Results suggest that the mobile HCG enabled participants to occupy their leisure time but the information contributed was perceived to be not as relevant. Implications of this study are discussed.

Categories and Subject Descriptors

H.5.2. Information interfaces and presentation (e.g., HCI); Evaluation/methodology; K.8.0. General: Games

General Terms

Design, Human Factors.

Keywords

Human Computation Games, Location-based Information, Mobile Devices, User Study.

1. INTRODUCTION

Mobile Human Computer Games (HCGs) generate useful computations as a byproduct of gameplay [2]. In the present work, we use mobile HCGs to foster the sharing of location-based content. In contrast to other mobile content sharing applications, players are able to derive fun while generating useful content. As a result, a number of applications have used this approach to collect useful information that could help humans in a variety of ways such as exploring one's surroundings [1, 4].

Harnessing the enjoyment and entertainment brought about by games with the aim to solve problems results in a user experience that is unique from other mobile content sharing applications. Ideally, the game mechanics in mobile HCGs should engage users to contribute location-based content [2] and at the same time, such content should be useful for others [4]. One thread of current research on user perceptions focuses on comparing user perceptions of engagement [5] in the different genres of Web-based HCGs [1] and has uncovered motivations like competition and killing time. Further, information quality is crucial in influencing users' intention to use and factors like completeness and timeliness have been identified in prior research. Little attention, however, has been given towards users' perceptions of engagement and information quality in mobile HCGs.

This work aims to address the abovementioned gap by comparing users' perceptions of engagement and information quality while using a mobile HCGs and a non-game-based mobile content sharing application through an experiment.

JCDL'12, June 10–14, 2012, Washington, DC, USA.
ACM 978-1-4503-1154-0/12/06.

2. METHODOLOGY

Two Android-based mobile applications were developed for the study: a mobile HCG and a non-game-based mobile content sharing application (CS). In both applications, location-based content comprises of text, images and rating. The mobile HCG uses a pet-based game genre in which players "feed" content to virtual pets. A pet's appearance and behavior are affected by the type of information fed. Specifically, the amount, quality and sentiment of the content affects its the size and movement, color and expressiveness. Figure 1 provides some examples of how pets would appear depending on the content fed. The content is accessed through a map-based interface with pets indicating the location (Figure 2). Similarly, content is accessed through a map-based interface in the CS application (Figure 3).

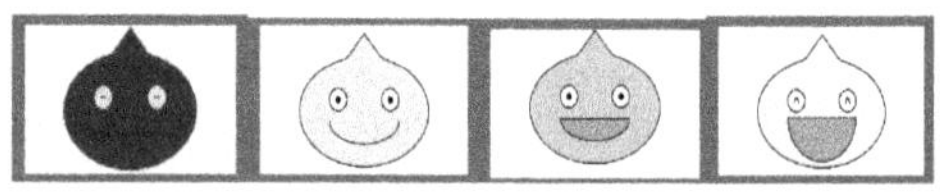

Figure 1. Different pets with varying sentiment, quality and volume of location-based information fed by players

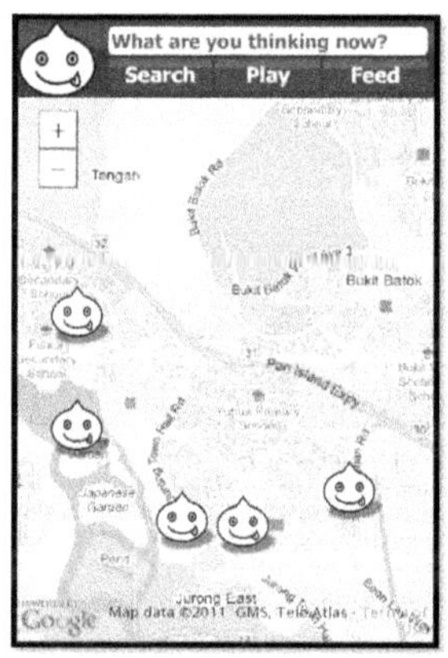

Figure 2. Pets on the map indicate available content in the mobile HCG.

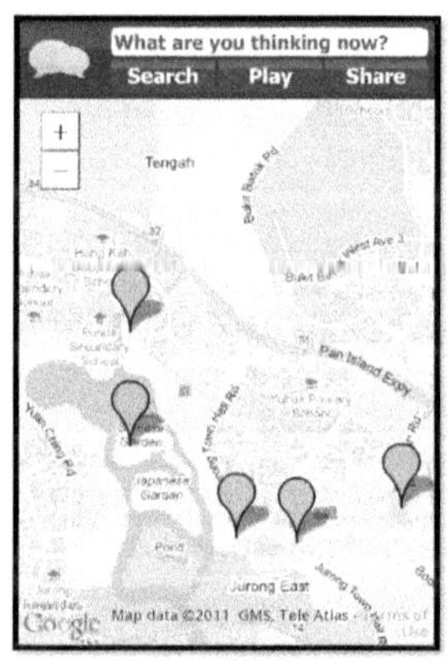

Figure 3. Map markers indicate available content in the mobile CS application.

A within-subjects experimental design was adopted. For each application, participants created and rated content at two pre-selected locations. Participants also completed a questionnaire that elicited their perceptions of the engagement and information quality of the two applications, and their intention to use them. Questions were in a form of affirmative statements and rated on a scale of 1 (strongly disagree) to 5 (strongly agree). Perceptions of engagement [5] were measured along the factors of leisure, control and immersion. Perceptions of information quality [3] were operationalized as relevancy, timeliness and completeness.

3. RESULTS

A total of 121 participants, of which 53 were female, were recruited. Their ages ranged from 17 to 65 years (M=30 years old, SD=7.39). Participants were from diverse backgrounds such as Computer Science/Information Technology (53.7%) and Engineering (16.5%). They were typical mobile phone users who frequently use the mobile phone to surf the Web, access social media applications, capture media and play games.

Table 1 shows the means and standard deviations of the variables used in the study. Seven paired sample T-tests were conducted to compare the perceptions of the two applications. Significant differences were observed for the leisure [$t(120)=2.103$, $p<0.05$] and relevancy variables [$t(120)=2.343$, $p<0.05$].

Table 1. Means and standard deviations of perceptions of engagement, information quality and intention to use.

Variables	HCG (N = 121) Mean (SD)	CS (N = 121) Mean (SD)
Leisure *	2.62 (1.03)	2.42 (0.89)
Control	2.87 (0.88)	2.85 (0.79)
Immersion	2.93 (0.75)	2.99 (0.63)
Relevancy *	2.47 (0.87)	2.71 (1.03)
Timeliness	2.53 (0.85)	2.67 (0.77)
Completeness	2.56 (0.79)	2.54 (0.85)
Intention to Use	2.76 (1.04)	2.77 (1.03)

* Statistically significant difference at $p<0.05$

Two multiple regression analyses were conducted to investigate the influence of participants' perceptions on their intention to use the applications. Table 2 summarizes the results. For the HCG, the independent variables described 79.1% of its variance and was statistically significant [$F(4,116)=71.994$, $p<0.001$]. In this model, participants' perception of leisure ($ß=0.647$, $p<0.001$) and control ($ß=0.146$, $p<0.05$) were significant predictors for intention to use. Additionally, the perception of completeness was also a significant predictor for intention to use the HCG ($ß=0.133$, $p<0.05$). In contrast, the independent variables for the CS application accounted for 55% of the variance and the regression model was statistically significant [$F(4,116)=23.241$, $p<0.001$]. Only the variable leisure was a significant predictor of intention to use ($ß=0.456$, $p<0.001$).

4. DISCUSSION AND CONCLUSION

The experiment yielded the following findings. First, participants found the mobile HCG entertaining. They might have received immediate gratification as they were able to see the changes in the pet after feeding them, and this could have created positive feelings towards the game. In contrast, the CS application did not provide any form of feedback that was perceived to be enjoyable. Interestingly, the game did not appear to instill confidence that its content would be relevant, implying that participants were less trusting of content generated by games. Put differently, participants did not seem to equate quality content with fun. They might have perceived that such content is susceptible to people who might game the system to solely reap rewards [1].

Next, the regression analyses showed that the perceptions of leisure and control were positively associated with the mobile HCG while the perception of leisure was positively associated with the CS application. It is not surprising that leisure was the common theme, suggesting that participants were able to alleviate boredom, highlighting the inclination for people to readily share their thoughts using mobile devices. For the mobile HCG, control was another variable that was significant, indicating that participants liked being able to bring about immediate changes to their pets' appearance from their contributions.

Table 2. Multiple regression analyses for engagement and information quality on dependent variable intention to use.

Independent variables	HCG (N = 121) β	HCG (N = 121) t	CS (N = 121) β	CS (N = 121) t
Leisure	0.647	10.404**	0.456	6.206**
Control	0.146	2.258*	0.085	1.113
Immersion	0.070	1.399	0.074	1.051
Relevancy	0.016	0.257	0.163	1.643
Timeliness	0.032	0.456	0.121	1.207
Completeness	0.133	2.168*	0.079	0.741
Adj R^2	0.791		0.550	
F-Value	71.994**		23.241**	

Statistically significant values: *$p<0.05$, **$p<0.001$

Finally, the perception of completeness was positively associated with the mobile HCG, suggesting the importance of accessing content with sufficient detail as users would lose their trust in the application if content was incomplete [3]. Surprisingly for the CS application, none of the variables were significant, indicating that being able to access to quality content is not a strong motivator as other factors could be more pertinent.

In conclusion, our results demonstrate the appeal of games in the generation of location-based content. In particular, mobile HCGs are perceived to embody factors of engagement and information quality that encourage further usage. Nevertheless, our work has limitations that should be addressed. For instance, individual differences, such as gender and social media experience, and game genres could influence perceptions of the application.

5. ACKNOWLEDGMENTS

This work was supported by the Singapore National Research Foundation Interactive Digital Media R&D Program, under research Grant NRF NRF2008IDM-IDM004-012.

6. REFERENCES

[1] Bell, M., Reeves, S., Brown, B., Sherwood, S., McMillan, D., Ferguson, J. and Chalmers, M. 2009. Eyespy: Supporting navigation through play. In *Proceedings of the 27th SIGCHI conference*. ACM, New York, 123-132.

[2] Goh, D. H.-L., Ang, R. P., Lee, C. S. and Chua, A. Y. K. 2011a. Fight or unite: Investigating game genres for image tagging. *JASIST*, 62, 7, 1131-1124.

[3] Kim, B. and Han, I. 2009. The role of trust belief and its antecedents in a community-driven knowledge environment. *JASIST*, 60, 5, 1012-1026.

[4] Lee, C. S., Goh, D. H.-L., Chua, A. Y. K. and Ang, R. P. 2010. Indagator: Investigating perceived gratifications of an application that blends mobile content sharing with gameplay. *JASIST*, 61, 6, 1244-1257.

[5] O`Brien, H. L and Toms, E. G. 2008. The development and evaluation of a survey to measure user engagement in e-commerce environments. *JASIST*, 59, 6, 938-955.

Lessons Learned from Developing and Evaluating a Comprehensive Digital Library for Engineering Education

Yunlu Zhang
Wuhan University
Hubei,China,430079
zhangyunlu850527@gmail.com

Alice Merner Agogino
University of California, Berkeley
California, 94720-1764
agogino@berkeley.edu

Shijun Li
Wuhan University
Hubei,China,430079
shjli@whu.edu.cn

ABSTRACT

Educating the engineering education community in today's digital world requires straightforward yet flexible access to high-quality educational resources. The Teach Engineering and NEEDS (National Engineering Education Delivery System) digital libraries collaborated in 2005 to create and steward the K-Gray Engineering Pathway (EP), a premier portal to comprehensive engineering and computing education resources within the greater National Science Digital Library (NSDL). We collaborated to design navigation, implement features, and find imagery that could effectively address both K-12 and higher education audiences. A system was designed to serve both target audiences, including an expanded simple search on every page to include grade/audience level search fields. This search, on all main pages, also includes a choice of learning resource type and a link to the Advanced Search with expanded search fields. EP tailored many features such as community pages and cataloging to be distinguishable by K-12 versus higher education users. Evaluation studies show that our current strength is a consistent interface with strong usability features. In this paper, we a provide retrospective and summarize our lessons learned and evaluation results, along with our directions for future research and development.

Categories and Subject Descriptors

H.4 [**Information Systems Applications**]: Miscellaneous; H.3.7 [**Information Storage and Retrieval**]: Digital Libraries—*User issues, Collection*

General Terms

Management, Design, Performance

Keywords

Digital Library; Engineering Education; education community

1. INTRODUCTION

The K-Gray Engineering Pathway (EP), hosted at UC Berkeley, is a multi-university effort to improve teaching and learning in engineering and computing. EP provides comprehensive high-quality teaching and learning resources in applied science and math, engineering, computer science /information technology, and engineering technology for use by K-12 and university educators and students. EP hosts 16 different collections, including the Broadening Participation in Computing (BPC) Portal [1] and PR2OVE-IT (Peer Reviewed Research Offering Validation of Effective and Innovative Teaching)[2], and has approximately 15,000 metadata records of educational resources. EP maintains social networking and community services, including a blog, Facebook and Twitter integration, search and news widgets and disciplinary communities.

Launched in 2005, EP is the engineering "wing" of the National Science Digital Library (NSDL.org), serving resource providers and users from a broad spectrum of constituencies: elementary, middle and high schools; two/four-year undergraduate programs; graduate and professional schools; and lifelong learners. Key stewardship goals are to merge the NEEDS (National Engineering Education Delivery System) [4] and TE (Teach Engineering)[3] digital libraries into a unified K-Gray Engineering Pathway, significantly and sustainably grow the Engineering Pathway, align EP's curricula with appropriate undergraduate or K-12 educational standards, increase the number of EP content providers and users, develop and implement interoperable quality control and review protocols for all EP content, and create a non-profit strategy and partnership for sustaining the K-Gray Engineering Pathway. In support of these goals, design of the site was given careful attention.The homepage is as shown in Figure 1.

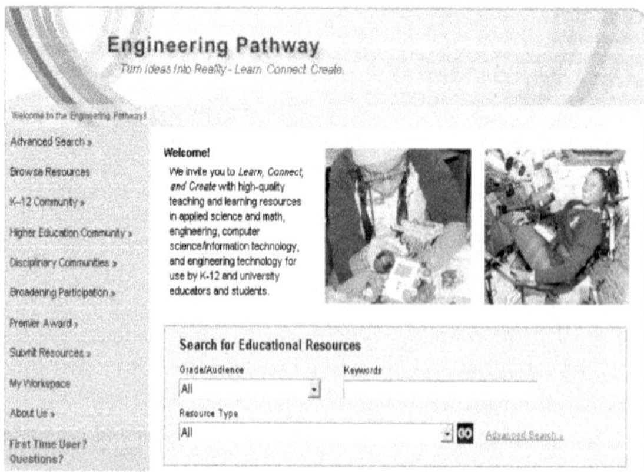

Figure 1: EP Homepage

JCDL'12, June 10–14, 2012, Washington, DC, USA.
ACM 978-1-4503-1154-0/12/06.

2. EVALUATION

2.1 Qualitative Evaluation

Our evaluation of EP draws on human-centered design qualitative methods of observations and interviews. Our qualitative formative evaluation studies show that our current strength is a consistent interface with strong usability features and quality content [5]. The highest priority of our users was the precision in the search for high quality and relevant educational resources. Based on this formative feedback, the search capabilities on high-level pages were changed to highlight a simple search that included the highest priority search fields: keyword, grade/audience and learning resource type. All other pages have grade/audience and keywords in the upper banner. K-12 users said "less was more"and wanted to reduce the number of options in both search and cataloging. In response to this feedback, we designed our K-12 catalog form and K-12 search form with fields limited to a subset of the learning resource type (LRT) options available to higher education users: curricular unit, interactive, lesson plan, hands-on activity, real-world data, and educational research paper and reference material.

EP provides services for a number of external collections and thus we included collection owners and faculty in our evaluation. We were told that faculty and collection owners appreciate codifying relationships between resources as important value-added services.The relational operators we implemented are: "part of," "references," "based on," "formats" and "requires" with the first two being the most heavily used. At the end of 2011, we had approximately 5,000 relations between resources. (30 % of all resources).

2.2 Quantitative Evaluation

EP substantially grew its user base over the past 6 years in both content and functionality. The number of catalog records increased by seven-fold from 2,408 engineering-relevant resources in 2005 to 16,855 in 2011. We have more than 9,000 registered users and average approximately one million page views a month. The EP blog, which does have original content, continued to show growth, ending 2011 with over 1 million page views as opposed to 450,000 in 2009. Our disciplinary pages are typically in the top 10 for all major ABET disciplines under both Google and Yahoo searches.

As connecting users to educational resources is EP's primary goal, we are interested in the views of the catalog records for these resources as well as how many of these views lead to linking to or downloading the resource. At the end of 2011, the cumulative number of views and downloads for our catalog records were approximately 9 million and 860,000, respectively. A "view"is defined as viewing the catalog record; a "download" is defined as linking to the actual resource or downloading a document, file or executable. In recent years, approximately 10% of the views lead to a download. Based on Google Analytics for the past year, visitors came from 166 countries, with the top five visitor countries and their percentage: United States (51.86%), India (9.17%), United Kingdom (3.67%), Canada (3.52%), Malaysia (2.27%).

3. SEARCH PATTERNS

EP has 40,907 distinct keywords and the majority of direct searches over our site are associated with browse terms such as "Premier Award" or "Associate Editor's Choice", showing a preference for quality and higher rated resources. Over half of the EP higher education users come from search engine referrals (53 %) or from the NSDL (13%). A significant percent are also from direct links from other sites, including our blog (14%). The keywords from search engines tend to be disciplinary, such as "electrical engineering education" or oriented towards learning resources, such as "engineering graphic tutorials" or "examples of simple machines."

For the K-12 TeachEngineering digital library, use patterns during the day and year closely follow the school calendar and clock. For example, periods of lower use are in the summer and after school hours. A significant portion of the hits are coming from K-12 schools and districts. Each month, users searched on an average of 7,000+ keywords and 10,000+ key phrases using external (non-TE) search engines. The curriculum pages receive the highest hit rates and the most popular search terms are "simple machines," "bridge(s)," "engineering," "energy," "electricity," "aerodynamics," "water," "math," "kindergarten" and "sound."

4. LESSONS LEARNED & FUTURE WORK

We learned and implemented the lesson of keeping apace of emerging web development techniques while merging the NEEDS and TeachEngineering digital libraries into Engineering Pathway in 2005. By making a clear distinction between content and format and transitioning to cascading style sheets (CSS), we allowed for much more flexibility in tailoring our content to various audiences, both then and continuing forward. This was especially helpful in responding to another ongoing lesson: understand your users' needs. Another lesson that must inform our future work is that technology and user expectations continually progress, and we must adapt and expand our features accordingly, such as expanding our social network and mobile learning features.

Our future research on educational digital libraries involves its use for mobile learning environments, we are designing, building and evaluating the GreenHat mobile augmented reality (AR) application to help students learn about biodiversity and sustainability issues in their natural environment [6].

5. REFERENCES

[1] Broadening participation in computing portal, http://www.bpcportal.org/.

[2] Pr2ove-it (peer reviewed research offering validation of effective and innovative teaching), http://www.pr2ove-it.org/proveit/.

[3] Teach engineering, http://www.teachengineering.org/.

[4] A. M. Agogino and B. Muramatsu. The national engineering education delivery system (needs): A multimedia digital library of coursewaree. *International J. of Engineering Education.*, 13(5), 1998.

[5] S. Robinson. A usability assessment of the engineering pathway educational digital library. *MS Report*, 2008.

[6] L. O. Ryokai, K. and A. Agogino(2011). Green hat: Exploring the natural environment through experts perspectives. *MS Report*, ACM CHI '11:Proceedings of the 29th International Conference on Human factors in Computing Systems:2149–2152.

Meta-Line: Lineage Information for Improved Metadata Quality

Sascha Tönnies
L3S Research Center
Appelstrasse 9a
30167 Hannover
Germany
toennies@l3s.de

Benjamin Köhncke
L3S Research Center
Appelstrasse 9a
30167 Hannover
Germany
koehncke@l3s.de

Wolf-Tilo Balke
IFIS TU Braunschweig
Mühlenpfordtstrasse 23
38106 Braunschweig
Germany
balke@ifis.cs.tu-bs.de

ABSTRACT

Controlled content quality also in terms of indexing is one of the major advantages of using digital libraries in contrast to general Web sources or Web search engines. However, considering today's information flood the mostly manual effort in acquiring new sources and creating suitable (semantic) metadata for content indexing and retrieval is already prohibitive. A recent solution is given by automatic generation of metadata, where various methods currently become more widespread. But in this case neglecting quality assurance is even more problematic, because heuristic generation often fails and the resulting low-quality metadata will directly diminish the quality of service that a digital library provides. To address this problem, we propose a metadata quality model to determine the overall quality of a metadata set and validate individual requirements imposed on that metadata set. Furthermore, lineage information is provided to trace the quality evolution of a metadata set.

Categories and Subject Descriptors

H.3.3 [**Information Systems**]: Information Storage and Retrieval – *Information Search and Retrieval.*

General Terms

Design, Performance, Experimentation.

Keywords

Metadata Quality, Quality Lineage, Model

1. INTRODUCTION

With the growth of the Internet as a publication platform and especially with the growing number of open access journals and 'grey literature'/preprint servers, more and more high quality content is made available constantly. Beside the content that is provided by domain specific publishers also this Web content is increasingly important for digital library users. Hence many digital libraries have extended their collections by harvesting content from the Web. However, unlike the controlled content that arrives from traditional publishers, assessing the quality of harvested content poses severe challenges. Whereas the general quality of each item or Web information source can usually be assessed quite well by the community of users (e.g. using feedback in Web 2.0 interfaces), the problem of correctly indexing the new content for retrieval with both bibliographic data and content-based index terms remains with the digital library provider. Whereas gathering information from the Web has often been compared to 'trying to drink from a fire hydrant', indexing all this information with controlled quality seems like 'trying to drink from a fire hydrant while assessing the water quality of each sip'. This leads to a trade-off for digital libraries between offering broad and up-to-date document collections and providing high quality metadata for retrieval.

We propose that information about the generation process of (not only semantic) metadata is essential and that in practice this kind of information is not available. To solve this problem, we have to trace the evolution of metadata records during their life cycle. Furthermore, this information must be globally available and machine readable to use it during automatic metadata enrichment and quality checks. This entails that we have to define a unique standard with the power to describe this kind of information. It seems obvious to reuse an established concept from the domain of data warehousing the so called data lineage [1] or data provenance [2]. Information stored in data warehouses is collected from many different sources and integrated as materialize views in local databases. One can clearly see the similarities to our scenario. Also digital libraries collect data from different sources and integrate them into their repository. With the usage of lineage information, it would be possible to trace the evolution of metadata records. But how could such lineage information look like? All the more if we consider the different requirements of the different domains, e.g. chemistry, computer science, architecture or mechanical engineering, do we have to confess that finding the "one size fits all" solution will not work?

Considering related work already done in the field of data provenance, we can see that this kind of information is always highly domain dependent. Thus, we can find literature about lineage models in specific domains, e.g. [3], or based on well-defined workflow engines, e.g. [4]. Emphasizing the main objective, i.e. the automatic quality assessment of metadata records, we may reduce this overwhelming problem of defining a global and domain spanning metadata lineage schema into a smaller one. We need a generic quality model which makes it possible to determine the quality of a specific metadata record in a specific version at any time.

JCDL'12, June 10–14, 2012, Washington, DC, USA.
ACM 978-1-4503-1154-0/12/06.

2. QUALITY MODEL

Data quality can be measured by several metrics. These metrics are objective or subjective and highly tasked dependent. This implies that a quality model has to integrate the concept of a metric as well as the concept of individual requirements. Our model (see Figure 1) is divided into three areas: *local*, *local*/global, and *global*. In this case, global means that the respective model parts are universally valid and therefore have to be globally available. The local part includes information that is highly content dependent and should therefore be stored within the respective organization, i.e. digital library. For the parts assigned to *global/local* such a strict allocation is not possible. Here, we have to decide case-by-case.

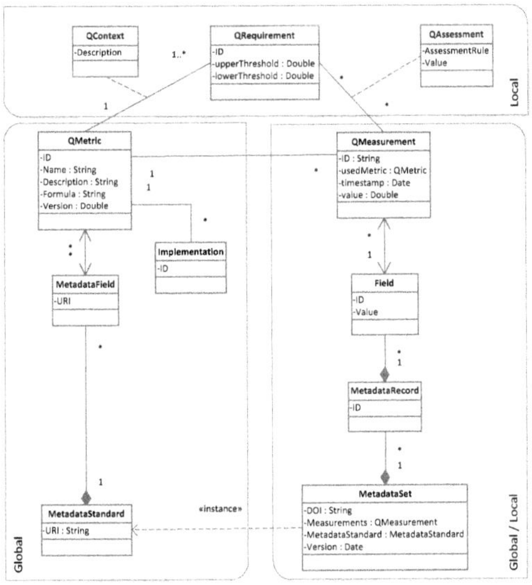

Figure 1: Metadata Quality Model

Global When talking about digital libraries and document collections, we have to consider different *metadata standards*. Taking also semantic metadata into account, the list of possible standards gets even longer. Every single one is uniquely identifiable by its URI, and defines several metadata fields. Each field has a unique identifier, i.e. its URI.

As already mentioned, the contents vary and so does the quality assessment from field to field. Therefore, it must be possible to assign different metrics to each individual *metadata field* and not only one "global" metric for a whole metadata standard. In our model this is achieved by a quality metric instance associated with a metadata field. Such a quality metric (*QMetric*) is defined as a quantifiable inspection criterion. Therefore, each QMetric has to have a name, a verbal description, the actual formula. Due to compatibility reasons, the outcome of each metric should be normalized to [0,1]. In addition, we can also store references to concrete implementations of the metric.

Global/Local In a next step, we need to measure the quality for individual instances of the metadata standard, i.e. metadata set. This set can differ depending on the version. Thus, it is essential for the model, that each set in a specific version can be identified. This can be achieved by assigning a digital object identifier (DOI®) to each set. Now, it is possible to perform a measurement for a specific metric in relation to a metadata set. The reference to the used metric is stored within the *QMeasurement* object. Each QMeasurement has been executed at a specific timestamp and the outcome is a value between [0,1]. Based on these concepts, we are already able to specify the overall quality of a metadata set.

Local After we can globally quantify the quality of a specific metadata set, we have to judge this value in the context of a specific digital library. By means of *QRequirement* the quality that a QMetric should have for a metadata field is specified. Typically it defines a set of thresholds which will be used during the quality assessment. It is important that each QRequirement is only valid for a specific context which is verbally described. In this way we will be able to accommodate different users or decision making contexts that have different criteria for assessing the data quality levels that are appropriate for their particular task. After we defined quality requirements for a specific context and we conducted some measurements, we are ready to apply our assessment rules. A *QAssessment* is the result of applying such a rule. Utilizing this model, we are now able to specify and reference one or more metrics for a specific metadata field. In addition, each information provider can use this knowledge to actually perform measurements of owning metadata sets and judge the quality according to his requirements.

Finally, we can adopt the well-known ETL workflow from the area of data warehousing and combine it with a central quality repository. By using a centralized repository, we are able to reuse measurements, thus the quality assessment is faster. This repository can be integrated into a workflow, to evaluate the metadata sets and automatically determine their quality.

3. CONCLUSION

We discussed the concept of data lineage process and showed that it is unlikely to come up with a domain spanning lineage model. Still, our main objective, the automatic quality assessment, could be solved by introducing our fine-grained quality model. Our introduced quality model distinguishes between the general metadata standard and concrete instances of this standard. Therefore, we can define several quality metrics for each field of the standard and we can perform concrete measurements of metadata records based on these metrics. In addition, each library can define its own requirements and assess them. For our future work we plan to establish a community based portal for developing quality metrics. The functionality could be similar to the functionality of the *myExperiment* portal. That implies building domain dependent communities, finding, sharing, and creating standards for semantic metadata and their related metrics.

4. REFERENCES

[1] Y. Cui and J. Widom, "Practical lineage tracing in data warehouses," in Proceedings of 16th International Conference on Data Engineering, 2000, pp. 367-378.

[2] P. Buneman, A. Chapman, and J. Cheney, "Provenance management in curated databases," in Proceedings of the 2006 ACM SIGMOD international conference on Management of data - SIGMOD '06, New York, New York, USA: ACM Press, 2006, pp. 539-550.

[3] R. Bose and J. Frew, "Composing lineage metadata with XML for custom satellite-derived data products," in Production, 2004, vol. 16, pp. 275 - 284.

[4] P. Missier, K. B. Jjame, J. Zhao, and C. Goble, "Data lineage model for Taverna workflows with lightweight annotation requirements," in IPAW, 2008, vol. 5272/2008, pp. 17-30.

Multi-Views of the ACM Classification System

Xia Lin, Mi Zhang, Haozhen Zhao
College of Information Science and Technology
Drexel University
3141 Chestnut Street, Philadelphia, PA19104
{xlin, mz349, hz58}@drexel.edu

Jan Buzydlowski
jbuzydlowski@acm.org

ABSTRACT

The ACM Computing Classification System (CCS) is a hierarchical classification system used to index and classify all the published literature of ACM. They reflect major areas and topics of the computing field and they often serve as an overview and navigational guide to the field. However, similar to all the traditional classification systems and subject domain thesauri, such an overview and navigational guide is static and sketchy, representing only a top-down representation of a domain. In this paper, we look into a 10-year period of ACM literature and examine how the CCS terms are actually used in the ACM digital library and how the patterns of term usages show different term relationships than those defined in the CCS. By comparing the dynamic statistical patterns of term usage with the static hierarchical structures of the terms, we show that much can be gained by integrating both of them into an interactive interface to provide better overview maps and navigational guides to the domain of computing.

Categories and Subject Descriptors

H.5. [**Information Interfaces and Presentations**]

H.5.3. [**Group and Organization Interfaces**]
Evaluation/methodology; Organizational design.

General Terms

Design, Documentation, Standardization.

Keywords

Classification Systems, Co-occurrence analysis, Visual Interfaces.

1. INTRODUCTION

The ACM Computing Classification System (CCS) is a main hierarchical classification system used to index and classify all the ACM published literature. The current version of ACM CCS is the 1998 version [1]. Its basic framework was established in 1982, with revisions in 1983, 1987, 1991, and 1998 [2]. The terms and hierarchy of CCS are selected and organized by domain experts. They reflect major areas and topics of the field of computing, and they can be used as an overview and navigational guide to the field.

The original ACM CCS was designed to meet the classification and indexing need of the traditional paper-based library environment. While the ACM has successfully moved to the digital library environment, its CCS is still a simple hierarchical list of pre-defined subject terms that does not take advantage of the digital and networked environment. The 1998 CCS Updated Committee has recognized this limitation and reported that some CCS structure "does not match well the literature and major subject areas of the discipline today" [3]. This is in part due to the fact that the list of CCS terms is completely isolated from the literature and the hierarchical structure was static and does not directly reflect content of the ACM published literature.

We are seeking to explore new roles and new applications of the ACM CCS in the digital environment. Toward this goal, we got permission to download a 10-year ACM digital library data set, including the classification categories and bibliographic descriptions of all the documents published between 1999 and 2009, the ten years after the current version of CCS is in use. The data downloaded are in XML format and broken into 31 different files. There are a total of 333,923 records under analysis, and the primary and secondary descriptors of CCS were used in the analysis of the subject terms and their usages. For each subject term, we counted how often it has been assigned to documents, how often it has been used as the primary descriptor of a document, how often it has been co-occurred with other terms, etc.

2. Analysis of ACM CCS Terms

The CCS classification scheme includes a hierarchical tree of three levels of coded concepts or categories plus a fourth level of uncoded subject descriptors. The top level includes 11 categories, coded from A to K. Through some term frequency and co-occurrence analysis, we observed that:

- The CCS tree structure is a relatively simple, unbalanced hierarchical tree. Some categories (i.e., Category A, E, and J) have limited numbers of sub-nodes (4, 7, and 9 respectively) and have not been used often in the past 10 years.
- The top-level categories are generic in nature and the concepts they represent overlap with each other significantly. This is inevitable when using a simple hierarchical structure to represent a complex conceptual space.
- The occurrence frequency shows the majority of ACM literature falls in categories C, G, H, and I. This reflects the authors and indexers' choice yet is not reflected in the static CCS.
- The top 10 most often used categories is a good representation of the "hot topics" in the field of computing. It is, however, a surprise to see the most often used category is the category F.2.2, "non-numerical algorithms and problems." (Table 1).

- Using the term co-occurrence data, associative relationships of the terms can be mapped to reveal how the sub-fields of computing are related to each other. (Figure 1).

Table 1. The most-often used CCS categories

Most used categories		
Code	**Category**	**Frequency**
F.2.2	Nonnumerical Algorithms and Problems	27285
C.2.1	Network Architecture and Design	24701
I.5.2	Design Methodology	18163
H.5.2	User Interfaces	17612
G.2.2	Graph Theory	15847
I.2.8	Problem Solving, Control Methods, and Search	14773
H.3.3	Information Search and Retrieval	14716
B.7.1	Types and Design Styles	13507
F.2.1	Numerical Algorithms and Problems	13071
G.1.6	Optimization	12731

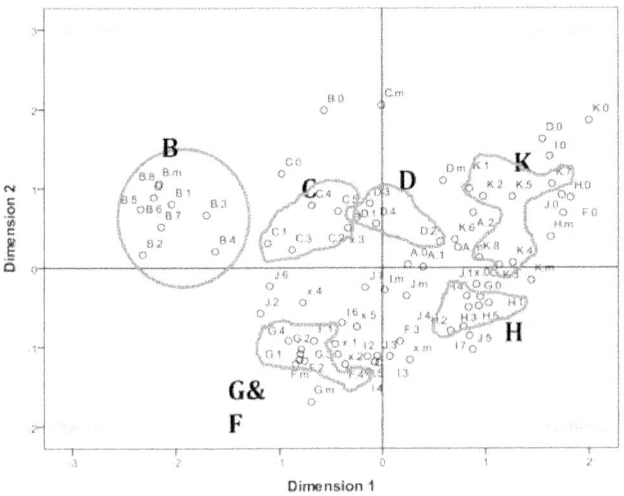

Figure 1. Two-dimensional map of subject terms at the 2nd level

3. An Interactive Interface of ACM CCS

To take advantages of both the hierarchical and associative relationships of the CCS terms, we develop an interactive interface to let users explore the ACM conceptual space.

Figure 2 shows an example of the interface. After sending a query, a user can choose to explore either the hierarchical list or associated map (generated by the PathFinder algorithm[4]). When the user moves the mouse over a subject term on the map, the term and its location on the hierarchical list will automatically identified and highlighted. The user can also click on a (graphic) node of a subject term to generate a new associative map for the clicked term, or click on the term itself to show all the children terms of the clicked term. Many other interactive functions are implemented as well to support user's searching and browsing.

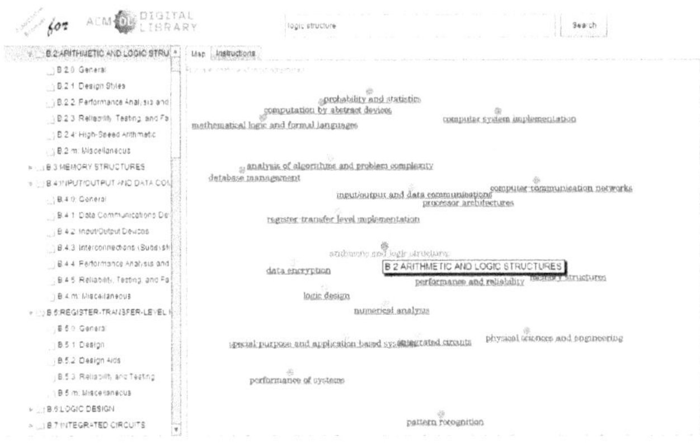

Figure 2. Interactive Interface for the ACM Classification System

4. Discussion

This article presents our initial exploration on effective use of the ACM CCS in the digital environment. The central question is how to move the static hierarchical representation of the classification system to a dynamic and interactive environment. Our results indicate that an interactive interface needs to become an essential part of the classification system. The interface should fully integrate the classification system with the document collections, should provide tools and algorithms to derive semantic relationships dynamically, and should let users perform "deep analysis" of associative relationships of the terms, categories, and documents. We will demonstrate the interactive system during the conference. We will also run experiments to test how effective users can use the interface to find ACM terms to index their documents or retrieve documents most relevant to their own papers.

ACKNOWLEDGMENTS

This work is partially supported by NSF Award No. 0935942 and by IMLS doctoral fellowships. Our thanks to ACM and Professor Lillian Cassel of Villanova University for making the data available for this research.

5. REFERENCES

[1] ACM CCS. (n.d.). The 1998 ACM Computing Classification System. Available at: http://www.acm.org/about/class/ccs98-html

[2] ACM. (n.d.) Introduction to the ACM Computing Classification System [1998 Version]. Available at: http://www.acm.org/about/class/ccs98-intro

[3] Coulter, N. et al. (1998). Computing Classification system 1998: Current status and future maintenance report of the CCS update committee. Computing Reviews, (January 1998). Available at: http://www.acm.org/about/class/ccsup.pdf

[4] Schvaneveldt, R. W. (1990). Properties of Pathfinder Networks. *Pathfinder Associative Networks: Studies in Knowledge Organization.* Ablex Pub.

National Digital Newspaper Program: A Case Study in Sharing, Linking, and Using Data

Nathan Yarasavage
Library of Congress
101 Independence Ave SE
Washington, DC
202-707-2954
nyarasavage@loc.gov

Robin Butterhof
Library of Congress
101 Independence Ave SE
Washington, DC
202-707-8172
robu@loc.gov

Christopher Ehrman
Library of Congress
101 Independence Ave SE
Washington, DC
202-707-0223
cehr@loc.gov

ABSTRACT
This poster presents a case study describing how the National Digital Newspaper Program's (NDNP) metadata specification and public website, Chronicling America, have been designed to promote a wide range of data sharing. Through use of the website's extensive application programming interface (API) and open-source software counterpart, several institutions are benefiting from the publicly-funded program's data.

Categories and Subject Descriptors
H.3.5 [**Information Systems**]: Information Storage and Retrieval – On-line Information Services – Data sharing.
H.3.7 [**Information Systems**]: Information Storage and Retrieval - Digital Libraries - Collection, Standards.

General Terms
Documentation, Design, Standardization.

Keywords
Application Programming Interface, Digitization, Historical Newspapers, National Digital Newspaper Program

1. INTRODUCTION
The National Digital Newspaper Program (NDNP) is a partnership between the National Endowment for the Humanities (NEH) and the Library of Congress (LC) to create and maintain an Internet-based, freely-accessible, searchable database of U.S. newspaper information and select digitized pages. Chronicling America is the website providing access to these resources: 140,114 newspaper records, 723 digitized titles, 399 title essays, and almost 5 million digitized pages at time of writing. NDNP is a distributed project modeled after the United States Newspaper Program (USNP), a national effort to inventory, catalog, and preserve on microfilm select at-risk original newsprint. The NDNP project builds upon the valuable bibliographic and microfilm assets created under the USNP. NEH provides 2-year grants for state institutions (awardees) to digitize 100,000 pages of microfilmed newsprint, published between 1836 and 1922. Post-1922 content is not considered in the public domain and is therefore outside the scope of this program. LC describes the digitization specifications and provides technical assistance to awardees. To date, 28 states have contributed to the program. Eventually data will be contributed from all states and territories. Awardees select titles, arrange for either in-house or vendor-based digitization, and complete quality assurance of the data using the LC provided Digital Viewer and Validator (DVV), a JSTOR/Harvard Object Validation Environment (JHOVE) based tool allowing viewing of NDNP data and validation of select technical aspects of the files [1][2][3].

JCDL'12, June 10–14, 2012, Washington, DC, USA.
ACM 978-1-4503-1154-0/12/06.

2. NDNP METADATA SPECIFICATION
In 2005, the NDNP standard for metadata describing digitized newspapers was proposed by LC [4]. The NDNP metadata specification utilizes the Metadata Encoding and Transmission Standard (METS) to carry descriptive, administrative, and structural metadata about the newspaper's title, page, and reel information. Title (descriptive) information is mapped from existing Machine Readable Cataloging (MARC) metadata into the Metadata Object Description Schema (MODS) format. Optical Character Recognition (OCR) text is encoded with a METS extension schema known as Analyzed Layout and Text Object (ALTO) XML schema. The combination use of METS and ALTO, commonly referred to as METS/ALTO, has been widely adopted by many large-scale national newspaper digitization projects around the world including the Australian Newspapers Digitisation Program, the British Newspaper Archive, and the Bibliothèque nacionale de France [5][6]. During validation by the DVV, digital signatures and technical metadata describing the original source microfilm and digital assets are encoded in the METS files as PREservation Metadata: Implementation Strategies (PREMIS) and Metadata for Images in XML (MIX) metadata [1].

3. NDNP API
Using common Web protocols and linked data principles, the NDNP development team has designed an API for Chronicling America that promotes a wide range of potential data use. Through the API, several views of the digitized content and its metadata are publicly visible, with no restrictions to access [7]. Searching across the Chronicling America Newspaper Directory [2] of over 140,000 newspaper MARC title records is possible using the OpenSearch protocol and the OpenSearch Description document describing Chronicling America's search engine. Resource Description Framework (RDF) representations of the resources, using existing and new vocabulary terms, have been employed. A resource map of all newspapers is available for clients interested in harvesting NDNP objects. All NDNP data

submitted by awardees, except archival TIFF (Tagged Image File Format) images, are packaged using the BagIt File Packaging Format [8] and made freely available to data harvesters via hypertext transfer protocol (http) [9]. Chronicling America has been constructed to integrate with third-party JavaScript applications, with support for both Cross-Origin Resource Sharing (CORS) and JavaScript Object Notation with padding (JSONP) responses [7]. Finally, Chronicling America follows the Sitemap protocol, providing an index of URLs linked from the site's robots.txt file [10].

4. USING NDNP DATA

While Chronicling America shares data freely through its API, the project also relies on outside data, namely, MARC records gathered via the WorldCat Search API [11]. These records comprise the bulk of the newspaper directory, a comprehensive listing of American newspapers published from 1690 to present. These records ensure up-to-date holdings information and represent a full catalog of U.S. newspapers. Chronicling America has welcomed academic research by providing API documentation on the site as well as joining the list of repositories for the NEH-sponsored Digging into Data Challenge [12]. For a 2011 Challenge award, researchers from the Virginia Polytechnic Institute and the University of Toronto will mine the OCR text to examine public opinion and information dissemination during the 1918 Influenza Pandemic. In a visualization project, Stanford researchers used MARC records from the newspaper directory to map the growth of American newspapers [13]. Chronicling America also inspired a visualization project on the evolution of individual newspaper titles through mergers and acquisitions [14]. Linkypedia, a project developed by Ed Summers, shows how Chronicling America content has been reused or linked within Wikipedia [15]. Opening Chronicling America's data to internet search engines and commercial users greatly increased the project's visibility and site traffic. In June 2009, the project reached a milestone of one million pages of content, and a site redesign added API access and crawler support. Site traffic doubled overall, and search engine referrals multiplied fifty-fold. A May 2011 redesign added social media sharing tools, increasing the direct linking capabilities of the site. Chronicling America has also been harvested by commercial users and integrated into proprietary databases. One subscription genealogy site now refers about 5% of total traffic.

5. LC NEWSPAPER VIEWER

To further the goal of providing open access to historical newspapers, in 2010, the NDNP development team at LC released an open source version of the software underlying Chronicling America. Coined the LC Newspaper Viewer, the application is architected using Apache HTTPd, Django, MySQL, and Apache Solr and is available for download via Sourceforge. The LC Newspaper Viewer Software is available under a Berkeley Software Distribution (BSD) style license for use by individuals or organizations wishing to provide access to or view data produced to the NDNP specification. Customization of the software has enabled non-NDNP content creators to make use of it as well [16]. Current public-facing use of the software includes the University of Oregon [17]. Several other awardees report using the software locally at their institutions for internal quality review purposes.

6. ACKNOWLEDGMENTS

The NDNP is funded by the National Endowment for the Humanities and supported by LC. Chronicling America, including its API and the LC Newspaper Viewer software, has been developed by the Repository Development Center (RDC) at LC. Special acknowledgements include: Leslie Johnston and the staff of the RDC; Teri Sierra; Mark Sweeney; and Deborah Thomas.

7. REFERENCES

[1] Library of Congress. National Digital Newspaper Program. Accessed Jan. 30, 2012. http://www.loc.gov/ndnp/.

[2] Library of Congress. Chronicling America. Accessed Jan. 30, 2012. http://chroniclingamerica.loc.gov/.

[3] Littman, J. 2006. A Technical Approach and Distributed Model for Validation of Digital Objects, *D-Lib Magazine*, 12, 5.

[4] Murray, R. 2005. Toward a Metadata Standard for Digitized Historical Newspapers. *Proceedings of the 5th ACM/IEEE-CS Joint Conference on Digital Libraries*, 330-331.

[5] The British Newspaper Archive. Accessed Jan. 30, 2012. http://www.britishnewspaperarchive.co.uk/.

[6] Klijn, E. 2008. The Current State-of-Art in Newspaper Digitization: A Market Perspective. *D-Lib Magazine*, 14, 1/2.

[7] Library of Congress. Chronicling America. About the Site and API. Accessed Jan. 30, 2012. http://chroniclingamerica.loc.gov/about/api/.

[8] Library of Congress. BagIt Specification. Accessed Jan. 30, 2012. http://www.digitalpreservation.gov/documents/bagitspec.pdf.

[9] Library of Congress. Chronicling America. Data. Accessed Jan. 30, 2012. http://chroniclingamerica.loc.gov/data/.

[10] Sitemaps.org. Accessed Jan. 30, 2012. http://www.sitemaps.org/.

[11] WorldCat Search API. Accessed Jan. 30, 2012. http://www.worldcat.org/affiliate/tools?atype=wcapi.

[12] Digging Into Data Challenge. Accessed Jan. 30, 2012. http://www.diggingintodata.org.

[13] Stanford University. Data Visualization: Journalism's Voyage West. Accessed Jan. 30, 2012. http://www.stanford.edu/group/ruralwest/cgi-bin/drupal/visualizations/us_newspapers.

[14] BeingNumerous. Genealogies of Old newspapers. Accessed Jan. 30, 2012. http://beingnumero.us/blog/2010/05/genealogies-of-old-newspapers/.

[15] Github. Linkypedia. Accessed Jan. 30, 2012. https://github.com/edsu/linkypedia.

[16] Sourceforge. LC Newspaper Viewer. Accessed Jan. 30, 2012. http://sourceforge.net/apps/trac/loc-ndnp/.

[17] University of Oregon. Historic Oregon Newspapers. Accessed Jan. 30, 2012. http://oregonnews.uoregon.edu/.

Responsibility for Research Data Quality in Open Access: A Slovenian Case

Janez Štebe
Social Science Data Archives
University of Ljubljana
Kardeljeva pl. 5
1000 Ljubljana, Slovenia
386(0)1 5805 292
Janez.Stebe@FDV.Uni-Lj.Si

ABSTRACT
In the framework of a project aiming to realize a strategy of open research data access in Slovenia in accordance with OECD principles, we conducted a series of interviews with different target audiences in order to assess the initial conditions in the area of data handling. The data creators and data services expressed a high level of awareness about data quality issues, especially in relation to good publication potential. Barriers to ensuring the greater accessibility of data in the future include the little recognition and reputation for doing the related extra work involved in preparing data and documentation, the need for financial rewards for such additional work, and the undeveloped culture of data exchange in general. The motivation to provide open access to such data will involve a combination of requirements prescribed for data delivery, and the provision of support services and financial rewards, in particular changing the views held by the professional scientific community about the benefits of open data for research activities.

Categories and Subject Descriptors
E.0 [**Data**]: Policy, Quality; Interviews

Keywords
Data Quality; Stakeholders Attitudes; Open Data; Culture

1. INTRODUCTION
A current Slovene national applied research call project, entitled »Open data – action plan delivery for the open access system of research data financed from public resources« [1], began its work with an overview of the current situation of handling data. In particular, we were interested in the understanding and willingness of different actors to resolve problems related to mutual responsibilities and expectations, according to the roles they play through various phases of the data life cycle, with an emphasis on data access. A model of roles, rights, responsibilities and relations will be used for a discussion on three preconditions of working data infrastructure (see [2]). These are an explicit support of research founding organizations, willingness and capacity of the members of the scientific community to participate and a sufficient level of skills, and professionalization of data scientist and data librarians to ensure a high quality service delivery.

JCDL'12, June 10–14, 2012, Washington, DC, USA.
ACM 978-1-4503-1154-0/12/06.

The semi-structured interviewing method was used on a purposefully selected sample of target group representatives. The interview started with a schematic overview of the roles and phases in the data life cycle, thereby introducing the framework of problems discussed later on during the interview. The selection of 22 interviewees altogether was balanced so as to cover representatives of different disciplines, researchers and leadership positions, those who create and use data, and those who already run some nascent data services activities. We searched for positive role models, those who are active and have good knowledge about problems and are already thinking about solutions.

Data quality in the context of open access depends on the evaluation of the potential of data for further use. If open research data arrangement is sought in advance of data creation, this influence more careful execution of procedures that ensures high quality data product. Narrow professional competencies are important for understanding data quality since they form a basis for decisions about the content of data collections, the details of defining and following data creation procedures, and in decisions about data cleaning and documentation. Thus, narrow professional fields are the most important when it comes to defining and following high quality measures. In the following we will compare those narrow professional competencies with general purpose services such as data centers and research libraries. Specifically we will address critical and skeptical views about the role professional libraries can play in introducing an open data access system that we encounter during interviews.

2. PRINCIPLES, HABITS AND PROBLEMS OF DELIVERING QUALITY DATA
Generally, strong concerns about data quality were expressed at both the level of awareness and in knowledge of the criteria and procedures (Table 1).

Table 1. Data creation issues (excerpts from semi-structured interviews)

1.	*"Researchers who have a look at the data collection immediately see whether the data is in order or not" (Andrej Blejec, Biologist).*
2.	*"What I would like to put an emphasis on are those metadata that complement recorded materials. I think the profession has accomplished things quite well here." (Audio archive researcher).*

The evaluation and selection of data based on quality are not as self-evident as with publications. Bad data can also be interesting (Table 2). Actually this claim calls for a diversified data publication arrangements. There is a general consensus that it would be hard to formalize quality data selection by analogy to a peer review for articles. What are good or useful data is more a point of reaching a consensus within the scientific community. Further, a sole criterion for what is good quality is based on certain self-evident beliefs about good practices that are established within the scientific community. A scientific value of data is coupled with the researchers esteem, his previous publication record and integrity, therefore what is evaluated is scientific value potential of publically available data, similar to evaluation of research proposal. Skepticism is common about the possibility of externally evaluating what are good data: for example, that library institution would take over the evaluation by some kind of editorship. This is something that a researcher himself has to deal with. Even if a librarian possesses a more universal set of competencies that limit their ability to evaluate content data quality, they can apply formal criteria and selections. The contribution of librarians could reflect the fact that they are experts in general metadata.

Table 2: Data selection issues excerpts

1.	*"Well, data are so and so, but everything is included in because bad data also say something. If data are missing you are repeatedly trying to discover and reveal why they haven't been included. Better bad data than no data." (Miran Hladnik, Slovene Literature).*
2.	*"Simple, this is very simple. A good researcher has good data, a bad researcher has bad data." (Head of a research library).*

The most important conclusion regarding data quality in the creation phase is that, despite the lower quality level in absolute terms, it can still be useful. Data are only as good as it is possible to achieve, taking into account a researcher's capacities, their assistants, laboratory equipment and financial constraints. Also important for further use is, that the information about the formal level of quality is transferred along with data to its usage stage. Data that are not sufficiently cleaned and documented present a common barrier to more open access and here general expertise of data librarians could come forward. It is a common perception that the value of data lies in the fact that they are meant for a particular end, namely, publication, a conclusion not different from others studies when identifying low data sharing culture environments. When discussing the possibility of open data access, the interviewees identified different barriers such as a lack of time and little motivation for the additional work needed for the data preparation and documentation.

Table 3: Motivation for open access

1.	*"As I see at the institute, some of the required preservation or preparation of data for general availability would be considered by our researchers as an extra obligation and additional administration unless they are given additional resources..." (Sciences Institute Director's Adviser).*
2.	*"Nowhere is this seen as an honourable job, it is slave labour (...)" (Miran Hladnik, Slovene Literature).*
3.	*"Often the general atmosphere is that this is mine and that someone else will find something in the data that I have not seen. It isn't necessarily the case that this is fine with everyone." (Andrej Blejec, Biologist).*

As we have seen, this is not so much related to a lack of knowledge of procedures. Researchers usually know what needs to be done. This findings are in accord to [3] conclusions about low reputation of data related activities and related career and specialized education investments prospect. Not only is there a division in roles esteem between science librarians and science staff in general, but also among members of scientific community there are long established 'paradigm' disputes about the role and value of data related activities, e.g. persistent in social science and humanities. The consequences of such attitudes are that for many researchers it seems natural to monopolize the data access until its cognitive potential has been exhausted. The data sharing culture is generally at a low level. In establishing an open data system, in the future it is necessary to respect the legitimate interests of the primary researchers to use their data for publications. It would also be necessary to ensure greater motivation to prepare data as a product in itself, for example by giving credit to the data producer when the data are used further. All such incentives were positively evaluated during the interviews when trying to challenge the prevailing perceived right of exclusive data use that is still deeply rooted in researchers habits.

3. CONCLUSIONS

In our contacts with scientists and institutional leaders the notion prevails, when challenged with the prospect of open data requirements, that making data available for public use would gain support if it were seen as a requirement for all. Still, in support of an open data access policy further incentives should include financial rewards for related additional work, the establishment of stable support services, and that the creating of data products is regarded as an equivalent to publication in research evaluations. There is also a problem of reputation and recognition inside a scientific community if this is solely linked to publications. A change in the power relations could occur if a reputation can also be built on the work involved in the creation and preparation of data for access.

What is thus needed is that, parallel to adequate financing and authorship rewards, beliefs about the need of that work become more widespread in terms of their usefulness for the scientific community, and for individual researchers.

4. REFERENCES

[1] Štebe, J. 2010. Arhiv družboslovnih podatkov in storitve prostega dostopa do znanstvenih podatkov v Republiki Sloveniji [*Social Science Data Archives and Open Data Services in the Republic of Slovenia*]. In *Božič, M., Zemljič, I. Open access to the achievements of Slovenian scientists.* Zveza bibliotekarskih društev Slovenije, 2010. http://www.dlib.si/?URN=URN:NBN:SI:DOC-JGYFFYW7

[2] Lyon, L. .2007. *Dealing with Data: Roles, Rights, Responsibilities and Relationships.* http://www.jisc.ac.uk/media/documents/programmes/digitalrepositories/dealing_with_data_report final.pdf

[3] Swan A. and Brown S. 2008. *To Share or not to Share: Publication and Quality Assurance of Research Data Outputs.* Retrieved Decembre 1, 2011, from http://www.rin.ac.uk/system/files/attachments/To-share-data-outputs-report.pdf

Scientific Cyberlearning Resources Referential Metadata Creation Via Information Retrieval

Xiaozhong Liu
School of Library and Information Science, Indiana University Bloomington
liu237@indiana.edu

Han Jia
School of Library and Information Science, Indiana University Bloomington
hanjia@imail.iu.edu

ABSTRACT

The goal of this research is to describe an innovative method of creating scientific referential metadata for a cyberinfrastructure-enabled learning environment to enhance student and scholar learning experiences. By using information retrieval and meta-search approaches, different types of referential metadata, such as related Wikipedia Pages, Datasets, Source Code, Video Lectures, Presentation Slides, and (online) Tutorials, for an assortment of publications and scientific topics will be automatically retrieved, associated, and ranked.

Categories and Subject Descriptors: H.3.3

[**Information Storage and Retrieval**] Information Search and Retrieval; *Search process*

Keywords

Metadata Generation, Metadata, Cyberlearning Resource

1. INTRODUCTION AND MOTIVATION

While rapid access to digital publications can accelerate research, some challenges must be addressed. For instance, the sheer volume of scholarly publications available online makes it impossible for a researcher to absorb all the new information available. Hence, researchers and students need to find innovative ways of quickly learning and understanding new scientific topics and publications. Some recent exciting developments have illustrated the possibility of utilizing multimedia content—i.e. videos and images—to help students and scholars understand scientific content [1, 6, 7]. Nevertheless, online open resources typically lack clear quality assurances. This is now recognized as a major concern with online open resources [4]. Meanwhile, the cost of generating sophisticated cyberlearning resources for large-scale scientific topics or publications is prohibitive.

Despite the promise of a more exciting cyberlearning experience given the rich content of online open resources, which provide open access to materials bearing upon specific scientific topics or publications, many scholars, instructors, and students have difficulty finding high quality and relevant resources. For this research, we assumed that cyberlearning resources were available on Internet and tried to automatically retrieve, associate, and rank resources based on their "importance" for each scientific topic or publication. In other words, we conceptualized the problem of generating cyberlearning referential metadata as an information retrieval problem amenable to automation using meta-search and retrieval algorithms, which have been studied in [2, 3, 8].

JCDL'12, June 10–14, 2012, Washington, DC, USA.
ACM 978-1-4503-1154-0/12/06.

2. CYBERLEARNING REFERENTIAL METADATA CREATION

In this research we used author-assigned keywords to represent each scientific research topic in a given domain of study, namely, information retrieval. For example, for this paper, six keywords—metadata generation, information retrieval, referential metadata, cyberlearning resource, user, and scientific publication—were used to represent six research topics.

In order effectively to generate referential metadata for each topic, we used information retrieval and meta-search approaches, where a Boolean query was sent to one or more search engines for each scientific keyword and cyberlearning resource type. The detailed query list for each resource type is listed in the Table 1. The first column is the cyberlearning resource type. For each type the target query was sent to one or more search engines. For example, in order to get tutorial resources for a keyword, the query "[Keyword] AND Tutorial NOT Video" (column 3) was sent to Google (column 2), where [Keyword] was replaced with the target keyword content. Similarly, for video resources, the query "[Keyword]" was sent to YouTube, TED, and Videolecture. For slides and source code, different queries were sent to different search engines. For example, for slides the queries "[Keyword] AND (filetype:ppt OR slides)" and "[keyword]" were sent to Google and Slideshare, respectively. For performance reasons, we indexed the Wikipedia page dump locally.

Resource type	*Search engines*	*Query (Keyword task)*
Wikipedia page	Wikipedia dump (local database)	[Keyword]
Tutorial	Google	[Keyword] AND Tutorial NOT Video
Slides	Google, Slideshare	Google: [Keyword] AND (filetype:ppt OR slides) Slidesshare: [Keyword]
Video	YouTube, TED, Videolecture	[Keyword]
Dataset	Google	[Keyword] AND Dataset
Source code	Google, SourceForge	Google: [Keyword] AND (Source Code OR Toolkit OR Java OR C++ OR Python) SourceForge: [Keyword]

Table 1: Meta-search query for different kind of resources

Based on Table 1, a list of queries were sent to different search engines to retrieve candidate resources. In our experiment, we used the top 15 retrieved results from each search engine to aggregate the final result collection for each resource category. In most cases, the result collection was a combination of informative resources and noisy results. Experience in information retrieval reveals that since different search engines return very diverse and erratic results for the same query, irrelevant data may pollute the search results and mislead users. To address this problem, we used the information retrieval ranking algorithm, language model, to prioritize those informative resources for the target scientific keywords while filtering out the irrelevant information.

For scientific publication metadata resource generation, the most straightforward method is to search for the paper title (exact match) in different search engines. However, this method has two major limitations. First, given a relatively long publication title, if we use exact string match, search engines can hardly find any results. We also found that the quality of resources was not good. A large portion consisted of publisher or digital library access pages for the target publication, which are not helpful for scholars and students to understand the paper. Second, the cost of this method is quite high. Given the very large potential publication collection, we needed to send multiple queries for each publication. For example, based on Table 1, for each keyword or publication, we needed to send four queries to Google. However, most search engines restrict the number of automatic visits, which makes this method inefficient.

In this research we used a more economical method to cope with this problem. We assumed each publication was composed of a list of topics, with each topic represented by an author-assigned keyword. We then used the results keywords to estimate the publication resources. For each resource type, we first aggregated all resources retrieved using the publication keywords and then used a ranking algorithm to identify the most important resources based on publication content. Such resources are highly likely to be relevant to the publication content and could help students or scholars understand the essence of the publication. For this method, we assumed that helping scholars or students understand the topics (keywords) of the paper will eventually help them to understand the paper itself.

In practice, the ranking algorithm for publication resources consists of two parts: first, the importance of the keyword for the publication, and second, the importance of the resource for the keyword. So, the ranking score is calculated as:

$$S(paper, resource) = S(paper, key_{resource}) \cdot S(key_{resource}, resource),$$

where $key_{resource}$ is the keyword that the resource belongs to.

In above formula, $S(paper, resource)$ is the importance of this resource for the target paper, $S(paper, key_{resource})$ weighs the importance of the keyword for the paper (based on keyword IDF), and $S(key_{resource}, resource)$ is the resource importance score for the keyword from the last section (3.1). We can interpret the algorithm in this way: If a resource is important for a keyword, and this keyword is also important for a paper, then this resource is highly likely important for this paper.

3. EXPERIMENTS

To test and compare different methods of cyberlearning resource metadata generation, we designed an experiment with information retrieval topics and publications. As we needed to judge whether *a resource could effectively help scholars or students understand the essence of a scientific topic or publication*, we used graduate students with basic knowledge in information retrieval for this experiment. Some evaluation participants of this experiment did not have programming experience, and so could hardly provide judgments for source code resources. As a result, participants only evaluated 5 categories of resources in this experiment: Wikipedia Pages, Video Lectures, Tutorials, Datasets, and Slides.

For topic evaluation, we sampled 70 publications and 45 keywords. For each keyword, we designed a web evaluation page. Likewise, we designed an evaluation for each publication.

On each evaluation page, the keyword or publication title and abstract was presented at the top and the retrieved top cyberlearning resources were offered with actual resource links. Users could access these resources via a popup window by clicking the hyperlink. Each student was asked to evaluate resource quality by using a dropdown menu. In this evaluation, students were asked to judge whether the cyberlearning resource could help them understand the essence of the scientific keyword or publication. Possible evaluations were "not relevant" (score of 1), "low relevance" (2), "good relevance" (3), and "high relevance" (4). Before taking this evaluation task, we trained participants with examples of helpful and unhelpful resources.

Averagely, different types of resources' quality for two tasks is presented in the following table:

Resource type	*Keyword task*	*Publication task*
Wikipedia pages	2.83	2.12
Tutorials	2.85	2.27
Slides	2.77	2.24
Videos	2.83	2.35
Datasets	2.68	2.19
Overall	2.79	2.23
Score 4 = perfect; 3 = good; 2 = OK; 1 = not helpful		

Table 2: Resource quality for the keyword task

For ranking, we evaluate resource ranking performance by using nDCG [5], and the result is presented in table 3.

Resource type	*Keyword task*	*Publication task*
Wikipedia pages	0.871	0.900
Tutorials	0.742	0.899
Slides	0.821	0.866
Videos	0.797	0.870
Datasets	0.806	0.875

Table 3: Keyword nDCG@3 for different resource types

4. ANALYSIS AND CONCLUSION

This research focused on the problem of generating cyberlearning referential metadata for scientific keywords and publications. It was conceptualized as an information retrieval and use problem amenable to automation using meta-search methodologies. More specifically, this paper makes the following contributions: First, it offers a new method of creating cyberlearning-based scientific referential metadata for e-learning. Second, this research provides a generalizable methodology using sophisticated information retrieval and meta-search algorithms to create scientific metadata. Third, we employed user evaluation to validate the usefulness of different types metadata and aggregation ranking algorithms.

REFERENCES

[1] Agazio, J., and Buckley, S. K. 2009. An untapped resource: using YouTube in nursing education. Nurse Educ. 34:23–8.

[2] Aslam, J., and Montagus, M. 2001. Models for Metasearch. In Proceedings of the 24th annual international ACM SIGIR conference on Research and development in information retrieval. ACM.

[3] Dwork, C., Kumar, R., Naor, M., and Sivakumar, D. 2001. Rank aggregation methods for the Web. In Proceedings of the 10th international conference on World Wide Web.

[4] D'Antoni, S. 2009. Open educational resources: reviewing initiatives and issues. Open Learning, 24(1): 1-8.

[5] Iiyoshi, T. and Kumar, M. S. V. 2008. Opening up education: The collective advancement of education through open technology, open content, and open knowledge. Cambridge, MA: MIT Press.

[6] Lawrence, S. and Giles, C. L. 1998. Inquirus, the NECI meta search engine. In Proceedings of the Seventh International World Wide Web Conference, 95–10.

[7] Nikopoulou-Smyrni, P. and Nikopoulos, C. 2010. Evaluating the impact of video-based versus traditional lectures on student learning. Educational Research, 1(8): 304-311.

[8] Sah, M., and Wade V. 2011. Automatic mining of cognitive metadata using fuzzy inference. In P. De Bra & K. Grønbæk (Ed.) Proceedings of the 22nd ACM conference on Hypertext and hypermedia, pages 37-46. New York: ACM.

Sheer Curation for Experimental Data and Provenance

Tobias Blanke
Centre for e-Research
King's College London
26-29 Drury Lane
London, UK
tobias.blanke@kcl.ac.uk

Mark Hedges
Centre for e-Research
King's College London
26-29 Drury Lane
London, UK
mark.hedges@kcl.ac.uk

Categories and Subject Descriptors

H.3.7 [**Information Storage and Retrieval**]: Digital Libraries—*Standards, Collection*; E.2 [**Data Storage Representations**]: Linked representations

Keywords

data library, experimental data, sheer curation, provenance

1. BACKGROUND

This poster presents an approach to the curation of the experimental data and processes of a group of scientific researchers in the field of biophysics. Recent research [2] has demonstrated that carrying out digital curation and preservation activities in the *early* stages of data creation is more cost-effective compared to the potential loss that can be incurred through the destruction of data, for example because of the need to recreate the data, or the loss of an organisation's reputation. On the one hand, decisions taken during the early stages of a digital object's lifecycle frequently have consequences for the preservation strategies that can be applied at a later date; on the other hand, if digital objects are being preserved so that they can be reused in an informed manner, account has to be taken of the different practices of researchers across disciplines and the different characteristics of the data they create or gather.

One approach to integrate research processes into data management has been termed sheer curation[1]. Here, digital curation activities are integrated into the workflow of the researchers creating or capturing data. The word 'sheer' is used in the sense of 'lightweight and virtually transparent' way in which these curation processes are integrated with minimal disruption to their normal working practices[2]. This approach depends on data capture or ingest being embedded within the researchers' working practices, so that data capture is automatic and invisible to the researcher. Sheer curation is based on the principle that effective data management at the point of creation and initial use lays a firm foundation for subsequent data publication, sharing, reuse, curation and preservation activities.

This poster presents our sheer curation experiments in the fields of biophysics and structural biology, a multidisciplinary area that interacts and collaborates with several research groups, both within the institution (e.g. Asthma, Cardiovascular, Cancer) and with industrial partners such as pharmaceutical companies. We interviewed researchers from five separate research groups on their curation practices, for the implementation we focused our efforts on the use cases of two of the groups only: macromolecular crystallography and biological nanoimaging.

Macromolecular crystallography addresses the determination of the structure of large molecules, such as proteins, using X-ray diffraction In high-level terms, an X-ray beam is directed at a crystal of the substance under investigation from many angles, resulting in a set (typically 360, although sometimes more) of diffraction images. Each image contains several hundred spots, whose location and intensity are determined, using specialised software, and then combined to produce a model of the atomic co-ordinates of the protein. In this process a large number of files is created but only a small number of the resulting files are published and kept.

Biological nanoimaging involves the use of microscopes to capture high-resolution images of biological samples, on the one hand to carry out research into cell and tissue structures, and on the other to develop new methods of and algorithms for digital imaging and processing. The data include pseudo-3D representations, where the same datasets may frequently be processed many times using different image analysis techniques, and many raw images are processed when developing new analysis tools. Again, much of the information generated in this process is not currently curated or retained.

2. IMPLEMENTATION RESULTS

Our first implementation objective was to develop a sheer curation environment by embedding digital library services within the experimental workflows of the targeted researchers, so that, as far as possible, capture of data and metadata occurs automatically as datasets are generated and is invisible to the researcher. The story of the experiment is represented implicitly in a variety of information such as the location of files in a directory hierarchy, metadata embedded opaquely in binary files, filenames, the contents of log files, and so on. However, the semantics of the collection as a whole is lost in this *post hoc* curation model, and it is unlikely that the researcher would have the time or the ability to explain it in great detail. In the model of sheer curation that we have

[1]By Alistair Miles of the Science and Technology Facilities Council

[2]http://alimanfoo.wordpress.com/2007/06/27/zoological-case-studies-in-digital-curation-dcc-scarp-imagestore/, Accessed 29 January 2012

JCDL'12, June 10–14, 2012, Washington, DC, USA.
ACM 978-1-4503-1154-0/12/06.

been following, the researchers' knowledge is elicited beforehand and encoded in software that processes the information as it is captured.

A major challenge faced by the project was to bridge the gap between the 'wild', ad hoc and independent environment of the researcher's desktop, and the managed and curated environment of the digital library. The tools used by the researchers are typically developed by people working within the discipline, either by the researcher communities themselves, or by suppliers of laboratory equipment, and they are designed to operate in the researchers' local environment using data that is accessible via the local file system (although there are some web-based services).

In all the scenarios addressed in our work, the scientist works through the processing of an experiment at the same desktop machine; indeed, as all processing is done locally, this was only to be expected. This simplified the implementation by allowing us to focus on capturing the researcher's process, i.e. restricting ourselves to looking at information flow in one direction only – from the desktop to the data library – during the processing of the data. This implementation used a lightweight client, running on the researcher's computer, to 'scavenge' information from the researcher's work area and transfer it to the digital library environment. This made it possible to capture automatically domain-specific metadata and other contextual information that is available when research is undertaken.

Specifically, each time that a file is created, modified or deleted within the monitored directory, the file is copied (for creations and modifications) and a message sent to the data library describing the type of action, original pathname and timestamp. On the curation environment side, this information is interpreted and used as the basis for creating digital objects, extracting domain-specific metadata from the objects, and inferring relationships between objects, which are then ingested into the data library. Much of the processing that takes place is concerned with analysing the information that is available and exploiting it to infer the details of the researcher's workflow. Although this workflow is outside our control, in any particular category of scenario (in our case, either macromolecular crystallography or nanoimaging) its structure is broadly known at a high level. This means that certain files are expected at certain stages, and in addition the workflow generates as a by-product a lot of information that can be used to infer inter-object relationships, for example in file headers and log files.

This approach can also be made to work in situations where it is not possible to use the monitoring client on the researcher's desktop. To implement this, the directory is submitted for deposit in its entirety at the end of the experiment, and the files are transferred to the data library one by one in timestamp order, thus simulating the live creation of the files. This approach was successful because the large majority files are simply created once and not updated subsequently, although some modifications had to be made to the software to handle those few files that were updated, mainly log files to which tools append status information each time they were executed.

Our second major objective was to manage not just individual datasets but entire experimental workflows, modelled as compound objects incorporating data, metadata and provenance information. This makes it possible to verify published results or reproduce the processing and data on which the conclusions are based and which justify them. Data provenance is a particular kind of metadata that describes the derivation history of digital objects. The Open Provenance Model (OPM) is an emerging standard for modelling provenance that aims to enable the digital representation of the provenance of any object, whether itself digital or not, in a generic manner so as to support the exchange of provenance information between different systems, the building of common tools etc. (see [1]for more details).

To publish the experimental processes, we have used a linked data model, with URIs resolving to a representation of the digital objects that are connected by links described using the OPM vocabulary, and potentially other ontologies. To bundle these composite objects together for Web publication, we use OAI-ORE (Open Archives Initiative Object Reuse and Exchange), which 'defines standards for the description and exchange of aggregations of Web resources'[3]. The experimental workflows that we have been addressing are regarded as aggregations in OAI-ORE terminology, and in our case the digital objects described by the resource maps include not only the files generated, but also the objects corresponding to OPM processes and agents, and the digital object that describes the experiment itself. Note that, in addition, the aggregation may aggregate additional objects that are outside the repository, for example publications or presentations based on the research, and (for the crystallography users) entries in the Protein Data Bank[4].

Our work has shown the advantages of a sheer curation approach for involving research processes in the management of data, not just for preservation but also for publication purposes. However, sheer curation also involves a large prior investment into capturing and formalising research processes.

3. REFERENCES

[1] Moreau, L., Cliord, B., Freire, J., Futrelle, J., Gil, Y., Groth, P., Kwasnikowska, N., Miles, S., Missier, P., Myers, J., Plale, B., Simmhan, Y., Stephan, E., den Bussche, J.V.: The open provenance model core specification (v1.1). Future Generation Computer Systems 27(6), 743–756 (2011)

[2] Rumsey, A.S.e.: Sustainable economics for a digital planet: Ensuring long-term access to digital information, final report of the blue ribbon task force on sustainable digital preservation and access. Tech. rep. (2010), `http://goo.gl/LBYU`

[3] http://www.openarchives.org/ore/

[4] http://www.rcsb.org/pdb/home/home.do

Web2MARC: Sharing and Using STEM Digital Content in School Libraries

Marcia A. Mardis, Casey McLaughlin, Grant Gingell
The Florida State University
School of Library and Information Studies
College of Communication & Information
+01 850.644.3392
mmardis,cam02h,ggingell @fsu.edu

ABSTRACT
Digital content can benefit K-12 science, technology, engineering, and mathematics (STEM) teaching and learning, but it is not widely integrated. Many school librarians are not sure how to build upon their expertise to share and link digital learning resources in their roles as resource providers and instructional collaborators. This poster will present Web2MARC, a web-based application for integration of digital resources into school library collections. Further work on the state of school library STEM collections, survey analysis, and Web2MARC is slated to be complete in 2013.

Categories and Subject Descriptors
J.1. [**Computer Applications**]: Administrative Data Processing; H.5. [**Information Systems**]: Information Interfaces and Presentation

Keywords
MARC, cataloging, digital resources, school libraries

1. INTRODUCTION
Myriad science, technology, engineering, and mathematics (STEM) digital library projects have exemplary collections for elementary and secondary educators and students. The prevalence digital media available in these collections offers new opportunities to diversify school library collections with open content such as downloadable and editable digital video and audio, data sets, interactives, simulations, and hypertext resources.

Many of these projects have offered workshops to enable rich implementation of their resources. Despite these efforts, school use of STEM digital library content remains nascent. Results of prior research devoted to examining the implementation process has suggested that to achieve deep and lasting digital library content integration in schools, support beyond professional development is needed and school-based actors beyond students and classroom teachers must be included. We need to know more about the complications inherent in the process of integrating STEM content in school library activities.

A key actor not targeted by many STEM digital library projects is the school librarian. School librarians have a 1:60 ratio to teachers in U.S. schools [3] and provide a virtually untapped local expert for dissemination of and instructional support for digital open content resources and techniques that can have a direct positive impact on teaching and learning. School librarians play many roles in schools, but a primary role is building and maintaining a resource base for teaching and learning. School librarians locate and organize materials that support the curriculum and student interest and make them findable through instructional collaboration and the Online Public Access Catalog (OPAC), today's card catalog.

Many school librarians do not know how to leverage their resource expertise and collaborative roles to foster engaged learning through open content. Recent studies show that while many students prefer to learn STEM concepts with digital content, few teachers infuse it into practice. School librarians are the needed catalyst for teachers and students to engage in innovative learning.

This project's aim is to explore ways in which school librarians can use digital library open content to expand and enrich the school library's resource base and instructional support. This project helps school librarians to identify digital library open content, integrate open content metadata into their catalogs.

Guided by the overarching question "How can school libraries support strong STEM achievement with digital library open content," the researcher is investigating a framework for promotion of open content use in schools through the following research questions:

1. To what extent is are school librarians able to integrate physical and digital STEM collection development?

2. How does the Web2MARC metadata distribution tool promote integration of open content and physical resources?

2. DIGITAL COLLECTIONS IN SCHOOL LIBRARIES
With the advent of the first OPACs in the mid-1970s to replace traditional card catalogs [2], librarians began, in essence, building and maintaining their own vast metadata repositories that included bibliographic information with features like holdings information and request services [1]. Traditionally, OPACs have pointed to only physical resources, but they have the technical capacity to include records that point to a range of media. OPACs are thus a building block for greater distribution and increased awareness of open content. While the value of digital content for teaching and learning is clear, knowledge of current digital collection development practices and strategies for effective implementation are not widely documented.

In response, the Digital Libraries to School Libraries (DL2SL) project, funded by the Institute for Museum and Library Services, aimed to 1) enhance current knowledge about school library collection of digital resources through a survey; and 2) develop a tool, Web2MARC, to aid the integration of digital resources in school libraries. Figure

JCDL'12, June 10–14, 2012, Washington, DC, USA.
ACM 978-1-4503-1154-0/12/06.

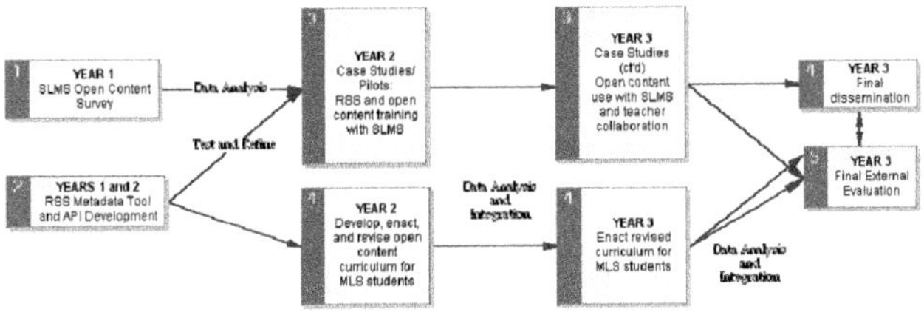

Figure 1. Overview of the Digital Libraries to School Libraries (DL2SL) Project Phases.

2.1 Digital Collection Practices Survey

The first phase of the DL2SL project included a national survey of school librarians' digital collection development practices. While they survey analysis is not reached complete, early results from the sample (N=1192) indicated that not only do many school librarians report that they are substantially or fully involved in supporting English Language Arts (n=919 or 77%) and social studies (n=899 or 75.5%) with technology, far fewer are very involved in supporting science (n=612 or 51.3%) or mathematics (n=559 or 46.9%) with technology, many also report that substantial or full involvement (n=632 or 53%) with in digital resource acquisition. The early survey results also indicated that while most school librarians (n=710 or 59.6%) evaluated the effectiveness of digital resources. Far fewer (n=583 or 48.9%) integrated digital resources into their catalogs, as seen in Figure 4.

These early analyses suggest that school librarians are far less likely to connect with STEM teachers and learners through their collections and not frequently or consistently including digital resources into the collection development strategies that they use for print resources.

2.2 Web2MARC Tool for Digital Content Integration

While the survey results do not foretell a perfect solution to increasing school librarians' integration of digital resources into their support and collection development strategies, a possible so approach is to build on the ideas that digital STEM resources are preferred by students, beyond the solo implementation of teachers, and often left out of school librarians' support strategies.

2.2.1 *Overview of tool function*

In response to these factors, Web2MARC (http://dl2lsl.org/web2marc) was developed as a way to allow school librarians to quickly and easily generate machine-readable catalog (MARC) records for their library catalogs. Figure 2 provides a graphical overview of the main functions of the tool.

Figure 2. Main Functions of the Web2MARC Tool.

This example will use the link to a video in an online collection called Teachers' Domain (http://teachersdomain.org). The video is named Tenths and Decimals. As Figure 3 shows, the tool's interface is straightforward and only requires the user to paste the Uniform Resource Locator (URL) for the video to generate a record.

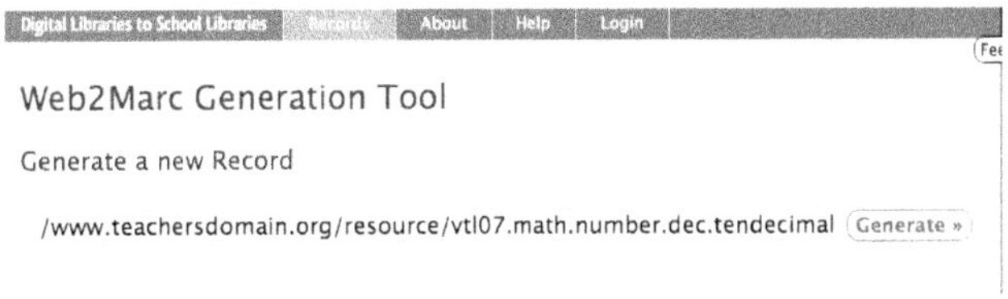

Figure 3. Start Page of Web2MARC Tool.

Once a user clicks the Generate button, the API visits the URL, scrapes content from the page and populates a MARC record. The record is then displayed to the user for editing. Users can edit the description of the resource to fit local needs, add curriculum standards, keywords, and use the Assist tool to add a Library of Congress or Dewey Decimal Call Number. Library of Congress (LC) legal subjects headings can also be assigned through a "suggest" function that completes terms that the user types with LC subject headings. One the record is edited, the user can then view and export the MARC record, as Figure 4 shows.

Figure 4. Web2MARC Tool MARC Record View and Export.

2.3 Future Work

Development is continuing on the Web2MARC tool based on input from users in testing sessions. Features will include greater scarping support for various types of media URLs; streamlined standards assignment; simplified call number assignment; batch record downloading; and RSS-based subscription to enable registered users to view and download records created by others. Tool development is expected to conclude in summer 2013.

3. ACKNOWLEDGMENTS

This work is supported by IMLS grant RE-04-09-0055-09.

4. REFERENCES

[1] Kaplan, A. G. (2004). *Meta-what? Metadata and information management for school library media collections.* Paper presented at the 27th American Educational Communications and Technology [AECT] Conference, October 19-23, 2004, Chicago, IL.

[2] Large, A., & Beheshti, J. (1997). OPAC: A research review. *LISR, 19*(2), 111-133.

[3] Mardis, M. A., & Hoffman, E. S. (2008). The status of technology, science and mathematics in U.S. middle school media centers. *Michigan Science Teacher Association (MSTA) Journal, 53*(2).

Social Network-based Recommendation: A Graph Random Walk Kernel Approach

Xin Li, Xin Su, Mengyue Wang
Department of Information Systems
City University of Hong Kong
Hong Kong

Xin.Li@cityu.edu.hk, kevinsuxin@gmail.com, menwang@cityu.edu.hk

ABSTRACT

Traditional recommender system research often explores customer, product, and transaction information in providing recommendations. Social relationships in social networks are related to individuals' preferences. This study investigates the product recommendation problem based solely on people's social network information. Taking a kernel-based approach, we capture consumer social influence similarities into a graph random walk kernel and build SVR models to predict consumer opinions. In experiments on a dataset from a movie review website, our proposed model outperforms trust-based models and state-of-the-art graph kernels.

Categories and Subject Descriptors

H.3.3 [**Information Search and Retrieval**]: Information Search and Retrieval – *Retrieval models*

Keywords

Social network, recommendation, graph kernel, random walk.

1. INTRODUCTION

Traditional recommender system research often explores customer, product, and transaction information in providing recommendations. Social networking, one of the most popular services in Web 2.0, provides a great resource to generate recommendations and personalize services [1]. This study focuses on the social network-based recommendation problem, which explores consumer social network information for product recommendation.

In social network-based recommendation, the dominant approach is to assess interpersonal influence through social trust. One's rating can be estimated by the average of his/her trusted persons' weighted by trust level [3]. Social trust can be transferred between indirectly connected individuals and calculated at social network level [8]. Trust has also been combined with other features, such as people's domain expertise trail level [6], for recommendation. In addition to trust, homophily is also a popular approach, where similar users are granted similar preferences. User homophily is usually compiled based on demographic information [7].

In this research, we try to blend these two approaches and capture homophily of consumers' social influence for recommendation. We develop a graph random walk kernel in a kernel-based machine-learning framework for this purpose. We proved the kernel's validity and evaluated its performance using a dataset collected from a movie review website.

JCDL'12, June 10–14, 2012, Washington, DC, USA.
ACM 978-1-4503-1154-0/12/06.

2. METHODOLOGY

For social network-based recommendation, we adopt a kernel-based approach to estimate consumer rating of products. We model consumer portfolios (as reflected by social network) using kernel functions and apply SVR as a kernel machine for each product to build a rating estimation model. These models are trained using each product's ratings. The key problem of this task is how to design an appropriate graph kernel to capture information embedded in social networks that are relevant to consumer preferences.

As stated in previous research, social influence plays a critical role in social network-based recommendation. Instead of directly assessing influence between persons, we look at the homophily of people's social influence. (In our unidirectional social network setting, this is the same as social influence received from others.) We predict people with similar (coverage and intensity of) social influence on others would make similar product assessments.

To assess people's social influence in the network, we conduct random walks with restart on the graph. For each node i, we conduct random walks from i and let it transmit to node i's neighborhood with a transition probability that is proportional to edge weights. Such random walks are conducted iteratively to farther nodes; at each step, there is a probability 1-α for the random walk stop and restart. The stationary transition probability $r_{i,j}$ of random walks reflects how much node i's opinions can reach node j. We then define the graph random walk kernel through a distance mea-sure defined on stationary transition probabilities.

Mathematically, we define the single-step transition probability matrix as P^T. Each element of the matrix is the relative transition probability from node i to j, $p_{ij}=P(s(t+1)=j|s(t)=i)=a_{ij}/\Sigma_j a_{ij}$, where a_{ij} is elements of the network's adjacency matrix. For a random walk starting from i at the t step, let's represent its probability to reach each node as a vector $r_i(t)$, thus: $r_i(t)=\alpha P^T r_i(t-1)+(1-\alpha)e_i$ $r_i(0)=e_i$, where e_i is the unit vector. By solving this equation, we get: $r_i(t)=(\Sigma^t_{k=0}(\alpha P^T)^k-\alpha\Sigma^{t-1}_{k=0}(\alpha P^T)^k)e_i$. Since $\lim_{t\to\infty}\sum_{k=0}^{t}(\alpha P^T)^k = (I-\alpha P^T)^{-1}$, the converged stationary transition probability vector is: $r_i=(1-\alpha)(I-\alpha P^T)^{-1}e_i$, i.e., $r_{ik}=e_k^T(1-\alpha)(I-\alpha P^T)^{-1}e_i$ and $R=\{r_{ik}\}=(1-\alpha)(I-\alpha P^T)^{-1}$. Matrix R is not symmetric and thus is not a valid kernel. However, using r_i to represent node i, we can define a valid random walk-based distance measure between nodes: $d_{ij}=\Sigma^n_{k=1}(r_{ik}-r_{jk})^2=||R(e_i-e_j)||^2=(e_i-e_j)^T R^T(e_i-e_j)$. Based on this valid distance measure, we can define a graph random walk kernel: $K_{RWR}=R^T R$.

In K_{RWR}, for any vector $x!=0$, $x^T K_{RWR} x = (Rx)^T(Rx)>=0$, so K_{RWR} is positive semidefinite and thus is a valid kernel.

3. EXPERIMENTAL STUDY

We collected data from www.mtime.com, one of the largest movie review websites in China. The website allows users to rate movies using a 1 to 10 scale. In the year 2009, there were 5,232 movies posted on the website. As of November 2010, when we collected data, 29,527 users had reviewed them. We chose the 452 movies with more than 100 reviews and conducted snowball sampling to get reviewers that are within two steps of friendship to two randomly selected friend users. The final user set contains 9,785 users with 143,141 inter-user edges. The 514 users who did not rate any of the 452 movies in our dataset are included in the social network but excluded from performance calculation.

We adopt the mean absolute error (MAE) measure as an evaluation metric. We also convert the problem to binary classification on whether the user likes the movie (i.e., rating higher than 5) and adopt the accuracy measure for evaluation.

We used five baselines in this paper, including social influence models and state-of-the-art graph kernels.

- Neighbor influence model (NI) predicts a user's rating of a movie based on the average of his/her friends' ratings.
- Multi-level neighbor influence model (MNI) extends NI and includes indirect friends with a dumping effect.
- The exponential diffusion kernel (KED) [5] accounts for social closeness and uses the relative distances between nodes as an indicator of user similarity. It takes an exponential dumping effect on different lengths of paths between nodes. $K_{ED}=e^{\alpha A}$, where A is the adjacency matrix of the social network and α is the dumping factor between 0 and 1.
- The von Neumann diffusion kernel (KVND) [4] is similar to the exponential diffusion kernel with a different path weighting mechanism, $K_{VND}=(I-\alpha A)^{-1}$.
- The commute time kernel (KCT) [2] is based on the average commute time of random walks between nodes. $K_{CT}=L^{+}$, which is the Moore-Penrose pseudo-inverse of the Laplacian matrix of the graph. It is on bidirectional social closeness.

We conduct user-level 10-fold cross validation to verify predictions on each movie's ratings. For the (multi-level) neighbor influence models, the rating can be directly predicted. For the kernel-based algorithms, we use SVR to build models for each movie and estimate the rating in the testing dataset. We tune the parameters for the best performance of each model.

Table 1. Comparison of Prediction Performance

Nature	Method	MAE	Accuracy
Influence	NI	1.2856	0.8848
Influence	MNI	2.4208	0.8902
Social closeness	KED	2.8501	0.8398
Social closeness	KVND	4.4793	0.3750
Social closeness	KCT	4.4855	0.4397
Social influence homophily	KRWK	**0.9944**	**0.9032**

As shown in Table 1, our proposed random walk kernel performs the best. In a 1 to 10 prediction, our proposed model achieves a MAE of about 0.99. It also has significantly better performance than baseline models in binary classification. The performance of the multi-level neighbor influence model is similar to that of the exponential diffusion kernel. The other two kernels barely provide any usable prediction. It should be noted that the neighbor influence model can only generate predictions on about 35% of movies for each user, those reviewed by their direct friends.

Furthermore, we investigate the performance of the algorithms on different types of users. Figure 1 shows the average MAE according to numbers of friends. In general, most models show an increasing performance according to number of friends for users with a small number of friends. Our proposed graph random walk kernel keeps this trend to users with less than 300 friends. It is more effective in inferring the opinion of users with more friends (who are usually opinion leaders in a network) than other models.

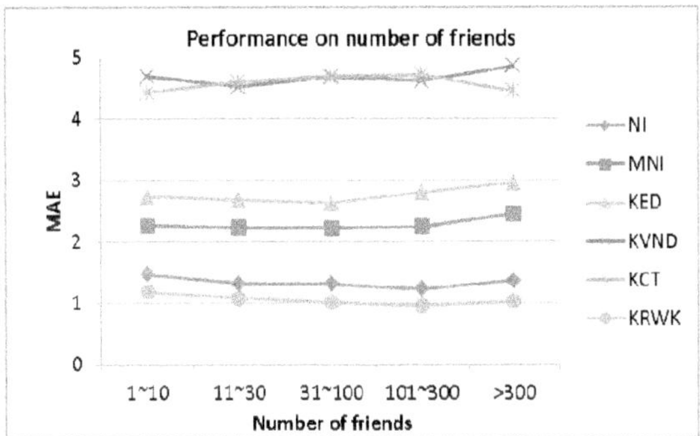

Figure 1. MAE of users with different numbers of friends

4. CONCLUSION

This paper proposes a graph random walk kernel for social network-based recommendation. The graph random walk kernel captures similarities of users' social influence as reflected by their social network to infer user interests and recommend products. We evaluate our proposed method on a movie rating dataset collected from a movie review website. The experimental results show that our proposed method is more effective than traditional influence/trust-based models and state-of-the-art graph kernels.

5. ACKNOWLEDGMENTS

Supported by CityU SRG 7002625, 7002518, and StUp 7200170.

6. REFERENCES

[1] Bonhard, P. 2005. Who do trust? Combining recommender systems and social networking for better advice. In *the Beyond Personalization Workshop*, San Diego.

[2] Fouss, F., Pirotte, A., Renders, J. M., and Saerens, M. 2007. Random-walk computation of similarities between nodes of a graph with application to collaborative recommendation. *IEEE T Knowl Data En*. 19: 355-369.

[3] Golbeck, J., and Hendler, J. 2006. FilmTrust: Movie recommendations using trust in Web-based social networks. In *IEEE CCNC '06*.

[4] Kandola, J., N. Cristianini, and Shawe-Taylor, J. 2002. Learning semantic similarity. In *NIPS '02*.

[5] Kondor, R. I., and Lafferty, J. 2002. Diffusion kernels on graphs and other discrete structures. In *ICML '02*.

[6] Sarda, K., Gupta, P., Mukherjee, D., Padhy, S., and Saran, H. 2008. A distributed trust-based recommendation system on social networks. In *HotWeb '08*.

[7] Siersdorfer, S., and Sizov, S. 2009. Social recommender systems for Web 2.0 folksonomies. In *HT '09*.

[8] Walter, F., Battiston, S., and Schweitzer, F. 2009. Personalised and dynamic trust in social networks. In *Recsys '09*.

The David Livingstone Spectral Imaging Project

Stephen Davison
University of California, Los Angeles
Digital Library Program
Box 957201, 390 Powell
Los Angeles, CA 90095
+1 310-267-5135
sdavison@library.ucla.edu

Adrian Wisnicki
Indiana University of Pennsylvania
Leonard Hall 114B
421 North Walk
Indiana, PA 15705-1094
+1 724-357-3965
Adrian.Wisnicki@iup.edu

Elizabeth McAulay
University of California, Los Angeles
Digital Library Program
Box 957201, 390 Powell
Los Angeles, CA 90095
+1 310-825-7657
emcaulay@library.ucla.edu

ABSTRACT

The David Livingstone Spectral Imaging Project is a collaborative, international effort to use spectral imaging technology and digital publishing to make available a series of faded, illegible texts produced by the famous Victorian explorer when he was stranded without ink or writing paper in Central Africa. The poster describes existing achievements of the project, plans for an innovative portal providing access to images and data, and preservation challenges.

Categories and Subject Descriptors

I.4.1 [**Image Processing and Computer Vision**]: Digitization and Image Capture

General Terms

Management, Documentation, Design, Standardization.

Keywords

Spectral imaging, digital libraries, palimpsests

1. INTRODUCTION

Presenting enhanced access to materials through innovative imaging technology and online representation is one goal of digital libraries. A recent electronic publication, *Livingstone's 1871 Field Diary: A Multispectral Critical Edition*, achieves this goal by making available images, transcriptions, and criticism of a previously illegible manuscript. (1) The diary was written by David Livingstone, a British explorer in Africa, after he had run out of both paper and ink. With homemade ink he wrote cross-wise on an old newspaper that he had fashioned into a small book. The newspaper is now fragile and the ink Livingstone used has faded extensively, making the manuscript exceptionally difficult to read. See Figure 1. Dr. Adrian Wisnicki, a specialist on Livingstone and nineteenth-century British literature, collaborated with scholars, imaging scientists, and the staff of the UCLA Digital Library Program to recover and publish this lost text. This poster reviews the imaging process used to create the images that became the basis for the electronic edition and accompanying spectral image archive. (2)

2. IMAGING and PROCESSING

The imaging, image processing, and data management work for the Livingstone project was conducted by a team of specialists who had developed these techniques during ten years of imaging of the celebrated Archimedes Palimpsest. (3) First, each folio of the 1871 field diary was illuminated by a series of successive wavelengths of light—starting with ultraviolet, working through the visible spectrum, and concluding with infrared—and each illumination was captured by a high-resolution digital camera (39 megapixel). The resulting images were then processed using tailored mathematical algorithms in order to manipulate and enhance raw spectral image data to differentiate the two inks—the homemade reddish ink that Livingstone used and the black ink of the newspaper over which he wrote. These two inks behave differently under different wavelengths of light. The printed text remains stable through the different illuminations; Livingstone's ink fades to total invisibility as wavelengths of light increase. Imaging scientists were able to enhance and invert this behavior to restore Livingstone's otherwise nearly illegible text. See Figure 2.

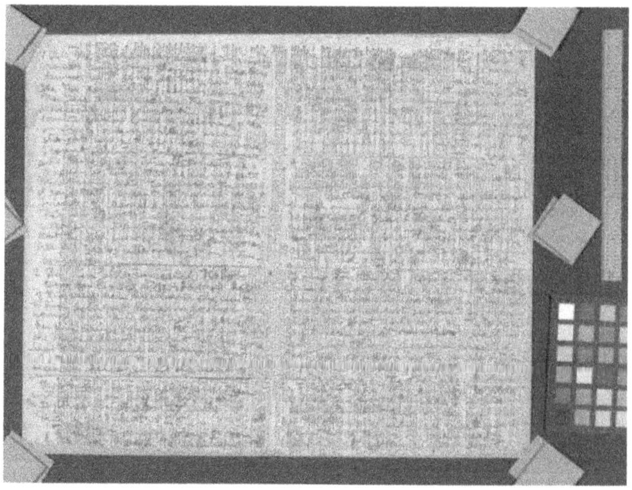

Figure 1. The 1871 Field Diary, 297b/149-146 in color.

The imaging scientists first used principal component analysis (PCA) to study the Livingstone images. The PCA technique uses combinations of an original set of images to construct an equivalent set of images ordered by statistical variance. If the images contain objects that differ in color, they may be distinguished ("segmented") in the set of principal components Once the PC images are produced, the scientists examine the images to identify those that show different inks and insert these images into the red, green, and blue channels (RGB) of a "pseudocolor" (false color) image. If the handwritten ink appears as "light" in one of the PC images and "dark" in another, then the corresponding pixels may exhibit a color tone in the pseudocolor image that allows easier differentiation between the handwritten and printed texts. If necessary, the scientists further manipulate the pseudocolor image by using appropriate software.

JCDL'12, June 10–14, 2012, Washington, DC, USA.
ACM 978-1-4503-1154-0/12/06.

For the 1871 Field Diary, scholars also worked with the imaging scientists to develop additional processing techniques. One of these techniques focused on exploiting the variant behavior of the inks, thereby suppressing the printed text and making Livingstone's handwriting very visible. Another technique focused on reducing bleedthrough text from the reverse side of the page. The resulting image displayed the recto text in cyan-blue and the verso text in green-yellow, a combination that significantly enhanced the legibility of the recto text. Finally, one of the imaging scientists also developed a "toolbox" for ImageJ, an open-source image processing application. (4) This toolbox facilitates the work of scholars who wish to fine-tune processed spectral images batch-produced by scientists. Ultimately, the work of the scientists resulted in the creation of a variety of spectral image processing techniques to recover the text of Livingstone's 1871 Field Diary. (5) As a result of these processing efforts, some ninety-nine percent of the diary's original text was recovered, and Livingstone's text has now been made available for the first time in 140 years.

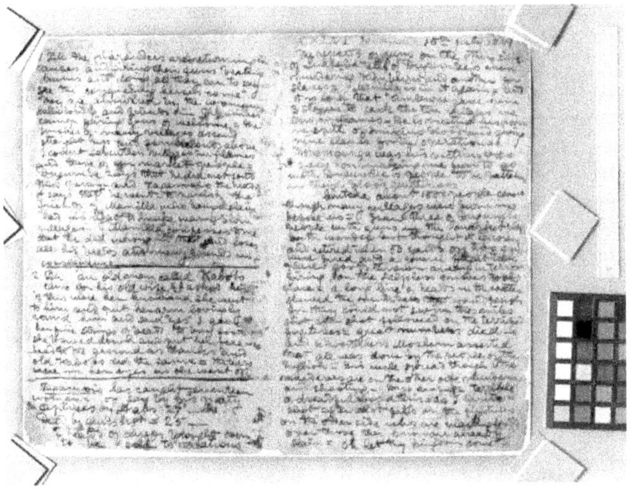

Figure 2. The 1871 Field Diary, 297b/149/146 and spectral ratio image.

3. RESULTS

While the rediscovery and publication of Livingstone's original writings were the objective of this project and the team has produced a sophisticated electronic edition, the Livingstone project also generated a significant amount of image data. This data has now also been published as a standalone dataset, the Livingstone Spectral Image Archive. This archive provides easy access to all the raw and processed spectral images and contains registered spectral TIFF images with metadata embedded in the header; metadata files in plain text; TEI/XML P5 transcriptions when available; and MD5 checksum files to ensure image and transcription fixity. In most cases, the XML transcriptions include spatial data linking lines of text to corresponding spectral image areas.

As part of the Livingstone Project, the open source toolbox in ImageJ for processing spectral data has been customized to facilitate basic image processing by non-experts and is now extensible for ongoing development. The use of ImageJ and the collaborative scholar-scientist model developed by the Livingstone team will facilitate the application of spectral imaging in U.S. collections by extending image processing – normally the province of scientists – to include significant input from scholars, historians and archivists who are familiar with the documents under consideration. (6)

4. DATA CURATION

As mentioned above, the resulting archive of images and associated files has been published online, but the data archive must also be curated and preserved as a digital asset. Therefore, following France et al.'s recommendation, the UCLA Library keeps a second copy of the dataset as a preservation master, which will soon be migrated to the Library's Fedora repository. (7) The preservation of this archive has been facilitated by careful preparation, which includes explicit filenaming, hierarchical organization of files into folders in a predictable structure, the creation of extensive metadata both embedded into the TIFF 6 files and available separately in plain text files, and the inclusion of extensive documentation outlining data standards, file specifications, and technologies used to produce the archive.

5. CONCLUSION

The use of spectral imaging enabled the rediscovery of the text of Livingstone's original 1871 field diary, the first significant nineteenth-century British manuscript to be studied with this technology. The application of this technology to medieval manuscripts continues, and digital libraries are well positioned to publish such work in a manner that invites readers to examine all the resulting images and participate in the reclamation of text. Next steps will include developing more sophisticated viewing interfaces (via web or app) that allow the user to delve into the rich image data that this method produces.

5. REFERENCES

[1] http://livingstone.library.ucla.edu/

[2] http://livingstone.library.ucla.edu/1871diary/ and http://livingstone.library.ucla.edu/livingstone_archive/

[3] http://www.archimedespalimpsest.org/

[4] http://rsb.info.nih.gov/ij/

[5] See "Note on Spectral Images" (http://livingstone.library.ucla.edu/1871diary/spectral_notes.htm) for the full list of techniques.

[6] The electronic edition of the 1871 Field Diary also includes a comprehensive "Project History & Archive" that chronicles in detail the collaborative work that recovered Livingstone's text. In addition, the project archive contains over 60 downloadable documents and files produced in the course of the project that collectively provide an intimate and comprehensive look into the production of the electronic edition.

[7] France, Fenella G., Doug Emery, and Michael B. Toth. "The Convergence of Information Technology, Data and Management in a Library Imaging Program." *Library Quarterly* 80, no. 1 (2010): 43.

The Logical Form of the Proposition Expressed by a Metadata Record

Karen M. Wickett and Allen H. Renear
Center for Informatics Research in Science and Scholarship
Graduate School of Library and Information Science
University of Illinois at Urbana-Champaign
501 E. Daniel St, Champaign, IL 61820
wickett2@illinois.edu, renear@illinois.edu

ABSTRACT

Metadata records are a ubiquitous and foundational feature of contemporary information systems. However, while their simple surface structure may lead us to think that the semantics of a metadata record is unproblematic and easily discerned, our analysis of an example record suggests otherwise. We show three possibilities for the logical form of the proposition expressed by a metadata record. All three are substantially different in the first order constructs utilized, and no two can be recognized as equivalent for the purposes of information organization. The semantics of the common metadata record is elusive. The main source of this problem appears to be the identifier attribute. Although identifier attributes have the syntactic appearance of any other attribute in the metadata vocabulary, this uniformity conceals their potential for assuming a distinctive semantic role, and one which appears to cross the traditional object language / metalanguage boundary, suggesting that translation of colloquial metadata records into logic-based knowledge representations does not take place entirely at a first-order level.

Categories and Subject Descriptors

I.2.4 [**Knowledge Representation Formalisms and Methods**]: Predicate Logic; H.3.7 [**Digital Libraries**]: Systems issues

General Terms

Theory

Keywords

Metadata, Identifiers, Semantic Web, Linked Open Data

1. THE PROBLEM

Integrating information from multiple sources and supporting inferencing for discovery and analysis requires that information be articulated explicitly and in comparable formats. In many cases the information we need to make accessible in digital library applications is stored in "colloquial" metadata records – records that are presented in a serialization language that has delimiter conventions and a vocabulary of attributes and values, but which does not have an associated formal semantics that determines how the information carried by the delimited tokens within a record should be expressed in a logic-based knowledge representation language (such as RDF or some dialect of first order logic).

Although the syntax of such languages is often rigorously defined by a formal meta-grammars such as BNF or XML / XSD, there is rarely any comparably formal specification of what the terms mean and precisely how they are to be used to make informative statements. These records are typically recognized as being a sequence of delimited attribute/value pairs, usually with one pair providing an "identifier" for the resource. This is a structure so straightforward and apparently obvious in intended interpretation that determining semantics would seem to be a trivial matter.

We argue that, despite appearances, it is not at all clear what the correct understanding of the logical semantics of a metadata record actually is. We show that the number of expressive first order constructs necessary to secure the anticipated entailments is greater and more varied than one might think, and involves some famously troublesome notions. More specifically we show that the identifier attributes commonly found in records, although they have the appearance of any other attribute, pose a particular challenge to formalization. There is no clear convention for treating this critical attribute and the alternatives are substantially different in nature.

2. METHOD

The information expressed by a metadata record is assumed to be propositional in nature, where a proposition is the language-independent content expressed by a symbol structure. Propositions in this sense are the things that may be considered true or false strictly speaking, whereas metadata records are only true or false in a derivative sense, depending on whether the proposition they express is true or false. Alternatively propositions might be considered the sorts of things that are the proper objects of epistemic attitudes, such as belief or doubt.

To determine the logical form of the proposition expressed by a metadata record we first select a characteristic metadata record as an example. We then list the important logical entailments of the proposition expressed by that record and represent each entailment in a fragment of first order logic supplied with the relevant vocabulary of predicates and individual constants. Next we consider conjectured translations of the metadata record into first order logic expres-

JCDL'12, June 10–14, 2012, Washington, DC, USA.
ACM 978-1-4503-1154-0/12/06.

sions. If an FOL translation has all of the same entailments formally (according to the rules of first order logic) that the colloquial metadata record has intuitively, and no entailments that the colloquial record does not have, then we will say that that translation reveals the *logical form* of the proposition expressed by that record.

Below is our example metadata record, in a general form.

R : Identifier : LNG42121.4
Title : Mother Rose
Creator : Dorothea Lange
Date : 1941

From the record and the standard interpretation of identifier elements, we conclude that with respect to some particular context, (E1) there is exactly one resource with the identifier "LNG42121.4", and that (E2) the resource described by the record is that resource. Based on natural readings of these metadata elements, we conclude that (E3) the title of the resource that is described by the record is "Mother Rose" and that it was created by Dorothea Lange (E4) in 1941 (E5).

3. FORMAL ACCOUNTS

The poster shows four formal accounts – R_S, R_Q, R_{QI}, and R_C – and their logical relationships to the entailments and each other. All of the accounts use the mechanisms of first order logic and binary predication to represent several attribute-value pairs for the same object. R_S uses the logical form of an open sentence, where the object of description is represented with an individual variable, and any object for which the attribute-value statements are all true will satisfy the description.

In R_Q and R_{QI}, the same basic form is followed for the attribute-values pairs, and the entire conjunctive statement is bound by a single existential quantifier. R_Q and R_{QI} are accounts that take a metadata record to be an assertion that at least one thing with the specified properties exists. R_{QI} takes the claim one step further with the identity statement, which means that the entire conjunctive statement is true of exactly one individual: the object LNG42121.4.

The R_C has the logical form of a conjunction of binary predications about the object of description. Therefore it is, in a sense, more specific than either R_Q (the existential claim without the binding identity statement that appears in R_{QI}) or the open sentence account in R_S. In fact, the existential claim in R_Q can be deduced from R_C in most systems for first order logic by existential generalization since if we know of a specific object with the given properties, we can conclude the general fact that such an object exists. In addition, R_C can be generated as a substitution instance of R_Q.

4. THE ENTAILMENTS

R_S is an open sentence, and in first order logic, open sentences do not themselves have truth values. Rather, an open sentence is said to be satisfiable if it is possible to assign constants to the individual variables in a way that results in a true sentence. We can construct an interpretation I_1 where the domain contains (at least) all of the objects referred to in the record and names are assigned as they appear in a formalization of the entailments. Then in I_1, R_S will be satisfied when x is assigned to the object of description, which in this case is the resource named by "LNG42121.4".

It follows from the existential claim given by R_Q that there is some single thing that has each of the properties ascribed to the resource by our record, but this claim operates at the level of a general existential claim. It does not follow as a matter of logic that it is LNG42121.4 which has these properties; only that there is such a resource.

With an axiom that specifies uniqueness for identifiers, R_Q does formally entail E1. R_Q does not deliver all of the entailments because uniqueness of the identifier does not, by itself, deliver "LNG42121.4" as an individual constant that can be substituted for x within the scope of the existential quantifier. One way to address this issue is to add an identity statement that directly asserts that thing that we have been describing generally as existing is, in fact, LNG42121.4. Adding this additional clause gives R_{QI}.

The formalization given by R_C entails all of the entailments, as long as we assume an axiom that specifies uniqueness for identifiers. While R_{QI} and R_C deliver our entailments, both formalizations interpret the identifier attribute/value pair in R as simultaneously providing (i) an individual constant and (ii) the name of that constant. This suggests that the meaning of R involves both object language and metalanguage assertions, something which is typically problematic in formal languages.

An alternative, which would avoid individual constants in the first argument position, is to reconsider the logical form of the entailments from the record. Instead of treating them as statements using an individual name, we can treat them as having the form of existential statements. In this approach we do not take the identifier element from the record to be giving us an individual constant that we can use to refer to the object of description. Instead, we treat the identifier element as providing the definite description "the object with the identifier LNG42121.4". All of the entailments reached this way follow directly from R_Q if we assume an axiom for identifier uniqueness.

But is it really the case that in logic-based representations of the propositions expressed by metadata records, the proper-name based references to resources are to be re-expressed as definite descriptions rather than as individual constants? If so this is a result apparently at odds with the direction being taken by the Linked Open Data and Semantic Web Communities, where URIs clearly function as individual constants referring to resources. Or are these URIs to be understand as being "really" unanalyzed definite descriptions? We believe that the problems here are deep and not at all specific to metadata records – they are in fact at the heart of logic-based knowledge representation. When, in logic-based representation, should we use logical constants and when not?

Acknowledgements
This work reflects contributions from Richard J. Urban, and originated in the Collection/Item Metadata Relationships project, which was supported by a 2007 IMLS NLG Research & Demonstration grant as part of the IMLS Digital Collections and Content project, Principal Investigator, Carole L. Palmer, Center for Informatics Research in Science and Scholarship (CIRSS). Additional support was provided by a National Science Foundation grant (OCI-0830976) to the Data Conservancy.

Toponym Extraction and Resolution in a Digital Library

James Creel
Department of Computer Science and Engineering
Texas A&M University
jcreel@tamu.edu

Katherine Weimer
Map and GIS Collections and Services
Texas A&M University Libraries
Texas A&M University
k-weimer@library.tamu.edu

ABSTRACT

Geospatial metadata enable rich and varied interfaces to digital collections, and present unique challenges and affordances for automated extraction. We describe our findings developing and utilizing a geoparser for the Texas A&M University Libraries' Institutional Repository.

Categories and Subject Descriptors

H.3.1 [**Information Systems**]: Content Analysis and Indexing; H.3.7 [**Information Storage and Retrieval**]: Digital Libraries—*collection, user issues*

General Terms

Algorithms

Keywords

Geographic Information Systems, Metadata Assignment, Named Entity Recognition, Named Entity Resolution, Geoparsing, Geotagging, Georeferencing, Georesolution

1. INTRODUCTION

In the recent literature, the designation *geoparser* or *geotagger* has come to refer to systems for automatically annotating documents with geospatial metadata based on their content. A geoparser typically operates in at least two stages: First, *toponyms*, i.e. place names, are identified as the geographic topics or subjects of a text; second, the toponyms are disambiguated in accordance with a name-authority such as a gazetteer. The disambiguation component of a geoparser is often termed a *georesolver*. Researchers at the Texas A&M University Libraries have developed a prototype geoparsing system to automate the generation of geospatial metadata for Library collections.

2. RELATED WORK

Recent years have seen a proliferation of geoparsing and georeferencing projects for digital collections. We can survey only a few representative projects in this space.

Martins et al. describe a prototype information extraction service in the context of the DIGMAP digital library of old maps[4]. This geoparser recognizes toponyms via word tokenization and gazetteer lookups. The toponyms are disambiguated on the basis of several heuristics that involve favoring larger and otherwise more prominent locations and relying on proximity of geographic feature-type designations in the text.

Grover et al. describe the Edinburgh geoparser and its application to several specialized collections of XML documents produced from optical character recognition on historic records[3]. Words in the document are looked up in gazetteers appropriate to the collections and disambiguated according to a variety of heuristics, including locations' geographic feature-type, population, surrounding text, and clustering of locations.

The MetaCarta commercial software suite[1] offers a variety of GIS capabilities, including the GeoTag component which extracts toponyms or "geographic references" and disambiguates them with numeric confidence values. Although the MetaCarta division of the Qbase corporation offers us little in the way of academic publications, the support FAQ at `http://www.metacarta.com/support-faqs.htm` mentions some heuristics found elsewhere in the literature, such as the use of surrounding text as context clues for disambiguating toponyms.

GEOLocate is a platform for georesolution of text descriptions associated with natural history and biodiversity collections[2]. In contrast to the other systems reviewed here which extract geographic references from free text, the GEOLocate software relies on "locality descriptions" already present in the metadata of natural history collections, for example, "Arkansas River at River Mile 10 boat landing., USA, Arkansas, Desha". The georeferencing algorithm identifies compass directions, distance descriptions, and toponyms occurring in a description.

3. THE TAMU LIBRARIES GEOPARSER

The Texas A&M Institutional Repository provides researchers and other TAMU System stakeholders a robust platform for preservation and dissemination of scholarly works. By the end of 2011, the repository contained approximately 47,000 items served by the DSpace digital repository software. Starting with the version 1.7 release, the DSpace digital repository software includes a framework for *curation tasks*, a simple, extensible means of performing operations on repository content. Curation tasks are encoded as custom Java programs that can modify any DSpace object and are available through the administrative interface.

The current geoparser prototype includes three DSpace curation tasks, `Suggest New Metadata` which invokes the

JCDL'12, June 10–14, 2012, Washington, DC, USA.
ACM 978-1-4503-1154-0/12/06.

geoparser proper, **Clear Suggested Metadata**, a utility to clear the geoparser results, and **Generate KML** which outputs the geospatial metadata to a new KML file attached to the item.

The **Suggest New Metadata** curation task recognizes names with with the OpenNLP maximum-entropy software library[1]. Then, the geoparser queries the GeoNames webservice [2] to obtain a listing of potential referents of the names. As of this writing, we have implemented several heuristics presented elsewhere in the literature, taking particular inspiration from the Edinburgh geoparser[3].

First, we rely on the "one-document, one-sense" heuristic that all occurrences of a particular toponym in a document refer to the same location. A document can surely refer to Paris, Texas as well as to Paris, France in the same sentence, but we expect most exceptions to this heuristic to manifest in the context of linguistic analyses, such as in documents about disambiguation of toponyms.

The contrived example of the preceding paragraph presents us with another obvious heuristic: that location information is often composited with a particular toponym by conventional linguistic constructions. The toponym "Paris, Texas" is, for example, composed of the two toponyms "Paris" and "Texas" in a conventional manner to unambiguously specify the context of the former toponym via the latter. Myriad examples of disambiguating context-clues are far less amenable to automatic parsing due to their own ambiguity, such as "by the river", or "off the highway". We are in the process of enumerating and formalizing the more obvious cases, recapitulating previous work described in the literature[2].

Other heuristics are less dependent on context. For example, supposing nothing is known about the topical content or provenance of a particular document containing repeated occurrences of the toponym "Paris", it is wise to assume that the referent is Paris, France. Some general observations support this assumption. First, locations of higher population are more frequently referenced ([3, p 3883] note that "for newspaper text, we found that more than 90% could be identified using this alone"). In addition, certain features of the landscape are more frequently referenced than others; for instance, cities are more commonly referenced than wilderness areas. The MetaCarta FAQ mentions these two heuristics as part of it's georesolution algorithm[1]. As it happens, the GeoNames webservice tends to return the most highly populated polities as the first results for toponym queries.

In addition, we have implemented a document-level contextual heuristic adapted from [3, p 3883], according to which the places to which a document refers tend to be close to one another, i.e. to be clustered in particular regions. Finally, on the basis of a similar intuition, we have implemented a heuristic similar to that described in [4, p 30]. According to this heuristic, if a candidate location for a toponym contains another candidate location for another toponym in the document, then it is a bit more likely to be topical to the document.

The **Suggest New Metadata** curation task applies heuristics in groups we call *refinement iterations*, the idea being that heuristics can produce better results on cleaner input data. In this way, we can apply contextual heuristics (using, for example, proximate geographic feature-types and other toponyms in the text) before applying non-contextual heuristics (such as favoring locations of higher population).

[1]http://incubator.apache.org/opennlp/
[2]http://www.geonames.org

3.1 Geospatial Visualization

The **Generate KML** curation task creates a KML file with annotated point markers for each location detected by the geoparser. The generated file can then be viewed in an application such as Google Earth[3] or OpenLayers[4].

4. FUTURE WORK

While the prototype already offers a valuable service to digital library cataloguers, our labours are best directed at improving the effectiveness of the georesolver prior to any formal evaluation. Additional work is needed on a variety of components. We are examining rule-based and document-code-analysis techniques to pre-process target documents in order to partition them into sections that are likely to contain relevant toponyms versus those that likely do not (such as vitas and bibliographies) Finally, we see great promise in the use of statistical classifiers beyond the simple heuristics and clustering of the current prototype. Specifically, once a given repository collection has been annotated with geospatial metadata, a supervised learning algorithm can learn a disambiguation function (i.e. classifier) using the collection as training data. Some approaches, such as naive Bayes classifiers and support vector machines, figure so prominently in the machine learning literature as to have become standard in undergraduate curricula. We intend to research the theory and advance the practice of supervised learning in the geoparsing domain, and report our findings in the sequel. Finally, we have manually annotated several hundred theses and dissertations from the Institutional Repository with ground-truth location references. These annotations will provide a basis for future evaluation of the tool as well as training data for a supervised classifier.

5. ACKNOWLEDGEMENTS

The authors would like to thank Scott Phillips for technical advice and editing assistance, and Doug Hahn and Michael Bolton of Texas A&M University Libraries for making this work possible.

6. REFERENCES

[1] MetaCarta, a Division of Qbase. `http://www.metacarta.com/`.

[2] H. Bart Jr. et al. GEOLocate - Software for Georeferencing Natural History Data . `http://www.museum.tulane.edu/geolocate/default.html`. [Online; accessed 29-January-2011].

[3] C. Grover, R. Tobin, K. Byrne, M. Wollard, J. Reid, S. Dunn, and J. Ball. Use of the Edinburgh geoparser for georeferencing digitized historical collections. *Philosophical Transactions of the Royal Society A*, 368:3875–3889, 2010.

[4] B. Martins, H. Manguinhas, J. Borbinha, and W. Siabato. A geo-temporal information extraction service for processing descriptive metadata in digital libraries. *e-Perimetron*, 4(1):25–37, 2009.

[3]http://www.google.com/earth/index.html
[4]http://www.openlayers.org

Pinterest: Social Collecting for #linking #using #sharing

Michael Zarro
College of Information Science and Technology
Drexel University
3141 Chestnut Street
Philadelphia, PA 19104
mzarro@drexel.edu

Catherine Hall
College of Information Science and Technology
Drexel University
3141 Chestnut Street
Philadelphia, PA 19104
ceh48@drexel.edu

Categories and Subject Descriptors

H.3.5 **[Information Storage and Retrieval]**: On-line information services – Web-based services

General Terms

Design, Human Factors, Standardization.

Keywords

Social collecting, annotations, linking, sharing, Pinterest.

1. INTRODUCTION

Information is collected and organized on a massive scale by the general public using social media websites for tagging, blogging, and photo sharing. Institutions have adopted social media efforts like the Flickr Commons or adding user-tagging capabilities to websites in recent years. In a similar vein, the website Pinterest allows users to annotate digital objects in their own personal collections (www.pinterest.com). A key difference between the Pinterest model and previous efforts is that images are copied from the source website to the user's Pinterest collection, creating a new digital surrogate. Pinterest combines the annotating features of tagging websites with the collecting and describing features of photo sharing and blogging websites. Digital libraries and other organizations can take advantage of these developments to expand the reach of their material, allowing users to create personalized collections incorporating their content.

1.1 Social Collecting

We define a site like Pinterest, that combines social and collecting capabilities, as a "*social collecting*" website. Social collecting is the collection, categorization, and representation of a digital object in a system that is accessible via the Web. Social collecting can expose a user-centered perspective of organizing or describing information resources in a digital library or website. Users of a social collecting site create and annotate surrogates of digital objects found on the Web, such as photographs or webpages. These surrogates are then saved in personal collections, called "pinboards" on Pinterest.

Social collecting has both personal and public facets. Users maintain collections using their own idiosyncratic methods, while their collections can be viewed by any other user of the system or unregistered visitors to the website. Digital libraries can leverage the work of user-curators to extend the reach of library to resources across the social web, and collect user-centered metadata from social collectors. Social collecting sites represent a path towards digital libraries getting a "social life" [10] by providing tools to curate and share collections.

1.1.1 Introduction to Pinterest.com

Pinterest is described as a "virtual pinboard" where people can "organize and share the beautiful things" found on the web. Launched in March 2010, Pinterest gained significant traction in late 2011, receiving 4.5 million unique visits in October and November [4] and is now one of the most popular social media websites, surpassing Delicious.com other established sites.

Pinterest users organize objects by selecting an image from the webpage where the object exists using a browser bookmarklet (or by uploading an image from their computer). This technological affordance [3] makes it easy to reuse and share images. Images uploaded via the bookmarklet contain a link back to the source website, but perhaps not to the original, as images may be used and reused several times on the Web. Pinterest also has many social components: users add boards to subject categories,'repin' objects from other users to their own boards, "like" or comment on objects, and "follow" boards and other user's activity.

1.2 Social Media and Libraries

The Smithsonian Institution [1] and Library of Congress [5] both report positive results from pilot projects collecting tags and image annotations using the Flickr Commons. In some cases, user contributions have been imported into the Library catalog, demonstrating the usefulness of the user's wisdom. Additional examples of library social efforts include: *Steve.museum* [6], a long-term project investigating the collecting and use of user tags in online library collections, and *Tag-It-Tuesdays* at the US National Archives which is part of the "citizen archivist dashboard" that also allows citizens to transcribe historical documents or upload their own digital copies of Archive records. Many libraries also maintain a presence on social sites like twitter or Facebook.

2. RESEARCH QUESTIONS

Exploring the Pinterest website and social media literature led to the following preliminary research questions: 1) How can we characterize activity of patron-curators on the social collecting website Pinterest.com, in relation to traditional library service models? 2) How do social collectors represent digital library holdings?

3. DISCUSSION

Annotation is a required feature of Pinterest. Users are collecting, annotating, and sharing digital objects from commercial entities, libraries, and other organizations. We downloaded pins on 12-16-2011 for three Pinterest categories: Food and Drink, Technology, and Travel. The captured data represents approximately 490 pins

JCDL'12, June 10–14, 2012, Washington, DC, USA.
ACM 978-1-4503-1154-0/12/06.

in each category, including the URL, pin description, number of likes and repins, name of the board to which the pin belongs, community comments. Additionally, we explored content from cultural organizations represented on Pinterest.

Social-collecting activity taken by a presumably untrained lay-user can be related to that of a trained librarian. Users "pin" images selected from the World Wide Web (often e-commerce websites and blogs) to a "pinboard" while assigning a short comment. Selecting an item to pin is equivalent to collection development. The Pinterest user is choosing an extremely small subset of objects from the World Wide Web to collect, and some discrimination necessarily occurs. The act of pinning and commenting is analogous to indexing and abstracting. The image is the surrogate the user chooses to represent her concept or object. Creating a pinboard and assigning it to a top-level category is analogous to defining a category in a hierarchy, and placing items in it. Social collecting activities may offer institutions a new way of viewing user-centered categories, much like that provided by earlier work with folksonomies and tagging [2].

Table 1. Pinterest activity compared to library services

Pinerest Activity	Library Service
Create and name pinboard	Taxonomy development
Assign pinboard to top-level category	Cataloging
Select a website with images suitable for pinning	Collection development
Select image to pin	Surrogate and Representing
Pin item to pinboard and comment	Indexing and Abstracting

3.1 Institutional Collections

Institutional content can be collected on Pinterest in two ways. First, the organization itself can create an account, set up Pinboards, and add pins. Second, Pinterest users can pin an organization's content to their personal pinboards. This activity does not require the consent or knowledge of the organization, and the context of social collecting allows reusing other's materials [3]. A key point of distinction between previous efforts like the Flickr Commons and Pinterest is that the "curator" of the social collections found on Pinterest is the user, not a librarian. The act of pinning creates a new digital surrogate and metadata for the object, thus a single item may be represented multiple times across the social web, with no direct link readily accessible between the various representations. This propagation introduces challenges for collecting potentially helpful user-contributed metadata. The following example shows how an image from the Smithsonian collection can be added to Pinterest, three levels away from the original digital photo found on the Smithsonian website:

Level 0: Smithsonian posts the image to their online digital collection (digital image of original print).

Level 1: Flickr Commons: The Smithsonian adds a copy of the image to their Flickr photostream.

Level 2: The design blog apartmenttherapy.com posts copy of the digital photo from Flickr.com to their post "historic interiors."

Level 3: A Pinterest user adds the copy from the blog apartmenttherapy.com to their personal pinboard.

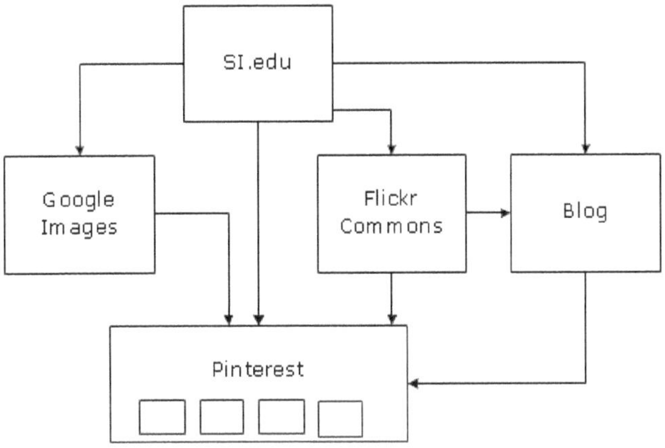

Figure 1. The propagation of resources as they are replicated across the social web, where provenance may be unknown.

4. CONCLUSION AND FUTURE WORK

In this work we introduced social collecting and the website Pinterest as an exemplar of the concept. Social collecting is indicative information organization, use, and sharing in a social web environment. This exploratory work describes technology that may prove useful for supporting digital library services.

Social collecting empowers users to act as curators and catalogers. Following the traditional cataloging model, only highly trained professionals are able to create surrogates of objects often while adhering to strict organization guidelines and policies. In contrast, the cataloger and patron roles are one and the same in the social collecting model. Currently, no methods exist to coordinate the collecting and annotation of resources across the social web. Future work will explore the benefits of Pinterest and similar sites to libraries and other institutions, as well as implications of policy decisions and interface design on user activity.

5. REFERENCES

[1] Kalfatovic, M.R., Kapsalis, E., Spiess, K.P., Van Camp, A. and Edson, M. 2009. Smithsonian team Flickr: A library, archives, and museums collaboration in web 2.0 space. *Archival Science*. 8, 4 (2009), 267–277.

[2] Marlow, C., Naaman, M., Boyd, D. and Davis, M. 2006. HT06, tagging paper, taxonomy, Flickr, academic article, to read. *Proceedings of the seventeenth conference on Hypertext and hypermedia* (New York, NY, USA, 2006), 31–40.

[3] Marshall, C.C. and Shipman, F.M. 2011. The ownership and reuse of visual media. *Proceeding of the 11th annual international ACM/IEEE joint conference on Digital libraries* (2011), 157–166.

[4] Pinterest And Quora: Why Facebook's "Like" Button Is So 2011. Forbes: 2012. *http://www.forbes.com/sites/victoriabarret/2012/01/04/pinterest-and-quora-why-facebooks-like-button-is-so-2011/*. Accessed: 2012-01-15.

[5] Springer, M., Dulabahn, B., Michel, P., Natanson, B., Reser, D., Woodward, D. and Zinkham, H. 2008. *For the Common Good: The Library of Congress Flickr Pilot Project*. Library of Congress.

[6] Trant, J. 2009. Studying social tagging and folksonomy: A review and framework. (2009).

YADDA2 – Assemble Your Own Digital Library Application from Lego Bricks

Wojtek Sylwestrzak
Centre for Open Science
ICM, Univ. of Warsaw
ul. Prosta 69
00-838 Warszawa, Poland
w.sylwestrzak@icm.edu.pl

Tomasz Rosiek
Centre for Open Science
ICM, Univ. of Warsaw
ul. Prosta 69
00-838 Warszawa, Poland
t.rosiek@icm.edu.pl

Łukasz Bolikowski
Centre for Open Science
ICM, Univ. of Warsaw
ul. Prosta 69
00-838 Warszawa, Poland
l.bolikowski@icm.edu.pl

ABSTRACT

YADDA2 is an open software platform which facilitates creation of digital library applications. It consists of versatile building blocks providing, among others: storage, relational and full-text indexing, process management, and asynchronous communication. Its loosely-coupled service-oriented architecture enables deployment of highly-scalable, distributed systems.

Categories and Subject Descriptors

H.3.7 [**Information Storage and Retrieval**]: Digital Libraries

General Terms

Design, Performance

1. INTRODUCTION

The document presents the recent results in development of an open, flexible, high-performance software platform for digital library applications, which we named YADDA2.

1.1 Motivation

Since the late 1990s, Interdisciplinary Centre for Mathematical and Computational Modelling (ICM) at the University of Warsaw has been providing access to full texts of major scientific publishers (Elsevier, Springer, and recently IEEE) for the Polish scientific community. We realized very quickly that maintaining individual publishers' platforms is expensive and cumbersome, and we started building our own software, named YADDA, to provide a full text search engine and a single point of access to the heterogeneous content. Components of the YADDA software found their way into a number of other digital library systems, including D-NET (the DRIVER Network Evolution Toolkit software suite [1]) or EuDML (the European Digital Mathematics Library [7]). As both the software and the collections of documents grew, the original design could no longer meet our needs, especially in terms of flexibility and scalability. Based on lessons learned and careful examination of other available solutions, we have designed and are currently developing a modular software platform named YADDA2, which could then be used to build concrete DL applications by us and by others alike.

JCDL'12, June 10–14, 2012, Washington, DC, USA.
ACM 978-1-4503-1154-0/12/06.

1.2 Related work

There are already several products and software frameworks, often mature, often distributed under open-source licenses, which boast high flexibility, modularity, and ability to work with third-party systems. Notable examples include: aDORe federation architecture [8], capable of storing hundreds of millions of digital objects and terabytes of image files; CiteSeerX [4], a database of research publications in computer and information science and related areas; dLibra Digital Library Framework [6] developed at Poznan Supercomputing and Networking Center; D-NET (DRIVER Network Evolution Toolkit) [5], originally created for the DRIVER repository infrastructure; Greenstone [10, 9], produced by the New Zealand Digital Library Project at the University of Waikato; H2O platform infrastructure, launched by HighWire Press[1]; INVENIO[2], originally developed at CERN; NCore [2], powered by Fedora [3], a framework for creation, management, and preservation of digital content.

2. SOFTWARE PLATFORM

2.1 Design goals

Design of the YADDA2 software platform was driven by a need for high flexibility and scalability. We needed a software platform that would facilitate creation of several types of products: *stand-alone repositories* with a web front-end and a publishing application in the back-end; *repository federations* containing of multiple autonomous collections, accessed though a central front-end; *publication data warehouses* aggregating content from multiple repositories in order to provide long-term preservation of data and access for researchers and analysts.

Ideally, building a new product should be reduced to assembling reusable, configurable components. Generic services such as metadata and content storages, full-text index, relational index, batch processing engine, or authorization and authentication should be readily available, their configuration and assembly should be straightforward. At the same time, an option to build custom compontents (in various programming languages) and bridges should be retained.

[1]See: http://highwire.stanford.edu/publishers/H2O.dtl
[2]See: http://invenio-software.org/

The platform should be able to handle objects of various types (documents, data sets, audio-visual content) and in various formats. Typically, components should be prepared to handle tens or hundreds of millions of objects. It should be easy to deploy distributed systems in a way that would be transparent to the individual components. Finally, the platform should seamlessly interoperate with third-party systems by embracing open protocols and standards for information exchange.

2.2 Architecture

YADDA2 allows to build distributed heterogeneous systems with multi-layer architecture. In most cases, an architecture of a YADDA2 based system would consist of two tiers: the base services tier and the applications tier. The base services provide generic functionalities which are independent of the type of content being stored or otherwise processed. The applications, on the other hand, use base services to provide business logic and user interface.

YADDA2 architecture was designed in order to provide high performance and scalability, with Service-Oriented Architecture making it easy to seamlessly plug in additional processing resources or mass storage to existing production environments. At the same time it offers the flexibility of open architecture. Users of the platform can easily add new services or adapt applications to their specific needs. One of the main features of the YADDA2 architecture is its ability to be deployed it in distributed environment, spreading across multiple organizations with different licencing and authentication policies. The platform satisfies the requirement of flexible maintenance and security issues management in infrastructure managed by more than one institution. YADDA2 includes advanced security context management tools and allows to manage either fine-gained security policies within particular application or coarse-grained licensing and authentication policies related to the access to particular services by particular institutions. The ability to effectively access the platform's resources not only with front-end applications but also with internal APIs, allows to easily create ad-hoc analysis and data post-processing tools by researchers.

From the technical point of view, YADDA2 architecture identifies the following components comprising the hosting platform: *hosting infrastructure* – service registries and service containers, responsible for instantiating, managing and communication between individual services; *core services* – components providing particular low level aspects of the platform's functionality (the current version of the platform includes Metadata and Content Storage, Full-text Index, Similarity Index, Batch Processing Engine, Relational Index, and User Annotation Service); and *platform clients* – software components using the services of the infrastructure.

YADDA2 is based on the Java language and supports a number of communication standards including HTTP, REST, SOAP and RMI. In addition, applications created on a base of YADDA2 support interfaces specific to digital libraries like OAI-PMH and OpenSearch.

3. SUMMARY

We have presented YADDA2, a new software platform for digital libraries. One differentiating factor is its open, modular, loosely-coupled design. Another one is its scalability, not only in the sense of large amounts of data or large traffic volumes that the derived applications can reliably handle, but also its multi-scale capabilities, making it particularly easy to tailor the size of an application to the specific needs, from a small, local (or embedded) repository implementation, to large scale, complex distributed systems handling heterogeneous content and services.

4. ACKNOWLEDGEMENTS

This work is supported by the National Centre for Research and Development (NCBiR) under Grant No. SP/I/1/77065/10 by the Strategic scientific research and experimental development program: "Interdisciplinary System for Interactive Scientific and Scientific-Technical Information".

5. REFERENCES

[1] M. Artini, L. Candela, D. Castelli, P. Manghi, M. Mikulicic, and P. Pagano. Sustainable Digital Library Systems over the DRIVER Repository Infrastructure. *Lecture Notes in Computer Science*, 5173:227–231, 2008.

[2] D. B. Krafft, A. Birkland, and E. J. Cramer. Ncore: architecture and implementation of a flexible, collaborative digital library. In *Proceedings of the 8th ACM/IEEE-CS joint conference on Digital libraries - JCDL '08*, page 313, New York, New York, USA, 2008. ACM Press.

[3] C. Lagoze, S. Payette, E. Shin, and C. Wilper. Fedora: an architecture for complex objects and their relationships. *International Journal on Digital Libraries*, 6(2):124–138, Dec. 2005.

[4] H. Li, I. Councill, W.-C. Lee, and C. L. Giles. CiteSeerx: An architecture and Web service design for an academic document search engine. In *Proceedings of the 15th international conference on World Wide Web - WWW '06*, page 883, New York, New York, USA, 2006. ACM Press.

[5] P. Manghi, M. Mikulicic, L. Candela, D. Castelli, and P. Pagano. Realizing and Maintaining Aggregative Digital Library Systems: D-NET Software Toolkit and OAIster System. *D-Lib Magazine*, 16(3/4), Mar. 2010.

[6] C. Mazurek, T. Parkoła, and M. Werla. Distributed Digital Libraries Platform in the PIONIER Network. *Lecture Notes in Computer Science*, 4172:488–491, 2006.

[7] W. Sylwestrzak, J. Borbinha, T. Bouche, A. Nowiński, and P. Sojka. EuDML—Towards the European Digital Mathematics Library. In *Towards a Digital Mathematics Library*, pages 11–26, 2010.

[8] H. Van de Sompel, R. Chute, and P. Hochstenbach. The aDORe federation architecture: digital repositories at scale. *International Journal on Digital Libraries*, 9(2):83–100, Oct. 2008.

[9] I. H. Witten, D. Bainbridge, and D. M. Nichols. *How to Build a Digital Library*. Morgan Kaufmann, 2nd edition, 2009.

[10] I. H. Witten, S. J. Boddie, D. Bainbridge, and R. J. McNab. Greenstone: a comprehensive open-source digital library software system. In *Proceedings of the fifth ACM conference on Digital libraries - DL '00*, pages 113–121, New York, New York, USA, 2000. ACM Press.

An Integrated Participatory Platform for Human Evaluation of Machine Translation

Jiangping Chen
University of North Texas
Denton, Texas, 76203
Jiangping.Chen@unt.edu

Olajumoke Azogu
University of North Texas
Denton, Texas, 76203
Olajumoke.Azogu@unt.edu

Wenqian Zhao
University of North Texas
Denton, Texas, 76203
WenqianZhao@my.unt.edu

ABSTRACT

We describe the functions of HeMT, a multilingual participatory platform for Human Evaluation of Machine Translation. HeMT is used by three types of users including translators, evaluators, and reviewers. It consists of six major modules: User Management, Manual Translation, User Training, Evaluation, Result Visualization, and Multilingual Lexicon Management. HeMT can be used by Digital Libraries and Machine Translation communities for conducting manual translation, machine translation evaluation, and computer-assisted translation tasks.

Categories and Subject Descriptors

H.3.7 [**Information Storage and Retrieval**]: Digital Libraries – *Collection, Dissemination, User Issues*

General Terms

Algorithms, Design, Experimentation.

Keywords

Digital Libraries, Metadata Records Translation, Human Evaluation of Machine Translation, Multilingual Information Systems, User Studies, Crowdsourcing, Web Database System

1. INTRODUCTION TO HeMT

We present HeMT (http://txcdk-v10.unt.edu/HeMT/), a Human Evaluation of Machine Translation system, developed as part of a larger study investigating the translation and evaluation of metadata records for digital collections. HeMT is designed to facilitate manual translation and human evaluation of machine translation (MT). It is a web-based participatory platform developed with open-source tools including PHP and MySQL.

HeMT supports three types of users: Translators, Reviewers and Evaluators. They are international and multilingual. Currently, HeMT users speak one or more of the following languages: English, Simplified Chinese, and Spanish.

2. HeMT SYSTEM FUNCTIONALITY

Our goal for HeMT is to design a system so that different types of research participants can seamlessly work together to perform high quality manual translation and evaluation. Figure 1 shows the system functions and their associations. In current implementation, HeMT accepts English metadata records and presents them to multiple translators for translating them manually into Simplified Chinese and Spanish. It also accepts the translation results of these records from three machine translation systems. The manual translations and MT translation results are then presented to evaluators for assessing the MT performance.

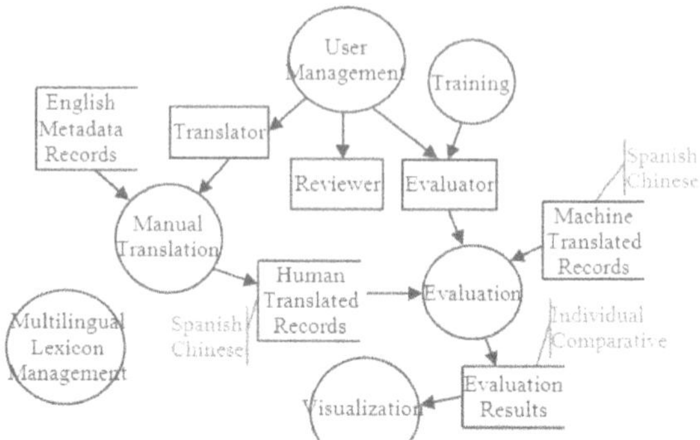

Figure 1. HeMT Functionality.

HeMT therefore consists of six functional modules. Each module interacts with the users in multiple languages. The six modules include: (1) User Management. This module allows users to register, login, and revise their profiles. It also requests the reviewers to approve or deny new users; (2) Multilingual Lexicon Management. This module allows reviewers to generate multilingual terminologies that are used by HeMT webpages. It makes HeMT language-independent that new language can be conveniently added to it; (3) Manual Translation. This module generates reference translations for evaluation. Translators are presented the original English metadata records and prompted to translate them into Chinese or Spanish. HeMT allows the translators to edit their translations later, and presents the same interface for the reviewers to approve, edit, or deny a translation; (4) User Training. (5) Evaluation. (6) Result Visualization. The last three modules are discussed in more detail below.

2.1. User Training

Human evaluation of MT may generate diverse judgments from evaluators [1, 2, 3]. Recently, a crowdsourcing approach using Amazon's Mechanical Turk was explored and issues raised about the quality of the evaluation results from the crowds [1]. HeMT introduced a controlled crowdsourcing approach in which evaluators will be trained. The training module consists of a number of short pages that explain the background of the project, registration, evaluation types, measures, and methods of dealing with specific situations. It ends with a quiz, and only those who pass the quiz can be accepted as evaluators. HeMT currently provides user training in three languages: English, Simplified Chinese, and Spanish.

2.2. Evaluation

Human evaluation of MT has been well applied by the MT community and is an interesting research area itself [1, 2]. The Evaluation module in HeMT applies both the traditional accuracy-adequacy approach and the comparative approach for evaluation. Evaluators are presented with individual metadata records to judge the extent to which MT records accurately and completely express meanings in the target language. Evaluators judge the performance of three freely available MT systems in two ways: (1) Individual evaluation, which compares of machine translation (MT) results with two reference translations using two measures: Adequacy and Fluency; (2) Comparative evaluation, which compares the performance of three machine translation systems (System 1, System 2 and System 3) to determine which system provides the best translation and which the worst. Both evaluation methods allow evaluators to comment on the process.

Figure 2 presents the individual evaluation page - a metadata record in Chinese translated by the first MT system is displayed, along with two reference translations, to an evaluator for assessment. This particular metadata record has five elements: Title, Creator, Subject, Description, and Coverage. The evaluator will judge the translation for each element, and will come up with the overall judgment for the whole record in terms of fluency and adequacy. The process is repeated for the other two MT systems.

Figure 2. Individual Evaluation – An Example in Chinese

Evaluators are encouraged to return to related training pages during the process for questions, or contact the research team. It takes about 2-4 minutes for an evaluator to complete the evaluation of one metadata record.

Evaluators take a survey to describe their evaluation experience and provide feedback on the usability of HeMT after evaluation.

2.3. Evaluation Result Visualization

This module aims to present evaluation result visually, which will help the research team to monitor the evaluation process during the evaluation, and for presenting the project to the public after the evaluation is completed. For example, Figure 4 shows the results of comparative evaluations of Chinese translations. It presents the frequency and relative frequency for each system on the two measurements: best performance and worst performance. More advanced analysis of the evaluation, such as inter-coder reliability and test statistics may be added in the future.

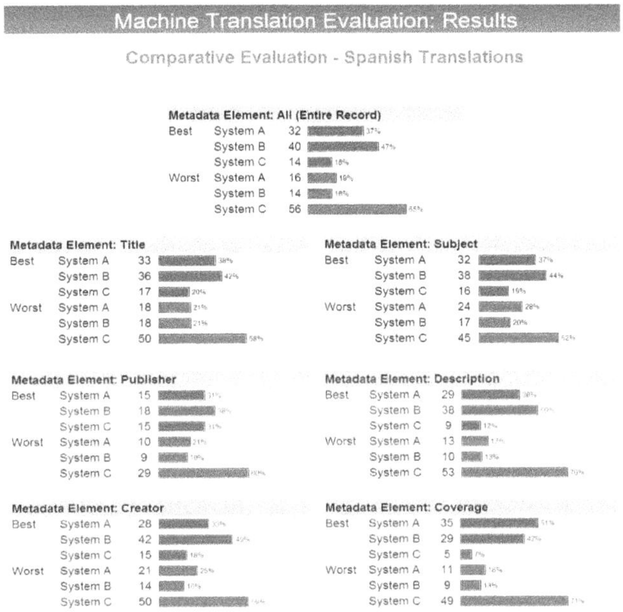

Figure 3. Comparative Evaluation - Results

3. USABILITY TESTING

We have conducted four rounds usability testing with 16 students who were either native speakers of Chinese or Spanish. The tests were conducted in laboratory settings in which testing participants were observed. During the testing, participants took the training lesson, registered to HeMT, and performed both types of evaluation for 2-10 records. They also filled out a post-task survey. The testing protocol ensured that all parts of HeMT were used. Feedback from each round of testing led to changes in the system before the next round. Consequently, current HeMT interfaces are significantly different from the initial ones.

4. CONCLUSION AND ACKNOWLEDGMENT

HeMT (http://txcdk-v10.unt.edu/HeMT/) is developed to enable the human evaluation of MT metadata records, and to contribute to finding effective strategies for metadata records translation for digital collections. It is readily extensible to other textual types and other languages. HeMT will be released as an open-source system when our project is completed. It can be used as a sample Web database system for students in Library and Information Science.

This work is supported by U.S. Institute of Museum and Library Services (http://www.imls.gov/) Grant LG-06-10-0162-10. We thank Ryan Knudson for editing this paper.

5. REFERENCES

[1] Callison-Burch, etc. Findings of the 2010 workshop on statistical machine translation and metrics for machine translation. In *Proceedings of WMT2010,* July, 2010, Uppsala, Sweden, 17-53.

[2] Lavie, A. 2010. Evaluating the output of machine translation systems. In *Proceedings of AMTA* 2010, Denver, Colorado.

[3] Chen, J.; Ding, R.; & Jiang, S. (2011). Metadata records translation: the case of the Portal to Texas History. *Library and Information Service.* 54(2), 16-20.

'Erasmus': An Organization- and User-Centered Dublin Core Metadata Tool

Michael Khoo, Craig M. MacDonald, Joon Park
The iSchool at Drexel University
3141 Chestnut Street
Philadelphia PA 19104
+1 215 895 1230
{khoo, cmm353, sp347}@drexel.edu

ABSTRACT
Digital library interoperability is supported by good quality metadata. The design of metadata creation and management tools is therefore an important component of overall digital library design. A number of factors affect metadata tool usability, including task complexity, interface usability, and organizational context of use. These issues are being addressed in the user-centered design of a metadata tool for the Internet Public Library.

Categories and Subject Descriptors
H.3.7 Digital Libraries – *collection, standards, user issues.*

General Terms
Design, Human Factors

Keywords
Dublin Core, metadata, metadata tool, user-centered design

1. INTRODUCTION
The Internet Public Library (ipl2: http://www.ipl.org/) receives 8 million visits and 22 million page views a year. Its catalog indexes approximately 40,000 resources, aimed at K-12 and informal education audiences. ipl2 has crosswalked its metadata to Dublin Core and has added this metadata to a Fedora Commons database, and a new tool for metadata creation and administration, *Erasmus*, has been developed. *Erasmus* supports the creation and editing of DC records by ipl2 volunteers, and graduate students in LIS classes, and allows ipl2 administrators to build customized cataloging interfaces. Metadata tool usability is important and can impact the quality of the metadata produced by that tool [1, 2, 3, 4, 6, 8, 9]. Metadata tool users engage in a set of demanding tasks, reviewing the resource to be cataloged, referring to metadata guidelines and collection scope, and using the metadata tool itself [4]. A number of factors affect metadata tool usability, such as task complexity, interface usability, and organizational context of use. To address these issues, the development of *Erasmus is* following an organization- and user-centered design process.

2. ERASMUS
The initial requirements work was carried out by students in a graduate 'Introduction to HCI' class. In teams, 24 students researched digital libraries and metadata tools, practiced using the existing tool, and developed sketches and paper prototypes of a new tool. They then tested their prototypes in class with heuristic evaluation and think alouds [7], and compiled their findings into usability reports. A doctoral student working with ipl2 used the reports to develop and refine an initial HTML prototype, and ipl2 developers then built a high-fidelity prototype, a forerunner of the interface shown in Figure 1. Two doctoral students then performed expert evaluations of this prototype, while at the same time drafting a user manual (these two activities were synergetic). Many of the usability problems found were related to the how the tool represented the complex knowledge required for cataloging in an uncluttered and easily accessible form in the interface itself. This led to the design and development of a variety of dropdown 'tooltip' boxes, such as those describing the cataloging requirements of particular metadata fields.

Organizational requirements were also gathered in the form of interviews with project members regarding their understanding of metadata work in ipl2. One finding here was that some of the difficulty with working with the original (pre-Dublin Core) metadata arose because the organizational knowledge associated with this metadata (such as why a particular field had been created and defined in a particular way) had not been explicitly recorded and so had been lost over time [c.f. 8]. It was often difficult to understand why particular metadata fields or vocabularies had been created and applied in particular ways. The documentation of these past decisions would have been useful for present-day catalogers, but it simply did not exist. An organizational (rather than technical) requirement for the tool was therefore that it be able to record the decisions underlying choices of metadata schema, elements, and definitions.

The new *Erasmus* tool is accessible in a Web browser. There are two basic modes, user and administrative. In user mode, the user logs in, and chooses whether they are creating or editing a record. After checking the URL for duplicates, the user is prompted to add the resource to a particular ipl2 collection, before beginning to catalog the resource in the interface shown in Figure 1. The metadata entry tool is shown on the left, and the web resource being cataloged on the right. The tool on the left has fields for metadata entry, and AJAX-scripted dropdowns provide further information about each metadata field and the associated cataloging policy. It should be noted that the elements of the tool seen in the left of the figure – the number and type of fields and their name and order, and the associated information in the dropdowns – are not hard-coded, but rather are stored in and generated from a MySQL database previously populated by an ipl2 administrator in administrative mode. *Erasmus* can thus be configured to allow any flavors of Dublin Core to be represented in the tool (Figure 2).

JCDL'12, June 10–14, 2012, Washington, DC, USA.
ACM 978-1-4503-1154-0/12/06

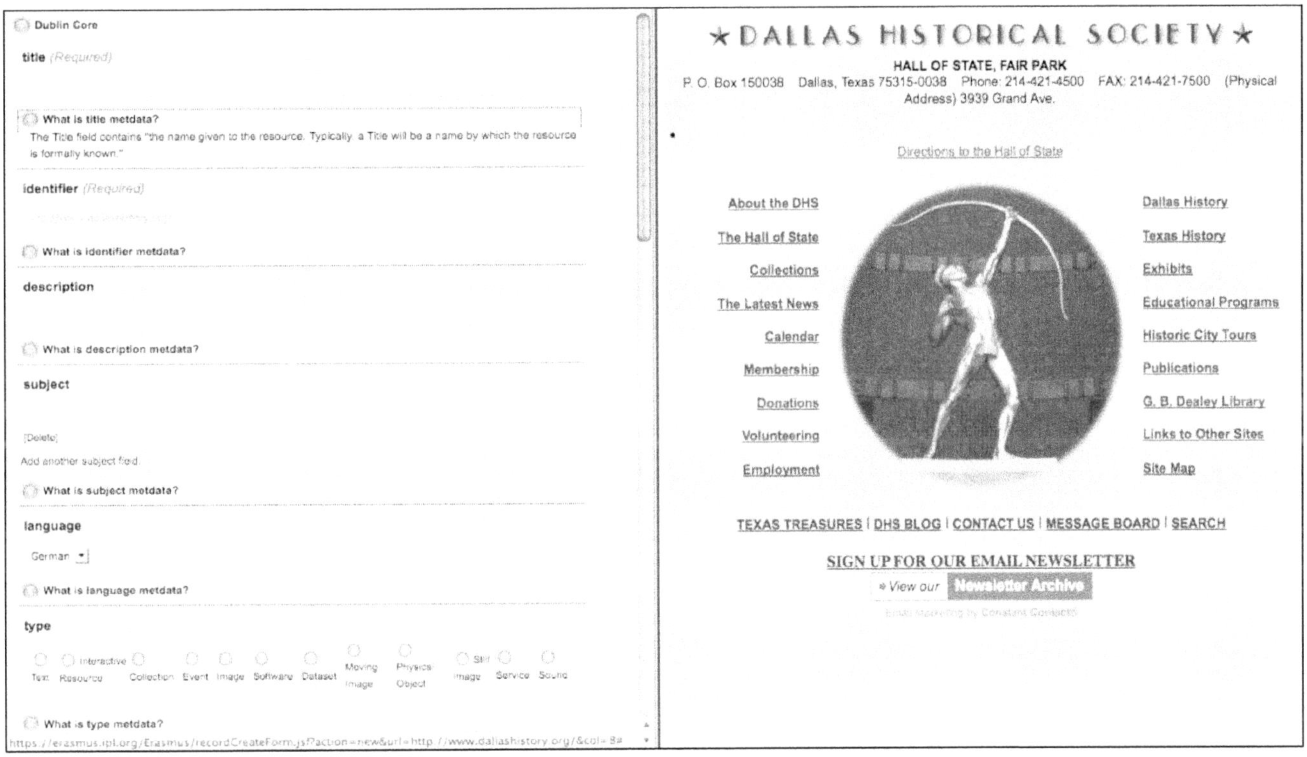

Figure 1. Screen shot of the *Erasmus* Web interface

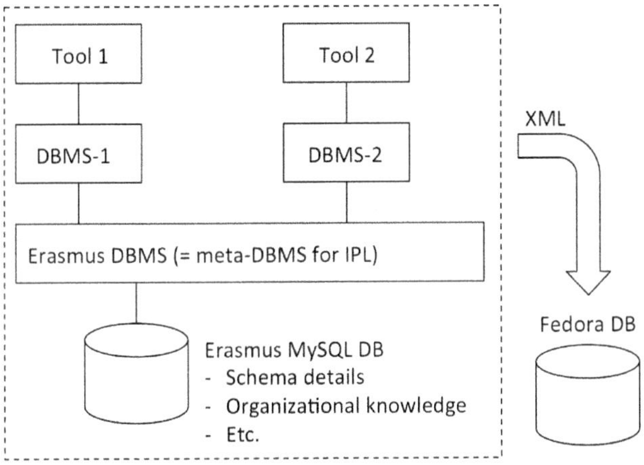

Figure 2. High level metadata flow in Erasmus

The user-centered design of *Erasmus* supports administrators to build schemas for any 'flavor' of Dublin Core, including qualified and administrative metadata, with relatively little effort. By using MySQL to store the schema information and documentation, the components of the tool are modular and extensible, and new schemas can be created easily. Next steps in the work include refining and user testing with students in LIS and cataloging classes, as well as refining the user manual.

3. ACKNOWLEDGMENTS

The authors thank the OCLC and ALISE Library and Information Science Research Grants Program for supporting this work.

4. REFERENCES

[1] Crystal, A. (2003). Interface design for metadata creation. CHI '03 extended abstracts, pp. 1038-1039.

[2] Crystal, A., & Greenberg, J. (2005). Usability of a metadata creation application for resource authors. Library & Information Science Research 27 (2005), 177-189.

[3] Greenberg, J., Crystal, A., Robertson, W. D., & Leadem, E. (2003). Iterative design of metadata creation tools for resource authors. Dublin Core 2003, September 28 - October 2, Seattle, WA, USA.

[4] Khoo, M., Devaul, H., and Sumner, T. 2002. Functional Requirements for Groupware to Support Community-Led Collections Building. ECDL '02, pp. 190-203.

[5] Khoo, M., & Hall, C. 2011. Merging Metadata: A Sociotechnical Study of Crosswalking and Interoperability. JCDL 2010, pp. 361-364.

[6] Nasoz, F., Bryce, R., Palmer, C., & Rugg, D. 2011. A user-centric metadata tool for preserving the nation's ecological data. International Conference on Human Interface and the Management of Information. HI'11. Pp. 361-364.

[7] Nielsen, J. 2005. Ten Heuristics for Interface Design. http://www.useit.com/papers/heuristic/heuristic_list.html

[8] Waugh, A. 1998. Specifying metadata standards for metadata tool configuration. Proc. World Wide Web 7 (WWW7). DOI: 10.1016/S0169-7552(98)00102-0

[9] Wilson, A. 2007. Toward releasing the metadata bottleneck: a baseline evaluation of contributor-supplied metadata. *Library Resources and Technical Services* 51(1), 16-28.

Faceted Search for Heterogeneous Digital Collections

Hui Zhang
Digital Library Program
Indiana University
Bloomington, Indiana USA
hz3@indiana.edu

Jon Dunn, Will Cowan
Digital Library Program
Indiana University
Bloomington, Indiana USA
{jwd, wgcowan}@indiana.edu

Mike Durbin, Brian Wheeler
Digital Library Program
Indiana University
Bloomington, Indiana USA
{midurbin, bdwheeler}@indiana.edu

ABSTRACT

The idea of faceted search has received growing attentions in the digital library field for its potential of improving user satisfaction by combing the query and browse strategies interactively. Furthermore, with the trend of using digital repositories as the central infrastructure for curation and preservation, there is a demand for a single search interface providing public access to all the diversified content stored in the repositories. In this demo, we present *Digital Collections Search*, a system that is designed to assist users who are unfamiliar with the subject of their information needs locating relevant items as well exploring related but unknown collections in the repository.

Categories and Subject Descriptors

H.3.7 [**Information Search and Retrieval**]: Digital Libraries

General Terms

Management, Design, Human Factors.

Keywords

Faceted search, discovery interface, fedora common, solr, blacklight, disseminator.

1. INTRODUCTION

A common challenge to discovery interface design is that the average users of digital library systems cannot specify their information needs appropriately due to the lack of knowledge on the subject. The problem is only intensified when libraries keep adding digitized contents of various types and from different domains into their repositories. For instance, the repository maintained by Indiana University's Digital Library Program (DLP) holds more than 100 collections with a variety of content types such as images, manuscripts, and sheet music. Although some of the collections have their own public websites, it is impractical to exploit this rich resource without a unified discovery interface because otherwise a potential user will have to search his topics on every single collection individually.

In this paper, we demonstrate *Digital Collections Search* (DCS), a system developed by DLP that supports exploratory search across collections preserved in its Fedora Commons repository.

JCDL'12, June 10–14, 2012, Washington, DC, USA.
ACM 978-1-4503-1154-0/12/06..

Although a faceted search interface to a union catalog is not a new idea, for instance the North Carolina State University Library's OPAC (Online Public Access Catalog), the DCS system is innovative in its supporting of contents generated from different metadata standards (e.g., EAD and MODS) and complicated workflows (e.g., flexible collection branding) by: creating an index framework serving as the middleware to synchronize the repository and discovery interface, developing Fedora services to "normalize" the digitized items and provide standardized output through web service.

2. SYSTEM OVERVIEW

2.1 Architecture

The general procedure of creating Solr index for the collections in Fedora will be briefly described in this section. Figure 1 illustrates the system architecture, which includes three layers: the back-end layer of Fedora repository, the middle layer of index framework, and the front-end layer of faceted discovery interface. The repository layer is responsible for providing MODS record for each digitized item, using a locally developed Fedora disseminator called getMODS, as input for the index layer. The middle layer of index service, called Fedora-index-service framework [1], is in charge of creating the Solr and Lucene indices for the MODS records. The framework is implemented as a RESTful web service application written specially to generate index for digitized items with complex structures (e.g., journals and books) while in sync with the Fedora repository. However, this framework does not support searching and browsing the index, therefore a discovery interface is developed in separate to allow public access to the indexed contents. The next two sections will discuss in details on how the Solr index is created and the design of the discovery interface.

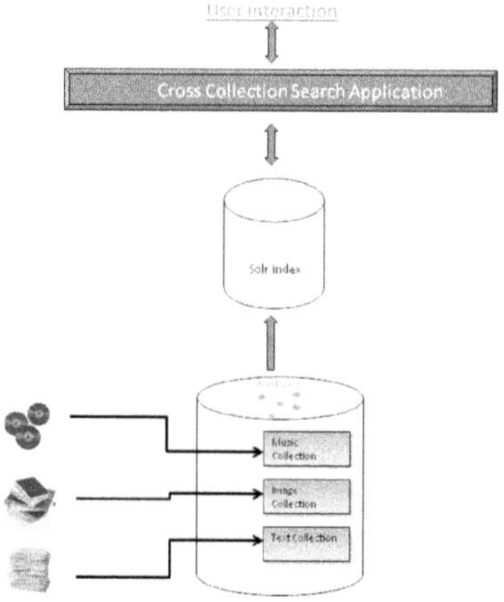

Figure 1: System Architecture

2.2 Building the Solr Index

Solr, an open source index server, is chosen as the framework for building the index because of its robustness and support for faceted search. Items in Fedora that will be included in the Solr index must associate themselves with the getMODS disseminator so the indexing routine only needs to handle one format no matter what metadata standards were used during the cataloging process. The generated MODS records will then be converted into a XML-style format that is native to Solr and indexed. All the input and output files for indexing are delivered as streams of raw bytes to save processing time and storage space.

Quality control and live update are two major challenges of incorporating the Solr index service with DLP's production system. Quality control, the procedure of keeping the indexed content correct and up-to-date, is involved across the whole workflow of indexing. For instance, an item may have to be removed from the index because it is unrelated with the collection. Therefore, the index service must implement routines to restrict problematic item from public access. Several measures are added to ensure this goal: a new field called *recordStatus* is created in MODS to register whether the item has completed the cataloging process; a Fedora service is created to confirm whether an item is eligible for public view; and the indexing program will check certain MODS fields to make sure they meet the expected pattern.

Live update is a customer raised feature that argues a digitized item should become available for the public view as soon as it has been cataloged. It requires that the Solr indexing speed must match the Fedora ingestion speed; it also demands a communication mechanism in between so that Fedora is able to notify the index service once an update to the repository is made. Through experiments, it is clear that the indexing process is slowed down mostly because of the Solr commit operation, and the solution is to specify the *maxTime* property of Solr's *autoCommit* configuration to the value (30000 ms) that will trigger the commit operation only when there were documents updated in the last five minutes. This change in Solr configuration is important to keep the repository and the index in synchronization especially during massive Fedora ingestion when thousands of digitized items are imported into the repository in batch mode.

The communication mechanism between Fedora and Solr indexer is built with the Java Message Service (JMS), where the Fedora server is specified as publisher and the index service is setup as the listener. Fedora will broadcast notice when an item is added or updated, and the indexing routine subscribed to the messages will in response start the process of (re) indexing that item.

2.3 The Discovery Interface

The discovery interface at the front-end is designed with the goal of assisting non-expert users in locating relevant items without the knowledge of the subject. Blacklight, an open source online public access catalog project, is chosen as the platform to develop the search interface because it is developed primarily for library usage and supports search with Solr index out-of-box.

Identifying the facet fields is a vital task for discovery interface design. All the facets used in DCS are data driven, which means their values are stored in Fedora and exposed using disseminator. After all, seven index fields are chosen as facets, where three of them, namely *Format*, *Collection*, and *Source*, are extracted from Fedora and passed directly to the indexer. In contrast, the other four facets are translated from the corresponding MODS fields based on the following mapping patterns:

- Topic facet: mods:subject|mods:topic
- Creator facet: mods:namepart
- Genre facet: mods:genre
- Year facet: mods:originalInfo[@keyDate and @w3cdtf]

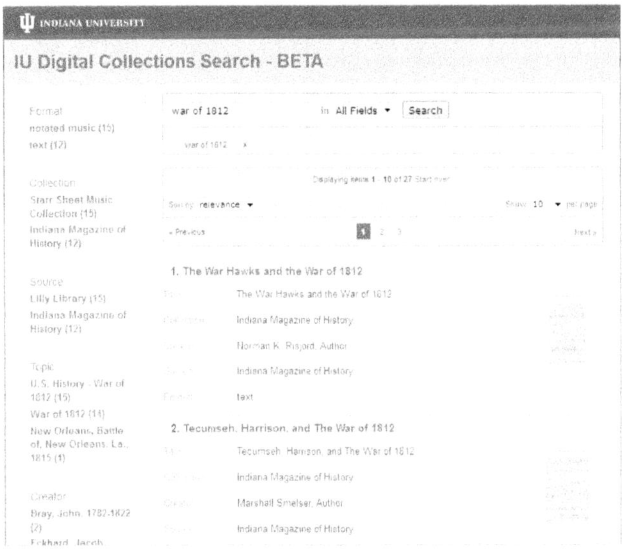

Figure 2. Snapshot of IU Digital Collections Search

A snapshot of the faceted search interface is depicted in Figure 2. In this example, it provides results to a keyword search of *war of 1812*, where the user can choose either narrowing down his request or exploring new items by picking the appropriate facets (e.g., picking a *topic* facet to specify requirement or a different *collection* to explore the repository) shown in the left pane. Selecting a different facet will initiate a new Solr search and the results will be rendered in the primary window on the right, and a click on the item title or its thumbnail will redirect the user to a webpage that will show the item in its full details.

3. FUTURE PLAN

DCS is still at Beta stage; we are adding new collections and collecting user feedbacks at this time. There is a plan for improvement and new features on top of the list are: supporting full-text search, recognizing and indexing new Fedora collections automatically. We also want to explore the possibility of integrating DCS with traditional library catalog and using it for video search.

4. REFERENCES

[1] Durbin, M. and Dunn, J. (2008) Accommodating Diverse Search Requirements over a Fedora Repository. In: Third international Conference on Open Repositories 2008. 1-4 April 2008, Southampton, United Kingdom.

NLM Video Search

John P. Doyle
U.S. National Library of Medicine
8600 Rockville Pike
Bethesda, MD 20894 USA
+1 301 496 4003
doylejo@mail.nlm.nih.gov

Doron Shalvi
U.S. National Library of Medicine
(contractor)
8600 Rockville Pike
Bethesda, MD 20894 USA
+1 301 496 8434
shalvid@mail.nlm.nih.gov

Edward C. Luczak
U.S. National Library of Medicine
(contractor)
8600 Rockville Pike
Bethesda, MD 20894 USA
+1 301 594 3668
luczake@mail.nih.gov

ABSTRACT
In this demo, we will demonstrate usage of NLM Video Search, open-source software which facilitates the dissemination of video content by combining traditional web video playback controls with on-demand seeking using text selected from a corresponding transcript (see Figure 1). NLM Video Search has been implemented in NLM's Fedora-based digital repository, which provides preservation and access to a growing number of rare, historical films and digitized texts.

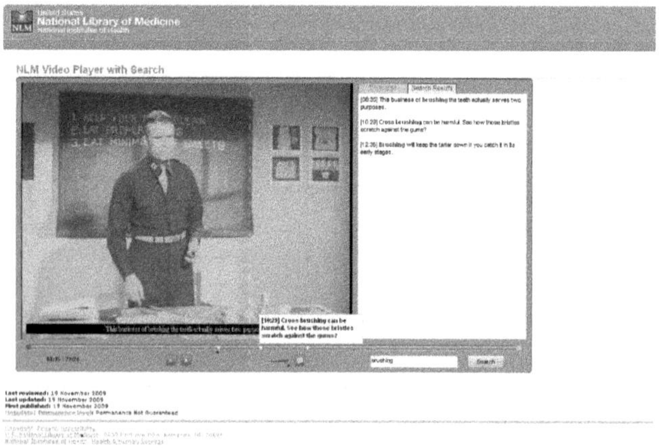

Figure 1 Text-driven seeking of video

Categories and Subject Descriptors
H.3.7 [**Information Storage and Retrieval**]: Digital Libraries – *Dissemination, Systems issue, User issues*

General Terms
Performance, Design.

Keywords
Digitized Video, Digital Library, Accessibility.

JCDL'12, June 10–14, 2012, Washington, DC, USA.
ACM 978-1-4503-1154-0/12/06.

1. OVERVIEW
Since its launch in September 2010, thousands of users from more than 100 countries have visited NLM's *Digital Collections*[1] to view hundreds of minutes of rare historical public health films via NLM Video Search. In this demo, we will demonstrate usage of NLM Video Search for searching, seeking, reading the transcript, and playback with and without captioning. We will also demonstrate integration of NLM Video Search within the overall *Digital Collections* website and its underlying Fedora Repository-driven functionality.

All the films can be searched, viewed, and downloaded freely without copyright restrictions. The films are available in a variety of video formats to accommodate a wide range of playback devices, including mobile devices. In addition to offering a full-text search of a film's transcript, the tool graphically displays where a search word or phrase occurs within the timeline of a film. Clicking the timeline results takes the user immediately to the appropriate portion of the film where the result appears.

2. TECHNOLOGY
NLM Video Search has been developed as free, open source software that can be easily adopted by other institutions that want to provide searchable, 508-compliant[2] captioned video content to their web users. Searchable video content can improve the user experience for nearly any user. Informational or training videos, lectures and speeches, or other video content can become much more usable when its transcript can be easily searched, and locations within the video can be quickly accessed.

To use NLM Video Search, web users need only have the free Adobe Flash Player software installed with their web browser. The NLM Video Search software is loaded dynamically with the web page that contains it; no prior software installation is required. NLM Video Search software has been successfully tested with the Internet Explorer, Firefox, and Chrome browsers on PC platforms, and Safari on Mac platforms.

NLM Video Search can be easily integrated with customized agency web sites, digital repositories, or other web applications. Many video playback and search applications can use the existing NLM Video Search software as is, without any software modifications. Video content is provided as H.264 compressed video files, and caption/transcript files are provided in the W3C

[1] http://collections.nlm.nih.gov

[2] http://www.section508.gov/

standard DFXP format. Caption/transcript files can be created using WGBH's free MAGpie authoring tool, which NLM has used for this purpose. Web developers can optionally use an NLM-provided JSP wrapper web page, and then easily modify its banner, colors, etc., to customize the look and feel. Developers who would like to customize the core software for their own applications can modify the ActionScript 3 code using the Adobe Flash Professional tool suite.

3. CONTENT

The initial group of historical films made accessible via NLM Video Search includes the topics of World War II-era public health and tropical diseases. These films – alongside dozens more to be made accessible via NLM Video Search through *Digital Collections* – stand among the 30,000 plus titles in the Library's collection, which, in light of its depth and breadth, ranks as the foremost medical film archive in the world. Dating from the 1910s to the present, the collection originates from many sources, including government agencies—notably the Public Health Service, and especially the Center for Disease Control and Prevention (CDC). Other films come from private health organizations, and from groups such as the American Dental Association. As these institutions move their productions from film to video and digital, they often wish to have their materials preserved and accessible at the NLM.

As a cost- and technically-efficient resource, and one that directly enables individuals with disabilities, NLM Video Search will be an integral resource in the future of research and learning. More audiences are becoming interested in medical and public health history, and NLM Video Search provides opportunities to broaden and deepen understanding of the past, present, and future of medicine and public health. This understanding helps refine critical thinking about medicine and science, promote deeper knowledge of medical and scientific concepts, and generally humanize medicine and public health by revealing the implications of disease and healthcare for individuals and communities in the United States and around the world.

4. ACKNOWLEDGEMENTS

We thank our several colleagues at the National Library of Medicine for their contributions to the NLM Video Search and the related digitization and digital library activities. NLM, the world's largest library of the health sciences, is a component of the National Institutes of Health, U.S. Department of Health and Human Services. We also thank the US Department of Health and Human Services for recognizing NLM Video Search in Round 3 of the HHS*innovates* departmental awards program.

Research Discovery through Linked Open Data

Paul Albert
Weill Cornell Medical Library
Weill Cornell Medical College
New York, NY
paa2013@med.cornell.edu

Kristi L. Holmes
Washington University in St. Louis
St. Louis, MO 63110
holmeskr@wustl.edu

Katy Börner
Indiana University
School of Library and Information Science
Bloomington, IN
katy@indiana.edu

Mike Conlon
University of Florida
Gainesville, FL
mconlon@ufl.edu

VIVO Collaboration

ABSTRACT
VIVO is an open source semantic web platform that contains information about scholars and their interests and activities. This demonstration will highlight the platform and ontology, data sources, features of the software and the ways that VIVO data can be leveraged for a variety of purposes within and beyond an institution to facilitate collaboration and research discovery.

Categories and Subject Descriptors
D.0 [**Software**]: General

Keywords
VIVO, Semantic Web, Open Source, Ontology, Research Representation, Profiles

1. BACKGROUND
VIVO [1] is an open source semantic web platform that enables the discovery of research and scholarship across disciplinary and administrative boundaries through interlinked profiles of people and other data relevant to researchers (Figure 1). VIVO allows researchers to highlight areas of expertise, display academic credentials, visualize academic and social networks, and display information such as publications, grants, teaching, service, awards, and more. Profile information can be programmatically imported from authoritative data sources such as institutional sources as well as bibliographic and grants databases. By storing and exposing data as RDF and using standard ontologies, the information in VIVO can either be displayed in a human-readable web page or delivered to other systems as RDF, allowing researcher metadata in VIVO to be harvested, aggregated, and integrated into the Linked Open Data cloud. Data reuse and repurposing enhances the accuracy and currency of the data while increasing efficiencies across an organization.

JCDL'12, June 10–14, 2012, Washington, DC, USA.
ACM 978-1-4503-1154-0/12/06.

VIVO was originally developed at Cornell University and is being expanded as a platform to support national and international research networking via semantic web standards with funding from the National Institutes of Health to the University of Florida, Cornell University, Indiana University and implemented at Ponce School of Medicine, Scripps Research Institute, Washington University in St. Louis, and Weill Cornell Medical College. Each site has a local installation that shares data in flexible and openly accessible ways to facilitate research discovery.

2. DATA
VIVO gathers data from a variety of sources: internal data sources such as human resources databases, course listings and university calendars can be programmatically harvested

Figure 1. A VIVO profile.

and leveraged to provide a good perspective of the local environment; award, funding, and publication data can be harvested from external systems; and individuals and their proxies can supplement the profile with additional information. A number of sites are working to highlight the efforts of their researchers contributions to Open Access journals, and VIVO offers institutions an elegant way for sites to highlight their institutional repository as a critical campus resource. By leveraging the data in an institutional repository and prioritizing resources for content, VIVO can serve as an ideal gateway for scholars to access the content that they need throughout the course of their scholarly activity. Open Access articles can result in greater impact of the work than may otherwise occur in traditional journals. [2] A number of institutions successfully leverage their individual institutional repository platforms (e.g. DSpace, Berkeley Electronic Press) and integrate the data into their VIVO.

3. RESEARCH DISCOVERY

VIVO promotes discovery in several key ways. Because profiles are rich in content and the data are highly structured, VIVO profiles will rank higher in general internet searches than typical webpages or social networking sites. Research discovery is facilitated via content browsing and the structured data lends itself to a variety of applications that can use these data. Data are repurposed and reused in a variety of tools and settings. Across institutions, VIVO provides a uniform semantic structure to enable a new class of tools that can use the data to advance science. Among some of the most compelling applications are VIVO Search [3], a deep semantic search which facilitates discovery of people, papers, grants, and more across VIVO sites; VIVO Searchlight [4] finds people whose work is related to the material on any web page allowing readers to find experts for collaboration, media requests, foundation relations, and more; An inter-institutional collaboration explorer [5] depicts co-authored papers across selected schools and organizations; and VIVO widgets for Drupal, WordPress and OpenSocial provide easy reuse of VIVO data.

Research discovery is facilitated via content browsing and the structured data lends itself to a variety of applications that can make use of these data. A SPARQL query builder

Figure 2. Map of Science visualization for the University of Florida.

is part of the standard VIVO distribution and allows for end-user data requests from a VIVO implementation, enabling access to data for subsequent analysis, evaluation, and visualization of the research enterprise. One new promising option is the Linked Data API [6], which provides a configurable way to access RDF data for many potential uses.

One of the most visible ways of leveraging VIVO data is through the network analysis and visualization tools available in the VIVO platform itself [7]. Visualizations of networks of co-authors and co-investigators on grants have recently been complimented by novel science map visualizations that support the comparison of publication profiles of up to three people, groups, or organizations (Figure 2). Visualizations are interactive and offer options for export as images or data. VIVO enables high quality data to be revealed about researchers, their collaborators, their funding sources, and more. These data can serve as the foundation for further network analyses and elegant visualizations of the research enterprise on the individual, local, and global levels.

4. THE VIVO COMMUNITY

VIVO enjoys a robust open source, open community space on SourceForge. The site offers a comprehensive project wiki, focused topic listservs, and ways of connecting with other VIVO project members such as event listings and collaborative phone calls. The VIVO software and ontology are publicly available at the SourceForge site, along with content that supports implementation, adoption, and development efforts at sites around the world. For more information, visit http://vivo.sourceforge,net.

VIVO and other compatible applications produce a rich network of information across institutions, agencies, and other organizations that can be searched to foster collaboration and enable open research discovery. The VIVO software and ontology are publicly available at http://vivo.sourceforge.net along with content that supports implementation, adoption, and development efforts around the world. To learn more about VIVO, please visit http://vivoweb.org/. VIVO is supported by NIH Award U24 RR029822.

5. ACKNOWLEDGMENTS

VIVO is supported by NIH Award U24 RR029822.

6. REFERENCES

[1] http://vivoweb.org/

[2] The effect of open access and downloads ('hits') on citation impact: a bibliography of studies. http://opcit.eprints.org/oacitation-biblio.html (accessed 30 January 2012)

[3] http://vivosearch.org/

[4] http://vivosearchlight.org/

[5] http://xcite.hackerceo.org/VIVOviz/visualization.html

[6] http://code.google.com/p/linked-data-api/

[7] http://vivo.cns.iu.edu/gallery.html

[8] http://vivo.sourceforge,net.

Structured Audio Content Analysis and Metadata in a Digital Library

David Bainbridge
University of Waikato
Hamilton, New Zealand
davidb@cs.waikato.ac.nz

J. Stephen Downie
University of Illinois
Urbana-Champaign, USA
jdownie@illinois.edu

Andreas F. Ehmann
University of Illinois
Urbana-Champaign, USA
aehmann@illinois.edu

ABSTRACT

This work illustrates how audio content analysis of music and manually assigned structural temporal metadata can be used to form a digital library designed for musicological exploration. In addition to text-based searching and browsing, the document view is enriched with an interactive structured audio time-line that shows ground-truth data representing the logical segments to the song, and a version that was automatically generated for comparison. A self-similarity "heat" map is also displayed, and is interactive. Clicking within the map at a co-ordinate (x, y) results in the audio being played simultaneous at time offset x and y, panned left and right, respectively, to make it easier for the listener to separate out the differences. The musicologist can also initiate an audio content based query starting at any point in the song. This produces a ranked result set which can be further studied through their respective document views. Alternatively they can perform a musical structure search (for example, for songs that contain the structure *b, b, c, b, c*).

Categories and Subject Descriptors

H.3.7 [**Information storage & retrieval**]: Digital Libraries

General Terms

Design and Experimentation

Keywords

Digital Libraries, Audio Content Analysis, Structured Metadata

Introduction

In this paper we present a digital library designed for musicologists that exploits structured audio metadata and content analysis to go beyond the traditional methods of text-based searching and browsing provided by a DL. Starting with a set of music files identified as worthy of study, the approach devised allows a music scholar to ingest this content into a DL collection that is enhanced with content analysis, processing, and searching services. All the usual digital library tools are at the scholar's disposal to form and manage the collection over time. Title and artist metadata, for instance, can be extracted from the audio files directly at the point of ingest if present/reliable, otherwise manual metadata can be assigned. This metadata can then be used to form browsing and searching options to the DL collection.

JCDL'12, June 10–14, 2012, Washington, DC, USA.
ACM 978-1-4503-1154-0/12/06.

A Digital Library for Musicologists

In Figure 1 we join the scholar after they have browsed their way by title to the song *Candela* to study its structure. Naturally from this page the user is able to play the song, as one would expect of any digital library of music content; however this is largely of secondary importance to the other functionality that is accessible through this page.

The most striking visual component to this page is the self-similarity "heat map" where the duration of the song forms both the x- and y-axis, and a red pixel located at a given (x, y) co-ordinate represents a location where two parts of the song are strongly similar, proportionally shifting hue to blue to represent where they are dissimilar. The similarity between time-instants in the song is based on a feature called chroma. A chroma feature measures how strongly frequencies pertaining to each of the twelve western-scale musical notes are "activated" at any given instance of time. In this implementation, the song is segmented into overlapping segments. Each segment has a duration of approximately 0.74 seconds, and the segments are overlapped by 50%. The cosine distance is used to measure similarity/dissimilarity. For further details on musical structural analysis and feature representations see [1].

In the heat-map, the leading diagonal to the matrix ($x = y$) is always coloured red as this represents the comparison of song segments with itself. When the user moves the mouse cursor around the self-similarity map a highlighting circle is shown to emphasize the area the user is over; annotated vertically and horizontally are the two time-offsets into the song that the mouse-position represents. Clicking the cursor at this point results in the audio being played *simultaneously* from these two time-offsets, where one part is panned to the left speaker, and the other to the right. In our figure, the musicologist has zeroed in the location $x = 33$, $y = 97$ which corresponds to the start of a strong red diagonal that occurs some distance off the leading diagonal. Listening to the two sounds played they hear that these two sections of the song are indeed repeating sections of the guitar piece *Candela* with a minor variation in the latter section where a recorder is also playing in the arrangement.

The structured audio time-lines (labeled A, B, ..., and 6, 5, 2, ... in the figure) located above the self-similarity map are

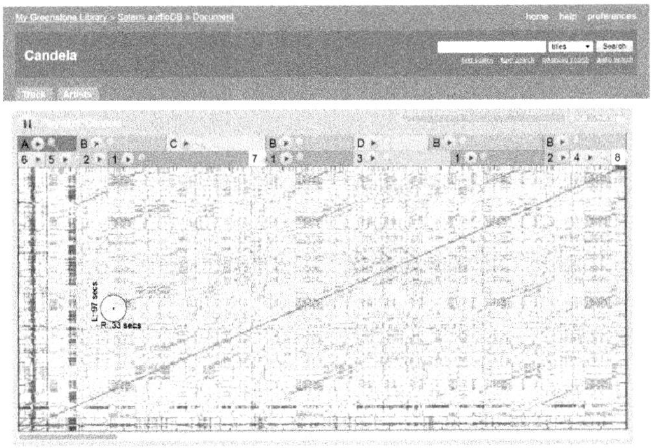

Figure 1: The musicologically enriched document view for *Candela*.

(a) (b)

Figure 2: Audio content based search results: (a) the result list from an audio content based query; and (b) the result of a structured music search.

another area of enriched musical content in the DL. The upper line shows the human-annotated ground-truth data for this song as decribed in [3]; the lower line is generated by an algorithmically based content analysis algorithm (with this particular algorithm choosing to label structural segments numerically as opposed to the more standard alphabetical labeling). While there is some agreement between these two lines, there are also differences. The play button within each structured time-line segment allows the user to investigate these divisions by playing the respective sections of the song. Furthermore, with the time-line width matched to be the same as the self-similarity map, there is the also the opportunity to study what is happening at these locations through the pan-left and pan-right functionality.

The time-line segments also have a magnifying glass button, and clicking on this initiates an audio content based query from that part of the song. In Figure 2a our musicologist has moved on to study *Michelle* by The Beatles, and the figure shows the result of searching the collection for content that matches the "I want you ..." refrain from this song. Not surprisingly *Michelle* is returned as the top hit (at 92.1%)—this is because the system has found several sections of the song that matched the query—the next hit being *Bigger Than JC* at 74.4%, and so on down, where only one hit per song occurs. From here the user can dip in to any of these songs and explore the reasons for the match in more detail. Note, when a music document is viewed after an audio content search, an additional time-line is added corresponding to the location(s) where the match occurred.

A further form of musical content-based searching is available through the main header to the digital library. Instead of searching by title or artist (which are also available) the user can click on the "search by" menu next to the quick-search text box and select "ground-truth structure" instead. Figure 2b shows the result of using this option, where the user has entered "b b c b c" as the query, in other words searching for songs that have two sections in a row the same, then a new section, then returning to the original section, before progressing to a recurrence of the second distinct section. In pop and rock music this is a popular sequence corresponding to verse, verse, chorus, verse, chorus. A more intriguing framing of a query along these lines—equally possible to construct in the digital library—would be to use the fielded search page to the DL and enter the same music structure query, but this time combine it with other fielded terms: Genre=Blues OR Jazz, Year<1950. Results from this compound query would let the musicologist seek out evidence of this pattern of sections being used in two of the key musical genres that influenced the development of Rock and Roll music.

Implementation details

In terms of implementation, the digital library framework used was Greenstone 3 [4], and the core interactive elements in the document view were implemented using SVG combined with Javascript. The left- and right-panning was implemented by processing raw audio streams, made accessible by the Firefox Audio extension API.[1]

AudioDB [2] content based searching was integrated into Greenstone through two components of the digital library software architecture: its build-time document processing plugin system, and its runtime message-passing service-base framework. The new search service took the form of a proxy, accepting messages in the XML syntax used by Greenstone, turning them into the necessary calls to the AudioDB command-line interface, and then converting the output from AudioDB back into the XML syntax expected by the digital library architecture. Finally, the two parts were packaged to operate as a Greenstone extension; the software is available at: http://trac.greenstone.org/gs3-extensions/audioDB/. The ground truth data for segmented songs was produced by the SALAMI project [3].

1. REFERENCES

[1] J. Paulus, M. Müller, and A. Klapuri. State of the art report: Audio-based music structure analysis. In *ISMIR*, pages 625–636, 2010.

[2] C. Rhodes, T. Crawford, M. Casey, and M. d'Inverno. Investigating music collections at different scales with AudioDB. *Journal of New Music Research*, 39(4):337–348, 2010.

[3] J. Smith, J. Burgoyne, I. Fujinaga, D. De Roure, and J. Downie. Design and creation of a large-scale database of structural annotations. In *ISMIR*, pages 555–560, 2011.

[4] I. H. Witten and D. Bainbridge. The Greenstone digital library software. *Handbook of Research on Digital Libraries*, pages 61–72, 2009.

[1] https://wiki.mozilla.org/Audio_Data_API

The *Profiles in Science* Digital Library: Behind the Scenes

Marie E. Gallagher
U.S. National Library of Medicine
8600 Rockville Pike
Bethesda, MD 20894 USA
+1 301 435 3252
mgallagher@mail.nih.gov

Christie Moffatt
U.S. National Library of Medicine
8600 Rockville Pike
Bethesda, MD 20894 USA
+1 301 496 9136
moffattc@mail.nih.gov

ABSTRACT

This demonstration shows the *Profiles in Science®* digital library. *Profiles in Science* contains digitized selections from the personal manuscript collections of prominent biomedical researchers, medical practitioners, and those fostering science and health. The *Profiles in Science* Web site[1] is the delivery mechanism for content derived from the digital library system. The system is designed according to our basic principles for digital library development [1]. The digital library includes the rules and software used for digitizing items, creating and editing database records and performing quality control as well as serving the digital content to the public. Among the types of data managed by the digital library are detailed item-level, collection-level and cross-collection metadata, digitized photographs, papers, audio clips, movies, born-digital electronic files, optical character recognized (OCR) text, and annotations (see Figure 1). The digital library also tracks the status of each item, including digitization quality, sensitivity of content, and copyright. Only items satisfying all required criteria are released to the public through the World Wide Web. External factors have influenced all aspects of the digital library's infrastructure.

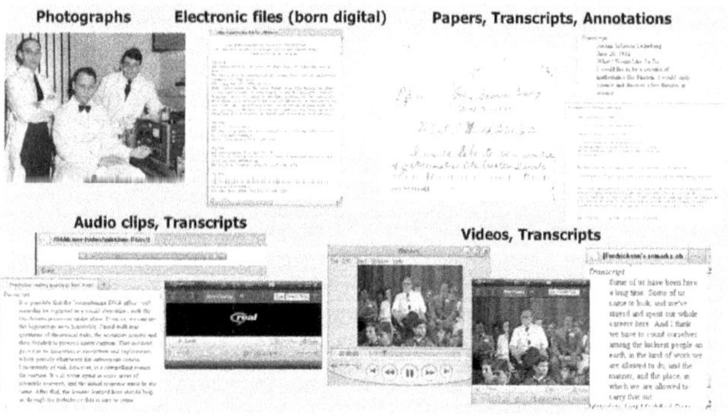

Figure 1. Samples of items in *Profiles in Science*

Categories and Subject Descriptors

H.3.7 [**Information Storage and Retrieval**]: Digital Libraries – *Collection, Dissemination, Systems issues*

[1] http://profiles.nlm.nih.gov/

JCDL'12, June 10–14, 2012, Washington, DC, USA.
ACM 978-1-4503-1154-0/12/06.

General Terms

Design, Legal Aspects

Keywords

Digital Library, Information System, Digitized Manuscripts, Adaptability

1. INTRODUCTION

The U.S. National Library of Medicine (NLM) is the world's largest biomedical library. In addition to published books and journals, NLM collects unpublished items belonging to groups and individuals who have made significant contributions and discoveries. NLM's History of Medicine Division (HMD) is the repository for these special collections. The Web provides an ideal route for making NLM's unique and extraordinary collections available worldwide to researchers, educators and students. Making available digital reproductions of historical items also decreases some of the need for handling the fragile originals. In 1997, the HMD and NLM's Lister Hill National Center for Biomedical Communications (LHNCBC) partnered to build a prototype digital collection that demonstrated the promise of delivering historical manuscript collections over the Web. Having anytime/anywhere access to high quality digital copies of their selected manuscripts, laboratory notebooks, drawings, diaries, photographs, audiovisuals and other materials encouraged the Nobel Prize-winning National Institutes of Health (NIH) scientists to donate their papers to NLM for digitization.

The prototype digital collection grew into a digital library system designed to manage digitized items and their associated metadata for the long-term. The digital library system became known as *Profiles in Science* and is delivered to the public through its Web site. NLM continues to organize, describe, digitize and add collections to *Profiles in Science*. The additions expanded to include other manuscript collections donated to NLM as well as collections held by other institutions through collaboration. Some of the items in *Profiles in Science* are: Joshua Lederberg's earliest known autograph, a photograph of Julius Axelrod at age 3, Francis Crick's drawing of the double helix, Albert Szent-Gyorgyi discussing cancer research, and Marshall Nirenberg's laboratory notebooks showing his work deciphering the genetic code. Currently thirty-six collections are available to the public. These include 142,180 image pages that constitute 27,042 digital items. Users can browse by navigating through the Web site, or search the metadata and OCR text to find items of interest. The project is staffed with computer scientists, archivists, a historian, and a library technician.

2. BEHIND THE SCENES

2.1 Data Creation

At the heart of the *Profiles in Science* digital library system is the metadata database [2]. The database contains descriptive, administrative and technical metadata about each item in the digital library. Software detects technical information about each file and updates the database automatically. Trained digital archivists enter most descriptive information and some administrative information using the *Profiles in Science* data entry program. The program guides the archivist by providing options and pull-down lists of standard vocabularies rather than free text input wherever possible, alerting the user when required information is missing, tracking workflow such as quality control status and copyright research status, and providing customized access so each user can edit only what s/he is authorized to edit. The program automatically generates unique identifiers that forever bind the metadata to the digital item. Item-level metadata includes most of the fifteen Dublin Core metadata elements[2] as well as extensive metadata regarding sensitivity, copyright permission status, quality control, physical condition, and final disposition. Collection-level metadata describes the subject and overall contents of the collection, exhibit sections, a brief chronology, and the collection's physical (boxes and folders) and logical (series and folders) structure. Some metadata spans all collections such as lists of organization names, personal names, journal names, languages, Medical Subject Headings (MeSH)[3] and document types[4].

2.2 Quality Control

Profiles in Science has a quality control and reporting tool known as the Diagnostic Server. The Diagnostic Server provides a read-only view of the metadata from various perspectives. The archivist uses the tool to compare and spot inconsistencies within the detailed information associated with an item, within collections, and across collections. For example, within any collection or across all collections, the archivist can see which metadata records and which digitized items are pending review. The archivist may also see which items have a particular copyright research status. S/he may choose to include all items or filter for items that are marked for public release. The archivist may also use the Diagnostic Server to review items to ensure that their descriptions are standard, consistent, and meet internally developed guidelines.

2.3 Data Dissemination

When we add items to the *Profiles in Science* digital library, we intend for them to become publicly available. Copyright law places U.S. Government works, including the notebooks and correspondence authored by the NIH Nobel laureates, in the public domain per U.S. Code Title 17 Section 105. When manuscript collections are donated to the NLM, the copyrights of the donor are usually transferred to the public domain through the Deed of Gift. Copyrights held by others, such as authors of correspondence sent to the NIH Nobel laureates, remain unchanged. Permissions to release these items to the public must be sought. Occasionally, although infrequently, the request is denied. In a few cases the copyright status of an item has changed when a previously unidentified copyright holder came forward. Over time we discovered that some items could not be released until sometime in the future. Such works include personnel recommendations, voting records, grant applications, research proposals, inquiries from patients, and items whose copyright status will change. Among the most complex changes to our digital library system are the additional rules that prevent accidental release of protected items and implement the permissions status tracking workflow.

2.4 External Factors

In response to external factors, the *Profiles in Science* digital library system's software components undergo constant modifications. One external factor we have experienced is software obsolescence. For example, our original search engine was a commercial product whose support ended. It was replaced by in-house software and will eventually be replaced by open source software. Another factor is security policies that dictate or prohibit the use of certain software, hardware, and configurations. Because security policies necessarily evolve, we must change or replace our software and configurations to comply; sometimes this happens on short notice due to imminent unforeseen security threats. We expect that policies and regulations requiring more space-saving and energy efficient hardware will become increasingly important for future hardware choices. Another external factor is the rapidly increasing number and variety of mobile devices; rather than providing custom interfaces for different devices, we wish to develop a universally-usable, standards-compliant, device-independent interface. We must also ensure that we comply with standards for implementing Section 508 of the Rehabilitation Act which are also undergoing change[5].

3. ACKNOWLEDGMENTS

We thank our dedicated and creative colleagues at the National Library of Medicine for their work on this project, as well as the collaborators who made it possible to include their collections in *Profiles in Science*. This work is supported by the Intramural Research Program of the NIH, National Library of Medicine. The Library, the world's largest library of the health sciences, is a component of the National Institutes of Health, U.S. Department of Health and Human Services.

4. REFERENCES

[1] McCray, A. T. and Gallagher, M. E. 2001. Principles for digital library development. *Commun. ACM* 44, 5 (May 2001), 48-54. DOI= http://doi.acm.org/10.1145/374308.374339.

[2] McCray, A. T., Gallagher, M. E. and Flannick, M. A. 1999. Extending the Role of Metadata in a Digital Library System. In *Proceedings of the IEEE Forum on Research and Technology Advances in Digital Libraries* (Baltimore, MD, March 19 - 21, 1999). ADL '99. IEEE Computer Society, Washington, DC, USA, 190-199. DOI= http://doi.ieeecomputersociety.org/10.1109/ADL.1999.777714.

[2] http://dublincore.org/documents/dces/

[3] http://www.nlm.nih.gov/mesh/

[4] http://www.getty.edu/research/tools/vocabularies/aat/

[5] http://www.access-board.gov/508.htm

The ResultsSpace Collaborative Search Environment

Robert Capra, Jaime Arguello, Annie T. Chen, Katie Hawthorne, Gary Marchionini, Lee Shaw
University of North Carolina
School of Information and Library Science
Chapel Hill, NC

rcapra, jarguell, atchen, kathryne, march, ledshaw {@email.unc.edu}

ABSTRACT

The ResultsSpace Collaborative Search Environment is a tool to support asynchronous collaborative information retrieval among a small group of collaborators. It is designed to promote awareness of collaborators' searches and the documents they have rated. Awareness is supported through several mechanisms: an area that shows a history of queries, a summary display of collaborators' ratings next to each search result, and changes in the visual salience of search results based on their aggregate rating from all collaborators. Faceted controls allow users to filter results based on specific ratings (relevant, not relevant, and maybe) and on specific collaborator(s) who have rated an item. We describe features of the system, how they are implemented, and give insights into the design rationale.

Categories and Subject Descriptors

H5.m Information interfaces and presentation; H3.3 Information search and retrieval

General Terms

Design, Human Factors.

Keywords

Collaborative search, collaborative information retrieval.

1. INTRODUCTION

A recent focus in information retrieval and information science communities is research on systems that can support information needs that span multiple search sessions and involve multiple people contributing to a final set of search results. The phrases "collaborative information retrieval" "collaborative information seeking" "collaborative information behavior" and "collaborative search" all refer to related work in these areas. Workshops have recently been held on these topics at JCDL 2008, CSCW 2010, GROUP 2009, GROUP 2010, ASIS&T 2011, and CIKM 2011.

Much of the research to date has focused on synchronous collaborative search, in which people sit at different computers, but conduct searches at the same time. However, several recent surveys have shown that people do a significant amount of asynchronous collaborative searching [2][4] and that existing tools do not support this activity well [1]. Many users rely on simple "tools-at-hand" such as email and text documents to organize their collaborative searches [1]. In this project, we set out to study asynchronous collaborative search activities.

JCDL'12, June 10–14, 2012, Washington, DC, USA.
ACM 978-1-4503-1154-0/12/06.

In addition, most studies of collaborative search have used tasks that asked participants to search on the open web, making computations of group precision and recall difficult (there are exceptions, e.g., [7]). The system we have developed uses an Indri search engine back-end that we can use to index specific, known corpora. To start, we have indexed news articles from the AQUAINT corpus. By using the AQUAINT corpus along with TREC tasks, we are developing an experimental system from which we can compute group-level recall and precision measures based on established tasks and relevancy ratings.

2. RELATED SYSTEMS

A complete review of collaborative search systems is outside the scope of this paper. However, we highlight several related systems – SearchTogether [3], CoSense [6], Coagmento [9], and Querium [8] – and refer readers to the excellent summary of collaborative search research in [5]. Prior systems have included collaborative awareness features such as query histories, integrated chat/IM, and relevance rating displays. Our system utilizes a subset of these mechanisms and explores new designs for tightly integrating collaborative awareness information within search result displays.

3. RESULTSSPACE SYSTEM

In this section, we outline major features of the ResultsSpace Collaborative Search Environment and describe design rationale.

Query histories – On the right side of the screen are two query history displays, one that shows collaborators' recent queries, and one that shows the user's own recent queries. Clicking on any of the queries re-issues that query and resets filters from previously active queries.

Faceted filters – Along the left side of the screen are controls that allow the user to filter results by User and Relevance Ratings.

Query display – Above the results is an area (shown in grey in Figure 1) that summarizes information about the current query including the query string and any filters that have been applied.

Relevance ratings and controls – To the left of each item in the results list, there is a set of three icons that correspond to three relevance ratings supported by the system: "relevant" = a green upwards arrow, "maybe" = a yellow box, and "not relevant" = a red downwards arrow. Users can click these icons to indicate their rating for each item or may leave an item unrated. Numbers are displayed inside each icon to show how many collaborators' have rated an item with that rating and mouse hover-over is used to show which specific collaborators made the rating. Icons with no numbers have zero ratings. This contrast between items with numbers and without helps to improve the task of scanning the list. The rating of the currently logged in user is indicated with a black bar under the rating. Figure 1 illustrates an example situation in which three collaborators (Rob, Gary, and Jaime) have been conducting searches on the topic of population growth.

Results displays – The items in the results list are generated using Indri and consist of the article title and a snippet of text with the search terms highlighted. The presentation of items is highlighted or diminished based on the combined relevance ratings. Items with an overall positive rating are highlighted with a light green background. Items with an overall negative rating are displayed with a lighter hue font color to give them a "faded out" appearance. If an item has multiple negative ratings, it is faded out even further, making it difficult to read. Items with no ratings or with a neutral rating have no highlight or fading out. In Figure 1, the first result has an overall positive rating (green highlight). Further down, result #5 was rated "not relevant" by two collaborators and is faded out. Result #6 is rated negatively, but less so than result #5, so it is faded out to a lesser degree.

4. SUMMARY

The ResultsSpace Collaborative Search Environment is a system to help support and study collaborative information retrieval among small groups of collaborators. It includes collaborative awareness features including highlighting and fading out of results based on collaborators' relevance ratings. We plan to examine the effects of these awareness mechanisms to determine how they affect collaborative information retrieval including group recall, group overlap, and awareness of collaborators' actions.

5. ACKNOWLEDGMENTS

This work was supported by the National Science Foundation grant IIS 0812363. We thank Gene Golovchinsky and Chirag Shah for discussions related to this project.

6. REFERENCES

[1] Capra, R., Marchionini, G., Velasco-Martin, J., & Muller, K. (2010). Tools-at-hand and learning in multi-session, collaborative search. In *Proc. CHI 2010.* ACM, New York, 951-960.

[2] Capra, R., Velasco-Martin, J. and Sams, B. (2011). Collaborative information seeking by the numbers. In *Proc. of the 3rd International Workshop on Collaborative Information Retrieval (CIR '11)*. ACM, New York, 7-10.

[3] Morris, M. R., & Horvitz, E. (2007). SearchTogether: an interface for collaborative web search. In *Proc. UIST 2007.* ACM, New York, 3-12.

[4] Morris, M. R. (2008). A survey of collaborative web search practices. In *Proc. CHI 2008.* ACM, New York, 1657–1660.

[5] Morris, M. R., & Teevan, J. (2009). *Collaborative Web Search: Who, What, Where, When, and Why. Synthesis Lectures on Information Concepts, Retrieval, and Services #14.* Morgan & Claypool.

[6] Paul, S. A., & Morris, M. R. (2009). CoSense: enhancing sensemaking for collaborative web search. In *Proc. CHI 2009.* ACM, New York, 1771–1780.

[7] Pickens, J., Golovchinsky, G., Shah, C., Qvarfordt, P., & Back, M. (2008). Algorithmic mediation for collaborative exploratory search. In *Proc. SIGIR 2008.* ACM, New York, 315-322.

[8] Golovchinsky, G., Diriye, A., Pickens, J. (2011). Designing for collaboration in information seeking. In *Proc. Fifth Workshop on Human-Computer Interaction and Information Retrieval (HCIR 2011)*, Oct. 20, 2011, Mountain View, CA.

[9] Shah, C., & Marchionini, G. (2010). Awareness in collaborative information seeking. *Journal of the American Society for Information Science and Technology, 61*(10), 1970-1986.

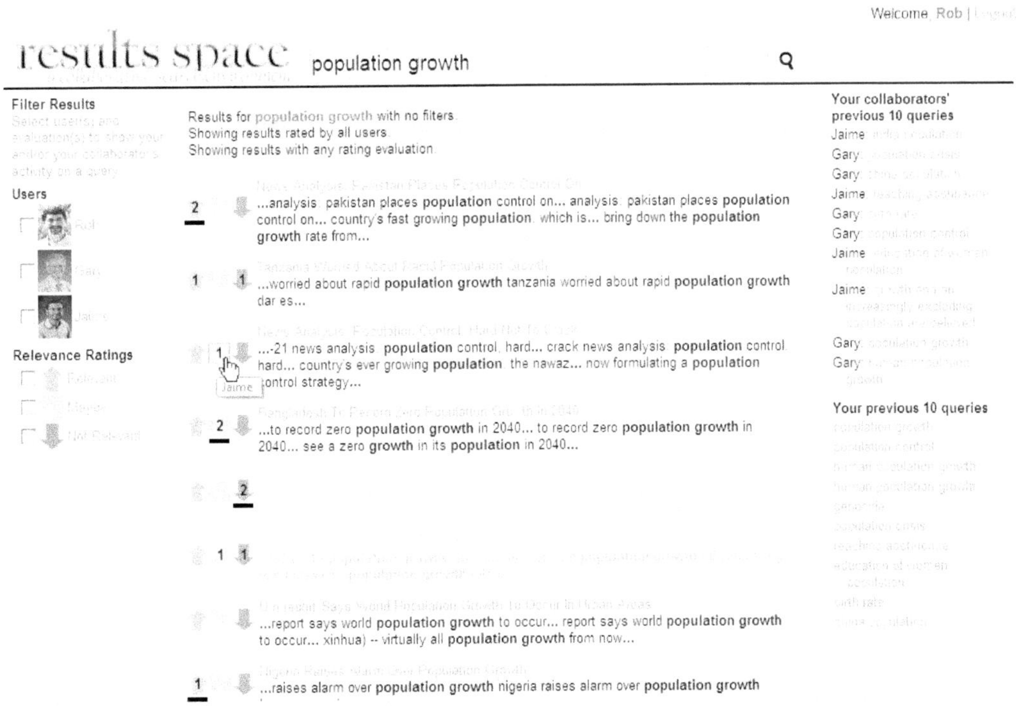

Figure 1. ResultsSpace Collaborative Search Environment

WARCreate - Create Wayback-Consumable WARC Files from Any Webpage

Mat Kelly
Department of Computer Science
Old Dominion University
Norfolk, Virginia
mkelly@cs.odu.edu

Michele C. Weigle
Department of Computer Science
Old Dominion University
Norfolk, Virginia
mweigle@cs.odu.edu

ABSTRACT

The Internet Archive's Wayback Machine is the most common way that typical users interact with web archives. The Internet Archive uses the Heritrix web crawler to transform pages on the publicly available web into Web ARChive (WARC) files, which can then be accessed using the Wayback Machine. Because Heritrix can only access the publicly available web, many personal pages (*e.g.*, password-protected pages, social media pages) cannot be easily archived into the standard WARC format. We have created a Google Chrome extension, WARCreate, that allows a user to create a WARC file from any webpage. Using this tool, content that might have been otherwise lost in time can be archived in a standard format by any user. This tool provides a way for casual users to easily create archives of personal online content. This is one of the first steps in resolving issues of "long term storage, maintenance, and access of personal digital assets that have emotional, intellectual, and historical value to individuals" [3].

Categories and Subject Descriptors

H.3.4 [**Information Storage and Retrieval**]: Systems and Software; H.3.7 [**Digital Libraries**]: Personal Web Archiving

General Terms

Design

Keywords

Personal Web Archiving, WARC, Browser, Wayback Machine, Internet Archive

1. INTRODUCTION

The Internet Archive, along with web archives at other libraries and institutions, has done a remarkable job at archiving the public web. But in recent years, the web has become a home for a significant amount of original user-generated content, such as that posted on social media sites. Users are becoming increasingly aware of the need for personal web archiving [4, 5]. Unfortunately, this content is largely unavailable to standard web archives because it lives behind the "walled garden" of authentication and is part of the "deep web" [1]. Our goal is to allow users, once past authentication, to generate their own archives that can be browse-able in a user-friendly manner.

The Internet Archive's Wayback Machine is the most well-known interface for accessing web archives. The archived pages are stored in the standard Web ARChive (WARC) format [2] and are generated by the Heritrix[1] crawler. Unfortunately, Heritrix is limited to crawling only publicly accessible pages, so many personal pages (*e.g.*, password-protected pages, social media pages) cannot be easily archived. In addition, for pages that are location or user-agent aware, the version archived at Internet Archive is the one that the Heritrix crawler (run from San Francisco) sees. For example, the most recently available version[2] of http://www.craigslist.org redirects to http://sfbay.craigslist.org.

In an effort to facilitate the use of the standard WARC format for personal web archives, we have developed a tool to allow a user to archive any page, edit its metadata, and submit it to an instance of the Wayback Machine (from here on referred to as Wayback).

2. WARCREATE

WARCreate[3] is an extension for the Google Chrome web browser that allows a user to generate a WARC file from the current webpage. In addition to creating a valid WARC that can be viewed in Wayback, the extension provides options that address privacy concerns (*e.g.*, a user might want the data encrypted in some way), potential bleed over (*e.g.*, two different users see different content at http://facebook.com), and other issues that may not be relevant to conventional web archiving as performed by Heritrix and the Internet Archive.

To create a WARC file from the current webpage, the user clicks on the browser extension's icon in the address bar and then presses the Generate WARC button (see Figure 1). The browser extension gathers the resources (including external scripts, CSS and images) and HTTP headers normally used by the web browser to generate a webpage and adds metadata (the *warcinfo* records) to generate a WARC file that conforms to the standard's specification (Figure 2). Adherence to the specification allows the WARC to be read by Wayback.

When the compilation of the WARC file is complete, the file is downloaded to the local file system. The browser ex-

[1] https://webarchive.jira.com/wiki/display/Heritrix/Heritrix
[2] Archived on July 25, 2011
[3] http://matkelly.com/warcreate

JCDL'12, June 10–14, 2012, Washington, DC, USA.
ACM 978-1-4503-1154-0/12/06.

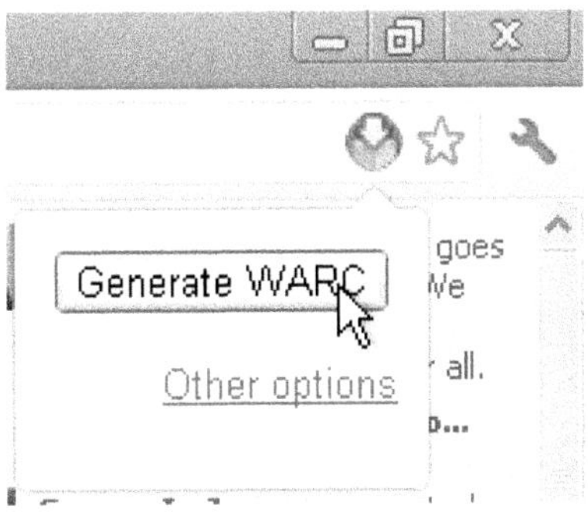

Figure 1: Creating a WARC is as simple as selecting the extension's icon and pressing the Generate WARC button. Other options can be selected for further customization of the generated file.

tension also allows a user to open an existing WARC file generated by the tool to make modifications. Any changes to the WARC file must be accounted for in the *content-length* WARC fields to ensure compatibility with the WARC standard. This overcomes the potential corruption of the WARC records that might occur if the file is edited with a simple text editor. Further functionality is being developed to allow the extension to read in, interpret and allow modification of any arbitrary WARC file. This would require comprehensive implementation of the WARC specification.

Unlike a web crawler, this tool archives only the single webpage that the user is visiting. In the future, we intend to add more of a crawling-like functionality. For now, the current extension can append the archive of the current page to an existing WARC file. This allows links to content from separate archiving sessions to be resolvable by Wayback.

```
WARC/1.0
WARC-Type: warcinfo
WARC-Date: 2012-01-18T22:12:49.445Z
WARC-Filename: MY_WARC.warc
WARC-Record-ID: <urn:uuid:98187a24-8d74-a2b8-ec19-fbb6a958db9e>
Content-Type: application/warc-fields
Content-Length: 541

Software: WARCreate/0.4.1 http://matkelly.com/warcreate
ip: 128.82.5.133
hostname: cs.odu.edu
format: WARC File Format 1.0
conformsTo: http://bibnum.bnf.fr/WARC/WARC_ISO_28500_version1_latestdraft.pdf
```

Figure 2: A generated WARC file is prefixed with a *warcinfo* record that conforms to a liberally attributed template while still maintaining minimum requirements.

3. OTHER CONSIDERATIONS

There are many facets of this type of personal web archiving that we leave for future exploration. The main issues we will investigate are ensuring privacy, maintaining archive integrity, preventing bleed over, and developing a service to consume the potentially private WARCs generated by the extension.

3.1 Privacy Concerns

Much of the data in personal web archives is of a sensitive or personal nature, thus the data placed in a WARC file must be protected. One way to achieve this is to encrypt the data so that only the recipient can interpret the archive. There are several issues to consider, such as ease of decryption, decentralization, increased space and time complexity, and loss of access when a central authority disappears. In the current Chrome extension, we have implemented a simple key-based encryption/decryption scheme for users that wish to test the reliability of this preliminary technique.

3.2 Archive Integrity

Heritrix subtly manipulates content in an archive for ease of navigation and to allow a webpage to be viewed in the modified context of the Wayback Machine user interface. Because data is manipulated, the integrity of the archive is compromised, as the page is not retained exactly in its original form. In future work, we hope to expand on the WARC format (and demonstrate this with an implementation) to provide WARC records containing the differential of how the webpage was manipulated. By utilizing this differential, the original content can be re-created much in the same way that software versioning uses differentials to store and revert to older versions of code.

3.3 Bleed Over

An issue that is not as common on the surface web as on the personalized deep web is that of a single URI referring to potentially different information. This can be seen when two users access a social media website while each is logged in (*e.g.*, http://www.facebook.com). The website uses authentication to provide customized information to each user. If two users were to create an archive of the same page, the resulting WARCs should be different and each user should only be able to access the WARC they created. This bleed over issue will be addressed in future work.

3.4 Service to Consume WARCs

Making WARC files accessible to the end user is just the first step. Unless a user has a personally deployed instance of Wayback, little can be done with the resulting file. We will investigate the feasibility of rapid deployment of a personal instance of Wayback or of finding an alternative for quick replay of small archives that were created with the Chrome extension. Initial approaches to accomplish this will attempt to decouple the code used to interpret WARC files from the open source Wayback and minimize the need for reinvention of these procedures while maintaining consistency of implementation with future versions of Wayback.

4. REFERENCES

[1] M. K. Bergman. The deep web: Surfacing the hidden value. *Journal of Electronic Publishing*, 2000.

[2] ISO. Information and documentation - WARC file format, 2009.

[3] C. C. Marshall. Rethinking Personal Digital Archiving, Part 1: Four Challenges from the Field. *DLib Magazine*, 14(3/4):2, 2008.

[4] C. C. Marshall, S. A. Bly, and F. Brun-Cottan. The long term fate of our digital belongings: Toward a service model for personal archives. In *Proceedings of IS&T Archiving*, pages 25–30, 2006.

[5] C. C. Marshall, F. McCown, and M. L. Nelson. Evaluating personal archiving strategies for internet-based information. In *Proceedings of IS&T Archiving*, pages 151–156, 2007.

Author Index

Abels, Eileen G. 339
Agogino, Alice Merner 393
Agosti, Maristella 11
Akbar, Monika 43
Albert, Paul 429
Almas, Bridget 213
AlNoamany, Yasmin 15
Arguello, Jaime 435
Au Yeung, Ching-man 351
Azogu, Olajumoke 421
Babeu, Alison 213
Bahsoun, Wahiba 61
Bainbridge, David 81, 431
Bakalov, Anton 237
Balagopalan, Arun 195
Balke, Wolf-Tilo 355, 395
Bamman, David 213
Barth, Bill 389
Ben Jabeur, Lamjed 61
Bernard, Jürgen 139
Blanke, Tobias 405
Bogacewicz, Roman 381
Bogen II, Paul Logasa 121, 157
Bolikowski, Łukasz 381, 419
Borbinha, José 171
Borgman, Christine L. 19
Börner, Katy 429
Britell, Scott 377
Buchanan, George 325
Busemeyer, Jerome 385
Butterhof, Robin 399
Buzydlowski, Jan 397
Calado, Pável 171, 387
Capra, Robert 435
Cassel, Lillian N. 121, 377
Cerrato, Lisa 213
Chell, Lindsay 367
Chen, Annie T. 435
Chen, Hui-Pin 337
Chen, Jiangping 421
Chen, Xue-wen 101
Chen, Ya-Ning 337
Chen, Yinlin 121
Chen, Yuxin 101
Chitturi, Kiran 341
Choi, Gilok 367
Chua, Alton Y.K. 391
Cole, Timothy W. 111
Conlon, Mike 429
Cowan, Will 425
Crane, Gregory 213
Creel, James 415
Cunningham, Sally Jo 305
Czeczko, Artur 381
Davison, Brian D. 371
Davison, Stephen 411
Delcambre, Lois M.L. 377
Deng, Hongbo 71
Denton, Patrick 101
Devaul, Holly 35
Diakoff, Harry 213
Dibie, Ogheneovo 27
Dichev, Christo 31
Dicheva, Darina 31
Ding, Ying 385
Downie, J. Stephen 431
Doyle, John P. 427
Draxler, Bridget 203
Dudley, Nicole J. 203
Dunn, Jon 425
Durbin, Mike 425
Ehmann, Andreas F. 431
Ehrich, Roger W. 285
Ehrman, Christopher 399
Elsherbiny, Noha 335
Esteva, Maria 389
Farrell, Dean 375
Ferreira, Anderson A. 175
Foltyn, Tomas 383
Foster, James M. 35
Fox, Edward A. 43, 121, 285, 335, 341, 377
Francisco-Revilla, Luis 365
Freire, Nuno 171
Furuta, Richard 157, 377
Gallagher, Marie E. 433
Gao, Liangcai 295
Gertz, Michael 223
Gharib Farag, Mohamed Magdy 341
Gibson, Jon 389
Giersch, Sarah 47
Giles, C. Lee 167, 185, 277, 343
Gingell, Grant 407
Goh, Dion H. 391
Gollapalli, Sujatha Das 167
Gonçalves, Marcos André 175
Gozali, Jesse Prabawa 315
Gregory, Lisa 375
Guo, Chun 359
Hagedorn, Kat 195
Hall, Catherine 417
Hall, Robert H. 23
Han, Jiawei 71
Han, Myung-Ja K. 111
Hanson, Ladd 389
Harrington, Matthew 213
Hawthorne, Katie 435
Hedges, Mark 405
Hinze, Annika 305
Holmes, Kristi L. 429
Hsieh, Haowei 121, 203
Hu, Xiao 129
Huang, Congrui 51
Huggett, Michael 233
Ishihara, Tatsuya 91
Itoko, Toshinari 91
Jameel, Shoaib 351
Jatowt, Adam 353
Jia, Han 403
Jiangqin, Wu 357

Jordan, Christopher 389
Kalfatovic, Martin 361
Kan, Min-Yen 315
Kang, Ji Hei 373
Kelly, Mat 437
Khabsa, Madian 185, 343
Khoo, Michael 423
Kim, Hae Min 339
King, Irwin 71
Kocourek, Pavel 383
Kohlhammer, Jörn 139
Köhncke, Benjamin 355, 395
Laender, Alberto H. F. 175
Lam, Wai 351
Lazorchak, Butch 369
Lee, Chei Sian 391
Lee, Dong Joon 363
Lee, Jin Ha 129
Lee, Sunshin 335
Lei, Zhen 281
Lhotak, Martin 383
Li, Junyan 101
Li, Shijun 393
Li, Xiaoming 51
Li, Xin 409
Liang, Feng 267
Lin, Xia 397
Lin, Xiaofan 295
Liu, Xiaozhong 359, 403
Liu, Ying 295
Luczak, Edward C. 427
Luo, Bo 101
Lyu, Michael R. 71
MacDonald, Craig M. 423
Manus, Susan 369
Marchionini, Gary 435
Mardis, Marcia A. 407
Markson, Christopher 345
Marshall, Catherine C. 1
Martins, Bruno 387
Martins de Matos, David 387
Maull, Keith E. 27
McAulay, Elizabeth 411
McCallum, Andrew 237
McKay, Dana 305
McLaughlin, Casey 407
McMartin, Flora 47
Meng, Yuanliang 101
Mercer, Robert E. 263
Miller, Matthew 367
Mimno, David 237
Misra, Dharitri 23
Mitra, Prasenjit 167, 277, 281
Mitrelis, Angelos 347
Moffatt, Christie 433
Nelson, Michael L. 0
Newman, David 195
Noh, Youn 195
Nomoto, Tadashi 125
Oh, Sooyoung 281
Okoye, Ifeyinwa 35
Oksanen, Suvi 199
Organisciak, Peter 349
Orio, Nicola 11
Owen, Tom 325
Padia, Kalpesh 15
Pan, Jing 249
Papachristopoulos, Leonidas 347
Papatheodorou, Christos 347
Park, Joon 423
Park, Sung Hee 285
Payne, Susan M. 23
Pearson, Jennifer 325
Pengcheng, Gao 357
Powell, Dever 369
Qi, Xixi 295
Qian, Xiaojun 351
Qiang, Runwei 267
Rasmussen, Edie 233
Razikin, Khasfariyati 391
Renear, Allen H. 413
Rinaldo, Constance 361
Rosiek, Tomasz 419
Roüast, Maxime 81
Rudersdorf, Amy 375
Ruppert, Tobias 139
Rusek, Krzysztof 381
Sanderson, Robert 379
Sandler, Trish-Rose 361
Sands, Ashley 19
Sato, Daisuke 91
Scherer, Maximilian 139
Schopf, Jennifer M. 153
Schreck, Tobias 139
Selden, Paul 101
Shaffer, Clifford A. 43
Shalvi, Doron 427
Shams, Rushdi 263
Shaw, Lee 435
Shipman, Frank M. 1, 157
Shuai, Xin 385
Shumar, Wesley 47
Silva, Rodrigo 175
Song, Min 241, 259, 345
Soulier, Laure 61
Štebe, Janez 401
Strötgen, Jannik 223
Stvilia, Besiki 363
Su, Xin 409
Sultan, Md. Arafat 35
Sumner, Tamara 27, 35
Sundaram, Hari 315
Sylwestrzak, Wojtek 419
Takagi, Hironobu 91
Tamine, Lynda 61
Tanaka, Katsumi 353
Tanapaisankit, Prat 259
Tang, Jie 51
Tang, Zhi 295
Teregowda, Pradeep B. 343
Thimbleby, Harold 325
Thoma, George R. 23
Thompson, Keri 361
Timpany, Claire 305
Tkaczyk, Dominika 381
Tönnies, Sascha 355, 395

Traweek, Sharon 19
Treeratpituk, Pucktada 185
Tront, Joseph 47
Tsakonas, Giannis 347
Tu, Fei-Yen 337
Tuarob, Suppawong 277
Tzadok, Asaf 91
Ulate, William 361
Vakkari, Pertti 199
Vanderschantz, Nicholas 305
Vannoy, Jordan A. 111
Vaz, Paula Cristina 387
Veloso, Adriano 175
Wallach, Hanna 237
Wallis, Jillian C. 19
Wang, Chong 241
Wang, Mengyue 409
Watrous-deVersterre, Lori 241, 259
Wei, Baogang 249
Weigle, Michele C. 15, 437
Weimer, Katherine 415
Wheeler, Brian 425
Wickett, Karen M. 413
Wilson, Gregory 341
Winet, Jon 203
Wisnicki, Adrian 411
Witt, Michael 149
Wu, Shuheng 363
Wynholds, Laura A. 19
Yan, Rui 51
Yang, Christopher C. 339
Yang, Jianwu 267
Yang, Seungwon 341
Yang, Xia 357
Yang, Zaihan 371
Yarasavage, Nathan 399
Yen, John 281
Yi, Deng 249
Yi, Yong Jeong 373
Yin, Yanfei 249
Yu, Haihan 249
Yu, Yongyang 149
Yuan, Lin 357
Zarro, Michael 417
Zhang, Hui 425
Zhang, Jane 369
Zhang, Jinsong 359
Zhang, Mi 339, 397
Zhang, Yan 51
Zhang, Yin 249
Zhang, Yunlu 393
Zhao, Haozhen 397
Zhao, Wenqian 421

www.ingramcontent.com/pod-product-compliance
Ingram Content Group UK Ltd.
Pitfield, Milton Keynes, MK11 3LW, UK
UKHW051413290926
15471UKWH00009B/1572

9 781450 317313